Directions for Use

Part I. Author, Title and Subject Index. In this Part there will be found entries under author, title and subject. The author entry is the main entry for the play and includes the following information: name of the author, title of the play, a descriptive phrase, the number of acts and scenes, the size of the cast and the number of sets required. In the case of single plays the publisher and date are given. If the play is part of a collection the name of the collection is given.

Sample entry:

> **Anouilh, Jean**
> The waltz of the toreadors; tr. by Lucienne Hill. [Acting ed] French 1958
> 80p illus
> Social comedy. Difficulties of General St Pé, his nagging wife and his sweetheart, recently returned after 17 years absence. 3 acts 5 scenes 4m 7w 1 setting
> —Same
> *In* Plays of the year v8

This entry tells us that a play by Jean Anouilh entitled "The Waltz of the Toreadors" is published separately by French and also appears in a collection entitled "Plays of the Year v8." (For full information about the collection cited see Part II of this Volume.) The play has five scenes and three acts, requires a cast of four men and seven women, and requires one setting for production.

For radio and television plays the size of the cast is given but the number of scenes and settings is omitted. For puppet plays the cast is given only as a number of characters.

All plays are also listed under their titles followed by the name of the author. Full information on the play can be obtained by consulting the author entry.

Sample entry:

> The **Waltz** of the toreadors. Anouilh, J.

All plays which deal in whole or part with a particular subject are listed under that subject. Again full information will be found by consulting the main entry under the author's name.

Sample entry:

> **Christmas**
> Allan, D. C. Eyes that see not
> *c* Asbrand, K. Light up the world
> Brings, L. M. ed. The modern treasury of Christmas plays (22 plays)

Some collections may have the same subject for each play. In such cases the entry under that subject gives the editor or author and title of the collection followed by the number of plays. Thus in the sample subject entry above "The modern treasury of Christmas plays" contains twenty-two plays. The symbol *c* for Asbrand, "Light up the world" indicates that it is a play for children.

Plays in a distinctive form such as masques, mysteries and miracle plays, one act plays, pageants, pantomimes, puppet plays, plays in verse, radio plays and television plays are entered under the form as well as under subject.

Part II. List of Collections Indexed. Here can be found complete information concerning the collections indexed including publisher, date and paging.

Part III. Cast Analysis. Directions for use of this section appear at the beginning of Part III.

Part IV. Directory of Publishers. This gives full information including address of the publishers which are indicated only by abbreviation in Part I.

PLAY INDEX

1953-1960

PLAY INDEX

1953-1960

AN INDEX TO 4592 PLAYS IN
1735 VOLUMES

Edited by
Estelle A. Fidell
Dorothy Margaret Peake

NEW YORK
THE H. W. WILSON COMPANY
1963

Published 1963

Printed in the U.S.A.

Library of Congress Catalog Card No. (53-8990)

PREFACE

This volume indexes 4592 plays in 1735 volumes published during the period 1953-1960, and thus supplements the *Play Index: 1949-1952*, edited by Dorothy Herbert West and Dorothy Margaret Peake.

The policies and principles which were followed in the *Play Index: 1949-1952* have been continued in the preparation of this volume with two exceptions. In line with the practice in the Standard Catalog Series and Wilson Catalog Cards we have used title page form of the author's name. Exception to this has been made in the case of some foreign names where transliteration seemed advisable and in these cases we have followed Library of Congress. Also in the case of well-known authors, such as Shaw, Bernard, we have used one form with references from other forms. Also we have indexed all volumes of condensations in series, such as "Best Plays" and "Broadway's Best," by author and title only and the entry has been marked "condensation." We have omitted the cast and the note since these plays were not in a form suitable or intended for production. With these exceptions the policies outlined in the Preface to the *Play Index: 1949-1952* still prevail.

The publisher and editors wish to express their appreciation to those publishers who have supplied us with copies of their publications for indexing. Appreciation is also expressed to the various members of the staff who have assisted in the work, especially to Mrs. Agnes Bryceland who has had the chief responsibility of preparing copy for publication.

Part I
Author, Title and Subject Index

Directions for Use

Part I. **Author, Title and Subject Index.** In this Part there will be found entries under author, title and subject. The author entry is the main entry for the play and includes the following information: name of the author, title of the play, a descriptive phrase, the number of acts and scenes, the size of the cast and the number of sets required. In the case of single plays the publisher and date are given. If the play is part of a collection the name of the collection is given.

Sample entry:

Anouilh, Jean
The waltz of the toreadors; tr. by Lucienne Hill. [Acting ed] French 1958
80p illus
Social comedy. Difficulties of General St Pé, his nagging wife and his sweetheart, recently returned after 17 years absence. 3 acts 5 scenes 4m 7w 1 setting
—Same
In Plays of the year v8

This entry tells us that a play by Jean Anouilh entitled "The Waltz of the Toreadors" is published separately by French and also appears in a collection entitled "Plays of the Year v8." (For full information about the collection cited see Part II of this Volume.) The play has five scenes and three acts, requires a cast of four men and seven women, and requires one setting for production.

For radio and television plays the size of the cast is given but the number of scenes and settings is omitted. For puppet plays the cast is given only as a number of characters.

All plays are also listed under their titles followed by the name of the author. Full information on the play can be obtained by consulting the author entry.

Sample entry:

The **Waltz** of the toreadors. Anouilh, J.

All plays which deal in whole or part with a particular subject are listed under that subject. Again full information will be found by consulting the main entry under the author's name.

Sample entry:

Christmas
Allan, D. C. Eyes that see not
c Asbrand, K. Light up the world
Brings, L. M. ed. The modern treasury of Christmas plays (22 plays)

Some collections may have the same subject for each play. In such cases the entry under that subject gives the editor or author and title of the collection followed by the number of plays. Thus in the sample subject entry above "The modern treasury of Christmas plays" contains twenty-two plays. The symbol c for Asbrand, "Light up the world" indicates that it is a play for children.

Plays in a distinctive form such as masques, mysteries and miracle plays, one act plays, pageants, pantomimes, puppet plays, plays in verse, radio plays and television plays are entered under the form as well as under subject.

Part II. **List of Collections Indexed.** Here can be found complete information concerning the collections indexed including publisher, date and paging.

Part III. **Cast Analysis.** Directions for use of this section appear at the beginning of Part III.

Part IV. **Directory of Publishers.** This gives full information including address of the publishers which are indicated only by abbreviation in Part I.

Play Index, 1953-1960

Part I

Author, Title and Subject Index

A is for apple. LePelley, G.

A. A. Milne's The Red House mystery. Sergel, R.

A B C for safety. Hark, M. and Mc-Queen, N.

Abailard, Pierre
Forsyth, J. Héloise

Abandoned children. See Foundlings

Abbott, George. See Adler, R. and Ross, J. Damn Yankees; The pajama game; Bock, J. Fiorello; Merrill, B. New girl in town

Abbots
Ridge, A. Three mice for the abbot

Abe Lincoln goes to school. Very, A.

Abe Lincoln in Illinois. Sherwood, R. E.

Abe Lincoln—New Salem days. Chorpenning, C. B.

Abel, Lionel
Absalom
Philosophical Biblical tragedy about King David who transcends his situation by sacrificing his son Absalom. 3 acts 8 scenes 11m 1w extras 2 interiors 2 exteriors
In Machiz, H. ed. Artists' Theatre: four plays
The death of Odysseus
Odysseus, master of Ithaca after his return, is faced with fatal dilemma. 4m 1w extras 1 interior
In Playbook: five plays for a new theatre

Abelard, Peter. See Abailard, Pierre

Abe's winkin' eye. Fisher, A.

Abigail Adams. Spamer, C.

Abner Crane from Hayseed Lane. Dias, E. J.

"Abortion." O'Neill, E.

About time, too. Carter, C.

Abraham and Isaac (Brome manuscript)
Abraham and Isaac
Bible. Old Testament. Genesis. 15th century English mystery play about Abraham's sacrifice of Isaac. Verse play in Middle English with modernized spelling. 4 scenes 5m 1 interior 3 exteriors
Same as: The sacrifice of Isaac
In Everyman, and medieval miracle plays
Abraham and Isaac (dramatization) See Malcolmson, A. Abraham and Isaac
The sacrifice of Isaac
Same as: Abraham and Isaac
In Browne, E. M. ed. Religious drama, 2

Abraham, the patriarch
Abraham and Isaac (Brome manuscript) Abraham and Isaac
Abraham and Isaac (Brome manuscript) The sacrifice of Isaac
Daviot, G. The little dry thorn
Gassner, J. The Brome Abraham and Isaac

Abraham and Isaac. Abraham and Isaac (Brome manuscript)

Abraham and Isaac. Malcolmson, A.

Abraham Lincoln: with malice toward none. Kissen, F.

Absalom. Abel, L.

Absolutely horrid. Ilian, C.

Absolutely murder. LePelley, G.

Absolutism. See Despotism

Abstance, Louise. See Abstance, P. jt. auth.

Abstance, Polly, and Abstance, Louise
Aunt Vonnie on vexation
Comical pantomime about woman who gives advice to the lovelorn. 6m 10w 1 interior
In Abstance, P. and Abstance, L. Light-hearted pantomimes
Corny confessions
Humorous pantomime of girl's broken romance. 2m 2w 1 exterior
In Abstance, P. and Abstance, L. Light-hearted pantomimes
Cotton Road
Comical pantomime of humble farmers and a big landowner in deep South. 5m 2w 1 exterior
In Abstance, P. and Abstance, L. Light-hearted pantomimes
Feudin' in the mountains
Comical pantomime of mountaineer life. Verse play. 7m 2w 1 exterior
In Abstance, P. and Abstance, L. Light-hearted pantomimes
Gold in the West
Farcical pantomime. Sheriff captures villainous cowboys in old West. Verse play. 5m 1w extras 1 interior
In Abstance, P. and Abstance, L. Light-hearted pantomimes
A Hallowe'en adventure
Halloween pantomime. Three teenagers visit haunted house. Verse play. 3m 2w extras 1 interior
In Abstance, P. and Abstance, L. Light-hearted pantomimes
The hold-up at Hoecake Junction
Comical pantomime of old lady demolishing two gangsters with umbrella in old time general store. Verse play. 9m 2w 1 interior
In Abstance, P. and Abstance, L. Light-hearted pantomimes

Abstance, P. and Abstance, L.—*Continued*

Murder at the manor
   Humorous pantomime of melodrama wherein rich old uncle is mysteriously shot. 7m 4w 1 interior
   In Abstance, P. and Abstance, L. Lighthearted pantomimes

The pigskin parade
   Comical pantomine of football season at local high school. 9m 1w extras no setting
   In Abstance, P. and Abstance, L. Lighthearted pantomimes

Slender Ella
   Comical pantomime parody of fairy tale. Cinderella. 3 scenes 3m 5w extras 2 interiors
   In Abstance, P. and Abstance, L. Lighthearted pantomimes

Soapera
   Comical pantomime parody on soap opera: a mother-in-law comes to visit a couple. Verse play. 3m 2w 1 interior
   In Abstance, P. and Abstance, L. Lighthearted pantomimes

The valiant Valentine
   Comical melodramatic pantomime for Valentine's Day. Hero captures villain who stole his sweetheart's jewels. Verse play. 3m 2w 1 interior
   In Abstance, P. and Abstance, L. Lighthearted pantomimes

The **accident** of birth. Fisher, A. and Rabe, O.

Accident prevention. See Accidents—Prevention

Accidents
   Anthony, R. Jackknife
   Howe, C. V. The long fall
      See also First aid in illness and injury; School accidents

   Prevention
c Blossom, L. The safety elves
   Chorpenning, C. B. Radio rescue
c Close, E. The land of the traffic goblins
c Fisher, A. Many a slip
c Patterson, L. The safety school
c Stees, L. Red for danger
      See also Safety education

According to law. Houston, N.

Account rendered. Chown, H.

Achard, Marcel
   Rollo (adaptation) See Douglas, F. Rollo

The **Acharnians.** Aristophanes

Ackland, Rodney
   A dead secret. ₍French's Acting ed₎ French (London) 1958 102p illus
      Mystery. Miserly Miss Lummus died. Was it murder? 9m 6w extras 1 setting
   In Plays of the year v16

Acrobats
   Welles, R. The man of the house

Act without words, I. Beckett, S.

Act without words, II. Beckett, S.

Acting
   Armer, A. and Grauman, W. E. Final curtain
   Bissell, R.; Burrows, A. and Bissell, M. Say, darling

Dias, E. J. Stage bore
Howells, W. D. Yorick's love
   See also Theater

Acting for parts. Curtis, P. D.

The **actor.** Weiss, M. J.

Actors
   Dalzell, W. and Mitzman, N. Father's been to Mars
   Granby, F. Resort Hotel
   Keeney, C. H. Once an actor
   Kelly, G. The flattering word
   Lee, J. Career
   Massinger, P. The Roman actor
   Melville, A. Simon and Laura
   Pirandello, L. The mountain giants
   Priestley, J. B. Private rooms
   Rattigan, T. Harlequinade
   Roberts, M. A palm tree in a rose garden
   Rodgers, R. Me and Juliet
   Williams, N. The mountain
      See also Actresses; Strolling players; Theater

Actresses
   Anouilh, J. Mademoiselle Colombe
   Armer, A. and Grauman, W. E. Whatever became of Lola Woods
   Beloin, E. and Garson, H. In any language
   Bowen, T. Star dust
   Campion, C. On the road
   Curtis, P. D. Acting for parts
   Curtis, P. D. Autograph hunters
   Daily, D. T. Displaced
   Dias, E. J. Stage bore
   Gottlieb, A. Wake up, darling
   Granby, F. Resort Hotel
   Healy, J. Summer and stock
   Inge, W. A loss of roses
   Johnson, P. Ladies and females
   Jones, T. Saben revisited
   Krasna, N. Kind sir
   Martens, A. C. The grandma bandit
   Melville, A. Simon and Laura
   Mosel, T. Star in the summer night
   Posegate, E. D. The Christmas star
   Priestley, J. B. Private rooms
   Rattigan, T. Harlequinade
   Reach, J. Beautiful dreamers
   Richards, S. Half-hour, please
   Roberts, C. Mr Gaylord remembers
   Rodgers, R. Me and Juliet
   Thomas, B. Two of everything
      See also Actors; Strolling players; Theater

Adam (Biblical character)
   York plays. The creation of Adam and Eve
   York plays. The creation of man
   York plays. The Garden of Eden

Adamov, Arthur
   Ping-pong; tr. by Richard Howard. Grove 1959 153p
      Life in the metaphor of a ping pong game. its hits and misses, with constant improvements suggested by the players. 2 acts 12 scenes 5m 2w 7 interiors 1 exterior

Adamov, Arthur—*Continued*
  Professor Taranne; tr. by Albert Bermel
    Character study of eccentric professor.
    10m 4w 1 interior
    In Four modern French comedies
Adams, Abigail (Smith)
  Spamer, C. Abigail Adams
Adams, John, President U.S.
  Probst, G. Nature's most precious gift
  Wishengrad, M. The ground of justice
Adams, Samuel Hopkins
  Night bus (moving picture adaptation) See
    Riskin, R. It happened one night
Adam's rib hurts. Kirkpatrick, J.
Addams, Jane
  Kissen, F. Jane Addams: the good neighbor
Addis, Hazel
  Drama
    Burlesque of melodramas of fifty years
    ago. Verse play. 1 act 2 scenes 5m 2w
    1 exterior
    In Addis, H. On with the show
  The fishermen's dream
    Comedy. Two fishermen catch a mermaid. 1 act 2m 1w 1 exterior
    In Addis, H. On with the show
  Off the rocks
    Old man tells small boy about his former
    work as lighthouse keeper. 1 act 1m 1b
    1 exterior
    In Addis, H. On with the show
  Open house
    Domestic comedy. Neighbors come to
    visit a family that has just moved in.
    1 act 2 scenes 5m 4w 1 interior
    In Addis, H. On with the show
  St George's Day
    Boy remains true to his Boy Scout
    pledge, following the example of St
    George. 1 act 3m 1b 1 interior
    In Addis, H. On with the show
  Sellevision
    Parody of Shakespeare is used on a
    television program for sponsor's advertising. 1 act 3m 2w 1 exterior
    In Addis, H. On with the show
  What ho for the open road
    Farce. British road inspector visits
    group of indolent highway repair men,
    in search of a missing hole. Cockney
    dialect. 1 act 5m 1 exterior
    In Addis, H. On with the show
Addyman, Elizabeth
  Over the garden fence. English Theatre
    1955 94p (Guild Lib)
    Domestic comedy. Neighboring families
    in British suburb finally solve difficult
    problems which arise from two mothers'
    overindulgence of their respective teenaged sons. 3 acts 5 scenes 4m 4w 3 interiors
  The secret tent. English Theatre 1955 84p
    illus (Guild Lib)
    Sympathetic detective investigating murder of a woman discovers her past; he
    and her mother-in-law decide to keep it
    from the husband. 3 acts 4 scenes 3m 4w
    1 interior
Adjustment, Social. See Social adjustment
Adler, Marjorie Duhan
  Too much springtime. Dramatic 1955 82p
    illus
    Comedy. Dramatization of the novel:
    The mating season, by P. G. Wodehouse.
    Bertie Wooster needs the help of Jeeves,
    his valet to prevent romantic troubles.
    3 acts 4 scenes 7m 9w 2 interiors

Adler, Richard, and Ross, Jerry
  Damn. Yankees; a new musical. Book by
    George Abbott and Douglass Wallop,
    music and lyrics by Richard Adler and
    Jerry Ross. Random House 1956 164p
    illus
    Fantasy. Musical comedy based on the
    novel: The year the Yankees lost the
    pennant, by Douglass Wallop. Baseball
    fan sells soul to Devil so that his favorite
    team can beat the New York Yankees.
    2 acts 21 scenes 13m 7w extras 8 interiors
    1 exterior
  The pajama game; book by George Abbott and Richard Bissell. Music and
    lyrics by Richard Adler and Jerry Ross.
    Random House 1954 180p illus
    Musical comedy based on the novel:
    7½ cents, by Richard Bissell. Labor
    trouble in a midwestern pajama factory.
    2 acts 17 scenes 12m 6w extras 7 interiors
    3 exteriors
  The pajama game (condensation)
    In Theatre, 1954
The admirable Bashville. Shaw, B.
The admirable Crichton. Barrie, J. M.
Adolescence
  Anderson, R. A. and Sweeney, R. L.
    Boris and the spaceman
  Armer, A. and Grauman, W. E. Love
    lesson for Scotty
  Armer, A. and Grauman, W. E. No time
    for dames
  Burgess, C. V. Ken looks ahead
  Burgess, C. V. Trouble at "The Blue
    Lantern"
  Chase, M. Bernardine
  Dalzell, W. and Martens, A. C. Onions
    in the stew
  Dias, E. J. Out of this world
  Dias, E. J. The sands of time
  Dunlop, R. S. An overpraised season
  Faust, E. Oh, to be sixteen again!
  Fisher, A. and Rabe, O. Anonymous
    letter
  Foote, H. A young lady of property
  Greth, Le R. E. Miss President, please!
  Kent, W. Seventeen
  McCullers, C. The member of the wedding
  Martens, A. C. Battle of the budget
  Martens, A. C. Drag race
  Martens, A. C. Nobody loves a fat boy
  Payton, D. Father says no!
  Rattigan, T. Love in idleness
  Roskam, C. The puzzle
  Snyder, W. H. The departing
  Sommer, E. A roomful of roses
  Weiss, M. J. The actor
  Weiss, M. J. Greetings from . . .
  Weiss, M. J. Her big crush
  Weiss, M. J. Money talks
  Welch, R. Let's get out of here
  Williams, T. This property is condemned
    See also Boys; Girls; Youth
Adopted by Santa Claus. Page, F. R.
Adoption
  Chetham-Strode, W. The pet shop
  Fields, J. and De Vries, P. The tunnel
    of love
  Sergel, C. The family nobody wanted
A adventure. Davis, J. P.

Adventure and adventurers
  Emmons, D. G. John Jewitt, the slave
  Howard, V. Around the world—by way of America
  Olfson, L. Around the world in eighty days
  Olfson, L. Quentin Durward
  Warnick, C. and Pahl, M. Adventures of Marco Polo
Adventure story. Rattigan, T.
Adventurers. See Adventure and adventurers
Adventures in camp. Priestley, F.
Adventures of Marco Polo. Warnick, C. and Pahl, M.
The **adventures** of Tom Sawyer. Olfson, L.
The **adventurous** balloon. Spamer, C.
Advertising
  Howells, J. H. Good-bye, Gray Flannel
    See also Publicity
Advertising, Television in. See Television in advertising
Aelfgifu, Wife of Edwy, King of England
  Arblay, Madame d'. Edwy and Elgiva
Aeroplanes
  Johnston, D. A fourth for bridge
  Wilson, D. Flight of the dove
Aeschylus
  Agamemnon
    First play in the trilogy: Oresteia. Greek classical tragedy. Based on legend of murder of Agamemnon by his wife and her lover after the Trojan war. Verse play. 1 act 2 scenes 4m 2w extras 1 exterior
  In Eleven plays of the Greek dramatists
  —Same; tr. by Richmond Lattimore
  In Grene, D. and Lattimore, R. eds. The complete Greek tragedies v 1
  In Grene, D. and Lattimore, R. eds. Greek tragedies v 1
  —Same; [tr. by F. L. Lucas]
  In Lucas, F. L. ed. Greek drama for everyman
  —Same; tr. by Louis MacNeice
  In Dean, L. F. ed. Nine great plays. 1956 edition
  In Fitts, D. ed. Four Greek plays
  In Lind, L. R. ed. Ten Greek plays in contemporary translations
  —Same; tr. by George Thomson
  In Fitts, D. ed. Six Greek plays in modern translation
  —Same; tr. by Philip Vellacott
  In Aeschylus. The Oresteian trilogy
  Agamemnon (adaptation) See Alfred, W. Agamemnon
  Choephoroe
    Sequel to Agamemnon. Second play in the trilogy: Oresteia. Greek classical tragedy. Based on legend of Orestes and Electra, son and daughter of Agamemnon, telling how they avenged their father's murder. Verse play 1 act 2 scenes 5m 3w extras 2 exteriors
    Same as: The libation bearers
  In Eleven plays of the Greek dramatists
  —Same; tr. by George Thomson
  In Fitts, D. ed. Six Greek plays in modern translation

  In Robinson, C. A. ed. An anthology of Greek drama. 2d ser
  —Same; tr. by P. Vellacott
  In Aeschylus. The Oresteian trilogy
  The Eumenides
    Greek classical tragedy. Third part of the Oresteian trilogy. Sequel to: The libation bearers, or Choephoroe. Based on legend of Orestes and the Furies (Eumenides) the goddesses of retribution, who refused to absolve him of murder of his mother. Verse play. 3m 3w extras 1 exterior
  In Eleven plays of the Greek dramatists
  —Same; tr. by Richmond Lattimore
  In Grene, D. and Lattimore, R. eds. The complete Greek tragedies v 1
  In Grene, D. and Lattimore, R. eds. Greek tragedies v3
  —Same; tr. by George Thomson
  In Fitts, D. ed. Six Greek plays in modern translation
  In Robinson, C. A. ed. An anthology of Greek drama. 2d ser.
  —Same; tr. by Philip Vellacott
  In Aeschylus. The Oresteian trilogy
  The libation bearers
    Same as: Choephoroe
  In Grene, D. and Lattimore, R. eds. Greek tragedies v2
  In Grene, D. and Lattimore, R. eds. The complete Greek tragedies v 1

  Oresteia; tr. from the Greek by E. D. A. Morshead
    Verse play. Abridged stage version of the trilogy, made up of Agamemnon, The choephoroi; or, The libation bearers, and the Eumenides. Theme is the fate of the house of Orestes. Crime, revenge, and final forgiveness by the gods. 3 acts 7 scenes 8m 6w extras 2 interiors 3 exteriors
  In Griffin, A. V. Living theatre

  The Persians; tr. and with an introduction by Seth G. Benardete
    Historical. Defeat of Persians by Greeks at Salamis, 480 B.C. Verse play. 3m 1w extras 1 exterior
  In Grene, D. and Lattimore, R. eds. The complete Greek tragedies v 1

  Prometheus bound
    Greek classical tragedy. Based on the legend of demi-god who stole fire from heaven to help man. Verse play. 6m 1w extras 1 exterior
  In Lucas, F. L. ed. Greek drama for everyman
  —Same; tr. and with an introduction by David Grene
  In Grene, D. and Lattimore, R. eds. The complete Greek tragedies v 1
  In Grene, D. and Lattimore, R. eds. Greek tragedies v 1
  —Same; tr. by Edith Hamilton
  In Downer, A. S. ed. The art of the play
  —Same; tr. by Clarence W. Mendell
  In Robinson, C. A. ed. An anthology of Greek drama. 2d ser.
  —Same; tr. by Rex Warner
  In Lind, L. R. ed. Ten Greek plays in contemporary translations

Aeschylus—*Continued*
Seven against Thebes; tr. and with an
introduction by David Grene
> Tragedy. Battle between sons of Oedi-
> pus for sovereignty of Thebes. Verse
> play. 2m 2w extras 1 exterior

In Grene, D. and Lattimore, R. eds.
The complete Greek tragedies **v** 1
The suppliant maidens; tr.' and with an
introduction by Seth E. Benardete
> Greek legend of the Danaïdes, 50 daugh-
> ters of Danaus, who fled from Egypt to
> escape forced marriage. Verse play. 3m
> extras 1 exterior

In Grene, D. and Lattimore, R. eds.
The complete Greek tragedies **v** 1
About
Aristophanes. The frogs

Aesop
The fox and the grapes (dramatization)
See Moore, S. S. The fox and the
grapes
The hare and the tortoise (dramatization)
See Moore, S. S. The hare and the
tortoise
The lion and the mouse (dramatization)
See Moore, S. S. The lion and the
mouse
The miller, his son, and their ass (dramatization) See Moore, S. S. The miller,
his son, and their ass
The shepherd-boy and the wolf (dramatization) See Moore, S. S. The shepherd-boy and the wolf
The travellers and the bear (dramatization) See Moore, S. S. The travellers
and the bear

Affairs of state. Verneuil, L.

Affection. See Friendship

Afraid of the dark. Reach, J.

Africa, Central
Howard, V. The spear
Africa, South
Anderson, M. Lost in the stars
Race question
Komai, F. Cry, the beloved country

African folk-lore. See Folk-lore, African

Agamemnon (Mythology)
Aeschylus. Agamemnon
Alfred, W. Agamemnon
Euripides. Iphigenia in Aulis

Agamemnon. Aeschylus

Agamemnon. Alfred, W.

Aged, Killing of
Shoub, M. Ashes in the wind

Agg, Howard
Autumn term. [French's Acting ed]
French (London) 1953 20p
> Headmistress of English school realizes
> she must retire. 1 act 6w 1 interior

The happy day. [French's Acting ed]
French (London) 1953 22p illus (Little
plays of Sicily)
> In a convent orphanage in Sicily, a
> mute fourteen year old girl, miraculous-
> ly speaks her first word on Saint Rosa-
> lia's feast day. 1 act 7w 1 interior

Red plush. [French's Acting ed] French
(London) 1953 24p illus
> Romantic comedy. Daughter of English
> gentleman falls in love with footman, a
> nobleman in disguise. 1 act 3m 3w 1 in-
> terior

Silk and sawdust. [French's Acting ed]
French (London) 1953 33p illus (Little
plays of Sicily)
> Sicilian puppeteer, loyal to family tradi-
> tion, uses ruse to keep son from for-
> saking the profession. 1 act 3m 3w 1b
> 1 interior

Winter sunrise. [French's Acting ed]
French (London) 1954 25p illus
> Embittered woman changes her attitude
> toward daughter before it is too late.
> 1 act 6w 1 interior

Agnew, Edith J
Beyond Good Friday. Friendship Press
1953 24p
> At Easter dawn service in New Mexico,
> a young man, member of Penitentes, a
> local society of Flagellants, finds new
> meaning in Christ's atonement. 1 act
> 2m 2w lg 1 interior

Agrarian question. See Land tenure

Agricultural laborers

Great Britain

Wesker, A. Roots

Agricultural pests
c Miller, H. L. Garden hold-up

Agriculture
c Ahrens, C. Jon's helpers
Emurian, E. K. Stewards of the soil

Aguirre, Isidora
Express for Santiago; adapted by Stanley
Richards
> Farce. After a couple have left on a
> trip the wife is afraid she left a pan
> of water boiling on her stove. 3m 2w
> extras 1 exterior

In The Best short plays, 1959-1960

Ah, men! Brown, A. M.

Ah, wilderness! O'Neill, E.

Ah, yesterday! Reach, J.

Ahrens, Carsten
c Jon's helpers
> A boy who wants to be a farmer is
> visited by soil, wind, rain, and other
> elements. 1b extras 1 exterior

In Birdsall, R. ed. Creative plays for
every school month

Ah-yo-ka. Spamer, C.

Aiken, Conrad
Mr Arcularis. Harvard Univ. Press 1957
83p
> Fantasy. Based on the author's short
> story. Man under anesthesia dreams of
> a cruise during which he comes to
> understand his dead mother's affair with
> his uncle. Background music 2 acts 8
> scenes 10m 5w 4 interiors 1 exterior

Air pilots
Rattigan, T. Flare path

Air rescue service. See Search and rescue
operations

Air sea rescue. Webber, J.

Air travel
c Vandenburgh, M. A "globester" trip

Airmail from Cyprus. Hall, W.

Ajax. Sophocles

Akutagawa, Ryunosuke. See Kanin, F. and
Kanin, M. Rashomon

Aladdin. Newman, D.

Aladdin steps out. Hark, M. and
McQueen, N.

Alamo

Siege, 1836

Yelvington, R. A cloud of witnesses

Alaska

Peterson, L. Stand-in for a murderer

The **Albany** depot. Howells, W. D.

Albee, Edward

The death of Bessie Smith

Set in the South. Emotional conflict between an interne and a nurse in hospital for white people. 8 scenes 5m 2w 4 interiors

In Albee, E. The zoo story; The death of Bessie Smith; The sandbox

The sandbox

A couple go to the beach with the wife's aged mother. 1 act 3m 2w 1 exterior

In Albee, E. The zoo story; The death of Bessie Smith; The sandbox

In The Best short plays, 1959-1960

The zoo story

A mentally disturbed man forms a terrible plan when he sees a placid man reading newspaper on park bench. 1 act 2m 1 exterior

In Albee, E. The zoo story; The death of Bessie Smith; The sandbox

Albert, consort of Queen Victoria

Housman, L. "A good lesson!"

Albery, James

Two roses

Proud impoverished father and the effect of suddenly acquired wealth on his two daughters. 3 acts 3 scenes 5m 4w 2 interiors 1 exterior

In Rowell, G. ed. Nineteenth century plays

Albery, Peter

Anne Boleyn

Historical tragedy. Marriage of Anne Boleyn and Henry VIII, King of England, and her downfall. 4 acts 11 scenes 8m 5w extras 5 interiors

In Plays of the year v14

Alcestis. Euripides

The **alchemist.** Jonson, B.

Alchemy

Jonson, B. The alchemist

Alcoholics

Arden, J. The party

Freeman, L. The answer

Inge, W. Come back, Little Sheba

Neuenburg, E. Distant thunder

O'Neill, E. A moon for the misbegotten

Sheffield, J. The forgotten land

Alcott, Louisa May

Little women (dramatization) See Howard, V. Happy holidays for little women

Little women (dramatization) See Morley, O. J. Little women

About

Spamer, C. Louisa May Alcott

Alden, Priscilla (Mullins)

Howells, W. D. Priscilla

Spamer, C. Priscilla Alden

Alden, Raymond

The Christmas Tree Forest (dramatization) See Clark, I. S. The Christmas Tree Forest

Aleichem, Sholem

Perl, A. Tevya and the first daughter

Tevya stories (dramatization) See Perl, A. Tevya and his daughters

For a play about this author see Rabinowitz, Shalom

Alexander the Great

Lee, N. The rival queens

Rattigan, T. Adventure story

Williams, N. Night of storm

Alexander, Alex

Cute as a button. Bakers Plays 1954 96p (Baker's Royalty plays)

Farce. Improvident social climber tries to promote wealthy marriages for her children. 3 acts 4 scenes 4m 6w 1 interior

Right under your nose. Bakers Plays 1954 99p illus (Baker's Royalty plays)

Domestic comedy. Widow with wild ideas for occupying her time, finally finds solution to her problems. 3 acts 4 scenes 4m 6w 1 interior

Alexander, Ronald

Grand prize. Dramatists 1955 77p front

Farce. Career girl wins TV contest, reward of which is being "Boss for a day." 3 acts 4 scenes 6m 3w 1 interior

Holiday for lovers. Dramatists 1957 80p illus

Romantic comedy. European tour of American family brings romance and happiness to all. 2 acts 5 scenes 4m 5w 4 interiors

Time out for Ginger. [Rev] Acting ed. Dramatists 1953 86p illus

Domestic comedy. Father's views on gym classes and daughter's place on football team bring notoriety to the family. 3 acts 4 scenes 5m 5w 1 interior

Alfonso III (VIII) King of Castile

Grillparzer, F. The Jewess of Toledo

Alfonso VIII, King of Castile. See Alfonso III (VIII) King of Castile

Alfred, William

Agamemnon. Knopf 1954 88p

Adaptation of the tragedy by Aeschylus. Based on legend of murder of Agamemnon by his wife and her lover after the Trojan War. Verse play. 4 acts 10 scenes 9m 4w extras 4 interiors

Algerian folk-lore. See Folk-lore, Algerian

Ali Baba and the forty thieves. Klein, M. W.

Alice in Bibleland. Wills, G.

Alice in Puzzleland. Fisher, A. and Rabe, O.

Alice in Wonderland. Miller, M.

Aliens

Anderson, W. "Me, Candido!"

Apstein, T. Come share my house

Brickenden, C. Zanorin

All aboard for Christmas. Hark, M. and McQueen, N.

The **all-American tour.** Newman, D.

All for love. Dryden, J.

"All hail the power of Jesus' name." Schofield, J. A. and Joudry, R. C.

All Hallows' Eve. See Halloween

All in the family. Hatlen, T. W.

All in the UN. Fisher, A. and Rabe, O.

All my sons. Miller, A.

All of a sudden. Raynor, M.

All out for Halloween. Hark, M. and McQueen, N.

All summer long. Anderson, R.

All that fall. Beckett, S.

All that glitters. Asbrand, K.

All that money can buy. Totheroh, D. and Benét, S. V.

All the king's men. Warren, R. P.

All the world around. Fisher, A. and Rabe, O.

All the world's a stage. Sinclair, L.

All this and Alan, too. Allred, J.

All this and jumble too. Dinner, W. and Morum, W.

Allan, Dorothy C.
Eyes that see not
  Allegory in verse. On Christmas Day blind man spurns boy's plea to turn from hard road of wordly amibtion to pleasant road leading to their Father's home. Choral music. 2m 1b 1 exterior
  In Cahill, E. M. ed. Celebrating Christmas

Allegories
Allan, D. C. Eyes that see not
Camus, A. State of siege
Čapek, J. and Čapek, K. The world we live in
Dekker, T. The Whore of Babylon
Everyman. Everyman
Everyman. The moral pay of Everyman
Everyman. The summoning of Everyman
Greene, N. D. The seekers
Howard, P. The dictator's slippers
Howard, P. We are tomorrow
Johnston, R. A. Everyman
Saroyan, W. The man with the heart in the highlands
Schloss, M. F. Totentanz
Weinstock, D. Dawn will come
Wilder, T. The skin of our teeth
Williams, T. Camino Real
Zeiger, H. Five days

Allegro. Rodgers, R. and Hammerstein, O.

Allen, Janet
Kind cousin. Deane 1955 56p illus ("Deane's" Ser. of plays)
  Ghost of dead aunt prevents jealous cousin from enjoying use of old English family mansion she connived to wrest from dead aunt's sister. Background music. 2 acts 4 scenes 2m 5w 1 interior

Allen, Mark
Turn any stone. Formative Press 1954 105p
  Romantic comedy. Successful young writer of detective stories turns to serious writing, helps father, a retired sea captain, return to sea, and wins girl he loves. 2 acts 5m 3w 1 interior

Allensworth, Carl
Ring once for Central
  Comedy. Busybody Vermont woman, listening in on party wire, sends search parties out in storm for supposedly lost girl. 1 act 3m 2w 1 interior
  In Smith, B. and others, eds. A treasury of non-royalty one-act plays

Allred, Joan
All this and Alan, too
  When Diane discovers that shy girlfriend Lennie likes her escort Alan, she pretends to be sick so Lennie can go to college dance with him. 1 act 5w 1 interior
  In Kamerman, S. E. ed. Blue-ribbon plays for girls

Allred, Pearl, and Allred, Thatcher
To the lovely Margaret
  Comedy. Brainy co-ed is left dateless at last moment for Prom but another young man comforts her. 1 act 2m 3w 1 interior
  In Smith, B. and others, eds. A treasury of non-royalty one-act plays

Allred, Thatcher. See Allred, P. jt. auth.

An **almanac** of liberty. Rose, R.

Almshouses
  Ireland
Gregory, Lady. The workhouse ward

Alone. Lantz, J. E. and Lantz, R. C.

Along came a blackbird. Hopper, V. S.

Altogether! Heave! Carlson, B. W.

Ama (condensation) Kwanze, M.

Amateur journalism
Gordon, K. The babbling Brooks

Amateur radio stations
Chorpenning, C. B. Radio rescue

Amateur theatricals
Crane, B. Stage-stricken
c Goldburg, N. and Goldburg, R. What's Chanuko without a play?

Ambition
Eliot, T. S. The confidential clerk
Mosel, T. The presence of the enemy
Olfson, L. Macbeth

Amelia Earhart. Spamer, C.

America remembers. Chandler, R.

America sings. Shrout, B. L.

America the Beautiful. Emurian, E. K.

American drama

  Colonial period
Custis, G. W. P. Pocahontas; or, The settlers of Virginia
Godfrey, T. The prince of Parthia

  Revolutionary period
Dunlap, W. André
Tyler, R. The contrast

  Early 19th century
Barker, J. N. Superstition
Bird, R. M. The broker of Bogota
Payne, J. H. and Irving, W. Charles the Second
Willis, N. P. Tortesa the usurer

American Education Week
c Woolsey, J. and Sechrist, E. H. The good old days

American folk-drama. See Folk-drama, American

American folk-lore. See Folk-lore, American

American portrait. Lavery, E.

The **American** spirit. Hennessy, M. A.

Americans in England
Gattey, C. N. and Bramley-Moore, Z. Mrs Adams and Eve
Rattigan, T. The sleeping prince

Americans in Europe
Bolton, G. Child of fortune

Americans in Italy
Hayes, A. The girl on the Via Flaminia
Laurents, A. The time of the cuckoo

Americans in Japan
Wincelberg, S. The conqueror

Americans in Okinawa
Patrick, J. The Teahouse of the August
Moon

Americans in Switzerland
Yaffe, J. The deadly game

Americans in Yugoslavia
Hivnor, R. The ticklish acrobat

Amicable parting. Kaufman, G. S. and
MacGrath, L.

Amish Mennonites. See Mennonites

The amorous goldfish. Voysey, M.

The amorous prawn. Kimmins, A.

Amusement parks
Richards, S. Tunnel of Love

Anastasia. Maurette, M.

Anastasiia Nikolaevna, Grand Duchess of
Russia
Maurette, M. Anastasia

Anatol. Schnitzler, A.

Anatomists
Thomas, D. The doctor and the devils

The anchor. Speare, E. G.

And a song was born. Marston, J.

And it's Christmas! Atherton, M.

And so say all of us! Cooper, D. S.

And there was light. Nappier, P.

Andersen, Hans Christian
Elves and the shoemaker (dramatization)
See Chadwick, E. Shoes for a queen
The Emperor's new clothes (dramatiza-
tion) See Newman, D. The Emperor's
new clothes
The Emperor's nightingale (dramatiza-
tion) See Windsor, H. J. The Em-
peror's nightingale
The little fir tree (dramatization) See
Very, A. The little fir tree
Little Ida and the flowers (dramatization)
See Ormandy, E. Little Ida and the
flowers
The princess on the pea (dramatization)
See Miller, H. L. The real princess
The real Princess (dramatization) See
Newman, D. The real Princess
The red shoes (dramatization) See Short,
R. The red shoes
The Snow Queen (dramatization) See
Magito, S. and Weil, R. The Snow
Queen
The tinder box (dramatization) See Dil-
lon, F. The tinder box

Anderson, Bruce F.
Prejudice unlimited
Radio play. Prejudiced American who
hates all other nationalities, para-
doxically finds it difficult to exist with-
out their contributions to civilization.
Background music. 3m
In Prescott, H. ed. Patrioscript

Anderson, Don
Watermelon
Radio play. Kind people in small town
try to help save life of child stricken
with rare blood disease. Background
music. 6m 1w
In Prescott, H. ed. Patrioscript

Anderson, Maxwell
Bad seed. [Rev] Dramatists 1957 84p illus
Dramatization of the novel by William
March. Mother discovering her eight-
year-old daughter has inherited homicidal tendencies and is a murderess,
tries to protect society in her own way,
but fails. Background music. 2 acts 8
scenes 7m 4w 1g 1 interior
Trade edition published by Dodd

The bad seed (condensation)
In The Best plays of 1954-1955
In Theatre, 1955

Elizabeth the Queen
Verse play. Political entanglements and
tragic outcome of love affair of Eliza-
beth I of England and Earl of Essex.
Play within a play. 3 acts 7 scenes 19m
5w extras 4 interiors
In Anderson, M. Four verse plays
In A Treasury of the theatre

The feast of Ortolans
Tragedy. Dinner party of nobles is interrupted by outbreak of French Revolution. 1 act 14m 3w extras 1 interior
In Smith, B. and others, eds. A treasury
of non-royalty one-act plays

High Tor
Fantasy, partly in verse. Ghosts of
Dutch crew help save ancestral moun-
tain top of Van Dorn near Tappan Zee
in New York State. 3 acts 6 scenes
16m 2w 1 exterior
In Anderson, M. Four verse plays
In Gaver, J. ed. Critics' choice

Lost in the stars
Tragedy. Dramatization of Alan Paton's novel "Cry the beloved country"
about an African Negro preacher's
search for his wayward son. 2 acts
18 scenes 26m 8w 9 interiors 2 exteriors
In Hewes, H. ed. Famous American
plays of the 1940's

Mary of Scotland
Life of Mary Stuart, Queen of the
Scots, from her arrival in Scotland to
claim her throne until her imprison-
ment by Elizabeth I of England. Verse
play. 3 acts 7 scenes 25m 6w extras
4 interiors 1 exterior
In Anderson, M. Four verse plays

The miracle of the Danube
Radio play. A miracle wrought by appa-
rition of Jesus Christ frees political prisoners. 7m
In The Best short plays, 1957

Winterset
Verse play. Social injustice based on
Sacco-Vanzetti case. Son of "framed"
man realizes futility of revenge. 3 acts
5 scenes 15m 4w extras 1 interior 1 ex-
terior
In Anderson, M. Four verse plays
In Gaver, J. ed. Critics' choice
In Griffin, A. V. Living theatre
In Quinn, A. H. ed. Representative
American plays
See also Stallings, Laurence, jt. auth.

Anderson, R. A. and Sweeney, R. L.
Boris and the briefcase. Eldridge 1959
25p (Eldridge Popular one-act playscripts)
Domestic comedy. A boy finds a briefcase filled with secret documents, but
his family refuses to believe him. 1 act
4m 3w extras 1 interior

Anderson, R. A. and Sweeney, R. L.—*Cont.*
Boris and the spaceman. Eldridge 1958
22p (Eldridge Popular one-act playscripts)
Domestic comedy. The magic tricks thirteen year old Boris learns from a visiting spaceman throw family into confusion. 1 act 3m 4w extras 1 interior
True blue and trusted. Eldridge 1959 29p
(Eldridge Novelties)
Burlesque of old fashioned melodrama.
Grandma knocks out villain just as he
is about to marry heroine thus saving
the day for the hero. 1 act 2 scenes
4m 4w 1 interior 1 exterior

Anderson, Robert
All summer long. French 1955 138p front
Based on the novel: A wreath and a
curse, by Donald Wetzel. Only his
crippled older brother is willing to help
an eleven-year-old boy in his efforts to
save their family's riverbank house,
threatened by flood. 2 acts 9 scenes 3m
3w 1b 1 setting
Also published in trade edition
Silent night, lonely night. French 1958
76p illus
A lonely man and woman by chance
spend Christmas Eve together in an inn
in New England. 2 acts 4 scenes 3m 3w
1 interior
Trade edition published by Random
House
Tea and sympathy. French 1955 92p illus
Boy in New England preparatory school
is unjustly accused of homosexuality.
3 acts 4 scenes 9m 2w 1 interior
Trade edition published by Random
House
—Same
In Best American plays; 4th ser
In New voices in the American theatre
Tea and sympathy (condensation)
In The Best plays of 1953-1954
In Theatre, 1954

Anderson, Sherwood
The triumph of the egg
Dramatization of episodes in author's
book of short stories. Restaurant owner
entertains customer with egg tricks. 2m
1w 1b extras 1 setting
In The Best short plays, 1957
The triumph of the egg (dramatization)
See O'Neil, R. The triumph of the egg

Anderson, Walt
"Me, Candido!" Dramatists 1958 77p illus
Puerto Rican family, alcoholic Irish-
man, and lonely old woman get into
trouble with law when they try to take
care of Puerto Rican orphan boy. 2 acts
10 scenes 8m 6w 1b 1g 6 interiors 1 exterior
The **Andersonville** trial. Levitt, S.

André, John
Dunlap, W. André
Fisher, A. and Rabe, O. Not for sale
André. Dunlap, W.

Andreev, Leonid
He who gets slapped; tr. from the Rus-
sian by Gregory Zilboorg
Tragic love of circus clown for a beauti-
ful young equestrienne. 3 acts 10m 3w
extras 1 interior
In Tucker, S. M. ed. Twenty-five mod-
ern plays
Androcles and the lion. Shaw, B.
Andromachê. Euripides
Andromache. Racine, J.
Andy Hardy. Rouverol, A.

Andy's gun. Spamer, C.
Angel in the looking-glass. Fisher, A.
The **angel** in the window. Preston, E. E.
Angels
c Hollinshead, L. M. Thank you, God for
everything
Hope, A. J.; Mary Francis, Sister, and
Birder, D. The complaining angel
Preston, E. E. The angel in the window
The **angry** alphabet. Curtis, P. D.
Animal coloration. See Color of animals
Animal locomotion
c Spamer, C. Hippety hop
Animals
c Carpenter, F. A day of good deeds
c Carpenter, F. Doctor Fox
c Carpenter, F. The magic owl
c Carpenter, F. The sick fox
c Carpenter, F. The tale of good faith
c Carpenter, F. Tiger in the wood
c Miller, H. L. Who's who at the zoo
Rees, P. Mix-up-atosis
c Spamer, C. The constable's duty
c Spamer, C. Friends
c Spamer, C. The mystery
c Spamer, C. Our dumb friends
c Spamer, C. The plight of the tree
c Very, A. The cock and the fox
c Werner, S. Home, sweet home
See also names of various animals
Animals, Color of. See Color of animals
Animals, Cruelty to. See Animals, Treat-
ment of
Animals, Movements of. See Animal loco-
motion
Animals, Treatment of
Williams, T. The strangest kind of ro-
mance
c Woolsey, J. and Sechrist, E. H. Mother
Goose gives advice
Anna Christie. O'Neill, E.
Annajanska, the Bolshevik Empress. Shaw,
B.
**Anne Boleyn, consort of Henry VIII, King
of England**
Albery, P. Anne Boleyn
Anne Boleyn. Albery, P.
Anniversary Day. Bate, S.
Anniversary waltz. Chodorov, J. and
Fields, J.
The **Annunciation.** Coventry plays
Annunciation of the Virgin Mary. See Mary,
Virgin—Annunciation
Anonymous letter. Fisher, A. and Rabe, O.
Anonyms and pseudonyms
Carmichael, F. More than meets the eye
Another life. Feutinger, J.
Another part of the forest. Hellman, L.
Another summer. Snyder, W. H.
Anouilh, Jean
Antigone; adapted and tr. by Lewis
Galantière
Tragedy. Adaptation of "Antigone" by
Sophocles. Based on Greek legend of
Antigone's loyalty to her rebel brother,
Polynices, against Creon, King of Thebes.
8m 4w extras 1 setting
In Anouilh, J. Five plays **v 1**

Anouilh, Jean—*Continued*

In Watson, E. B. and Pressey, B. eds.
Contemporary drama: eleven plays

Ardèle; tr. from Ardèle; ou, La Marguerite, by Lucienne Hill
French bedroom farce set in a large country house inhabited by retired general with amorous ideas, his nagging invalid wife, his sister, her lover, and others. 3 acts 4m 4w 1b 1g 1 interior

In Anouilh, J. Five plays v2

In Cordell, R. A. and Matson, L. eds.
The off-Broadway theatre

Becket; or, The honor of God; tr. by Lucienne Hill. Coward-McCann 1960 128p
Historical drama. Personalities of Thomas Becket and King Henry II in 12th century England dramatize rivalry between church and state. 4 acts 13m 3w 3 interiors 1 exterior

Cecile; or, The school for fathers; English version by Luce and Arthur Klein
Courtship in 17th century France. Hypocritical father protects his daughter's reputation. 1 act 3m 2w extras 1 exterior

In Bentley, E. ed. From the modern repertoire; ser. 3

The ermine (L'Hermine) tr. by Miriam John
Tragedy. Impoverished young Frenchman murders his sweetheart's wealthy aunt. 3 acts 8m 7w 3 interiors

In Anouilh, J. Five plays v1

In Plays of the year v13

Eurydice (Legend of lovers) tr. by Kitty Black
Modernized version in French setting of legend of Orpheus who failed to fulfil the necessary condition for bringing wife, Eurydice, back from the dead. 3 acts 10m 5w extras 2 interiors

In Anouilh, J. Five plays v 1

The fighting cock; adapted by Lucienne Hill. Coward-McCann 1960 121p
Comedy. Principled general with Spartan temperament learns that life has to be lived. 2 acts 3 scenes 10m 4w 1 interior 1 exterior

The lark; adapted by Lillian Hellman. [Acting ed] Dramatists 1957 59p illus
Joan of Arc's life and her part in French history portrayed in flashbacks at her trial. Musical background. 2 acts 15m 5w extras 1 setting
Trade edition published by Random House

In Anouilh, J. Five plays v2

In Gassner, J. ed. Twenty best European plays on the American stage

In A Treasury of the theatre
—Same; tr. by Christopher Fry. Oxford 1956 [c1955] 103p

The lark (condensation)
In The Best plays of 1955-1956
In Theatre, 1956

Mademoiselle Colombe; adapted by Louis Kronenberger. [Acting ed] French 1954 111p illus
Romantic comedy. Happiness of young couple jeopardized by wife's success in a play starring her mother-in-law. Set in early 20th century Paris. 2 acts 4 scenes 10m 5w 3 interiors
Trade edition published by Coward-McCann
—Same
In Anouilh, J. Five plays v2

Medea; English version by Lothian Small
Tragedy. based on the Greek legend of a jealous woman's revenge. 4m 2w extras 2 exteriors

In Plays of the year v15

The rehearsal; tr. by Lucienne Hill
During a rehearsal of a play for a charity ball a French countess finds way to break up her husband's affair with girl of lower middle class. 3 acts 5 scenes 4m 3w 2 interiors

In Anouilh, J. Five plays v 1

Restless heart; tr. by Lucienne Hill
A girl, whose family conducts a small orchestra in cheap hotel, falls in love with wealthy man but her family's crude manners prevent her happiness. 3 acts 6m 9w extras 1 interior

In Anouilh, J. Five plays v2

Romeo and Jeannette; tr. by Miriam John
Young Frenchman falls in love with his fiancée's sister. 4 acts 4m 3w 2 interiors

In Anouilh, J. Five plays v 1

Thieves' carnival; English version by Lucienne Hill
Comedy. Hilarious situations involving two rich young ladies, two fortune hunters and three pickpockets in various disguises. 4 acts 7m 3w 1g extras 2 interiors 1 exterior

In Bentley, E. ed. The modern theatre v3

Time remembered. English version by Patricia Moyes. French 1959 82p illus
Romantic comedy. Young milliner bears striking resemblance to a prince's dead sweetheart. 2 acts 5 scenes 14m 3w 2 interiors 2 exteriors
Trade edition published by Coward-McCann
—Same
In Anouilh, J. Five plays v2

Time remembered (condensation)
In The Best plays of 1957-1958
In Broadway's best, 1958

The waltz of the toreadors; tr. by Lucienne Hill. [Acting ed] French 1958 80p illus
Social comedy. Difficulties of General St Pé, his nagging wife and his sweetheart, recently returned after 17 years absence. 3 acts 5 scenes 4m 7w 1 setting
Trade and paper editions published by Coward-McCann
—Same
In Plays of the year, v8

The waltz of the toreadors (condensation)
In The Best plays of 1956-1957
In Broadway's best, 1957

Ansky, S.
The Dybbuk; in the English version by Henry G. Alsberg
Yiddish drama. Tragedy concerned with superstitious belief in demoniacal possession and exorcism. Based on a Jewish folk tale. 4 acts 21m 13w extras 2 interiors 1 exterior

In Gassner, J. ed. Twenty best European plays on the American stage

The **answer.** Freeman, L.

The **answer.** Smith, W. S.

Answering the call. Emmons, D. G.

The **ant** bed. Emery, C.

Anthony, Rock
Jackknife. French 1957 80p
Romantic comedy. Three people pretend to have been injured in accident in order to collect insurance money. 3 acts 4 scenes 7m 2w 1 interior

Anthony of Padua, Saint
Maeterlinck, M. A miracle of Saint Antony

Anthony, Susan Brownell
Spamer, C. Susan B. Anthony

Antigone. Anouilh, J.

Antigone. Sophocles

Anti-Nazi movement
Hellman, L. Watch on the Rhine

Antipathies. See Prejudices and antipathies

Antisemitism
Marlowe, C. The Jew of Malta
See also Jewish question

Antonius, Marcus
Olfson, L. Julius Caesar
Shakespeare, W. Antony and Cleopatra

Antony, Marc. See Antonius, Marcus

Antony and Cleopatra. Shakespeare, W.

Antony of Padua, Saint. See Anthony of Padua, Saint

Ants
Spewack, S. Under the sycamore tree

Any old toys. Chitty, A. W. I.

Any other business. Ross, G. and Singer, C.

Anything for father. Asbrand, K.

Aoi no uye. Komparu, Z. U.

Apache Indians

Wars, 1883-1886
Nichols, D. Stagecoach

Apartment houses
Woskoff, V. Castle in the village

Apollo
Euripides. Ion

The **Apollo** of Bellac. Giraudoux, J.

Apostle of freedom. Fisher, A. and Rabe, O.

Apostles
Emurian, E. K. The first breakfast
Emurian, E. K. The Last Supper
Emurian, E. K. The living dramatization of the Beatitudes
Phillips, J. B. The calling of the disciples
Phillips, J. B. Christ the Son of God
Phillips, J. B. Jesus returns to Galilee
c Spamer, C. M. Jesus and the fishermen

Apothecaries. See Pharmacists

Apparitions
Kwanze, M. Suma Genji
Williams, T. The purification
See also Ghosts

Appell, Don
Lullaby. Dramatists 1954 72p illus
Dominating mother almost ruins her son's marriage. 2 acts 4 scenes 2m 2w 2 interiors

The **apple** cart. Shaw, B.

Applegarth, Margaret T.
Color blind
An artist discovers that children of every race and nationality are children of God. Hymn singing. 3 acts 3w 1b 1g extras 1 interior
In Breck, F. E. ed. Playlets and poems for church school

Home Sweet Home
Grandma Moses paints picture to show how a Maine farmer decided to help refugees. Background music. 2 scenes 1m 2w extras 1 interior
In Applegarth, M. T.; Daily, D. T. and Wolfe, B. S. Four playettes

Were you there?
Church congregation is rebuked for discriminating against Negro Christian visitor from Nigeria. Background music. 2 scenes 1m 1w extras 1 interior
In Applegarth, M. T.; Daily, D. T. and Wolfe, B. S. Four playettes

Apples in the wilderness. McCaslin, N.

Appleseed, Johnny. See Chapman, John

The **Appletons** and the UN. Garver, J.

Appointment in Eden. Verity, E. and Allen, V.

The **apprentice.** Murphy, A.

Apprentices
Murphy. A. The apprentice

April Fool's Day
c Martens, A. C. Weather or not
c Newman, D. The magic goose

Apstein, Theodore
The beams of our house
Wanton Mexican woman who deserts her husband returns to find her place taken by another. Background music. 3 scenes 4m 3w extras 1 setting
In The Best short plays, 1952-1953

Come share my house. French 1960 80p illus
American student brings Mexican wife back to New York where they face poverty and hostility. 3 acts 7m 7w extras 2 interiors

Fortunata writes a letter
Domestic comedy set in Central America. Woman offers chickens to feed war orphans. 1 act 2m 1w 1 interior
In The Best short plays, 1957

A remittance from Spain
Aging beauty lives by her wits in Mexican resort hotels. Background music. 1 act 3m 3w 1 interior
In The Best short plays of 1953-1954

Arab-Jewish relations. See Jewish-Arab relations

Arabian folk-lore. See Folk-lore, Arabian

Arabian Nights
Ali Baba and the forty thieves (dramatization) See Klein, M. W. Ali Baba and the forty thieves

Arabian Nights (as subject)
c Newman, D. Aladdin

Aranda tribe
Peterson, L. Sticks and stones

Arason, Jón, Bp.
Sveinbjörnsson, T. Bishop Jón Arason

Arbie, the bug boy. Conkle, E. P.

The **arbitration.** Menander

Arblay, Frances (Burney) d'
Robinson, R. Fanny Burney's resignation
For a play by this author see Arblay, Madame d'

Arblay, Madame d'
Edwy and Elgiva; ed. with an introduction by Miriam J. Benkovitz. Shoe String 1957 93p
Tragedy of 10th century Anglo-Saxon England. Conflict between church and state is focussed on church's opposition, led by Archbishop Dunstan, to King Edwy's marriage to Elgiva. 5 acts 75 scenes 15m 2w extras 3 interiors 1 exterior

Arbor Day
c Fisher, A. On strike
c Hark, M. and McQueen, N. A day for trees
c Levofsky, R. A house for Duke
c Newman, D. In honor of trees
c Woolsey, J. and Sechrist, E. H. The great Tree Council

Archaeologists, English
Trease, G. Letters of gold

Architects
Ibsen, H. The master builder
O'Neill, E. The great God Brown

Archy and Mehitabel. Kleinsinger, G.

Ardèle. Anouilh, J.

Arden, Jane
The party
At her seventeenth birthday party, a girl learns how much alcoholic father needs her sympathetic understanding. 2 acts 5 scenes 3m 3w 1 interior
In Plays of the year v18

Ardrey, Robert
Sing me no lullaby. Dramatists 1955 68p
At reunion, college friends face problem of conflicting loyalties when they learn one of their members is object of federal security investigation. 3 acts 6m 3w 1 interior

Ardvorlich's wife. Bottomley, G.

Are teachers human? Reach, J.

Are you thrifty? Russell, S. P.

Arise, thy light is come! DeWitt, R. H.

Aristocracy
Chekhov, A. The cherry orchard
Probst, G. Nature's most precious gift
Williams, N. The king decides

Aristophanes
The Acharnians
Greek classical comedy. Athenian farmer makes a separate peace treaty all by himself with Sparta. 16m 4w extras 1 interior 1 exterior
In Casson, L. ed. Masters of ancient comedy
The birds; an English version by Dudley Fitts. Harcourt 1957 181p
Greek classical comedy. Fantasy. Two Athenians persuade birds to build a city called Cloudcuckooland, in the air to cut off the gods from men. 20m 2w extras 1 exterior
—Same
In Fitts, D. ed. Four Greek plays
In Fitts, D. ed. Six Greek plays in modern translation
—Same; with an introduction by Dudley Fitts and illus. by Marian Parry. Heritage 1959 52p illus
Bound (inverted) with the author's "The frogs"
—Same; tr. by Benjamin Bickley Rogers
In Aristophanes. Five comedies

The clouds; tr. by Benjamin Bickley Rogers
Greek classical satire in verse on sophistical system of Socrates' educational methods as contrasted to the Men of Marathon or Right and Wrong Logic. 1 act 10m extras 1 exterior
In Aristophanes. Five comedies
In Eleven plays of the Greek dramatists
In Lucas, F. L. ed. Greek drama for everyman
In Robinson, C. A. ed. Anthology of Greek drama. 2d ser.
The frogs; an English version by Dudley Fitts. Harcourt 1955 166p
Greek satirical fantasy in verse. Dionysius, patron of theater, went to underworld to choose a great poet and had to decide between Aeschylus and Euripides. 9m 3w extras 4 exteriors
—Same; tr. from the Greek by William James Hickie, with an introduction by Gilbert Seldes and wood-engravings by John Austen. Heritage 1959 62p illus
Bound (inverted) with the author's "The birds"
—Same; tr. by Benjamin Bickley Rogers
In Aristophanes. Five comedies
In Robinson, C. A. ed. Anthology of Greek drama. 2d ser.
also in Eleven plays of the Greek dramatists
Ladies' day; an English version by Dudley Fitts. Harcourt 1959 134p
Greek classical comedy. Burlesques the dramatist Euripides and also the eternal battle of the sexes. 11 parts 9m 4w extras 1 interior 1 exterior
Lysistrata; an English version by Dudley Fitts. Harcourt 1954 132p
Greek classical farce in verse. To end war Athenian women organize a sex strike. 1 act 4m 5w extras 1 exterior
—Same; tr. by Doros Alastos
In Aristophanes. Two plays: Peace and Lysistrata
—Same; tr. by Charles T. Murphy
In Lind, L. R. ed. Ten Greek plays in contemporary translations
—Same; tr. by Benjamin Bickley Rogers
In Aristophanes. Five comedies
also in Eleven plays of the Greek dramatists
Peace; tr. by Doros Alastos
Greek classical drama. To end Peloponnesian War, Peace, who has been buried by War, is rescued by Greek farmers, under the leadership of Trygaios. Done in modern English. 3 acts 14m 2w extras 3 exteriors
In Aristophanes. Two plays: Peace and Lysistrata
The wasps
Greek classical satire on demagogues. Philocleon's passion for lawsuits is checked when his son, Bdelycleon, turns their house into law court. Verse play 8m 2w extras 1 exterior
In Aristophanes. Five comedies

Arithmetic
c Armstrong, J. B. No more arithmetic
c Miller, H. L. Not for girls

Arizona
Sherwood, R. E. The petrified forest

Ark, Noah's. See Noah's ark

Arlett, Vera I.

c The people who came to an inn. Epworth 1955 16p
  Fantasy. Jim rescues angel expelled from Heaven. Includes tableau of Nativity scene. Background carols. 1 act 4m 2b extras 1 exterior

c Young Richard Whittington. Pitman (London) 1953 27p
  Romantic comedy. Adaptation of the English folk-tale about Dick Whittington and his cat, who brings him fortune and the girl he loves. 1 act 4m 4w 1 interior

Arlington, Virginia. Tomb of the Unknowns

c Jeffrey, H. K. and Walls, D. A. Veterans Day

Armer, Alan, and Grauman, Walter E.

The beast lies dormant
  Television play. Romantic comedy. Meek suitor of successful business woman turns into tough "muscles" man. 1m 1w
  In Armer, A. and Grauman, W. E. Vest pocket theatre

Black star
  Television play. Effect of theft of black diamond in Johannesburg, Africa upon life of dissolute woman. 1m 1w
  In Armer, A. and Grauman, W. E. Vest pocket theatre

Closing time
  Television play. Waitress in cheap cafe uses music of juke box to save herself from a knife-killer. 1m 1w
  In Armer, A. and Grauman, W. E. Vest pocket theatre

Coral
  Television play. Man whom dance hall hostess hopes to marry proves to be veteran she jilted because of his scarred face. 1m 1w
  In Armer, A. and Grauman, W. E. Vest pocket theatre

Country cousin
  Television comedy. Young man gets acquainted with attractive young woman while both are waiting to meet their blind dates. 1m 1w
  In Armer, A. and Grauman, W. E. Vest pocket theatre

Dead weight
  Television play. Wife employs psychology to make her crippled husband realize his disability is only imaginary. 1m 1w
  In Armer, A. and Grauman, W. E. Vest pocket theatre

Final curtain
  Television play. To improve actress' technique in love scene her director pretends to be in love with her. 1m 2w extras
  In Armer, A. and Grauman, W. E. Vest pocket theatre

Glass slipper
  Television play. At a Y.M.C.A. dance a girl who pretends to be popular and wealthy loses a prospective admirer. 1m 1w
  In Armer, A. and Grauman, W. E. Vest pocket theatre

In darkened rooms
  Television play. Man who murders his blind wife discovers she has provided police with clue. 2m 1w
  In Armer, A. and Grauman, W. E. Vest pocket theatre

The last straw
  Television play. Ethical problem confronts partners in pharmaceutical company when they receive laboratory report showing recently manufactured drug is toxic. 1m 1w
  In Armer, A. and Grauman, W. E. Vest pocket theatre

Love lesson for Scotty
  Television play. Teen-age girl shows backward youth how to be success with the girls. 1m 1w
  In Armer, A. and Grauman, W. E. Vest pocket theatre

Love scores a touchdown
  Television comedy. Attractive young woman tries to persuade star football player to change colleges. 1m 1w
  In Armer, A. and Grauman, W. E. Vest pocket theatre

No time for dames
  Television play. Fourteen year old boy changes his mind about girls when he meets one of his sister's friends. 1m 2w
  In Armer, A. and Grauman, W. E. Vest pocket theatre

One year after
  Television play. Supernatural. "Murdered" husband returns on night when his wife planned to marry another man. 1m 1w
  In Armer, A. and Grauman, W. E. Vest pocket theatre

Sure as fate
  Television play. Tragic outcome of effort of ex-convict's wife to make him face life courageously. 1m 1w
  In Armer, A. and Grauman, W. E. Vest pocket theatre

Time out for dreams
  Television comedy. Young secretary realizes her dream of being invited out to dinner by her boss. 1m 1w
  In Armer, A. and Grauman, W. E. Vest pocket theatre

Timeless second
  Television play. In last second before midnight on New Year's Eve, Broadway producer has glimpse of his future. 1m 1w
  In Armer, A. and Grauman, W. E. Vest pocket theatre

To be alone
  Television play. In self defense a survivor of a final atomic war kills her insane companion. 1m 1w
  In Armer, A. and Grauman, W. E. Vest pocket theatre

Whatever became of Lola Woods
  Television play. Aging Hollywood star faces realization that her career is over. 1m 1w
  In Armer, A. and Grauman, W. E. Vest pocket theatre

Arms and the man. Shaw, B.

Armstrong, J. Byron

c No more arithmetic
  Boy who hates arithmetic finds that he couldn't do a lot of things if all the numbers disappeared. 6b extras 1 interior
  In Birdsall, R. ed. Creative plays for every school month

Armstrong, W. F.

Haunted rooms. Dramatic 1955 17p illus
  Farce. Ghosts try to convince psychiatrist of their existence. 1 act 8w 1 interior

Army life. See United States. Army—Military life

The **Army** takes over. Burgess, C. V.

Arnold, Benedict
Fisher, A. and Rabe, O. Not for sale

Arnold, H. G.
Sam Pollard. Epworth 1955 39p
Episodes in life of pioneer missionary and translator in China. 8 acts 14m 8w 5 interiors 1 exterior

Arnold, James W.
The sheriff. French (London) 1955 29p illus
Tragedy. Sheriff meets death believing himself a failure. 1 act 6m 1w 1 interior

Around the world—by way of America. Howard, V.

Around the world in eighty days. Olfson, L.

Arrabal
The automobile graveyard
Modern Passion Play whose Christ is a jazz musician and whose world is a hotel-brothel set in junkyard of old cars. 2 acts 5m 2w 1 exterior
In Arrabel. The automobile graveyard; and, The two executioners

The two executioners
Relationship of mentally unbalanced woman with husband and sons. 1 act 5m 1w 1 interior
In Arrabel. The automobile graveyard; and, The two executioners

The **arrest** in the garden. Phillips, J. B.

Arson
Vidal, G. Barn burning
Williams, T. 27 wagons full of cotton

Art
Forgeries
See Forgery of works of art

Art for art's sake. Sutherland, D.

Art forgeries. See Forgery of works of art

Art with a capital "A." Dennys, J.

Arthur, King
Olfson, L. A Connecticut Yankee in King Arthur's court

Arthur, King (Romances, etc.)
c Howard, V. Sir Galahad and the maidens
Mantle, M. Gareth triumphs

Arthur I, duke of Brittany
Boyd, A. K. Prince Arthur and Hubert

Arthur, Kay
The long view. French 1954 30p illus
Love and understanding of students means more to old professor than being made head of department. 1 act 5m 3w 1 interior

Artists
Dennys, J. Art with a capital "A"
Li, Y. M. Heaven challenges
Li, Y. M. The woman painter
Sergel, R. A cup of tea

Arunta tribe. See Aranda tribe

As long as they're happy. Sylvaine, V.

As pretty does. Aschmann, H. T.

As silent as the ocean. Manning, S. A.

As you desire me. Pirandello, L.

As you like it. Olfson, L.

Asbrand, Karin
All that glitters
Little shepherd of today sits on the hillside with his guitar as he watches his sheep on Christmas night. 1 tableau 1m 1w 1b chorus 1 exterior
In Asbrand, K. Hark, the little angels speak

Anything for father
Children decide best Father's Day present is to do things without being told. 3b 3g 1 interior
In Asbrand, K. Rehearsal-less fun

The beautiful queen
The Old Testament story of Esther, Queen of Persia, whose courage saved her people, the Jews, from destruction. 3 scenes 8w 2 interiors
In Asbrand, K. Easy church plays for women and girls

Brotherhood
After the Civil War a Northerner and a Southerner discover spirit of brotherhood. Background music. 1 act 3m 1 interior
In Asbrand, K. Rehearsal-less fun

Candle in the window
A woman, bitter over husband's death realizes at Christmas time that other people need her. Carols. 2m 7w 1 interior
In Asbrand, K. Rehearsal-less fun

c Children of the Bible
Easter sketch. Biblical children talk to children of today. 6m 2w 3g 1 setting
In Asbrand, K. S. The children's program book

Christmas rose
A crippled teenager is able to take a few steps when she reaches for a rose from the church altar at Christmastime. 1m 3w 1 interior
In Asbrand, K. Hark, the little angels speak

Christmas satellite
A scientist is so excited about satellite he is working on that he forgets Christmas. 1m 2w 1b 3g 1 interior
In Asbrand, K. Hark, the little angels speak

c Christmas snowman
Christmas snowman is lonely until all the children visit him with holly and mistletoe. Includes songs with musical scores. Verse play. Large mixed cast 1 exterior
In Asbrand, K. Hark, the little angels speak

c Christmas wishes
A star fairy grants two little girls their Christmas wishes. 1m 2g extras 1 interior
In Asbrand, K. S. Easy programs for church holidays

c Come to Bethlehem
Christmas. In a dream, two little girls see a pageant of the Nativity. Includes background music by a children's chorus. 2g extras chorus 1 setting
In Asbrand, K. S. Easy programs for church holidays

c "Come to my party"
A little girl is too snobbish to invite little foreign girl to her Christmas party. 5b 6g 1 interior
In Asbrand, K. Hark, the little angels speak

Count your blessings
On Thanksgiving, mother reads Biblical parable of the Prodigal Son from the Gospel of Luke to influence children. 1w 1b 2g 1 interior
In Asbrand, K. Rehearsal-less fun

Asbrand, Karin—*Continued*

c Crooked dime
Four children on way to Sunday School at Easter are described. 2b 2g 1 exterior

In Asbrand, K. S. The children's program book

A day of thankful prayer
Pilgrim family invites an Indian boy for Thanksgiving dinner. 1m 1w 3b 2g 1 interior

In Asbrand, K. Rehearsal-less fun

c The Easter egg's dilemma
Peter Rabbit delivers Easter eggs and chicks to good children. 8g 1b 1 setting

In Asbrand, K. S. The children's program book

Easy as pie. Bakers Plays 1953 30p
Comedy. Teen-age girl's friends help her cook a dinner for her boy friend. 1 act 3m 7w 1 interior

The Farmer in the Dell
Farce. Farmer and his associates tell about their humorous activities. Singing 1m 3w extras 1 interior

In Asbrand, K. Rehearsal-less fun

c Florrie's fortune
When girl tastes witches' brew on Halloween magic things happen. 6m 2w 1g 1 exterior

In Asbrand, K. S. The children's program book

Gifts of gold
Teen age girl who thinks giving Christmas gifts is silly, dreams of the Three Wise Men bringing gifts to the Christ Child. 3m 3w 1 interior

In Asbrand, K. Hark, the little angels speak

c Hi ho! Christmas
Snow White and seven dwarfs learn about Christmas customs around the world from children in various countries. Includes songs with background music and a Nativity tableau. 3m 2w 7b 1g extras 1 setting

In Asbrand, K. S. Easy programs for church holidays

c The image of Christmas. Bakers Plays 1958 8p
Christmas spirit depicted in its meaning to people, from a tiny child to a grandmother. 9 tableaux 3m 5w 3g

It happened at Christmas
At Christmastime a shopkeeper listens to his conscience and forgives man who robbed him. 3m 1w 1b 1g extras 1 interior

In Asbrand, K. Hark, the little angels speak

It's time for remembering. Bakers Plays 1956 7p
A pageant using marching groups. Two children talk about the meaning of Memorial Day. 3b 10g extras 1 interior

c Let's be valentines
Valentine Fairy tells five little girls how to make someone happy. Songs, dance. 1w 6g 1 setting

In Asbrand, K. S. The children's program book

Liberty Belle
Betsy Ross' daughter, niece, and nephew are visited by George Washington as they sew flags for his inauguration. 1 act 4m 4w extras 1 interior

In Asbrand, K. Rehearsal-less fun

c Light up the world
Christmas. The significance of different kinds of light in relation to Christmas. Unidentified cast 7 characters 1 setting

In Cahill, E. M. ed. Celebrating Christmas

c Little Christmas guest
Special guests from several countries visit little Lois. They sing Christmas songs and do Christmas dances. 1 act 8g 1 interior

In Kamerman, S. E. ed. Blue-ribbon plays for girls

c Masquerade
On Thanksgiving some orphans wish someone would adopt them. 1w 1b 4g 1 interior

In Asbrand, K. S. The children's program book

The miracle maker
Because of her daughter's faith a lame woman is cured when Jesus Christ passes her house. 6w 1 interior

In Asbrand, K. Easy church plays for women and girls

More blessed to give
Hardworking woman gives her much longed for new dress to poor young veteran's wife. 4w 1 interior

In Asbrand, K. Easy church plays for women and girls

Mothers
Mother's Day. Ten famous mothers portrayed in tableaux. Choral music. 11w extras 10 tableaux

In Asbrand, K. Easy church plays for women and girls

Mothers of yore
Tableau. Some famous mothers of history speak. Songs. 1m 4w 3b extras 1 interior

In Asbrand, K. Rehearsal-less fun

c The music mart
Spirits of Music and Dance help music store owner increase his sales by bringing to life in song and dance various pieces of music. 2m 1w 2b 3g 1 interior

In Asbrand, K. S. Easy programs for church holidays

Neighbors should be neighborly
Two women find new bride is a good neighbor. 3w 1 exterior

In Asbrand, K. Rehearsal-less fun

On earth peace
On Christmas Eve a young wife and child, on way to join husband, stop for refuge in a barn shared by two quarreling women. 5w 1 interior

In Asbrand, K. Easy church plays for women and girls

c Our little Christmas angels
On Christmas Eve three children become Christmas angels. 1m 1w 3g 1 interior

In Asbrand, K. S. The children's program book

The Prince of Peace
Christmas Nativity play. Innkeeper's daughter persuades her mother to let Mary and Joseph lodge in the stable. Includes a tableau and choral music. 2 scenes 5m 5w extras 1 interior

In Asbrand, K. Easy church plays for women and girls

Reach for the moon
Little girl from big city doesn't think Halloween in small town will be fun. 2w 2g 1 interior

In Asbrand, K. Rehearsal-less fun

School daze
Farce. High school girls dressed as boys, and boys as girls, parody day in teacher's life. Singing, background music. 1 act 7m 5w 1b 1 interior

In Asbrand, K. Rehearsal-less fun

Asbrand, Karin—*Continued*

Sight to see
Parsimonious wealthy woman threatened with blindness gets new light on Christian life when she begins to read the Bible. 2 acts 9w 1 interior
In Asbrand, K. Easy church plays for women and girls

So it's Christmas again. Bakers Plays 1956 11p
Christmas. Retelling of the Nativity with background of familiar Christmas hymns. 7m 6w 1b 1 interior 2 exteriors

Spring fever
Three small town women teach city friend about gardening. 4w 1 interior
In Asbrand, K. Rehearsal-less fun

c The stars celebrate Christmas
Six little stars tell what they did on the first Christmas night. Includes song with musical score. Verse play. 6g 1 exterior
In Asbrand, K. Hark, the little angels speak

c Story book Christmas
On Christmas Eve. Mother Goose characters visit little boy and girl while they sleep. Includes directions for dances. 1b 1g extras 1 interior
In Asbrand, K. Hark, the little angels speak

c Strangers at the gate
Christmas. In Bethlehem, an innkeeper and his household are convinced that the babe born in their stable is the Messiah. Includes background music and a Nativity tableau. 4m 4w extras 1 interior
In Asbrand, K. S. Easy programs for church holidays

The three Marys
Easter. News of Christ's Resurrection brings comfort to mother of one of the thieves who had been crucified with Christ. Choir music. 1m 4w extras 1 interior
In Asbrand, K. Easy church plays for women and girls

c Valentine box. Bakers Plays 1956 11p
One little girl refuses to give a valentine to anyone in her class she doesn't like. Then the Flower Fairies come to help decorate the valentines. 3b 13g extras 1 interior

A valentine for Grandma
Lonely old lady in home for the aged gets many valentines. Song. 3w 1 interior
In Asbrand, K. Rehearsal-less fun

The week before Christmas! Bakers Plays 1958 7p
Farce. Pantomine showing activity of each family member a week before Christmas. 2 parts 4m 4w 1b 1g 1 interior

c When America was young
Little girl raised by Indians is found again by her Pilgrim father. Singing. 3m 1w 1g extras 1 exterior
In Asbrand, K. S. The children's program book

c When daddy comes home
Children tell their father how much he means to them on Father's Day. Verse play. 1m 1w 3b 2g 1 interior
In Asbrand, K. S. The children's program book

c Witches' brew. Bakers Plays 1956 11p music
Boy and girl meet witches and hobgoblins who recall mean things they did on Halloween, and confess the nice things they can do. 1b 1g extras 1 exterior

Youth serves the church
Visitor at Young People's Club, meeting at a local church, learns of club's varied activities. 14w 1 interior
In Asbrand, K. Easy church plays for women and girls

The **Ascension.** Phillips, J. B.

The **Ascension.** York plays

Ascension of Christ. See Jesus Christ—Ascension

The **ascent** of F6. Auden, W. H. and Isherwood, C.

Aschmann, Helen T.
As pretty does. Eldridge 1953 23p (Eldridge Popular one-act playscripts)
Farce. Fate takes a hand when boys plan to bring in girls from next town to attend prom. Background music. 1 act 3m 6w extras 1 interior

Ashbery, John
The heroes
Modern version of the myth of Theseus set at weekend party with the characters dressed in white tennis clothes. 7m 5w 1 interior
In Machiz, H. ed. Artists' Theatre: four plays

Ashermann, Otto
Shakespeare. French 1956 29p illus
Based upon a German farce on "Goethe." Young man must pass examination on Shakespeare to enter college. Shakespeare appears to help him. 1 act 4m 3w 1 interior

Ashes in the wind. Shoub, M.

Ashton, E. Bruce
The beggarman's bride. Pitman 1953 21p
From an incident in Charles Kingsley's: Hereward the Wake. Knight of the court returns from battle disguised as beggar to test his lady's love. 1 act 2m 7w 1 interior

To serve a king. Pitman (London) 1954 30p
Romantic comedy. During Louis XIV's reign in 17th century France clever young woman helps lover apprehend a Spanish spy. 1 act 3m 4w 1b extras 1 interior

Ashton, Elizabeth Bruce. See Ashton, E. Bruce

Ashton, Leonora Sill
Bethlehem's Field. Eldridge 1958 13p (Eldridge Christmas entertainments)
Man who has lost his entire family is bitter about continuing his annual part in community Christmas plans. 1 act 2 scenes 6m 2w 1 exterior

Christmas story
Fantasy. Lost modern-day children encounter a shepherd of Biblical Bethlehem. 1 act 4b 3g 1 exterior
In Brings, L. M. ed. The modern treasury of Christmas plays

The phantom postman. Eldridge 1953 23p (Eldridge Popular one-act playscripts)
Romantic comedy. At party in supposedly haunted house a lost letter, which had caused so much unhappiness is found and returned to its owner. 1 act 2 scenes 4m 4w 1 interior

Asia

Description and travel
c Jordan, L. M. and Garber, H. W. Traveler to Cathay

History
Marlowe, C. Tamburlaine the Great

Ask Mr Jefferson. Fisher, A. and Rabe, O.

Aske, Lake
Too young. French (London) 1953 33p
illus
> Headmaster in English coeducational grammar school finds it difficult to enforce the rule of non-fraternization between teen-age boys and girls. 1 act 5m 6w extras 1 interior

Asmodée. Mauriac, F.

Assault and battery
Bevan, M. Inquest on Monday

Asses and mules
c Woolsey, J. and Sechrist, E. H. The donkey's mission

Assinder, Peter
The paying guest. Kenyon House Press 1954 18p
> Miss Rathbone, acquitted of one murder, plans another until evidence of first murder is discovered. 1 act 2 scenes 4w 1 interior

Assisi, Francis of, Saint. See Francis of Assisi, Saint

Aste, Ippolito Tito d'
Sansone (adaptation) See Howells, W. D. Samson

Astor, John Jacob
Emmons, D. G. Astor's bid for empire

Astor's bid for empire. Emmons, D. G.

Astronomy
c Miller, H. L. Star Cadets

At liberty. Williams, T.

At the foot of the Mount. Casey, B. M.

At the hawk's well. Yeats, W. B.

Athaliah, Queen of Judah
Racine, J. Athaliah

Athaliah. Racine, J.

The atheist's tragedy. Tourneur, C.

Athelstan, King of England
The Welsh embassador

Athelstane, King of England. See Athelstan, King of England

Atherton, Marguerite
And it's Christmas! Eldridge 1958 9p (Eldridge Christmas entertainments)
> In dream, young girl is visited by the traditions of Christmas from Christmas Pudding to Mistletoe. Carols. 1 act 6m 3w extras 1 interior

c Jack-in-the-box
> How a toymaker invents the "Jack-in-the-box." 3 acts 1m 4w 7b 5g 1 interior 1 exterior

In 'Round the year plays for the grades

Athletes
Howard, V. Athletes all
Lindsay, H. and Crouse, R. Tall story

Athletes all. Howard, V.

Atkinson, Alex
Four winds. French (London) 1954 67p illus
> Murder mystery. Police inspector apprehends real criminal in case of doctor's wife found murdered, holding in her hand half a torn letter from another man. 3 acts 5m 4w 1 interior

Atomic energy
c Fisher, A. Caves of the earth
Fisher, A. Three and the dragon
Schary, D. The highest tree

Atomic journey. Eaton, J. J. and Juste, M.

Atonement
Agnew, E. J. Beyond Good Friday

Atsumori. Kwanze, M.

Attila
Corneille, P. Attila

Attila, king of the Huns. See Attila

Attila. Corneille, P.

Attley, Marian. See Sprenger, C. H. jt. auth.

Atwater, Richard, and Atwater, Florence
Mr Popper's penguins (dramatization) See Wright, L. Mr Popper's penguins

Atwell, Rosemary, and Virden, Helen
c Christmas in the forest
> Christmas. Boy and girl go to forest to select Christmas tree. Verse play. 1b 1g extras no setting

In Atwell, R. and Virden, H. Play-time

c Mother of the Year
> Mother's Day. A classroom contest to select the Woman of the Year. Verse play. 1 act 3m 1w 6b 4g 1 interior

In Atwell, R. and Virden, H. Play-time

A pound of prevention. Dramatic 1955 20p illus
> Comedy. Safety Society for Secret Stuffers demonstrates that the best way to lose a pound of weight is a pound of prevention. 1 act 12w 1 interior

c Thanksgiving in Mother Goose land
> A boy and girl try to select Mother Goose characters as guests at Thanksgiving dinner. Verse play. 1 act 5m 2w 4b 2g no setting

In Atwell, R. and Virden, H. Play-time

c Valentine from Mars
> Valentine's Day. Students send valentimes to various countries, but a Martian brings his response in person. Verse play. 1 act 6b 5g no setting

In Atwell, R. and Virden, H. Play-time

c Witch hunt
> Halloween. Small boys hunt witches on Halloween night. Verse play. 1 act 4b extras no setting

In Atwell, R. and Virden, H. Play-time

Au revoir. Priestley, H. E.

Auden, W. H.
The Play of Daniel. See The Play of Daniel

Auden, W. H. and Isherwood, Christopher
The ascent of F6
> Satire on futility of man's search for meaning of life. Mountain F6 is climbed by Englishman who is found dead on summit. 2 acts 7 scenes 12m 3w 3 interiors 4 exteriors

In Auden, W. H. and Isherwood, C. Two great plays

The dog beneath the skin; or, Where is Francis?
> Farcical satire on modern society, with pointed references to England. Verse play. 3 acts 15 scenes Large mixed cast 8 interiors 5 exteriors

In Auden, W. H. and Isherwood, C. Two great plays

Audubon, John James
c Mathews, J. Audubon's America

Audubon's America. Mathews, J.

Augier, Emile
Olympe's marriage; English version by Barrett H. Clark
> Moral drama defending marriage and domesticity which revolves around the withheld secret that the Countess de Puygiron is the notorious woman, Olympe Taverny. 3 acts 5m 4w 2 interiors

In Stanton, S. S. ed. Camille, and other plays

Augustus, Emperor of Rome
Lee, N. Gloriana
Augustus does his bit. Shaw, B.
Aunt Lizzie lives it up! Kalen, E.
Aunt Martha. Lea, G.
Aunt Min drops in. Sutton, T.
Aunt Vonnie on vexation. Abstance, P. and Abstance, L.
Auntie Mame. Lawrence, J. and Lee, R. E.
Aunts
Peavey, H. Teen antics
The **aunt's** sake. Sakanishi, S. tr.
Aurthur, Robert Alan
Man on the mountaintop
> Neurotic young man, who had been child prodigy, becomes readjusted to life through his love for a young woman. 5m 2w
In Vidal, G. ed. Best television plays
A very special baby. Dramatists 1957 72p illus
> Resentment over wife's death at birth of son and son's incapacity for professional career cause father to thwart son's ambitions. 2 acts 5 scenes 5m 1w 1 setting
A very special baby (condensation)
In The Best plays of 1956-1957
Austen, Jane
Pride and prejudice (dramatization) See Jerome, H. Pride and prejudice
Pride and prejudice (radio adaptation) See Newman, D. Pride and prejudice
Austin, Clara L.
c Mrs Santa proves a point
> Santa doesn't believe Mrs Santa has as much to do as he, so they change places for an afternoon. 16 characters 1 interior
In Birdsall, R. ed. Creative plays for every school month
Australia
Lawler, R. Summer of the seventeenth doll
Peterson, L. Sticks and stones
Australian folk-lore. See Folk-lore, Australian
Austria
Delderfield, R. F. The Mayerling affair
> History—Revolutionary, 1848-1849
Fry, C. The dark is light enough
Authors
Carmichael, F. More than meets the eye
Collier, E. Dark lady
Davis, J. P. A adventure
Pirandello, L. When someone is somebody
Rosten, H. The happy housewife
Saroyan, W. Once around the block
Schulberg, B. and Breit, H. The disenchanted
> *See also* Novelists; *also* names of individual authors
Authorship
Chenery, M. Lesson for today
Houston, N. She writes a roof
Radin, B'. A seacoast in Bohemia
Autobiography
O'Casey, S. I knock at the door
O'Casey, S. Pictures in the hallway

Auto-da-fé. Williams, T.
Autograph hunters. Curtis, P. D.
Autographs
Curtis, P. D. Autograph hunters
Automata
Čapek, K. R. U. R.
c Fisher, A. Robots to the rescue
Automobile drivers
Martens, A. C. Drag race
Martens, A. C. Hold your horsepower!
The **automobile** graveyard. Arrabal
Automobiles
> Touring
c Woolsey, J. and Sechrist, E. H. Let's travel by auto
Autumn
c Pottow, D. Preparing for winter
c Spamer, C. Silly, a leaf
c Very, A. Getting ready for winter
Autumn in the air. Lockwood, L.
Autumn term. Agg, H.
Avarice
Bannerman, H. K. My last duchess
Becque, H. The vultures
Dekker, T. If this be not a good play, the Devil is in it
Emery, C. Madame Vulture
Greene, N. D. The seekers
Grundy, S. A pair of spectacles
Hellman, L. Another part of the forest
Hellman, L. The little foxes
Holm, J. C. The southwest corner
Howard, S. The late Christopher Bean
c Howard, V. The strange tale of King Midas
Jonson, B. The alchemist
Jonson, B. Volpone
Latham, J. L. The nightmare
Levin, I. Interlock
Marlowe, C. The Jew of Malta
Mauermann, G. A cup of kindness
O'Casey, S. Time to go
Ridge, A. Three mice for the abbot
Tourneur, C. The atheist's tragedy
Williams, T. Cat on a hot tin roof
c Woolsey, J. and Sechrist, E. H. Saint Peter and the birds
Zweig, S. Volpone
> *See also* Misers
Avery, Ira
Matilda. French 1953 105p illus
> Farce. Officious maid fired, but restored to place in household when family realizes how her talents have served them. 3 acts 5 scenes 5m 3w 1 interior
Aviators. See Air pilots
Awake and sing! Odets, C.
Away in a manger (Hymn)
Lorenz, E. J. A Christmas gift for Hans
Awoi no uye. Komparu, Z. U.
Axelrod, George
Goodbye Charlie. French 1959 69p illus
> Farce. A famous lover and man of the world dies and is reincarnated as a woman but has trouble developing his feminine personality. 2 acts 5 scenes 4m 3w 1 interior

Axelrod, George—*Continued*

The seven year itch. [Rev] Dramatists
1956 76p illus
  Comedy. While his wife and son are
  away New York City summer bachelor
  has affair with actress who lives upstairs. Background music. 3 acts 5 scenes
  5m 6w 1 interior
    Trade edition published by Random House
—Same
  In Best American plays; 4th ser
  In New voices in the American theatre
The seven year itch (condensation)
  In Theatre, 1953
Will success spoil Rock Hunter? French
1957 77p illus
  Farcical fantasy satirizing moving picture industry. Reporter, who has sold
  his soul to Devil in guise of movie
  agent, is rescued by playwright. 3 acts
  4 scenes 6m 2w 2 interiors
    Trade edition published by Random House

Aya no tsuzumi. Kwanze, M.

Aymé, Marcel

Clérambard; English version by Alvin
  Sapinsley and Leo Kerz; basic translation from the French by Norman Denny.
  French 1958 102p illus
  Comedy. Satirizes attempt of man to
  live life of saint, though reality doesn't
  permit it. Members of impoverished
  family of French nobility work at man-
  ufacturing highly colored pullovers on
  knitting machines in their living room.
  4 acts 9m 7w 2 interiors 1 exterior
—Same
  In Four modern French comedies

B

Bab buys a car. Carlton, J.

The **babbling** Brooks. Gordon, K.

Baby Doll. Williams, T.

A **baby** for Brenda. Emery, C.

The **baby** Moses. Spamer, C. M.

Baby-sitters
  Hark, M. and McQueen, N. Star baby-
    sitter
  McCoy, P. A rumpus on rampage
  Martens, A. C. Who's that knocking on
    my door?
  Weiss, M. J. Parents are people

The **Bacchae**. Euripides

The **Bacchanals**. Euripides

Bacchus. See Dionysus

The **bachelor**. Turgenev, I.

The **bachelor** party. Chayefsky, P.

Back to Bethlehem. Miller, C. H.

Backward children. See Children, Abnormal
  and backward

The **bad** children. Jackson, S.

The **bad** seed. Anderson, M.

The **bad**-tempered man. Menander

Baden, Renetta

The Christmas Eve visitor
  Biblical pageant in which a stranger
  re-creates story of birth of Christ for
  two children waiting for Santa Claus

to arrive. Includes singing of carols by
soloists and choral singing 1 act 9
scenes 19m 5w 3b 1g extras choir 2
interiors 2 exteriors
  In Brings, L. M. ed. The modern
    treasury of Christmas plays

Badger, Alexander

Before the dawn
  Woman reporter's investigation results
  in last minute pardon for condemned
  man. 1 act 3m 2w 1 interior
  In Brings, L. M. comp. The golden
    book of church plays
The bomb. Bakers Plays 1958 24p (Baker's
  Royalty plays)
  Mystery. The police receive a tip that
  a bomb has been planted in the office of
  a fashion importer. 1 act 4m 3w 1 interior
Willie's secret weapon. Bakers Plays
1957 64p illus (Baker's Royalty plays)
  Comedy. To win university scholarship
  contest in science, boy constructs secret weapon which inadvertently traps
  two foreign agents. Background music.
  3 acts 6m 9w extras 1 interior

The **bag** of parting. Sakanishi, S. tr.

A **bag** of tangerines. Sakanishi, S. tr.

Bagnold, Enid

The chalk garden. French 1956 117p
  Changes wrought in household of English socialite, an amateur gardener, by
  the ex-convict she unwittingly employs
  as governess to her 16 year-old granddaughter. 3 acts 2m 7w 1 interior
    Trade edition published by Random
    House
The chalk garden (condensation)
  In The Best plays of the year 1955-1956
  In Theatre, 1956

Bailey, Anne Howard

Impersonation
  Television play. A teenage bandit meets
  an understanding older woman in a
  train. 4m 1w extras
  In Roberts, E. B. Television writing
    and selling
The narrow man
  Television play. College president turns
  down a financial offer in face of college's bankruptcy because of prejudice
  of donor against foreign-born. 4m 1w
  In Burack, A. S. ed. Television plays
    for writers

Bailey, Hazel F.

"Better than seven sons"
  Pantomime of Biblical story of Ruth to
  illustrate love between modern young
  woman and her mother-in-law. 5w 1 in-
  terior
  In Bailey, H. F. Simple chancel dramas
Christmas Eve candle vespers
  Christmas candlelight worship service
  including scenes of the Nativity; with
  music by women's choir and soloists.
  3m 11w extras
  In Bailey, H. F. Simple chancel dramas
The Feast of the Ingathering
  Thanksgiving worship service. Includes
  dramatic episodes based on the Old
  Testament accounts of Sukkoth. Choral
  music. Large mixed cast
  In Bailey, H. F. Simple chancel dramas
A manger lowly
  Worship program for Christmas of the
  Nativity. The shepherds and the Wise
  Men come to worship the Infant Jesus.
  Choral singing and carols. 3 acts 14m
  1w extras 1 exterior 1 interior
  In Bailey, H. F. Simple chancel dramas

Bailey, Hazel F.—*Continued*

The picture window frames Christmas
Christmas play including a pantomime of trimming the tree and hiding gifts. A family shelters a poor old man on Christmas Eve. Carols. 3 scenes 3m 2w 1b 1g 1 interior
In Bailey, H. F. Simple chancel dramas

c Roses for the King. Bakers Plays 1954 15p illus
Christmas fantasy. Story of Granny's rose tree which blossoms on Christmas Day. Background music. 1 act 2m 2w extras 1 interior

The singing children
Worship service for Palm Sunday. Singing children precede Jesus on His entry into Jerusalem. Music. 1m 1b 1g extras 1 interior
In Bailey, H. F. Simple chancel dramas

"There was a garden"
Worship service. Dramatization of the events of first Easter morning. Based on the New Testament accounts in the Gospels. Background music; children's choir. 8m 7w 1b 1g
In Bailey, H. F. Simple chancel dramas

Walk in the light
Worship service. Includes both a dramatization of the New Testament story of Bartimaeus the blind beggar and a candlelight service. 10m extras 1 interior
In Bailey, H. F. Simple chancel dramas

"We bring this child unto the Lord"
Worship service, including a dramatization of the Old Testament story of how Samuel's mother dedicated him to the Lord's service. Choral singing. 2 acts 2m 1w 1b extras 1 interior
In Bailey, H. F. Simple chancel dramas

The **bait.** Merrill, J.

Bake a cherry pie. Hark, M. and Mcqueen, N.

Bakeless, Katherine Little
c Most memorable voyage
Columbus' crew on the Pinta is restless and he tries to convince them they will soon reach land. 1 act 8m 2b extras 1 exterior
In Burack, A. S. ed. Four-star plays for boys

Baker, Hendrik. See Hulme-Beaman, S. B. The cruise of the "Toytown Belle"

Baker, Loveday Goldie
Conspiracy at "The Crayfish." Deane 1955 60p illus ("Deane's" Ser. of plays)
Comedy. English widower. an innkeeper, puts ad in matrimonial paper, with amusing results. Background music. 3 acts 6 scenes 6m 7w 1 interior

Baker's Roaring twenties scrapbook; a gay, naughty, wild and mad collection of material to provide any group with a full evening revue of the Roaring Twenties; ed. by John G. Fuller. Bakers Plays 1960 58p
Musical revue, portraying various phases of American life in the 1920's. Includes additional sketches for each act and a list of appropriate songs. 2 acts 14 scenes Large mixed cast 1 setting

Baker (Walter H.) Company
Baker's Roaring twenties scrapbook

The **bald** soprano. Ionesco, E.

Baldwin, Robert
Cross, E. W. The patriots

Ballad opera
Brecht, B. The threepenny opera

Ballads
c Marston, M. A. The robbers

England
See Ballads, English

Scotland
See Ballads, Scottish

United States
See Ballads, American

Ballads, American
Kreymborg, A. There's a nation

Ballads, English
c Holmes, R. V. King John and the Abbott of Canterbury
c Marston, M. A. The riddling knight

Ballads, Scottish
Bottomley, G. Towie Castle

The **ballet** dancer. Priestley, F.

Ballet dancing
Priestley, F. The ballet dancer

Balloons
c Spamer, C. The adventurous balloon

The **Balwhinnie** bomb. Daviot, G.

Bandits. See Brigands and robbers

Bands (Music)
Willson, M. The music man

Bangham, Mary Dickerson
"Come, see the place. . ." Bakers Plays 1959 15p
Easter tableaux of events connected with burial of Christ and the Resurrection. Background music. 6 tableaux Large mixed cast
Come to the manger. Bakers Plays 1959 16p
Christmas worship program. Includes a Nativity pageant with choral music. 8 tableaux. Large mixed cast

Bank clerks. See Bank employees

Bank employees
Kaiser, G. From morn to midnight

Bankruptcy
Beach, L. The goose hangs high

Banks, Frances. See Claiborne, R. jt. auth.

Banks, Lynne Reid
It never rains. Deane 1954 75p front ("Deane's" Ser. of plays)
Domestic comedy. Yorkshire factory worker, crippled in an accident, and his family have series of misfortunes until he learns to face his disability bravely. 3 acts 4 scenes 5m 5w 1 interior
The killer dies twice. Deane 1956 63p illus ("Deane's" Ser. of plays)
Murder mystery. Murder of hated sadist in ski resort in Austrian Alps is baffling to detective. Music. 3 acts 5 scenes 4m 4w 1 interior
See also Maddern, V. jt. auth.

Bannerman, H. K.
My last duchess. Dramatic 1955 26p
Based on Robert Browning's poem. In 16th century Italy, clever young woman averts marriage to greedy duke when she discovers true story behind famous portrait of his wife. 1 act 3m 2w 1 interior

Bannerman, Helen
Story of Little Black Sambo (dramatization). See Chorpenning, C. B. Rama and the tigers

The **baptism** of Jesus. Phillips, J. B.

The **baptism** of Jesus. Spamer, C. M.

The Bar-None Trading Post. Miller H. L.

Barabbas
 Ghelderode, M. de. Barabbas

Barabbas. Ghelderode, M. de

Barasch, Norman, and Moore, Carroll
 Make a million. French 1959 86p illus
  Romantic comedy. Plans of quiz show
  producer who needs money to remarry
  his first wife are complicated by un-
  predictable contestant. 3 acts 17m 4w
  extras 1 interior

Barbee, Lindsey
 Beggars can't be choosers
  Schoolgirls contribute their cherished
  possessions to a Christmas box for a
  poor ministers family. 1 act 1m 8w
  1 setting
  In Brings, L. M. ed. The modern treasury of Christmas plays
 Christmas for Cinderella
  Four cousins mysteriously invited to
  Christmas party in rich cousin's house
  find their secret hopes come true. 1 act
  7w 1 interior
  In Brings, L. M. ed. The modern
   treasury of Christmas plays
 The Friday Foursome packs a box
  Christmas. Girls club tries to make the
  box they prepare for a poor family more
  like a Christmas gift than charity. 1 act
  1w 6g 1 interior
  In Kamerman, S. E. ed. Blue-ribbon
   plays for girls
 A letter to Lincoln
  In 1862 two little girls help slaves escape through secret tunnel to a free
  state, and receive a letter from Abraham Lincoln in acknowledgement of
  deed. 1 act 3 scenes 1w 6g 1 interior
  In Kamerman, S. E. ed. Blue-ribbon
   plays for girls

The **barber** and the donkey. Webber, C. E.

Barbers
 c Miller, H. L. The busy barbers

Barchester Towers. Draper, J.

A **bargain's** a bargain. Carlson, B. W.

Barham, Richard Harris
 The jackdaw of Rheims (dramatization)
  See Marston, M. A. The jackdaw of
  Rheims

Barkentin, Marjorie
 James Joyce's Ulysses in nighttown.
 Random House 1958 119p (Modern Lib
 Paperbacks)
  Based on the novel: Ulysses, by James
  Joyce. A panorama of Dublin life cen-
  tered around a father's search for his
  son. Scenes, incidents and characters
  parallel those in Homer's Odyssey. 2
  acts Large mixed cast 1 setting
 —Same
  In Cordell, R. A. and Matson, L. eds.
   The off-Broadway theatre

Barker, James Nelson
 Superstition
  Early 19th century tragedy. Witchcraft,
  persecution and sorcery in colonial New
  England. 5 acts 9 scenes 15m 4w 1b
  extras 1 interior 4 exteriors
  In Quinn, A. H. ed. Representative
   American plays

Barn burning. Vidal, G.

Barnes, Emily Ann, and Young, Bess M.
 c The magic fishbone
  Dramatization of story by Charles Dickens. King Watkins who has no money
  and nineteen children is given magic
  fishbone by a fairy. 6 scenes 3m 4w 1b
  3 interiors 1 exterior
  In Fenner, P. and Hughes, A. comps.
   Entrances and exits
 c Sokar and the crocodile
  A dramatization of book by Alice
  Howard about little boy in ancient
  Egypt who was promised by a magic
  crocodile that he would become a prince.
  4 scenes 2m 2w 1b extras 2 exteriors
  In Fenner, P. and Hughes, A. comps.
   Entrances and exits

Barnett, Morris
 Yankee peddler; or, Old times in Virginia
  Farce. Conniving peddler wins money
  and wife and unites two lovers. 1 act
  3 scenes 7m 3w 1 exterior
  In Smith, B. and others, eds. A treasury of non-royalty one-act plays

Barnharrow. Daviot, G.

Barr, June
 c The lazy little raindrop
  One little raindrop refuses to go with
  the others until he realizes how important his job is. 1 act 12g 1 exterior
  In Kamerman, S. E. ed. Blue-ribbon
   plays for girls

Barrett, Jean Smith. See Smith, L. B. jt.
 auth.

The **Barretts** of Wimpole Street. Besier, R.

Barrie, James M.
 The admirable Crichton
  Satire on British class distinction in
  19th century. When a group of aristo-
  crats is shipwrecked on an island, the
  butler takes over. 4 acts 7m 6w extras
  2 interiors 1 exterior
  In Sper, F. ed. Favorite modern plays
  In A Treasury of the theatre
  In Warnock, R. Representative modern
   plays, British
 Little minister (condensation)
  In The Best plays of 1894-1899
 The old lady shows her medals (adapta-
  tion) See Bucci, M. The old lady
  shows her medals

The **barrier.** McGreevey, J.

Barrow, William
 Peaceful evening. Deane 1955 22p
 ("Deane's" Ser. of plays)
  Exploits of dissolute son kept from dot-
  ing mother by daughter who sacrifices
  her life's savings to this end. 1 act
  3w 1 exterior

Barry, Mae Howley
 Come live in my house. Dramatic 1955
 27p illus
  Farce. Complications arise over widow's
  ad for companion to live with her. 1 act
  7w 1 interior
 The nautical approach. Dramatic 1955 22p
  Farce. Seaman, trying to make first
  date with pretty nurse, is involved in
  some amusing complications in mater-
  nity ward. 1 act 3m 4w 1 interior

Baum, L. Frank
c The Wizard of Oz (dramatization) See
Thane, A. The Wizard of Oz

Baxter, A. M.
A pageant of Christmas
> Nativity play. Shepherds and the three
> wise men set off to visit Christ Child.
> 12m choir 1 exterior
In Cameo plays: bk 19

Bayard, J. F. A. See Scribe, E. jt. auth.

Bayer, Eleanor, and Bayer, Leo
Third best sport. Dramatists 1959 102p
illus
> Farce. Bride taken on honeymoon to
> business convention in Florida. 7m 4w
> 1 interior

Bayer, Leo. See Bayer, E. jt. auth.

Bayliss, A. E. M.
My hat!
> Comedy about a hat that gets around
> too much. 1 act 3m 2w 1 exterior
In Cameo plays: bk 19

What make?
> The admiral's gardener and a faulty
> lawn mower throw everything into con-
> fusion. 3m 1w 1 exterior
In Cameo plays: bk 19

Bayliss, R. G.
c The burglar alarm. Paxton 1956 31p
> Domestic comedy. Grandfather and
> grandson with the aid of policeman
> succeed in plot to snare burglars and
> earn reward. 3 scenes 8m 2w 1 interior

The Gentlemen Smugglers. Paxton 1954
21p
> Leader of smugglers turns table on
> troopers who have trapped them in cave.
> 3 scenes 14m 1 interior

Be good, sweet maid. Webber, C. E.

Be happy? Go wacky! Tobias, J.

Be my ghost. Murray, J.

Be my guest. Taggart, T.

Be my "walentine". Miller, H. L.

Be nice to the Easter bunny. Martens, A. C.

Be your age. Orr, M. and Denham, R.

Be yourself! Pierce, C. W.

Beach, Lewis
The goose hangs high
> Sacrifices of parents for their college
> age children; crisis occurs at Christmas
> when father is suddenly bankrupt and
> they cannot return to college. 3 acts
> 7m 6w 1 interior
In Keyes, R. K. and Roth, H. M. eds.
Comparative comedies, present and
past

Beacon of strength. Brenner, M.

The beaded buckle. Patton, F. G.

Beale, Jack. See Cargill, P. jt. auth.

Beaman, S. B. Hulme- See Hulme-Beaman,
S. B.

The beams of our house. Apstein, T.

Bean, Valentine
I created Santa Claus. Bakers Plays 1958
22p
> Modern and biblical scenes promote
> theme of blessedness of giving. Nativity
> tableau. Music. 1 act Large mixed cast
> 1 interior

Beany's private eye. Miller, H. L.

Beard
Tobias, J. The Katz' whiskers

Bears
c Scott, L. B. The three bears
c Spamer, C. The three bears
c Very, A. The callers

The **beast** lies dormant. Armer, A. and
Grauman, W. E.

Beatitudes
Emurian, E. K. The living dramatization
of the Beatitudes

Beaumont, Francis, and Fletcher, John
The maid's tragedy
> Jacobean tragedy of revenge and murder
> set in Rhodes. Verse play with a brief
> masque in the first act. 5 acts 12 scenes
> 11m 7w extras 1 setting
In McIlwraith, A. K. ed. Five Stuart
tragedies

Beautiful dreamers. Reach, J.

The **beautiful** queen. Asbrand, K.

Beauty, Personal
Rodman, H. A thing of beauty

Beauty and the Beast. Beers, J.

Beauty and the Beast. MacAlvay, N.

The **beaux'** stratagem. Farquhar, G.

Becket, Thomas à. See Thomas à Becket,
Saint, Abp. of Canterbury

Becket. Tennyson, A.

Becket; or, The honor of God. Anouilh, J.

Beckett, Samuel
Act without words, I
> Mime for one player. A man is alter-
> nately successful and frustrated in at-
> tempts to perform certain actions. 1m
> 1 setting
In Beckett, S. Krapp's last tape, and
other dramatic pieces
In Beckett, S. Endgame; followed by
Act without words, a mime for
one player

Act without words, II
> Mime for two players contrasts actions
> of the two. 2m 1 setting
In Beckett, S. Krapp's last tape, and
other dramatic pieces

All that fall. Grove 1957 59p
> Old woman going to railway station
> meets variety of people. When train is
> late she imagines the worst. Background
> music 6m 2w 1b 1g 1 exterior
—Same
In Beckett, S. Krapp's last tape, and
other dramatic pieces

Embers
> Radio play. In ramblings of old man and
> wife, commonplace situation becomes
> drama. Background music. 3m 1w
In Beckett, S. Krapp's last tape, and
other dramatic pieces

Endgame; followed by Act without words,
a mime for one player; tr. from the
French by the author. Grove 1958 91p
> Fantasy. Four characters are trapped in
> a room to await death. 1 act 2m 2w 1
> interior

Krapp's last tape
> Man thinks about meaning of Life and
> his own life as he listens to tape record-
> ings of his memories. 1 act 1m 1 in-
> terior
In Beckett, S. Krapp's last tape, and
other dramatic pieces

Beckett, Samuel—*Continued*

Wating for Godot. Grove 1954 60p
> Tragicomedy. Two old tramps wait on
> lonely road for Godot. Nothing happens
> as this is the point of stand-still. 2 acts
> 4m 1b 1 exterior
> Trade edition also published by Grove
> Press. Paper edition published in Eng-
> land by French

Waiting for Godot (condensation)
In The Best plays of 1955-1956

Becque, Henry

The vultures; tr. from the French by
Freeman Tilden
> When the father of a wealthy family
> dies, his business partner and attorney
> gather like vultures to enrich them-
> selves on his estate. 3 acts 12m 6w 1 in-
> terior

In A Treasury of the theatre

Woman of Paris
> Social comedy in 19th century Paris.
> Government official's wife uses lover's
> influence to secure husband's promotion.
> 3 acts 3m 2w 1 interior

In Bentley, E. ed. The modern theatre
v 1

Bedtime story. O'Casey, S.

Beers, Jesse
c Beauty and the Beast. French 1954 48p
illus
> Adaptation of German folk tale. 3 acts
> 6m 4w 1 setting

Before the dawn. Badger, A.

The beggar of Basra. Bateson, D.

The beggarman's bride. Ashton, E. B.

Beggars can't be choosers. Lindsey, B.

Begging
c Bateson, D. The beggar of Basra

Beginning of the way. Raeburn, H.

Behan, Brendan

The hostage. Grove 1958 92p
> In a disreputable Dublin boarding house,
> young British soldier is held as a hos-
> tage for an Irish Republican Army man
> held under sentence of death by Brit-
> ish. Singing and dancing. 3 acts 6m 7w
> extras 1 interior

The quare fellow. Grove 1956 86p
> Talk in an English prison before "the
> quare fellow" is hanged. 3 acts 4 scenes
> 22m 1 exterior 1 interior
> Also published in trade edition

Behavior. See Conduct of life

Behold the body. Federspiel, J. A. D.

Behrman, S. N.

Biography
> Sophisticated social comedy. Marion
> Froude, born in a village, ventures to
> New York and London. 3 acts 5m 3w
> 1 interior

In Behrman, S. N. 4 plays

The cold wind and the warm. French
1959 100p illus
> Jewish man, loved by girl, can't forget
> his love for another woman and finally
> kills himself. Background music. 3 acts
> 9 scenes 8m 4w 2 settings
> Trade edition published by Random
> House

The cold wind and the warm (condensa-
tion)
In The Best plays of 1958-1959
In Broadway's best, 1959

End of summer
> Futile life of wealthy woman and its
> effects upon daughter's search for pur-
> pose in her own life. 3 acts 7m 3w 1
> interior

In Behrman, S. N. 4 plays

Jane. French 1953 109p illus
> Comedy of manners based on story of
> same title by W. Somerset Maugham.
> English lady becomes toast of London
> society because of her disarming hon-
> esty. 3 acts 5m 4w 1 interior

Rain from heaven
> Lady Violet harbors in her Berlin home,
> a Jewish musician, a Russian scholar
> and a Russian pianist. 3 acts 6m 4w
> 1 interior

In Behrman, S. N. 4 plays

The second man
> Sophisticated comedy. Novelist in love
> with two women. 3 acts 4 scenes 3m
> 2w 1 interior

In Behrman, S. N. 4 plays
See also Rome, H. Fanny

Behrman, Samuel Nathaniel. See Behrman,
S. N.

Beich, Albert, and Wright, William H.

The man in the dog suit. Dramatists 1959
82p
> Based on the novel: Three ways to
> Mecca, by Edwin Corle. Shy, ineffectual
> young man interested in tree surgery
> finds that when he dons dog suit mas-
> querade costume he can outface his
> wife's relatives who are pushing him
> into banking. 3 acts 6m 4w 1 interior

Belasco, David

The heart of Maryland (condensation)
In The Best plays of 1894-1899

Madame Butterfly
> An adaptation of the story by John
> Luther Long. Sentimental tragedy o'
> American officer who abandons Japanese
> sweetheart. 1 act 6m 4w 1 interior

In Quinn, A. H. ed. Representative
American plays

Belgium

History—1555-1648
Goethe, J. W. von. Egmont

Belief and doubt. See Faith

Bell, Anita

Egad, what a cad! or, Virtue triumphs
over villainy. French 1953 40p
> Melodrama. Virtue triumphs over vil-
> lainy when Constant is saved from
> Bertram by Manly. 1 act 2 scenes 3m
> 4w 1 interior

Bell, Ruth E.

Through a glass darkly. French 1954 30p
illus
> New pastor invites congregation to his
> study to plan activities. Mixed quartet
> offstage. 1 act 5m 4w 1b extras 1 in-
> terior

The bell of St Hildegarde. Quinn, A. H. and
Quinn, K. C.

The bell that couldn't ring. Spamer, C.

The Bell Witch of Tennessee. McCaslin, N.

Bellamy, Francis Rufus
Emurian, E. K. I pledge allegiance

Belle. Gross, E. and Gross, N.

Bells
c Spamer, C. The bells

The bells. Lewis, L.

The bells. Spamer, C.

Bells are ringing. Styne, J.

The **bells** of the city. Tennant, K.

Beloin, Edmund, and Garson, Henry
In any language. Acting ed. Dramatists 1953 64p illus
  Comedy. From story by Henry Garson. Hollywood actress, on location in Italy, brings about reconciliation with her husband. Music. 3 acts 4 scenes 13m 6w 1b 1g 1 interior

Benavente, Jacinto
La malquerida ┌The passion flower┐ tr. from the Spanish by John Garrett Underhill
  Tragedy. Love of a girl for her stepfather. Set in rural Spain. 3 acts 6m 9w 2 interiors
  In Gassner, J. ed. Twenty best European plays on the American stage
  In Tucker, S. M. ed. Twenty-five modern plays

Benchley, Nathaniel
The frogs of Spring. French 1954 98p
  Domestic comedy adapted from author's novel "Side Street." Experiences of two families living in New York City garden apartments. 3 acts 6 scenes 5m 3w 4b 1 exterior
Side Street (dramatization) See Benchley, N. The frogs of Spring

Beneath this spire. Trick, O. B.

Benedetti, Aldo de
Two dozen red roses; adapted from the Italian of Aldo de Benedetti, by Kenneth Horne. Acting ed. Dramatists 1953 91p front
  Domestic comedy. Complications arise when husband, in spirit of fun, anonymously sends roses to his wife. 3 acts 3m 2w 1 interior

Beneke, Angelin
c Symbols of Christmas. Eldridge 1958 15p (Eldridge Christmas entertainments)
  In dream, teenager is visited by groups representing Christmas bells, cards, trees, stockings, explaining origin of Christmas symbols. Background music and carols. 2 scenes 3m 2w extras 1 interior

Benét, Stephen Vincent
The Devil and Daniel Webster
  Based on the author's story. Lawyer Webster rescues the soul of a New Hampshire farmer from the Devil. 1 act 11m 1w extras 1 interior
  In Cerf, B. and Cartmell, V. H. eds. 24 favorite one-act plays
The Devil and Daniel Webster (moving picture adaptation) See Totheroh, D. and Benét, S. V. All that money can buy
  See also Totheroh, D. jt. auth.

Benfield, Derek
The way the wind blows. Deane 1954 66p illus ("Deane's" Ser. of plays)
  Domestic comedy. English family reunited for Christmas enjoys typical holiday and solves problems. Background carols. 3 acts 4 scenes 6m 5w 1 interior

Benjamin, James, and Kellerman, Don
No man is an island
  Television play. A dramatization of story by Helen Kroner about the friendship of two men, one of whom is a Negro, and the difficulties they overcome. 6m 1w
  In Look up and live (Television program) The seeking years

Benjamin Franklin. Feder, B.

Benjamin Franklin: statesman and inventor. Kissen, F.

Benkei on the bridge. Hiyoshi, Y.

Bennett, Rowena
c Puss in Boots. French 1954 71p illus
  Dramatization of old fairy tale. Mouse is puppet. Music offstage. 3 acts 9m 3w 3 exteriors
c The runaway pirate
  Verse play. A would-be pirate gets cold feet at the last moment. 1 act 4m extras 1 interior
  In Burack, A. S. ed. Four-star plays for boys

Bennett, Violet Ellen
Shadows walk softly. Nat. Union of Townswomen's Guilds 1953 19p
  Young widow's dream of ancestor's visit gives her courage to face problems. 1 act 9w 1 interior

Benny goes to Mistletonia. Rawe, M. S.

Benson, Sally
The young and beautiful. French 1956 87p illus
  Based on "The Saturday Evening Post" 'Josephine' short stories by F. Scott Fitzgerald
  A teen age girl frantically in search of romance, uses her talents to attract boy friends, to the exclusion of other sensibilities. Set in 1914. 3 acts 5 scenes 6m 5w 1 interior
  See also Kent, W. Seventeen

Benten the thief. Kawatake, M.

Beppo and Beth. Wilson, E.

Bequests. See Inheritance and succession; Wills

Berenice
  Racine, J. Berenice

Berenice, Queen of Palestine. See Berenice

Berenice. Racine, J.

Berg, Dick
The drop of a hat. Dramatists 1957 40p illus
  Intrigue and double dealing in the continuous fight for editorial control of a woman's fashion magazine. 1 act 9w 2 interiors

Berger, Earl of Bjalbo. See Birger of Bjalbo, Regent of Sweden

Berggren, Joyce
The harp that was silent
  Bible. Old Testament. Story of David, King of Israel and Bathsheba after she became his queen. 4m 4w 1 interior
  In Bryant, A. comp. Religious plays that click

Bergh, Haakon
Old King Cole. Book and lyrics by Joe Grenzeback; music by Haakon Bergh. French 1955 67p illus music
  Musical. King Cole can't celebrate his daughter's coming-out party, without jester's help, because magician has cast a spell on the fiddles. 2 acts 3 scenes 9m 7w 1 interior

Bergman, Ingmar
The magician
  Moving picture play set in mid-nineteenth century Sweden. The hazardous journey of a nefarious magician and his company on their way to Stockholm to perform at the Royal Palace. 9m 7w
  In Bergman, I. Four screenplays

Bergman, Ingmar—*Continued*

The seventh seal
Moving picture play. An agnostic knight returns from a holy crusade to play chess with Death. 12m 6w
In Bergman, I. Four screenplays

Smiles of a summer night
Moving picture play. Social comedy. Successful actress plots to regain a former lover. 4m 7w
In Bergman, I. Four screenplays

Wild strawberries
Moving picture play. On the day he is to become a Jubilee Doctor, seventy-six year old Professor Isak Borg reviews his family's life as he has known it through three generations. 12m 14w
In Bergman, I. Four screenplays

Berkey, Ralph. See Denker, H. jt. auth.

Berlin
Neuenburg, E. Fear is a murderer
Van Druten, J. I am a camera

History—Allied occupation, 1945-
Mannheimer, A. and Kohner, F. Stalin Allee

Bernadette Soubirous, Saint. See Soubirous, Bernadette, Saint

Bernard Shaw in heaven. Rubinstein, H. F.

Bernardine. Chase, M.

Berney, William. See Richardson, H. jt. auth.

Bernice, Princess of Judea. See Berenice

Berns, Julie, and Elman, Irving
Uncle Willie. French 1958 90p front
Domestic comedy. Life among Irish and Jewish inhabitants of the Bronx, early 20th century. 3 acts 6m 4w 3g 1 exterior

Bernstein, Leonard
Candide; book by Lilian Hellman; lyrics by Richard Wilbur; other lyrics by John Latouche and Dorothy Parker. Random House 1957 143p
Musical comedy based on Voltaire's novel. Satirizes the creed of Candide's tutor that "All is for the best in this best of all possible worlds." Portrays changing fortunes and disillusionment of Candide as he travels around Europe and to South America in search of his lost love. 2 acts 11 scenes Large mixed cast 3 interiors 8 exteriors

Candide (condensation)
In The Best plays of 1956-1957
In Broadway's best, 1957

West Side story; a musical (based on a conception of Jerome Robbins); book by Arthur Laurents; music by Leonard Bernstein; lyrics by Stephen Sondheim. Random House 1958 143p illus
Libretto of a musical comedy set in New York City. The tragic outcome of the rivalry between two teenage gangs. Musical scores published by G. Schirmer, and Chappell & Company. 2 acts Large mixed cast 6 interiors 6 exteriors

West Side story (condensation)
In Broadway's best, 1958

Wonderful town; book by Joseph Fields and Jerome Chodorov; music by Leonard Bernstein; lyrics by Betty Comden and Adolph Green. Random House 1953 173p illus
Musical comedy based on play: My sister Eileen, by Joseph Fields and Jerome Chodorov, and the stories by Ruth Mc-

Kenney. Adventures of two sisters from Ohio in New York City's Greenwich Village in 1930's. 2 acts 13 scenes 15m 5w extras 4 exteriors 4 interiors

Wonderful town (condensation)
In The Best plays of 1952-1953
In Theatre, 1953

Besier, Rudolf
The Barretts of Wimpole Street
Dramatization of the romance between Robert Browning and Elizabeth Barrett, complicated by domineering father and her illness. 5 acts 4 scenes 13m 4w 1 interior
In Sper, F. Favorite modern plays

Best bargain in the world. Fisher, A. and Rabe, O.

The **best** man. Vidal, G.

The **best** of the Old West. Howard, V.

The **best** part of Christmas. Newman, D.

Best trip ever. Manley, F.

Bethlehem. Ketchum, A.

Bethlehem's Field. Ashton, L. S.

Betrothal
Howells, W. D. A previous engagement

Betsy's first report card. Lynch, P.

"Better than seven sons." Bailey, H. F.

Betti, Ugo
The burnt flower-bed (L'aiuola bruciata) tr. by Henry Reed. ᵣFrench's Acting edᵢ French (London) 1957 57p
Futile negotiations and death on a frontier among those who vaguely feel the power of faith and love in humanity. 3 acts 5m 2w extras 1 interior
—Same
In Betti, U. Three plays

The queen and the rebels (La regina e gli insorti) tr. by Henry Reed ᵣFrench's Acting edᵢ French (London) 1957 60p illus
Symbolism. During revolution woman lets police think she is the hunted Queen, while real Queen suffers from fear. 4 acts 7m 3w extras 1 interior
—Same
In Betti, U. Three plays

Summertime
Girl pursues man, gets him out of scrape, wins him, then almost decides he is too weak to be good husband. 3 acts 5m 6w 1 interior 2 exteriors
In Betti, U. Three plays

Betting. See Gambling

Betty gets a new dress. Quinlan, M. E.

Between two thieves. LeRoy, W.

Bevan, Mark
Inquest on Monday. ᵣFrench's Acting edᵢ French (London) 1954 24p illus
Old gentleman hears different versions of same assault and battery case. 1 act 7m 2w 1 exterior

Beware the bear! Crary, M.

Beyond Good Friday. Agnew, E. J.

Beyond the horizon. O'Neill, E.

Bibi. Nathan, P. S.

Bible

Criticism, interpretation, etc.
Wills, G. Alice in Bibleland

Drama
See Mysteries and miracle plays—English

Bible—*Continued*

History of Biblical events
Racine, J. Athaliah

Miracles
See Jesus Christ—Miracles

Parables
See Jesus Christ—Parables

Prophecies
Estes, S. In quest of power through prophecy

Prophecies—Messiah
See Messiah—Prophecies

Bible. Old Testament
Bailey, H. F. The Feast of the Ingathering
Berggren, J. The harp that was silent
Estes, S. In quest of power through faith
Howard, V. The search
Lawrence, D. H. David
    See also names of Biblical characters and events

Bible. Old Testament. Apocrypha. Judith
Giraudoux, J. Judith

Bible. Old Testament. Daniel
The Play of Daniel
c Spamer, C. M. Daniel in the lions' den

Bible. Old Testament. Esther
Asbrand, K. The beautiful queen

Bible. Old Testament. Exodus
c Spamer, C. M. The baby Moses
c Spamer, C. M. The flight out of Egypt

Bible. Old Testament. Genesis
Abraham and Isaac (Brome manuscript) Abraham and Isaac
Abraham and Isaac (Brome manuscript) The sacrifice of Isaac
Blazer, F. The well of Dothan
Chester plays. Noah's flood
Coventry plays. Cain and Abel
Daviot, G. The little dry thorn
Estes, S. In quest of power through divine guidance
Fry, C. The firstborn
Gassner, J. The Brome Abraham and Isaac
Obey, A. Noah
c Spamer, C. M. Noah's ark
c Spamer, C. M. The Pharaoh's dream
York plays. The creation, and The fall of Lucifer
York plays. The creation of Adam and Eve
York plays. The creation of man
York plays. The creation of the heavenly beings: The fall of Lucifer
York plays. The fall of man
York plays. The Garden of Eden

Bible. Old Testament. Hosea
Nicholson, N. A match for the Devil

Bible. Old Testament. Job
Corey, O. The Book of Job
MacLeish, A. J.B.

Bible. Old Testament. Jonah
Mankowitz, W. It should happen to a dog
Nathan, R. Jezebel's husband

Bible. Old Testament. Joshua
Estes, S. In quest of power through decision
c Spamer, C. M. The walls of Jericho

Bible. Old Testament. Judges
Howells, W. D. Samson
Morris, T. B. The watcher of the road
c Spamer, C. M. Gideon and the angel
c Spamer, C. M. Samson and Delilah

Bible. Old Testament. Kings
Estes, S. In quest of power through wisdom
Racine, J. Athaliah
c Spamer, C. M. Elijah, the prophet
c Spamer, C. M. Elisha cures Naaman
c Spamer, C. M. Solomon's Temple

Bible. Old Testament. Ruth
Bailey, H. F. "Better than seven sons"
Estes, S. In quest of power through obedience
c Spamer, C. M. Ruth

Bible. Old Testament. Samuel
Abel, L. Absalom
Bailey, H. F. "We bring this child unto the Lord"
Dimondstein, B. David and Bath-Sheba
Estes, S. In quest of power through dedication
Howard, V. David and Goliath
c Spamer, C. M. David and Goliath
c Spamer, C. M. Jonathan's son
c Spamer, C. M. Saul and the ghost

Bible. New Testament
Howard, V. The search
York plays. The judgment
York plays. The last judgment
    See also Jesus Christ—Nativity

Bible. New Testament. Acts
Estes, S. In quest of power through courage
Estes, S. In quest of power through witnessing
Johnston, R. A. The Digby Conversion of St Paul
Knox, A. He knew the Master
Phillips, J. B. The Ascension
Phillips, J. B. The gift of the Holy Spirit
York plays. The Ascension

Bible. New Testament. Apocrypha. Nicodemus
Harrowing of hell. The harrowing of hell

Bible. New Testament. Gospels
Bailey, H. F. A manger lowly
Bailey, H. F. "There was a garden"
Bailey, H. F. Walk in the light
Estes, S. In quest of power through humility
Ghelderode, M. de. Barabbas
Hollinshead, L. M. Publican and sinner
Johnston, R. A. The York Resurrection
Phillips, J. B. The arrest in the garden
Phillips, J. B. The baptism of Jesus
Phillips, J. B. The calling of the disciples
Phillips, J. B. The centurion's servant
Phillips, J. B. Christ enters Jerusalem
Phillips, J. B. Christ the Son of God
Phillips, J. B. The cleansing of the Temple
Phillips, J. B. The death of Jesus and the promise of the Resurrection

Bible. New Testament. Gospels—*Continued*
Phillips, J. B. The healing of the paralyzed man
Phillips, J. B. Jesus appears to His disciples
Phillips, J. B. The journey to Jerusalem
Phillips, J. B. The Last Supper
Phillips, J. B. A man called Jesus (26 plays)
Phillips, J. B. The parable of the last judgment
Phillips, J. B. The temptation of Jesus
Phillips, J. B. The Transfiguration
Phillips, J. B. The trial before Pilate
c Spamer, C. M. The baptism of Jesus
c Spamer, C. M. Christ lives again
c Spamer, C. M. Jairus' daughter
c Spamer, C. M. The Last Supper
c Spamer, C. M. The loaves and the fishes
c Spamer, C. M. The parable of the sower
The three Maries
York plays. The Crucifixion
York plays. Palm Sunday
York plays. The Resurrection
York plays. The second trial before Pilate: The scourging and condemnation
York plays. The temptation of Christ

Bible. New Testament. John
Coventry plays. The woman taken in adultery
Phillips, J. B. The healing at the Pool of Bethesda
Phillips, J. B. The healing of the man born blind
Phillips, J. B. Jesus appears in Galilee
Phillips, J. B. The Resurrection of Jesus

Bible. New Testament. Luke
Asbrand, K. Count your blessings
Coventry plays. The Annunciation
Coventry plays. The parliament of heaven: The Annunciation and Conception
Estes, S. In quest of power through prophecy
Parker, M. M. The prodigal comes home
Phillips, J. B. The boyhood of Jesus
Phillips, J. B. The parable of the Pharisee and the tax collector
Raeburn, H. The green wood
c Spamer, C. M. The boy Jesus visits Jerusalem
c Spamer, C. M. The Christ child in the temple
c Spamer, C. M. Gabriel visits Mary
c Spamer, C. M. The good Samaritan
c Spamer, C. M. Jesus and the fishermen
c Spamer, C. M. Jesus is born
c Spamer, C. M. The widow's son
Towneley plays. The play of the shepherds
Towneley plays. The Wakefield Second shepherds' pageant

Bible. New Testament. Mark
Phillips, J. B. Jesus returns to Galilee

Bible. New Testament. Matthew
Coventry plays. Herod and the kings
Emurian, E. K. Inasmuch
Emurian, E. K. The living dramatization of the Beatitudes
Phillips, J. B. The Lord's prayer

c Spamer, C. M. The wise men
Towneley plays. The Wakefield Pageant of Herod the Great
Bickerstaff, Isaac, pseud. See Swift, Jonathan
Bicycles and tricycles
c Miller, H. L. The case of the balky bike
Biddle, Anthony Joseph Drexel
Crichton, K. The happiest millionaire
Biddle, Cordelia Drexel, and Crichton, Kyle
My Philadelphia father (dramatization) See Crichton, K. The happiest millionaire
Bielby, Morwenna R.
I was in prison. Epworth 1955 72p
    Quaker Elizabeth Fry's reforms in English prisons for women. 3 acts 4m 12w 2b extras 1 interior 1 exterior
The **big** deal. Chayefsky, P.
The **big** decision. Hauser, W.
The **big** melodrama. Howard, V.
The **big** middle. Corey, O. R.
Big shot. Hartley, R.
Big top circus. Sognefest, A.
Bill and Sue. Brenner, M.
Bill of Rights (U.S.) See United States. Constitution. 1st-10th amendments
Bill visits Mexico. McGee, A.
Billboards. See Signs and signboards
The **billion** dollar saint. White, N. E.
Billy Adams, American. Case, T. W.
Billy Budd. Coxe, L. O. and Chapman, R.
Billy the Kid. See Bonney, William Harrison
Biography. Behrman, S. N.
Bird, Robert Montgomery
The broker of Bogota
    Tragic conflict between father and the son who betrays him, set in a Spanish colony in the New World. Verse play. 5 acts 16 scenes 8m 2w extras 3 interiors 3 exteriors
In Quinn, A. H. ed. Representative American plays
The **bird-catcher** in hell. Enami, S.
A **bird** in the bush. Martens, A. C.
Birds
c Mathews, J. Audubon's America
c Spamer, C. The terrible grood
c Woolsey, J. and Sechrist, E. H. Saint Peter and the birds
The **birds.** Aristophanes
The **birds** and the boys. Davidson, W.
The **Birds'** Christmas Carol. Miller, H. L.
Birger de Bielbo. See Birger of Bjalbo, Regent of Sweden
Birger of Bjalbo, Regent of Sweden
Strindberg, A. Earl Birger of Bjälbo
The **birth** of Christ. York plays
Birthday honours. Jones, P.
A **birthday** long ago. Ruth, G. J.
A **birthday** through the centuries. Lowe, E.
Birthdays
c Miller, H. L. Wait and see
Rosenthal, A. Red letter day
c Woolsey, J. and Sechrist, E. H. Johnny's birthday surprise

Bishop Jón Arason. Sveinbjörnsson, T.

Bishops
Ghelderode, M. de. Chronicles of hell

The Bishop's bonfire. O'Casey, S.

The Bishop's candlesticks. Olfson, L.

Bissell, Marian. See Bissell, R. jt. auth.

Bissell, Richard
7 ½ cents (dramatization) See Adler, R. and Ross, J. The pajama game

Bissell, Richard; Burrows, Abe, and Bissell, Marian
Say, darling. Little 1958 182p (An Atlantic Monthly press bk)
    Comedy based on the novel by Richard Bissell. Experiences of an author called to New York to assist in production of musical play based on his best-selling novel. 3 acts 13 scenes 19m 8w extras 9 interiors

A bit of peace and quiet. Burgess, C. V.

Black, Franklyn
c The heartless princess. French (London) 1954 74p (French's Juvenile ser)
    Fairy tale. With help of clever fox, Prince Alexis uncovers plot to overthrow king and wins his princess. 3 acts 8 scenes 4m 8w extras 2 interiors 1 exterior

Black-ey'd Susan. Jerrold, D.

Black limelight. Sherry, G.

The black mask
    Mysterious character warns group of boys to cancel their Halloween party. Incidental music. 1 act 5b extras 1 interior
In 'Round the year plays for the grades

Black star. Armer, A. and Grauman, W. E.

The blackbird. Howard, V.

Blacklock, Jack
A time of minor miracles. Bakers Plays 1960 26p
    Busload of travelers marooned at home of embittered radio commentator at Christmas help restore his faith. Background music. 1 act 6m 3w 1 interior

Blackmail. See Extortion

Blackmore, Peter
Down came a blackbird. Deane 1954 86p illus ("Deane's" Ser. of plays)
    Comedy. Efficient secretary to Egyptologist has plastic surgery to correct ugly nose. 2 acts 5 scenes 4m 4w 1 interior
Mad about men. Deane 1956 78p ("Deane's" Ser. of plays)
    Romantic comedy. Mermaid impersonates her Cornish cousin for two weeks. 3 acts 6 scenes 5m 5w 1 interior

Blackmore, Richard Doddridge
Lorna Doone (radio adaptation) See Miller, H. L. Lorna Doone

The blacks: a clown show. Genet, J.

Blake, Lisabeth. See Violett, E. jt. auth.

Blake, Richard
What hath God wrought
    Television play. Samuel Morse faces problems in attempt to construct the telegraph. 8m 1w extras
In Roberts, E. B. Television writing and selling

Blake's decision. McCarty, R. K.

Bland, Margaret
Pink and patches (dramatization) See Bucci, M. A pink party dress

Blankfort, Dorothy, and Blankfort, Michael
Monique. French 1957 93p
    Murder mystery based on novel: Celle qui n'était plus: The woman who was no more, by Pierre Boileau and Thomas Narcejac. Crafty woman doctor, psychological destruction, suicide, and surprise ending. 2 acts 6 scenes 5m 6w 1 interior

Blankfort, Michael. See Blankfort, D. jt. auth.

Blankman, Howard
By hex. Book by John Rengier; music and lyrics by Howard Blankman; some additional lyrics by Richard Gehman and John Rengier. Dramatists 1956 60p illus
    Musical comedy. Young couple flout Amish tradition only to find there is more peace in the old ways. 2 acts 8 scenes 8m 5w 5 exteriors 1 interior

Blazer, Frances
The prodigal mother. Bakers Plays 1958 23p (Baker's Royalty plays)
    Mother who has never told anyone that son has serious illness, is accused of selfishness. 1 act 3m 2w 1 interior
The well of Dothan. Bakers Plays 1958 19p illus
    Bible. Old Testament. Genesis. Joseph's resentment towards his brothers ends when he heeds advice of his father. Jacob. 1 act 2 scenes 4m 1w 2b 1 exterior

The bleeding heart of Wee Jon. Campbell, J. G.

Blewett, Dorothy
Quiet night. [Rev. and rewritten acting ed] French (London) 1953 56p
    One night's activities in hospital ward in Australia. 3 acts 3m 11w 1 interior

Blind
Armer, A. and Grauman, W. E. In darkened rooms
Cullinan, G. The Republic of the Blind
Ghelderode, M. de. The blind men
c Hollinshead, L. M. Thank you, God for everything
Lumsden, M. The gift
Phillips, M. K. Grandma and mistletoe
Sakanishi, S. tr. Plop! Click!

The blind men. Ghelderode, M. de

Blindness
George, M. Symphonie pastorale
Gibson, W. The miracle worker
Horne, K. A. This dark world and wide
Schulman, S. H. Turn my face toward the east

Bliss, Philip Paul
Emurian, E. K. It is well with my soul

Blithe spirit. Coward, N.

Blobo's boy. Zuckerman, A. J.

Blood wedding. García Lorca, F.

The bloody tenet. Schevill, J.

Blossom, Lena
c The safety elves
    The safety elves tell the children how to avoid accidents. 13 characters 1 interior
    In Birdsall, R. ed. Creative plays for every school month

Blue concerto. Seiger, M. L.

Blue denim. Herlihy, J. L. and Noble, W.

The blue serge suit. Howard, V.

Blue stocking. Sergel, R.

Blueprint, U.S.A. Porter, J. C.

Blyton, Enid
c Finding the tickets. Evans 1955 10p
  Comedy. Last minute search for railroad tickets causes three boys to miss train. 1 scene 3b 1 interior
c Mr Sly-One and the cats. Evans 1955 12p
  Fairy tale. Pixies, pretending to be cats, outwit old man who stole their boots. Singing and dancing. 1 scene 1m 5b 1 exterior
c The mothers' meeting. Evans 1955 11p
  Comedy. Mr Muddle disturbs the quiet of mothers' meeting by awakening their babies. 1 scene 1m 6w 1 interior
c Who will hold the giant? Evans 1955 12p
  Fairy tale. Fairies and gnomes plot to imprison destructive giant. 1 scene Unidentified cast 1 exterior

Boarding-houses. See Hotels, taverns, etc.

Boarding schools
  Kendall, K. Darling girl
  See also Schools

Bobby and the Lincoln speech. Hark, M. and McQueen, N.

Bobby and the time machine. Wallerstein, J. S.

Bock, Jerry
  The body beautiful; a musical comedy; book by Joseph Stein and Will Glickman; music by Jerry Bock; lyrics by Sheldon Harnick. French 1957 79p illus (French's Musical lib)
    A fight manager gets an Ivy League graduate who wants to be a prize fighter but can't fight. 2 acts 18 scenes 21m 6w extras 7 interiors 4 exteriors
  Fiorello! Book by Jerome Weidman and George Abbott; music by Jerry Bock; lyrics by Sheldon Harnick. Random House 1960 147p illus
    Musical comedy. Fiorello La Guardia's political rise and election as mayor of New York City. 2 acts Large mixed cast 4 interiors 5 exteriors
  Fiorello! (condensation)
    In The Best plays of 1959-1960
    In Broadway's best, 1960

The **body** beautiful. Bock, J.

Body-snatching
  Thomas, D. The doctor and the devils

The **body** was well nourished. See Launder, F. and Gilliat, S. Meet a body

Boegehold, Betty
c The shoemaker's Christmas
    Fairy tale. While shoemaker sleeps, elves make shoes for him so that he will have money for Christmas presents. 3 scenes 3m 4w extras 1 interior
    In Birdsall, R. ed. Creative plays for every school month

Boileau, Pierre
  The woman who was no more: Celle qui n'était plus (dramatization) See Blankfort, D. and Blankfort, M. Monique

Boker, George Henry
  Francesca da Rimini
    Tragedy in 14th century Italy. Relations between two noble families: two brothers are rivals for the daughter of the Lord of Ravenna. Verse play. 5 acts 13 scenes 7m 2w extras 5 interiors 4 exteriors
    In Quinn, A. H. ed. Representative American plays

Boland, Bridget
  The prisoner. Dramatists 1956 69p illus
    Psychological methods (brainwashing) employed in extracting a "confession" from Catholic Cardinal imprisoned in mid-European country. 3 acts 10 scenes 8m 1w 2 interiors
  —Same
    In Plays of the year v10
  The return
    A middle aged nun who leaves convent after thirty-six years faces adjustment to a completely changed world. 3 acts 6 scenes 3m 3w 2 interiors
    In Plays of the year v9

Boleyn, Anne. See Anne Boleyn, consort of Henry VIII, King of England

Boli, Lois
c They found Christmas. Eldridge 1953 7p (Eldridge Christmas entertainments)
    Fantasy. Children learn origin of Christmas customs. Carols. 1 act 1w 1b 1g extras

Bolivar, Simón
  Ullman, S. S. The youth, Bolivar

Bollans, G. E.
  The crooked courtship. Deane 1955 30p ("Deane's" Ser. of plays)
    Comedy. Widow's marriage to younger man foiled by her daughter, a policewoman trainee. 1 act 5w 1 interior
  Wedding bells for Clara? Deane 1956 28p ("Deane's" Ser. of plays)
    Romantic comedy. Woman's pen-friend suitor turns out to be married man. 1 act 6w 1 interior

A **bolt** from heaven. Weiss, H.

Bolton, Guy
  Child of fortune. Dramatists 1957 82p illus
    Adapted from novel: The wings of the dove, by Henry James. Man's feigned love for invalid American heiress in Europe develops into real devotion. 3 acts 5 scenes 6m 5w 2 interiors

Bolton, Guy, and McGowan, John
  Girl crazy; a straight play version adapted by Anne Coulter Martens, Newt Mitzman and William Dalzell from the musical comedy. Dramatic 1954 93p illus
    Romantic comedy. Eastern young man operating dude ranch in Arizona wins Western girl. 3 acts 5 scenes 10m 8w 1 interior

The **bomb.** Badger, A.

A **bomb** for Santa. Mattice, I.

Bombs
  Daviot, G. The Balwhinnie bomb

Bond, Christopher
  The food of love ("The sweetest canticle") Deane 1955 71p ("Deane's" Ser. of plays)
    Romantic comedy. Music-master in English public school finally acclaimed as great musician and benefactor to school. Background music. 3 acts 4 scenes 6m 3w 1 interior

Bond, Nelson
  Mr Mergenthwirker's lobblies. French 1957 93p illus
    Romantic comedy of fantasy and mystery. Shy man's two imaginary companions help identify murderer. 3 acts 4 scenes 7m 3w extras 2 interiors
  State of mind. French 1958 76p illus
    Comedy. Owner of large estate, fed up with taxes and regimentation, secedes from the Union. 3 acts 12 scenes 7m 5w 1b extras 3 settings

The **bonehead** case. Garry, J. F.

Bonheur, Rosa
Spamer, C. Rosa Bonheur

Bonn, Myrtle
c Magical letters. Nat. Educ. 1955 15p
    Pictures of seven famous Americans
    come to life to show American ideals.
    Singing. 4 acts 6m 2w 4b 3g extras
    1 interior

Bonney, William Harrison
Smith, B. and Webb, C. Mañana bandits
Vidal, G. The death of Billy the Kid

Bontsche Schweig. See Perl, A. The world
of Sholom Aleichem

The **Book** of Job. Corey, O. R.

The **book** revue. Hark, M. and McQueen, N.

Book Week
c Fisher, A. Once upon a time
c Fisher, A. Treasure hunt
c Hark, M. and McQueen, N. The book
  revue
c Hark, M. and McQueen, N. Off the shelf
c Lunnon, B. S. Johnny has comicopia
c Miller, H. L. Boys in books
c Miller, H. L. Girls in books
c Miller, H. L. The library circus
c Miller, H. L. The miraculous tea party
  Miller, H. L. Spooks in books
c Miller, H. L. Turning the tables
c Newman, D. Aladdin
c Newman, D. The Emperor's new clothes
c Newman, D. A gift to the world
c Newman, D. The real Princess
c Spamer, C. Little blank book
c Spamer, C. The new book
c Thompson, B. J. Pleasant dreams
c Woolsey, J. and Sechrist, E. H. The
  wonder world of books

Books
Miller, H. L. Spooks in books

          Defacement
    See Books—Mutilation, defacement,
etc.

     Mutilation, defacement, etc.
c Hark, M. and McQueen, N. Off the shelf
c Spamer, C. The new book

Books and crooks. Mitzman, N. and Dalzell, W.

Books and reading
Hark, M. and McQueen, N. Books are
  bridges

Books are bridges. Hark, M. and
McQueen, N.

Booksellers and bookselling
Mauermann, G. A cup of kindness

The **boor**. Chekhov, A.

Booth, Edwin
Geiger, M. Edwin Booth

Boots and shoes
c Miller, H. L. New shoes
c Short, R. The red shoes

A **bore** for breakfast. Burgess, C. V.

Borer, Mary Cathcart. See Ridley, A. jt.
auth.

Boretz, Alvin
The trial of Poznan
    Television play. Trial of three Polish
    youths charged with murdering police
    officer during the Posen (Poznan) riots
    of 1956. 8m
  In Best television plays, 1957

Borgers, Edward. See Borgers, P. jt. auth.

Borgers, Pamela, and Borgers, Edward
c The strange case of Mother Goose: words
  by Mother Goose, Pamela and Edward
  Borgers; music by Pamela and Edward
  Borgers. Children's Theatre 1957 74p
music
    Musical revue based on the story of the
    first edition of Mother Goose rhymes
    published by Thomas Fleet. 2 acts 9m 6w
    extras 1 interior

Borgia, Cesare
Lee, N. Caesar Borgia

Sisson, R. A. The splendid outcasts

Borgia, Lucrezia
Sisson, R. A. The splendid outcasts

Boris and the briefcase. Anderson, R. A.
and Sweeney, R. L.

Boris and the spaceman. Anderson, R. A.
and Sweeney, R. L.

Boris Godunov, Czar of Russia
Pushkin, A. Boris Godunov

Boris Godunov. Pushkin, A.

Bornstein, Marilyn and Cole, Gloria
c Paul in food land
    Little boy who won't eat the right foods
    has a dream in which he learns about
    nutrition. Includes songs. 1m 1w 10b
    extras 1 interior
  In Birdsall, R. ed. Creative plays for
  every school month

Boruff, John
The loud red Patrick. French 1956 104p
illus
    Romantic comedy suggested by novel
    by Ruth McKenney. 17 year old girl
    turns tables on over-bearing father by
    using family council he instituted to
    secure his consent to her marriage. 3 acts
    4m 3w 2g 1 interior

The **boss**. Howard, P.

The **boss**. Sheldon, E.

Bost, Pierre. See Cannan, D. jt. auth.

Boston
     Social life and customs
Howells, W. D. Five o'clock tea
Howells, W. D. Out of the question

Boston Tea Party, 1773
Woolsey, J. and Sechrist, E. H. Paul
Revere, Boston patriot

Botany
c Spamer, C. The orange tree

Both ends meet. Macrae, A.

Bottomley, Gordon
Ardvorlich's wife
    Verse play based on a historical episode
    in: The legend of Montrose, by Sir
    Walter Scott. In 16th century Scotland
    the Lady of Ardvorlich becomes insane
    when her brother is murdered by the
    feuding MacGregor clan. Includes a
    women's dance and words and music
    of a song. 8w 1 exterior
  In Bottomley, G. Poems and plays

Deirdre
    Based on a version of the Irish Deirdre
    legend in: Deirdire, and The lay of the
    children of Uisne, translated by Alex-
    ander Carmichael. 4 acts 10 scenes 8m
    7w 2 interiors 7 exteriors
  In Bottomley, G. Poems and plays

Bottomley, Gordon—*Continued*

Fire at Callart
> Historical verse play set in 16th century Scotland. Mary Cameron, daughter of the Laird of Callart, is the only one of her family to survive the plague. 9m 4w 2 interiors

In Bottomley, G. Poems and plays

Gruach
> Lord and Lady Macbeth, chief characters in Shakespeare's play: Macbeth, are portrayed in their youth when young Macbeth arrives as the king's messenger and meets his future wife. Verse play. 2 scenes 6m 7w 1 interior

In Bottomley, G. Poems and plays

King Lear's wife
> Concerns the leading characters in Shakespeare's King Lear. The daughter of a dying queen kills her father's mistress. Verse play 2m 7w 1 interior

In Bottomley, G. Poems and plays

Marsaili's weeping
> Historical tragedy in verse set in 16th century Scotland. The chief of Clan Mackintosh, rejected lover of a woman of the Camerons of Rannoch, murders her three children. 3m 5w 1 exterior

In Bottomley, G. Poems and plays

The riding to Lithend
> Dramatization of an episode from the Njála saga. A wife takes revenge on her husband for striking her. Verse play set in Iceland in 990. 9m 9w extras 1 interior

In Bottomley, G. Poems and plays

Towie Castle
> Historical verse play based on the Scottish ballad: Edom o'Gordon. Set in 16th century Scotland during the civil wars. 1m 4w 1 exterior

In Bottomley, G. Poems and plays

The white widow
> Episodes from the life of Mary Stuart. Queen of the Scots. Verse play. 8m 11w 1 interior 1 exterior

In Bottomley, G. Poems and plays

The woman from the voe
> Dramatization of legend of the Shetland Islands about people from beneath the sea who sometimes intermarry with human beings on land. Verse play. 3m 7w 1 interior 1 exterior

In Bottomley, G. Poems and plays

Boucicault, Dion

The Colleen Bawn
> Nineteenth century Ireland. A man rues his rash first marriage, when he realizes a better one, with an heiress, could have been made. Incidental music. 3 acts 14 scenes 9m 6w extras 6 interiors 6 exteriors

In Rowell, G. ed. Nineteenth century plays

The octoroon; or, Life in Louisiana
> Octoroon daughter of bankrupt planter commits suicide when she is bought by a cunning overseer. 5 acts 8 scenes 8m 3w extras 2 interiors 5 exteriors

In Quinn, A. H. ed. Representative American plays

Bowen, Terence

Star dust. ⌈French's Acting ed⌉ French 1954 31p illus
> Farce. Actress attempts to get interview with producer. 1 act 2m 4w 1 interior

Bowie, Lynn

"You heard me!" Bakers Plays 1954 96p illus (Baker's Royalty plays)
> Farce. Mild-mannered man mistaken for criminal tries disguise. 3 acts 4 scenes 5m 8w 1 interior

Bowles, Jane

In the summer house. Random House 1954 122p illus
> Social comedy. Mother and daughter have boarding house near Mexican border. 2 acts 5 scenes 5m 10w extras 1 interior 2 exteriors

In the summer house (condensation)
> *In* The Best plays of 1953-1954

Bowles, Paul

No exit (adaptation) See Sartre, J. P. No exit

Box and Cox. Morton, J. M.

Boxes

Richards, I. A. A leak in the universe

Boxing

Bock, J. The body beautiful

Corrie, J. Love and the boxer

Odets, C. Golden boy

Serling, R. Requiem for a heavyweight

Boy appeal. Franklin, C.

The boy friend. Wilson, S.

The boy Jesus visits Jerusalem. Spamer, C. M.

Boy meets girl in Washington. Taggart, T.

A boy named Beulah. Tobias, J.

The boy next door. Murray, J.

Boy of mine. Thomas, D.

Boy Scouts

Addis, H. St George's Day

c Clark, M. G. Columbus and a Boy Scout

c Gow, R. Under the skull and bones

c Spamer, C. N. The honored ones

c Woolsey, J. and Sechrist, E. H. Radios versus doughnuts

The boy who changed the world, Malango, P.

The boy who had no gravity. Spamer, C.

The boy who knew Jesus. Harrington, H.

Boyd, A. K.

Clive's fear, unique
> Based on incident in Robert Clive's life described in Browning's poem: Clive. Duel over cheating at cards. 11m 1 interior

In Boyd, A. K. An hour to play

Fighting Bob
> Adapted from Sheridan's play: The rivals. Comedy of manners in 18th century England. Bob Acres challenges Beverley to duel over Lady Lydia. 2 scenes 4m 1 interior 1 exterior

In Boyd, A. K. An hour to play

Half hour on the "Asia"
> Based on an incident recorded in "Anson's voyage round the world" by Richard Walter. American Indians mutiny on board the Spanish man-of-war "Asia." 1 interior

In Boyd, A. K. An hour to play

The mock doctor
> Abridged from the play of the same title by Fielding, after Molière's 'Le médecin malgré lui'. Satirical farce. Woodcutter, posing as doctor, achieves success and promotes a romance, to the chagrin of his wife. 4 scenes 7m 3w 1 interior 1 exterior

In Boyd, A. K. An hour to play

Boyd, A. K.—*Continued*

Pip and the convict
  Adaptation of an incident in "Great expectations" by Dickens. The orphan boy, Pip, befriends an escaped convict. 4 scenes 5m 1w 1b 1 interior 1 exterior
  In Boyd, A. K. An hour to play

Prince Arthur and Hubert
  Adapted from Shakespeare's play: King John. In prison, Arthur of Brittany pleads with Hubert de Burgh not to execute King John's order to burn Arthur's eyes out. Elizabethan dialect. 4m 1 interior
  In Boyd, A. K. An hour to play

Robbery at Gadshill
  Adapted from Shakespeare's play: King Henry IV, Part I. Comedy. Henry, Prince of Wales and his friend Poins set trap for Falstaff. Elizabethan dialect. 2 scenes 6m 1 interior 1 exterior
  In Boyd, A. K. An hour to play

The **boyhood** of Jesus. Phillips, J. B.

Boyle, Hal
  Ettlinger, D. The thousand-yard look

Boys
  Anderson, R. All summer long
  DuBois, G. Huckleberry Finn
  Foote, H. John Turner Davis
  Hartley, R. Big shot
  Hastings, C. Uncertain joy
c Howard, V. Oliver Twist asks for more
c Lunnon, B. S. Johnny has comicopia
  McCarty, R. K. Longing for Christmas
  MacDougall, R. The facts of life
  Olfson, L. The adventures of Tom Sawyer
  Panetta, G. Comic strip
  Phillips, M. K. Hold that Indian
  Rouverol, A. Andy Hardy
c Schoneman, E. T. The wish machine
  Snyder, W. H. Another summer
  York, M. A. Treasure Island

Boys in books. Miller, H. L.

Brabazon, Francis
  The bridge
    Philosophical verse play in which old man shows others the futility of war. 4m extras 1 exterior
  In Brabazon, F. Singing threshold

  Happy monody
    Verse play for children. Four shop keepers and others discuss life in a philosophical vein. 11m 2w no scenery
  In Brabazon, F. Singing threshold

  The madmen
    Philosophical verse play about a man who discovers the meaning of sainthood. 1m extras 1 exterior
  In Brabazon, F. Singing threshold

  The moon
    Philosophical verse play about a man who learns to give up everything in order to follow God. 2m 1w extras 1 exterior
  In Brabazon, F. Singing threshold

  The quest
    Verse play. Philosophical drama about different people who seek God, or an ultimate reality. 5 scenes 11m extras 1 interior 1 exterior
  In Brabazon, F. Singing threshold

  Singing threshold
    Several years in life of young farmer's widow. Verse play. 4 acts 7 scenes Large mixed cast 3 interiors 3 exteriors
  In Brabazon, F. Singing threshold

The stranger
    Philosophical verse play about the necessity for each human being to be aware of the continual presence of God. 1m 1w extras 1 exterior
  In Brabazon, F. Singing threshold

Bradbury, A. J.
c The King's anniversary. Paxton 1954 24p
    Romantic comedy. Keeper of King's Duster uses magic paint to decorate court chambers and almost ruins plans for marriage of king's daughter. Background music. 3 acts 10m 5w extras 1 interior

Bradbury, Parnell
  The come back. Deane 1955 52p ("Deane's" Ser. of plays)
    Domestic comedy. Man believing in reincarnation, thinks he is a bigamist, because in previous existence he was a Mormon. 3 acts 2m 5w 1 interior

Braddon, Mary Elizabeth. See Hazlewood, C. H.

Bradley, Anne
  This England. National Union of Townswomen's Guilds 1953 7p
    Comedy. Mother, daughter, aunt bicycle out to country to picnic. 3w 1 exterior

The **braggart.** Lathrop, D.

Braille, Louis
  Schulman, S. H. Turn my face toward the east

Brain-washing
  Boland, B. The prisoner
  Crouch, A. Not by might

The **brains** of the family. Clandon, L.

Bramley-Moore, Z. See Gattey, C. N. jt. auth.

Brampton, Joan
  Dilemma. Dramatists 1958 78p illus
    A man marries girl for the money she will inherit and when she dies tries to trick her grandfather with an impostor in her place. 3 acts 3m 3w 1 interior

Brand, Mona
  Strangers in the land
    Psychological drama about changes in some rubber planters' characters and ideals as a result of guerilla war in Malaya after World War II. 2 acts 4 scenes 6m 4w 1 interior
  In Two plays about Malaya

Brand. Ibsen, H.

The **brass** ring. Elman, I.

Bratt, H.
  Sprechstunde (adaptation) See Roffey, J. and Harbord, G. Night of the fourth

Braun, Wilbur
  Drop dead! Bakers Plays 1956 32p
    Mystery comedy. Detective, with aid of clever newspaper woman, solves so-called murder. 1 act 2 scenes 3m 3w 1 interior
    For other plays by this author see Chadwicke, Alice; Faust, Esther; Fernway, Peggy

Bravery. See Courage

Brazil
  Ullman, S. S. A democratic emperor

Bread
c Miller, H. L. The Bread and Butter Shop

The **Bread** and Butter Shop. Miller, H. L.

Break of noon. Claudel, P.

Breakdown. Werry, W.

Brecht, Bertolt

The Caucasian chalk circle
Based on a 14th century Chinese play: The circle of chalk, by Hui-lan-ki. In a medieval Caucasian city, wily judge uses ancient chalk circle test to prove that young woman who rescued a child abandoned by its mother during a war deserves to keep child. 2 parts 5 scenes Large mixed cast 9 interiors 3 exteriors

In Brecht, B. Two plays

The good woman of Setzuan
Parable of the conflict of good and evil as seen in the life of a poor woman who tries to follow commandment, love thy neighbor. Set in provincial China. Includes songs. 18 scenes 13m 10w extras 5 interiors 3 exteriors

In Brecht, B. Two plays

Mother Courage; English version by Eric Bentley
The tragedy of war reflected in the experiences of a camp follower and her family during the Thirty Years' War. Includes musical scores and words of songs, and ballads. 12 scenes Large mixed cast 2 interiors 10 exteriors

In Bentley, E. ed. The modern theatre v2

Saint Joan of the stockyards; English version by Frank Jones
Business manipulation, industrial strife, and labor trouble in Chicago's stockyards. Verse play. 11 acts 21 scenes 9m 4w extras 6 interiors 9 exteriors

In Bentley, E. ed. From the modern repertoire; ser. 3

The threepenny opera
Ballad opera based on John Gay's: The beggar's opera, and poems of François Villon. Satirizes corrupt political conditions in 17th century England. Features exploits of Captain MacHeath, alias Mackie the Knife. Songs, background music. 3 acts 9 scenes 20m 12w 6 interiors

In Bentley, E. ed. The modern theatre v 1

Breck, Flora E.

One Father of mankind
Four girls discover that a girl of another race is nice person to know. 4w 1 interior

In Breck, F. E. ed. Playlets and poems for church school

Breeches from Bond Street. Gowan, E. P.

Breit, Harvey. See Schulberg, B. jt. auth.

Bremer, Ward

Nothing but nonsense. French 1957 69p
Musical comedy revue. Ten skits, interspersed with musical specialties, parodying television programs. 2 acts Large mixed cast 1 setting

Brenner, Alfred

Survival
Television play. Based on the trial of David Holmes, American merchant seaman, who in 1842 threw twelve men overboard in order to save the others in his overcrowded lifeboat. 3 acts 11m 5w

In Best television plays, 1957

Brenner, Marlene

Beacon of strength. Bakers Plays 1957 15p (Baker's Royalty plays)
Juliette Low's Girl Scouts prove their worth by rescuing drowning girl. 1 act 3w 5g 1 interior

Bill and Sue. Bakers Plays 1961 27p (Baker's Royalty plays)
Comedy. A group of young women looking for husbands arrive at famous resort hotel. 1 act 3m 4w 1 interior

The gentle one. Bakers Plays 1960 24p (Baker's Royalty plays)
Question of faith in one day in lives of five women, each of whom wants something. 1 act 6w 1 exterior

The golden land. Bakers Plays 1957 25p (Baker's Royalty plays)
Struggle between sisters when one tries to cheat other of inheritance. 1 act 5w 1 exterior

Love and Miss Dodie. Bakers Plays 1955 28p (Baker's Royalty plays)
Pathetic love story unfolds as old lady secretly treats accident victim. 1 act 5 women 1 interior

Middle of nowhere. Bakers Plays 1959 31p (Baker's Royalty plays)
Mystery comedy. One of the guests at isolated motel is an escaped homicidal maniac. 1 act 5w 1 interior

My Aunt Agatha. Bakers Plays 1954 25p (Baker's Royalty plays)
Domestic comedy. Planning to settle her estate before her death, aunt brings nieces together to test their sincerity. 1 act 5w 1 interior

The physical threat. Bakers Plays 1957 27p (Baker's Royalty plays)
Romantic comedy. Family uses jealousy to force a proposal. 1 act 7m 2w 1 interior

The roof. Bakers Plays 1954 23p (Baker's Royalty plays)
Women discuss murder of neighbor little realizing murderer is one of their own group and that they are involved in subversive activity. 1 act 6w 1 exterior

The wait. Bakers Plays 1958 24p (Baker's Royalty plays)
While women wait for word of relatives trapped in mine their true natures show. 1 act 6w 1 interior

Brewsie and Willie. Violett, E. and Blake, L.

Brickenden, Catharine

Zanorin. French (Toronto) 1958 26p illus
Romantic comedy. An invalid spinster's foreign gardener turns out to be a famous violinist. 1 act 2m 3w 1 exterior

—Same

In Richards, S. ed. Canada on stage

The **bridal** bouquet. Spence, W.

Bride roses. Howells, W. D.

The **bridge.** Brabazon, F.

Bridger, James

c Carlson, B. W. Jim Bridger and his eight-hour echo

Bridges

Howe, C. V. The long fall

Brigands and robbers

Boyd, A. K. Robbery at Gadshill
Hesketh, J. Mr Owl
Howard, V. Don Quixote saves the day
c Marston, M. A. The robbers
Miller, H. L. Lorna Doone
Miyamasu. Eboshi-ori
Parr, R. The flying machine
Sakanishi, S. tr. Literate highwaymen
Sherwood, R. E. The petrified forest
Trease, G. Letters of gold
Wolfe, T. The return of Buck Gavin
See also Burglary; Crime and criminals; Thieves

Brighten every corner. Herman, G.

Bring on the angels. Sloane, A.

Bringing up father. Fisher, A. and Rabe, O.

Britannia's honor. Dekker, T.

Britannicus
Racine, J. Britannicus

Britannicus. Racine, J.

British Guiana
Hart, M. The climate of Eden

British in Tahiti
Giraudoux, J. The virtuous island

The **broken** broomstick. Miller, H. L.

The **broken** heart. Ford, J.

The **broker** of Bogota. Bird, R. M.

The **Brome Abraham and Isaac.** See Abraham and Isaac (Brome manuscript); Gassner, John

Brontë, Charlotte
Jane Eyre (radio adaptation) See Olfson, L. Jane Eyre

About
Malone, M. A letter for Charlotte
Spamer, C. Charlotte Bronte

Brontë, Emily
Wuthering Heights (dramatization) See Jacoby, L. Wuthering Heights
Wuthering Heights (radio adaptation) See Olfson, L. Wuthering Heights

Brooke, Eleanor. See Kerr, J. jt. auth.

Brooks, Patricia
Meet George. Deane 1955 23p ("Deane's" Ser. of plays)
  Domestic comedy. Because of insinuations of town gossip, wife spends anxious afternoon waiting for husband to come home. 1 act 6w 1 interior
The only prison. Deane 1955 59p illus ("Deane's" Ser. of plays)
  Women confined in Japanese prison camp in World War II learn real value of freedom. 3 acts 5 scenes 8w 1 interior

Brooks, Phillips, Bp.
Emurian, E. K. Three skits for Christmas

The **broom** and the groom. Gordon, K.

Brotherhood
Asbrand, K. Brotherhood
c Carlson, B. W. Thanksgiving is the time
Fisher, A. Three and the dragon
Kelsey, R. W. Who is my neighbor?
Leslie, A. E. In as much
National Recreation Association. Who are we of the United States

Brotherhood. Asbrand, K.

Brotherhood Week
c Woolsey, J. and Sechrist, E. H. Mars calling!

Brothers
Farquhar, G. The twin-rivals
Pinter, H. The caretaker
Tumarin, B. and Sydow, J. Dostoyevsky's The brothers Karamazov
  See also Brothers and sisters

The **brothers.** Terence

Brothers and sisters
Camché, N. The orphans
Hellman, L. Toys in the attic
Hughes, R. The sisters' tragedy
Miller, H. L. "N" for nuisance

Nash, N. R. Girls of summer
Savory, G. A likely tale
Shakespeare, W. Twelfth night

The **brothers** Karamazov. See Tumarin, B. and Sydow, J. Dostoyevsky's The brothers Karamazov

Broughton, James
The last word
  During last few moments of their lives before extermination by bombs, a husband and wife face each other for the first time as persons. 1m 1w 1 interior
  In Halverson, M. ed. Religious drama, 3
Summer fury
  Tragedy of anti-Mexican feeling in Los Angeles. 3m 5w 1 exterior
  In The Best short plays, 1957

Brown, Albert M.
Ah, men! Bakers Plays 1959 13p
  Comedy. Group of men prove they discuss diets, children, and gossip even more than women do. Singing. 1 act 6m 1 interior

Brown, Francisca Emerson
The educated school house
  Radio play. Little one room schoolhouse is unhappy when the big new schoolhouse is built, until townspeople find new uses for him. Background music. 4m 3w extras
  In Prescott, H. ed. Patrioscript

Brown, Lionel
Stolen waters. Deane 1954 58p illus ("Deane's" Ser. of plays)
  Jewish background concealed in marriage, revealed when inheritance is at stake. 3 acts 4 scenes 4m 5w 1 interior
This year—next year. Deane 1956 66p illus ("Deane's" Ser. of plays)
  Murder. Wealthy mother plans estate so children can avoid payment of inheritance tax. 3 acts 4 scenes 4m 7w 1 interior

Brown, Martha. See Very, A. jt. auth.

Brown, Ruth M.
Freedom is our heritage
  Pageant for grades six through eight. Portrays the American way of life and love of liberty. 11 episodes 7 tableaux Large mixed cast
  In Birdsall, R. ed. Creative plays for every school month

Brown dog—black dog. Priestley, F.

Browning, Elizabeth (Barrett)
Besier, R. The Barretts of Wimpole Street
Holland, N. Crisis in Wimpole Street

Browning, Robert
Clive (dramatization) See Boyd, A. K. Clive's fear, unique
My last duchess (dramatization) See Bannerman, H. K. My last duchess
The Pied Piper of Hamelin (dramatization) See Marston, M. A. The Pied Piper of Hamelin
c The Pied Piper of Hamlin (dramatization) See Dunbar, T. M. The Pied Piper of Hamlin

About
Besier, R. The Barretts of Wimpole Street

The **Browning** version. Rattigan, T.

The **bruising** of Satan. Simmons, A.

Brumbaugh, Patrick
c Simple Simon. French 1959 85p illus
Comedy. The king, worried by his enemy and his own traitorous adviser, is disappointed that his son Prince Simon seems too simple and shy to help run the kingdom. 3 acts 9m 4w extras 1 interior

A **brush** with the enemy. Webber, J.

The **brute**. Chekhov, A.

Brutus, Lucius Junius
Lee, N. Lucius Junius Brutus

Brydon, Margaret Wylie, and Ziegler, Esther
The reluctant ghost
Some girls trying to save their neighbor's house from sale inadvertently succeed. 1 act 2w 8g 1 interior
In Kamerman, S. E. ed. Blue-ribbon plays for girls

Buaku. Sakanishi, S. tr.

Bucci, Mark
Chain of jade. Lyrics and adaptation by David Rogers. Music by Mark Bucci. Vocal score ed. by Lockrem Johnson. French 1960 43p music
Musical play based on "The stolen prince" by Dan Totheroh, written in the style of the classic Chinese theater, about a little lost prince who is brought up by a poor fisherman. 1 act 6m 2w 2b 1g 1 interior
The old lady shows her medals; adaptation and lyrics by David Rogers; music by Mark Bucci. French 1960 67p music
Musical comedy. An adaptation of J. M. Barrie's play about a lonely charwoman who pretends she has a son away at the war. Set in London during World War I. Vocal score and libretto. 1 act 3 scenes 2m 4w 1 interior
A pink party dress; a musical comedy by David Rogers and Mark Bucci; music by Mark Bucci; adaptation and lyrics by David Rogers. French 1960 47p music
A musical play based on Margaret Bland's "Pink and patches" about young mountain girl who yearns to escape life of drudgery when she observes people at a fashionable hotel. Includes words and music. 1m 3w 1 exterior

Büchner, Georg
Leonce and Lena; English version by Eric Bentley
Bored Prince philosophizes over trivialities and profundities as he approaches marriage. 3 acts 11 scenes 9m 3w extras 4 interiors 6 exteriors
In Bentley, E. ed. From the modern repertoire; ser. 3
Woyzeck
Tragedy. Young German soldier murders his faithless mistress. Songs and dances, background music. 26 scenes 16m 4w 1b 3g extras 8 interiors 6 exteriors
In Bentley, E. ed. The modern theatre v 1

Buck, Pearl
The good earth (moving picture adaptation) See Jennings, T.; Slesinger, T. and West, C. The good earth

Buckingham, George Villiers, 2d duke of.
See Villiers, George

Buddha and Buddhism
Enami, S. Ukai
Komparu, Z. Hatsuyuki
Komparu, Z. U. Bashō

Kwanze, K. Eguchi
Kwanze, M. Kakitsubata
Kwanze, M. Tōboku

Buddhism. See Buddha and Buddhism

Buddhist sects. See Zen (Sect)

Buell, Hester
Fat woman picnic. French 1955 24p illus music
Domestic comedy. Fourth of July picnic. Late 19th century Kansas. Music. 1 act 3m 2w 1 interior

Buffon, Georges Louis Leclerc, comte de
Geiger, M. Light and liberty

Bugbee, Willis N.
Life starts at thirty-five; or, "Those fussy maids." Bugbee 1953 18p
Romantic comedy. Young man and his wife scheme to bring romance to three spinsters. 1 act 4m 5w 1 interior

Building
Howe, C. V. The long fall

Building as a profession
Chayefsky, P. The big deal

Bulgarian-Serbian War, 1885. See Serbo-Bulgarian War, 1885

Bullfight. Stevens, L.

Bullfighters
Robinson, C. R. The white dove
Stevens, L. Bullfight

Bulwer-Lytton, Edward
Money
Satire on money and the greed and hypocrisy it breeds; set in 19th century England among aristocracy. 5 acts 11 scenes 18m 3w extras 6 interiors
In Rowell, G. ed. Nineteenth century plays

Bunnies and bonnets. Miller, H. L.

The **bunnies'** dilemma. Spamer, C.

Bunny of the year. Newman, D.

Bunyan, Paul
McCaslin, N. Giant of the timber

The **bunyip** lives again! Carlson, B. W.

Burgess, C. V.
The Army takes over
Young Englishman who resents being drafted talks with friend who has enjoyed his military service. 4m 2w 1 interior
In Burgess, C. V. Talking of the Taylors
A bit of peace and quiet
Family members argue because several of them feel that their privacy has been invaded. 3m 2w 1 interior
In Burgess, C. V. Talking of the Taylors
A bore for breakfast
British teen-age girl makes discourteous remark to very boring woman, causing mother's insistence that hypocrisy is sometimes socially necessary. 3m 3w 1 interior
In Burgess, C. V. Talking of the Taylors
Chris is sent to Coventry
When young Englishman refuses to strike with other workers, no one will speak to him. 3m 2w 1 interior
In Burgess, C. V. Talking of the Taylors

Burgess, C. V.—*Continued*

Doers and viewers
A boy withdraws his membership from committee at youth club because he feels he has done most of the work. 3m 2w 1 interior
In Burgess, C. V. Talking of the Taylors

Ken changes his mind
Young man cancels weekend camping trip with his friend when he receives an invitation for the week end from son of his wealthy employer. 4m 2w 1 interior
In Burgess, C. V. Talking of the Taylors

Ken looks ahead
Young British boy decides to quit school and learn a trade, despite father's wishes. 3m 2w 1 interior
In Burgess, C. V. Talking of the Taylors

Reports in the garden
British teen-age boy tries to convince his family that his classes in literature at school are a waste of time. 3m 2w 1 exterior
In Burgess, C. V. Talking of the Taylors

Susan to the rescue
British family discovers that all of its members could be more thrifty in different ways. 3m 2w 1 interior
In Burgess, C. V. Talking of the Taylors

The Taylors in the never-never land
Members of British family don't agree about buying on the instalment plan. 3m 2w 1 interior
In Burgess, C. V. Talking of the Taylors

Trouble at "The Blue Lantern"
British teen age boy questions his parents' right to know where he is and who his friends are. 3m 2w 1 interior
In Burgess, C. V. Talking of the Taylors

The virtues of Thelma
Girl is angry because her family compares her unfavorably with her cousin who does not smoke or wear make up. 3m 3w 1 interior
In Burgess, C. V. Talking of the Taylors

Burgh, Hubert de, earl of Kent
Boyd, A. K. Prince Arthur and Hubert

The **burglar** alarm. Bayliss, R. G.

The **burglar** alarm. Waugh, J. R.

Burglary
c Bayliss, R. G. The burglar alarm
Sutherland, D. Trying to take things quietly
See also Brigands and robbers; Larceny; Thieves

Burgoyne, John
Shaw, B. The Devil's disciple

Burial service. See Funeral sermons

Buried treasure. See Treasure-trove

Burke, Natalie
The girl who had everything. French 1957 89p illus
Romantic comedy. Complications and impersonation when housekeeper rents house during owner's absence. 3 acts 4 scenes 3m 8w extras 1 interior

Burlesque
Addis, H. Drama

Burlingame, Cora
Yellow fever
Major Walter Reed and other members of the Army Medical Corps search for cure for yellow fever. 1 act 12m 1 interior
In Burack, A. S. ed. Four-star plays for boys

Burma

Politics and government—1945-
Nu, U. The people win through

Burner of the Bugle. Wattron, F. and Walker, P.

Burney, Fanny. See Arblay, Frances (Burney) d'

The **burning** glass. Morgan, C.

Burns, Robert
Crozier, E. Rab the rhymer

The **burnt** flower-bed. Betti, U.

Burr Conspiracy, 1805-1807
Raiden, E. Mr Jefferson's Burr

Burrows, Abe. See Bissell, R. jt. auth.

Bus stations. See Motor bus lines—Stations

Bus stop. Inge, W.

Buses. See Motor buses

Business
Lusk, D. Girls are better than ever
Regan, S. The fifth season

Business consultants
Newbold, H. Joanie on the spot

Business ethics
Armer, A. and Grauman, W. E. The last straw
Berg, D. The drop of a hat
Howells, W. D. and Kester, P. The rise of Silas Lapham
Miller, S. One bright day
Reach, J. Patterns
Ross, G. and Singer, C. Any other business
Sheldon, E. The boss

Business men. See Businessmen

Businessmen
Keeney, C. H. Old Skin Flint

Bussy D'Ambois. Chapman, G.

Busu. Sakanishi, S. tr.

The **busy** barbers. Miller, H. L.

But I know what I like. Sinclair, L.

But this I know. McCarty, R. K.

Butler, Ivan
Tranquil House. Stacey Publications 1954 78p illus
Young girl comes to work in old age home. 3 acts 6 scenes 3m 7w 1 interior
The wise children. Stacey Publications 1953 80p illus
Family drama concerning choice confronting a woman and her two grown-up children when ex-husband returns from abroad suffering from an incurable disease. Gramaphone music. 3 acts 4 scenes 4m 5w 1 interior
See also Cary, F. L. jt. auth.

Buttle, Myra
  Toynbee in Elysium. Sagamore 1959 96p
    Satirical fantasy on Arnold Toynbee's
    concept of history as judged in Elysium
    by ghosts of famous historians. 3 scenes
    10m 1w extras no scenery
Buy Jupiter! Davidson, W.
Buzzell, Ann M.
  c "The man on the street"
    Christmas. Two men broadcast an out-
    door radio program to see how many
    shoppers know the origin of Christmas
    customs. 5m 7w 2b extras 1 exterior
    In Birdsall, R. ed. Creative plays for
      every school month
By Christ alone. Smith, W. S.
By hex. Blankman, H.
By order of the king. Fisher, A.
Bye bye birdie (condensation). Strouse, C.
Byron, Anne Isabella (Milbanke) Byron,
    baroness
  Vooght, C. Nineteen, The Beacon
Byzantine emperors
  Corneille, P. Héraclius
Byzantine Empire
  Corneille, P. Pulchérie

C

Cabana Blues. Hark, M. and McQueen, N.
A **cabin** by the lake. Waldau, R. S.
The **cactus** wildcat. Wallerstein, J. S.
Caesar, Caius Julius
  Corneille, P. La mort de Pompée
  Olfson, L. Julius Caesar
  Shakespeare, W. Antony and Cleopatra
  Shaw, B. Caesar and Cleopatra
Caesar and Cleopatra. Shaw, B.
Caesar Borgia. Lee, N.
Caiaphas, Joseph (Jewish high priest)
  York plays. The second trial before
    Pilate: The scourging and condemna-
    tion
Cain
  Coventry plays. Cain and Abel
Cain and Abel. Coventry plays
The **Caine** mutiny court-martial. Wouk, H.
Cake
  c Fisher, A. The Christmas cake
Calais
          Siege, 1346
  Shaw, B. The six of Calais
Calderón
  Life is a dream; tr. and introduction by
    William E. Colford. Barrons Educ.
    Ser. 1958 101p
    Drama of 17th century Spain: intrigue,
    imprisonment, honor; attempt of one
    man to triumph over predicted fate.
    Verse play. Background music. 3 acts
    41 scenes 5m 2w extras 2 settings
Caligula. Camus, A.
Ca'line. Harris, B. K.

Calitri, Princine M.
  One love had Mary. Bakers Plays 1958
    20p (Baker's Royalty plays)
    Mary Todd's family considers her love.
    Abraham Lincoln, an ungainly back-
    woodsman. 1 act 7w 1 interior
Call me a liar. Mortimer, J.
The **callers.** Very, A.
Callie goes to camp. Porter, E. W.
The **calling** of the disciples. Phillips, J. B.
Calvary. Yeats, W. B.
Camché, Nancy
  The orphans. French 1955 15p illus
    Son's and daughter's responsibility for
    care of aged mother resolved by her
    death. 1 act 3m 2w 1g 1 interior
Camille. Dumas, A.
Camino Real. William, T.
The **camouflage** shop. Spamer, C.
The **camp.** Ferguson, J.
Camp followers
  Brecht, B. Mother Courage
Campbell, J. Gounod
  The bleeding heart of Wee Jon
    Comic fantasy with pseudo-oriental flavor
    about a dragon and a man who wants
    to marry Lord Sou Poo's daughter. 4m
    1w extras 1 exterior
    In Richards, S. ed. Canada on stage
Camping
  c Carlson, B. W. It's a—!
  Crary, M. Beware the bear!
  Hill, K. Midnight burial
  Porter, E. W. Callie goes to camp
  Priestley, F. Adventures in camp
  c Wallerstein, J. S. Windigo Island
  c Woolsey, J. and Sechrist, E. H. Catching
    the ghost
Campion, Cyril
  On the road. Acting ed. French (Lon-
    don) 1954 76p illus
    Escaped thief, joining traveling troupe of
    actresses, is exposed. 2 acts 4 scenes
    11w 1 interior
  Wayward women. [French's Acting ed]
    French (London) 1958 72p
    Tragedy. Mother tells story of daughter's
    life in underworld of Hampstead, Eng-
    land. 13w 1 interior
Camps
  Gross, E. and Gross, N. Marko goes a
    courtin'
Campton, David
  The laboratory. Miller, J.G. 1955 29p
    illus
    Farce. In small apothecary shop in Italy
    three people who come to buy poison
    are sold love potions instead. 1 act
    2m 3w 1 interior
Camus, Albert
  Caligula. Adapted from the French by
    Justin O'Brien. French 1961 86p
    A study in tyranny. Caesar demands the
    impossible from his subjects and meets
    his death. 2 acts 4 scenes 13m 2w
    2 interiors
  —Same; tr. by Stuart Gilbert
    In Camus, A. Caligula & three other
      plays
  Caligula (condensation)
    In The Best plays of 1959-1960

Camus, Albert—*Continued*

The just assassins
Tragedy on theme of whether murder is justified in service of a lofty ideal. A terrorist group assassinates a Roman nobleman. 5 acts 7m 2w 2 interiors
In Camus, A. Caligula & three other plays

The misunderstanding
Tragedy. Son returns to his homeland after many years only to be murdered for his money by his mother and sister who do not recognize him. 3 acts 2m 3w 2 interiors
In Camus, A. Caligula & three other plays

The possessed; tr. from the French by Justin O'Brien. Knopf 1960 182p
A dramatization of Dostoevsky's novel, 19th century Russia. Psychological study of individuals and their interest in revolutionary national and political ideas. 3 parts 22 scenes 19m 5w 5 interiors 2 exteriors

State of siege
Allegory. The people in a city are thrown into confusion by appearance of The Plague who arrives in person to become their leader. 3 parts 14m 4w extras 2 exteriors
In Camus, A. Caligula & three other plays

Can this be love? Owen, A.

Canada
History—Rebellion. 1837-1838
Cross, E. W. The patriots

Candida. Shaw, B.

Candide. Bernstein, L.

Candide. Hellman, L.

The **candle.** Spamer, C.

Candle in the window. Asbrand, K.

The **candle** in the window. Childs, C.

A **candle**-lighting service. Holbrook, M.

Candlelight services
Bailey, H. F. Christmas Eve candle vespers
Bailey, H. F. Walk in the light

Candles for sale. Curtis, P. D.

Candy. See Confectionery

Cannan, Dennis, and Bost, Pierre
The power and the glory. [Acting ed] French 1959 90p illus
A dramatized version of the novel by Graham Greene. A Mexican priest, fleeing from police, is too weak to resist drinking, but not to risk his life ministering to poverty-stricken peasants. 3 acts 12 scenes 21m 7w 2b 1g extras 4 interiors 3 exteriors

Canterbury Cathedral
Sayers, D. The zeal of Thy house

Čapek, Josef, and Čapek, Karel
The world we live in; in the adaptation by Owen Davis
Allegorical fantasy. Human conduct and aims presented as a picture of insect life in the dream of a dying vagrant. 3 acts 5 scenes Large mixed cast 2 exteriors
In Gassner, J. ed. Twenty best European plays on the American stage

Čapek, Karel
R. U. R. English version by Paul Selver and Nigel Playfair
Fantasy. Robots revolt against their human masters. 3 acts 13m 4w 2 interiors
In A Treasury of the theatre
—Same; tr. from the Czech by Paul Selver
In Tucker, S. M. ed. Twenty-five modern plays
See also Čapek, J. jt. auth.

Capitalism
Howard, P. The boss
Shaw, B. Major Barbara

Capitalists and financiers
Howells, W. D. A hazard of new fortunes

Capote, Truman
The grass harp. Dramatists 1954 71p illus
Comedy. An idyll about the pure in heart who, like the meek, inherit the earth. 2 acts 5 scenes 10m 8w 1 interior 1 exterior

Caprice. Musset, A. de

Captains Courageous. Olfson, L.

Cardinals
Boland, B. The prisoner
c Marston, M. A. The jackdaw of Rheims

Cards
Gogol, N. Gamblers

Cards of identity. Dennis, N.

Cardsharping
Boyd, A. K. Clive's fear, unique

Career, Lee, J.

The **caretaker.** Pinter, H.

Carey, Ernestine Gilbreth
Jumping Jupiter (dramatization) See Davidson, W. Buy Jupiter!

Cargill, Patrick, and Beale, Jack
Ring for Catty. [French's Acting ed] French (London) 1956 85p illus
A Cockney bank clerk, an ex-airman, a miner and a young boy in a sanatorium ruled over by nurse Catty. 6m 6w 1 interior

Carlos, Prince of Asturias
Schiller, F. von. Don Carlos

Carlos, Don. See Carlos, Prince of Asturias

Carlson, Bernice Wells
c Altogether! Heave!
When a sergeant in the Revolutionary Army thinks his job is beneath him, George Washington stops to help lift fallen tree off the road. 6m extras 1 exterior
In Carlson, B. W. The right play for you
c A bargain's a bargain
A worker who has tricked two others, is cunningly tricked in turn. 4m extras 1 exterior
In Carlson, B. W. The right play for you
c The bunyip lives again!
Comedy. Photographer constructs legendary monster in Australia in order to photograph it, but complications ensue when fortune hunters discover the monster. 9m extras 1 exterior
In Carlson, B. W. The right play for you

Carlson, Bernice W.—*Continued*

c Don't tell a soul!
> During the Revolutionary War, two patriot children left alone with valuable bundle, refuse to give it up to Tory spy. 2 acts 2m 1w 1b 1g 1 interior

> *In* Carlson, B. W. The right play for you

c For soldiers everywhere
> Weary doctor during Civil War who has run out of supplies is rescued by Clara Barton's arrival with wagonload of food and medicine. 5m 4w 1 exterior

> *In* Carlson, B. W. The right play for you

c It's a—!
> Short comedy sketch. Two boys camping out in their tent become afraid of the dark. 2b extras 1 exterior

> *In* Carlson, B. W. The right play for you

c Jes' too lazy!
> Comedy sketch about a hound that sat on a tack and was too lazy to move. 1m 1w 1b 1g 1 exterior

> *In* Carlson, B. W. The right play for you

c Jim Bridger and his eight-hour echo
> When pioneer woman wants to take her clock along on trip west, guide tells her there is a special echo in the west which tells time. 2m 1w 1 exterior

> *In* Carlson, B. W. The right play for you

c Just as strong
> Comedy. When Grandpa arrives for visit everyone tries to take care of him although he wants to be independent. 2m 1w 2b 1g 1 exterior

> *In* Carlson, B. W. The right play for you

c The lady who put salt in her coffee
> Based on a story "The Peterkin Papers" by Lucretia P. Hale about a woman who puts salt instead of sugar into her coffee and doesn't know what to do about it. 3m 3w 3b 1g 1 interior

> *In* Carlson, B. W. The right play for you

c Litterbug convention
> Different kinds of litterbugs hold convention but are routed by all the "clean-uppers." Unidentified cast 6 characters extras 1 interior

> *In* Carlson, B. W. The right play for you

c Mystery of the glittering gem
> Farce. A woman wants to give a gem she found in old trunk to most original costume at her Halloween party. 2m 2w 1b 2g extras 1 interior

> *In* Carlson, B. W. The right play for you

c Near mutiny on the "Santa Maria"
> Christopher Columbus' men are near mutiny when suddenly land is sighted. 5m 1b 1 exterior

> *In* Carlson, B. W. The right play for you

c Not me!
> Short farce about old man who listens to accident description to see if he was in it. 3m 1 interior

> *In* Carlson, B. W. The right play for you

c On the bat
> Farce. Three old ladies get all mixed up about baseball and want to have Babe Ruth arrested. 3w 1 interior

> *In* Carlson, B. W. The right play for you

c St Nicholas just the same
> Adaptation of early American folk tale from New Amsterdam. Mysterious stranger who gives some gold to poor Dutch family turns out to be Saint Nicholas. 2m 1w 1b 1g extras 1 interior

> *In* Carlson, B. W. The right play for you

c Thanksgiving is the time
> Some Americans find that Thanksgiving is time to share with citizens of foreign backgrounds. 3m 5w 2b 3g extras 1 interior

> *In* Carlson, B. W. The right play for you

c A traitor's reward
> In ancient times, schoolteacher who betrayed his city by giving the young boys he taught to the enemy, was given a traitor's reward. 5m 1b extras 1 interior

> *In* Carlson, B. W. The right play for you

c Who's stronger?
> The North Wind and the Sun have a contest to see which of them can make a man take off his coat. 1m extras 1 exterior

> *In* Carlson, B. W. The right play for you

Carlson, Margaret Mattison
> Christmas in many nations. Augustana 1955 24p music
>> Christmas pageant depicting customs from Scandinavian countries, England, Germany, Mexico. Christmas carols. 7 scenes Large mixed cast 3 interiors

Carlton, Joseph
> Bab buys a car. Bakers Plays 953 32p illus
>> Teenage tomboy who doesn't want to go to party her family has arranged, rebels on afternoon of the party by taking her jalopy out for a trial run. 1 act 5m 5w 1 interior

Carlyle, Jane Baillie (Welsh)
> Spamer, C. Jane Welsh

Carmelites
> Mary Francis, Sister. La madre

Carmichael, Alexander
> Deirdire (adaptation). See Bottomley, G. Deirdire
> (tr.) Deirdire, and The lay of the children of Uisne (dramatization) See Bottomley, G. Deirdire

Carmichael, Fred
> Divorce granted. Bakers Plays 1959 25p (Baker's Royalty plays)
>> Comedy. Women in judge's chamber wait to be called for their divorce hearings. 1 act 7w 1 interior
> Four for the money. Bakers Plays 1956 27p
>> Wealthy widow about to make will poses as housekeeper to determine which of her daughters-in-law should inherit her estate. 1 act 6w 1 interior
> He's having a baby. French 1953 19p illus
>> Farce. What would happen if men had babies and women paced maternity ward. 1 act 5w 1 interior

Carmichael, Fred—*Continued*

Inside Lester. French 1955 107p illus
Mystery comedy. Mystery writer who swallows diamond received by mail is kidnapped along with secretary and her niece, but outwits criminals. 3 acts 4 scenes 4m 5w 2 interiors

Luxury cruise. French 1960 89p illus
Romantic comedy. Three couples on a cruise. Each act traces each pair through the cruise and tells their story. 3 acts 7 scenes 3m 6w 1 interior

More than meets the eye. French 1954 119p illus
Domestic comedy. Young author who writes children's stories under pseudonym "Grandma Letty," runs into trouble when chosen "Grandmother of the Year." 3 acts 5m 6w 1 interior

The night is my enemy. French 1956 92p illus
Mystery. British doctor, mentally unbalanced, takes life into his own hands to rid world of all who are imperfect. 3 acts 5 scenes 5m 5w 1 interior

The pen is deadlier. French 1960 85p illus
Murder mystery. More than one person wishes hateful Hollywood gossip columnist dead but someone else is killed instead. 3 acts 5 scenes 4m 6w 1 interior

Petey's choice. French 1958 100p illus music
Domestic comedy. The public discovers that man about to be appointed president of a college was once a singer of popular songs. Contains song, music and lyrics. 3 acts 5 scenes 4m 5w 1 interior

She-sickness. Bakers Plays 1954 24p
Romantic comedy. Former suitor disguised as steward succeeds in breaking up plans for his former sweetheart's shipboard marriage. 1 act 2m 2w 1 interior

Carney, Frank

The righteous are bold. French 1956 88p
Young Irish woman, emotionally disturbed, returns home after having worked as spiritualist's contact in England during World War II. Family priest, through faith, exorcises demons from the haunted girl. 3 acts 6m 4w 1 interior

Carnival

Olson, E. The carnival of animals

Carnival king. Treece, H.

The **carnival** of animals. Olson, E.

Carols

Conkle, E. P. A bauble for the baby

c Marston, M. A. A Christmas carol

Carousel. Rodgers, R. and Hammerstein, O.

Carpenter, Frank

c A day of good deeds
Rabbit gets into trouble when he trys to spend one day doing good deeds. 7 characters 1 exterior

In Carpenter, F. Six animal plays

c Doctor Fox
Fox and Duck try to sell pills to the other animals. 5 characters 1 exterior

In Carpenter, F. Six animal plays

c The magic owl
The owl learns to work magic on all the other animals. 6 characters 1 exterior

In Carpenter, F. Six animal plays

The setting sun. French (London) 1953 31p illus
Verse play. Young woman visits gipsy encampment to get love potion but listens to the old gipsy woman's tragic tale instead. 1 act 3m 3w 1 exterior

c The sick fox
A clever rabbit outwits a cunning fox. 6 characters 1 exterior

In Carpenter, F. Six animal plays

c The tale of good faith
Five animal characters try to find whether there is any good faith in the world. 5 characters 1 exterior

In Carpenter, F. Six animal plays

c Tiger in the wood
Though all the animals in the wood are afraid of him, tiger turns out to be their best friend. 6 characters 1 exterior

In Carpenter, F. Six animal plays

Carpio, Lope de Vega. See Vega Carpio, Lope de

Carrière, Albert

Danbury Fair
Tragedy. Excitement, love, and death on the concession grounds in the hurly-burly of a state fair. 1 act 13m 11w 1b extras 1 exterior

In Smith, B. and others, eds. A treasury of non-royalty one-act plays

It's about time
Farce. Scoffing history professor is duped into buying a time machine. 1 act 2m 3w extras 1 interior

In Smith, B. and others, eds. A treasury of non-royalty one-act plays

Mystery at the depot
Railroad detective traps thief and murderer in freight station. 1 act 6m 1 interior

In Smith, B. and others, eds. A treasury of non-royalty one-act plays

Carrington, V. C. Christie, D. and Christie, C.

Carroll, Lewis

Alice in Wonderland (dramatization) See Miller, M. Alice in Wonderland

Carroll, Paul Vincent

The wayward saint. Dramatists 1955 67p illus
Comedy about an old Irish priest whom the bishop has moved to a small parish because of his "supernatural caperings." 3 acts 7m 4w 1 interior

The wise have not spoken. Dramatists 1954 68p illus
Poor Irish family personifies the unsettled conditions in the country after the war for Irish freedom. 3 acts 4 scenes 8m 2w extras 1 interior

Carroll, Walter

Comin' for to carry
Negro folk fantasy. An angel brings a girl back to the straight and narrow path. 1 act 5m 1w 1 exterior

In Smith, B. and others, eds. A treasury of non-royalty one-act plays

Carruthers, Jeanne

Fear not. Friendship Press 1955 32p music
Indian professor embraces Christianity and with renewed faith in non-violence he turns back mob without fear. Background music. 1 act 7m 1w extras 1 exterior

Physician in charge. Friendship Press 1954 32p illus
Missionary doctor and native nurse dedicate their lives to help people of India although some natives misunderstand their motives. 1 act 7 scenes 9m 3w 3 interiors

Carry and borrow. Spamer, C.

Carter, Arthur P.

Operation Mad Ball. [Rev. and rewritten] French 1960 115p

Comedy. Americans abroad. Soldiers wanting to fraternize with nurses smuggle off base everything necessary for a ball in off-limits bar. 3 acts 13 scenes 27m 4w 8 interiors

Carter, Beatrix

The sermon. Kenyon House Press 1954 15p

Comedy. Woman tries to give worldy possessions to poor but the harder she tries the more money she accumulates. 1 act 5w 1 interior

The witch hunt. Kenyon House Press 1954 12p illus

Social comedy. A whispering campaign and an accident bring young man's snobbish mother and his fiancie together. 1 act 4w 1 interior

Carter, Conrad

About time, too

Comedy. English girl seeks approval of her suitor's domineering mother. 2w 1 interior

In Carter, C. About time, too, and five other playlets

A chocolate

Comedy. Two elderly English sisters recall their girlhood quarrel over a man. 4w 1 interior

In Carter, C. About time, too, and five other playlets

Don't argue!

Comedy. Wife tries to persuade husband to investigate when she thinks she hears a burglar at night. 2m 1w 1 interior

In Carter, C. About time, too, and five other playlets

Good-bye, Aunt Mildred!

Comedy. Mixed emotions are felt by women of an English family as they see visiting relative off on her homeward journey. 6w 1 exterior

In Carter, C. About time, too, and five other playlets

Stick up for yourself

Domestic comedy. Young man tries to avoid becoming a henpecked husband like his father. 2m 2w 1 interior

In Carter, C. About time, too, and five other playlets

Such ado about something

Farce. Satire on the triangle problem in marriage. Verse play. 2m 2w 1 interior

In Carter, C. About time, too, and five other playlets

Carving (Art industries)   See Wood-carving

Cary, Falkland L.

Live and let love. Stacey Pubs. 1955 72p illus

Romantic comedy about a young woman who surprises friend trying to force her into matrimony. 3 acts 5 scenes 9w 1 interior

Murder out of tune. [French's Acting ed] French (London) 1953 71p illus

Doctor under suspicion of murder is helped by old friend. Background music 3 acts 3m 6w 1 interior

Pitfall. Stacey Pubs. 1955 64p front

Mystery. Married man involved in the investigation of murder of a young woman, finds peace when he decides to aid the police in administering justice. 3 acts 5 scenes 3m 4w 1 interior

See also King, P. jt. auth.

Cary, Falkland L. and Butler, Ivan

The paper chain. [French's Acting ed] French (London) 1953 76p illus

Communist agent, who murders British government worker to prevent an exposé, apprehended by Scotland Yard detectives. 3 acts 6 scenes 3m 6w 1 interior

Case, Theodore W.

Billy Adams, American

Television play. After World War II, embittered German tries to get his little son to America as stowaway. 9m 3w 1b

In Roberts, E. B. Television writing and selling

A case for Mrs Hudson. Murray, J.

A case for two detectives. Murray, J.

The case of rebellious Susan. Jones, H. A.

The case of the balky bike. Miller, H. L.

The case of the misbehaving toys. Thompson, R.

The case of the missing pearls. Dias, E. J.

The case of the missing poet. Murray, J.

The case of the sea-lion flippers. Sinclair, L.

Casey, Beatrice Marie

At the foot of the Mount

Interpretation of what Sermon on the Mount meant to the people who heard it. 13m 9w extras 1 exterior

In Casey, B. M. Good things for church groups

The Christmas loaf

Poor couple who share what they have at Christmas time with one, more unfortunate, find their blessings multiplied. 3m 3w 1 interior

In Casey, B. M. Good things for church groups

Church notices

Verse play. A young couple away from home read the church news. 6m 6w 1 interior

In Casey, B. M. Good things for church groups

Dawn in the garden

An interpretation of the Resurrection of Christ with spoken chorus. 2m 1w chorus 1 exterior

In Casey, B. M. Good things for church groups

Excuse for living. Elridge 1959 11p (Elridge Church entertainments)

New horizons open for her when doctor tells wealthy woman there is nothing wrong with her but selfishness. 1 act 2m 2w 1 interior

The flower of hope

During an Easter play at church one woman helps another overcome her lack of faith. 7w extras 1 interior

In Casey, B. M. Good things for church groups

God so loved the world

Woman who has had great tragedy in her life loses her bitterness at Christmastime in helping at an orphanage. 2w 1g 1 interior

In Casey, B. M. Good things for church groups

Casey, Beatrice M.—*Continued*

Green eyes

A girl almost breaks off her engagement because she is jealous of a rich but superficial woman, who has lost her faith in God. 1 act 2m 2w 1 interior

In Casey, B. M. Good things for church groups

The guest at Cana

Failure in marriage is shown to be failure to instill a Christian spirit in marriage. 10m 10w extras 1 interior

In Casey, B. M. Good things for church groups

The hand of God

Hotel manager refuses to rent a room to Negro missionary. 2m 1 interior

In Casey, B. M. Good things for church groups

High polish

A family tries to impress a famous aunt they have never seen. 3m 5w 1 interior

In Casey, B. M. Good things for church groups

His and hers

Two couples compete in a humorous way with the projects they are doing for the church. 2m 2w 1 interior

In Casey, B. M. Good things for church groups

Important business

A husband is impressed when wife's church work scores success for him in his business. 1m 1w 1 interior

In Casey, B. M. Good things for church groups

The jewel beyond price

Man tries to find which of God's gifts is the best. Verse play with songs. 7m 7w extras 1 interior

In Casey, B. M. Good things for church groups

The lamp in the night

In a dream a church worker realizes the important work of foreign missions. 4m 2w extras 1 interior

In Casey, B. M. Good things for church groups

The land afar

Verse play. An old missionary explains the importance of his work in many parts of the world. 2m 1w extras 1 interior

In Casey, B. M. Good things for church groups

Lilies bloom at Easter

At Easter-time a thoughtless woman realizes the harm she has been doing her family. 2m 3w 1 interior

In Casey, B. M. Good things for church groups

The little things

Bored teenager finds that it is the little things in life that keep her closer to God. 5m 4w extras 1 interior

In Casey, B. M. Good things for church groups

The love of Ruth

In family crisis young widow helps her father-in-law regain his Christian faith. 1 act 4m 4w 1 interior

In Brings, L. M. comp. The golden book of church plays

The main road

Members of high school orchestra are faced with the choice of taking their big chance or giving benefit for unfortunate family. 4m 4w 1 interior

In Casey, B. M. Good things for church groups

The manger

Flu epidemic at army post helps a romance between a lieutenant and an army nurse at Christmastime. Christmas songs. 4m 4w extras 1 interior

In Casey, B. M. Good things for church groups

My neighbor

A man is jealous of another man in his church. 2m 1w 1 exterior

In Casey, B. M. Good things for church groups

Myself and I

A businessman who is about to go into illegal business venture has a talk with his conscience. 2m 1 interior

In Casey, B. M. Good things for church groups

One day for mother

Two couples realize the importance of spending more time with their elderly mothers. 3m 3w 1 interior

In Casey, B. M. Good things for church groups

One song for Christmas

Young singer who is very interested in her career thinks she is too busy to go home for Christmas. 3w 1 interior

In Casey, B. M. Good things for church groups

The other nine

At Thanksgiving, a man is bitter because he finds that his son wants to be a doctor rather than stay on family farm. 4m 4w 1 interior

In Casey, B. M. Good things for church groups

The portrait

A Sunday School teacher finds how her teachings have reached the lives of her former students. 4m 5w 1 interior

In Casey, B. M. Good things for church groups

The promised one

When a prophet says the star of Bethlehem announces the birth of the Messiah, a woman thinks she has been struck blind for her disbelief. Set in Biblical times. 7m 6w chorus 1 exterior

In Casey, B. M. Good things for church groups

A red carpet for the bishop

Group of church workers are nervous about their reception for new bishop when their pastor is suddenly called away. 4m 4w 1 interior

In Casey, B. M. Good things for church groups

Second chance

Smug, successful businessman is asked how he would change his past life if he could. 2m 1 interior

In Casey, B. M. Good things for church groups

The servant of the King

Group of men and boys realize from one of the parables Jesus told, the importance of coming to church. 13m 1 exterior

In Casey, B. M. Good things for church groups

Casey, Beatrice M.—*Continued*
Seventy times seven
A woman who is hated by another tries
to return good for evil. 3w 1 interior
In Casey, B. M. Good things for church
groups
Sunday morning
A husband and wife are so concerned
about what to wear to church that they
have an argument. 2m 1w 1 interior
In Casey, B. M. Good things for church
groups
Sweetness and light
A man forgets the Christian teaching of
loving one's neighbor when he becomes
angry with his brother. 1 act 1m 2w
1 interior
In Casey, B. M. Good things for church
groups
The tears of Madelon
All the shepherds take gifts to the newborn Christ. But an impoverished woman has nothing to give. 1 act 3m 3w
1 exterior
In Casey, B. M. Good things for church
groups
They say
A woman tries, by spreading malicious
gossip, to part two friends. 4w 2 interiors
In Casey, B. M. Good things for church
groups
A welcome for mother
A man and his wife are not happy about
his mother coming to live with them
until they read the fourth commandment.
1m 2w 1 interior
In Casey, B. M. Good things for church
groups
Casey, Michael
A soul in fine array. French 1954 31p
illus
Shortly after receiving final vows young
nun is sent to infirmary because of incurable disease. 1 act 2 scenes 9w 1 in-
terior
Casey, Rosemary
Late love. French 1954 110p illus
Romantic comedy. Painter arrives at
country home to paint portrait of its
owner, stays long enough to foster a
love affair, and find romance herself.
3 acts 3m 4w 1 interior
Castaways. See Survival (after aeroplane
accidents, shipwrecks, etc.)
Caste. Robertson, T. W.
Castle in the village. Woskoff, V.
Casual labor. See Migrant labor
The **cat** and the fiddle. De Francquen, L.
The **cat** and the moon. Yeats, W. B.
A **cat** has nine. Parker, K.
Cat on a hot tin roof. Williams, T.
The **cat** who wanted to ride on a broom.
Very, A.
Catastrophe Clarence. Shore, M.
Catch as catch can. Fisher, A.
Catching the ghost. Woolsey, J. and Sechrist,
E. H.
Catharine II, Empress of Russia
Shaw, B. Great Catherine
Catherine of Valois, consort of Henry V,
King of England
Sisson, R. A. The queen and the Welsh-
man

Catherine the Great. See Catharine II, Em-
press of Russia
Cathleen ni Houlihan. Yeats, W. B.
Catholic Church
Hartke, G. V. The little world of Don
Camillo
Herman, G. A smell of cinnamon
Mary Francis, Sister. Counted as mine
Mary Francis, Sister. Smallest of all
Clergy
Jackson, H. H. S. God's ambassador
Olfson, L. The Bishop's candlesticks
See also Bishops; Cardinals
Catholic Church in Iceland
Sveinbjornsson, T. Bishop Jón Arason
Catholics in Ireland
O'Casey, S. Red roses for me
Cats
c Goulding, D. J. The master cat
c Hark, M. and McQueen, N. Too many
kittens
Kleinsinger, G. Archy and Mehitabel
c Lewis, M. R. Dick Whittington
c Miller, H. L. The country store cat
c Miller, H. L. Three little kittens
c Miller, M. Puss in Boots
c Spamer, C. The foolish kitten
c Very, A. Puss-in-Boots
c Very, A. Three little kittens go to school
Cattle market. See Stockyards
The **Caucasian** chalk circle. Brecht, B.
Caught between. Kromer, H.
Caught in a web. St Clair, R.
Cavalcade. Coward, N.
Cavalcade of human rights. Fisher, A. and
Rabe, O.
Cavalleria rusticana. Verga, G.
The **cave** dwellers. Saroyan, W.
Caverhill, William Melville. See Melville,
Alan
Caves of the earth. Fisher, A.
Cayphas, Joseph (Jewish high priest) See
Caiaphas, Joseph (Jewish high priest)
Cecile. Anouilh, J.
The **Celestina.** Rojas, F. de
Célimare. Labiche, E. and Delacour
The **cell.** Kirn, J.
Central America
Apstein, T. Fortunata writes a letter
Social life and customs
Ullman, S. S. El gallo
The **centurion's** servant. Phillips, J. B.
Cepeda, Teresa de. See Teresa, Saint
A **certain** man had two sons. Finch, R.
A **certain** star. Cooper, F. A.
Cervantes Saavedra, Miguel de
Don Quixote (dramatization) See Seiler,
C. The wonderful adventures of Don
Quixote
Don Quixote de la Mancha (dramatiza-
tion) See Howard, V. Don Quixote
saves the day

Chad, Saint
Lehman, L. Saint Chad of the seven wells

Chadwick, Eva
c Shoes for a queen. Paxton 1953 11p music
    Dramatization of the fairy tale: The elves and the shoemaker, by Hans Christian Andersen. Elves help poor shoemaker become chief shoemaker for the king. Includes music for songs and dances. 2 acts 4m 3w extras 1 interior

Chadwick, Vivienne Charlton
The invisible line. French 1960 28p illus
    When girl's finance leaves her without explanation, she goes to spend summer at lonely cottage where she meets mysterious stranger sought by the police. 1 act 2m 3w 1 interior

Chadwicke, Alice
Davy Crockett. French 1956 105p illus
    Comedy. Davy Crockett's life from the time he starts noticing girls to his entry into politics. 3 acts 5 scenes 6m 8w 1 interior

Pudd'nhead Wilson. French 1958 104p illus
    Based on novel by Mark Twain. Pudd'nhead Wilson uses his knowledge of fingerprinting to detect a murder. 3 acts 5 scenes 7m 6w 1 interior

    For other plays by this author see Braun, Wilbur; Faust, Esther; Fernway, Peggy

Chain of jade. Bucci, M.

The **chairs**; tr. by Donald M. Allen. Ionesco, E.

The **chalk** garden. Bagnold, E.

The **chameleon** complex. See Beloin, E. and Garson, H. In any language

Champagne complex. Stevens, L.

Champagne sec. Easton, C.

Champions of democracy. Fisher, A. and Rabe, O.

Chandler, Ruth
c America remembers
    Thanksgiving Day. Some children of today tell a Pilgrim family how much their early struggles are respected by people of today. 1m 1w 1b 2g extras 1 interior
    In Birdsall, R. ed. Creative plays for every school month

The **changeling**. Middleton, T. and Rowley, W.

The **changeling**. Stephens, P. J.

Chanson de Roland
Nicholson, A. and Chorpenning, C. B. The magic horn

Chanukah. See Hannukah (Feast of Lights)

Chapman, George
Bussy D'Ambois
    Jacobean verse play. Intrigue at court of Henry III of France, specifically, Tragic love affair of Bussy D'Ambois, adventurer, and Tamyra, Countess of Montsurry. 5 acts 12 scenes 17m 7w extras 1 setting
    In McIlwraith, A. K. ed. Five Stuart tragedies

Chapman, John
c Crank, H. P. The promise lily

Fisher, A. and Rabe, O. Johnny Appleseed's vision

c Hark, M. and McQueen, N. Visit of Johnny Appleseed

Howard, V. Johnny Appleseed in danger

McCaslin, N. Apples in the wilderness

Young, S. The sound of apples

Chapman, Robert. See Coxe, L. O. jt. auth.

Character
    Plays listed here have a particular interest as character studies
Adamov, A. Professor Taranne
Beckett, S. Krapp's last tape
Chekhov, A. Uncle Vanya
Ford, J. The broken heart
Fry, C. The dark is light enough
García-Lorca, F. The house of Bernarda Alba
Ibsen, H. The master builder
Jonson, B. Volpone
Lawrence, J. and Lee, R. E. Auntie Mame
Marlowe, C. The Jew of Malta
Miller, J. P. The rabbit trap
Olfson, L. David Copperfield and Uriah Heep
O'Neill, E. Hughie
O'Neill, E. A touch of the poet
Pomerantz, E. Only a game
Zweig, S. Volpone

Characters and characteristics in literature
Hark, M. and McQueen, N. Aladdin steps out

Charities. See Disaster relief

Charity
Preston, E. E. The voice that failed
Priestley, F. The Good Samaritans

Charlemagne (Romances, etc.)
Nicholson, A. and Chorpenning, C. B. The magic horn

Charles IX, King of France
Lee, N. The massacre of Paris

Charles the Second. Payne, J. H. and Irving, W.

Charles Wesley. Emurian, E. K.

The **Charleston** craze. Friend, M.

Charlie's May basket. Woolsey, J. and Sechrist, E. H.

Charlotte Augusta, of Wales, consort of Prince Leopold of Saxe-Coburg-Saalfeld
Ginsbury, N. The first gentleman

Charlotte Bronte. Spamer, C.

The **charm.** Engle, J. D.

Charwomen and cleaners
Sutherland, D. The clean up

Chase, Mary
Bernardine. ⌐Rev. acting ed⌐ Dramatists 1954 92p illus
    Comedy about teen-age boys which projects the real world of adolescents and relationship between themselves and grown-ups. 2 acts 10 scenes 13m 6w extras 1 exterior 4 interiors
    Published in trade edition by Oxford
Bernardine (condensation)
    In The Best plays of 1952-1953
    In Theatre 1953

Harvey; illus. by Blechman. Oxford 1953 89p illus
    Fantasy which debunks psychiatry, as it characterizes an amiable drunk with his imaginary companion, Harvey, an oversize rabbit. 3 acts 5 scenes 6m 6w 2 interiors

Chase, Mary—*Continued*

Mrs McThing. [Rev acting ed] Dramatists 1954 72p illus
> Witch's revenge for the unkind treatment of her daughter helps little boy turn the tables on his snobbish, dictatorial mother. 2 acts 5 scenes 8m 8w 1b 1g 2 interiors

The plum tree (dramatization) See McMahon, L. and Sergel, R. The plum tree

Chaucer, Geoffrey. See Very, A. The cock and the fox

Chayefsky, Paddy

The bachelor party
> Television play. Five men go on a night about town in honor of co-worker's impending marriage. 6m 6w

> *In* Chayefsky, P. Television plays

The big deal
> Television play. Former successful building contractor, bankrupt for fifteen years, accepts a $3,600-a-year building inspector's job in order not to sponge any longer on daughter. 9m 12w

> *In* Chayefsky, P. Television plays

Holiday song
> Television play. Cantor loses faith in God and refuses to sing for High Holy Days, but his faith is restored when he unwittingly becomes responsible for bringing together couple whom war had separated. 7m 4w extras

> *In* Chayefsky, P. Television plays

Marty
> Television play. Harassed by friends and relatives to get married, a plain 36 year old Italian bachelor finally decides to marry a plain spinster of 29. 7m 7w extras

> *In* Chayefsky, P. Television plays

Middle of the night. French 1957 82p illus
> Romantic comedy. Widower, aged 53 falls in love with young married woman, aged 24 and they have to surmount families opposition and their own misgivings. 3 acts 8 scenes 3m 8w 2 interiors
> Trade edition published by Random House

The mother
> Television play. Married, self-sacrificing daughter tries to take care of aged mother, but the mother insists on independence. 2m 8w

> *In* Chayefsky, P. Television plays

> *In* Vidal, G. ed. Best television plays

Printer's measure
> Television play. Old-time printer refuses to adjust to technological progress in the form of a linotype machine. 9m 5w extras

> *In* Chayefsky, P. Television plays

The tenth man. French 1960 104p
> Men in a synagogue believing that the daughter of one is possessed by dybbuk (a lost soul), ceremoniously exorcise the dybbuk. 3 acts 4 scenes 12m 1w 1 interior
> Trade edition published by Random House

The tenth man (condensation)
> *In* The Best plays of 1959-1960
> *In* Broadway's best, 1960

Cheating at cards. See Cardsharping

Cheating cheaters. Relonde, M.

Cheerfulness
c Spamer, C. The mirror children

Chekhov, Anton

The boor; English version by H. R. Baukhage and Barrett H. Clark
> Romantic comedy. Landowner tries to collect debt from neighbor in czarist Russia, but collects young widow instead. 1 act 2m 1w extras 1 interior
> Same as: The brute

> *In* Smith, B. and others, eds. A treasury of non-royalty one-act plays

The brute; English version by Eric Bentley. French 1956 21p
> Same as: The boor

The cherry orchard
> Effect of poverty on Russian aristocrats, their friends and servants. 4 acts 10m 5w extras 2 interiors 1 exterior

> *In* Heffner, H. The nature of drama

> *In* Stallman, R. W. and Watters, R. E. The creative reader

—Same; tr. by George Calderon
> *In* Tucker, S. M. ed. Twenty-five modern plays

—Same; tr. from the Russian by Constance Garnett
> *In* Cubeta, P. M. ed. Modern drama for analysis. 1955 edition

> *In* A Treasury of the theatre

—Same; tr. by Stark Young
> *In* Chekhov, A. Best plays

A country scandal (Platonov) tr. and adapted by Alex Szogyi. Coward-McCann 1960 127p
> Farce set in 19th century Russia with the principal character a young tutor. 4 acts 74 scenes 11m 5w 2 interiors 2 exteriors
> Also published in trade edition

A marriage proposal
> Hypochondriacal suitor quarrels with the girl he wants to marry, but she accepts him. 1 act 2m 1w 1 interior

> *In* Cerf, B. and Cartmell, V. H. eds. 24 favorite one-act plays

The seagull; tr. by D. Iliffe. French (London) 1953 53p illus
> Symbolic. Tragic outcome of young actress' love for a selfish playwright. Russia, 19th century. 4 acts 7m 7w 2 interiors 2 exteriors

—Same; tr. by Stark Young
> *In* Chekhov, A. Best plays

> *In* Downer, A. S. ed. The art of the play

> *In* Gassner, J. ed. Twenty best European plays on the American stage

> *In* Griffin, A. V. Living theatre

The three sisters; tr. by Stark Young
> Life of the intelligensia in 19th century Russia reflected in unhappy lives of a Moscow family stranded in a small city. 4 acts 9m 5w 2 interiors 1 exterior

> *In* Chekhov, A. Best plays

Uncle Vanya; tr. by Stark Young. French 1956 61p
> Country life in 19th century Russia and character contrast between selfish, intellectual professor and his brother-in-law, owner of country estate. 4 acts 5m 4w 3 interiors 1 exterior

—Same
> *In* Chekhov, A. Best plays

—Same; tr. by Marian Fell
> *In* Watson, E. B. ed. Contemporary drama: fifteen plays

Chenery, M.
Lesson for today. Deane 1956 27p ("Deane's" Ser. of plays)
Comedy. Writer learns about the modern woman when his wife, daughters, and secretary "blackmail" him. 1 act 1m 4w 1 interior

Chenery, Muriel Sybil. See Chenery, M.

Cherokee Indians
Kissen, F. Sam Houston: brother of the Cherokees

The **cherry** orchard. Chekhov, A.

The **cherry** tree. Spamer, C.

Chester plays
The deluge (adaptation) See Malcolmson, A. Noah's flood

Noah's flood; The Chester Pageant of the Water-Leaders and Drawers in Dee
14th or early 15th century English mystery play. Based on the Old Testament story from the Book of Genesis about Noah and the ark. Verse play in Middle English with modernized spelling. 5m 5w 1 setting
In Browne, E. M. ed. Religious drama, 2
In Everyman, and medieval miracle plays

Chesterton, G. K.
The surprise. Sheed 1953 63p
Play within a play. To prove his philosophy that happiness is dependent upon surprise, author presents a puppet play to a friar. 2 acts 6 scenes 6m 2w 2 exteriors

Chetham-Strode, Warren
The pet shop. [French's Acting ed] French (London) 1955 67p illus
Domestic comedy. Mother overwhelms adopted daughter with love and protection. 3 act 4m 6w 2 interiors

Chettle, Henry. See Dekker, T. jt. auth.

Chevigny, Hector
Daniel Webster
Television play. Daniel Webster foregoes presidential ambition to negotiate treaty with Britain. Musical background. 3 acts 11m 1w extras
In The Best television plays v3

Cheyney, Peter
The urgent hangman (dramatization) See Verner, G. Meet Mr Callaghan

Chiari, Joseph
Mary Stuart. Oxford 1955 71p
Verse play. Three incidents in life of Mary Stuart, Queen of Scotland. 3 acts 7 scenes 16m 5w extras 6 interiors 1 exterior

Chicago
Brecht, B. Saint Joan of the Stockyards

Child of fortune. Bolton, G.

Child psychology. See Adolescence; Boys; Children; Girls; Youth

Children
Applegarth, M. T. Color blind
c Asbrand, K. S. When daddy comes home
c Barton, E. The third lamb
c Close, E. The land of the traffic goblins
c Fisher, A. Caves of the earth
Hark, M. and McQueen, N. The place to begin
c Martens, A. C. The time machine
Miller, H. L. Three cheers for mother
c Seiler, C. Let's go to the moon
c Spamer, C. The joy givers

Children, Abnormal and backward. See Exceptional children

Children of darkness. Mayer, E. J.

The **children** of Herakles. Euripides

Children of the Americas. National Recreation Association

Children of the Bible. Asbrand, K. S.

Children of the ladybug. Thom, R.

The **children** who forgot. Spamer, C.

Children's clubs
c Woolsey, J. and Sechrist, E. H. Pumpkin is the password

The **children's** hour. Hellman, L.

Children's literature
c Lunnon, B. S. Johnny has comicopia

Children's plays
Birdsall, R. ed. Creative plays for every school month (87 plays)
Carlson, B. W. The right play for you (19 plays)
Easy juvenile grab bag (13 plays)
Fenner, P. and Hughes, A. comps. Entrances and exits (14 plays)
Hurt, F. The weather imp; and, The King of Nowhere (2 plays)
Ilian, C. Absolutely horrid
Ilian, C. Time for a play (6 plays)
Miller, H. L. First plays for children (26 plays)
Moore, S. S. Six playlets from Aesop's fables (6 plays)
'Round the year plays for the grades (16 plays)
Spamer, C. Easy science plays for grade school (15 plays)
Spamer, C. Juvenile treasure chest (16 plays)
Tennant, K. The bells of the city, and other plays (5 plays)

Children's praises. Nystrom, D.

Childs, Clara
c The candle in the window
Christ Child visits three children in guise of Little Boy when the children put candle in the window on Christmas eve. Includes carol singing. 1 act 1w 5b 5g 1 interior
In Brings, L. M. ed. The modern treasury of Christmas plays

Chimpanzees
Tarpley, V. and Tarpley, K. Jump over the moon

China
Arnold, H. G. Sam Pollard
Hagy, L. Fire in a paper
c Totheroh, D. The stolen prince
Williams, N. A battle of wits

History—1945-
Li, Y. M. The modern bridge

Social life and customs
Brecht, B. The good woman of Setzuan
Fisk, D. M. The secondary wife
Hui-lan-ki. The story of the circle of chalk
Jennings, T.; Slesinger, T. and West, C. The good earth
Kao-Tong-Kia. Lute song
Li, Y. M. The grand garden
Li, Y. M. Heaven challenges
Li, Y. M. The woman painter
Williams, N. A battle of wits

Chinese drama
Hui-lan-ki. The story of the circle of chalk
Kao-Tong-Kia. Lute song
Li, Y. M. The grand garden
Li, Y. M. Heaven challenges
Li, Y. M. The modern bridge
Li, Y. M. The woman painter
Chinese in the United States
Rodgers, R. Flower drum song
Chippewa Indians
McCaslin, N. The star that never moves
Chitty, A. W. I.
c Any old toys. Paxton 1953 16p music
Wizard encounters toy-mender and helps old man to make old toys new again. Words and music for songs. 4m 2w 1b 1g extras 1 exterior
c The bath-room folks party. Paxton 1953 9p music
Soap, toothbrush and others encourage children to form good health habits. Includes words and music for song. Unidentified cast 8 characters no scenery
Chivalry
Howard, V. Don Quixote saves the day
A **chocolate**. Carter, C.
The **chocolate** bunny. Spamer, C.
Chodorov, Edward
Oh, men! Oh, women! French 1955 89p illus
Romantic comedy. Psychoanalyst accidentally learns about his fiancee's past life from two of his patients. 3 acts 5m 3w 3 interiors
Oh, men! Oh, women! (condensation)
In Theatre, 1954
The spa. Dramatists 1957 72p illus
Romantic comedy based on play by Ferenc Molnar. Story of Olympia, princess of the Austrian-Hungarian empire, who falls in love with Captain Kovacs, an imposter, while visiting a spa with mother. Background music. 3 acts 6m 3w 1 interior
See also Bernstein, L. Wonderful town; Fields, J. jt. auth.
Chodorov, Jerome, and Fields, Joseph
Anniversary waltz. Dramatists 1957 82p illus
Domestic comedy. Trials and tribulations of couple celebrating their fifteenth wedding anniversary. 3 acts 5 scenes 7m 5w 1 interior
Trade edition published by Random House
The **Choephori**. Aeschylus
Choëphoroe. Aeschylus
Chorio. Kwanze, K. N.
Chorpenning, Charlotte B.
Abe Lincoln—New Salem days. Coach House Press 1954 80p illus music
Historical play. Episode in Lincoln's life at New Salem from 1831-1837. Music included. 3 acts 9m 7w 1b 2g 1 interior
Lincoln's secret messenger. Coach House Press 1955 64p illus
President Lincoln's young messenger proves his loyalty and prevents catastrophe from befalling the Union Army. Background music. 3 acts 8m 2w extras 1 exterior 1 interior
The prince and the pauper. Childrens Theatre 1954 60p illus
Dramatization of novel by Mark Twain. Adventures of Edward Tudor, Prince of Wales afterwards Edward VI, King of England, and Tom Canty, poor boy with whom he inadvertently changed places. 3 acts 11 scenes 17m 10w 3b 2g extras 4 interiors 3 exteriors
Radio rescue. Coach House Press 1954 50p illus
Comedy. Amateur radio operators avert wreck. 3 acts 6m 6w 2 interiors 1 exterior
Rama and the tigers. Coach House Press 1954 64p illus
Fairy tale. Based on the "story of Little Black Sambo," by Helen Bannerman. Little boy's adventures with some tigers in the jungle result in getting butter his mother needs to make pancakes. 3 acts 4 scenes 1m 1w 1b extras 2 exteriors
Rip Van Winkle. Coach House Press 1954 64p illus
A dramatization of the story by Washington Irving about the man who slept for twenty years. 3 acts 4 scenes 7m 4w 4b 6g extras 2 interiors 1 exterior
See also Nicholson, A. jt. auth.
Chown, Herbert
Account rendered. Pitman 1953 27p
Man, about to die in nursing-home is visited by a member of "Facts finding commission" whose acquaintances examine sick man's credits and debits for eternity. 1 act 5m 4w 1 interior
Chris is sent to Coventry. Burgess, C. V.
The **Christ** child in the temple. Spamer, C. M.
Christ enters Jerusalem. Phillips, J. B.
Christ lives again. Spamer, C. M.
Christ the Son of God. Phillips, J. B.
Christian life
Applegarth, M. T. Were you there?
Asbrand, K. Sight to see
Casey, B. M. Green eyes
Casey, B. M. The jewel beyond price
Casey, B. M. My neighbor
Casey, B. M. Myself and I
Casey, B. M. Second chance
Casey, B. M. Seventy times seven
Casey, B. M. Sweetness and light
Casey, B. M. A welcome for mother
Corey, O. R. The big middle
Kromer, H. Take any street
St Clair, R. The happy life
Stanley-Wrench, M. The splendid burden
Stricker, E. B. What is the church?
Wolfe, B. S. Watch your step
See also Christianity; Faith; Stewardship
Christian stewardship. See Stewardship, Christian
Christianity
Carruthers, J. Fear not
Casey, B. M. The guest at Cana
Casey, B. M. They say
Cockram, R. Shadow of the eagle
Cruse, C. Son of Stephen
Howard, V. The spear
Kirn, J. The cell
Kromer, H. They made a path
Lehman, L. Saint Chad of the Seven Wells
Marlowe, C. The tragedy of Doctor Faustus
Rodman, H. The will to win
Shaw, B. Androcles and the lion
Wilson, D. C. The return of Chandra

Christianity—*Continued*

History
See Church history

Christianity and other religions
Fry, C. Thor, with angels
Osgood, P. E. Midwinter-Eve fire

Christie, Agatha
Towards zero. ₁Acting ed₁ French 1957 75p illus
> Dramatization of author's mystery. Invalid old lady who has invited odd assortment of guests to house-party is murdered. Family lawyer and Superintendent Battle prove this was inevitable. 3 acts 6 scenes 7m 4w 1 interior

—Same. Dramatists 1957 86p illus

Witness for the prosecution. French 1954 112p
> Murder trial in which wife gives evidence against husband, then perjures herself to free him despite his actual guilt. 3 acts 4 scenes Large mixed cast 2 interiors

Witness for the prosecution (condensation)
> *In* The Best plays of 1954-1955
> *In* Theatre, 1955

Christie, Campbell. See Christie, D. jt. auth .

Christie, Dorothy, and Christie, Campbell
Carrington, V. C. French (London) 1954 88n
> British army officer court martialed for taking money from his unit's funds. 3 acts 16m 2w 4 interiors

The touch of fear. ₁French's Acting ed₁ French 1957 83p illus
> Dilys the governess is murdered. 3 acts 5m 4w 1 interior

Christmas
Allan, D. C. Eyes that see not
Anderson, R. Silent night, lonely night
c Arlett, V. I. The people who came to an inn
Asbrand, K. All that glitters
Asbrand, K. Candle in the window
Asbrand, K. Christmas rose
Asbrand, K. Christmas satellite
c Asbrand, K. Christmas snowman
c Asbrand, K. Christmas wishes
c Asbrand, K. Come to Bethlehem
c Asbrand, K. "Come to my party"
Asbrand, K. Easy church plays for women and girls (9 plays)
Asbrand, K. Gifts of gold
Asbrand, K. Hark, the little angels speak (9 plays)
c Asbrand, K. Hi ho! Christmas
c Asbrand, K. The image of Christmas
Asbrand, K. It happened at Christmas
c Asbrand, K. Light up the world
c Asbrand, K. Little Christmas guest
Asbrand, K. On earth peace
c Asbrand, K. Our little Christmas angels
Asbrand, K. The Prince of Peace
Asbrand, K. So it's Christmas again
c Asbrand, K. The stars celebrate Christmas
c Asbrand, K. Story book Christmas
c Asbrand, K. Strangers at the gate
Asbrand, K. The week before Christmas
Ashton, L. S. Bethlehem's Field
Ashton, L. S. Christmas story

Atherton, M. And it's Christmas!
c Austin, C. L. Mrs Santa proves a point
Baden, R. The Christmas Eve visitor
Bailey, H. F. Christmas Eve candle vespers
Bailey, H. F. A manger lowly
Bailey, H. F. The picture window frames Christmas
c Bailey, H. F. Roses for the King
Bangham, M. D. Come to the manger
Barbee, L. Christmas for Cinderella
Barbee, L. The Friday Foursome packs a box
Baugham, R. K. A modern Christmas carol
Baxter, A. M. A pageant of Christmas
Bean, V. I created Santa Claus
c Beneke, A. Symbols of Christmas
Benfield, D. The way the wind blows
Blacklock, J. A time of minor miracles
c Boegehold, B. The shoemaker's Christmas
c Boli, L. They found Christmas
Brings, L. M. ed. The modern treasury of Christmas plays (22 plays)
c Buzzell, A. M. "The man on the street"
c Carlson, B. W. St Nicholas just the same
Carlson, M. M. Christmas in many nations
Casey, B. M. The Christmas loaf
Casey, B. M. God so loved the world
Casey, B. M. The manger
Casey, B. M. One song for Christmas
c Childs, C. The candle in the window
Christmas in art
c Christmas old—Christmas new
c Clark, I. S. The Christmas Tree Forest
Conkle, E. P. A bauble for the baby
Cooper, F. A. A certain star
Cooper, F. A. If thine enemy
Cowen, W. J. Little friend
Crouch, M. Christmas in her eyes
Cruse, C. Healing in its wings
Cruse, I. R. To bear the message
Daily, D. T. The Christmas party
c Davis, J. A. Santa's spectacles
DeWitt, R. H. Arise, thy light is come!
Drapkin, I. Lucy
Duff, A. A play for Christmas Eve
c Duggar, F. December's gifts
c Dunbar, T. M. Girls are so useless!
c Early, L. S. Everywhere, Christmas
Emery, C. The Christmas stranger
Emurian, E. K. Christmas traditions
Emurian, E. K. Inasmuch
Emurian, E. K. Three skits for Christmas
Emurian, E. K. 'Twas the night before Christmas
Faust, J. P. To us a son
Fearheiley, D. A star too far
c Feder, L. Christmas in the melting pot
Fisher, A. Angel in the looking-glass
c Fisher, A. The Christmas cake
c Fisher, A. A Christmas tree for Kitty
Fisher, A. The Merry Christmas elf
c Fisher, A. The Spirit of Christmas
c Fisher, A. Time out for Christmas
Fleming, T. Miracle at midnight

Christmas—*Continued*

c Fluckey, J. O. Davy's star
c Fluckey, J. O. The little blue angel
c Fluckey, J. O. Santa and the space men
Fuller, R. The Noël candle
George, L. D. When the little angel sang
Gruwell, B. G. O holy night
Hare, W. B. A Christmas carol
Hare, W. B. The white Christmas
Hark, M. and McQueen, N. All aboard for Christmas
c Hark, M. and McQueen, N. Christmas Eve news
c Hark, M. and McQueen, N. Christmas in the woods
Hark, M. and McQueen, N. Christmas recaptured
c Hark, M. and McQueen, N. Junction Santa Claus
Hark, M. and McQueen, N. Reindeer on the roof
c Hark, M. and McQueen, N. The Santa Claus parade
Hark, M. and McQueen, N. The Teen Club's Christmas
Hark, M. and McQueen, N. Tomorrow is Christmas
c Hastings, M. L. C. Christmas in other lands
Hatcher, H. B. The holy Nativity
Hawse, A. The cradle
Hawse, A. Seeing the star
Hazeltine, A. I. Madelon
Heicher, M. and St Clair, R. The lost star
Hein, R. Receive your King!
Hellier, E. B. He who walks in love
c Hoggan, M. H. The toymakers' pledge
c Holbrook, M. A candle-lighting service
c Hondelink, M. E. Christmas cards
Horn Book Magazine. Four Christmas plays (4 plays)
c Howard, D. Christmas doings
Howells, W. D. The night before Christmas
c Ilian, C. A Christmas miracle
Jorgenson, E. S. The message of Christmas
c Joy to the world
c Kent, M. The Nativity
Kerr, M. L. His star
c Kerr, M. L. The wonderful Child
Ketchum, A. Bethlehem
Kimes, B. The lost Christmas
c Kinkhead, J. B. Let us adore Him
Knox, J. The shepherd of Bethlehem
Liggat, J. Friendly relations
Lindsey, B. Beggars can't be choosers
Lorenz, E. J. A Christmas gift for Hans
Lorenzen, R. F. The scarf from Smyrna
Lowe, E. A birthday through the centuries
Lynch, P. The Christmas angel
Lynch, P. Just a little something for Christmas
McCarty, R. K. Longing for Christmas
McCaslin, N. The legend of the Christmas candle
McCaslin, N. St Nicholas of New Amsterdam

MacDonald, D. M. Let nothing ye dismay
McGreevey, J. Coins of His kingdom
McGreevey, J. The shepherd who stayed away
McMartin, E. L. The tree
McMullen, J. C. I don't believe in Christmas
Magary, F. A. Rest, ye merry gentlemen!
c Manthorn, R. A. A Christmas box
Marcelline, Sister M. Silver beads
Marston, J. And a song was born
c Marston, M. A. A Christmas carol
Martens, A. C. Christmas is too old-fashioned
Martens, A. C. A cool Yule
Martens, A. C. The fantastic Mr C.
Martens, A. C. Home for Christmas
c Martens, A. C. The tiniest Christmas tree
Martens, G. M. The hopeful travelers
Mary Francis, Sister. Christmas at Greccio
c Matthews, E. Teddy's own Santa
c Mattice, I. A bomb for Santa
Mattson, J. A Sunday school Christmas program
Miller, C. H. Back to Bethlehem
c Miller, H. L. The Birds' Christmas Carol
Miller, H. L. The Christmas oboe
c Miller, H. L. The Christmas runaways
c Miller, H. L. The Christmas umbrella
Miller, H. L. The coming of the Prince
Miller, H. L. The left-over reindeer
c Miller, H. L. The Santa Claus twins
c Miller, H. L. Wake up, Santa Claus!
c Moore, D. O. Christmas comes to Santa's workshop
Morley, O. J. Little women
National Recreation Association. Plays, pageants and ceremonials for the Christmas season (10 plays)
c National Recreation Association. The runaway sled
c National Recreation Association. The St George play
c National Recreation Association. Santa Claus visits Mars
Neilson, P. Christmas unusual
Neilson, P. The star still shines
Neilson, P. To hear the angels sing
c Newman, D. The best part of Christmas
c Newman, D. Christmas at the Cratchits
c Newman, D. The Christmas tree surprise
c Newman, D. Long ago in Bethlehem
c Newman, D. The way to the inn
O'Brien, F. B. The guardian
O'Connell, M. O. Sister. One red rose
Olfson, L. Which of the nine?
c Olson, E. E. Lighting the way
Osgood, P. E. Midwinter-Eve fire
Owen, V. The wanderers
c Page, F. R. Adopted by Santa Claus
Paige, M. C. Father trims the tree
Peery, R. R. The glory of His coming
Phillips, A. L. The shepherds and the wise men
Phillips, M. K. Grandma and mistletoe
Phillips, M. K. The woman who didn't want Christmas
Piersel, W. G. A town is born

Church, Richard
The prodigal. Staples Press 1953 139p
Life and death of poet Christopher Marlowe, depicting also character of his parents, a prosperous shoemaker and his wife. 4 scenes Large mixed cast 2 interiors

Church
Casey, B. M. Church notices
Casey, B. M. The servant of the King
Casey, B. M. Sunday morning
Trick, O. B. Beneath this spire

Church and social problems
Wefer, M. This Thine house

Church and state in England. See Church and state in Great Britain

Church and state in Great Britain
Anouilh, J. Becket
Arblay, Madame d'. Edwy and Elgiva
Duncannon, F. E. N. P. viscount. Like stars appearing
Eliot, T. S. Murder in the cathedral
Tennyson, A. Becket

Church history
Stanley-Wrench, M. The splendid burden

Primitive and early church
c Morris, T. B. The sleeping fires
The church in the wildwood. Emurian, E. K.

Church notices. Casey, B. M.

Church of England

Clergy
Draper, J. Barchester Towers

Church schools
Casey, B. M. The portrait

Church societies
Asbrand, K. Youth serves the church

Church work
Bell, R. E. Through a glass darkly
Casey, B. M. His and hers
Casey, B. M. Important business
Casey, B. M. The lamp in the night
Casey, B. M. A red carpet for the bishop
Emurian, E. K. The radiance streaming

Church work with youth
Smith, A. C. Greater than any man

Le **Cid.** Corneille, P.

Cid Campeador
Corneille, P. Le Cid

Cinderella. Palmer, K. and Palmer, W.

Cinderella's friends. Spamer, C.

The **circle.** Maugham, W. S.

The **circle** of chalk. See Hui-lan-ki. The story of the circle of chalk

Circus
Andreev, L. He who gets slapped
c Colson, J. G. Top of the bill
Deval, J. Tonight in Samarkand
Devany, E. H. The red and yellow ark
c Harris, A. Circus in the wind
c Nicholson, M. A. The crying clown
Seiler, C. The clown and his circus
c Slattery, M. The circus stars' mistake
c Sognefest, A. Big top circus

Circus in the wind. Harris, A.

The **circus** stars' mistake. Slattery, M.

Cities and towns
c Flavelle, I. B. Giants of the city
c Hauser, W. The big decision
c Pennington, L. and Kaeyer, M. Our home town

Citizenship
c Carlson, B. W. Litterbug convention
Fisher, A. and Rabe, O. Johnny on the spot
Fisher, A. and Rabe, O. Shipmates
Fisher, A. and Rabe, O. Wheels within wheels
c Hauser, W. The big decision
c Miller, H. L. The curious quest
c Pennington, L. and Kaeyer, M. Our home town
c Porter, H. W. Election Day
Thompson, M. A. The conquered, the unconquerable, and I

Civil liberty. See Liberty

Civil rights
Rose, R. An almanac of liberty
See also Liberty

Civil War

United States
See United States—History—Civil War

Civil War, American. See United States History—Civil War

Civilization
c Marcus, I. H. To you the torch

Civilization, Greek
Sinclair, L. When Greek meets Greek

Civilization, Modern
Rutenborn, G. The sign of Jonah

Civilization and war. See War and civilization

Claflin, Merle
Saturday at the Cohens. French 1957 35p
Domestic comedy. Old Jewish couple coming to live with successful son cause distress in household that has forgotten religion. 1 act 2 scenes 3m 5w 1 interior

Claiborne, Ross, and Banks, Frances
The last leaf. French 1959 89p illus
Domestic comedy. Old lady whose eccentricities are constant source of embarrassment to her children, decides to have her funeral while she is alive to enjoy it. 3 acts 4 scenes 4m 5w 1 interior

Clandon, Laura
The brains of the family. Dramatic 1956 20p illus
Domestic comedy. TV talent scout chooses young sister with brains rather than "actress" of family. 1 act 2m 4w 1 interior

Clapp, Patricia
Edie-across-the-street. Bakers Plays 1960 78p
Comedy. Shy girl, embarrassed at meeting local hero is struck by a car, and local young people hold benefit for her expenses. 3 acts 4m 9w 1 interior
Peggy's on the phone. Dramatic 1956 21p illus
Domestic comedy. Whole family cooperates to help the second oldest daughter when she thinks her escort has disappointed her for dance date. 1 act 4w 1 interior

Clara Barton. Spamer, C.

Clara Barton: angel of the battlefield. Kissen, F.

Clara paints the town. McCoy, P. S.

Clare, Nora
  Surprise packet. Kenyon House Press 1954 17p illus
    Comedy. Chest bought at auction aids in capture of thief. 1 act 5w 1 interior
  The windfall. Kenyon House Press 1954 15p illus
    Comedy. Young man finds unique way of subsidizing two impoverished old school teachers. 1 act 2m 2w 1 interior
Clarence Gate. Robinson, R.
Clark, Al W.
  Graves ghost. Art Craft 1956 92p illus
    Mystery. Storm forces passengers of a bus to seek shelter with a cemetery caretaker and his inhospitable wife, who has reason to be inhospitable. 3 acts 3m 5w 1 interior
Clark, Barrett H.
  Fires at Valley Forge
    Teen age soldiers fight with George Washington at Valley Forge. 1 act 9m 1 exterior
  In Burack, A. S. ed. Four-star plays for boys
  In Smith, B. and others, eds. A treasury of non-royalty one-act plays
Clark, Isabel S.
c The Christmas Tree Forest. French 1959 31p illus
    Based on story by Raymond Alden. Inhabitants of Great Walled Country who never grow up enter Christmas Tree Forest each year to gather presents for each other. 1 act 22m 3w 5b 5g 1 interior
Clark, Margaret Goff
c Columbus and a Boy Scout
    Columbus Day. When Boy Scout has to earn money to buy his own uniform, he learns Columbus' motto of perseverance. 2 scenes 2w 6b 1 interior
  In Birdsall, R. ed. Creative plays for every school month
  My wife, Henry. Eldridge 1954 24p (Eldridge Popular one-act playscripts)
    Comedy. Real identity disclosed, writers discover they can continue careers using right names. 1 act 2m 3w 1 interior
Clark, Sarah Grames
  21 good neighbors
    Girl who has been living in South America tells friends about work of Organization of American States. 6g 1 interior
  In Birdsall, R. ed. Creative plays for every school month
Clarke, Mary Frances, Mother
  Herman, G. A smell of cinnamon
Class distinction
  Anouilh, J. The ermine
  Anouilh, J. The rehearsal
  Anouilh, J. Restless heart
  Barry, P. Holiday
  Boucicault, D. The Colleen Bawn
  Camus, A. The just assassins
  Chodorov, E. The spa
  Goodchild, R. The grand duchess
  Hale, R. and Hale, N. Love comes in many colors
  Howells, W. D. Out of the question
  Howells, W. D. and Kester, P. The rise of Silas Lapham
  Lessing. Emilia Galotti
  Phillips, I. Gown of glory
  Rattigan, T. The sleeping prince
  Robertson, T. W. Caste

  Shaw, B. Misalliance
  Strindberg, A. Miss Julie
  Stuart, A. Lace on her petticoat
  Taylor, S. Sabrina Fair
  Williams, H. and Williams, M. Plaintiff in a pretty hat
  Williams, N. The king decides
    See also Middle classes

Great Britain
  Barrie, J. M. The admirable Crichton
  Galsworthy, J. Loyalties
Classical drama
  Aeschylus. Agamemnon
  Aeschylus. Choephoroe
  Aeschylus. The Eumenides
  Aeschylus. The libation bearers
  Aeschylus. The Oresteian trilogy (3 plays)
  Aeschylus. Prometheus bound
  Aristophanes. The Acharnians
  Aristophanes. The birds
  Aristophanes. The clouds
  Aristophanes. The frogs
  Aristophanes. Lysistrata
  Aristophanes. Peace
  Aristophanes. The wasps
  Euripides. Alcestis
  Euripides. Andromachê
  Euripides. The Bacchae
  Euripides. The children of Herakles
  Euripides. The Cyclops
  Euripides. Electra
  Euripides. Hecuba
  Euripides. Helen
  Euripides. Hippolytus
  Euripides. Ion
  Euripides. Iphigeneia at Aulis
  Euripides. Iphigeneia in Taurica
  Euripides. Iphigenia in Tauris
  Euripides. The madness of Herakles
  Euripides. Medea
  Euripides. Orestes
  Euripides. The Phoenician maidens
  Euripides. Rhesus
  Euripides. Suppliants
  Euripides. The Trojan women
  Euripides. The women of Troy
  Menander. The bad-tempered man
  Menander. She who was shorn
  Plautus, T. M. Mostellaria
  Sophocles. Ajax
  Sophocles. Antigone
  Sophocles. Electra
  Sophocles. Oedipus at Colonus
  Sophocles. Oedipus Rex
  Sophocles. Oedipus the King
  Sophocles. Philoctetes
  Sophocles. Three Theban plays (3 plays)
  Sophocles. Women of Trachis
    See also Greek drama; Greek drama (Comedy); Greek drama (Tragedy); Latin drama (Comedy); Latin drama (Tragedy)
Claudel, Paul
  Break of noon; tr. by W. Fowlie
    Philosophical tragedy about meaning of love as seen in experiences of husband and wife, and wife's two lovers. 3 acts 3m 1w 1 interior 2 exteriors
  In Claudel, P. Two dramas

Claudel, Paul—*Continued*
The tidings brought to Mary; tr. by W. Fowlie
Supernatural representation of death and rebirth centered around relationship between two sisters, one good and one evil. Set in 15th century France. 4 acts 3m 3w extras 1 interior 2 exteriors
In Claudel, P. Two dramas
—Same; tr. from the French by Louise Morgan Sill
In A Treasury of the theatre

A **clean** kill. Gilbert, M.

The **clean** up. Sutherland, D.

Clean-up time. Jones, C.

The **cleansing** of the Temple. Phillips, J. B.

A **clearing** in the woods. Laurents, A.

Clemens, Samuel L.
The prince and the pauper (dramatization) See Chorpenning, C. B. The prince and the pauper
See also Howells, W. D. jt. auth.
For another play by this author see Twain, Mark

Cleopatra, Queen of Egypt
Shakespeare, W. Antony and Cleopatra
Shaw, B. Caesar and Cleopatra

Clérambard, Aymé, M.

Clergy
Anderson, M. Lost in the stars
Delderfield, R. F. Golden rain
Emurian, E. K. Charles Wesley
George, M. Symphonie pastorale
Hawtrey, C. The private secretary
Kelly, G. The flattering word
King, P. Serious charge
McGreevey, J. Papa was a preacher
Perrini, A. Once a thief
Phillips, I. Gown of glory
Sandberg, L. M. The Pastor's guiding hand
Sherriff, R. C. The telescope
Simpson, H. Miss Matty in mischief
Thomas, D. and Slocumb, P. Next-to-last rites
Weiss, H. A bolt from heaven
Willis, C. The velvet plain
See also Catholic church—Clergy; *also* names of individual clergymen, e.g. Marshall, Peter

Catholic Church
Carroll, P. V. The wayward saint

Clerks
Mortimer, J. Call me a liar

The **climate** of Eden. Hart, M.

Climenhaga, Joel
Heathen pioneer. French 1956 25p illus
Comedy. Influenced by revival meeting young man heads for South Dakota to "convert the heathen," his first convert being man who comes to arrest him for stealing. 1 act 2m 2w 1 exterior

Clinton-Baddeley, V. C.
Jack and the beanstalk; or, Love conquers all; with music by Gavin Gordon. [French's Acting ed] French (London) 1953 80p
Libretto of a musical comedy. Modernized version of the fairy tale. 2 acts 22 scenes 18m 6w extras 6 interiors 8 exteriors

Clive, Robert Clive, baron
Boyd, A. K. Clive's fear, unique

Clive's fear, unique. Boyd, A. K.

The **clock**. Spamer, C.

Cloisters. See Convents and nunneries

Close, Eunice
c Germs versus Fairy Good-Health. Paxton 1954
Fairy tale. Good health fairies assisted by brownies win the battle against germs. Verse play. 1 scene Large mixed cast
c The land of the traffic goblins. Paxton 1958 11p
Two children caught playing in street are picked up by traffic goblins. 2 scenes 14m 5b 3g 1 interior 1 exterior

Closing time. Armer, A. and Grauman, W. E.

Clothing and dress
Asbrand, K. More blessed to give
c Field, R. Polly Patchwork
Howard, V. The blue serge suit
Phillips, M. K. A flair for fashion
Regan, S. The fifth season
Russell, M. A fashion revue
See also Fashion

Clothing trade
George, C. Fanny, the frivolous flapper

A **cloud** of witnesses. Yelvington, R.

Cloud seven. Wilk, M.

Clouds
c Spamer, C. The little clouds

The **clouds**. Aristophanes

The **clown** and his circus. Seiler, C.

The **clown** out west. Seiler, C.

The **clown** Prince of Wanderlust. Parkhirst, D.

Clowns
Seiler, C. The clown and his circus

Club-foot. See Foot—Abnormities and deformities

Clubs
Burgess, C. V. Doers and viewers
Gibson, M. N. Will the ladies please come to order
Kirkpatrick, J. The clubwoman's club
c Miller, H. L. Ten pennies for Lincoln
Sheridan, E. One bit of glory
See also Children's clubs; Woman—Societies and clubs

The **clubwoman's** club. Kirkpatrick, J.

The **clumsy** fairy. Spamer, C.

Coaching (Athletics)
Conkle, E. P. Poor Old Bongo!

Coast-guard (Great Britain)
Webber, J. Air sea rescue
Webber, J. Lights on the coast

A **coat** of many colors. Thompson, M. A.

The **cock** and the fox. Very, A.
Cockney dialect. See Dialect—English—
Cockney
Cockram, Ronald
Shadow of the eagle. ₁Acting ed₎ French
(London) 1953 41p illus
Peter, the apostle, visits house of Jacob
and wins more followers. 2 acts 4 scenes
5m 4w 1g 1 interior
Cockroaches
Kleinsinger, G. Archy and Mehitabel
Cocteau, Jean
The infernal machine; tr. from the French
by Carl Wildman
Tragedy depicting inevitability of fate.
Based on Greek legend in which incest
is unwittingly committed by Oedipus, King
of Thebes. 4 acts 12m 3w 1b 1g 1 setting
In Tucker, S. M. ed. Twenty-five
modern plays
Intimate relations; English version by
Charles Frank
Overprotective, emotional mother com-
mits suicide when she cannot prevent
son from marrying. 3 acts 2m 3w 2 in-
teriors
In Bentley, E. ed. From the modern
repertoire, ser. 3
Coddled Egbert. Tobias, J.
Coeducation
Aske, L. Too young
See also Education; Education of
women
Coffee for one. Last, J.
Coins of His kingdom. McGreevey, J.
Cold (Disease)
c Spamer, C. The cold twins
The **cold** twins. Spamer, C.
The **cold** wind and the warm. Behrman,
S. N.
Cole, Gloria. See Bornstein, M. jt. auth.
Coleridge, Samuel
The rime of the ancient mariner (dramati-
zation) See Jagendorf, M. The rime of
the ancient mariner
Colette
Gigi (dramatization) See Loos, A. Gigi
Collaborationists. See Treason
The **Colleen** Bawn. Boucicault, D.
College and school drama
Gibson, M. N. Senior play
Howard, V. There's talent tonight
Reach, J. Are teachers human?
College and school journalism
Fisher, A. and Rabe, O. Anonymous let-
ter
Gran, J. M. A nose for news
Wattron, F. and Walker, P. Burner of the
Bugle
College journalism. See College and school
journalism
College life. See Students
College students. See Students
Colleges. See Universities and colleges
Collier, Edwin
Dark lady. Reynolds & Co. ₁1955₎ 82p
Comedy. Playwright, who intends to
make a play from pompous friend's pop-
ular novel, uses strategy to make author
accept dramatic version of the novel.
3 acts 4m 4w 1 interior

Collins, Bessie F.
Grand jury
Radio play. Reactions of several people
called for jury duty exposes lack of
sense of civic duty. Background music.
6m 3w 1b extras
In Prescott, H. ed. Patrioscript
Collins, Daniel
Summer brings gifts. French 1957 90p
illus
Romantic comedy. Young woman's conflict between desire for a career versus
marriage to the man she loves, set in
background of loving Colorado family
in the summer of 1913. 3 acts 5 scenes
5m 6w 1g 1 interior
Collins, Floyd
Shaw, D. Rescue
Collodi, Carl
Pinocchio (dramatization) See Miller, M.
Pinocchio
Colombo, Cristoforo
c Bakeless, K. L. Most memorable voyage
c Fisher, A. Day of destiny
c Fisher, A. The weaver's son
c Kramer, C. The voyage
c Martens, A. C. You are watching!
c Newman, D. A compass for Christopher
c Very, A. The return of Columbus
c Woolsey, J. and Sechrist, E. H. This
dream came true
Colonel Sellers as a scientist. Howells, W.
D. and Clemens, S. L.
Color
c Curtis, P. D. The colours clash
c Hark, M. and McQueen, N. Rainbow
colors
Color blind. Applegarth, M. T.
Color of animals
c Spamer, C. The camouflage shop
Colored people (American) See Negroes
Colour bar. Corrie, J.
The **colours** clash. Curtis, P. D.
Colson, J. G.
c The green ball. Paxton 1954 16p
Comedy. Prince Jolly's tutor proves to
doubting King Irate the value of his
new method of education. 1 scene 6m
4w 1 interior
c Robin Hood in Sherwood Forest
Robin Hood and his men discover two
spies in their midst sent by Sheriff of
Nottingham. 1 act 14m 1 exterior
In Burack, A. S. ed. Four-star plays
for boys
c Top of the bill
Two clowns are depressed about their
unsuccessful act, when two boys sneak
into the ring and put on their own act.
1 act 3m 2b 1 interior
In Burack, A. S. ed. Four-star plays
for boys
Columbia, the gem of the ocean. Emurian,
E. K.
Columbus, Christopher. See Colombo,
Cristoforo
Columbus and a Boy Scout. Clark, M. G.
Columbus Day
c Carlson, B. W. Near mutiny on the
"Santa Maria"
c Clark, M. G. Columbus and a Boy Scout
c Fisher, A. Day of destiny
c Fisher, A. The weaver's son
c Kramer, C. The voyage

Columbus Day—*Continued*

c Martens, A. C. You are watching!
c Newman, D. A compass for Christopher
c Very, A. The return of Columbus
c Woolsey, J. and Sechrist, E. H. This dream came true
    See also Colombo, Cristoforo

Comden, Betty. See Bernstein, L. Wonderful town; Styne, J. Bells are ringing

The come back. Bradbury, P.

Come back, Little Sheba. Inge, W.

Come back Peter. Dearsley, A. P.

Come, fill the cup. Harig, P.

Come live in my house. Barry, M. H.

Come live with me. Vooght, C.

"Come, see the place. . ." Bangham, M. D.

Come share my house. Apstein, T.

Come to Bethlehem. Asbrand, K.

"Come to my party." Asbrand, K.

Come to the manger. Bangham, M. D.

Come to the stable. DeVier, H. E.

Comedy
    This subject is used for non-tragic plays dealing with humorous situations or characters. Plays of broad or slapstick humor are entered under Farce

Addis, H. The fishermen's dream
Adler, M. D. Too much springtime
Anderson, M. High Tor
Anouilh, J. Thieves' carnival
Armer, A. and Grauman, W. E. Country cousin
Armer, A. and Grauman, W. E. Love scores a touchdown
Armer, A and Grauman, W. E. Time out for dreams
Asbrand, K. Easy as pie
Atwell, R. A pound of prevention
Axelrod, G. The seven year itch
Aymé, M. Clérambard
Badger, A. Willie's secret weapon
Baker, L. G. Conspiracy at "The Crayfish"
Bayliss, A. E. M. My hat!
Bayliss, A. E. M. What make?
Beich, A and Wright, W. H. The man in the dog suit
Beloin, E. and Garson, H. In any language
Bissell, R.; Burrows, A. and Bissell, M. Say, darling
Blackmore, P. Down came a blackbird
c Blyton, E. Finding the tickets
c Blyton, E. The mothers' meeting
Bollans, G. E. The crooked courtship
Bond, N. State of mind
Boyd, A. K. Robbery at Gadshill
Bradley, A. This England
Brenner, M. Middle of nowhere
Brown, A. M. Ah, men!
c Brumbaugh, P. Simple Simon
Capote, T. The grass harp
c Carlson, B. W. The bunyip lives again!
c Carlson, B. W. It's a—!
c Carlson, B. W. Jes' too lazy!
c Carlson, B. W. On the bat
Carmichael, F. Inside Lester

Carroll, P. V. The wayward saint
Carter, A. P. Operation Mad Ball
Carter, B. The sermon
Carter, C. About time, too
Carter, C. About time, too, and five other playlets (6 plays)
Carter, C. A chocolate
Carter, C. Don't argue!
Carter, C. Good-bye, Aunt Mildred!
Chadwicke, A. Davy Crockett
Chenery, M. Lesson for today
Clapp, P. Edie-across-the-street
Clare, N. Surprise packet
Clare, N. The windfall
Clark, M. G. My wife, Henry
Climenhaga, J. Heathen pioneer
Collier, E. Dark lady
c Colson, J. G. The green ball
Conkle, E. P. Son-of-a-biscuit-eater
Cooper, D. S. And so say all of us!
Coward, N. Ways and means
Crary, M. Beware tne bear!
Crone, R. New girl in town
D'Abbes, I. and Sherie, F. Murder in motley
Dalzell, W. and Martens, A. C. Onions in the stew
Davidson, W. The birds and the boys
Davidson, W. Buy Jupiter!
Daviot, G. Lady Charing is cross
Daviot, G. The pomp of Mr Pomfret
Daviot, G. The staff-room
Davis, J. P. A adventure
Delderfield, R. F. Golden rain
Delderfield, R. F. The guinea-pigs
Dennys, J. Art with a capital "A"
Devany, E. H. The cow-catcher on the caboose
Dinner, W. and Morum, W. All this and jumble too
Dinner, W. and Morum, W. Ladies' bar
Douglas, J. Just off Broadway
Draper, J. Barchester Towers
Elam, R. C. Duchess of Dogwood Lane
Elward, J. Paper foxhole
Emery, C. A private affair
Erhard, T. The high white star
Faust, E. Oh, to be sixteen again!
Federspiel, J. A. D. Behold the body
Fernway, P. "I never said a word, but—!"
Fields, J. and Chodorov, J. The Ponder heart
Fields, J. and De Vries, P. The tunnel of love
Frost, R. Small hotel
Gattey, C. N. and Bramley-Moore, Z. Mrs Adams and Eve
Gehman, H. M. For the love of Pete
Gibson, M. N. Will the ladies please come to order
Ginnes, A. S. and Wallach, I. Drink to me only
Glickman, W. and Stein, J. Mrs Gibbons' boys
Gordon, K. The babbling Brooks
Gordon, K. Money mad
Gowan, E. P. Breeches from Bond Street
Grable, M. What price murder?
Green, P. Quare medicine
Greth, Le R. E. Host to a ghost

Comedy—*Continued*

Greth, Le R. E. The kid from Mars
Greth, Le R. E. Miss Robin Crusoe
Greth, Le R. E. The sky's the limit
Gross, E. and Gross, N. Marko goes a courtin'
Gross, E. and Gross, N. A party is born
Hark, M. and McQueen, N. On your own feet
Hark, M. and McQueen, N. Star baby-sitter
c Harris, A. Circus in the wind
Harris, B. K. Ca'line
Henderson, J. A midsummer night's scream
Howard, V. The mayor
Howard, V. The valentine box
Howard, V. The women from Kentucky
Howells, J. H. Good-bye, Gray Flannel
Howells, W. D. The smoking car
c Ilian, C. The nut tree
Ionesco, E. The bald soprano
Ionesco, E. Jack
Ionesco, E. The lesson
Jeans, R. Double take
Jerome, P. Goin' round the hoop
Johnson, P. Success story
Johnson, P. The witching hour
Jonson, B. Three plays
Jonson, B. Volpone
Kesler, H. O. Line of scrimmage
Kesler, H. O. Million-dollar maybe
Kimmins, A. The amorous prawn
Kirkpatrick, J. A summer for the Indians
Koch, F. Wash Carver's mouse trap
Kurnitz, H. Once more, with feeling
Labiche, E. and Delacour. Célimare
Labiche, E. and Marc-Michel. An Italian straw hat
Last, J. Coffee for one
Last, J. Make it murder
Lathrop, D. The braggart
Lathrop, D. Forever Eve
c Lawrence, G. B. The king's shirt
Lawrence, J. and Lee, R. E. Auntie Mame
Lawrence, J. and Lee, R. E. Only in America
LePelley, G. Absolutely murder
Leydon, B. Johnny Jones, space cadet!
Lindsay, H. and Crouse, R. The Great Sebastians
Lindsay, H. and Crouse, R. The Prescott proposals
Lisle V. The merry matchmaker
Lockwood, L. Autumn in the air
Lynch, P. To open, pry cover
McCleery, W. The lady chooses
McCoy, P. S. Susan steps out
McCreary, B. and McCreary, M. Three needles in a haystack
MacLeod, R. Kate
Maddern, V. and Banks, L. R. Miss Pringle plays Portia
Malango, P. The boy who changed the world
Manion, D. Girl wanted
Manning, S. A. As silent as the ocean
Mansur, F. L. Train for Sherwood

Marchant, W. The desk set
Marr Johnson, D. Never say die
Martens, A. C. Pajama party
Martens, A. C. The search for Wildcat McGillicuddy
Martens, A. C. Shoot if you will
Martens, A. C. Sing a song of something
Martens, A. C. Step lively, please
Martens, A. C. What's the matter with TV?
Martens, A. C. Who's that knocking on my door?
Martens, A. C. Witch Hazel
Mathers, A. Flapper girls
Mauermann, G. A cup of kindness
Mauermann, W. G. Just us girls
Menander. The arbitration
Menander. The bad-tempered man
Menander. The grouch
Menander. She who was shorn
Miller, H. L. Beany's private eye
Miller, H. L. A hooky holiday
Miller, H. L. "N" for nuisance
Mills, O. Goose in the kitchen
Mills, O. In the soot
Mitchell, B. E. and Rose, Le R. Mountain gal
Mitzman, N. and Dalzell, W. Books and crooks
Mitzman, N. and Dalzell, W. In 25 words —or death
Molière, J. B. P. The critique of The school for wives
Molière, J. B. P. The Versailles impromptu
Morris, T. B. The nine days
Mortimer, J. The dock brief
Mortimer, J. I spy
Mortimer, J. What shall we tell Caroline?
Musset, A. de. Fantasio
Nicholson, H. Port and a pistol
Niss, S. The penny
Olfson, L. The adventures of Tom Sawyer
Olfson, L. The Pickwick papers
Olfson, L. The tempest
O'Neill, E. "The movie man"
Osborne, S. If you ask me—
Parish, J. Mystery, mayhem, and murder!
Parker, J. W. Sleep on, Lemuel
Patrick, J. The Teahouse of the August Moon
Patton, F. G. The beaded buckle
Payton, D. Father says no!
Payton, D. The hanging of Uncle Dilby
Payton, D. He tried with his boots on
Peach, L. du G. A horse! A horse!
Peach, L. du G. and Hay, I. The white sheep of the family
Peavey, H. Teen antics
Percy, E. and Denham, L. The man with expensive tastes
Perl, A. Tevya and the first daughter
Perrini, A. Once a thief
Perry, M. The fifth wheel
Pertwee, R. Dirty work
Phillips, M. K. Hold that Indian
Pierce, C. W. Mum's the word
Plautus. The haunted house
Plautus. The rope

Comedy—*Continued*

Price, O. Out of the mist
Protter, N. Follow the gleam
Pryor, C. Just my speed
Quinn, C. For want of a character
Rattigan, T. French without tears
Reach, J. Are teachers human?
Reach, J. Beautiful dreamers
Reach, J. It walks at midnight
Reach, J. Stranger in town
Reach, J. Terror at Black Oaks
Ready, S. Ladies at sea
Rees, P. Mix-up-atosis
Regan, S. The fifth season
Ridley, A. and Borer, M. C. Tabitha
Roberts, C. Mr Gaylord remembers
Rogers, A. B. Tiger on his toes
Rose, Le R. Spooks alive
Rose, S. The Edgar Bergen show
St Clair, R. Caught in a web
St Clair, R. Mark Twain's A double barrelled detective story
St Clair, R. Susie and the F.B.I.
Sakanishi, S. tr. The aunt's sake
Sakanishi, S. tr. Busu
Sakanishi, S. tr. The Deva King
Sakanishi, S. tr. The family quarrel
Sakanishi, S. tr. Gargoyle
Sakanishi, S. tr. The letter "I"
Sakanishi, S. tr. Literate highwaymen
Sakanishi, S. tr. The magic mallet of the Devil
Sakanishi, S. tr. The melon thief
Sakanishi, S. tr. Plop! Click!
Sakanishi, S. tr. Seed of hōjō
Sakanishi, S. tr. The wounded highwayman
Saroyan, W. Once around the block
Savory, G. A month of Sundays
c Seiler, C. The clown out west
Seiler, C. The stronger sex
Seiler, C. What's wrong with the girls
Seiler, G. The Princess and the swineherd
Sergel, K. My little Margie
Shaw, B. The Inca of Perusalem
Shaw, B. O'Flaherty V. C.
Shaw, B. The six of Calais
Shaw, B. Why she would not
Sheridan, R. B. The critic
Shore, M. Catastrophe Clarence
Smith, B. and Webb, C. Lawyer Lincoln
Snyder, W. The old school bell
Spargrove, D. One for the book
Spence, W. How Betsy butted in
Spewack, S. and Spewack, B. L. My three angels
Sprague, M. Murder comes in threes
Stephens, C. G. The matter with Mildred
Stern, L. and Zelinka, S. The $99,000 answer
Storey, R. Touch it light
Strong, L. A. G. It's not very nice
Sutherland, D. Art for art's sake
Sutherland, D. The clean up
Sutherland, D. Father's economy drive
Sutherland, D. The man who understood women
Sutherland, D. Scherzo in two flats

Sutherland, D. Six more miniatures (6 plays)
Sutherland, D. Trying to take things quietly
Synge, J. M. The playboy of the western world
Synge, J. M. The tinker's wedding
Taggart, T. Boy meets girl in Washington
Taggart, T. Follow simple directions
Taggart, T. The gross story conference
Taggart, T. Morning of a private eye
Taggart, T. Oily to rise
Taggart, T. Punky Doodle
Taggart, T. Two in the balcony
Taggart, T. When mothers meet
Taggart, T. and Reach, J. Dear Phoebe
Taylor, G. Kill or cure
Tedlock, D. Oil wells and wedding bells
Terence. The brothers
Terence. Phormio
Tobias, J. The crazy mixed-up Kidds
Tobias, J. The Katz' whiskers
Turgenev, I. A poor gentleman
Turgenev, I. A provincial lady
Tyson, A. Millie, the beautiful working girl
Verity, E. and Last, J. Cove Cottage
Villiers, G. and others. The rehearsal
Wallace, N. Speed, bonnie boat
c Wallerstein, J. S. The cactus wildcat
Watkyn, A. Not in the book
Waugh, J. R. The burglar alarm
Waugh, J. R. The ebony box
Waugh, J. R. The missing formula
c Webber, C. E. The barber and the donkey
Webber, J. Dial 999
The Welsh embassador
Werfel, F. Jacobowsky and the colonel
Westgate, T. Petticoat handicap
Wilde, P. Salt for savor
Williams, N. A battle of wits
Williams, P. Commencement
Williams, T. The Lady of Larkspur Lotion
Wilson, E. Beppo and Beth
Yeats, W. B. The pot of broth

　　　See also Farces; Greek drama (Comedy); Latin drama (Comedy); Satire; Tragicomedy

Domestic

Addis, H. Open house
Addyman, E. Over the garden fence
Alexander, A. Right under your nose
Alexander, R. Time out for Ginger
Anderson, R. A. and Sweeney, R. L. Boris and the briefcase
Anderson, R. A. and Sweeney, R. L. Boris and the spaceman
Anouilh, J. Cecile
Apstein, T. Fortunata writes a letter
Banks, L. R. It never rains
Barry, S. Cupid's bow
Bates, S. Granny takes the helm
Bauer, P. The last straw
c Bayliss, R. G. The burglar alarm
Benchley, N. The frogs of Spring
Benedetti, A. de. Two dozen red roses
Benfield, D. The way the wind blows
Berns, J. and Elman, I. Uncle Willie

Congreve, William—*Continued*

Love for love
Restoration comedy of manners. Son competes with father for hand of Angelica who loves son and finally saves son's inheritance. Songs 5 acts 13 scenes 10m 6w extras 6 interiors

In Congreve, W. Complete plays

In Kronenberger, L. ed. Cavalcade of comedy

The mourning bride
Tragedy. Restoration drama. 5 acts 13 scenes 8m 3w extras 4 interiors

In Congreve, W. Complete plays

The old bachelor
Comedy of manners. Late Restoration drama. Songs and dancing. 5 acts 20 scenes 11m 6w extras 5 interiors 6 exteriors

In Congreve, W. Complete plays

The way of the world; ed. by Vincent F. Hopper and Gerald B. Lahey. Barrons Educ. Ser. 1958 195p illus (Theatre classics for the modern reader)
Restoration comedy of manners. Satire on 17th century London society. Aunt forgives niece's lover after he helps extricate her from intrigue. Songs and a dance. 5 acts 12 scenes 6m 8w extras 6 interiors 1 exterior

—Same

In Congreve, W. Complete plays

In Dean, L. F. ed. Nine great plays. 1956 edition

In Kronenberger, L. ed. Cavalcade of comedy

In Restoration plays

Conjuring
Lillington, K. The Devil's grandson

Conkle, E. P.

Arbie, the bug boy
Romantic farce. Zealous exterminator visits his girl's family. 3m 2w 1 interior

In The Best short plays, 1952-1953

A bauble for the baby. French 1955 22p illus
Christmas. Father fashions present for his two-months old baby. Carol singing. 1 act 1m 3w extras 1 interior

Granny's little cheery room. French 1960 21p illus
Comedy. Farm woman gets ready to go to heaven and then decides to stay on earth for awhile. 1 act 1m 3w 1 interior

Heaven is a long time to wait
Four orphans, about to be separated by adoption into different families, review their happy life when their parents were alive. 1w 1b 2g 1 interior

In The Best short plays, 1958-1959

Lavender gloves
Comedy. Unconventional detective mystery set in provincial English inn. 1 act 4m 3w 1 interior

In Richards, S. ed. Canada on stage

No more wars but the moon. French 1955 23p illus
Comedy. New widow in town puts vitality into Ladies' Aid Society by starting crusade for world peace. 1 act 6w 1 interior

Poor Old Bongo! French 1954 22p illus
Farce. New coach dispels memories of former coach. 1 act 8m 7w 1 interior

The reticent one. Bakers Plays 1955 21p (Baker's Royalty plays)
Supernatural. Women waiting to be called to their reward are surprised when the one they gossiped about is called first. 1 act 6w extras 1 interior

Son-of-a-biscuit-eater. French 1958 20p illus
A teenager teaches his father and grandfather something about "women folks." 1 act 3m 1w 1 exterior

Conkle, Ellsworth Prouty. See Conkle, E. P.

Conkling, Louise

Let 'em eat steak. French 1958 78p illus
Satirical comedy about current trend of substituting research for teaching in many universities. 2 acts 6m 5w 1 interior

A **Connecticut** Yankee in King Arthur's court Olfson, L.

The **connection.** Gelber, J.

Connelly, Marc

The green pastures
Fantasy. Negro religious folk-drama. 2 parts 18 scenes Large mixed cast 6 interiors 9 exteriors

In A Treasury of the theatre

In Watson, E. B. and Pressey, W. B. eds. Contemporary drama: eleven plays

The traveler
Satire. Subway rider breaks travel pattern by taking railroad train. 1 act 3m 1 interior

In Cerf, B. and Cartmell, V. H. eds. 24 favorite one-act plays

The **conquered,** the unconquerable, and I. Thompson, M. A.

The **conqueror.** Wincelberg, S.

Conrad, Joseph

One day more
Insane old sea captain insisting that his son, who ran away to sea as a boy, will return, has picked out a wife for him. 1 act 4m 1w 1 exterior

In Bentley, E. ed. The modern theatre v3

Conscience
Ferguson, J. The camp
Miller, S. One bright day
See also Guilt

Conspiracies
Otway, T. Venice preserved

Conspiracy at "The Crayfish." Baker, L. G.

The **constable's** duty. Spamer, C.

The **constant** couple. Farquhar, G.

The **constant** wife. Maugham, W. S.

Constantine the Great. Lee, N.

Constantinus I, the Great, Emperor of Rome
Lee, N. Constantine the Great

Construction. See Building

Construction industry. See Building as a profession

Contentiousness. See Quarreling

Contests, Prize in advertising. See Prize contests in advertising

Contraband trade. See Smuggling

Contract bridge
Martens, A. C. Cross your bridge

The **contrast**. Tyler, R.

Conventions. See Congresses and conventions

Convents and nunneries
Boland, B. The return
Herman, G. Brighten every corner
Hope, A. J.; Mary Francis, Sister, and Birder, D. The complaining angel
O'Connell, M. O. Sister. One red nose
Trease, G. The unquiet cloister
White, N. E. Seven nuns at Las Vegas

Conversion
Climenhaga, J. Heathen pioneer
Wilde, O. La sainte courtisane

Conversion of St Paul. See Johnston, R. A. The Digby Conversion of St Paul

Convicts. See Crime and criminals; Prisoners

Cookery
Asbrand, K. Easy as pie
Delderfield, R. F. The guinea-pigs
Howard, V. Million dollar recipe
Mills, O. Goose in the kitchen
Sheridan, E. One bit of glory

Cooking. See Cookery

Cooks. See Servants

A **cool** yule. Martens, A. C.

Coolidge, Jane Toy
Mrs Parker's portrait. Bakers Plays 1960 21p (Baker's Royalty plays)
Woman born January 1, 1900, recalls the highpoints of her life as wife, mother and civic worker. 1 act 3w 1 interior

Cooney, Patrick
The perfect aurora. Longmans 1955 31p illus (Plays for to-day)
Romantic comedy. Writer's fiancée becomes jealous of his fictional heroine, and takes steps to break up "romance." 1 act 1m 3w 1 interior

Cooper, Dorothy S.
And so say all of us! Acting ed. French (London) 1953 29p illus
Comedy. Plot to condemn cottages thwarted by one tenant. Piano music off stage. 1 act 6w 1 interior

Cooper, Frank A.
A certain star. Row 1953 27p illus
Christmas legend. Story of the Nativity and the Christmas star that broke the chain of evil which bound five persons. 1 act 2m 3w 1 exterior
If thine enemy. Eldridge Pub. 1958 40p (Eldridge Christmas entertainments)
Angel disguised as young farmer helps little girl straighten out neighborhood problem. 1 act 3m 2w 1g 1 interior 1 exterior
Worlds apart. Eldridge Pub. 1954 22p (Eldridge Popular one-act playscripts)
Fantasy. Space men prevent earth's destruction. 1 act 5m 1b 1 interior

Coppel, Alec
The gazebo. Dramatists 1959 63p illus
Melodrama. Writer with an eye to inventing almost-perfect crime is forced to commit real murder. 2 acts 9m 3w 1 interior

Coral. Armer, A. and Grauman, W. E.

The **coral**. Kaiser, G.

Corey, Orlin R.
The big middle. Broadman 1960 28p
The church, its pastor and businessman face momentous decision when another church wishes to buy land next door. 1 act 3m 4w 2 interiors
The Book of Job. Childrens Theatre 1960 73p illus
Bible. Old Testament. Job. Biblical text adapted for the stage. Musical background. 1 act 5m 5w 1 interior

Corinth House. Johnson, P. H.

Corle, Edwin
Three ways to Mecca (dramatization) See Beich, A. and Wright, W. H. The man in the dog suit

Corneille, Pierre
Attila
Historical French classical drama. Tyranny of barbarian king Attila toward conquered. 5 acts 4m 3w extras 1 exterior
In Corneille, P. Moot plays of Corneille
Le Cid; tr. and ed. by John C. Lapp. Appleton 1955 71p
French classical tragicomedy in verse. Chimene is torn between love and filial duty prior to marriage to Cid Campeador in 11th century Spain. 5 acts 29 scenes 8m 4w 1 setting
—Same; tr. by Rosalie Feltenstein. Barrons Educ. Ser. 1953 66p
Don Sanche d'Aragon (Don Sancho of Aragon)
Romantic tragicomedy in verse. Young soldier of unknown origin turns out to be Don Sancho, rightful king of Aragon. 5 acts 5m 4w extras 1 interior
In Corneille, P. Moot plays of Corneille
Héraclius
Historical French classical drama in verse. Question of identity between two men, one of whom is son of rightful emperor. Set in 7th century Eastern Roman Empire. 5 acts 7m 3w extras 1 interior
In Corneille, P. Moot plays of Corneille
La mort de Pompé (The death of Pompey)
Historical French classical drama. Ancient Egypt wars with the Roman Empire. Cornelia remains bitter towards magnanimous Caesar over the death of husband. Pompey. 5 acts 9m 3w extras 1 interior
In Corneille, P. Moot plays of Corneille
Othon (Otho)
Historical French classical tragedy in verse. Court intrigue around an aging monarch, set in 1st century B.C. Roman Empire. 5 acts 9m 3w extras 1 interior
In Corneille, P. Moot plays of Corneille
Pulchérie (Pulcheria)
Historical French classical drama in verse. Young woman renounces man she loves for good of her country. Set in 5th century Eastern Roman Empire. 5 acts 3m 3w 1 interior
In Corneille, P. Moot plays of Corneille
Sertorius
Historical French classical tragedy in verse. Ambition, rivalry and love among the Roman generals and noblewomen. Set in Spain, first century B.C. 5 acts 6m 3w extras 1 interior
In Corneille, P. Moot plays of Corneille
Suréna
Historical French classical drama in verse. Two lovers for whom marriage is impossible, try to conceal their love. Set in Parthia, 1st century B.C. 5 acts 4m 3w 1 interior
In Corneille, P. Moot plays of Corneille

Cornelia. Daviot, G.

Cornish drama
David and Bathsheba
David takes the shoots to Jerusalem
The three Maries

Corny confessions. Abstance, P. and Abstance, L.

Corporations
Teichmann, H. and Kaufman, G. S. The solid gold Cadillac

Corpulence
Atwell, R. A pound of prevention

Corrie, Joe
Colour bar. ₁French's Acting ed₁ French 1954 23p illus
Father preaches racial equality until daughter falls in love with Negro. 1 act 2 scenes 2m 4w 1 interior 1 exterior
Love and the boxer. ₁French's Acting ed₁ French (London) 1954 27p illus
Farce. A prize-fighter zig-zags in his courtship of two sisters. 1 act 4m 4w 1 interior
The theft. ₁Acting ed₁ French (London) 1954 28p illus
Snobbish family's reputation saved by sacrifice of one they snubbed. 1 act 3m 4w 1 interior

Corrigan, Lloyd
Whosoever believeth. French 1956 21p illus
Faith versus common sense as told in story of what might have happened after the Last Supper. 1 act 3m 1 interior

Corruption (in politics)
Brecht, B. The threepenny opera
Edmunds, M. Moon of my delight
Getzinger, E. W. Let your light so shine
Lawrence, J. and Lee, R. E. The gang's all here
Sayre, G. W. Final edition
Sheldon, E. The boss
Thomas, A. The witching hour
Warren, R. P. All the king's men

Corwin, Norman
The rivalry. Acting ed. Dramatists 1960 79p illus
Dramatization of debates between Lincoln and Stephen Douglas. 2 acts 2m 1w extras 1 interior
The rivalry (condensation)
In Broadway's best, 1959

Cost and standard of living
Weiss, M. J. The actor

Costa du Rels, Adolfo
The king's standards; tr. by Helen A. Gaubert. French 1958 72p illus
Set in France, 1953. Struggle faced by two worker-priests as to whether to continue re-Christianizing the Marxist-geared proletariat, or obey wishes of their church. 3 acts 4m 2w 1 interior

Costigan, James
Little moon of Alban
Television play. When girl's fiancee is killed she become volunteer nurse in religious order, only to be assigned to care for his wounded killer. Set in Ireland during political troubles of the 1920's. 3 acts 10m 8w
In Costigan, J. Little moon of Alban & A wind from the south

A wind from the south
Television play. A girl whose brother runs hotel in Ireland has brief romance with an unhappily married American summer tourist. 3 acts 5m 4w extras
In Costigan, J. Little moon of Alban & A wind from the south

A **costly** gold hunt. Emmons, D. G.

The **costume** dance. Spamer, G.

Cottages
Copper, D. S. And so say all of us!

Cotton ginning. See Cotton gins and ginning

Cotton gins and ginning
c McMillin, M. The young whittler
Williams, T. 27 wagons full of cotton

Cotton Road. Abstance, P. and Abstance, L.

The **Count** of Monte Cristo. Olfson, L.

Count your blessings. Asbrand, K.

Count your blessings. Jeans, R.

Counted as mine. Mary Francis, Sister

A **counterfeit** presentment. Howells, W. D.

The **countess** Cathleen. Yeats, W. B.

Countess Mizzie. Schnitzler, A.

Country cousin. Armer, A. and Grauman, W. E.

Country life
See also Farm life

Carolina
Harris, B. K. Ca'line

Great Britain
Scriven, R. C. The inward eye: boy 1913

Russia
Chekhov, A. P. Uncle Vanya

United States
Bucci, M. A pink party dress

A **country** scandal. Chekov, A.

The **country** store cat. Miller, H. L.

Country stores. See General stores

The **country** wife. Wycherley, W.

Courage
Damico, J. A storm is breaking
Foote, H. The trip to Bountiful
Foss, J. Courage, '53
Goldina, M. The courageous one
c Hark, M. and McQueen, N. The stuff of heroes
Howe, C. V. The long fall
Joy, R. P. Hour of honor
Keeney, C. H. Major Milliron reports
Kleist, H. von. The Prince of Homburg
Lake, G. Incident at a grave
Ridge, A. Emhammed of the red slippers
Rose, R. Thunder on Sycamore Street
Trick, O. B. The frontier

Courage, '53. Foss, J.

The **courageous** one. Goldina, M.

Court fools. See Fools and jesters

Court martial. See Courts-martial and courts of inquiry

The **court** of hearts. Diffin, L. T.

Courteline, Georges
The commissioner; tr. by Albert Bermel
Comedy about petty magistrates who have no real concept of administering legal justice to fellowmen. 8m 1w 1 interior
In Four modern French comedies

These Cornfields (Les boulingrens) English version by Eric Bentley
Farce. A man comes to tea at home of couple he has just met. 2m 2w 1 interior
In Bentley, E. ed. Let's get a divorce! and other plays

Courtesy
Burgess, C. V. A bore for breakfast
Hackett, W. A dress affair
c Hark, M. and McQueen, N. Doctor Manners
Howard, V. Your manners and mine
c Miller, H. L. A visit to Goldilocks
Steele, J. Tea for six

Courting. See Courtship

The courting of Marie Jenvrin. Ringwood, G. P.

Courting trouble. Fisher, A.

Courts and courtiers
c Bradbury, A. J. The King's anniversary
c Colson, J. G. The green ball
Olfson, L. Infanta
See also Names of countries with subdivision Courts and courtiers, e.g. Russia—Courts and courtiers

Courts-martial and courts of inquiry
Anderson, M. The miracle of the Danube
Christie, D. and Christie, C. Carrington, V. C.
Wouk, H. The Caine mutiny court-martial

Courtship
Anouilh, J. Cecile
Besier, R. The Barretts of Wimpole Street
Betti, U. Summertime
Chekhov, A. The boor
Chekhov, A. A marriage proposal
Collins, D. Summer brings gifts
Dayton, M. Whirlwind courtship
Dekker, T. The wonder of a kingdom
Delmar, V. Warm Wednesday
Fleece, J. The first oyster
Foote, H. The midnight caller
Hanig, D. Give us time to sing
Howells, W. D. Her opinion of his story
Howells, W. D. An Indian giver
Howells, W. D. Parting friends
Howells, W. D. Priscilla
Labiche, E. and Martin, E. A trip abroad
McCleery, W. The guest cottage
Molière, J. B. P. The school for wives
Musset, A. de. It's impossible to think of everything
Olfson, L. Much ado about nothing
Orr, M. and Denham, R. Be your age
Popplewell, J. Dear delinquent
Postance, N. Surprise!
Reach, J. Ah, yesterday!
Reeves, T. Wedding breakfast
Richardson, H. and Berney, W. Dark of the moon

Ringwood, G. P. The courting of Marie Jenvrin
Seidel, N. Keeping company
Sergel, R. A New England nun
Sheridan, R. B. St Patrick's Day
Spargrove, D. One for the book
Sterling, A. Kissin' cousins
Stevens, E. The little nuisance
Stout, W. In Dixon's kitchen
Strong, L. A. G. It's not very nice
c Very, A. The three sillies
Williams, M. Invitation to breakfast
See also Dating (Social customs); Love; Marriage

Cove Cottage. Verity, E. and Last, J.

Covenanters
Daviot, G. Barnharrow

Covenants (Church history). See Covenanters

Coventry mysteries. See Coventry plays

Coventry Nativity play. Coventry plays. See Coventry plays. The pageant of the Shearmen and Taylors—The Coventry Nativity play

Coventry plays
The Annunciation; The Coventry Pageant of the Shearmen and Tailors
Bible. New Testament. Luke. First part of 15th century English mystery play of the Nativity. Comprises prologue by Isaiah, Annunciation to Mary, Doubt of Joseph, and Journey to Bethlehem. Verse play in Middle English with modernized spelling. 2 scenes 4m 1w 1 interior 2 exteriors
In Everyman, and medieval miracle plays

Cain and Abel; The N. Town cycle
14th century English mystery play ascribed to Coventry plays, part of cycle, performed at "N. Town" an unidentified place. Based on Old Testament Book of Genesis wherein Cain murders his brother Abel. Verse play in Middle English with modernized spelling. 3 scenes 4m 1 interior 2 exteriors
In Everyman, and medieval miracle plays

Herod and the kings; Coventry Shearmen and Tailors' play
Bible. New Testament. Matthew. 15th century English mystery play. Role of Herod in visit of the Magi to infant Jesus, and Massacre of the Holy Innocents. Verse play in Middle English with modernized spelling. 10m 4w extras 1 setting
In Browne, E. M. ed. Religious drama, 2

The Magi, Herod and the slaughter of the Innocents (adaptation) See Malcolmson, A. Herod and the Magi

The pageant of the Shearmen and Taylors —The Coventry Nativity play [ed. by John Piers Allen]
15th century English mystery play of the Nativity. This version done in Middle English with modernized spelling. Includes songs. Verse play. 4 parts 19 scenes 16m 6w 1 setting
In Allen, J. P. ed. Three medieval plays v 1

The parliament of heaven: The Annunciation and Conception; Hegge cycle
Part of 15th century English mystery play of the Nativity. Mercy, Truth, Justice and Peace beseech God to save man from eternal punishment. God's

Coventry plays—*Continued*
answer is the Annunciation and the Immaculate Conception as related in Luke's Gospel. Verse play in Middle English with modernized spelling. 5m 5w 1 setting
In Browne, E. M. ed. Religious drama, 2

The woman taken in adultery; Hegge cycle
Bible. New Testament. John. 15th century mystery play. The battle of wits between Christ and the Pharisees. Verse play in Middle English with modernized spelling. 5m 1w 1 setting
—Same; The N. Town cycle
In Browne, E. M. ed. Religious drama, 2

Covetousness. See Avarice

Covington, W. P.
Shirt-tail boy
Abe Lincoln's stepmother persuades his father to let Abe have books and go to school. 1 act 3m 2w 1b 1 interior
In Smith, B. and others, eds. A treasury of non-royalty one-act plays

The **cow-catcher** on the caboose. Devany, E. H.

Coward, Noël
Blithe spirit
Farce. Medium evokes spirit of Charles' former wife causing frustrating, embarrassing experiences in Charles' current marriage. 3 acts 7 scenes 2m 5w 1 interior
In Kronenberger, L. ed. Cavalcade of comedy
In A Treasury of the theatre
In Warnock, R. Representative modern plays, British

Cavalcade
Changes in British social life from 1899-1930 as seen in fortunes of two English families of different classes. Songs, music and dancing. 3 parts 21 scenes Large mixed cast 10 interiors 5 exteriors
In Voaden, H. ed. Two good plays to read and act

Fallen angels. French 1958 65p illus
Romantic comedy. Two happily married women are visited by man they were both once in love with. 3 acts 3m 3w 1 interior

Fumed oak
Domestic comedy. Browbeaten man living with his daughter, wife and her mother suddenly announces he is leaving forever. 1 act 1m 3w 1 interior
In Cooper, C. W. Preface to drama

Hands across the sea
Sophisticated drawingroom Londoners entertain former hosts from rubber plantation whom they hardly remember. 1 act 5m 4w 1 interior
In Cerf, B. and Cartmell, V. H. eds. 24 favorite one-act plays

Nude with violin. ₍Rev. acting ed₎ French 1958 92p illus
Comedy. Complications arise for everyone concerned when will of rich painter is read. 3 acts 5 scenes 8m 6w 1 interior
Trade edition published by Doubleday

Quadrille. Doubleday 1955 ₍1952₎ 191p
Social comedy. Marital and extramarital problems of two couples, one American and other English. Incidental music. 3 acts 7 scenes 8m 7w extras 3 interiors

Ways and means
Comedy. Improvident young British couple secure much needed funds through fortuitous aid of burglar. 3 scenes 5m 4w 1 interior
In Watson, E. B. and Pressey, B. eds. Contemporary drama: eleven plays

Cowboy dialect. See Dialect—Cowboy

Cowboys
Finch, R. and Smith, B. Western night
c Miller, H. L. The half-pint cowboy
c Miller, H. L. Jiminy Cinders
See also Ranch life

Cowen, William Joyce
Little friend. French 1953 63p illus
Christmas. Little girl in small French town learns that love of God and love of one's neighbors can work miracles but one must not bargain. Carol singing. 3 acts 9 scenes 5m 4w 1b 1g extras 2 interiors

Cox, Patricia
Myself when young. Deane 1954 25p ("Deane's" Ser. of plays)
Images conjured up from memory prove to middle-aged married woman that she has become very stodgy and is no longer attractive. 1 act 7w 1 interior

Cox, William Norment
The Scuffletown outlaws
Bitterness between Croatan Indian chief and white man in North Carolina in 1870 set off Indian's revenge. 2 scenes 5m 2w 1 interior
In Walser, R. ed. North Carolina drama

Coxcombs in petticoats. Molière, J. B. P.

Coxe, Louis O. and Chapman, Robert
Billy Budd
Based on novel by Herman Melville. Symbolic struggle between good and evil on British warship in 1798. 3 acts 9 scenes 23m 1b extras 2 interiors 1 exterior
In Halverson, M. ed. Religious drama, 3
In Stallman, R. W. and Watters, R. E. The creative reader

Coyle, Rollin W.
Unto thy doors
Christmas story with Nativity tableaux. Joseph asks at shops and even at temple for room and is refused. 1 act 5m 3w extras 1 exterior
In Powers, V. E. ed. Plays for players, and a guide to play production

Cracker money. Gethers, S.

The **cradle.** Hawse, A.

Crane, Burton
Stage-stricken. Bakers Plays 1953 34p (Baker's Royalty plays)
Farce. Everything goes wrong backstage in little theatre production. 1 act 6m 3w 1 interior

Visiting celebrity. Bakers Plays 1953 26p (Baker's Royalty plays)
Farce. Announcer from local radio station helps ladies in rebellion against president of women's club. 1 act 7w extras 1 interior

Cranes
Kinoshita, J. Twilight crane

Crank, Harriett P.
c The promise lily
In early 19th century, Johnny Appleseed helps pioneer children plant apple trees which one day prove very valuable to them. 2 scenes 2m 1w 3b 4g extras 2 exteriors
In Birdsall, R. ed. Creative plays for every school month

Cranks. See Eccentrics and eccentricities

Crary, Margaret
Beware the bear! Row 1953 48p music
Comedy. Campers capture "intruder" mistaking him for escaped convict. 1 act 8w 1 interior

Crawford, Arch
c A visit with the firemen
Each fireman explains his special job to children. 6m 3b 3g 1 interior
In Birdsall, R. ed. Creative plays for every school month

Crawford, Eskel. See Tomkins, B. No, no, a million times no; Pistol-packin' Sal

The **crazy** mixed-up Kidds. Tobias, J.

Crean, Robert J.
The trial. Bakers Plays 1960 42p (Baker's Royalty plays)
Trial of cloistered nun accused of turning her back on family and problems of world to pursue life of prayer. 1 act 3m 6w 1 interior

Creation
York plays. The creation, and The fall of Lucifer
York plays. The creation of the heavenly beings: The fall of Lucifer

The **creation**, and The fall of Lucifer. York plays

The **creation** of Adam and Eve. York plays

The **creation** of man. York plays

The **creation** of the heavenly beings: The fall of Lucifer. York plays

Creditors. Strindberg, A.

Credulity
Richards, S. Gin and bitterness

Creighton, Anthony. See Osborne, J. jt. auth.

The **Cretan** woman. Jeffers, R.

Crewcuts and longhairs. Taggart, T.

Crichton, Kyle
The happiest millionaire. Dramatists 1957 89p illus
Suggested by the book, "My Philadelphia father" by Cordelia Drexel Biddle and Kyle Critchton. Domestic comedy. Colonel Anthony J. Drexel Biddle's propensity for putting whole heart into any undertaking had definite effect on his family. 2 acts 5 scenes 9m 6w 1 interior

The **crier** calls. Swann, D. L.

Crime and crime. Strindberg, A.

Crime and criminals
Armer, A. and Grauman, W. E. Closing time
Campion, C. Wayward women
Carmichael, F. Inside Lester
Daviot, G. Reckoning
Delderfield, R. F. The offending hand
Golden, E. Great expectations
Hayes, J. The desperate hours
c Howard, V. The treasure of Monte Cristo
Hughes, K. Sammy
Latham, J. L. The nightmare
Levin, M. Compulsion
Martens, A. C. A bird in the bush
Martens, A. C. The grandma bandit
Morrison, D. Mirage
Nash, N. R. Handful of fire
Parker, K. T. Double identity
Peach, L. du G. and Hay, I. The white sheep of the family
Pinter, H. The dumb waiter
Popplewell, J. Dear delinquent
Saroyan, W. Hello out there
Spewack, S. and Spewack, B. L. My three angels
Stoler, S. A. End of the rainbow
Taylor, D. Five in judgment
Taylor, T. The ticket-of-leave man
Tumarin, B. and Sydow, J. Dostoyevsky's The brothers Karamazov
See also Brigands and robbers; Detectives; Fraud; Gambling; Gangs; Impostures and imposture; Juvenile delinquency; Larceny; Murder; Pirates; Prisons; Smuggling; Thieves; Treason

Identification
Chadwicke, A. Pudd'nhead Wilson

Crime and insanity. See Insane, Criminal and dangerous

Crime in the streets. Rose, R.

The **crime** in the Whistler room. Wilson, E.

Criminal intent
Emery, C. Tiger Lily

Cripples
Batson, G. House on the cliff

Crisis in Wimpole Street. Holland, N.

Crispin the tailor. Douglas, L.

The **critic.** Sheridan, R. B.

The **critique** of The school for wives. Molière, J. B. P.

Croatan Indians
Cox, W. N. The Scuffletown outlaws

Crockett, David
Chadwicke, A. Davy Crockett
McCaslin, N. With the sunrise in his pocket

Crockett, Davy. See Crockett, David

Crocodiles
c Barnes, E. A. and Young, B. M. Sokar and the crocodile

Crone, Raymond
New girl in town. French 1954 101p illus
Comedy. New girl in town complicates local love affair. 3 acts 4 scenes 3m 8w 1 interior

The **crooked** courtship. Bollans, G. E.

Crooked dime. Asbrand, K. S.

Crosby, Millard
Readin', 'ritin', and 'rithmetic. French 1954 36p illus
Farce. Teacher's experiences with class of teenagers. 1 act 5m 6w 1 interior

Cross, Eric W.
The patriots. Ryerson Press 1955 106p illus
Robert Baldwin defends leader in Canadian Rebellion of 1837. 3 acts 11 scenes 14m 6w 3 interiors

Cross, Frank L. See Wilson, R. C. Strangers in Bethlehem

Cross, Mary Ann (Evans) See Eliot, George

Cross and crosses

Legends

David takes the shoots to Jerusalem

Cross your bridge. Martens, A. C.

Crosses on the hill. Lamphere, E. A.

Crossing the street. Spamer, C.

Crosspatch and Cupid. Miller, H. L.

Crothers, Rachel

He and she
> Husband and wife in their struggle between duty to careers versus family. 3 acts 3 scenes 3m 4w 2 interiors

In Quinn, A. H. ed. Representative American plays

Crouch, Archie

Not by might. Friendship Press 1956 40p music
> Account of spiritual freedom through faith. Communists try brainwashing to secure confession from prisoner held in French-Indochinese camp after war of "liberation." Incidental music 1 act 7m 2w 1 interior

Crouch, Mabel

Christmas in her eyes
> Hometown girls are snubbed by returning city girl who has no Christmas sentiment. 1 act 7w 1 interior

In Brings, L. M. ed. The modern treasury of Christmas plays

Crouse, Russel. See Lindsay, H. jt. auth.

Crowds. See Mobs

Crows

c Marston, M. A. The jackdaw of Rheims

Crozier, Eric

Rab the Rhymer. Miller, J.G. 1953 64p front
> Dramatizes critical period in Burn's life when he was at peak of his creative energy. Accented by the use of twenty-eight of his songs. 3 acts 4 scenes 5m 2w 2 interiors

The **crucible.** Miller, A.

The **Crucifixion.** York plays

Crucifixion of Christ. See Jesus Christ—Crucifixion

The **cruise** of the "Toytown Belle." Hulme-Beaman, S. B.

Cruse, Clyde

Healing in its wings. Bakers Plays 1957 21p
> Christmas. Dress rehearsal for Christmas pageant at which time a child is believed to be lost; includes the presentation of pageant itself. Background music. 1 act 2 parts 7m 4w 1b 1g extras 1 interior

Son of Stephen. Bakers Plays 1959 11p
> Son of Stephen, first person to die for his Christian faith, vows vengeance but then is won over to his father's faith. 1 act 3m 3w 1 interior

Cruse, Irma Russell

To bear the message. Eldridge 1959 13p (Eldridge Christmas entertainments)
> Two people try to instill in members of their church true spirit of olden time Christmas. 1 act 6m 7w choir 1 interior

Cry on my shoulder. Parker, K. T.

Cry, the beloved country. Komai, F.

The **crying** clown. Nicholson, M. A.

The **cuckoo.** Murdoch, M.

Cullen, Alan

c Niccolo and Nicollette; or, The puppet prince. Childrens Theatre 1957 54p illus
> Prince who is turned into puppet by evil magician is rescued by leprechaun. 5 scenes 7m 3w extras 3 interiors 2 exteriors

Cullinan, Gerald

The Republic of the Blind
> Radio play. Fantasy. At an inn in strange town, a man discovers that all inhabitants are blind veterans from different wars. Background music. 8m

In Prescott, H. ed. Patrioscript

Culture

Goldschmidt, W. ed. Ways of mankind (13 plays)

Sinclair, L. But I know what I like

Cummings, E. E.

Santa Claus
> Modern morality play about Santa Claus who wishes to give and Death who wishes to take. 5 scenes 2m 1w 1g extras 1 interior

In Halverson, M. ed. Religious drama, 3

Cuny, Therese Marie. See Shelby, K. jt. auth.

The **cup.** Tennyson, A.

A **cup** of kindness. Mauermann, W. G.

A **cup** of tea. Parker, K. T.

A **cup** of tea. Sergel, R.

Cupid's bow. Barry, S.

Cupid's post office. Hark, M. and McQueen, N.

Cupies and hearts. Hark, M. and McQueen, N.

Curiosity

Inge, W The tiny closet

The **curious** quest. Miller, H. L.

The **curse** and the crown. McCourt, G. M.

Curtis, P. D.

Acting for parts
> When several girls are auditioning for parts in a play, two girls get parts by tricking the others with a Cockney accent. 1 act 2w 6g 1 interior

In Curtis, P. D. Three short humorous sketches

c The angry alphabet. Paxton 1953 8p
> Young boy incurs anger of the alphabet by saying that spelling doesn't count; Alphabet proves him wrong and presents him with dictionary. 1w 1b 1g extras 1 interior

Autograph hunters
> Girls try to get autograph of an actress they believe will be a future star. 2w 6g 1 interior

In Curtis, P. D. Three short humorous sketches

Candles for sale
> Farce. Shopkeeper sells surplus candles by tricking her customers, when suddenly trick backfires. 9w 1g 1 interior

In Curtis, P. D. Three short humorous sketches

c The colours clash. Paxton 1954 8p
> The colors come to aid of court painter who is afraid of being beheaded if king disapproves of his portrait of princess. 3m 1w extras 1 interior

The experts
> Farce. Shaving brush in flower pot enables small boy to mystify botanical experts. 6m 1b 1 interior

In Curtis, P. D. Three short humorous sketches

Curtis, P. D.—*Continued*
Fair deals
Headmaster and dealer try to track down schoolboy who mistakenly bought world famous stamp. 4m 4b 1 interior
In Curtis, P. D. Three short humorous sketches
c The hours on strike. Paxton 1953 8p
Young boy of ten accused of wasting time is found guilty by Father Time but is given chance to redeem himself. 5m 1b extras 1 interior
Picking the team
Farce. Small boy uses trick to persuade football club to put his brother on the team. 6b 1 interior
In Curtis, P. D. Three short humorous sketches
The trial of Mr Newall. Paxton 1960 11p
Teacher who views both his students and history with stern eye, is reprimanded in dream by some ancient kings of England. 9m 1w 1 interior

Cusack, Dymphna
The golden girls. Deane 1955 70p illus ("Deane's" Ser. of plays)
Tyranny of wealthy mercenary father continues after his death when eldest daughter takes control over her two unmarried sisters. 3 acts 9 scenes 5m 5w 1 interior

Custis, George Washington Parke
Pocahontas; or, The settlers of Virginia
Early American dramatization of the Pocahontas legend in which she saves the life of John Smith. 3 acts 15 scenes 11m 3w 2 interiors 8 exteriors
In Quinn, A. H. ed. Representative American plays

Cute as a button. Alexander, A.

The **Cyclops.** Euripides

Cyprian's prayer. Wilson, E.

Cyrano de Bergerac, Savinien
Olfson, L. Cyrano de Bergerac
Rostand, E. Cyrano de Bergerac

Cyrano de Bergerac. Olfson, L.

Cyrano de Bergerac. Rostand, E.

Czechoslovak Republic
Lindsay, H. and Crouse, R. The Great Sebastians

D

D'Abbes, Ingram, and Sherie, Fenn
Murder in motley. French 1953 68p illus
Comedy. Manager eludes detective when he stages pretended murder to get publicity for play. 3 acts 12m 5w extras 1 interior

Dace, Wallace
We commit this body
Thirst and starvation on an early 19th century American slave ship in the tropics. 6m extras 1 exterior
In The Best short plays, 1959-1960

Daily, Dorothy Tinsley
The Christmas party. Friendship Press 1955 31p illus
Young Puerto Rican wife inspired by Christmas Eve play at church shares her feeling of good will with neighbors. Background carols. 1 act 3m 2w 1 interior

Displaced
Polish refugee helps young American actress find herself. 4w 1 interior
In Applegarth, M. T., Daily, D. T. and Wolfe, B. S. Four playettes

D'Alton, Louis
The Devil a saint would be. French 1952 90p illus
Morality. Woman visited by saint who turns out to be the Devil; then real saint visits her. 3 acts 4 scenes 7m 3w extras 1 interior

Dalzell, William. See Mitzman, N. jt. auth.

Dalzell, William, and Martens, Anne Coulter
Onions in the stew. Dramatic 1956 102p
Comedy. Based on book by Betty MacDonald. Puget Sound home has charm in spite of summer outsiders. 3 acts 5 scenes 7m 11w extras 1 interior

Dalzell, Wiliam, and Mitzman, Newt
Father's been to Mars. French 1954 90p illus
Farce. TV actor finds it hard to adjust to change each evening from space hero to husband and father. 3 acts 4 scenes 3m 8w 1 interior

The **damask** drum. Mishima, Y.

Dame Robin Hood. Ilian, C.

Damico, Jim
A storm is breaking. French 1954 14p illus
Young boy courageously defends his belief in protecting little things against interfering stranger. 1 act 1m 1w 1b 1 exterior

Damn Yankees. Adler, R. and Ross, J.

Danaïdes
Aeschylus. The suppliant maidens

Danbury, Connecticut

Fair
Carrière, A. Danbury Fair

Danbury Fair. Carrière, A.

Dance of death. See Schloss, M. F. Totentanz

The **dance** of death. Strindberg, A.

A **dance** with our Miss Brooks. Martens, A. C.

Dancers
Shaw, D. Native dancer

The **dancers.** Foote, H.

Dancing
c Knight, C. Patch upon patch
Lynch, P. The teen age party
Parker, K. T. Shall we dance?
Savage, G. I won't dance!

Folk and national
c Mitchell, L. F. Music! Music! Everywhere!

The **dancing** children. Very, A.

The **dancing** ghost. Greth, Le R. E.

The **dancing** school
Grandma's deafness creates a mix-up in her grandchildren's lives. 1 act 1m 2w 6b 5g 1 interior
In 'Round the year plays for the grades

Danger from the sky. Ressieb, G.

The **danger** of freedom. Wishengrad, M.

Danger—pixies at work. Howard, V.

Dangerous Jack. Millet, M.

Daniel, the prophet
  The Play of Daniel
c Spamer, C. M. Daniel in the lions' den
Daniel in the lions' den. Spamer, C. M.
Daniel Webster. Chevigny, H.
Daniels, Elva S. See Noon, E. F. jt. auth.
Danks, Hart Pease
  Emurian, E. K. Silver threads among the gold
D'Arblay, Frances Burney. See Arblay, Madame d'
D'Arblay, Madame. See Arblay, Madame d'
The **dark** at the top of the stars. Inge, W.
The **dark** at the top of the stairs (condensation) Inge, W.
Dark interlude. Emery, C.
The **dark** is light enough. Fry, C.
Dark lady. Collier, E.
Dark of the moon. Richardson, H. and Berney, W.
Dark possession. Vidal, G.
Darkness at noon. Kingsley, S.
Darling girl. Kendall, K.
A **dash** of bitters. Denham, R. and Smith, C. S.
A **dash** of Santa Claus. Richards, S. and Slocumb, P.
The **dashing** white sergeant. Gairdner, C. C. and Pilcher, R.
Date-time. Gross, E. and Gross, N.
A **date** with April. See Batson, G. I found April
Dating (Social customs)
  Weiss, M. J. Guidance through drama
  Weiss, M. J. Her big crush
The **daughters** of Troy. Euripides
David, King of Israel
  Berggren, J. The harp that was silent
  David and Bathsheba
  David takes the shoots to Jerusalem
  Dimondstein, B. David and Bath-Sheba
  Howard, V. David and Goliath
  Lawrence, D. H. David
c Spamer, C. M. David and Goliath
c Spamer, C. M. Jonathan's son
David. Lawrence, D. H.
David and Bathsheba
  Part of ancient Cornish mystery play based on legend of the rood. Story of David and Bathsheba and of David's death. Verse play. 8m 1w 1 setting
  In Browne, E. M. ed. Religious drama, 2
David and Bath-Sheba. Dimondstein, B.
David and Goliath. Howard, V.
David and Goliath. Spamer, C. M.
David Copperfield and Uriah Heep. Olfson, L.
David takes the shoots to Jerusalem
  Part of ancient Cornish mystery play on legend of the rood. About the origin of the wood of Christ's cross. Verse play. 7m 1 setting
  In Browne, E. M. ed. Religious drama, 2

Davidson, Mary Richmond
  On the road to Egypt
    Christmas. Holy Family finds shelter in cave occupied by a thief and a poor man. 3m 1w 1 interior
  In Cahill, E. M. ed. Celebrating Christmas
Davidson, William
  The birds and the boys. Dramatic 1956 92p illus
    Teen-age comedy involving young married woman's successful efforts to make community accept juvenile delinquents from nearby reform school. 3 acts 6m 10w 1g 1 interior
  Buy Jupiter! Dramatic 1954 85p
    Based on book Jumping Jupiter, by Ernestine Gilbreth Carey. A comedy about a department store in which head of toy department, Kay, her sister, and their friends carry out unusual sales promotion. 3 acts 4 scenes 6m 12w extras 1 interior
Davies, Robertson
  Overlaid
    When old farmer who loves opera receives thousand dollars, he considers going to opera in New York for first time in his life, but daughter wants money for tombstone. 1 act 2m 1w 1 interior
  In Richards, S. ed. Canada on stage
Davies, Rhys
  No escape
    Based on author's novel, Under the rose. When a man who jilted spinster returns to taunt her she kills him. Set in rural Wales. 3 acts 6 scenes 3m 4w 1 interior
  In Ring up the curtain
  Under the rose (dramatization) See Davies, R. No escape
Daviot, Gordon
  The Balwhinnie bomb
    Post office bomb scare in a small Scotch village proves to be a hoax. 1 act 3m 1w 1 interior
  In Daviot, G. Plays v2
  Barnharrow
    Tragic incident during the Covenanters' uprising in the 1680's. Set in western Scotland. 1 act 3m 2w 1 interior
  In Daviot, G. Plays v3
  Cornelia
    Romantic comedy. Forthright young woman from Labrador visits her guardian, wealthy English socialite. 3 acts 4m 2w 1 interior
  In Daviot, G. Plays v2
  Dickon
    Through series of maneuvers, Richard III becomes King of England. Set in England between 1483-1485. 2 acts 16m 3w extras 9 interiors
  In Daviot, G. Plays v 1
  Lady Charing is cross
    Satirical comedy. In early 20th century England, a titled lady endeavours to make over an uncouth, independent Socialist. 3 acts 4 scenes 2m 3w 2 interiors
  In Daviot, G. Plays v3
  The little dry thorn
    The Old Testament story of Abraham. 3 acts 6m 4w 1b 1 interior
  In Daviot, G. Plays v 1
  Patria
    Some nationalists, led by an American poet, attempt to foment revolution in small, prosperous European country, long part of an empire. 2 acts 9 scenes 13m 6w 2b 2 interiors
  In Daviot, G. Plays v2

Daviot, Gordon—*Continued*

The pen of my aunt
French lady and her maid, workers in the Resistance movement, help French soldier escape capture by Germans in Occupied France. 1 act 2m 2w 1 interior

In Daviot, G. Plays v2

The pomp of Mr Pomfret
Comedy. Pompous, inconsiderate social climber pays dearly for his rudeness to fellow-Englishman, unpretentious, self-made millionaire. 3 acts 6 scenes 9m 2w 3 interiors

In Daviot, G. Plays v2

The princess who liked cherry pie
Romantic fairy tale. The successful suitor of princess had to be persuaded to like her favorite pie. 1 act 7m 4w extras 1 interior

In Daviot, G. Plays v2

Reckoning
Tragic outcome of young Englishwoman's love for burglar who betrays his friend for murder he himself had committed. 2 acts 3 scenes 11m 2w 1b 2 interiors

In Daviot, G. Plays v3

The staff-room
Comedy. His Majesty's Inspector of Schools makes unexpected official visit to an English girls' high school. 1 act 1m 5w 1 interior

In Daviot, G. Plays v3

Sweet coz
Romantic comedy. Young Englishwoman, a doctor, who gets intoxicated at hospital's charity ball, brings home an unsuccessful young architect. 3 acts 2m 3w 1 interior

In Daviot, G. Plays v3

Valerius
Life in Roman garrison in Britain where soldiers hold the great wall against the barbarians. Set in 196 A.D. 2 acts 4 scenes 15m extras 1 interior 1 exterior

In Daviot, G. Plays v 1

Davis, Donald. See Davis, O. jt. auth.

Davis, James P.

A adventure. ₁Rev₁ French 1960 77p illus
Comedy set in Boston in 1907. Eccentric socialite writes libelous novels about leading figures. 3 acts 9m 5w 1 interior

Davis, Jeanne A.

c Santa's spectacles. Bakers Plays 1955 27p music
Cranky old lady smiles only while wearing Santa's glasses but when Santa needed them, kindly elf gives her smile as Christmas present. Carol singing. 3 scenes 1m 1w extras 1 interior

Davis, John

The package for Ponsonby
Comedy. Granny from County Home arranges financial support for poor composer and wife in resort town. 1 act 3m 4w 1 interior

In Smith, B. and others, eds. A treasury of non-royalty one-act plays

Davis, Luther. See Wright, R. and Forrest, G. Kismet

Davis, Owen, and Davis, Donald

Ethan Frome. ₁Rev. acting ed₁ Dramatists 1954 92p illus
Based on Edith Wharton's novel. A play of retribution in which the main characters are a discouraged New England farmer, his hypochondriac wife, and a girl who still finds joy in living. 3 acts 10 scenes 7m 4w extras 2 interiors 3 exteriors

Davy Crockett. Chadwicke, A.

Davy's star. Fluckey, J. O.

Dawn in the garden Casey, B. M.

The **dawn** must break Sek, M.

Dawn will come. Weinstock, D.

Day, Philip F.

Simeon, the faithful servant. Bakers Plays 1958 24p
Portrays Biblical character Simeon and shows the Jewish hope for a Messiah. 1 act 2 scenes 7m 2w extras 1 exterior

A **day** for trees. Hark, M. and McQueen, N.

Day of destiny. Fisher, A.

A **day** of good deeds. Carpenter, F.

A **day** of thankful prayer. Asbrand, K.

A **day** with Stevenson. Stevenson, F. K.

Days and days. Woolsey, J. and Sechrist, E H.

Dayton, Miles

Sweetie. French 1955 96p
Farce. To secure job, man gets actress to act as wife, but complications arise when actress' prize-fighter suitor appears. 3 acts 4 scenes 4m 6w 1 interior

Whirlwind courtship. Bakers Plays 1957 84p illus (Baker's Royalty plays)
Romantic farce. Love at first sight has ups and downs but is proven true—not once but twice. 3 acts 4 scenes 4m 6w 1 interior

Dead on nine. Popplewell, J.

A **dead** secret. Ackland, R.

Dead weight. Armer, A. and Grauman, W. E.

Deadly Ernest. Payton, D.

The **deadly** game. Yaffe, J.

Deadwood. Lee, W. C.

Deadwood Dick. Taggart, T.

Deaf

c The dancing school
Gibson, W. The miracle worker

Dean, Elsie

Stood up. Dramatic 1954 20p illus
Comedy. Young girl disappointed by escort of her choice finally attends junior prom with faithful beau. 1 act 3m 4w 1b 1 interior

Deans (in schools)

Radin, B. A seacoast in Bohemia

Dear Charles. Melville, A.

Dear delinquent. Popplewell, J.

Dear Phoebe. Taggart, T. and Reach, J.

Dearsley, A. P.

Come back Peter. ₁French's Acting ed₁ French (London) 1954 92p illus
Comedy. Grown children return to overflow small house their parents bought after they had all left home. 3 acts 5 scenes 6m 4w 1 interior

Death

Albee, E. The sandbox
Anouilh, J. Eurydice
Bergman, I. The seventh seal
Dimondstein, B. The lost victory
Dimondstein, B. Mister Gultz
Everyman. Everyman
Everyman. The moral play of Everyman
Everyman. The summoning of Everyman
Foote, H. The death of the old man
Herman, G. An echo of wings

Death—*Continued*

Johnston, R. A. Everyman

Maeterlinck, M. The intruder

Manley, F. Best trip ever

Pirandello, L. Lazarus

Pirandello, L. The life I gave you

Schloss, M. F. Totentanz

Wilder, T. Our town

Williams, N. Dreams

Death of a salesman. Miller, A.

The **death** of Bessie Smith. Albee, E.

The **death** of Billy the Kidd. Vidal, G.

The **death** of Cuchulain. Yeats, W. B.

The **death** of Jesus and the promise of the Resurrection. Phillips, J. B.

The **death** of Odysseus. Abel, L.

The **death** of Satan. Duncan, R.

The **death** of the hired man. Gould, J. R.

The **death** of the old man. Foote, H.

The **death** of Wallenstein. See Schiller, F. von. Wallenstein

Death on the line. Jones-Evans, E.

Debby's dilemma. Weiss, M. J.

De Benedetti, Aldo. See Benedetti, Aldo de

De Bielbo, Birger. See Birger of Bjalbo, Regent of Sweden

De Burgh, Hubert, earl of Kent. See Burgh, Hubert de, earl of Kent

Decadence. See Degeneration

Deceit. See Fraud

December bride. Duffield, B.

December's gifts. Duggar, F.

Decision for freedom. Greene, R. S.

Declaration of Independence. See United States. Declaration of Independence

The **deep** blue sea. Rattigan, T.

Deep freeze. McMullen, J. C.

Defalcation. See Embezzlement

Defoe, Daniel

Robinson Crusoe (dramatization) See Miller, M. Robinson Crusoe

Deformities

Emery, C. Dark interlude

De Francquen, Leonard

The cat and the fiddle. Deane 1956 20p ("Deane's" Ser. of plays)

Aunt in British boarding house foregoes cherished role in Christmas pantomime to allow niece to accept music scholarship. 1 act 6w 1 interior

Three bags full. Deane 1954 30p ("Deane's" Ser. of plays)

Farce. Psychiatrist, under guise of curing patient, joins her in her stealing and pranks. 1 act 8w 1 interior

Degeneration

Williams, T. Cat on a hot tin roof

Williams, T. 27 wagons full of cotton

De Hartog, Jan. See Hartog, Jan de

Deirdire. Bottomley, G.

Deirdre. Yeats, W. B.

Deirdre of the sorrows. Synge, J. M.

Dekker, Thomas

Britannia's honor

Seventeenth century pageant given by the Society of Skinner's at inauguration of Richard Deane as Mayor of London in 1628. Large mixed cast

In Dekker, T. The dramatic works of Thomas Dekker v4

The honest whore; part 2

Sequel to: The honest whore, part I, by Thomas Dekker and Thomas Middleton. Post-Elizabethan verse play. Aided by her father, reformed courtesan successfully resists attempts to make her return to former life. 5 acts 13 scenes 14m 7w extras 1 setting

In Dekker, T. The dramatic works of Thomas Dekker v2

If this be not a good play, the Devil is in it

Seventeenth century English morality play in verse. Covetousness has usurped the place of knowledge. 5 acts 17 scenes 27m 1w extras 1 setting

In Dekker, T. The dramatic works of Thomas Dekker v3

London's tempe

Seventeenth century pageant given at the inauguration of James Campbell as Mayor of London on October 29, 1629 by the Ironmongers Guild. Large mixed cast

In Dekker, T. The dramatic works of Thomas Dekker v4

The magnificent entertainment given to King James

Pageant given for King James I, Queen Anne, his wife, and Henry Frederick, Prince of Wales, on day of their triumphant passage through London, March 15, 1603. No formal arrangement of acts, scenes, or cast. Large mixed cast

In Dekker, T. The dramatic works of Thomas Dekker v2

Match me in London

Seventeenth century English melodrama verse. Young woman elopes with Cordolente and remains faithful to him despite King's advances to her. 5 acts 22 scenes 15m 3w extras 1 setting

In Dekker, T. The dramatic works of Thomas Dekker v3

Old Fortunatus

Elizabethan fantasy in verse. Based on the folk tale: Fortunatus and the purse. Beggar's choice of gift of wealth from the goddess. Fortune, leads to misfortune. 5 acts 10 scenes 15m 4w extras 1 interior 3 exteriors

In Dekker, T. The dramatic works of Thomas Dekker v 1

Satiromastix

Elizabethan verse play. A satire in a romantic setting on Ben Jonson's: Poetaster, a thinly disguised attack on the characters of Jonson's fellow playwrights. Thomas Dekker and John Marston. 5 acts 11 scenes 13m 5w extras 1 setting

In Dekker, T. The dramatic works of Thomas Dekker v 1

The shoemakers' holiday

Elizabethan romantic comedy in verse. Success story of Simon Eyre, 15th century craftsman who became Lord Mayor of London. Songs and dancing. 5 acts 25 scenes 18m 4w extras 1 setting

In Dekker, T. The dramatic works of Thomas Dekker v 1

Dekker, Thomas—*Continued*

Troia-nova triumphans
Seventeenth century pageant presented October 29, 1612 in honor of Sir John Swinnerton, Mayor of London. Divided into four sections, called land triumphs, which incorporate encomiums by Neptune, Virtue, Envy and Fame. Includes songs. Large mixed cast

In Dekker, T. The dramatic works of Thomas Dekker v3

The Welsh embassador. See The Welsh embassador

The Whore of Babylon
Post-Elizabethan verse drama. An allegory showing greatness and other virtues of Queen Elizabeth I, personified in Titania, Queen of the Fairies, as opposed to treacherous religious and political machinations of the Church of Rome, personified in the Whore of Babylon. 5 acts 17 scenes 23m 6w extras 1 setting

In Dekker, T. The dramatic works of Thomas Dekker v2

The wonder of a kingdom
Seventeenth century English romantic comedy in verse. After some adventures and setbacks, daughter of a Florentine duke is permitted to marry man of her choice. 5 acts 15 scenes 21m 5w extras 1 setting

In Dekker, T. The dramatic works of Thomas Dekker v3

See also Massinger, P. jt. auth., Middleton, T. jt. auth. *also* Marlowe, C. Lust's dominion; Rowley, S. The noble Spanish soldier; Rowley, W. and others. The witch of Edmonton

Dekker, Thomas, and Ford, John

The Sun's darling
Elizabethan masque in verse. The Sun selects Spring as a bride for his favorite son. Includes songs and dances. 5 acts 8 scenes 19m 8w extras 1 setting

In Dekker, T. The dramatic works of Thomas Dekker v4

Dekker, Thomas, and Middleton, Thomas

The honest whore; part I
Elizabethan tragicomedy. Reformed courtesan helps reunite lovers separated by family feud, while shrewish wife tries to rouse patient husband to a show of anger. 5 acts 15 scenes 20m 4w extras 8 interiors 3 exteriors

In Dekker, T. The dramatic works of Thomas Dekker v2

Dekker, Thomas, and Webster, John

Northward ho
Post-Elizabethan verse play. Husband takes revenge upon man who has falsely represented the former's wife as faithless. 5 acts 11 scenes 18m 4w extras 1 setting

In Dekker, T. The dramatic works of Thomas Dekker v2

Sir Thomas Wyatt
Sir Thomas Wyatt is executed because he withdraws loyalty from Queen Mary when she contemplates marriage to King Philip of Spain. Verse play set in 16th century England. 5 acts 17 scenes 21m 3w extras 1 setting

In Dekker, T. The dramatic works of Thomas Dekker v 1

Westward ho
Post-Elizabethan social comedy in verse. Three wives on flirtatious adventure which turns out to be quite innocent. 5 acts 15 scenes 20m 5w extras 1 setting

In Dekker, T. The dramatic works of Thomas Dekker v2

Dekker, Thomas; Chettle, Henry, and Haughton, William

Patient Grissil
Elizabethan romantic comedy in verse. Nobleman marries commoner's daughter and deliberately subjects her to trials and indignities which she weathers well. 5 act 11 scenes 16m 4w extras 1 setting

In Dekker, T. The dramatic works of Thomas Dekker v 1

Delacour. See Labiche, E. jt. auth.

Delaney, Shelagh

A taste of honey. Grove 1959 87p
Young impoverished English girl's experiences with her amoral mother, Negro sailor who gets her pregnant, and homosexual who takes care of her. 2 acts 3m 2w 1 interior

De la Ramée, Louise

The Nürnberg stove (dramatization) See Siks, G. B. The Nuremberg stove

Delderfield, R. F.

Golden rain. [French's Acting ed] French 1953 80p illus
Comedy. Young English rector sincerely sticks to his beliefs and effects some needed reforms even in those close to him. 3 acts 5 scenes 5m 4w 1 interior

The guinea-pigs. Deane 1954 24p ("Deane's" Ser. of plays)
Women of English Women's Institute, calling to secure use of barn for church gatherings, become unwilling partakers of hostess' individualistic cookery. 1 act 7w 1 interior

The Mayerling affair. [French's Acting ed] French (London) 1958 86p illus
Tragedy. Death of Rudolf, Crown Prince of Austria and his mistress. 3 acts 6m 5w 2 interiors

The offending hand. Deane 1955 64p illus ("Deane's" Ser. of plays)
British young man, released from prison, rejoins gang of burglars and almost wrecks the lives of all concerned with him. 3 acts 4 scenes 4m 4w 1 interior

The orchard walls. [French's Acting ed] French (London) 1954 68p illus
Comedy. Warm-hearted school principal of an English girls' school aids two young people in love and finds her own happiness. 3 acts 4 scenes 4m 5w 1 interior

The Rounderlay tradition. Deane 1954 32p ("Deane's" Ser. of plays)
Ghosts of young English girl's ancestors help save her from unhappy marriage. 8w 1 interior

Smoke in the valley. [French's Acting ed] French (London) 1953 26p illus
English lord's spoiled daughter, Elaine, selfishly persuades father to give the railroads right of way but it is not to her advantage. 1 act 2m 3w 1 interior

Delilah
Morris, T. B. The watcher of the road

Delinquency, Juvenile. See Juvenile delinquency

Delinquent girls. See Unmarried mothers

Delirium
c Woolsey, J. and Sechrist, E. H. Jerry and the Skweegees

Delmar, Viña

Mid-summer. French 1954 99p illus
Domestic comedy. Kind, uneducated mother of precocious child sacrifices dream of security for teacher-husband's desire to write for vaudeville. 3 acts 5 scenes 6m 3w 2b 1g 1 interior

Warm Wednesday. French 1959 73p
Romantic comedy. Girl disappears on eve of her wedding and coincidentally the man she once jilted, returns to town. 3 acts 5m 5w 1 interior

Deluge
Chester plays. Noah's flood
Delva, Josephine G.
c The rise of a nation
How George Washington and the dele-
gates from the states wrote the American
Constitution. 15m extras 1 interior
In Birdsall, R. ed. Creative plays for
every school month
Dementia praecox. See Schizophrenia
A **democratic** emperor. Ullman, S. S.
Democracy
Fisher, A. and Rabe, O. Champions of
democracy
Fisher, A. and Rabe, O. Johnny on the
spot
Flaten, M. Testing ground for democracy
Johnston, D. The golden cuckoo
Probst, G. Nature's most precious gift
The **democrat** and the commissar. Geiger, M.
Demonology
Kwanze, K. N. The maple viewing
See also Apparitions; Exorcism;
Ghosts; Witchcraft
De Musset, Alfred. See Musset, Alfred de
Denham, Lilian. See Percy, E. jt. auth.
Denham, Reginald. See Orr, M. jt. auth.
Denham, Reginald, and Smith, Conrad Sutton
A dash of bitters. Acting ed. Dramatists
1955 81p
Adapted from story: The perfectionist,
by Margaret St Clair. Old lady still suf-
fering from unrequited love poisons erst-
while lover's son. 3 acts 7 scenes 2m 2w
1 interior
Denker, Henry, and Berkey, Ralph
Time limit. French 1956 96p illus
In hearing to determine advisability of
court-martial trial. Colonel proves that
American major charged with treason in
Communist prison during Korean War,
acted to protect lives of his fellow
prisoners. 3 acts 17m 2w 1 setting
Time limit! (condensation)
In Theatre, 1956
Dennis, Nigel
Cards of identity
Comical satire. An identity club is
founded to create and define new and
more suitable identities for its members.
3 acts 7 scenes 16m 4w 2 interiors
In Dennis, N. Two plays and a preface
The making of moo
Comical satire on man's tribal customs
and beliefs. 3 acts 2 scenes 12m 1w
1 interior
In Dennis, N. Two plays and a preface
Dennis, Patrick
Auntie Mame (dramatization) See Law-
rence, J. and Lee, R. E. Auntie Mame
Dennys, Joyce
Art with a capital "A." French (London)
1953 22p illus
Comedy. Artists at outdoor art exhibi-
tion reveal their true natures. 1 act 2m
5w 1 exterior
The lawn. Deane 1954 22p ("Deane's"
Ser. of plays)
Family ghosts prepare old lady for death.
1 act 6w 1 exterior
Lear of Albion Crescent. Deane 1956 24p
("Deane's" Ser. of plays)
Comedy. Father of four daughters, who
has heart set on a boy, gets erroneous
call from hospital saying new baby is a
girl. 1 act 1m 4w 1 interior

Dentistry. See Teeth
The **departing.** Snyder, W. H.
Department stores
Davidson, W. Buy Jupiter!
Dighton, J. Man alive
Depressions
1929—United States
Wilson, E. Beppo and Beth
Desert soliloquy. Peterson, L.
The **deserted** house. Morris, T. B.
Design for murder. Batson, G.
Desire under the elms. O'Neill, E.
The **desk** set. Marchant, W.
The **desperate** hours. Hayes, J.
Despotism
Camus, A. Caligula
Massinger, P. The Roman actor
Saroyan, W. The slaughter of innocents
See also Dictators
Destiny. See Fate and fatalism
Desvallieres, Maurice. See Feydeau, G. jt.
auth.
Detectives
Addyman, E. The secret tent
Atkinson, A. Four winds
Badger, A. The bomb
Braun, W. Drop dead!
Carmichael, F. The pen is deadlier
Carrière, A. Mystery at the depot
Cary, F. L. Murder out of tune
Cary, F. L. and Butler, I. The paper chain
Christie, A. Towards zero
D'Abbes, I. and Sherie, F. Murder in
motley
Knott, F. Dial "M" for murder
Lewis, E. A screw loose
Miller, H. L. Beany's private eye
Miller, H. L. The Christmas oboe
Mortimer, J. I spy
Murray, J. The impossible room
Reach, J. Murder is my business
Roffey, J. and Harbord, G. Night of the
fourth
Sprague, M. Murder comes in threes
Taggart, T. Morning of a private eye
The **Deva** King. Sakanishi, S. tr.
Deval, Jacques
Tonight in Samarkand; adapted by Lorenzo
Semple, Jr. French 1956 87p
Tragedy ensues for young woman, the
tiger tamer in circus, when the third
vision of disaster that she has seen in a
seer's crystal ball, proves to be reality.
3 acts 7m 5w 1 interior
Devany, Edward H.
The cow-catcher on the caboose
Comedy. Aged, incompetent but lovable,
railroad employee fights retirement. 2
scenes 6m 1w 1 interior
In The Best short plays, 1958-1959
The red and yellow ark
Circus roustabout endangers his life to
help boy fly his treasured kite. 1 act
4 scenes 4m 1w 1b extras 1 exterior
In The Best short plays of 1957-1958
DeVega, Lope Carpio. See Vega Carpio,
Lope de

De Vier, Herman E.
Come to the stable
    Nativity drama. After permitting Mary and Joseph to stay in his stable, greedy innkeeper realizes how selfish he has been in the past. 3 acts 6 scenes 7m 6w 1 exterior
    In Bryant, A. comp. Religious plays that click

Devil
Adler, R. and Ross, J. Damn Yankees
Axelrod, G. Will success spoil Rock Hunter?
Benét, S. V. The Devil and Daniel Webster
Carroll, P. V. The wayward saint
D'Alton, L. The Devil a saint would be
Dekker, T. If this be not a good play, the Devil is in it
Goethe, J. W. von. Faust, part 1
Goethe, J. W. von. Faust, part II
Goethe, J. W. von. The Urfaust
Gregory, H. and Henneberger, J. The thousand flerbs
Harrowing of hell. The harrowing of hell
Howard, S. Madam, will you walk?
Julian, J. The Devil and the dream
Lillington, K. The Devil's grandson
Marlowe, C. The tragedy of Doctor Faustus
Marlowe, C. The tragical history of Doctor Faustus
Olson, E. Faust: a masque
Perrini, A. Once a thief
Sakanishi, S. tr. The magic mallet of the Devil
Stone, W. Devil take a whittler
Totheroh, D. and Benét, S. V. All that money can buy
York plays. The creation, and The fall of Lucifer
York plays. The creation of the heavenly beings: The fall of Lucifer
York plays. The temptation of Christ
The **Devil** a saint would be. D'Alton, L.
The **Devil** and Daniel Webster. Benét, S. V.
The **Devil** and the dream. Julian, J.
Devil take a whittler. Stone, W.
The **Devil** was sick. Horne, K.
The **Devil's** disciple. Shaw, B.
The **Devil's** grandson. Lillington, K.

De Vries, Peter
The tunnel of love (dramatization) See Fields, J. and De Vries, P. The tunnel of love
    See also Fields, J. jt. auth.

DeWitt, Robert Hanna
Arise, thy light is come! Broadman 1957 11p music
    Christmas pageant which begins with the power of Jesus in the present day and turns a backward glance at the Nativity. Background music. 17m 1w extras

Dial "M" for murder. Knott, F.
Dial 999. Webber, J.

Dialect
            Cockney
    See Dialect—English—Cockney
            Cowboy
Finch, R. and Smith, B. Western night
Rodgers, R. and Hammerstein, O. Oklahoma!

            English
Vooght, C. Come live with me
            English—Cockney
Addis, H. What ho for the open road
Bollans, G. E. The crooked courtship
Bollans, G. E. Wedding bells for Clara?
Carter, C. Stick up for yourself
Collier, E. Dark lady
Cooper, D. S. And so say all of us!
Kennedy, C. R. The terrible meek
Sutherland, D. The clean up

            English—Early modern
Dryden, J. and Lee, N. The Duke of Guise
Dryden, J. and Lee, N. Oedipus
Lee, N. Caesar Borgia
Lee, N. Constantine the Great
Lee, N. Gloriana
Lee, N. Lucius Junius Brutus
Lee, N. The massacre of Paris
Lee, N. Mithridates, King of Pontus
Lee, N. The Princess of Cleve
Lee, N. The rival queens
Lee, N. Sophonisba
Lee, N. Theodosius
Lee, N. The tragedy of Nero, Emperour of Rome
Lee, N. The works of Nathaniel Lee (13 plays)

            English—Elizabethan
Addis, H. Sellevision
Beaumont, F. and Fletcher, J. The maid's tragedy
Boyd, A. K. Prince Arthur and Hubert
Boyd, A. K. Robbery at Gadshill
Chapman, G. Bussy D'Ambois
Dekker, T. Britannia's honor
Dekker, T. The dramatic works of Thomas Dekker (24 plays)
Dekker, T. The honest whore; part 2
Dekker, T. If this be not a good play, the Devil is in it
Dekker, T. London's tempe
Dekker, T. The magnificent entertainment given to King James
Dekker, T. Match me in London
Dekker, T. Old Fortunatus
Dekker, T. Satiromastix
Dekker, T. The shoemakers' holiday
Dekker, T. Troia-nova triumphans
Dekker, T. The Whore of Babylon
Dekker, T. The wonder of a kingdom
Dekker, T. and Ford, J. The Sun's darling
Dekker, T. and Middleton, T. The honest whore; part I
Dekker, T. and Webster, J. Northward ho
Dekker, T. and Webster, J. Sir Thomas Wyatt
Dekker, T. and Webster, J. Westward ho
Dekker, T.; Chettle, H. and Haughton, W. Patient Grissil
Ford, J. The broken heart
Ford, J. Five plays
Ford, J. The lover's melancholy
Ford, J. Love's sacrifice
Ford, J. Perkin Warbeck
Ford, J. 'Tis pity she's a whore
Heywood, T. A woman killed with kindness
Jonson, B. The alchemist
Jonson, B. Bartholomew Fair

Dialect—English—Elizabethan—*Continued*

Jonson, B. Five plays
Jonson, B. Sejanus, his fall
Jonson, B. Three plays
Jonson, B. Volpone
McIlwraith, A. K. ed. Five Stuart tragedies (5 plays)
Marlowe, C. Edward the Second
Marlowe, C. The Jew of Malta
Marlowe, C. Lust's dominion
Marlowe, C. Tamburlaine the Great: part I
Marlowe, C. The tragedy of Doctor Faustus
Marlowe, C. The tragical history of Doctor Faustus
Massinger, P. The Roman actor
Massinger, P. and Dekker, T. The virgin martyr
Middleton, T. and Dekker, T. The Roaring Girl
Rowley, S. The noble Spanish soldier
Rowley, W. and others. The witch of Edmonton
Webster, J. The Duchess of Malfi
Webster, J. The Duchess of Malfy
The Welsh embassador

English—Middle English

Abraham and Isaac (Brome manuscript) Abraham and Isaac
Abraham and Isaac (Brome manuscript) The sacrifice of Isaac
Browne, E. M. ed. Religious drama, 2 (22 plays)
Chester plays. Noah's flood
Coventry plays. The Annunciation
Coventry plays. Cain and Abel
Coventry plays. Herod and the kings
Coventry plays. The pageant of the Shearmen and Taylors—The Coventry Nativity play
Coventry plays. The parliament of heaven: The Annunciation and Conception
Coventry plays. The woman taken in adultery
Everyman. Everyman
Everyman. The moral play of Everyman
Everyman. The summoning of Everyman
Everyman, and medieval miracle plays (16 plays)
Harrowing of hell. The harrowing of hell
Towneley plays. The play of the shepherds; Wakefield cycle; secunda pastorum
Towneley plays. The Wakefield Pageant of Herod the Great
Towneley plays. The Wakefield Second shepherds' pageant
York plays. The Ascension
York plays. The birth of Christ; York Tile-Thatchers' play
York plays. The creation, and The fall of Lucifer
York plays. The creation of Adam and Eve
York plays. The creation of man
York plays. The creation of the heavenly beings: The fall of Lucifer
York plays. The Crucifixion
York plays. The fall of man

York plays. The Garden of Eden
York plays. The judgment
York plays. The last judgement; York Mercers' play
York plays. Palm Sunday
York plays. The Resurrection
York plays. The second trial before Pilate: The scourging and condemnation
York plays. The temptation of Christ

English—Norfolk
Wesker, A. Roots

English—Slang
Sutherland, D. Trying to take things quietly

English—Yorkshire
Ratcliffe, D. U. Jingling Lane

German-American
Blankman, H. By hex
Hague, A. Plain and fancy
Miller, H. L. Be my "walentine"

Irish
Carney, F. The righteous are bold
Carroll, P. V. The wise have not spoken
Ervine, St J. John Ferguson
Gregory, Lady. The workhouse ward
O'Casey, S. Bedtime story
O'Casey, S. The Bishop's bonfire
O'Casey, S. The drums of Father Ned
O'Casey, S. The end of the beginning
O'Casey, S. Hall of healing
O'Casey, S. Juno and the paycock
O'Casey, S. The plough and the stars
O'Casey, S. A pound on demand
O'Casey, S. Purple dust
O'Casey, S. Red roses for me
O'Casey, S. The shadow of a gunman
O'Casey, S. The Silver Tassie
O'Casey, S. Three plays
O'Casey, S. Time to go
O'Casey, S. Within the gates
O'Neill, E. A touch of the poet
Purkey, R. A. The leprechaun
Shaw, B. O'Flaherty V. C.
Synge, J. M. Deirdre of the sorrows
Synge, J M. In the shadow of the glen
Synge, J. M. The playboy of the western world
Synge, J. M. Riders to the sea
Synge, J. M. The tinker's wedding
Synge, J. M. The well of the saints

Italian-American
Panetta, G. Comic strip
Poverman, H. Easy money
Williams, T. The rose tattoo

Middle English
See Dialect—English—Middle English

Midwestern
Smith, B. and Webb, C. Lawyer Lincoln

Mountain whites (Southern States)
Chadwicke, A. Davy Crockett
Conkle, E. P. Granny's little cheery room
Covington, W. P. Shirt-tail boy
Green, P. Quare medicine
Hughes, E. W. The wishful taw
Jerome, P. Goin' round the hoop
Koch, F. These doggone elections
Koch, F. Wash Carver's mouse trap

Dialect—Mountain whites (Southern States)
—*Continued*

McMahon, L. E. I smell smoke
Mitchell, B. E. and Rose, Le R. Mountain gal
Richardson, H. and Berney, W. Dark of the moon
Rose, Le R. Headin' for a weddin'
Schweikert, C. P. Hessie of the hills
Schweikert, C. P. Hoax of Hogan's Holler
Sheffield, J. The forgotten land
Shelby, K. and Cuny, T. M. Giving goes on
Stone, W. Devil take a whittler
Stout, W. In Dixon's kitchen
Wolfe, T. The return of Buck Gavin

Negro
Boucicault, D. The octoroon
Carroll, W. Comin' for to carry
Chadwicke, A. Pudd'nhead Wilson
Green, P. The No 'Count Boy
McCaslin, N. John Henry
Parker, J. W. Sleep on, Lemuel

New England
Applegarth, M. T. Home Sweet Home
Herne, J. A. Shore Acres
O'Neill, E. Desire under the elms
Sergel, R. The revolt of mother

Old English
See Dialect—English—Middle English

Sailor
Jerrold, D. Black-ey'd Susan
O'Neill, E. The moon of the Caribbees

Scottish
Crozier, E. Rab the Rhymer

Southern States
Barnett, M. Yankee peddler
Eaton, C. E. Sea psalm
Foote, H. John Turner Davis
McMahon, B. The Ming thing
Patton, F. G. The beaded buckle
Williams, T. Cat on a hot tin roof
Williams, T. The last of my solid gold watches
Williams, T. 27 wagons full of cotton

Southern States (Mountain whites)
See Dialect—Mountain whites (Southern States)

Welsh
Stephens, P. J. The changeling
Thomas, D. Under Milk Wood

Western
Asbrand, K. The Farmer in the Dell
Payton, D. He tried with his boots on
Riggs, L. Roadside
Shaw, B. The shewing-up of Blanco Posnet
Tomkins, B. Pistol-packin' Sal

Diamond cut diamond. Williamson, H. R.
Diamonds
Armer, A. and Grauman, W. E. Black star
Diaries
Miller, H. L. The judge's diary
Payton, D. Nearly beloved
The diary of a scoundrel. Ostrovsky, A.
The diary of Anne Frank. Goodrich, F. and Hackett, A.

Dias, Earl J.
Abner Crane from Hayseed Lane
Supposed country bumpkin of the 1890's outwits suave city villain who tries to marry his girl. 4 scenes 4m 5w 2 interiors 1 exterior
In Dias, E. J. Melodramas and farces for young actors
The case of the missing pearls
Shellack Homes solves theft of pearls and exonerates butler. 2 scenes 6m 4w 1 interior
In Dias, E. J. Melodramas and farces for young actors
The face is familiar
When his cousin wires that she cannot chaperone college party, Joel drafts roommate Wally to impersonate her. 1 scene 4m 3w extras 1 setting
In Dias, E. J. Melodramas and farces for young actors
Feudin' fun
Two feuding hillbilly families are united after the discovery that disputed land belongs to neither family. 2 scenes 5m 3w 1 interior
In Dias, E. J. Melodramas and farces for young actors
The natives are restless tonight
Daughter of vaudeville-type British family disappears in African jungle, and is rescued by handsome young hunting guide. 2 scenes 10m 3w 1 setting
In Dias, E. J. Melodramas and farces for young actors
Out of this world
Teen-ager is cured of his infatuation for a 22 year old girl when she theatrically simulates infirmities of old age. 1 scene 2m 4w 1 setting
In Dias, E. J. Melodramas and farces for young actors
The sands of time
A 16-year-old girl loses her crush on her older sister's beau when he pretends to be afflicted with old age ailments. 2 scenes 3m 3w 1 interior
In Dias, E. J. Melodramas and farces for young actors
Stage bore
Young understudy, gets an opening night chance to star in a play when leading lady breaks her ankle on banana peel. 3 scenes 2m 5w 1 setting
In Dias, E. J. Melodramas and farces for young actors
Stop the presses!
Scholarly cub reporter gets big story which hard-boiled city editor couldn't get. 2 scenes 6m 2w 1 interior
In Dias, E. J. Melodramas and farces for young actors
Strong and silent
Harvard man turns out to be United States marshall who saves Bar Nothing ranch from rustlers. 4 scenes 4m 3w 3 interiors 1 exterior
In Dias, E. J. Melodramas and farces for young actors
Way, way down east
Spoof on the American melodrama of 1890's in which mortgage is *not* foreclosed. 4 scenes 5m 3w extras 1 interior 2 exteriors
In Dias, E. J. Melodramas and farces for young actors
What ho!
American lad, David Dauntless, is falsely accused of theft by Lady Hightone who at first refuses to let him marry her daughter. 2 scenes 6m 4w 1 setting
In Dias, E. J. Melodramas and farces for young actors

Discontent
  Lee, J. Career
Disease, Mental. See Mental illness
The **disenchanted.** Schulberg, B. and Breit, H.
Disguises
  Agg, H. Red plush
  Ashton, E. B. The beggarman's bride
  Bowie, L. "You heard me!"
  Carmichael, F. She-sickness
  Emery, C. Portrait of Deborah
  Farquhar, G. The beaux' stratagem
  Farquhar, G. The recruiting officer
  Ford, J. The lover's melancholy
c Ilian, C. Dame Robin Hood
  Jonson, B. Bartholomew Fair
  Kirkpatrick, J. Adam's rib hurts
  LePelley, G. A is for apple
  Mantle, M. Gareth triumphs
  Middleton, T. and Dekker, T. The Roaring Girl
  Molière, J. B. P. Coxcombs in petticoats
  Molière, J. B. P. The precious damsels
  Molière, J. B. P. The pretentious ladies
  Olfson, L. As you like it
  Olfson, L. Monsieur Beaucaire
  Tydeman, R. Duet with dowagers
  The Welsh embassador
A **dish** of green peas. Fisher, A. and Rabe, O.
Dishonesty. See Honesty
Disorders of the personality. See Personality, Disorders of
Displaced. Daily, D. T.
Displaced persons (World War, 1939-1945)
  See Refugees
A **distant** bell. Morrill, K.
Distant thunder. Neuenburg, E.
Divided we stand. Wishengrad, M.
Divine healing. See Faith cure
The **divine** miracle. Trick, O. B.
Divorce
  Butler, I. The wise children
  Carmichael, F. Divorce granted
  Mitchell, L. The New York idea
  Owen, A. Can this be love?
  Sardou, V. and Najac, É. de. Let's get a divorce!
Divorce granted. Carmichael, F.
Dixie. Emurian, E. K.
Do-it-yourself. Martens, A. C.
Do-Nothing Dan. Murdoch, W.
Do—or die! Taggart, T.
The **dock** brief. Mortimer, J.
The **doctor** and the devils. Thomas, D.
Doctor Fox. Carpenter, F.
Dr Hudson's secret journal. Martens, A. C.
Dr Knock. Romains, J.
Doctor Manners. Hark, M. and McQueen, N.
Doctor Time's office. Very, A.
Doctors. See Physicians
Doctor's delight. Jackson, B.
The **doctor's** dilemma. Shaw, B.
Dodge, Mary (Mapes)
c Mason, M. E. Mary Elizabeth's wonderful dream
  Spamer, C. Mary Mapes Dodge

Doers and viewers. Burgess, C. V.
The **dog** beneath the skin. Auden, W. H. and Isherwood, C.
The **dog** Toby. Priestley, H. E.
Dogs
c Carlson, B. W. Jes' too lazy!
  Faust, E. Gone to the dogs
  Holland, N. Crisis in Wimpole Street
  Priestley, F. Brown dog—black dog
  Priestley, H. E. The dog Toby
  Robinson, T. The visitor (Lassie)
  Shore, J. and Lincoln, R. The soldier who became a Great Dane
c Very, A. Three little kittens go to school
Dolls
c Goulding, D. J. Mr Bunch's toys
c Hark, M. and McQueen, N. The dolls
  Miller, H. L. Dolly saves the day
  Preston, E. E. The Christmas dolls' revue
c Spamer, C. The playroom
c Woolsey, J. and Sechrist, E. H. The Feast of the Dolls
Dolls, Feast of
c Woolsey, J. and Sechrist, E. H. The Feast of the Dolls
The **dolls.** Hark, M. and McQueen, N.
Doll's Festival. See Dolls, Feast of
A **doll's** house. Ibsen, H.
Dolly Madison. Spamer, C.
Dolly saves the day. Miller, H. L.
Dom Pedro II. See Pedro II, Emperor of Brazil
Domestic animals. See names of domestic animals, e.g. Cats; Dogs
Domestic relations. See Comedy—Domestic; Family
Domitian, Titus Flavius, Emperor of Rome
  Massinger, P. The Roman actor
Don Carlos. Schiller, F. von
Don Juan. Molière, J. B. P.
Don Quixote saves the day. Howard, V.
Don Sanche d'Aragon. Corneille, P.
Donerblitz. Spamer, C.
Donisthorpe, G. Sheila
  Fruit of the tree. [French's Acting ed] French (London) 1957 55p illus
    Jealous teen-ager murders her rival who has past history of bad heart, and death is certified as heart failure, but evidence of evil is revealed to real mother of the illegitimately-born murderess. 3 acts 3m 4w 1 interior
Donkeys. See Asses and mules
The **donkey's** mission. Woolsey, J. and Sechrist, E. H.
Don't argue! Carter, C.
Don't tell a soul! Carlson, B. W.
Don't tell your father. McMahon, L.
Dooley and the amateur hour. Gross, E. and Gross, N.
The **door.** Murray, J.
A **door** should be either open or shut. Musset, A. de
Dope! Lee, M.
Doren, Mark van. See Van Doren, Mark
Dorothea, Saint
  Massinger, P. and Dekker, T. The virgin martyr

Dorothy of Cappadocia, Saint. See Dorothea, Saint
Doss, Helen Grigsby
The family nobody wanted (dramatization) See Sergel, C. The family nobody wanted
Dostoevsky, Fedor
The possessed (dramatization) See Camus, A. The possessed
Dostoyevsky's The brothers Karamazov. Tumarin, B. and Sydow, J.
Double consciousness. See Personality, Disorders of
The **double-dealer.** Congreve, W.
Double identity. Parker, K. T.
Double take. Jeans, R.
Double yolk. Williams, H. and Williams, M.
Dough for dopes. Pierce, C. W.
Douglas, Don
Just off Broadway. Bakers Plays 1953 73p (Baker's Edition of plays)
> Comedy. When Toby Jones, the imaginary sweetheart Carol had invented appeared at her mother's theatrical boarding house he caused quite a stir. 3 acts 5 scenes 4m 5w 1 interior

Douglas, Felicity
It's never too late. French 1956 114p illus
> Domestic comedy. Woman whose family doesn't appreciate her decides to become a writer. 2 acts 5 scenes 6m 6w 2 interiors

—Same
In Ring up the curtain
Rollo
> Adaptation of play by Marcel Archard. Frenchman's lifelong jealousy of his successful friend leads him to seek revenge for imaginary wrongs. 3 acts 3m 3w 2 interiors

In Plays of the year v20
Douglas, Lilian
c Crispin the tailor
> A tailor and a magic bird drive away some witches and restore the count's lost daughter. 6 scenes 7m 4w 4 interiors 2 exteriors

In Cameo plays: bk 19
Douglas, Lloyd C.
Dr Hudson's secret journal (dramatization) See Martens, A. C. Dr Hudson's secret journal
Home for Christmas (dramatization) See Martens, A. C. Home for Christmas
The Robe (dramatization) See McGreevey, J. Coins of His kingdom
Douglas, Stephen Arnold
Corwin, N. The rivalry
Douglas, William Orville
An almanac of liberty (dramatization) See Rose, R. An almanac of liberty
Dowling, Jennette
The young Elizabeth; by Jennette Dowling in collaboration with Francis Letton
> Historical drama covering turbulent years in life of Queen Elizabeth I prior to her accession to English throne. 2 acts 13 scenes 15m 6w 7 interiors

In Plays of the year v7
Down, Oliphant
The maker of dreams
> Pierrette weeps in unrequited love until the Manufacturer of Dreams opens Pierrot's eyes to her love. 1 act 2m 1w 1 interior

In Cerf, B. and Cartmell, V. H. eds. **24 favorite one-act plays**

Down came a blackbird. Blackmore, P.
Downing, Robert
Sticks and stones
> Because the Senior Scholarship Award of the high school was scheduled to go to Helen, jealous Abbie starts malicious gossip about her. 1 act 3m 5w 1 interior

In Kamerman, S. E. ed. Blue-ribbon plays for graduation
Dozier, Robert
A real fine cutting edge
> Television play. Army sergeant attempts to break high I.Q. draftee. 6m extras

In Burack, A. S. ed. Television plays for writers
Draft, Military. See Military service, Compulsory
Drag race. Martens, A. C.
Dragnet. Reach, J.
Dragons
Howard, V. Drexel
c Tennant, K. The prince who met a dragon
Dragon's mouth. Hawkes, J. and Priestley, J. B.
Drama. See Classical drama; Comedy; Drama, Medieval; Folk-drama; Historical drama; Melodrama; Plays in verse; Tragedy; Tragicomedy; *also* various national dramas, e.g. English drama; French drama; Spanish drama
Drama. Addis, H.
Drama, Classical. See Classical drama
Drama, Historical. See names of countries with subdivision History
Drama, Medieval
The Play of Daniel
Dramatists
Axelrod, G. Will success spoil Rock Hunter?
Collier, E. Dark lady
Gottlieb, A. Wake up, darling
Kanin, F. and Kanin, M. His and hers
Lee, J. Career
Molnar, F. The play's the thing
Osborne, J. and Creighton, A. Epitaph for George Dillon
Quinn, C. For want of a character
Strindberg, A. Crime and crime
Villiers, G. and others. The rehearsal
Draper, John
Barchester Towers. Vosper, M. 1953 69p illus
> Based on novel by Anthony Trollope. Portrays the innermost circles of a 19th century English Cathedral community and the machinations for his own advancement of the bishop's chaplain. 3 acts 4 scenes 8m 4w 3 interiors

Drapkin, Ida
Lucy
> Christmas play. Young girl decides not to be adopted by rich Aunt but to remain with own poor family. 1 act 4w 1g 1 interior

In Smith, B. and others, eds. A treasury of non-royalty one-act plays
Dream a little dream. Kesler, H. O.
The **dream** of Peter Mann. Kops, B.
A **dream** play. Strindberg, A.
The **dream** unwinds. Harris, N.
The **dreaming** dust. Johnston, D.

The **dreaming** of the bones. Yeats, W. B.

Dreams
  Aiken, C. Mr Arcularis
  Asbrand, K. Gifts of gold
  Atherton, M. And it's Christmas!
c Beneke, A. Symbols of Christmas
  Bennett, V. E. Shadows walk softly
c Bornstein, M. and Cole, G. Paul in food
    land
  Čapek, J. and Čapek, K. The world we
    live in
  Curtis, P. D. The trial of Mr Newall
  Dimondstein, B. Eva
  Fry, C. A sleep of prisoners
  Gibson, M. N. Return engagement
  Ireland, I. A. This angel business
  Kantan
  Kops, B. The dream of Peter Mann
  Lathrop, D. Something new in murder
c Lunnon, B. S. Johnny has comicopia
  Manning, M. Passages from Finnegans
    wake
  Mishima, Y. Kantan
  Moreno, R. A horse play
  Parr, R. The flying machine
c Rawe, M. S. Benny goes to Mistletonia
c Thompson, B. J. Pleasant dreams
  Trick, O. B. Beneath this spire
c Very, A. Too much turkey
  Williams, T. Camino Real

Dreams. Williams, N.

Dreiser, Theodore
  The girl in the coffin
    Tragedy. Labor leader interrupts mourn-
    ing for daughter's death to address
    workers in crucial textile mill strike.
    1 act 4m 3w 1 interior
    In Smith, B. and others, eds. A treasury
      of non-royalty one-act plays

A **dress** affair. Hackett, W.

Dress shops. See Clothing trade

Drexel. Howard, V.

Dreyfus, Alfred
  Herald, H.; Herczeg, G. and Raine, N. R.
    The life of Emile Zola

Drink to me only. Ginnes, A. S. and Wal-
    lach, I.

Driscoll, Reed
  The whiz bang minstrel show. Bakers
    Plays 1954 111p
    Minstrel show. Includes production notes.
    Large mixed cast 1 setting

Driver education. See Automobile drivers

Droit du seigneur. See Jus primae noctis

Drop dead! Braun, W.

The **drop** of a hat. Berg, D.

Drug addicts. See Narcotic addicts

Drugs. See Pharmacy

Druids and Druidism
  Osgood, P. E. Midwinter-Eve fire

The **drums** of Father Ned. O'Casey, S.

Druten, John Van. See Druten, John

Dryden, John
  All for love; or, The world well lost
    English Restoration tragedy. Adaptation
    of Shakespeare's "Anthony and Cleo-
    patra" done in blank verse. Background
    music. 5 acts 7 scenes 6m 4w 2g extras
    1 interior
    In Morrell, J. M. ed. Four English
      tragedies of the 16th and 17th
      centuries
    In Restoration plays

Dryden, John, and Lee, Nathaniel
  The Duke of Guise
    Restoration historical tragedy in verse.
    In 16th century France, the Duke of
    Guise leads a revolt against King Henry
    III. Includes songs with musical scores.
    5 acts 12 scenes. 20m 4w extras 5 in-
    teriors 1 exterior
    In Lee, N. The works of Nathaniel Lee
      v2
  Oedipus
    Restoration tragedy in verse. Based on
    the Greek legend of Oedipus, King of
    Thebes, who was doomed by fate to
    marry his own mother. 5 acts 12m 3w
    extras 1 interior 2 exteriors
    In Lee, N. The works of Nathaniel Lee
      v 1

Dublin
  Barkentin, M. James Joyce's Ulysses in
    nighttown

Du Bois, Graham
  His hand and pen
    In 1861 the Bartons buy a desk from
    Abraham Lincoln's family. Only Mrs
    Barton knows of secret drawer which
    contains some of Lincoln's letters. 1 act
    4w 1 interior
    In Kamerman, S. E. ed. Blue-ribbon
      plays for girls
  Huckleberry Finn
    Radio adaptation of first part of novel
    by Mark Twain. Kidnapped from Widow
    Douglas by his mean father, the boy
    Huck Finn escapes and then helps Jim,
    a runaway slave, escape on a raft down
    Mississippi River. Background music.
    4m 1w
    In Burack, A. S. ed. Four-star radio
      plays for teen-agers

Duchess of Dogwood Lane. Elam, R. C.

The **Duchess** of Malfi. Webster, J.

The **Duchess** of Malfy. Webster, J.

The **Duchess** of Padua. Wilde, O.

Duckbills
c Spamer, C. The mystery

Dude ranches
  Bolton, G. and McGowan, J. Girl crazy
  Gordon, K. That's my cousin

Duel of angels. Giraudoux, J.

Dueling
  Boyd, A. K. Clive's fear, unique
  Boyd, A. K. Fighting Bob
  Kimes, B. The duelling Oakes

The **duelling** Oakes. Kimes, B.

The **Duenna.** Sheridan, R. B.

Duerrenmatt, Frederick
  Traps (dramatization) See Yaffe, J. The
    deadly game
  The visit; adapted by Maurice Valency.
    French 1958 108p illus
    Wealthy woman returning to native vil-
    lage announces she will give a large sum
    of money if one man, who once loved
    and then rejected her, is murdered. 3 acts
    Large mixed cast 3 interiors
    Trade edition published by Random
    House
  The visit (condensation)
    In The Best plays of 1957-1958
    In Broadway's best, 1958

Duet with dowagers. Tydeman, R.

Duff, Annis
A play for Christmas Eve
Christmas Nativity play in verse with background choir music. The shepherds and the Wise Men bring gifts to the Christ Child. 2 scenes 7m 1w 1b extras 1 setting
In Horn Book Magazine. Four Christmas plays

Duffield, Brainerd
Christmas at Lourdes. Dramatic n.d. 26p
Based on novel: The song of Bernadette, by Franz Werfel which tells of the appearance of the Virgin Mary to Saint Bernadette at Lourdes in France. 1 act 4m 7w 1 interior

December bride; adapted from the television series created by Parke Levy. Dramatic 1956 94p
Domestic comedy. Lily, a widow, marries an old beau and has mother-in-law problem. 3 acts 6 scenes 4m 5w 1 interior

The war of the worlds. Dramatic 1955 79p
Science fiction. Based on novel by H. G. Wells, which treats of possible invasion from Mars. 2 acts 12m 8w extras 1 setting

Duggar, Frances
c December's gifts
Mother Nature distributes gifts to each month with December receiving something special. Christmas. 1 act 14g extras 1 exterior
In Kamerman, S. E. ed. Blue-ribbon plays for girls

The **Duke** of Guise. Dryden, J. and Lee, N.

Dumas, Alexandre
Camille; English version by Edith Reynolds and Nigel Playfair
The erring woman and her relation to society: a beautiful courtesan is capable of an unselfish love. Set in France, 1848. 5 acts 11m 7w 4 interiors
In Stanton, S. S. ed. Camille, and other plays

c The Count of Monte Cristo (dramatization) See Howard, V. The treasure of Monte Cristo

The Count of Monte Cristo (radio adaptation) See Olfson, L. The Count of Monte Cristo

The **dumb** waiter. Pinter, H.

Du Maurier, Daphne
Rebecca (moving picture adaptation) See Sherwood, R. E. and Harrison, J. Rebecca

Dunbar, T. M.
c Girls are so useless! Paxton 1954 9p
On Christmas Eve an 8 year-old girl captures burglar posing as Father Christmas. 1 act 5m 1g 1 interior

c The Piped Piper of Hamlin. Paxton 1953 12p
Verse play. Dramatization of poem by Robert Browning which in turn was based on old German legend. 2 scenes 7m 2w 1b extras 1 interior

Duncan, Ronald
The death of Satan. Faber 1955 110p
Comedy. Witty fantasy set in hell. Satan discovers that modern man no longer suffers because he no longer has any ideals. Verse play. 2 acts 6 scenes 9m 5w 3 interiors 1 exterior

Duncannon, Frederick Edward Neuflize Ponsonby, viscount
Like stars appearing. Heinemann 1953 97p music
Conflict between church and state in England during thirteenth century in which Henry III, builder of Westminster Abbey and Richard, Bishop of Chichester are protagonists. 2 acts 10 scenes 14m 3w 1b extras 6 interiors 1 exterior

Dunlap, William
André
Revolutionary war tragedy. Several people plead for life of the captured spy, Major André, during Revolutionary War. Verse play. 5 acts 16 scenes 9m 2w 1b 1g extras 3 interiors 3 exteriors
In Quinn, A. H. ed. Representative American plays

Dunlop, Richard S.
Four bells means glory! French 1960 30p illus
Farce. Young fireman is going to be dropped from the force because his station hasn't been called in seven years. 1 act 5m 2w 1 interior

An overpraised season. French 1960 29p
Dramatization of problems confronting three adolescents. 1 act 3m 3w 1 interior

Dunsany, Edward John Moreton Drax Plunkett, 18th baron. See Dunsany, Lord

Dunsany, Lord
The jest of Hahalaba
Hoping to become wealthy through advance information conjured up by genie, a man reads of his own death. 1 act 4m 1 interior
In Cerf, B. and Cartmell, V. H. eds. 24 favorite one-act plays

Dunstan, Saint, Abp. of Canterbury
Arblay, Madame d'. Edwy and Elgiva

Du Rels, Adolfo Costa. See Costa du Rels, Adolfo

Du Rels, Costa. See Costa du Rels, Adolfo

Durrell, Lawrence
Sappho. Dutton [1958] 187p
Events in the life of the Greek poetess Sappho, her lovers, her poetry and her part in the imperialistic wars of the Greek islands. Verse play. 9 scenes 10m 8w extras 3 interiors 2 exteriors

Dürrenmatt, Friedrich. See Duerrenmatt, Frederick

D'Usseau, Arnaud. See Parker, D. jt. auth.
Dutch treat. Lynch, P.

Dutch treat. Van Kampen, B.

Duty
Collins, B. F. Grand jury

Dwarfs
Olfson, L. Infanta

Dwellings
Brydon, M. W. and Ziegler, E. The reluctant ghost

The **Dybbuk.** Ansky, S.

Dyke, Henry Van. See Van Dyke, Henry

E

Each star a state. Woolsey, J. and Sechrist, E. H.

Earhart, Amelia
Spamer, C. Amelia Earhart

Earl Birger of Bjälbo. Strindberg, A.

Early, Lillian Soldan
c Everywhere, Christmas
    Christmas scenes from different homes in different centuries all over the world. Choral music. 8 scenes Large mixed cast choir 6 interiors 2 exteriors
    In Birdsall, R. ed. Creative plays for every school month
Early frost. Parkhirst, D.
Earth
c Spamer, C. Raindrops
Earthenware stoves. See Stoves, Earthenware
East and West
    Spiegelgass, L. A majority of one
Easter
    Agnew, E. J. Beyond Good Friday
c Asbrand, K. Children of the Bible
c Asbrand, K. Crooked dime
c Asbrand, K. The Easter egg's dilemma
    Asbrand, K. The three Marys
    Bailey, H. F. "There was a garden"
    Bangham, M. D. "Come, see the place..."
    Casey, B. M. The flower of hope
    Casey, B. M. Lilies bloom at Easter
    Emurian, E. K. The first breakfast
    Emurian, E. K. The Resurrection
    Fearheiley, D. M. Mourning before morning
    Finian, Brother. The Light of the World
    Getzinger, E. W. Promise of the angels
c Gilbert, J. Community Easter parade
c Hark, M. and McQueen, N. Father's Easter hat
    Ingebretson, A. Sister; Miller, J. Sister, and Roberts, M. Sister. The living Saviour
    Johnston, R. A. The York Resurrection
    Lamphere, E. A. Crosses on the hill
    Lilyers, J. The risen Christ
    McCann, K. Out of despair
    McCarty, R. K. But this I know
    McCourt, G. M. The curse and the crown
c Martens, A. C. Be nice to the Easter bunny
    Martens, A. C. Radiant morning
    Martens, A. C. The three faces of Easter
c Matthews, E. Mr Blanchard—Easter bunny
    Mattson, J. M. I saw the cross
c Miller, H. L. The bashful bunny
c Miller, H. L. Bunnies and bonnets
c Miller, H. L. The rabbits who changed their minds
    Miller, H. L. The vanishing Easter egg
c Newman, D. Bunny of the year
    Nystrom, D. Children's praises
    Posegate, E. D. Read me a story
    Schofield, J. A. and Joudry, R. C. "All hail the power of Jesus' name"
    Schofield, J. A. and Joudry, R. C. "Many infallible proofs"
    Schofield, J. A. and Joudry, R. C. Three Easter playlets for children and young adults
    Schofield, J. A. and Joudry, R. C. "Who is this?"
    Sebby, S. R. Easter fantasia
    Simmons, A. The bruising of Satan
    Smith, W. S. By Christ alone

c Spamer, C. The bunnies' dilemma
c Spamer, C. The chocolate bunny
c Spamer, C. A place for all
    Strindberg, A. Easter
    Tashjian, V. The Easter story
    The three Maries
    Trick, O. B. The divine miracle
    Wilson, R. C. Easter witnesses
c Woolsey, J. and Sechrist, E. H. The donkey's mission
    York, E. B. The kindled flame
    York plays. The Resurrection
Easter. Strindberg, A.
The **Easter** egg's dilemma. Asbrand, K. S.
Easter fantasia. Sebby, S. R.
The **Easter** story. Tashjian, V.
Easter witnesses. Wilson, R. C.
Eastern Empire. See Byzantine Empire
Easton, Carol
    Champagne sec. French 1956 22p illus
    Social comedy. Silver wedding anniversary party is interrupted by appearance of first wife who was reported dead 27 years before. 1 act 2m 2w 1 interior
Easy as pie. Asbrand, K.
Easy money. Poverman, H.
Eaton, Charles Edward
    Sea psalm
    Young girl's sweetheart is drowned at sea and she thinks she hears him calling her. 1m 3w 1 interior
    In Walser, R. ed. North Carolina drama
Eaton, James J. and Juste, Michael
    Atomic journey. Michael Houghton 1954 60p
    Super-Fascist invasion is foiled by the international police as space ship on an interstellar journey is grounded. 3 acts 7 scenes 12m 4w 2 interiors 1 exterior
The **ebony** box. Waugh, J. R.
Eboshi-Ori. Miyamasu
Eccentricities. See Eccentrics and eccentricities
Eccentrics and eccentricities
    Adamov, A. Professor Taranne
    Fields, J. and Chodorov, J. The Ponder heart
    Giraudoux, J. The Madwoman of Chaillot
    Hart, M. and Kaufman, G. S. You can't take it with you
    Howard, V. The mad Doctor Zing
    Jonson, B. Epicœne
    Lawrence, J. and Lee, R. E. Auntie Mame
    LePelley, G. A is for apple
    Reach, J. It walks at midnight
    Saroyan, W. The time of your life
    Teichmann, H. The girls in 509
c Woolsey, J. and Sechrist, E. H. Jerry and the Skweegees
An **echo** of wings. Herman, G.
Economy. See Saving and thrift
Eden
    York plays. The Garden of Eden
The **Edgar** Bergen show. Rose, S.
Edie-across-the-street. Clapp, P.

Edmunds, Murrell
Moon of my delight. Yoseloff 1960 144p
Racial discrimination in the South in which cheap politician's crusade of hatred ends in murder of Negro boy. 3 acts 13m 4w 1 exterior

The **educated** schoolhouse. Brown, F. E.

Education
Aristophanes. The clouds
c Colson, J. G. The green ball
Geiger, M. The university of the United States
Peterson, L. Desert soliloquy
Weiss, M. J. Money talks
Wilson, D. C. That heaven of freedom
See also Coeducation; Education of women; Universities and colleges

Elementary
c Matthews, E. On to seventh grade!

Primary
c Gill, M. L. Treasure hunt

Education of women
Molière, J. B. P. The learned ladies

Education Week. See American Education Week

Educators. See Teachers

Edward II, King of England
Marlowe, C. Edward the Second
Treece, H. Carnival king

Edward III, King of England
Shaw, B. The six of Calais

Edward VI, King of England
Chorpenning, C. B. The prince and the pauper
Newman, D. The prince and the pauper

Edward the Second. Marlowe, C.

The **Edwardians.** Gow R.

Edwards, George Graveley. See Graveley, George

Edwin Booth. Geiger, M.

Edwy, King of England
Arblay, Madame d'. Edwy and Elgiva

Edwy and Elgiva. Arblay, Madame d'

Egad, what a cad! Bell, A.

Egelykke. Munk, K.

The **egghead.** Kazan, M.

Egmont, Lamoral count
Goethe, J. W. von. Egmont

Egmont. Goethe, J. W. von

Egoism
Kerr, J and Brooke, E. King of hearts
Wedekind, F. The tenor
See also Self-interest

Eguchi. Kwanze, K.

Egypt
c Barnes, E. A. and Young, B. M. Sokar and the crocodile
Corneille, P. La mort de Pompée
Fisher, A. and Rabe, O. What happened in Egypt
Shaw, B. Caesar and Cleopatra
Stevenson, B. E. A King in Babylon

Eighteenth summer. Martin, B.

Elam, Rebecca Cole
Duchess of Dogwood Lane
Before her grandchildren can interfere, elderly, impoverished widow makes her own plans for disposing of her big house. 1m 3w 1 interior
In Twelve half-hours with the Winthrop Theater

The **elder** statesman. Eliot, T. S.

Eldridge, Muriel T.
Conference eve. French 1957 16p
Farcical pantomime depicting emergencies encountered before women's club convenes. Verse play. 1 act 6 scenes 1m 7w extras 1 interior

Election Day
Fisher, A. The voice of liberty
c Fisher, A. Voting Day
c Newman, D. Election Day in the U.S.A.
c Porter, H. W. Election Day

Election Day. Porter, H. W.

Election Day in the U.S.A. Newman, D.

Elections
Fisher, A. and Rabe, O. May the best man win
c Miller, H L. Vicky gets the vote
See also Voting

Electra, daughter of Agamemnon
Aeschylus. Choephoroe
Aeschylus. The libation bearers
Euripides. Electra
Euripides. Orestes
Giraudoux, J. Electra
Sartre, J. P. The flies
Sophocles. Electra

Electra. Euripides

Electra. Giraudoux, J.

Electra. Sophocles

Electricity
c Spamer, C. The bell that couldn't ring

Electronic brains. See Electronic calculating-machines

Electronic calculating-machines
Marchant, W. The desk set

Electronic computers. See Electronic calculating-machines

The **elevator.** Howells, W. D.

Elgiva. See Aelfgifu, Wife of Edwy, King of England

Elijah, The prophet
c Spamer, C. M. Elijah, the prophet

Elijah, the prophet. Spamer, C. M.

Eliot, George, pseud.
Silas Marner (radio adaptation) See Olfson, L. Silas Marner

About
Spamer, C. George Eliot

Eliot, T. S.
The confidential clerk. French 1954 106p
Satirical play in verse about British financier who is thwarted in desire to have a son to carry on his business just as he had failed in his youthful ambition to become a potter. 3 acts 4m 3w 2 interiors
Trade edition published by Harcourt
The confidential clerk (condensation)
In The Best plays of 1953-1954
In Theatre, 1954

Eliot, T. S.—*Continued*
The elder statesman. Farrar, Straus 1959
132p
Retired British statesman, who has risen
to a position of honor, is confronted by
two people he had wronged in his youth.
Verse play. 3 acts 5m 3w 1 interior
1 exterior
Murder in the cathedral
Conflict between church and state in 12th
century England culminates in murder of
Thomas à Becket in Canterbury Ca-
thedral. Verse play. 2 parts 4 scenes
13m extras women's speaking chorus
2 interiors
In Dean, L. F. ed. Nine great plays.
1956 edition
In Tucker, S. M. ed. Twenty-five mod-
ern plays
In Warnock, R. Representative modern
plays, British
In Watson, E. B. ed. Contemporary
drama: fifteen plays
Eliot, Thomas Stearns. See Eliot, T. S.
Elisha, the prophet
c Spamer, C. M. Elisha cures Naaman
Elisha and the long knives. Wasserman, D.
and Balch, J.
Elisha cures Naaman. Spamer, C. M.
Elizabeth I, Queen of England
Anderson, M. Elizabeth the Queen
Dowling, J. The young Elizabeth
Letton, J. and Letton, F. The young
Elizabeth
Trease, G. The shadow of Spain
Elizabeth the Queen. Anderson, M.
Elizabeth Zane saves Fort Henry. Woolsey,
J. and Sechrist, E. H.
Elizabethan dialect. See Dialect—English—
Elizabethan
Elizabethan drama. See English drama—
Early modern and Elizabethan
Elizabethan English. See Dialect—English
—Elizabethan
Elman, Irving
The brass ring. Dramatists 1953 73p
American businessman creates dream
world as escape. 2 acts 6m 5w 1 setting
See also Berns, J. jt. auth.
Elves. See Fairies
Elward, James
Paper foxhole
Television comedy. In order to speed up
return home at end of World War II,
American soldiers in non-combat zone
in Pacific stage fake attack by Japanese
guerrillas. 10m
In Writers Guild of America. The prize
plays of television and radio, 1956
Embers. Beckett, S.
Embezzlement
Kaiser, G. From morn to midnight
Ridley, A. You, my guests!
The emerald. Jones, E. M.
Emergencies. See First aid in illness and
injury
Emery, Charles
The ant bed. French 1958 32p illus
Farce. Neglected wife persuades gang-
ster to pretend to be old flame, while
husband persuades gangster's moll to
pose as old girl friend. 1 act 2m 2w
1 interior

A baby for Brenda. French 1960 29p illus
Domestic comedy. Couple pretend they
have a baby in order to receive five
thousand dollars from rich uncle. 1 act
2m 4w 1 interior
The Christmas stranger. French 1955 28p
illus
Because a stranger (Christ) passes their
way, the lives of small New England
family are completely changed on Christmas afternoon. 1 act 1m 3w 1 interior
Dark interlude. Bakers Plays 1958 30p
(Baker's Royalty plays)
Deformed housekeeper of hunchback is
jealous of beautiful girl he loves. 1 act
3m 3w 1 interior
Madame Vulture. French 1960 35p illus
Greedy woman wishes one nephew to remain single, her other to end marriage
so she can control their inheritance.
1 act 2m 3w 1 interior
Portrait of Deborah. French 1959 78p
illus music
Set in New England. Young girl disguises herself as a man and joins the
army during the Revolutionary War.
3 acts 6 scenes 7m 7w extras 4 interiors
A private affair. French 1958 36p illus
Comedy. Confusion reigns in hotel for
problem child, lady psychiatrist, and
innocent man whom she mistakes for
patient. 1 act 3m 4w 1 interior
Tiger Lily. French 1954 35p
Lily and her friend, Quinny, almost suc-
ceed in their plot to kill Derek and his
sister, Nina, in order to collect Derek's
insurance. 1 act 3m 2w 1 interior
Emhammed of the red slippers. Ridge, A.
Emigration and immigration
Fisher, A. and Rabe, O. Immigrants all,
Americans all
Emilia Galotti. Lessing
Emmett, Daniel Decatur
Emurian, E. K. Dixie
Emmons, Della Gould
Answering the call
Marcus Whitman and his wife become
missionaries in the northwest United
States in the 1830's. 3 scenes 13m 4w
extras 2 interiors 1 exterior
In Emmons, D. G. Northwest history
in action
Astor's bid for empire
John Jacob Astor attempts to build his
business in fur trading in the Northwest.
4 scenes 19m extras 2 interiors 2 exteriors
In Emmons, D. G. Northwest history
in action
A costly gold hunt
When settlers searching for gold were
taken prisoner by Indians, the govern-
ment decided to ransom them. 3 scenes
9m 1w extras 1 interior 1 exterior
In Emmons, D. G. Northwest history
in action
John Jewitt, the slave
Young English boy is taken slave by an
Indian chief. 5m 1w
In Emmons, D. G. Northwest history
in action
Joint occupation, joint celebration
Missionaries and settlers gradually
awaken interest of United States government in Northwest Territory. 3 scenes
21m 2w 3b 3 exteriors
In Emmons, D. G. Northwest history
in action

Emmons, Della G.—*Continued*

Ours to the forty-ninth
    Pageant showing highlights in history of northwestern United States. 8 episodes Large mixed cast 5 interiors 3 exteriors
    In Emmons, D. G. Northwest history in action

Out to win
    Highlights of Lewis and Clark exploring expedition. 3 scenes 13m 1w extras 3 exteriors
    In Emmons, D. G. Northwest history in action

Statehood for Washington
    Washington Territory is created the state of Washington. 5 scenes 19m 5w extras 4 interiors 1 exterior
    In Emmons, D. G. Northwest history in action

A territory is born
    Events leading to founding of the Washington Territory in middle 19th century. 4 scenes Large mixed cast 2 interiors 1 exterior
    In Emmons, D. G. Northwest history in action

Through Naches Pass
    19th century settlers in Northwest build a road as link with civilization. 3 scenes 8m 6w 1b extras 1 interior 2 exteriors
    In Emmons, D. G. Northwest history in action

A toehold for the U.S.A.
    After Revolutionary War several American sea captains decide to strike out on trading ventures around the world. 4 scenes 16m 1b extras 1 interior 2 exteriors
    In Emmons, D. G. Northwest history in action

Who's for the Divide?
    Settlers and missionaries in Northwest Territory of United States in the 1830's feel need for some kind of government. 4 scenes 12m 1w extras 1 interior 2 exteriors
    In Emmons, D. G. Northwest history in action

The **Emperor** Jones. O'Neill, E.

Emperors. See Byzantine Emperors; *also* names of individual kings and rulers

The **Emperor's** clothes. Tabori, G.

The **Emperor's** new clothes. Newman, D.

The **Emperor's** nightingale. Windsor, H. J.

Empty bowls. Fisher, A. and Rabe, O.

Emurian, Ernest K.

America the beautiful
    Dramatization of how Katherine Lee Bates wrote the words for the patriotic hymn: America, the Beautiful. 5w chorus 1 interior
    In Emurian, E. K. Plays and pageants for many occasions

Battle hymn of the Republic
    Dramatization of how a song from a Georgia camp meeting became the fighting song for North during the Civil War. 1 act 6m 2w male quartet 2 interiors
    In Emurian, E. K. More Plays and pageants for many occasions

Charles Wesley
    A brief dramatization of life of English clergyman. 1 act 2 scenes 5m 2b extras 1 interior 1 exterior
    In Emurian, E. K. Ten new plays for church and school

Christmas traditions
    On Christmas Eve the Jackson family discusses Christmas traditions and their origins. 1 act 3m 3w 1 interior
    In Emurian, E. K. Plays and pageants for many occasions

The church in the wildwood
    How William Savage Pitts came to write words and music for hymn: The little brown church in the vale. 3 scenes 8m 3w extras 2 exteriors
    In Emurian, E. K. More Plays and pageants for many occasions

Columbia, the gem of the ocean
    Dramatization of how Thomas à Becket wrote the song: Columbia, the gem of the ocean. 5m 2w 1 interior
    In Emurian, E. K. Plays and pageants for many occasions

Dixie
    Dramatization of how Daniel Emmett wrote the famous song. 4m 1w 1 interior
    In Emurian, E. K. Plays and pageants for many occasions

Famous families
    Scenes of family life from the lives of the patriarch Jacob, Saint Joseph, Martin Luther and Samuel Wesley. 1 act 4 scenes 15m 5w 4b 3g 4 interiors
    In Emurian, E. K. Ten new plays for church and school

Famous fathers
    Famous fathers of history are pictured in their homes, as is a typical father of today. 4 scenes 18m 1w extras 3 interiors 1 exterior
    In Emurian, E. K. More Plays and pageants for many occasions

The first breakfast
    Dramatizes events leading up to and including Lord's first breakfast with disciples after His Resurrection. 1 act 8m 1 interior
    In Emurian, E. K. Ten new plays for church and school

God of our fathers
    How Reverend Daniel Crane Roberts wrote the words to the well-known hymn. 12m 2w extras 1 interior
    In Emurian, E. K. More Plays and pageants for many occasions

Great women of history
    A Mother's Day pageant portraying six women. With chorus and appropriate songs. 6 scenes 5m 6w extras 1 setting
    In Emurian, E. K. Plays and pageants for many occasions

Home sweet home
    How John Howard Payne wrote famous song. 2 acts 4 scenes 19m 4w 1 interior 3 exteriors
    In Emurian, E. K. More Plays and pageants for many occasions

I pledge allegiance
    Depicts creation of American flag, Francis Bellamy's writing of the pledge of allegiance to the flag, and the origin of Christian flag. 3 acts 4 scenes 14m 2w extras 4 interiors
    In Emurian, E. K. Plays and pageants for many occasions

I'll take you home again, Kathleen
    Grieving over the tragic death of his wife a man writes the words and music of song. 1 act 5m 1w male quartet 1 exterior
    In Emurian, E. K. Ten new plays for church and school

Emurian, Ernest K.—*Continued*

Inasmuch
Old man is visited by several strangers at Christmas. Illustrates the Biblical theme "Unto the least of these" found in the Gospel of Matthew. 1 act 5m 1w 4b 3g 1 interior

In Emurian, E. K. Ten new plays for church and school

It is well with my soul
Scenes from the lives of Horatio G. Spafford and Philip Paul Bliss who wrote the words and music for many hymns in the nineteenth century. 1 act 6m 1b 2 interiors

In Emurian, E. K. Ten new plays for church and school

The Last Supper
Pageant of Leonardo da Vinci's painting of The Last Supper in which each apostle gives his name and tells his relationship to Jesus. 1 tableau 16m 1 interior

In Emurian, E. K. More Plays and pageants for many occasions

The living dramatization of the Beatitudes
Each of the twelve apostles explains one of the Beatitudes. 1 act 13m extras 1 exterior

In Emurian, E. K. Ten new plays for church and school

The new colossus
How Emma Lazzarus, American Jewish poetess, came to write her poem in honor of the Statue of Liberty. 4m 5w extras 1 interior

In Emurian, E. K. More Plays and pageants for many occasions

The radiance streaming
Shows closeness and fellowship prevailing as men, women and children of church participate in its various activities. 4 scenes 8m 9w extras 3 interiors 1 exterior

In Emurian, E. K. More Plays and pageants for many occasions

The Resurrection
Pageant with Easter hymns and New Testament text. 15m 3w choir 1 exterior

In Emurian, E. K. Plays and pageants for many occasions

Silver threads among the gold
How Hart Pease Danks came to write the music for well-known song. 4m 1w 1 interior

In Emurian, E. K. More Plays and pageants for many occasions

The Star Spangled Banner
How the words and music to the Star Spangled Banner came to be written. 2 scenes 17m extras 1 interior 1 exterior

In Emurian, E. K. More Plays and pageants for many occasions

Stewards of the soil
How farmers throughout the ages have praised God for harvests they have reaped. 1 act 4 scenes 7m 1w extras 2 interiors 1 exterior

In Emurian, E. K. Ten new plays for church and school

Thanksgiving through the ages
Spirit of Thanksgiving is portrayed among different people since Biblical times. 4 scenes 10m 4w 1b extras 3 interiors

In Emurian, E. K. Plays and pageants for many occasions

Three skits for Christmas
Origin of two Christmas songs and a Christmas flower, the poinsettia. 1 act 3 scenes 8m 2w extras 2 interiors 1 exterior

In Emurian, E. K. Ten new plays for church and school

'Twas the night before Christmas
Dramatizes the true story of the writing of the memorable poem. 1 act 7m 1w 1b 2g extras 1 interior

In Emurian, E. K. Plays and pageants for many occasions

Uncle Sam
High school students present play depicting origin of the term Uncle Sam. 1 act 15m 2w extras 1 interior

In Emurian, E. K. Ten new plays for church and school

Yankee Doodle
Various theories as to origin of American song Yankee Doodle, sung during the French and Indian War in 1755. 7m extras 1 exterior

In Emurian, E. K. More plays and pageants for many occasions

En route to the UN. Fisher, D.

Enami, Sayemon

The bird-catcher in hades (Esashi Jûwô)
Farce used as an interlude in a Japanese Nō drama. Satire on Nō plays dealing with heaven and hell. The king of Hades finds roast bird so delicious that he permits the bird-catcher to return to life. Verse play. 2m extras 1 setting
Same as: The bird-catcher in hell

In Sakanishi, S. tr. Japanese folk-plays

The bird-catcher in hell (Esashi Jūō)
Same as: The bird-catcher in hades

In Waley, A. The Nō plays of Japan

Ukai (The cormorant-fisher)
Japanese Nō verse drama. Because he once befriended a priest, the soul of cormorant fisher is sent to Place of Buddha instead of Deepest Pit. 4m extras 1 exterior

In Waley, A. The Nō plays of Japan

The enchanted. Giraudoux, J.

The enchanted pumpkin. Fowler, M. G.

End of summer. Behrman, S. N.

The end of the beginning. O'Casey, S.

The end of the line. Murray, J.

End of the rainbow. Stoler, S. A.

End of the world
Purkey, R. A. Hangs over thy head

Endgame. Beckett, S.

An enemy of the people. Ibsen, H.

Engagement. See Betrothal

England. See Great Britain

Engle, John D.

The charm, by John D. Engle, Jr. Eldridge 1958 22p (Eldridge Popular one-act playscripts)
Eastern Kentucky folk-tale. Blacksmith's daughter in love with son of woman believed to be a witch. 1 act 3m 3w 1 interior

English drama

Medieval

Abraham and Isaac (Brome manuscript)
Abraham and Isaac

Abraham and Isaac (Brome manuscript)
The sacrifice of Isaac

Chester plays. Noah's flood

English drama—Restoration—*Continued*
Dryden, J. All for love
Dryden, J. and Lee, N. The Duke of Guise
Dryden, J. and Lee, N. Oedipus
Etherege, Sir G. The man of mode
Farquhar, G. The beaux' stratagem
Farquhar, G. The constant couple
Farquhar, G The recruiting officer
Farquhar, G. The twin-rivals
Lee, N. Caesar Borgia
Lee, N. Constantine the Great
Lee, N. Gloriana
Lee, N. Lucius Junius Brutus
Lee, N. The massacre of Paris
Lee, N. Mithridates, King of Pontus
Lee, N. The Princess of Cleve
Lee, N. The rival queens
Lee, N. Sophonisba
Lee, N. Theodosius
Lee, N. The tragedy of Nero, Emperour of Rome
Lee, N. The works of Nathaniel Lee (13 plays)
Otway, T. Venice preserved
Restoration plays (8 plays)
Vanbrugh, Sir J. The confederacy
Vanbrugh, Sir J. The relapse
Villiers, G. and others. The rehearsal
Wycherley, W. The country wife

18th century
Goldsmith, O. The good natur'd man
Goldsmith, O. She stoops to conquer
Murphy, A. The apprentice
Murphy, A. Know your own mind
Murphy, A. The old maid
Murphy, A. Three weeks after marriage
Murphy, A. The upholsterer
Murphy, A. The way to keep him
Murphy, A. The way to keep him & five other plays (6 plays)
Sheridan, R. B. The critic
Sheridan, R. B. The Duenna
Sheridan, R. B. The rivals
Sheridan, R. B. St Patrick's Day
Sheridan, R. B. The school for scandal
Sheridan, R. B. Six plays
Sheridan, R. B. A trip to Scarborough
English folk-lore. See Folk-lore, English
English in Tahiti. See British in Tahiti
English language

Orthography and spelling
c Curtis, P. D. The angry alphabet
Enlistment. See Recruiting and enlistment
Entail. See Land tenure
Enter George Washington. Hark, M. and McQueen, N.
The **entertainer.** Osborne, J.
Entertainers
Magnau, K. Goodbye, Texas—Broadway, hello!
Osborne, J. The entertainer
See also Magicians
Entertaining
Gross, E. and Gross, N. A party is born
Mosel, T. The lawn party

Ephron, Phoebe
"Howie." [Rev. acting ed] French 1959 96p illus
   Domestic comedy. Obnoxious son-in-law who can't hold a job gets on a quiz show where amazing things happen. 3 acts 5 scenes 10m 6w 2 interiors
Epicœne. Jonson, B.
Epitaph for George Dillon. Osborne, J. and Creighton, A.
Equal protection of the law. See Equality before the law
Equality before the law

United States
Wishengrad, M. The ground of justice
Erhard, Tom
The high white star. Eldridge 1958 72p (Eldridge 3-act play-scripts)
   Comedy. School life. Effects on various students when English teacher catches them cheating on test. 3 acts 4m 9w 2 interiors
The **ermine.** Anouilh, J.
Ernie Barger is fifty. Mosel, T.
Ervine, St John
John Ferguson
   Tragedy. Irish farmer sustained by faith when son kills man who wronged his daughter. 4 acts 9m 2w 1 interior
   In Tucker, S. M. ed. Twenty-five modern plays
Escape. Galsworthy, J.
Escape to fear. Bate, S.
Escapes
Daviot, G. The pen of my aunt
DuBois, G. Huckleberry Finn
Galsworthy, J. Escape
McConnell, J. The red cloak
Olfson, L. The Count of Monte Cristo
   See also Prisoners
Especially mother. Royle, S. and Renavent, G.
Espionage. See Spies
Essex, Robert Devereux, earl of
Anderson, M. Elizabeth the Queen
Estes, Susan
In quest of power through courage
   Dramatization from New Testament of the martyrdom of Saint Stephen. 4m extras no scenery
   In Estes, S. In quest of power
In quest of power through decision
   The Old Testament story of how Joshua and his people made decision to worship the God of Israel. Musical solo. Speech choir. 4m extras no scenery
   In Estes, S. In quest of power
In quest of power through dedication
   Old Testament story of the dedication of Samuel in the temple. 2m 2w 1b extras no scenery
   In Estes, S. In quest of power
In quest of power through divine guidance
   Old Testament story of how Rebekah becomes Isaac's wife. Musical solo. 6m 2w extras no scenery
   In Estes, S. In quest of power
In quest of power through faith
   Several Old Testament characters illustrate the power of faith. Musical solo. 10m extras no scenery
   In Estes, S. In quest of power

Estes, Susan—*Continued*

In quest of power through humility
Bible. New Testament. Gospels. Birth and mission of Saint John the Baptist. Background music. 5m 1w extras no scenery
In Estes, S. In quest of power

In quest of power through obedience
A short dramatization of Old Testament story of Ruth. Speech choir and musical solo. 1m 3w extras no scenery
In Estes, S. In quest of power

In quest of power through prayer
Three Biblical characters illustrate the power of prayer. Speech choir. Background music. 4m 2w extras no scenery
In Estes, S. In quest of power

In quest of power through prophecy
How the Old Testament prophecy of Isaiah concerning the birth of Christ was fulfilled in the New Testament account of the Gospel of Luke. 5m 3w no scenery
In Estes, S. In quest of power

In quest of power through the Holy Spirit
How Simon Peter and his followers experience the power of the Holy Spirit. 6m extras no scenery
In Estes, S. In quest of power

In quest of power through wisdom
The wisdom of Solomon becomes applicable to a modern day family. 6m 3w 1 interior
In Estes, S. In quest of power

In quest of power through witnessing
St Paul the apostle witnesses for Christ at court of King Agrippa. Musical solo. 5m 1w extras no scenery
In Estes, S. In quest of power

Esther, Queen of Persia
Asbrand, K. The beautiful queen

Esther, Feast of. See Purim (Feast of Esther)

Estrada, Doris
Three on a bench. Row 1953 30p illus
Romantic comedy. In pursuing her favorite role as cupid, middle-aged widow finds new romance herself. 1 act 2m 2w 1 exterior
—Same
In Powers, V. E. ed. Plays for players, and a guide to play production

Ethan Frome. Davis, O. and Davis, D.

Etherege, Sir George
The man of mode; or, Sir Fopling Flutter
Plotless comedy of manners of London society's love affairs introducing Sir Fopling Flutter, the epitome of foppery. Singing, music and dancing. 5 acts 11 scenes 7m 8w extras 5 interiors 1 exterior
In Kronenberger, L. ed. Cavalcade of comedy
In Restoration plays

Ethics
Augier, E. Olympe's marriage
Galsworthy, J. Escape
Gethers, S. Cracker money
Getzinger, E. W. Let your light so shine
Howard, P. The dictator's slippers
Howard, P. We are tomorrow
Millar, R. Waiting for Gillian
Pagnol. Topaze

Pathelin. The farce of Master Pierre Pathelin
Rice, E. The winner
See also Communist ethics; Friendship; Guilt; Honor; Journalistic ethics; Medical ethics; Political ethics

Ethics, Communist. See Communist ethics

Ethics, Journalistic. See Journalistic ethics

Ethics, Medical. See Medical ethics

Ethics, Political. See Political ethics

Ethics, Practical. See Conduct of life

Etiquette
c Spamer, C. Tea party
See also Courtesy; Dating (Social customs)

Ettlinger, Don
The thousand-yard look
Documentary television play based on dispatches of correspondent Hal Boyle about a group of American soldiers in the Korean War. 10m extras
In Roberts, E. B. Televison writing and selling

Eumenides. See Furies

The **Eumenides.** Aeschylus

Euripides
Alcestis; tr. by Richard Aldington
Greek classical drama. Based on legend of Alcestis who pledged herself to die in place of her husband. Verse play. 6m 2w 1b extras 1 exterior
In Lind, L. R. ed. Ten Greek plays in contemporary translations
—Same; tr. by Dudley Fitts and Robert Fitzgerald
In Fitts, D. ed. Four Greek plays
—Same; tr. by Richmond Lattimore
In Grene, D. and Lattimore, R. eds. The complete Greek tragedies v3
In Grene, D. and Lattimore, R. eds. Greek tragedies v3
—Same; tr. by A. S. Way
In Euripides. Plays v 1
Andromache; tr. by Van L. Johnson
Greek classical tragedy. Legend relating how Andromachê and her son were saved from a death plot instigated by Hermione and Menelaus. 4m 5w 1b extras 1 exterior
In Fitts, D. ed. Six Greek plays in modern translation
—Same; tr. by L. R. Lind
In Lind, L. R. ed. Ten Greek plays in contemporary translations
—Same; tr. and with an introduction by John Frederick Nims
In Grene, D. and Lattimore, R. eds. The complete Greek tragedies v3
—Same; tr. by A. S. Way
In Euripides. Plays v 1
Andromache (adaptation) See Racine, J. Andromache
The Bacchae; tr. by William Arrowsmith
Greek classical tragedy. Punishment of Pentheus, King of Thebes, by Dionysus, god of wine for refusing to permit Bacchanalian revels in Thebes. Verse play. 1 act 7m 1w extras 1 exterior
In Grene, D. and **Lattimore, R. eds.** The complete Greek tragedies v4
In Grene, D. and Lattimore, R. eds. Greek tragedies v3

Euripides—*Continued*

—Same; tr. by Henry Birkhead

In Lind, L. R. ed. Ten Greek plays in contemporary translations

—Same; tr. by F. L. Lucas

In Lucas, F. L. ed. Greek drama for everyman

—Same; tr. by Henry Hart Milman

In Robinson, C. A. ed. Anthology of Greek drama. 2d ser.

—Same; tr. by Philip Vellacott

In Euripides. The Bacchae, and other plays

The Bacchanals; tr. by A. S. Way
 Same as: The Bacchae

In Euripides. Plays v2

The children of Herakles; tr. by A. S. Way
 Greek classical tragedy. Legendary account of the war resulting from the refusal of Demophon, King of Athens to surrender the children of Herakles to their enemy, Eursytheus, King of Argos. Verse play. 1 act 7m 2w extras 1 exterior
 Same as: The Heracleidae

In Euripides. Plays v 1

The Cylops
 Greek satyr play. Based on Homer's story of Odysseus' escape from the cave of the Cyclops, Polyphemus. Verse play. 4m extras 1 exterior

In Eleven plays of the Greek dramatists

—Same; tr. and with an introduction by William Arrowsmith

In Greene, D. and Lattimore, R. eds. The complete Greek tragedies v3

—Same; tr. by Percy Bysshe Shelley

In Euripides. Plays v2

The daughters of Troy; tr. by A. S. Way
 Greek classical tragedy. Fate of the women of Troy after city was captured by Greeks in Trojan War. Verse play. 3m 5w extras 1 exterior
 Same as: The women of Troy

In Euripides. Plays v 1

Electra; tr. and with an introduction by Emily Townsend Vermeule
 Greek classical tragedy. Based on the legend of Orestes and Electra, son and daughter of Agamemnon, telling how they avenged their father's murder. Verse play. 7m 2w extras 1 exterior

In Grene, D. and Lattimore, R. eds. The complete Greek tragedies v4

—Same; tr. by A. S. Way

In Euripides. Plays v 1

Hecuba; tr. and with an introduction by William Arrowsmith
 Greek classical tragedy. Based on legend relating how Hecuba, wife of Priam, King of Troy, avenged murder of their son by Polymestor, King of Thrace. Verse play. 5m 3w extras 1 exterior

In Grene, D. and Lattimore, R. eds. The complete Greek tragedies v3

—Same; tr. by A. S. Way

In Euripides. Plays v 1

Helen; tr. and with an introduction by Richmond Lattimore
 Greek classical melodrama in verse. Based on legend that only the wraith of Helen of Troy had caused Trojan War, Helen herself being in Egypt. Verse play. 7m 3w extras 1 exterior

In Grene, D. and Lattimore, R. eds. The complete Greek tragedies v3

—Same; tr. by Philip Vellacott

In Euripides. The Bacchae, and other plays

—Same; tr. by A. S. Way

In Euripides. Plays v2

The Heracleidae; tr. and with an introduction by Ralph Gladstone
 Same as: The children of Herakles

In Grene, D. and Lattimore, R. eds. The complete Greek tragedies v3

Heracles; tr. and with an introduction by William Arrowsmith
 Greek classical tragedy. Based on legend about Herakles who, in a fit of temporary insanity, kills his wife and children whom he has come to save from the tyrant Lycus. Verse play. 6m 2w extras 1 exterior
 Same as: The madness of Herakles

In Grene, D. and Lattimore, R. eds. The complete Greek drama v3

Hippolytus; tr. and with an introduction by David Grene
 Greek classical tragedy. Based on legend telling how Aphrodite, angry at Hippolytus for worshipping Artemis, plotted the youth's destruction. Verse play. 4m 4w extras 1 exterior

In Grene, D. and Lattimore, R. eds. The complete Greek tragedies v3

In Grene, D. and Lattimore, R. eds. Greek tragedies v 1

—Same; tr. by F. L. Lucas

In Lucas, F. L. ed. Greek drama for everyman

—Same; tr. by A. S. Way

In Euripides. Plays v2

Hippolytus (adaptation) See Jeffers, R. Cretan woman

Ion; tr. by Philip Vellacott
 Greek classical tragedy in verse. Legend of origin of Ionian division of Greek people through Ion, mortal son of the god Apollo. 5m 3w extras 1 exterior

In Euripides. The Bacchae, and other plays

—Same; tr. by A. S. Way

In Euripides. Plays v 1

—Same; tr. and with an introduction by Ronald Frederick Willetts

In Grene, D. and Lattimore, R. eds. The complete Greek tragedies v4

Iphigeneia at Aulis; tr. by A. S. Way
 Greek classical tragedy. Based on legend of sacrifice of Iphigenia, daughter of Agamemnon, to help Greek cause in Trojan War. Verse play. 1 act 5m 2w extras 1 exterior
 Same as: Iphigenia in Aulis

In Euripides. Plays v2

Iphigenia in Aulis; tr. and with an introduction by Charles R. Walker
 Same as: Iphigeneia at Aulis

In Grene, D. and Lattimore, R. eds. The complete Greek tragedies v4

Iphigeneia in Taurica; tr. by A. S. Way
 Greek classical tragedy. Legend relating how Iphigenia, while serving as priestess of Artemis plots to save her brother, Orestes, from being sacrificed to the goddess. Verse play. 5m 2w extras 1 exterior
 Same as: Iphigenia in Taurus

In Euripides. Plays v2

Euripides—*Continued*
Iphigenia in Tauris
Same as: Iphigeneia in Taurica
In Eleven plays of the Greek dramatists
—Same; tr. by Witter Bynner
In Grene, D. and Lattimore, R. eds.
The complete Greek tragedies v3
In Grene, D. and Lattimore, R. eds.
Greek tragedies v2
The madness of Herakles; tr. by A. S.
Way
Same as: Heracles
In Euripides. Plays v2
The Medea; tr. and with an introduction
by Rex Warner
Greek classical tragedy. Based on legend
of Medea's revenge against husband
Jason for deserting her. Verse play.
5m 2w 2b extras 1 exterior
In Grene, D. and Lattimore, R. eds.
The complete Greek tragedies v3
—Same; tr. by A. S. Way
In Euripides. Plays v 1
Orestes; tr. and with an introduction by
William Arrowsmith
Greek classical tragedy. Based on legend
about Apollo's intervention to save
Orestes and Electra after they had been
condemned to death for revenge slaying
of their mother. Verse play 7m 3w ex-
tras 1 setting
In Grene, D. and Lattimore, R. eds.
The complete Greek tragedies v4
—Same; tr. by A. S. Way
In Euripides. Plays v2
The Phoenician maidens; tr. by A. S.
Way
Greek classical tragedy. Eteokles and
Polyneikes, sons of Oedipus, King of
Thebes, kill each other in battle for
Theban sovereignty. Verse play. 8m 2w
extras 1 setting
Same as: The Phoenician women
In Euripides. Plays v2
The Phoenician women; tr. and with an
introduction by Elizabeth Wyckoff
Same as: The Phoenician maidens
In Grene, D. and Lattimore, R. eds.
The complete Greek tragedies v4
Rhesus; tr. and with an introduction by
Richmond Lattimore
Greek classical tragedy. Based on legend
of Trojan War, concerning the slaying,
by Greek spies, of Rhesus, King of
Thrace and an ally of the Trojans. Verse
play. 9m 2w extras 1 exterior
In Grene, D. and Lattimore, R. eds.
The complete Greek tragedies v4
—Same; tr. by A. S. Way
In Euripides. Plays v2
The suppliant women; tr. and with an in-
troduction by Frank William Jones
Greek classical tragedy. Based on legend
of Argive women who invoked aid of the
gods in recovering from the Thebans
bodies of the Argive warriors slain in
battle against Thebes. Verse play. 5m
3w 7b extras 1 exterior
Same as: Suppliants
In Grene, D. and Lattimore, R. eds.
The complete Greek tragedies v4
Suppliants; tr. by L. R. Lind
Same as: The suppliant women
In Lind, L. R. ed. Ten Greek plays in
contemporary translations
—Same; tr. by A. S. Way
In Euripides. Plays v 1

The Trojan women; tr. and with an in-
troduction by Richmond Lattimore
Greek classical tragedy. Portrays de-
struction of Troy and enslavement of
Trojan women immediately after the fall
of Troy. Anti-militaristic in tone. Verse
play. 1 act 4m 5w extras 1 exterior
In Grene, D. and Lattimore, R. eds.
The complete Greek tragedies v3
In Grene, D. and Lattimore, R. eds.
Greek tragedies v2
—Same; tr. by Isabelle K. and Antony E.
Raubitschek with the assistance of
Anne L. McCabe
In Robinson, C. A. ed. Anthology of
Greek drama
—Same; tr. by Philip Vellacott
In Euripides. The Bacchae and other
plays
See also Aristophanes. Ladies' day

About
Aristophanes. The frogs
European War, 1914-1918
O'Casey, S. The Silver Tassie
Sherriff, R. C. Journey's end
Stallings, L. and Anderson, M. What
price glory?

Great Britain
Bucci, M The old lady shows her medals
Naval operations
O'Neill E. In the zone
Eurydice, wife of Orpheus
Anouilh, J. Eurydice
Eurydice. Anouilh, J.
Euthanasia. See Aged, Killing of
Eva. Dimondstein, B.
Evans, Eric Jones- See Jones-Evans, Eric
Evening dress. Howells, W. D.
Every man in his humour. Jonson, B.
Everyman
Everyman
15th century morality play. Allegory of
death. Verse play in Middle English
with modernized spelling. 15m 2w extras
1 setting
Same as: The moral play of Everyman;
The summoning of Everyman
In Browne, E. M. ed. Religious drama, 2
In Griffin, A. V. Living theatre
Everyman (adaptation) See Sorell, W.
Everyman today
The moral play of Everyman
Same as: Everyman; The summoning of
Everyman
In Everyman, and medieval miracle
plays
The summoning of Everyman
Same as: Everyman; The moral play of
Everyman
In Allen, J. P. ed. Three medieval plays
v2
Everyman. Johnston, R. A.
Everyman today. Sorell, W.
Everywhere, Christmas. Early, L. S.
Everywhere Christmas. Very, A.
Evil. See Good and evil
Evil spirits. See Demonology

Evolution
Lawrence, J. and Lee, R. E. Inherit the wind
Examinations
Ashermann, O. Shakespeare
Erhard, T. The high white star
Exceptional children
Gurney, A. R. Three people
See also Gifted children
Exclusive model. McQuade, W.
Excuse for living. Casey, B. M.
Exorcism
Ansky, S. The Dybbuk
Carney, F. The righteous are bold
Komparu, Z. U. Awoi no uye
Expectant relations. Foote, H.
The experiment of a free press. Probst, G.
The experts. Curtis, P. D.
Explosions
Parker, K. T. Voice of the machines
Express for Santiago. Aguirre, I.
Expressionism
Kaiser, G. The coral
Kaiser, G. Gas (I)
Kaiser, G. Gas—Part II
Extermination of pests. See Pests—Extermination
Extortion
Hamilton, P. The man upstairs
Watkyn, A. Not in the book
Eye
Surgery
Scriven, R. C. A single taper
Eyes that see not. Allan, D. C.
Eyre, Simon
Dekker, T. The shoemakers' holiday

F

Fabbri, Diego
Processeo a Gesu (adaptation) See LeRoy, W. Between two thieves
Fables
c Carpenter, F. A day of good deeds
c Carpenter, F. Doctor Fox
c Carpenter, F. The magic owl
c Carpenter, F. The sick fox
c Carpenter, F. The tale of good faith
c Carpenter, F. Tiger in the wood
c Moore, S. S. The fox and the grapes
c Moore, S. S. The hare and the tortoise
c Moore, S. S. The lion and the mouse
c Moore, S. S. The miller, his son, and their ass
c Moore, S. S. The shepherd-boy and the wolf
c Moore, S. S. Six playlets from Aesop's Fables (6 plays)
c Moore, S. S. The travellers and the bear
See also Allegories; Folk-lore; Parables
A fabulous tale. Stockton, R. F.
A face in the crowd. Schulberg, B.
The face is familiar. Dias, E. J.

The facts of life. MacDougall, R.
Fair deals. Curtis, P. D.
Fair game. Locke, S.
Fairchild, William
The sound of murder
Murder mystery. A woman and her lover plan to murder husband but latter's secretary records their conversation on tape recorder. 3 acts 6 scenes 4m 2w 1 interior
In Plays of the year v20
Fairies
c Blossom, L. The safety elves
c Blyton, E. Mr Sly-One and the cats
Blyton, E. Who will hold the giant?
Chadwick, E. Shoes for a queen
Fisher, A. The Merry Christmas elf
c Jones, B. M. The magic spinning-wheel
c Marston, M. A. Goblin market
c Mattice, I. A bomb for Santa
Olfson, L. A midsummer night's dream
c Peterson, M. N. Ten helpful elves
Purkey, R. A. The leprechaun
Ratcliffe, D. U. Jingling Lane
c Spamer, C. The adventurous balloon
c Spamer, C. The clumsy fairy
c Spamer, C. The hatless snowmen
c Spamer, C. The May fairies
c Spamer, C. The parasols
c Very, A. The fairy circus
Wilde, P. Salt for savor
Fairs
Jonson, B. Bartholomew Fair
See also Danbury, Connecticut—Fair
The fairy circus. Very, A.
Fairy tales
c Barnes, E. A. and Young, B. M. The magic fishbone
c Bennett, R. Puss in Boots
c Black, F. The heartless princess
c Blyton, E. Mr Sly-One and the cats
c Blyton, E. Who will hold the giant?
c Boegehold, B. The shoemaker's Christmas
c Bradbury, A. J. The King's anniversary
Chadwick, E. Shoes for a queen
Chorpenning, C. B. Rama and the tigers
Clinton-Baddeley, V. C. Jack and the beanstalk
c Close, E. Germs versus Fairy Good-Health
c Cullen, A. Niccolo and Nicollette
Daviot, G. The princess who liked cherry pie
c Diffin, L. T. The court of hearts
Dillon, F. The tinder box
c Douglas, L. Crispin the tailor
c Fisher, A. Hearts, tarts, and valentines
c Floyd, B. Once upon a time
c Fluckey, J. O. The heart of the forest
Giraudoux, J. Ondine
c Goulding, D. J. The master cat
c Harding, M. The Sea King's daughter
c Harris, A. The plain Princess
c Hollinshead, L. M. In honour bound
c Holloway, Sister M. M. The last of the leprechauns
c Hopper, V. S. Along came a blackbird
c Hourihane, U. Lucinda and the birthday ball
Hughes, G. The magic apple

Fairy tales—*Continued*

c Hulme-Beaman, S. B. The cruise of the "Toytown Belle"
c Jackson, S. The bad children
  Jonson, M. Greensleeves' magic
c Kane, E. B. The magic word
c Lawrence, G. B. The king's shirt
c Leuser, E. The King of the Golden River
c MacAlvay, N. Beauty and the Beast
c Magito, S. and Weil, R. The Snow Queen
c Masters, R. and Masters, L. The mystery of the ming tree
c Miller, H. L. The real princess
c Miller, M. Pinocchio
c Miller, M. The princess and the swine-herd
c Miller, M. Puss in Boots
c Miller, M. Snow White and Rose Red
c Molloy, L. L. The fortune of Merrylegs and Tawny-Whiskers
c Newman, D. Aladdin
c Newman, D. The Emperor's new clothes
c Newman, D. A gift to the world
c Newman, D. The magic goose
c Newman, D. The real Princess
c Ormandy, E. Little Ida and the flowers
c Palmer, C. K. Hop o' my thumb
c Palmer, K. and Palmer, W. Cinderella
c Palmer, K. and Palmer, W. The magic mountain
c Parkhirst, D. The Clown Princess of Wanderlust
c Seiler, C. Let's go to the moon
  Seiler, G. The Princess and the swine-herd
c Short, R. The red shoes
c Spamer, C. Cinderella's friends
c Spamer, C. The gingerbread house
c Spamer, C. The gold spinner
c Spamer, C. The king's cooks
c Sprenger, C. H. and Attley, M. Snow White and the seven dwarfs
c Tennant, K. The magic fat baby
c Tennant, K. The prince who met a dragon
c Thane, A. The Wizard of Oz
c Very, A. Jack and the beanstalk
c Very, A. The little fir tree
c Very, A. Puss-in-Boots
c Very, A. The shoemaker and the elves
c Wallerstein, J. S. Raymond and the monster
c Watkins, D. Frost-Bite and the eleven Fidgets
  Windsor, H. J. the Emperor's nightingale
c Woolsey, J. and Sechrist, E. H. I wish I were a queen
c Woolsey, J. and Sechrist, E. H. The Queen of Hearts' party
    See also Folk-lore

Faith

  Asbrand, K. The miracle maker
  Blacklock, J. A time of minor miracles
  Brenner, M. The gentle one
  Casey, B. M. The love of Ruth
  Chayefsky, P. Holiday song
  Corrigan, L. Whosoever believeth
  Cowen, W. J. Little friend

  Crouch, A. Not by might
  Delderfield, R. F. Golden rain
  Ervine, St J. John Ferguson
  Estes, S. In quest of power through faith
  Getzinger, E. W. Not without honor
  Greene, G. The living room
  Greene, G. The potting shed
  Hawse, A. Seeing the star
  McCann, K. Out of despair
  McCarty, R. K. But this I know
  MacLeish, A. J.B.
  Neuenburg, E. Distant thunder
  Obey, A. Noah
c Palmer, K. and Palmer, W. The magic mountain
  Pirandello, L. Lazarus
  Quinn, A. H. and Qunin, K. C. The bell of St Hildegarde
  Rodman, H. The faith hawker
  St Clair, R. The happy life
  Trick, O. B. The divine miracle
  Van Druten, J. I've got sixpence
  Williams, C. Grab and grace
  Yeats, W. B. The cat and the moon

Faith-cure

  Moody, W. V. The faith healer
  Smith, W. S. The answer
    See also Miracles

The **faith** hawker. Rodman, H.

The **faith** healer. Moody, W. V.

The **falcon.** Tennyson, A.

Fall of man

  York plays. The fall of man

The **fall** of the city. MacLeish, A.

Fallen angels. Coward, N.

False personation. See Impostors and im-posture

Family

  Alexander, R. Holiday for lovers
  Alexander, R. Time out for Ginger
  Anderson, R. All summer long
  Anouilh, J. Restless heart
  Arrabal. The two executioners
  Asbrand, K. The week before Christmas
  Avery, I. Matilda
  Banks, L. R. It never rains
  Benchley, N. The frogs of Spring
  Bergman, I. Wild strawberries
  Burgess, C. V. A bit of peace and quiet
  Burgess, C. V. Reports in the garden
  Burgess, C. V. Susan to the rescue
  Burgess, C. V. The Taylors in the never-never land
  Burgess, C. V. Trouble at "The Blue Lan-tern"
  Butler, I. The wise children
c Carlson, B. W. Just as strong
  Carroll, P. V. The wise have not spoken
  Casey, B. M High polish
  Casey, B. M. Lilies bloom at Easter
  Chodorov, J. and Fields, J. Anniversary waltz
  Clandon, L. The brains of the family
  Clapp, P. Peggy's on the phone
  Collins, D. Summer brings gifts
  Coward, N. Fumed oak

Fantasy—*Continued*

Chorpenning, C. B. Rip Van Winkle
Connelly, M. Green pastures
Cooper, F. A. Worlds apart
Cullinan, G. The Republic of the Blind
c Curtis, P. D. The hours on strike
Dekker, T. Old Fortunatus
Dighton, J. Man alive
Down, O. The maker of dreams
Duncan, R. The death of Satan
Dunsany, Lord. The jest of Hahalaba
Ferrini, V. Telling of the North Star
Finch, R. and Smith, B. Western night
Fleming, T. Miracle at midnight
c Floyd, B. Pinky Winky's trip to the moon
Giraudoux, J. The enchanted
Giraudoux, J. The madwoman of Chaillot
Goethe, J. W. von. Faust, part II
Golden, E. Gulliver's travels in Lilliput Land
c Goulding, D. J. Pagan magic
Gregory, H. and Henneberger, J. The thousand flerbs
Hark, M. and McQueen, N. Aladdin steps out
c Hollinshead, L. M. Thank you, God for everything
Hope, A. J.; Mary Francis, Sister, and Birder, D. The complaining angel
Howard, P. We are tomorrow
Howard, S. Madam, will you walk?
Howard, V. Gulliver wins his freedom
Ibsen, H. Peer Gynt
Ionesco, E. The future is in eggs
Jagendorf, M. The rime of the ancient mariner
Jefferson, J. Rip Van Winkle
c John, C. Sea shells
Lathrop, D. A page of destiny
Laurents, A. A clearing in the woods
MacKaye, P. The scarecrow
McNeely, J. The staring match
Maeterlinck, M. A miracle of Saint Antony
c Marcus, I. H. To you the torch
Martens, G.-M. The hopeful travellers
Merrill, J. The immortal husband
Miller, M. Alice in Wonderland
c Milne, A. A. Winnie-the-Pooh
Mishima, Y. The Lady Aoi
Mizer, J. Golden slippers
Molnar, F. Fantasy
Moreno, R. A horse play
Niggli, J. Miracle at Blaise
O'Casey, S. Time to go
Orth, R. For heaven's sake
Ouzts, J. D. Happy Pagan
Philp, P. Love and lunacy
Pirandello, L. The mountain giants
Purkey, R. A. The leprechaun
Ratcliffe, D. U. Jingling Lane
c Ratcliffe, D. U. Robinetta
Richards, I. A. A leak in the universe
Rodgers, R. and Hammerstein, O. Carousel
Rose, R. An almanac of liberty
Rose, R. The incredible world of Horace Ford
Rubinstein, H. F. Bernard Shaw in heaven

Saroyan, W. The man with the heart in the highlands
c Seiler, C. The clown out west
Sherriff, R. C. The white carnation
c Spamer, C. The mouse and the moon
c Spamer, C. The playroom
Spring, H. St George at the Dragon
Stockton, R. F. A fabulous tale
Stone, W. Devil take a whittler
Strindberg, A. A dream play
Strindberg, A. Ghost sonata
Strindberg, A. Swanwhite
Taggart, T. Oily to rise
c Thane, A. The Wizard of Oz
c Totheroh, D. The stolen prince
Tree, J. The fisherman
Ustinov, P. The love of four colonels
Vidal, G. Visit to a small planet
Viereck, P. The tree witch
White, N. E. The billion dollar saint
White, N. E. Seven nuns at Las Vegas
Wilder, T. The long Christmas dinner
Wilder, T. Our town
Wilder, T. The skin of our teeth
Wilson, E. The crime in the Whistler room
Wilson, E. Cyprian's prayer
Wilson, E. The little blue light
c Woolsey, J. and Sechrist, E. H. The Santa Claus court
Yeats, W. B. The King of the Great Clock Tower
Yeats, W. B. The Land of Heart's Desire
Yeats, W. B. The player queen
Yeats, W. B. Purgatory
　　See also Fairy tales; Ghosts; Science fiction

The **Farce** of Master Pierre Pathelin. Pathelin

Farces
　　In this index the subject "Farces" has been used for broad or slapstick humor

Abstance, P. and Abstance, L. Murder at the manor
Addis, H. What ho for the open road
Aguirre, I. Express for Santiago
Alexander, A. Cute as a button
Alexander, R. Grand prize
Anouilh, J. Ardèle
Aristophanes. Lysistrata
Armstrong, W. F. Haunted rooms
Asbrand, K. The Farmer in the Dell
Asbrand, K. School daze
Asbrand, K. The week before Christmas!
Aschmann, H. T. As pretty does
Ashermann, O. Shakespeare
Auden, W. H. and Isherwood, C. The dog beneath the skin
Avery, I. Matilda
Axelrod, G. Goodbye Charlie
Axelrod, G. Will success spoil Rock Hunter?
Barnett, M. Yankee peddler
Barry, M. H. Come live in my house
Barry, M. H. The nautical approach
Bate, S. Anniversary Day
Bate, S. Holiday haunts
Bate, S. A mouse! A mouse!
Bayer, E. and Bayer, L. Third best sport

Farces—*Continued*

Lathrop, D. Romeo and Juliet
Levin, I. No time for sergeants
LePelley, G. A is for apple
Lindsay, H. and Crouse, R. Life with Father
Lynn, K. S. Who killed Cock Robin?
McCleery, W. The guest cottage
MacDonagh, D. Step-in-the-hollow
McMahon, B. The Ming thing
McMahon, B. Publicity on the fifteenth
McMahon, L. E. Half-Pint Windom rides west
McMahon, L. E. I smell smoke
McQuade, W. Exclusive model
Malleson, M. Sganarelle
Manheim, M. Comedy of roses
Manning, H. Seeing double
Manning, H. That's my baby
Martens, A. C. Cross your bridge
Martens, A. C. Now it can be told
Martens, A. C. The search for Wildcat McGillicuddy
Martens, A. C. Who stole third base?
Melville, A. Mrs Willie
Melvyn, G. The love match
Molière, J. B. P. The physician in spite of himself
Molière, J. B. P. The reluctant doctor
Molière, J. B. P. Scapin the scamp
Molière, J. B. P. That scoundrel Scapin
Molière, J. B. P. The would-be invalid
Moross, J. The golden apple
Morris, F. H. Reel George
Morton, J. M. Box and Cox
Murphy, A. The apprentice
Murphy, A. The old maid
Murphy, A. Three weeks after marriage
Murphy, A. The upholsterer
Murray, J. A case for two detectives
Murray, W. A night in . . .
c National Recreation Association. The St George play
O'Casey, S. Bedtime story
O'Casey, S. The end of the beginning
O'Casey, S. Hall of healing
O'Casey, S. A pound on demand
O'Casey, S. Purple dust
Olfson, L. The taming of the shrew
Orth, R. Two have dreamed
Parker, K. T. Cry on my shoulder
Pathelin. The farce of Master Pierre Pathelin
Pinero, A. W. The magistrate
Prévert, J. A united family
Reach, J. Afraid of the dark
Reach, J. Open house
Ready, S. Peril at the post office
Relonde, M. Cheating cheaters
Rose, Le R. Headin' for a weddin'
Roussin, A. The little hut
Sakanishi, S. tr. A bag of tangerines
Sakanishi, S. tr. Buaku
Sakanishi, S. tr. The fox mound
Sakanishi, S. tr. Mr Dumbtaro
Sakanishi, S. tr. The ribs and the cover
Sakanishi, S. tr. Thunder God
Sakanishi, S. tr. An unfair exchange

Schaefer, L. Song for a hero
Schweikert, C. P. Hessie of the hills
Scribe, E. and Bayard, J. F. A. A peculiar position
Sharp, A. Nightmare Abbey
Shaw, B. The admirable Bashville
Shaw, B. Annajanska, the Bolshevik Empress
Shaw, B. Augustus does his bit
Shaw, B. Too true to be good
Sheridan, R. B. St Patrick's Day
Shore, J. and Lincoln, R. The soldier who became a Great Dane
Smith, B. Freedom's bird
Spencer, G. Six ladies in waiting
Spewack, S. Under the sycamore tree
Stevens, L. Champagne complex
Strauss, J. Golden butterfly
Sutton, T. Aunt Min drops in
Sylvaine, V. As long as they're happy
Taggart, T. Be my guest
Taggart, T. Crewcuts and longhairs
Tarpley, V. and Tarpley, K. Jump over the moon
Thompson, D. The shoemaker's wife
Tilford, H. Miss Dill from Dippyville
Tobias, J. Be happy? go wacky!
Tobias, J. A boy named Beulah
Tobias, J. Coddled Egbert
Tobias, J. Pick a Dilly
Tobias, J. Tune in on terror
Travers, B. Wild horses
Tree, J. The fisherman
Wattron, F. and Walker, P. Burner of the Bugle
Waugh, J. R. Food for thought
Waugh, J. R. Spots of bother
Weaver, V. B. The reign of Minnie Belle
Webber, J. A brush with the enemy
Welles, R. The man of the house
Wetmore, A. The pedlar
White, N. E. The billion dollar saint
White, N. E. Seven nuns at Las Vegas
Wilde, P. Salt for savor
Wilder, T. The happy journey
Wilder, T. Happy journey to Trenton and Camden
Wilder, T. The matchmaker
Wimberly, R. L. Willy Velvet, homicide detective

See also Burlesque; Comedy; Satire

Farm laborers. See Agricultural laborers

Farm life

Brabazon, F. Singing threshold
Conkle, E. P. Granny's little cheery room
O'Neill, E. Beyond the horizon
Savory, G. A month of Sundays
Tennyson, A. The promise of May
Warnick, C. Heidi

The **Farmer** in the Dell. Asbrand, K.

Farming. See Agriculture

Farquhar, George

The beaux' stratagem
> Late Restoration comedy of manners.
> Fortune-hunting nobleman employs disguise to win a rich wife. Includes words for songs. 5 acts 16 scenes 11m 5w extras 6 interiors

In Farquhar, G. George Farquhar

In Restoration plays

Farquhar, George—*Continued*

The constant couple; or, A trip to the jubilee
> Late Restoration comedy of manners. A rake's adventures in London. 5 acts 21 scenes 8m 4w extras 6 interiors 5 exteriors

In Farquhar, G. George Farquhar

The recruiting officer
> Late Restoration comedy of manners. Sergeant, disguised as fortune-teller promotes enlistment campaign for the British army during Queen Anne's reign. Contains words for songs. 5 acts 19 scenes 12m 4w extras 6 interiors 3 exteriors

In Farquhar, G. George Farquhar

The twin-rivals
> Late Restoration comedy of manners, set in early 18th century England. Twin brothers dispute over inheritance. 5 acts 20 scenes 10m 4w extras 5 interiors 3 exteriors

In Farquhar, G. George Farquhar

Farrow, Natalie

Spring prom magic. French 1954 108p illus
> Comedy. Seventeen-year-old Terry Allister is finally escorted to Spring prom by popular Warren Spade despite unfair tactics of her rival. 3 acts 4 scenes 9m 12w 1 interior

Fascism

Pirandello, L. The new colony

Fashion

Russell, M. A fashion revue

Fashion. Ritchie, A. C. M.

A fashion revue. Russell, M.

Fasts and feasts
> *See also* Religious life and customs under names of countries, e.g. Sicily—Religious life and customs

Judaism
See Passover

Fat woman picnic. Buell, H.

Fate and fatalism

Calderón. Life is a dream

Cocteau, J. The infernal machine

Maeterlinck, M. Pelléas and Mélisande

The father. Strindberg, A.

Father keeps house. Hark, M. and McQueen, N.

Father knows best. Sergel, K.

Father lives with seven women. Garver, J.

Father says no! Payton, D.

Father trims the tree. Paige, M. C.

Fathers

Besier, R. The Barretts of Wimpole Street

Dennys, J. Lear of Albion Crescent

Emurian, E. K. Famous fathers

c Hark, M. and McQueen, N. Father keeps house

Howard, V. A hobby for Dad

McLiam, J. The sin of Pat Muldoon

Sergel, K. My little Margie
> *See also* Parent and child

Father's been to Mars. Dalzell, W. and Mitzman, N.

Father's Day

Asbrand, K. Anything for father

c Asbrand, K. When daddy comes home

c Sprague, G. W. A man's point of view

c Woolsey, J. and Sechrist, E. H. A picnic for father

Father's Easter hat. Hark, M. and McQueen, N.

Father's economy drive. Sutherland, D.

Fauchois, René

Prenez garde à la peinture (adaptation) See Howard, S. The late Christopher Bean

Faulkner, William

Barn burning (adaptation) See Vidal, G. Barn burning

Requiem for a nun (dramatization) See Ford, R. Requiem for a nun

Smoke (adaptation) See Vidal, G. Smoke
> *See also* Ford, R. jt. auth.

Faust, Esther

Gone to the dogs. French 1953 96p
> Farce. Wealthy and eccentric spinster wills fortune to pair of Pekinese dogs. 3 acts 4m 6w 4 scenes 1 interior

Oh, to be sixteen again! French 1954 106p
> Comedy. Escapades—romantic and otherwise—of sixteen-year old Mindy. 3 acts 4 scenes 4m 7w 1 interior

For other plays by this author see Braun, Wilbur; Chadwicke, Alice; Fernway, Peggy

Faust, J. Paul

To us a son. Bakers Plays 1954 19p illus
> Nativity play. When shepherds arrive Jewish innkeeper and his family are convinced that baby born in their stable is the Messiah. Background music. 2 scenes 5m 6w extras 1 interior

See also Sollitt, K. W. jt. auth.

Faust. See Goethe. Urfaust

Faust: a masque. Olson, E.

Faust, part 1. Goethe, J. W. von

Faust, part II. Goethe, J. W. von

Fear

Betti, U. The Queen and the rebels

Inge, W. The dark at the top of the stairs

Kanin, F. and Kanin, M. Rashomon

Sherriff, R. C. Journey's end

Fear is a murderer. Neuenburg, E.

Fear not. Carruthers, J.

Fearheiley, Don M.

Mourning before morning. Bakers Plays 1956 22p illus
> Easter. Mother's death teaches unbelieving son true meaning of the Resurrection. 1 act 3m 3w 1 interior

A star too far. Broadman 1957 27p illus
> Estrangement of proud father and bitter son ends when son is released from prison on Christmas Eve. Background carols. 1 scene 3m 2w 1 interior

Feast of Esther. See Purim (Feast of Esther)

Feast of Lights. See Hannukah (Feast of Lights)

The feast of Ortolans. Anderson, M.

The feast of the dolls. Woolsey, J. and Sechrist, E. H.

The Feast of the Ingathering. Bailey, H. F.

A February failure. Miller, H. L.

February frenzy. Miller, H. L.

Feder, Bayleh
c Benjamin Franklin
When classmates have to gather information about Benjamin Franklin's life, they meet several colonial people who help them. 2 acts 3m 2w 7b 5g extras 1 interior 1 exterior
In Birdsall, R. ed. Creative plays for every school month

Feder, Laura
c Christmas in the melting pot
How children celebrate Christmas in varied parts of the United States. Includes a Nativity tableaux. 8 scenes 1m 3w 4b 10g extras 3 interiors 5 exteriors
In Birdsall, R. ed. Creative plays for every school month
c Gifts for mother
Children discover a lot of things they could do for mother on Mother's Day. 3b 2g extras 1 interior
In Birdsall, R. ed. Creative plays for every school month

Federspiel, Jo Ann Deason
Behold the body
Mystery comedy. When Aunt Ella disappears the family suspects Aunt Susie may have had something to do with it. 3m 4w 1 interior
In Twelve half-hours with the Winthrop Theater

Felipe II, King of Spain. See Philip II, King of Spain

Female impersonators. See Impersonators, Female

Feminism. See Woman

Fenwick, Robert
Toys and science
Television play. Scientific explanation of many mechanical toys by toymaker to boy. 2m 1b
In Settel, I. ed. Top TV shows of the year, 1954-1955

Ferguson, John
The camp. Epworth 1956 23p
Nativity play in verse set in refugee camp where camp commandant personifies conscience of mankind. 1 act 4m 4w extras 1 exterior

Fernway, Peggy
"I never said a word, but—!" French 1956 33p illus
Comedy. Gossip spreads false story of elopement. 1 act 2 scenes 8w 1 interior
For other plays by this author see Braun, Wilbur; Chadwicke, Alice; Faust, Esther

Ferrini, Vincent
Telling of the North Star
Fantasy in verse. Ghosts of sea captain and his crew return for his great granddaughter. 7m 2w extras 1 setting
In The Best short plays, 1953-1954

The festival. Spewack, S. and Spewack, B.

Festivals. See Dolls, Feast of

Feudin' fun. Dias, E. J.

Feudin' in the mountains. Abstance, P. and Abstance, L.

Feuds. See Vendetta

Feutinger, Josephine
Another life. French 1956 81p illus
Rendezvous with old sweetheart convinces suburban matron that she has always had the happiness she was seeking. Background music. 3 acts 4 scenes 4m 4w 2 interiors

Feydeau, Georges
Keep an eye on Amélie! English version by Brainerd Duffield
Everyone keeps getting involved with wrong people in this farce about marriage. 3 acts 2 scenes 16m 9w 1g extras 4 interiors
In Bentley, E. ed. Let's get a divorce! and other plays

Feydeau, Georges, and Desvallieres, Maurice
Hotel Paradiso. English tr. by Peter Glenville. French 1957 130p illus
Farce. Assortment of refined people intent on assignations in cheap hotel are intercepted by police raid. 3 acts 13m 8w extras 2 interiors
Hotel Paradiso (condensation)
In Broadway's best, 1957

Fichter, Helen G.
c To soap or not to soap
Halloween. Two boys who intend to play mean tricks on people on Halloween suddenly discover several reasons why they shouldn't. 1m 1w 5b 2g extras 1 exterior
In Birdsall, R. ed. Creative plays for every school month

Field, Eugene
The coming of the Prince (radio adaptation) See Miller, H. L. The coming of the Prince

Field, Rachel
c Polly Patchwork
Polly's dress, made from patchwork quilt, helps her win spelling match. Set in colonial America. 3 scenes 2m 3w 1b 2g 2 interiors
In Fenner, P. and Hughes, A. comps. Entrances and exits

Fielding, Henry
Mock doctor (adaptation) See Boyd, A. K. The mock doctor

Fields, Joseph. See Bernstein, L. Wonderful town; also Chodorov, J. jt. auth.

Fields, Joseph, and Chodorov, Jerome
The Ponder heart. French 1956 96p
Dramatization of Eudora Welty's novel. Uncle Daniel Ponder, wealthy, eccentric, warm of heart but weak in the head, is brought to trial for murder of his 17 year old wife. 3 acts 15m 8w 5b 2g 2 interiors 1 exterior
Trade edition published by Random House
The Ponder heart (condensation)
In The Best plays of 1955-1956
In Theatre, 1956

Fields, Joseph, and De Vries, Peter
The tunnel of love. French 1957 120p illus
Comedy based on novel by Peter De Vries. Complications arise when couple trying to adopt baby asks couple next door to vouch for their suitability as parents. 3 acts 5 scenes 2m 4w 1 interior
Trade edition published by Little

The fifth season. Regan, S.

The fifth wheel. Perry, M.

Fighting Bob. Boyd, A. K.

The fighting cock. Anouilh, J.

Final curtain. Armer, A. and Grauman, W. E.

The final curtain. Murray, J.

Final edition. Owens, R. J.

Final edition. Sayre, G. W.

Financiers. See Capitalists and financiers

Finch, Robert
A certain man had two sons
Set on a modern farm; plot follows story line of Biblical parable of the prodigal son. 1 act 3m 2w 1 interior
In Brings, L. M. comp. The golden book of church plays
From Paradise to Butte
Comedy. Rancher changes his mind about leaving his wife when city-bred cowboy threatens to displace him. 1 act 3m 1b 1 setting
In Smith, B. and others, eds. A treasury of non-royalty one-act plays
The return
Tragedy. City-loving daughter decides to return to Montana valley home to live with dying mother. 1 act 3w 1 interior
In Smith, B. and others, eds. A treasury of non-royalty one-act plays

Finch, Robert, and Smith, Betty
Western night
Fantasy. Death takes injured cowboy home to Iowa. 1 act 6m 1 interior
In Smith, B. and others, eds. A treasury of non-royalty one-act plays

Finding the tickets. Blyton, E.

Fine wagon. See Green, P. Wings for to fly

Fingerprints
Chadwicke, A. Pudd'nhead Wilson

Finian, Brother
The Light of the World
Easter play. Passion and Resurrection of Jesus Christ. Background music. 9 scenes 17m extras 3 interiors 2 exteriors
In Brings, L. M. comp. The golden book of church plays

Finney, Jack
Telephone roulette. Dramatic 1956 22p
Romantic comedy. Telephone date with unknown young man is too much for Gloria but not for her roommate. 1 act 1m 2w 1 interior

Fiorello! Bock, J.

Fire at Callart. Bottomley, G.

Fire at the Fieldings. Woolsey, J. and Sechrist, E. H.

The fire demons. Woolsey, J. and Sechrist, E. H.

Fire in a paper. Hagy, L.

Fire prevention
c Fisher, A. What happened on Clutter Street
c Miller, H. L. The polka dot pup
c Newman, D. The fire-safe town
c Woolsey, J. and Sechrist, E. H. The fire demons

The fire-safe town. Newman, D.

Firemen
c Crawford, A. A visit with the firemen
Dunlop, R. S. Four bells means glory!
c Woolsey, J. and Sechrist, E. H. Fire at the Fieldings

Fires
Kaufman, G. S. The still alarm
c Woolsey, J. and Sechrist, E. H. Fire at the Fieldings

Fires at Valley Forge. Clark, B. H.

First aid in illness and injury
c Fisher, A. Old Mr Fixit
Woolsey, J. and Sechrist, E. H. First aid in the first troop

First aid in the first troop. Woolsey, J. and Sechrist, E. H.

The first breakfast. Emurian, E. K.

The first cat on Mars. Harper, J. M.

The first Christmas tree. Spamer, C.

The first gentleman. Ginsbury, N.

First in peace. Hark, M. and McQueen, N.

The first jack-o-lanterns. Spamer, C.

The first oyster. Fleece, J.

The first Thanksgiving. Newman, D.

The firstborn. Fry, C.

The fish that wished to live on land. Spamer, C.

Fisher, Aileen
Abe's winkin' eye
Childhood of twelve-year-old Abraham Lincoln with his new family after his father remarries. 3m 3w 1b 1g 1 interior
In Fisher, A. Holiday programs for boys and girls
Angel in the looking-glass
When little girl in angel costume knocks at doors of several people in apartment building they realize how their selfishness has destroyed their Christmas spirit. 1m 4w 2b 1g 3 interiors
In Fisher, A. Holiday programs for boys and girls
c By order of the king
The king decides to banish everything that would make kingdom unsafe for his children but they still want to learn about safety. 6m 2w 2b 2g extras 1 interior
In Fisher, A. Health and safety plays and programs
c Catch as catch can
The viruses are disappointed when children find out how not to catch cold. Unidentified cast 5 characters extras 1 interior
In Fisher, A. Health and safety plays and programs
c Caves of the earth
People of the earth prepare to enter caves for fear of atomic disaster, but children prove that the world should unite instead. 3m 1w 1b 1g extras 1 exterior
In Fisher, A. Holiday programs for boys and girls
c The Christmas cake
Husband is worried that his wife will be angry when he forgets to put her cake into oven, but his omission turns out well. 1m 1w 1b extras 1 interior
In Fisher, A. Holiday programs for boys and girls
A Christmas tree for Kitty
Some children trim Christmas tree for a new baby. 1w 2b 2g extras 1 interior
In Fisher, A. Holiday programs for boys and girls
c Courting trouble
Mother Goose characters tell how they could have been more careful in promoting safety. 2m extras 1 interior
In Fisher, A. Health and safety plays and programs

Fisher, Aileen—*Continued*

c Day of destiny
> On board the Santa Maria in 1492, Columbus' men agree to sail only two more days before forcing him to turn back if land is not sighted. 8m 2b 1 exterior

In Fisher, A. Holiday programs for boys and girls

c Full of vim
> Boys and girls with letters spelling out "vitamins" tell how important they are. Verse play. 4b 4g extras 1 interior

In Fisher, A. Health and safety plays and programs

c Getting it straight
> Girl mystifies her classmates with special way for learning good posture. 2b 3g extras 1 interior

In Fisher, A. Health and safety plays and programs

Ghosts on guard
> Some teenagers intending to play mean Halloween tricks, are themselves frightened by a ghost. Verse play 2 scenes 3m 3w 1b 1 interior 1 exterior

In Fisher, A. Holiday programs for boys and girls

c Hearts, tarts, and valentines
> The king is angry when someone steals the tarts made for him by Queen of Hearts and refuses to let Princess of Diamonds marry his son, Jack of Hearts. 5m 2w extras 1 interior

In Fisher, A. Holiday programs for boys and girls

c Hidden meanings
> Boys and girls quiz each other about vitamins hidden in different foods. Verse play. 4b 4g extras 1 interior

In Fisher, A. Health and safety plays and programs

c The king's toothache
> Two children read story about wise man who tells the king how to take care of his teeth. 12m 1b 1g 1 interior

In Fisher, A. Health and safety plays and programs

c Leave it to Gramps
> Grandpa asks the children some riddles about vitamins. Verse play. 2m 1w 1b 1g 1 interior

In Fisher, A. Health and safety plays and programs

c Long live father
> Children decide to write down rules of health and safety as birthday present for father. 2 scenes 1m 1w 1b 2g extras 1 interior

In Fisher, A. Health and safety plays and programs

Luck takes a holiday
> Two families show how they are going to depend on safety rules rather than luck to prevent accidents. 7m 3w extras 2 interiors

In Fisher, A. Health and safety plays and programs

c The magic formula
> Professor is disappointed when he finds that his magic formula is not any more healthful for children than plain milk. 4m 3w 1 interior

In Fisher, A. Health and safety plays and programs

c Many a slip
> Objects in the house explain how children have been careless and have caused accidents. 1w 1b 1g extras 1 interior

In Fisher, A. Health and safety plays and programs

The Merry Christmas elf
> A writer discovers elf who is the Spirit of Christmas and who rushes around changing a lot of people. 3m 1w 3b 4g extras 1 exterior

In Fenner, P. and Hughes, A. comps. Entrances and exits

In Fisher, A. Holiday programs for boys and girls

Mr Do and Mr Don't
> Boys and girls learn the do's and don'ts about safety. Verse play. 6b 6g extras 1 interior

In Fisher, A. Health and safety plays and programs

c Mother of Thanksgiving
> Radio play. Life of Sarah Josepha Hale who was instrumental in having Thanksgiving proclaimed national holiday in 1864. 5m 4w 3b 2g extras

In Fisher, A. Holiday programs for boys and girls

c Mother's Day off and on
> A father and his children think that taking over mother's job on Mother's Day will be easy. 1m 1w 1b 2g 2 interiors

In Fisher, A. Holiday programs for boys and girls

c Murder in the kitchen
> Children find an unusual way of telling their mothers how important it is to conserve vitamins in cooking vegetables. 2w 2b 2g extras 2 interiors

In Fisher, A. Health and safety plays and programs

c New hearts for old
> Children convince their father how important it is to buy mother a valentine. Verse play. 1m 1w 2b 2g 1 interior

In Fisher, A. Holiday programs for boys and girls

c The not-so-crooked man
> Mother Goose characters tell crooked man how they obey the rules of health. Unidentified cast 8 characters 1 interior

In Fisher, A. Health and safety plays and programs

c Nothing ever happens!
> When policemen go through a family's house, they explain the different things they find that could be dangerous. 2m 1w 3b 3g extras 1 interior

In Fisher, A. Health and safety plays and programs

c Old Mr Fixit
> Old man who is hard of hearing misinterprets children's conversation and ends up giving them a lesson in first aid. 1m 2b 2g 1 interior

In Fisher, A. Health and safety plays and programs

On Halloween
> Halloween verse play with witches, ghosts and goblins. Large mixed cast no scenery

In Fisher, A. Holiday programs for boys and girls

c On strike
> The tree and woodland animals are angry because a farmer doesn't realize the importance of trees. 3 scenes 8 characters 1 exterior

In Fisher, A. Holiday programs for boys and girls

Fisher, Aileen—*Continued*

c Once upon a time
> Characters from famous children's stories tell stories to children of "Old Woman Who Lived in a Shoe." 5m 1w extras 1 interior

> *In* Fisher, A. Holiday programs for boys and girls

A play without a name
> Two teenagers discover that problems delegates faced in uniting American states in 1787 are similar to those faced by United Nations today in uniting the world. 9m 5w extras no scenery

> *In* Fisher, A. Holiday programs for boys and girls

c Robots to the rescue
> After man has some robots made they emphasize how much more wonderful the human body is and that it must be properly taken care of. 2 scenes 5m extras 1 interior

> *In* Fisher, A. Health and safety plays and programs

The safety parade
> Humorous pantomimes illustrating safety rules. 7b 7g extras no scenery

> *In* Fisher, A. Health and safety plays and programs

c The spirit of Christmas
> Christmas Spirit shows how selfish people send him away but unselfish people let him stay with them. Verse play. 2m 2w 2g extras no scenery

> *In* Fisher, A. Holiday programs for boys and girls

c Standing up for Santa
> All the other children try to convince Eleanor that there is a Santa Claus. 1 act 12g extras 1 interior

> *In* Kamerman, S. E. ed. Blue-ribbon plays for girls

c Sure cure
> A policeman tells children how he takes care of them. Verse play. 1m 1w 1b 1 interior

> *In* Fisher, A. Health and safety plays and programs

Three and the dragon
> Three families, each in its own way, show selfish unconcern for other people in the world, not realizing the danger to all from the "atomic dragon." Verse play. 4m 3w 1b extras 1 exterior

> *In* Fisher, A. Holiday programs for boys and girls

c Time out for Christmas
> Last year's toys tell the twenty four days of December why they don't want Christmas to come this year. 28 characters 1 interior

> *In* Fisher, A. Holiday programs for boys and girls

c Treasure hunt
> The children in classroom decide that books are treasures and dress in costumes of famous book characters to surprise their teacher. 2 scenes 1w 5b 4g extras 1 interior 1 exterior

> *In* Fisher, A. Holiday programs for boys and girls

Unexpected guests
> Pilgrims who expected ten Indians to share their Thanksgiving feast are surprised when ninety arrive. 2m 2w 4b 4g 1 interior

> *In* Fisher, A. Holiday programs for boys and girls

The voice of liberty
> On Election Day a family is not interested in voting until son reminds them of history of the Liberty Bell and how it symbolizes freedom. 2m 4w 4b 1 interior

> *In* Fisher, A. Holiday programs for boys and girls

c Voices
> Boys and girls hold letters spelling out "health" with verses on how they can keep it. Verse play. 3b 3g 1 interior

> *In* Fisher, A. Health and safety plays and programs

c Voting Day
> Boys and girls holding letters of word "voting" tell what it means and why it is important. Large mixed cast no scenery

> *In* Fisher, A. Holiday programs for boys and girls

Washington marches on
> Scenes showing highlights from the life of George Washington. 14 scenes. Large mixed cast 1 interior

> *In* Fisher, A. Holiday programs for boys and girls

c The weaver's son
> The boy, Christopher Columbus, a weaver's son is reprimanded for spending his time watching ships. 3m 1w 1g 1 interior

> *In* Fisher, A. Holiday programs for boys and girls

c What happened on Clutter Street
> Some children clearing away litter for better fire prevention meet the fire fiends. 4m extras 1 exterior

> *In* Fisher, A. Health and safety plays and programs

c Why the sleepy Dormouse
> Parody on Alice in Wonderland characters. Alice tells the Dormouse how boys and girls need eleven hours of sleep daily. Unidentified cast 6 characters 1 exterior

> *In* Fisher, A. Health and safety plays and programs

Fisher, Aileen, and Rabe, Olive

The accident of birth
> What the United Nations does to help the two hundred thousand children born in the world each day. 3m 2b 2g extras 1 interior

> *In* Fisher, A. and Rabe, O. United Nations plays and programs

Alice in Puzzleland
> Sketch using characters from Lewis Carroll's Alice in Wonderland. Alice figures out riddle which tells about the activities of the United Nations. Unidentified cast 13 characters 1 exterior

> *In* Fisher, A. and Rabe, O. United Nations plays and programs

All in the UN
> Some boys and girls discuss the number of countries which belong to the United Nations. 11b 10g 1 interior

> *In* Fisher, A. and Rabe, O. United Nations plays and programs

All the world around
> Work of United Nations in education, agriculture and medicine is seen in three countries. 3m 2w 5b 2g chorus 3 exteriors

> *In* Fisher, A. and Rabe, O. United Nations plays and programs

Fisher, A. and Rabe, O.—*Continued*

Anonymous letter
Eighth grade students intend to write letter about teacher in gossip column of the school newspaper, when someone writes a letter about one of them. 2m 2w extras 1 interior

In Fisher, A. and Rabe, O. Patriotic plays and programs

Apostle of freedom
Roger Williams fights for freedom of religion in the American colonies. 3m 2w 1 interior

In Fisher, A. and Rabe, O. Patriotic plays and programs

Ask Mr Jefferson
Modern day students assigned to gather information about Thomas Jefferson are surprised to find him sitting in library. 2 scenes 2b 2g extras 2 interiors

In Fisher, A. and Rabe, O. Patriotic plays and programs

Best bargain in the world
Man who doesn't approve of the United Nations because he is ignorant of its activities, is enlightened. 2m 1w 1b 1g 1 interior

In Fisher, A. and Rabe, O. United Nations plays and programs

Bringing up father
Children find humorous way of showing their father the important things that taxes he pays get for him. 1m 1w 2b 2g 1 interior

In Fisher, A. and Rabe, O. Patriotic plays and programs

Cavalcade of human rights
Historical episodes from history, spanning ancient Egypt to Germany under Hitler, showing oppressed man's fight for dignity and freedom. 24m 8w extras chorus no scenery

In Fisher, A. and Rabe, O. United Nations plays and programs

In Kamerman, S. E. ed. Blue-ribbon plays for graduation

Champions of democracy
Radio play. How democracy evolved since colonial times in America. 17m 4w 1b extras

In Fisher, A. and Rabe, O. Patriotic plays and programs

A dish of green peas
Two women find themselves involved in plot to find traitor to the American cause in Revolutionary War. 2 scenes 3m 2w 1 interior

In Fisher, A. and Rabe, O. Patriotic plays and programs

c **Empty bowls**
Children tell about the work of the United Nations Children's Fund. 11b 11g extras 1 interior

In Fisher, A. and Rabe, O. United Nations plays and programs

Flag of freedom
Examples of two people who risked lives for freedom in Civil War and Second World War. 3m 1w 1b 2g 1 interior 1 exterior

In Fisher, A. and Rabe, O. Patriotic plays and programs

A fresco for UNESCO
A group of children draw on blackboard their ideas about United Nations Educational, Scientific and Cultural Organization. 1b 1g chorus extras 1 interior

In Fisher, A. and Rabe, O. United Nations plays and programs

The get-together dinner
Man who thinks that the United States can stand alone is shown how many items he eats that come from other countries. 2m 1w 1b 1g 1 interior

In Fisher, A. and Rabe, O. United Nations plays and programs

c **Getting in line**
Children with letters spelling out the United Nations show the meaning of unification. 7b 6g 1 interior

In Fisher, A. and Rabe, O. United Nations plays and programs

Haym Salomon's battle
Jewish businessman in Philadelphia gives indispensable aid to Treasury of the new country after the Revolutionary War. 2 scenes 9m 5w extras 1 interior 1 exterior

In Fisher, A. and Rabe, O. Patriotic plays and programs

Honest Abe Lincoln
A friend tries to get Abraham Lincoln to sneak out of town because he owes many debts, but Lincoln refuses. 2m 1w 2b 3g 1 exterior

In Fisher, A. and Rabe, O. Patriotic plays and programs

Immigrants all, Americans all
Radio play. Scenes showing what America has meant to immigrants from all over the world since colonial days. 4m 3w 6b 4g extras

In Fisher, A. and Rabe, O. Patriotic plays and programs

Invasion from the stratosphere
Invaders from another planet decide to take over earth because people are always divided until they find that people are united in the United Nations. 4m 2w extras 1 interior

In Fisher, A. and Rabe, O. United Nations plays and programs

Johnny Appleseed's vision
Johnny Appleseed visits a pioneer family. Verse play. 2m 1w 1b 2g extras 1 exterior

In Fisher, A. and Rabe, O. Patriotic plays and programs

Johnny on the spot
Boys and girls assure spirit of the future that they have confidence in freedom and democratic spirit of America. 2 scenes 2m 1w 2b 1g extras 1 interior 1 exterior

In Fisher, A. and Rabe, O. Patriotic plays and programs

Let there be bread
Pictures some activities of the United Nations to combat hunger throughout world. 13m 8w 2b 1g extras no scenery

In Fisher, A. and Rabe, O. United Nations plays and programs

Long may it wave
Shelling of Fort McHenry in 1812 inspires Francis Scott Key to write words to Star Spangled Banner. 2m 2w chorus 1 interior

In Fisher, A. and Rabe, O. Patriotic plays and programs

May the best man win
Boys and girls discuss whom they should support in school election. 3b 3g 1 interior

In Fisher, A. and Rabe, O. Patriotic plays and programs

"Molly Pitcher"
Molly Pitcher inspires tired troops at Battle of Monmouth during the Revolutionary War. 3m 1w extras 1 exterior

In Fisher, A. and Rabe, O. Patriotic plays and programs

Fisk, Dorothy M.
  The secondary wife. Deane 1956 26p
  ("Deane's" Ser. of plays)
    Meeting of wife and prospective secondary
    wife of wealthy Chinese. Background
    music. 1 act 4m 2w 1 interior

Fitch, Clyde
  The girl with the green eyes
    Social comedy. Wife's needless jealousy
    almost wrecks marriage. 4 acts 5 scenes
    10m 16w 3 interiors
    In Quinn, A. H. ed. Representative
      American plays

Fitzgerald, F. Scott
  Three hours between planes (dramatization) See Winer, E. Three hours between planes
    See also Benson, S. The young and
    beautiful

Five boys and a Santa. Howard, V.
The **five** buttons. Murray, J.
Five days. Zieger, H.
The **five** dollar bill. Mosel, T.
Five finger exercise. Shaffer, P.
Five in judgment. Taylor, D.
Five Nations. See Iroquois Indians
Five o'clock tea. Howells, W. D.
The **five** senses. Hark, M. and McQueen, N.

Flag Day
  c Larkin, E. Mistress Betsy and the flag
  Miller, H. L. The talking flag
  c Newman, D. The stars and stripes
  c Spamer, C. The stars and stripes
  c Woolsey, J. and Sechrist, E. H. Each star
    a state

Flag of freedom. Fisher, A. and Rabe, O.

Flagellants and flagellation
  Agnew, E. J. Beyond Good Friday

Flagellation. See Flagellants and flagellation

Flags
                United States
  Emurian, E. K. I pledge allegiance
  Fisher, A. and Rabe, O. Pledge to the
    flag
  Fisher, A. and Rabe, O. A star for Old
    Glory
  c Miller, H. L. Old Glory grows up
  c Spamer, C. The stars and stripes
  c Woolsey, J. and Sechrist, E. H. Each star
    a state

A **flair** for fashion. Phillips, M. K.

Flapper girls. Mathers, A.

Flare path. Rattigan, T.

Flaten, Mary
  Testing ground for democracy
    Verse play about education in a de-
    mocracy compared to system in total-
    itarian country. 1 act 3 scenes 4m 1w
    extras 1 exterior
    In Kamerman, S. E. ed. Blue-ribbon
      plays for graduation

The **flattering** word. Kelly, G.

Flavelle, Irene B.
  c Giants of the city
    Boy and girl learn about great sources
    of power in their city. 1m 1b 1g extras
    1 interior
    In Birdsall, R. ed. Creative plays for
      every school month
  c Vacation in the city
    Little girl is unhappy at prospect of
    spending summer vacation in city until
    she discovers the many activities avail-
    able. 6m 1w 1b 3g 1 exterior
    In Birdsall, R. ed. Creative plays for
      every school month

Die **Fledermaus** (adaptation) See Strauss,
  J. Golden butterfly

Fleece, Jeffrey
  The first oyster. Bakers Plays 1960 23p
  (Baker's Royalty plays)
    Domestic comedy. A mother, concerned
    about son's indifference to marriage,
    concocts plot concerning a non-existent
    beautiful girl. 1 act 2m 2w 1 interior

Fleet, Thomas
  c Borgers, P. and Borgers, E. The strange
    case of Mother Goose

Fleming, Tom
  Miracle at midnight. Epworth 1954 70p
    Christmas fantasy in verse. Man at
    Christmas time should become, like the
    Prince of Peace, a child again. 1 scene
    3m 3w chorus 1 exterior

Fletcher, John. See Beaumont, F. jt. auth.

Fletcher, Lucille
  Sorry, wrong number
    Horror. Crossed wires cause neurotic
    woman to overhear plans for her own
    murder. 1 act 5m 9w 1 interior
    In Cerf, B. and Cartmell, V. H. eds. 24
      favorite one-act plays

The **flies.** Sartre, J. P.
Flight. Foote, H.
Flight crews. See Air pilots
Flight into Egypt. Tabori, G.
Flight of the dove. Wilson, D.
The **flight** out of Egypt. Spamer, C. M.
Flood, Biblical. See Deluge
Floods
  Anderson, R. All summer long
Florence
  Wilde, O. A Florentine tragedy
Florence Nightingale. Spamer, C.
A **Florentine** tragedy. Wilde, O.
Florrie's fortune. Asbrand, K.
Flower drum song. Rodgers, R.
A **flower** for Mother's Day. MacLellan, E.
  and Schroll, C. V.
The **flower** garden. Very, A.
The **flower** of hope. Casey, B. M.
The **flowering** peach. Odets, C.
Flowers
  Asbrand, K. Christmas rose
  Howells, W. D. Bride roses
  c MacLellan, E. and Schroll, C. V. A flower
    for Mother's Day
  c Ormandy, E. Little Ida and the flowers
  c Spamer, C. The tulip garden
  c Very, A. The flower garden
  c Very, A. The Mayflower

Floyd, Barbara

c Once upon a time. Bakers Plays 1957 22p
Humorous parody of fairy tales: wicked
stepmother tries to keep young shepherd
and sweetheart apart. 2 acts 5 scenes 9m
10w extras 1 interior 3 exteriors

c Pinky Winky's trip to the moon. Bakers
Plays 1957 23p
Fantasy. Little boy on way to Man in
the Moon meets baby stars, Milky Way
and others. 7 scenes Large mixed cast
1 setting

Fluckey, James O.

c Davy's star; script by Edith Quick; music
by James O. Fluckey. Eldridge 1958 56p
music
Christmas operetta with music. Children
at an orphanage present Christmas program. One little boy, left out because
he is deaf, hopes to be invited to someone's home for Christmas. Includes libretto and lyrics. 3 acts 3m 2w 4b 5g
extras 1 interior

c He said he was Santa; script by Edith
Quick; music by James O. Fluckey.
Eldridge 1953 58p music
Christmas operetta. When Santa gets
lost in Swiss Alps he is rescued by
gnomes who decide to cut off his hair
and give him a shave while he is asleep.
Includes libretto and lyrics. 3 acts Large
mixed cast 1 interior

c The heart of the forest; music by James
O. Fluckey; script by Edith Quick. Eldridge 1953 56p music
Operetta. Grelda, a selfish little girl, has
her heart taken away by Good Witch
but redeems it by a deed of kindness.
Contains words and music for songs.
3 acts 1m 5w 5g extras 1 interior 1
exterior

c The little blue angel; script by Edith
Quick; music by James O. Fluckey.
Eldridge 1954 60p music
Operetta. A little boy and a beautiful
princess wait for blue angel that always
appears at midnight on top of Christmas tree. Includes libretto and lyrics.
3 acts. 3b 4g extras 1 interior

c Santa and the space men; script by Edith
Quick; music by James O. Fluckey. Eldridge 1956 56p music
Operetta. Early on Christmas Eve Santa
Claus has forced emergency landing because of reindeer trouble up in the
sky, caused by spacemen who want to
kidnap Santa. Includes libretto and
lyrics. 3 acts 7b 7g extras 1 interior

The **flying** machine. Parr, R.

The **flying** prince. Harris, A.

Flying saucers
Cooper, F. A. Worlds apart

Foard, John. See Ford, John

Fog on the bay. Wardall, C.

Folk-drama

American

Hughes, E. W. The wishful taw
Jefferson, J. Rip Van Winkle
McCaslin, N. The gift of corn
McCaslin, N. The star that never moves
McCaslin, N. The Yankee Peddler
Richardson, H. and Berney, W. Dark of
the moon
Riggs, L. Roadside
Rodgers, R. and Hammerstein, O. Okla-
homa!

Irish

Synge, J. M. The playboy of the western
world

Japanese

Sakanishi, S. tr. The aunt's sake
Sakanishi, S. tr. The bag of parting
Sakanishi, S. tr. A bag of tangerines
Sakanishi, S. tr. Buaku
Sakanishi, S. tr. Busu
Sakanishi, S. tr. The Deva King
Sakanishi, S. tr. The family quarrel
Sakanishi, S. tr. The fox mound
Sakanishi, S. tr. Gargoyle
Sakanishi, S. tr. The ink-smeared lady
Sakanishi, S. tr. Japanese folk-plays (22
plays)
Sakanishi, S. tr. The letter "I"
Sakanishi, S. tr. Literate highwaymen
Sakanishi, S. tr. The magic mallet of the
Devil
Sakanishi, S. tr. The melon thief
Sakanishi, S. tr. Mr Dumbtaro
Sakanishi, S. tr. Plop! Click!
Sakanishi, S. tr. The ribs and the cover
Sakanishi, S. tr. Seed of hōjō
Sakanishi, S. tr. Thunder God
Sakanishi, S. tr. An unfair exchange
Sakanishi, S. tr. The wounded highway-
man

Negro

Connelly, M. Green pastures

Spanish

García Lorca, F. Blood wedding

Folk-lore
Dekker, T. Old Fortunatus
Engle, J. D. The charm
c Goldsmith, S. L. How Boots befooled the
king
c Goldsmith, S. L. The staff and the fiddle
Smith, B. and Webb, C. Mañana bandits
    See also Fairies; Legends—United
States

African

Ridge, A. Hare and the field of millet
Ridge, A. Under the monkey-bread tree

Algerian

Ridge, A. Emhammed of the red slippers

American

Benét, S. V. The Devil and Daniel Web-
ster
c Carlson, B. W. St. Nicholas just the same
c Hess, M. N. Folk-o-rama U.S.A.
McCaslin, N. The Bell Witch of Tennes-
see
McCaslin, N. Giant of the timber
McCaslin, N. He traveled the world
McCaslin, N. St Nicholas of New Amster-
dam
McCaslin, N. Seafaring giant
McCaslin, N. Tall Bill and his big ideas
Totheroh, D. and Benét, S. V. All that
money can buy

Arabic

c Klein, M. W. Ali Baba and the forty
thieves

Australian

c Carlson, B. W. The bunyip lives again!

English

c Arlett, V. I. Young Richard Whittington
c Spamer, C. The three bears

Folk-lore—*Continued*

German

c Beers, J. Beauty and the Beast
Hughes, G. The magic apple
c Jagendorf, M. Merry Tyll
c Melanos, J. A. Rapunzel and the witch

Indic

c Harris, A. The flying prince

Irish

Yeats, W. B. The Land of Heart's Desire

Japanese

Kinoshita, J. Twilight crane

Jews

Ansky, S. The Dybbuk
Perl, A. The world of Sholom Aleichem

Negro

McCaslin, N. John Henry

Russian

c Woolsey, J. and Sechrist, E. H. The legend of Babouska

Folk-o-rama U.S.A. Hess, M. N.

Folk-plays. See Folk-drama

Folk-songs
c Mitchell, L. F. Music! Music! Everywhere!

Folk tales. See Folk-lore

Follow simple directions. Taggart, T.

Follow the girls. Renno, E. L.

Follow the gleam. Protter, N.

Food
Howard, V. Herman's temptation

Food for thought. Waugh, J. R.

The food of love. Bond, C.

The foolish kitten. Spamer, C.

Fools and jesters
Bergh, H. Old King Cole

Fool's paradise. Lynch, P.

Foot
Abnormities and deformities
Kolb, K. She walks in beauty

Football
Abstance, P. and Abstance L. The pigskin parade
Curtis, P. D. Picking the team
Kesler, H. O. Line of scrimmage
Renno, E. L. Follow the girls
White, N. E. The billion dollar saint

Foote, Horton
The dancers
Television play. Teen-age boy lacking self-confidence meets girl with similar handicap and together they attend first dance. 3 acts 3m 7w 4 interiors 1 exterior
In Foote, H. Harrison, **Texas**
In Foote, H. A young lady of property
The death of the old man
Television play. Old man who is dying, worries about what will happen to his daughter until a cousin offers her a home. 2 acts 4m 3w
In Foote, H. Harrison, **Texas**
In Foote, H. A young lady of property

Expectant relations
Television play. Two nieces are mercenary rivals for their aged uncle's fortune, but he outwits them. 3 acts 4m 5w
In Foote, H. Harrison, Texas
Flight
Television play. Young woman leaves family after revealing secret marriage to man who has fled town. 1m 5w
In Burack, A. S. ed. Television plays for writers
John Turner Davis
Television play. Boy abandoned by parents finds home. Southern dialect. 6m 4w extras
In The Best short plays of 1953-1954
In Foote, H. Harrison, Texas
In Foote, H. A young lady of property
The midnight caller. [Rev] Dramatists 1959 28p
Effect of girl's stormy romance upon other female members of her boarding house. 1 act 2m 5w 1 interior
—Same
In Foote, H. Harrison, Texas
The oil well
Man dreams of finding oil on his land while his wife thinks in terms of crops on the land. 5m 3w 1 interior 1 exterior
In Foote, H. A young lady of property
The old beginning
Young man attempts to break away from domineering father. 7m 4w 2 interiors 1 exterior
In Foote, H. A young lady of property
The tears of my sister
Television play. Young woman feels obliged to marry older but wealthy man in order to help her family. 2 acts 2m 4w
In Foote, H. Harrison, Texas
The traveling lady. Dramatists 1955 68p illus
Wife and daughter, rejected by ex-convict husband, turn to widower. 3 acts 4 scenes 4m 5w 1g 1 exterior
The trip to Bountiful. Dramatists 1954 72p illus
Aging widow living with son and selfish daughter-in-law, runs away to her old home. 3 acts 4 scenes 6m 3w extras 1 interior 2 exteriors
—Same;
In Foote, H. Harrison, Texas
A young lady of property
Television play. Teen-age girl whose only interest in life is house she inherited from her dead mother, finds that her father intends to sell it when he remarries. 3 acts 3m 6w
In Foote, H. Harrison, Texas
In Foote, H. A young lady of property
In Vidal, G. ed. Best television plays

For better, for worse. Watkyn, A.

For God so loved the world. Smith, M. G.

For heaven's sake. Morton, E.

For heaven's sake. Orth, R.

For love of a house. Gray, M.

For our mother Malaya! Richardson, L.

For soldiers everywhere. Carlson, B. W.

For the love of Pete. Gehman, H. M.

For want of a character. Quinn, C.

Ford, John
The broken heart
Jacobean tragedy in verse set at court of Laconia in Sparta. Revenge of Orgilus against ambitious Ithocles who forced his sister, Penthea, into unhappy marriage. Vocal and instrumental music and dancing. 5 acts 18 scenes 13m 6w extras 10 interiors 2 exteriors
In Ford, J. Five plays
The lover's melancholy
Jacobean tragicomedy in verse. Prince's melancholy is dispelled by discovery that strange youth is really beautiful girl in disguise. Includes a masque. 5 acts 12 scenes 12m 4w extras 6 interiors
In Ford, J. Five plays
Love's sacrifice
Jacobean tragedy in verse set in Renaissance Italy. Fatal outcome of a courtier's love for virtuous wife of elderly Duke of Pavia. Dancing with background music. 5 acts 15 scenes 11m 5w extras 11 interiors
In Ford, J. Five plays
Perkin Warbeck
Jacobean historical tragedy in verse. Chronicle play about Perkin Warbeck, pretender to English throne during reign of Henry VII. 5 acts 18 scenes 21m 3w extras 7 interiors 6 exteriors
In Ford, J. Five plays
'Tis pity she's a whore
Jacobean tragedy in verse, set in Renaissance Italy. Disastrous consequences of young man's incestuous love for sister. 5 acts 27 scenes 22m 8w extras 1 setting
In Ford, J. Five plays
In McIlwraith, A. K. ed. Five Stuart tragedies
See also Dekker, T. jt. auth.

Ford, Ruth
Requiem for a nun. Random House 1959 105p illus
Based on novel by William Faulkner. Negro woman is tried for murder of white child she was caring for. Set in deep South. 3 acts 5m 2w 3 interiors

Ford, Ruth, and Faulkner, William
Requiem for a nun (condensation)
In The Best plays of 1958-1959

A foregone conclusion. Howells, W. D. and Poel, W.

Foreigners. See Aliens

The foresters. Tennyson, A.

Forever Eve. Lathrop, D.

Forever Judy. Lindsay, H. C.

Forgery
Percy, E. and Denham, L. The man with expensive tastes

Forgery of works of art
Kurnitz, H. Reclining figure

The forgotten factor. Thornhill, A.

The forgotten hero. Miller, H. L.

The forgotten land. Sheffield, J.

Forrest, George. See Wright, R. jt. auth.

Forsyth, James
Héloise. Theatre Arts 1958 84p front (The Drama lib)
12th century love story of Héloïse and Abelard. Set in France. 3 acts 7m 2w 3 interiors 4 exteriors
—Same;
In Cordell, R. A. and Matson, L. eds. The off-Broadway theatre

Forsythe, Anthony
No mother to guide her; or, More to be pitied than censured. French 1955 101p
Melodrama. Villain tries to drug heroine. 3 acts 5m 8w 1 interior

Fortunata writes a letter. Apstein, T.

Fortunatus and the purse (dramatization) See Dekker, T. Old Fortunatus

The fortune of Merrylegs and Tawny-Whiskers. Molloy, L. L.

Fortune-telling
Deval, J. Tonight in Samarkand
Jonson, B. The alchemist
Parker, K. T. A cup of tea
See also Dreams

Foss, Jack
Courage, '53
Radio play. American soldiers fighting in Korean War exhibit courage without being able to define it. Background music. 7m 1w
In Prescott, H. ed. Patrioscript

Foster, Stephen Collins
Green, P. The Stephen Foster story
Woolsey, J. and Sechrist, E. H. Stephen Foster, beautiful dreamer

Foster home care
Foote, H. John Turner Davis
See also Adoption

The founders. Green, P.

Foundlings
Olfson, L. Silas Marner

Fouquier-Tinville, Antoine Quentin
Hochwaelder, F. The public prosecutor

Four bells means glory! Dunlop, R. S.

Four for the money. Carmichael, F.

Four frightened sisters. Spence, W.

Four winds. Atkinson, A.

The fourposter. Hartog, J. de

A fourth for bridge. Johnston, D.

Fourth of July
Buell, H. Fat woman picnic
Emurian, E. K. God of our fathers

Fowler, Mary G.
c The enchanted pumpkin
Halloween. A little boy learns that wicked witch changed another little boy into pumpkin. 2 scenes 1b extras 2 interiors
In Birdsall, R. ed. Creative plays for every school month

Fox, Frank
My little Margie (adaptation) See Sergel, K. My little Margie

The fox. See Jonson, B. Volpone

The fox and the grapes. Moore, S. S.

The fox mound. Sakanishi, S. tr.

Fraidy cat. Martens, A. C.

France
History—House of Valois, 1328-1589
Anouilh, J. The lark
Chapman, G. Bussy D'Ambois
History—16th century
Dryden, J. and Lee, N. The Duke of Guise

France—*Continued*

History—Revolution, 1789-1794
Anderson, M. The feast of Ortolans
Graveley, G. The mountain flock
Hochwaelder, F. The public prosecutor
McConnell, J. The red cloak

History—Restoration, 1814-1830
Scribe, E. The queen's gambit

History—German occupation, 1940-1945
Kneale, N. Mrs Wickens in the fall

Politics and government—Third Republic, 1870-1940
Herald, H.; Herczeg, G. and Raine, N. R. The life of Émile Zola

Social conditions
Mindel, J. Freeing the land

Social life and customs—House of Valois, 1328-1589
Olfson, L. Quentin Durward

Social life and customs—Bourbons, 1579-1789
Ashton, E. B. To serve a king
Jackson, B. Doctor's delight
Malleson, M. The misanthrope
Malleson, M. Sganarelle
Mills, H. The little glass clock
Molière, J. B. P. Coxcombs in petticoats
Molière, J. B. P. Five plays
Molière, J. B. P. The imaginary invalid
Molière, J. B. P. The learned ladies
Molière, J. B. P. Love's the best doctor
Molière, J. B. P. The middle-class gentleman
Molière, J. B. P. The misanthrope
Molière, J. B. P. The miser
Molière, J. B. P. The miser, and Coxcombs in petticoats (2 plays)
Molière, J. B. P. The physician in spite of himself
Molière, J. B. P. The precious damsels
Molière, J. B. P. The pretentious young ladies
Molière, J. B. P. The reluctant doctor
Molière, J. B. P. The school for wives
Molière, J. B. P. The self-made gentleman
Molière, J. B. P. Six prose comedies (6 plays)
Molière, J. B. P. The slave of truth
Molière, J. B. P. The slave of truth; Tartuffe; The imaginary invalid (3 plays)
Molière, J. B. P. Tartuffe
Molière, J. B. P. The would-be gentleman
Molière, J. B. P. The would-be invalid
Olfson, L. Cyrano de Bergerac
Rostand, E. Cyrano de Bergerac

Social life and customs—17th century
See France—Social life and customs—Bourbons, 1589-1789

Social life and customs—1789-1900
Musset, A. de. Caprice
Musset, A. de. A comedy and two proverbs (3 plays)

Musset, A. de. A door should be either open or shut
Musset, A. de. It's impossible to think of everything

Francesca da Rimini. Boker, G. H.

Francesco d'Assisi, Saint
Mary Francis, Sister. Christmas at Greccio
Swann, M. The Little Poor Man of Assisi
White, N. E. The billion dollar saint

Francis of Assisi, Saint. See Francesco d'Assisi, Saint

Francquen, Leonard de. See De Francquen, Leonard

Frank Anne
Anne Frank: diary of a young girl (dramatization) See Goodrich, F. and Hackett, A. The diary of Anne Frank

Frankel, Betty S.
c 'Way out West
A group of children spend the summer with their uncle on his cattle ranch. 3 acts 8m 3w 4b 4g 2 exteriors
In Birdsall, R. ed. Creative plays for every school month

Frankie and Albert. Hughes, E.

Franklin, Benjamin
c Feder, B. Benjamin Franklin
Green, P. Franklin and the King
Kissen, F. Benjamin Franklin: statesman and inventor

Franklin, Clay
Boy appeal. Dramatic 1956 75p illus
Domestic comedy. Father's prize cow changes family fortune and shows teenager, Sally, how to use brain to attract boys. 3 acts 5 scenes 6m 10w 1 interior

Franklin and the King. Green, P.

Fraud
Kober, A. and Oppenheimer, G. A mighty man is he
Miller, H. L. The Lincoln cupboard
Olfson, L. David Copperfield and Uriah Heep
Reach, J. Patterns
See also Imposters and imposture; Swindlers and swindling

Fray Junípero Serra. Helm, M.

Freedom. See Liberty

Freedom is our heritage. Brown, R. M.

Freedom of the press. See Liberty of the press

Freedom's bird. Smith, B.

Freeing the land. Mindel, J.

Freeman, Leonard
The answer. French 1958 28p illus
Derelict who frequents bar on New York's East Side is writing a play which he says has answer to world peace. 1 act 7m 1w 1 interior

Freeman, Mary Wilkins
A New England nun (dramatization) See Sergel, R. A New England nun
The revolt of mother (dramatization) See Sergel, R. The revolt of mother

French and Indian War. See United States —History—French and Indian War, 1755-1763

French drama
Medieval
Pathelin. The farce of Master Pierre Pathelin
17th century
Corneille, P. Attila
Corneille, P. Don Sanche d'Aragon
Corneille, P. Héraclius
Corneille, P. La mort de Pompée
Corneille, P. Othon
Corneille, P. Pulchérie
Corneille, P. Sertorius
Corneille, P. Suréna
Molière, J. B. P. The critique of The school for wives
Molière, J. B. P. The Versailles impromptu
Racine, J. B. Phaedra
French Guinea. See Guinea, French
French in England
Olfson, L. Monsieur Beaucaire
French language
Study and teaching
Rattigan, T. French without tears
French Revolution. See France—History—Revolution, 1789-1794
French without tears. Rattigan, T.
A **fresco** for UNESCO. Fisher, A. and Rabe, O.
The **Friday** Foursome packs a box. Barbee, L.
Friedberg, William. See Warnick C. Heidi; Warnick, C. and Pahl, M. Adventures of Marco Polo
Friend, Milton
The Charleston craze. French 1956 35p
    Romantic comedy. Teen-age girl's romance with her partner in dance contest is almost wrecked when he apparently elopes with another girl. 1 act 2m 5w extras 1 interior
Friendly relations. Liggat, J.
Friends. Spamer, C.
Friends, Society of
Bielby, M. R. I was in prison
Friendship
Asbrand, K. Neighbors should be neighborly
Burgess, C. V. Ken changes his mind
Gregory, Lady. The workhouse ward
c Hark, M. and McQueen, N. Good neighbors
Ridley, A. You, my guests!
Scholl, R. The golden axe
Frings, Ketti
Look homeward, angel. French 1958 99p illus
    Domestic comedy. Based on novel by Thomas Wolfe. Emotional conflicts between members of family in which individualistic young boy struggles to break away. 3 acts 5 scenes 10m 9w 1 interior 1 exterior
    Trade edition published by Scribner
—Same;
In Watson, E. B. ed. Contemporary drama: fifteen plays
Look homeward, angel (condensation)
In The Best plays of 1957-1958
In Broadway's best, 1958

Frogs
c Spamer, C. The fish that wished to live on land
The frogs. Aristophanes
The frogs of Spring. Benchley, N.
From morn to midnight. Kaiser, G.
From Paradise to Butte. Finch, R.
The frontier. Trick, O. B.
Frontier and pioneer life
Emmons, D. G. A costly gold hunt
Emmons, D. G. Joint occupation, joint celebration
Emmons, D. G. Ours to the forty-ninth
Emmons, D. G. Through Naches Pass
Emmons, D. G. Who's for the Divide?
c Quinlan, M. E. Pete of the rancho
Wasserman, D. and Balch, J. Elisha and the long knives
Canada
Gowan, E. P. Breeches from Bond Street
Indian Territory
Riggs, L. Roadside
Rodgers, R. and Hammerstein, O. Oklahoma!
Kentucky
Wetmore, A. The pedlar
Middle West
Howard, V. Johnny Appleseed in danger
Southwest, New
Nichols, D. Stagecoach
Tennessee
Chadwicke, A. Davy Crockett
The West
c Carlson, B. W. Jim Bridger and his eight-hour echo
McCaslin, N. Tall Bill and his big ideas
Shaw, B. The shewing-up of Blanco Posnet
Frost, Rex
Small hotel. [French's Acting ed] French (London) 1956 73p illus
    Comedy. In British residence hotel. the manager attempts to fire elderly but esteemed waiter. 3 acts 5m 6w 1 interior
—Same;
In Plays of the year v13
Frost, Robert
The death of the hired man (dramatization) See Gould, J. R. The death of the hired man
Frost-Bite and the eleven Fidgets. Watkins, D.
Fruit of the tree. Donisthorpe, G. S.
Fry, Christopher
The dark is light enough. Dramatists 1957 120p illus music
    Verse play based on incident in Hungarian revolt against the Austro-Hungarian Empire, 1848-1849. Character study of courageous Austrian countess who sheltered ne'er-do-well ex-son-in-law, deserter from Hungarian army. 3 acts 12m 3w 1 interior
    Trade edition published by Oxford
The dark is light enough (condensation)
In The Best plays of 1954-1955

Fry, Christopher—*Continued*
The firstborn. Dramatists 1958 92p illus
Verse play based on Old Testament
account of conflict between Moses and
Pharaoh. 3 acts 10m 3w 1 interior
Trade edition published by Oxford
—Same;
In Halverson, M. ed. Religious drama 1

A phoenix too frequent. ₍Rev. acting ed₎
Dramatists 1953 50p illus
Romantic comedy in verse. Ephesus'
widow is determined to die upon hus-
band's tomb, but changes her mind
when she falls in love with a corporal.
Based on the story: Widow of Ephesus,
by Petronius. 1m 2w 1 interior
Trade edition illustrated by Ronald
Searle published by Oxford
—Same;
In Warnock, R. Representative modern
plays, British

A sleep of prisoners. ₍Rev. acting ed₎
Dramatists 1953 64p
Modern mystery play in verse. Four
men, in series of dreams wrapped in
Biblical lore, review man's struggle
against outer and inner conflicts. 4m
1 interior

Thor, with angels. ₍Rev. acting ed₎
Dramatists 1953 57p illus
Verse play set in Jutish farmstead near
Canterbury in 596. Young Briton, captured by Jutes in battle, shows his
captors the difference between Christianity and their pagan beliefs. 1 act
8m 3w 1 setting

Venus observed. ₍Rev. acting ed₎ Dramatists 1953 92p illus
Romantic comedy in verse. Rivalry of
father and son for love of daughter of
father's bailiff. 3 acts 4 scenes 6m 4w
2 interiors
—Same;
In Watson, E. B. and Pressey, B. eds.
Contemporary drama: eleven plays

Fry, Elizabeth (Gurney)
Bielby, M. R. I was in prison

Fuente ovejuna. Vega, L. de.

Fugitives from justice. See Escapes

A full moon in March. Yeats, W. B.

Full of vim. Fisher, A.

Fuller, John G. ed. See Baker's Roaring
twenties scrapbook

Fuller, Ruth
The Noël candle; dramatized from the
story by Clement C. Moore. Dramatic
1956 28p illus
Christmas. Play based on legend that
a light in the window on Christmas Eve
will attract the Christ Child. 1 act 2m
5w 1b 1 interior

Fumed oak. Coward, N.

Funa-Benkei. Kwanze, K. N.

Fund raising
c Woolsey, J. and Sechrist, E. H. Pumpkin
is the password

Funeral sermons
Thomas, D. and Slocumb, P. Next-to-last
rites

Funeral service
Claiborne, R. and Banks, F. The last
leaf

Funt, Julian
The magic and the loss. ₍Acting ed₎
French 1954 87p illus
Career girl trying to secure Madison
Avenue vice presidency, finds life of a
professional woman hard and lonely.
3 acts 5 scenes 4m 2w 1 interior
The magic and the loss (condensation)
In The Best plays of 1953-1954

Fur trade
Emmons, D. G. Astor's bid for empire

Furies
Aeschylus. The Eumenides

Future
Armer, A. and Grauman, W. E. To be
alone
The future is in eggs. Ionesco, E.

Future life
Chown, H. Account rendered

G

G for Gettysburg. Hark, M. and McQueen,
N.

Gabriel visits Mary. Spamer, C. M.

Gairdner, Charles Campbell, and Pilcher,
Rosamunde
The dashing white sergeant. Acting ed.
Evans 1955 80p illus
Spoiled girl faces life on her seventeenth
birthday. Scene laid in 20th century
Scotland. 3 acts 5 scenes 4m 2w 1 in-
terior

El gallo. Ullman, S. S.

Galsworthy, John
Escape
Escaped convict presents ethical problems to people with whom he seeks refuge, especially the parson of small
church. 9 episodes 17m 8w 1g 3 interiors
5 exteriors
In A Treasury of the theatre
Loyalties
Various class loyalties in British society
create conflict and discrimination against
"outsiders." 3 acts 7 scenes 17m 3w 5
interiors
In Sper, F. ed. Favorite modern plays
In Warnock, R. Representative modern
plays, British

Gamblers. Gogol, N.

Gambling
Gogol, N. Gamblers
MacDougall, R. The facts of life
Semple, L. Golden fleecing
See also Cardsharping

A game of chess. Murray, J.

Games
c Spamer, C. Fishermen

Gangs
Bernstein, L. West Side story
The gang's all here. Lawrence, J. and Lee,
R. E.

Gangsters. See Brigands and robbers

Garber, Helen Whitmer. See Jordan, L. M.
jt. auth.

García Lorca, Federico
  Blood wedding; tr. from the Spanish by
    Graham-Luján and Richard L. O'Con-
    nell
      Symbolic tragic folk drama. Marriage
      to unwilling bride brings death to both
      bridegroom and former suitor. 3 acts 7
      scenes 4m 7w extras 5 interiors 2 ex-
      teriors
    In Bierman, J.; Hart, J. and Johnson,
      S., eds. The dramatic experience
    In García Lorca, F. Three tragedies of
      Federico García Lorca
    In A Treasury of the theatre
    In Watson, E. B. ed. Contemporary
      drama: fifteen plays
  The house of Bernarda Alba
      Tragedy. Tyrannical proud provincial
      Spanish mother guards family honor as
      five unhappy spinster daughters lan-
      guish under her roof. 3 acts 10w extras
      1 interior 1 exterior
    In García Lorca, F. Three tragedies of
      Federico García Lorca
  Yerma
      Tragedy in verse. Childless woman final-
      ly kills husband who denies her the
      children she craves. 3 acts 6 scenes 6m
      17w 1b 2 interiors 3 exteriors
    In García Lorca, F. Three tragedies of
      Federico García Lorca
Garden hold-up. Miller, H. L.
A garden in Verona. Morris, T. B.
The Garden of Eden. York plays
Gardening
  Asbrand, K. Spring fever
  Bagnold, E. The chalk garden
    See also Agricultural pests
Gareth triumphs. Mantle, M.
Gargoyle. Sakanishi, S. tr.
Garis, Roger
  The Inn
      Television play. Man who stops in
      small town is immediately imprisoned
      for murder although he has never been
      there before. 14m 3w extras
    In Roberts, E. B. Television writing
      and selling
The garroters. Howells, W. D.
Garry, James Francis
  The bonehead case. Eldridge 1954 15p
    (Eldridge Novelties)
      Farce. Lawyer persuades athlete Phyneas
      Q. Bonehead to sue college for lack of
      education. 3 scenes 6m 2w 2 interiors
      1 exterior
Garson, Henry. See Beloin, E. jt. auth.
Garver, Juliet
c The Appletons and the UN
      Parents of quarreling children decide to
      start using United Nations procedures
      in their own home. 3 acts 3m 1w 2g
      1 interior
    In Birdsall, R. ed. Creative plays for
      every school month
  Father lives with seven women. Eldridge
    1955 26p (Eldridge Popular one-act play-
    scripts)
      Domestic comedy. Father's book describ-
      ing how he lives with his wife and six
      daughters becomes best seller. 1 act 3m
      13w 1 interior

Honest to goodness. Art Craft 1953 25p
      Domestic comedy. Young girl, wishing
      to have the bedroom to herself, invents
      truth powder to prod her older sister's
      fiance into matrimony. 1 act 3m 3w
      1 interior
Gas (I). Kaiser, G.
Gas—Part II. Kaiser, G.
Gassner, John
  The Brome Abraham and Isaac; an acting
    version in modern English, by John
    Gassner, with original music by Thomas
    Matthews
      15th century English miracle play based
      on Biblical story of sacrifice of Isaac.
      Verse play with background music. 4m
      1 exterior
    In Switz, T. M. and Johnston, R. A. eds.
      Great Christian plays
Gattey, C. Neilson, and Bramley-Moore, Z.
  Mrs Adams and Eve. Deane 1955 36p
    ("Deane's" Ser. of plays)
      Comedy. American thrift-shop operator
      makes deal with Mrs Adams, English
      dealer in second hand clothes. 1 act
      7w 1 interior
  Mrs Griggs loses her bed. Deane 1955
    28p ("Deane's" Ser. of plays)
      Domestic comedy. Young man gets rid
      of unwelcome mother-in-law and has
      pleasant surprise for his faithful wife.
      1 act 1m 5w 1 interior
  Treasure from France. Deane 1956 27p
    ("Deane's" Ser. of plays)
      Romantic comedy. England, 1793. All
      except one guest who have come to
      surprise party for exiled French vicomte,
      leave when they discover he is penniless.
      1 act 10w 1 interior
Gay, John
  Beggar's opera (adaptation) See Brecht,
    B. The threepenny opera
The gazebo. Coppel, A.
Gazzo, Michael V.
  A hatful of rain. French 1956 118p
      Young veteran, determined to conquer
      his drug habit, receives help and under-
      standing from his wife. 3 acts 6 scenes
      7m 2w 1 interior
      Trade edition published by Random
      House
  —Same;
    In Best American plays; 4th ser.
  A hatful of rain (condensation)
    In Theatre, 1956
Gehman, Helen M.
  For the love of Pete. Eldridge 1955 22p
    (Eldridge Popular one-act playscripts)
      Comedy. Young woman just barely
      escapes mistake of overdressing for her
      prospective date. 1 act 6w 1 interior
Gehman, Richard. See Blankman, H. By
  hex
Geiger, Milton
  The democrat and the commissar
      Radio play. Thomas Jefferson, in a
      posthumous appearance, points out to
      Russian commissar differences between
      American and Communist theories of
      revolution. Background music. 5m
    In Jeffersonian Heritage (Radio pro-
      gram) The Jefferson heritage
  Edwin Booth. Dramatists 1959 70p illus
      Edwin Booth while a boy caring for his
      ranting, hard-drinking actor father,
      develops his own ideas of acting Shake-
      spearean plays. 3 acts 5m 3w 1b 1 setting

Geiger, Milton—*Continued*
Light and liberty
Radio play. Thomas Jefferson refutes erroneous statements of French naturalist, Comte de Buffon, concerning United States. 5m extras
In Jeffersonian Heritage (Radio program) The Jefferson heritage

The return of a patriot
Radio play. In 1789 Thomas Jefferson is asked by President Washington to become the first United States Secretary of State. Background music. 5m 2w
In Jeffersonian Heritage (Radio program) The Jefferson heritage

The university of the United States
Radio play. Thomas Jefferson describes his life long fight for public education. Background music. 6m extras
In Jeffersonian Heritage (Radio program) The Jefferson heritage

Geishas
Patrick, J. The Teahouse of the August Moon

Gelber, Jack
The connection. Grove 1960 96p illus (Evergreen original)
Nightmarish world of the heroin addict. 2 acts 14m 1w 1 interior

General George. Very, A.

General stores
c Miller, H. L. The country store cat

Genet, Jean
The blacks: a clown show; tr. from the French by Bernard Frechtman. Grove 1960 128p
Attack on white supremacy with elements of comic fantasy: Negroes, as caricatures of white types, act out murder of a white man in play within a play. 8m 5w 1 interior

The maids; tr. from the French by Bernard Frechtman. Grove 1954 102p (An Evergreen bk)
Tragedy. Two maids both love and hate their mistress against whom they conspire, even to attempting murder. 1 act 3w 1 interior
—Same;
In Gassner, J. ed. A treasury of the theatre

Genius. See Gifted children

Genjō. Kongō, Y.

The **gentle** assassin. Spring, H.

The **gentle** gunman. MacDougall, R.

The **gentle** one. Brenner, M.

The **gentleman** walks outside. Yudkoff, A.

A **gentleman's** daughters. Stuart, A.

The **Gentlemen** Smugglers. Bayliss, R. G.

Gently does it. Green, J.

Geology. See Mountains; Volcanoes

George, Saint
Addis, H. St George's Day

George III, King of Great Britain
Green, P. Franklin and the King

George IV, King of Great Britain
Ginsbury, N. The first gentleman

George, Charles
Fanny, the frivolous flapper; book, lyrics and music by Charles George. French 1960 72p illus music
Musical comedy set in the 1920's. "Flappers," their boyfriends, and activities centering around French dress shop. Includes songs with musical scores. 1 act 6m 4w 1 interior

Golden butterfly. See Strauss, J. Golden butterfly

George, Lillian Dunlap
When the little angel sang
A little angel comes to Bethlehem to sing about birth of Christ. 1 act 2m 3w 1 exterior
In Brings, L. M. ed. The modern treasury of Christmas plays

George, Millicent
Symphonie pastorale. De Wolfe & Stone 1954 75p
Tragedy based on story by Gide. Protestant pastor fails ministry and family when he falls in love with blind orphan girl he takes into his home. Background music. 3 acts 3m 3w 1 interior

George Eliot. Spamer, C.

The **George** Gobel show. Kanter, H. and others

George Washington: father of his country. Kissen, F.

George Washington serves his country. Woolsey, J. and Sechrist, E. H.

German-American dialect. See Dialect—German-American

German folk-lore. See Folk-lore, German

Germans in the United States
Miller, H. L. Be my "walentine"

Germany
History—1618-1648
See Thirty Years' War, 1618-1648

History—Allied occupation, 1945-
Ustinov, P. The love of four colonels

Social conditions
Becque, H. The weavers
Van Druten, J. I am a camera

Social life and customs—18th century
Schiller, F. von. Intrigue and love

Germs versus Fairy Good-Health. Close, E.

The **get-together** dinner. Fisher, A. and Rabe, O.

Gethers, Steven
Cracker money
Television play. Inadequate salary poses ethical problems for high school teacher. 9m 4w
In Best television plays, 1957

Getting in line. Fisher, A. and Rabe, O.

Getting it straight. Fisher, A.

Getting married. Shaw, B.

Getting ready for winter. Very, A.

Gettysburg. National Military Park
McMahon, B. Guided tour

Gettysburg, Battle of, 1863
Sapinsley, A. Lee at Gettysburg

Getzinger, Elaine Walker

Let your light so shine
    Honest candidate, defeated by corrupt
    political machine, is tempted to abandon
    high ethical code. 3 scenes 2m 2w 1 in-
    terior
    In Brings, L. M. comp. The golden
        book of church plays

Not without honor
    A lame girl of Nazareth is healed through
    faith in Jesus Christ. 3 scenes 10w
    1 interior
    In Brings, L. M. comp. The golden
        book of church plays

Promise of the angels
    Easter play. Woman's faith in Jesus
    Christ is vindicated by his Resurrection.
    4 scenes 2m 3w 1 interior 1 exterior
    In Brings, L. M. comp. The golden
        book of church plays

Ghelderode, Michel de

Barabbas; tr. by George Hauger
    Effect of Christ's Crucifixion on Barab-
    bas, the criminal chosen by the crowd
    to be released instead of Christ. Based
    on the New Testament accounts in the
    Gospels of the Crucifixion. 3 acts 14m
    3w extras 1 interior 2 exteriors
    In Ghelderode, M. de. Seven plays

The blind men (Les aveugles) tr. by
    George Hauger
    Three Flemish blind men on pilgrimage
    to Rome perish because greed and dis-
    trust leads them to refuse offer of help.
    A dramatic interpretation of Pieter
    Breughel the Elder's painting: The par-
    able of the blind men. 1 act 4m 1 exterior
    In Ghelderode, M. de. Seven plays

Chronicles of hell (Fastes d'Enfer) tr. by
    George Hauger
    In medieval Flanders the death of a
    Catholic bishop, hated by his colleagues
    but adored by his parish, reveals the
    worst side of human nature. 1 act 10m
    1w extras 1 interior
    In Ghelderode, M. de. Seven plays

Lord Halewyn (Sire Halewijn) tr. by
    Gerard Hopkins
    Based on Flemish romance about an
    insane young nobleman who used magic
    powers to lure young maids to their
    death. 14 scenes 11m 5w extras 6 in-
    teriors 2 exteriors
    In Ghelderode, M. de. Seven plays

Pantagleize; tr. by George Hauger
    Tragedy. A philosopher and dreamer
    inadvertently gives long awaited signal
    for revolution. 3 acts 9 scenes 1m extras
    6 interiors 3 exteriors
    In Ghelderode, M. de. Seven plays

Three actors and their drama (Trois ac-
    teurs, un drame) tr. by George Hauger
    Play within a play. Triangle situation
    among cast of a play is not resolved
    as playwright had planned. 1 act 4m 1w
    1 interior
    In Ghelderode, M. de. Seven plays

The women at the tomb (Les femmes au
    tombeau) tr. by George Hauger
    Except for grief-stricken Virgin Mary,
    all the women waiting to visit Christ's
    tomb are eager to gain some personal
    advantage. 1 act 1m 11w 1 interior
    In Ghelderode, M. de. Seven plays

The **ghost** from outer space. Greth, Le R. E.

A **ghost** of distinction. Spence, W.

The **ghost** sonata. Strindberg, A.

The **ghost** tiger. Tennant, K.

Ghosts

Allen, J. Kind cousin
Anderson, M. High Tor
Armstrong, W. F. Haunted rooms
Bate, S. Holiday haunts
Brydon, M. W. and Ziegler, E. The re-
    luctant ghost
Clark, A. W. Graves ghost
Delderfield, R. F. The Rounderlay tradi-
    tion
Dennys, J. The lawn
Ferrini, V. Telling of the North Star
Greth, Le R. E. Host to a ghost
Hare, W. B. A Christmas carol
Hennessy, M. A. The American spirit
Jones-Evans, E. Death on the line
Komparu, Z. U. Kumasaka
Kwanze, K. Eguchi
Kwanze, K. Funa-Benkei
Kwanze, K. Kayoi Komachi
Kwanze, M. Aya no tsuzumi
Kwanze, M. Kiyotsune
Kwanze, M. Nishikigi
Kwanze, M. Tamura
Kyd, T. The Spanish tragedy
Mishima, Y. The damask drum
Mizer, J. Golden slippers
Murray, J. The door
Olfson, L. Hamlet
Rose, Le R. Spooks alive
Sherriff, R. C. The white carnation
Spence, W. A ghost of distinction
Spielman, F. The stingiest man in town
Tobias, J. The crazy mixed-up Kidds
Vidal, G. The turn of the screw
    See also Apparitions; Horror tales;
    Spiritualism

Ghosts. Ibsen, H.

Ghosts on guard. Fisher, A.

Giant of the timber. McCaslin, N.

Giants of the city. Flavelle, I. B.

Giblin, James

My bus is always late. Dramatic 1955
    23p illus
    Old lady waiting for bus in suburban
    bus station befriends a vagrant and
    reconciles a young couple. 1 act 5m 3w
    1 setting

Gibson, Martha Norwood

Return engagement. French 1958 16p illus
    A teenager at a dance, a wallflower, has
    day dream that she is a movie star. 1
    act 8m 6w 1 interior

Senior play. French 1959 23p illus
    Teacher has to resist pressure to give
    lead in class play to daughter of in-
    fluential family, when she considers
    another girl more talented. 1 act 2m 5w
    1 interior

Will the ladies please come to order.
    French 1958 16p illus
    Comedy. At a meeting of ladies' club,
    the true natures of four club officers
    are revealed. 1 act 8w 1 interior

Gibson, William

The miracle worker. Knopf 1957 131p
    Television play. The childhood of Helen
    Keller, as she first rebels against her
    teacher, Anne Macy Sullivan. 5m 3w 1b
    2g extras

The miracle worker (condensation)
    In Broadway's best, 1960

Gibson, William—*Continued*

Two for the seesaw. French 1960 104p illus
> Poor young man decides to return to his wealthy wife after affair with New York City dancer. 3 acts 9 scenes 1m 1w 2 interiors

—Same;
> *In* Gibson, W. The seesaw log

Two for the seesaw (condensation)
> *In* Broadway's best, 1958

Gide, André

The immoralist (dramatization) See Goetz, R. and Goetz, A. The immoralist

Symphonie pastorale (dramatization) See George, M. Symphonie pastorale

Gideon (Biblical character)

c Spamer, C. M. Gideon and the angel

Gideon and the angel. Spamer, C. M.

The **gift.** Lumsden, M.

The **gift** of corn. McCaslin, N.

The **gift** of Tenyin. Tumpane, J. D.

The **gift** of the drum. Goulding, D. J.

The **gift** of the Holy Spirit. Phillips, J. B.

A **gift** to the world. Newman, D.

Gifted children

Delmar, V. Mid-summer

Gifts

Asbrand, K. More blessed to give

Lynch, P. Just a little something for Christmas

McMullen, J. C. Deep freeze

Gifts for mother. Feder, L.

Gifts for the elves. Woolsey, J. and Sechrist, E. H.

Gifts for young Abe. Very, A.

Gifts of gold. Asbrand, K.

Gigi. Loos, A.

Gilbert, Jane

c Community Easter parade
> Verses written to familiar songs tell how various people in community make Easter a pleasant holiday for everyone. Large mixed cast

> *In* Birdsall, R. ed. Creative plays for every school month

Gilbert, Michael

A clean kill
> When a woman dies suddenly of poisoning, estranged husband is accused of murdering her with newly invented cleaning fluid. 3 acts 5m 3w 1 interior

> *In* Plays of the year v21

Gilbert, W. S. See Sullivan, A. Ruddigore

Gill, Mildred L.

c Treasure hunt
> On the last day of primary school children tell about the different educational treasures they found in school. Large mixed cast 1 interior

> *In* Birdsall, R. ed. Creative plays for every school month

Gillette, William

Secret Service
> The affairs of Northern spy and his Southern sweetheart in Richmond, during the time when Union forces were besieging city. 4 acts 4 scenes 12m 5w extras 2 interiors

> *In* Quinn, A. H. ed. Representative American plays

Secret Service (condensation)
> *In* The Best plays of 1894-1899

Gilliat, Sidney. See Launder, F. jt. auth.

Gin (Cotton machinery) See Cotton gins and ginning

Gin and bitterness. Richards, S.

The **gingerbread** house. Spamer, C.

Ginnes, Abram S. and Wallach, Ira

Drink to me only. French 1958 78p illus
> Comedy. Lawyer, defending playboy who shot his seventh wife has to prove possibility of remaining conscious after two bottles of whiskey. 3 acts 10m 8w 2 interiors

Ginsbury, Norman

The first gentleman. Dramatists 1957 95p illus
> Historical drama. Early 19th century England is setting for struggle between Prince Regent and daughter over marriage choice. 3 acts 7 scenes 10m 11w extras 5 interiors

Gipsies

Carpenter, F. The setting sun

Giraudoux, Jean

The Apollo of Bellac. Adapted by Maurice Valency from the French. French 1954 37p illus
> Comedy. Shy girl looking for a job meets nondescript little man who teaches her to use flattery on men to gain success. 1 act 9m 3w 1 interior

—Same
> *In* Cerf, B. and Cartmell, V. H. eds. 24 favorite one-act plays

> *In* Giraudoux, J. Four plays

Duel of angels (Pour Lucrèce) tr. by Christopher Fry. Oxford 1959 [c1958] 66p
> Domestic comedy about virtue and vice as portrayed by two women. Complications arise when a virtuous woman is supposedly seduced by modern day Don Juan. 3 acts 8m 5w extras 2 interiors 1 exterior

Duel of angels (condensation)
> *In* The Best plays of 1959-1960
> *In* Broadway's best, 1960

Electra
> Tragedy. Based on Greek legend of Orestes and Electra, son and daughter of Agamemnon, who avenged their father's murder. 2 acts 23 scenes 7m 7w 3g extras 1 exterior

> *In* Bentley, E. ed. The modern theatre v 1

The enchanted
> Government inspector in provincial French town tries unsuccessfully to convince a young girl she must rid herself of her belief in spirits and make-believe. Then she falls in love and immediately believes in the real world. 3 acts 9m 3w 7g 1 interior 1 exterior

> *In* Giraudoux, J. Four plays

Judith; English version by John K. Savacool
> Modernized version of the apocryphal Old Testament Book of Judith. During siege of city of Shechem by Assyrians, Judith, beautiful young Jewish widow, succeeds in delivering her people by murdering Assyrian general, Holofernes. 3 acts 10m 3w 1b extras 2 interiors

> *In* Bentley, E. ed. The modern theatre v3

Giraudoux, Jean—*Continued*
The madwoman of Chaillot; adapted, and
with introduction by Maurice Valency
Farcical fantasy. Eccentric Parisian
countess and her friends foil plot to
raze Paris in order to get oil which
prospectors believe is beneath it. 2 acts
17m 8w extras 1 interior 1 exterior
In Gassner, J. ed. Twenty best Euro-
pean plays on the American stage
In Giraudoux, J. Four plays
In Griffin, A. V. Living theatre
In A Treasury of the theatre
In Watson, E. B. and Pressey, B. eds.
Contemporary drama: eleven plays
Ondine; adapted by Maurice Valency.
[Acting ed] French 1956 96p
Fairy tale based on German traditional
tale of water sprite who married a
knight but could only live on earth as
long as he was faithful to her. 3 acts
17m 12w 2 interiors 1 exterior
Trade edition published by Random
House
—Same
In Gassner, J. ed. Twenty best Euro-
pean plays on the American stage
In Giraudoux, J. Four plays
Ondine (condensation)
In Theatre, 1954
A supplement to Cook's voyage (adapta-
tion) See Valency, M. The virtuous
island
Tiger at the gates; tr. by Christopher Fry.
[Acting ed] French 1956 78p illus music
Treatise on war based on Greek legend
of Trojan War. Hector, the Trojan
warrior, meets Ulysses, emissary of the
Greeks in effort to prevent war. Back-
ground music. 2 acts 15m 6w 1g 1 in-
terior 1 exterior
Trade edition published by Oxford
—Same
In Gassner, J. ed. Twenty best Euro-
pean plays on the American stage
Tiger at the gates (condensation)
In The Best plays of 1955-1956
In Theatre, 1956
The virtuous island. French 1956 44p
illus
Adapted by Maurice Valency from "A
supplement to Cook's voyage" Comedy.
When Captain Cook's ship puts in at
a South Seas island in 1769, two proper
passengers are put ashore to teach na-
tives about morality. 1 act 10m 4w ex-
tras 1 exterior
A girl can tell. Herbert, F. H.
Girl chases boy. Stanton, R.
Girl crazy. Bolton, G. and McGowan, J.
The girl in the coffin. Dreiser, T.
The girl on the Via Flaminia. Hayes, A.
Girl Scouts
Brenner, M. Beacon of strength
c Thompson, B. J. Pleasant dreams
Woolsey, J. and Sechrist, E. H. First aid
in the first troop
Girl wanted. Manion, D.
The girl who had everything. Burke, N.
The girl with the green eyes. Fitch, C.

Girls
Alexander, R. Time out for Ginger
Asbrand, K. Christmas rose
Asbrand, K. Reach for the moon
Bagnold, E. The chalk garden
Burgess, C. V. The virtues of Thelma
Carlton, J. Bab buys a car
c Dunbar, T. M. Girls are so useless!
Farrow, N. Spring prom magic
Hayes, M. and Hayes, J. Penny
Kendall, K. Darling girl
Kesler, H. O. Dream a little dream
Kuehl, W. A. Sunstroke
Lisle, V. The merry matchmaker
McCoy, P. S. The Lieutenant pays his
respects
Martens, A. C. Sugar and spite
Miller, H. L. Heart throbs
Miller, H. L. Just what the doctor ordered
Morris, T. B. A garden in Verona
Murdoch, M. The cuckoo
Paradis, M. B. Midge rings the bell
Payton, D. Nearly beloved
Protter, N. Follow the gleam
Pryor, C. Just my speed
Ratcliffe, D. U. Jingling Lane
Reach, J. Beautiful dreamers
Stuart, A. Lace on her petticoat
Tolkin, M. and Kallen, L. Maybe Tues-
day
See also Adolescence; Children; Youth
Education
See Coeducation
Girls are better than ever. Lusk, D.
Girls are so useless! Dunbar, T. M.
Girls in books. Miller, H. L.
The girls in 509. Teichmann, H.
Girls of summer. Nash, N. R.
Gittings, Robert
Man's estate
Verse play about the boyhood of Saint
Richard of Chichester, of his temptations
and his resistance to them. 1m 3b 2g
chorus 1 exterior
In Two saints' plays
Give us time to sing. Hanig, D.
Giveaway. Kay, I.
Giving goes on. Shelby, K. and Cuny,
T. M.
Gizzlegump. Howard, V.
Glaspell, Susan
Trifles
Discerning sheriff's wife and friend solve
murder but reveal nothing because of
sympathy. 1 act 3m 2w 1 interior
In Cerf, B. and Cartmell, V. H. eds.
24 favorite one-act plays
The glass menagerie. Williams, T.
A glass of bitter. Priestley, J. B.
The glass of water. Scribe, E.
Glass slipper. Armer, A. and Grauman,
W. E.
Glickman, Will. See Bock, J. The body
beautiful; Hague, A. Plain and fancy

Glickman, Will, and Stein, Joseph
Mrs Gibbon's boys. [French's Acting ed]
French (London) 1958 64p
Comedy. Sons break jail causing embarrassment to mother on the wedding day of her second marriage. 3 acts 8m 2w 1 interior

A "globester" trip. Vandenburgh, M.

Gloriana. Lee, N.

Glory in the flower. Inge, W.

The glory of His coming. Peery, R. R.

Gnomes. See Fairies

Goblin market. Marston, M. A.

Goblins. See Fairies

God and Kate Murphy (condensation) Tunney, K. and Synge, J.

God of our fathers. Emurian, E. K.

God so loved the world. Casey, B. M.

Godfrey, Thomas
The Prince of Parthia
Heroic drama in style of Dryden. Dissension between King of Parthia and his sons: murder, revenge and suicide. 5 acts 10 scenes 5m 4w extras 4 interiors 1 exterior
In Quinn, A. H. ed. Representative American plays

Gods
Fisher, A. and Rabe, O. Of gods and men

God's ambassador. Jackson, H. H. S.

Godunov, Boris. See Boris Godunov, Czar of Russia

Goethe, Johann Wolfgang von
Egmont; tr. from the German by Willard R. Trask. Barrons Educ. Ser. 1960 120p
Tragedy. Historical drama of Count Egmont who led 16th century Flemish revolt in the Netherlands. 5 acts 15m 4w extras 6 interiors 3 exteriors
—Same; English version by Michael Hamburger
In Bentley, E. ed. The classic theatre v2
Faust, part 1; tr. by C. F. MacIntyre. New Directions 1957 [c1949] 188p music
Poetic tragedy based on Faust legend of man who sold his soul to the Devil. Aged scholar, transformed by Devil into handsome youth, seduces devout young woman. Songs, music, dancing. 25 scenes Large mixed cast 8 interiors 10 exteriors
—Same; tr. by Alice Raphael; introduction and notes by Jacques Barzun. Rinehart 1955 210p
—Same; tr. by Sir Theodore Martin
In Goethe, J. W. von. Goethe's Faust, parts I and II
Faust, part II; tr. by Sir Theodore Martin
Fantasy based on Faust legend. Faust tastes every form of intellectual and world power but fails to find way to redeem his soul from Devil until at last he promotes a reclamation project that will benefit many people. Music, singing and dancing. 5 acts 27 scenes Large mixed cast 9 interiors 14 exteriors
In Goethe, J. W. von. Goethe's Faust, parts I and II
Iphigenia in Tauris; tr. by Sidney E. Kaplan. Barrons Educ. Ser. 1953 58p
Based on Greek legend of Iphigenia who, while serving as priestess of Artemis, saved her brother, Orestes, from being sacrificed to the goddess. 5 acts 20 scenes 4m 1w 1 exterior

Torquato Tasso; a new tr. with an introduction by Ben Kimpel and T. C. Duncan Eaves. Univ. of Ark. 1956 76p
Tragedy in verse. Based on legend about Italian poet, Tasso, whose unrequited love for a princess drove him insane. 5 acts 24 scenes 3m 2w 2 interiors 1 exterior
The Urfaust; tr. and introduction by Douglas M. Scott. Barrons Educ. Ser. 1958 71p
The author's Faust in its original form. Scholar who has made pact with Devil seduces devout young woman. 10m 4w extras 9 interiors 9 exteriors

Goetz, Augustus. See Goetz, R. jt. auth.

Goetz, Ruth, and Goetz, Augustus
The hidden river. Dramatists 1957 76p illus
Psychological play based on novel by Storm Jameson depicting hatreds and suspicions of a well-to-do French family involved in Underground movement during World War II. 3 acts 5 scenes 7m 3w 1 interior
The hidden river (condensation)
In Broadway's best, 1957
The immoralist. Dramatists 1954 126p illus
A dramatization of novel by André Gide. Couple tries to make a go of their marriage despite the man's homosexuality. Set in France and North Africa in 1900. 3 acts 8 scenes 6m 2w 2 interiors
The immoralist (condensation)
In The Best plays of 1953-1954
In Theatre, 1954

Goggan, John Patrick. See Patrick, John

Gogol, Nikolai
Gamblers; English version by Eric Bentley
Farce. Professional card shark is himself cheated by his colleagues in a complicated maneuver. 1 act 9m 1 interior
In Bentley, E. ed. The modern theatre v3

Goin' round the hoop. Jerome, P.

Gold in the West. Abstance, P. and Abstance, L.

The gold spinner. Spamer, C.

Golden, Edward
Great expectations
Radio adaptation of novel by Charles Dickens. In 19th century England Pip, a poor orphan, reared as gentleman eventually marries proud adopted daughter of rich woman and discovers that his benefactor is a convict he once helped. Background music. 5m 4w
In Burack, A. S. ed. Four-star radio plays for teen-agers
Gulliver's travels in Lilliput Land
Radio adaptation of part of novel by Jonathan Swift. Fantasy satirizing 17th and 18th century European politics. Background music. 15m 1w
In Burack, A. S. ed. Four-star radio plays for teen-agers
The Lady of the Lake
Radio adaptation of poem by Sir Walter Scott. Based on legend of 16th century Scotland concerning suitors of Ellen Douglas, the lady of Loch Katrine. Background music; some ballad singing. 6m 3w chorus extras
In Burack, A. S. ed. Four-star radio plays for teen-agers

Golden, Harry
Only in America (dramatization) See Lawrence, J. and Lee, R. E. Only in America

The **golden** apple. Moross, J.

The **golden** axe. School, R.

A **golden** bell for mother. Very, A.

Golden boy. Odets, C.

Golden butterfly. Strauss, J.

The **golden** cuckoo. Johnston, D.

Golden fleecing. Semple, L.

The **golden** girls. Cusack, D.

The **golden** land. Brenner, M.

Golden rain. Delderfield, R. F.

Golden river. Tarpley, V. and Tarpley, K.

Golden slippers. Mizer, J.

Goldilocks. Kerr, W. and Kerr, J.

Goldilocks and the three bears (dramatization) See Scott, L. B. The three bears

Goldina, Miriam
The courageous one; tr. by Miriam Goldina and Helen Choat. French 1958 85p illus 1
An adaptation of Maxim Gorky's Meshtchane. Emphasizes necessity of courageous, vital stand in life. Contrast between strong people and weak. 3 acts 4 scenes 7m 6w 1 interior

Goldman, Paul
Mermaid Avenue is the world
Dreams and aspirations of people in boarding house in Coney Island. 3m 4w 1 setting
In The Best short plays, 1959-1960

Goldschmidt, Walter, and Sinclair, Lister
A word in your ear
Radio play showing relationship between language and culture by means of examples taken from languages all over the world. Background music. 11m 3w
In The Best short plays of 1953-1954

Goldsmith, Clifford
Your every wish. Dramatists 1957 76p illus
A group of parents, disgusted with comparisons their teenage children are always making, exchange children to teach them a lesson, but the children like their new homes. 3 acts 5 scenes 8m 4w 2 interiors

Goldsmith, Oliver
The good natur'd man
Romantic comedy. 18th century London. Disguised intentions and thwarted love affairs. 5 acts 10m 5w 3 interiors
In Goldsmith, O. Oliver Goldsmith

She stoops to conquer. Barrons Educ. Ser. 1958 157p illus (Theatre classics for the modern reader)
Comedy. 18th century England. Friend of young man, bashful with ladies, leads him to mistake house of his prospective bride as an inn. 5 acts 10 scenes 6m 4w extras 3 interiors 1 exterior

—Same; or, The mistakes of a night
In Goldsmith, O. Oliver Goldsmith

In Keyes, R. K. and Roth, H. M. eds. Comparative comedies, present and past

In Kronenberger, L. ed. Cavalcade of **comedy**

Goldsmith, Sophie L.
c How Boots befooled the king
Based on story by Howard Pyle. Folk tale about king who offers daughter's hand in marriage to anyone who can trick him. 3 acts 7 scenes 11m 9w 3 interiors 1 exterior
In Fenner, P. and Hughes, A. comps. Entrances and exits

c The staff and the fiddle
Based on story by Howard Pyle. Folk tale about fiddler who wins the hand of the princess. 3 acts 8 scenes 8m 4w 4 interiors 1 exterior
In Fenner, P. and Hughes, A. comps. Entrances and exits

Goldstone, Jean Stock, and Reich, John
Mary Stuart. Dramatists 1958 86p illus
An adaptation of play by Friedrich Schiller with title Maria Stuart. The last two months in life of Scottish queen as her death becomes a certainty. 6 scenes 11m 3w 2 interiors 1 exterior

Gone to the dogs. Faust, E.

Good and evil
Brecht, B. The good woman of Setzuan
Claudel, P. The tidings brought to Mary
Cooper, F. A. A certain star
Giraudoux, J. Duel of angels
McNeely, J. The staring match
Rutenborn, G. The sign of Jonah
Strindberg, A. Crime and crime
Strindberg, A. Swanwhite
See also Guilt

Good-bye, Aunt Mildred! Carter, C.

Good-bye, Gray Flannel. Howells J. H.

Good-bye to the clown. Kinoy, E.

The **good** earth. Jennings, T.; Slesinger, T. and West, C.

The **Good** Hope. Heijermans, H.

"A **good** lesson!" Housman, L.

The **good** natur'd man. Goldsmith, O.

Good neighbors. Hark, M. and McQueen, N.

Good neighbors. Herman, S. W.

The **good** old days. Woolsey, J. and Sechrist, E. H.

Good Samaritan (Parable)
c Spamer, C. M. The good Samaritan
The **good** Samaritan. Spamer, C. M.
The **good** Samaritans. Priestley, F.
The **good** woman of Setzuan. Brecht, B.

Goodbye Charlie. Axelrod, G.

Goodbye, Texas—Broadway, hello! Magnau, K.

Goodchild, Roland
The grand duchess
Elderly duchess reluctantly discovers she has a lot in common with young actress who is going to marry her grandson. 1 act 2m 2w 1 interior
In Richards, S. ed. Canada on stage

Goodhue, Nelson
Little Nell, the orphan girl; or, A fight for a woman's honor! Bakers Plays 1957 96p illus
Romantic melodrama. Villain jealous of Nell's love for hero, kills secretary and tries to throw the blame on Nell. 3 acts 4 scenes 4m 8w 1 interior

Goodrich, Frances. See Hackett, A. jt. auth.

Goodrich, Frances, and Hackett, Albert
The diary of Anne Frank. Dramatists
1958 121p illus music
>Dramatization of book "Anne Frank:
diary of a young girl." Attempts of
young Jewish girl's family to remain
hidden during German occupation of
Holland. 2 acts 10 scenes 5m 5w 1 interior
>Trade edition published by Random
House

The diary of Anne Frank (condensation)
In The Best plays of 1955-1956

The goose hangs high. Beach, L.

Goose in the kitchen. Mills, O.

Gordon, Kurtz
The babbling Brooks. French 1955 110p
illus
>Comedy. Teenage daughter of gossiping
mother uses conversation overheard in
family living room as frontpage murder
story for her own neighborhood newspaper. 3 acts 4 scenes 4m 10w 1 interior

The broom and the groom. French 1958
89p illus
>Domestic comedy. When young bride
receives broom as gift she turns out to
be a witch. 3 acts 5 scenes 5m 5w 1 interior

Money mad. Dramatists 1954 74p illus
>Comedy. High school senior and his girlfriend save their college funds from loss
through poor investment by their fathers.
3 acts 5 scenes 9m 9w 1 interior

That's my cousin. Dramatists 1957 81p
illus
>Romantic comedy. Adventures of young
woman who tries to put defunct dude
ranch on paying basis. 3 acts 4 scenes
8m 10w extras 1 interior

Gorki, Maxim. See Gorky, Maxim

Gorky, Maxim
The lower depths; tr. from the Russian by
Jenny Covan
>Philosophical. Life among outcasts, murderers, thieves, prostitutes, etc. in a
Russian cellar lodging. 4 acts 13m 4w
extras 1 interior 1 exterior
In A Treasury of the theatre
In Tucker, S. M. ed. Twenty-five modern plays

Meshtchane (adaptation) See Goldina, M.
The courageous one

The **Gospel** Witch. Phelps, L.

Gossip
Brooks, P. Meet George
Casey, B. M. They say
Conkle, E. P. The reticent one
Fernway, P. "I never said a word, but—!"
Fisher, A. and Rabe, O. Anonymous letter
Gordon, K. The babbling Brooks
Hellman, L. The children's hour
Kirkpatrick, J. It takes a woman
Martens, A. C. Sugar and spite
Sheridan, R. B. The school for scandal

Gottlieb, Alex
Wake up, darling. Dramatists 1956 82p
illus music
>Domestic comedy. Successful advertising
man who wants to be playwright versus
wife who has been chosen to star in
musical. 2 acts 5 scenes 5m 6w 1 interior
See also Fisher, S. jt. auth.

Gould, Jay Reid
The death of the hired man. Dramatic
1956 21p
>Based on the poem by Robert Frost.
Vagrant hired man comes back to die in
the only home he has ever known. 1 act
2m 2w 1 exterior

Steps from beyond. Row 1954 31p illus
>Melodrama. French-Canadian widow has
sealed letter left her by her dead son
and suddenly imposter appears claiming letter is for him. 1 act 3m 2w 1 interior
—Same
In Powers, V. E. ed. Plays for players,
and a guide to play production

Goulding, Dorothy Jane
c The gift of the drum
>Adaptation of old Zuñi Indian legend.
Because Indians had nothing to amuse
themselves with, a great god sent them
a drum. 3m extras 1 exterior
In Goulding, D. J. The master cat, and
other plays

c The master cat
>A dramatization of Perrault's fairy tale
"Puss in Boots." Includes five songs with
musical scores. 6 scenes 4m 1w extras
2 interiors 3 exteriors
In Goulding, D. J. The master cat, and
other plays

c Mr Bunch's toys
>Little girl who hasn't quite enough
money to buy present in toyshop for her
sister is helped by all the toys. 3 scenes
1m 1g extras 1 interior
In Goulding, D. J. The master cat, and
other plays

The Nativity
>Nativity pageant with speaking chorus.
5 tableaux 2m 2w chorus extras 1 setting
In Goulding, D. J. The master cat, and
other plays

c Pagan magic
>Pantomime fantasy about little girl who
is rescued from bad spirits in trees by
good spirits. Verse play. 1m 1w extras
1 exterior
In Goulding, D. J. The master cat, and
other plays

c Pirates!!
>In a haunted cave on beach five pirates
capture governess and her young charges.
5m 1w 6b 3g 1 exterior
In Goulding, D. J. The master cat, and
other plays

Governesses. See Servants

Gow, Ronald
The Edwardians
>Comedy based on novel by V. Sackville-West. Cynical young duke falls in love
with middle-aged woman. 3 acts 8m 6w
1 exterior
In Plays of the year v20

c Under the skull and bones
>Two Boy Scouts fall asleep and dream
they are captured by ship full of pirates.
3 scenes 8m 2b extras 2 exteriors
In Fenner, P. and Hughes, A. comps.
Entrances and exits

Gowan, Elsie Park
Breeches from Bond Street. French 1952
24p
>Comedy. To a Canadian border town in
1880 comes a polished Englishman and
a mail-order bride for town's gambler.
4m 2w 1 exterior

Gown of glory. Phillips, I.

Grab and grace. Williams, C.

Grable, Marsha
What price murder? French 1957 32p illus
Man disapproves daughter's engagement
to reporter and after receiving anonymous threatening note, disappears and
reporter solves mystery. 1 act 2 scenes
3m 5w 1 interior

Graduation present. Orme, F.

Graft (in politics) See Corruption (in politics)

Grafton, Edith, and Grafton, Samuel
Mock trial
Television play. Law student's mock trial
of town officials reveals irregularities.
13m 4w
In Burack, A. S. ed. Television plays
for writers

Grafton, Samuel. See Grafton, E. jt. auth.

Graham, Allan
Wherever she may roam. Bakers Plays
1954 67p illus (Baker's Royalty plays)
Domestic comedy. Granny solves some
financial problems and some affairs of
the heart on annual visit with her son
and his family. 3 acts 4 scenes 5m 6w
1 interior

Graham, Manta S.
c The promotion
Eight-year-old George Washington thinks
he is too big to ride with lead rein
attached to his mother's horse. 1w 2b 1g
extras 1 exterior
In Birdsall, R. ed. Creative plays for
every school month

Graham-Campbell, Alison. See Jay, M. jt.
auth.

Gran, John M.
A nose for news. Northwestern Press 1953
68p illus
Farce. Teacher in charge of school publication initiates staff into the Loyal
and Secret Order of Type Lice. 3 acts
6m 7w 1 interior

Granby, Fay
Resort Hotel. French 1956 90p illus
Romantic farce. Knowledge of wealthy
girl's intended elopement gives two impoverished actors and an actress, who
impersonate her and her retinue, an
anxious holiday at Resort Hotel. 3 acts
4m 8w 1 interior

The **grand** duchess. Goodchild, R.

The **grand** garden. Li, Y. M.

Grand jury. Collins, B. F.

Grand prize. Alexander, R.

Grandfathers. See Grandparents

Grandma and mistletoe. Phillips, M. K.

The **grandma** bandit. Martens, A. C.

Grandma Moses. See Moses, Anna Mary
(Robertson)

Grandmothers. See Grandparents

Grandparents
Asbrand, K. A valentine for Grandma
Bate, S. Granny takes the helm
Bayliss, R. G. The burglar alarm
Carmichael, F. More than meets the eye
c The dancing school
Graham, A. Wherever she may roam
Hark, M. and McQueen, N. Who's old-
fashioned?
c Knight, C. Patch upon patch
Phillips, M. K. Grandma and mistletoe
Snyder, W. H. Another summer

Granny takes the helm. Bate, S.

Granny's little cheery room. Conkle, E. P.

Grant, Neil
Situations vacant. [French's Acting ed]
French (London) 1953 16p illus
Romantic comedy. Young business woman mistakes man she met on vacation
for applicant of office job. 1 act 1m 1w
1 interior

The **grass** harp. Capote, T.

The **grass** is greener. Williams, H. and Williams, M.

The **grass** that's greener. Kesler, H. O.

Grauman, Walter E. See Armer, A. jt. auth.

Graveley, George
The mountain flock. Campfield Press 1960
112p
France, during the Revolution. Priest
who has refused to take new civil oath
to the state, and an enlightened member
of revolutionists, finally succumb to ruth-
lessness and bigotry that surround them.
3 acts 6 scenes 7m 4w 2 interiors

Graves ghost. Clark, A. W.

Gravity
c Spamer, C. The boy who had no gravity

Gray, Dulcie
Love affair. [French's Acting ed] French
(London) 1957 70p illus
Love affairs of an artist break up mar-
riages of others. 2 acts 5m 4w 1 interior

Gray, Marjorie
For love of a house. Longmans 1954 32p
illus
Housekeeper with eye on old lady's will
tries to poison her but is thwarted by
cousin. 1 act 4w 1 interior

Great Britain

Army
Burgess, C. V. The Army takes over

Farm life
See Farm life—Great Britain

History—Roman period, 55 B.C.-449 A.D.
Daviot, G. Valerius
Sherriff, R. C. The long sunset

History—Anglo-Saxon period, 449-1066
Arblay, Madame d' Edwy and Elgiva
Tennyson, A. Harold

History—Medieval period, 1066-1485
Anouilh, J. Becket
Eliot, T. S. Murder in the Cathedral

History—Angevin period, 1154-1216
Boyd, A. K. Prince Arthur and Hubert

History—13th century
Marlowe, C. Edward the Second

History—14th century
Treece, H. Carnival king

History—Lancaster and York, 1399-1485
Greene, N. D. The seekers

History—House of Lancaster, 1399-1461
Sisson, R. A. The queen and the Welshman

History—House of York, 1461-1485
Daviot, G. Dickon

History—Tudors, 1485-1603
Albery, P. Anne Boleyn
Chiari, J. Mary Stuart

Great Britain—History—Tudors, 1485-1603
—*Continued*

Dekker, T. and Webster, J. Sir Thomas Wyatt
Dowling, J. The young Elizabeth
Ford, J. Perkin Warbeck
Goldstone, J. S. and Reich, J. Mary Stuart
Letton, J. and Letton, F. The young Elizabeth
Schiller, F. von. Mary Stuart
Tennyson, A. Queen Mary
Williamson, H. R. His Eminence of England

History—Stuarts, 1603-1714
Miller, H. L. Lorna Doone

History—19th century
Ginsbury, N. The first gentleman

Middle classes
See Middle classes—Great Britain

Navy
Coxe, L. O. and Chapman, R. Billy Budd
Jerrold, D. Black-ey'd Susan

Police
See Police—Great Britain

Politics and government
Anderson, M. Elizabeth the Queen
Daviot, G. Lady Charing is cross
Jones, P. and Jowett, J. The party spirit

Social conditions
Newman, D. The prince and the pauper
Wesker, A. Roots

Social life and customs
Agg, H. Red plush
Rattigan, T. While the sun shines

Social life and customs—449-1066
Olfson, L. A Connecticut Yankee in King Arthur's court

Social life and customs—Medieval period, 1066-1485
Ashton, E. B. The beggarman's bride

Social life and customs—14th century
Boyd, A. K. Robbery at Gadshill

Social life and customs—Lancaster and York, 1399-1485
Dekker, T. The shoemakers' holiday

Social life and customs—Tudors, 1485-1603
Chorpenning, C. B. The prince and the pauper
Gressieker, H. Royal gambit
Jonson, B. Every man in his humour
Stafford, K. Tinker? Tailor? Soldier?
c Totheroh, D. Master Will

Social life and customs—Early Stuarts, 1603-1649
Dekker, T. and Webster, J. Northward ho
Jonson, B. The alchemist
Jonson, B. Bartholomew Fair
Jonson, B. Epicœne
Middleton, T. The Roaring Girl
Rowley, W. and others. The witch of Edmonton

Social life and customs—Restoration, 1660-1688
Congreve, W. The way of the world
Etherege, Sir G. The man of mode
Wycherley, W. The country wife

Social life and customs—1689-1714
Brecht, B. The threepenny opera
Congreve, W. The double-dealer
Congreve, W. Love for love
Congreve, W. The mourning bride
Congreve, W. The old bachelor
Farquhar, G. The beaux' stratagem
Farquhar, G. The constant couple
Farquhar, G. The recruiting officer
Farquhar, G. The twin-rivals
Vanbrugh, Sir J. The relapse

Social life and customs—1789-1820
Johnson, P. Ladies and females
Murch, E. The thin red line
Newman, D. Pride and prejudice

Social life and customs—18th century
Boyd, A. K. Fighting Bob
Gattey, C. N. and Bramley-Moore, Z. Treasure from France
Jacoby, L. Wuthering Heights
Jerome, H. Pride and prejudice
Olfson, L. Monsieur Beaucaire
Scribe, E. The glass of water
Sheridan, R. B. The rivals
Sheridan, R. B. The school for scandal

Social life and customs—19th century
Albery, J. Two roses
Barrie, J. M. The admirable Crichton
Boyd, A. K. Pip and the convict
Bulwer-Lytton, E. Money
Delderfield, R. F. Smoke in the valley
Draper, J. Barchester Towers
Golden, E. Great expectations
Nicholson, H. Port and a pistol
Olfson, L. David Copperfield and Uriah Heep
Olfson, L. The importance of being Earnest
Olfson, L. Jane Eyre
Olfson, L. The Pickwick papers
Olfson, L. Silas Marner
Olfson, L. Wuthering Heights
Robertson, T. W. Caste
Sharp, A. Nightmare Abbey
Simpson, H. Miss Matty in mischief
Simpson, H. Miss Matty in society
Taylor, T. The ticket-of-leave man
Taylor, T. and Reade, C. Masks and faces
Tydeman, R. Duet with dowagers
Wilde, O. An ideal husband
Wilde, O. The importance of being Earnest
Wilde, O. Lady Windermere's fan

Social life and customs—20th century
Adler, M. D. Too much springtime
Addyman, E. Over the garden fence
Baker, L. G. Conspiracy at "The Crayfish"
Behrman, S. N. Jane
Benfield, D. The way the wind blows
Coward, N. Cavalcade
Daviot, G. Cornelia
Daviot, G. The pomp of Mr Pomfret

Great Britain—Social life and customs—20th century—*Continued*

Gow, R. The Edwardians
Home, W. D. The reluctant debutante
Horne, K. The Devil was sick
Kops, B. The dream of Peter Mann
Loewe, F. My fair lady
Shaw, B. Heartbreak house
Shaw, B. Pygmalion

Great Catherine. Shaw, B.

The **Great** Divide. Moody, W. V.

Great expectations. Golden, E.

The **great** God Brown. O'Neill, E.

Great-grandfather was an immigrant. Salinger, H.

The **great** highway. Strindberg, A.

The **Great** Sebastians. Lindsay, H. and Crouse, R.

The **great** Tree Council. Woolsey, J. and Sechrist, E. H.

Great women of history. Emurian, E. K.

Greater than any man. Smith, A. C.

Greece

Civilization

See Civilization, Greek

History

Durrell, L. Sappho

History—Peloponnesian War, 431-404 B.C.

Aristophanes. Peace

Greed. See Avarice

The **greedy** goblin. Miller, H. L.

Greek drama

Euripides. Helen
Euripides. The Heracleidae
Fitts, D. ed. Six Greek plays in modern translation (6 plays)
Lind, L. R. ed. Ten Greek plays in contemporary translations (10 plays)

Greek drama (Comedy)

Aristophanes. The Acharnians
Aristophanes. The birds
Aristophanes. The clouds
Aristophanes. The frogs
Aristophanes. Ladies' day
Aristophanes. Lysistrata
Aristophanes. The wasps
Menander. The arbitration
Menander. The bad-tempered man
Menander. The grouch
Menander. She who was shorn

Greek drama (Satyr play)

Euripides. The Cyclops

Greek drama (Tragedy)

Aeschylus. Agamemnon
Aeschylus. Choephoroe
Aeschylus. The Eumenides
Aeschylus. The libation bearers
Aeschylus. The Persians
Aeschylus. Prometheus bound
Aeschylus. Seven against Thebes
Aeschylus. The suppliant maidens
Euripides. Alcestis
Euripides. Andromachê
Euripides. The Bacchae
Euripides. The children of Herakles
Euripides. Electra

Euripides. Hecuba
Euripides. Heracles
Euripides. Hippolytus
Euripides. Iphigenia in Aulis
Euripides. Iphigenia in Tauris
Euripides. The madness of Herakles
Euripides. **The Medea**
Euripides. The Phoenician women
Euripides. Rhesus
Euripides. The suppliant women
Euripides. Suppliants
Euripides. The Trojan women
Euripides. The women of Troy
Grene, D. and Lattimore, R. eds. The complete Greek tragedies (33 plays)
Sophocles. Ajax
Sophocles. Antigone
Sophocles. Electra
Sophocles. Oedipus at Colonus
Sophocles. Oedipus Rex
Sophocles. Oedipus the King
Sophocles. Philoctetes
Sophocles. Three Theban plays (3 plays)
Sophocles. The women of Trachis

Greek letter societies

Lewis, J. Return engagement

Greek mythology. See Mythology, Greek

Green, Adolph. See Bernstein, L. Wonderful town; Styne, J. Bells are ringing

Green, Carolyn

Janus. French 1956 84p illus
> Midwest tycoon discovers that his wife and her lover, New York teacher have been meeting once a year to turn out their annual best seller. 3 acts 4 scenes 3m 2w 1 interior
> Trade edition published by Random House

Green, Janet

Gently does it. Dramatists 1954 89p illus
> English melodrama. Money-mad young man who made the murder of his aging, wealthy wife appear as an accidental death, schemes to kill her sister and heir. 2 acts 6 scenes 2m 4w 1 interior
> Same as: Murder mistaken

Murder mistaken
> Same as: Gently does it
> *In* Plays of the year v8

Green, Julian

South
> Tragic outcome of U.S. Army officer's love for his host's daughter. Setting: South Carolina plantation house just before Civil War. 3 acts 11 scenes 6m 6w 2b 1 interior
> *In* Plays of the year v12

Green, Paul

The confederacy. French 1959 123p
> Symphonic outdoor drama of Robert E. Lee during Civil War and how he decided to throw in his lot with his native state. Uses choral and background music and dance. 2 acts 13 scenes Large mixed cast 4 interiors 6 exteriors

The founders. Jamestown Festival ed. 1607-1957. French 1957 210p
> A symphonic outdoor drama. Tells in dialogue, song, dance and pantomime the dangers that beset the Jamestown colony. Many scenes Large mixed cast 1 exterior

Franklin and the King
> Historical drama. Benjamin Franklin is unable to dissuade King George III and Lord North from declaring war against colonies. 1 act 5m 1w extras 1 interior
> *In* Smith, B. and others. eds. A treasury of non-royalty one-act plays

Green, Paul—*Continued*

In Abraham's bosom
  Miscegenation. Sensitive mulatto son of Southern plantation owner struggles to rise above his station. 1 act 6m 1w 1 exterior
  In Smith, B. and others, eds. A treasury of non-royalty one-act plays

The lost colony. Roanoke Island ed. Univ. of N.C. Press 1954 70p illus
  Symphonic outdoor panorama. Story of faith and courage of people of fated colony founded by Sir Walter Raleigh at Roanoke, Virginia. Background music. 2 acts 11 scenes Large mixed cast, chorus

The No 'Count Boy. [Rev. and rewritten] French 1953 29p illus
  Romantic comedy. Concerns young Negro girl, her hard working boy friend and the wandering, dreamy boy who enchants her with his tunes and stories. 2m 2w 1 exterior
—Same
  In Walser, R. ed. North Carolina drama

Quare medicine
  Local quack's patent medicine proves useful to henpecked husband in southern mountains. 3m 1w 1 interior
  In Walser, R. ed. North Carolina drama

The Stephen Foster story. French 1960 107p
  Symphonic outdoor drama about Stephen Foster. His music is sung and used as background music. 2 acts 9 scenes Large mixed cast 4 interiors 4 exteriors

This Declaration. French 1954 18p illus music
  Thomas Jefferson composes the Declaration of Independence. 1 act 7m 1w 1 interior

Wilderness Road. French 1956 166p illus
  A symphonic outdoor drama. Music, dance, pantomime and pageantry. Impact of Civil war on idealistic schoolteacher in mountains of Kentucky. Many scenes Large mixed cast 1 exterior

Wings for to fly. French 1959 77p music
  Three short sketches showing gulf of misunderstanding between white and black in the South: Fine wagon, Lay this body down, The thirsting heart. Includes words and music for songs. 3 parts 14m 9w 1b 3 interiors

The **green** ball. Colson, J. G.

Green eyes. Casey, B. M.

The **green** helmet. Yeats, W. B.

Green pastures. Connelly, M.

The **Green** wood. Raeburn, H.

Greenberg, Noah
  (ed.) The Play of Daniel. See The Play of Daniel

Greene, Graham
  The living room. [Acting ed] French 1955 82p illus
    Tragedy. Young Catholic girl in love with married man fails to get understanding from her psychologist-lover, her fear-ridden aunts or her uncle, an invalid priest. 2 acts 5 scenes 2m 5w 1 interior
    Trade edition published by Viking

  The living room (condensation)
    In The Best plays of 1954-1955

The potting shed. French 1957 93p illus
  Conflict between religious miracle and rationalist beliefs as middle-aged man tries to reconstruct traumatic event in his early life. 3 acts 6m 5w 3 interiors
  Trade edition published by Viking

The potting shed (condensation)
  In The Best plays of 1956-1957
  In Broadway's best, 1957

The power and the glory (dramatization) See Cannan, D. and Bost, P. The power and the glory

Greene, Neil D.
  The seekers
    Allegory set in medieval England. Three men find a treasure chest and each plots the destruction of the other. 1 act 8m 2 exteriors
    In Powers, V. E. ed. Plays for players, and a guide to play production

Greene, Robert S.
  Decision for freedom
    Radio play. When Communists take over village in northern Vietnam, young native and wife flee to southern Vietnam. 5m 2w
    In Writers Guild of America. The prize plays of television and radio, 1956

Greensleeves' magic. Jonson, M.

Greenwich Village, New York (City) See New York (City)—Greenwich Village

Greetings from . . . Weiss, M. J.

Gregory, Howard, and Henneberger, John
  The thousand flerbs. Eldridge 1958 16p (Eldridge Popular one-act playscripts)
    Fantasy. Mousey little man gets rich by selling his soul to the Devil. 1 act 5m 2w extras 1 interior

Gregory, Isabella Augusta (Persse) Lady. See Gregory, Lady

Gregory, Lady
  Spreading the news
    A "rumor factory" creates a non-existent murder which snowballs at an Irish Fair. 1 act 7m 3w 1 exterior
    In Cerf, B. and Cartmell, V. H. eds. 24 favorite one-act plays
  The workhouse ward
    Elderly inmate of Irish almshouse refuses to be separated from his friend when his sister offers him home. Irish dialect. 1 scene 2m 1w 1 interior
    In A Treasury of the theatre

Greg's gruesome gadgets. Walsh, R. G.

Grenzeback, Joe. See Bergh, H. Old King Cole

Gressieker, Hermann
  Royal gambit; tr. and adapted by George White. French 1959 70p
    Sixteenth century England of blustering amoral Henry VIII and six of his eight wives. 5 acts 1m 6w 4 interiors 1 exterior

Greth, Le Roma Eshbach
  The dancing ghost. Bakers Plays 1961 61p (Baker's Royalty plays)
    Mystery. Group of tourists in Western ghost town are trapped in an old theater which is to be blown up at dawn. 3 acts 5m 6w 1 interior

  The ghost from outer space. Bakers Plays 1958 28p
    Family is visited by guest from outer space. 1 act 3m 4w 1 interior

  The happy haunting ground. Bakers Plays 1959 67p (Baker's Royalty plays)
    Indian ghost that haunts their house during rodeo days upsets Brison family and their numerous guests. 3 acts 8m 9w 1 interior

Greth, Le R. E.—*Continued*

Host to a ghost. Eldridge 1958 73p illus (Eldridge 3-act playscripts)
Comedy-mystery. Plot concerns weeping ghost who uses knock-out drops and a two hundred year old secret. 3 acts 6m 6w extras 1 interior

The kid from Mars. Bakers Plays 1957 22p
Comedy. Teen-agers try to fool each other with make-believe Martians but plot boomerangs. 1 act 3m 3w 1 interior

Miss President, please! Eldridge 1956 75p illus (Eldridge 3-act playscripts)
Domestic comedy. Young girl upsets whole family in efforts to get older sister to the prom. 3 acts 5m 8w extras 1 interior

Miss Robin Crusoe. Bakers Plays 1960 22p
Comedy. Some girls, separated from their dates, are marooned on island where mysterious lights are seen and footsteps are heard. 1 act 5w 1 exterior

The sky's the limit. Eldridge 1959 73p (Eldridge 3-act playscripts)
Science fiction comedy. Two girls from another planet run out of fuel and land space ship in garden of Congressional aspirant. 3 acts 6m 8w 1 interior

Sweet? sixteen. Bakers Plays 1957 24p
Farce. Sister tries to interest 16-year-old brother in girls. 2m 5w 1 interior

Grillparzer, Franz

The Jewess of Toledo
Tragic consequences of romance between Alfonso III, King of Castile and daughter of his Jewish Minister of Finance. Set in 12th century Spain. 5 acts 6m 5w extras 2 interiors 2 exteriors

In Grillparzer, F. The Jewess of Toledo [and] Esther

Medea; tr. by Arthur Burkhard. [Rev. ed] Register Press 1956 120p
Tragedy in verse. Based on Greek legend of Medea's revenge against Jason for deserting her. 5 acts 4m 3w 2b extras 1 interior 3 exteriors

Sappho; tr. by Arthur Burkhard. Register Press 1953 99p
Tragedy. Based on legend in which poetess Sappho commits suicide when a man rejects her love for that of younger woman. 5 acts 3m 3w 1 exterior

Grimm, Jacob

Hansel and Gretel (dramatization) See Jackson, S. The bad children

Rumpelstiltskin (dramatization) See Hollinshead, L. M. In honour bound

The shoemaker and the elves (dramatization) See Very, A. The shoemaker and the elves

Snow White and the seven dwarfs (dramatization) See Sprenger, C. H. and Attley, M. Snow White and the seven dwarfs

Grimm, Jacob and Grimm, Wilhelm

The nose (dramatization) See Hughes, G. The magic apple

c Snow White and Rose Red (dramatization) See Miller, M. Snow White and Rose Red

Grimm, Jakob Ludwig Karl

c Newman, D. A gift to the world

Grimm, Wilhelm. See Grimm, J. jt. auth.

Grimm, Wilhelm Karl

c Newman, D. A gift to the world

Gross, Edwin, and Gross, Nathalie

Belle
Comedy. Teen-agers in drug store question soda fountain girl about fraternity pin. 1 act 7m 7w 1g 1 interior

In Gross, E. and Gross, N. Teen theater

Date-time
Comedy. Father tries to assert himself on daughter's curfew but boy friend disarms him by flattery. 1 act 2m 2w 1b 1 interior

In Gross, E. and Gross, N. Teen theater

Dooley and the amateur hour
A dramatization of short story by Charles Alden Peterson. Farce. Teenage doorman at movies pinch-hits as master of ceremonies on amateur night, gets girl and salary increase. 1 act 3 scenes 3m 6w extras 2 interiors

In Gross, E. and Gross, N. Teen theater

Marko goes a courtin'
Comedy. Summer camp girls rebel against counsellor, then accept her. 1 act 6w 1 interior

In Gross, E. and Gross, N. Teen theater

A party is born
Sweet sixteen party is saved when eight State University boys decide to attend at last moment. 1 act 5m 5w 1 interior

In Gross, E. and Gross, N. Teen theater

She loves him yes
Comedy. Noted authoress gives high school interviewer lesson on use of coincidence in writing play. 1 act 4m 5w 1b 1 interior

In Gross, E. and Gross, N. Teen theater

Gross, Nathalie. See Gross, E. jt. auth.

The **gross** story conference. Taggart, T.

The **grouch.** Menander

The **ground** of justice. Wishengrad, M.

Grow up! Lamson, P.

Gruach. Bottomley, G.

Gruber, Franz Xaver

Marston, J. And a song was born

Grundtvig, Nikolai Frederik Severin

Munk, K. Egelykke

Grundy, Sydney

A pair of spectacles
Generous man, embittered by false friends, attempts to become like his miserly brother but finally recovers his faith in human nature. 3 acts 3 scenes 8m 3w 1 interior

In Rowell, G. ed. Nineteenth century plays

Gruwell, Betty Grey

O holy night. French 1959 15p
Pageant and Christmas devotional service, in pantomime, with carols. Large mixed cast 1 interior

The **guardian.** O'Brien, F. B.

Guardian and ward

Hastings, C. Uncertain joy

Guareschi, Giovanni

The little world of Don Camillo (dramatization) See Hartke, G. V. The little world of Don Camillo

Guerrillas

Richardson, L. For our mother Malaya!

The **guest** at Cana. Casey, B. M.

The **guest** cottage. McCleery, W.

Guided tour. McMahon, B.

Guillaume de Sens

Sayers, D. The zeal of Thy house

Guilt

Serling, R. Noon on Doomsday

Guinea, French
Spewack, S. and Spewack, B. L. My three angels

The **guinea-pigs.** Delderfield, R. F.

Guise, Henri I de Lorraine, 3d duc de
Dryden, J. and Lee, N. The Duke of Guise
Lee, N. The massacre of Paris

Gulliver wins his freedom. Howard, V.

Gulliver's travels in Lilliput Land. Golden, E.

Gurney, A. R.
Three people
    Involvement of university teacher and wife with their mentally deficient baby. 1 act 1m 1w 1 interior
    In The Best short plays of 1955-1956
Turn of the century
    Elderly lady lives in gracious manner of past unconcerned about dwindling family funds. 1 act 4m 6w 1 interior
    In The Best short plays of 1957-1958

Gustaf I Vasa, King of Sweden
Strindberg, A. The regent

Gustavus I. See Gustaf I Vasa, King of Sweden

Gustavus Adolphus. See Gustaf I Vasa, King of Sweden

Guy Domville. James, H.

Gypsy. Styne, J.

H

Hachi no ki. Kwanze, M.

Hackett, Albert. See Goodrich, F. jt. auth.

Hackett, Albert, and Goodrich, Frances
The diary of Anne Frank (condensation)
    In Theatre, 1956

Hackett, Walter
A dress affair. Bakers Plays 1955 16p
    Comedy. Boy from other side of the tracks is saved from embarrassment by teen-ager at her party. 1 act 3m 4w 1 interior
The outgoing tide
    When class valedictorian writes pessimistic speech about world and its future, several people change his viewpoint. 1 act 2 scenes 4m 3w 1 interior
    In Kamerman, S. E. ed. Blue-ribbon plays for graduation
The way the ball bounces. Bakers Plays 1958 20p
    Teenager becomes very conceited when he is offered contract for his singing but finally decides to go to college instead. 1 act 3m 4w 1 interior

Hagoromo. Kwanze, M.

Hague, Albert
Plain and fancy. Book by Joseph Stein and Will Glickman; music by Albert Hague; lyrics by Arnold B. Horwitt. French 1956 112p illus
    Musical comedy. New Yorker and his girlfriend learn about life among the "Pennsylvania Dutch" of the Amish country. 2 acts 18 scenes 18m 11w extras 3 interiors 12 exteriors
    Trade edition published by Random House

Hagy, Loleta
Fire in a paper
    In China long ago two daughters-in-law learn to obey their mother-in-law and discover how to bring her fire in a paper (a lantern) and wind in a paper (a fan). 1 act 3 scenes 5w 2 interiors
    In Kamerman, S. E. ed. Blue-ribbon plays for girls

Haines, William Wister
Command decision
    Based on the author's novel. Efforts of American Air Force commander to achieve military objective in spite of military and political interference. England during World War II. 3 acts 4 scenes 18m 1 interior
    In Quinn, A. H. ed. Representative American plays

Hair. See Beard

Haircutting
c Miller, H. L. The busy barbers

The **hairy** ape. O'Neill, E.

Haku Rakuten. Kwanze, M.

Hale, Lucretia P.
The Peterkin Papers (dramatization) See Carlson, B. W. The lady who put salt in her coffee

Hale, Nathan. See Hale, R. jt. auth.

Hale, Ruth, and Hale, Nathan
Lilacs in the rain. French 1957 84p
    Romantic comedy. Story of John Lambert's four daughters and their sweet but turbulent romances. 3 acts 4 scenes 5m 6w 1 interior
Love comes in many colors. French 1959 82p illus
    Domestic comedy. When father suggests to daughter that she invite to their home a girl of different background, he sets off a chain reaction that ends in daughter's leaving home. 3 acts 5m 6w 1 interior

Hale, Sarah Josepha (Buell)
c Fisher, A. Mother of Thanksgiving

Half hour on the "Asia." Boyd, A. K.

Half-hour, please. Richards, S.

The **half-pint** cowboy. Miller, H. L.

Half-Pint Windom rides west. McMahon, L. E.

Hall, Willis
Airmail from Cyprus
    Television play. Emotional effect of murder on three people involved. 2m 4w
    In British Broadcasting Corporation. The television playwright

Hall of healing. O'Casey, S.

Hallman, Eugene S.
Survival
    Radio play. An airplane crashes in the Arctic and its inhabitants survive because one of them is young Eskimo who knows traditional survival techniques. 4m
    In Goldschmidt, W. ed. Ways of mankind

Halloween
Abstance, P. and Abstance, L. A Hallowe'en adventure
c Asbrand, K. Florrie's fortune
Asbrand, K. Reach for the moon
c Asbrand, K. Witches' brew
c Atwell, R. and Virden, H. Witch hunt
c The black mask

Halloween—*Continued*

c Carlson, B. W. Mystery of the glittering gem

c Fichter, H. G. To soap or not to soap

Fisher, A. Ghosts on guard

Fisher, A. On Halloween

c Fowler, M. G. The enchanted pumpkin

Halloween assembly

c Halloween trial

Hark, M. and McQueen, N. All out for Halloween

Hark, M. and McQueen, N. Halloween luck

c Hark, M. and McQueen, N. The house is haunted

c Hark, M. and McQueen, N. Meet Mr Witch

c Hark, M. and McQueen, N. The new broom

Hark, M. and McQueen, N. Who's scared of ghosts?

Howard, V. Spook shop

c Leuser, E. The litttle witch who tried

Lynch, P. Off with his head

c Martens, A. C. The magic broom

c Miller, H. L. The broken broomstick

c Miller, H. L. The greedy goblin

Miller, H. L. The haunted clothesline

c Miller, H. L. A school for scaring

Miller, H. L. Spooky spectacles

c Miller, H. L. Spunky Punky

c Moore, H. G. Storybook Halloween

c Newman, D. The Pumpkineaters' pumpkin

c Norman, D. Something new for Halloween

c Olson, E. E. The Hallowe'en party

c Spamer, C. The first jack-o'-lanterns

c Spamer, C. The little goblins

c Spamer, C. Pumpkin Ghost

c Spamer, C. A pumpkin's fate

c Spamer, C. Washout

c Very, A. The cat who wanted to ride on a broom

c Very, A. Old Lady Witch's party

c Woolsey, J. and Sechrist, E. H. A Halloween surprise package

c Woolsey, J. and Sechrist, E. H. The witches' complaint

A **Hallowe'en** adventure. Abstance, P. and Abstance, L.

Halloween assembly
> Outline for school assembly program into which can be fitted appropriate songs, dances and dramatic readings. 1 act Large mixed cast 2 interiors
>
> *In* 'Round the year plays for the grades

Halloween luck. Hark, M. and McQueen, N.

The **Hallowe'en** party. Olson, E. E.

A **Halloween** surprise package. Woolsey, J. and Sechrist, E. H.

Halloween trial
> Two children learn not to play harmful tricks on Halloween. 1 act 8 characters 1 interior
>
> *In* 'Round the year plays for the grades

Hallowell, Hilda

The widow's choice. [French's Acting ed] French (London) 1953 24p music
> Romantic comedy. Widow shopkeeper tests two suitors, a bankrupt gentleman and a penniless player, to see which to choose. Songs. 1 scene 2m 3w 1 interior

Halman, Doris

Johnny Pickup
> Television play. Romance of lame youth and timid girl he meets on Coney Island beach. 2 acts 2m 2w
>
> *In* The Best television plays v3

Hamaguchi Gohei. Tennant, K.

Hamilton, Alexander

Kingsley, S. The patriots

Hamilton, Patrick

The man upstairs. Constable 1954 105p
> His friend's sound recording machine helps Englishman outwit blackmailing gang. 3 acts 4m 3w 1 interior

Hamlet. Olfson, L.

Hammerstein, Oscar. See Rodgers, R. Flower drum song; Me and Juliet; Pipe dream; *also* Rodgers, R. jt. auth.

Hanakatami (condensation) Kwanze, K.

The **hand** of God. Casey, B. M.

Handful of fire. Nash, N. R.

Handicapped. See Disabled

Hands across the sea. Coward, N.

Hanging

Behan, B. The quare fellow

The **hanging** of Uncle Dilby. Payton, D.

Hangs over thy head. Purkey, R. A.

Hanig, David

Give us time to sing
> Romantic comedy. Lonely shoemaker succumbs to love of determined woman baker. 1 act 3m 2w 1 interior
>
> *In* Smith, B. and others. eds. A treasury of non-royalty one-act plays

Hanjo. Mishima, Y.

Hannibal

Lee, N. Sophonisba

Hansberry, Lorraine

A raisin in the sun. Random House 1959 142p illus
> Tensions erupt in middle class Chicago Negro family when they come into possession of legacy. 3 acts 6 scenes 7m 3w 1b 1 interior

A raisin in the sun (condensation)
> *In* The Best plays of 1958-1959
>
> *In* Broadway's best, 1959

Hanukkah (Feast of Lights)

c Goldburg, N. and Goldburg, R. What's Chanuko without a play?

c Peterson, M. N. Happy Chanukah

The **happiest** millionaire. Crichton, K.

Happiness

c Hark, M. and McQueen, N. The princess and the rose-colored glasses

Ouzts, J. D. Happy Pagan

Happy birthday to you! Karchmer, S.

Happy Chanukah. Peterson, M. N.

The **happy** day. Agg, H.

The **happy** haunting ground. Greth, Le R. E.

Happy holidays. Newman, D.

Happy holidays for little women. Howard, V.

The **happy** housewife. Rosten, H.

The **happy** journey. Wilder, T.

The **happy** journey to Trenton and Camden. Wilder, T.

The **happy** life. St Clair, R.

The **happy** man. Williams, H. and Williams, M.

Happy monody. Brabazon, F.

Happy New Year. Spamer, C.

Happy Pagan. Ouzts, J. D.

Harbord, Gordon. See Roffey, J. jt. auth.

Harding, Margaret
c The Sea King's daughter. (French's Juvenile ed) French (London) 1953 44p
At Shakespeare's behest, three young playwrights produce their new fairy tale play by exercising powers of make-believe. 2 acts 5 scenes 11m 7w 5b 3g extras 1 setting

Hare, Walter Ben
A Christmas carol
Based on Charles Dickens' story. Includes words and music of: Christmas carol. 1 act 3 scenes 10m 7w 4b 2g extras 1 interior
In Brings, L. M. ed. The modern treasury of Christmas plays

The white Christmas
Worship program. Nativity play designed to show the origin of custom of giving Christmas gifts. 8m 6w extras choir
In Brings, L. M. ed. The modern treasury of Christmas plays

Hare and the field of millet. Ridge, A.

The **hare** and the tortoise. Moore, S. S.

Hares
Ridge, A. Hare and the field of millet
Ridge, A. Under the monkey-bread tree

Harig, Peg
Come, fill the cup. French 1957 39p illus
Domestic comedy. Young woman introduces conservative, wealthy fiancé to her Greenwich Village family. 1 act 2 scenes 1m 6w 1 interior 1 exterior

Hark, Mildred, and McQueen, Noel
c A B C for safety
All the tools and other objects involved in children's accidents tell them how to be careful. 1 act 3b 3g extras 1 interior
In Hark, M. and McQueen, N. Junior plays for all occasions

Aladdin steps out
Fantasy. Literary characters come to life in fantasy after mother berates family for not reading enough. 1 act 7m 1w 3b 3g 1 interior
In Hark, M. and McQueen, N. Teenage plays for all occasions

All aboard for Christmas
Arrival of new baby settles question of having electric trains set up for Christmas display. Carol singing. 1 act 3m 2w 1b 2g extras 1 interior
In Hark, M. and McQueen, N. Teenage plays for all occasions

All out for Halloween. Bakers Plays 1955 19p
Teenage boy prevents group of children from turning Halloween pranks into vandalism. 1 act 6m 3w 1b 2g extras 1 interior

Bake a cherry pie
Town baker makes donation to Washington's Birthday celebration in return for housewife's pie recipe. 1 act 3m 3w 1b 1 interior
In Hark, M. and McQueen, N. Teenage plays for all occasions

c Bobby and the Lincoln speech
Little boy in Lincoln's Day program meets man who is writing a book about Lincoln. 1 act 2m 2w 1b 1g 1 interior
In Hark, M. and McQueen, N. Junior plays for all occasions

c The book revue
Boys and girls try to choose the book they like best from all book characters they know. 1 act 3b 3g extras 1 interior
In Hark, M. and McQueen, N. Junior plays for all occasions

Books are bridges
Comedy. Visiting author-lecturer shows practical value of books to family whose mother is away. 1 act 2m 1w 2g 1 interior
In Hark, M. and McQueen, N. Teenage plays for all occasions

Cabana Blues
High school principal clears new boy suspected of stealing dance record. Background music. 1 act 4m 3w 1 interior
In Hark, M. and McQueen, N. Teenage plays for all occasions

c Christmas Eve news
Newsboys find that everyone wants to buy newspaper with story of Christmas in it. 1 act 18m 8w 1g extras 1 exterior
In Hark, M. and McQueen, N. Junior plays for all occasions

c Christmas in the woods
Children make Christmas tree for animals and birds in the forest. 1 act 1b 1g extras 1 exterior
In Hark, M. and McQueen, N. Junior plays for all occasions

Christmas recaptured
Christmas spirit is revived when Aunt Mathilda arrives and family gifts are reappraised. Background carols. 1 act 3m 4w 1b 1 interior
In Hark, M. and McQueen, N. Teenage plays for all occasions

c Cupid's post office
Dan Cupid delivers valentines to all kinds of people. 1 act 7m 4b 4g extras 1 interior
In Hark, M. and McQueen, N. Junior plays for all occasions

c Cupies and hearts
Several children save up soap wrappers to send away for Valentine's Day present for parents. 1 act 1m 2w 1b 2g 1 interior
In Hark, M. and McQueen, N. Junior plays for all occasions

c A day for trees
Animals are surprised by a group of children who come to the woods for an Arbor Day lesson. 1 act 1w 2b 2g extras 1 interior
In Hark, M. and McQueen, N. Junior plays for all occasions

c Doctor Manners
Doctor has mysterious ways of showing rude children how they should behave. 1 act 1m 1w 2b 3g 1 interior
In Hark, M. and McQueen, N. Junior plays for all occasions

Hark, M. and McQueen, N.—*Continued*

c The new broom
Halloween play. Salesman tries to sell family a haunted house. 1 act 2m 2w 1b 1g extras 1 interior
In Hark, M. and McQueen, N. Junior plays for all occasions

c New-fangled Thanksgiving
Family who decided to have Thanksgiving dinner in hotel instead of at home finds enthusiasm waning. 1 act 3m 3w 1b 1 interior
In Hark, M. and McQueen, N. Junior plays for all occasions

c Not fit for man or beast
Comedy melodrama. Paw leaves his family to look for gold in the Klondike. 1 act 4m 3w 1 interior
In Hark, M. and McQueen, N. Junior plays for all occasions

c Nothing to be thankful for
Family is disappointed that Thanksgiving plans are going wrong, until near-tragedy makes them realize how thankful they should be. 1 act 2m 2w 1b extras 1 interior
In Hark, M. and McQueen, N. Junior plays for all occasions

c Nursery rhyme diet
The Mother Goose characters explain the importance of vitamins to Jack Sprat. 1 act Unidentified cast 14 characters 1 interior
In Hark, M. and McQueen, N. Junior plays for all occasions

An ode to Spring
Comedy. High school students are happy to learn that spring prom has not been cancelled. 1 act 5m 6w 1 interior
In Hark, M. and McQueen, N. Teen-age plays for all occasions

c Off the shelf
During Book Week the books in the library complain because children treat them carelessly. 1 act Unidentified cast 8 characters 1 interior
In Hark, M. and McQueen, N. Junior plays for all occasions

On your own feet. Bakers Plays 1960 18p
When Dad says that children should stand on their own feet, they start selling neighborhood services complete with fringe benefits and rest periods. 1 act 6m 5w 2b 2g extras 1 interior

c Our own four walls
While their parents are away four children decide to repaint living room. 1 act 2m 2w 1b 1g 1 interior
In Hark, M. and McQueen, N. Junior plays for all occasions

The place to begin
Having finished medical training, young doctor visits rural parents who are disappointed to learn he is planning pediatrics career in city. 1 act 2m 2w 1b 1g 1 interior
In Kamerman, S. E. ed. Blue-ribbon plays for graduation

c Pleasant dreams
Fat boy and thin boy both decide they need lots of vitamins to grow strong. 1 act 2b extras 1 interior
In Hark, M. and McQueen, N. Junior plays for all occasions

Portrait of an American
Comedy. Father is pleased with townspeople who make him symbol of heroism in historic home. 1 act 3m 4w 1b 1 interior
In Hark, M. and McQueen, N. Teen-age plays for all occasions

c The princess and the rose-colored glasses
Princess becomes happy only when she learns to look at bright side of things through mysterious glasses. 1 act 7m 3w 1g 1 interior
In Hark, M. and McQueen, N. Junior plays for all occasions

c A prize for mother
Children enter a contest to win prize to give mother on Mother's Day. 1 act 2m 2w 1b 1g extras 1 interior
In Hark, M. and McQueen, N. Junior plays for all occasions

c Rainbow colors
The colors appear to tell boys and girls how they are formed. 1 act 2b 2g extras 1 exterior
In Hark, M. and McQueen, N. Junior plays for all occasions

Reindeer on the roof
Mother's simple display wins competition for best Christmas decoration where father's spectacular fails. Background carols. 1 act 5m 4w 1b 1 interior
In Hark, M. and McQueen, N. Teen-age plays for all occasions

Romance for Dad. Baker, W.H. 1959 18p
Domestic comedy. Four teenage children decide that their widower-father needs wife and start campaign to find one. 1 act 3m 5w 1 interior

c The Santa Claus parade
Santa Claus takes big Christmas parade to visit little sick boy. 1 act Large mixed cast 1 exterior
In Hark, M. and McQueen, N. Junior plays for all occasions

Shy Charlie. Bakers Plays 1954 24p
Shy high school boy's dating problems. 1 act 2m 3w 1g 1 interior

Spring daze
Comedy. Mother helps teen-age son out of multiple dates by arranging house party. 1 act 2m 2w 1 interior
In Hark, M. and McQueen, N. Teen-age plays for all occasions

c Spring is here
Spring and all her helpers have hard time persuading Old Man Winter to leave. 1 act Unidentified cast 19 characters extras 1 exterior
In Hark, M. and McQueen, N. Junior plays for all occasions

Star baby-sitter. Eldridge 1955 23p
(Eldridge Popular one-act playscripts)
Comedy. Football star with failing grade in English and important game coming up, inadvertently becomes baby sitter for principal of his school. 1 act 3m 3w 1 girl 1 interior

c The stuff of heroes
Little boy saves his friend from drowning but thinks himself coward because he was afraid. 1 act 1m 3b 1g 1 interior
In Hark, M. and McQueen, N. Junior plays for all occasions

c T for turkey
Children make up verses about what they are thankful for as they help prepare Thanksgiving dinner. 1 act 1m 1w 3b 3g 1 interior
In Hark, M. and McQueen, N. Junior plays for all occasions

The Teen Club's Christmas. Bakers Plays 1954 22p
Domestic comedy. Family living room becomes workshop for son's Teen Club project of repairing broken toys for needy children at Christmas. 1 act 5m 5w 1 interior

Hark, M. and McQueen, N.—*Continued*

c Three wishes for mother
    Children find good fairy who will grant mother's three wishes for Mother's Day. Verse play. 1 act 1w 1b 2g extras 1 exterior
    In Hark, M. and McQueen, N. Junior plays for all occasions

To my valentine
    Mixed up valentine cards cause temporary embarrassment to Taylor family. 1 act 4m 2w 1 interior
    In Hark, M. and McQueen, N. Teen-age plays for all occasions

Tomorrow is Christmas. Bakers Plays 1958 24p
    Neighbors and other occurrences keep delaying family who are to spend Christmas at Grandpa's and Grandma's. 1 act 3m 3w extras 1 interior

c Too many kittens
    Complications arise when family tries to give away four kittens. 1 act 1m 2w 1b 4g 1 interior
    In Hark, M. and McQueen, N. Junior plays for all occasions

c Visit of Johnny Appleseed
    Johnny Appleseed arrives to visit pioneer family whose little boy has fallen ill. Verse play. 1 act 1m 1w 2b 2g 1 interior
    In Hark, M. and McQueen, N. Junior plays for all occasions

Vote for your hero
    Comedy. Average man gets help from his illustrious children and friends in mayoralty campaign. 1 act 4m 3w 1b 1 interior
    In Hark, M. and McQueen, N. Teen-age plays for all occasions

What, no venison?
    Comedy. Employer changes his mind about younger generation at Thanksgiving dinner in employee's home. 1 act 3m 3w 1b 1g 1 interior
    In Hark, M. and McQueen, N. Teen-age plays for all occasions

c When do we eat?
    Little boy invites two new teachers home on day his mother is housecleaning. 1 act 1m 4w 1b 2g 1 interior
    In Hark, M. and McQueen, N. Junior plays for all occasions

Who's old-fashioned?
    Comedy. Grandpa guarantees success of high school graduation party when he calls the square dances. 1 act 3m 3w 1b 1 interior

Who's scared of ghosts? Eldridge 1959 21p (Eldridge Popular one-act play-scripts)
    On Halloween night in deserted house, two teenagers meet ghosts whose one ambition has been to see people. 1 act 3m 3w 1 interior 1 exterior
    In Hark, M. and McQueen, N. Teen-age plays for all occasions

Harlem, New York (City). See New York (City)—Harlem

Harlequinade. Rattigan, T.

Harnick, Sheldon. See Bock, J. Fiorello!

Harold II, King of the English
    Tennyson, A. Harold

Harold. Tennyson, A.

The harp that was silent. Berggren, J.

Harper, James Macpherson

c The first cat on Mars
    Crew of rocket ship is taking supplies to colonists on Mars. 1 act 9m 1 interior
    In Burack, A. S. ed. Four-star plays for boys

Harriet Beecher Stowe. Spamer, C.

Harrington, Helen
    The boy who knew Jesus. Bakers Plays 1960 22p
    A crippled boy grows up in the time of Jesus. Background music. 1 act 7m 3w extras 1 exterior

Harris, Aurand

c Circus in the wind. [Rev. and rewritten] French 1960 43p
    Comedy. Small boy, accidentally carried off by the circus, is pursued by grandfather who also has trouble tearing himself away. Background music. 3 acts 4m 1w 1b 1g extras 1 interior 1 exterior

c The flying prince. French 1958 43p
    Dramatization of folk tale of India about princess who is kidnapped by bandit and prince who turns himself into a bird to rescue her. 2 acts 7m 8w extras 1 interior 3 exteriors

c The plain Princess. Childrens Theatre 1955 49p music
    Dramatization of fairy tale by Phyllis McGinley. Ugly princess becomes beautiful when she learns to be unselfish. 3 acts 4 scenes 6m 7w 2 interiors

c Simple Simon. Childrens Theatre 1953 50p illus music
    As exponent of personal liberty Simple Simon almost forfeits his life in a totalitarian kingdom. Singing and dancing with background music. 3 acts 10m 4w extras 1 exterior

We were young that year. French 1954 86p illus music
    Young girl's first love, set in mountain summer resort. Singing and dancing with background music. 3 acts 7m 9w 1b 1g 1 setting

Harris, Bernice Kelly
    Ca'line
    Comedy. Impoverished servant woman looks down upon discomforts of rural life after she becomes resident of county poorhouse. 1 act 4m 3w extras 1 interior
    In Walser, R. ed. North Carolina drama

Harris, Neil
    The dream unwinds. French 1953 35p illus
    Young migrant worker's dream of home shattered by reality when he returns for visit. 1 act 4m 2w 1 setting

Harrison, Joan. See Sherwood, R. E. jt. auth.

Harrowing of hell
    The harrowing of hell; The Chester Pageant of the Cooks and Innkeepers
    14th or early 15th century mystery play based on apocryphal New Testament Gospel of Nicodemus. Christ's descent into hell to take to heaven the good souls. Final scene about "an offending ale-wife . . . may well be a later addition." Verse play in Middle English with modernized spelling. Singing. 3 scenes 14m 1w 1 interior 1 exterior
    In Everyman, and medieval miracle plays
    —Same; York Saddlers' play
    In Browne, E. M. ed. Religious drama, 2

The **harrowing** of hell; The Chester Pageant of the Cooks and Innkeepers. Harrowing of hell

The **harrowing** of hell; York Saddlers' play. Harrowing of hell

Hart, Moss
The climate of Eden. Random House 1953 177p
　Based on Edgar Mittelhölzer's novel: Shadows move among them. Missionary of naturalistic religion establishes free thinking community in British Guiana. 2 acts 8m 5w extras 1 setting

The climate of Eden (condensation)
　In The Best plays of 1952-1953
　In Theatre 1953

Hart, Moss, and Kaufman, George S.
You can't take it with you
　Highly individualistic people in eccentric New York City home convert conventional outsider who marries daughter of household. 3 acts 4 scenes 12m 7w 1 interior
　In Sper, F. ed. Living American plays

Hartke, Gilbert V.
The little world of Don Camillo. Dramatic 1957 117p
　Dramatization of novel by Giovanni Guareschi. Catholic priest's troubles with his wayward flock, especially the Communist mayor of Italian village. 3 acts 9 scenes 17m 8w 1 interior 2 exteriors

Hartley, Ray
Big shot. French 1953 34p illus
　Comedy. Teenage boy whose mother is afraid of dogs secretly harbors sick stray dog in cellar. 1 act 2 scenes 3m 4w 1 interior

Hartog, Jan de
The fourposter. [Acting ed] French 1954 77p illus
　Domestic comedy. Chronicle of stormy but happy marriage. 3 acts 6 scenes 1m 1w 1 interior
—Same
　In Best American plays; 4th ser.

Harvey. Chase, M.

Hastings, Charlotte
Uncertain joy
　Ten-year old boy, mistreated by father, poses many problems for his would-be-guardian. 3 acts 5 scenes 4m 1b 4w 1 interior
　In Plays of the year v12

Hastings, M. Louise C.
Christmas in other lands
　A mother tells her children about Christmas in other lands. 3 tableaux 1w 1b 1g extras
　In National Recreation Association. Plays, pageants and ceremonials for the Christmas season

c A May Day pageant
　Pageant showing how May Day was celebrated in medieval England. Includes pantomimes and a Maypole dance. 3m 3w 1b extras 1 exterior
　In Birdsall, R. ed. Creative plays for every school month

Hatcher, Harvey B.
The holy Nativity. Broadman 1957 27p illus music
　Christmas pantomime of the Nativity. 12 tableaux with background music or organ, trumpets, string quartet, choir with soloists and a girls' choir. 12 scenes Large mixed cast

Hate. See Hatred

A **hatful** of rain. Gazzo, M. V.

Hatlen, Theodore W.
All in the family. Row 1954 112p
　Domestic comedy. Teenage boy's Back-to-the-Home campaign leads to a not-so-quiet evening at home for his family. 3 acts 7m 6w 1 interior

The **hatless** snowmen. Spamer, C.

Hatred
Genet, J. The maids
Goetz, R. and Goetz, A. The hidden river
Horne, K. A. This dark world and wide

Hats
Bayliss, A. E. M. My hat!
c Hark, M. and McQueen, N. Father's Easter hat
Johnson, P. Success story
Labiche, E. and Marc-Michel. An Italian straw hat
Lynch, P. Fishing hat
Osborne, S. If you ask me—
Righter, N. F. Hold onto your hat

Hatsuyuki. Komparu, Z.

Haughton, William. See Dekker, T. jt. auth.

The **haunted** clothesline. Miller, H. L.

The **haunted** house. Plautus

Haunted houses. See Ghosts

Haunted rooms. Armstrong, W. F.

Hauptmann, Gerhart
The rats; tr. from the German by Ludwig Lewisohn
　Tragedy. Unmarried woman tries to regain possession of her baby. 5 acts 10m 8w 2 interiors 1 exterior
　In Tucker, S. M. ed. Twenty-five modern plays

The weavers; tr. from the German by Mary Morison
　Tragedy. Revolt of textile workers in mid-nineteenth century Germany. 5 acts Large mixed cast 5 interiors
　In A Treasury of the theatre

Hauser, Winifred
c The big decision
　For primary grades. Shows that city needs many different kinds of workers. 20m 7w 1 interior
　In Birdsall, R. ed. Creative plays for every school month

The **haven.** Mosel, T.

Hawkes, Jacquetta, and Priestley, J. B.
Dragon's mouth
　Written for platform reading. Four people, one of whom is doomed to die, arrive at self revelations about themselves and each other. 2 parts 2m 2w no scenery
　In Cordell, R. A. and Matson, L. eds. The off-Broadway theatre

Hawse, Alberta
The cradle. Eldridge 1956 36p music (Eldridge Christmas entertainments)
　Christmas. Effect of birth of Jesus upon owner of Bethlehem stable who had become selfish as he guarded a cradle for the Messiah. Solos. Background music. 3 acts 3m 4w 1 interior

Seeing the star. Eldridge 1954 28p (Eldridge Christmas entertainments)
　Christmas play within a play. Young man regains his faith as he watches the rehearsal of Christmas play. Solos and background music. 3 acts 5m 4w 1 interior

Hawthorne, Nathaniel
Feather top (dramatization) See Mac-Kaye, P. The scarecrow
The house of the Seven Gables (radio adaptation) See Olfson, L. The house of the Seven Gables

Hawtrey, Charles
The private secretary. Rev. version by Hugh Miller. [French's Acting ed] French (London) 1954 [c1907] 82p illus
Victorian farce. In 1884, a meek clergyman, recently employed as private secretary, finds that employer's nephew is trying to pass off one of his own friends as secretary. 3 acts 9m 4w 2 interiors

Hay, Ian. See Peach, L. du G. jt. auth.

Haycox, Ernest
Stage to Lordsburg (moving picture adaptation) See Nichols, D. Stagecoach

Hayes, Alfred
The girl on the Via Flaminia. French 1954 90p
Based on author's novel. Tragic story of affair between American soldier and Italian girl in Rome in last year of World War II. 3 acts 2 scenes 7m 4w 2 interiors
—Same
In Cordell, R. A. and Matson, L. eds. The off-Broadway theatre
The girl on the Via Flaminia (condensation)
In The Best plays of 1953-1954

Hayes, Joseph
The desperate hours. French 1956 184p
Based on author's novel. Three escaped convicts take over the Hilliard home in Indianapolis and hold family hostage. 3 acts 24 scenes 10m 3w 1b 2 settings
Trade edition published by Random House
—Same
In Bierman, J.; Hart, J. and Johnson, S. eds. The dramatic experience
The desperate hours (condensation)
In The Best plays of 1954-1955
In Theatre, 1955
See also Hayes, M. jt. auth.

Hayes, Marrijane and Hayes, Joseph
Mister Peepers. French 1953 103p illus
Based on the television program: Mr Peepers. Over one weekend Mr Peepers, amiable, quiet schoolteacher, receives good offer from business firm and also falls in love. 3 acts 7m 7w extras 1 interior
Penny. French 1954 84p illus
Domestic comedy based on the comic strip: Penny, by Harry Haenigsen. Effects upon her parents, friends, and townspeople of publication of Penny's reply to her father's editorial on women's wiles. 3 acts 5 scenes 6m 6w extras 1 exterior

Haym Salomon's battle. Fisher, A. and Rabe, O.

A **hazard** of new fortunes. Howells, W. D.

Hazel Kirke. MacKaye, S.

Hazeltine, Alice Isabel
Madelon
Christmas Nativity play. Based on legend of the first Christmas roses which sprang by miracle from tears of little girl who had no gift for Christ Child.

Play in verse with songs and background choir music. 2 scenes 7m 1g 1 interior 1 exterior
In Horn Book Magazine. Four Christmas plays

Hazlewood, C. H.
Lady Audley's secret
19th century murder mystery. Mysterious disappearance of visitor at home of country squire. 2 acts 6 scenes 4m 3w extras 2 interiors 3 exteriors
In Rowell, G. ed. Nineteenth century plays

He and she. Crothers, R.

He is come! The Messiah! Wagner, N.

He knew the master. Knox, A.

He said he was Santa. Fluckey, J. O.

He traveled the world. McCaslin, N.

He tried with his boots on. Payton, D.

He who gets slapped. Andreev, L.

He who walks in love. Hellier, E. B.

Headin' for a weddin'. Rose, Le R.

Healey, Robert M.
Nobody knows. Bakers Plays 1958 17p (Baker's Royalty plays)
Negro drama student refuses to act in a play because of the way it depicts Negro in the South. 1 act 3m 1 interior

The **healing** at the Pool of Bethesda. Phillips, J. B.

Healing in its wings. Cruse, C.

The **healing** of the man born blind. Phillips, J. B.

The **healing** of the paralyzed man. Phillips, J. B.

Health. See Hygiene

Health farms. See Health resorts, watering places, etc.

Health resorts, watering-places, etc.
Chodorov, E. The spa
Howard, V. A rest for Mr Winkle
Tobias, J. A boy named Beulah

Health Week
c Woolsey, J. and Sechrist, E. H. The imps' defeat

Healy, John
The matching piece. Eldridge 1958 21p (Eldridge Popular one-act playscripts)
Farce. Confusion breaks out when a young husband starts making plaster masks for masquerade party. 1 act 3m 3w 1 interior
Nero fiddles. French 1958 22p
Comedy. Members of Emperor Nero's household promote some of their own interests when they discover his supposedly secret plan to burn Rome. 1 act 2m 6w 1 interior
Summer and stock. Eldridge 1959 18p (Eldridge Popular one-act playscripts)
Farce. Self centered girl is so determined to be a star, that indulgent parents buy the stock company. 1 act 3m 4w extras 1 interior

Hearn, Lafcadio. See Tennant, K. Hamaguchi Gohei

Heart of Bruce. Williamson, H. R.

The **heart** of Maryland. Belasco, D.

The **heart** of the forest. Fluckey, J. O.

Heart throbs. Miller, H. L.

Heart trouble. Hark, M. and McQueen, N.

Heartbreak house. Shaw, B.

The **heartless** princess. Black, F.

Hearts and flowers for mother. Hark, M. and McQueen, N.

Hearts, tarts, and valentines. Fisher, A.

Heathen pioneer. Climenhaga, J.

Heaven
Orth, R. For heaven's sake
Tree, J. The fisherman

Heaven challenges. Li, Y. M.

Heaven is a long time to wait. Conkle, E. P.

Heavenly stars. Spamer, C.

Heayes, Neil
Morning air. Deane 1955 66p illus
("Deane's" Ser. of plays)
Domestic comedy. Discovery of formula for elixir of life, developed by former owner of their cottage, causes complications in lives of young newlyweds. 3 acts 4m 3w 1 interior

Hebbel, Friedrich
Maria Magdalena; tr. by Paula Green
Tragedy. Pharisaical middle class father's attitude drives son from home, and causes daughter's suicide. 3 acts 24 scenes 7m 3w 1b 2 interiors
In Griffin, A. V. Living theatre

Hecuba, wife of Priam, King of Troy
Euripides. Hecuba
Euripides. The Trojan women

Hecuba. Euripides

Hedda Gabler. Ibsen, H.

Heger, Kathryn
Somebody special. French 1958 19p illus
Young man spends vacation at resort hotel hoping to meet special girl but he runs into complications. 1 act 2m 6w extras 1 interior

Hegge cycle. See Coventry plays

Heicher, Merlo
The meaning of Christmas Day
Nativity play helps young moderns discover the meaning of Christmas Day. Includes three tableaux and choral singing. 1 act 8 scenes 8m 4w extras choir 1 setting
In Brings, L. M. ed. The modern treasury of Christmas plays

Heicher, Merlo, and St Clair, Robert
The lost star
Three wise men argue amongst themselves as to which one will be favored by Christ Child. 1 act 4 scenes 14m 4w extras 3 interiors 1 exterior
In Brings, L. M. ed. The modern treasury of Christmas plays

Heidi. Warnick, C.

Heijermans, Herman
The Good Hope; tr. from the Dutch by Lilian Saunders and Caroline Heijermans-Houwink
Tragedy. Pitiful plight of poor families of crew of an unseaworthy fishing schooner sent out by greedy shipowner. 4 acts 11m 7w 2 interiors
In Gassner, J. ed. Twenty best European plays on the American stage

Hein, Robert F.
Receive your King! Warburg Press 1954 23p music
Christmas worship program. Nativity scenes with choral music and a tableau. 5 parts Large mixed cast 2 interiors

Heinlein, Mary Virginia
c The panda and the spy. Childrens Theatre 1954 59p
Runaway circus panda, hidden by some children in their home, helps catch spy trying to steal secret papers from their father. 3 acts 3m 9w 11b 1g 1 interior

Heirs. See Inheritance and succession

Helen. Euripides

Helen of Troy
Euripides. Helen
Euripides. The Trojan women
Moross, J. The golden apple

Hell
Sartre, J. P. No exit

Hellier, Elizabeth B.
He who walks in love. Eldridge 1953 17p
(Eldridge Christmas entertainments)
Christmas Nativity play. Slave girl at inn in Bethlehem helps Holy Family. Choir and soloist; background music. 4 scenes 7m 4w 1b 1g extras 1 setting

Hellman, Lillian
Another part of the forest
Concerns the Hubbard family of "The little foxes." Set twenty years earlier, it reveals how Ben Hubbard wrested family wealth from tyrannical father. 3 acts 8m 5w 1 interior 1 exterior
In Watson, E. B. and Pressey, B. eds. Contemporary drama: eleven plays
Candide (condensation)
In The Best plays of 1956-1957
The children's hour. Acting ed. Dramatists 1953 75p illus
Tragedy ensues for two young women teachers when pupil in their boarding school spreads story that they have an abnormal attachment for each other. 3 acts 4 scenes 2m 14w 2 interiors
—Same
In Plays of the year v5
The little foxes
Psychological study of greed. Set in small southern town about 1900, two brothers and a sister attempt to swindle each other. 3 acts 6m 4w 1 interior
In A Treasury of the theatre
Toys in the attic. Random House 1960 116p illus
Two sisters who support corrupt brother are almost disappointed when he suddenly becomes rich through an illegal deal with local tyrant. Set in deep South. 3 acts 4m 4w extras 1 interior 1 exterior
Toys in the attic (condensation)
In The Best plays of 1959-1960
In Broadway's best, 1960
Watch on the Rhine
German refugee, an anti-Nazi, kills blackmailing Nazi agent in Washington, D.C. shortly before World War II. 3 acts 4m 4w 2b 1g 1 interior
In Gaver, J. ed. Critics' choice
See also Bernstein, L. Candide

Hello from Bertha. Williams, T.

Hello, Mr Groundhog. Miller, H. L.

Hello out there. Saroyan, W.

Helm, MacKinley
Fray Junípero Serra; the great walker. Stanford Univ. Press 1956 86p front
The life of an eighteenth century Franciscan friar, Junipero Serra, in Mexico, and in California where he founded missions. Choral music, songs and dances. 1 act 47 scenes 7m chorus 1 setting

Héloïse. Forsyth, J.

Helpers. Spamer, C.

Henderson, John
A midsummer night's scream. Eldridge 1954 72p music (Eldridge 3-act play-scripts)
    Comedy. Teenagers' attempt to stage play in deserted and supposedly haunted theater belonging to their town's grouchy millionaire. Background music 3 acts 4 scenes 6m 7w 1 interior

Henneberger, John. See Gregory, II. jt. auth.

Hennessy, Michael A.
The American spirit. Bakers Plays 1958 27p (Baker's Royalty plays)
    Boy Scout, assigned to blow bugle at Memorial Day ceremony in cemetery, suddenly finds himself surrounded by ghosts of great American patriots. Background music. 1 act 15m 1w 1 exterior

Henry II, King of England
Anouilh, J. Becket
Eliot, T. S. Murder in the Cathedral

Henry III, King of England
Duncannon, F. E. N. P. viscount. Like stars appearing

Henry III, King of France
Dryden, J. and Lee, N. The Duke of Guise

Henry VIII, King of England
Albery, P. Anne Boleyn
Gressieker, H. Royal gambit

Henry, John. See John Henry

Henry, Virginia
c May Day in the woods. Eldridge 1958 18p music
    May Day operetta for primary grades. Children dance at festival in which woodland creatures and flowers crown the May Flower as their Queen of May. Includes music for songs. Large mixed cast 1 exterior

"Henry IV." Pirandello, L.

Henry Van Dyke's The Other Wise Man. Sergel, R.

Henschel, George. See Howells, W. D. A sea change

Her big crush. Weiss, M. J.

Her husband's consent. Leonard, E. S.

Her opinion of his story. Howells, W. D.

Heracleidae. See Heraclidae

The **Heracleidae.** Euripides

Heracles. See Hercules

Heracles. Euripides

Heraclidae
Euripides. The children of Herakles
Euripides. The Heracleidae

Heraclius. Corneille, P.

Herakles. See Hercules

Herald, Heinz; Herczeg, Geza, and Raine, Norman Reilly
The life of Emile Zola
    Moving picture play based on book: Zola and his time, by Matthew Josephson. After winning fame and fortune, the 19th century French novelist is brought to trial for efforts to clear Alfred Dreyfus. 8 parts 20m 3w
    In Gassner, J. and Nichols, D. eds. Great film plays

Herbert, F. Hugh
A girl can tell. Dramatists 1954 96p illus
    Romantic comedy. While looking through old scrapbook a mother tells her 15-year old daughter how she chose her husband from among six suitors. 3 acts 6 scenes 10m 5w 3 interiors

The moon is blue. Acting ed. Dramatists 1953 76p
    Romantic comedy of naive girl's experiences in sophisticated New York. 3 acts 5 scenes 3m 1w 1 interior 1 exterior
    Trade edition published by Random House

Hercules
Euripides. Heracles
Euripides. The madness of Herakles
Sophocles. The women of Trachis

Herczeg, Geza. See Herald, H. jt. auth.

Here we are. Parker, D.

Heredity
Anderson, M. Bad seed
Ibsen, H. Ghosts

Herefordshire dialect. See Dialect—English—Herefordshire

Herlihy, James Leo, and Noble, William
Blue denim. French 1958 105p illus
    Parents of teen-age son suddenly discover he is to be father of his sweetheart's child. 3 acts 3m 3w 1 interior
    Trade edition published by Random House

Herman, George
Brighten every corner. French 1958 34p illus
    At death of a nun, various people, from a deranged laborer to a state legislator, recall constructive influence she had on their lives. Background music. 1 act Large mixed cast 1 interior
An echo of wings. French 1960 45p illus
    Fantasy. School fire takes lives of many teachers and children and one man asking why, talks to those who died. 1 act 13m 6w 2b 1g 1 setting
A simple little affair. French 1960 39p illus
    Emotions of everyone concerned at a wedding prevent it from being a simple little affair and it becomes an act of great courage and hope. 1 act 9m 5w 1 interior
A smell of cinnamon. French 1958 80p
    Problems of Cardinal Perelli, assigned to present to the Vatican the case for cannonization of Mother Mary Frances Clarke, founder of the Sisters of Charity of the Blessed Virgin Mary, at Dubuque, Iowa. 2 acts 4m 8w 1 interior

Herman, Sema Williams
c Good neighbors
    Group of primary school children talk about neighborliness and tell how they learn about different kinds of people. Includes songs with musical scores. 9b 8g extras 1 exterior
    In Birdsall, R. ed. Creative plays for every school month

Herman's temptation. Howard, V.

Herne, James A.
Margaret Fleming
    Realism. Wealthy mill owner attempts to keep his mistress and her child a secret from his wife. 4 acts 5 scenes 7m 5w 3 interiors
    In Quinn, A. H. ed. Representative American plays
Shore Acres
    Set in Maine, 1880. Emotional conflict among members of a seafaring family. 4 acts 19m 10w 1g 2 interiors 2 exteriors
    In Downer, A. S. ed. American drama

The **herne's** egg. Yeats, W. B.

Herod I, the Great, King of Judea
Coventry plays. Herod and the kings
Coventry plays. The pageant of the Shearmen and Taylors—The Coventry Nativity play

Herod I, the Great, King of Judea—*Cont.*
St Clair, R. The holy search
Towneley plays. The Wakefield Pageant of Herod the Great

Herod and the kings. Coventry plays

Herod and the Magi. Malcolmson, A.

Heroes
Miller, H. L. Pin-up pals
Schaefer, L. Song for a hero
See also Courage; Martyrs; Mythology

The heroes. Ashbery, J.

Heroic verse, English
Lee, N. Gloriana
Lee, N. Sophonisba

Heroism. See Courage

A hero's homecoming. Miller, H. L.

He's having a baby. Carmichael, F.

Hesketh, James
Mr Owl. ₍French's Acting ed₎ French (London) 1953 46p illus
In early 19th century England, innkeeper's daughter helps Bow Street runner of London Police apprehend highwayman. 2 acts 11m 1w 1 interior

Hess, Marian Nichols
c Folk-o-rama U.S.A.
While on picnic a boy and girl meet the Spirit of America who introduces them to many characters from our history and folklore. Includes songs and folk dances. 10m 1w 1b 1g extras 1 exterior
In Birdsall, R. ed. Creative plays for every school month

Hessie of the hills. Schweikert, C. P.

Heywood, Thomas
A woman killed with kindness
Elizabethan domestic tragedy. Husband forgives wife's infidelity. Verse play. Music and dancing. 5 acts 19 scenes 17m 3w extras 1 setting
In Morrell, J. M. ed. Four English tragedies of the 16th and 17th centuries

Hi ho! Christmas. Asbrand, K.

Hiawatha. Norris, J.

Hidden meanings. Fisher, A.

The hidden river. Goetz, R. and Goetz, A.

High polish. Casey, B. M.

The high school. See Perl, A. The world of Sholom Aleichem

High schools
Abstance, P. and Abstance, L. The pigskin parade
Aschmann, H. T. As pretty does
McCoy, P. S. Susan steps out
Miller, H. L. The Shakespearean touch
Miller, H. L. What makes it tick?
Reach, J. Are teachers human?
Reach, J. Meet me at the prom
Williams, P. Commencement
See also Boarding schools; Schools

High schools (Endowed)

England
Daviot, G. The staff-room

High Tor. Anderson, M.

High treason. See Treason

The high white star. Erhard, T.

High window. Powers, V.

The highest tree. Schary, D.

Highly seasoned. Knapp, B.

Highwaymen. See Brigands and robbers

Hilarius
Ludus super iconia Sancti Nicolai (adaptation) See Malcolmson, A. The statue of Saint Nicholas

Hill, George Roy, and Whedon, John
A night to remember
Television play. A documentary of happenings on board the steamship "Titanic" when she hit an iceberg and sank, April 14, 1912. Based on book by Walter Lord. Large mixed cast
In Writers Guild of America. The prize plays of television and radio, 1956

Hill, Kay
Midnight burial
Comedy. A girl at camp inadvertently receives cake made with rat poison instead of vanilla and runs into complications when she tries to bury it. 1 act 8g 1 exterior
In Kamerman, S. E. ed. Blue-ribbon plays for girls

Hill, Lucienne. See Regnier, M. Paddle your own canoe

Hippety hop. Spamer, C.

Hippolytus
Euripides. Hippolytus

Hippolytus. Euripides

Hiraoka, Kimitake. See Mishima, Yukio

His and hers. Casey, B. M.

His and hers. Kanin, F. and Kanin, M.

His Eminence of England. Williamson, H. R.

His hand and pen. Du Bois, G.

His star. Kerr, M. L.

His wonders to perform. Posegate, E. D.

History, Biblical. See Bible—History of Biblical events

Histrionics. See Acting

Hitler's victims. Dimondstein, B.

Hivnor, Robert
The ticklish acrobat
Satire on Americans in their attempt to help and understand impoverished Europeans, and vice versa. 8m 5w 1 exterior
In Playbook: five plays for a new theatre

Hiyoshi, Sa-ami Yasukiyo. See Hiyoshi, Yasukiyo

Hiyoshi, Yasukiyo
Benkei on the bridge (Hashi-Benkei)
Japanese Nō verse drama. Noble youth defeats priest in duel and wins him as loyal follower. 3m extras 1 exterior
In Waley, A. The Nō plays of Japan

Hoax of Hogan's Holler. Schweikert, C.

Hoaxes
Shakespeare, W. Twelfth night

The hobble-de-hoy. Richards, S. and Slocumb, P.

A hobby for Dad. Howard, V.

Hochwaelder, Fritz
The public prosecutor; tr. by Kitty Black. ₍French's Acting ed₎ French (London) 1958 63p illus
The end of Reign of Terror in France with trial of Fonquier-Tinville. 3 acts 9m 1w 1 interior
—Same
In Plays of the year v16

Hochwaelder, Fritz—*Continued*

The strong are lonely. French 1954 99p illus

"Play from the German of Fritz Hochwaelder, adapted by Eva Le Gallienne from the French version by Jean Mercure and Richard Theiberger." Spanish king's order of 1767 that the Jesuit abandon their mission, a utopian state, in Paraguay, leads to Indian uprising. 2 acts 5 scenes 20m extras 1 interior

—Same

In Plays of the year, v14

Hochwälder, Fritz. See Hochwaelder, Fritz

Hoggan, Mable Hunter

c The toymakers' pledge. Eldridge 1956 18p music (Eldridge Christmas entertainments)

Christmas. Toymakers invoke aid of Santa Claus in providing gift for rich little Rosalie. Includes songs and a Nativity pantomime with children's chorus. 2 scenes 6m 2w 3g 2b extras 2 interiors

The **hōka** priests. Komparu, Z. U.

Holbrook, Marion

c A candle-lighting service

Christmas worship program with Madonna and Child. 1 tableau Unidentified cast 9 characters

In National Recreation Association. Plays, pageants and ceremonials for the Christmas season

Hold onto your hat. Righter, N. F.

Hold that Indian. Phillips, M. K.

The **hold**-up at Hoecake Junction. Abstance, P. and Abstance, L.

Hold your horsepower! Martens, A. C.

A **hole** in the head. Schulman, A.

Holiday. Barry, P.

Holiday for lovers. Alexander, R.

Holiday haunts. Bate, S.

Holiday song. Chayefsky, P.

Holidays

c Newman, D. Happy holidays

c Woolsey, J. and Sechrist, E. H. Days and days

See also names of individual holidays, e.g. Arbor Day; Christmas; Easter

Holland, Norman

Crisis in Wimpole Street. [French's Acting ed] French (London) 1953 22p illus

Just before her secret marriage to Robert Browning, Elizabeth Barrett's pet spaniel, Flush, is kidnapped and returned in September 1846. 1 act 7w extras 1 interior

Widow of Charles Dickens. [French's Acting ed] French 1953 22p illus

A meeting, on the day after Dickens' death, of the four women who had been closest to him. 1 act 6w 1 interior

Will and testament. [French's Acting ed] French 1954 21p illus

Young man is freed from domineering mother when uncle's will opens an unexpected way to independence and romance. 1 act 4m 1w 1 interior

Hollinshead, Letitia M.

c In honour bound. Bakers Plays 1957 25p

Based on the Grimm fairy tale, Rumpelstiltskin. 1 act 3 scenes 5m 2w 2b 2 interiors

Publican and sinner. Bakers Plays 1955 38p

How Levi, the publican, became Matthew, the Apostle; based on New Testament accounts. 2 acts 5 scenes 4m 5w 1g 1 interior 1 exterior

c Thank you, God for everything. Bakers Plays 1955 18p

Fantasy. Two little angels who restore blind girl's sight also teach her to accept the real world which is not as beautiful as she had imagined it. 2 scenes 2m 2w 3b 1g 1 interior

Holloway, Sister Marcella Marie

c The last of the leprechauns. French 1958 54p illus music

Cathy, lost Princess of Ireland, overcomes opposition and wins Prince Michael with help of leprechaun leader. Songs. 3 acts 3 scenes 5m 4w 1 interior 1 exterior

Holm, John Cecil

The southwest corner. Dramatists 1955 74p illus

Based on the novel of the same title by Mildred Walker. Elderly Vermont widow almost loses her home to aggressive, avaricious companion. 3 acts 6 scenes 4m 3w 1 interior

Holmes, Marion

Jungle prize. Friendship Press 1955 32p illus

Based on incident in Communist guerilla warfare in Malaya, 1952. A Chinese Malayan youth who had joined Communists is sent to slash rubber trees in his own village. 1 act 5m 1w 1 interior

Holmes, Oliver Wendell

Lavery, E. The magnificent Yankee

Holmes, Ruth Vickery

c King John and the Abbott of Canterbury

Adaptation of old English ballad about shepherd who outwitted King John of England. 4 scenes 7m 2 interiors

In Burack, A. S. ed. Four-star plays for boys

In Fenner, P. and Hughes, A. comps. Entrances and exits

Holt, Nelle A.

The willing spirit. Bakers Plays 1954 21p

Narrator relates story of one family's work for the church as example of true Christian stewardship. 1 act 12m 10w 2g 1 interior

Holy Innocents, Massacre of the

Coventry plays. Herod and the kings

Coventry plays. The pageant of the Shearmen and Taylors—The Coventry Nativity play

Towneley plays. The Wakefield Pageant of Herod the Great

The **Holy** Nativity. Hatcher, H. B.

The **holy** search. St Clair, R.

Holy Spirit

Estes, S. In quest of power through the Holy Spirit

See also Pentecost

Holy Week

Getzinger, E. W. Promise of the angels

See also Easter

Home, William Douglas

The reluctant debutante. French 1957 106p

English debutante upsets snobbish mother's matchmaking plans by setting her heart on charming but apparently penniless youth. 2 acts 4 scenes 3m 5w 1 interior

Home, William D.—*Continued*
The reluctant debutante (condensation)
In Broadway's best, 1957

Home. See Family

Home economics
c Peterson, M. N. Ten helpful elves
Richmond, S. S. Homemakers have a way
c Spamer, C. Helpers
See also House cleaning

Home for Christmas. Martens, A. C.

Home of the brave. Laurents, A.

Home rule (Ireland) See Irish question

Home Sweet Home. Applegarth, M. T.

Home sweet home. Emurian, E. K.

Home, sweet home. Peterson, L.

Home, sweet home. Werner, S.

The **homecoming.** Hark, M. and McQueen, N.

Homecoming. O'Neill, E.

Homemakers have a way. Richmond, S. S.

Homes for the aged. See Old age homes

Homesickness. See Nostalgia

Homosexuality
Anderson, R. W. Tea and sympathy
Delaney, S. A taste of honey
Goetz, R. and Goetz, A. The immoralist
King, P. Serious charge
See also Lesbianism

Hondelink, Margaret E.
c Christmas cards
Christmas operetta. Includes 15 tableaux representing Christmas cards. 2m 2w 1g extras choir
In Birdsall, R. ed. Creative plays for every school month

Honest Abe Lincoln. Fisher, A. and Rabe, O.

Honest to goodness. Garver, J.

The **honest** whore; part I. Dekker, T. and Middleton, T.

The **honest** whore; part 2. Dekker, T.

Honesty
Fisher, A. and Rabe, O. Honest Abe Lincoln
Malleson, M. The misanthrope
Molière, J. B. P. The misanthrope
Molière, J. B. P. The slave of truth
Poverman, H. Easy money
Ullman, S. S. The reward
See also Business ethics

The **honeymooners;** a letter to the boss. Marx, M. and others

Honor
Vidal, G. Honor

Honor. Vidal, G.

The **honored** ones. Olson, E. E.

A **hooky** holiday. Miller, H. L.

Hop o' my thumb. Palmer, C. K.

Hope, Arthur J.; Mary Francis, Sister, and Birder, Dudley
The complaining angel; a farce with music; book by Natalie E. White; lyrics by John D. Tumpane; Sister Mary Francis ₁and₁ Natalie E. White; music

by Arthur J. Hope; Sister Mary Francis ₁and₁ Dudley Birder. French 1957 53p front
Sequel to: Seven nuns at Las Vegas by N. E. White. Musical farce and fantasy about guardian angel of deceased actress who has been reassigned to a nun and finds convent life difficult. Piano score available separately. 2 acts 12 scenes 1m 8w women's chorus 1 setting

The **hopeful** travellers. Martens, G. M.

Hopi Indians
Peterson, L. Desert soliloquy

Hopper, Virginia Shearer
c Along came a blackbird
Blackbird steals the nose of pretty maid in royal palace. 1 act 2 scenes 4m 2w 1g 1 interior
In 'Round the year plays for the grades

Horgan, Paul
One red rose for Christmas (dramatization)` See O'Connell, M. O. Sister. One red rose

Horne, Kay Annette
This dark world and wide
Condemned prisoner who has had her eyes removed as gift to blind, learns that her hated sister is recipient. 3m 2w 1 interior
In Twelve half-hours with the Winthrop Theater

Horne, Kenneth
The Devil was sick. ₁French's Acting ed₁ French (London) 1957 89p illus
Farce centered around an English vicarage, marriage entanglements and a legacy. 3 acts 4m 4w 1 interior
Trial and error
Romantic comedy. Man marries attractive widow, who was acquitted of pushing her first husband off an ocean liner, but the latter suddenly returns, very much alive. 3 acts 4 scenes 3m 4w 1 interior
In Plays of the year v9
See also Benedetti, A. de. Two dozen red roses

Horror tales
Fletcher, L. Sorry, wrong number
Parker, K. T. Stand up to death
Pinter, H. The dumb waiter
Thomas, D. The doctor and the devils
See also Ghosts

A **horse!** A horse! Peach, L. du G.

A **horse** play. Moreno, R.

Horse stealing
Shaw, B. The shewing-up of Blanco Posnet

Horses
Peach, L. du G. A horse! A horse!

Horwitt, Arnold B. See Hague, A. Plain and fancy

Hospitals
Albee, E. The death of Bessie Smith
Blewett, D. Quiet night
Martens, A. C. Dr Hudson's secret journal
See also Sanatoriums

Host to a ghost. Greth, Le R. E.

The **hostage.** Behan, B.

Hotel Paradiso. Feydeau, G. and Desvallieres, M.

Hotels, taverns, etc.
Baker, L. G. Conspiracy at "The Cray-fish"
Costigan, J. A wind from the south
De Francquen, L. The cat and the fiddle
Frings, K. Look homeward, angel
Frost, R. Small hotel
Goldman, P. Mermaid Avenue is the world
Heger, K. Somebody special
Howells, W. D. Room forty-five
Johnson, P. H. Corinth House
Kirkpatrick, J. A summer for the Indians
Nichols, J. 'Twas such a night
Parker, D. and D'Usseau, A. The ladies of the corridor
Rattigan, T. Separate tables
Saroyan, W. The time of your life
Schulman, A. A hole in the head
Tedlock, D. Oil wells and wedding bells
Williams, T. The Lady of Larkspur Lotion

Hotoke no hara (condensation) Kwanze, M.

The **hour**-glass. Yeats, W. B.

Hour of honor. Joy, R. P.

Hourihane, Ursula
c Lucinda and the birthday ball. Paxton 1954 15p (Paxton Playlets)
Fairy tale based on Cinderella story. Fairies help kind village maiden become bride of prince. Background music with dancing. 3 scenes 4m 22w 1 interior 2 exteriors

Hours (Time) See Time

The **hours** on strike. Curtis, P. D.

The **house** by the lake. Mills, H.

The **house** by the stable. Williams, C.

House cleaning
c Hark, M. and McQueen, N. When do we eat?
c Jones, C. Clean-up time

A **house** for Duke. Levofsky, R.

The **house** is haunted. Hark, M. and McQueen, N.

The **house** is still. Smith, L. B. and Barrett, J. S.

The **house** of Bernarda Alba. García Lorca, F.

The **house** of Sugawara. Takeda, I.; Miyoshi, S. and Namiki, S.

The **house** of the Seven Gables. Olfson, L.

House on the cliff. Batson, G.

Housekeepers. See Servants

Housekeeping. See Home economics

Housemaids. See Servants

Houses. See Dwellings

Houses, Apartment. See Apartment houses

Housman, Laurence
"A good lesson!"
A segment of: Victoria Regina. Albert asserts his independence. 1 act 4m 1 interior
In Cooper, C. W. Preface to drama

Houston, Noel
According to law
Courtroom drama. Prejudiced court tries and unjustly convicts Negro for rape. 1 act 10m extras 1 interior
In Smith, B. and others, eds. A treasury of non-royalty one-act plays
She writes a roof
Comedy. Mother writes successful fiction based on incidents in own household, despite daughter's objections. 1 act 4w 1 interior
In Smith, B. and others, eds. A treasury of non-royalty one-act plays

Houston, Sam
Kissen, F. Sam Houston: brother of the Cherokees

Hovick, Rose Louise. See Lee, Gypsy Rose

How Betsy butted in. Spence, W.

How Boots befooled the king. Goldsmith, S. L.

How does your garden grow? Zahn, M.

Howard, Alice
Sokar and the crocodile (dramatization) See Barnes, E. A. and Young, B. M. Sokar and the crocodile

Howard, Bronson
Shenandoah
Sentimental drama of Northern officer and Southern sweetheart; danger, heroism, and happy ending. 4 acts 4 scenes 13m 7w 2 interiors 1 exterior
In Quinn, A. H. ed. Representative American plays

Howard, Doris
c Christmas doings
Christmas pantomime for primary grades: trimming tree, building snowmen, etc. Christmas songs. 4 episodes Large mixed cast 1 interior
In Birdsall, R. ed. Creative plays for every school month

Howard, Peter
The boss. Blandford 1954 75p
Conflict between Marxian and capitalist ideologies centered around threatened strike in plant of successful industrialist. 3 acts 6m 2w 1 interior
The dictator's slippers. Blandford 1954 58p
Allegory. Joint successors to a deceased dictator discuss new technique of international cooperation, based on determining what, not who, is right. 2 acts 7m extras 1 interior
The man with the key. Blandford 1954 74p
At informal meeting, delegates to international peace conference learn about new idea for achieving unity. 3 acts 6m 3w 1 interior
The real news. Blandford 1954 68p
Young reporter refuses to write a scoop story which would violate journalistic ethics. 3 acts 9m 3w 1 interior
We are tomorrow. Blandford 1954 100p
Allegorical fantasy. College student's projected idea of peaceful world based on absolute moral standards becomes reality at future date. 2 acts 3 scenes 7m 2w 1 interior

Howard, Sidney
The late Christopher Bean
Adaptation of the play: Prenez garde à la peinture, by René Fauchois. New England doctor's family reveals innate greed when posthumous fame of artist

Howard, Sidney—*Continued*

they had sheltered causes his paintings, left in their home, to become extremely valuable. 3 acts 5m 4w 1 interior

In Gassner, J. ed. Twenty best European plays on the American stage

In Sper, F. ed. Living American plays

Madam, will you walk? Dramatists 1955 110p illus

Fantasy and romantic comedy combined in an improvisation of the Faust theme. The Devil, in the guise of a doctor, helps unhappy daughter of disgraced Tammany politician find true love. 3 acts 5 scenes 11m 4w extras 2 interiors 2 exteriors

Madam, will you walk (condensation)

In Theatre, 1954

The silver cord

Sons and the mother who dominates them. 4 acts 4 scenes 2m 4w 2 interiors

In Quinn, A. H. ed. Representative American plays

Howard, Vernon

Around the world—by way of America

Based on incident in: Around the world in eighty days, by Jules Verne. Englishman attempting to travel around world in eighty days is delayed in West when Indians attack his train. 2 acts 9m 2w 2b 1g extras 1 interior 1 exterior

In Howard, V. Short plays from the great classics

Athletes all

Farce. Students put on amusing school show to display prowess in athletics. 11b 1 interior

In Howard, V. Short plays for all-boy casts

The best of the Old West

Farce. Amusing characters from typical western melodrama. 6m 2w 1 interior

In Howard, V. Short plays for all-boy casts

The big melodrama

Farce based on parody of characters in old time melodrama: hero rescues helpless heroine from villain's clutches. 4m 2w 1 interior

In Howard, V. Short plays for all-boy casts

The blackbird

Farce. Simple-minded soldier catches notorious spy. 3m 2w 1 interior

In Howard, V. Short plays for all-boy casts

The blue serge suit

Farce. Two salesmen sell strange collection of garments to naive customer. 6m 1 interior

In Howard, V. Short plays for all-boy casts

c Danger—pixies at work

Farce. Strange things happen when boys try to cook and sew to surprise their mother for Mother's Day. 1m 6b 1 interior

In Howard, V. Short plays for all-boy casts

David and Goliath

Bible. Old Testament. Samuel. David saves Israel from Philistines by killing Goliath. 7m 5w extras 1 exterior

In Howard, V. Short plays from the great classics

Don Quixote saves the day

Based on incident in: Don Quixote, by Miguel de Cervantes Saavedra. In 16th century Spain, chivalrous knight rescues ladies from group of bandits. 10m 4w extras 1 exterior

In Howard, V. Short plays from the great classics

Drexel

Farce. Four boys find nervous dragon in the woods. 4b extras 1 exterior

In Howard, V. Short plays for all-boy casts

Five boys and a Santa

Santa brings wrong presents because by mistake one little boy mails him grocery list. 5b extras 1 interior

In Howard, V. Short plays for all-boy casts

Gizzlegump

Farce. A man visits a town where everything is done backwards. 6m 1 exterior

In Howard, V. Short plays for all-boy casts

Gulliver wins his freedom

Based on incident in: Gulliver's travels, by Jonathan Swift. Fantasy. Gulliver's adventures with tiny people of Lilliput. 2 acts 13m 2w extras 2 exteriors

In Howard, V. Short plays from the great classics

Happy holidays for little women

Based on incident in: Little women, by Louisa May Alcott. Four March sisters receive invitation to a New Year's party. Set in New England during Civil War. 5m 5w 1 interior

In Howard, V. Short plays from the great classics

Herman's temptation

Farce. Boys make ineffectual attempts to help overweight friend go on diet. 5b 1 exterior

In Howard, V. Short plays for all-boy casts

A hobby for Dad

Farce. When fathers visit school, they break things and get in trouble with principal. 5m 3b 1 interior

In Howard, V. Short plays for all-boy casts

I resolve

Farce. New Year's resolutions made by several people don't turn out as they should. 7m 1w 1 interior

In Howard, V. Short plays for all-boy casts

The inventor's clinic

Farce. Three eccentric inventors try to sell their secret inventions. 5m 1 interior

In Howard, V. Short plays for all-boy casts

Johnny Appleseed in danger

Set on the midwestern frontier in early 18th century. How Johnny Appleseed (John Chapman) prevented Indian attack on settlers by introducing apple seed planting to Indians. 6m 3w 2b 1g extras 1 exterior

In Howard, V. Short plays from the great classics

The mad Doctor Zing

Farce. Mad doctor develops formula that makes people think they are dogs. 6m 1 interior

In Howard, V. Short plays for all-boy casts

Howard, Vernon—*Continued*

The women from Kentucky
Comedy. What Lincoln and his men think is secret message is really recipe for peach pie. 2 acts 4m 4w 1 interior

In Howard, V. Easy plays for church and school

Your manners and mine
Farce. Unusual things happen when four boys enroll in charm school. 1m 4b 1 interior

In Howard, V. Short plays for all-boy casts

Your money or your life
Farce. Master of ceremonies plays tricks on unsuspecting contestant. 4m 1 interior

In Howard, V. Short plays for all-boy casts

Howe, Carroll V.

The long fall
Fatal accident on bridge under construction tests courage of engineer's son. 1 act 8m 1 exterior

In The Best short plays

Howe, Julia (Ward)

Emurian, E. K. Battle hymn of the Republic

Spamer, C. Julia Ward Howe

Howe, William Howe, 5th viscount

Sherwood, R. E. Small war on Murray Hill

Howells, J. Harvey

Good-bye, Gray Flannel
Television comedy. New York advertising man who retires to Connecticut to raise apples finds himself promoting local fruit growing industry. 8m 2w extras

In Writers Guild of America. The prize plays of television and radio, 1956

Howells, W. D.

The Albany depot
Comedy. Man who goes to meet his cook at railway station keeps mistaking someone else for her. 1 act 5 scenes 4m 5w 1 interior

In Howells, W. D. Complete plays

Bride roses
Two women and young man in a florist's shop buy flowers for different reasons. 1 act 2m 2w 1 interior

In Howells, W. D. Complete plays

A counterfeit presentment
Girl at hotel becomes acquainted with man who resembles former sweetheart who betrayed her. 4 acts 3m 2w 1 interior

In Howells, W. D. Complete plays

The elevator
Farce, set in the 1880's, about group of young people trapped in stalled elevator. 1 act 8m 5w 3 interiors

In Howells, W. D. Complete plays

Evening dress
Domestic farce. To satisfy wife's ideas of social duty, tired man tries to get ready for evening musical. 1 act 3 scenes 2m 3w 1 interior

In Howells, W. D. Complete plays

Five o'clock tea
Satire on Boston society women of the 1880's. 1 act 5m 6w 1 interior

In Howells, W. D. Complete plays

The garroters
Farce based on J. M. Morton's "Who stole the pocket-book." Absent-minded man knocks down inoffensive old man whom he mistakes for daring pickpocket. 1 act 3 scenes 5m 4w 2 interiors

In Howells, W. D. Complete plays

A hazard of new fortunes
Based on author's novel. Farmer turns financier, and backs new magazine so that son can get business experience on its staff. 3 act 7 scenes 7m 5w 5 interiors 1 exterior

In Howells, W. D. Complete plays

Her opinion of his story
Man tries to court young woman by telling her about romantic story he is writing. 1 act 1m 2w 1 exterior

In Howells, W. D. Complete plays

The impossible
When their dinner guests all send last minute regrets, socialite couple are told by strange voice from telephone to invite people from breadlines. 1 act 2m 1w 1 interior

In Howells, W. D. Complete plays

An Indian giver
Romantic comedy. Young lady describes most eligible man around to her house guest and reluctantly "gives" him to her before he arrives. Set in the 1890's. 1 act 1m 3w 1 interior

In Howells, W. D. Complete plays

A letter of introduction
Farce. Absent-minded man posts two letters in the wrong envelopes. 1 act 3m 3w 1 interior

In Howells, W. D. Complete plays

A likely story
Comedy. Mix-up of love letter and replies to invitation for garden party complicate lives of young man and fiancée. 1 act 2m 4w 1 interior

In Howells, W. D. Complete plays

In Smith, B. and others, eds. A treasury of non-royalty one-act plays

A masterpiece of diplomacy
Farce. When two doctors arrive at same time, a family tries to keep each unaware of other. 1 act 5m 2w 1b 1 interior

In Howells, W. D. Complete plays

The mother and the father
The emotions of father and mother at the birth, marriage and death of their daughter. 3 parts 1m 1w 1 interior

In Howells, W. D. Complete plays

The mouse trap
Farce. Mouse gets loose in fashionable drawing room. 1 act 1m 6w 1 interior

In Howells, W. D. Complete plays

The night before Christmas
Couple preparing Christmas tree for their children, think that Christmas is filled with hypocrisy, but soon change their minds. 1 act 2m 3w 2b 1g 1 interior

In Howells, W. D. Complete plays

Out of the question
Comedy about three strata of Boston society in the 1870's. 6 acts 4m 5w 1 interior 1 exterior

In Howells, W. D. Complete plays

The parlor car
Romantic comedy set in parlor car of New York Central Railroad in the 1870's wherein young woman renews her broken engagement. 1 act 3m 1w 1 interior

In Howells, W. D. Complete plays

Howells, W. D.—*Continued*

Parting friends
Farce. Crowd aboard a steamer leaving for Europe prevents shy young man from saying goodbye to sweetheart. 1 act 3m 5w extras 1 interior

In Howells, W. D. Complete plays

Previous engagement
Comedy about engaged couple set on Long Island in the 1890's. 1 act 2m 2w 1 interior

In Howells, W. D. Complete plays

Priscilla
Verse play based on Longfellow's "The courtship of Miles Standish." 3 acts 9m 3w 1 interior 1 exterior

In Howells, W. D. Complete plays

The register
Farce set in boarding house in the 1880's about girl who hears young man describing her, through the register between their rooms. 1 act 2m 2w 2 interiors

In Howells, W. D. Complete plays

Room forty-five
Farce. Loud snoring in hotel room below throws temperamental woman into frenzy. 1 act 3m 2w 1 interior

In Howells, W. D. Complete plays

Samson
Adaptation of "Sansone," by I. T. d'Aste. Verse play based on Old Testament story in Book of Judges, of Samson and Delilah. 5 acts 7m 2w 2 interiors 2 exteriors

In Howells, W. D. Complete plays

Saved
Satirical melodrama with characters saved from sin and evil partly through efforts of little child. 1 act 5m 2w 1g 1 interior

In Howells, W. D. Complete plays

A sea change; or, Love's stowaway; lyrics by W. D. Howells; music by George Henschel
Humorous operetta about romance on passenger ship at sea. 2 acts 4m 3w extras 1 exterior

In Howells, W. D. Complete plays

Self-sacrifice
Romantic comedy set around 1910 which hinges upon shocking display of girl pretending to smoke cigarettes and drink cocktails. 1 act 1m 2w 1 interior

In Howells, W. D. Complete plays

The sleeping car
Farce set in the 1880's in sleeping car, about people who look in wrong berths for their relatives. 1 act 7m 2w 1 interior

In Howells, W. D. Complete plays

The smoking car
Comedy. When strange woman in railway car leaves baby with young man for a few moments, his brother-in-law convinces him that she has abandoned it. 1 act 4m 3w 1 interior

In Howells, W. D. Complete plays

A true hero
Melodrama. Idealistic young man tries to "save" older woman who has stolen some jewelry. 1 act 3m 1w 1 interior

In Howells, W. D. Complete plays

The unexpected guests
Comedy. Unexpected arrival of two guests precipitates polite lie. 1 act 4m 7w 1 interior

In Howells, W. D. Complete plays

Yorick's love
Verse play adapted from the Spanish play "Un nuevo drama," by M. Tamayo y Baus. Domestic tragedy among actors involving murder and suicide. Play within a play. 3 acts 4 scenes 10m 2w 3 interiors 1 exterior

In Howells, W. D. Complete plays

Howells, W. D. and Clemens, S. L.
Colonel Sellers as a scientist
Farce about bumbling dreamer who thinks he is a scientist. 3 acts 5 scenes 8m 3w 1 interior

In Howells, W. D. Complete plays

Howells, W. D. and Kester, Paul
The rise of Silas Lapham
Based on Howells' novel. Self-made man, whose family tries to get into Boston society, risks fortune when he refuses to take advantage of dishonest business deal. 4 acts 9m 6w 3 interiors 1 exterior

In Howells, W. D. Complete plays

Howells, W. D. and Poel, William
A foregone conclusion
Based on Howells' novel. Tragedy befalls an Italian priest in Venice who is drawn toward American girl. 4 acts 4m 5w 3 interiors

In Howells, W. D. Complete plays

"Howie." Ephron, P.

Huckleberry Finn. DuBois, G.

Hughes, Elizabeth Wilson
The wishful taw
Folk drama. Musical play with dancing. Ozark Mountain wedding tragedy. Includes songs with musical scores. 2 acts 8m 8w extras 1 exterior

In The Best short plays of 1953-1954

Hughes, Elwil
Frankie and Albert
Based on ballad about Frankie who shot her unfaithful lover, Albert (or Johnny). Piano music and songs. 2 scenes 7m 5w 1 interior

In The Best short plays, 1957

Hughes, Glenn
The magic apple. French 1954 58p illus
Dramatization of German folk tale from story "The nose," by the Brothers Grimm. Music, singing, and dancing. 5 scenes 6m 5w extras 1 interior 1 exterior

Hughes, John
The ship of dreams
Young boy whose domineering father wants him to work in family store, dreams of running away to sea. Set in Wales. 1 act 4m 3w 2 interiors

In Richards, S. ed. Canada on stage

Hughes, Ken
Sammy
Television play. Small time criminal frantically tries to get money he owes another criminal. 2m

In British Broadcasting Corporation. The television playwright

Hughes, Langston
Simple takes a wife (dramatization) See Martin, D. Simply heavenly

Hughes, Richard
The sisters' tragedy. Bakers Plays 1956 23p (Baker's Royalty plays)
Tragedy. Young girl allows her blind, deaf-mute brother to drown in order to free two sisters of his care. 1 act 2m 3w 1 interior

Hughie. O'Neill, E.

Hugo, Victor
The Bishop's candlesticks (radio adaptation) See Olfson, L. The Bishop's candlesticks

Huguenots in France
Lee, N. The massacre of Paris

Hui-lan-ki
The story of the circle of chalk; tr. by Frances Hume, with illus. by John Buckland-Wright. Rodale ₁1954₁ 124p illus
In 14th century China, provincial governor uses clever stratagem to arrive at truth during trial of a second wife accused of murdering her husband and kidnapping his first wife's child. 4 acts 32 scenes 9m 5w extras 4 interiors

Hulme-Beaman, S. B.
c The cruise of the "Toytown Belle" . . . adapted by Hendrik Baker from the play written for broadcasting by S. B. Hulme-Beaman. French (London) 1953 62p illus
Fairy tale. Inhabitants of Toytown, including the Mayor, Larry the Lamb, and the magician, embark on voyage in search of hidden treasure. 3 acts 6 scenes 13m extras 1 interior 4 exteriors

Human relations. See Interpersonal relations

Human sacrifice. See Sacrifice, Human

Humanity
Čapek, J. and Čapek, K. The world we live in
Coxe, L. O. and Chapman, R. Billy Budd
Fisher, A. and Rabe, O. Cavalcade of human rights
Gorky, M. The lower depths
Kaiser, G. The coral
Kaiser, G. Gas (I)
Kaiser, G. Gas—part II
Lagerkvist, P. Let man live
Miller, A. A memory of two Mondays
O'Casey, S. Within the gates
Saroyan, W. The cave dwellers
Saroyan, W. The man with the heart in the highlands
Schary, D. The highest tree
Spewack, S. Under the sycamore tree
Strindberg, A. A dream play
Strindberg, A. The great highway
Whiting, J. Marching song
Wilder, T. Our town
Wilder, T. The skin of our teeth
Williams, T. Camino Real

Humphrys, Ruth
No trouble at all. French 1959 36p (Canadian playwright ser)
Domestic comedy. Professor and family moving into a new home, play hosts to a series of unwelcome guests. 1 act 7m 4w 1b 3g 1 interior

Humpty Heart. Spamer, C.

Hunchbacks
Emery, C. Dark interlude

Hundred Years' War, 1339-1453. See Calais —Siege, 1346

The **hunted.** Senior, E.

Hurt, Freda
c The King of Nowhere
North Wind crowns snowman the King of Nowhere. 1m 1b 1g extras 1 exterior
In Hurt, F. The weather imp; and, The King of Nowhere

c The weather imp
Mischievous weather imp works havoc with weather by calling the seasons to reign at wrong time. 2m 1w 1b 1g extras 1 exterior
In Hurt, F. The weather imp; and, The King of Nowhere

Husband and wife
Aguirre, I. Express for Santiago
Anouilh, J. Mademoiselle Colombe
Appell, D. Lullaby
Apstein, T. Fortunata writes a letter
Armer, A. and Grauman, W. E. Dead weight
Armer, A. and Grauman, W. E. Sure as fate
Bauer, P. The last straw
Beckett, S. Embers
Benedetti, A. de. Two dozen red roses
Boker, G. H. Francesca da Rimini
Bradbury, P. The come back
Brooks, P. Meet George
Broughton, J. The last word
Carter, C. Don't argue!
Crothers, R. He and she
Dekker, T. and Webster, J. Northward ho
Dekker, T. and Webster, J. Westward ho
Emery, C. The ant bed
Emurian, E. K. I'll take you home again, Kathleen
Fields, J. and De Vries, P. The tunnel of love
Fisher, S. and Gottlieb, A. Susan slept here
Foote, H. The traveling lady
Gazzo, M. V. A hatful of rain
George, M. Symphonie pastorale
Giraudoux, J. Duel of angels
Gottlieb, A. Wake up, darling
Herne, J. A. Margaret Fleming
Heywood, T. Woman killed with kindness
Ibsen, H. A doll's house
Ibsen, H. John Gabriel Borkman
Ibsen, H. Little Eyolf
Inge, W. Come back, Little Sheba
Jones, P. Birthday honours
Kanin, F. and Kanin, M. Rashomon
Kaufman, G. S. and MacGrath, L. Amicable parting
Kay, I. Giveaway
Kober, A. and Oppenheimer, G. A mighty man is he
Kwanze, M. Izutsu
Kwanze, M. Kinuta
Kwanze, M. Kiyotsune
Lynch, P. Neglected husbands' sewing club
McCullers, C. The square root of wonderful
MacKaye, S. Hazel Kirke
Melville, A. Simon and Laura
Millar, R. Waiting for Gillian
Molière, J. B. P. The physician in spite of himself
Molière, J. B. P. The reluctant doctor
Morgan, E. You're a long time dead
Musset, A. de. Caprice
Nicholson, N. A match for the Devil
Niss, S. The penny
O'Neill, E. "A wife for a life"
Parker, K. T. Star minded
Pirandello, L. The rules of the game

Husband and wife—*Continued*
  Priestley, J. B. A glass of bitter
  Sakanishi, S. tr. The bag of parting
  Sakanishi, S. tr. The ink-smeared lady
  Schaefer, L. The little flaw of Ernesto Lippi
  Seidelhuber, G. The lavender kite
  Seiger, M. L. Blue concerto
  Shaw, G. B. Candida
  Sheldon, E. The boss
  Shirley, R. Time the sad jester
  Stein, H. A sight for sore thoughts
  Strindberg, A. The dance of death
  Strindberg, A. The father
  Synge, J. M. In the shadow of the glen
  Taylor, G. Kill or cure
  Thomas, D. and Slocumb, P. Next-to-last rites
  Wilk, M. Cloud seven
    See also Divorce; Family; Marriage
Husson, Albert
  La cuisine des anges (adaptation) See Spewack, S. and Spewack, B. My three angels
Hutton, Michael Clayton
  Silver wedding. ₁French's Acting ed₁ French (London) 1958 75p illus
    On silver wedding anniversary wife presents diplomat husband with packet of letters he wrote to other women, then leaves. 3 acts 2m 4w 1 interior
Hygiene
c Chitty, A. W. I. The bath-room folks party
c Close, E. Germs versus Fairy Good-Health
c Fisher, A. Catch as catch can
c Fisher, A. Long live father
c Fisher, A. The not-so-crooked man
c Fisher, A. Robots to the rescue
c Fisher, A. Voices
c Fisher, A. Why the sleepy Dormouse
c Miller, H. L. It's a problem
c Newman, D. Kachoo!
c Oh, can you help the princess?
c Ringe, M. The land of good health
c Zahn, M. How does your garden grow?
    See also Posture
Hygiene, Public
c Carlson, B. W. Litterbug convention
  Ibsen, H. An enemy of the people
Hyman, Mac
  No time for sergeants (dramatization) See Levin, I. No time for sergeants
Hymns
  Emurian, E. K. It is well with my soul
Hypnotism
  Martens, A. C. The search for Wildcat McGillicuddy
  Mills, H. The house by the lake
  Taggart, T. Crewcuts and longhairs
Hypochondria
  Jackson, B. Doctor's delight
  Molière, J. B. P. The imaginary invalid
  Molière, J. B. P. The would-be invalid

Hypocrisy
  Burgess, C. V. A bore for breakfast
  Miller, A. All my sons
  Molière, J. B. P. Tartuffe
  O'Casey, S. The Bishop's bonfire

I

I am a camera. Van Druten, J.
I created Santa Claus. Bean, V.
I don't believe in Christmas. McMullen, J. C.
I found April. Batson, G.
I hear America singing! National Recreation Association
I knock at the door. O'Casey, S.
"I never said a word, but—!" Fernway, P.
I pledge allegiance. Emurian, E. K.
I remember mama. Van Druten, J.
I resolve. Howard, V.
I saw the cross. Mattson, J. M.
I smell smoke. McMahon, L. E.
I spy. Mortimer, J.
I was in prison. Bielby, M. R.
I wish I were a queen. Woolsey, J. and Sechrist, E. H.
I won't dance! Savage, G.
I-ami
  Tango-monogurui (condensation)
    In Waley, A. The Nō plays of Japan
Ibsen, Henrik
  Brand; newly tr. from the Norwegian by Michael Meyer. Doubleday 1960 157p (Anchor bks)
    Priest spends life seeking salvation of the world. 5 acts 8 scenes 12m 4w extras 1 interior 6 exteriors
  A doll's house; tr. by Eva Le Gallienne
    Symbolism. Woman's right to be an individual in spite of marriage. 3 acts 4m 4w extras 1 interior
    In Ibsen, H. Six plays
  An enemy of the people
    Social reform. Doctor who advocates community sanitation regarded as radical. Norway, late 19th century. 5 acts 7m 2w 1b extras 4 interiors
    In Dean, L. F. ed. Nine great plays. 1956 edition
    In Ibsen, H. Four plays
    —Same; tr. by Eva Le Gallienne
    In Ibsen, H. Six plays
    —Same; tr. by James Walter McFarlane
    In Ibsen, H. Ibsen
  Ghosts
    Problem play, exposing conventions of marriage and specifically dealing with syphilitic hereditary taints. 3 acts 20 scenes 3m 2w 1 interior
    In Downer, A. S. ed. The art of the play
    —Same; tr. from the Norwegian by William Archer
    In A Treasury of the theatre
    —Same; tr. by Eva Le Gallienne
    In Ibsen, H. Six plays
    In Levin, R. Tragedy: plays, theory, and criticism

Ibsen, Henrik—*Continued*

Hedda Gabler; with a preface and a new tr. of the play by Eva Le Gallienne. N.Y. Univ. Press 1953 202p front
Tragedy. Discontented woman evades consequences of her connection with lover's death. 4 acts 3m 4w 1 interior

—Same

In Four modern plays

In Ibsen, H. Four plays

—Same; tr. by Edmund Gosse and William Archer

In Griffin, A. V. Living theatre

In A Treasury of the theatre

In Watson, E. B. ed. Contemporary drama: fifteen plays

—Same; tr. by Eva Le Gallienne

In Ibsen, H. Six plays

—Same; tr. by Michael Meyer

In Ibsen, H. The lady from the sea; The master builder; John Gabriel Borkman ₍and₎ When we dead awaken

John Gabriel Borkman
Man is caught between claims of two women: his wife and her twin sister. 4 acts 3m 5w 2 interiors

In Ibsen, H. The last plays

—Same; tr. by Michael Meyer

In Ibsen, H. The lady from the sea; The master builder; John Gabriel Borkman ₍and₎ When we dead awaken

The lady from the sea
Strange man from the sea exerts mysterious power over a woman but when given freedom of choice by her husband she rejects former. 5 acts 5m 3w 1 interior 4 exteriors

In Ibsen, H. Four plays

—Same; tr. by Michael Meyer

In Ibsen, H. The lady from the sea; The master builder; John Gabriel Borkman ₍and₎ When we dead awaken

Little Eyolf
Psychological study of relations between husband and wife after the death of their child. 3 acts 2m 3w 1b 1 interior 2 exteriors

In Ibsen, H. The last plays

The master builder; a new tr. by Eva Le Gallienne with a prefatory study. N.Y. Univ. Press 1955 222p
Symbolic tragedy. Character study of ruthless, successful architect, fearful of being supplanted by younger man. 3 acts 4m 3w extras 2 interiors 1 exterior

—Same;

In Ibsen, H. Six plays

—Same; tr. by Michael Meyer

In Ibsen, H. The lady from the sea; The master builder; John Gabriel Borkman ₍and₎ When we dead awaken

Peer Gynt; tr. with an introduction by William and Charles Archer; illus. by Per Krohg. Heritage 1957 314, xxiii p illus
Satirical fantasy. Norwegian farm lad embarks on series of adventures before returning home for final reckoning of his life. Verse play with music and dancing. 5 acts 38 scenes Large mixed cast 29 exteriors 3 interiors

—Same. Philosophical Lib. 1955 197p

Rosmersholm; tr. from the Norwegian by William Archer
Tragedy. Influence of a strong-minded emancipated woman upon weak-spirited idealist. 4 acts 4m 2w 2 interiors

In Tucker, S. M. ed. Twenty-five modern plays

—Same; tr. by Eva Le Gallienne

In Ibsen, H. Six plays

—Same; tr. by James Walter McFarlane

In Ibsen, H. Ibsen

When we dead awaken; tr. by William Archer
Psychological symbolism. In 19th century Norway, sculptor meets woman who felt she had died after being the inspiration for his masterpiece many years before. 3 acts 3m 3w extras 2 exteriors

In Ibsen, H. The last plays

—Same; tr. by Michael Meyer

In Ibsen, H. The lady from the sea; The master builder; John Gabriel Borkman ₍and₎ When we dead awaken

The wild duck
Symbolic tragedy about morality, the confusion between "ideals" and "illusions" demonstrated in lives wrecked because of misguided idealism of would-be reformer. 5 acts 18m 3w extras 2 interiors

In Cubeta, P. M. ed. Modern drama for analysis. 1955 edition

In Heffner, H. The nature of drama

In Ibsen, H. Four plays

In Stallman, R. W. and Watters, R. E. The creative reader

—Same; tr. by Frances E. Archer

In Bierman, J., Hart, J. and Johnson, S. eds. The dramatic experience

—Same; tr. by James Walter McFarlane

In Ibsen, H. Ibsen

Iceland

Bottomley, G. The riding to Lithend

Icelandic and Old Norse literature

Bottomley, G. The riding to Lithend

"I'd be glad to." Mason, J.

An **ideal** husband. Wilde, O.

Idealism

Ibsen, H. The wild duck

Miller, A. All my sons

Teichmann, H. Miss Lonelyhearts

Identification

Corneille, P. Héraclius

Identity, Personal. See Personality

If thine enemy. Cooper, F. A.

If this be not a good play, the Devil is in it. Dekker, T.

If we only could cook. Hark, M. and McQueen, N.

If you ask me— Osborne, S.

Ikeniye. Kwanze, M.

Ikuta. Komparu, Z.

Ilian, C.

c Absolutely horrid
Fairy tale based on Mother Goose rhyme about little girl who had a little curl. 7m 3w 1 interior

In Ilian, C. Time for a play

Ilian, C.—*Continued*

c A Christmas miracle
    Children get their wish for miracle when
    their little lame brother is healed on
    Christmas Eve. 2w 4b 1g 1 interior
    In Ilian, C. Time for a play

c Dame Robin Hood
    Two children help Robin Hood disguise
    himself as woman in order to escape
    capture by the King's men. 4m 1b 1g
    extras 1 interior
    In Ilian, C. Time for a play

c Lazy Jack
    Based on Mother Goose rhyme about the
    Old Woman who lived in a shoe. 1w 1b
    extras 1 interior
    In Ilian, C. Time for a play

c The nut tree
    Comedy based on the Mother Goose
    rhyme: I had a little nut tree. 4m 2w
    1 interior
    In Ilian, C. Time for a play

c The two woodcarvers
    Adapted from old German legend. Strange
    old woman saves the work of an honest
    woodcarver from his jealous rival.
    2 scenes 4m 2w 1 interior
    In Ilian, C. Time for a play

I'll eat my hat! Miller, H. L.

I'll take you home again, Kathleen. Emurian, E. K.

Illegitimacy
    Pinero, A. W. The thunderbolt
    See also Unmarried mothers

The **Illusionists.** Olson, E.

The **image** of Christmas. Asbrand, K.

The **imaginary** invalid. Molière, J. B. P.

Immaculate Conception
    Coventry plays. The parliament of heaven: The Annunciation and Conception

Immigrants. See Emigration and immigration

Immigrants all, Americans all. Fisher, A. and Rabe, O.

The **immoralist.** Goetz, R. and Goetz, A.

The **immortal** husband. Merrill, J.

Immortality
    Merrill, J. The immortal husband

Impersonation
    Anouilh, J. Time remembered
    Blackmore, P. Mad about men
    Bucci, M. The old lady shows her medals
    Burke, N. The girl who had everything
    Dias, E. J. The face is familiar
    Granby, F. Resort Hotel
    McCoy, P. A rumpus on rampage
    Manion, D. Girl wanted
    Payne, J. H. and Irving, W. Charles the Second
    Taggart, T. Be my guest
    Taylor, T. and Reade, C. Masks and faces
        See also Imposters and imposture

Impersonation. Bailey, A. H.

Impersonators, Female
    Jonson, B. Epicœne

The **imploring** flame. Sheffield, J.

The **importance** of being Earnest. Olfson, L.

The **importance** of being Earnest. Wilde, O.

Important business. Casey, B. M.

The **impossible.** Howells, W. D.

The **impossible** room. Murray, J.

Imposters and imposture
    Bate, S. A mouse! A mouse!
    Brampton, J. Dilemma
    Chodorov, E. The spa
    Emery, C. A baby for Brenda
    Gould, J. R. Steps from beyond
    McMahon, B. Publicity on the fifteenth
    Maurette, M. Anastasia
    Newman, D. The prince and the pauper
    Pushkin, A. Boris Godunov
    Ready, S. Ladies at sea
    Spence, W. The locked room
        See also Fraud; Impersonation;
    Swindlers and swindling

Improvisation. Ionesco, E.

The **imps'** defeat. Woolsey, J. and Sechrist, E. H.

In Abraham's bosom. Green, P.

In any language. Beloin, E. and Garson, H.

In as much. Leslie, A. E.

In darkened rooms. Armer, A. and Grauman, W. E.

In Dixon's kitchen. Stout, W.

In honor of trees. Newman, D.

In honor of Washington. Hark, M. and McQueen, N.

In honour bound. Hollinshead, L.

In quest of power through courage. Estes, S.

In quest of power through decision. Estes, S.

In quest of power through dedication. Estes, S.

In quest of power through divine guidance. Estes, S.

In quest of power through faith. Estes, S.

In quest of power through humility. Estes, S.

In quest of power through obedience. Estes, S.

In quest of power through prayer. Estes, S.

In quest of power through prophecy. Estes, S.

In quest of power through the Holy Spirit. Estes, S.

In quest of power through wisdom. Estes, S.

In quest of power through witnessing. Estes, S.

In the chains of life. Dimondstein, B.

In the shadow of the glen. Synge, J. M.

In the soot. Mills, O.

In the summer house. Bowles, J.

In the zone. O'Neill, E.

In 25 words—or death. Mitzman, N. and Dalzell, W.

Inasmuch. Emurian, E. K.

The **Inca** of Perusalem. Shaw, B.

Incendiarism. See Arson

Incest
    Cocteau, J. The infernal machine
    Ford, J. 'Tis pity she's a whore
    Williams, T. The purification

Incident at a grave. Lake, G.

Income tax
    Lynch, P. The income tax

The **income** tax. Lynch, P.

The **incredible** world of Horace Ford. Rose, R.
Independence Day. See Fourth of July
India
  Carruthers, J. Fear not
  Wilson, D. C. That heaven of freedom
An **Indian** giver. Howells, W. D.
Indians of North America
  Maher, R. When the fire dies
    See also names of individual tribes, e.g. Cherokee Indians; Chippewa Indians; Hopi Indians, Tlingit Indians; Zuñi Indians; etc.

              Legends
  c Very, A. The dancing children
Indians of South America
  Hochwaelder, F. The strong are lonely
Indic folk-lore. See Folk-lore, Indic
An **indoor** tree-lighting service. Schofield, J.
Industrial relations
  Burgess, C. V. Chris is sent to Coventry
  Reach, J. Patterns
  Thornhill, A. The forgotten factor
    See also Labor disputes
Infanta. Olfson, L.
Infantile paralysis. See Poliomyelitis
Infants
  Oxton, C. Late arrival
The **infernal** machine. Cocteau, J.
Ingathering, Feast of the. See Sukkoth
Inge, William
  Bus stop. Dramatists 1956 71p
    Romantic comedy. Young cowboy successfully woos night club singer while their bus is stranded overnight by snowstorm. 3 acts 5m 3w 1 interior
    Trade edition published by Random House
  —Same
    In Best American plays; 4th ser.
    In Inge, W. 4 plays
  Bus stop (condensation)
    In The Best plays of 1954-1955
    In Theatre, 1955
  Come back, Little Sheba
    Despite disappointment in marriage, alcoholic struggles to regain normal living. 2 acts 6 scenes 8m 3w 1 interior
    In Cubeta, P. M. ed. Modern drama for analysis. 1955 edition
    In Inge, W. 4 plays
    In New voices in the American theatre
    In Watson, E. B. ed. Contemporary drama: fifteen plays
  The dark at the top of the stairs
    Set in small Oklahoma town in early 1920's. Explores man's hidden fears in drama of traveling salesman's family. 3 acts 5m 4w 2b 1 interior
    In Inge, W. 4 plays
  The dark at the top of the stairs (condensation)
    In The Best plays of 1957-1958
    In Broadway's best, 1958
  Glory in the flower
    Re-kindling of old love in Midwestern town, but the spark dies. 1 act 5m 1w extras 1 interior
    In Cerf, B. and Cartmell, V. H. eds. 24 favorite one-act plays

A **loss** of roses; with a foreword by the author. Random House 1960 127p illus
    Shattered illusions of aging tent show actress. 2 acts 5 scenes 4m 4w 1 interior
A loss of roses (condensation)
    In Broadway's best, 1960
Picnic. Dramatists 1955 77p illus
    Beautiful small town Kansas girl leaves home to follow worthless but virile lover. 3 acts 4 scenes 4m 7w 1 exterior
    Trade edition published by Random House
—Same
    In Best American plays; 4th ser.
    In Gaver, J. ed. Critics' choice
    In Inge, W. 4 plays
Picnic (condensation)
    In The Best plays of 1952-1953
    In Theatre 1953
The tiny closet
    Inquisitive landlady breaks her promise to boarder regarding his locked closet. 3m 1 interior
    In The Best short plays, 1958-1959
Inge, William Motter. See Inge, William
Ingebretson, Arlene, Sister; Miller, Jean, Sister, and Roberts, Margaret, Sister
  The living Saviour. Augustana 1955 16p illus music
    Easter missionary service for church school. Hymn singing with musical accompaniment. 2 parts Large mixed cast 1 setting
Inherit the wind. Lawrence, J. and Lee, R. E.
Inheritance and succession
  Allen, J. Kind cousin
  Brampton, J. Dilemma
  Brown, L. This year—next year
  Carmichael, F. Four for the money
  Farquhar, G. The twin-rivals
  Foote, H. Expectant relations
  Kesler, H. O. Million-dollar maybe
  Latham, J. L. The nightmare
  Maddern, V. and Banks, L. R. Miss Pringle plays Portia
  Pilgrim, F. The skeleton at the party
  Pinero, A. W. The thunderbolt
  Roche, D. My wife's lodger
  Taggart, T. Punky Doodle
  Tobias, J. Pick a Dilly
  Vidal, G. Smoke
  Williams, T. Suddenly last summer
    See also Legacies; Wills
Injuries. See First aid in illness and injury
The **ink-smeared** lady. Sakanishi, S. tr.
The **Inn.** Garis, R.
Innocents, Massacre of the Holy. See Holy Innocents, Massacre of the
Inns. See Hotels, taverns, etc.
Inquest on Monday. Bevan, M.
Inquisitiveness. See Curiosity
Insane
            Hospitals
  Martens, A. C. Quiet, please
Insane, Criminal and dangerous
  Sherry, G. Black limelight
Insanity
  Albee, E. The zoo story
  Armer, A. and Grauman, W. E. To be alone

Insanity—*Continued*
  Arrabal. The two executioners
  Carmichael, F. The night is my enemy
  Conrad, J. One day more
  Euripides. Heracles
  Euripides. The madness of Herakles
  Goethe, J. W. von. Torquato Tasso
  Green, J. Gently does it
  Green, J. Murder mistaken
  McGreevey, J. The barrier
  Mishima, Y. Hanjo
  Morrill, K. A distant bell
  Murray, J. A game of chess
  Nash, N. R. See the jaguar
  Olfson, L. **Jane Eyre**
  Olfson, L. **King Lear**
  Oliver, W. I. The stallion
  Pirandello, L. "Henry IV"
  Strindberg, A. The father
  Williams, E. Vigil
  Williams, T. Portrait of a Madonna
  Williams, T. A streetcar named Desire
  Yeats, W. B. Purgatory
    See also Schizophrenia
Insanity and crime. See Insane, Criminal and dangerous
Insects
  Čapek, J. and Čapek, K. The world we live in
Inside Lester. Carmichael, F.
Inside the earth. Spamer, C.
Inspector Hart's experiment. Webber, J.
Instalment plan
  Burgess, C. V. The Taylors in the never-never land
Intellectuals
  Chekhov, A. Uncle Vanya
  Sharp, A. Nightmare Abbey
  Wilson, A. The mulberry bush
Interlock. Levin, I.
International cooperation
  Clark, S. G. 21 good neighbors
  Howard, P. The dictator's slippers
International police
  Eaton, J. J. and Juste, M. Atomic journey
International relations
  Betti, U. The burnt flower-bed
Interplanetary voyages
c Seiler, C. Let's go to the moon
  Tuson, N. Moon rocket
    See also Science fiction
Intimate relations. Cocteau, J.
Intolerance. See Toleration
Intrigue and love. Schiller, F. von
Introducing Judy. Priestley, H. E.
The **intruder.** Maeterlinck, M.
Invasion from the stratosphere. Fisher, A. and Rabe, O.
Inventions
  Howard, V. The inventor's clinic
Inventors
  Walsh, R. G. Greg's gruesome gadgets
The **inventor's** clinic. Howard, V.
Investments
  Gordon, K. Money mad
The **invisible** line. Chadwick, V. C.

Invitation to breakfast. Williams, M.
The **inward** eye: boy 1913. Scriven, R. C.
Ion. Euripides
Ionesco, Eugène
  The bald soprano; tr. by Donald M. Allen
    Comedy satirizing English middle class life. 3m 3w 1 interior
    In Ionesco, E. Four plays
  The chairs; tr. by Donald M. Allen
    Avante garde drama in which old couple receive many imaginary guests who have come to hear the old man's great pronouncement. 1 scene 2m 1w 1 interior
    In Gassner, J. ed. A treasury of the theatre
    In Ionesco, E. Four plays
  The future is in eggs; or, It takes all sorts to make a world
    Comical fantasy. Couple must produce eggs destined to become intellectuals. 1 act 4m 5w 1 interior
    In Ionesco, E. Rhinoceros, and other plays
  Improvisation; or, The shepherd's chameleon; tr. by Donald Watson
    Ionesco himself appears as the chief character who is writing a play. 4m 1w 1 interior
    In Ionesco, E. The killer, and other plays
  Jack; or, The submission; tr. by Donald M. Allen
    Comedy. Sulky young man disappoints his family by refusing to marry girl they have chosen for him. 4m 5w 1 interior
    In Ionesco, E. Four plays
  The killer; tr. by Donald Watson
    Satire on artificiality and regimentation of modern life, set in lovely housing development where a killer is slowly disposing of inhabitants. 3 acts 14m 2w extras 1 interior
    In Ionesco, E. The killer, and other plays
  The leader
    Satire on mass adulation of political leaders. 4m 2w 1 exterior
    In Ionesco, E. Rhinoceros, and other plays
  The lesson; tr. by Donald M. Allen
    Comedy. Bizarre lesson ends with elderly teacher murdering his young student. 2m 1w extras 1 interior
    In Ionesco, E. Four plays
  Maid to marry; tr. by Donald Watson
    Short comical farce with no plot about modern civilization. 1m 2w 1 interior
    In Ionesco, E. The killer, and other plays
  Rhinoceros
    Satire. Absurdity of society made tolerable by self delusion. All citizens but one turn into rhinoceroses. 3 acts 4 scenes 11m 6w extras 2 interiors 1 exterior
    In Ionesco, E. Rhinoceros, and other plays

  About
  Ionesco, E. Improvisation
Iphigeneia at Aulis. Euripides
Iphigeneia in Taurica. Euripides
Iphigenia, daughter of Agamemnon
  Euripides. Iphigeneia at Aulis
  Euripides. Iphigeneia in Taurica
  Euripides. Iphigenia in Aulis
  Euripides. Iphigenia in Tauris
  Goethe, J. W. von. Iphigenia in Tauris

Iphigenia in Aulis. Euripides
Iphigenia in Tauris. Euripides
Iphigenia in Tauris. Goethe, J. W. von
Ireland, Ivy A.
This angel business. National Union of
Townswomen's Guilds 1955 23p
Mother's dream helps clarify reasons for
unconventional conduct of her own
daughter and another young woman.
1 act 6w 1 interior
Ireland
Behan, B. The hostage
Costigan, J. A wind from the south
Ervine, St J. John Ferguson
Manning, M. Passages from Finnegans
wake
Murray, J. Will-O'-Wisp
O'Casey, S. The drums of Father Ned
c Pierce, G. M. The story of March 17
Synge, J. M. Deirdre of the sorrows
Synge, J. M. In the shadow of the glen
Synge, J. M. The playboy of the western
world
Synge, J. M. Riders to the sea
Synge, J. M. The tinker's wedding
Synge, J. M. The well of the saints
Yeats, W. B. The Countess Cathleen

History—Rebellion of 1798
Yeats, W. B. Cathleen ni Houlihan

History—Sinn Fein Rebellion. 1916
O'Casey, S. The plough and the stars

History—1920-
Costigan, J. Little moon of Alban
O'Casey, S. The shadow of a gunman
O'Conor, J. The iron harp

History—Civil War. 1922-1923
O'Casey, S. Juno and the paycock

Politics and government
MacDonagh, D. Step-in-the-hollow
O'Casey, S. Juno and the paycock

Social conditions
O'Casey, S. Red roses for me

Social life and customs
Boucicault, D. The Colleen Bawn
Carney, F. The righteous are bold
Carroll, P. V. The wayward saint
Johnston, D. The moon in the Yellow
River
O'Casey, S. I knock at the door
O'Casey, S. Pictures in the hallway
Shaw, B. O'Flaherty V. C.
Irish dialect. See Dialect—Irish
Irish folk-drama. See Folk-drama, Irish
Irish folk-lore. See Folk-lore, Irish
Irish in Massachusetts
O'Neill, E. A touch of the poet
Irish in New York (City)
Berns, J. and Elman, I. Uncle Willie
Irish question
MacDougall, R. The gentle gunman
The **iron harp.** O'Conor, J.
Irony. See Satire
Iroquois Indians
Sinclair, L. Legend of the long house
c Norris, J. Hiawatha

Irving, Washington
Rip Van Winkle (dramatization) See
Chorpenning, C. B. Rip Van Winkle;
also Howard, V. The return of Rip
Van Winkle; Jefferson, J. Rip Van
Winkle
See also Payne, J. H. jt. auth.
Irving Stone's Love is eternal. Sergel, R.
Isaac, the Patriarch
Estes, S. In quest of power through
divine guidance
Isherwood, Christopher
Berlin stories (dramatization) See Van
Druten, J. I am a camera
See also Auden, W. H. jt. auth.
The **island.** Thon, F.
It happened at Christmas. Asbrand, K.
It happened one night. Riskin, R.
It is well with my soul. Emurian, E. K.
It never rains. Banks, L. R.
It should happen to a dog. Mankowitz, W.
It takes a woman. Kirkpatrick, J.
It walks at midnight. Reach, J.
Italian-American dialect. See Dialect—
Italian-American
An **Italian** straw hat. Labiche, E. and Marc-
Michel
Italians in the United States
Chayefsky, P. Marty
Miller, A. A view from the bridge
Panetta, G. Comic strip
Schaefer, L. The little flaw of Ernesto
Lippi
Italy
Ford, J. Love's sacrifice
Ford, J. 'Tis pity she's a whore
Tennyson, A. The falcon

History—1492-1559
Lee, N. Caesar Borgia
Sisson, R. A. The splendid outcasts
Webster, J. The Duchess of Malfi

History—16th century
Webster, J. The white devil

Politics and government
Pirandello, L. The new colony

Social life and customs
Beloin, E. and Garson, H. In any lan-
guage
Laurents, A. The time of the cuckoo

**Social life and customs—Ancient,
to 476 A.D.**
c Morris, T. B. The sleeping fires

Social life and customs—16th century
Bannerman, H. K. My last duchess
It's a—! Carlson, B. W.
It's a problem. Miller, H. L.
It's about time. Carrière, A.
It's great to be crazy. Payton, D.
It's impossible to think of everything. **Mus-**
set, A. de.
It's never too late. Douglas, F.
It's not very nice. Strong, L. A. G.

It's time for remembering. Asbrand, K.
I've got sixpence. Van Druten, J.
Izutsu. Kwanze, M.
Izutsu (condensation) Kwanze, M.

J

J.B. MacLeish, A.
Jack. Ionesco, E.
Jack and the beanstalk. Clinton-Baddeley, V. C.
Jack and the beanstalk. Very, A.
Jack and the beanstalk (dramatization) See Clinton-Baddeley, V. C. Jack and the beanstalk
Jack-in-the-box. Atherton, M.
The jackdaw of Rheims. Marston, M. A.
Jackknife. Anthony, R.
Jackson, Barry
  Doctor's delight
    Comedy translated and adapted from Moliere's "La malade imaginaire." Hypochondriacal father wants a doctor as son-in-law. Set in 17th century France. 3 acts 8m 4w 1 interior
    In Plays of the year v5
Jackson, Harold H. S.
  God's ambassador. Epworth 1955 20p (An Epworth play)
    Based on story told in Victor Hugo's "Les Miserables," about bishop who helps discharged convict. 3 acts 6m 2w 1 interior
Jackson, Mabel-Ruth
c Meet Father Time
    Father Time visits boys and girls to show them how we measure time. 4b 4g extras 1 interior
    In Birdsall, R. ed. Creative plays for every school month
Jackson, Maud C.
  Perfect understanding
    Domestic comedy. The Marlowes think they live in perfect understanding until their antique clock is sold twice and daughter's crazy hat is carried off to a rummage sale. 1 act 7w 1 interior
    In Kamerman, S. E. ed. Blue-ribbon plays for girls
Jackson, Shirley
c The bad children. Dramatic 1959 36p illus
    Modern version of Hansel and Gretel in which two problem children contend with witch, a charming girl with college degree. 1 act 2m 2w 1b 1g extras 1 exterior
Jacob, the Patriarch
  Blazer, F. The well of Dothan
  Emurian, E. K. Famous families
Jacobowsky and the colonel. Werfel, F.
Jacoby, Lois
  Wuthering Heights
    Television play adapted from novel by Emily Brontë. 7m 3w 2b 1g extras
    In Roberts, E. B. Television writing and selling

Jagendorf, M.
c Merry Tyll
    Based on episode from author's book: Tyll Ulenspiegel's merry pranks, about the German folklore character. 8m 2w 1b 2g extras 1 exterior
    In Fenner, P. and Hughes, A. comps. Entrances and exits
  The rime of the ancient mariner
    Dramatic version of Coleridge's ballad fantasy. Verse play. 1 act 9m 1w 1b extras 1 setting
    In Smith, B. and others, eds. A treasury of non-royalty one-act plays
Jairus' daughter. Spamer, C. M.
James, Edward
  Father knows best (adaptation) See Sergel, K. Father knows best
James, Henry
  Guy Domville. Lippincott 1960 220p (Keystone bks)
    Naive young man, forced to forego his entrance into religious life, becomes worldly sophisticate before coming to his senses. 3 acts 5m 4w extras 2 interiors 1 exterior
  The turn of the screw (adaptation) See Vidal, G. The turn of the screw
  Wings of the dove (dramatization) See Bolton, G. Child of fortune
James V, King of Scotland
  Golden, E. The Lady of the Lake
James Joyce's Ulysses in nighttown. Barkentin, M.
Jameson, Storm
  Hidden river (dramatization) See Goetz, R. and Goetz, A. The hidden river
Jamestown, Virginia
  Green, P. The founders
Jane. Behrman, S. N.
Jane Addams. Kissen, F.
Jane Eyre. Olfson, L.
Jane finds her cousins. Priestley, F.
Jane Welsh. Spamer, C.
Janus. Green, C.
Japan
  Kinoshita, J. Twilight crane
c Tennant, K. Hamaguchi Gohei
  Williams, N. Protest
    History—Allied occupation, 1945-1952
  Wincelberg, S. The conqueror
    Social life and customs
  Kanin, F. and Kanin, M. Rashomon
  Wincelberg, S. The conqueror
c Woolsey, J. and Sechrist, E. H. The Feast of the Dolls
Japanese drama
  Ernst, E. ed. Three Japanese plays
  Mishima, Y. The damask drum
  Mishima, Y. Five modern Nō plays
  Mishima, Y. Hanjo
  Mishima, Y. Kantan
  Mishima, Y. The Lady Aoi
  Mishima, Y. Sotoba Komachi
  Takeda, I.; Miyoshi, S. and Namiki, S. The house of Sugawara
    See also Kabuki (Japanese drama and theater); Kyōgen (Japanese drama and theater); Nō (Japanese drama and theater)

Japanese folk-drama. See Folk-drama, Japanese

Japanese folk-lore. See Folk-lore, Japanese

Japanese in the United States
Robinson, T. The visitor (Lassie)

Jarry, Alfred
Ubu Roi; tr. from the French by Barbara Wright
    Satirical farce. Père Ubu makes himself king of Poland. Pokes fun at middle class conservatism and human stupidity. 5 acts Large mixed cast 1 interior
In Four modern French comedies

Jay, Marion, and Graham-Campbell, Alison
With this sword. Miller, J.G. 1954 60p
    Progress of feminism in Great Britain portrayed in series of pantomimes and dramatic scenes. 38 scenes Large mixed cast choir 1 setting

Jealousy
Allen, J. Kind cousin
Anouilh, J. Medea
Batson, G. I found April
Berg, D. The drop of a hat
Brenner, M. The golden land
Brenner, M. The physical threat
Cooney, P. The perfect aurora
Donisthorpe, G. S. Fruit of the tree
Douglas, F. Rollo
Downing, R. Sticks and stones
Emery, C. Dark interlude
Fitch, C. The girl with the green eyes
Komparu, Z. U. Awoi no uye
Lee, N. The rival queens
Miller, A. A view from the bridge
Mishima, Y. The Lady of Aoi
Racine, J. Andromache
Roos, A. and Roos, W. Speaking of murder
Wycherley, W. The country wife

Jeans, Ronald
Count your blessings
    Comedy. Married couple explore divorce possibilities to capitalize on clause in aunt's will. 2 acts 4 scenes 3m 6w 1 interior
In Plays of the year v5
Double take (produced at the Aldwych Theatre, London, under the title, Three-way switch) [French's Acting ed] French (London) 1959 70p illus
    Comedy. Couple faced with bankruptcy individually plan fake robbery. 3 acts 6m 3w 1 interior

Jeffers, Robinson
The Cretan woman
    Based on Hippolytus of Euripides. Vengeful Aphrodite uses Theseus to destroy his son Hippolytus who rejects love of young stepmother Phaedra. 1 act 4m 3w extras 1 exterior
In Bentley, E. ed. From the modern repertoire; ser. 3

Jefferson, Joseph
Rip Van Winkle
    Based on Washington Irving's tale of man who slept for twenty years. 4 acts 7 scenes 7m 3w extras 2 interiors 2 exteriors
In Quinn, A. H. ed. Representative American plays

Jefferson, Thomas, President U.S.
Fisher, A. and Rabe, O. Ask Mr Jefferson
Geiger, M. The democrat and the commissar

Geiger, M. Light and liberty
Geiger, M. The return of a patriot
Geiger, M. The university of the United States
Green, P. This Declaration
Kingsley, S. The patriots
Kissen, F. Thomas Jefferson
Mindel, J. Freeing the land
Mindel, J. To secure these rights
Probst, G. The experiment of a free press
Probst, G. Nature's most precious gift
Wishengrad, M. The danger of freedom
Wishengrad, M. Divided we stand
Wishengrad, M. The ground of justice
Wishengrad, M. The living declaration

Jeffrey, Helen K. and Walls, David A.
c Veterans Day
    Two children learn the origin of Tomb of the Unknown Soldier at Arlington. Virginia. 2m 1w 2b 2g extras 1 interior
In Birdsall, R. ed. Creative plays for every school month

Jennings, Talbot; Slesinger, Tess, and West, Claudine
The good earth
    Moving picture play based on novel by Pearl Buck. Life of Chinese peasant and family in the early 20th century as they struggle to keep their land despite drought and famine. 8 parts 7m 5w 2b 1g extras
In Gassner, J. and Nichols, D. eds. Great film plays

Jenny Lind. Spamer, C.

Jerome, Helen
Pride and prejudice
    Dramatization of novel by Jane Austen. Romantic comedy set in 18th century England. 3 acts 7 scenes 11m 7w extras 3 interiors
In Voaden, H. Two good plays

Jerome, Peter
Goin' round the hoop. Bakers Plays 1953 39p (Baker's Royalty plays)
    Comedy. Poor widow in southern mountains unexpectedly finds way to save her home. 1 act 2m 2w 1 interior

Jerrold, Douglas
Black-ey'd Susan
    Melodrama. 19th century England. Wicked landlord and dishonorable naval officer victimize helpless sailor and sweetheart. Incidental music. 3 acts 13 scenes 14m 2w extras 5 interiors 6 exteriors
In Rowell, G. ed. Nineteenth century plays

Jerry and the Skweegees. Woolsey, J. and Sechrist, E. H.

Jes' too lazy! Carlson, B. W.

The jest of Hahalaba. Dunsany, Lord

Jesuits in Paraguay
Hochwaelder, F. The strong are lonely

Jesus and the fishermen. Spamer, C. M.

Jesus appears in Galilee. Phillips, J. B.

Jesus appears to His disciples. Phillips, J. B.

Jesus Christ
c Barton, E. The third lamb
c Childs, C. The candle in the window
Coventry plays. The woman taken in adultery
Emery, C. The Christmas stranger
Emurian, E. K. The Last Supper
Raeburn, H. The green wood
c Spamer, C. M. Jesus and the fishermen

Jesus Christ—Nativity—*Continued*
Heicher, M. The meaning of Christmas Day
Hein, R. Receive your King!
Hellier, E. E. He who walks in love
c Hoggan, M. H. The toymakers' pledge
Horn Book Magazine. Four Christmas plays (4 plays)
Jones, E. M. The emerald
Jorgenson, E. S. The message of Christmas
c Kent, M. The Nativity
c Kerr, M. L. The wonderful Child
Ketchum, A. Bethlehem
c Kinkead, J. B. Let us adore Him
Knox, J. The shepherd of Bethlehem
Lord, D. A. Joy for the world
Marcelline, Sister M. Silver beads
Mary Francis, Sister. Christmas at Greccio
Neilson, P. Room for the King
Osgood, P. E. Midwinter-Eve fire
Phillips, A. L. The shepherds and the wise men
Russell, M. The three women of the Nativity
c Ruth, G. J. A birthday long ago
St Clair, R. The holy search
St Clair, R. Joy to the world
Sergel, R. No star to guide them
Sollitt, K. W. and Faust, J. P. The soldier and the Prince of Peace
c Spamer, C. M. Jesus is born
c Spamer, C. M. The wise men
Towneley plays. The play of the shepherds
Towneley plays. The Wakefield Pageant of Herod the Great
Towneley plays. The Wakefield Second shepherds' pageant
Wagner, N. He is come! The Messiah!
Williams, C. The house by the stable
York, E. B. The silver star of Christmas
York plays. The birth of Christ
See also Holy Innocents, Massacre of the

Nativity—Art
See Jesus Christ—Art

Parables
Phillips, J. B. The parable of the Pharisee and the tax collector
c Spamer, C. M. The good Samaritan
c Spamer, C. M. The parable of the sower

Passion
Finian, Brother. The Light of the World
Mattson, J. M. I saw the cross
See also Holy Week

Prayers
See Lord's Prayer

Resurrection
Asbrand, K. The three Marys
Bailey, H. F. "There was a garden"
Casey, B. M. Dawn in the garden
Emurian, E. K. The first breakfast
Fearheiley, D. M. Mourning before morning
Finian, Brother. The Light of the World
Getzinger, E. W. Promise of the angels

Johnston, R. A. The York Resurrection
McGreevey, J. Out of the darkness
Mattson, J. M. I saw the cross
Phillips, J. B. The Resurrection of Jesus
Posegate, E. D. Read me a story
Schofield, J. A. and Joudry, R. C. "All hail the power of Jesus' name"
Schofield, J. A. and Joudry, R. C. "Many infallible proofs"
Simmons, A. The bruising of Satan
c Spamer, C. M. Christ lives again
Tashjian, V. The Easter story
The three Maries
Yeats, W. B. The Resurrection
York, E. B. The kindled flame
York plays. The Resurrection

Significance
Yeats, W. B. Calvary

Teachings
Casey, B. M. At the foot of the Mount

Temptation
Phillips, J. B. The temptation of Jesus
York plays. The temptation of Christ

Transfiguration
Phillips, J. B. The Transfiguration

Trial
Phillips, J. B. The trial before Pilate
York plays. The second trial before Pilate: The scourging and condemnation

Jesus Christ in art. See Jesus Christ—Art
Jesus is born. Spamer, C. M.
Jesus returns to Galilee. Phillips, J. B.
The **Jew** of Malta. Marlowe, C.
The **jewel** beyond price. Casey, B. M.
The **Jewess** of Toledo. Grillparzer, F.
Jewish-Arab relations
Dimondstein, B. Miracle from heaven
Jewish folk-lore. See Folk-lore—Jews
Jewish philosophy. See Philosophy, Jewish
Jewish question
Brown, L. Stolen waters
Jews
Folk-lore
See Folk-lore—Jews
Persecutions
Dimondstein, B. Hitler's victims
Goodrich, F. and Hackett, A. The diary of Anne Frank
Religion
See Judaism
Jews in Japan
Spiegelgass, L. A majority of one
Jews in Malta
Marlowe, C. The Jew of Malta
Jews in New York (City)
Berns, J. and Elman, I. Uncle Willie
Chayefsky, P. The tenth man
Odets, C. Awake and sing!
Richards, S. Through a glass, darkly
Jews in Pennsylvania
Fisher, A. and Rabe, O. Haym Salomon's battle

Jews in Russia
Perl, A. Tevya and his daughters
Perl, A. Tevya and the first daughter
Perl, A. The world of Sholom Aleichem
Jews in Spain
Grillparzer, F. The Jewess of Toledo
Jews in the United States
Behrman, S. N. The cold wind and the warm
Lawrence, J. and Lee, R. E. Only in America
Jezebel's husband. Nathan, R.
Jill and Perry go military. Splaver, S.
Jim Bridger and his eight-hour echo. Carlson, B. W.
Jiminy Cinders. Miller, H. L.
Jimmy and the same old stuff. Martens, A. C.
Jingling Lane. Ratcliffe, D. U.
Jinny Morgan. Spring, H.
Joan of Arc, Saint
Anouilh, J. The lark
Shaw, B. Saint Joan
Spamer, C. Joan of Arc
Joan, Princess of Wales
Lewis, S. Siwan
Joan of Arc. Spamer, C.
Joanie on the spot. Newbold, H.
Job, the Patriarch
Corey, O. The Book of Job
MacLeish, A. J.B.
Joe Tracy. Rigney, W. J.
John the Baptist, Saint
Estes, S. In quest of power through humility
St Clair, R. The promised ones
Wilde, O. Salomé
John, King of England
c Holmes, R. V. King John and the Abbott of Canterbury
John, C.
c Sea shells. Paxton 1954 21p music (Paxton Playlets)
Fantasy. Magic sea shell enables two boys to help Neptune recover trident, stolen by pirates. Song with musical score. 1 scene 7m 1w 2b 1 exterior
John, Charles. See John, C.
John Crown's legacy. Suerken, E. H.
John Ferguson. Ervine, St J.
John Gabriel Borkman. Ibsen, H.
John Grumlie. Very, A.
John Henry
McCaslin, N. John Henry
John Jewitt, the slave. Emmons, D. G.
John Turner Davis. Foote, H.
Johnnie jump up. Hark, M. and McQueen, N.
Johnny Aladdin. Wallerstein, J. S.
Johnny Appleseed. See Chapman, John
Johnny Appleseed in danger. Howard, V.
Johnny Appleseed's vision. Fisher, A. and Rabe, O.
Johnny has comicopia. Lunnon, B. S.
Johnny Jones, space cadet! Leydon, B.
Johnny on the spot. Fisher, A. and Rabe, O.
Johnny Pickup. Halman, D.

Johnny's birthday surprise. Woolsey, J. and Sechrist, E. H.
Johnson, Diana Marr. See Marr Johnson, Diana
Johnson, Pamela Hansford
Corinth House. St Martins 1954 143p
Psychological drama set in English boarding school, centering around conflict between retired teacher and former student whom she expelled. 3 acts 4 scenes 1m 6w 2 interiors
Johnson, Philip
Ladies and females. [French's Acting ed] French (London) 1953 27p illus
Effect of young actress' devotion to her calling upon village society leader. England about 1800. 1 act 7w 1 interior
No weeds for the widow. [French's Acting ed] French (London) 1954 29p illus
Romantic comedy. Penniless widow upsets her married daughter's scheme to place her as companion to an invalid. 1 act 2m 4w 1 interior
Success story. [French's Acting ed] French (London) 1953 24p illus
Comedy. Her charwoman's hat helps bankrupt London milliner stay in business. 1 act 6w 1 interior
The witching hour. [French's Acting ed] French (London) 1954 29p illus
Comedy. Servants in London house try to discover source of midnight tapping on wall of their sitting room. 1 act 6w 1 interior
Johnston, Denis
The dreaming dust
Dramatization of some controversial episodes in life of Jonathan Swift. 1 act 5m 3w 1 interior
In Johnston, D. The golden cuckoo, and other plays
A fourth for bridge
Based on actual incident during World War II. Several men from different sides of the war spend time together amicably in an airplane. 1 act 7m 1 interior
In Johnston, D. The golden cuckoo, and other plays
The golden cuckoo
Philosophical farce. Old man establishes one-man republic in protest against abuses of present day democratic society. 3 acts 5 scenes 10m 4w 3 interiors 1 exterior
In Johnston, E. The golden cuckoo, and other plays
The moon in the Yellow River
Comedy. Impact of science upon ancient way of simple people. Set in Ireland. 3 acts 7m 3w 2 interiors
In Browne, E. M. ed. Three Irish plays
Johnston, Robert A.
The Digby Conversion of St Paul; an acting version in modern English, by Robert A. Johnston with original music by Thomas Matthews
Late 15th century English mystery play from the Digby cycle. Based on Biblical account of conversion of the Jew, Saul of Tarsus, to Christianity. Verse play with musical background. 5 scenes 14m 2 interiors 2 exteriors
In Switz, T. M. and Johnston, R. A. eds. Great Christian plays
Everyman; an acting version in modern English, by Robert A. Johnston with original music by Thomas Matthews
15th century English morality play in verse. Allegory of death. Background music. 13m 4w 1 exterior
In Switz, T. M. and Johnston, R. A. eds. Great Christian plays

Johnston, Robert A.—*Continued*

The York Resurrection; an acting version in modern English, by Robert A. Johnston, with original music by Thomas Matthews

Easter. 14th century English mystery play, from the York cycle, about the Resurrection of Christ. Verse play with background music. 4 scenes 10m 3w 1 interior 2 exteriors

In Switz, T. M. and Johnston, R. A. eds. Great Christian plays

Joint occupation, joint celebration. Emmons, D. G.

Jokai, Maurus

Which of the nine? (radio adaptation) See Olfson, L. Which of the nine?

Jokai, Mor. See Jokai, Maurus

Jonah, the prophet

Mankowitz, W. It should happen to a dog

Jonathan's son. Spamer, C. M.

Jonathan's Thanksgiving. Very, A.

Jones, Beryl M.

c The magic spinning-wheel

Farmer's new maid who is excellent spinner, turns out to be a fairy. 6 scenes 2m 5w extras 1 interior 2 exteriors

In Cameo plays: bk 19

Jones, Chrystal

c Clean-up time

Pantomime. Using shadow screen, Mother Goose characters pantomime appropriate house cleaning activities for "clean-up-week." 19 characters 1 interior

In Birdsall, R. ed. Creative plays for every school month

Jones, Corinne Bullard

c Thanksgiving at Mother Hubbards

Story book characters from Mother Goose fill up Mother Hubbard's cupboard for Thanksgiving. 1 act 15 characters 1 interior

In 'Round the year plays for the grades

Jones, E. M.

The emerald

Influence of jewel that one of the three kings laid before Christ Child at His birth. 2 scenes 5m 1 interior

In Cameo plays: bk 19

Jones, Gwenyth

The Mayor of Torontal. [French's Acting ed] French (London) 1953 46p illus

Romantic comedy. Bachelor mayor of small East-Central European town acts on townspeople's complaints that new resident, charming widow, is disturber of peace. 1 act 4m 5w 1 interior

Jones, Henry Arthur

The case of rebellious Susan (condensation)

In The Best plays of 1894-1899

Jones, Paul

Birthday honours

Domestic comedy. When doctor's wife begins seeing another man the doctor becomes interested in his attractive secretary. 3 acts 2m 4w 1 interior

In Plays of the year, v9

Jones, Peter, and Jowett, John

The party spirit

Satirical farce about British politics. Centers around back-of-the-scenes competition between leaders of two major parties. 3 acts 4 scenes 8m 4w 2 interiors

In Plays of the year v11

Jones, Tom

Saben revisited. French 1955 24p

Play within a play. Successful actress returns to visit college where she received dramatic training. 1 act 3m 5w extras 1 interior

Jones-Evans, Eric

Death on the line. Pitman 1954 26p

Based on story: The signalman, by Charles Dickens. Ghost warns the signalman of an impending train wreck. 1 act 5m 1 interior

Jon's helpers. Ahrens, C.

Jonson, Ben

The alchemist

Jacobean comedy. Cheaters are cheated when they use "philosopher's stone" for swindling scheme. Verse play. 5 acts 11 scenes 11m 2w extras 6 interiors 2 exteriors

In Jonson, B. Five plays

In Jonson, B. Three plays

In Kronenberger, L. ed. Cavalcade of comedy

Bartholomew Fair; ed. by E. A. Horsman. Harvard Univ. Press 1960 xxxiv, 177p illus (The Revels plays)

Jacobean satirical comedy set in 17th century London. Events, farcical and romantic, ensue when justice of the peace goes to Fair in disguise to seek out criminals. Includes a puppet show. Verse play. 5 acts 10 scenes 21m 7w extras 1 interior 5 exteriors

—Same

In Jonson, B. Five plays

Epicœne; or, The silent woman

Jacobean farce ridiculing 17th century English society. Verse play. 5 acts 10 scenes 11m 5w 1b extras 5 interiors 1 exterior

In Jonson, B. Three plays

Every man in his humour

Jacobean comedy satirizing 16th century English society. Verse play. 5 acts 21 scenes 13m 3w 6 interiors 5 exteriors

In Jonson, B. Five plays

Sejanus, his fall

Jacobean tragedy of high treason in Rome during reign of Emperor Tiberius. Sejanus comes to violent end when Emperor discovers his plot to usurp the throne. 5 acts 22 scenes 32m 3w extras 18 interiors 5 exteriors

In Jonson, B. Five plays

Volpone; or, The fox. Appleton 1958 111p (Crofts Classics)

Jacobean drama. Play in verse. Songs. Servant and master play on greed of master's friends. 5 acts 39 scenes 21m 2w extras 4 interiors 2 exteriors

—Same. Barrons Educ. Ser. 1959 218p illus (Theatre classics for the modern reader)

—*also*

In Dean, L. F. ed. Nine great plays. 1956 edition

In Jonson, B. Five plays

In Jonson, B. Three plays

In Kronenberger, L. ed. Cavalcade of comedy

Volpone (adaptation) See Zweig, S. Volpone

Jonson, Marian
  Greensleeves' magic. The Coach House Press 1954 64p music
    Fairy tale. Ballad singer teaches three princesses magic way to free their land from power of wicked Duchess. Singing and dancing. 3 acts 6m 5w extras 1 exterior

Jordan, Lillie M. and Garber, Helen Whitmer
  Traveler to Cathay
    Scenes from life of Marco Polo, his childhood, his journey to court of Kublai Khan, and return home. 5 acts 4 scenes 8m 3w 1b extras 2 interiors 1 exterior
    In Birdsall, R. ed. Creative plays for every school month

Jorgenson, Effie Sandstrom
  The message of Christmas. Augustana 1955 24p illus music
    Christmas worship program to be enacted by the Sunday School. Includes a Nativity pageant with hymn singing by children's choir. Large mixed cast

Joseph, Saint
  Emurian, E. K. Famous families

Joseph, the Patriarch
  Blazer, F. The well of Dothan
  Howard, V. The Pharaoh's silver
c Spamer, C. M. The Pharaoh's dream

Josephson, Matthew
  Zola and his time (moving picture adaptation) See Herald, H.; Herczeg, G. and Raine, N. R. The life of Emile Zola

Joshua, son of Nun
  Estes, S. In quest of power through decision

Joudry, Patricia
  Teach me how to cry. Dramatists 1955 78p
    Troubled teenage girl saved from withdrawal into world of fantasy by love of lonely boy. 3 acts 10 scenes 3m 7w extras 1 setting

Journalism. See Journalists; Reporters and reporting

Journalistic ethics
  Howard, P. The real news

Journalists
  Howells, W. D. A hazard of new fortunes

Journey of promise. Kozlenko, W.

The **journey** to Jerusalem. Phillips, J. B.

Journey's end. Sherriff, R. C.

Jowett, John. See Jones, P. jt. auth.

Joy, Ralph Paul
  Hour of honor. Row 1954 16p
    Father finds courage to tell truth about embezzlement for which son was sent to prison. 1 act 2m 3w 1 interior
  —Same
    In Powers, V. E. ed. Plays for players, and a guide to play production

Joy, Valeska
c The milkmaid and her pail
    Betty learns meaning of proverb: Never cry over spilled milk. 1 act 3g extras 1 exterior
    In Kamerman, S. E. ed. Blue-ribbon plays for girls

Joy for the world. Lord, D. A.

The **joy** givers. Spamer, C.

Joy to the world
    Christmas pageant and worship program using Christmas carols. Nativity scenes with shepherds and angels. 4 tableaux 5m 1w extras 1 interior

    In National Recreation Association. Plays, pageants and ceremonials for the Christmas season

Joy to the world. St Clair, R.

Joyce, James
  Finnegans wake (dramatization) See Manning, M. Passages from Finnegans wake
  Ulysses (dramatization) See Barkentin, M. James Joyce's Ulysses in Nighttown

Judaism
  Claflin, M. Saturday at the Cohens
  Shaber, D. The youngest shall ask

Judas Iscariot
  Phillips, J. B. The parable of the last judgment
  Sigmund, J. G. and Smith, B. The silvered rope
  Smith, W. S. By Christ alone

Judges
  Howard, V. No order in the court
  MacDonagh, D. Step-in-the-hollow

The **judge's** diary. Miller, H. L.

Judgment, Last. See Judgment Day

The **judgment.** York plays

Judgment Day
  York plays. The judgment
  York plays. The last judgement

Judicial error
  Anderson, M. Winterset

Judith. Giraudoux, J.

Julia Ward Howe. Spamer, C.

Julian, Joseph
  The Devil and the dream. Anti-Defamation League. 1957 15p music
    The Devil tries to sow seeds of racial hatred among group of high school students. Includes words and music of a song. 2 scenes 6m 1w extras 1 setting

Juliana's birthday. Woolsey, J. and Sechrist, E. H.

Julius Caesar. Olfson, L.

Jump for George. Miller, H. L.

Jump over the moon. Tarpley, V. and Tarpley, K.

Junction Santa Claus. Hark, M. and McQueen, N.

Jungle prize. Holmes, M.

Juno and the paycock. O'Casey, S.

Jury
  Latham, J. and Lord, B. One in twelve
  Rose, R. Twelve angry men
  Rose, R. Twelve angry men; stage version by Sherman L. Sergel
    See also Trials

Jus primae noctis
  Stevens, L. The lovers

Just a little something for Christmas. Lynch, P.

Just a matter of timing. Nappier, P.

Just a picture. Ouzts, J. D.

Just as strong. Carlson, B. W.

The **just** assassins. Camus, A.

Just my speed. Pryor, C.

Just off Brodway. Douglas, D.

Just us girls. Mauermann, W. G.

Just what the doctor ordered. Miller, H. L.

Juste, Michael. See Eaton, J. J. jt. auth.

Justice. See Equality before the law

Justice, Miscarriage of. See Judicial error

Justices of the peace
Jonson, B. Bartholomew Fair

Jutes
Fry, C. Thor, with angels

Juvenile delinquency
Davidson, W. The birds and the boys
Kromer, H. Stolen goods
Rose, R. Crime in the streets
Sheffield, J. The imploring flame
Sherriff, R. C. The telescope

K

Kabuki (Japanese drama and theater)
Kawatake, M. Benten the thief

Kachoo! Newman, D.

Kaeyer, Malvina. See Pennington, L. jt. auth.

Kagekiyo. Kwanze, M.

Kaiser, Georg
The coral; tr. from the German by Winifred Katzin
> First part of expressionistic trilogy dealing with problems of humanity in an industrial world, leading to collapse of society. Followed by: Gas (I). 5 acts 14m 5w 3 interiors 2 exteriors

In Tucker, S. M. ed. Twenty-five modern plays
From morn to midnight; tr. from the German by Ashley Dukes
> Expressionistic tragedy. Provincial bank cashier, in revolt against dull existence, embezzles large sum and tries to find happiness in gay, metropolitan life. 7 scenes Large mixed cast 5 interiors 2 exteriors

In Gassner, J. ed. Twenty best European plays on the American stage
Gas (I); tr. by Herman Scheffauer with an introduction by Victor Lange. Ungar 1957 96p (Milestones of thought)
> Sequel to: The coral. Second part of the author's expressionistic trilogy dealing with problems of man in industrial society. 5 acts 15m 4w extras 2 interiors

—Same
In Tucker, S. M. ed. Twenty-five modern plays
Gas—part II; tr. from the German by Winifred Katzin
> Sequel to Gas (1); Third part of trilogy. Industrialization brings about collapse of society. 3 acts 16m extras 2 interiors

In Tucker, S. M. ed. Twenty-five modern plays

Kakitsubata. Kwanze, M.

Kakitsubata (condensation) Kwanze, M.

Kalen, Elsa
Aunt Lizzie lives it up! French 1954 96p
> Romantic farce. Wealthy eccentric woman insists that niece, who is secretly married, accompany her on ocean voyage. 3 acts 4 scenes 5m 8w 1 interior

Kallen, Lucille. See Tolkin, M. jt. auth.

Kampen, Barbara van. See Van Kampen, Barbara

Kane, Eleanora Bowling
c The magic word. Bakers Plays 1953 16p
> Fairy tale. Black Ogre takes over village infested with evil deeds but magic word, kindness, saves it. 1 act 7m 2w 1b 1g extras 1 exterior

Kanin, Fay, and Kanin, Michael
His and hers. [Acting ed] French 1954 143p illus
> Romantic comedy. Divorced couple collaborate in writing a play. 3 acts 6 scenes 10m 4w 2 interiors
> Published also in trade edition
Rashomon. French 1959 66p illus
> Based on stories by Ryunosuke Akutagawa. In medieval Japan, a samurai is killed and his wife assaulted by bandit. The bandit's trial reveals, through flashbacks, three contradictory accounts given by the bandit, the wife and the samurai. 2 acts 6m 3w 1 setting
> Trade edition published by Random House

Kanin, Michael. See Kanin, F. jt. auth.

Kantan
> Japanese Nō verse drama. A traveler sleeps on magic pillow and dreams of life as Emperor of China. Includes traditional dances. 7m 1w extras 1 setting

In Waley, A. The Nō plays of Japan

Kantan. Mishima, Y.

Kantan (adaptation) See Mishima, Y. Kantan

Kanter, Hal, and others
The George Gobel show
> Television play in the series featuring comedian Gobel. Domestic comedy illustrating wife's diverse roles as housekeeper, accountant and sweetheart. 2m 5w

In Writers Guild of America. The prize plays of television and radio, 1956

Kanze, Motomasa Jūrō. See Kwanze, Motomasa Jūrō

Kanze, Nobumitsu. See Kwanze, Kojirō Nobumitsu

Kao-Tong-Kia
Lute song; adapted for Broadway presentation by Will Irwin and Sidney Howard; acting version arranged by Ruth Sergel. Dramatic 1954 82p
> Chinese drama. Love story of ancient China about impecunious youth who left wife and parents to become high official at imperial court. 3 acts 11 scenes 9m 6w extras 1 setting

Karchmer, Sylvan
Happy birthday to you! French 1953 20p
> Aged woman's children and grandchildren try to persuade her to sell her home. 1 act 3m 6w 1 interior

Karma. Kocher, E.

Kataki. Wincelberg, S.

Kate. MacLeod, R.

Katherine of Valois. See Catharine of Valois, consort of Henry V, King of England

The Katz' whiskers. Tobias, J.

Kauffmann, Stanley
The more the merrier
> Farce. Couples become engaged, separated, and re-engaged in process of shutting out rest of world. 1 act 2m 2w extras 1 interior

In Smith, B. and others, eds. A treasury of non-royalty one-act plays
For another play by this author see Barry, Spranger

Kaufman, George S.
The still alarm
Farce. Men entertain firemen calmly as hotel burns. 1 act 5m 1 interior
In Cerf, B. and Cartmell, V. H. eds. 24 favorite one-act plays
See also Hart, M. jt. auth.; Teichmann, H. jt. auth.

Kaufman, George S. and MacGrath, Leueen
Amicable parting. Dramatists 1957 16p
Domestic comedy. Young couple, planning to separate, quarrel over division of their possessions. 1 scene 1m 1w 1 interior

Kawatake, Mokuami
Benten the thief (Aoto zōshi hana no nishikie) Tr. by Yukuo Uyehara; English version by Earle Ernst
Japanese Kabuki drama. Tragicomic antics of thief who torments others and eventually kills himself. 3 acts 7 scenes 13m 1w extras 2 interiors 5 exteriors
In Ernst, E. ed. Three Japanese plays

Kay, Ian
Giveaway. Bakers Plays 1957 16p (Baker's Royalty plays)
Worthless husband's lies force his wife to choose between him and rich brother who has been supporting them. 1 act 2m 1w 1 interior

Kayoi Komachi. Kwanze, K.

Kazan, Molly
The egghead. Dramatists 1958 88p
College professor who champions former student being investigated for Communist activities, is shocked to find accusations are true. 3 acts 7m 4w 1b 1 interior

Keeney, C. H.
Major Milliron reports
During World War II in Europe, American army officer inspires frightened young son with courage to fight and die bravely. 1 act 5m 1 interior 1 exterior
In Keeney, C. H. Curtain time
Old Skin Flint
Eventful day in life of crochety old business man involves an elderly employee's accidental injury, and his granddaughter's elopement. 1 act 3m 2w 1 interior
In Keeney, C. H. On stage tonight
Once an actor
Romantic comedy. Elderly down-at-the-heels actor tries to promote wealthy marriage for son. 1 act 4m 2w 1 interior
In Keeney, C. H. On stage tonight
Pity the poor fish
Domestic comedy. Family plans for first fishing weekend seem doomed when mother invites a popular novelist to visit. 1 act 2m 2w 1b 1g 1 interior
In Keeney, C. H. On stage tonight

Keep an eye on Amélie! Feydeau, G.

Keeping company. Seidel, N.

Keller, Helen Adams
Gibson, W. The miracle worker

Kellerman, Don. See Benjamin, J. jt. auth.

Kelly, George
The flattering word
Actor's flattery wins support of scoffing minister. 1 act 2m 3w extras 1 interior
In Cerf, B. and Cartmell, V. H. eds. 24 favorite one-act plays
The show-off
Comedy. Fast-talking braggart finally becomes successful when he sells brother-in-law's invention. 3 acts 6m 3w 1 interior
In Kronenberger, L. ed. Cavalcade of comedy

Kelsey, Ruth W.
Who is my neighbor?
Bossy and snobbish old woman forbids her family to be neighborly until near tragedy forces them to rebel. 3 scenes 5w 2g 1 interior
In Bryant, A. comp. Religious plays that click

Kemble, Sarah. See Siddons, Sarah (Kemble)

Ken changes his mind. Burgess, C. V.

Ken looks ahead. Burgess, C. V.

Kendall, Kate
Darling girl. Dramatists 1955 87p illus
Problems of teenage girls at boarding school in New Hampshire. 3 acts 5 scenes 4m 10w 1 interior 1 exterior

Kennedy, Charles Rann
The terrible meek
Tragedy. Miracle anti-war play based on Christ's execution. 1 act 2m 1w 1 exterior
In Smith, B. and others, eds. A treasury of non-royalty one-act plays

Kent, Margaret
c The Nativity. Paxton 1955 8p music
Christmas. Nativity play with choral music. 3 parts 3 scenes 9m 1w 1g extras 1 interior 2 exteriors
c When queens cook. Paxton 1953 12p music
Musical play based on nursery rhyme: Little Jack Horner. Jack finds Queen's ring in pie she baked. 1 scene 5m 1w 1 interior

Kent, Walter
Seventeen; a musical comedy based on Booth Tarkington's "Seventeen." Book by Sally Benson; lyrics by Kim Gannon; music by Walter Kent. French 1954 98p illus
Boy's first love. Set in Indianapolis in 1907. 2 acts 12 scenes 15m 10w 1g 1 interior 7 exteriors
Vocal and piano score also published by French

Kentucky
Green, P. Wilderness Road

Kerr, Jean, and Brooke, Eleanor
King of hearts. Dramatists 1954 84p illus
Romantic comedy. Successful, egotistical comicstrip artist loses fiancée to his new assistant. 3 acts 6m 2w 2b extra 1 interior
Trade edition published by Doubleday

Kerr, Mildred Lewis
His star. Lorenz 1955 11p music
Christmas worship service with choral music. Large mixed cast
c The wonderful Child. Lorenz 1956 15p music
Christmas. Nativity pageant with choral music. 4 scenes 4m 1w 3b 6g choir 1 interior 3 exteriors

Kerr, Walter and Kerr, Jean
Goldilocks. Doubleday 1959 120p
A humorous satire of motion picture industry in its infancy. 2 acts 12 scenes 7m 3w 5 interiors 7 exteriors

Kesler, Hal O'Neil
Dream a little dream. French 1956 100p
Domestic comedy. Teenage girl's daydreams intensify fear of social ostracism because of her father's unorthodox political views. 3 acts 13m 15w extras 1 interior
The grass that's greener. French 1955 92p illus
Domestic farce. Father's mayorality campaign complicated by problems of lovesick teenage daughter and her stagestruck brother. 3 acts 7m 7w 1 interior

Kesler, Hal O.—*Continued*

Line of scrimmage; ed. by Verne E. Powers. Row 1954 104p illus
Comedy. Football so dominates school that scholarship becomes necessary evil to evade. 3 acts 10m 11w 1 interior

Million-dollar maybe. Row 1953 93p illus
When wealthy man dies, his niece and nephew find that his dog and not they, has inherited fortune. Requires three real dogs. 3 acts 4 scenes 7m 8w 1 interior

Kester, Paul. See Howells, W. D. jt. auth.

Ketchum, Arthur

Bethlehem
Christmas. The sheperds and the Magi come to Bethlehem at Christ's Nativity. Verse play with choir music. 7m 1w 1b choir 1 setting
In Horn Book Magazine. Four Christmas plays

Key, Francis Scott

Emurian, E. K. The Star Spangled Banner

Fisher, A. and Rabe, O. Long may it wave

The **keys** to peace. Newman, D.

The **kid** from Mars. Greth, Le R. E.

Kielland, Trygve

Queen Margaret of Norway; tr. from the Norwegian by Constance Malleson
Early in her career. Margrete, Scandinavian queen, succeeded in making herself supreme power in 14th century Norway. 5 acts 11 scenes Large mixed cast 7 interiors 1 exterior
In Modern Scandinavian plays

Kill or cure. Taylor, G.

The **killer.** Ionesco, E.

The **killer** dies twice. Banks, L. R.

Killing of the aged. See Aged, Killing of

Kimes, Bruce

The duelling Oakes. French 1957 36p
Domestic comedy. Newlyweds attempt to settle argument by duel. 1 act 3m 2w 1 interior

The lost Christmas. French 1953 32p
On Christmas Eve, an embittered, middle-aged spinster receives long lost letter from her girlhood sweetheart. 1 act 4m 3w 1 interior

Kimmins, Anthony

The amorous prawn
Comedy. General's wife turns their official residence into guest house to make money for his retirement. 3 acts 8m 3w 1 interior
In Plays of the year v21

Kind cousin. Allen, J.

Kind sir. Krasna, N.

The **kindled** flame. York, E. B.

Kindness

Anderson, D. Watermelon
c Fluckey, J. O. The heart of the forest
Foote, H. John Turner Davis
Jackson, H. H. S. God's ambassador
c Kane, E. B. The magic word
Kwanze, M. Hachi no ki
Lee, W. C. Deadwood
Olfson, L. The Bishop's candlesticks

Kindness to animals. See Animals, Treatment of

King, Norman

The shadow of doubt
Exoneration of famous British nuclear physicist who has served sentence for supposed treason. 3 acts 5m 3w 1 interior
In Plays of the year v12

King, Philip

Serious charge
To conceal his betrayal of young woman, English youth accuses his vicar of homosexuality. 3 acts 5m 4w 2 interiors
In Plays of the year v11

King, Philip, and Cary, Falkland

Sailor, beware! [French's Acting ed] French (London) 1958 96p illus
Domestic comedy. Bridegroom insists on entering marriage on own terms thereby thwarting domineering mother-in-law. 3 acts 4 scenes 4m 5w 1 interior
—Same
In Plays of the year v12

The **King** and I. Rodgers, R. and Hammerstein, O.

The **king** decides. Williams, N.

A **king** in Babylon. Stevenson, B. E.

King John and the Abbot of Canterbury. Holmes, R. V.

King Lear. Olfson, L.

King Lear's wife. Bottomley, G.

King of hearts. Kerr, J. and Brooke, E.

The **King** of Nowhere. Hurt, F.

The **King** of the Golden River. Leuser, E.

The **King** of the Great Clock Tower. Yeats, W. B.

King Sun. Spamer, C.

King Winter. Very, A.

Kings and rulers

Beaumont, F. and Fletcher, J. The maid's tragedy
c Brumbaugh, P. Simple Simon
c Goldsmith, S. L. How Boots befooled the king
c Holmes, R. V. King John and the Abbot of Canterbury
O'Neill, E. The Emperor Jones
Rattigan, T. The sleeping prince
Shaw, B. The apple cart
Shaw, B. The Inca of Perusalem
Waugh, J. R. The wise counsellor
See also Regency—Sweden

Succession

Ford, J. Perkin Warbeck

The **King's** anniversary. Bradbury, A. J.

The **king's** cooks. Spamer, C.

The **king's** shirt. Lawrence, G. B.

The **king's** standards. Costa du Rels, A.

The **king's** threshold. Yeats, W. B.

The **king's** toothache. Fisher, A.

Kingsley, Charles

Hereward the Wake (dramatization) See Ashton, E. B. The beggarman's bride

Kingsley, Sidney

Darkness at noon
Reminiscences of Communist during his 1937 trial prior to execution in Russian prison. 3 acts 18m 3w extras 17 interiors 1 exterior
In Gaver, J. ed. Critics' choice
Lunatics and lovers (condensation)
In Theatre, 1955

Kingsley, Sidney—*Continued*

The patriots
    Thomas Jefferson as secretary of state
    in the chaotic days of infant Republic
    clashes with Alexander Hamilton. 3 acts
    7 scenes prologue 18m 5w extras 4 in-
    teriors 1 exterior
    In Gaver, J. ed. Critics' choice

Kinkead, Jane B.
c Let us adore Him
    The first Christmas. Includes readings
    from the Bible and 2 tableaux. Vocal
    and instrumental music. 4 scenes 12m 1w
    extras choir 1 interior 1 exterior
    In Birdsall, R. ed. Creative plays for
        every school month

Kinoshita, Junji
Twilight crane; tr. by A. C. Scott
    Based on Japanese folklore. A wounded
    crane, rescued by simple peasant turns
    mortal and becomes his wife. 3m 1w
    extras 1 exterior
    In Playbook: five plays for a new the-
        atre

Kinoy, Ernest
Good-bye to the clown. French 1954 26p
    Psychological problem involved in little
    girl's failure to distinguish between real
    and make-believe. 1 act 2 scenes 3m 1w
    1g 2 interiors

Kinuta. Kwanze, M.

Kipling, Rudyard
Captains Courageous (radio adaptation)
    See Olfson, L. Captains Courageous

Kirkpatrick, John
Adam's rib hurts. French 1954 34p illus
    Romantic farce. Merchants bankrupted
    when youth, disguised as elderly profes-
    sor sells women non-buying economy
    program. 1 act 2m 6w 1 interior
The clubwoman's club. French 1959 32p
    Farce. Unscrupulous governor won't
    permit flower planting on highways, so
    ladies' club concocts scheme. 1 act 2m
    5w 1 interior
It takes a woman. French 1959 30p illus
    Farce. A man's family doesn't like his
    fiancée who has already jilted him for
    someone else, hiding in the closet. 1 act
    3m 4w 1 interior
The mind of a killer. French 1960 32p
illus
    Drama of suspense. Woman acquitted
    of murdering her husband thinks she has
    discovered the real killer. 1 act 3m 2w
    1 interior
Splint for a broken heart. French 1955
36p
    Romantic comedy. Teenage girl promotes
    quarrel to mend sister's broken heart.
    1 act 2m 4w 1 interior
A summer for the Indians. French 1960
29p illus
    Comedy. Woman owner of small Maine
    hotel does something about troublesome
    Indian Summer romances. 1 act 7w 1 in-
    terior

Kirn, John
The cell. Broadman 1960 37p
    Attempts to portray early Christian
    martyrs as human beings with human
    weaknesses. 1 act 7m 1w 1 interior

Kismet. Wright, R. and Forrest, G.

Kiss me Kate. Porter, C.

Kissen, Fan
Abraham Lincoln: with malice toward
none
    Abraham Lincoln pardons very young
    soldier who was sentenced to be shot for
    sleeping while on sentry duty. 3 scenes
    8m 1w 3 interiors
    In Kissen, F. They helped make Amer-
        ica

Benjamin Franklin: statesman and inven-
tor
    Highlights of Benjamin Franklin's life,
    including his scientific experiments and
    his work in England on behalf of colo-
    nists. 4 scenes 14m 4w extras 3 interiors
    1 exterior
    In Kissen, F. They helped make Amer-
        ica
Clara Barton: angel of the battlefield
    Clara Barton goes to front lines as nurse
    in Civil War and eventually founds
    American Red Cross. 4 scenes 14m 7w
    extras 4 interiors
    In Kissen, F. They helped make Amer-
        ica
George Washington: father of his coun-
try
    Washington defeats British at Trenton.
    4 scenes 18m 5w 3 interiors 2 exteriors
    In Kissen, F. They helped make Amer-
        ica
Jane Addams: the good neighbor
    Saddened by the poverty she saw around
    her as a child, Jane Addams moves into
    slums to work among poor. 4 scenes 4m
    11w extras 2 interiors 1 exterior
    In Kissen, F. They helped make Amer-
        ica
Paul Revere: patriot and craftsman
    How Paul Revere helped countrymen in
    Revolutionary War and War of 1812.
    4 scenes 8m 5w 5 interiors
    In Kissen, F. They helped make Amer-
        ica
Robert E. Lee: Virginia's valiant son
    Robert E. Lee surrenders southern forces
    to General Grant at end of Civil War.
    3 scenes 11m 3w 1 interior 1 exterior
    In Kissen, F. They helped make Amer-
        ica
Sacajawea: guide in the wilderness
    Sacajawea, of Mandan Indian tribe, leads
    Lewis and Clark expedition and finds her
    long lost brother. 4 scenes 7m 3w 2b
    extras 4 exteriors
    In Kissen, F. They helped make Amer-
        ica
Sam Houston: brother of the Cherokees
    Sam Houston, "adopted" brother of
    Cherokee Indians, is instrumental in
    persuading them to remain at peace with
    United States government. 4 scenes
    10m 2w 2 interiors 2 exteriors
    In Kissen, F. They helped make Amer-
        ica
Thomas Jefferson: defender of liberty
    Jefferson's beliefs about education, re-
    ligious freedom and his role in drafting
    Declaration of Independence. 3 scenes
    11m 5w 2 interiors 1 exterior
    In Kissen, F. They helped make Amer-
        ica
William Penn: brother to all men
    William Penn forms colony of Pennsyl-
    vania with group of Quakers and estab-
    lishes principle of religious freedom.
    3 scenes 16m 4w 1 interior 2 exteriors
    In Kissen, F. They helped make Amer-
        ica

Kissin' cousins. Sterling, A.

Kites
Devany, E. H. The red and yellow ark

Kiyotsune. Kwanze, M.

Klein, Muriel Walzer
c Ali Baba and the forty thieves
    Based on folk tale from Arabian Nights.
    Ali Baba discovers robbers' cave filled
    with treasure. 10 scenes 12m 7w 1g
    extras 4 interiors 1 exterior
    In Fenner, P. and Young, B. M. comps.
        Entrances and exits

Kleinsinger, George
Archy and Mehitabel; play and lyrics by
Joe Darion; music by George Klein-
singer
　Musical play based on book by Don
　Marquis. Poetic cockroach typewrites
　doings of his alley cat friend. 1 act 3m
　1w extras 1 interior
In The Best short plays of 1957-1958

Kleist, Heinrich von
Penthesilea; English version by Humphry
Trevelyan
　Classical mythology. Penthesilea, Queen
　of Amazons loves Achilles but kills him
　in order not to be subject to him. Verse
　play. 1 act 24 scenes 5m 4w extras 1 ex-
　terior
In Bentley, E. ed. The classic theatre v2

The Prince of Homburg; tr. with an introduction by Charles E. Passage. Liberal Arts Press 1956 xxviii, 83p
　Historical drama. Mainly concerns the
　Prince of Homburg's fate in relation to
　Prussian ideals of heroism, discipline and
　courage in warfare. Verse play. 5 acts
　36 scenes 13m 2w extras 6 interiors 3 ex-
　teriors
—Same; English version by James Kirkup
In Bentley, E. ed. The classic theatre v2

Kleptomania
De Francquen, L. Three bags full

Knapp, Bettye
Highly seasoned. Bakers Plays 1953 71p
(Baker's Royalty plays)
　Domestic comedy. Teenage girl publishes
　novel based on her father's letters to her
　mother during his early career as travel-
　ing salesman. 3 acts 5 scenes 6m 6w
　1 exterior

Three men on a string. Bakers Plays 1953
74p (Baker's Royalty plays)
　Romantic comedy. Popular nubile young
　woman is faced with problem of selecting
　husband. 3 acts 5 scenes 12m 8w 1 in-
　terior

Wonder boy. Eldridge 1953 78p (Eldridge
3-act playscripts)
　Domestic farce. Shy, modest high school
　senior undergoes change of personality
　when he comes out of coma due to con-
　cussion. 3 acts 5 scenes 6m 8w 1 interior

Kneale, Nigel
Mrs Wickens in the fall
　Television play. American tourist couple
　see psychological effects upon French
　family of German occupation in World
　War II. 15m 5w
In British Broadcasting Corporation.
　The television playwright

Knight, Charlotte
c Patch upon patch
　A reenactment of dance incidents con-
　nected with stories of some pieces in
　Grandmother's patchwork quilt. Includes
　variety of dances. 1 scene 2m 9w extras
　1 interior
In Easy juvenile grab bag

Knight, Emily M.
c What happened in 1776? Eldridge 1959
10p (Eldridge Special day material)
　Children of today discover that two great
　events that shaped history happened on
　the east and west coast of this country.
　16m 1w 2b 2g extras 1 interior

Knights and knighthood
c Howard, V. Sir Galahad and the maidens

Knott, Frederick
Dial "M" for murder. [Acting ed] Dramatists 1954 79p illus
　Good detective work saves wife whose
　husband had plotted to have her con-
　victed of murder. 3 acts 6 scenes 5m 1w
　1 interior
　Trade edition published by Random
　House

Dial "M" for murder (condensation)
In The Best plays of 1952-1953
In Theatre, 1953

Know your own mind. Murphy, A.

Knox, Avon
He knew the Master. Bakers Plays 1954
38p illus
　Based on New Testament account of
　martyrdom of St Stephen. 3 acts 4 scenes
　3m 4w 1 exterior

Knox, Janet
The shepherd of Bethlehem
　Nativity play. Abigail's mother saves
　infant Jesus from King Herod's searching
　soldiers. 1 act 8m 2w 3g extras 1 interior
In Brings, L. M. ed. The modern treas-
　ury of Christmas plays

Kober, Arthur, and Logan, Joshua
Wish you were here (condensation)
In Theatre, 1953

Kober, Arthur, and Oppenheimer, George
A mighty man is he. Dramatists 1960
82p music
　Domestic comedy. Husband's infidelities,
　uncovered by wife and first mistress,
　precipitates a cooperative course of ac-
　tion. 3 acts 4m 5w 1 interior

Koch, Fred
These doggone elections
　Farce. Hillbillies in North Carolina ar-
　range to have a dog vote. 1 act 4m 1w
　1 interior
In Smith, B. and others, eds. A treas-
　ury of non-royalty one-act plays

Wash Carver's mouse trap
　Comedy. A mountaineer and a small
　time New York business man try to
　outwit each other. 2m 2w 1 interior
In Walser, R. ed. North Carolina drama

Koch, Frederick Henry. See Koch, Fred

Kocher, Eric
Karma
　During Trinidad Coolie hosein festival,
　plantation owner becomes incarnate soul
　of coolie he whipped. Music and dancing.
　3m 1w extras 1 interior
In The Best short plays of 1953-1954

A medal for Julien
　Expectant unwed mother helps Korean
　War casualty find reason for living.
　3m 3w 1 interior
In The Best short plays of 1954-1955

Koestler, Arthur
Darkness at noon (dramatization) See
　Kingsley, S. Darkness at noon

Kohner, Frederick. See Mannheimer, A. jt.
auth.

Kolb, Kenneth
She walks in beauty
　Television play. Girl's love of poetry
　helps her see value of operation for club-
　foot. 4m 1w 1b 1g extras
In Writers Guild of America. The prize
　plays of television and radio, 1956

Komai, Felicia
Cry, the beloved country, by Felicia Komai with the collaboration of Josephine Douglas. Friendship Press 1955 [c1954] 79p
> Based on novel by Alan Paton. Tragedy in verse concerned with injustice shown South African Negroes. Background drum music. 3 acts 9 scenes 15m 7w 2b extras 4 interiors 2 exteriors

Komparu, Zembō Motoyasu. See Komparu, Zempō

Komparu, Zempō
Hatsuyuki (Early Snow)
> Japanese Nō verse drama. Because of lady's prayers to Amida Buddha, soul of her pet bird is reborn in Paradise. Includes temple dances. 6m 1w extras 1 interior

In Waley, A. The Nō plays of Japan

Ikkaku Sennin: The One-Horned Rishi (condensation)
In Waley, A. The Nō plays of Japan

Ikuta
> Japanese Nō verse drama. In answer to his prayer, son of slain warrior is vouchsafed vision of his father. 2m 1b extras 1 setting

In Waley, A. The Nō plays of Japan

Komparu, Zenchiku Ujinobu
Aoi no uye (Princess Hollyhock)
> Japanese Nō drama. Exorcists drive out demon, jealousy, from Lady Awoi, wife of Prince Genji. 3m 2w extras 1 interior
> Same as: Awoi no uye

In Waley, A. The Nō plays of Japan

Awoi no uye
> Same as: Aoi no uye
In Pound, E. and Fenollosa, E. The classic Noh theatre of Japan

Awoi no uye (adaptation) See Mishima, Y. The lady Aoi

Bashō
> Japanese Nō verse drama. Woman, who is the spirit of bashō tree, performs dance to show her gratitude for being allowed to hear Buddhist hermit recite "Lotus Sutra." 2 parts 2m 2w 1 exterior
In The Japan Society for the Promotion of Science. The Noh drama

The hōka priests (Hōkazō)
> Japanese Nō verse drama. Two brothers, disguised as hōka priests, kill their father's murderer by taking advantage of his interest in Zen. Includes two traditional dances. 4m extras 1 setting
In Waley, A. The Nō plays of Japan

Kumasaka
> Japanese Nō drama of 15th century. Ghost of the brigand, Kumasaka, tells priest how a brave young man killed him. Includes a warrior dance. 2m extras 1 exterior
In Pound, E. and Fenollosa, E. The classic Noh theatre of Japan
In Waley, A. The Nō plays of Japan

Taniko (The valley-hurling)
> Japanese Nō verse drama. In accordance with ancient custom, boy who becomes ill on a mountain-climbing pilgrimage is hurled into valley. 2m 1w 1b extras 1 setting
In Waley, A. The Nō plays of Japan

Yamauba: The Dame of the Mountains (condensation)
In Waley, A. The Nō plays of Japan

Kongō, Yagorō
Genjo
> Japanese Nō verse drama based on a story by Utai Kimmō Zuye. Japanese musician en route to China is stopped by spirit of Japanese emperor, also a musician. Includes playing a Japanese lute. 5m 1w extras 1 exterior
In Pound, E. and Fenollosa, E. The classic Noh theatre of Japan

Tori-oi (condensation)
In Waley, A. The Nō plays of Japan

Kopit, Arthur L.
Oh, Dad, poor Dad, Mamma's hung you in the closet and I'm feelin' so sad; a pseudo-classical tragifarce in a bastard French tradition. Hill & Wang 1960 89p (A Spotlight dramabook)
> Tragicomedy. Farce satirizing possessive mother as exemplified in relationship between wealthy, snobbish, overprotective mother and pampered, adolescent son. 3 scenes 2m 2w extras 1 interior

Kops, Bernard
The dream of Peter Mann; with an introduction by Mervyn Jones. Penguin 1960 92p
> Cynical view of contemporary society and its problems by British working class. Dream sequences. Songs. 3 acts 10m 6w extras 2 exteriors

Korean War, 1950-1953
Ettlinger, D. The thousand-yard look
Foss, J. Courage, '53
Serling, R. The strike

Prisoners and prisons
Denker, H. and Berkey, R. Time limit

Kozlenko, William
Journey of promise. Bakers Plays 1953 24p (Baker's Royalty plays)
> Refugee stowaway and his wife discover time bomb in hold of ship taking them to America. 1 act 7m 1w extras 1 interior

Kramer, Clara
c The voyage
> Radio announcer pretends to broadcast from Spain the day Columbus embarks on his voyage to New World. 9m 2w 2 exteriors
In Birdsall, R. ed. Creative plays for every school month

Krapp's last tape. Beckett, S.

Krasna, Norman
Kind sir. Dramatists 1954 73p illus
> Actress uses feminine wiles to win reluctant suitor. 3 acts 6 scenes 3m 3w 1 interior
> Trade edition also published

Who was that lady I saw you with? Dramatists 1959 104p illus
> Farce. Chemistry professor caught kissing a student. 2 acts 13 scenes 15m 6w 6 interiors 1 exterior
> Trade edition published by Random House

Kreymborg, Alfred
There's a nation
> Ballad play in which Uncle Sam reviews glorious history of United States. Children's chorus. 1 act 6m 2w chorus 1 setting
In Smith, B. and others, eds. A treasury of non-royalty one-act plays

Kromer, Helen
Caught between. Friendship Press 1955 24p illus
> Educated, teenage Indian boy rebels against ways of his people. 1 act 8m 2w extras 1 exterior

Kromer, Helen—*Continued*

No man is an island (dramatization) See Benjamin, J. and Kellerman, D. No man is an island

Stolen goods. Friendship Press 1956 32p illus
Juvenile delinquency in a small town involving two boys, one the son of prominent church member. 1 act 8m 4w 1 interior

Take any street. Friendship Press 1954 31p
When their grandchild is found to have leukemia, prosperous family gets new conception of Christian life. 1 act 2m 5w 1 interior

They made a path. Friendship Press 1953 64p illus music
Pageant drama based on book: Forward through the ages, by Basil Mathews. Story of expansion of Christian Church throughout world from time of Saint Paul to modern Siam and Korea. 8 scenes Large mixed cast 2 interiors 1 exterior

Kublai Khan, Emperor of China
c Jordan, L. M. and Garber, H. W. Traveler to Cathay

Kuehl, William A.

Sunstroke
Farce. A teenager invites her friends to a rain party on her lawn. Unfortunately it doesn't rain. 1 act 2m 6w 1 exterior
In Powers, V. E. ed. Plays for players, and a guide to play production

Kumasaka. Komparu, Z. U.

Kurnitz, Harry

Once more, with feeling. Random House 1959 106p illus
Comedy. Domestic difficulties of an eccentric symphony orchestra conductor. 3 acts 5 scenes 8m 1w 3 interiors

Reclining figure. Dramatists 1955 72p illus
Romantic comedy. Forged Renoir brings young art dealer a wife as well as a chastened millionaire father-in-law. 3 acts 9m 1w 1 interior
Trade edition published by Random House

Kwanami. See Kwanze, Kiyotsugu

Kwanami Kiyotsugu. See Kwanze, Kiyotsugu

Kwanze, Kiyotsugu

Eguchi
Japanese Nō verse drama. Traveling priest monk sees ghost of the Lady of Eguchi, famous courtesan, credited with being incarnation of Bodhisattva Fugen. Includes songs and dances. 2 parts 4m 4w 1 exterior
In The Japan Society for the Promotion of Science. The Noh drama

Hanakatami: The flower basket (condensation)
In Waley, A. The Nō plays of Japan

Kayoi Komachi
Japanese Nō verse drama. Ghosts of two lovers, separated by a difference of religion, reunited by Buddhist priest. 2m 1w extras 1 exterior
In Pound, E. and Fenollosa, E. The classic Noh theatre of Japan

Matsukaze (condensation)
In Waley, A. The Nō plays of Japan

Sotoba Komachi
Japanese Nō verse drama. At wayside shrine two itinerant priests meet old woman haunted by ghost of her girlhood lover. 2m 1w 1 exterior
In Pound, E. and Fenollosa, E. The classic Noh theatre of Japan
—Same
In Waley, A. The Nō plays of Japan
Sotoba Komachi (adaptation) See Mishima, Y. Sotoba Komachi

Kwanze, Kojirō Nobumitsu

Chorio
Japanese Nō drama. In ancient China, old man, who turns out to have been famous warrior, promises to teach a younger one secrets of warfare. 2 parts 4m extras 1 exterior
In Pound, E. and Fenollosa, E. The classic Noh theatre of Japan

Funa-Benkei (Benkei in the boat)
Japanese Nō verse drama. Victorious warrior lord, fleeing jealous brother, parts from his mistress. Then Benkei, his faithful retainer, fights the ghost of drowned enemy chief who tries to sink their boat. Includes dances. 2 parts 6m 1w 1 interior 1 exterior
In The Japan Society for the Promotion of Science. The Noh drama

The maple viewing (Momijigari) English version by Meredith Weatherby
Japanese Nō verse drama. Demon disguised as beautiful woman attempts to lure great general to his destruction. 2 parts 1m 2w extras 1 exterior
In Ernst, E. ed. Three Japanese plays

Kwanze, Motokiyo

Ama: The fisher-girl (condensation)
In Waley, A. The Nō plays of Japan

Atsumori
Japanese Nō verse drama. Warrior turned Buddhist priest, meets ghost of Atsumori, an enemy he killed in battle and prays for latter's salvation. 3m extras 1 exterior
In Waley, A. The Nō plays of Japan

Aya no tsuzumi (The damask drum)
Japanese Nō verse drama. Princess is possessed by ghost of aged gardener who committed suicide after learning she had falsely led him to hope for her love. 2m 1w extras 1 setting
In Waley, A. The Nō plays of Japan
Aya no tsuzumi (adaptation) See Mishima, Y. The damask drum

Hachi no ki
Japanese Nō verse drama. Impoverished retainer is rewarded for his kindness in sheltering his lord, disguised as priest, during snowstorm. 3m 1w extras 1 interior 1 exterior
In Waley, A. The Nō plays of Japan

Hagoromo
Japanese Nō verse drama. Priest agrees to return a spirit's magic mantle if she will teach him her dance. 2m 1w extras 1 exterior
In Pound, E. and Fenollosa, E. The classic Noh theatre of Japan
In Waley, A. The Nō plays of Japan

Haku Rakuten
Japanese Nō verse drama. By their dancing Japanese gods of poetry create wind that blows back to his own country the ship of Chinese poet, Haku Rakuten. 3m extras 1 exterior
In Waley, A. The Nō plays of Japan

Hanako (adaptation) See Mishima, Y. Hanjo

Kwanze, Motokiyo—*Continued*

Hotoke no hara (condensation)
In Waley, A. The Nō plays of Japan

Ikeniye (The Pool-sacrifice)
Japanese Nō verse drama. Daughter of
family traveling to the East is selected
as the human sacrifice to Dragon of the
Pool in wayside village. 4m 2w extras
1 setting
In Waley, A. The Nō plays of Japan

Izutsu (Well curb)
Japanese Nō drama. Traveling priest
recalls love story of Narihara and his
childhood sweetheart, and later sees
ghost of wife who performs traditional
dance. 2 parts 2m 2w extras 1 exterior
In The Japan Society for the Promotion
of Science. The Noh drama

Izutsu (condensation)
In Waley, A. The Nō plays of Japan

Kagekiyo
Japanese Nō verse drama. Girl finds her
exiled father, old and blind, but he
wishes her to leave him again. 2m 2w
extras 1 exterior
In Pound, E. and Fenollosa, E. The
classic Noh theatre of Japan
In Waley, A. The Nō plays of Japan

Kakitsubata
Japanese Nō verse drama. Priest meets
flower spirit of one of ladies of Narikari,
an ancient sage and musician who had
been the incarnation of a high spirit.
Includes dancing with background music.
1m 1w extras 1 exterior
In Pound, E. and Fenollosa, E. The
classic Noh theatre of Japan

Kakitsubata (condensation)
In Waley, A. The Nō plays of Japan

Kinuta
Japanese Nō verse drama. Woman dies
lamenting husband's long absence, and
her ghost returns to reproach him. 1m 3w
chorus 1 interior
In Pound, E. and Fenollosa, E. The
classic Noh theatre of Japan

Kiyotsune
Japanese Nō verse drama. Lieutenant in
Heike army, which had suffered many
defeats, commits suicide and his ghost
appears to sorrowing wife. 2m 1w 1 interior
In The Japan Society for the Promotion of Science. The Noh drama

Mari: The football (condensation)
In Waley, A. The Nō plays of Japan

Nishikigi
Japanese Nō verse drama. Ghosts of two
lovers who had died unmarried are united
by pious priest. 2 parts 2m 1w extras
1 exterior
In Pound, E. and Fenollosa, E. The
classic Noh theatre of Japan

Ominameshi (condensation)
In Waley, A. The Nō plays of Japan

Sanemori
Japanese Nō verse drama. Traveling
priest performs special rites for salvation of warrior's tormented soul, seen
in shape of simple rustic. Includes warrior's dance. 2 parts 6m chorus 1 exterior
In The Japan Society for the Promotion of Science. The Noh drama

Shunkwan (condensation)
In Waley, A. The Nō plays of Japan

Suma Genji
Japanese Nō verse drama. Wandering
priest watches two apparitions of hero.
Genji. 3m chorus 1 exterior
In Pound, E. and Fenollosa, E. The
classic Noh theatre of Japan

Takasago
Japanese Nō verse drama. Based on
legend of two pines of Sumiyoshi and
Takasago which personify ancient devoted couple separated by sea and mountain. Includes instrumental music.
classical dances and a god-dance. 2 parts
6m 1w extras 2 exteriors
In The Japan Society for the Promotion of Science. The Noh drama

Take no yuki: Snow on the bamboos
(condensation)
In Waley, A. The Nō plays of Japan

Tamura
Japanese Nō verse drama. Ghost of a
famous warrior appears at temple he
erected in honor of goddess Kwannon,
to tell how goddess helped him in martial
career. 2 parts 5 scenes 6m extras 1 exterior
In The Japan Society for the Promotion of Science. The Noh drama
In Pound, E. and Fenollosa, E. The
classic Noh theatre of Japan

Tōboku
Japanese Nō verse drama based on legend
of Lady Izumi, famous poet. Wandering
monk sees ghost of long dead poetess
who tells him how she became a Bodhisattva of song and dance. Includes a
traditional dance. 2 parts 4m 2w 1 exterior
In The Japan Society for the Promotion of Science. The Noh drama

Tōru (condensation)
In Waley, A. The Nō plays of Japan

Tsunemasa
Japanese Nō verse play. Priest invokes
spirit of dead warrior who tells of his
happy youth. 2m extras 1 exterior
In Pound, E. and Fenollosa, E. The
classic Noh theatre of Japan
In Waley, A. The Nō plays of Japan

Kwanze, Motomasa Jūrō

Sumidagawa (The Sumida River)
Japanese Nō verse tragedy. Distraught
mother, searching for son, kidnapped by
slaver, finds he has died and been buried
by kind villagers whom she joins in a
memorial service. 2m 1w 1b extras 1 exterior
In The Japan Society for the Promotion of Science. The Noh drama

Kyd, Thomas

The Spanish tragedy; ed. by Philip Edwards. Harvard Univ. Press 1959 lxx,
153p (The Revels plays)
Elizabethan tragedy of revenge set in
16th century Spain and Portugal. Verse
play. 4 acts 29 scenes Large mixed cast
8 interiors 4 exteriors

Kyōgen (Japanese drama and theater)

Enami, S. The bird-catcher in hell
Sakanishi, S. tr. The aunt's sake
Sakanishi, S. tr. The bag of parting
Sakanishi, S. tr. A bag of tangerines
Sakanishi, S. tr. Buaku
Sakanishi, S. tr. Busu
Sakanishi, S. tr. The Deva King
Sakanishi, S. tr. The family quarrel

Kyōgen (Japanese drama and theater)—
—*Continued*
Sakanishi, S. tr. The fox mound
Sakanishi, S. tr. Gargoyle
Sakanishi, S. tr. The ink-smeared lady
Sakanishi, S. tr. Japanese folk-plays (22 plays)
Sakanishi, S. tr. The letter "I"
Sakanishi, S. tr. Literate highwaymen
Sakanishi, S. tr. The magic mallet of the Devil
Sakanishi, S. tr. The melon thief
Sakanishi, S. tr. Mr Dumbtaro
Sakanishi, S. tr. Plop! Click!
Sakanishi, S. tr. The ribs and the cover
Sakanishi, S. tr. Seed of hōjō
Sakanishi, S. tr. Thunder God
Sakanishi, S. tr. An unfair exchange
Sakanishi, S. tr. The wounded highwayman

L

Labiche, Eugène, and Delacour
Célimare (Célimare le bien-aimé) English version by Lynn and Theodore Hoffman
> Comedy about extra-marital affairs of several people. Set in Paris. 1863. Includes songs. 3 acts 5m 3w extras 3 interiors

In Bentley, E. ed. Let's get a divorce! and other plays
Labiche, Eugène, and Marc-Michel
An Italian straw hat; English version by Lynn and Theodore Hoffman
> Hilarious complications arise when horse of man who is about to be married eats hat of strange young lady. 5 acts 11m 6w extras 4 interiors 1 exterior

In Bentley, E. ed. The modern theatre v3
Labiche, Eugène, and Martin, Édouard
A trip abroad (Le voyage de Monsieur Perrichon) English version by R. H. Ward
> Romantic comedy. Two men court beautiful girl. Set in Paris. 1860. 2 acts 4 scenes 10m 2w extras 3 interiors

In Bentley, E. ed. Let's get a divorce! and other plays
Labor, Organized. See Trade-unions
Labor and capital. See Industrial relations
Labor and laboring classes
Becque, H. The weavers
Howard, P. The boss
See also Migrant labor
Labor disputes
Chicago
Brecht, B. Saint Joan of the stockyards
Labor unions. See Trade-unions
The laboratory. Campton, D.
Lace on her petticoat. Stuart, A.
Lacey's last garland. Miller, H. L.
Ladies and females. Johnson, P.
Ladies at sea. Ready, S.
Ladies' bar. Dinner, W. and Morum, W.
Ladies' day. Aristophanes

The ladies of the corridor. Parker, D. and D'Usseau, A.
The Lady Aoi. Mishima, Y.
Lady Audley's secret. Hazlewood, C. H.
Lady Charing is cross. Daviot, G.
The lady chooses. McCleery, W.
The lady from the sea. Ibsen, H.
The Lady of Larkspur Lotion. Williams, T.
The Lady of the Lake. Golden, E.
The lady who put salt in her coffee. Carlson, B. W.
Lady Windermere's fan. Wilde, O.
Lagerkvist, Pär
Let man live
> Theme is man's inhumanity to man. Sixteen victims ranging from early Christian martyr to underground figure of World War II. 1 act 10m 4w 1 interior

In Halverson, M. ed. Religious drama, 3
Lagerlöf, Selma
Christ legends (dramatization) See Sergel, R. No star to guide them
Lagman, John H.
The sweetheart of Broadway. Christopher 1958 182p
> Show business. Woman's fight for success in the theater. 4 acts 5 scenes 13m 6w 5 interiors

La Guardia, Fiorello Henry
Bock, J. Fiorello!
Lake, Goldie
Incident at a grave
> Man, grieving over death of son in battle, finds courage to face life. 3m 3w 1 exterior

In The Best short plays, 1952-1953
Lamkin, Speed
Comes a day. Dramatists 1959 77p
> Romantic comedy. Daughter tries to recoup family fortune by marrying for money, but love wins out. 3 acts 8m 5w 1 setting

The lamp in the night. Casey, B. M.
Lamphere, Eula A.
Crosses on the hill. French 1959 86p illus
> Man attempts to disprove Easter by staging the Crucifixion instead of Easter pageant. 3 acts 18m 7w 1g 6 interiors

Lamson, Peggy
Grow up! French 1959 34p illus
> Teen age boy faces problems as he emerges into adult world but younger brother shows him the way. 1 act 3m 2w 1 interior

Lancashire dialect. See Dialect—English—Lancashire
The land afar. Casey, B. M.
The land of good health. Ringe, M.
The Land of Heart's Desire. Yeats, W. B.
The land of lost toys. Simmons, C.
The land of the traffic goblins. Close, E.
Land questions. See Land tenure
Land tenure
Mindel, J. Freeing the land
Landlord and tenant
Ridley, A. and Borer, M. C. Tabitha
Shaw, B. Widowers' houses
Landon, Margaret
Anna and the King of Siam (dramatization) See Rodgers, R. and Hammerstein, O. The King and I

Language and languages
Goldschmidt, W. and Sinclair, L. A word in your ear
c Hark, M. and McQueen, N. Mind your P's and Q's
c Miller, H. L. The Petrified Prince
Sinclair, L. A word in your ear

Lantz, J. Edward, and Lantz, Ruth C.
Alone
    Young woman must decide whether or not to marry the man whose child she is to bear. 1 act 3m 2w 1 interior
    In Lantz, J. E. and Lantz, R. C. Plays for happier homes
Marriage for love
    Bride faints during wedding ceremony due to her mental anguish over different faith of her groom. 1 act 3m 3w 1 interior
    In Lantz, J. E. and Lantz, R. C. Plays for happier homes
Marriage—not legal
    Problem of in-laws interference in marriage. 1 act 3m 3w 1g 1 interior
    In Lantz, J. E. and Lantz, R. C. Plays for happier homes
Reluctantly yours
    Comedy. Elderly couple can't decide whether or not to get married. 1 act 3m 2w 1 interior
    In Lantz, J. E. and Lantz, R. C. Plays for happier homes
Two too many
    Problem of incompatibility in marriage. 1 act 3m 3w 1 interior
    In Lantz, J. E. and Lantz, R. C. Plays for happier homes

Lantz, Ruth C. See Lantz, J. E. jt. auth.

Larceny
Armer, A. and Grauman, W. E. Black star
Howells, W. D. The garroters
Joy, R. P. Hour of honor
McCreary, B. and McCreary, M. Three needles in a haystack
    See also Burglary; Stealing; Thieves

Lardner, Ring
The tridget of Greva
    Disconnected trivia in humorous dialogue by three fishermen in three boats. 1 act 3m 1 exterior
    In Cerf, B. and Cartmell, V. H. eds. 24 favorite one-act plays

The lark. Anouilh, J.

Larkin, Elizabeth
c Mistress Betsy and the flag
    Flag Day. George Washington asks Betsy Ross to make flag for United States of America. 3 acts 4m 3w extras 1 interior
    In Birdsall, R. ed. Creative plays for every school month

Larson, Victor, and Magary, Frank A.
Message from Mars. Dramatic 1954 78p illus
    Science fiction. At United States Air Force base, spy for the Martians almost succeeds in helping the latter to destroy base. 3 acts 5 scenes 6m 7w extras 1 interior

Lassie (Television program)
Robinson, T. The visitor (Lassie)

Last, Jack
Coffee for one. Deane 1955 32p ("Deane's" Ser. of plays)
    One sister tries to poison the other and points blame to housekeeper. 6w 1 interior
Make it murder. Deane 1959 59p illus
    Mystery comedy. Soon after man is told by his lawyer that he is bankrupt he is found mysteriously murdered. Set in England. 3 acts 5m 5w 1 interior
Mr Mason. Deane 1955 63p ("Deane's" Ser. of plays)
    Mystery. Ruthless businessman who dominates his home finds himself accused of poisoning a widow who has been a guest. Set in England in 1908. 3 acts 4 scenes 4m 3w 1 interior
Two black sheep. Deane 1954 26p ("Deane's" Ser. of plays)
    With a pact never to let any relatives stay with them, two women share a house. Trouble begins when inadvertently one invites as house guest the other's sister who is just out of prison. 1 act 6w 1 interior
    See also Verity, E. jt. auth.

The last days of Lincoln. Van Doren, M.

Last Judgment. See Judgment Day

The last judgement. York plays

The last leaf. Claiborne, R. and Banks, F.

The last of my solid gold watches. Williams, T.

The last of the knights. Strindberg, A.

The last of the leprechauns. Holloway, Sister M. M.

The last straw. Armer, A. and Grauman, W. E.

The last straw. Bauer, P.

Last Supper. See Lord's Supper

The Last Supper. Emurian, E. K.

The Last Supper. Phillips, J. B.

The Last Supper. Spamer, C. M.

The last word. Broughton, J.

Late arrival. Oxton, C.

The late Christopher Bean. Howard, S.

Late love. Casey, R.

Latham, Jean Lee
The nightmare. French 1953 84p illus
    When an old man dies and leaves fortune to granddaughter, his son-in-law connives to get fortune, by murder made to seem a suicide. 3 acts 4m 3w 1 interior

Latham, John, and Lord, Betty
One in twelve
    Television play. Importance of fair trial by jury. 3m 2w
    In The Best television plays v3

Lathrop, Don
The braggart. Bakers Plays 1955 23p (Baker's Royalty plays)
    A brother and his fiancée who see his sister falling in love with a man who constantly tells tall tales, decide to trap braggart. 1 act 2m 2w 1 interior
Forever Eve. Bakers Plays 1958 40p (Baker's Royalty plays)
    Comedy. Girl at school is unjustly accused of being out all night, and in clearing herself, becomes romantically entangled with a Marine sergeant. 1 act 7w 1 interior

Lathrop, Don—*Continued*

A page of destiny. Bakers Plays 1956 34p
(Baker's Royalty plays)
> Romantic comedy. A poor spirit is disappointed because his mother was supposed to have met his father twenty years ago so that he could have existed. 1 act 4m 4w 1 exterior

Romeo and Julia. Bakers Plays 1957 31p
> Farce. Joe deals romantically with three sisters. 1 act 2m 4w extras 1 interior

Something new in murder. French 1957
47p illus
> Romantic comedy. Harassed playwright who must produce a play in a week falls asleep and dreams a satisfying plot. 1 act 3m 5w 1 interior

The Winslow girl. Bakers Plays 1957 31p
(Baker's Royalty plays)
> Romantic comedy. Teen-aged girl attempts dating older men but has a valid change of heart. 1 act 2m 3w 1 interior

Latin drama (Comedy)

Plautus. The haunted house

Plautus. Mostellaria

Plautus. The rope

Terence. The brothers

Terence. Phormio

Latin drama (Tragedy)

Seneca. Oedipus

Latouche, John. See Moross, J. The golden apple

Lattimore, Richmond. See Grene, D. jt. ed.

The **laughed**-at monkey. Spamer, C.

The **laughing** cavalier. White, J. K.

Laughter
c Spamer, C. The laughed-at monkey

Launder, Frank, and Gilliat, Sidney

Meet a body
> Revised version of "The body was well nourished"
> Romantic melodrama. Young vacuum cleaner salesman foils plot to murder government official. 3 acts 5 scenes 9m 4w 4 interiors

In Plays of the year v10

Laurents, Arthur

A clearing in the woods. Dramatists 1957
170p illus
> Fantasy. Virginia reviews her life to discover why she cannot find peace. 2 acts 5m 4w 1g 1 setting
> Trade edition published by Random House

A clearing in the woods (condensation)
In The Best plays of 1956-1957

Home of the brave
> When several soldiers volunteer for a dangerous mission, Jewish soldier feeling prejudice and guilt develops psychological paralysis. Set in Pacific during World War II. 3 acts 8 scenes 6m 2 interiors 2 exteriors

In Hewes, H. ed. Famous American plays of the 1940s

The time of the cuckoo. [Acting ed]
French 1954 105p illus
> American spinster's love affair with shopkeeper in Venice. 2 acts 6 scenes 5m 5w 1 exterior
> Trade edition published by Random House

The time of the cuckoo (condensation)
In The Best plays of 1952-1953

In Theatre, 1953

See also Styne, J. Gypsy

Lavender gloves. Conkle, E. P.

The **lavender** kite. Seidelhuber, G.

Lavery, Emmet

American portrait. French 1959 70p
music
> Covers one hundred years of American life from Emerson and Thoreau to rise of Hitler. Features reading and singing of famous poems and songs. 2 parts Large mixed cast chorus orchestra no scenery

The magnificent Yankee
> Oliver Wendell Holmes' life as Justice of the United States Supreme Court from Theodore Roosevelt's presidency to Franklin D. Roosevelt's. 3 acts 7 scenes 14m 2w 1 interior

In Sper, F. ed. Living American plays

Lawler, Ray

Summer of the seventeenth doll. French
1957 110p illus
> Set in Australia. Two itinerant canecutters who have spent the past sixteen summers with two barmaids find that this is the year for change. 3 acts 5 scenes 3m 4w 1 interior
> Trade edition published by Random House

Summer of the 17th doll (condensation)
In The Best plays of 1957-1958

The **lawn.** Dennys, J.

The **lawn** party. Mosel, T.

Lawrence, D. H.

David
> Episodes in life of David before he became King of Israel. Based on Old Testament accounts in the Books of Samuel. 16 scenes 15m 4w 3 interiors 10 exteriors

In Halverson, M. Religious drama 1

Lawrence, George B.

c The king's shirt; a very grim fairy story, rewritten by George B. Lawrence. Paxton 1953 15p music
> Fairy tale. A tramp is only one who succeeds in making king laugh. Includes songs. 3 scenes 6m 2w extras 1 exterior 1 interior

Lawrence, Jerome, and Lee, Robert E.

Auntie Mame. [Rev] Dramatists 1960 123p
front music
> Comedy based on novel by Patrick Dennis. Young Pat. orphaned at ten, is brought up by his gay, warmhearted but eccentric aunt. 2 acts 25 scenes Large mixed cast 10 interiors 4 exteriors
> Published in trade edition by Vanguard

The gang's all here. French 1960 111p
illus
> Satire on politics. Spineless man is elected to Presidency and takes his corrupt friends with him, only to be disillusioned. 3 acts 15m 4w 4 interiors
> Trade edition published by World Pub.

Inherit the wind. [Rev] Dramatists 1958
104p illus
> Based on Tennessee trial in 1925, of John Thomas Scopes who was charged with teaching evolution in the schools. The case hinged on modernist-fundamentalist controversy in Christianity. Includes group singing. 3 acts 5 scenes 23m 7w extras 1 setting
> Trade edition published by Random House

—Same
In Best American plays; 4th ser.

Inherit the wind (condensation)
In The Best plays of 1954-1955

In Theatre, 1955

Lawrence, J. and Lee, R. E.—*Continued*

Only in America. French 1960 96p illus

Comedy. Based on the book by Harry
Golden. Harry's newspaper is so successful he is asked to serve on school board
but can't because he was once in prison.
3 acts 18m 6w 1 interior 1 exterior

Lawyer Lincoln. Smith, B. and Webb, C.

Lawyers

Chadwicke, A. Pudd'nhead Wilson

Christie, A. Towards zero

Christie, A. Witness for the prosecution

Garry, J. F. The bonehead case

Ginnes, A. S. and Wallach, I. Drink to me only

Latham, J. and Lord, B. One in twelve

Mortimer, J. The dock brief

Murray, J. The boy next door

Pathelin. The farce of Master Pierre Pathelin

Reach, J. You, the jury

Yaffe, J. The deadly game

Lay this body down. See Green, P. Wings for to fly

Lazarus, Emma

Emurian, E. K. The new colossus

Lazarus. Pirandello, L.

The **lazy** little raindrop. Barr, J.

Lea, Gordon

Aunt Martha. Deane 1954 28p ("Deane's" Ser. of plays)

Reading Aunt Martha's will upsets those
assembled, for everything goes to Mary,
and Grannie tells Mary why. 1 act 8w
1 interior

The **leader.** Ionesco, E.

A **leak** in the universe. Richards, I. A.

Lear of Albion Crescent. Dennys, J.

The **learned** ladies. Molière, J. B. P.

Leave it to Gramps. Fisher, A.

Leaves

c Spamer, C. The costume dance

Lederer, Charles. See Wright, R. and Forrest, G. Kismet

Lee, C. Y.

Flower drum song (dramatization) See Rodgers, R. Flower drum song

Lee, Gypsy Rose

Styne, J. Gypsy

Lee, James

Career. French 1957 89p

After years of hard work and bitter dis-
appointment an actor finally gets break
and wonders if it was worth it. 3 acts
11m 4w 1 interior

Trade edition published by Random
House

—Same

In Cordell, R. A. and Matson, L. eds.
The off-Broadway theatre

Lee, Maryat

Dope! French 1953 23p

Drug addiction among teen-agers of New
York's Harlem. Music and dancing. 6m
6w extras 1 exterior

—Same;

In The Best short plays, 1952-1953

Lee, Nathaniel

Caesar Borgia

Restoration historical tragedy in verse.
In early 16th century Italy. Cesare Borgia
sacrifices woman he loves in order to
overthrow his enemies. Includes songs.
5 acts 7 scenes 14m 2w extras 1 setting

In Lee, N. The works of Nathaniel Lee
v2

Constantine the Great

Restoration historical tragedy in verse.
While consolidating his position as Emperor of Rome, Constantine I also deals
with problem of son's love for the woman
Constantine himself expected to marry.
5 acts 9 scenes 9m 2w extras 1 setting

In Lee, N. The works of Nathaniel Lee
v2

Gloriana; or, The Court of Augustus Cæsar

Restoration tragedy in heroic verse. The
love of Augustus Caesar, Emperor of
Rome, for his son's mistress. Includes
songs. 5 acts 7 scenes 9m 3w extras 5 interiors 2 exteriors

In Lee, N. The works of Nathaniel Lee
v 1

Lucius Junius Brutus; father of his coun-try

Restoration historical tragedy in verse.
Founder of Roman Republic is faced with
defection of his sons who conspire to
restore the Tarquin king. 5 acts 8 scenes
19m 5w extras 1 setting

In Lee, N. The works of Nathaniel Lee
v2

The massacre of Paris

Restoration historical tragedy in verse.
Charles IX, vacillating king of France,
assents to massacre of the Huguenots on
St Bartholomew's Day, 1572, as planned
by Queen Mother, Duke of Guise, and
others. 5 acts 12 scenes 21m 5w extras
6 interiors 2 exteriors

In Lee, N. The works of Nathaniel Lee
v2

Mithridates, King of Pontus

Restoration historical tragedy in verse.
In first century B.C. while Mithridates VI
fought to throw off the yoke of Rome, he
discovered that one of his sons was his
rival in love. 5 acts 6 scenes 9m 2w
extras 1 setting

In Lee, N. The works of Nathaniel Lee
v 1

The Princess of Cleve

Restoration comedy in verse, satirizing
the licentiousness of 17th century Parisian
society. Includes songs and dancing with
instrumental music. 5 acts 14 scenes 9m
7w extras 3 interiors

In Lee, N. The works of Nathaniel Lee
v2

The rival queens; or, The death of Alex-ander the Great

Restoration tragedy in verse. First wife
of Alexander the Great murders his
second wife, while his followers plot to
poison him. 5 acts 13m 4w extras 1 setting

In Lee, N. The works of Nathaniel Lee
v 1

Sophonisba; or, Hannibal's overthrow

Restoration historical tragedy in heroic
verse. Hannibal's defeat in Second Punic
War and tragic consequences. 5 acts
9 scenes 11m 6w extras 1 setting

In Lee, N. The works of Nathaniel Lee
v 1

Lee, Nathaniel—*Continued*

Theodosius; or, The force of love
Restoration drama in verse. Tragedy ensues when Theodosius II, Emperor of the East, and friend, a Persian prince, fall in love with the same woman. Includes songs with musical scores. 5 acts 10 scenes 7m 6w extras 1 setting

In Lee, N. The works of Nathaniel Lee v2

The tragedy of Nero, Emperour of Rome
Restoration tragedy in verse. Closing events in public and private life of Nero, Emperor of Rome. 5 acts 15 scenes 12m 5w extras 1 setting

In Lee, N. The works of Nathaniel Lee v 1

See also Dryden, J. jt. auth.

Lee, Robert E. See Lawrence, J. jt. auth.

Lee, Robert Edward
Green, P. The confederacy
Kissen, F. Robert E. Lee: Virginia's valiant son
Sapinsley, A. Lee at Gettysburg

Lee, Wayne C.
Deadwood
Poor, elderly woman, considered deadwood by modern neighbors, helps flood victims. 1 act 1m 4w 1 interior

In Brings, L. M. comp. The golden book of church plays

Lee at Gettysburg. Sapinsley, A.

The left-over reindeer. Miller, H. L.

Legacies
Brenner, M. The golden land
Brenner, M. My Aunt Agatha
See also Wills

Legend. Wilde, P.

The **legend** of Babouska. Woolsey, J. and Sechrist, E. H.

The **legend** of St Basil. Ridge, A.

The **legend** of the Christmas candle. McCaslin, N.

Legend of the long house. Sinclair, L.

Legends
Cooper, F. A. A certain star
Fuller, R. The Noël candle
Goethe, J. W. von. Faust, part 1
Goethe, J. W. von. Faust, part II
Hazeltine, A. I. Madelon
Marlowe, C. The tragedy of Doctor Faustus
Marlowe, C. Tragical history of Doctor Faustus
c Spamer, C. Why the evergreen trees never lose their branches
See also Folk-lore

England
c Lewis, M. R. Dick Whittington

France
Nicholson, A. and Chorpenning, C. B. The magic horn

Germany
c Dunbar, T. M. The Pied Piper of Hamlin
c Ilian, C. The two woodcarvers
c Marston, M. A. The pied piper of Hamelin

Greece
Ridge, A. The legend of Saint Basil

Holland
See Legends—Netherlands

Ireland
Bottomley, G. Deirdire
Yeats, W. B. At the hawk's well
Yeats, W. B. The death of Cuchulain
Yeats, W. B. Deirdre
Yeats, W. B. The dreaming of the bones
Yeats, W. B. A full moon in March
Yeats, W. B. The green helmet
Yeats, W. B. The herne's egg
Yeats, W. B. On baile's strand
Yeats, W. B. The only jealousy of Emer

Japan
Kwanze, M. Takasago

Mexican
Ullman, S. S. Princess of the snows

Netherlands
Ridge, A. Three mice for the abbot

New York (State)
Howard, V. The return of Rip Van Winkle

Provence
Ridge, A. Saint Martha and the Tarasque of Tarascon

Scotland
Golden, E. The Lady of the Lake

Shetland Islands
Bottomley, G. The woman from the voe

Spain
Molière, J. B. P. Don Juan

United States
Fisher, A. and Rabe, O. Johnny Appleseed's vision
McCaslin, N. Apples in the wilderness
McCaslin, N. With the sunrise in his pocket

Legislative hearings

United States
Zuckerman, A. J. Blobo's boy

Lehar, Franz
The merry widow; music by Franz Lehar; new book and lyrics by Charles George. French 1954 160p music
Adaptation with modern settings of Franz Lehar's operetta, about romance of dashing young prince of Alturia and American widow. Vocal score and libretto. 2 acts 6m 12w chorus 1 interior

Lehman, Leo
Saint Chad of the seven wells; or, The bewildered hart
Chad, Bishop of Licetfield and his effort to preach gospel of Christianity in 7th century England. 3 acts 9 scenes 9m 2w 2 interiors

In Two saints' plays

Thirty pieces of silver
Television play. Friends pressure refugee German Jewish woman to apply for compensation money from German government. 4m 4w

In British Broadcasting Corporation. The television playwright

Leonard, E. Stanley
Her husband's consent
Sophisticated comedy. Considerate husband helps wife secure second husband, as he himself arranges divorce. 1 act 3m 1w 1 interior

In Smith, B. and others, eds. A treasury of non-royalty one-act plays

Leonardo da Vinci
Emurian, E. K. The Last Supper

Leonce and Lena. Büchner, G.

LePelley, Guernsey
A is for apple. Bakers Plays 1953 86p illus (Baker's Royalty plays)
Farce. Football player, disguised as a doctor, tries to secure large scholarship donation for his college from eccentric old lady. 3 acts 4 scenes 5m 7w 1 interior
Absolutely murder. Bakers Plays 1955 93p (Baker's Royalty plays)
Mystery comedy set in abandoned mill, about a walking corpse, a one-handed murderer and an undecided girl. 3 acts 4m 8w 1 interior

The **leprechaun.** Purkey, R. A.

Leprechauns. See Fairies

Lerner, Alan Jay. See Loewe, F. My fair lady

LeRoy, Warner
Between two thieves. French 1959 68p illus
A group of Jews accuse Jesus of being subversive in both politics and religion. Then one points out that only Jesus was not found wanting in a crisis. 2 acts 9m 4w 1 exterior

Lesbianism
Hellman, L. The children's hour
See also Homosexuality

Lesley, Richardson
For our mother Malaya!

Leslie, Alice E.
In as much
When poor Italian family moves into new neighborhood, members of church try to make them welcome. 3 scenes 4m 8w 2b 2g extras 1 interior 1 exterior
In Bryant, A. comp. Religious plays that click

Lessing
Emilia Galotti; introduction and tr. by Anna Johanna Gode von Aesch. Barrons Educ. Ser. 1959 104p
Tragedy of class distinction set in 18th century Italy. When a prince tries to seduce his daughter, middle class father stabs her to save "honor." 5 acts 43 scenes 7m 3w extras 3 interiors

The **lesson.** Ionesco, E.

Lesson for today. Chenery, M.

Let 'em eat steak. Conkling, L.

Let man live. Lagerkvist, P.

Let nothing ye dismay. MacDonald, D. M.

Let them eat cake. Lonsdale, F.

Let there be bread. Fisher, A. and Rabe, O.

Let there be farce. Walsh, N.

Let us adore Him. Kinkead, J. B.

Let your light so shine. Getzinger, E. W.

Let's be valentines. Asbrand, K. S.

Let's get a divorce! Sardou, V. and Najac, É. de

Let's get out of here. Welch, R.

Let's go to the moon. Seiler, C.

Let's have a covered dish. Virden, H.

Let's travel by auto. Woolsey, J. and Sechrist, E. H.

Let's travel by bus. Woolsey, J. and Sechrist, E. H.

Let's travel by train. Woolsey, J. and Sechrist, E. H.

A **letter** for Charlotte. Malone, M.

The **letter** "I". Sakanishi, S. tr.

A **letter** is mailed. Woolsey, J. and Sechrist, E. H.

A **letter** of introduction. Howells, W. D.

A **letter** to Lincoln. Barbee, L.

Letters
Gould, J. R. Steps from beyond
Howells, W. D. A letter of introduction
Howells, W. D. A likely story
Sardou, V. A scrap of paper

Letters of gold. Trease, G.

Letton, Francis. See Letton, J. jt. auth.

Letton, Jennette, and Letton, Francis
The young Elizabeth. Dramatists 1955 92p illus
Life of Elizabeth I, Queen of England from death of her father until her accession to throne. 2 acts 16m 6w 5 interiors

Leuser, Eleanore
c The King of the Golden River
Radio adaptation of fairy tale by John Ruskin. Background music. 6m extras
In Burack, A. S. ed. Four-star radio plays for teen-agers

c The little witch who tried
Winnie, the witch, tries to become a real girl but reverts in time for big Halloween broomstick ride. 1 act 8g 1 interior
In Kamerman, S. E. ed. Blue-ribbon plays for girls

Levi. See Matthew, Saint, Apostle

Levin, Ira
Interlock. Dramatists 1958 75p
German refugee girl who brings together her fiance, struggling pianist and her employer, a wealthy invalid woman is abandoned in favor of woman's wealth. 3 acts 2m 3w 1 interior
No time for sergeants. [Acting ed] Dramatists 1958 82p front
Farce adapted from novel by Mac Hyman. Trials and tribulations of Southern Mountaineer inductee in the U.S. Army. 2 acts Large mixed cast 2 interiors 2 exteriors
Trade edition published by Random House
—Same
In Best American plays; 4th ser.
No time for sergeants (condensation)
In The Best plays of 1955-1956
In Theatre, 1956

Levin, Meyer
Compulsion. Simon & Schuster 1959 132p
Dramatization of Leopold and Loeb murder case of the 1920's. 3 acts 27 scenes Large mixed cast 14 interiors 2 exteriors
Compulsion (condensation)
In Broadway's best, 1958

Levitt, Saul
The Andersonville trial. Random House 1960 120p front
Based on trial of Henry Wirz who was tried for cruelty and negligence of his duties at notorious prison camp for Northern soldiers during Civil War. 2 acts 27m 1 interior
The Andersonville trial (condensation)
In The Best plays of 1959-1960
In Broadway's best, 1960

Levofsky, Regina
c A house for Duke
> Arbor Day. Little boy who says he built a doghouse all by himself finds that many people are needed to prepare lumber. 2 scenes 2m 1b 1g extras 1 exterior

In Birdsall, R. ed. Creative plays for every school month

Lewis, Edward
A screw loose. Paxton 1960 15p
> Satire on murder mystery. Detective accidentally murders prospective buyer of heavily mortgaged ancestral home. 3 scenes 6m 1w 1 interior

Lewis, Grover
Wait for morning, child. French 1958 48p illus
> Man who returns home after many years remembers the injustice done to his brother by his father. 1 act 2m 1w 2 interiors

Lewis, Jean
Return engagement. Eldridge 1958 27p (Eldridge Popular one-act playscripts)
> Squabbles among sorority sisters over sorority's dance. 1 act 2m 6w 1 interior

Lewis, Leopold
The bells
> Alsace. 19th century. Psychological study of murderer haunted by his guilt. 3 acts 3 scenes 11m 3w 3 interiors

In Rowell, G. ed. Nineteenth century plays

Lewis, Mary Rea
c Dick Whittington
> With the help of his cat, Dick Whittington, a poor penniless orphan boy, becomes Lord Mayor of London. 3 acts 4 scenes 9m 5w 3 interiors 2 exteriors

In Fenner, P. and Hughes, A. comps. Entrances and exits

Lewis, Saunders
Siwan; tr. by Emyr Humphreys
> Love affair between Princess Siwan and Gwilym de Breos and his execution at hands of her husband Prince Llywelen. Verse play set in Wales. 1230. 3 acts 2m 2w extras 2 interiors

In Plays of the year, v21

Lewis and Clark Expedition
Emmons, D. G. Out to win
Kissen, F. Sacajawea: guide in the wilderness

Leydon, Bob
Johnny Jones, space cadet! French 1953 98p illus
> Comedy. Young boy with driving ambition to fly to the moon meets mysterious girl from Mars and becomes a hero. 3 acts 4 scenes 4m 7w 1 interior

Li, Chin-yang. See Lee, C. Y.

Li, Yu-chu Man-kuei
The grand garden
> Symbolism. Decline of Chinese family in 1930's. Various members represent traditional life while son alone struggles to re-establish his family in new way of life. 4 acts 17 scenes 3m 14w extras 2 interiors 2 exteriors

In Li, Y. M. The grand garden and other plays

Heaven challenges
> Talented woman artist faces divorce, personal criticism and jealousy before winning independence and respect in society. Set in China in 1940's. 5 acts 2 scenes 3m 4w 1 interior

In Li, Y. M. The grand garden and other plays

The modern bridge
> Communist infiltration into group of Chinese teachers by capitalizing on human emotions and weaknesses. Set in China, 1949. 5 acts 10m 5w 2 interiors 1 exterior

In Li, Y. M. The grand garden and other plays

The woman painter
> A later version of "Heaven challenges" entered above with the last three acts completely changed. Woman painter, stabbed in the arm by jealous girl, can no longer paint, and vows to spend rest of her life making others happy. Set in China. 5 acts 4 scenes 4m 5w 1 interior

In Li, Y. M. The grand garden and other plays

The **libation** bearers. Aeschylus

Liberty
Brooks, P. The only prison
Brown, R. M. Freedom is our heritage
Fisher, A. The voice of liberty
Fisher, A. and Rabe, O. Ask Mr Jefferson
Fisher, A. and Rabe, O. Flag of freedom
Fisher, A. and Rabe, O. Rocket to freedom
Fisher, A. and Rabe, O. When freedom was news
c Harris, A. Simple Simon
Houston, N. According to law
Howard, V. What is an American?
Powers, V. The wall
Saroyan, W. The slaughter of the innocents
Schiller, F. William Tell
Wishengrad, M. The danger of freedom
Yelvington, R. A cloud of witnesses
> *See also* Liberty of the press; Religious liberty

Liberty Belle. Asbrand, K.

Liberty of the press
Probst, G. The experiment of a free press
Thompson, M. A. The witch hunters

Librarians
Marchant, W. The desk set

The **library** circus. Miller, H. L.

The **Lieutenant** pays his respects. McCay, P. S.

The **life** I gave you. Pirandello, L.

Life is a dream. Calderon

The **life** of an artist. Dimondstein, B.

The **life** of Emile Zola. Herald, H.; Herczeg, G. and Raine, N. R.

The **life** of Lincoln. Tyson, R. H.

Life starts at thirty-five. Bugbee, W. N.

Liggat, James
Friendly relations. [French's Acting ed] French (London) 1953 76p illus
> Romantic comedy. To help promote international understanding, visiting Australian is invited to English home for Christmas. 3 acts 5 scenes 3m 5w 1 interior

Light
c Miller, H. L. The story of light

Light and liberty. Geiger, M.

Light-o'-love. Schnitzler, A.

The **Light** of the World. Finian, Brother

Light up the world. Asbrand, K. S.

Lighthouses
  Addis, H. Off the rocks
Lighting the way. Olson, E. E.
Lightning
c Spamer, C. The rebellious lightning bolt
Lights on the coast. Webber, J.
Like stars appearing. Duncannon, F. E. N. P. viscount
A **likely** story. Howells, W. D.
A **likely** tale. Savory, G.
Lilacs in the rain. Hale, R. and Hale, N.
Lilies bloom at Easter. Casey, B. M.
Liliom. Molnar, F.
Lillington, Kenneth
  The Devil's grandson
    Unpopular magician performer in English music-hall outwits Devil who tries to buy his soul. 4m 1w 1 interior
  In The Second book of one-act plays
Lilyers, Jean
  The risen Christ. Augustana 1954 15p music
    Easter. On street in Jerusalem three children talk over Christ's entry into Jerusalem, and His Crucifixion. Then an older brother brings them news of His Resurrection. Includes words and music for hymns. 3m 3w 2b 1g 1 exterior
Lincoln, Abraham, President U.S.
  Barbee, L. A letter to Lincoln
  Chorpenning, C. B. Abe Lincoln—New Salem days
  Chorpenning, C. B. Lincoln's secret messenger
  Corwin, N. The rivalry
  Covington, W. P. Shirt-tail boy
  Du Bois, G. His hand and pen
  Fisher, A. Abe's winkin' eye
  Fisher, A. and Rabe, O. Honest Abe Lincoln
  Howard, V. The women from Kentucky
  Kissen, F. Abraham Lincoln: with malice toward none
c Martens, A. C. Pictures in the fire
c Miller, H. L. A February failure
  Miller, H. L. I'll eat my hat!
  Miller, H. L. The Lincoln cupboard
c Miller, H. L. A Lincoln museum
c Miller, H. L. Mystery at Knob Creek Farm
c Newman, D. Mr Lincoln's beard
c Newman, D. A present from Abe
  Sherwood, R. E. Abe Lincoln in Illinois
  Smith, B. and Webb, C. Lawyer Lincoln
c Tyson, R. H. The life of Lincoln
  Van Doren, M. The last days of Lincoln
c Very, A. Abe Lincoln goes to school
c Woolsey, J. and Sechrist, E. H. Lincoln's secret journey
Lincoln, Mary (Todd)
  Calitri, P. M. One love had Mary
  Sergel, R. Irving Stone's Love is eternal
Lincoln, Richard. See Shore, J. jt. auth.
The **Lincoln** cupboard. Miller, H. L.
Lincoln Day
  Chorpenning, C. B. Lincoln's secret messenger
  Fisher, A. Abe's winkin' eye

c Hark, M. and McQueen, N. Bobby and the Lincoln speech
c Hark, M. and McQueen, N. Lincoln reminders
c Miller, H. L. A February failure
  Miller, H. L. I'll eat my hat!
  Miller, H. L. The Lincoln cupboard
c Miller, H. L. A Lincoln museum
c Miller, H. L. Melody for Lincoln
c Miller, H. L. Ten pennies for Lincoln
c Newman, D. Mr Lincoln's beard
c Newman, D. A present from Abe
c Tyson, R. H. The life of Lincoln
c Very, A. Abe Lincoln goes to school
c Very, A. Gifts for young Abe
c Woolsey, J. and Sechrist, E. H. Lincoln's secret journey
A **Lincoln** Museum. Miller, H. L.
Lincoln reminders. Hark, M. and McQueen, N.
Lincoln's birthday. See Lincoln Day
Lincoln's secret journey. Woolsey, J. and Sechrist, E. H.
Lincoln's secret messenger. Chorpenning, C. B.
Lind, Jenny
  Spamer, C. Jenny Lind
Lindsay, Howard, and Crouse, Russel
  The Great Sebastians. [Acting ed] Dramatists 1957 102p
    Comedy. Vaudeville team of mind-reading act are caught behind the Iron Curtain in Czechoslovakia when their friend Masaryk dies. 3 acts 4 scenes 15m 6w 3 interiors
    Trade edition published by Random House
  Life with father
    Domestic farce about life in large family. Set in Victorian New York. 3 acts 8 scenes 7m 8w 1b 1 interior
  In Cooper, C. W. Preface to drama
  In Sper, F. ed. Favorite modern plays
  The Prescott proposals. Dramatists 1954 80p illus
    Comedy. Charming American woman finds her work on United Nations Committee jeopardized by Communist intrigue. 3 acts 4 scenes 11m 4w extras 2 interiors
    Trade edition published by Random House
  Tall story. [Acting ed] Dramatists 1960 95p illus
    Romantic comedy. The outcome of a crucial college game depends on not-too-bright athlete who finds himself mysteriously involved with gangsters. 3 acts 9 scenes 21m 8w 1b 5 interiors
    Trade edition published by Random House
Lindsay, Kathleen, and Lindsay, Robert Howard
  Miracle at Potter's farm. French 1956 43p illus
    When five children are orphaned, aggressive relatives want to break up family, but youngest child finds an innocent solution through his prayers. 7 scenes 11m 4w 2 interiors 1 exterior
Lindsay, Robert Howard. See Lindsay, K. jt. auth.
Lindsey, Henry C.
  Forever Judy. French 1953 23p illus
    Domestic comedy. Teenage girl and boyfriend to whom family object are caught rehearsing love scene for school play by maid who misunderstands. 1 act 2m 3w 1 interior

Lindsey, Henry C.—*Continued*
Mr Sweeney's conversion. French 1955
22p illus
Domestic comedy. Meek man mistakenly
thinks he has inherited some money.
tells off his domineering wife and boss.
1 act 4m 1w 1 interior

Line of scrimmage. Kesler, H. O.

Lineberger, James
A sometime thing. French 1959 31p illus
Man encourages affection of widow in
order to steal her savings. but the love
his young son feels for her is real. 1 act
2m 1w 1 interior 1 exterior

The **lion** and the mouse. Moore, S. S.

Lisle, Vera
The merry matchmaker. Bakers Plays
1953 91p illus (Baker's Royalty plays)
Comedy. Matchmaking girl manages to
marry off her brother to girl she thinks
is suited for him, and herself to man
determined not to get married. 3 acts
3m 7w 1 interior

Literary forgeries and mystifications
Williams, T. Lord Byron's love letter

Literary frauds. See Literary forgeries and
mystifications

Literate highwaymen. Sakanishi, S. tr.

Litterbug convention. Carlson, B. W.

Litterbugs on trial. Ryan, M. A.

Little blank book. Spamer, C.

The **little** blue angel. Fluckey, J. O.

The **little** blue light. Wilson, E.

Little boy's clock. Spamer, C.

The **little brown church in the vale (Hymn)**
Emurian, E. K. The church in the wildwood

Little Christmas guest. Asbrand, K.

Little cloud. Spamer, C.

The **little** clouds. Spamer, C.

The **little** dry thorn. Daviot, G.

Little Eyolf. Ibsen, H.

The **little** fir tree. Very, A.

The **little** flaw of Ernesto Lippi. Schaefer, L.

The **little** foxes. Hellman, L.

Little friend. Cowen, W. J.

Little friends. Very, A.

The **little** girl laughed. See Batson, G.
I found April

The **little** glass clock. Mills, H.

The **little** goblins. Spamer, C.

The **little** green worker. Spamer, C.

The **little** hut. Roussin, A.

Little icicle. Spamer, C.

Little Ida and the flowers. Ormandy, E.

Little lost leprechaun. Martens, A. C.

The **little** minister. Barrie, J. M.

Little moon of Alban. Costigan, J.

Little Nell, the orphan girl. Goodhue, N.

The **little** nuisance. Stevens, E.

The **Little** Poor Man of Assisi. Swann, M.

The **little** things. Casey, B. M.

The **little** witch who tried. Leuser, E.

Little women. Morley, O. J.

The **little** world of Don Camillo. Hartke,
G. V.

Live and let love. Cary, F. L.

Living, Cost of. See Cost and standard of
living

The **living** declaration. Wishengrad, M.

The **living** dramatization of the Beatitudes.
Emurian, E. K.

The **living** room. Greene, G.

The **living** Saviour. Ingebretson, A. Sister;
Miller, J. Sister, and Roberts, M. Sister

Livingston, Shirley. See Miller, G. jt. auth.

Livingstone, David
Howard, V. The spear

Llwelyn ab Iorwerth, Prince of Wales
Lewis, S. Siwan

Llwelyn the Great. See Llwelyn ab Iorwerth, Prince of Wales

The **loaves** and the fishes. Spamer, C. M.

Locke, Sam
Fair game. Dramatists 1958 91p front
Romantic comedy. Young divorcee who
arrives in New York City to study psychology finds herself fair game for all
"wolves" in town. 3 acts 8 scenes 8m 6w
5 interiors

The **locked** room. Spence, W.

Lockwood, Lyn
Autumn in the air. [French's Acting ed]
French (London) 1956 74p illus
Comedy. Elizabeth, unhappily married
for fourteen years, hopes to regain former
suitor, only to discover that he now loves
her niece. 3 acts 5m 4w 1 interior

Loesser, Frank
Most happy fella (condensation)
In Theatre, 1956

Loewe, Frederick
My fair lady; adaptation and lyrics by
Alan Jay Lerner; music by Frederick
Loewe. Coward-McCann 1956 186p
Musical comedy. Based on: Pygmalion,
by Bernard Shaw. British professor of
phonetics transforms Covent Garden
flower girl into semblance of a duchess
2 acts 18 scenes Large mixed cast chorus
5 interiors 6 exteriors
Paper edition published by The New
American Library. English trade edition
published by Constable
My fair lady (condensation)
In The Best plays of 1955-1956

Logan, Joshua. See Rodgers, R. and Hammerstein, O. South Pacific; Rome, H.
Fanny; *also* Kober, A. jt. auth.

London
Maugham, W. S. The circle
c Tennant, K. The bells of the city
Social life and customs
c Arlett, V. I. Young Richard Whittington
Coward, N. Hands across the sea

London triumphing. See Dekker, T.
Troia-nova triumphans

London's tempe. Dekker, T.

Long, John Luther
Madame Butterfly (dramatization) See
Belasco, D. Madame Butterfly

Long ago in Bethlehem. Newman, D.

The **long** Christmas dinner. Wilder, T.

Long day's journey into night. O'Neill, E.

The **long** fall. Howe, C. V.

The **long** goodbye. Williams, T.

Long live father. Fisher, A.

Long may it wave. Fisher, A. and Rabe, O.

The **long** sunset. Sherriff, R. C.

The **long** view. Arthur, K.

The **long** voyage home. O'Neill, E.

Longfellow, Henry Wadsworth
A Christmas carol (dramatization) See Marston, M. A. A Christmas carol
The courtship of Miles Standish (dramatization) See Howells, W. D. Priscilla

Longing for Christmas. McCarty, R. K.

Lonsdale, Frederick
Let them eat cake
  Romantic comedy. Intrigues and love affairs among several members of English nobility in 1920. 3 acts 9m 5w 1 interior
In Plays of the year v19

Look back in anger. Osborne, J.

Look homeward, angel. Frings, K.

Look who's laughing. Randall, J.

Loos, Anita
Gigi. [Acting ed] French 1953 102p illus
  Based on the novel by Colette. Set in early 20th century Paris. Gigi, brought up to be prosperous demimondaine, maneuvers proposal of marriage from sophisticated man-about-town. 2 acts 6 scenes 2m 4w 2 interiors
  Trade edition published by Random House

Lorca, Federico García. See García Lorca, Federico

Lord, Betty. See Latham, J. jt. auth.

Lord, Daniel A.
Joy for the world. Eucharistic Crusade of the Knights and Handmaids of the Blessed Sacrament 1954 55p
  Musical dramatic presentation of Virgin Mary in scripture, history, legend, and the heart of our times. Includes scenes of the Nativity and Crucifixion. Choral and solo singing, ballet and other dances, and pantomimes. 2 acts 18 scenes Large mixed cast 1 setting

Lord, Walter
A night to remember (dramatization) See Hill, G. R. and Whedon, J. A night to remember

Lord Byron's love letter. Williams, T.

Lord Halewyn. Ghelderode, M. de

Lord's prayer
Phillips, J. B. The Lord's prayer
The **Lord's** prayer. Phillips, J. B.

Lord's Supper
Corrigan, L. Whosoever believeth
Phillips, J. B. The Last Supper
Smith, W. S. They that walk in darkness
c Spamer, C. M. The Last Supper

Lorenz, Jane Ellen
A Christmas gift for Hans. Lorenz 1955 32p music
  Christmas drama with German carols. In 16th century Germany Martin Luther writes hymn: Away in a manger, as gift for his son. 2m 4w 3b 4g chorus extras 1 **interior**

Lorenzen, Ronald F.
The scarf from Smyrna. Dramatic 1953 20p illus
  Christmas. According to legend, daughter of Innkeeper at Bethlehem stole a scarf given to Christ Child, which in turn was stolen from her. 1 act 3m 5w 1 interior

Lorna Doone. Miller, H. L.

Los Angeles
      Race question
Broughton, J. Summer fury

A **loss** of roses. Inge, W.

The **lost** bouquet. Spamer, C.

The **lost** Christmas. Kimes, B.

The **lost** Christmas cards. Miller, H. L.

The **lost** colony. Green, P.

Lost in the stars. Anderson, M.

The **lost** star. Heicher, M. and St Clair, R.

The **lost** victory. Dimondstein, B.

The **loud** red Patrick. Boruff, J.

Louisa May Alcott. Spamer, C.

Love, Charles R.
Proof of a man
  Tragedy. Son forbidden to play football by overly anxious mother is driven into frenzy. 1 act 4 scenes 4m 2w 1 setting
In Powers, V. E. ed. Plays for players, and a guide to play production

Love
Down, O. The maker of dreams
Procunier, E. R. Two sides of darkness
Schnitzler, A. Anatol
Thompson, D. The shoemaker's wife
  See also Courtship; Friendship; Marriage

Love, Maternal
Addyman, E. Over the garden fence
Appell, D. Lullaby
Brecht, B. The Caucasion chalk circle
Cocteau, J. Intimate relations
Pirandello, L. The life I gave you

Love, Platonic
Saroyan, W. The cave dwellers

Love affair. Gray, D.

Love and Alexander Botts. Upson, W. H.

Love and lunacy. Philp, P.

Love and Miss Dodie. Brenner, M.

Love and the boxer. Corrie, J.

Love comes in many colors. Hale, R. and Hale, N.

Love errant. Nail, R.

Love for love. Congreve, W.

Love in idleness. Rattigan, T.

Love is eternal. See Sergel, R. Irving Stone's Love is eternal

Love lesson for Scotty. Armer, A. and Grauman, W. E.

The **love** match. Melvyn, G.

The **love** of four colonels. Ustinov, P.

The **love** of Ruth. Casey, B. M.

Love scores a touchdown. Armer, A. and Grauman, W. E.

The **lovers**. Stevens, L.

The **lover's** melancholy. Ford, J.

Love's sacrifice. Ford, J.

Love's the best doctor. Molière, J. B. P.

Low, Juliette (Gordon)
Brenner, M. Beacon of strength

Lowe, Eloise
A birthday through the centuries. Eldridge 1959 7p (Eldridge Christmas entertainments)
Christmas worship program. 1m chorus

The **lower** depths. Gorky, M.

Loyalties. Galsworthy, J.

Loyalty, Political. See Allegiance

Loyalty-security program, 1947-
Ardrey, R. Sing me no lullaby

Lucifer. See Devil

Lucinda and the birthday ball. Hourihane, U.

Lucius Junius Brutus. Lee, N.

Luck takes a holiday. Fisher, A.

Lucy. Drapkin, I.

Lullaby. Appell, D.

Lumbering
c Levofsky, R. A house for Duke

Lumsden, Mary
The gift. French (London) 1953 73p illus
Englishwoman sacrifices one of her eyes so that younger sister may have the corneal graft needed in an eye operation. 2 acts 4 scenes 2m 4w 1 interior

Lunatic asylums. See Insane—Hospitals

Lunatics and lovers. Kingsley, S.

Lunnon, Betty Sheehan
c Johnny has comicopia
Book Week. Boy who wants to read only comic books dreams about several books and comic book characters. 2 scenes 1w 2b extras 1 interior
    In Birdsall, R. ed. Creative plays for every school month

Lusk, Donald
Girls are better than ever. French 1953 95p illus
Romantic comedy. Man refuses to do business with female clients but when negotiating sale of business by letter, his partner turns out to be beautiful woman. 3 acts 4 scenes 4m 6w 1 interior

Lust's dominion. Marlowe, C.

Lute song. Kao-Tong-Kia

Luther, Martin
Emurian, E. K. Famous families
Lorenz, E. J. A Christmas gift for Hans

Lutherans in Iceland
Sveinbjörnsson, T. Bishop Jón Arason

Luxury cruise. Carmichael, F.

Lying. See Truthfulness and falsehood

Lynch, Peg
Betsy's first report card. French 1960 17p
Domestic comedy. Couple is shocked when their child's first report card designates her as average. 1 act 1m 1w 1g 1 interior
The Christmas angel. French 1956 23p
Domestic comedy. At Christmastime when a man retaliates small boys' snowballs, he breaks parsonage window and runs away. 1 act 3m 2w 4b extras 1 interior
Dutch treat
Domestic comedy. Impatient husband wanting to get to movies on time tries to help wife figure out luncheon fees for her bridge club. 1m 1w 1 interior
    In Lynch, P. Ethel and Albert comedies

Fishing hat
Domestic comedy. Wife gets into trouble when she throws away husband's favorite but decrepit fishing hat and buys him new one. 1m 1w 1 interior
    In Lynch, P. Ethel and Albert comedies
Fool's paradise. French 1955 19p
Domestic comedy. Couple go out to dinner at swank restaurant where the man suddenly discovers they have brought along the wrong gift: the garbage! 1 act 6m 4w 1 interior
The income tax. French 1955 28p
Domestic comedy. Couple suddenly gets mysterious notice that the government is coming to check last year's income tax returns. 1 act 3m 2w 1 interior
Just a little something for Christmas
Domestic comedy. Husband and wife receive some unexpected visitors on Christmas and frantically wrap gift for them intended for someone else. 2m 1w 1 interior
    In Lynch, P. Ethel and Albert comedies
Neglected husbands' sewing club. French 1956 24p
Domestic comedy. When several neglected husbands feel that their wives are too busy with bridge, they form club to darn socks and talk about hairdo's. 1 act 6m 5w 1 interior
Off with his head. French 1955 21p
Domestic comedy. During preparations for Halloween party, man slips pumpkin over his head and finds it won't come off. 1 act 3m 2w 1 interior
The teen age party. French 1955 29p
Domestic comedy. Middle aged man thinks that he is quite a dancer until he and his wife chaperone teenage dance. 1 act 6m 5w extras 1 interior
To open, pry cover
Comedy. When a man can't pry the lid off jar of pickles, he writes an irate letter to manufacturer. 2m 1w 1 interior
    In Lynch, P. Ethel and Albert comedies
What's that tune?
Domestic comedy. Husband and wife hear workman whistling a tune. Complications ensue when they can't agree on name of song. 2m 1w 1 interior
    In Lynch, P. Ethel and Albert comedies

Lynn, Kenneth S.
Who killed Cock Robin? French 1955 122p illus
Farce. Television executive is proud of his success with the ladies, until a Congressman appears on the scene to investigate television. 2 acts 7m 5w 1 interior

Lysistrata. Aristophanes

Lytton, Edward George Earle Lytton Bulwer Lytton, 1st baron. See Bulwer-Lytton, E.

M

MacAlvay, Nora
c Beauty and the Beast. Coach House Press 1955 64p illus music
Fairy tale. Singing and dancing with background music. 3 acts 4 scenes 6m 7w extras 1 interior

Macbeth, King of Scotland
Olfson, L. Macbeth

Macbeth. Olfson, L.

Macbeth a la mode. Taggart, T.

McCann, Kitty

Out of despair. Bakers Plays 1960 12p

    Easter story. Simple country woman shows meaning of Christ's Resurrection in her life. 2m 2w extras 1 interior

McCarty, E. Clayton

The moon's still yellow. French 1956 126p illus

    Romantic comedy. Teen age girl feels that life in her home is terribly trivial and monotonous except for mysterious flowers that arrive daily for her sister. 3 acts 7m 7w 1 interior

McCarty, Rega Kramer

Blake's decision. Rodeheaver 1953 16p

    Saved by Chinese natives and missionary family, ex-soldier Blake is determined to return to China as medical missionary despite opposition of family and fiancée. 3 acts 6m 4w 1b 1 interior

But this I know. Rodeheaver 1953 16p

    Easter play. Faith of Army chaplain, threatened with blindness, helps other patients in Army hospital find new faith. 3 acts 5m 3w 1g 1 interior

Longing for Christmas. Rodeheaver 1955 16p

    When Christmas plans are interrupted by grandparents possible visit, pastor's visit, and disappearance of their turkey, the Palmers discover essence of Christmas. 3 acts 2m 3w 1b 3g 1 interior

McCaslin, Nellie

Apples in the wilderness

    How Johnny Appleseed spent his life planting apple seeds throughout middle west in first half of nineteenth century. 2 scenes 10m 4w 1b 1g extras 1 interior

    In McCaslin, N. Tall tales and tall men

The Bell Witch of Tennessee

    Tennessee folk tale. Witch plagues farming family for years with noises and strange accidents and then falls in love with the daughter. 3 scenes 4m 4w 2b extras 1 interior

    In McCaslin, N. Tall tales and tall men

Giant of the timber

    American folk tale about how Paul Bunyan worked as logger with his blue ox, Babe. 14m 1w extras 1 exterior

    In McCaslin, N. Tall tales and tall men

The gift of corn

    Traditional Ottawa Indian legend about first appearance of corn on earth. 2 scenes 9m 5w extras 1 interior

    In McCaslin, N. Tall tales and tall men

He traveled the world

    Mormon folk tale about mysterious traveller who is treated kindly by a family and turns out to be Jesus. 2 scenes 3m 1w 2b 1 interior

    In McCaslin, N. Tall tales and tall men

John Henry

    Radio play. Exploits of the gigantic legendary Negro folk hero. Southern folk tale. 11m 2w extras

    In McCaslin, N. Tall tales and tall men

The legend of the Christmas candle

    On Christmas Eve in 15th century France, two children who place their only gift, a lighted candle in window receive great gift from the Christ Child. Songs and folk dancing. 2 scenes 1m 1w 2b 1g extras 1 interior 1 exterior

    In Cahill, E. M. ed. Celebrating Christmas

St Nicholas of New Amsterdam

    Old American version of Dutch folk tale about poor family who shares meager supper with Saint Nicholas. 3m 1w 2b 1g 1 interior

    In McCaslin, N. Tall tales and tall men

Seafaring giant

    Radio play. Account of some seagoing exploits of folk hero, Stormalong, gigantic sailor. 8m extras

    In McCaslin, N. Tall tales and tall men

The star that never moves

    Traditional Ojibwa Indian legend about North Star. 2 scenes 7m 1w extras 2 exteriors

    In McCaslin, N. Tall tales and tall men

Tall Bill and his big ideas

    How long ago in the West Pecos Bill taught cowboys to rope and brand cattle. 7m 2w 1b 1g extras 1 exterior

    In McCaslin, N. Tall tales and tall men

With the sunrise in his pocket

    Radio play. Combination of several short tales about Davy Crockett. 4m extras

    In McCaslin, N. Tall tales and tall men

The Yankee Peddler

    The Yankee Peddler visits country store in New England long ago. 7m 2w 2g extras 1 interior

    In McCaslin, N. Tall tales and tall men

McCauley, Mary (Ludwig) Hays

Fisher, A. and Rabe, O. "Molly Pitcher"

Woolsey, J. and Sechrist, E. H. Molly Pitcher, heroine of Monmouth

McCleery, William

The family man. French 1953 73p illus

    Domestic comedy. Teen age girl tries to impress beaus with her sophistication, and they mistake her hard-working client for "older man." 3 acts 4m 6w 1 interior

The guest cottage. French 1956 76p illus

    Farce. Girl is caught between her forceful intellectual fiancé who wants her to marry him at once and her domineering father who objects. 3 acts 3m 6w 1 interior

The lady chooses. French 1956 88p illus

    Comedy. Suburban wife decides to revitalize her marriage by running for Congress. 3 acts 4m 7w 1 interior

McConnell, Jean

The red cloak. Deane 1955 22p ("Deane's" Ser. of plays)

    Countess completes thrilling escape from prison during French Revolution. 1 act 6w 1 interior

MacCormick, Iain

The small victory

    Television play. Communist soldiers in North Korea imprison a priest, nun, a reporter and British vice consul and try to force them to sign false statements. 8m

    In British Broadcasting Corporation. The television playwright

McCourt, Gleness M.

The curse and the crown. Eldridge 1959 19p (Eldridge Church entertainments)

    Story of one of the cynical soldiers who crucified Christ. 2 acts 3m 2w 1 exterior

McCoy, Paul S.

Clara paints the town. Eldridge 1955 29p (Eldridge Popular one-act playscripts)

    Domestic comedy. When teenage girl gives party, she disapproves when mother wants to show her latest painting. Father decides to hide the painting. 1 act 3m 4w 1 interior

The Lieutenant pays his respects

    Romantic comedy. When handsome young lieutenant comes home Betty finally gets a date with him despite young sister's interference. 1 act 6w 1 interior

    In Kamerman, S. E. ed. Blue-ribbon plays for girls

McCoy, Paul S.—*Continued*

A rumpus on rampage. Eldridge 1956 28p
(Eldridge Popular one-act playscripts)
Comedy. Teen age girl takes baby
sitting job to impress her rich aunt, but
her young charge sneaks off to movies.
Boyfriend agrees to impersonate "baby."
1 act 3m 4w 1 interior

Susan steps out. Art Craft 1956 104p illus
Comedy. Teen-age girl persuades rich
old bachelor to donate money to high
school but his condition is that she
comes from an old fashioned family.
3 acts 5m 7w 1 interior

Two dates for tonight. Eldridge 1953 89p
illus (Eldridge 3-act playscripts)
Romantic comedy. Kidnapping, mistaken
identity and general pandemonium break
out when teen age girl tries to avoid
prom date her parents arranged for her.
3 acts 6m 8w 1 interior

McCreary, Bill, and McCreary, Marcie

Three needles in a haystack. [Rev] French
1960 54p
Comedy. Three of Miss Myles' students
had opportunity to steal money out of her
cash box for senior trip; she stages mock
trial in history class to find culprit.
3 acts 9m 7w 1 interior

McCullers, Carson

The member of the wedding
Study of loneliness and day-dreaming of
small town adolescent girl in Georgia,
and crisis which occurs at her brother's
wedding. 3 acts 5 scenes 5m 7w 1b
1 setting
In Gaver, J. ed. Critics' choice
In Hewes, H. ed. Famous American
plays of the 1940s

The square root of wonderful. Houghton
1958 159p
When woman falls in love with architect,
her unsuccessful writer husband who had
abandoned her returns. 3 acts 4 scenes
4m 4w 1b 1 interior

MacDonagh, Donagh

Step-in-the-hollow
Farce about amoral judge who is more
rogue than most of those he tries. Set
in Ireland. Verse play. 3 acts 4 scenes
7m 4w 2 interiors
In Browne, E. M. ed. Three Irish plays

MacDonald, Betty

Onions in the stew (dramatization) See
Dalzell, W. and Martens, A. C. Onions
in the stew

MacDonald, Dora Mary

Let nothing ye dismay
Untenanted, old mansion comes alive
again on Christmas Eve, thanks to lonely
celebrant and caretaker. 1 act 2m 2w
extras 1 interior
In Brings, L. M. ed. The modern treasury of Christmas plays

MacDougall, Roger

The facts of life
Domestic comedy. Two busy parents
discover that their somewhat neglected
son is mathematical genius and runs
flourishing gambling concern at dog
tracks. 2 acts 4 scenes 4m 4w 1 interior
In Ring up the curtain

The gentle gunman
English judge and Irish doctor argue
merits of Irish independence as they are
drawn into intrigues of the I.R.A. men.
Set in northern Ireland, 1942. 3 acts
4 scenes 15m 2w 2 interiors
In Plays of the year v5

Macedonia

History—Ancient to 168 B.C.
Rattigan, T. Adventure story

McGee, Ann

c Bill visits Mexico
Pan-American Day. Boys and girls of
Mexico explain their country to little boy
from United States. 3 scenes 1w 6b 3g
extras 2 interiors 1 exterior
In Birdsall, R. ed. Creative plays for
every school month

McGinley, Phyllis

The plain Princess (dramatization) See
Harris, A. The plain Princess

McGowan, John. See Bolton, G. jt. auth.

MacGrath, Leueen. See Kaufman, G. S. jt.
auth.

McGreevey, John

The barrier. Dramatic 1954 24p
Insane man who hates doctor whom he
holds responsible for his wife's death,
comes back to kill doctor's wife. 1 act
4m 1w 1 interior

Coins of His kingdom. Dramatic 1954 25p
illus
Christmas. Based on scenes from novel,
The Robe, by Lloyd C. Douglas. The robe
which Christ wore at His crucifixion
plays mystical part in life of young Roman. 1 act 5m 3w 2g 1 exterior

A man called Peter. Dramatic 1955 91p
illus
Based on the biography, by Catherine
Marshall. A young minister who has
devoted his life to his work is criticized
for his firm convictions. 3 acts 7m 8w
1 interior

Out of the darkness
Miracle occurs when Roman soldier
admits he lied about Christ's Resurrection. 1 act 4m 3w extras 1 exterior
In Brings, L. M. Golden book of church
plays

Papa was a preacher. Dramatic 1954 74p
illus
Domestic comedy. Dramatization of book
by Alyene Porter, about minister's family
and some parishioners who try to run the
parish. 3 acts 5 scenes 7m 8w 1 interior

The shepherd who stayed away. Bakers
Plays 1956 22p
Christmas drama. A shepherd is bitter
about the illness of son but his wife
tries to have faith in God. As she prays
a bright light appears and great chorus
announces that the Messiah has come.
1 act 3m 3w extras 1 exterior

Machinery and civilization. See Technology
and civilization

MacKaye, Percy

The scarecrow
Dramatization of Nathaniel Hawthorne's
story "Feathertop." Symbolic play of
hypocrisy and truth, reality and fantasy
about scarecrow who became a man.
4 acts 4 scenes 10m 5w 2 interiors
In Quinn, A. H. ed. Representative
American plays

MacKaye, Steele

Hazel Kirke
Peer marries miller's daughter over objections of her father and elderly suitor.
4 acts 4 scenes 9m 5w extras 2 interiors
1 exterior
In Quinn, A. H. ed. Representative
American plays

McKechnie, Jean Lyttleton. See Knox,
Janet

McKenny, Ruth

The loud red Patrick (dramatization) See
Boruff, J. The loud red Patrick

Mackie, Philip

The whole truth
> Murder mystery in which assassin goes to great lengths to incriminate innocent man. 3 acts 4 scenes 6m 2w 2 interiors

In Plays of the year v13

Mackintosh, Elizabeth. See Daviot, Gordon

McLaughlin, Miriam Love

The mind's construction
> Tragedy. College girl disappears because she believes she has inherited her mother's mental illness. 5w 1 interior

In Twelve half-hours with the Winthrop Theater

MacLeish, Archibald

The fall of the city
> Radio play in verse. A dictator's pattern of conquest. 7m 1w extras

In The Best short plays, 1957

J.B. French 1958 113p front
> Verse play. Dramatization of the theme of the Book of Job. Prosperous business-man loses his wealth, health and family, but maintains his faith in God. 2 acts 11m 6w 1b 3g 1 interior
> Trade edition published by Houghton

J.B. (condensation)
In The Best plays of 1958-1959
In Broadway's best, 1959

This music crept by me upon the waters. Harvard Univ. Press 1953 38p (The Poets' theatre ser)
> Verse play set on Caribbean island. Married couples search for true happiness. 1 act 5m 5w 1 exterior

—Same
In The Best short plays of 1955-1956

MacLellan, Esther, and Schroll, Catherine V.

c A flower for Mother's Day
> Each of the flowers wants to be chosen the Mother's Day flower. 1 act 2w 12g 1 exterior

In Kamerman, S. E. ed. Blue-ribbon plays for girls

MacLeod, Robert

Kate. Deane 1955 22p ("Deane's" Ser. of plays)
> As going away presents, Kate, a cleaning woman, gives each of the people she serves exact present he most desires. 1 act 3m 4w 1 interior

McLiam, John

The sin of Pat Muldoon. Dramatists 1957 77p illus
> Deep love between family members, although they are plagued with bitterness and unreasonable behavior of the father. 3 acts 5 scenes 8m 3w 1 interior

McMahon, Bernice

Guided tour
> Radio play. Young boy is impressed by historical events about which he learns on visit to Gettysburg National Military Park. Background music. 5m 3w 1b

In Prescott, H. ed. Patrioscript

The Ming thing. Dramatic 1953 25p illus
> Domestic farce. Aunt who gave the Smith family a Ming vase arrives unexpectedly just after vase has been loaned to a friend. 1 act 3m 4w 1 interior

Publicity on the fifteenth. Eldridge 1953 17p (Eldridge Popular one-act play-scripts)
> When young woman mistakes famous opera star for a cook, the star decides to take on the job. 1 act 1m 4w 1 interior

McMahon, Luella E.

Don't tell your father. Dramatic 1956 74p illus
> Domestic comedy. Man with three teen-age children of his own is long suffering employee of arrogant newspaperman with an equally arrogant sixteen year old son. 3 acts 7m 7w extras 1 interior

Half-Pint Windom rides west. Dramatic 1955 25p illus
> Farce for women. Half-Pint rides into town amid clatter of hoofs and banging of guns to avenge death of his father, Pint. 1 act 19w extras no scenery

I smell smoke. Dramatic 1955 19p illus
> Farce set in the Ozarks. Visit of young son of feuding neighbor awakens men of a family who have slept through forest fire that threatened their cabin. 1 act 4m 2w 1 exterior

The people versus Maxine Lowe. Dramatic 1955 87p illus
> Woman on trial for murdering her husband, strangely refuses to defend herself as evidence piles up against her, until mysterious witness takes the stand. 3 acts 10m 13w extras 1 interior

School bus romance. Dramatic 1956 23p illus
> Twenty minute cross section of life on a school bus. 1 act 3m 3w extras 1 exterior

McMahon, Luella E. and Sergel, Ruth

The plum tree. Dramatic 1953 30p illus
> A dramatization of story by Mary Ellen Chase about three elderly women who have been committed to a state hospital and how each is affected. 7w 1 interior

McMartin, Ellen Laura

The tree
> Christmas. Teen-agers who pretend not to be interested in Christmas tree surprise their mother with four trees. 1 act 4m 4w 1 interior

In Brings, L. M. ed. The modern treasury of Christmas plays

McMaster, Alison

Upstairs and downstairs. Deane 1955 57p illus ("Deane's" Ser. of plays)
> Romantic comedy. When English widow rents two rooms to increase family income, some surprising events ensue. 3 acts 4 scenes 4m 3w 1 interior

McMillin, Martha

c The young whittler
> How Eli Whitney invented cotton gin. 2 scenes 5m 2w 1b 1 interior

In Birdsall, R. ed. Creative plays for every school month

McMullen, J. C.

Deep freeze. Bakers Plays 1953 29p illus
> Domestic comedy. Newlyweds in small apartment receive an oversize freezer as gift from bride's rich aunt. When they try to dispose of it they get word that she is coming to visit. 1 act 4m 5w 1 interior

I don't believe in Christmas
> Grandmother's Christmas dinner proves to her family, especially one son, that Christmas has a real meaning. 2 scenes 2m 8w 1b 1 interior

In Cahill, E. M. ed. Celebrating Christmas

Son of Erin. Bakers Plays 1953 89p illus (Baker's Royalty plays)
> Domestic comedy. Becoming millionaires has created a divided family life but father discovers how to put his house in order. 3 acts 6m 5w 1 interior

McNeely, Jerry
The staring match. Dramatists 1957 35p
illus
Fantasy. Two mysterious strangers appear in town, one in a black suit. the other in white, and claim to be angels of the Lord, but no one can tell which one is. 2 acts 6m 2w 1g extras 1 interior

McQuade, William
Exclusive model
Farce. Marital crisis is averted when two women see maid wearing dress identical with theirs. 1 act 2m 3w 1 interior
In Smith, B. and others, eds. A treasury of non-royalty one-act plays

McQueen. Noel. See Hark, M. jt. auth.

Macrae, Arthur
Both ends meet
Satirical comedy. British socialites, who unwittingly reveal their favorite methods of tax evasion in presence of income tax collector, help promote young actor's romance. 3 acts 4 scenes 6m 2w 1 interior
In Plays of the year v10

Macy, Anne (Sullivan)
Gibson, W. The miracle worker

Mad about men. Blackmore, P.

The **mad** Doctor Zing. Howard, V.

Madam, will you walk? Howard, S.

Madame Butterfly. Belasco, D.

Madame Vulture. Emery, C.

Maddern, Victor, and Banks, Lynne Reid
Miss Pringle plays Portia. Deane 1955 27p ("Deane's" Ser. of plays)
Comedy. Man claims the playing field presented by his uncle to village thirty years before, but at town meeting he is shrewdly outwitted by clever spinster. 1 act 3m 5w extras 1 interior

Madelon. Hazeltine, A. I.

Mademoiselle Colombe. Anouilh, J.

Madison, Dorothy (Payne) Todd
Spamer, C. Dolly Madison

The **madmen.** Brabazon, F.

Madness. See Insanity

The **madness** of Herakles. Euripides

La **madre.** Mary Francis, Sister

The **madwoman** of Chaillot. Giraudoux, J.

Maeterlinck, Maurice
The intruder
Blind old man senses presence of death before nurse comes to announce that his daughter has died. 4m 3w 1 interior
In A Treasury of the theatre
A miracle of Saint Antony; tr. by Ralph Roeder
Satirical fantasy. St Antony revives wealthy old lady, displeasing her heirs. 1 act 2 scenes 7m 3w extras 2 interiors
In Smith, B. and others, eds. A treasury of non-royalty one-act plays
Pelléas and Mélisande; tr. from the French by Richard Hovey
Tragedy. Based on story of Paola and Francesca in Dante's "Inferno." Fateful romance of Mélisande and Prince Pelléas, younger brother of her husband. 5 acts 20 scenes 5m 2w 1b 8 interiors 3 exteriors
In Tucker, S. M. ed. Twenty-five modern plays

Magary, Frank A.
Rest, ye merry gentlemen! Eldridge 1958 60p (Eldridge 3-act playscripts)
Romantic comedy. Professor who made public speech to the effect that keeping house is simple accepts young widow's challenge to manage her household during Christmas week. 3 acts 4 scenes 3m 8w 1b 1 interior
See also Larson, V. jt. auth.

Magazine publishing. See Periodicals, Publishing of

Magee, Catherine
Radio Jerusalem, the story of Jesus
Radio play. Events in life of Jesus Christ used as subject of imaginary radio newscast. Background music. 2m 2w extras
In Brings, L. M. comp. The golden book of church plays

Magi
Coventry plays. Herod and the kings
Coventry plays. The pageant of the Shearmen and Taylors—The Coventry Nativity play
Heicher, M. and St Clair, R. The lost star
Malcolmson, A. Herod and the Magi
St Clair, R. The holy search
Sergel, R. Henry Van Dyke's The Other Wise Man
c Spamer, C. M. The wise men
Towneley plays. The Wakefield Pageant of Herod the Great

Magic
c Barnes, E. A. and Young, B. M. Sokar and the crocodile
Bergh, H. Old King Cole
c Chitty, A. W. I. Any old toys
c Cullen, A. Niccolo and Nicollette
c John, C. Sea shells
c Miller, H. L. The wishing stream
Olfson, L. A midsummer night's dream
Olfson, L. The tempest
Olson, E. The sorcerer's apprentices
c Taylor, F. The magic doughnuts
c Tennant, K. The magic fat baby
c Wallerstein, J. S. Johnny Aladdin
Waugh, J. R. The silver idol
Wilson, E. Cyprian's prayer
See also Alchemy; Conjuring; Witchcraft

The **magic** and the loss. Funt, J.

The **magic** apple. Hughes, G.

The **magic** broom. Martens, A. C.

The **magic** carpet sweeper. Miller, H. L.

The **magic** doughnuts. Taylor, F.

The **magic** fat baby. Tennant, K.

The **magic** fishbone. Barnes, E. A. and Young, B. M.

The **magic** formula. Fisher, A.

The **magic** goose. Newman, D.

The **magic** horn. Nicholson, A. and Chorpenning, C. B.

The **magic** mallet of the Devil. Sakanishi, S. tr.

The **magic** mountain. Palmer, K. and Palmer, W.

The **magic** owl. Carpenter, F.

The **magic** spinning-wheel. Jones, B. M.

The **magic** word. Kane, E. B.

Magical letters. Bonn, M.

The **magician**. Bergman, I.

Magicians
  Bergman, I. The magician
  Olson, E. The carnival of animals

The **magistrate**. Pinero, A. W.

Magito, Suria, and Weil, Rudolf
  c The Snow Queen. Theatre Arts 1960 85p
    music (The Drama lib)
      A dramatization of Hans Christian An-
      dersen's fairy tale about adventures of
      two children in the realm of the Snow
      Queen. Contains songs with musical
      scores. 2 acts 9 scenes 5m 3w 2b 3g
      extras 4 interiors 4 exteriors

Magnau, Katherine
  Goodbye, Texas—Broadway, hello! Hum-
    phries 1956 24p
      Two young lovers, stars of a traveling
      hillbilly musical show, almost lose each
      other when show is partially broken up.
      1 act 13 scenes 19m 6w extras 8 interiors
      1 exterior

The **magnificent** entertainment given to King
  James. Dekker, T.

The **magnificent** Yankee. Lavery, E.

Maher, Ramona
  When the fire dies. French 1955 24p illus
      Young Indian girl returning from govern-
      ment school to her home on reservation,
      has trouble adapting to old ways. 1 act
      1m 4w 1 interior

Maid to marry. Ionesco, E.

The **maids**. Genet, J.

The **maid's** tragedy. Beaumont, F. and
  Fletcher, J.

Mai-Guruma (condensation) Miyamasu

The **main** road. Casey, B. M.

Maine
  Herne, J. A. Shore Acres

Major Barbara. Shaw, B.

Major Milliron reports. Keeney, C. H.

Majorca
  Thon, F. The island

A **majority** of one. Spigelgass, L.

Make a million. Barasch, N. and Moore, C.

Make His name glorious. Sumerau, D. L.

Make it murder. Last, J.

The **maker** of dreams. Down, O.

The **making** of moo. Dennis, N.

Makowsky, Lucile
  The New World
      Immigrant's progress in America. 1 act
      6 scenes 9m 8w 1b 1g 1 setting
    In The Best short plays of 1957-1958

Maladjusted children. See Problem children

Malango, Patricia
  The boy who changed the world. French
    1959 75p illus
      Fantasy set in prehistoric era. Teen age
      cave boy, unpopular because he doesn't
      like survival skills, is saved from exile
      when he invents music, painting, and the
      wheel. 3 acts 8m 6w extras 1 interior
      2 exteriors

Malaya
  Brand, M. Strangers in the land
  Holmes, M. Jungle prize
  Richardson, L. For our mother Malaya!

Malcolm, Ian
  A moment of existence
      Philosophic drama on existentialist
      themes. Man's place in society; his in-
      ability to communicate with others. 1 act
      5m 1 interior
    In Richards, S. ed. Canada on stage

Malcolmson, Anne
  Abraham and Isaac
      English miracle play in verse done in
      modern English from the medieval Brome
      play. The theme is from Old Testament
      story. 4 scenes 4m 1b 1 exterior
    In Malcolmson, A. Miracle plays

  Herod and the Magi
      English medieval miracle play in verse
      done in modern English from the Magi,
      Herod and the slaughter of the Innocents
      of the Coventry play. 7 scenes 6m 1w
      extras 2 interiors 2 exteriors
    In Malcolmson, A. Miracle plays

  The Nativity
      English medieval miracle play in verse
      done in modern English from the York
      Nativity play. 1m 1w 1 exterior
    In Malcolmson, A. Miracle plays

  Noah's flood
      English medieval miracle play in verse,
      done in modern English from the Chester
      play, The deluge. The theme is from the
      Old Testament. 4 scenes 4m 4w extras
      1 exterior
    In Malcolmson, A. Miracle plays

  Saint Nicholas and the three scholars
      Medieval miracle play in verse done in
      modern English from Tres clerici. It
      tells about an old couple who kill three
      scholars for their gold. 5m 1w 1 exterior
    In Malcolmson, A. Miracle plays

  The shepherds' play
      English medieval miracle play in verse
      done in modern English from the Secunda
      pastorum of the Wakefield Cycle. 8 scenes
      4m 2w extras 1 exterior
    In Malcolmson, A. Miracle plays

  The statue of Saint Nicholas
      Medieval miracle play in verse done in
      modern English from the Latin "Ludus
      super iconia Sancti Nicolai" by Hilarius,
      about statue of Saint Nicholas which
      comes to life and foils band of thieves.
      2m extras 1 exterior
    In Malcolmson, A. Miracle plays

The **male** animal. Thurber, J. and Nugent, E.

Malleson, Miles
  The misanthrope, by Molière; a new
    adaptation by Miles Malleson
      Satirical comedy of manners. In 17th
      century Paris, young gentleman's obses-
      sion with ideal of honesty alienates him-
      self from his friends and the girl he
      loves. Background music. 2 acts 8m 3w
      1 interior
    In Plays of the year v11

  Sganarelle; a farce in one act by Molière
    in a free English version by Miles Mal-
    leson
      Farce. Misunderstanding between two
      lovers and a man and wife due to young
      woman's loss of locket containing lover's
      picture. Set in 17th century Paris. 1 act
      4m 3w 1 exterior
    In Plays of the year v11

Malone, Mary
  A letter for Charlotte
      Charlotte Bronte is encouraged to write
      by her sisters, and receives her first
      letter of encouragement from publisher.
      1 act 2 scenes 3w 1 interior
    In Kamerman, S. E. ed. Blue-ribbon
      plays for girls

La **malquerida** [The passion flower] Benavente, J.

Malta
Marlowe, C. The Jew of Malta

Man
Adamov, A. Ping-pong
Camus, A. State of siege
Cummings, E. E. Santa Claus
Dennis, N. The making of moo
Duncan, R. The death of Satan
Fisher, A. and Rabe, O. Cavalcade of human rights
Ionesco, E. The killer
Lagerkvist, P. Let man live
MacLeish, A. J.B.
Malcolm, I. A moment of existence
Wilson, D. C. Peace on Mars

Man, Fall of. See Fall of man

Man, Prehistoric
Malango, P. The boy who changed the world
c Tennant, K. The ghost tiger

Man alive. Dighton, J.

Man and superman. Shaw, B.

A **man** called Peter. McGreevey, J.

The **man** in the dog suit. Beich, A. and Wright, W. H.

Man of arts. Wehner, E.

The **man** of mode. Etherege, Sir G.

The **man** of the house. Welles, R.

The **man** on a stick. Ware, L. and Ware, H.

Man on the mountaintop. Aurthur, R. A.

"The **man** on the street." Buzzell, A. M.

The **man** upstairs. Hamilton, P.

The **man** who understood women. Sutherland, D.

The **man** with expensive tastes. Percy, E. and Denham, L.

The **man** with the heart in the highlands. Saroyan, W.

The **man** with the key. Howard, P.

Mañana bandits. Smith, B. and Webb, C.

Mandan Indians
Kissen, F. Sacajawea: guide in the wilderness

The **manger**. Casey, B. M.

A **manger** lowly. Bailey, H. F.

Manheim, Mannie
Comedy of roses. French 1957 27p illus
Farce. Driver is accused of negligence when the Queen's float overturns at the annual Tournament of Roses parade. 1 act 7m 6w 1 interior

Manion, Dale
Girl wanted. French 1957 32p
Comedy. Woman's employer demands that she find a girl to go to the dance with her nephew. 1 act 7w 1 interior

Mankowitz, Wolf
It should happen to a dog
Comic development of Biblical story of Jonah. God directs Jonah to vocation he doesn't want. 1 act 6 scenes 2m 1 exterior
In Halverson, M. ed. Religious drama, 3

Manley, Frederic
Best trip ever
Television play. A trip to Miami is won by two women one of whom, although she doesn't know it, is dying of incurable disease. 4m 2w 1g
In Roberts, E. B. Television writing and selling

The **mannequin** parade. Priestley, F.

Mannheimer, Albert, and Kohner, Frederick
Stalin Allee. French 1957 118p illus
Domestic comedy in Communist East Berlin where father hopes to get Communist luxury apartment, daughter loves an American, and grandmother schemes. 3 acts 4 scenes 9m 4w 1g extras 1 interior

Manning, Hilda
Seeing double. French 1955 79p illus
Farce. Identical twins, enroute to new school meet with accident which forces one to keep her face bandaged for awhile; they pretend to be one person at school. 3 acts 7 scenes 3m 10w 2 interiors
That's my baby. French 1953 77p illus
Domestic farce. Couple invite the husband's employer to dinner with hopes of promotion but he turns out to be allergic to their baby. 3 acts 5m 6w 1 interior
Wonderful summer. French 1957 38p illus
Romantic comedy. When widower and his two teenage children arrive at their resort home, the summer holds something special for each of them. 3 acts 5 scenes 4m 7w 1 interior
For other plays by this author see Reach, James; Sutton, Thomas; Williams, Pete

Manning, Mary
Passages from Finnegans wake, by James Joyce. Harvard Univ. Press 1957 75p (The Poets' theatre ser)
A dramatization of parts of James Joyce's novel. An attempt to reproduce the half conscious world of dream sensation in sleeping mind of Dublin pub owner. 6 scenes 4m 1w extras 2 interiors

Manning, Sally Ann
As silent as the ocean
Comedy. Young man visits his eccentric aunt to solve mystery of his missing uncle. 1m 2w 1 interior
In Twelve half-hours with the Winthrop Theater

Man's estate. Gittings, R.

A **man's** point of view. Sprague, G. W.

Mansfield, Katherine
A cup of tea (dramatization) See Sergel, R. A cup of tea

Mansur, Frank L.
Train for Sherwood. Bakers Plays 1954 25p (Baker's Royalty plays)
Comedy. Two thieves who stole necklace meet some comical people in railroad station, who make their getaway difficult. 1 act 5m 2w 1 interior

Manthorn, Ruth A.
c A Christmas box
Mother Goose characters prepare Christmas gifts for the children of the old woman who lived in a shoe. 20 characters 1 interior
In Birdsall, R. ed. Creative plays for every school month

Mantle, Margaret
Gareth triumphs
Dramatization of Gareth and Lynette, one of the Idylls of the King, by Alfred Tennyson. 4m 4w 1b 1 interior
In Birdsall, R. ed. Creative plays for every school month

Many a slip. Fisher, A.
"Many infallible proofs." Schofield, J. A. and Joudry, R. C.
Many thanks. Hark, M. and McQueen, N.
The maple viewing. Kwanze, K. N.
Marc-Michel. See Labische, E. jt. auth.
Marcelline, Sister M.
Silver beads. St Anthony Guild 1953 33p
Christmas. The children of Bethlehem wish to fight to help free Israel from Romans, but desist when they hear message of peace from angel choir announcing birth of Christ. 3 acts 7m 6w 3b 1g extras 1 interior 1 exterior
March, William
Bad seed (dramatization) See Anderson, M. Bad seed
A march of dimes. Miller, G. and Livingston, S.
Marchant, William
The desk set. French 1956 90p illus
Reference librarian with encyclopedic knowledge is temporarily thwarted by efficiency expert who installs electronic brain. 3 acts 8m 8w 2 interiors
Marching song. Whiting, J.
Marco Polo. See Polo, Marco
Marcus, Irving H.
c To you the torch
Fantasy contrasting civilization and problems of the world of children with those in world of men. 1 act 6m 2b 2g extras 1 exterior
In Kamerman, S. E. ed. Blue-ribbon plays for graduation
Margaret, Queen of Denmark, Norway and Sweden. See Margrete, Queen of Denmark, Norway and Sweden
Margaret Fleming. Herne, J. A.
Margrete, Queen of Denmark, Norway and Sweden
Kielland, T. Queen Margaret of Norway
Maria Magdalena. Hebbel, F.
Marie Antoinette, consort of Louis XVI, King of France
Spamer, C. Marie Antoinette
Marie Antoinette. Spamer, C.
Mark Antony. See Antonius, Marcus
Mark Twain. See Twain, Mark
Mark Twain's A double barrelled detective story. St Clair, R.
Marketing (Home economics)
c Spamer, C. The store
Marko goes a courtin'. Gross, E. and Gross, N.
Marloe, Christopher. See Marlowe, Christopher
Marlowe, Christopher
Edward the Second
Elizabethan historical tragedy. Murder of King Edward II in 13th century England. Verse play. 5 acts 24 scenes 26m 2w extras 8 interiors 11 exteriors
In Marlowe, C. Five plays
In Morrell, J. M. ed. Four English tragedies
The Jew of Malta
Elizabethan historical tragedy. Disintegration of character of avaricious Jew who sacrificed his only daughter in attempted revenge against Christian enemies. Verse play. 5 acts 23 scenes 16m 6w extras 5 interiors 7 exteriors
In Marlowe, C. Five plays

Lust's dominion
Partially written by Thomas Dekker Seventeenth century tragedy in verse. The love affair between Eugenia, Queen Mother of Spain and Eleazar, Prince of Barbary. 5 acts 16 scenes 19m 3w extras 1 setting
In Dekker, T. The dramatic works of Thomas Dekker v4
Tamburlaine the Great; part I
Elizabethan historical tragedy. Career of Timur the Great, 14th century conqueror of Asia from his first military conquest to his marriage. Verse play. 5 acts 17 scenes 21m 4w extras 1 setting
In Marlowe, C. Five plays
Tamburlaine the Great; part II
Elizabethan historical tragedy. Completes life story of Timur the Great; Part I, entered above. Verse play. 5 acts 19 scenes 25m 2w extras 1 setting
In Marlowe, C. Five plays
The tragedy of Doctor Faustus. Washington Sq. Press 1959 li, 78p illus (A Folger Library General reader's ed)
Elizabethan tragedy. Faust legend about man who sold his soul to the Devil. Verse play. 1 act 15 scenes 28m 3w extras 6 interiors 4 exteriors
Same as: The tragical history of Doctor Faustus
The tragical history of Doctor Faustus
Same as: The tragedy of Doctor Faustus
In Downer, A. S. ed. The art of the play
In Griffin, A. V. Living theatre
In Marlowe, C. Five plays
See also Church, R. The prodigal
Marquis, Don
Archy and Mehitabel (dramatization) See Kleinsinger, G. Archy and Mehitabel
Marr Johnson, Diana
Never say die. [French's Acting ed] French (London) 1958 63p
Comedy. River House, social settlement in London's East End, is on verge of being closed when at a party, new benefactor is found after several lemonades spiked with gin. 3 acts 6m 5w 1 interior
Marriage
Anouilh, J. Ardèle
Apstein, T. Come share my house
Augier, E. Olympe's marriage
Barry, P. Paris bound
Cary, F. L. Live and let love
Casey, B. M. The guest at Cana
Chayefsky, P. The bachelor party
Chodorov, J. and Fields, J. Anniversary waltz
Coward, N. Fallen angels
Coward, N. Quadrille
Davis, O. and Davis, D. Ethan Frome
Dekker, T. Match me in London
Feydeau, G. Keep an eye on Amélie!
Fisk, D. M. The secondary wife
Foote, H. Flight
Gibson, W. Two for the seesaw
Goetz, R. and Goetz, A. The immoralist
Gray, D. Love affair
Greene, G. The living room
Hartog, J. de. The fourposter
Horne, K. Trial and error
Hutton, M. C. Silver wedding
Kanin, F. and Kanin, M. His and hers
Lantz, J. E. and Lantz, R. C. Marriage for love

Marriage—*Continued*

Lantz, J. E. and Lantz, R. C. Marriage—not legal

Lantz, J. E. and Lantz, R. C. Reluctantly yours

Lantz, J. E. and Lantz, R. C. Two too many

Lockwood, L. Autumn in the air

Martin, D. Simply heavenly

Maugham, W. S. The constant wife

Moody, W. V. The Great Divide

Morrison, D. Mirage

O'Hara, F. Try! Try!

Olfson, L. The taming of the shrew

O'Neill, E. "Servitude"

Parker, D. Here we are

Perl, A. Tevya and his daughters

Rattigan, T. The Browning version

Reach, J. Open house

Richards, S. Tunnel of Love

Rosten, H. The happy housewife

Roussin, A. The little hut

Shaw, B. Candida

Shaw, B. Getting married

Shulman, M. and Smith, R. P. The tender trap

Stevens, L. The marriage-go-round

Strindberg, A. Creditors

Synge, J. M. The tinker's wedding

Tilford, H. Miss Dill from Dippyville

Turgenev, I. The bachelor

Williams, T. Baby Doll

Williams, T. Period of adjustment

   See also Courtship; Divorce; Family; Husband and wife; Love

Marriage for love. Lantz, J. E. and Lantz, R. C.

The **marriage**-go-round. Stevens, L.

Marriage law

Tolstoy, L. Redemption

Marriage—not legal. Lantz, J. E. and Lantz, R. C.

A **marriage** proposal. Chekhov, A.

Marriage proposals

Musset, A. de. A door should be either open or shut

Spencer, H. Priscilla and John

Waldau, R. S. A cabin by the lake

Marriages, Mixed

Brown, L. Stolen waters

Mars calling! Woolsey, J. and Sechrist, E. H.

Marsaili's weeping. Bottomley, G.

Marseilles, France

Rome, H. J. Fanny

Marshall, Catherine

A man called Peter (dramatization) See McGreevey, J. A man called Peter

Marshall, Peter

McGreevey, J. A man called Peter

Marston, John

And a song was born. French 1953 23p
   How Franz Xaver Gruber came to write the music for Christmas carol "Silent night." 1 act 6m 4w 1 interior

Marston, Millicent A.

A Christmas carol
   Christmas. Pantomime of Longfellow's paraphrase of a carol from the Old French, with choral music. Large mixed cast no setting
   In Marston, M. A. Mimes with crowds

c Goblin market
   Pantomime of Christina Rossetti's poem about young woman who brought fruit from the goblins for one of her golden curls. 1m 2w extras no setting
   In Marston, M. A. Mimes with crowds

c The jackdaw of Rheims
   Pantomime of Richard Barham's poem about the Cardinal of Rheims' pet crow who stole his master's ring. 5m 6b extras 1 setting
   In Marston, M. A. Mimes with crowds

c The Pied Piper of Hamelin
   Pantomime of Browning's poem based on German legend about piper who freed Hamelin of its rats. Large mixed cast 1 setting
   In Marston, M. A. Mimes with crowds

c The riddling knight
   Pantomime. Adaptation of old English ballad, also known as "Riddles wisely expounded" telling how youngest of three sisters won knight for a husband by guessing his riddles. 1m 3w extras no setting
   In Marston, M. A. Mimes with crowds

c The robbers
   Pantomime. Adaptation of old poem about lady beset by robbers. 2m 1w extras no setting
   In Marston, M. A. Mimes with crowds

c The roving journeyman
   Pantomime. Adaptation of old ballad about mayor's daughter who fell in love with itinerant worker. 3m 7w no setting
   In Marston, M. A. Mimes with crowds

Martens, Anne Coulter

Battle of the budget. Bakers Plays 1954 28p
   Domestic comedy. When father refuses to raise adolescent children's allowances, they devise scheme to persuade him. 1 act 2 scenes 4m 4w 1 interior

c Be nice to the Easter bunny. Bakers Plays 1956 8p
   Easter Bunny and his helpers are shocked when they hear on radio program that two children don't believe in them. 1b 1g extras 1 interior

A bird in the bush
   Pantomime comedy. Escaped convict poses as bird watcher. 1 act 1m 5w 1 exterior
   In Martens, A. C. We're speechless

Christmas is too old-fashioned. Dramatic 1953 28p illus
   Posing as tired shopper, elderly woman helps promote nephew's romance with successful personal shopper. 1 act 7w 1g 1 interior

A cool Yule. Bakers Plays 1959 23p
   Young girl thinks that old-fashioned Christmases should be modernized. 1 act 7w 1g 1 interior

Cross your bridge
   Farcical pantomime. Lady tries to teach her friends contract bridge from mail order book. 5w 1 interior
   In Martens, A. C. We're speechless

A dance with our Miss Brooks. Dramatic 1954 82p illus
   Romantic comedy based on characters created by R. J. Mann. Pretty high school English teacher runs into trouble preparing for big dance of the year. 3 acts 6m 14w 1 interior

Do-it-yourself. Dramatic 1955 26p illus
   Domestic comedy. In family addicted to do-it-yourself projects older daughter, a hold out, is concerned with Senior Prom. 1 act 4m 5w 1 interior

Martens, Anne C.—*Continued*

Dr Hudson's secret journal. Dramatic 1956 77p illus
> Based on novel by Lloyd C. Douglas. Dr Hudson finds that a religious feeling often comes to him in crisis and awaits this feeling when daughter is involved in serious accident. 3 acts 5 scenes 6m 10w 1b 2g extras 1 interior

Drag race. Bakers Plays 1958 21p
> Group of teenagers is arrested for drag racing. 1 act 5m 4w 1 interior

The fantastic Mr C. Dramatic 1954 27p illus
> Comedy. Mr C. alias Santa Claus, reads book by famous psychologist on importance of debunking Christmas, and decides to quit. 1 act 7m 7w 1 interior

Fraidy cat. Dramatic 1953 62p illus
> Romantic comedy. At summer resort, shy young writer of murder mysteries saves girl he loves from two dangerous crooks. 3 acts 4m 7w extras 1 interior

Girl crazy (adaptation) See Bolton, G. and McGowan, J. Girl crazy

The grandma bandit. Bakers Plays 1960 23p (Baker's Royalty plays)
> Actress who thinks nothing ever happens in her small town is visited suddenly by old lady who is a bandit. 1 act 6w 1 interior

Hold your horsepower! Dramatic 1956 27p illus
> Safe driving. Several high school students discover what they have learned in driving course suddenly becomes matter of life or death. 1 act 9m 7w 2 interiors

Home for Christmas. Dramatic 1954 59p illus
> Based on novel by Lloyd C. Douglas. One sister brings widely scattered family home for what may be their mother's last Christmas. 2 acts 3m 7w extras 1 interior

Jimmy and the same old stuff. Bakers Plays 1956 8p
> Rebellious at having to rehearse for Thanksgiving pageant. Jimmy falls asleep and his dream shows him much to be thankful for. 2 scenes 1w 2b 3g extras 1 interior

c Little lost leprechaun. Bakers Plays 1957 12p
> Two children receive a little leprechaun for present on Saint Patrick's Day. 1w 2b 1g extras 1 interior

c The magic broom. Bakers Plays 1956 8p
> Little girl who wishes she could ride a broom on Halloween gets her chance. 1m 2w 4b 4g extras 1 interior

Mothers on strike. Bakers Plays 1956 6p
> To protest always doing chores on Mother's Day, mothers plan to go on strike, while children plan for different Mother's Day celebration. 1 scene 4w 2b 2g 1 interior

Nobody loves a fat boy. Bakers Plays 1956 27p
> Comedy. Overweight teen-ager must lose weight before Sophomore Hop in order to fit into suit. 1 act 4m 4w extras 1 interior

Now it can be told
> Farcical pantomime based on: Sleeping beauty. Modern young man wakens princess from hundred-year sleep. 2 scenes 4m 4w 1 interior
>
> *In* Martens, A. C. We're speechless

Once in a blue moon. Dramatic 1954 21p illus
> Romantic comedy. A threatening blue mass is approaching the moon while in radio station, broadcasters wait to learn its meaning. 1 act 5m 4w extras 1 interior

Pajama party. Dramatic 1955 25p illus
> Comedy. Alerted by police who are searching for Blue Light Burglar, girls at slumber party suspect stranger who claims to be a cousin. 1 act 10w 1 interior

People to people. Bakers Plays 1957 15p
> Satire on popular TV program. Guest reveals his real self not knowing that he is being televised. 1 act 2m 7w 1 interior

c Pictures in the fire. Bakers Plays 1956 7p
> Nine-year-old Abraham Lincoln and his mother see pictures of his future in the fire of fireplace. Background reading of Gettysburg address and music. 1m 1w 1b extras 1 interior

Pow wow. Bakers Plays 1955 23p
> Romantic comedy. Girl's younger sisters plot to get rid of her old boy friend because new one has a convertible and a swimming pool. 1 act 2m 7w 6b 1 interior

Quiet, please
> Pantomime. Young woman mistakes library of a hospital for the insane for public library. 8w 1 interior
>
> *In* Martens, A. C. We're speechless

Radiant morning. Dramatic 1956 23p illus
> Easter. The mother of Jesus and two other mothers who have lost sons meet accidentally. 1 act 1m 5w extras 1 exterior

The search for Wildcat McGillicuddy. Dramatic 1956 31p illus
> Comedy. Students explore the past of hypnotized Wildcat Willie until they reach Battle of Boyne in 1690 in Ireland. 1 act 5m 5w extras 1 interior

Shoot if you will
> Comedy. Two women hanging clothes outdoors misinterpret when they overhear two nature photographers talk about "shooting." 6w 1 exterior
>
> *In* Martens, A. C. We're speechless

Sing a song of something
> Comedy. Difficulties arise when Women's Social Club and Women's Singing Society meet in adjoining rooms. Background music. 17w extras 1 interior
>
> *In* Martens, A. C. We're speechless

Step lively, please. Dramatic 1953 26p illus
> Teenage comedy. Gail, aided by her friends, uses feminine guile to secure keys to family's car from competitive brother. 1 act 3m 4w 1 interior

Sugar and spite. Bakers Plays 1955 26p
> High-school girl who has always been first in everything suddenly has to cope with a threatening rival. 1 act 17w 1 interior

The three faces of Easter. Bakers Plays 1958 20p
> Teen-age girl sees that Easter has three meanings: festivities for children, fashion for adults and its true religious meaning. 1 act 3m 7w extras 1 interior

c The time machine. Bakers Plays 1957 10p
> For the grades. On the last day of school some children find time machine, and try to peer into future, but by mistake it goes into reverse. Large mixed cast 1 interior

c The tiniest Christmas tree. Bakers Plays 1956 10p
> On Christmas Eve the tiniest Christmas tree finds happiness in being selected for sick little girl. 2w 2b 2g extras 1 exterior

c A visit from Washington. Bakers Plays 1956 65p
> Pageant for Washington's Birthday using groups of marchers such as Cub Scouts. Two children explain to George Washington why we celebrate his birthday. 2b 1g 1 exterior

Martens, Anne C.—*Continued*

c Weather or not. Bakers Plays 1956 8p
  A boy and girl sneak into World Weather
  Bureau and push all the buttons, sending
  snow to African jungle and heat wave to
  Arctic. 5b 5g 1 interior

What's the matter with TV? Bakers
  Plays 1953 33p (Baker's Royalty plays)
  Comedy. Grandmother in family goes on
  strike against television because it has
  become so important that everybody is
  forgetting his manners. Then the
  championship fight comes on. 1 act 5m
  8w extras 1 interior

c Who sent the comic valentine? Bakers
  Plays 1956 8p
  Princess of the Land of Hearts is in
  tears because she received comic valentine. 5m 4w extras 1 interior

Who stole third base?
  Farcical pantomime of women's baseball
  game. 13w extras 1 exterior
  In Martens, A. C. We're speechless

Who's that knocking on my door? Bakers
  Plays 1954 38p (Baker's Royalty plays)
  A girl thinks she has ideal baby-sitting
  job until children refuse to go to bed, her
  boyfriend announces he has tickets for a
  play, and a strange woman arrives. 1 act
  2m 5w 1b 1g 1 interior

Witch Hazel. Dramatic 1955 28p
  Comedy. A girl buys a strange chair and
  ignores warning that its former owner
  was a witch. 1 act 8w 1 interior

c You are watching! Bakers Plays 1956 8p
  Television program pretends to interview
  Christopher Columbus before he sets off
  on what he thought was voyage to India.
  5m 2b 1g extras no scenery
  See also Dalzell, W. jt. auth.

Martens, G. M.
  The hopeful travellers (Les gueux au
  paradis) Adapted by André Obey and
  tr. by Iris Capell. Miller, J. G. 1953
  77p
  A fantasy about two Flemish rascals
  who are killed at Christmastime, escape
  from hell and try to bluff their way into
  heaven. 3 acts 4 scenes Large mixed cast
  4 interiors

Martha, Saint
  Ridge, A. Saint Martha and the Tarasque
  of Tarascon

Martha Washington. Spamer, C.

Martin, Bernice
  Eighteenth summer. French 1959 76p illus
  Molly and her friends wrestle with conflicting loyalties the summer that Molly's
  selfish, unprincipled cousin visits her.
  3 acts 6m 6w 1 exterior

Martin, David
  Simply heavenly; book and lyrics by
  Langston Hughes; music by David
  Martin. Dramatists 1959 87p
  Musical comedy set in Harlem. Based on
  Langston Hughes' novel "Simple takes
  a wife" about an ordinary Negro and
  his problems in getting married. 2 acts
  11m 8w 4 interiors 1 exterior

Martin, Édouard. See Labiche, E. jt. auth.

Marty. Chayefsky, P.

Martyrs
  Cruse, C. Son of Stephen

  Kirn, J. The cell

  Lagerkvist, P. Let man live

Marx, Marvin, and others
  The honeymooners; a letter to the boss
  Domestic comedy. Episode from television
  program "The honeymooners" starring
  Jackie Gleason. When a man is fired he
  writes nasty letter to ex-employer. 2m 1w
  In Settel, I. ed. Top TV shows of the
  year, 1954-55

Marxism. See Communism

Mary, Virgin
  Coventry plays. The parliament of heav-
  en: The Annunciation and Conception

  Lord, D. A. Joy for the world

  Mary Francis, Sister. Counted as mine

  Mary Francis, Sister. Smallest of all

  Annunciation
  Coventry plays. The Annunciation

  Coventry plays. The pageant of the Shearmen and Taylors—The Coventry Nativity play

  St Clair, R. The promised ones

c Spamer, C. M. Gabriel visits Mary

  Apparitions and miracles (Modern)
  Duffield, B. Christmas at Lourdes

Mary I, Queen of England
  Tennyson, A. Queen Mary

Mary Stuart, Queen of the Scots
  Anderson, M. Mary of Scotland

  Bottomley, G. The white widow

  Chiari, J. Mary Stuart

  Goldstone, J. S. and Reich, J. Mary Stuart

  Schiller, F. von. Mary Stuart

Mary Francis, Sister
  Christmas at Greccio. French 1959 30p
  St Francis of Assisi originates idea of
  Christmas Crib in thirteenth century.
  1 act 6m 2w 1g 1 exterior

  Counted as mine. French 1954 57p
  Mexico. 16th century. Dramatization of
  appearance of the Blessed Virgin to an
  Indian. 3 acts 6 scenes 10m 2w choir 1
  interior 2 exteriors

  La madre. French 1959 143p front music
  Episodes in life of St Teresa of Avila
  and her part in Carmelite reform movement. 3 acts 5 scenes 4m 8w 2 interiors

  Smallest of all. French 1958 80p illus
  Youth of Bernadette Soubirous when both
  priest and police for a time tried to make
  her admit that her vision of the Virgin
  was untrue. Set in Lourdes, France in
  1858. 3 acts 5 scenes 4m 4w extras
  1 interior 1 exterior

Mary Elizabeth's wonderful dream. Mason,
  M. E.

Mary Mapes Dodge. Spamer, C.

Mary of Scotland. Anderson, M.

Mary Stuart. Chiari, J.

Mary Stuart. Goldstone, J. S. and Reich, J.

Mary Stuart. Schiller, F. von

Mary's invitation. Miller, H. L.

Masks (Plays) See Masques

Masks and faces. Taylor, T. and Reade, C.

Mason, Jane
c "I'd be glad to"
  Parents and students finally take time
  out to tell busy teacher how much they
  appreciate her. 1m 5w 5b 6g extras
  1 interior
  In Birdsall, R. ed. Creative plays for
  every school month

Mason, Miriam E.
Mary Elizabeth's wonderful dream
    Two children, finding old copies of St
    Nicholas magazine, try to reconstruct life
    when Mary Mapes, an editor of magazine,
    was young girl. 1 act 2 scenes 2w 9g
    1 interior
In Kamerman, S. E. ed. Blue-ribbon
    plays for girls
Masquerade. Asbrand, K.
Masques
Dekker, T. and Ford, J. The Sun's darling
Massachusetts

    History—Colonial period
Schevill, J. The bloody tenet
The **massacre** of Paris. Lee, N.
Massacre of the Holy Innocents. See Holy
Innocents, Massacre of the
Massinger, Philip
The Roman actor
    Jacobean historical tragedy in verse.
    Reign of tyrant Domitian. Emperor of
    Rome and its effects, especially upon his
    wife and the actor she loved. Includes
    two plays within the play. 5 acts 11
    scenes 20m 5w extras 1 setting
In McIlwraith, A. K. ed. Five Stuart
    tragedies
Massinger, Philip, and Dekker, Thomas
The virgin martyr
    Seventeenth century English tragedy in
    verse. Martyrdom of Dorothea of Cappa-
    docia, later Saint Dorothea, during reign
    of Diocletian, Emperor of Rome. 5 acts
    12 scenes 16m 4w extras 1 setting
In Dekker, T. The dramatic works of
    Thomas Dekker v3
The **master** builder. Ibsen, H.
The **master** cat. Goulding, D. J.
Master Will. Totheroh, D.
Masteroff, Joe
The warm peninsula. French 1960 84p
    Comedy. Lives and loves of a plain girl
    and a beautiful girl who meet and be-
    come roommates in Miami Beach. 2 acts
    4m 3w 2 interiors
A **masterpiece** of diplomacy. Howells,
W. D.
Masters, Lillian. See Masters, R. jt. auth.
Masters, Robert, and Masters, Lillian
c The mystery of the ming tree. French
    1958 59p
    Dramatization of Chinese fairy tale.
    Wicked sorcerer forces Mandarin to
    send away his three daughters who must
    find three strange gifts before they can
    return. 2 acts 10m 3w no scenery
A **match** for the Devil. Nicholson, N.
Match me in London. Dekker, T.
The **matching** piece. Healy, J.
The **matchmaker.** Wilder, T.
Materialism
Miller, A. All my sons
O'Neill, E. The great God Brown
Maternal love. See Love, Maternal
Mathers, Anita
Flapper girls. French 1955 32p illus
    Comedy. When girl is disappointed be-
    cause rival gets title "Miss Flapper Girl
    of 1927", younger sister goes into action.
    1 act 8w 1 interior
Mathews, Basil
Forward through the ages (dramatization)
    See Kromer, H. They made a path

Mathews, June
c Audubon's America
    Scenes from life of John James Audubon
    and his work in gathering information
    about birds of America. 3 scenes 8m 1w
    2b 2g 3 interiors
In Birdsall, R. ed. Creative plays for
    every school month
Matilda. Avery, I.
The **mating** season. See Adler, M. D. Too
much springtime
Matrimony. See Marriage
Matson, Lowell. See Cordell, R. A. jt. ed.
Matsukaze (condensation) Kwanze, K.
A **matter** of record. Morrison, D.
The **matter** with Mildred. Stephens, C. G.
Matthew, Saint, Apostle
Hollinshead, L. M. Publican and sinner
Matthews, Elizabeth
c Mr Blanchard—Easter bunny
    Orphans decide to give up annual trip
    to city in order to buy Easter baskets
    for littlest children in their orphanage.
    3 scenes 1m 1w 5b 4g 2 interiors
In Birdsall, R. ed. Creative plays for
    every school month
c On to seventh grade!
    Boys and girls graduating from elemen-
    tary school tell what they have learned
    in first six years of school. 7b 6g 1 in-
    terior
In Birdsall, R. ed. Creative plays for
    every school month
c Teddy's own Santa
    Children plan Christmas surprise for poor
    little boy. 3 acts 1m 1w 4b 2g 2 interiors
In Birdsall, R. ed. Creative plays for
    every school month
Mattice, Imogene
c A bomb for Santa
    Christmas. One of elves in Santa's work-
    shop is angry because he doesn't get
    more time off. Includes songs and musical
    scores. 9 characters, extras 1 interior
In Birdsall, R. ed. Creative plays for
    every school month
Mattson, Jean M.
I saw the cross
    Easter play. Reactions of Judas, Peter,
    Caiaphas, Pilate, Roman soldiers and
    others to Passion and Resurrection of
    Jesus Christ. Background music 5 scenes
    17m 5w extras 3 interiors 2 exteriors
In Brings, L. M. comp. The golden
    book of church plays

A Sunday school Christmas program.
    Eldridge 1954 10p (Eldridge Christmas
    entertainments)
    Traditional story of the Nativity as well
    as present day ideas about Christmas.
    9m 7w 1b 1g choir 4 interiors 1 exterior
Maudie and the opposite sex. Sergel, K.
Mauermann, W. Gordon
A cup of kindness. Row 1953 32p
    Comedy. Bookseller contrives to give
    vauable book, sought by greedy custom-
    ers, to his needy friend's daughter. 1 act
    3m 3w 1 interior

Just us girls. Art Craft 1953 29p illus
    Widow's prospective second marriage
    proves to be chief item discussed at
    meeting of Garden Club's social com-
    mittee. 1 act 4w 1 interior

Maugham, W. Somerset
The circle
Drawing room comedy. English country life. Two triangles involving people who do not learn from sad example. 3 acts 4m 3w 1 interior
In Kronenberger, L. ed. Cavalcade of comedy
In A Treasury of the theatre
The constant wife
Clever wife outwits solicitous friends and philandering husband when she challenges single moral standard. 3 acts 4m 5w 1 interior
In Warnock, R. Representative modern plays, British
Maugham, William Somerset. See Maugham, W. Somerset
Maurette, Marcelle
Anastasia. English adaptation by Guy Bolton. [Acting ed] French 1956 99p illus
Syndicate trains young girl to impersonate murdered daughter of last Russian emperor in order to collect dead Tsar's fortune. 3 acts 7m 5w 2 interiors
Trade edition published by Random House
—Same
In Plays of the year v9
Anastasia. (condensation)
In Theatre, 1955
Mauriac, François
Asmodée. French 1957 92p illus music
Emotional conflict among members of aristocratic French family brought on by arrival of young English student. 3 acts 5 scenes 5m 4w 1 interior
Maxwell, Mary Elizabeth (Braddon) See Hazelwood, C. H.
May Day
c Hastings, M. L. C. A May Day pageant
c Henry, V. May Day in the woods
c Miller, H. L. May Day for mother
c Woolsey, J. and Sechrist, E. H. Charlie's May basket
May Day for mother. Miller, H. L.
May Day in the woods. Henry, V.
A **May** Day pageant. Hastings, M. L. C.
The **May** fairies. Spamer, C.
May the best man win. Fisher, A. and Rabe, O.
Maybe Tuesday. Tolkin, M. and Kallen, L.
Mayer, Edwin Justus
Children of darkness
Comedy. Originally titled "Jailor's Wench." Based in part on last 24 hours of life before his execution of Jonathan Wild, highwayman. 3 acts 7m 1w extras 1 interior
In Kronenberger, L. ed. Cavalcade of comedy
The **Mayerling** affair. Delderfield, R. F.
The **Mayflower.** Very, A.
The **mayor.** Howard, V.
The **Mayor** of Torontal. Jones, G.
Me and Juliet. Rodgers, R.
"Me, Candido!" Anderson, W.
The **meaning** of Christmas Day. Heicher, M.
A **medal** for Julien. Kocher, E.
Medea. Anouilh, J.
The **Medea.** Euripides

Medea. Grillparzer, F.
Medical ethics
Shaw, B. The doctor's dilemma
Medical missions. See Missions, Medical
Medical profession. See Physicians
Medical research
Burlingame, C. Yellow fever
Medicine
O'Casey, S. Hall of healing
See also Pharmacy
Medicine, Patent, proprietory, etc.
Green, P. Quare medicine
Medieval drama. See Drama, Medieval
Mediums
Coward, N. Blithe spirit
Meet a body. Launder, F. and Gilliat, S.
Meet Father Time. Jackson, M. R.
Meet George. Brooks, P.
Meet me at the prom. Reach, J.
Meet Mr Callaghan. Verner, G.
Meet Mr Witch. Hark, M. and McQueen, N.
The **melancholy** princess. Taylor, F.
Melanos, Jack A.
c Rapunzel and the witch. Childrens Theatre 1957 53p music
German folk tale about Rapunzel, whose long golden hair enabled prince to rescue her from tower in which she was held prisoner by witch. Songs and background music 3 acts 5 scenes 2m 3w extras 2 exteriors
Melodrama
Abstance, P. and Abstance, L. Murder at the manor
Abstance, P. and Abstance, L. The valiant Valentine
Addis, H. Drama
Anderson, R. A. and Sweeney, R. L. True blue and trusted
Bell, A. Egad, what a cad!
Coppel, A. The gazebo
Dekker, T. Match me in London
Forsythe, A. No mother to guide her
Goodhue, N. Little Nell, the orphan girl
Gould, J. R. Steps from beyond
Green, J. Gently does it
c Hark, M. and McQueen, N. Not fit for man or beast
Hazelwood, C. H. Lady Audley's secret
Howard, V. The big melodrama
Howells, W. D. Saved
Howells, W. D. A true hero
Jerrold, D. Black-ey'd Susan
Last, J. Mr Mason
Launder, F. and Gilliat, S. Meet a body
Moody, W. V. The Great Divide
Roos, A. and Roos, W. Speaking of murder
Sherwood, R. E. The petrified forest
Stevenson, B. E. A King in Babylon
Taggart, T. Deadwood Dick
Tomkins, B. No, no, a million times no!
Tyson, A. Millie, the beautiful working girl
Melody for Lincoln. Miller, H. L.
The **melon** thief. Sakanishi, S. tr.

Melville, Alan
Dear Charles
Social comedy adapted from "Les enfants d'Edouard," by Marc-Gilbert Sauvajon and Frederick Jackson. Three grown children of unwed French authoress insist that she choose one of their fathers as husband. 3 acts 7m 5w 1 interior

In Plays of the year v8
Mrs Willie. [French's Acting ed] French London 1957 72p illus
Farce. Balkan queen in exile maneuvers to claim throne for son. 3 acts 6m 5w 1 interior
Simon and Laura
Domestic comedy. Quarreling husband and wife acting team become stars of television program about happily married couple. 3 acts 8m 5w 1b 1 interior

In Plays of the year v11

Melville, Herman
Billy Budd (dramatization) See Coxe, L. O. and Chapman, R. Billy Budd

Melvyn, Glenn
The love match. [French's Acting ed] French (London) 1957 74p illus
Farce. English railroad engineer and his enthusiasm for football. 3 acts 5m 3w 1 interior

The **member** of the wedding. McCullers, C.

Memorial Day
Asbrand, K. It's time for remembering
Miller, H. L. The judge's diary
Miller, H. L. Lacey's last garland
Miller, H. L. The pink parasol
c Miller, H. L. The teddy bear hero
c Newman, D. Memorial Day for the Blue and Gray
Olson, E. E. The honored ones
c Spamer, C. Andy's gun
c Wilcox, E. M. We caught the torch
Memorial Day for the Blue and Gray. Newman, D.

Memory
Beckett, S. Krapp's last tape
A **memory** of two Mondays. Miller, A.

Men
Brown, A. M. Ah, men!

Menander
The arbitration
Greek classical drama. The extant portion of domestic comedy based on a man's suspicions that wife has been unfaithful. 5 acts 6m 3w 1 exterior

In Casson, L. ed. Masters of ancient comedy
The bad-tempered man; or, The misanthrope; tr. by Philip Vellacott. Oxford 1960 50p
Same as The grouch, and The misanthrope. Greek classical comedy about old grouch who hates everybody, and a young Athenian man-about-town who wants to marry grouch's daughter. 5 scenes 10m 2w extras 1 exterior
The grouch
Same as: The bad-tempered man; The misanthrope

In Casson, L. ed. Masters of ancient comedy
She who was shorn
Nearly complete fragment of Greek classical comedy. Tangled love affairs of twins who as foundlings were reared, one by a rich, and the other, by poor woman. 5 acts 5m 3w 1 exterior

In Casson, L. ed. Masters of ancient comedy

Mencken, Henry Louis
Sloane, A. Bring on the angels

Menelaus
Euripides. The Trojan women

Mennonites
Blankman, H. By hex
Hague, A. Plain and fancy

Menotti, Gian Carlo
The Saint of Bleecker Street (condensation)

In Theatre, 1955

Mental illness
Carney, F. The righteous are bold
Gelber, J. The connection
Parker, K. The surrounding mist
Parkhirst, D. Early frost
Tobias, J. Coddled Egbert
Williams, T. Hello from Bertha
Williams, T. Suddenly last summer
Wishengrad, M. The rope dancers

Mental philosophy. See Philosophy

Merchant marine

Great Britain
O'Neill, E. In the zone

The **merchant** of Yonkers. See Wilder, T. The matchmaker

Merchant ships. See Merchant marine

Mermaid Avenue is the world. Goldman, P.

Mermaids
Addis, H. The fishermen's dream
Blackmore, P. Mad about men

Merrill, Bob
New girl in town; a new musical (based on the play Anna Christie, by Eugene O'Neill; book by George Abbott; music and lyrics by Bob Merrill. Random House 1958 146p illus
Musical comedy. New York waterfront at turn of the century. 2 acts 16m 13w extras

Merrill, James
The bait
Love affair involving people so introspective that they do not understand each other at all. Verse play. 4m 1w 1 exterior

In Machiz, H. ed. Artists' Theatre: four plays
The immortal husband
Fantasy based on Greek myth of Tithonus and Aurora, who persuaded Zeus to give her lover immortality but failed to ask for eternal youth. 8m 9w 1 interior 2 exteriors

In Playbook: five plays for a new theatre

The **Merry** Christmas elf. Fisher, A.

Merry-go-round. Schnitzler, A.

The **merry** matchmaker. Lisle, V.

Merry Tyll. Jagendorf, M.

The **merry** widow. Lehar, F.

The **message.** Howard, V.

A **message** from John. Spence, W.

Message from Mars. Larson, V. and Magary, F. A.

A **message** from Thankful
Two little girls hear story of a brave little pioneer girl. 1 act 1w 4g 1 interior

In 'Round the year plays for the grades

The message of Christmas. Jorgenson, E. S.

Messenger, Philip. See Massinger, Philip

Messiah
Prophecies
Day, P. F. Simeon, the faithful servant
Estes, S. In quest of power through prophecy

Meteorology
c Spamer, C. The weather man
See also Weather

A **Mexican** holiday. Woolsey, J. and Sechrist, E. H.

Mexicans in the United States
Broughton, J. Summer fury

Mexico
Apstein, T. The beams of our house
Cannan, D. and Bost, P. The power and the glory
Fisher, A. and Rabe, O. The story of a well
Nash, N. R. Handful of fire
Stevens, L. Bullfight
History—1910-1946
Niggli, J. The ring of General Macías
Social life and customs
c McGee, A. Bill visits Mexico
c Woolsey, J. and Sechrist, E. H. A Mexican holiday

Mice
Howells, W. D. The mouse trap
c Spamer, C. The mouse and the moon

Michel, Marc Antoine Amédée. See Marc-Michel

Michener, James A.
Tales of the South Pacific (dramatization) See Rodgers, R. and Hammerstein, O. South Pacific

Middle age
Cox, P. Myself when young
Lynch, P. The teen age party
Mosel, T. Ernie Barger is fifty
Priestley, J. B. Private rooms
Spigelgass, L. A majority of one
Vining, D. The one that got away
The middle-class gentleman. Molière, J. B. P.

Middle classes
Great Britain
Ionesco, E. The bald soprano
Osborne, J. Look back in anger

Middle English dialect. See Dialect—English—Middle English

Middle of nowhere. Brenner, M.

Middle of the night. Chayefsky, P.

Middleton, Thomas. See Dekker, T. jt. auth.

Middleton, Thomas, and Dekker, Thomas
The Roaring Girl; or, Moll Cut-Purse
Seventeenth century English romantic comedy in verse, set in early 17th century England. Mary Firth, alias Moll Cut-Purse, knowledgeable London woman, dressed as man and armed, helps young couple get married despite parental opposition. 5 acts 11 scenes 19m 2w 4 interiors 1 exterior
In Dekker, T. The dramatic works of Thomas Dekker v3

Middleton, Thomas, and Rowley, William
The changeling; ed. by N. W. Bawcutt. Harvard Univ. Press 1958 140p (The Revels plays)
Jacobean psychological tragedy in verse. Because she loves another man, fickle young woman has her fiancé murdered by deformed servant who loves her. 5 acts 14 scenes 11m 3w extras 3 interiors

Midge rings the bell. Paradis, M. B.

Midnight burial. Hill, K.

The midnight caller. Foote, H.

A midnight ride. Wilcox, E. M.

The midnight ride of Tex O'Coco. Taggart, T.

Mid-summer. Delmar, V.

A midsummer night's dream. Olfson, L.

A midsummer night's scream. Henderson, J.

Midwestern dialect. See Dialect—Midwestern

Midwinter-Eve fire. Osgood, P. E.

A mighty man is he. Kober, A. and Oppenheimer, G.

Migrant labor
Foote, H. John Turner Davis
Steinbeck, J. Of mice and men

Migratory workers. See Migrant labor

Military life. See Soldiers; and subdivision Military life under armies; e.g., U.S. Army—Military life

Military service, Compulsory
Weiss, M. J. Greetings from . . .

The milkmaid and her pail. Joy, V.

Millar, Ronald
Waiting for Gillian
Young married couple reach better understanding of each other and of ethical values after wife's automobile accident. 3 acts 6 scenes 5m 4w 2 interiors
In Plays of the year, v10

Miller, Arthur
All my sons
Materialism of profiteering American arms manufacturer contrasted with idealism of soldier sons. 3 acts 5m 4w 1b 1 exterior
In Gaver, J. ed. Critics' choice
In Hewes, H. ed. Famous American plays of the 1940s
In Miller, A. Arthur Miller's Collected plays
The crucible. Dramatists 1953 95p
Story of trial for witchcraft in Salem, Massachusetts in 1692. 2 acts 5 scenes 11m 10w 4 interiors 1 exterior
Trade edition published by Viking
—Same
In Best American plays; 4th ser.
In Cooper, C. W. Preface to drama
In Miller, A. Arthur Miller's Collected plays
In Watson, E. B. ed. Contemporary drama: fifteen plays
The crucible (condensation)
In The Best plays of 1952-1953
In Theatre, 1953

Miller, Arthur—*Continued*

Death of a salesman
Mediocre salesman, after life of self-deception, realizes his failure and commits suicide to leave his family insurance money. 2 acts 8m 5w 1 setting

In Bierman, J.; Hart, J. and Johnson, S. eds. The dramatic experience

In Four modern plays

In Gaver, J. ed. Critics' choice

In Miller, A. Arthur Miller's Collected plays

In New voices in the American theatre

In A Treasury of the theatre

In Tucker, S. M. ed. Twenty-five modern plays

In Watson, E. B. and Pressey, B. eds. Contemporary drama: eleven plays

A memory of two Mondays. Dramatists 1956 51p
Workaday life in an auto parts warehouse. New York City in the 1930's. 1 act 12m 2w 1 interior

—Same

In Cerf, B. and Cartmell, V. H. eds. 24 favorite one-act plays

In Miller, A. Arthur Miller's Collected plays

In Miller, A. A view from the bridge; two one-act plays

A view from the bridge. Dramatists 1957 70p illus
Tragedy. An Italian, warped by jealous love for wife's niece, brings disaster upon himself and two illegal Italian immigrants hiding out in his Brooklyn home. 2 acts 12m 3w 1 setting

—Same

In Best American plays; 4th ser.

In Miller, A. Arthur Miller's Collected plays

In Miller, A. A view from the bridge; two one-act plays

A view from the bridge (condensation)

In The Best plays of 1955-1956

Miller, Clara Hooker

Back to Bethlehem. Eldridge 1955 17p (Eldridge Christmas entertainments)
Christmas Nativity play. Grandmother helps wandering family find interest and time for Christmas. 4 acts 6m 4w extras chorus 1 interior 1 tableau

Miller, Clifford L.

Wings over dark waters. Great-Concord Publishers 1954 270p
Documents contributions of and events in history of Negro people in United States since colonial times. 5 parts 57 scenes Large mixed cast 6 interiors 15 exteriors

Miller, Grace, and Livingston, Shirley

c A march of dimes
Eighteen dimes tell people why they should support the March of Dimes program. 18 characters no scenery

In Birdsall, R. ed. Creative plays for every school month

Miller, Helen Louise

c The Bar-None Trading Post
Visit to trading post is opportunity for children to barter and use several kinds of money and credit. 1m 1w 6b 5g 1 interior

In Miller, H. L. Plays for living and learning

c The bashful bunny
Easter Bunny's son is too bashful to recite his poem at Easter Egg hunt. 1 act 1m 2w 2b 1g 1 exterior

In Miller, H. L. Gold medal plays for holidays

Be my "walentine"
German-American farm girl's father surprises her on Valentine's Day. 1 act 2 scenes 5m 5w 1 interior

In Miller, H. L. Prize plays for teenagers

Beany's private eye
Comedy. Two boys keep everyone upset with their amateur detective course. 1 act 6m 4w 1 interior

In Miller, H. L. Prize plays for teenagers

c The Birds' Christmas Carol
Adaptation of an episode in story by Kate Douglas Wiggin. Little invalid girl celebrates Christmas. 1 act 4 scenes 2m 4w 3b 1g extras chorus 3 interiors

In Miller, H. L. Gold medal plays for holidays

c Boys in books
Boy characters from several books dramatize incidents. 14b 1 interior

In Miller, H. L. Plays for living and learning

c The Bread and Butter Shop
Granny shows how children all over the world have something in common because they all eat bread. 1m 1w 11b 9g extras 1 interior

In Miller, H. L. Plays for living and learning

c The broken broomstick
Halloween. With help of her friends, little witch gets new broom. 14 characters extras 1 exterior

In Miller, H. L. First plays for children

c Bunnies and bonnets
Easter Bunny comes to television studio to distribute Easter eggs to performers. 1 act 1m 5w 5b 4g extras 1 interior

In Miller, H. L. Gold medal plays for holidays

c The busy barbers
Barbers show boys and girls how they cut hair. Large mixed cast 1 interior

In Miller, H. L. First plays for children

c The case of the balky bike
Mysterious bicycle in police station remains unclaimed. No one can ride it until Bicycle Safety Squad shows up. 3m 8b 3g 1 interior

In Miller, H. L. Plays for living and learning

The Christmas oboe
Comedy. Beany, an amateur detective, picks wrong suspects when he tries to locate missing oboe on Christmas Eve. 1 act 5m 2w 1 interior

In Miller, H. L. Prize plays for teenagers

c The Christmas runaways
When two children run away at Christmastime from their uncle and aunt, they meet other runaways. 1 act 1w 4b 1g 1 interior

In Miller, H. L. Gold medal plays for holidays

c The Christmas umbrella
Santa's elves discover that by mistake Santa took box of old umbrellas instead of box of toys to children on Christmas Eve. 1 act 2 scenes 2m 3w 5b 4g extras 1 interior

In Miller, H. L. Gold medal plays for holidays

Miller, Helen L.—*Continued*

The coming of the Prince
Radio adaptation of story by Eugene Field.
On Christmas Eve, the Prince whose
coming is forgotten by busy world, is
found in forest by poor little girl. Background music including carols and hymns.
9m 3w 5b 6g chorus extras
In Burack, A. S. ed. Four-star radio
plays for teen-agers

c The country store cat
Children playing store, help nearsighted
cat catch a mouse. Includes songs. 14b
6g extras 1 interior
In Miller, H. L. First plays for children

Crosspatch and Cupid
Crosspatch wants to make boys and girls
bad, but Cupid tries to make them good.
1 act 1w 5b 5g extras 1 interior
In Miller, H. L. Gold medal plays for
holidays

c The curious quest
Girl's father points out to her and her
friends some of duties and responsibilities
of citizens in a democracy. 1m 5b 3g
1 interior
In Miller, H. L. Plays for living and
learning

c Dolly saves the day
Little girl and her doll save some important papers from destruction during
American Revolution. 1 act 3m 1w 1b
1g 1 exterior
In Miller, H. L. Gold medal plays for
holidays

c A February failure
Abraham Lincoln's formula for persever-
ance impresses boy who feels he is not
doing well in school. 1w 1b extras 1 interior
In Miller, H. L. Plays for living and
learning

February frenzy
German exchange student learns about
Americans when they celebrate birthdays
of Washington and Lincoln. 1 act 4m
4w extras 1 interior
In Miller, H. L. Prize plays for teen-
agers

c The forgotten hero
On Veterans Day children discover that
school janitor was hero in the war. 1m
1w 4b 4g 1 interior
In Miller, H. L. Gold medal plays for
holidays

c Garden hold-up
Farmers teach young gardeners how to
deal with animal and insect pests. 2
scenes 5m 6b extras 1 exterior
In Miller, H. L. First plays for children

c Girls in books
Girl characters from several books dramatize incidents. 13g 1 interior
In Miller, H. L. Plays for living and
learning

c The greedy goblin
Boys set a trap for goblin who keeps
stealing all the pumpkin pies. 1 act 2m
1w 3b 2g 1 interior
In Miller, H. L. Gold medal plays for
holidays

c The half-pint cowboy
In old West, small cowboy averts an
Indian attack by befriending Indian
chief's son. 22m 1b 1 exterior
In Miller, H. L. First plays for children

The haunted clothesline
On Halloween a boy and girl are able to
reconcile their feuding families with
help of friendly ghost. 1 act 4m 3w 1 exterior
In Miller, H. L. Prize plays for teen-
agers

Heart throbs
By mistake a teenager mixes comic
valentines with her mother's club an-
nouncements. 1 act 2 scenes 1m 15w
2 interiors
In Miller, H. L. Prize plays for teen-
agers

c Hello, Mr Groundhog
Children learn about weather and weather flags while waiting for groundhog
to come out of his hole. 15b 15g 1 exterior
In Miller, H. L. Plays for living and
learning

A hero's homecoming
Disillusioned war veteran finds he can
be of greatest use in his community by
becoming a teacher. 1 act 3m 5w 1 interior
In Miller, H. L. Prize plays for teen-
agers

A hooky holiday
Comedy. Because the whole family took
day off from their various jobs, their
teenage son has no witness to prove he
didn't play hooky from school. 1 act 5m
5w 1 interior
In Miller, H. L. Prize plays for teen-
agers

I'll eat my hat!
Teacher has to eat his hat when his
class makes the honor roll in the state
Lincoln Tests. 1 act 2 scenes 6m 4w
extras 1 interior
In Miller, H. L. Prize plays for teen-
agers

c It's a problem
Health principles concerning cleanliness,
good nutrition, and rest. 7b 8g 1 interior
In Miller, H. L. Plays for living and
learning

c Jimmy Cinders
Little cowboy's wicked step brothers,
who are cattle rustlers, refuse to take
him to rodeo. 1 act 7m 1b 1 interior
In Burack, A. S. ed. Four-star plays for
boys

The judge's diary
Teen-agers who are preparing Civil War
exhibit for Memorial Day decide that
war isn't "romantic" when they read
soldier's diary. 1 act 3m 4w 2b 1g 1 interior
In Miller, H. L. Prize plays for teen-
agers

Jump for George
A girl who is considered thoughtless
by her fellow students, shows true merit
on Washington's Birthday. 1 act 6m
11w extras 1 interior
In Miller, H. L. Prize plays for teen-
agers

Just what the doctor ordered
Shy girl surprises everyone when she
goes to a party with the football team.
1 act 14m 3w 1 interior
In Miller, H. L. Prize plays for teen-
agers

Lacey's last garland
Little southern girl teaches family a
lesson when she puts flowers on graves
of northern soldiers on Memorial Day.
1 act 1m 2w 1b 3g 1 interior
In Miller, H. L. Gold medal plays for
holidays

Miller, Helen L.—*Continued*

The left-over reindeer
Man who doesn't like Christmas refuses to let his children read story of Saint Nicholas. 1 act 5m 3w 4b 3g 1 interior
In Miller, H. L. Prize plays for teen-agers

c The library circus
Book Week. Animals of Bookland step out of their books to present a circus for children. Background music. 7m extras 1 interior
In Miller, H. L. First plays for children

The Lincoln cupboard
Young man inspired by Lincoln's ideals exposes fraudulent antique dealer. 1 act 4m 2w 1 interior
In Miller, H. L. Prize plays for teen-agers

c A Lincoln museum
Students bring items to make a Lincoln museum and tell about the significance of each. 11b 10g 1 interior
In Miller, H. L. Plays for living and learning

Lorna Doone
Radio adaptation of novel by Richard Doddridge Blackmore. Romantic love story set in 17th century England. Lorna, held captive by the outlaw Doones, is rescued by John Ridd, an honest farmer. Background music. 8m 3w 1g extras
In Burack, A. S. ed. Four-star radio plays for teen-agers

c The lost Christmas cards
Postman tells school children how to prepare Christmas cards properly for mailing. Includes songs. 2 scenes 1m 6b 6g extras 1 interior 1 exterior
In Miller, H. L. First plays for children

The magic carpet sweeper
Children discover new kind of present for their mother on Mother's Day. 1 act 1w 3b 2g 1 interior
In Miller, H. L. Gold medal plays for holidays

c Mary's invitation
One little girl's friend doesn't want to visit school during Education Week because he isn't a parent. 1 act 2 scenes 2m 3w 1b 3g chorus 1 exterior
In Miller, H. L. Gold medal plays for holidays

c May Day for mother
Mother's Day. Little girl chosen Queen of the May wants honor conferred on her mother. Includes songs and a Maypole dance. 8m 7w 2b 3g extras 1 exterior
In Miller, H. L. First plays for children

c Melody for Lincoln
Little girl is sad when her teacher wants her to play the piano at Lincoln Festival, rather than be in the play. 1 act 1m 2w 1b 4g 1 interior
In Miller, H. L. Gold medal plays for holidays

c The miraculous tea party
Little girl discovers that books can be interesting friends. 1 act 2w 7b 6g 1 exterior
In Miller, H. L. Gold medal plays for holidays

c Mr Snow White's Thanksgiving
By Thanksgiving Day the family's turkey has become a pet and nobody wants to eat him. 1 act 2m 2w 1b 2g 1 interior
In Miller, H. L. Gold medal plays for holidays

Mother for mayor
When busy mother runs for mayor, complications develop in lives of her children. 1 act 4m 3w 1g 1 interior
In Miller, H. L. Prize plays for teen-agers

c The Mother Goose bakeshop
Mother Goose characters help their bakers remember who ordered a birthday cake. 5m 4w 2b 1g extras 1 interior
In Miller, H. L. First plays for children

c Mother's fairy godmother
Several children discover that their mother has a fairy godmother. 1 act 2w 2b 2g 1 interior
In Miller, H. L. Gold medal plays for holidays

c Mystery at Knob Creek Farm
On a visit to Lincoln's farm in Kentucky, children talk to a boy who seems to be young Abe Lincoln. 1 act 6b 5g 1 exterior
In Miller, H. L. Gold medal plays for holidays

c The mystery of turkey-lurkey
Family's Thanksgiving turkey runs away. Partially in verse with songs and rhythm instruments. 1 act 1m 2b 2g extras chorus 1 exterior
In Miller, H. L. Gold medal plays for holidays

"N" for nuisance
Comedy. Teen-ager Saralee thinks kid brothers are usually nuisances but hers is sometimes very useful. 1 act 3m 3w 1 interior
In Miller, H. L. Prize plays for teen-agers

c New shoes
Sixth grade graduation program with pantomime. At shoe store children are shown all shoes they have worn in the past and will wear in the future. 1 act 2m 1b 1g extras
In Kamerman, S. E. ed. Blue-ribbon plays for graduation
In Miller, H. L. Plays for living and learning

c Not for girls
Mr Wizard helps Dora do practical arithmetic and overcome anti-mathematics feeling. 3m 1w 1b 4g 1 interior
In Miller, H. L. Plays for living and learning

c Old Glory grows up
How American flag added a star for each new state admitted to the Union after original thirteen. Choral singing. 3m 1w 1b 1g extras, choir 1 setting
In Miller, H. L. First plays for children

c The Patriotic Teddy Bear and the UN
Teddy Bear and other toys learn about United Nations. 1 act 1m 6b 3g 1 interior
In Miller, H. L. Plays for living and learning

c Paul Revere rides again
History class studying Paul Revere decides to see what modern coverage of that day via radio and television would be like. 4 scenes 11m 2w 6b 7g 4 interiors
In Miller, H. L. Plays for living and learning

c The Petrified Prince
To revive the Petrified Prince, his subjects are required to write and speak correctly. 7b 7g 1 interior
In Miller, H. L. Plays for living and learning

Miller, Helen L.—*Continued*

c The teddy bear hero
> For his heroism in a recent war, a teddy bear is honored at the Teddy Bears' Memorial Day picnic. 1m 3b 3g 1 exterior

In Miller, H. L. First plays for children

c Ten pennies for Lincoln
> Lincoln's birthday. Prospective members of Lincoln Club tell how they earned ten pennies required for admission. 13b 8g 1 interior

In Miller, H. L. First plays for children

c Thankful's red beads
> Just before Thanksgiving Day a Puritan family in New England is saved from an Indian attack. 6m 2w 1b 1g 1 interior

In Miller, H. L. First plays for children

c Thanks to butter-fingers
> When two girls set table for Thanksgiving they find diamond inside a family heirloom. 1 act 2m 1w 2g 1 interior

In Miller, H. L. Gold medal plays for holidays

c A Thanksgiving riddle
> School children act out answers to riddles about what the Puritans did on Thanksgiving Day. 1w 5b 5g 1 interior

In Miller, H. L. First plays for children

Three cheers for mother
> When teen-agers offer to baby sit for all the neighborhood mothers, they get more than they bargained for. 1 act 2m 4w 4b 3g 1 interior

In Miller, H. L. Prize plays for teenagers

c Three little kittens
> Based on nursery rhyme: Three little kittens who lost their mittens. 1m 1b 1g extras no setting

In Miller, H. L. First plays for children

c A travel game
> Children play travel game naming various modes of travel throughout the world. 1m 15b 15g 1 interior

In Miller, H. L. Plays for living and learning

The tree of hearts
> Royal gardener develops special tree for prince's birthday on Valentine's Day. 2 scenes 5m 3w extras 1 exterior

In Miller, H. L. Gold medal plays for holidays

c Trouble in Tick-Tock Town
> Town council takes wrist watch from little boy who was causing trouble by his inability to tell time. 10m 1b extras 1 interior

In Miller, H. L. First plays for children

Turkey turns the tables
> Three teen-agers amass strange evidence against their misunderstood foreign houseguest. 1 act 2m 2w 1 interior

In Miller, H. L. Prize plays for teenagers

c Turning the tables
> Children in a library are bored with books when suddenly many famous book characters come to life and tell of their exploits. 1 act 1w 15b 8g 1 interior

In Miller, H. L. Gold medal plays for holidays

The vanishing Easter egg
> Three teenagers feel too grown up for chocolate eggs at Easter. 1 act 4m 4w 1 interior

In Miller, H. L. Prize plays for teenagers

c Vicky gets the vote
> During school election some children realize their responsibility in voting. 1 act 2m 3w 6b 4g 1 interior

In Miller, H. L. Gold medal plays for holidays

c A visit to Goldilocks
> Based on English folktale: Goldilocks and the three bears. The bears visit Goldilocks and find that she has learned to be polite. 2 scenes 1m 1w 1g extras 1 interior 1 exterior

In Miller, H. L. First plays for children

c Visitor to Mount Vernon
> Patriotic Teddy Bear visits Mount Vernon and is found asleep in George Washington's bed. 2 scenes 3m 1w 2b extras 1 interior 1 exterior

In Miller, H. L. Plays for living and learning

c Wait and see
> On her birthday the Wait-and-See Fairies show little girl how to overcome her impatience. Includes songs. 1m 1w 3b 4g extras 1 interior

In Miller, H. L. First plays for children

c Wake up, Santa Claus!
> When Santa Claus oversleeps on Christmas Eve, two Eskimo children finally rouse him. 3m 1w 1b 1g extras 1 interior

In Miller, H. L. First plays for children

The Washington shilling
> Modern boy learns valuable lesson from George Washington. 1 act 3 scenes 2m 1w 3b 5g extras 1 interior 1 exterior

In Miller, H. L. Gold medal plays for holidays

c Washington's leading lady
> Children try to decide which of the women in George Washington's life was most important. 1 act 2m 10w 3b 4g 1 interior

In Miller, H. L. Gold medal plays for holidays

c The weatherman on trial
> City children who put the weatherman on trial for spoiling their fun, learn about value of both rain and sunshine. Includes songs. 5m 1w 1g extras 1 interior

In Miller, H. L. First plays for children

What makes it tick?
> Principal and staff of a high school convince discontented students not to drop out of school. 1 act 5m 3w 1 interior

In Miller, H. L. Prize plays for teenagers

c Who's who at the zoo
> On trip to the zoo, class learns about animals from South America. 1m 8b 9g 1 exterior

In Miller, H. L. Plays for living and learning

c The wishing stream
> Four Chinese children make a wish at magic stream but only the unselfish wish of little sister is granted. 2 acts 5m 1w 1b 3g 1 setting

In Miller, H. L. First plays for children

Miller, Herman A.
A penny for Charon. French 1954 102p
illus
> Comedy. Gem cutter who can no longer
> find work because of his advancing age
> decides to steal. 3 acts 7m 2w 1 in-
> terior

Miller, J. P.
The rabbit trap
> After years of subordination office em-
> ployee finds the courage to stand up for
> his rights. 6m 2w

In Vidal, G. ed. Best television plays

Miller, Jean, Sister. See Ingebretson, A.
Sister, jt. auth.

Miller, Lee, and Miller, Lynde
'Sno haven. Banner 1953 96p illus
> Mystery. Guests stranded during snow-
> storm at winter resort hotel attempt to
> identify foreign saboteur in their midst.
> 3 acts 4 scenes 8m 11w 1 interior

Miller, Lynde. See Miller, Lee, jt. auth.

Miller, Madge
Alice in Wonderland. Childrens Theatre
1953 44p illus
> Fantasy adapted from Lewis Carroll's
> story. Alice finds the culprit who stole
> the Queen's tarts. Songs and dances.
> 2 parts 7 scenes 5m 2w 4b 2g 2 interiors
> 3 exteriors

c Pinocchio
> Puppet play based on fairy tale by Carl
> Collodi. The adventures of the talking
> wooden puppet, whose nose grew longer
> every time he told a lie. 2 parts 8 scenes
> 8 characters 3 interiors 3 exteriors

In Miller, M. Miniature plays

c The princess and the swineherd. Childrens Theatre 1956 48p music
> Comic version of fairy tale about the
> princess who had to learn true values
> from a swineherd. Singing and dancing
> with background music. 3 acts 4 scenes
> 2m 6w 1 interior 1 exterior

c Puss in boots
> Based on fairy tale by Charles Perrault.
> Clever cat wins both fortune and a royal
> bride for poor miller's son. 4 scenes 3m
> 2w 1b 1 interior 2 exteriors

In Miller, M. Miniature plays

c Robinson Crusoe
> Based on novel by Daniel Defoe. Crusoe,
> English castaway on desert island res-
> cues and domesticates a native. 2 parts
> 5m extras 2 exteriors

In Miller, M. Miniature plays

c Snow White and Rose Red
> Based on fairy tale by Brothers Grimm.
> Two peasant sisters befriend a bear and
> a fish near their home, thereby releasing
> two princes from evil enchantment.
> 2 parts 5 scenes 3m 3w 1 interior 1 ex-
> terior

In Miller, M. Miniature plays

Miller, Sigmund
One bright day
> Conscience versus business among the
> people of powerful drug company or-
> ganization. 3 acts 5 scenes 11m 4w 2
> interiors

In Plays of the year v14

Miller, William Burke
Shaw, D. Rescue

The **miller,** his son, and their ass. Moore,
S. S.

Millet, Martha
Dangerous Jack. Sierra Press 1953 78p
illus
> Philosophic verse play. A skeptic and in-
> dependent thinker wanders the range of
> time and place. 10 scenes Large mixed
> cast 3 interiors 7 exteriors

Millie, the beautiful working girl. Tyson, A.

Million-dollar maybe. Kesler, H. O.

Million dollar recipe. Howard, V.

The **millionairess.** Shaw, B.

Mills, Hugh
The house by the lake
> English psychiatrist tries murder by
> hypnosis on his wife, a former mental
> patient after she discovers an earlier
> homicide. 3 acts 4 scenes 4m 5w 1 in-
> terior

In Plays of the year, v14

The little glass clock
> Social comedy set in 17th century France.
> Beautiful bride of French army officer
> cleverly evades amorous attentions of the
> king. 3 acts 11m 2w 1 interior

In Plays of the year v11

Mills, Osbert
Goose in the kitchen. Deane 1956 20p
("Deane's" Ser. of plays)
> Comedy. Neighbors lay aside their fem-
> inist principles to help young bride who
> can't cook. 1 act 5w 1 interior

In the soot. Deane 1956 20p ("Deane's"
Ser. of plays)
> Comedy. While sweeping chimney for
> new tenant, a man discovers mysterious
> chest which he thinks contains treasure.
> 1 act 4m 3w 1 interior

Milne, A. A.
The Red House mystery (dramatization)
See Sergel, R. A. A. Milne's The Red
House mystery

The ugly duckling
> Their Royal Highnesses erroneously think
> their subterfuge has married off a plain
> daughter. 1 act 4m 3w 1 interior

In Cerf, B. and Cartmell, V. H. eds. 24
favorite one-act plays

c Winnie-the-Pooh. Dramatic 1957 62p illus
> Based on stories of A. A. Milne about
> Winnie-the-Pooh, a little bear, all his
> animal friends, and their adventures.
> 3 acts 13 characters 1 exterior

Mime. See Pantomimes

The **mind** of a killer. Kirkpatrick, J.

Mind your P's and Q's. Hark, M. and
McQueen, N.

Mindel, Joseph
Freeing the land
> Radio play. After observing poverty of
> French farmers and laborers, due chiefly
> to land tenure laws, Thomas Jefferson
> fought to abolish similar evils in Virginia
> laws. 8m 1w extras

In Jeffersonian Heritage (Radio program) The Jefferson heritage

To secure these rights
> Radio play. Thomas Jefferson shows how
> disunity of states under the Articles of
> the Confederation proved need for strong
> central government. Background music.
> 4m 1w extras

In Jeffersonian Heritage (Radio program) The Jefferson heritage

The **mind's** construction. McLaughlin,
M. L.

Mines and mining
Brenner, M. The wait
O'Neill, E. "A wife for a life"

The **Ming** thing. McMahon, B.

Ministers of the gospel. See Clergy

Minstrels. See Negro minstrels

Miracle at Blaise. Niggli, J.

Miracle at midnight. Fleming, T.

The miracle at Nain. Wareham, R. C.

Miracle at Potter's farm. Lindsay, K. and Lindsay, R. H.

Miracle from heaven. Dimondstein, B.

The miracle maker. Asbrand, K.

A miracle of Saint Antony. Maeterlinck, M.

The miracle of the Danube. Anderson, M.

Miracle of the Madonna. St Clair, R.

Miracle-plays. See Mysteries and miracle-plays

The miracle worker. Gibson, W.

Miracles
Agg, H. The happy day
Hazeltine, A. I. Madelon
c Ilian, C. A Christmas miracle
McGreevey, J. Out of the darkness
Mary Francis, Sister. Smallest of all
Morris, T. B. The nine days
Ridge, A. The legend of Saint Basil
St Clair, R. Miracle of the Madonna
Smith, W. S. The answer
Stockton, R. F. A fabulous tale
Synge, J. M. The well of the saints
Wilde, P. Legend
    See also Jesus Christ—Miracles

The miraculous tea party. Miller, H. L.

Mirage. Morrison, D.

Mirage. Thomas, T. C.

The mirror children. Spamer, C.

Mirrors
c Spamer, C. The mirror children

Misalliance. Shaw, B.

The misanthrope. Malleson, M.

The misanthrope. Molière, J. B. P.

The misanthrope. See Menander. The bad-tempered man; The grouch

Miscarriage of justice. See Judicial error

Miscegenation
Corrie, J. Colour bar
Green, P. In Abraham's bosom

The miser. Molière, J. B. P.

Misers
Molière, J. B. P. The miser
Olfson, L. Silas Marner
    See also Avarice

Mishima, Yukio
The damask drum; tr. by Donald Keene
    Modern Japanese tragedy based on Nō play: Aya no tsuzumi, by Motokiyo Kwanze. Elderly janitor falls in love with heartless young woman who leads him to believe she will love him if he beats a damask drum loudly enough for her to hear. 5m 3w 1 setting
    In Mishima, Y. Five modern Nō plays
Hanjo; tr. by Donald Keene
    Modern Japanese drama based on Nō play: Hanako, by Motokiyo Kwanze. Insane girl waits for man who abandoned her but does not recognize him when he comes. 1m 2w 1 interior
    In Mishima, Y. Five modern Nō plays
Kantan; tr. by Donald Keene
    Modern Japanese play based on Nō play. Traveler sleeps on magic pillow and dreams of a life as successful business-man. Includes dances. 2m 3w extras 1 interior
    In Mishima, Y. Five modern Nō plays

The Lady Aoi; tr. by Donald Keene
    Modern Japanese drama based on Nō play: Awoi no uye, by Zenchiku Ujnobu Komparu. Fantasy. Jealous woman tries to separate erstwhile lover from his sick wife by casting a spell of memory over him. 1m 3w 1 setting
    In Mishima, Y. Five modern Nō plays
Sotoba Komachi; tr. by Donald Keene
    Modern Japanese drama based on Nō play by Kiyotsugu Kwanze. In a park, old woman meets vagabond poet who sees her as she was when a young belle. 2m 1w extras 1 interior
    In Mishima, Y. Five modern Nō plays

Miss Dill from Dippyville. Tilford, H.

Miss Harper's birthday. Phillips, T. J.

Miss Julie. Strindberg, A.

Miss Lonelyhearts. Teichmann, H.

Miss Matty in mischief. Simpson, H.

Miss Matty in society. Simpson, H.

Miss Muffet's lunch. Spamer, C.

Miss President, please! Greth, Le R. E.

Miss Pringle plays Portia. Maddern, V. and Banks, L. R.

Miss Robin Crusoe. Greth, Le R. E.

Miss Senior High. Hark, M. and McQueen, N.

The missing formula. Waugh, J. R.

Missionaries
Casey, B. M. The hand of God
Emmons, D. G. Answering the call
McCarty, R. K. Blake's decision
Wilson, D. C. The return of Chandra

Missions
Casey, B. M. The lamp in the night
Casey, B. M. The land afar
Ingebretson, A. Sister; Miller, J. Sister, and Roberts, M. Sister. The living Saviour
Simpson, G. H. A time for love

California
Helm, M. Fray Junípero Serra

China
Arnold, H. G. Sam Pollard
Sumerau, D. L. Make His name glorious

India
Wilson, D. C. The return of Chandra

Missions, Medical
Carruthers, J. Physician in charge
India
Wilson, D. C. The return of Chandra

Mississippi River
DuBois, G. Huckleberry Finn

Mistaken identity
Murphy, A. The old maid
Winer, E. Three hours between planes

Mr Arcularis. Aiken, C.

Mr Blanchard—Easter bunny. Matthews, E.

Mr Bunch's toys. Goulding, D. J.

Mr Do and Mr Don't. Fisher, A.

Mr Dumbtaro. Sakanishi, S. tr.

Mr Gaylord remembers. Roberts, C.

Mister Gultz. Dimondstein, B.

Mr Jefferson's Burr. Raiden, E.

Mister Johnson. Rosten, N.

Mr Lincoln's beard. Newman, D.

Mr Mason. Last, J.

Mr Mergenthwirker's lobblies. Bond, N.

Mr Owl. Hesketh, J.

Mister Peepers. Hayes, M. and Hayes, J.

Mr Pickwick. Young, S.

Mr Popper's penguins. Wright, L.

Mr Sly-One and the cats. Blyton, E.

Mr Snow White's Thanksgiving. Miller, H. L.

Mr Sweeney's conversion. Lindsey, H. C.

Mrs Adams and Eve. Gattey, C. N. and Bramley-Moore, Z.

Mistress Betsy and the flag. Larkin, E.

Mrs Gibbons' boys. Glickman, W. and Stein, J.

Mrs Griggs loses her bed. Gattey, C. N. and Bramley-Moore, Z.

Mrs McThing. Chase, M.

Mrs Parker's portrait. Coolidge, J. T.

Mrs Santa proves a point. Austin, C. L.

Mrs Warren's profession. Shaw, G. B.

Mrs Wickens in the fall. Kneale, N.

Mrs Willie. Melville, A.

The misunderstanding. Camus, A.

Mitchell, B. E. and Rose, Le Roma
Mountain gal. Heuer 1953 72p
Comedy. In a hillbilly family, woman berates poor orphan servant girl until some tourists from the North want to take her to live with them. 3 acts 5m 5w 2 interiors

Mitchell, L. Frances
c Music! Music! Everywhere!
Music Week. Two children tell about folk-songs and dances they saw in Europe as two others explain American folk-songs and dances. 10m 2w 2b 2g extras 1 interior
In Birdsall, R. ed. Creative plays for every school month

Mitchell, Langdon
The New York idea
Social comedy. The effects of divorce laws upon a group of people; their respect for social values. 4 acts 4 scenes 9m 6w 3 interiors
In Quinn, A. H. ed. Representative American plays

Mittelhölzer, Edgar
Shadows move among them (dramatization) See Hart, M. The climate of Eden

Mitzman, Newt. See Dalzell, W. jt. auth.

Mitzman, Newt, and Dalzell, William
Books and crooks. Dramatic 1953 81p
Comedy. Pair of crooks enter school, tie up the principal; one of them impersonates him and runs the school for a while. 3 acts 7m 5w extras 2 interiors
In 25 words—or death. French 1955 96p
Mystery comedy. Winners in contest receive as reward an old-fashioned Thanksgiving in New England lodge, where they find some sinister happenings. 3 acts 4m 6w 1 interior

Mix-up-atosis. Rees, P.

Miyamasu
Eboshi-ori
Japanese Nō verse drama. Using his family's charm-sword, Ushiwaka, young nobleman who has taken service with some traveling merchants, kills Kumasaka, notorious brigand. 7m 1w extras 1 setting
In Waley, A. The Nō plays of Japan
Mai-guruma: The dance waggons (condensation)
In Waley, A. The Nō plays of Japan

Miyoshi, Shōraku. See Takeda, I. jt. auth.

Mizer, Jean
Golden slippers. Art Craft 1953 22p illus
Fantasy. Woman who has become a cold tyrannical executive because her fiance was killed in World War II is visited by his ghost. 1 act 1m 3w 1 interior

Mobs
Rose, R. Thunder on Sycamore Street
Rose, R. Tragedy in a temporary town

The mock doctor. Boyd, A. K.

Mock trial. Grafton, E. and Grafton, S.

Mock trials
Grafton, E. and Grafton, S. Mock trial
Rose, R. The remarkable incident at Carson Corners
Yaffe, J. The deadly game

The modern bridge. Li, Y. M.

A modern Christmas carol. Baughman, R. K.

Modern civilization. See Civilization, Modern

Modernist-fundamentalist controversy
Lawrence, J. and Lee, R. E. Inherit the wind

Molière, Jean Baptiste Poquelin
Coxcombs in petticoats (Les précieuses ridicules) English version by George Graveley
Comedy. Satire on pretentiousness in 17th century Paris society. Music and dancing. 1 act 8m 3w 1 interior
Same as: The precious damsels; The pretentious ladies
In Molière, J. B. P. The miser, and Coxcombs in petticoats
In Molière, J. B. P. Six prose comedies
The critique of The school for wives (La critique de L'école des femmes) tr. by Morris Bishop
Comedy. A study of "The school for wives" in which Molière explains his purpose and methods and defends the play, through its characters, against its critics. Set in Paris in the 17th century. 5m 2w 1 interior
In Molière, J. B. P. Eight plays
Don Juan; or, The statue at the feast (Don Juan; ou, Le festin de Pierre) tr. by John Wood
Based on Spanish legend of Don Juan, a profligate nobleman who is finally carried off to hell by supernatural means of statue of the man whom he had killed in a duel after seducing man's daughter. 5 acts 6 scenes 14m 3w extras 2 interiors 3 exteriors
Same as: Don Juan: or, The stone guest
In Molière, J. B. P. Don Juan, and Forced to be a doctor
In Molière, J. B. P. Six prose comedies

Molière, Jean B. P.—*Continued*

Don Juan; or, The stone guest (Don Juan; ou Le festin de Pierre) English version by George Graveley
Same as: Don Juan; or, The statue at the feast
In Molière, J. B. P. Five plays

Forced to be a doctor ¡Le médecin malgré lui¡ English version by George Graveley
Satirical farce. Woodcutter posing as a doctor achieves success. Set in 17th century France. 3 acts 8m 3w 1 interior 2 exteriors
Same as: The physician in spite of himself; The reluctant doctor
In Molière, J. B. P. Don Juan, and Forced to be a doctor

The imaginary invalid; new English version by Miles Malleson
Satirical comedy set in 17th century Paris. Hypochondriac wants to marry his daughter to a doctor in order to get free medical care. Music, songs, dancing. 3 acts 8m 4w extras 1 interior
Same as: The would-be invalid
In Molière, J. B. P. The slave of truth; Tartuffe; The imaginary invalid
In Plays of the year v19

The learned ladies (Les femmes savantes) tr. and introduction by Renée Waldinger. Barrons Educ. Ser. 1957 87p
A satire on education of women. Set in 17th century Paris. 5 acts 28 scenes 8m 5w 1 interior

Love's the best doctor (L'amour médecin) tr. by John Wood
Romantic comedy. Satire on medical profession in 17th century Paris. Singing and dancing. 3 scenes 11m 4w extras 1 interior
In Molière, J. B. P. Five plays

La malade imaginaire (adaptation) See Jackson, B. Doctor's delight

The middle-class gentleman (Le bourgeois gentilhomme) translation and introduction by Herma Briffault. Barrons Educ. Ser. 1957 111p
Satirical comedy. 17th century French parvenue has himself tutored in the ways of Parisian society. Singing and ballet. 5 acts 34 scenes 14m 4w extras 1 interior
Same as: The self-made gentleman; The would-be gentleman

The misanthrope; tr. and introduction by Bernard D. N. Grebanier. Barrons Educ. Ser. 1959 76p
Comedy of manners. Satire on 17th century Parisian society. 5 acts 29 scenes 8m 3w 1 interior
Same as: The slave of truth
—Same; comedy in five acts, 1666, done into English verse by Richard Wilbur. Drawings by Enrico Arno. Harcourt 1955 140p illus
—Same; tr. by Morris Bishop
In Molière, J. B. P. Eight plays
also in Griffith, A. V. Living theatre

The misanthrope (adaptation) See Malleson, M. The misanthrope

The miser (L'avare) English version by George Graveley
Comedy satirizing miserliness. Set in 17th century Paris. 5 acts 11m 4w 1 interior
In Molière, J. B. P. Six prose comedies
—Same; tr. by John Wood

In Molière, J. B. P. Five plays
In Molière, J. B. P. The miser, and Coxcombs in petticoats

The physician in spite of himself (Le médecin malgré lui) tr. by Morris Bishop
Same as: Forced to be a doctor: The reluctant doctor
In Molière, J. B. P. Eight plays

The precious damsels (Les prècieuses ridicules) tr. by Morris Bishop
Same as: Coxcombs in petticoats; The pretentious young ladies
In Molière, J. B. P. Eight plays

The pretentious young ladies <Les précieuses ridicules> translation and introduction by Herma Briffault. Barrons Educ. Ser. 1959 38p
Same as: Coxcombs in petticoats; The precious damsels

The reluctant doctor (Le médecin malgré lui) English version by George Graveley
Same as: Forced to be a doctor; The physician in spite of himself
In Molière, J. B. P. Six prose comedies

The ridiculous précieuses
Same as: Coxcombs in petticoats; The precious damsels; The pretentious young ladies
In Cooper, C. W. Preface to drama

Scapin the scamp (Les fourberies de Scapin) English version by George Graveley
Romantic farce set in 17th century Naples. Rogue Scapin tricks two wealthy, avaricious fathers into financing their children's marriages. 3 acts 9m 3w 1 exterior
Same as: That scoundrel Scapin
In Molière, J. B. P. Six prose comedies

The school for wives (L'école des femmes) tr. by Morris Bishop
Romantic comedy. Aged guardian versus young man as suitors of young woman. Set in 17th century France. 5 acts 37 scenes 7m 2w 1 exterior
In Molière, J. B. P. Eight plays
—Same; free version by Miles Malleson
In Plays of the year v10

The self-made gentleman (Le bourgeois gentilhomme) English version by George Graveley
Same as: The middle-class gentleman; The would-be gentleman
In Molière, J. B. P. Six prose comedies

Sganarelle (adaptation) See Malleson, M. Sganarelle

The slave of truth (Le misanthrope) new English version by Miles Malleson
Same as: The misanthrope
In Molière, J. B. P. The slave of truth; Tartuffe; The imaginary invalid

Tartuffe, the hypocrite; translation and introduction by Renée Waldinger. Barrons Educ. Ser. 1959 97p
Satirical comedy. Religious hypocrisy. 17th century France. 5 acts 32 scenes 7m 5w 1 interior
—Same; tr. by Morris Bishop
In Molière, J. B. P. Eight plays
—Same; tr. by Robert Hartle
In Downer, A. S. ed. The art of the play

Molière, Jean B. P.—*Continued*
—Same; new English version by Miles
    Malleson
    In Molière, J. B. P. The slave of truth;
        Tartuffe; The imaginary invalid
That scoundrel Scapin (Les fourberies de
    Scapin) tr. by John Wood
    Same as: Scapin the scamp
    In Molière, J. B. P. Five plays
The Versailles impromptu (L'impromptu
    de Versailles) tr. by Morris Bishop
        Comedy. Molière's actors rehearse his
        latest play. Their rehearsal is his answer
        to his critics, an explanation of some
        of his dramatic techniques, and bur-
        lesque of some of leading actors of the
        day. Set in 17th century France. 10m
        6w no scenery
    In Molière, J. B. P. Eight plays
The would-be gentleman (Le bourgeois
    gentilhomme) tr. by Morris Bishop
        Same as: The middle-class gentleman:
        The self-made gentleman
    In Molière, J. B. P. Eight plays
—Same; tr. by John Wood
    In Molière, J. B. P. Five plays
The would-be invalid; tr. and ed. by
    Morris Bishop
        Same as: The imaginary invalid
    In Dean, L. F. ed. Nine great plays,
        1956 edition
Molloy, Lida Lisle
c The fortune of Merrylegs and Tawny-
    Whiskers
        When boy finds a piece of silver every-
        one tries to give him advice. 1 act 7m 1b
        extras 1 interior
    In Burack, A. S. ed. Four-star plays
        for boys
"**Molly** Pitcher." Fisher, A. and Rabe, O.
Molly Pitcher, heroine of Monmouth.
    Woolsey, J. and Sechrist, E. H.
Molnar, Ferenc
    Liliom; tr. from the Hungarian by Ben-
        jamin F. Glazer
        Fantasy. Liliom, erstwhile circus barker
        is allowed to return to earth for one
        day to do something good. 1 act 7 scenes
        18m 5w 2 interiors 3 exteriors
    In A Treasury of the theatre
    In Tucker, S. M. ed. Twenty-five mod-
        ern plays
    Liliom (adaptation) See Rodgers, R. and
        Hammerstein, O. Carousel
    The play's the thing; in the adaptation
        by P. G. Wodehouse
        Romantic comedy. Playwrights compose
        a drama. Play within a play. 3 acts 8m
        1w 1 interior
    In Gassner, J. ed. Twenty best Euro-
        pean plays on the American stage
    See also Chodorov, E. The spa
A **moment** of existence. Malcolm, I.
Mom's perfect day. Hark, M. and Mc-
    Queen, N.
Monarchs. See Kings and rulers
Monasticism and religious orders
    Schaefer, L. Song for a hero
Monasticism and religious orders for women
    Casey, M. A soul in fine array
    Mary Francis, Sister. La madre
        See also Convents and nunneries

Money
    Carter, B. The sermon
c Miller, H.L. The Bar-None Trading Post
    Waugh, J. R. The ebony box
        See also Wealth
Money. Bulwer-Lytton, E.
Money mad. Gordon, K.
Money raising. See Fund raising
Money talks. Weiss, M. J.
Monique. Blankfort, D. and Blankfort, M.
Monkeys
c Spamer, C. The laughed-at monkey
        See also Chimpanzees
Monks. See Monasticism and religious
    orders
Monmouth, Battle of, 1778
    Woolsey, J. and Sechrist, E. H. Molly
        Pitcher, heroine of Monmouth
Monsieur Beaucaire. Olfson, L.
Montana
    Finch, R. The return
A **month** in the country. Turgenev, I.
A **month** of Sundays. Savory, G.
Months
c Duggar, F. December's gifts
Mooar, Caroline H.
c Washington's Birthday
        Mother and her children talk about
        George Washington. 1 act 1w 5b 4g 1 in-
        terior
    In 'Round the year plays for the grades
Moody, William Vaughn
    The faith healer
        Faith healer, who is also a religious
        man, faces opposition from medical sci-
        ence. 3 act 3 scenes 6m 4w 1g extras
        1 interior
    In Quinn, A. H. ed. Representative
        American plays
    The Great Divide
        Melodrama. Contrast between cultured
        eastern heroine and wild, woolly west-
        erner. 3 acts 11m 3w 3 interiors
    In Downer, A. S. ed. American drama
Moon, Charlotte
    Sumerau, D. L. Make His name glorious
Moon
    Martens, A. C. Once in a blue moon
    Philp, P. Love and lunacy
c Spamer, C. The visit to the moon
The **moon.** Brabazon, F.
A **moon** for the misbegotten. O'Neill, E.
The **moon** in the Yellow River. Johnston, D.
The **moon** is blue. Herbert, F. H.
Moon of my delight. Edmunds, M.
The **moon** of the Caribbees. O'Neill, E.
Moon rocket. Tuson, N.
The **moon's** still yellow. McCarty, E. C.
Moore, Carroll. See Barasch, N. jt. auth.
Moore, Clement Clarke
    The Noël candle (dramatization) See
        Fuller, R. The Noël candle
    'Twas the night before Christmas (drama-
        tization) See Emurian, E. K. 'Twas the
        night before Christmas

Moore, Doris O.
c Christmas comes to Santa's workshop.
Eldridge 1959 19p (Eldridge Christmas
entertainments)
> Toys in Santa's workshop come to life
> just before Christmas. Large mixed cast
> 1 interior

Moore, Horace Grady
c Storybook Halloween
> Mother Goose characters are afraid of
> gobblins. 1 act 9 characters 1 exterior

In 'Round the year plays for the grades

Moore, Stephen S.
c The fox and the grapes
> Based on Aesop's fable, showing how
> people rationalize that what is out of
> reach is undesirable. 3b 2g extras 1
> setting

In Moore, S. S. Six playlets from
Aesop's fables
c The hare and the tortoise
> Based on Aesop's fable of how slow but
> steady tortoise won a race. 2 scenes 5
> characters extras 2 exteriors

In Moore, S. S. Six playlets from
Aesop's fables
c The lion and the mouse
> Based on Aesop's fable. Little mouse
> saves life of lion who had been merci-
> ful to him. 2 scenes 2b extras 2 exteriors

In Moore, S. S. Six playlets from
Aesop's fables
c The miller, his son, and their ass
> Based on Aesop's fable about the
> father and son who lost their donkey
> by trying to please everyone. 1 scene 4m
> 2b 3g extras 1 exterior

In Moore, S. S. Six playlets from
Aesop's fables
c The shepherd-boy and the wolf
> Based on Aesop's fable about boy who
> cried for help as a joke once too often.
> 1 scene 4m 1w extras 1 exterior

In Moore, S. S. Six playlets from
Aesop's fables
c The travellers and the bear
> Based on Aesop's fable about boy who
> ran away and left his friend in danger.
> 1 scene 2b extras 1 exterior

In Moore, S. S. Six playlets from
Aesop's fables

The **moral** play of Everyman. Everyman
Moralities
Cummings, E. E. Santa Claus
D'Alton, L. The Devil a saint would be
Lamphere, E. A. Crosses on the hill
Schloss, M. F. Totentanz
Sorell, W. Everyman today
Williams, C. Grab and grace
Williams, C. The house by the stable
Yeats, W. B. The hour-glass

Moralities, English
Dekker, T. If this be not a good play,
the Devil is in it
Everyman. Everyman
Everyman. The moral play of Everyman
Everyman. The summoning of Everyman
Johnston, R. A. Everyman

Morality plays. See Moralities; Moralities,
English

Morals. See Conduct of life
More blessed to give. Asbrand, K.
More room for love. Stephens, C. G.
More than meets the eye. Carmichael, F.

The **more** the merrier. Kauffmann, S.
Moreno, Ralph
A horse play. Hartmus Handpress 1960
91p illus
> Tragic comic fantasy on dreams. When
> couple falls asleep, their dreams take
> over the action. 2 parts 1m 1w extras
> 2 interiors 6 exteriors

Morgan, Charles
The burning glass. St Martins 1954 155p
> Problem of young English scientist who
> discovers new way to harness solar
> energy, which may be used for the
> benefit or destruction of mankind. 3 acts
> 4 scenes 6m 2w 1 interior

Morgan, Elaine
You're a long time dead
> Television play. Man who plans to mur-
> der his wife suddenly discovers that he
> must change his plans. 11m 10w

In British Broadcasting Corporation.
The television playwright

Morley, Olive J.
Little women
> Dramatization of episode from novel by
> Louisa May Alcott. Four March sisters
> celebrate Christmas in 1862 while their
> father is away fighting in Civil War.
> 1 act 9w 1 interior

In Kamerman, S. E. ed. Blue-ribbon
plays for girls

Mormons and Mormonism. See Nephites
Morning air. Heayes, N.
Morning of a private eye. Taggart, T.
Morning's at seven. Osborn, P.

Moross, Jerome
The golden apple; a musical play written
by John Latouche; the music composed
by Jerome Moross. Random House
1954 133p illus (A Random House
Play)
> Musical farce. Story of Helen of Troy
> transferred to State of Washington in
> 1900. 2 acts 4 scenes 19m 5w extras 1
> exterior

The golden apple (condensation)
In The Best plays of 1953-1954
In Theatre, 1954

Morrill, Katherine
A distant bell. French 1960 89p
> Effect of charming but mentally un-
> balanced woman upon her children.
> 3 acts 8 scenes 5m 8w 1 interior

A distant bell (condensation)
In Broadway's best, 1960

Morris, Colin
The unloved
> Television play. Headmaster of English
> school for maladjusted children succeeds
> in helping new pupil. 20m 5w

In British Broadcasting Corporation.
The television playwright

Morris, Edmund
The wooden dish. Dramatists 1956 69p
illus
> When an elderly man's daughter-in-law
> refuses to keep him any longer, tensions
> arise among his children as to where
> he should stay. 3 acts 4 scenes 6m 4w
> 1 interior

Morris, Florence Huntington
Reel George. French 1953 12p
> Farce. Doting mother shows moving pic-
> ture sequence starring her son, which
> unfortunately runs backwards. 1 act 2m
> 2w 1 interior

Morris, T. B.

The deserted house. French (London)
1953 81p illus
> During World War II in France, young
> people work for the Resistance and
> make their headquarters in a strange,
> deserted house. 3 acts 4 scenes 7m 4w
> 1g 1 interior

A garden in Verona. [Acting ed] French
(London) 1954 24p illus
> Creation of the character of Rosaline,
> mentioned but never seen in Shake-
> speare's Romeo and Juliet, and of Ju-
> liet's life before she met Romeo. 1 act
> 7w 1 exterior

The nine days. [French's Acting ed]
French (London) 1953 76p illus
> Comedy. Girl who has been life-long
> cripple is mysteriously cured in a fall,
> and various townspeople try to capital-
> ize on "miracle." 3 acts 4m 7w 1 in-
> terior

c The sleeping fires. [Acting ed] French
(London) 1953 23p illus
> Group of wealthy Roman children in
> first century Italy tries to console Chris-
> tian slave when her father is imprisoned
> for his faith. 1 act 6w 5g 1 interior

The watcher of the road. [French's Acting
ed] French 1954 22p illus
> Based on Old Testament story in the
> Book of Judges. Delilah feels remorse
> after betraying Samson, as she waits
> for news of him. 1 act 7w 1 interior

Morrison, David

A matter of record. Bakers Plays 1958 21p
(Baker's Royalty plays)
> Man murders his cousin for her for-
> tune only to find that her tape recorder
> has made recording of his voice. 1 act
> 3m 3w 1 interior

Mirage. Bakers Plays 1956 24p (Baker's
Royalty plays)
> Man framed and sent to prison by an-
> other who also steals his fiancee, seeks
> revenge years later; his hatred softens
> when he sees the shrew that the woman
> has become. 1 act 2m 2w 1 interior

Morse, Samuel Finley Breese

Blake, R. What hath God wrought

La mort de Pompée. Corneille, P.

Mortimer, John

Call me a liar
> Television play. Lonely clerk gets into
> habit of making up false stories about
> the family and social life he doesn't
> have. 7m 6w

In British Broadcasting Corporation.
The television playwright

The dock brief
> Comedy. Unsuccessful lawyer defends
> man who cheerfully admits killing his
> wife. 2 scenes 2m 1 interior

In Mortimer, J. Three plays

In Plays of the year v17

I spy
> Comedy. Detective on case to find The
> Other Man in woman's life falls in love
> with her. 3m 2w 1 setting

In Mortimer, J. Three plays

What shall we tell Caroline?
> Comedy. Middle aged teacher and wife
> decide they must tell eighteen-year-old
> daughter about "life." 2 scenes 2m 2w
> 1 interior

In Mortimer, J. Three plays

In Plays of the year v17

Morton, Edward

For heaven's sake. Epworth 1953 79p
> Romantic comedy. Young diamond
> smuggler reforms after staying with
> English minister's family and falling in
> love with host's daughter. 3 acts 4
> scenes 5m 4w 1 interior

Morton, John Maddison

Box and Cox
> Farce. Printer and hatter share same
> rented room and learn they have been
> engaged to same woman. 1 act 2m 1w
> 1 interior

In Smith, B. and others, eds. A treasury
of non-royalty one-act plays

Who stole the pocket-book (adaptation)
See Howells, W. D. The garroters

Morum, William. See Dinner, W. jt. auth.

Mosel, Tad

Ernie Barger is fifty
> Television play. A man who at fifty, is
> losing his success in business and affec-
> tion of his son, wonders how to sal-
> vage his life. 3 acts 7m 2w

In Mosel, T. Other people's houses

The five dollar bill
> Television play. Teen-age boy's rebel-
> lion against his father's lack of under-
> standing leads to sudden impulse to
> steal. 3m 2w

In Best television plays, 1957

The haven
> Television play. Country place which
> had always meant solace to a family,
> fails to help them out of domestic crisis.
> 3 acts 4m 1w 1g

In Mosel, T. Other people's houses

The lawn party
> Television play. Small town woman's
> great desire to hold a formal lawn party
> is achieved. 3 acts 2m 3w

In Mosel, T. Other people's houses

My lost saints
> Selfish mother's feigned illness poses
> problem for daughter who does not want
> to leave the family whose maid she has
> been for many years. 1m 4w

In Vidal, G. Best television plays

Other people's houses
> Television play. Old man who lives with
> his children is a problem to them. 3 acts
> 3m 2w

In Mosel, T. Other people's houses

The out-of-towners
> Television play. Strangers, man and
> woman, meet at convention hotel. 5m 2w

In Burack, A. S. ed. Television plays
for writers

The presence of the enemy
> Television play. Two non-conformists
> versus their "family." 3m 2w

In The Best short plays of 1957-1958

Star in the summer night
> Television play. Once glamorous and
> successful actress faces with courage
> and charm, a world which has turned
> against her. 3 acts 9m 4w

In Mosel, T. Other people's houses

The waiting place
> Television play. Misunderstanding be-
> tween father, teen-age daughter and po-
> tential step-mother. 3 acts 2m 3w 2 in-
> teriors

In Mosel, T. Other people's houses

Moses, the Patriarch

Fry, C. The firstborn

c Spamer, C. M. The baby Moses

c Spamer, C. M. The flight out of Egypt

Moses, Anna Mary (Robertson)

Applegarth, M. T. Home Sweet Home

Motokiyo, Zeami. See Kwanze, Motokiyo

Motomasa, Jūrō. See Kwanze, Motomasa Jūrō

Motor bus lines

Stations

Giblin, J. My bus is always late

Motor buses

McMahon, L. E. School bus romance

c Woolsey, J. and Sechrist, E. H. Let's travel by bus

Motoyasu, Zembō. See Komparu, Zempō

The mountain. Williams, N.

Mountain climbing. See Mountaineering

The mountain flock. Graveley, G.

Mountain gal. Mitchell, B. E. and Rose, Le R.

The Mountain giants. Pirandello, L.

Mountain whites (Southern States)

Abstance, P. and Abstance, L. Feudin' in the mountains

Dias, E. J. Feudin' fun

Green, P. Quare medicine

Hughes, E. W. The wishful taw

Koch, F. Wash Carver's mouse trap

Mitchell, B. E. and Rose, Le R. Mountain gal

Rose, Le R. Headin' for a weddin'

St Clair, R. Caught in a web

Schweikert, C. P. Hessie of the hills

Schweikert, C. P. Hoax of Hogan's Holler

Shelby, K. and Cuny, T. M. Giving goes on

Vollmer, L. Sun-up

Dialect

See Dialect—Mountain whites (Southern States)

Mountaineering

Auden, W. H. and Isherwood, G. The ascent of F6

Mountains

c Spamer, C. Inside the earth

Mourning before morning. Fearheiley, D. M.

The mourning bride. Congreve, W.

A mouse! A mouse! Bate, S.

The mouse and the moon. Spamer, C.

The mouse trap. Howells, W. D.

Movements of animals. See Animal locomotion

"The movie man." O'Neill, E.

Moving-picture industry

Roberts, M. A palm tree in a rose garden

Moving-picture plays

Bergman, I. Four screenplays (4 plays)

Bergman, I. The magician

Bergman, I. The seventh seal

Bergman, I. Smiles of a summer night

Bergman, I. Wild strawberries

Gassner, J. and Nichols, D. eds. Great film plays (6 plays)

Herald, R.; Herczeg, G. and Raine, N. R. The life of Emile Zola

Nichols, D. Stagecoach

Riskin, R. It happened one night

Schulberg, B. A face in the crowd

Sherwood, R. E. and Harrison, J. Rebecca

Thomas, D. The doctor and the devils

Totheroh, D. and Benét, S. V. All that money can buy

Williams, T. Baby Doll

Moving-pictures

Axelrod, G. Will success spoil Rock Hunter?

Beloin, E. and Garson, H. In any language

Kerr, W. and Kerr, J. Goldilocks

Morris, F. H. Reel George

Nathan, R. The sleeping beauty

O'Neill, E. "The movie man"

Stevenson, B. E. A King in Babylon

Taggart, T. The gross story conference

Mowatt, Anna Cora (Ogden) See Ritchie, A. C. M.

Much ado about nothing. Olfson, L.

The mulberry bush. Wilson, A.

Mum's the word. Pierce, C. W.

Munk, Kaj

Egelykke; tr. from the Danish by Llewellyn Jones

Youthful infatuation of Nikolai Grundtvig for a married woman. 5 acts 4m 4w 1b 3 interiors 2 exteriors

In Modern Scandinavian plays

Murch, Edward

Spring flowers for Marguerite. Deane 1954 20p ("Deane's" Ser. of plays)

Mother and her son's godmother view with different eyes prospective visit of the son's widow. Set in England. 1 act 4w 1 interior

The thin red line. Deane 1954 30p front ("Deane's" Ser. of plays)

Romantic comedy. During the Napoleonic Wars a young girl hides an escaped French Army captain. Set in England in 1815. 1 act 3m 3w 1 interior

Murder

Addyman, E. The secret tent

Anderson, M. Bad seed

Anouilh, J. The ermine

Armer, A. and Grauman, W. E. In darkened rooms

Armer, A. and Grauman, W. E. One year after

Assinder, P. The paying guest

Atkinson, A. Four winds

Banks, L. R. The killer dies twice

Batson, G. Design for murder

Batson, G. House on the cliff

Beaumont, F. and Fletcher, J. The maid's tragedy

Brenner, M. The roof

Brown, L. This year—next year

Büchner, G. Woyzeck

Camus, A. The just assassins

Camus, A. The misunderstanding

Carmichael, F. The night is my enemy

Carmichael, F. The pen is deadlier

Cary, F. L. Murder out of tune

Cary, F. L. Pitfall

Cary, F. L. and Butler, I. The paper chain

Christie, A. Towards zero

Christie, D. and Christie, C. The touch of fear

Coppel, A. The gazebo

Murder—*Continued*

Davies, R. No escape
Donisthorpe, G. S. Fruit of the tree
Fairchild, W. The sound of murder
Garis, R. The Inn
Gilbert, M. A clean kill
Green, J. Gently does it
Green, J. Murder mistaken
Kanin, F. and Kanin, M. Rashomon
Knott, F. Dial "M" for murder
Last, J. Make it murder
LePelley, G. Absolutely murder
Levin, M. Compulsion
Lewis, E. A screw loose
Lewis, L. The bells
Mackie, P. The whole truth
Mills, H. The house by the lake
Morrison, D. A matter of record
Murray, J. The final curtain
Olfson, L. Hamlet
Olfson, L. Macbeth
Parker, K. T. Double identity
Reach, J. Dragnet
Reach, J. Murder for the bride
Reach, J. Women in white
Roos, A. and Roos, W. Speaking of murder
Saroyan, W. Hello out there
Senior, E. The hunted
Sherry, G. Black limelight
Sherwood, R. E. and Harrison, J. Rebecca
Thomas, D. The doctor and the devils
Tumarin, B. and Sydow, J. Dostoyevsky's The brothers Karamazov
Voysey, M. The amorous goldfish
Webster, J. The Duchess of Malfi
Wilde, O. The Duchess of Padua
Williams, E. Vigil
Yeats, W. B. Purgatory
   See also Poisoners

Murder at the manor. Abstance, P. and Abstance, L.

Murder comes in threes. Sprague, M.

Murder for the bride. Reach, J.

Murder in motley. D'Abbes, I. and Sherie, F.

Murder in the cathedral. Eliot, T. S.

Murder in the kitchen. Fisher, A.

Murder is my business. Reach, J.

Murder mistaken. Green, J.

Murder on arrival. Batson, G.

Murder out of tune. Cary, F. L.

Murder trials. See Trials (Murder)

Murdoch, Marion
The cuckoo
   Domestic comedy. Teen-age girl thwarts jealous plans of her mother's friend by devious methods. 1 act 7w 1 interior
   In Kamerman, S. E. ed. Blue-ribbon plays for girls

Murdoch, Wynn
Do-Nothing Dan. Bakers Plays 1955 95p (Baker's Edition of plays)
   Romantic comedy. Young man's family is disgusted that he won't work until he meets a girl and engages in an odd but successful business. 3 acts 3m 5w 1 interior

Murphy, Arthur
The apprentice
   Satire on 18th century London apprentices who neglect business to rehearse plays at spouting clubs. 7m 1w extras 4 interiors 1 exterior
   In Murphy, A. The way to keep him & five other plays
Know your own mind
   Comedy of several pairs of star-crossed lovers who, despite intrigue, are united. 8m 5w 3 interiors
   In Murphy, A. The way to keep him & five other plays
The old maid
   Situation comedy based on mistaken identity of two women who are sharp contrasts in personalities. 5m 3w 1 interior
   In Murphy, A. The way to keep him & five other plays
Three weeks after marriage
   Farce on marriage, centering on newly-weds' quarrel over whist game. First titled: What we must all come to. 4m 4w 2 interiors
   In Murphy, A. The way to keep him & five other plays
The upholsterer
   Satirizes 18th century English upholsterer's domestic life as he neglects business for petty politics. 9m 3w 3 interiors 2 exteriors
   In Murphy, A. The way to keep him & five other plays
The way to keep him
   London drawing room comedy. Two wives scheme to win back two difficult husbands. 6m 6w 4 interiors
   In Murphy, A. The way to keep him & five other plays

Murray, John
Be my ghost
   Girl who is sure her uncle left second will which would disinherit her greedy relatives, is helped by friendly skeleton. 1 act 5m 5w 1 interior
   In Murray, J. Mystery plays for young people
The boy next door
   Teen-ager finds that her family's trusted lawyer is responsible for mysterious tragedy which happened next door long ago. 1 act 2m 3w 1 interior
   In Murray, J. Mystery plays for young people
A case for Mrs Hudson
   When frantic family finds famous detective is out, his housekeeper surprisingly solves the case for them. 1 act 3m 3w 1 interior
   In Murray, J. Mystery plays for young people
A case for two detectives
   Farce. Armchair detective and Rivets O'Neill, typical American detective, both solve murder mystery the wrong way. 1 act 6m 6w 1 interior
   In Murray, J. Mystery plays for young people
The case of the missing poet
   Authority on rare books is missing together with one of his books. 1 act 5m 3w 1 interior
   In Murray, J. Mystery plays for young people
The door
   Nurse is called to attend patient she is not permitted to see. 1 act 1m 2w 1 interior
   In Murray, J. Mystery plays for young people

Murray, John—*Continued*

The end of the line
Girl who overhears man in her office plotting to kill her employer is trapped by him on subway train. 1 act 5m 3w 1 interior

In Murray, J. Mystery plays for young people

The final curtain
Various conflicts among the members of a hit show come to head when one of them is murdered during performance. 1 act 6m 5w 1 interior

In Murray, J. Mystery plays for young people

The five buttons
When wealthy man dies and leaves no money his daughter is bewildered until she finds paper that involves an old friend. 1 act 3m 4w 1 interior

In Murray, J. Mystery plays for young people

A game of chess
Young couple enter house during storm and find a lonely, eccentric old man. 1 act 2m 3w 1 interior

In Murray, J. Mystery plays for young people

The impossible room
Family consults criminologist on disappearance of their guest and find that he is actually jewel thief. 1 act 4m 4w 1 interior

In Murray, J. Mystery plays for young people

The mystery in the lab
Scientist discovers that some of his papers have been stolen. 1 act 4m 3w 1 interior

In Murray, J. Mystery plays for young people

The Swiss Chalet mystery
Two Americans find important papers from behind Iron Curtain at Swiss Chalet, but have trouble in getting them to American official. 1 act 5m 4w 1 interior

In Murray, J. Mystery plays for young people

Ups and downs
Man who has stolen fortune in bonds, seems to have disappeared inside an elevator. 1 act 4m 2w 1 interior

In Murray, J. Mystery plays for young people

When the hurlyburly's done
Students marooned in deserted house are visited by two men who have come to find treasure hidden there. 1 act 5m 6w 1 interior

In Murray, J. Mystery plays for young people

Will-O'-Wisp
Mystery surrounds the location of emerald hidden in old Irish Inn. 1 act 3m 3w 1 interior

In Murray, J. Mystery plays for young people

Murray, Warren

A night in . . . Bakers Plays 1954 22p illus (Baker's Royalty plays)
Farce. Hilarious situations develop when couple try to find the wife's old school friend in a strange town. 1 act 6m 4w extras 1 exterior

Music

Emurian, E. K. It is well with my soul

Music, Popular (Songs, etc.)
Emurian, E. K. I'll take you home again, Kathleen
Lynch, P. What's that tune?

The **music**-cure, Shaw, B.

Music-halls (Variety-theaters, cabarets, etc.)
Osborne, J. The entertainer
See also Vaudeville

The **music** man. Willson, M.

The **music** mart. Asbrand, K.

Music! Music! Everywhere! Mitchell, L. F.

Music teachers
Bond, C. The food of love

Music Week
c Mitchell, L. F. Music! Music! Everywhere!

Musical comedies. See Musical revues, comedies, etc.

Musical plays. See Musical revues, comedies, etc.

Musical revues, comedies, etc.
Adler, R. and Ross, J. Damn Yankees
Adler, R. and Ross, J. The pajama game
c Asbrand, K. The music mart
Baker's Roaring twenties scrapbook
Bergh, H. Old King Cole
Bernstein, L. Candide
Bernstein, L. West Side story
Bernstein,L. Wonderful town
Blankman, H. By hex
Bock, J. The body beautiful
Bock, J. Fiorello!
c Borgers, P. and Borgers, E. The strange case of Mother Goose
Bremer, W. Nothing but nonsense
Bucci, M. Chain of jade
Bucci, M. The old lady shows her medals
Bucci, M. A pink party dress
Clinton-Baddeley, V. C. Jack and the beanstalk
c Fluckey, J. O. Davy's star
c Fluckey, J. O. He said he was Santa
c Fluckey, J. O. The heart of the forest
c Fluckey, J. O. The little blue angel
c Fluckey, J. O. Santa and the space men
George, C. Fanny, the frivolous flapper
Hague, A. Plain and fancy
c Henry, V. May Day in the woods
c Hondelink, M. E. Christmas cards
Hope, A. J.; Mary Francis, Sister, and Birder, D. The complaining angel
Howells, W. D. A sea change
c Kent, M. When queens cook
Kent, W. Seventeen
Kleinsinger, G. Archy and Mehitabel
Lavery, E. American portrait
Lehar, F. The merry widow
Loewe, F. My fair lady
Magnau, K. Goodbye, Texas—Broadway, hello!
Merrill, B. New girl in town
Moross, J. The golden apple
c Palmer, K. and Palmer, W. The magic mountain
Porter, C. Kiss me Kate
Rodgers, R. Flower drum song
Rodgers, R. Me and Juliet
Rodgers, R. Pipe dream

Mystery—*Continued*

c Woolsey, J. and Sechrist, E. H. Mystery next door
    See also Murder

The **mystery**. Spamer, C.

Mystery at Knob Creek Farm. Miller, H. L.

Mystery at the depot. Carrière, A.

The **mystery** in the lab. Murray, J.

Mystery, mayhem, and murder! Parish, J.

Mystery next door. Woolsey, J. and Sechrist, E. H.

Mystery of the glittering gem. Carlson, B. W.

The **mystery** of the ming tree. Masters, R. and Masters, L.

The **mystery** of turkey-lurkey. Miller, H. L.

Mythology, Classical
    Kleist, H. von. Penthesilea
    See also Mythology, Greek

Mythology, Greek
    Aeschylus. Agamemnon
    Aeschylus. Choephoroe
    Aeschylus. Eumenides
    Aeschylus. The suppliant maidens
    Alfred, W. Agamemnon
    Anouilh, J. Antigone
    Anouilh, J. Medea
    Cocteau, J. The infernal machine
    Dryden, J. and Lee, N. Oedipus
    Euripides. Alcestis
    Euripides. Andromaché
    Euripides. The Bacchae
    Euripides. The children of Herakles
    Euripides. The Cyclops
    Euripides. Electra
    Euripides. Hecuba
    Euripides. Helen
    Euripides. The Heracleidae
    Euripides. Heracles
    Euripides. Hippolytus
    Euripides. Ion
    Euripides. Iphigeneia at Aulis
    Euripides. Iphigeneia in Taurica
    Euripides. Iphigenia in Aulis
    Euripides. The madness of Herakles
    Euripides. The Medea
    Euripides. Orestes
    Euripides. The Phoenician maidens
    Euripides. The Phoenician women
    Euripides. Rhesus
    Euripides. Suppliants
    Euripides. **The women of Troy**
    Giraudoux, J. Electra
    Giraudoux, J. Tiger at the gates
    Goethe, J. W. von. Iphigenia in Tauris
    Grillparzer, F. Medea
    c Howard, V. The strange tale of King Midas
    Jeffers, R. The Cretan woman
    Kleist, H. von. Penthesilea
    Lind, L. R. ed. Ten Greek plays in contemporary translations
    Merrill, J. The immortal husband
    Racine, J. Andromache
    Sartre, J. P. The flies
    Sophocles. Ajax
    Sophocles. Antigone
    Sophocles. Electra

Sophocles. Oedipus at Colonus
Sophocles. Oedipus Rex
Sophocles. Oedipus the King
Sophocles. Philoctetes
Sophocles. Three Theban plays
Sophocles. The women of Trachis

N

"N" for nuisance. Miller, H. L.

N. Towne cycle. See Coventry plays

Naaman, the Syrian
    c Spamer, C. M. Elisha cures Naaman

Nail, Robert
    Love errant. French 1954 36p
        Romantic comedy. High school girl and boy have gone steady so long, they try a change. but adverse experience reinforces their affection. 1 act 2m 2w 1 interior

Najac, Émile de. See Sardou, V. jt. auth.

Namiki, Senryū. See Namiki, Sōsuke

Namiki, Sōsuke. See Takeda, I. jt. auth.

Nappier, Patricia
    And there was light
        Mother who attempts to strengthen son's character finds that in doing so she has strengthened her own. 1m 4w 1 interior
        In Twelve half-hours with the Winthrop Theater
    Just a matter of timing
        Domestic comedy. During Civil War, grandmother, unaware of her soldier grandson's secret visits home to see his wife, makes elaborate preparations for his announced visit. 1m 5w 1 interior
        In Twelve half-hours with the Winthrop Theater

Narcotic addicts
    Gazzo, M. V. A hatful of rain
    Gelber, J. The connection
    Lee, M. Dope!

The **narrow man**. Bailey, A. H.

Nash, N. Richard
    Girls of summer. French 1957 122p illus
        Woman of thirty, sacrificing her life to rear younger brother and sisters, meets with multiple romance one summer. 3 acts 4m 4w 1 interior
    Handful of fire. [Acting ed] French 1959 86p
        Purity and corruption in Mexican border town. Poor photographer and his sweetheart are abused by owner of gambling casino. 3 acts 16m 6w 1 interior 1 exterior
    The rainmaker. [Acting ed] French 1955 102p illus
        Romantic comedy. Confidence man, claiming to be a rainmaker, visits drought-stricken ranch with some unexpectedly happy results. 3 acts 6m 1w 1 setting
        Trade edition published by Random House
    Rouge atomique. Dramatists 1955 18p
        Duel over teacups between wife and mistress of a man injured, perhaps fatally, in automobile accident. Verse play with background music. 1 act 2w 1 setting
        In The Best short plays of 1954-1955

Nash, N. R.—*Continued*

See the jaguar. Acting ed. Dramatists 1953 133p
    In remote village of American West a brutal man has completely dominated every living thing he possesses except his self-willed daughter. 3 acts 6 scenes 12m 3w extras 2 exteriors

Nathan, Paul S.

Bibi. French 1959 80p illus
    Romantic comedy. Lonely little girl whose father is busy traveling is befriended by foreigner attached to United Nations, and is heartbroken when he falls in love with her aunt. 3 acts 4m 1g 1 interior 1 exterior

Nathan, Robert

Jezebel's husband
    Satire based on the later years of the Biblical prophet Jonah. 2 acts 4 scenes 6m 5w 1 interior
    In Nathan, R. Jezebel's husband & The sleeping beauty

The sleeping beauty
    Satire. Naive young director and waitress friend contrasted with brash Hollywood types on studio filming lot. 3 acts 3 scenes Large mixed cast 1 interior
    In Nathan, R. Jezebel's husband & The sleeping beauty

National Health Week. See Health Week

National Recreation Association

Children of the Americas
    Scenes of American life with songs and dances from colonial days to present. 6 scenes Large mixed cast 1 interior 1 exterior
    In National Recreation Association. Pageants and programs for school, church and playground

I hear America singing!
    Walt Whitman and other famous Americans of the past tell what America means to them. 7m 2w 1b 1g extras chorus 1 interior
    In National Recreation Association. Pageants and programs for school, church and playground

c The runaway sled
    Little boy falls asleep and has strange dream after he writes letter to Santa Claus on Christmas Eve. 1m 1w 1b extras 1 interior 1 exterior
    In National Recreation Association. Plays, pageants and ceremonials for the Christmas season

c The St George play
    Christmas farce. Combination of two traditional English plays using mythical and legendary characters. Unidentified cast 6 characters 1 interior
    In National Recreation Association. Plays, pageants and ceremonials for the Christmas season

c Santa Claus visits Mars
    King of Mars, having no color on his planet, is visited by Santa and Earth children who dance for him at Christmastide. Unidentified cast 4 characters extras 1 interior
    In National Recreation Association. Plays, pageants and ceremonials for the Christmas season

Who are we of the United States
    One scene with speaking chorus and solo voices about the many races that make up the United States. Large mixed cast no scenery
    In National Recreation Association. Pageants and programs for school, church and playground

Native dancer. Shaw, D.

The **natives** are restless tonight. Dias, E. J.

The **Nativity.** Goulding, D. J.

The **Nativity.** Kent, M.

The **Nativity.** Malcolmson, A.

Natural history

United States

Geiger, M. Light and liberty

Natural resources. See Power resources

Nature study

c Pottow, D. Preparing for winter

Nature's most precious gift. Probst, G.

Nature's way. Wouk, H.

The **nautical** approach. Barry, M. H.

Navaho Indians

Kromer, H. Caught between

Near mutiny on the "Santa Maria." Carlson, B. W.

Nearly beloved. Payton, D.

Neglected husbands' sewing club. Lynch, P.

Negro dialect. See Dialect—Negro

Negro folk-drama. See Folk-drama, Negro

Negro folk-lore. See Folk-lore, Negro

Negro minstrels

Driscoll, R. The whiz bang minstrel show

Negroes

Albee, E. The death of Bessie Smith
Anderson, M. Lost in the stars
Applegarth, M. T. Were you there?
Benjamin, J. and Kellerman, D. No man is an island
Carroll, W. Comin' for to carry
Edmunds, M. Moon of my delight
Ford, R. Requiem for a nun
Genet, J. The blacks: a clown show
Green, P. The No 'Count Boy
Green, P. Wings for to fly
Hansberry, L. A raisin in the sun
Healey, R. M. Nobody knows
Martin, D. Simply heavenly
O'Neill, E. The Emperor Jones
Parker, J. W. Sleep on, Lemuel
Peterson, L. Take a giant step
Williams, N. Dreams
Willis, C. The velvet plain

History

Miller, C. L. Wings over dark waters

Religion

Connelly, M. Green pastures

Neighborliness

c Herman, S. W. Good neighbors
States, B. O. The tall grass

Neighbors should be neighborly. Asbrand, K.

Neilson, Pearl

Room for the King
    Nativity drama. While Mary and Joseph attempt to find room in the inn, shepherds watch their restless flocks and wait uneasily for something to happen. Speaking chorus. 9m 2w extras 1 interior 1 exterior
    In Bryant, A. comp. Religious plays that click

Neilson, Pearl—*Continued*

The star still shines. Rodeheaver 1954
16p
> Young people helping with Christmas
> decorations in church see what taking
> commercialism out of Christmas means
> to different people. 1 act 12m 5w extras
> 2 interiors

Nelson, Frances Herbert (Woodward) Nelson, viscountess
Vooght, C. Nineteen, The Beacon

Nephites
McCaslin, N. He traveled the world

Nero, Emperor of Rome
Healy, J. Nero fiddles
Lee, N. The tragedy of Nero, Emperour of Rome
Racine, J. Britannicus

Nero fiddles. Healy, J.

Netherlands

German occupation, 1940-1945
Goodrich, F. and Hackett, A. The diary of Anne Frank

Social life and customs
c Woolsey, J. and Sechrist, E. H. Juliana's birthday

Neuenburg, Evelyn
Distant thunder. Bakers Plays 1956 24p (Baker's Royalty plays)
> Strength of lonely person is tested when
> "cured" alcoholic wife is told she caused
> her husband's death. 1 act 1m 3w 2 interiors

Fear is a murderer. Bakers Plays 1958 18p (Baker's Royalty plays)
> Set in Communist East Berlin. Family
> members are divided in their political
> viewpoints. 1 act 4w 1 interior

Pinnacle. Bakers Plays 1957 28p (Baker's Royalty plays)
> Emotional dependency of grown woman
> on her mother. 1 act 4w 1 interior

The secret. Bakers Plays 1954 23p (Baker's Royalty plays)
> Three women of different personalities
> are in love with the same man, when
> one of them precipitates crisis. 1 act 5w
> extras 1 interior

Strange victory. Bakers Plays 1953 21p (Baker's Royalty plays)
> The infancy of Giuseppe Verdi; his
> mother and he take refuge in a tower
> during siege of their town. 1 act 1m 2w
> 1 interior

Susie was a vampire. Bakers Plays 1953 20p illus (Baker's Royalty plays)
> Domestic comedy. When young couple
> return from honeymoon they plan quiet
> evening at home but in-laws begin dropping in. 1 act 2m 4w 1 interior

Truth is for the Birds. Bakers Plays 1958 24p (Baker's Royalty plays)
> Domestic comedy. Husband is insulted
> when wife tells him what she really
> thinks about his prepared speech. 1 act
> 1m 4w 1 interior

Never say die. Marr Johnson, D.

The **new** book. Spamer, C.

The **new** broom. Hark, M. and McQueen, N.

The **new** colony. Pirandello, L.

The **new** colossus. Emurian, E. K.

New England
Davis, O. and Davis, D. Ethan Frome
O'Neill, E. Desire under the elms
O'Neill, E. Homecoming

Social life and customs
Howard, V. Happy holidays for little women
McCaslin, N. The Yankee Peddler

Social life and customs—*Colonial period*
Phelps, L. The gospel witch

New England dialect. See Dialect—New England

A **New** England nun. Sergel, R.

New England witchcraft. See Witchcraft—New England

New-fangled Thanksgiving. Hark, M. and McQueen, N.

New girl in town. Crone, R.

New girl in town. Merrill, B.

New Hampshire

19th century
Benét, S. V. The Devil and Daniel Webster
Totheroh, D. and Benét, S. V. All that money can buy

New hearts for old. Fisher, A.

New Orleans
Vidal, G. Visit to a small planet

New shoes. Miller, H. L.

The **new** Washington. Newman, D.

The **New** World. Makowsky, L.

New Year
Armer, A. and Grauman, W. E. Timeless second
Howard, V. I resolve
c Newman, D. Happy holidays
c Spamer, C. Happy New Year
c Very, A. Doctor Time's office
c Very, A. The twelve months

New York (City)
Bernstein, L. West Side story
Bock, J. Fiorello!
Locke, S. Fair game
Merrill, B. New girl in town
Panetta, G. Comic strip
Rice, E. L. Street scene
Tolkin, M. and Kallen, L. Maybe Tuesday
Wouk, H. Nature's way

Greenwich Village
Bernstein, L. Wonderful town

Harlem
Lee, M. Dope!

Social conditions
Miller, A. A memory of two Mondays

Social life and customs
Wilson, E. Beppo and Beth
Wilson, E. This room and this gin and these sandwiches

The **New** York idea. Mitchell, L.

Newbold, Hope
Joanie on the spot. Bakers Plays 1956 91p illus (Baker's Edition of plays)
> When man's business is failing he consults business analyst who turns out to
> be pretty girl. 3 acts 6m 6w 1 interior

Newlyweds. See Husband and wife; Marriage

Newman, Deborah

c Aladdin
Aladdin finds magic lamp and genie inside it fulfills Aladdin's wish to marry Sultan's daughter. 2 scenes 4m 4w extras 2 interiors

In Newman, D. Holiday plays for little players

c The all-American tour
Each airline passenger tells what life is like in his state. 10 characters extras 1 interior

In Newman, D. Holiday plays for little players

c The best part of Christmas
Everyone tries to decide what is nicest thing about Christmas. 18 characters extras 1 interior

In Newman, D. Holiday plays for little players

c Bunny of the year
How Mrs Hen becomes Bunny of the Year. 9 characters extras 1 exterior

In Newman, D. Holiday plays for little players

c Christmas at the Cratchits
Adaptation of part of Charles Dickens' "A Christmas carol." How a poor family celebrates Christmas. 1m 1w 3b 3g 1 interior

In Newman, D. Holiday plays for little players

c The Christmas tree surprise
Elves and Snowflakes surprise some poor children with a Christmas tree. 1m 1w 2b 2g extras 1 exterior

In Newman, D. Holiday plays for little players

c A compass for Christopher
Imaginary incident in Columbus' childhood wherein he expresses his desire to be a sailor when he grows up. 2m 4b 4g 1 exterior

In Newman, D. Holiday plays for little players

c Election Day in the U.S.A.
Ten ballot boxes tell voters about proper way of voting. 21 characters extras 1 interior

In Newman, D. Holiday plays for little players

c The Emperor's new clothes
Two weavers fool the Emperor with an invisible robe. 5m 3w extras 1 interior

In Newman, D. Holiday plays for little players

c The fire-safe town
Various characters from Mother Goose tell the Fire Chief how to prevent fires. 7m 3w 5b 4g extras 1 interior

In Newman, D. Holiday plays for little players

c The first Thanksgiving
A story of those who attended the first Thanksgiving. 3m 2w 2b 5g 1 interior

In Newman, D. Holiday plays for little players

c A gift to the world
How the Grimm brothers decided to write down all the old fairy tales. 2m 4w 5b 6g 1 interior

In Newman, D. Holiday plays for little players

c Happy holidays
The holidays and the months decide they like themselves just the way they are. 21 characters extras 1 interior

In Newman, D. Holiday plays for little players

c In honor of trees
Each tree wants to become the school-children's Arbor Day choice. 13 characters extras 1 interior

In Newman, D. Holiday plays for little players

c Kachoo!
The cold sprites tell the children how not to catch cold in rainy weather. 1 act 1w 7g extras 1 interior

In Kamerman, S. E. ed. Blue-ribbon plays for girls

c The keys to peace
The different virtues that promote peace instead of war are given voices to enlighten quarreling citizens. 2m 3w 1b 1g extras 1 interior

In Newman, D. Holiday plays for little players

c Long ago in Bethlehem
A story of the first Christmas. 1m 2w 3g extras 1 exterior

In Newman, D. Holiday plays for little players

c The magic goose
Simon wins the king's daughter. 8m 6w 1 exterior

In Newman, D. Holiday plays for little players

c Memorial Day for the Blue and Gray
Southern children decide to remember the northern as well as the southern soldiers. 2w 3b 5g 1 exterior

In Newman, D. Holiday plays for little players

c Mr Lincoln's beard
How a little girl persuaded Lincoln to grow a beard. 5m 4g extras chorus 1 exterior

In Newman, D. Holiday plays for little players

c The new Washington
New student unexpectedly takes the part of Washington in class play. 1w 4b 5g extras 1 interior

In Newman, D. Holiday plays for little players

c A present from Abe
Lincoln's early schooling in pioneer Kentucky. 1m 4b 4g extras 1 interior

In Newman, D. Holiday plays for little players

Pride and prejudice
Radio adaptation of novel by Jane Austen. Romantic comedy, set in early 19th century England, concerning the efforts of socially ambitious gentlewoman to secure wealthy husbands for her daughters. Background music. 5m 9w

In Burack, A. S. ed. Four-star radio plays for teen-agers

The prince and the pauper
Radio adaptation of novel by Mark Twain. In 16th century England, Edward, Prince of Wales (later King Edward VI) exchanges clothes with Tom Canty, a slum boy and later has difficulty proving his identity. Background music. 24m 8w extras

In Burack, A. S. ed. Four-star radio plays for teen-agers

c The prize shamrock
Tim Reilly wins contest to see who can grow the best shamrock. 7m 5w extras 1 exterior

In Newman, D. Holiday plays for little players

Newman, Deborah—*Continued*

c The Pumpkineaters' pumpkin
>Witches and goblins help Peter Pump-
kineater and his wife find a home. 1m
1w extras 1 exterior

In Newman, D. Holiday plays for little
>players

c The real princess
>The king searches for "real" princess to
marry his son. 2 scenes 1m 2w 3b 7g
1 interior

In Newman, D. Holiday plays for little
>players

c Roses for mother
>The roses are awakened just in time to
become a bouquet for Mother's Day.
15 characters 1 exterior

In Newman, D. Holiday plays for little
>players

c Somebody's valentine
>Story of valentine who wants to belong
to somebody. 1m 4w 2b 2g 1 interior

In Newman, D. Holiday plays for little
>players

c Something new for Halloween
>Lonely little witch finds her fairy god-
mother. 1m 3b 5g extras 1 interior

In Newman, D. Holiday plays for little
>players

c The stars and stripes
>Betsy Ross makes the first flag. 3m 5w
2b 4g 1 interior

In Newman, D. Holiday plays for little
>players

c The stolen heart
>The witch steals the magic heart and
learns how to be kind. 2w 7g 1 interior

In Kamerman, S. E. ed. Blue-ribbon
>plays for girls

In Newman, D. Holiday plays for little
>players

c Thanks for Thanksgiving
>First Thanksgiving for a new immigrant
family. 3b 9g extras 1 interior

In Newman, D. Holiday plays for little
>players

c Thanks to the Indians
>How the Indians helped Pilgrims at first
Thanksgiving. 3m 3b 5g 1 interior

In Newman, D. Holiday plays for little
>players

c Washington's gold button
>George Washington gives his gold button
to patriot's son. 1m 3w 1b 3g 1 interior

In Newman, D. Holiday plays for little
>players

c The way to the inn
>About those who first saw the star of
Bethlehem. 4m 3w 1b 2g extras 1 exterior

In Newman, D. Holiday plays for little
>players

Newspapers

Fisher, A. and Rabe, O. When freedom
was news

McMahon, L. Don't tell your father

Taggart, T. and Reach, J. Dear Phoebe
>*See also* Reporters and reporting

Next-to-last rites. Thomas, D. and Slocumb, P.

Niccolo and Nicollette. Cullen, A.

Nicholas, Bp. of Myra

c Woolsey, J. and Sechrist, E. H. The
Santa Claus court

Nichols, Dudley

Stagecoach
>Moving picture play based on the story:
Stagecoach to Lordsburg, by Ernest
Haycox. The eventful trip of stagecoach,
en route from Tonto, Arizona to Lordsburg, New Mexico in 1885, includes attack by Apache Indians. 4 parts 19m 6w
extras

In Gassner, J. and Nichols, D. eds.
>Great film plays

Nichols, Jane

'Twas such a night
>Legend says that long ago proprietess of
old inn murdered guests for their money.
During stormy night around 1900 the
legend is reenacted. 3m 4w 1 interior

In Twelve half-hours with the Winthrop
>Theater

**Nicholson, Anne, and Chorpenning, Char-
lotte B.**

The magic horn; a story of Roland and
Charlemagne. Coach House Press 1954
64p illus
>Young Roland, nephew of Emperor
Charlemagne, seeks to recover the latter's famous sword Durandal from sor-
ceress, Falerina. 3 acts 7m 5w 1 interior
1 exterior

Nicholson, Hubert

Port and a pistol
>Satirical comedy based on incident in
Nightmare Abbey, by Thomas Peacock.
In 19th century England impoverished
landowner tries to arrange wealthy marriage for pseudo-intellectual son. 1 act
2 scenes 5m 2w 2 interiors

In The Second book of one-act plays

Nicholson, Mary Ann

c The crying clown
>Circus owner is about to fire clown be-
cause his act isn't any good, when distracted by little boy sneaking into tent.
1 act 3m 1b 1 exterior

In Burack, A. S. ed. Four-star plays for
>boys

Nicholson, Norman

A match for the Devil. Faber 1955 83p
>Play, partly in verse, based on Old
Testament story of Hosea, a baker, who
takes back his unfaithful wife. 4 scenes
5m 4w 2 exteriors

A **nickel** and a dime. Fisher, A. and Rabe, O.

Nielson, Pearl

Christmas unusual. Art Craft 1956 23p
illus
>A recently widowed husband and two
grown children wonder what to do about
Christmas until daughter ascertains that
her mother would have wanted them to
share it with poor people. 1 act 4m 2w
1 interior

To hear the angels sing. Rodeheaver 1955
15p
>When harassed mother says she would
like to skip Christmas this year, her children and their grandmother take over
preparations. 3 scenes 5m 5w choir 1 interior

Niggli, Josephina

Miracle at Blaise
>Fantasy. French underground fighter is
saved from death at hands of Nazis by
miracle on Christmas Eve. 1 act 6w 1 interior

In Smith, B. and others, eds. A treasury
>of non-royalty one-act plays

The ring of General Macías
>Tragedy. General's wife poisons Mexican
revolutionary hero seeking safety in her
house. 1 act 3m 2w 1 interior

In Smith, B. and others, eds. A treasury
>of non-royalty one-act plays

The **night** before Christmas. Howells, W. D.

Night crossing. Rattray, B.

A **night** in . . . Murray, W.

The **night** is my enemy. Carmichael, F.

Night of storm. Williams, N.

Night of the auk. Oboler, A.

Night of the fourth. Roffey, J. and Harbord, G.

A **night** to remember. Hill, G. R. and Whedon, J.

Nightingale, Florence
Spamer, C. Florence Nightingale

The **nightmare**. Latham, J. L.

Nightmare Abbey. Sharp, A.

Nihilism
Wilde, O. Vera

Nihilists. See Nihilism

The **nine** days. Morris, T. B.

Nineteen, the beacon. Vooght, C.

The **$99,000** answer. Stern, L. and Zelinka, S.

Nishikigi. Kwanze, M.

Niss, Stanley
The penny
Television comedy. Police have difficulty when man, whose wife had him arrested after quarrel, is unwilling to accept bail. 9m 1w
In Writers Guild of America. The prize plays of television and radio, 1956

Nō (Japanese drama and theater)
Enami, S. Ukai
Hiyoshi, Y. Benkei on the bridge
The Japan Society for the Promotion of Science. The Noh drama (10 plays)
Kantan
Komparu, Z. Hatsuyuki
Komparu, Z. Ikuta
Komparu, Z. U. Awoi no uye
Komparu, Z. U. Bashō
Komparu, Z. U. The hōka priests
Komparu, Z. U. Kumasaka
Komparu, Z. U. Tanikō
Kongō, Y. Genjō
Kwanze, K. Eguchi
Kwanze, K. Kayoi Komachi
Kwanze, K. Sotoba Komachi
Kwanze, K. N. Chorio
Kwanze, K. N. Funa-Benkei
Kwanze, K. N. The maple viewing
Kwanze, M. Atsumori
Kwanze, M. Aya no tsuzumi
Kwanze, M. Hachi no ki
Kwanze, M. Hagoromo
Kwanze, M. Haku Rakuten
Kwanze, M. Ikeniye
Kwanze, M. Izutsu
Kwanze, M. Kagekiyo
Kwanze, M. Kakitsubata
Kwanze, M. Kinuta
Kwanze, M. Kiyotsune
Kwanze, M. Nishikigi
Kwanze, M. Sanemori
Kwanze, M. Suma Genji
Kwanze, M. Takasago
Kwanze, M. Tamura
Kwanze, M. Tōboku
Kwanze, M. Tsunemasa
Kwanze, M. J. Sumidagawa

Miyamasu. Eboshi-ori
Pound, E. and Fenollosa, E. The classic Noh theatre of Japan (14 plays)
Shojo
Waley, A. The Nō plays of Japan (36 plays)

The **No** 'Count Boy. Green, P.

No escape. Davies, R.

No exit. Sartre, J. P.

No man is an island. Benjamin, J. and Kellerman, D.

No more arithmetic. Armstrong, J. B.

No more wars but the moon. Conkle, E. P.

No mother to guide her. Forsythe, A.

No, no, a million times no! Tomkins, B.

No order in the court. Howard, V.

No star to guide them. Sergel, R.

No time for dames. Armer, A. and Grauman, W.E.

No time for sergeants. Levin, I.

No trouble, at all. Humphrys, R.

No weeds for the widow. Johnson, P.

Noah. Obey, A.

Noah's ark
Chester plays. Noah's flood
Obey, A. Noah
c Spamer, C. M. Noah's ark

Noah's ark. Spamer, C. M.

Noah's flood. Chester plays

Noah's flood. Malcolmson, A.

Noble, William. See Herlihy, J. L. jt. auth.

The **noble** Spanish soldier. Rowley, S.

Nobody knows. Healey, R. M.

Nobody loves a fat boy. Martens, A. C.

Nobumitsu, Kanze Kojirō. See Kwanze, Kojirō Nobumitsu

Nobumitsu, Kojirō. See Kwanze, Kojirō Nobumitsu

The **Noël** candle. Fuller, R.

Noh. See Nō (Japanese drama and theater)

Noises
Martens, A. C. Quiet, please

Nominations for office. See Political conventions

Noon, Elizabeth F. and Daniels, Elva S.
Our own United States
Joint program for grades one through six. Describes work done in various industries throughout United States. Includes dances and songs with musical scores. Large mixed cast 1 setting
In Birdsall, R. ed. Creative plays for every school month

Noon on Doomsday. Serling, R.

Norfolk dialect. See Dialect—English—Norfolk

Norris, James
c Hiawatha. Childrens Theatre 1953 44p illus music
Hiawatha, young Mohawk brave, persuades five warring tribes of the Iroquois to form a league for peace. Includes Indian chants and dances and two puppets. 3 acts 5 scenes 12m 2w 2b 1g extras 1 interior 4 exteriors

Northward ho. Dekker, T. and Webster, J.

Norway
History—1030-1397
Kielland, T. Queen Margaret of Norway

Norway—*Continued*

Social life and customs

c Woolsey, J. and Sechrist, E. H. A Norwegian mountain mystery

A **Norwegian** mountain mystery. Woolsey, J. and Sechrist, E. H.

Norwegians in the United States
Van Druten, J. I remember mama

Nose

Abnormities and deformities
Olfson, L. Cyrano de Bergerac
Rostand, E. Cyrano de Bergerac

A **nose** for news. Gran, J. M.

Nostalgia
Snyder, W. H. The departing

Not by might. Crouch, A.

Not fit for man or beast. Hark, M. and McQueen, N.

Not for girls. Miller, H. L.

Not for sale. Fisher, A. and Rabe, O.

Not in the book. Watkyn, A.

Not me! Carlson, B. W.

Not on the menu. Pyle, M. T.

The **not**-so-crooked man. Fisher, A.

Not without honor. Getzinger, E. W.

Nothing but nonsense. Bremer, W.

Nothing ever happens! Fisher, A.

Nothing to be thankful for. Hark, M. and McQueen, N.

Novelists
Batson, G. I found April
Green, C. Janus

Now it can be told. Martens, A. C.

Nu, U.
The people win through; with a long biographical introduction by Edward Hunter. Taplinger 1957 184p
   Burma's dilemma when youth—hotheaded and idealistic—attempt an insurrection against government. 8 scenes Large mixed cast 4 interiors 3 exteriors

Nude washing dishes. Seiler, C.

Nude with violin. Coward, N.

Nugent, Elliott. See Thurber, J. jt. auth.

Numerals
c Spamer, C. Carry and borrow

Nuns. See Convents and nunneries; Monasticism and religious orders for women

The **Nuremberg** stove. Siks, G. B.

Nursery rhyme diet. Hark, M. and McQueen, N.

Nursery rhymes
c Miller, H. L. Three little kittens
c Salisbury, E. Shoe children
   See also Mother Goose

Nurses and nursing
Bate, S. The nautical approach
Blewett, D. Quiet night
c Carlson, B. W. For soldiers everywhere
Carruthers, J. Physician in charge
Kissen, F. Clara Barton: angel of the battlefield
Reach, J. Women in white

The **nut** tree. Ilian, C.

Nutrition
c Bornstein, M. and Cole, G. Paul in food land
c Miller, H. L. It's a problem
   See also Food; Vitamins

Nystrom, Daniel
Children's praises. Augustana 1953 16p music
   Easter choral worship service for children. Large mixed cast

O

O holy night. Gruwell, B. G.

Obedience
c Spamer, C. The May fairies

Obesity. See Corpulence

Obey, André
The hopeful travellers (adaptation) See Martens, G. M. The hopeful travellers
Noah; in the adaptation by Arthur Wilmurt
   Based on Old Testament story in Book of Genesis. Noah's faith meets its supreme test when, after ark's safe landing on Mt Ararat, his passengers desert him. Background music of shepherd's pipes; also sounds made by various animals and birds. 3 acts 5 scenes 5m 4w extras 3 exteriors
   In Gassner, J. ed. Twenty best European plays on the American stage

The **oblong** circle. Rednour, H. P.

Oboler, Arch
Night of the auk. Horizon Press 1958 [c1956] 180p
   Verse play. Five passengers, one a famous scientist, come speeding back to earth from first landing on the moon to find earth destroyed. 3 acts 6 scenes 5m 1 interior

O'Brien, Frances Blazer
The guardian. French 1958 24p illus
   Events concerning the Nativity; Joseph is simple young carpenter who thinks at first that Mary, his betrothed, has betrayed him, but visit from angel of the Lord reassures him. 1 act 3m 3w chorus extras 4 interiors 3 exteriors

O'Brien, Liam
The remarkable Mr Pennypacker. French 1954 120p illus
   Domestic comedy. Wilmington, Delaware, 1890. A freethinker has two wives and seventeen children. 3 acts 4 scenes 9m 4w 4b 3g 1 interior
   Trade edition published by Random House

The remarkable Mr Pennypacker (condensation)
   In Theatre, 1954

O'Brien, Rose
c Trippy answers the phone
   Little boy who often answers phone for his mother finally gets a call himself. 3m 4w 2b extras 1 interior
   In Birdsall, R. ed. Creative plays for every school month

O'Casey, Sean
Bedtime story
   Naive young man's first experience with a mercenary light o' love. Includes songs with musical scores. 1 act 4m 3w 1 interior
   In O'Casey, S. Five one-act plays
   In O'Casey, S. Selected plays

O'Casey, Sean—*Continued*

The Bishop's bonfire. Macmillan (N Y) 1955 124p front music
> Subtitle: A sad play within the tune of a polka. Theme developed is the idea of joy and freedom crushed by the puritanism and covetousness of church. Set in Irish village, as villagers prepare for visit of Bishop. 3 acts 10m 2w 1 interior

The drums of Father Ned. St Martins 1960 109p front music
> Satire. Emphasizes enjoyment of life and youth and satirizing drabness of certain people who fear change. Set in Ireland in the 1920's. 3 acts 17m 3w extras 2 interiors 1 exterior

The end of the beginning
> Domestic farce. Irish life. Includes song with musical score. 1 act 2m 1w 1 interior

In O'Casey, S. Five one-act plays

Hall of healing
> Satirical farce. Medical care of the poor in Dublin dispensary. Includes songs with musical scores. 1 act 8m 3w 1 interior

In O'Casey, S. Five one-act plays

I knock at the door; adapted by Paul Shyre. Dramatists 1958 77p music
> Based on first in series of six autobiographical novels about O'Casey's life: his schooling, life with his mother and sister and his illnesses. Includes songs wtih musical scores. 2 acts 4m 2w no scenery

Juno and the paycock
> Study of tenement Dublin family is struggle between Free Staters and Republicans in 1922. Irish dialect. 3 acts 6m 4w extras 1 interior

In Cubeta, P. M. ed. Modern drama for analysis. 1955 edition

In Heffner, H. The nature of drama

In Kronenberger, L. ed. Cavalcade of comedy

In O'Casey, S. Juno and the paycock, and The plough and the stars

In O'Casey, S. Selected plays

In O'Casey, S. Three plays

In Warnock, R. Representative modern plays, British

Pictures in the hallway; adapted by Paul Shyre. French 1956 71p music
> Based on second of six autobiographical novels by O'Casey about his youth in Ireland: his first sweetheart, episodes in the rebellion in Ireland and first job. Includes songs with musical scores. 2 acts 18m 9w no scenery

The plough and the stars
> Tragedy. An incident in the Sinn Fein Rebellion, 1916. Irish dialect. 4 acts 10m 6w 3 interiors 1 exterior

In O'Casey, S. Juno and the paycock, and The plough and the stars

In O'Casey, S. Selected plays

In O'Casey, S. Three plays

In A Treasury of the theatre

In Tucker, S. M. ed. Twenty-five modern plays

A pound on demand
> Farce. Postal service. 1 act 3m 1w 1 interior

In O'Casey, S. Five one-act plays

Purple dust. Dramatists 1957 94p music
> Farce, satirical and symbolical. Two Englishmen attempt to revive grace of bygone age by rehabilitating obsolete Tudor house in Ireland. Songs with musical scores. Irish dialect. 3 acts 12m 3w 1 interior

—Same

In Cordell, R. A. and Matson, L. eds. The off-Broadway theatre

In O'Casey, S. Selected plays

In Watson, E. B. ed. Contemporary drama: fifteen plays

Red roses for me. Dramatists 1956 82p illus music
> Tragedy symbolizing poetic soul of Ireland torn by religious and political strife. Specifically, Dublin during 1913 strike. Songs with musical scores. 4 acts 21m 9w 1 interior 2 exteriors

—Same

In O'Casey, S. Selected plays

The shadow of a gunman
> Tragedy. Young Irish woman killed by Black and Tans during raid in Anglo-Irish War of 1920. Irish dialect. 2 acts 8m 3w 1 interior

In O'Casey, S. Selected plays

In O'Casey, S. Three plays

The Silver Tassie
> Crippled Irish veteran of World War 1, formerly football hero, disillusioned by return home. Songs with musical scores. 4 acts 18m 5w 3 interiors 1 exterior

In O'Casey, S. Selected plays

Time to go
> Fantasy. Mysterious young couple advocate doctrine of honest dealing to group of avaricious Irish country people. Includes songs with musical scores. 1 act 10m 3w 1 exterior

In O'Casey, S. Five one-act plays

In O'Casey, S. Selected plays

Within the gates
> Symbolic exposition of human problems. Songs with musical scores. 4 scenes 14m 6w extras 1 exterior

In O'Casey, S. Selected plays

Occupations
Clark, M. G. My wife, Henry

Ocean travel
Carmichael, F. Luxury cruise

Howells, W. D. A sea change

Rattray, B. Night crossing

Oceania
Valency, M. The virtuous island

O'Connell, Mary Olive, Sister
One red rose. Longmans 1954 63p
> Two lonely people, the Mother Superior of an orphanage and fifteen year old orphan girl find inner peace through understanding and power of forgiveness. 1 act 8 scenes 1m 6w extras 4 interiors

O'Conor, Joseph
The iron harp
> Tragedy. Ireland in the 1920's, during political trouble and bloodshed. Love of girl and soldier cannot transcend terror of their times. 3 acts 10m 1w 1 interior

In Browne, E. M. ed. Three Irish plays

In Plays of the year, v16

The **octoroon**. Boucicault, D.

An **ode** to Spring. Hark, M. and McQueen, N.

Odets, Clifford

Awake and sing!
> Jewish family in Bronx during depression years endures frustrations of their circumscribed lives. 3 acts 4 scenes 7m 2w 1 interior

In Griffin, A. V. Living theatre

The flowering peach (condensation)

In The Best plays of 1954-1955

Golden boy
> Tragedy. Young Italian violinist, turned prizefighter, is torn between love for his art and desire for wealth and fame. 3 acts 12 scenes 17m 2w 4 interiors 1 exterior

In A Treasury of the theatre

Odysseus

Abel, L. The death of Odysseus

Euripides. Rhesus

Sophocles. Ajax

Oedipus

Cocteau, J. The infernal machine

Dryden, J. and Lee, N. Oedipus

Seneca. Oedipus

Sophocles. Oedipus at Colonus

Sophocles. Oedipus Rex

Sophocles. Oedipus the King

Oedipus. Dryden, J. and Lee, N.

Oedipus. Seneca

Oedipus at Colonus. Sophocles

Oedipus Rex. Sophocles

Oedipus the King. Sophocles

Of gods and men. Fisher, A. and Rabe, O.

Of mice and men. Steinbeck, J.

Off the rocks. Addis, H.

Off the shelf. Hark, M. and McQueen, N.

Off with his head. Lynch, P.

The offending hand. Delderfield, R. F.

O'Flaherty V. C. Shaw, B.

Oh boy, what a girl! Roeder, L.

Oh, can you help the princess?
> King and Queen Perfect Posture look critically at posture of their subjects. 1 act 17 characters extras 1 interior

In 'Round the year plays for the grades

Oh, Dad, poor Dad, Mamma's hung you in the closet and I'm feelin' so sad. Kopit, A. L.

Oh, men! Oh, women! Chodorov, E.

Oh, to be sixteen again! Faust, E.

O'Hara, Frank

Try! Try!
> Korean War veteran returns home to find that wife has lover, and that life has no place for him. Verse play. 2m 1w 1 interior

In Machiz, H. ed. Artists' Theatre: four plays

The oil well. Foote, H.

Oil wells

Foote, H. The oil well

Oil wells and wedding bells. Tedlock, D.

Oily to rise. Taggart, T.

Ojibwa Indians. See Chippewa Indians

Okinawa

Patrick, J. The Teahouse of the August Moon

Oklahoma! Rodgers, R. and Hammerstein, O.

Old age

Albee, E. The sandbox

Beckett, S. All that fall

Beckett, S. Waiting for Godot

Brenner, M. Love and Miss Dodie

c Carlson, B. W. Just as strong

Claiborne, R. and Banks, F. The last leaf

Elam, R. C. Duchess of Dogwood Lane

Foote, H. The death of the old man

Foote, H. The trip to Bountiful

Holm, J. C. The southwest corner

Karchmer, S. Happy birthday to you!

Lantz, J. E. and Lantz, R. C. Reluctantly yours

Lee, W. C. Deadwood

McMahon, L. E. and Sergel, R. The plum tree

Morris, E. The wooden dish

Mosel, T. Other people's houses

Mosel, T. Star in the summer night

Williams, N. Protest

Old age homes

Butler, I. Tranquil House

Sugarman, J. The pint pot

The old bachelor. Congreve, W.

The old beginning. Foote, H.

Old-fashioned Thanksgiving. Roberts, H. M.

Old Fortunatus. Dekker, T.

Old Glory grows up. Miller, H. L.

Old King Cole. Bergh, H.

The old lady shows her medals. Bucci, M.

Old Lady Witch's party. Very, A.

The old maid. Murphy, A.

Old maids. See Spinsters

The old master. Schofield, S.

Old Mr Fixit. Fisher, A.

The old school bell. Snyder, W.

Old Skin Flint. Keeney, C. H.

The old woman and her pig. Very, A.

The Old Woman's day. Spamer, C.

Oldfield, Mary

Please communicate. Dramatists 1956 91p
> Driver in hit-and-run case discovers victim is his son. His wife thereafter lives to identify driver and avenge son. 3 acts 5 scenes 4m 3w 1 interior

Olfson, Lewy

The adventures of Tom Sawyer
> Radio adaptation of an incident in Mark Twain's novel, Runaway Tom Sawyer, Huckleberry Finn and Joe Harper return in time to hear their funeral sermon preached. Musical background. 4m 3w extras

In Olfson, L. Radio plays of famous stories

Around the world in eighty days
> Radio adaptation of novel by Jules Verne. Adventures of Englishman who, in late 19th century, took wager to travel around the world in eighty days. Background music. 18m 1w

In Burack, A. S. ed. Four-star radio plays for teen-agers

As you like it
> Radio adaptation of Shakespeare's romantic comedy. Two young people find their love tested by banishment, disguise and misfortune. Background music. 5m 2w

In Olfson, L. Radio plays from Shakespeare

Olfson, Lewy—*Continued*

The Bishop's candlesticks
Radio adaptation of part of Victor Hugo's novel, "Les Miserables" in which starving ex-convict, Jean Valjean, steals Bishop of Digne's silver candlesticks. Musical background. 7m 6w
In Olfson, L. Radio plays of famous stories

Captains Courageous
Radio adaptation of Kipling's novel. Musical background. 9m 3w
In Olfson, L. Radio plays of famous stories

A Connecticut Yankee in King Arthur's Court
Radio adaptation of Mark Twain's novel. Musical background. 7m 3w
In Olfson, L. Radio plays of famous stories

The Count of Monte Cristo
Radio adaptation of first part of novel by Alexandre Dumas. Edmond Dantès, Maltese seaman, escapes from prison and later manages to find Spada family treasure buried on isle of Monte Cristo. Set in 19th century France. Background music. 12m 1w
In Burack, A. S. ed. Four-star radio plays for teen-agers

Cyrano de Bergerac
Radio adaptation of the play by Edmond Rostand. Musical background. 5m 6w
In Olfson, L. Radio plays of famous stories

David Copperfield and Uriah Heep
Radio adaptation of parts of Dickens' novel, "David Copperfield," which tell how David prevented unscrupulous Uriah Heep from defrauding Mr Wickfield of his law firm. Musical background. 6m 3w
In Olfson, L. Radio plays of famous stories

Hamlet
Radio adaptation of Shakespeare's tragedy. In medieval Denmark, the rightful heir to the throne, incited by father's ghost, avenges the latter's murder. Play within a play. Verse play with background music. 10m 2w
In Olfson, L. Radio plays from Shakespeare

The house of the Seven Gables
Radio adaptation of Nathaniel Hawthorn's novel. Musical background. 8m 7w
In Olfson, L. Radio plays of famous stories

The importance of being Earnest
Radio adaptation of the play by Oscar Wilde. Musical background. 5m 4w
In Olfson, L. Radio plays of famous stories

Infanta. Row 1954 20p
A dramatization based on Oscar Wilde's story "The birthday of the Infanta" in which lonely princess learns about beauty and faith from ugly dwarf. 1 act 2m 3w 1 interior
—Same
In Powers, V. E. ed. Plays for players, and a guide to play production

Jane Eyre
Radio adaptation of Charlotte Brontë's novel. Musical background. 3m 4w
In Olfson, L. Radio plays of famous stories

Julius Caesar
Radio adaptation of Shakespeare's historical tragedy. The assassination of Caesar in 44 B.C. Rome followed by Mark Antony's funeral oration and Battle of Philippi. Background music. 12m 3w
In Olfson, L. Radio plays from Shakespeare

King Lear
Radio adaptation of Shakespeare's tragedy. Insanity prevents king from recognizing true devotion of his youngest daughter. Background music. 6m 3w
In Olfson, L. Radio plays from Shakespeare

Macbeth
Radio adaptation of Shakespeare's historical tragedy, in verse. Driven by ambition to secure throne, noble warrior and his wife commit murder. Set in 11th century Scotland. Background music. 10m 5w extras
In Olfson, L. Radio plays from Shakespeare

A midsummer night's dream
Radio adaptation of Shakespeare's verse play. Romantic comedy involving both mortals and fairies. Background music. 7m 2w
In Olfson, L. Radio plays from Shakespeare

Monsieur Beaucaire
Radio adaptation of Booth Tarkington's story. Musical background. 6m 7m extras
In Olfson, L. Radio plays of famous stories

Much ado about nothing
Radio adaptation of Shakespeare's romantic comedy. In medieval Italy two pairs of lovers face different problems. Background music. 6m 3w
In Olfson, L. Radio plays from Shakespeare

The Pickwick papers
Radio adaptation of an incident in Dickens' novel. Samuel Pickwick's encounter with his widowed landlady, Mrs Bardell. Musical background. 13m 2w
In Olfson, L. Radio plays of famous stories

Quentin Durward
Radio adaptation of incident in Sir Walter Scott's novel. Musical background. 11m 3w
In Olfson, L. Radio plays of famous stories

Romeo and Juliet
Radio adaptation of Shakespeare's tragedy. In 15th century Italy two young lovers, separated by their feuding families, commit suicide. Verse play with background music. 10m 2w
In Olfson, L. Radio plays from Shakespeare

Silas Marner
Radio adaptation of George Eliot's novel. Musical background. 4m 5w extras
In Olfson, L. Radio plays of famous stories

The taming of the shrew
Radio adaptation of Shakespeare's comedy. Farce about man who married and finally tamed shrewish woman. Background music. 8m 1w
In Olfson, L. Radio plays from Shakespeare

Olfson, Lewy—*Continued*

The tempest
    Radio adaptation of Shakespeare's comedy. Shipwrecked party of usurping Duke of Milan lands on island where they find real Duke of Milan, ruler of his domain by magic. Background music. 8m 2w
    In Olfson, L. Radio plays from Shakespeare
Which of the nine?
    Radio adaptation of Jókai Mór's short story. Poor cobbler and his nine children teach wealthy old man true meaning of Christmas. 7m 4b 5g
    In Olfson, L. Radio plays of famous stories
Wuthering Heights
    Radio adaptation of Emily Brontë's novel. Background music. 4m 2w
    In Olfson, L. Radio plays of famous stories

Oliver, William I.

The stallion
    Tragedy resulting from conflict between father and son when father tries to sell boy's horse. Background music. 6 scenes 3m 1w extras 3 exteriors
    In The Best short plays, 1957

Oliver Twist asks for more. Howard, V.

Olson, Elder

The carnival of animals
    Radio play. Magician's strange performance at carnival elicits varied responses from audience. Verse play. 8m 5w extras
    In Olson, E. Plays & poems, 1948-58
Faust: a masque
    Retelling of Faust legend. Man destroys his soul to regain youth. Verse play. 5m 1w extras 1 interior
    In Olson, E. Plays & poems, 1948-58
The illusionists
    Science fiction. Earth man visits another planet and discovers horrible way of life there. 7m 2w 1 interior
    In Olson, E. Plays & poems, 1948-58
The shepherd and the conqueror
    Satiric modern version of medieval mystery play. Verse play. 4m no scenery
    In Olson, E. Plays & poems, 1948-58
The sorcerer's apprentices
    Philosophic theme about two ignorant apprentices in magician's chamber who unleash terrible power they do not understand and are destroyed. Verse play. 2m 1 interior
    In Olson, E. Plays & poems, 1948-58

Olson, Esther E.

c The Hallowe'en party
    Halloween. Boys find friend's Halloween party more diverting than malicious mischief they had planned. 1 scene 4b 5g 1 interior
    In Easy juvenile grab bag
The honored ones
    Memorial Day. At American Legion program boy scout gives his cherished grandstand seat to wounded veteran. 1 scene 7m 1 exterior
    In Easy juvenile grab bag
c Lighting the way
    Christmas. Wealthy woman whose car breaks down on Christmas Eve, acts as Santa Claus to poor children. 2m 1w 2b 2g 1 interior
    In Cahill, E. M. ed. Celebrating Christmas

Olympe's marriage. Augier, E.

Ominameshi (condensation) Kwanze, M.

On baile's strand. Yeats, W. B

On earth peace. Asbrand, K.

On Halloween. Fisher, A.

On strike. Fisher, A.

On the bat. Carlson, B. W.

On the road. Campion, C.

On the road to Egypt. Davidson, M. R.

On to seventh grade! Matthews, E.

On your own feet. Hark, M. and McQueen, N.

Once a thief. Perrini, A.

Once an actor. Keeney, C. H.

Once around the block. Saroyan, W.

Once in a blue moon. Martens, A. C.

Once in September. Stephens, C. G.

Once more, with feeling. Kurnitz, H.

Once upon a time. Fisher, A.

Once upon a time. Floyd, B.

Ondine. Giraudoux, J.

One-act plays
    Adamov, A. Professor Taranne
    Agg, H. Autumn term
    Agg, H. The happy day
    Agg, H. Red plush
    Agg, H. Silk and sawdust
    Agg, H. Winter sunrise
    Agnew, E. J. Beyond Good Friday
    Albee, E. The sandbox
    Albee, E. The zoo story
    Allensworth, C. Ring once for Central
    Allred, J. All this and Alan, too
    Allred, P. and Allred, T. To the lovely Margaret
    Anderson, M. The feast of Ortolans
    Anderson, R. A. and Sweeney, R. L. Boris and the briefcase
    Anderson, R. A. and Sweeney, R. L. Boris and the spaceman
    Anderson, R. A. and Sweeney, R. L. True blue and trusted
    Anouilh, J. Cecile
    Apstein, T. Fortunata writes a letter
    c Arlett, V. I. The people who came to an inn
    c Arlett, V. I. Young Richard Whittington
    Armstrong, W. F. Haunted rooms
    Arnold, J. W. The sheriff
    Arrabal. The two executioners
    Arthur, K. The long view
    Asbrand, K. Easy as pie
    c Asbrand, K. Little Christmas guest
    Aschmann, H. T. As pretty does
    Ashermann, O. Shakespeare
    Ashton, E. B. The beggarman's bride
    Ashton, E. B. To serve a king
    Ashton, L. S. Bethlehem's Field
    Ashton, L. S. Christmas story
    Ashton, L. S. The phantom postman
    Aske, L. Too young
    Assinder, P. The paying guest
    Atherton, M. And it's Christmas!
    Atwell, R. A pound of prevention
    c Atwell, R. and Virden, H. Christmas in the forest
    c Atwell, R. and Virden, H. Mother of the Year
    c Atwell, R. and Virden, H. Play-time (5 plays)

One-act plays—*Continued*

Weiss, M. J. Parents are people
Welch, R. Let's get out of here
Welles, R. The man of the house
Wembley South Kenton Afternoon Towns-women's Guild, Drama Section. The sacred den
c Werner, S. Home, sweet home
Werry, W. Breakdown
Westgate, T. Petticoat handicap
Wilde, O. A Florentine tragedy
Wilde, O. La sainte courtisane
Wilde, O. Salomé
Wilde, P. Legend
Wilder, T. The happy journey
Wilder, T. The happy journey to Trenton and Camden
Williams, E. Vigil
Williams, N. A battle of wits
Williams, T. At liberty
Williams, T. Auto-da-fé
Williams, T. Camino real
Williams, T. Hello from Bertha
Williams, T. The Lady of Larkspur Lotion
Williams, T. The last of my solid gold watches
Williams, T. The long goodbye
Williams, T. Lord Byron's love letter
Williams, T. Portrait of a Madonna
Williams, T. The purification
Williams, T. The strangest kind of romance
Williams, T. Talk to me like the rain and let me listen . . .
Williams, T. This property is condemned
Williams, T. 27 wagons full of cotton
Williams, T. 27 wagons full of cotton, and other one-act plays (13 plays)
Wilson, D. C. Peace on Mars
Wilson, D. C. That heaven of freedom
Wimberly, R. L. Willy Velvet, homicide detective
Winer, E. Three hours between planes
c Woolsey, J. and Sechrist, E. H. The Santa Claus court
Yeats, W. B. Cathleen ni Houlihan
Yeats, W. B. The Land of Heart's Desire
York, E. B. The kindled flame
York, E. B. The silver star of Christmas
Young, S. The sound of apples
Yudkoff, A. The gentlemen walks outside
One bit of glory. Sheridan, E.
One bright day. Miller, S.
One day for mother. Casey, B. M.
One day more. Conrad, J.
One family sings. Trapp, M. A.
One Father of mankind. Breck, F. E.
One for the book. Spargrove, D.
One in twelve. Latham, J. and Lord, B.
One love had Mary. Calitri, P. M.
One red rose. O'Connell, M. O. Sister
One song for Christmas. Casey, B. M.
The one that got away. Vining, D.
One year after. Armer, A. and Grauman, W. E.

O'Neil, Raymond
The triumph of the egg
Dramatization of Sherwood Anderson's story. Midwestern couple is unsuccessful in chicken farming and restaurant keeping. 1 act 2m 1w 1b 1 interior
In Smith, B. and others, eds. A treasury of non-royalty one-act plays

O'Neill, Eugene
"Abortion"
Tragedy. Relationship between girl and selfish young man ends in suicide and death. 1 act 4m 3w 1 innterior
In O'Neill, E. Lost plays of Eugene O'Neill
Ah, wilderness!
Life of an average family in small town. Parents worry over son's radical ideas, then remember their own youth. 4 acts 6 scenes 9m 6w 3 interiors 1 exterior
In Watson, E. B. ed. Contemporary drama: fifteen plays
Anna Christie
Tragedy. The influence of sea upon the destiny of a barge captain's daughter. 4 acts 11m 3w 3 interiors
In Cubeta, P. M. ed. Modern drama for analysis. 1955 edition
In A Treasury of the theatre
Anna Christie (adaptation) See Merrill, B.
New girl in town
Beyond the horizon
Tragedy. Contrasting characters of two restless brothers on family farm. 3 acts 6 scenes 6m 4w 1 interior 2 exteriors
In Quinn, A. H. ed. Representative American plays
Desire under the elms
Tragedy. Middle aged man marries young bride. Set in New England, 1850. 3 parts 12 scenes 8m 2w 5 interiors 1 exterior
In O'Neill, E. Three plays
The Emperor Jones; with a study guide for the screen version of the play, by William Lewin [and] Max J. Herzberg. Students' ed. Appleton 1949 64p
Tragedy. Negro tyrant in West Indies, overthrown by natives. 8 scenes 3m 1w extras 1 interior 7 exteriors
—Same
In Downer, A. S. ed. The art of the play
In Four modern plays
The great God Brown
Symbolism. Conflict between artistic and materialistic ambitions of an architect. 4 acts 11 scenes 9m 5w extras 6 interiors
In Tucker, S. M. ed. Twenty-five modern plays
The hairy ape
Tragedy. Expressionistic play which follows the brutalization of Yank, stoker on transatlantic liner, searching for identity. 8 scenes 6m 2w 3 interiors
In Downer, A. S. ed. American drama
In Levin, R. Tragedy: plays, theory, and criticism
In A Treasury of the theatre
Homecoming
Tragedy of incest on the Agamemnon theme set in New England in 1865. 4 acts 7m 2w 2 interiors 1 exterior
In O'Neill, E. Three plays
Hughie. Yale Univ. Press 1959 37p
Unsuccessful Broadway gambler finds courage to start again as he reviews the life of deceased friend, a simple trusting man. 2m 1 interior

O'Neill, Eugene—*Continued*

In the zone
Seamen on board British merchant marine vessel in World War I suspect fellow worker of being a spy. 1 act 8m 1 interior
In The Best short plays, 1957

Long day's journey into night. Yale Univ. Press 1955 176p
Tragedy. Depicts O'Neill's boyhood and problems involved in his early family life. 4 acts 5 scenes 3m 2w 1 interior

Long day's journey into night (condensation)
In The Best plays of 1956-1957
In Broadway's best, 1957

The long voyage home
Sailor on the way home is tricked by scheming couple. 1 act 6m 3w extras 1 interior
In Cooper, C. W. Preface to drama

A moon for the misbegotten. [Acting ed] French 1958 106p illus
Tragedy. Huge, Connecticut farm woman who is almost a freak, tries to prevent lover, broken down actor, from drinking himself to death. 4 acts 4m 1w 1 interior

—Same
In Best American plays; 4th ser.

A moon for the misbegotten (condensation)
In The Best plays of 1956-1957
In Broadway's best, 1957

The moon of the Caribbees
Sailors on tramp steamer celebrate night in West Indies port with rum and women. 1 act 17m 4w extras 1 exterior
In Cerf, B. and Cartmell, V. H. eds. 24 favorite one-act plays

"The movie man"
Comedy ridiculing an eccentric Hollywood producer and photographer. Set in Mexico. 1 act 5m 1w 1 interior
In O'Neill, E. Lost plays of Eugene O'Neill

"Servitude"
Wife of famous writer mistakenly thinks he is interested in another woman. 3 acts 4m 2w 1b 1g 1 interior
In O'Neill, E. Lost plays of Eugene O'Neill

"The sniper"
Portrayal of destruction, panic, and death in war as seen through the eyes of a halfwit. Set in Belgium. 1 act 8m 1 interior
In O'Neill, E. Lost plays of Eugene O'Neill

Strange interlude
Psychological drama. Woman whose lover is dead, finds the fulfillment of her love in three different men. 9 acts 5m 3w 4 interiors 2 exteriors
In O'Neill, E. Three plays

A touch of the poet. Yale Univ. Press 1957 182p
Truculent, hard drinking, pretentious Irish immigrant in Massachusetts stands in way of daughter's marriage to an American. Irish dialect. 4 acts 7m 3w 1 interior

A touch of the poet (condensation)
In The Best plays of 1958-1959
In Broadway's best, 1959

"A wife for a life"
Young goldminer falls in love with girl who, unknown to him, is wife of another miner. Set in Arizona desert. 1 act 3m 1 exterior
In O'Neill, E. Lost plays of Eugene O'Neill

Onions in the stew. Dalzell, W. and Martens, A. C.

Only a game. Pomerantz, E.

Only in America. Lawrence, J. and Lee, R. E.

The **only** jealousy of Emer. Yeats, W. B.

The **only** prison. Brooks, P.

Open house. Addis, H.

Open house. Reach, J.

Operation Mad Ball. Carter, A. P.

Operettas. See Musical revues, comedies, etc.

Oppenheimer, George. See Kober, A. jt. auth.

Orange
c Spamer, C. The orange tree

The **orange** tree. Spamer, C.

The **orchard** walls. Delderfield, R. F.

Orestes, son of Agamemnon
Aeschylus. Choephoroe
Aeschylus. The Eumenides
Aeschylus. The libation bearers
Euripides. Electra
Euripides. Iphigenia in Tauris
Euripides. Orestes
Giraudoux, J. Electra
Goethe, J. W. von. Iphigenia in Tauris
Sartre, J. P. The flies
Sophocles. Electra

Orestes. Euripides

Organizations, International. See International cooperation

Oringer, Barry Ira
Son of the revolution. French 1957 20p
Study of two revolutionary leaders, one believing cause of freedom to be incorruptible and the other that every evil end stems from evil means. Set in South America. 1 act 3m 1w extras 1 interior

Ormandy, Edith
c Little Ida and the flowers
Dramatization of fairy tale by Hans Christian Andersen about flowers that dance in the moonlight. 1 act 1w 9g 1 interior
In Kamerman, S. E. ed. Blue-ribbon plays for girls

Orme, Frank
Graduation present
Orphan boy pretends that famous flyer is his father. 1 act 2 scenes 8m 1w 1 interior
In Kamerman, S. E. ed. Blue-ribbon plays for graduation

The **orphans.** Camché, N.

Orphans and orphan-asylums
Anderson, W. "Me, Candido!"
c Asbrand, K. Masquerade
Conkle, E. P. Heaven is a long time to wait
c Fluckey, J. O. Davy's star
c Matthews, E. Mr Blanchard—Easter bunny
O'Connell, M. O. Sister. One red rose
Orme, F. Graduation present

Orphans and orphan-asylums—*Continued*
Phillips, M. K. The woman who didn't want Christmas
Wasserman, D. and Balch, J. Elisha and the long knives
Orpheus
Anouilh, J. Eurydice
Orpheus descending. Williams, T.
Orr, Mary, and Denham, Reginald
Be your age. Acting ed. Dramatists 1953 83p front
Romantic comedy. Family tries to break up romance between college-age daughter and her middle-aged psychology professor. 3 acts 5 scenes 5m 6w 1 interior
Orth, Robert
For heaven's sake. Bakers Plays 1954 72p (Baker's Royalty plays)
Romantic comedy. Young girl-shy man is befriended by soul from heaven who comes down to advise him. 3 acts 5 scenes 8m 5w 2 interiors
Two have dreamed. Bakers Plays 1954 77p (Baker's Royalty plays)
Farce. Attempts of family to be neighborly to new neighbors results in chaos. 3 acts 5m 5w 1 interior
Osborn, Paul
Morning's at seven
Comedy. Middle class old people reveal hopes, ambitions, and frustrations in two backyards of adjoining houses. 3 acts 4m 5w 1 exterior
In Kronenberger, L. ed. Cavalcade of comedy
Osborne, John
The entertainer. Criterion Bks. 1958 89p
Third-rate unscrupulous music-hall entertainer on his way out drags those nearest him down with him. Set in English seaside resort. Includes vaudeville routines. 15 scenes 5m 3w 1 setting
The entertainer (condensation)
In The Best plays of 1957-1958
Look back in anger. Dramatic 1959 86p
Youth in postwar England. Angry Jimmy Porter rails against middle-class complacency, which is his wife's background. 3 acts 3m 2w 1 interior
Trade edition published by Criterion Bks.
Look back in anger (condensation)
In The Best plays of 1957-1958
In Broadway's best, 1958
Osborne, John, and Creighton, Anthony
Epitaph for George Dillon. Criterion Bks. 1958 94p
Emotional conflict between dedicated but unsuccessful playwright and different members of a family with whom he lives. 3 acts 4 scenes 5m 4w 1 interior
Epitaph for George Dillon (condensation)
In The Best plays of 1958-1959
Osborne, Shirley
If you ask me— Eldridge 1959 13p (Eldridge Popular one-act playscripts)
Comedy. Woman wears ridiculous hat to see if her friends will tell her the truth. 1 act 4w 1 interior
Osgood, Phillips Endecott
Midwinter-Eve fire
Christmas. On Midwinter Eve in Roman England, Celtic children learn from a Christian the difference between Druid and Christian beliefs. Includes tableau of the Nativity. 2m 4b 3g extras 1 exterior
In Horn Book Magazine. Four Christmas plays

Ostrovskiĭ, Aleksander Nĭkalaevich. See Ostrovsky, Alexander
Ostrovsky, Alexander
The diary of a scoundrel; English version by Rodney Ackland
Social comedy of 19th century Russia. Fortune hunter's schemes to marry wealthy girl upset by discovery of his diary. 3 acts 5 scenes 8m 7w 3 interiors
In Bentley, E. ed. The modern theatre v2
Otahiti. See Tahiti
Othello. Shakespeare, W.
The **other** nine. Casey, B. M.
Other people's houses. Mosel, T.
The **Other** Wise Man. Sergel, R. See Sergel, R. Henry Van Dyke's The Other Wise Man
Othon. Corneille, P.
Ottawa Indians
McCaslin, N. The gift of corn
Otway, Thomas
Venice preserved; or, A plot discovered
Restoration tragedy in blank verse, set in 17th century Venice. Young nobleman who joins conspiracy to overthrow state, brings disaster upon himself, fellow conspirators, and wife. 5 acts 12 scenes 17m 2w extras 5 interiors 2 exteriors
In Restoration plays
Our dumb friends. Spamer, C.
Our great Declaration. Fisher, A. and Rabe, O.
Our greatest gift. Voss, B. M.
Our home town. Pennington, L. and Kaeyer, M.
Our little Christmas angels. Asbrand, K.
Our own four walls. Hark, M. and McQueen, N.
Our own United States. Noon, E. F. and Daniels, E. S.
Our town. Wilder, T.
Ours to the forty-ninth. Emmons, D. G.
Out of despair. McCann, K.
Out of the darkness. McGreevey, J.
Out of the mist. Price, O.
Out of the question. Howells, W. D.
Out of this world. Dias, E. J.
The **out**-of-towners. Mosel, T.
Out to win. Emmons, D. G.
The **outgoing** tide. Hackett, W.
Outlaws. See Brigands and robbers
Ouzts, Joyce Diedrich
Happy Pagan
Fantasy. Girl dreams that she visits land of fairies and happiness, but Prince Charming cannot return to her world with her. 1m 3w 1 exterior
In Twelve half-hours with the Winthrop Theater
Just a picture
Romantic comedy. When two spinster sisters and orphaned niece decide to sell big house they live in, prospective buyer turns out to be old suitor of younger sister. 2m 3w 1 interior
In Twelve half-hours with the Winthrop Theater
Over the garden fence. Addyman, E.
Overlaid. Davies, R.

An overpraised season. Dunlop, R. S.

Owen, Armitage
Can this be love? [French's Acting ed]
French (London) 1954 60p front
Domestic comedy. Timid man persuades his friend to play up to tyrannical wife so that husband can have grounds for divorce. 3 acts 4 scenes 4m 3w 1 interior

Owen, Valerie
The wanderers. Paxton 1958 11p
At Christmastime long ago, group of strolling players is turned out of a city. 8m 6w 1 exterior

Owen Tudor. See Tudor, Owen

Owens, Rosemary J.
Final edition. Eldridge 1959 21p (Eldridge Popular one-act playscripts)
Newspapers in town have been harassed by little man from Mars who wants them to publish his peace plan. 1 act 2 scenes 2m 2w 1 interior

Ownership. See Property

Oxenford, John
A day well spent (adaptation) See Wilder, T. The matchmaker

Oxton, Charles
Late arrival. [Rev. version] French 1955 126p illus
Domestic comedy. Self centered and idealistic college-age girl is hurt and bewildered when informed her middle aged parents are expecting a baby. 3 acts 6 scenes 3m 6w 1 interior

P

Pacifism
Kennedy, C. R. The terrible meek
See also Peace

The **package** for Ponsonby. Davis, J.

Paddle your own canoe. Regnier, M.

Pagan magic. Goulding, D. J.

Page, Frank Russell
c Adopted by Santa Claus
Two children visiting Santa Claus's workshop on Christmas Eve see toys brought to life by Wizard of the North. 4m 1b 2g extras 1 interior
In Cahill, E. M. ed. Celebrating Christmas

A **page** of destiny. Lathrop, D.

A **pageant** of Christmas. Baxter, A. M.

The **pageant** of the Shearmen and Taylors— The Coventry Nativity play. Coventry plays

Pageants
Asbrand, K. All that glitters
c Asbrand, K. Come to Bethlehem
c Asbrand, K. The image of Christmas
Asbrand, K. It's time for remembering
Baden, R. The Christmas Eve visitor
Bangham, M. D. "Come, see the place..."
Bangham, M. D. Come to the manger
Brown, R. M. Freedom is our heritage
Carlson, M. M. Christmas in many nations
c Christmas old—Christmas new
Cruse, C. Healing in its wings
Dekker, T. Britannia's honor
Dekker, T. London's tempe
Dekker, T. The magnificent entertainment given to King James

Dekker, T. Troia-nova triumphans
DeWitt, R. H. Arise, thy light is come!
Emmons, D. G. Ours to the forty-ninth
Emurian, E. K. Great women of history
Emurian, E. K. The Last Supper
Emurian, E. K. The Resurrection
Goulding, D. J. The Nativity
Gruwell, B. G. O holy night
c Joy to the world
Kromer, H. They made a path
c Martens, A. C. A visit from Washington
Peery, R. R. The glory of His coming
c Salisbury, E. Shoe children
Smith, M. G. For God so loved the world
Waldrop, C. L. M. Unto us
Wilson, R. C. Easter witnesses
Wilson, R. C. Strangers in Bethlehem
See also Masques; Mysteries and miracle-plays

Pagnol
Topaz; tr. and introduction by Renée Waldinger. Barrons Educ. Ser. 1958 146p
Satirizes necessity of resorting to dishonesty in order to survive a predatory political system. Set in French boarding school in large city. 4 acts 43 scenes 10m 6w 11b 3 interiors

Pahl, Mel. See Warnick, C. jt. auth.

Paige, Milton C.
Father trims the tree
Christmas pantomime. Trimming Christmas tree proves difficult in spite of father's plans. 2m 1w 1b 1g 1 interior
In Cahill, E. M. ed. Celebrating Christmas

Painters
Casey, R. Late love
Coward, N. Nude with violin
c Curtis, P. D. The colours clash
Howard, S. The late Christopher Bean
Seiler, C. Nude washing dishes
Strindberg, A. Comrades

Painting
c Hark, M. and McQueen, N. Our own four walls
Miller, H. L. "N" for nuisance
Sutherland, D. Art for art's sake

Paintings
Howard, S. The late Christopher Bean
McCoy, P. S. Clara paints the town
Schofield, S. The old master
Travers, B. Wild horses

A **pair** of spectacles. Grundy, S.

The **pajama** game. Adler, R. and Ross, J.

Pajama party. Martens, A. C.

Palestine
History—To 70 A.D.
See Bible—History of Biblical events

Palm Sunday
Bailey, H. F. The singing children

Palm Sunday. York plays

A **palm** tree in a rose garden. Roberts, M.

Palmer, C. King
c Hop o' my thumb; libretto and lyrics by H. E. Priestley; music by C. King Palmer. Paxton 1958 27p
Pantomime based on Perrault's fairy tale. Singing and dancing. Musical score available separately. 4 scenes 14m 8w 6b chorus extras 2 interiors 2 exteriors

Palmer, King, and Palmer, Winifred
c Cinderella. Paxton 1954 20p
> Pantomime of folk tale based on Perrault's fairy tale. Singing and dancing. Musical score available separately. 4 scenes 6m 4w extras 2 interiors 1 exterior

c The magic mountain. Paxton 1954 15p music
> Operetta. Boy and girl use courage and faith to overcome goblins, which feat earns them privilege to ask favor of fairy queen. Includes music for songs. 3 scenes 6b 6g 1 exterior

Palmer, Winifred. See Palmer, K. jt. auth.

Paloma, Princess of Pluto. Howard, V.

Pan-American Day
Clark, S. G. 21 good neighbors
c McGee, A. Bill visits Mexico

The **panda** and the spy. Heinlein, M. V.

Pandas
Heinlein, M. V. The panda and the spy

Panetta, George
Comic strip. French 1958 83p illus
> Affairs of Italian family on Bleeker Street during era of Major LaGuardia's radio broadcasts. 3 acts 9m 3w 3b 3 interiors 1 exterior

Pantagleize. Ghelderode, M. de

Pantomimes
Abstance, P. and Abstance, L. Aunt Vonnie on vexation
Abstance, P. and Abstance, L. Corny confessions
Abstance, P. and Abstance, L. Cotton Road
Abstance, P. and Abstance, L. Feudin' in the mountains
Abstance, P. and Abstance, L. Gold in the West
Abstance, P. and Abstance, L. A Hallowe'en adventure
Abstance, P. and Abstance, L. The hold-up at Hoecake Junction
Abstance, P. and Abstance, L. Murder at the manor
Abstance, P. and Abstance, L. The pigskin parade
Abstance, P. and Abstance, L. Slender Ella
Abstance, P. and Abstance, L. Soapera
Abstance, P. and Abstance, L. The valiant Valentine
Asbrand, K. The week before Christmas
c Atwell, R. and Virden, H. Witch hunt
Bailey, H. F. "Better than seven sons"
Bailey, H. F. The picture window frames Christmas
Beckett, S. Act without words, I
Beckett, S, Act without words, II
Eldridge, M. T. Conference eve
Fisher, A. The safety parade
Fisher, A. and Rabe, O. Sing, America, sing
c Goulding, D. J. Pagan magic
Gruwell, B. G. O holy night
Hatcher, H. B. The holy Nativity
c Howard, D. Christmas doings
Jay, M. and Graham-Campbell, A. With this sword
c Jones, C. Clean-up time
Marston, M. A. A Christmas carol
Marston, M. A. Goblin market

Marston, M. A. The Jackdaw of Rheims
c Marston, M. A. Mimes with crowds
Marston, M. A. The Pied Piper of Hamelin
Marston, M. A. The riddling knight
Marston, M. A. The robbers
Marston, M. A. The roving journeyman
Martens, A. C. A bird in the bush
Martens, A. C. Cross your bridge
Martens, A. C. Now it can be told
Martens, A. C. Quiet, please
Martens, A. C. Shoot if you will
Martens, A. C. Sing a song of something
Martens, A. C. We're speechless (7 plays)
Martens, A. C. Who stole third base?
c Miller, H. L. New shoes
Paige, M. C. Father trims the tree
c Palmer, C. K. Hop o' my thumb
c Palmer, K. and Palmer, W. Cinderella
c Posso, M. E. Santa was so tired!
c Shrout, B. L. America sings
c Spamer, C. Helpers
c Swanson, V. A. What do you see in the manger?
Taggart, T. The midnight ride of Tex O'Coco
c Tyson, R. H. The life of Lincoln
Virden, H. Let's have a covered dish
Wagner, N. He is come! The Messiah!
c Walker, S. The seven gifts
Wilde, P. Legend
c Woolsey, J. and Sechrist, E, H. The legend of Babouska
c Woolsey, J. and Sechrist, E. H. Mother Goose's children
c Woolsey, J. and Sechrist, E. H. Saint Peter and the birds

Papa was a preacher. McGreevey, J.

The **paper** chain. Cary, F. L. and Butler, I.

Paper foxhole. Elward, J.

The **parable** of the last judgment. Phillips, J. B.

The **parable** of the Pharisee and the tax collector. Phillips, J. B.

The **parable** of the sower. Spamer, C. M.

Parables
Brecht, B. The good woman of Setzuan
> *See also* name of parable, e.g. Good Samaritan (Parable); Prodigal son (Parable); etc.

Paradis, Marjorie B.
Midge rings the bell
> Girl plays a prank at school but manages to win coveted scholarship anyway. 1 act 2 scenes 11w 2 interiors
> *In* Kamerman, S. E. ed. Blue-ribbon plays for graduation

Paraguay
Hochwaelder, F. The strong are lonely

The **parasols.** Spamer, C.

Parent and child
Addyman, E. Over the garden fence
Agg, H. Winter sunrise
Anderson, M. Lost in the stars
Arden, J. The party
Aurthur, R. A. A very special baby
Barrow, W. Peaceful evening
Beach, L. The goose hangs high
Bird, R. M. The broker of Bogota
Blazer, F. The prodigal mother

Parent and child—_Continued_

Boruff, J. The loud red Patrick
Camus, A. The misunderstanding
Chase, M. Bernardine
Chetham-Strode, W. The pet shop
Cusack, D. The golden girls
Delaney, S. A taste of honey
Dimondstein, B. Eva
Dimondstein, B. Mister Gultz
Fearheiley, D. A star too far
Foote, H. The death of the old man
Foote, H. The old beginning
Goldsmith, C. Your every wish
Hayes, M. and Hayes, J. Penny
Hebbel, F. Maria Magdalena
Hellman, L. Another part of the forest
Herlihy, J. L. and Noble, W. Blue denim
Holland, N. Will and testament
Howells, W. D. The mother and the father
Joy, R. P. Hour of honor
Kwanze, M. Kagekiyo
Lessing. Emilia Galotti
Lewis, G. Wait for morning, child
Lineberger, J. A sometime thing
Lynch, P. Betsy's first report card
MacKaye, S. Hazel Kirke
Morrill, K. A distant bell
Morris, C. The unloved
Mortimer, J. What shall we tell Caroline?
Mosel, T. The five dollar bill
Murch, E. Spring flowers for Marguerite
Nappier, P. And there was light
Olfson, L. King Lear
Oliver, W. I. The stallion
Posegate, E. D. Read me a story
c Quinlan, M. E. Betty gets a new dress
Richards, S. Through a glass, darkly
Roskam, C. Plenty of rein
Schiller, F. von. Intrigue and love
Schulman, A. A hole in the head
Shaber, D. The youngest shall ask
Shaffer, P. Five finger exercise
Shaw, B. Misalliance
Sheffield, J. The forgotten land
Shelby, K. and Cuny, T. M. Giving goes on
Spigelgass, L. A majority of one
Stephens, C. G. Once in September
Stuart, A. A gentleman's daughters
Taggart, T. Follow simple directions
Taylor, S. The pleasure of his company
Thom, R. Children of the ladybug
Thomas, D. Boy of mine
Vollmer, L. Sun-up
Vooght, C. Come live with me
Webber, C. E. Be good, sweet maid
Zuckerman, A. J. Blobo's boy
   See also Adolescence; Boys; Children; Family; Fathers; Girls; Mothers; Youth

Parents' and teachers' associations
c Miller, H. L. Mary's invitation

Parents are people. Weiss, M. J.

Paris
Becque, H. The vultures
Becque, H. Woman of Paris
Giraudoux, J. Madwoman of Chaillot
Loos, A. Gigi

Paris bound, Barry, P.

Parish, Jed
Mystery, mayhem, and murder! Bakers Plays 1954 102p (Baker's Edition of plays)
   Mystery comedy. When family moves into summer house, haunting laughter is heard, body is found in living room and mysterious stranger appears. 3 acts 4m 7w 1 interior

Parker, Dorothy
Here we are
   Newlyweds on train quarrel pointlessly on honeymoon. 1 scene 1m 1w 1 interior
   _In_ Cerf, B. and Cartmell, V. H. eds. 24 favorite one-act plays

Parker, Dorothy, and D'Usseau, Arnaud
The ladies of the corridor. French 1954 121p illus
   Social and moral problems of group of women living in New York residential hotel. 2 acts 12 scenes 7m 9w 6 interiors
   Trade edition published by Viking

Parker, John W.
Sleep on, Lemuel
   Set in North Carolina. A Negress conjure-doctor performs her tricks in order to bring two lovers together. 3m 2w 1 exterior
   _In_ Walser, R. ed. North Carolina drama

Parker, Ken
A cat has nine. Banner 1954 101p illus
   Domestic comedy. Man tries to run his family like an efficiency expert until his doctor reads wrong X-ray and tells him he hasn't long to live. 3 acts 5 scenes 3m 8w 1 interior

The surrounding mist. Northwestern Press 1956 100p illus (Royalty plays)
   Tragicomedy. A happy family, including ill father and fortune-telling grandmother faces crisis when the son who works in mental institution is attacked by patient. 3 acts 4 scenes 1m 5w 1 interior

Parker, Kenneth T.
Cry on my shoulder
   Television play. Romantic farce. Young theatrical agent falls in love with leading lady of unsuccessful play which he promoted. 5m 3w extras
   _In_ Parker, K. T. Parker's television plays

A cup of tea
   Television play. Clever fortune teller secures valuable ring from woman customer in tea shop. 2m 4w
   _In_ Parker, K. T. Parker's television plays

Double identity
   Television play. Murder mystery. Young man who resembles known criminal is used as dupe by criminal and his associates. 5m 3w extras
   _In_ Parker, K. T. Parker's television plays

Shall we dance?
   Television play. Romantic comedy. Young woman at dance studio gets chance to teach her older sister's former suitor. 4m 5w
   _In_ Parker, K. T. Parker's television plays

Stand up to death
   Television horror tale. Doctor tries to keep his daughter alive artificially after she died on her wedding night. 3m 2w
   _In_ Parker, K. T. Parker's television plays

Parker, Kenneth T.—*Continued*
Star minded
  Television play. Domestic comedy. Husband finds way to cure his wife of infatuation for movie star. 1m 4w
  In Parker, K. T. Parker's television plays
Voice of the machines
  Television drama of suspense. Life of young woman, apparently sole survivor of factory explosion, is endangered when she tells of the event. 4m 2w extras
  In Parker, K. T. Parker's television plays
Within the family
  Television tragedy. Policeman's integrity tested when he catches brother-in-law robbing store. 3m 3w
  In Parker, K. T. Parker's television plays
Parker, Mary Moncure
The prodigal comes home
  Based on Biblical parable of the prodigal son in the Gospel of Luke. 1 act 5m 3w 1 interior
  In Brings, L. M. comp. The golden book of church plays
Parkhirst, Douglass
c The Clown Prince of Wanderlust. French 1960 49p front music
  There is furious activity in kingdom of Wanderlust because someone must be able to help princess, who cannot laugh, before midnight. 2 acts 13m 12w extras 1 exterior
Early frost. French 1955 25p illus
  Mystery of two elderly sisters living alone in rambling house, one of whom was involved as a child in disappearance of little girl. Climax is reached when their little niece comes to live with them. 1 act 5w 1 interior
Safe harbor. French 1958 23p illus music
  Woman whose sweetheart is drowned at sea waits all her life for his return. Includes song with musical score. 1 act 3m 3w 1 interior
The **parliament** of heaven: The Annunciation and Conception. Coventry plays
The **parlor** car. Howells, W. D.
Parodies
  Bremer, W. Nothing but nonsense
c Floyd, B. Once upon a time
  Taggart, T. Macbeth a la mode
  Taggart, T. Two in the balcony
c Watkins, D. Frost-Bite and the eleven Fidgets
Parr, Ronald
The flying machine. Longmans 1955 22p illus (Plays for to-day)
  At isolated country inn, while waiting for his car to be repaired. English business man dreams of a highwayman's escape from that inn two hundred years before. 8m 3w 1 setting
Penny plain. Longmans 1955 23p illus
  While his sisters and brothers are at theatre with their uncle, a young invalid stages play in his toy theatre. 3m 2w 2b 2g 1 setting
Parties. See Entertaining
Parting friends. Howells, W. D.
The **party.** Arden, J.
A **party** is born. Gross, E. and Gross, N.
The **party** spirit. Jones, P. and Jowett, J.
Passages from Finnegans wake. Manning, M.
Passover
  Shaber, D. The youngest shall ask

The **pastor's** guiding hand. Sandberg, L. M.
Patch upon patch. Knight, C.
Patent medicines. See Medicines, Patent, proprietory, etc.
Pathelin
The farce of Master Pierre Pathelin; tr. by John Allen
  In 15th century France lawyer cheats a draper and in turn is victimized by same trick. 1 act 8 scenes 4m 1w 3 interiors 1 exterior
  In Allen, J. P. ed. Three medieval plays v3
Patient Grissil, Dekker, T.; Chettle, H. and Haughton, W.
Paton, Alan
Cry, the beloved country (dramatization) See Komai, F. Cry, the beloved country
Patria. Daviot, G.
Patrick, Saint
c Pierce, G. M. The story of March 17
Patrick, John
The Teahouse of the August Moon. Dramatists 1957 94p
  Satirical comedy based on novel by Vern Sneider. Captain of an Army team working to Americanize small Okinawan village faces problems engendered by official plans versus native culture. 3 acts 10 scenes 13m 4w 2b 1g extras 3 interiors 3 exteriors
  Trade edition published by Putnam
—Same
  In Gaver, J. ed. Critics' choice
Teahouse of the August Moon (condensation)
  In The Best plays of 1953-1954
  In Theatre, 1954
The **Patriotic** Teddy Bear and the UN. Miller, H. L.
Patriotism
  Fisher, A. and Rabe, O. Pledge to the flag
  Fisher, A. and Rabe, O. What is a patriot
  Hennessy, M. A. The American spirit
  Howard, V. What is an American?
  National Recreation Association. I hear America singing!
  Salinger, H. Great-grandfather was an immigrant
  Thompson, M. A. Young Doc Smith died tomorrow
The **patriots.** Cross, E. W.
The **patriots.** Kingsley, S.
Patterns. Reach, J.
Patterson, Leona
c The safety school
  School safety patrol is suddenly visited by special safety fairy who tells them how to prevent accidents. 5b 5g extras 1 interior
  In Birdsall, R. ed. Creative plays for every school month
Patton, Frances Gray
The beaded buckle
  Comedy. Small town socialite is accused of theft. 2m 4w 1 interior
  In Walser, R. ed. North Carolina drama
Paul, Saint, apostle
  Estes, S. In quest of power through witnessing
  Johnston, R. A. The Digby Conversion of St Paul

Paul in food land. Bornstein, M. and Cole, G.

Paul Revere, Boston patriot. Woolsey, J. and Sechrist, E. H.

Paul Revere: patriot and craftsman. Kissen, F,

Paul Revere rides again. Miller, H. L.

The **paying** guest. Assinder, P.

Payne, John Howard
Emurian, E. K. Home sweet home

Payne, John Howard, and Irving, Washington
Charles the Second
> Comedy of manners. King Charles II and Earl of Rochester disguise themselves as two rough sailors in a tavern. 3 acts 4 scenes 4m 2w 2 interiors 1 exterior

> *In* Quinn, A. H. ed. Representative American plays

Payton, Donald
Deadly Ernest. Art Craft 1953 79p illus
> Romantic comedy. Young man, fired from his job, has fight with his girl friend, then hires mysterious man named Ernest to put him out of his misery. 3 acts 5 scenes 6m 8w 1 interior

Father says no! Heuer 1953 28p
> Comedy. Father refuses to let his fourteen-year-old daughter have dates but grandmother circumvents orders. 1 act 4m 4w 1 interior

The hanging of Uncle Dilby. Art Craft 1953 29p illus
> Comedy. When family hears that old uncle is coming to visit they hasten to hang his portrait, but minor calamities intervene. 1 act 3m 3w 1 interior

He tried with his boots on. Art Craft 1953 31p illus
> Comedy. To escape from his parents and sister, Wilbur day dreams of living in Old West where he triumphs as Shoot-a-Mile Kid. 1 act 5m 5w 1 interior 1 exterior

It's great to be crazy. Art Craft 1953 80p illus
> Domestic comedy. Antics of three teenagers which include becoming amateur magicians and constructing fake family trees, taxes father's sanity. 3 acts 6m 9w 1 interior

Nearly beloved. Heuer 1953 79p
> Domestic comedy. Bored teenager keeps diary, full of terrible but non-existent events, which father secretly reads in order to know his children better. 3 acts 5m 8w 1 interior

Peace
Aristophanes. Peace
Conkle, E. P. No more wars but the moon
Freeman, L. The answer
Howard, P. The man with the key
Owens, R. J. Final edition

Peace. Aristophanes

Peace on Mars. Wilson, D. C.

Peaceful evening. Barrow, W.

Peach, L. du Garde
A horse! A horse! French (London) 1953 64p illus
> Comedy. When impoverished duke has trouble keeping estate together, his favorite horse suggests they form a circus group. 3 acts 3m 2w 1 interior

Peach, L. du Garde and Hay, Ian
The white sheep of the family. French 1953 112p illus
> Comedy. Family of criminals is shocked when the son wants to reform because of a girl, until her talent as safebreaker is revealed. 3 acts 4 scenes 5m 4w 1 interior

Peacock, Thomas Love
Nightmare Abbey (dramatization) See Sharp, A. Nightmare Abbey

Peasantry
China
Jennings, T.; Slesinger, T. and West, C. The good earth
Spain
Vega Carpio, L. de. Fuente ovejuna

Peasants. See Peasantry

Peavey, Hazel
Teen antics. French 1954 102p illus
> Comedy. When mother of two teen-age girls is called away on extended visit their two maiden aunts arrive to make life unbearable. 3 acts 4 scenes 4m 6w 1 interior

Pecos Bill
McCaslin, N. Tall Bill and his big ideas

A **peculiar** position. Scribe, E. and Bayard, J. F. A.

Peddlers and peddling
Barnett, M. Yankee peddler
> *See also* Salesmen and salesmanship

The **pedlar.** Wetmore, A.

Pedro II, Emperor of Brazil
Ullman, S. S. A democratic emperor

Peer Gynt. Ibsen, H.

Peery, Rob Roy
The glory of His coming. Lorenz 1956 32p music
> Christmas pageant about ancient world just before and after birth of Christ. 5 scenes 4 tableaux 16m 7w 1b extras chorus 2 interiors 2 exteriors

Peggy's on the phone. Clapp, P.

Pelléas and Mélisande. Maeterlinck, M.

Peloponnesian War, 431-404 B.C. See Greece —History—Peloponnesian War, 431-404 B.C.

The **pen** is deadlier. Carmichael, F.

The **pen** of my aunt. Daviot, G.

Penguins
c Wright, L. Mr Popper's penguins

Penitentes. See Flagellants and flagellation

Penn, William
Kissen, F. William Penn: brother to all men

Pennington, Lillian, and Kaeyer, Malvina
c Our home town
> Play for primary grades about jobs and responsibilities of all the people who live in a town. Includes songs and musical scores. 11m 3w extras 1 exterior

> *In* Birdsall, R. ed. Creative plays for every school month

Pennsylvania German dialect. See Dialect— German-American

Penny. Hayes, M. and Hayes, J.

The **penny.** Niss, S.

A **penny** for Charon. Miller, H. A.

Penny plain. Parr, R.

Pentecost
Phillips, J. B. The gift of the Holy Spirit

Penthesilea. Kleist, H. von

People to people. Martens, A. C.

The **people** versus Maxine Lowe. McMahon, L. E.

The **people** who came to an inn. Arlett, V. I.

The **people** win through. Nu, U.

Percy, Edward, and Denham, Lilian
The man with expensive tastes. English Theatre 1955 94p illus (Guild lib)
Mystery comedy about glamorous girl knife thrower, American detective and forger who must have money for his expensive tastes. Set in England. 3 acts 7m 3w 1 interior

The **perfect** aurora. Cooney, P.

Perfect understanding. Jackson, M. C.

Peril at the post office. Ready, S.

Period of adjustment. Williams, T.

Periodicals, Publishing of
Berg, D. The drop of a hat

Perl, Arnold
Tevya and his daughters. Dramatists 1958 54p
Comedy set in Czarist Russia, 1900. Adventures of Tevya, a poor Jew, his family, and how he marries off his daughters. 2 acts 6m 6w 1 interior

Tevya and the first daughter
Comedy based on the Tevya stories of Sholom Aleichem. In Czarist Russia, a poor Jew wishes to marry his daughter to rich suitor but she chooses poor tailor. 2 scenes 4m 6w 1 setting
In The Best short plays, 1959-1960

The world of Sholom Aleichem. Acting ed. Dramatists 1953 55p illus
These three acts may be produced as separate one-act plays. They all deal with Jews in Czarist Russia and are bound together by narrator. Mendele the Book Seller, actually Shalom Rabinowitz. The first act: the tale of Chelm, is based on Jewish folktale about village cheated of its quota of intelligence by angel who distributes souls. The second: Bontsche Schweig, is a fantasy about a poor, humble man who asked for only the most meager reward in heaven. The third, based on work by Sholom Aleichem, tells about Jewish parents who try to get son admitted to a non-religious school. 3 acts 16 scenes 20m 10w 3 interiors 1 exterior

Perrault, Charles
Cinderella (dramatization) See Palmer, K. and Palmer, W. Cinderella
Cinderella (dramatization) See Spamer, C. Cinderella's friends
Hop o' my thumb (dramatization) See Palmer, C. K. Hop o' my thumb
Puss in Boots (dramatization) See Goulding, D. J. The master cat; Miller, M. Puss in boots

Perrini, Alberto
Once a thief; tr. by Arline Labia
Comedy. Rector of small town, led by Devil, goes on soul-saving tour which ends in bank robbery. 3 scenes 9m 2w 2 interiors 1 exterior
In The Best short plays of 1955-1956

Perry, Marjean
The fifth wheel. French 1958 26p illus
Comedy. One woman member throws the Woman's Club into complete confusion during her six months membership. 1 act 5w 1 interior

A trap is a small place
Girl wants to marry and escape stifling relationship with another woman, but boy is dominated by his mother. 1 act 1m 3w 1 interior
In The Best short plays, 1952-1953
In The Best short plays, 1957

Two's company
Romantic comedy. Girl is torn between two suitors. 4 scenes 2m 1w 1 interior
In The Best short plays, 1959-1960

The **Persians**. Aeschylus

Personal liberty. See Liberty

Personality
Dennis, N. Cards of identity
Strindberg, A. The road to Damascus
See also Character; Individuality

Personality, Disorders of
Sieveking, L. The strange case of Dr Jekyll and Mr Hyde

Pertwee, Roland
Dirty work. English Theatre 1954 22p illus (Guild lib)
Mystery comedy. Two thieves make clever use of launderette to hide jewels stolen from store across the street. 1 act 7w 1g 1 interior

Pests

Extermination
Conkle, E. P. Arbie the bug boy

The **pet** shop. Chetham-Strode, W.

Pete of the rancho. Quinlan, M. E.

Peter, Saint, apostle
Cockram, R. Shadow of the eagle
Estes, S. In quest of power through the Holy Spirit
c Woolsey, J. and Sechrist, E. H. Saint Peter and the birds

Peterson, Charles Alden
Gross E. and Gross, N. Dooley and the amateur hour

Peterson, Len
Desert soliloquy
Radio play. Hopi Indian youth reviews training and ideas he received from his people in effort to decide whether to continue education in white man's world. 3m 5w 2b
In Goldschmidt, W. ed. Ways of mankind

Home, sweet home
Radio play. A Chinese-American visiting his relatives in China contrasts his family's customs in America with family structure in China. 5m 2w 1b
In Goldschmidt, W. ed. Ways of mankind

Stand-in for a murderer
Radio play. Act of ritual warfare ends in death for young noble of Tlingit Indian tribe in 19th-century Alaska. 6m
In Goldschmidt, W. ed. Ways of mankind

Sticks and stones
Radio play. Portrays some of religious and social customs of Arunta natives in Australia. 10m 1w 1b
In Goldschmidt, W. ed. Ways of mankind

Peterson, Louis
Take a giant step. French 1954 110p illus
Negro teen-ager is condemned by his family and at school when he contradicts teacher in her remarks about Negroes in the Civil War, but his grandmother defends him. 2 acts 6 scenes 9m 7w 4 interiors

Take a giant step (condensation)
In The Best plays of 1953-1954

Peterson, Mary Nygaard
c Happy Chanukah
>   Little boy learns about the origin of
>   Chanukah, the Jewish Feast of Lights.
>   3m 1w 2g 1 interior
>   *In* Birdsall, R. ed. Creative plays for
>   every school month

c Ten helpful elves
>   Lazy young wife whose house is un-
>   tidy, is visited by ten elves who show
>   her how to keep everything neat and
>   clean. 1m 1w extras 1 interior
>   *In* Birdsall, R. ed. Creative plays for
>   every school month

Petey's choice. Carmichael, F.

The **petrified** forest. Sherwood, R. E.

The **Petrified** Prince. Miller, H. L.

Petronius Arbiter
Widow of Ephesus (dramatization)   See
>   Fry, C. A phoenix too frequent

Petticoat handicap. Westgate, T.

Phaedra. Racine, J. B.

Phantasy. See Fantasy

Phantoms. See Apparitions

The **Pharaoh's** dream. Spamer, C. M.

The **Pharaoh's** silver. Howard, V.

Pharisees
Coventry plays. The woman taken in adultery

Pharmacists
Campton, D. The laboratory

Pharmacy
Armer, A. and Grauman, W. E. The last
straw

Phelps, Lyon
The Gospel Witch. Harvard Univ. Press
1955 94p
>   Dramatization of some events before
>   and during witchcraft trials in Salem,
>   Massachusetts in the 1690's. 10 scenes
>   9m 4w extras 8 interiors 1 exterior
—Same
>   *In* Halverson, M. ed. Religious drama, 3

Philadelphia

Social life and customs
Crichton, K. The happiest millionaire

Philip II, King of Macedonia
Williams, N. Night of storm

Philip II, King of Spain
Schiller, F. von. Don Carlos

Philippa, consort of Edward III, King of England
Shaw, B. The six of Calais

Philippine Islands
Fisher, A. and Rabe, O. Skills to share

Phillips, Addison Leroy
The shepherds and the wise men
>   The shepherds and three wise men meet
>   in Bethlehem to warn Joseph and Mary
>   of King Herod's intention to kill the in-
>   fant Jesus. Choral music. 1 act 10m 1w 1b
>   extras choir 1 setting
>   *In* Brings, L. M. ed. The modern treas-
>   ury of Christmas plays

Phillips, Irving
Gown of glory. Dramatic 1953 94p
>   Dramatization of novel by Agnes Sligh
>   Turnbull about poor Presbyterian min-
>   ister's family in small Pennsylvania vil-
>   lage of the early 1900's. 3 acts 10m 10w
>   1 interior

Phillips, J. B.
The arrest in the garden
>   Radio play. Based on Biblical accounts
>   in New Testament Gospels. Jesus prays
>   with His disciples in Garden of Geth-
>   semane where He is betrayed by Judas
>   Iscariot and arrested. 8m 2w
>   *In* Phillips, J. B. A man called Jesus

The Ascension
>   Radio play. Based on Biblical account
>   in New Testament Book of Acts. Forty
>   days after His Resurrection, as His dis-
>   ciples watch, Jesus ascends into heaven.
>   6m
>   *In* Phillips, J. B. A man called Jesus

The baptism of Jesus
>   Radio play. Based on Biblical accounts
>   in New Testament Gospels. Jesus comes
>   to the River Jordan to be baptized by
>   John. 4m 1b
>   *In* Phillips, J. B. A man called Jesus

The boyhood of Jesus
>   Radio play. Based on Biblical account in
>   New Testament Gospel of Luke. At age
>   of twelve Jesus visits the Temple at
>   Jerusalem. 6m 1w
>   *In* Phillips, J. B. A man called Jesus

The calling of the disciples
>   Radio play. Based on Biblical accounts
>   in New Testament Gospels. Andrew,
>   Peter, Philip and Nathanael become
>   the first disciples of Christ. 5m
>   *In* Phillips, J. B. A man called Jesus

The centurion's servant
>   Radio play. Based on Biblical accounts
>   in New Testament Gospels. Jesus heals
>   servant of Roman officer. 5m 1b
>   *In* Phillips, J. B. A man called Jesus

Christ enters Jerusalem
>   Radio play. Based on Biblical account
>   in New Testament Gospels. Jesus makes
>   triumphal entry into Jerusalem. 7m 1b
>   *In* Phillips, J. B. A man called Jesus

Christ the Son of God
>   Radio play. Based on Biblical accounts
>   in New Testament Gospels. Peter iden-
>   tifies Jesus as Messiah. 5m
>   *In* Phillips, J. B. A man called Jesus

The cleansing of the Temple
>   Radio play. Based on Biblical accounts
>   in New Testament Gospels. Jesus orders
>   the commercial enterprisers out of Tem-
>   ple at Jerusalem. 3m 1w
>   *In* Phillips, J. B. A man called Jesus

The death of Jesus and the promise of the
Resurrection
>   Radio play. Based on Biblical accounts
>   in New Testament Gospels. The Cruci-
>   fixion of Christ. 11m
>   *In* Phillips, J. B. A man called Jesus

The gift of the Holy Spirit
>   Radio play. Based on Biblical account
>   in New Testament Book of Acts. After
>   Jesus' death, on day of Pentecost Holy
>   Spirit descends upon His disciples. 8m
>   *In* Phillips, J. B. A man called Jesus

The healing at the pool of Bethesda
>   Radio play. Based on Biblical account
>   in New Testament Gospel of John. On
>   the Sabbath Jesus heals a lame man.
>   6m
>   *In* Phillips, J. B. A man called Jesus

The healing of the man born blind
>   Radio play. Based on Biblical account
>   in New Testament Gospel of John. On
>   the Sabbath Jesus sends blind man to
>   wash in Pool of Siloam and thus gain
>   sight. 6m
>   *In* Phillips, J. B. A man called Jesus

Phillips, J. B.—*Continued*

The healing of the paralyzed man
Radio play. Based on Biblical accounts in New Testament Gospels. Jesus heals paralytic whose friends have lowered him through hole in roof of house where Jesus is preaching. 14m 1w
In Phillips, J. B. A man called Jesus

Jesus appears in Galilee
Based on Biblical account in New Testament Gospel of John. As disciples fish in sea of Galilee, Jesus, after His Resurrection, appears to them. 5m
In Phillips, J. B. A man called Jesus

Jesus appears to His disciples
Radio play. Based on Biblical accounts in New Testament Gospels. After His Resurrection Jesus appears to two of His followers on road to Emmaus and later to disciples in closed room. 7m
In Phillips, J. B. A man called Jesus

Jesus returns to Galilee
Radio play. Based on Biblical account in New Testament Gospel of Mark. Jesus sends disciples out into world to preach. 13m
In Phillips, J. B. A man called Jesus

The journey to Jerusalem
Radio play. Based on Biblical accounts in New Testament Gospels. Jesus and disciples journey toward Jerusalem for Passover. 7m
In Phillips, J. B. A man called Jesus

The Last Supper
Radio play. Based on Biblical accounts in New Testament Gospels. Jesus gathers disciples together for Last Supper. 6m
In Phillips, J. B. A man called Jesus

The Lord's prayer
Radio play. Based on Biblical account in New Testament Gospel of Matthew. Jesus teaches disciples the Lord's prayer. 5m extras
In Phillips, J. B. A man called Jesus

The parable of the last judgment
Radio play. Based on Biblical accounts in New Testament Gospels. Jesus teaches about last judgment and later is betrayed to high priests by Judas. 9m
In Phillips, J. B. A man called Jesus

The parable of the Pharisee and the tax collector
Radio play. Based on Biblical account in New Testament Gospel of Luke. Jesus' parable about prayers of a Pharisee and a publican. 8m
In Phillips, J. B. A man called Jesus

The Resurrection of Jesus
Radio play. Based on Biblical account in New Testament Gospel of John. After His Resurrection Jesus appears to Mary Magdalene in garden near His tomb. 3m 1w
In Phillips, J. B. A man called Jesus

The temptation of Jesus
Radio play. Based on Biblical accounts in New Testament Gospels. Jesus is tempted by Satan during forty days in the wilderness. 2m
In Phillips, J. B. A man called Jesus

The Transfiguration
Radio play. Based on Biblical accounts in New Testament Gospels. Peter, James and John witness the Transfiguration of Christ. 4m
In Phillips, J. B. A man called Jesus

The trial before Pilate
Radio play. Based on Biblical accounts in New Testament Gospels. Jesus is tried before Pilate and condemned to be crucified. 8m extras
In Phillips, J. B. A man called Jesus

Phillips, Marguerite Kreger

A flair for fashion
An old client recognizes Daphne Kerr's grandmother as famous dressmaker who gave up career to care for Daphne. 1 act 6w 1 interior
In Kamerman, S. E. ed. Blue-ribbon plays for girls

Grandma and mistletoe
Blind grandmother reforms thief who kisses her under mistletoe. 1 act 1m 3w 1 interior
In Brings, L. M. ed. The modern treasury of Christmas plays

Hold that Indian. Eldridge 1955 19p (Eldridge Popular one-act playscripts)
Comedy. Three junior high students who run away from home to get into movies, are disillusioned to find guard at the gate of studio is an Indian working his way through college. 1 act 4m 4w 1 exterior

The woman who didn't want Christmas
Five orphans help cynical business woman find spirit of Christmas. 1 act 4w 5g 1 interior
In Kamerman, S. E. ed. Blue-ribbon plays for girls

Phillips, T. J.

Miss Harper's birthday. Bakers Plays 1955 22p
Two snobbish school teachers who have spent their lives meeting the right people must face reality when their young nephew comes to live with them. 1 act 2m 3w 1 interior

Philoctetes. Sophocles

Philosophers
Ghelderode, M. de. Pantagleize

Philosophers' stone. See Alchemy

Philosophy
Betti, U. The burnt flower-bed
Brabazon, F. The bridge
Brabazon, F. Happy monody
Brabazon, F. The madmen
Brabazon, F. The moon
Brabazon, F. The quest
Camus, A. Caligula
Camus, A. The just assassins
Claudel, P. Break of noon
Lagerkvist, P. Let man live
Malcolm, I. A moment of existence
Millet, M. Dangerous Jack
Olson, E. Faust: a masque
Oringer, B. I. Son of the revolution
Saroyan, W. The cave dwellers
Saroyan, W. The time of your life
Strindberg, A. The great highway
See also Ethics; Good and evil

Philosophy, Jewish
Chayefsky, P. Holiday song

Philp, Peter
Love and lunacy. Miller, J.G. 1955 125p front
Satire on our present and future world, from peace conferences to politicians, showing how Moon first brought love and lunacy to Earth. 3 acts 4m 2w extras 3 exteriors

The **Phoenician** maidens. Euripides

The **Phoenician** women. Euripides

Phoenix '55. Wallach, I.

A **phoenix** too frequent. Fry, C.

Phormio. Terence

The **physical** threat. Brenner, M.

Physician in charge. Carruthers, J.

The **physician** in spite of himself. Molière, J. B. P.

Physicians
Blankfort, D. and Blankfort, M. Monique
Blewett, D. Quiet night
Burlingame, C. Yellow fever
Carruthers, J. Physician in charge
Hark, M. and McQueen, N. The place to begin
Howells, W. D. A masterpiece of diplomacy
Ibsen, H. An enemy of the people
Martens, A. C. Dr Hudson's secret journal
Molière, J. B. P. Love's the best doctor
Molière, J. B. P. The would-be invalid
Priestley, H. E. Punch and the doctor
Rattigan, T. The deep blue sea
Rodgers, R. and Hammerstein, O. Allegro
Romains, J. Dr Knock

Physicists
King, N. The shadow of doubt

Pianists
Batson, G. I found April
Shaw, B. The music-cure
Spewack, S. and Spewack, B. The festival

The **Piccolominis.** Schiller, F. von. See Schiller, F. von. Wallenstein

Pick a Dilly. Tobias, J.

Picking the team. Curtis, P. D.

The **Pickwick** papers. Olfson, L.

Picnic. Inge, W.

A **picnic** for father. Woolsey, J. and Sechrist, E. H.

Picnicking
Bradley, A. This England
Buell, H. Fat woman picnic

The **picture** window frames Christmas. Bailey, H. F.

Pictures in the fire. Martens, A. C.

Pictures in the hallway. O'Casey, S.

The **Pied** Piper of Hamelin. Marston, M. A.

The **Pied** Piper of Hamlin. Dunbar, T. M.

Pierce, Carl Webster
Be yourself! Bakers Plays 1957 85p (Baker's Royalty plays)
Comedy. Under terms of will, snobbish woman and her son must live for a year with her lower class sister and her bus driver son to inherit half interest in hotel. 3 acts 6m 5w 1 interior
Dough for dopes. Bakers Plays 1954 96p illus (Baker's Royalty plays)
Domestic comedy. A woman's ambition in life to get acquainted with the town's social leader is fostered when she suddenly wins twenty-five thousand dollars on television show. 3 acts 7m 11w 1 interior
Mum's the word. Bakers Plays 1955 89p illus (Baker's Royalty plays)
Comedy. Young man, unpopular with his fiancee's mother, tries to correct attitude in unorthodox situations, involving owner of an antique shop, a trance medium and a young man who is turned into a mummy. 3 acts 6m 7w extras 2 interiors

Pierce, Georgiana M.
c The story of March 17
St Patrick's Day. How Saint Patrick escaped death and was permitted to continue preaching in Ireland. 2m 1b 1g extras 1 exterior
In Birdsall, R. ed. Creative plays for every school month

Pierpont, John
Emurian, E. K. Three skits for Christmas

Piersel, W. Guthrie
A town is born. Bakers Plays 1957 24p
Adapted from author's story. At Christmas Eve, on a train, five rough men build ideal imaginary town for little girl who is bored by inactivity. 1 act 6m 1g 1 interior

The **pigskin** parade. Abstance, P. and Abstance, L.

Pilcher, Rosamunde. See Gairdner, C. C. jt. auth.

Pilgrim, Frank
The skeleton at the party. Deane 1955 28p ("Deane's" Ser. of plays)
Comedy. In midst of girl's wedding festivities a strange woman arrives claiming to be her father's widow and heir to his estate. 1 act 6w 1 interior

Pilgrim Fathers
c Asbrand, K. When America was young
c Chandler, R. America remembers
c Warner, L. H. The thankful Pilgrims

Pilgrim parting. Miller, H. L.

Pin-up pals. Miller, H. L.

Pinero, Arthur W.
The magistrate
Concealment of a woman's real age in her second marriage causes embarrassment. 3 acts 4 scenes 12m 4w 4 interiors
In Bentley, E. ed. From the modern repertoire; ser. 3
The thunderbolt
Missing will drawn in favor of illegitimate daughter complicates inheritance. 4 acts 10m 9w 3 interiors
In Tucker, S. M. ed. Twenty-five modern plays
Trelawny of the Wells (condensation)
In The Best plays of 1894-1899

Ping-pong. Adamov, A.

The **pink** parasol. Miller, H. L.

A **pink** party dress. Bucci, M.

Pinky Winky's trip to the moon. Floyd, B.

Pinnacle. Neuenburg, E.

Pinocchio. Miller, M.

The **pint** pot. Sugarman, J.

Pinter, Harold
The caretaker
Tragedy of modern life. Tramp serves as catalytic agent in relationship of two diametrically opposite brothers. 3 acts 3m 1 interior
In Pinter, H. The caretaker and The dumb waiter
The dumb waiter
Horror tale. In basement of a run-down boarding house two gunmen await their next victim. 2m 1 interior
In Pinter, H. The caretaker and The dumb waiter

Pip and the convict. Boyd, A. K.

Pipe dream. Rodgers, R.

Pirandello, Luigi
As you desire me; tr. by Marta Abba
> Concerns identity of young woman believed to be the bride who, ten years before, had been carried away from her Italian home by Austrian officers during World War I. 3 acts 9m 7w 2 interiors

In Gassner, J. ed. Twenty best European plays on the American stage
"Henry IV"; tr. by Edward Storer
> Tragedy. Man who has masqueraded as insane for many years commits crime, compelling him to continue his pretended madness. 3 acts 11m 2w 2 interiors

In Watson, E. B. ed. Contemporary drama: fifteen plays
Lazarus; tr. by Frederick May
> Young seminarian has his faith restored to him through his father's resurrection. 3 acts 8m 3w 2 exteriors

In Pirandello, L. The rules of the game; The life I gave you; Lazarus
The life I gave you; tr. by Frederick May
> Tragic figure of a mother who, giving up her grandchild-to-be, loses her son a second time. Portrays life transferred from one to another by strength of love. 3 acts 3m 6w extras 1 interior

In Pirandello, L. The rules of the game; The life I gave you; Lazarus
The mountain giants
> Pirandello's last play. Notes indicate action in last, unfinished act. Characters are members of theatrical company, play is partly fable, partly real. 3 acts 10m 4w extras 1 interior 2 exteriors

In Pirandello, L. The mountain giants, and other plays
The new colony
> Political drama written as protest against the Fascist government of Italy under Benito Mussolini. 3 acts 10m 12w extras 1 interior 1 exterior

In Pirandello, L. The mountain giants, and other plays
Right you are; Cosí è (se vi pare) A stage version with an introduction and notes by Eric Bentley. Columbia Univ. Press 1954 165p illus (Columbia Bicentennial editions and studies)
> A man and his mother-in-law tell conflicting stories about their respective wife and daughter. Audience has to decide which is illusion and which is reality. 3 acts 24 scenes 9m 7w extras 2 interiors

The rules of the game; tr. by Robert Rietty
> Man appears indifferent to his wife's lover and refuses to fight for her so that her lover is killed instead. 3 acts 9m 4w 2 interiors

In Pirandello, L. The rules of the game; The life I gave you; Lazarus
Six characters in search of an author; tr. from the Italian by Edward Storer
> Play within a play. Play rehearsal interrupted by characters who claim they are being misrepresented by both author and actors. 3 acts 10m 7w 1b 1g extras 1 interior

In Heffner, H. The nature of drama
In A Treasury of the theatre
When someone is somebody
> Comedy portraying idolization of literary success in modern world. 3 acts 5 scenes 11m 6w extras 2 interiors 1 exterior

In Pirandello, L. The mountain giants, and other plays

Pirates
c Bennett, R. The runaway pirate
c Goulding, D. J. Pirates! !
c Gow, R. Under the skull and bones
c John, C. Sea shells
York, M. A. Treasure Island
Pirates! ! Goulding, D. J.
Pistol-packin' Sal. Tomkins, B.
Pitcher, Molly. See McCauley, Mary (Ludwig) Hays
Pitfall. Cary, F. L.
Pitts, William Savage
Emurian, E. K. The church in the wildwood
Pity the poor fish. Keeney, C. H.
Pixies. See Fairies
A **place** for all. Spamer, C.
The **place** to begin. Hark, M. and McQueen, N.
Plague
> ### Scotland
> Bottomley, G. Fire at Callart

Plain and fancy. Hague, A.
The **plain** Princess. Harris, A.
Plaintiff in a pretty hat. Williams, H. and Williams, M.
Planets
c Spamer, C. King Sun
Planting time. Very, A.
Platypus. See Duckbills
Plautus
The haunted house
> Latin comedy about a roguish servant and the complications that arise from his plots and intrigues. 5 acts 9m 3w 1 exterior

In Casson, L. ed. Masters of ancient comedy
Mostellaria; tr. by Lynn Boal Mitchell
> Comedy. Adventures of cunning slave and how he outwits his master. 5 acts 14m 5w 2 exteriors

The rope
> Latin comedy about a girl stolen from her father and adventures that befall them both before they are reunited. 5 acts 9m 4w extras 2 exteriors

In Casson, L. ed. Masters of ancient comedy

A **play** for Christmas Eve. Duff, A.
The **Play** of Daniel; ed. for modern performance by Noah Greenberg; narration by W. H. Auden. Oxford 1959 118p illus music
> 13th century liturgical drama based on British Museum's transcription of the Beauvais Play of Daniel. Life of Daniel, the prophet, as related in Old Testament Book of Daniel. Includes full musical scores. 11m 3w extras choir 1 setting

The **play** of the shepherds; Wakefield cycle: secunda pastorum. Towneley plays
Play production (Theater) See Theater—Production and direction
Play within a play
Anderson, M. Elizabeth the Queen
Chesterton, G. K. The surprise
Emurian, E. K. Uncle Sam
Genet, J. The blacks: a clown show
Ghelderode, M. de. Three actors and their drama

Plays in verse—*Continued*
c Spamer, C. The store
c Spamer, C. Tea party
Stanley-Wrench, M. The splendid burden
Switz, T. M. and Johnston, R. A. eds.
  Great Christian plays (5 plays)
Taggart, T. Macbeth a la mode
Thom, R. Children of the ladybug
The three Maries
Tourneur, C. The atheist's tragedy
Tourneur, C. The revenger's tragedy
Towneley plays. The play of the shepherds; Wakefield cycle: secunda pastorum
Towneley plays. The Wakefield Pageant
  of Herod the Great
Towneley plays. The Wakefield Second
  shepherds' pageant
c Very, A. The cat who wanted to ride on
  a broom
c Very, A. The dancing children
c Very, A. Doctor Time's office
c Very, A. The flower garden
c Very, A. Gifts for young Abe
c Very, A. A golden bell for mother
c Very, A. John Grumlie
c Very, A. The Mayflower
c Very, A. Old Lady Witch's party
c Very, A. The old woman and her pig
c Very, A. Planting time
c Very, A. The shoemaker and the elves
c Very, A. Thanksgiving Eve
c Very, A. Three little kittens go to school
c Very, A. The three sillies
c Very, A. Tick-tock
c Very, A. The trees at school
Viereck, P. The tree witch
Waley, A. The Nō plays of Japan (36
  plays)
Webster, J. The Duchess of Malfi
Webster, J. The white Devil
Webster, J. and Tourneur, C. Four plays
The Welsh embassador
Wilde, O. The Duchess of Padua
Wilde, O. La sainte courtisane
Williams, T. The purification
Willis, N. P. Tortesa the usurer
c Woolsey, J. and Sechrist, E. H. Mother
  Goose gives advice
Yeats, W. B. At the hawk's well
Yeats, W. B. Calvary
Yeats, W. B. The Countess Cathleen
Yeats, W. B. The death of Cuchulain
Yeats, W. B. Deirdre
Yeats, W. B. The dreaming of the bones
Yeats, W. B. A full moon in March
Yeats, W. B. The green helmet
Yeats, W. B. The herne's egg
Yeats, W. B. The King of the Great
  Clock Tower
Yeats, W. B. The king's threshold
Yeats, W. B. The Land of Heart's De-
  sire
Yeats, W. B. The only jealousy of Emer
Yeats, W. B. Purgatory
Yeats, W. B. The shadowy waters
Yelvington, R. A cloud of witnesses
York plays. The Ascension
York plays. The birth of Christ

York plays. The creation, and The fall
  of Lucifer
York plays. The creation of Adam and
  Eve
York plays. The creation of man
York plays. The creation of the heavenly
  beings: The fall of Lucifer; York Tan-
  ners' play
York plays. The Crucifixion
York plays. The fall of man
York plays. The Garden of Eden
York plays. The judgment
York plays. The last judgement; York
  Mercers' play
York plays. Palm Sunday
York plays. The Resurrection
York plays. The second trial before Pilate:
  The scourging and condemnation
York plays. The temptation of Christ
Young, S. The sound of apples
The play's the thing. Molnar, F.
Playwrights. See Dramatists
Pleasant dreams. Hark, M. and McQueen, N.
Pleasant dreams. Thompson, B. J.
Please communicate. Oldfield, M.
The **pleasure** of his company. Taylor, S.
Pledge to the flag. Fisher, A. and Rabe, O.
Plenty of rein. Roskam, C.
The **plight** of the tree. Spamer, C.
Plop! Click! Sakanishi, S. tr.
The **plough** and the stars. O'Casey, S.
The **plum** tree. McMahon, L. E. and
  Sergel, R.
Pocahontas. Custis, G. W. P.
Poel, William. See Howells, W. D. jt.
  auth.
Poetry
  Kwanze, M. Haku Rakuten
Poets
  Dekker, T. Satiromastix
  Emurian, E. K. The new colossus
  Grillparzer, F. Sappho
  Mishima, Y. Sotoba Komachi
  Yeats, W. B. The king's threshold
Poinsett, Joel Roberts
  Emurian, E. K. Three skits for Christ-
  mas
Poisoners
  Denham, R. and Smith, C. S. A dash of
  bitters
  See also Murder
Poisons
  Last, J. Mr Mason
Pole, Reginald, Cardinal
  Williamson, H. R. His Eminence of Eng-
  land
Police
c Bayliss, R. G. The burglar alarm
  Cary, F. L. Pitfall
c Fisher, A. Sure cure
  Niss, S. The penny
  Parker, K. T. Within the family
c Woolsey, J. and Sechrist, E. H. What
  happened to Billy?
  See also Detectives
  Great Britain
  Webber, J. Inspector Hart's experiment

Policewomen
Bollans, G. E. The crooked courtship

Poliomyelitis
c Miller, G. and Livingston, S. A march of dimes
Schary, D. Sunrise at Campobello

Politeness. See Courtesy

Political conventions
Vidal, G. The best man

Political ethics
Vidal, G. A sense of justice
See also Corruption (in politics)

Political refugees. See Refugees, Political

Politics, Practical
Bock, J. Fiorello!
Corwin, N. The rivalry
Hark, M. and McQueen, N. Vote for your hero
Ionesco, E. The leader
McCleery, W. The lady chooses
Shaw, B. The apple cart
Timpany, F. P. The storm at sea
Vidal, G. The best man
c Wallerstein, J. S. Johnny Aladdin
Warren, R. P. All the king's men
See also Corruption (in politics)

The **polka** dot pup. Miller, H. L.

Pollard, Samuel
Arnold, H. G. Sam Pollard

Polly patchwork. Field, R.

Pollywogs. Howard, V.

Polo, Marco
c Jordan, L. M. and Garber, H. W. Traveler to Cathay
Warnick, C. and Pahl, M. Adventures of Marco Polo

Polygamy
Easton, C. Champagne sec

Pomeranz, Edward
Only a game. French 1954 35p illus
A man whose philosophy of life is to keep people laughing at his jokes has no friends and cannot understand why he is dropped from a club. 1 act 5m 2w 1 interior

The **pomp** of Mr Pomfret. Daviot, G.

The **Ponder** heart. Fields, J. and Chodorov, J.

A **poor** gentleman. Turgenev, I.

Poor Old Bongo! Conkle, E. P.

Popocatepetl and Ixtaccihuatl. See Ullman, S. S. Princess of the snows

Popplewell, Jack
Dead on nine
Two other murders result from foiled plots of a husband and wife to kill each other. 3 acts 7 scenes 4m 3w 1 interior
In Plays of the year, v13

Dear delinquent. Dramatists 1958 90p illus
Romantic comedy. When pretty girl who is also a burglar, robs a man's apartment, he decides to reform her. 3 acts 4 scenes 5m 3w 1 interior
—Same
In Plays of the year v16

Port and a pistol. Nicholson, H.

Porter, Alyene
Papa was a preacher (dramatization)
See McGreevey, J. Papa was a preacher

Porter, Cole
Kiss me Kate; a musical play; book by Samuel and Bella Spewack; lyrics by Cole Porter. Knopf 1953 147p illus
Musical comedy. Adaptation of Shakespeare's "Taming of the shrew." During rehearsals for musical version of Shakespeare play, director and divorced wife, a Hollywood star, become reconciled. Play within a play. 2 acts 16 scenes 17m 5w extras 7 interiors 4 exteriors

Porter, Ella Williams
Callie goes to camp
New girl at camp seems queer and bookish until she beats the best tennis player in camp. 1 act 3 scenes 4g 2 interiors
In Kamerman, S. E. ed. Blue-ribbon plays for girls

Porter, Harriette Wilburr
c Election Day
Older man tells a younger how important it is for all citizens to vote. 2m extras 1 interior
In Birdsall, R. ed. Creative plays for every school month

Porter, Jack V.
Blueprint, U.S.A.
Radio play. Radio announcer broadcasts signing of Constitution of the United States at Constitutional Convention in Philadelphia, 1787. Background music. 11m
In Prescott, H. ed. Patrioscript

The **portrait.** Casey, B. M.

Portrait of a Madonna. Williams, T.

Portrait of an American. Hark, M. and McQueen, N.

Portrait of Deborah. Emery, C.

Portraits
Payton, D. The hanging of Uncle Dilby

Posegate, Ethel Durnal
The Christmas star
Movie actress finds she is fortunate to be stranded on Christmas Eve with Christian farmer's family during snow storm. 1 act 4 scenes 4m 4w 1g 1 setting
In Brings, L. M. ed. The modern treasury of Christmas plays

His wonders to perform. Rodeheaver 1953 15p
When young soldier returns home to family, they find that his experiences have imbued him with importance of prayer and unselfishness in celebrating Christmas. 3 acts 5m 4w 1g 1 interior

Putting first things first
Two young mothers get some good advice from wise old grandmother. 1 act 3w 1g 1 interior
In Brings, L. M. comp. The golden book of church plays

Read me a story. Rodeheaver 1954 16p
Easter drama. Two parents have little time for their neglected child who visits Christian home where story of Easter is read to her. 4 acts 3m 3w 1b 2g 3 interiors

Posen
Boretz, A. The trial of Poznan

The **possessed.** Camus, A.

Posso, Mary Estelle
c Santa was so tired!
Christmas pantomime. Santa almost fails to wake up in time to deliver Christmas toys. 4 characters extras 1 interior
In Birdsall, R. ed. Creative plays for every school month

Postage-stamps
Curtis, P. D. Fair deals
Postal service
United States
c Woolsey, J. and Sechrist, E. H. A letter
is mailed
Postance, Nancy
Surprise! French 1953 35p illus
Romantic comedy. Girl is determined to
marry a man despite mother's objections,
until other girls' pictures fall out of his
pockets. 1 act 2 scenes 5w 1 interior
Posture
c Fisher, A. Getting it straight
c Oh, can you help the princess?
The **pot** of broth. Yeats, W. B.
Potter, Dan S.
A touch of marble
Memory of incident involving psychotic
schoolmate causes frigidity in young
woman. 6 scenes 4m 3w 1 interior
In The Best short plays, 1958-1959
The **potting** shed. Greene, G.
Pottow, Dorothy
c Preparing for winter
Boy and girl learn about the ways the
animals, trees and flowers prepare for
winter. 2 scenes 1m 1w 1b 1g extras
2 exteriors
In Birdsall, R. ed. Creative plays for
every school month
A **pound** of prevention. Atwell, R.
A **pound** on demand. O'Casey, S.
Poverman, Helen
Easy money
Aged immigrant refuses to accept his
children's suggestions for getting benefits
from government by making false claims.
Italian-American dialect. 3m 1w extras
1 interior
In The Best short plays, 1958-1959
Poverty
Gorky, M. The lower depths
Shaw, B. Major Barbara
Pow wow. Martens, A. C.
Power (Mechanics) See Power resources
The **power** and the glory. Cannan, D. and
Bost, P.
The **power** of darkness. Tolstoy, L.
Power resources
c Flavelle, I. B. Giants of the city
Powers, Verne
High window. Row 1953 40p illus
Mystery. After his uncle falls to his
death from window, erstwhile carefree
young man falls under domination of
his shrewd aunt until curious news-
paperwoman solves mystery. 1 act 2m
3w 1 interior
The wall
In village that has been invaded, cour-
ageous man faces death for conspiring
against life of foreign captain. 1 act 5m
2w 1 exterior
In Powers, V. E. ed. Plays for players,
and a guide to play production
Powicke, Hilda Benson
The song and the star. Augustana 1953
23p music
Christmas worship program for children,
with choral music. Large mixed cast no
scenery
Poznan. See Posen
Practical politics. See Politics, Practical

Prayer
Estes, S. In quest of power through
prayer
Lindsay, K. and Lindsay, R. H. Miracle
at Potter's farm
Smith, W. S. The answer
The **precious** damsels. Molière, J. B. P.
Precocity. See Gifted children
Predestination. See Fate and fatalism
Prehistoric man. See Man, Prehistoric
Prejudice unlimited. Anderson, B. F.
Prejudices and antipathies
Anderson, B. F. Prejudice unlimited
Applegarth, M. T. Color blind
Bailey, A. H. The narrow man
Breck, F. E. One Father of mankind
Laurents, A. Home of the brave
Robinson, T. The visitor (Lassie)
Serling, R. Noon on Doomsday
Swann, D. L. The crier calls
See also Race discrimination
Preparing for winter. Pottow, D.
The **Prescott** proposals. Lindsay, H. and
Crouse, R.
The **presence** of the enemy. Mosel, T.
A **present** from Abe. Newman, D.
Pressey, Benfield. See Watson, E. B. jt. ed.
Prestidigitation. See Conjuring
Preston, Effa E.
The angel in the window
Angel in church window helps young
people with their problems. 1 act 7m 7w
choir 1 interior
In Brings, L. M. comp. The golden
book of church plays
The Christmas dolls' revue
Dolls from all over the world put on
show before Christmas in Santa's stock-
room. 1 act 20w extras 1 interior
In Brings, L. M. ed. The modern
treasury of Christmas plays
Star of wonder
Visitors to small town, delayed at rail-
road station, learn to appreciate Christ-
mas. 1 act 8m 8w 1b 1 interior
In Brings, L. M. ed. The modern
treasury of Christmas plays
The voice that failed
Church music committee helps young
singer regain her voice. Background
music. 1 act 4m 5w 1 interior
In Brings, L. M. comp. The golden
book of church plays
Pretenders. See Imposters and imposture
The **pretentious** young ladies. Molière,
J. B. P.
Prévert, Jacques
A united family (La famille tuyau de
poête) English version by J. D. Allen
Farce. A worker-priest in France goes
on a job in his own family's house.
4m 3w 1 interior
In Bentley, E. ed. Let's get a divorce!
and other plays
A **previous** engagement. Howells, W. D.
Price, Olive
Out of the mist. Eldridge 1953 65p
(Eldridge 3-act playscripts)
Comedy. Mysterious space man figures
in young man's plot to win back his
girlfriend from her absorption in astron-
omy. 3 acts 4 scenes 6m 6w 1 interior

Pride
Jerome, H. Pride and prejudice
Pride and prejudice. Jerome, H.
Pride and prejudice. Newman, D.
Pride and vanity
Fearheiley, D. A star too far
Newman, D. Pride and prejudice
Sayers, D. The zeal of Thy house
See also Snobs and snobbishness

Priestley, Florence
Adventures in camp
> At girls' camp, two groups are rivals for camp prize. 2 scenes 1m 7w 1 exterior

In Priestley, F. Six plays for girls
The ballet dancer
> Unexpected outcome of scholarship contest in school for ballet. 3 scenes 11w extras 1 interior

In Priestley, F. Six plays for girls
Brown dog—Black dog
> Just before pet show, two gypsies steal woman's prize dog and dye it black. 3 scenes 8w 3 exteriors

In Priestley, F. Six plays for girls
The Good Samaritans
> A girl is repaid in surprising way for good work she has done for others. 2 scenes 1m 6w 1 interior 1 exterior

In Priestley, F. Six plays for girls
Jane finds her cousins
> Episode from novel: Jane Eyre, by Charlotte Bronte. Jane discovers that she has a family after all. 2 scenes 1m 4w 1 interior

In Priestley, F. Six plays for girls
The mannequin parade
> Famous movie star comes to judge a girls' sewing club. 3 scenes 8w 1 interior

In Priestley, F. Six plays for girls

Priestley, H. E.
Au revoir
> Puppet play. Punch makes amends to the showman, the doctor, and his dog for being mean to them. 6 characters 1 setting

In Priestley, H. E. Six little Punch plays
Bathing the baby
> Puppet play. Punch helps Judy take care of their baby. 3 characters 1 setting

In Priestley, H. E. Six little Punch plays
The dog Toby
> Puppet play. Punch has trouble with his dog Toby. 3 characters 1 setting

In Priestley, H. E. Six little Punch plays
Introducing Judy
> Puppet play. Judy tries to bake fruit pie for Punch. 2 characters 1 setting

In Priestley, H. E. Six little Punch plays
Punch and the doctor
> Puppet play. Naughty Punch kicks the doctor who is trying to set his broken leg. 3 characters 1 setting

In Priestley, H. E. Six little Punch plays
Punch and the showman
> Puppet play. Punch fights to become his own showman. Background music. 2 characters 1 setting

In Priestley, H. E. Six little Punch plays

Priestley, J. B.
A glass of bitter. [French's Acting ed] French (London) 1954 19p illus
> Woman who has never told her husband that she once had an illegitimate son must face problem when he turns up in trouble with police. 1 act 3m 2w 1 interior

Mother's Day. [French's Acting ed] French (London) 1953 20p illus
> Comedy. Timid mother who is slave to her family has a strong minded friend, with magical powers, with whom she exchanges personalities for awhile. 1 act 2m 3w 1 interior

Private rooms. [French's Acting ed] French (London) 1953 28p illus
> Romantic comedy. In two private rooms of restaurant in central Europe around 1900, aging actor tries to impress young dancer, and middle aged actress entertains young poet. 1 act 3m 2w 2 interiors

Try it again. [French's Acting ed] French (London) 1953 21p illus
> Three women are arguing over a man: his mother, his wife and his mistress, while outside the window an interested film director is taking down the dialog. 1 act 2m 4w 1 interior

See also Hawkes, J. jt. auth.

Priests
Cannan, D. and Bost, P. The power and the glory
Carney, F. The righteous are bold
Costa du Rels, A. The king's standards
Graveley, G. The mountain flock
Greene, G. The living room
Hartke, G. V. The little world of Don Camillo
Howells, W. D. and Poel, W. A foregone conclusion
Ibsen, H. Brand
O'Casey, S. The Bishop's bonfire
Rigney, W. J. Joe Tracy
The **prince** and the pauper. Chorpenning, C. B.
The **prince** and the pauper. Newman, D.
Prince Arthur and Hubert. Boyd, A. K.
The **Prince** of Homburg. Kleist, H. von
The **Prince** of Parthia. Godfrey, T.
The **Prince** of Peace. Asbrand, K.
The **prince** who met a dragon. Tennant, K.

Princes
Bucci, M. Chain of jade
The **princess** and the rose-colored glasses. Hark, M. and McQueen, N.
The **princess** and the swineherd. Miller, M.
The **Princess** and the swineherd. Seiler, G.
The **Princess** of Cleve. Lee, N.
Princess of the snows. Ullman, S. S
Princess Victoria's twelfth birthday. Robinson, R.
The **princess** who liked cherry pie. Daviot, G.

Princesses
Olfson, L. Infanta
Principals, School. See School superintendents and principals
Printer's measure. Chayefsky, P.
Printing
Chayefsky, P. Printer's measure
Priscilla. Howells, W. D.
Priscilla Alden. Spamer, C.

Priscilla and John. Spencer, H.

Prison escapes. See Escapes

The prisoner. Boland, B.

Prisoners
Bate, S. Escape to fear
Behan, B. The quare fellow
Boland, B. The prisoner
Boyd, A. K. Pip and the convict
Crouch, A. Not by might
    See also Escapes

Prisoners of war
Zeiger, H. Five days

Prisons
Saroyan, W. Hello out there
Great Britain
Bielby, M. R. I was in prison

A private affair. Emery, C.

Private rooms. Priestley, J. B.

Private schools
Hellman, L. The children's hour
    See also Boarding schools
The private secretary. Hawtrey, C.

Prize contests in advertising
Mitzman, N. and Dalzell, W. In 25
  words—or death
Prize-fighting. See Boxing

A prize for mother. Hark, M. and Mc-
Queen, N.
The prize shamrock. Newman, D.

Problem children
Education
Morris, C. The unloved

Probst, George
The experiment of a free press
    Radio play. Thomas Jefferson explains
    why he fought for freedom of press in
    spite of bitter and slanderous opposition.
    Background music. 1m extras
  In Jeffersonian Heritage (Radio pro-
    gram) The Jefferson heritage
Nature's most precious gift
    Radio play. In their letters to each other
    Thomas Jefferson and John Adams de-
    bate aristocracy versus democracy.
    Background music. 2m
  In Jeffersonian Heritage (Radio pro-
    gram) The Jefferson heritage

Procunier, Edwin R.
Two sides of darkness
    Love and war remain the same through
    the ages. 3m 2w extras 1 setting
  In The Best short plays, 1958-1959
Voices of desire
    Waiter in Paris restaurant serves Cana-
    dian tourists whose problems range from
    comic to tragic. 1 act 4m 3w 1 exterior
  In Richards, S. ed. Canada on stage

The prodigal. Church, R.

The prodigal comes home. Parker, M. M.

The prodigal mother. Blazer, F.

Prodigal son (Parable)
Finch, R. The certain man had two sons
Parker, M. M. The prodigal comes home

Professor Taranne. Adamov, A.

Professors. See Teachers

Profiteering
Miller, A. All my sons

Prometheus bound. Aeschylus

The promise lily. Crank, H. P.

The promise of May. Tennyson, A.

Promise of the angels. Getzinger, E. W.

The promised one. Casey, B. M.

The promised ones. St Clair, R.

The promotion. Graham, M. S.

Proof of a man. Love, C. R.

Property
Scholl, R. The golden axe
Proposals of marriage. See Marriage pro-
posals
Prosecutors. See Law and lawyers

Prostitution
Williams, T. Hello from Bertha
Protest. Williams, N.

Protestants in Ireland
O'Casey, S. Red roses for me

Protter, Nancy
Follow the gleam. [Rev] French 1960 92p
illus
    Mad adventures of husband-hunting col-
    lege freshmen. 2 acts 12 scenes Large
    mixed cast 3 interiors 3 exteriors

Proverbs
c Joy, V. The milkmaid and her pail

A provincial lady. Turgenev, I.

Prussia
History—1640-1740
Kleist, H. von. The Prince of Homburg

Pryor, Carey
Just my speed. French 1956 87p illus
    Comedy. Though her stern aunt wants
    to take her, a young girl prefers her
    bachelor uncle, and sets out to find a
    wife for him. 3 acts 4 scenes 4m 7w 1
    interior

Pseudonyms. See Anonyms and pseudonyms

Psychiatrists
Chase, M. Harvey
De Francquen, L. Three bags full
Duerrenmatt, F. The visit
Emery, C. A private affair
Greene, G. The living room
Howard, V. Pollywogs
Roffey, J. and Harbord, G. Night of the
fourth
Sherman, R. W. Santa's neurosis

Psychoanalysis
Chodorov, E. Oh, men! Oh, women!

Psychology
    Plays listed here have particular em-
    phasis on psychological problems, con-
    flicts or situations
Armer, A. and Grauman, W. E. Dead
weight
Arrabal. The two executioners
Blankfort, D. and Blankfort, M. Monique
Brenner, M. The wait
Camus, A. The possessed
Hellman, L. The little foxes
Hellman, L. Toys in the attic
Ibsen, H. John Gabriel Borkman
Ibsen, H. The lady from the sea
Ibsen, H. Little Eyolf
Ibsen, H. When we dead awaken
Inge, W. A loss of roses
James, H. Guy Domville
Johnson, P. H. Corinth House
Kinoy, E. Good-bye to the clown
Kneale, N. Mrs Wickens in the fall
Laurents, A. Home of the brave
Lehman, L. Thirty pieces of silver

Psychology—*Continued*
  Love, C. R. Proof of a man
  Miller, A. The crucible
  Miller, A. Death of a salesman
  Mosel, T. Ernie Barger is fifty
  O'Neill, E. Strange interlude
  Strindberg, A. The road to Damascus
  Strindberg, A. There are crimes and crimes
  Webber, C. E. Be good, sweet maid
  Wishengrad, M. The rope dancers
Psychology, Applied
  Stephens, C. G. The matter with Mildred
  Taylor, G. Kill or cure
Public hygiene. See Hygiene, Public
The **public** prosecutor. Hochwaelder, F.
Publican and sinner. Hollinshead, L. M.
Publicity
  Howard, V. The publicity expert
The **publicity** expert. Howard, V.
Publicity on the fifteenth. McMahon, B.
Publishers and publishing. See Periodicals, Publishing of
Pudd'nhead Wilson. Chadwicke, A.
Puerto Ricans in the United States
  Anderson, W. "Me, Candido!"
Puget Sound
  Dalzell, W. and Martens, A. O. Onions in the stew
Pulchérie. Corneille, P.
Pumpkin Ghost. Spamer, C.
Pumpkin is the password. Woolsey, J. and Sechrist, E. H.
The **Pumpkineaters'** pumpkin. Newman, D.
A **pumpkin's** fate. Spamer, C.
Punch and Judy
  Priestley, H. E. Au revoir
  Priestley, H. E. Bathing the baby
  Priestley, H. E. The dog Toby
  Priestley, H. E. Introducing Judy
  Priestley, H. E. Punch and the doctor
  Priestley, H. E. Punch and the showman
  Priestley, H. E. Six little Punch plays (6 plays)
    See also Puppets and puppet plays
Punch and the doctor. Priestley, H. E.
Punch and the showman. Priestley, H. E.
Punic War, 2d, 218-201 B.C.
  Lee, N. Sophonisba
Punky doodle. Taggart, T.
Puppets and puppet-plays
  Agg, H. Silk and sawdust
  Chesterton, G. K. The surprise
  c Miller, M. Pinocchio
  Priestley, H. E. Au revoir
  Priestley, H. E. Bathing the baby
  Priestley, H. E. The dog Toby
  Priestley, H. E. Introducing Judy
  Priestley, H. E. Punch and the doctor
  Priestley, H. E. Punch and the showman
  Priestley, H. E. Six little Punch plays (6 plays)
  Shaw, B. Shakes versus Shav
  Takeda, I.; Miyoshi, S. and Namiki, S. The house of Sugawara
  c Woolsey, J. and Sechrist, E. H. The witches' complaint

Purgatory. Yeats, W. B.
The **purification.** Williams, T.
Puritans
  Miller, H. L. Thankful's red beads
  Olfson, L. The house of the Seven Gables
  Schevill, J. The bloody tenet
Purkey, Ruth Angell
  Hangs over thy head
    Playwright reads to actors unfinished play about end of world by H-bomb. 1 act 4m 2w 1 interior
    In The Best short plays of 1955-1956
  The leprechaun
    Fantasy about leprechaun in guise of shoemaker who falls in love with country belle. 1 act 3m 1w 1 interior
    In Powers, V. E. Plays for players, and a guide to play production
Purple dust. O'Casey, S.
Pushkin, Aleksander Sergeevich. See Pushkin, Alexander
Pushkin, Alexander
  Boris Godunov; Russian text with translation and notes by Philip L. Barbour. Columbia Univ. Press 1953 196p (Columbia Slavic studies)
    Historical tragedy in blank verse, set in Russia from 1598-1605. Boris Godunov, suspected of having caused murder of rightful heir to throne, becomes Czar, only to be deposed later by imposter. 22 scenes 25m 5w extras 10 interiors 8 exteriors
Puss in Boots. Bennett, R.
Puss in Boots. Miller, M.
Puss-in-Boots. Very, A.
Putnam, Amelia (Earhart) See Earhart, Amelia
Putting first things first. Posegate, E. D.
The **puzzle.** Roskam, C.
Pygmalion. Shaw, B.
Pyle, Howard
  How Boots befooled the king (dramatization) See Goldsmith, S. L. How Boots befooled the king
  The staff and the fiddle (dramatization) See Goldsmith, S. L. The staff and the fiddle
Pyle, Mary Thurman
  c Not on the menu
    Visiting aunt learns about family affairs from the children. 3w 3b 1g 1 interior
    In Fenner, P. and Hughes, A. comps. Entrances and exits

Q

Quacks and quackery
  Boyd, A. K. The mock doctor
  Molière, J. B. P. The physician in spite of himself
  Molière, J. B. P. The reluctant doctor
Quadrille. Coward, N.
Quakers. See Friends, Society of
The **quare** fellow. Behan, B.
Quare medicine. Green, P.

R

Quarreling
Asbrand, K. On earth peace
Kaufman, G. S. and MacGrath, L. Amicable parting
Kirkpatrick, J. Splint for a broken heart
Melville, A. Simon and Laura
Miller, H. L. The haunted clothesline
Murphy, A. Three weeks after marriage
Niss, S. The penny
Parker, D. Here we are
Schaefer, L. Song for a hero
c Spamer, C. Friends
c Spamer, C. Our dumb friends
The Queen and the rebels. Betti, U.
The queen and the Welshman. Sisson, R. A.
Queen Margaret of Norway. Kielland, T.
Queen Mary. Tennyson, A.
The Queen of Hearts' party. Woolsey, J. and Sechrist, E. H.
Queen Victoria. Spamer, C.
Queens
Betti, U. The Queen and the rebels
See also Kings and rulers; and names of individual queens, e.g. Mary Stuart, Queen of the Scots
The queen's gambit. Scribe, E.
Quentin Durward. Olfson, L.
The quest. Brabazon, F.
Quick, Edith. See Fluckey, J. O. Davy's star; He said he was Santa; The heart of the forest; The little blue angel; Santa and the space men
Quiet night. Blewett, D.
Quiet, please. Martens, A. C.
Quinlan, M. Eva
c Betty gets a new dress
Teen-age girl persuades mother to buy her new party dress. 1 scene 1w 1g 1 interior
In Easy juvenile grab bag
Pete of the rancho
Small daughter of pioneer family, captured by Indians, is rescued by her cowboy friend. 3 acts 6m 2w 1g 1 interior 1 exterior
In Easy juvenile grab bag
Quinn, Arthur Hobson, and Quinn, Kathleen Carberry
The bell of St Hildegarde. French 1954 26p illus
The triumph of faith over science in a small French village. 1 act 7m 5w extras 1 exterior
Quinn, Carolyn
For want of a character
Comedy. Young playwright in tavern attempts to write play about people he sees there. 4m 4w extras 1 interior
In Twelve half-hours with the Winthrop Theater
Quinn, Kathleen Carberry. See Quinn, A. H. jt. auth.
Quiz shows
Barasch, N. and Moore, C. Make a million
Ephron, P. "Howie"
Stern, L. and Zelinka, S. The $99,000 answer

R. U. R. Čapek, K.
Rab the rhymer. Crozier, E.
The rabbit trap. Miller, J. P.
Rabbits
Chase, M. Harvey
c Spamer, C. The bunnies' dilemma
The rabbits who changed their minds. Miller, H. L.
Rabe, Olive. See Fisher, A. jt. auth.
Rabinowitz, Shalom
Perl, A. The world of Sholom Aleichem
For plays by this author see Aleichem, Sholom
Race discrimination
Applegarth, M. T. Were you there?
Benjamin, J. and Kellerman, D. No man is an island
Casey, B. M. The hand of God
Julian, J. The Devil and the dream
Sergel, C. The family nobody wanted
See also Discrimination; Prejudices and antipathies; Race problems
Race problems
Albee, E. The death of Bessie Smith
Corrie, J. Colour bar
Edmunds, M. Moon of my delight
Ford, R. Requiem for a nun
Genet, J. The blacks: a clown show
Green, P. Wings for to fly
Healey, R. M. Nobody knows
Race question. See Race problems
Racial crossing. See Miscegenation
Racial discrimination. See Race discrimination
Racine, Jean
Andromache; tr. into English verse, and with an introduction by Kenneth Muir
Adaptation of Euripides' Andromache, based on a Greek legend. Tragedy in verse centered around Hermione's jealousy of Andromache because of the latter's betrothal to Pyrrhus. 5 acts 4m 4w extras 1 interior
In Racine, J. Five plays
Athaliah; tr. into English verse, and with an introduction by Kenneth Muir
Based on the Biblical account in the Old Testament second Book of Kings. The fate of Athaliah, Queen of Judah, who seized the throne after death of her son, King Ahaziah, and slew, as she supposed, all his sons. Verse play with choral singing. 5 acts 6m 5w 2b extras 1 interior
In Racine, J. Five plays
Berenice; tr. into English verse, and with an introduction by Kenneth Muir
Historical tragedy in verse. In first century Rome public policy prevents the Emperor Titus from marrying Berenice, a princess of Judea. 5 acts 5m 2w extras 1 interior
In Racine, J. Five plays
Britannicus; tr. into English verse, and with an introduction by Kenneth Muir
Historical tragedy in verse. Nero, Emperor of Rome, poisons half-brother, Britannicus, for having conspired, with aid of Nero's mother, to seize throne. 5 acts 4m 3w extras 1 interior
In Racine, J. Five plays

Racine, Jean—*Continued*

Phaedra; an English acting version; introduction and tr. by Bernard D. N. Grebanier. Barrons Educ. Ser. 1958 92p
  Tragedy. French neo-classic version of the Greek legend about queen who falls in love with stepson. 5 acts 3m 5w extras 1 interior

—Same; tr. and ed. by Oreste F. Pucciani. Appleton 1959 xxv, 69p (Crofts classics)

—Same; tr. into English verse, and with an introduction by Kenneth Muir

  In Racine, J. Five plays

The **radiance** streaming. Emurian, E. K.

Radiant morning. Martens, A. C.

Radin, Ben

A seacoast in Bohemia
  Television play. Conflict between student and teacher in play-writing course. 8m 5w 1b extras

  In The Best television plays v3

Radio broadcasting

c Buzzell, A. M. "The man on the street"

c Kramer, C. The voyage

  Westgate, T. Petticoat handicap

Radio Jerusalem, the story of Jesus. Magee, C.

Radio plays

Anderson, B. F. Prejudice unlimited

Anderson, D. Watermelon

Anderson, M. The miracle of the Danube

Beckett, S. Embers

Brown, F. E. The educated schoolhouse

Burack, A. S. ed. Four-star radio plays for teen-agers (12 plays)

Collins, B. F. Grand jury

Cullinan, G. The Republic of the Blind

Emmons, D. G. John Jewitt, the slave

c Fisher, A. Mother of Thanksgiving

Fisher, A. and Rabe, O. Champions of democracy

Fisher, A. and Rabe, O. Immigrants all, Americans all

Fisher, A. and Rabe, O. Our great Declaration

Fisher, A. and Rabe, O. Skills to share

Fisher, A. and Rabe, O. The story of a well

c Fisher, D. En route to the UN

Foss, J. Courage, '53

Geiger, M. The democrat and the commissar

Geiger, M. Light and liberty

Geiger, M. The return of a patriot

Geiger, M. The university of the United States

Goldschmidt, W. ed. Ways of mankind (13 plays)

Goldschmidt, W. and Sinclair, L. A word in your ear

Greene, R. S. Decision for freedom

Hallman, E. S. Survival

McCaslin, N. John Henry

McCaslin, N. Seafaring giant

McCaslin, N. With the sunrise in his pocket

MacLeish, A. The fall of the city

McMahon, B. Guided tour

Magee, C. Radio Jerusalem, the story of Jesus

Mindel, J. Freeing the land

Mindel, J. To secure these rights

Olfson, L. The adventures of Tom Sawyer

Olfson, L. As you like it

Olfson, L. The Bishop's candlesticks

Olfson, L. Captains Courageous

Olfson, L. A Connecticut Yankee in King Arthur's court

Olfson, L. Cyrano de Bergerac

Olfson, L. David Copperfield and Uriah Heep

Olfson, L. Hamlet

Olfson, L. The House of the Seven Gables

Olfson, L. The importance of being Earnest

Olfson, L. Jane Eyre

Olfson, L. Julius Caesar

Olfson, L. King Lear

Olfson, L. Macbeth

Olfson, L. A midsummer night's dream

Olfson, L. Monsieur Beaucaire

Olfson, L. Much ado about nothing

Olfson, L. The Pickwick papers

Olfson, L. Quentin Durward

Olfson, L. Radio plays from Shakespeare (10 plays)

Olfson, L. Radio plays of famous stories (15 plays)

Olfson, L. Romeo and Juliet

Olfson, L. Silas Marner

Olfson, L. The taming of the shrew

Olfson, L. The tempest

Olfson, L. Which of the nine?

Olfson, L. Wuthering Heights

Olson, E. The carnival of animals

Peterson, L. Home, sweet home

Peterson, L. Stand-in for a murderer

Peterson, L. Sticks and stones

Phillips, J. B. The arrest in the garden

Phillips, J. B. The Ascension

Phillips, J. B. The baptism of Jesus

Phillips, J. B. The boyhood of Jesus

Phillips, J. B. The calling of the disciples

Phillips, J. B. The centurion's servant

Phillips, J. B. Christ enters Jerusalem

Phillips, J. B. Christ the Son of God

Phillips, J. B. The cleansing of the Temple

Phillips, J. B. The death of Jesus and the promise of the Resurrection

Phillips, J. B. The gift of the Holy Spirit

Phillips, J. B. The healing at the Pool of Bethesda

Phillips, J. B. The healing of the man born blind

Phillips, J. B. The healing of the paralyzed man

Phillips, J. B. Jesus appears in Galilee

Phillips, J. B. Jesus appears to His disciples

Phillips, J. B. Jesus returns to Galilee

Phillips, J. B. The journey to Jerusalem

Phillips, J. B. The Last Supper

Phillips, J. B. The Lord's prayer

Phillips, J. B. A man called Jesus (26 plays)

Phillips, J. B. The parable of the last judgment

The rats. Hauptmann, G.

Rattigan, Terence

Adventure story

Alexander the Great's conquest of Asia Minor, and its effect on him personally. 2 acts 10 scenes 12m 5w extras 3 interiors 2 exteriors

In Rattigan, T. Collected plays v2

The Browning version

Ailing English schoolmaster aware of wife's infidelity, compromises with his situation. 1 act 5m 2w 1 interior

In Cerf, B. and Cartmell, V. H. eds. 24 favorite one-act plays

In Rattigan, T. Collected plays v2

The deep blue sea. French 1954 93p front

Middle-aged woman's failure to hold young lover leads her to attempt suicide, but refugee doctor restores desire to live. 3 acts 5m 3w 1 interior

—Same

In Rattigan, T. Collected plays v2

Flare path

Wartime rural England. Reunion of American actor and wife of an RAF pilot. 3 acts 4 scenes 7m 4w 1 interior

In Rattigan, T. Collected plays v 1

French without tears

Comedy of several embryonic British diplomats, learning French in seaside French town, distracted by love affairs. 3 acts 5 scenes 7m 3w 1 interior

In Rattigan, T. Collected plays v 1

Harlequinade

English comedy about rehearsal of play, with temperamental actors and directors. 1 act 10m 5w 1 interior

In Rattigan, T. Collected plays v2

Love in idleness

Domestic comedy. Boy finds his widowed mother living with man of whom he disapproves. 3 acts 3m 6w 2 interiors

In Rattigan, T. Collected plays v 1

Separate tables. French 1956 127p

Contains two separate plays: Table by the window, and Table number seven, about life among the occupants of a shabby hotel in England. 5 scenes 3m 8w 2 interiors

Trade edition published by Random House

Separate tables (condensation)

In The Best plays of 1956-1957

In Broadway's best, 1957

The sleeping prince. Dramatists 1959 97p illus

Social comedy set in London during coronation week of King George V. Romantic interlude in lives of Prince Regent of Carpathia and an American chorus girl. 2 acts 5 scenes 7m 6w 1 interior

Trade editions published by Random House and H. Hamilton

While the sun shines

Comedy of errors nearly breaks up impending marriage of English earl. 3 acts 4 scenes 5m 2w 1 interior

In Rattigan, T. Collected plays v 1

Who is Sylvia?

English comedy about extra-marital affairs of English nobleman forever seeking face of first love. 3 acts 6m 7w 1 interior

In Rattigan, T. Collected plays v2

The Winslow boy

Legal action for civil liberties in England which rapidly snowballs into country-wide controversy, is taken by a boy's father when son is expelled from school accused of theft. 3 acts 7m 4w 1 interior

In Sper, F. ed. Favorite modern plays

In Rattigan, T. Collected plays v 1

Rattray, Brenda

Night crossing. English Theatre 1955 23p illus (Guild lib)

Young woman, discouraged about her love affair, receives new hope from fellow passenger aboard ship crossing the English Channel. 1 act 7w 1 exterior

Rawe, Marcella S.

c Benny goes to Mistletonia

On Christmas Eve a little boy dreams that he takes a trip on Noah's Ark to see the Christ Child. Includes dances and familiar children's songs. 1w 1b extras choir 1 interior

In Birdsall, R. ed. Creative plays for every school month

Raymond and the monster. Wallerstein, J. S.

Raynor, Molly

All of a sudden. English Theatre 1954 30p illus (Guild lib)

Englishwomen, sorting clothes given to a voluntary agency for disaster relief, discover which of two sisters is real thief in nearby department store. 1 act 8w 1 interior

Reach, James

Afraid of the dark. French 1953 76p illus

Mystery-farce. Newly-weds decide to spend honeymoon in bridegroom's aunt's old deserted mansion where lights go off suddenly and weird assortment of characters appear. 3 acts 6m 7w 1 interior

Ah, yesterday! A nostalgic comedy of the twenties. French 1955 92p illus

Romantic comedy. A man looks back at his youth in 1920's when he was college student and spent the summer at resort where he courted three girls. 2 acts 3 scenes 5m 7w 1 interior

Are teachers human? French 1956 80p

Comedy. Complications in a high school when the new English teacher vies with the coach for extra-curricula time of Puddinghead, prize team player. 3 acts 6 scenes 6m 7w 1 interior

Beautiful dreamers. Bakers Plays 1956 77p illus (Baker's Royalty plays)

Comedy. The lives and loves of several girls in a Hollywood residence club for aspiring actresses. 3 acts 4 scenes 12w 1 interior

Dragnet. French 1956 80p

Mystery. Based on the radio and television series. Laboratory tests prove that supposed suicide could not possibly have fired the gun that killed him. 3 acts 7 scenes 5m 5w 2 interiors

It walks at midnight. Bakers Plays 1956 69p illus

Comedy mystery. Strange inhabitants turn up when honeymoon couple stay overnight in bride's family's remote country mansion. 3 acts 4 scenes 5m 6w 1 interior

Meet me at the prom. Bakers Plays 1955 71p illus

Comedy. High school life during Thanksgiving Week, which, with football game and prom, is high point of year. 3 acts 4 scenes 6m 10w 1 interior

Reach, James—*Continued*

Murder for the bride. Bakers Plays 1955 76p illus
Mystery. When young woman gives bridal shower for friend, lights go off suddenly and one woman is murdered with knife which was gift to bride. 3 acts 5 scenes 11w 1 interior

Murder is my business. French 1958 83p illus
Mystery. Michael Shayne's beautiful client tells him her brother has been murdered although another man claims to be brother. 3 acts 6m 5w 3 interiors

Open house. French 1954 78p illus
Farce. Man who poses as wealthy to girl he is marrying, invites trouble. 3 acts 5 scenes 5m 6w 1 interior

Patterns. French 1959 85p illus
Young executive comes into contact with the ruthless maneuvers used in his corporation to further its interests. 3 acts 6 scenes 7m 6w 1 interior

Stranger in town. French 1955 84p
Comedy-mystery. When business man brings home new young associate as boarder everybody's interest, especially daughter's is aroused, over the mystery of boarder's past. 3 acts 5 scenes 5m 5w 1 interior

Terror at Black Oaks. Dramatic 1953 68p illus
Mystery comedy. Family intrigue concerns a man, convicted of murdering his uncle, escaping from the penitentiary while his cousin and her handsome admirer try to prove his innocence. 3 acts 6m 7w 1 interior

Women in white. French 1953 82p illus
Mystery. One of the nurses in small city hospital is murdered at nurses' residence and case becomes policewoman's first assignment. 3 acts 4 scenes 11w 1 interior

You, the jury. French 1958 84p
Women on trial for murder of young man. Play permits audience to act as jury and decide her fate. 3 acts 4 scenes 7m 8w 1 interior

For other plays by this author see Manning, Hilda; Sutton, Thomas; Williams, Pete; *also* Taggart, T. jt. auth.

Reach for the moon. Asbrand, K.

Read me a story. Posegate, E. D.

Reade, Charles. See Taylor, T. jt. auth.

Readin', 'ritin', and 'rithmetic. Crosby, M.

Ready, Stuart

Ladies at sea. Deane 1955 57p illus ("Deane's" Ser. of plays)
Comedy. Relatives of old sea captain who was supposed to have hidden treasure, await wife, whom they have never seen; unscrupulous impostor arrives forcing real wife to pose as servant. 3 acts 4 scenes 10w 1 interior

Peril at the post office. Deane 1955 22p ("Deane's" Ser. of plays)
Farce. In small English village, a telegram is received that seems to imply an imminent attack, beginning with the post office building. 7w 1 interior

A **real** fine cutting edge. Dozier, R.

The **real** news. Howard, P.

The **real** princess. Miller, H. L.

The **real** princess. Newman, D.

Rebecca. Sherwood, R. E. and Harrison, J.

Rebekah
Estes, S. In quest of power through divine guidance

Rebellions. See Revolutions

The **rebellious** lightning bolt. Spamer, C.

Receive your King! Hein, R. F.

Reckoning. Daviot, G.

Reclining figure. Kurnitz, H.

Recording instruments
Beckett, S. Krapp's last tape

Recruiting and enlistment
Farquhar, G. The recruiting officer
Splaver, S. Jill and Perry go military
The **recruiting** officer. Farquhar, G.

Rectors. See Clergy

The **red** and yellow ark. Devany, E. H.

A **red** carpet for the bishop. Casey, B. M.

The **red** cloak. McConnell, J.

Red Cross. United States. American National Red Cross
Kissen, F. Clara Barton: angel of the battlefield

Red for danger. Stees, L.

Red letter day. Rosenthal, A.

Red plush. Agg, H.

Red roses for me. O'Casey, S.

The **red** shoes. Short, R.

Redemption. Tolstoy, L.

Rednour, Harold P.
The oblong circle. French 1954 75p illus
Mystery. When man seeks shelter in an old mansion from storm, a night begins wherein he must fight for his life against an unknown force. 3 acts 4 scenes 10m 2w 1 interior

Reducing (Body weight control) See Corpulence

Reed, Walter
Burlingame, C. Yellow fever

Reel George. Morris, F. H.

Rees, Phoebe
Mix-up-atosis. Deane 1955 20p ("Deane's" Ser. of plays)
Comedy. When man receives a package marked livestock his neighbors are convinced it contains rabbits suffering from Myxamatosis and force him to open it. 1 act 6w 1 interior

Reeves, Theodore
Wedding breakfast. [Rewritten and rev] French 1955 82p illus
When girl introduces career-girl sister to store clerk, career-girl tries to make professional man of him. 3 acts 2m 2w 1 interior

Reform, Social. See Social problems

Refugees
Applegarth, M. T. Home Sweet Home
Ferguson, J. The camp
Kozlenko, W. Journey of promise

Refugees, Austrian
Tabori, G. Flight into Egypt

Refugees, Jewish
Lehman, L. Thirty pieces of silver

Refugees, Polish
Daily, D. T. Displaced
Werfel, F. Jacobowsky and the colonel

Refugees, Political
Trick, O. B. The frontier

Refugees, Vietnamese
Greene, R. S. Decision for freedom

Refuse and refuse disposal
c Ryan, M. A. Litterbugs on trial

Regan, Sylvia
  The fifth season. [Acting ed] French 1953
    95p illus
      Comedy. Personal lives of members of an
      unsuccessful dress firm become entangled
      when they sell the whole line to buyer
      who really likes the glamorous models.
      3 acts 6 scenes 6m 7w 1 interior
Regency

                    Sweden
  Strindberg, A. The last of the knights
The **regent**. Strindberg, A.
The **register**. Howells, W. D.
Regnier, Max
  Paddle your own canoe; adapted by
    Lucienne Hill
      Romantic comedy, based on a scenario by
      Andre Gillois. Widow of man supposedly
      drowned in South American jungle con-
      tinues their successful canoe business,
      only to find him years later in Peru, with
      a business of his own. 3 acts 3m 2w 1 in-
      terior
    In Plays of the year v17
The **rehearsal**. Anouilh, J.
The **rehearsal**. Villiers, G. and others
Reich, John. See Goldstone, J. S. jt. auth.
The **reign** of Minnie Belle. Weaver, V. B.
Reincarnation
  Axelrod, G. Goodbye Charlie
  Bradbury, P. The come back
  Kocher, E. Karma
Reindeer on the roof. Hark, M. and Mc-
    Queen, N.
The **relapse**. Vanbrugh, Sir J.
Relatives. See Family
Release. Shaughnessy, A.
Religion
  Brabazon, F. The stranger
  Costigan, J. Little moon of Alban
  Emurian, E. K. Stewards of the soil
  Greene, G. The potting shed
  Hart, M. The climate of Eden
  Ibsen, H. Brand
  Lantz, J. E. and Lantz, R. C. Marriage
    for love
  Leslie, A. E. In as much
  Lindsay, K. and Lindsay, R. H. Miracle
    at Potter's farm
  Martens, A. C. Dr Hudson's secret journal
  Moody, W. V. The faith healer
  O'Casey, S. The Bishop's bonfire
  Pirandello, L. Lazarus
  Quinn, A. H. and Quinn, K. C. The bell
    of St Hildegarde
  Strindberg, A. Crime and crime
    See also Faith; Supernatural
Religion and communism. See Communism
    and religion
Religious belief. See Faith
Religious drama. See Moralities, English;
    Mysteries and miracle-plays
Religious freedom. See Religious liberty
Religious liberty
  Fisher, A. and Rabe, O. Apostle of free-
    dom
  Kissen, F. William Penn: brother to all
    men
  Wishengrad, M. Divided we stand
    See also subjects under Bible and
    Jesus Christ

Relonde, Maurice
  Cheating cheaters
      Farce. Quack cheats hired hands with
      ghost hauntings, until they scare him and
      get their wages. 1 act 3 scenes 4m 2w
      2 interiors
    In Smith, B. and others, eds. A treas-
      ury of non-royalty one-act plays
Rels, Adolfo Costa du. See Costa du Rels,
    Adolfo
Rels, Costa du. See Costa du Rels, Adolfo
The **reluctant** debutante. Home, W. D.
The **reluctant** doctor. Molière, J. B. P.
The **reluctant** ghost. Brydon, M. W. and
    Ziegler, E.
Reluctantly yours. Lantz, J. E. and Lantz,
    R. C.
The **remarkable** incident at Carson Corners.
    Rose, R.
The **remarkable** incident at Carson Corners.
    Sergel, K.
The **remarkable** Mr Pennypacker. O'Brien, L.
A **remittance** from Spain. Apstein, T.
Renavent, George. See Royle, Selena, jt.
    auth.
Rengier, John. See Blankman, H. By hex
Renno, Edward L.
  Follow the girls. Dramatic 1956 78p
      Romantic comedy. At a summer resort,
      several people vie with each other in
      persuading young man to play football
      for their respective colleges. 3 acts
      4 scenes 5m 6w extras 1 exterior
Repentance
  Tolstoy, L. The power of darkness
Reporters and reporting
  Badger, A. Before the dawn
  Braun, W. Drop dead!
  Dias, E. J. Stop the presses!
  Grable, M. What price murder?
  Howard, P. The real news
  Sayre, G. W. Final edition
  Sloane, A. Bring on the angels
  Taggart, T. and Reach, J. Dear Phoebe
  Teichmann, H. Miss Lonelyhearts
    See also Newspapers
Reports in the garden. Burgess, C. V.
The **Republic** of the Blind. Cullinan, G.
Requiem for a heavyweight. Serling, R.
Requiem for a nun. Ford, R.
Requiem for a nun (condensation) Ford, R.
    and Faulkner, W.
Rescue. Shaw, D.
Rescue work
  Shaw, D. Rescue
**Resistance movements (World War, 1939-
    1945)** See World War, 1939-1945—Un-
    derground movements
Resort Hotel. Granby, F.
Resorts. See Dude ranches; Health resorts;
    Summer resorts
The **respectful** prostitute. Sartre, J. P.
Ressieb, George
  Danger from the sky. French 1957 78p
    illus
      Mysterious countess comes to pay a call
      on family of top-flight physicist. 3 acts
      4 scenes 6m 6w 1 interior
A **rest** for Mr Winkle. Howard, V.
Rest, ye merry gentlemen! Magary, F. A.

Restaurants, lunch rooms, etc.
  Anderson, S. The triumph of the egg
  Lynch, P. Fool's paradise
  Procunier, E. R. Voices of desire

Restless heart. Anouilh, J.

Restoration drama. See English drama—
  Restoration

The **Resurrection.** Emurian, E. K.

The **Resurrection.** Yeats, W. B.

The **Resurrection.** York plays

Resurrection of Christ. See Jesus Christ—
  Resurrection

The **Resurrection** of Jesus. Phillips, J. B.

Retarded children. See Exceptional children

The **reticent** one. Conkle, E. P.

Retirement
  Devany, E. H. The cow-catcher on the caboose

The **return.** Boland, B.

The **return.** Finch, R.

Return engagement. Gibson, M. N.

Return engagement. Lewis, J.

The **return** of a patriot. Geiger, M.

The **return** of Buck Gavin. Wolfe, T.

The **return** of Chandra. Wilson, D. C.

The **return** of Columbus. Very, A.

The **return** of Rip Van Winkle. Howard, V.

Revenge
  Anouilh, J. Medea
  Douglas, F. Rollo
  Duerrenmatt, F. The visit
  Euripides. Medea
  Ford, J. The broken heart
  Grillparzer, F. Medea
  Komparu, Z. U. The hōka priests
  Kyd, T. The Spanish tragedy
  Oldfield, M. Please communicate
  Spence, W. The locked room
  Tourneur, C. The revenger's tragedy
  Vidal, G. Barn burning
  Webster, J. The Duchess of Malfi
  Webster, J. The Duchess of Malfy
  Williams, E. Someone waiting
  Zola, E. Thérèse Raquin
    See also Vendetta

The **revenger's** tragedy. Tourneur, C.

Revere, Paul
  Kissen, F. Paul Revere: patriot and craftsman
  c Wilcox, E. M. A midnight ride
  Woolsey, J. and Sechrist, E. H. Paul Revere, Boston patriot

Revivals
  Climenhaga, J. Heathen pioneer

The **revolt** of mother. Sergel, R.

Revolutionaries. See Revolutionists

Revolutionists
  Camus, A. The possessed
  Cannan, D. and Bost, P. The power and the glory
  Daviot, G. Patria
  Graveley, G. The mountain flock
    See also Revolutions

Revolutions
  Geiger, M. The democrat and the commissar
  Ghelderode, M. de. Pantagleize
  Shaw, B. Annajanska, the Bolshevik Empress

The **reward.** Ullman, S. S.

Rhesus. Euripides

Rhinoceros. Ionesco, E.

The **ribs** and the cover. Sakanishi, S. tr.

Rice, Elmer L.
  Street scene
    Tragedy. Sordid existence of occupants of New York City tenement house. 3 acts Large mixed cast 1 exterior
    In Griffin, A. V. Living theatre
  The winner. Dramatists 1954 127p illus
    Working girl, left a fortune by a rich man, is slandered by his wife, who contests the will. 1 act 4 scenes 8m 4w 2 interiors

Richard de Wyche, Saint
  Duncannon, F. E. N. P. viscount. Like stars appearing
  Gittings, R. Man's estate

Richard of Chichester, Saint. See Richard de Wyche, Saint

Richard III, King of England
  Daviot, G. Dickon

Richards, I. A.
  A leak in the universe
    Science-fiction fantasy about meaning of matter. Conjuror discovers objects placed in mysterious box cease to exist. 4m 1w 1 interior
    In Playbook: five plays for a new theatre

Richards, Stanley
  Gin and bitterness
    To prove his theory that guests at cocktail parties are over-credulous, host passes off as guest a restaurant worker disguised as an official from the United Nations. 3m 5w 1 interior
    In The Best short plays, 1958-1959
  Half-hour, please
    Young actress reviews her climb to Broadway. 4m 7w 1 setting
    In The Best short plays of 1954-1955
  Through a glass, darkly
    Brooklyn Jewish boy braves father's intolerance when he brings Christian bride home for a visit. 1 act 4m 3w 1 interior
    In The Best short plays, 1957
  Tunnel of Love. Banner 1953 29p
    Riding through Tunnel of Love at New York's Coney Island, a husband and wife review their twenty-five years of married life. 1 act 7m 4w 1 exterior
  —Same
    In The Best short plays, 1952-1953

Richards, Stanley, and Slocumb, Paul
  A dash of Santa Claus. Eldridge 1956 32p (Eldridge Christmas entertainments)
    Domestic comedy. Couple try to spend quiet Christmas Eve, but mysterious gifts appear suddenly and three Santa Clauses arrive, when their children refuse to believe in even one. 1 act 5m 3w 1b 1g 1 interior
  The hobble-de-hoy. [Rev. ed] Banner 1953 89p illus
    Romantic comedy. When handsome celebrity returns to his college campus the girl who heads reception committee is so upset at missing him that she disappears, leaving a farewell note. 3 acts 4 scenes 6m 6w extras 1 interior

Richardson, Howard, and Berney, William
Dark of the moon. Theatre Arts ₁1957?₁ 80p music (The Drama lib)
American folk-drama. A boy who is a witch is changed into a human and is destined to remain so if his sweetheart is faithful to him a year. Set in the Smoky Mountains. Songs with musical scores. 2 acts 9 scenes 14m 9w extras 3 interiors 4 exteriors

Richardson, Lesley
For our mother Malaya!
World War II. Malayans form successful anti-Japanese army after withdrawal of the British from Malaya and work for independence until the British destroy the "Peoples' Committees." Songs. 4 acts 9 scenes 20m 5w 1b 1g extras 2 interiors 2 exteriors

In Two plays about Malaya

Richmond, Samuel S.
Homemakers have a way
Teen age girls, needing a sponsor for their Homemakers Club, settle on Claire's rich Aunt Ida who doesn't really like home economics. 1 act 2 scenes 7w 1 interior

In Kamerman, S. E. ed. Blue-ribbon plays for girls

Richter, Conrad
The town (dramatization) See Sergel, R. Blue stocking

Riddles
c Marston, M. A. The riddling knight

Riddles wisely expounded. See Riddling knight

Riddling knight
c Marston, M. A. The riddling knight

The riddling knight. Marston, M. A.

Riders to the sea. Synge, J. M.

Ridge, Antonia
Emhammed of the red slippers
Radio adaptation of an Algerian folk tale. Little Emhammed wins badge of courage, a pair of red slippers, by rescuing his lost baby brother. 2m 2b extras

In Ridge, A. Six radio plays

Hare and the field of millet
Radio adaptation of an African folk tale about Mr Hare and the field of millet. 1m extras

In Ridge, A. Six radio plays

The legend of Saint Basil
Radio play. Based on a Greek legend of St Basil whose faith saved the city of Caesarea from destruction by Julian, Emperor of Rome. 10m 2b

In Ridge, A. Six plays

Saint Martha and the Tarasque of Tarascon
Radio adaptation of legend of Provence relating how St Martha subdued the beast of Tarascon. 4m 3w

In Ridge, A. Six radio plays

Three mice for the abbot
Radio adaptation of Dutch legend about an abbot who coveted beautiful things. 10m

In Ridge, A. Six radio plays

Under the monkey-bread tree
Radio adaptation of African folk tale. During a drought clever Mr Hare outwits the animals who try to take over spring he discovered. 1m extras

In Ridge, A. Six radio plays

The riding to Lithend. Bottomley, G.

Ridley, Arnold
You, my guests! ₁French's Acting ed₁ French (London) 1956 70p illus
Comedy. Three dear old ladies attempt to poison their landlady, who poisoned one lady's pet cat and habitually stole their whiskey. 3 acts 4m 5w 1 interior

Ridley, Arnold, and Borer, Mary Cathcart
Tabitha. ₁French's Acting ed₁ French (London) 1956 69p illus
Lawyer's selfish family refuses to help him when they learn he has embezzled profits from trust fund to satisfy their expensive tastes. 3 acts 5m 5w 1 interior

Riggs, Lynn
Green grow the lilacs (adaptation) See Rodgers, R. and Hammerstein, O. Oklahoma!

Roadside
Humorous folk-drama set in Indian Territory in 1905. Romance between a girl in covered wagon and a man of the West. Western dialect. 3 acts 4 scenes 8m 2w 1 interior 1 exterior

In Tucker, S. M. ed. Twenty-five modern plays

Right of adoption. Miller, H. L.

Right under your nose. Alexander, A.

Right you are. Pirandello, L.

The righteous are bold. Carney, F.

Righter, Norma Forman
Hold onto your hat
Young orphan girl antagonizes owner of hat shop when she becomes salesgirl there. 1 act 8w 1 interior

In Powers, V. E. ed. Plays for players, and a guide to play production

Rights, Civil. See Civil rights

Rigney, William J.
Joe Tracy. Bakers Plays 1955 22p (Baker's Royalty plays)
At graduation, young man tells his old teacher that he intends to become a priest but a girl who has always been interested in him vows she will prevent this. 1 act 4m 1w 1 interior

The rime of the ancient mariner. Jagendorf, M.

Ring for Catty. Cargill, P. and Beale, J.

The ring of General Macías. Niggli, J.

Ring once for Central. Allensworth, C.

Ringe, Mary
c The land of good health
King and queen of Healthland tell how to stay healthy. 1 act 12 characters 1 interior

In 'Round the year plays for the grades

Ringwood, Gwen Pharis
The courting of Marie Jenvrin
Romantic comedy. In remote Northwest Territories of Canada, waitress agrees to marry first man who can get a cow into the snowbound settlement. 1 act 5m 2w 1 interior

In Richards, S. ed. Canada on stage

Riots. See Mobs

Rip Van Winkle. Chorpenning, C. B.

Rip Van Winkle. Jefferson, J.

The rise of a nation. Delva, J. G.

The rise of Silas Lapham. Howells, W. D. and Kester, P.

The risen Christ. Lilyers, J.

Riskin, Robert
It happened one night
    Moving picture play based on the story: Night bus, by Samuel Hopkins Adams. Young newspaperman helps millionaire's daughter who ran away from father, when latter tries to annul her marriage to social climber. 9 parts 15m 3w
    In Gassner, J. and Nichols, D. eds. Great film plays

Ritchie, Anna Cora Mowatt
Fashion
    Social comedy on the fashionable world. French count becomes a social hit but turns out to be a cook. 5 acts 7 scenes 8m 5w extras 5 interiors
    In Quinn, A. H. ed. Representative American plays

Ritner, Ann
Summer brings gifts (dramatization) See Collins, D. Summer brings gifts

The **rival** queens. Lee, N.

The **rivalry.** Corwin, N.

The **rivals.** Sheridan, R. B.

Road signs. See Signs and signboards

The **road** to Damascus. Strindberg, A.

Roads
    Maintenance and repair
Addis, H. What ho for the open road

Roadside. Riggs, L.

Roanoke Island
Green, P. The lost colony

The **Roaring** Girl. Middleton, T. and Dekker, T.

The **roaring** twenties. Trigger, E.

Robberies
Murray, J. A case for Mrs Hudson
Murray, J. The mystery in the lab
O'Neill, E. The long voyage home
Perrini, A. Once a thief
    See also Trials (Robbery)

Robbers. See Brigands and robbers

The **robbers.** Marston, M. A.

Robbery. See Robberies

Robbery at Gadshill. Boyd, A. K.

Robert I, King of Scotland
Williamson, H. R. Heart of Bruce

Robert the Bruce. See Robert I, King of Scotland

Robert E. Lee: Virginia's valiant son. Kissen, F.

Roberts, Cyril
Mr Gaylord remembers. [French's Acting ed] French (London) 1954 27p
    Former bit player in theatrical company, is looked down upon by students she coaches until strange man drops in and tells her he remembers what an excellent actress she was in her youth. 1 act 1m 4w 1 exterior

Roberts, Daniel Crane
Emurian, E. K. God of our fathers

Roberts, Helen M.
Old-fashioned Thanksgiving
    Thanksgiving fantasy. Trying on some Pilgrim costumes in the attic two girls are transported back to days of first Thanksgiving. 1 act 6w 1 interior
    In Kamerman, S. E. ed. Blue-ribbon plays for girls

Roberts, Margaret, Sister. See Ingebretson, A. Sister, jt. auth.

Roberts, Meade
A palm tree in a rose garden. Dramatists 1958 66p illus
    Hollywood. Frustrations and disappointments involved in the movie industry. Contrast between its superficialty and the real sincerity of two people. 3 acts 6 scenes 3m 5w 1 interior

Robertson, T. W.
Caste
    Set in 19th century England. British peer marries ballet dancer and meets family disapproval. 3 acts 3 scenes 5m 3w 2 interiors
    In Rowell, G. ed. Nineteenth century plays

Robertson, Thomas William. See Robertson, T. W.

Robin Hood
c Colson, J. G. Robin Hood in Sherwood Forest
c Ilian, C. Dame Robin Hood
c Ratcliffe, D. U. Robinetta
Tennyson, A. The foresters

Robin Hood in Sherwood Forest. Colson, J. G.

Robinetta. Ratcliffe, D. U.

Robinson, Clarence R.
The white dove
    Tragedy. Set in Spain. A mother and a wife, one with resignation and the other with fear, face bullfighter's entrance into the ring. 1 act 3m 2w 1 interior
    In Powers, V. E. ed. Plays for players, and a guide to play production

Robinson, Dennis F.
Salt winds. Deane 1959 61p illus
    Domestic comedy. English family life. Serious scientific father is astounded at plans of stage struck daughter and frivolous son. 3 acts 6 scenes 4m 4w 1 exterior

Robinson, Ruth
Clarence Gate
    Sarah Siddons complains to the king that the new plans for Regent's Park will spoil the view from her window. Set in England. 6m 7w 1 interior
    In Robinson, R. Fanny Burney's resignation, and other plays

Fanny Burney's resignation
    Fanny Burney wishes to resign from her position at court, but in the end her popularity forces her to stay. Set in England. 6m 6w 1 exterior
    In Robinson, R. Fanny Burney's resignation, and other plays

Princess Victoria's twelfth birthday
    On her twelfth birthday the future Queen Victoria wishes for some independence from her domineering mother. 4m 7w 1 interior
    In Robinson, R. Fanny Burney's resignation, and other plays

Robinson, Thelma
The visitor (Lassie)
    A play in the television series: Lassie featuring the dog of the same name. Japanese boy visiting Lassie's American family encounters violent prejudice but Lassie helps him avert disaster. 4m 2w 5b
    In Writers Guild of America. The prize plays of television and radio, 1956

Robinson Crusoe. Miller, M.

Robots. See Automata

Robots to the rescue. Fisher, A.

Roche, Dominic

My wife's lodger. Deane 1954 53p illus
("Deane's" Ser. of plays)
> Comedy. British soldier returns from war
> to find his family disinterested in him.
> Then an American arrives with the news
> that he has inherited big ranch in Texas.
> 3 acts 5m 5w 1 interior

Rocket to freedom. Fisher, A. and Rabe, O.

Rodgers, Richard

Flower drum song; a musical play; music
by Richard Rodgers; lyrics by Oscar
Hammerstein, 2d; book by Oscar Hammerstein, 2d, and Joseph Fields; based
on the novel by C. Y. Lee. Farrar,
Straus 1959 141p illus
> Libretto of the musical comedy. Conflict
> between older generation of San Fran-
> cisco's Chinatown, who wish to preserve
> tradition, and younger one who become
> Americanized. 2 acts 14 scenes 11m 7w
> 10 interiors 3 exteriors

Flower drum song (condensation)
> *In* Broadway's best, 1959

Me and Juliet; music by Richard Rodgers;
book and lyrics by Oscar Hammerstein.
Random House 1953 142p illus
> Musical comedy. Love life of Broadway
> actors in a show within show. 2 acts
> 16 scenes 17m 13w extras 9 interiors 1
> exterior

—Same
> *In* Rodgers, R. and Hammerstein, O.
> 6 plays by Rodgers and Hammer-
> stein

Pipe dream; music by Richard Rodgers;
book and lyrics by Oscar Hammerstein
II. Viking 1956 158p illus music
> Based on the novel "Sweet Thursday"
> by John Steinbeck. Lives and love af-
> fairs of inhabitants of Cannery Row.
> 2 acts 18 scenes 16m 7w 6 interiors 1
> exterior

The sound of music; music by Richard
Rodgers; lyrics by Oscar Hammerstein
II; book by Howard Lindsay and Russel Crouse. Random House 1960 141p
illus
> Based on the story: The Trapp family
> singers by Maria Augusta Trapp. Libret-
> to of the musical comedy about the early
> professional life of Trapp family. 2 acts
> 20 scenes 8m 13w 1b 2g 8 interiors 4
> exteriors

Rodgers, Richard, and Hammerstein, Oscar
Allegro
> Musical comedy. Life of an American
> doctor from his birth to turning point of
> his career in his thirty-fifth year. 2 acts
> Large mixed cast 1 setting

> *In* Rodgers, R. and Hammerstein, O.
> 6 plays by Rodgers and Hammer-
> stein

Carousel
> Musical comedy based on the play:
> Liliom, by Ferenc Molnár. Fantasy. A
> circus barker who mistreated his wife,
> is allowed to return to earth some
> fifteen years after his death for one
> day to do one good deed. 2 acts
> 8 scenes 16m 14w extras 8 exteriors

> *In* Rodgers, R. and Hammerstein, O.
> 6 plays by Rodgers and Hammer-
> stein

The King and I
> Musical comedy based on book by Mar-
> garet Landon. Experiences of English
> governess at the court of Siam in 19th
> century. 2 acts 17 scenes 9m 4w ex-
> tras 6 interiors 3 exteriors

> *In* Rodgers, R. and Hammerstein, O.
> 6 plays by Rodgers and Hammer-
> stein

Oklahoma!
> Musical comedy based on the play:
> Green grow the lilacs, by Lynn Riggs.
> Folk drama of the Indian territory. In-
> cludes cowboy songs. 2 acts 6 scenes
> 14m 9w 1 interior 5 exteriors

> *In* Rodgers, R. and Hammerstein, O.
> 6 plays by Rodgers and Hammer-
> stein

South Pacific
> A dramatization of Tales of the South
> Pacific by James A. Michener. Romantic
> comedy about sailors in the South Pa-
> cific during World War II. 2 acts 20m 5w
> 1b 1g extras 5 interiors 6 exteriors

> *In* Quinn, A. H. ed. Representative
> American plays

> *In* Rodgers, R. and Hammerstein, O.
> 6 plays by Rodgers and Hammer-
> stein

Rodman, Howard

The faith hawker
> Television play. Cynical young man
> learns meaning of faith when his sweet-
> heart is struck with a deadly disease.
> 3m 2w

> *In* Look up and live (Television pro-
> gram) The seeking years

A thing of beauty
> Television play. Beautiful girl is dis-
> satisfied because people see only her
> beauty and an ugly girl wishes only
> to be beautiful. 4m 3w

> *In* Look up and live (Television pro-
> gram) The seeking years

The will to win
> Television play. Young man who says
> that principles of Christianity are old
> fashioned, almost brings disaster upon
> himself and his friends. 6m 2w

> *In* Look up and live (Television pro-
> gram) The seeking years

Roeder, Leslie

Oh boy, what a girl! Bakers Plays 1956
83p (Baker's Royalty plays)
> Romantic comedy. Young girl comes to
> visit in haughty but financially em-
> barrassed family. Complications de-
> velop when the snobbish daughter's
> beau becomes interested in visitor.
> 3 acts 4 scenes 4m 7w 1 interior

Roepke, Gabriela

A white butterfly; tr. from the Spanish
by Thomas M. Patterson
> Middle aged office manager is too busy
> to notice his lonely secretary. 5m 4w
> 1 interior

> *In* The Best short plays, 1959-1960

Roffey, Jack, and Harbord, Gordon

Night of the fourth. [French's Acting ed]
French (London) 1957 80p illus
> Adapted from the play: Sprechstunde
> by H. Pratt. Psychiatrist helps detec-
> tive who believes that during a period
> of amnesia he committed the murder in
> case he is trying to solve. 3 acts 10m 1w
> 2 interiors

Rogers, Alice B.
Tiger on his toes. Dramatic 1954 86p illus
>Comedy. Father of an artistic boy invents a football-playing twin son to influence his old uncle, because the old man likes athletes and father wishes to inherit his money. 3 acts 8m 8w 1 interior

Rogers, David. See Bucci, M. Chain of jade; The old lady shows her medals; A pink party dress

Rogues and vagabonds
Molière, J. B. P. Scapin the scamp
Molière, J. B. P. That scoundrel Scapin
Williams, T. Orpheus descending

Rojas, Fernando de
The Celestina; tr. from the Spanish by Lesley Byrd Simpson. Univ. of Calif. Press 1955 162p
>Spanish tragedy. Nobleman, Calisto, with aid of procuress, Celestina, seduces Melibea, and retribution sets in. 16 acts 32 scenes 7m 6w 5 interiors 2 exteriors

—Same; tr. from the Spanish by Mack Hendricks Singleton. Univ. of Wis. Press 1958 299p

Rollo. Douglas, F.

Romains, Jules
Dr Knock; English version by Harley Granville-Barker
>Doctor buys a profitless country practice which soon flourishes thanks to psychology and modern propaganda techniques. 3 acts 3 scenes 9m 5w 2 interiors 1 exterior

In Bentley, E. ed. From the modern repertoire, ser. 3

The Roman actor. Massinger, P.

Roman Catholic Church. See Catholic Church

Romance for Dad. Hark, M. and McQueen, N.

Romances, Flemish
Ghelderode, M. de. Lord Halewyn

Romanoff and Juliet. Ustinov, P.

Romans in Great Britain
Daviot, G. Valerius
>*See also* Great Britain—History—Roman period, 55 B.C.-449 A.D.

Rome, Harold
Fanny. Random House 1954 143p illus
>Musical play by S. N. Behrman and Joshua Logan based on trilogy of Marcel Pagnol. Music and lyrics by Harold Rome. Lure of sea defeats Fanny's hope of marriage to Marius but not her love for him. Marseilles setting. 2 acts 16 scenes Large mixed cast 9 interiors 5 exteriors

Fanny (condensation)
In Theatre, 1955

Rome
Tennyson, A. The cup

History—Republic, 510-265 B.C.
c Carlson, B. W. A traitor's reward

History—Republic, 510-30 B.C.
Lee, N. Lucius Junius Brutus
Lee, N. Mithridates, King of Pontus

History—Republic, 265-30 B.C.
Corneille, P. Othon
Olfson, L. Julius Caesar

History—Empire, 30 B.C.-476 A.D.
Shaw, B. Androcles and the lion

History—Empire, 30 B.C.-284 A.D.
Healy, J. Nero fiddles
Jonson, B. Sejanus, his fall
Lee, N. The tragedy of Nero, Emperour of Rome
Massinger, P. The Roman actor
Racine, J. Berenice
Racine, J. Britannicus

History—Empire, 284-476
Lee, N. Constantine the Great

Romeo and Jeannette. Anouilh, J.

Romeo and Julia. Lathrop, D.

Romeo and Juliet. Olfson, L.

Romeo and Juliet. Shakespeare, W.

La ronde. Schnitzler, A.

The roof. Brenner, M.

Room for Mary. Thurston, M. B.

Room for the King. Neilson, P.

Room forty-five. Howells, W. D.

A roomful of roses. Sommer, E.

Rooming houses. See Hotels, taverns, etc.

Roos, Audrey, and Roos, William
Speaking of murder. French 1957 90p illus
>Drama of suspense. Woman in love with Charles Ashton kills his first wife, blackmails her own governess into secrecy, and with Charles' remarriage, plots to kill his second wife. 3 acts 5 scenes 2m 4w 1b 1g 1 interior

Roos, William. See Roos, Audrey, jt. auth.

Roosevelt, Franklin Delano, President U.S.
Schary, D. Sunrise at Campobello

Roosevelt family
Schary, D. Sunrise at Campobello

The rooster. See Ullman, S. S. El gallo

Roots. Wesker, A.

The rope. Plautus

The rope dancers. Wishengrad, M.

Rosa Bonheur. Spamer, C.

Rose, Le Roma
Headin' for a weddin'. Heuer 1953 79p
>Farce. Teen-age hillbilly with a picturesque family strikes up correspondence with a rich debutante and tells her he is a gentleman farmer. Heiress descends on family unexpectedly. 3 acts 5m 10w 1 interior

Spooks alive. Art Craft 1953 77p (An Art Craft play)
>Comedy-mystery. Strange things happen when professor and his family go to live in an abandoned prison. 3 acts 7m 8w 1 interior

See also Mitchell, B. E. jt. auth.

Rose, Reginald
An almanac of liberty
>Television play based on an event described in: An almanac of liberty, by W. O. Douglas. Fantasy. While time stands still, group of citizens discover that recent attack on stranger who voiced his own political views was violation of civil rights. 15m 6w 1b 1g

In Rose, R. Six television plays
Crime in the streets
>Television play. Social worker succeeds in turning young gang leader away from life of crime. 12m 1w 1b

In Rose, R. Six television plays

Rose, Reginald—*Continued*

Dino; stage version by Kristin Sergel. Adapted from the television show of the same name. Dramatic 1956 71p
Social case-worker at settlement house helps a teen-age boy, paroled from state reformatory, make a good social adjustment. 3 acts 7m 11w extras 1 setting

—Same

In The Best short plays of 1955-1956

The incredible world of Horace Ford
Television play. Psychological fantasy about man's preoccupation with his childhood memories. 8m 5w 4b

In Rose, R. Six television plays

The remarkable incident at Carson Corners
Television play. School children invite their parents to mock trial of janitor to determine cause of accident which killed one of their classmates. 11m 6w 3b 2g

In Rose, R. Six television plays

The remarkable incident at Carson Corners (adaptation) See Sergel, K. The remarkable incident at Carson Corners

Thunder on Sycamore Street
Television play. Ex-convict courageously faces mob of neighbors who are determined to drive him and his family out of the community. 7m 6w

In Rose, R. Six television plays

In Vidal, G. ed. Best television plays

Tragedy in a temporary town
Television play. Trailer camp men try to lynch innocent Puerto Rican who is accused of frightening a high-strung girl. 11m 3w

In Burack, A. S. ed. Television plays for writers

Twelve angry men. Dramatic 1955 63p front
Television play. Juror, intent on fair verdict, insists that jury review significance of evidence in case of youth on trial for murder. 14m

—Same

In Rose, R. Six television plays

Rose, Si

The Edgar Bergen show
Radio play. Comedy skits from the radio program: The Edgar Bergen show, featuring the ventriloquist, Edgar Bergen and his three puppets, Charlie McCarthy, Mortimer Snerd and Effie Klinker; also the Mellomen quartette and Carol Richards, singer. 6m extras

In Writers Guild of America. The prize plays of television and radio, 1956

The rose tattoo. Williams, T.

Rosenthal, A.

Third person
Unsettled young veteran's prolonged visit to his former commanding officer causes crisis in the latter's married life. 2 acts 4 scenes 3m 2w 1g 1 interior

In Plays of the year, v7

Rosenthal, Andrew

Red letter day. [French's Acting ed] French (London) 1953 65p
A woman is unhappy as her fiftieth birthday approaches because her husband spends so much time away from home. 3 acts 4m 6w 1 interior

Roses for mother. Newman, D.

Roses for the King. Bailey, H. F.

Roskam, Clair

Plenty of rein
Television play. Two parents find it difficult to permit their teen-age children to make their own decisions. 3m 2w

In Look up and live (Television program) The seeking years

The puzzle
Television play. Although he says he is innocent, teen-age boy is accused of stealing money in a drugstore. 4m 1w

In Look up and live (Television program) The seeking years

Rosmersholm. Ibsen, H.

Ross, Betsy. See Ross, Elizabeth (Griscom)

Ross, Elizabeth (Griscom)

Asbrand, K. Liberty Belle

Fisher, A. and Rabe, O. A star for Old Glory

c Larkin, E. Mistress Betsy and the flag

c Newman, D. The stars and stripes

Ross, George, and Singer, Campbell

Any other business. French (London) 1959 83p illus
A British company's Board of Directors suspects one of its members of betraying their company to competitor. 3 acts 4 scenes 10m 1w 1 interior

—Same

In Plays of the year, v18

Ross, Jerry. See Adler, R. jt. auth.

Rossetti, Christina Georgina

Goblin market (dramatization) See Marston, M. A. Goblin market

Rostand, Edmond

Cyrano de Bergerac; a new version in English verse by Brian Hooker
French poet of the 17th century handicapped by long nose strives to secure the happiness of the woman he loves. 5 acts Large mixed cast 2 interiors 3 exteriors

In A Treasury of the theatre

—Same; tr. from the French by Gertrude Hall

In Tucker, S. M. ed. Twenty-five modern plays

Cyrano de Bergerac (radio adaptation) See Olfson, L. Cyrano de Bergerac

Rosten, Hedda

The happy housewife
Television play. Domestic comedy. Young publisher persuades his wife to give up domesticity for career. 3m 4w 1b 1g

In The Best television plays v3

Rosten, Norman

Mister Johnson (condensation)

In Theatre, 1956

Rouge atomique. Nash, N. R.

The Rounderlay tradition. Delderfield, R. F.

Roussin, Andre

The little hut. Dramatists 1953 70p
Satirical comedy of manners. Triangle problem among some British castaways on desert island. 3 acts 4m 1w 1 exterior
Trade edition published by Random House

Rouverol, Aurania

Andy Hardy. French 1953 99p
Romantic comedy revolving around teenager Andy's new scheme for dating girls, his father's insistence on retiring, and his sister's career-versus-marriage situation. 3 acts 4 scenes 9m 9w 1 interior

The **roving** journeyman. Marston, M. A.

Rowley, Samuel
The noble Spanish soldier
> Probably written largely by Thomas Dekker
> Seventeenth century tragedy in verse. Perfidious King of Spain becomes victim of his own plot to murder his contracted bride and her son in order to validate his marriage to a Florentine. 5 acts 12 scenes 17m 3w 1 setting
>
> *In* Dekker, T. The dramatic works of Thomas Dekker v4

Rowley, William, and others
The witch of Edmonton, by William Rowley, Thomas Dekker, John Ford, etc.
> Seventeenth century English tragedy in verse. Based on Henry Goodcole's account of Elizabeth Sawyer, condemned for witchcraft in 1621. 5 acts 14 scenes 13m 5w 3 interiors 6 exteriors
>
> *In* Dekker, T. The dramatic works of Thomas Dekker v3
> *See also* Middleton, T. jt. auth.

Royal-Dawson, Felicity. See Douglas, Felicity

Royal gambit. Gressieker, H.

Royalty. See Kings and rulers

Royle, Selena, and Renavent, George
Especially mother. [Rev. ed] Banner 1953 96p illus
> Domestic comedy. When widow finds herself no longer wealthy, her life changes and her teen-age children develop a few ideas of their own. 3 acts 5m 2w 1 interior

Rubber plantation workers
Brand, M. Strangers in the land

Rubber workers. See Rubber plantation workers

Rubinstein, H. F.
Bernard Shaw in heaven
> Fantasy. Shakespeare and Shaw meet in heaven and discuss their work as playwrights. 1 act 8m 3w 1 exterior
>
> *In* The Second book of one-act plays

Ruddigore. Sullivan, A.

Rulers. See Kings and rulers

The **rules** of the game. Pirandello, L.

Rumor
Gregory, Lady. Spreading the news

A **rumpus** on rampage. McCoy, P.

The **runaway** pirate. Bennett, R.

The **runaway** sled. National Recreation Association

Rural life. See Country life

Ruskin, John
c The King of the Golden River (radio adaptation) See Leuser, E. The King of the Golden River

Russell, Mary
A fashion revue; or, Styles old and new. Bakers Plays 1959 16p
> Humorous portrayal of fashions years ago and today for bathers, brides and grandmothers. Includes singing and dancing. 12 scenes Large mixed cast 1 interior

The three women of the Nativity. Bakers Plays 1960 15p
> Drama concerning three women in the Bible, Mary, Elizabeth and Anna, who were emotionally connected with the Nativity. 3 scenes 2m 5w extras 3 interiors

Russell, Solveig Paulson
c Are you thrifty?
> Two boys make bet on how many of their friends will be thrifty with money. 1w 5b 6g 1 exterior
>
> *In* Birdsall, R. ed. Creative plays for every school month

Russia
Courts and courtiers
Shaw, B. Great Catherine
History—1533-1605
Pushkin, A. Boris Godunov
Politics and government—19th century
Wilde, O. Vera
Social conditions
Camus, A. The possessed
Chekhov, A. The cherry orchard
Social life and customs
Goldina, M. The courageous one
Social life and customs—19th century
Chekhov, A. The brute
Chekhov, A. A country scandal
Chekhov, A. The sea gull
Chekhov, A. The three sisters
Chekhov, A. Uncle Vanya
Ostrovsky, A. The diary of a scoundrel
Turgenev, I. The bachelor
Turgenev, I. A month in the country
Turgenev, I. The poor gentleman
Turgenev, I. A provincial lady
Turgenev, I. Three famous plays (3 plays)

Russian folk-lore. See Folk-lore, Russian

Rutenborn, Guenter
The sign of Jonah; tr. from the German by George White. Nelson 1960 91p
> Centers around a modern day Jonah who is placed in situation similar to that of the Biblical prophet. 9 scenes 9m 2w 1 interior

Ruth, Gladys J.
c A birthday long ago
> Christmas. Three little boys take presents to the Christ Child. 1w 3b 1 interior
>
> *In* Birdsall, R. ed. Creative plays for every school month

Ruth (Biblical character)
Bailey, H. F. "Better than seven sons"
Estes, S. In quest of power through obedience
c Spamer, C. M. Ruth

Ruth. Spamer, C. M.

Ryan, Margaret A.
c Litterbugs on trial
> Several "litterbugs" are tried in court for leaving refuse at picnic grounds and on street. 14m 2w 2w 1 interior
>
> *In* Birdsall, R. ed. Creative plays for every school month

S

Saben revisited. Jones, T.

Sabrina fair. Taylor, S.

Sacagawea
Emmons, D. G. Out to win
Kissen, F. Sacajawea: guide in the wilderness

Sacajawea. See Sacagawea

Sacajawea: guide in the wilderness. Kissen, F.

Sacco-Vanzetti case
Anderson, M. Winterset

Sachs, Hans
"Der Todte Mann" ("The Dead Man")
(adaptation) See Thompson, D. The
shoemaker's wife

Sackville-West, V.
The Edwardians (dramatization) See
Gow, R. The Edwardians

The sacred den. Wembley South Kenton
Afternoon Townswomen's Guild. Drama
Section

Sacrifice, Human
Kwanze, M. Ikeniye

The sacrifice of Isaac. Abraham and Isaac
(Brome manuscript)

Sadism
Banks, L. R. The killer dies twice

Safe harbor. Parkhirst, D.

The safety clinic. Miller, H. L.

Safety education
c Blossom, L. The safety elves
c Fisher, A. By order of the king
c Fisher, A. Courting trouble
c Fisher, A. Long live father
Fisher, A. Luck takes a holiday
Fisher, A. Mr Do and Mr Don't
c Fisher, A. Nothing ever happens!
Fisher, A. The safety parade
c Hark, M. and McQueen, N.   A B C for
safety
c Miller, H. L. The safety clinic
c Patterson, L. The safety school
c Spamer, C. Crossing the street
c Stees, L. Red for danger

The safety elves. Blossom, L.

The safety parade. Fisher, A.

The safety school. Patterson, L.

Sagas. See Icelandic and Old Norse literature

Sailor, beware! King, P. and Cary, F. L.

Sailors. See Seamen

Sailor's life. See Seafaring life

St Bartholomew's Day, Massacre of, 1572
Lee, N. The massacre of Paris

Saint Chad of the seven wells. Lehman, L.

St Clair, Margaret
The perfectionist (dramatization) See
Denham, R. and Smith, C. S. A dash
of bitters

St Clair, Robert
Caught in a web. Eldridge 1955 88p
(Eldridge 3-act playscripts)
Mystery comedy. Young newspaperman
and girl try to solve disappearance of
three people but get involved with some
strange backwoods mountaineers. 3 acts
5 scenes 6m 7w 1 interior 2 exteriors
The happy life
Young Christian businessman and his
family face disaster with faith and courage. 3 scenes 4m 2w extras 2 interiors
In Brings, L. M. comp. The golden
book of church plays

The holy search
Nativity play. Wicked King Herod tries
to find out from the three wise men
where the Christ Child is hidden. 1 act
4 scenes 8m 3w extras 2 interiors
In Brings, L. M. ed. The modern treasury of Christmas plays

Joy to the world
Nativity play. The shepherds greet the
infant Jesus as the newborn King in
Bethlehem when Mary and Joseph set
out for Jerusalem. 3 scenes 2m 2w 1b
extras 2 interiors 1 exterior
In Brings, L. M. ed. The modern treasury of Christmas plays

Mark Twain's A double barrelled detective story. Manuscript editing and general revisions by Verne E. Powers.
Row 1954 144p illus
Mystery-comedy. Orphan boy comes to
mining town to find his father's killer
when suddenly Sherlock Holmes himself
appears to conduct the investigation.
3 acts 8m 7w extras 2 interiors

Miracle of the Madonna
Christmas play with three tableaux about
a girl who gets the coveted part in the
church play and is then stricken with
polio. 1 act 4 scenes 4m 5w extras 3 interiors
In Powers, V. E. ed. Plays for players,
and a guide to play production

The promised ones
The announcement to Joachim of forthcoming birth of John the Baptist, and
Annunciation of the Virgin Mary. 1 act
3 scenes 5m 3w 2 interiors
In Brings, L. M. comp. The golden
book of church plays

Susie and the F.B.I. Bakers Plays 1958
83p illus (Baker's Edition of plays)
Comedy. Spy drama set in hotel with
15-year-old daughter of the owner tracking the suspects. 3 acts 4m 6w 1 interior
See also Heicher, M. jt. auth.

St George at the Dragon. Spring, H.

The St George play. National Recreation
Association

St George's Day. Addis, H.

Saint Joan. Shaw, B.

Saint Joan of the stockyards. Brecht, B.

Saint Martha and the Tarasque of Tarascon. Ridge, A.

Saint Nicholas and the three scholars. Malcolmson, A.

St Nicholas just the same. Carlson, B. W.

St Nicholas of New Amsterdam. McCaslin, N.

Saint of Bleecker Street. Menotti, G. C.

St Patrick's Day
c Martens, A. C. Little lost leprechaun
c Newman, D. The prize shamrock
c Pierce, G. M. The story of March 17

St Patrick's Day. Sheridan, R. B.

Saint Peter and the birds. Woolsey, J. and
Sechrist, E. H.

St Valentine's Day. See Valentine's Day

Saint Valentine's surprise. Very, A. and
Brown, M.

La sainte courtisane. Wilde, O.

Sakanishi, Shio
(tr.) The aunt's sake (Oba ga sake)
Japanese comic interlude. Man, pretending to be a devil, steals some wine from
his aunt. 1m 1w 1 interior
In Sakanishi, S. tr. Japanese folk-plays

Sakanishi, Shio—*Continued*

(tr.) The bag of parting (Itoma-bakuro)
Japanese comic interlude. While his wife is away, husband tries to divorce her but she returns to play a trick on him. 2m 1w 1 interior

In Sakanishi, S. tr. Japanese folk-plays

(tr.) A bag of tangerines (Koji-dawara)
Japanese farcical interlude. A farmer's son pretends to be a devil inside a bag of tangerines. 3m 1 interior

In Sakanishi, S. tr. Japanese folk-plays

(tr.) Buaku
Japanese farcical interlude. Clever servant outwits his master who has sent a fellow servant to kill him. 3m 1 interior

In Sakanishi, S. tr. Japanese folk-plays

(tr.) Busu
Japanese comic interlude. Two servant boys play trick on their master. 3m 1 interior

In Sakanishi, S. tr. Japanese folk-plays

(tr.) The Deva King (Niwō)
Japanese comic interlude. Poor man who receives much money when he impersonates a god unfortunately tries the trick once too often. 2m extras 1 exterior

In Sakanishi, S. tr. Japanese folk-plays

(tr.) The family quarrel (Mizu-ron muko)
Japanese comic interlude. Man and his son-in-law alternately divert the water from each other's rice fields. 2m 1w 1 exterior

In Sakanishi, S. tr. Japanese folk-plays

(tr.) The fox mound (Kitsune-zuka)
Japanese farcical interlude. Servant sent to guard master's farm from wild beasts mistakes his master and fellow servant for foxes. 3m 1 exterior

In Sakanishi, S. tr. Japanese folk-plays

(tr.) Gargoyle (Oni-gewari)
Japanese comic interlude. Man becomes homesick for wife when ugly gargoyle on the temple reminds him of her. 2m 1 exterior

In Sakanishi, S. tr. Japanese folk-plays

(tr.) The ink-smeared lady (Suminuri onna)
Japanese interlude. Domestic comedy about a great lord who discovers wife's deceit by trick he plays on her. 2m 1w 1 interior

In Sakanishi, S. tr. Japanese folk-plays

(tr.) The letter "I." (I-moji)
Japanese comic interlude. A great lord decides to take a wife. 3m 1w 1 interior

In Sakanishi, S. tr. Japanese folk-plays

(tr.) Literate highwaymen (Fumi yama-dachi)
Japanese comic interlude. Two highwaymen quarrel, decide to kill each other and then think better of it. 2m 1 exterior

In Sakanishi, S. tr. Japanese folk-plays

(tr.) The magic mallet of the Devil (Oni no Tsuchi)
Japanese comic interlude. While the Devil sleeps, two men fight over his magic mallet. 3m extras 1 interior

In Sakanishi, S. tr. Japanese folk-plays

(tr.) The melon thief (Uri nusubito)
Japanese comic interlude. Farmer, whose melons have been stolen, sets trap for thief by pretending to be scarecrow. 2m 1 exterior

In Sakanishi, S. tr. Japanese folk-plays

(tr.) Mr Dumbtaro (Dontaro)
Japanese farcical interlude. When a man's two mistresses reject him he decides to enter monastery. 1m 2w 1 setting

In Sakanishi, S. tr. Japanese folk-plays

(tr.) Plop! Click! (Dobu kacchiri)
Japanese comic interlude. A passer-by plays trick on two blindmen. 3m 1 exterior

In Sakanishi, S. tr. Japanese folk-plays

(tr.) The ribs and the cover (Hone-kawa)
Japanese farcical interlude. In temple a novice continually confuses the priest's orders and says the wrong thing to everyone. 5m 1 interior

In Sakanishi, S. tr. Japanese folk-plays

(tr.) Seed of hōjō (Hōjō no tane)
Japanese comic interlude. An uncle and nephew try to outwit each other with tall stories. 2m 1 exterior

In Sakanishi, S. tr. Japanese folk-plays

(tr.) Thunder God (Kaminari)
Japanese comic interlude. A man cures the Thunder God of palsy. 1m extras 1 exterior

In Sakanishi, S. tr. Japanese folk-plays

(tr.) An unfair exchange (Sarugai Kōtō)
Japanese farcical interlude. Man steals a blind man's wife and puts monkey in her place. 2m 1w 1 setting

In Sakanishi, S. tr. Japanese folk-plays

(tr.) The wounded highwayman (Teo yamadachi)
Japanese comic interlude. A priest thinks he has murdered a highwayman and goes to spend the night in the latter's house. 2m 1w 1 interior 1 setting

In Sakanishi, S. tr. Japanese folk-plays

Salamis, Battle of, 480 B.C.
Aeschylus. The Persians

Salem, Massachusetts
Olfson, L. The house of the Seven Gables

Salesmanship. See Salesmen and salesmanship

Salesmen and salesmanship
Curtis, P. D. Candles for sale
Inge, W. The dark at the top of the stairs
McCaslin, N. The Yankee Peddler
Miller, A. Death of a salesman
Webber, P. A brush with the enemy

Salinger, Herman
Great-grandfather was an immigrant
Radio play. A German immigrant is shown patriotically defending America against a fellow immigrant who constantly criticizes the United States. Background music. 8m 2w 3b

In Prescott, H. ed. Patrioscript

Salisbury, Elsie
c Shoe children
Outdoor pageant for grades one to four with dances, using characters from nursery rhymes. Large mixed cast 1 exterior

In Birdsall, R. ed. Creative plays for every school month

Salomé. Wilde, O.

Saloons. See Hotels, taverns, etc.

Salt for savor. Wilde, P.

Salt winds. Robinson, D. F.

Salverson, George
You are not alone
Radio play. On a subway ride two men realize that life all over the world from big cities to primitive societies is lived in terms of groups. 5m 2w

In Goldschmidt, W. ed. Ways of mankind

Sam Houston: brother of the Cherokees. Kissen, F.

Sam Pollard. Arnold, H. G.

Sammy. Hughes, K.

Sammy Bushytail. Spamer, C. M.

Samson, Judge of Israel
Howells, W. D. Samson
c Spamer, C. M. Samson and Delilah
Samson. Howells, W. D.
Samson and Delilah. Spamer, C. M.

Samuel, Judge of Israel
Bailey, H. F. "We bring this child unto the Lord"
Estes, S. In quest of power through dedication

Sanatoriums
Cargill, P. and Beale, J. Ring for Catty
See also Hospitals

Sand Cave, Kentucky
Shaw, D. Rescue

Sandberg, Lois M.
The pastor's guiding hand. Bakers Plays 1957 30p (Baker's Royalty plays)
One day in the life of New England clergyman in 1872 as he settles quarrels and problems, and is mainstay of his parish. 2 acts 4m 4w 1 interior
The sandbox. Albee, E.

Sanders, Betty Lenoir
What's cookin'?
Domestic comedy. The whole family is drawn into big preparations for daughter's wedding, when daughter calls to say she has just eloped. 1 act 1m 5w 1 interior
In Twelve half-hours with the Winthrop Theater
The sands of time. Dias, E. J.
Sanemori. Kwanze, M.

San Francisco
Social life and customs
Rodgers, R. Flower drum song

Santa and the space men. Fluckey, J. O.

Santa Claus
c Austin, C. L. Mrs Santa proves a point
c Davis, J. A. Santa's spectacles
c Fisher, A. Standing up for Santa
c Fluckey, J. O. He said he was Santa
c Fluckey, J. O. Santa and the space men
c Hark, M. and McQueen, N. The Santa Claus parade
Howard, V. Five boys and a Santa
Martens, A. C. The fantastic Mr C.
c Matthews, E. Teddy's own Santa
c Mattice, I. A bomb for Santa
Miller, H. L. The left-over reindeer
c Miller, H. L. Santa Claus for president
c Miller, H. L. Softy the Snow Man
c Miller, H. L. Wake up, Santa Claus!
c Posso, M. E. Santa was so tired!
c Spamer, C. Donerblitz
c Woolsey, J. and Sechrist, E. H. Gifts for the elves
See also Christmas

Santa Claus. Cummings, E. E.
The Santa Claus court. Woolsey, J. and Sechrist, E. H.
Santa Claus for president. Miller, H. L.
The Santa Claus parade. Hark, M. and McQueen, N.
The Santa Claus twins. Miller, H. L.
Santa Claus visits Mars. National Recreation Association

Santa was so tired! Posso, M. E.
Santa's neurosis. Sherman, R. W.
Santa's spectacles. Davis, J. A.

Sapinsley, Alvin
Lee at Gettysburg
Television play. Robert E. Lee's plan for the Battle of Gettysburg thwarted by deliberate delay of Generals Longstreet and Stuart in obeying his orders. 16m
In Best television plays, 1957

Sappho
Durrell, L. Sappho
Grillparzer, F. Sappho
Sappho. Durrell, L.
Sappho. Grillparzer, F.

Sardou, Victorien
A scrap of paper; English version by Léonie Gilmour
Romantic comedy. Old love letter creates confusion when it comes belatedly into possession of a man whose sweetheart is now married to someone else. Set in mid-nineteenth century France. 3 acts 7m 6w 3 interiors
In Stanton, S. S. ed. Camille, and other plays

Sardou, Victorien, and Najac, Émile de
Let's get a divorce! English version by Angela and Robert Goldsby
Domestic comedy. Complications arise when unhappily married couple decide to get a divorce. Set in France in 1880. 3 acts 7m 5w extras 1 interior 1 exterior
In Bentley, E. ed. Let's get a divorce! and other plays

Saroyan, William
The cave dwellers. French 1958 126p
Group of down and out people live in abandoned lower East Side theater while waiting for wrecking crew. Theme is love as motivating force in human life. 2 acts 10 scenes 9m 5w 1 interior
Also published in trade edition by Putnam
The cave dwellers (condensation)
In Broadway's best, 1958
Hello out there
Murder of young prisoner held for sex crime. 5m 2w 1 interior
In Watson, E. B. and Pressey, B. eds. Contemporary drama: eleven plays
The man with the heart in the highlands
Allegorical fantasy revealing man's yearning for beauty and affection. Poet and his son are visited by an old Shakespearean actor. 6 scenes 11m 3w 2b extras 2 interiors 1 exterior
Same as: My heart's in the Highlands
In The Best short plays, 1957
My heart's in the Highlands
Same as: The man with the heart in the Highlands
In A Treasury of the theatre
Once around the block. [Rev] French 1959 20p
A successful but tired writer advises his young protege to tire himself by running around the block in order to win a girl who admires the writer. 1 act 3m 1w 1 interior
The slaughter of the innocents. French 1958 59p illus
People are afraid to protest at police state's trials without juries until a child is tried. 2 acts 5 scenes 17m 6w 1b 1 interior
—Same
In Saroyan, W. The William Saroyan Reader

Saroyan, William—*Continued*

The time of your life
  Study of inner lives in waterfront saloon in San Francisco where people drink, gamble, and try to help other lost souls. 3 acts 5 scenes 18m 8w 2 interiors
  In Bierman, J., Hart, J. and Johnson, S. eds. The dramatic experience
  In Gaver, J. ed. Critics' choice
  In Saroyan, W. The William Saroyan Reader

Sartre, Jean Paul

Dirty hands (Les mains sales)
  Tragedy. Young intellectual, a Communist Party worker in mid-European country during World War II, caught between theories and actions. 7 acts 10m 2w 1 interior
  In Sartre, J. P. No exit, and three other plays

The flies (Les mouches); tr. from the French by Stuart Gilbert
  Symbolical treatment in modern idiom of the Greek legend of Orestes and Electra. 3 acts 4 scenes 7m 6w 1b extras 2 interiors 2 exteriors
  In Gassner, J. ed. A treasury of the theatre
  In Sartre, J. P. No exit, and three other plays

No exit. French 1958 54p illus
  Two women and a man consigned to windowless room in hell torture each other with their confessions. 1 act 2m 2w 1 interior
—Same
  In Sartre, J. P. No exit, and three other plays
—Same; tr. by Stuart Gilbert
  In Gassner, J. ed. Twenty best European plays on the American stage

The respectful prostitute (La putain respectueuse)
  Woman's unsuccessful attempt to prevent a southern lynching. 2 scenes 5m 1w extras 1 interior
  In Sartre, J. P. No exit, and three other plays

Satan. See Devil

Satellites

Asbrand, K. Christmas satellite
c Spamer, C. Heavenly stars

Satire

Aristophanes. The clouds
Aristophanes. The frogs
Aristophanes. Peace
Aristophanes. The wasps
Ashbery, J. The heroes
Auden, W. H. and Isherwood, C. The ascent of F6
Auden, W. H. and Isherwood, C. The dog beneath the skin
Barrie, J. M. The admirable Crichton
Bernstein, L. Candide
Boyd, A. K. The mock doctor
Brecht, B. The threepenny opera
Bulwer-Lytton, E. Money
Buttle, M. Toynbee in Elysium
Congreve, W. The way of the world
Connelly, M. The traveler
Daviot, G. Lady Charing is cross
Dekker, T. Satiromastix
Dennis, N. Cards of identity
Dennis, N. The making of moo

Eliot, T. S. The confidential clerk
Giraudoux, J. The Apollo of Bellac
Giraudoux, J. The virtuous island
Golden, E. Gulliver's travels in Lilliput Land
Howells, W. D. Saved
Ibsen, H. Peer Gynt
Ionesco, E. The bald soprano
Ionesco, E. The killer
Ionesco, E. The leader
Ionesco, E. Rhinoceros
Jarry, A. Ubu Roi
Jones, P. and Jowett, J. The party spirit
Jonson, B. The alchemist
Jonson, B. Every man in his humour
Kerr, W. and Kerr, J. Goldilocks
Kopit, A. L. Oh, Dad, poor Dad, Mamma's hung you in the closet and I'm feelin' so sad
Lawrence, J. and Lee, R. E. The gang's all here
Lee, N. The Princess of Cleve
Lewis, E. A screw loose
Macrae, A. Both ends meet
Maeterlinck, M. A miracle of Saint Antony
Malleson, M. The misanthrope
Martens, A. C. People to people
Molière, J. B. P. Coxcombs in petticoats
Molière, J. B. P. Five plays
Molière, J. B. P. The imaginary invalid
Molière, J. B. P. The learned ladies
Molière, J. B. P. Love's the best doctor
Molière, J. B. P. The middle-class gentleman
Molière, J. B. P. The misanthrope
Molière, J. B. P. The miser
Molière, J. B. P. The miser, and Coxcombs in petticoats (2 plays)
Molière, J. B. P. The physician in spite of himself
Molière, J. B. P. The precious damsels
Molière, J. B. P. The pretentious ladies
Molière, J. B. P. The reluctant doctor
Molière, J. B. P. The self-made gentleman
Molière, J. B. P. Six prose comedies (6 plays)
Molière, J. B. P. The slave of truth
Molière, J. B. P. The slave of truth; Tartuffe; The imaginary invalid (3 plays)
Molière, J. B. P. Tartuffe
Molière, J. B. P. That scoundrel Scapin
Molière, J. B. P. The would-be gentleman
Molière, J. B. P. The would-be invalid
Musset, A. de. A door should be either open or shut
Nathan, R. Jezebel's husband
Nathan, R. The sleeping beauty
Nicholson, H. Port and a pistol
O'Casey, S. The drums of Father Ned
O'Casey, S. Purple dust
Pagnol. Topaze
Patrick, J. The Teahouse of the August Moon
Philp, P. Love and lunacy
Roussin, A. The little hut
Schnitzler, A. Countess Mizzie
Seiler, C. The wonderful adventures of Don Quixote

Satire—*Continued*

Sharp, A. Nightmare Abbey
Shaw, B. Androcles and the lion
Shaw, B. The apple cart
Shaw, B. Arms and the man
Shaw, B. Augustus does his bit
Shaw, B. The doctor's dilemma
Shaw, B. Getting married
Shaw, B. Major Barbara
Sheridan, R. B. The critic
Sheridan, R. B. The rivals
Spewack, S. Under the sycamore tree
Teichmann, H. and Kaufman, G. S. The solid gold Cadillac
Tyler, R. The contrast
Ustinov, P. The love of four colonels
Valency, M. The virtuous island
Vanbrugh, Sir J. The relapse
Vidal, G. Summer pavilion
Vidal, G. Visit to a small planet
Villiers, G. and others. The rehearsal
Wallach, I. Phoenix '55
Wimberley, R. L. Willy Velvet, homicide detective

Satiromastix. Dekker, T.

Saturday at the Cohens. Claflin, M.

Satyric drama, Greek. See Greek drama (Satyr play)

Saul, King of Israel
c Spamer, C. M. Saul and the ghost

Saul and the ghost. Spamer, C. M.

Saul of Tarsus. See Paul, Saint, apostle

Sauvajon, Marc-Gilbert, and Jackson, Frederick
Les enfants d'Edouard (adaptation) See Melville, A. Dear Charles

Savage, George
I won't dance! Eldridge 1954 24p (Eldridge Popular one-act playscripts)
Romantic comedy. When teenage boy refuses to learn to dance his family is upset until shy girl with same problem moves in next door. 1 act 4m 4w 1 interior

Saved. Howells, W. D.

Saving and thrift
Burgess, C. V. Susan to the rescue
c Hark, M. and McQueen, N. Lincoln reminders
Kirkpatrick, J. Adam's rib hurts
c Miller, H. L. The Bar-None Trading Post
c Russell, S. P. Are you thrifty?
Sutherland, D. Father's economy drive

Savory, Gerald
A likely tale. [French's Acting ed] French (London) 72p illus
Dying old man keeps changing his will to the dismay of his three elderly children who fear he will make it in favor of their younger brother or their maid. 3 acts 3m 3w 1 interior
A month of Sundays. [French's Acting ed] French (London) 1957 83p illus
To delight of his family, a visitor and a new farm hand succeed in proving to Mr Sylvester that running a farm in Cornwall as his grandfather did is not conducive to comfortable living. 3 acts 3m 4w 1 interior

Sawyer, Elizabeth
Rowley, W. and others. The witch of Edmonton

Say, darling. Bissell, R.; Burrows, A. and Bissell, M.

Sayemon, Enami no. See Enami, Sayemon

Sayers, Dorothy
The zeal of Thy house
In 12th century England William of Sens, (Guillaume de Sens) a French architect brought over to reconstruct the choir section of Canterbury Cathedral, suffers divine punishment for his sin of pride. Choral music. 4 scenes 23m 1w 2b extras choir 1 setting
In Halverson, M. ed. Religious drama 1

Sayre, George Wallace
Final edition
A group of reporters expose corrupt politician. 1 act 2 scenes 8m 1 interior
In Burack, A. S. ed. Four-star plays for boys

Sayre, Tom
A town is born (adaptation) See Piersel, W. G. A town is born

Scapin the scamp. Molière, J. B. P.

The scarecrow. MacKaye, P.

The scarf from Smyrna. Lorenzen, R. F.

Schaefer, Lee
The little flaw of Ernesto Lippi
Italian - American domestic comedy. 5 scenes 3m 6w 2 interiors
In The Best short plays of 1953-1954
Song for a hero
Farce. Contentious monks compose song for wedding of village hero. Guitar music. 6 scenes 9m 1w 3g 1 interior
In The Best short plays of 1954-1955

Schary, Dore
The highest tree. Random House 1960 130p illus
Physicist who discovers he has leukemia must break the news to his sweetheart, and decides to spend remaining days in abolishing atomic weapon experiments. 3 acts 5 scenes 9m 6w 1 interior
Sunrise at Campobello. Random House 1958 109p illus
Franklin Delano Roosevelt's personal and family life from 1921-1924 when he fought his way back to active life after attack of infantile paralysis. 3 acts 8 scenes 16m 5w 3b 4 interiors
Also published in the New American Library as A Signet book
Sunrise at Campobello (condensation)
In The Best plays of 1957-1958
In Broadway's best, 1958

Scherzo in two flats. Sutherland, D.

Schevill, James
The bloody tenet
Conflict between the preaching of Roger Williams and established doctrine of the Puritans leads to his trial in colonial Massachusetts. 5 scenes 8m 2w 4 interiors
In Halverson, M. ed. Religious drama 1

Schiller, Friedrich von
Don Carlos, infante of Spain; tr. by Charles E. Passage. Ungar 1959 xxvii, 216p
Historical tragedy. 16th century Spain. Psychological study of Don Carlos and his conflict with father, King Philip. 5 acts 11m 5w 1b 1g extras 12 interiors 2 exteriors
—Same; English version by James Kirkup
In Bentley, E. ed. The classic theatre v2

Schiller, Friedrich von—*Continued*

Intrigue and love (Kabale und Liebe) tr. by Guenther Reinhardt. Barrons Educ. Ser. 1953 133p
> Tragedy. Cruel father uses political influence to separate his son from the girl he loves. Set in 18th century Germany. 5 acts 37 scenes 8m 4w extras 5 interiors

Maria Stuart (adaptation) See Goldstone, J. S. and Reich, J. Mary Stuart

Mary Stuart; a tragedy; a new, unabridged translation with an introduction by Sophie Wilkins. Barrons Educ. Ser. 1959 166p (Foreign language classics in English)
> Tragedy. Last three days in the life of Mary Stuart, Queen of Scotland. Verse play. 5 acts 52 scenes 14m 6w extras 4 interiors 1 exterior

—Same; tr. by Joseph Mellish and adapted by Eric Bentley

In Bentley, E. ed. The classic theatre v2

Wallenstein; a historical drama in three parts: Wallenstein's camp, The Piccolominis, The death of Wallenstein; tr. by Charles E. Passage. Ungar 1958 xxxix, 275p
> Set in Bohemia during the Thirty Years' War. Events of the winter of 1633-1634 which culminated in the assassination of the German general, Albrecht von Wallenstein. 3 parts 10 acts Large mixed cast 4 interiors 1 exterior
> Trade edition also published

William Tell; tr. by Sidney E. Kaplan. Barron's Educ. Ser. 1954 125p
> In 15th century Switzerland William Tell fights for rights of free men against the tyrant, Gessler. 5 acts 15 scenes Large mixed cast 4 interiors 10 exteriors

Schizophrenia
Vidal, G. Dark possession

Schloss, Martin F.
Totentanz [Dance of death] in a modern version; tr. from the German by Margaret Trinklein
> Allegorical medieval morality play. Death calls all mankind, rich and poor, old and young, good and bad to dance to his fiddle. Verse play with violin music. 8m 6w 1 exterior

In Switz, T. M. and Johnston, R. A. eds. Great Christian plays

Schnitzler, Arthur
Anatol; English version by Harley Granville-Barker
> Remembrance, analysis, and classification of past and present loves by romantic intellectuals in Vienna. 7 scenes 4m 7w 4 interiors 1 exterior

In Bentley, E. ed. From the modern repertoire; ser. 3

Countess Mizzie; or, The family reunion; tr. by Edwin Björkman
> Sophisticated satire. Viennese Prince acknowledges his natural son by daughter of friend, a Count whose own mistress is leaving him. 1 act 7m 2w 1 exterior

In Smith, B. and others, eds. A treasury of non-royalty one-act plays

Light-o'-love; tr. from the German by Bayard Quincy Morgan
> Tragedy. Woman discovers her lover has been killed in duel over wife of another man. 3 acts 4m 3w 1g 2 interiors

In Tucker, S. M. ed. Twenty-five modern plays

Merry-go-round. Weidenfeld 1953 90p illus
> Manners and morals on various levels of 19th century Viennese society, as revealed in several sex episodes. 10 scenes 10m 10w 8 interiors 2 exteriors
> Same as: La ronde

La ronde; English version by Eric Bentley
> Same as: Merry-go-round

In Bentley, E. ed. The modern theatre v2

Schofield, Jessie
c An indoor tree-lighting service
> Boys and girls talk about all the customs associated with Christmas tree. Christmas carols. 7b 4g extras 1 interior

In National Recreation Association. Plays, pageants and ceremonials for the Christmas season

Schofield, Joseph Anderson, and Joudry, Robert Clyde
"All hail the power of Jesus' name"
> Easter play. The events of the Crucifixion and Resurrection as seen by several of Jesus' friends. 3 acts 11m 8w choir extras 1 interior 2 exteriors

In Schofield, J. A. and Joudry, R. C. Three Easter plays

"Many infallible proofs"
> Easter. Several children in Jerusalem discuss the news of Christ's Resurrection. 3b 3g 1 exterior

In Schofield, J. A. and Joudry, R. C. Three Easter playlets for children and young people

"Who is this?"
> Easter play. Several children watch Jesus ride into Jerusalem on the first Palm Sunday. 3b 3g 1 exterior

In Schofield, J. A. and Joudry, R. C. Three Easter playlets for children and young people

Schofield, Stephen
The old master. Deane 1954 29p ("Deane's" Ser. of plays)
> Among the effects of cottage to be sold is valuable but stolen painting. Several people go to great lengths to get it. 1 act 2m 4w 1 interior

Scholarships
Paradis, M. B. Midge rings the bell

Scholl, Ralph
The golden axe
> Axe-wielding billboard hater foils calculating widow. 1 act 2m 1w 1 interior

In The Best short plays of 1957-1958

Schoneman, Ethel T.
c The wish machine
> Science fiction. A group of boys find a machine from outer space that will make any wish come true. 17b extras 1 interior

In Birdsall, R. ed. Creative plays for every school month

School accidents
Rose, R. The remarkable incident at Carson Corners

School bus romance. McMahon, L. E.

School buses. See Motor buses

School daze. Asbrand, K.

School discipline
Lathrop, D. Forever Eve
Taggart, T. When mothers meet

The school for scandal. Sheridan, R. B.

A school for scaring. Miller, H. L.

The school for wives. Molière, J. B. P.

School-houses
Brown, F. E. The educated schoolhouse
School journalism. See College and school journalism
School life. See Students
School plays. See Children's plays; College and school drama
School superintendents and principals
Delderfield, R. F. The orchard walls
Mitzman, N. and Dalzell, W. Books and crooks
Williams, P. Commencement
Schools
Flaten, M. Testing ground for democracy
Hark, M. and McQueen, N. G for Gettysburg
c Miller, H. L. Mary's invitation
See also Boarding schools; Universities and colleges

England
Aske, L. Too young
Bond, C. The food of love
Delderfield, R. F. The orchard walls
Rattigan, T. The Winslow boy

Great Britain
See Schools—England

United States
c Gill, M. L. Treasure hunt
c Matthews, E. On to seventh grade!
Schoolteachers. See Teachers
Schroll, Catherine V. See MacLellan, E. jt. auth.
Schulberg, Budd
The disenchanted (dramatization) See Schulberg, B. and Breit, H. The disenchanted
A face in the crowd. Random House 1957 172p front
Based on the author's short story: Your Arkansas traveler. A moving picture play depicting rise of drunken derelict from an Arkansas jail to television stardom, and his destruction by the woman responsible for his success. 9m 2w extras
Your Arkansas traveler (moving picture dramatization) See Schulberg, B. A face in the crowd
Schulberg, Budd, and Breit, Harvey
The disenchanted. French 1959 80p illus
Based on novel by Budd Schulberg. A man, trying to make a comeback as novelist but currently doing work he dislikes in motion pictures, finds that there is no second chance for anyone. 3 acts 7 scenes 10m 4w extras 3 interiors
Trade edition published by Random House
The disenchanted (condensation)
In The Best plays of 1958-1959
In Broadway's best, 1959
Schulman, Arnold
A hole in the head. French 1957 94p front
Comedy. Man and his young son try to run a shabby hotel in Florida against increasing odds. 2 acts 6 scenes 7m 5w 1b 1 exterior
Also published in trade edition by Random House
Schulman, Susan H.
Turn my face toward the east. French 1959 21p
Struggles of Louis Braille to get his system for teaching the blind to read accepted. 1 act 4m 3w 1g extras 1 interior

Schweikert, Clarissa P.
Hessie of the hills. Eldridge 1953 48p (Eldridge 3-act playscripts)
Farce. Daughter of mountaineer family runs away to the city presumably with visiting agricultural experimentalist. 3 acts 5m 6w 1 interior
Hoax of Hogan's Holler. Eldridge 1955 50p (Eldridge 3-act playscripts)
Comedy. Not only is a hillbilly family bothered by ghost haunting their cabin, but mysterious city boy appears and begins courting daughter of family. 3 acts 5m 8w 1 interior
Science
Fenwick, R. Toys and science
c Spamer, C. Little cloud
c Spamer, C. Little icicle
c Spamer, C. Raindrops
c Spamer, C. The rebellious lightning bolt

Experiments
Badger, A. Willie's secret weapon
Science fiction
Duffield, B. The war of the worlds
Fisher, A. and Rabe, O. Invasion from the stratosphere
Fisher, A. and Rabe, O. Rocket to freedom
Greth, Le R. E. The ghost from outer space
Greth, Le R. E. The kid from Mars
Greth, Le R. E. The sky's the limit
c Harper, J. M. The first cat on Mars
Howard, V. Paloma, Princess of Pluto
Larson, V. and Magary, F. A. Message from Mars
Leydon, B. Johnny Jones, space cadet!
c Martens, A. C. The time machine
Oboler, A. Night of the auk
Olson, E. The illusionists
Owens, R. J. Final edition
Ressieb, G. Danger from the sky
c Schoneman, E. T. The wish machine
Shore, M. Catastrophe Clarence
Tuson, N. Moon rocket
Vidal, G. Visit to a small planet
c Wallerstein, J. S. Bobby and the time machine
Scientists
Howells, W. D. and Clemens, S. L. Colonel Sellers as a scientist
Morgan, C. The burning glass
Schary, D. The highest tree
Scotch in France
Olfson, L. Quentin Durward
Scotland
Wallace, N. Speed, bonnie boat

History—To 1057
Olfson, L. Macbeth

History—War of Independence, 1285-1371
Williamson, H. R. Heart of Bruce

History—16th century
Anderson, M. Mary of Scotland
Bottomley, G. Ardvorlich's wife
Bottomley, G. Fire at Callart
Bottomley, G. Marsaili's weeping
Bottomley, G. Towie Castle

History—1660-1688
Daviot, G. Barnharrow

Seeing the star. Hawse, A.

The **seekers.** Greene, N. D.

Seidel, Nora

Keeping company. Bakers Plays 1953 96p illus (Baker's Royalty plays)
Domestic comedy. Spinster who has been going steady for nineteen years and her two teenage wards plot to get her beau to propose. 3 acts 5m 6w 1 interior

Seidelhuber, Gladys

The lavender kite. French 1955 19p illus
Sensitive young wife grieving over death of her child is unable to understand the harshness of her husband. 1 act 2m 1w 1 interior

Seiger, Marvin L.

Blue concerto
Young woman's decision to remain with crippled husband, releasing trumpet playing lover. Trumpet music in background. 1 act 2m 2w 1 interior
In The Best short plays of 1955-1956

Seiler, Conrad

The clown and his circus. Longmans 1953 66p music
When circus moves on leaving Dodo the clown behind, he meets several remarkable friends and has some strange adventures. 3 acts 6m 6w 1b 4g no scenery

c The clown out west. Longmans 1959 82p
Comedy. Clown and his horse take trip out west where they meet a bandit and have some amusing adventures. 3 acts 4 scenes 7m 3w 2b 3g extras 3 exteriors

c Let's go to the moon. French 1956 58p illus
Little boy who doesn't like fairy tales meets a space man and goes on a dream trip to moon. 3 acts 7b 5g 1 interior 1 exterior

Nude washing dishes
A painter is angry when his friends look at his painting from a commercial rather than an artistic viewpoint. 4m 3w 1 interior
In The Best short plays, 1959-1960

The stronger sex. Dramatists 1958 20p
Comedy. Speaker who is extolling the good old days when woman knew her place, gets his come-uppance. 1 act 3m 2w 1 interior

What's wrong with the girls. Dramatists 1956 32p
Comedy. Expert on the female of the species begins his lecture on them with acted demonstrations, perpetrating the unexpected. 1 act 4m 3w no scenery

The wonderful adventures of Don Quixote. Dramatists 1956 64p
Based on Cervantes' novel about the man who thinks he lives in the days of chivalry and goes off to perform deeds of honor. Set in 17th century Spain. 3 acts 5 scenes 12m 10w extras 1 exterior

Seiler, Gwendolen

The Princess and the swineherd; lyrics and incidental music by Conrad Seiler. [Rev. ed] French 1954 69p music
Comedy. The prince disguised as swineherd wins the princess with aid of magic cooking-pot. Includes songs with musical scores. 3 acts 18m 5w 2 interiors 1 exterior

Sejanus, his fall. Jonson, B.

Sek, Misha

The dawn must break. The Peasant Jugoslavia, Ltd. 1959 118p
Family and friends in Yugoslavia, and how their lives were effected by political changes in last 40 years. 4 acts 7m 2w 3 interiors

Self-interest

Aurthur, R. A. A very special baby

Benson, S. The young and beautiful

Casey, B. M. Excuse for living

Fisher, A. Angel in the looking-glass

Foote, H. The trip to Bountiful

Funt, J. The magic and the loss

George, M. Symphonie pastorale

Ghelderode, M. de. The women at the tomb

Howards, S. The silver cord

c Miller, H. L. The wishing stream

Mosel, T. My lost saints

Ridley, A. You, my guests!

Rodman, H. The will to win

Sergel, R. A cup of tea

Williams, N. The mountain
See also Egoism

The **self**-made gentleman. Molière, J. B. P.

Self-sacrifice

Barrow, W. Peaceful evening

Corneille, P. Pulchérie

De Francquen, L. The cat and the fiddle

Self-sacrifice. Howells, W. D.

Sellevision. Addis, H.

Semple, Lorenzo

Golden fleecing, by Lorenzo Semple, Jr. French 1958 103p
Farce. Three American gamblers with a walkie-talkie and an electronic computer attempt to win at roulette, in Venice, but run into trouble with an Admiral. 3 acts 4 scenes 11m 2w 1 interior

Seneca

Oedipus; tr. by Clarence W. Mendell
Latin classical tragedy, Oedipus legend. Fate preordains that Oedipus must kill his father and marry his mother. Verse play. 4 scenes 7m 2w extras 1 exterior
In Levin, R. Tragedy: plays, theory, and criticism

Senior, Edward

The hunted
After murdering fifteen-year old girl he loved, man commits suicide while awaiting sheriff's posse. 6m 3w extras 1 setting
In The Best short plays, 1958-1959

Senior play. Gibson, M. N.

A **sense** of justice. Vidal, G.

Senses and sensation

c Hark, M. and McQueen, N. The five senses

Separate tables. Rattigan, T.

Sequoya, Cherokee Indian

Spamer, C. Ah-yo-ka

Serbo-Bulgarian War, 1885

Shaw, B. Arms and the man

Sergel, C.

The family nobody wanted. Dramatic 1957 109p illus
Based on the book by Helen Grigsby Doss. Teenager who has several oriental brothers and sisters by adoption, has trouble being accepted by his girlfriend's family. 3 acts 7m 10w 1 interior

Sergel, Kristin

Father knows best. Dramatic 1954 75p illus
Domestic comedy. Father who suddenly decides that teenagers should be watched, creates a lot of confusion when he forces his own to stay at home. 3 acts 4 scenes 7m 10w 1 interior

Sergel, Kristin—*Continued*

Maudie and the opposite sex. Dramatic 1955 71p illus
> Romantic comedy. Based on the "Maudie" stories by Graeme and Sarah Lorimer about teenager whose parents separate her from boyfriend by going to distant resort, and how she launches counterattack. 3 acts 4 scenes 5m 9w 1 exterior

My little Margie. Dramatic 1953 75p illus
> A comedy based on television program by Frank Fox. Father who dislikes daughter's boyfriend pretends to like him a great deal thinking contrarily that she might lose interest. 3 acts 4 scenes 6m 6w 1 interior

The remarkable incident at Carson Corners. Dramatic 1955 70p illus
> Using members of audience as jury, students conduct trial to investigate the death of fellow-student and the responsibility of various members of the community in it. 3 acts 13m 13w no scenery

See also Rose, R. Dino

Sergel, Ruth

A. A. Milne's The Red House mystery. Dramatic 1956 96p illus
> Based on mystery story by A. A. Milne. During house party at Red House, the owner's brother is killed and the host disappears. Police think it clear case of homicide but one guest notices tell-tale clues. 3 acts 4 scenes 7m 8w 1 interior

Blue stocking. Dramatic 1953 25p illus
> Domestic comedy based on incident in novel: The town, by Conrad Richter. A cultured relative makes a frontier family feel awkward. Set in Ohio just after the Revolutionary War. 2m 5w 1 interior

A cup of tea. Dramatic 1954 28p illus
> An adaptation of Katherine Mansfield's story. Starving but beautiful young artist asks for cup of tea from wealthy young society matron who decides to help her as a gesture to enhance her own ego. 2m 4w 1 interior

Henry Van Dyke's The Other Wise Man. Dramatic 1955 40p illus
> Based on Henry Van Dyke's story about a man who wanted to bring gifts for the new born Christ child but spent his life searching for him. 4 scenes 11m 14w extras no scenery

Irving Stone's Love is eternal. Dramatic 1955 103p
> Based on novel by Irving Stone. The story of Mary Todd's youth, her marriage to Lincoln and her life through the Civil War. 3 acts 4 scenes 14m 16w 3 interiors

A New England nun; dramatized by Ruth Sergel. Dramatic 1955 28p illus
> Based on story by Mary Wilkins Freeman about woman whose reaction is unusual when she discovers fiance of fourteen years no longer loves her. 1 act 1m 4w 1 interior

No star to guide them. Dramatic 1956 36p illus
> Based on: Christ legends, by Selma Lagerlöf. The three kings who have journeyed from the East to see the Christ Child are shocked to find only a poor man's son. Includes singing by soloists or choir. 1 act 2 scenes 8m 5w 2g extras 2 interiors 1 exterior

The revolt of mother. Dramatic 1954 28p illus
> Domestic comedy. Based on story by Mary Wilkins Freeman. On the eve of her daughter's wedding New England farmer's wife revolts against husband's tyranny, after he has promised her a new house for years. 1 act 3m 3w 1 interior

See also McMahon, L. E. jt. auth.

Serious charge. King, P.

Serling, Rod

Noon on Doomsday
> Television play. Freed killer and his townspeople are forced to face their guilt after a prejudiced trial. 7m 4w

In Burack, A. S. ed. Television plays for writers

Requiem for a heavyweight
> Television play. Injured "might-have-been champion" prizefighter is saved from becoming a derelict by young woman in an employment agency. 17m 2w 1b extras

In Best television plays, 1957

In Writers Guild of America. The prize plays of television and radio, 1956

The strike
> During the Korean War, American army officer has to decide between saving the remnant of five hundred men in his command or a twenty man patrol marooned in enemy territory. 27m

In Vidal, G. ed. Best television plays

The sermon. Carter, B.

Serra, Junípero

Helm, M. Fray Junípero Serra

Sertorius. Corneille, P.

The servant of the King. Casey, B. M.

Servants

Avery, I. Matilda

Bagnold, E. The chalk garden

Barrie, J. M. The admirable Crichton

Burke, N. The girl who had everything

Gray, M. For love of a house

Howells, W. D. The Albany depot

MacLeod, R. Kate

Molière, J. B. P. The would-be invalid

"Servitude." O'Neill, E.

The setting sun. Carpenter, F.

Settlements, Social. See Social settlements

Seven against Thebes. Aeschylus

The seven gifts. Walker, S.

Seven nuns at Las Vegas. White, N. E.

The seven year itch. Axelrod, G.

Seventeen. Kent, W.

The seventh seal. Bergman, I.

Seventy times seven. Casey, B. M.

Sewing

Priestley, F. The mannequin parade

Sex

Racine, J. B. Phaedra

Schnitzler, A. Merry-go-round

Sganarelle. Malleson, M.

Shaber, David

The youngest shall ask
> Son rebels against Judaism during celebration of Passover. 2m 1w 1 interior

In The Best short plays, 1952-1953

The shadow of a gunman. O'Casey, S.

The shadow of doubt. King, N.

The shadow of Spain. Trease, G.

Shadow of the eagle. Cockram, R.

Shadows walk softly. Bennett, V. E.

The shadowy waters. Yeats, W. B.

Shaffer, Peter

Five finger exercise. Harcourt 1958 110p
None of members of a family understands each other, but with arrival of a young German tutor who is really seeking a home, each comes to grips with himself. 2 acts 4 scenes 3m 2w 1 interior
Trade editions also published by H. Hamilton and Harcourt

Five finger exercise (condensation)
In The Best plays of 1959-1960
In Broadway's best, 1960

Shakes versus Shav. Shaw, B.

Shakespeare, William

Antony and Cleopatra
The tragic war of Antony versus Caesar. with Cleopatra as Antony's love. 5 acts 16 scenes 30m 4w extras 1 setting
In Downer, A. S. ed. The art of the play

Antony and Cleopatra (adaptation) See Dryden, J. All for love

As you like it (radio adaptation) See Olfson, L. As you like it

Hamlet (radio adaptation) See Olfson, L. Hamlet

Julius Caesar (radio adaptation). See Olfson, L. Julius Caesar

King Henry IV, Part I (adaptation) See Boyd, A. K. Robbery at Gadshill

King John (adaptation) See Boyd, A. K. Prince Arthur and Hubert

King Lear (radio adaptation) See Olfson, L. King Lear

Macbeth (radio adaptation) See Olfson, L. Macbeth

A midsummer night's dream (radio adaptation) See Olfson, L. A midsummer night's dream

Much ado about nothing (radio adaptation) See Olfson, L. Much ado about nothing

Othello
Tragedy. Moorish nobleman is victim of a plot instigated by his evil assistant. Verse play. 5 acts 15 scenes 10m 3w extras 3 interiors 5 exteriors
In Bierman, J.; Hart, J. and Johnson, S. eds. The dramatic experience
In Cooper, C. W. Preface to drama
In Levin, R. Tragedy: plays, theory, and criticism

Romeo and Juliet
An edited version of the play by Shakespeare. Lovers, separated by feuding families, commit suicide. Set in Renaissance Italy. Verse play. 5 acts 23 scenes 21m 4w extras 4 interiors 6 exteriors
In Griffin, A. V. Living theatre

Romeo and Juliet (radio adaptation) See Olfson, L. Romeo and Juliet

The taming of the shrew (radio adaptation) See Olfson, L. The taming of the shrew

The tempest
Comedy. The party of the usurping Duke of Milan is shipwrecked on island where they find the real Duke of Milan, his daughter, the spirits of the air, and the brutish Caliban. 5 acts 9 scenes 14m 4w extras 4 exteriors
In Stallman, R. W. and Watters, R. E. The creative reader

The tempest (radio adaptation) See Olfson, L. The tempest

Twelfth night; or, What you will
Romantic comedy. Mistaken identity theme revolving about twin brother and sister; subordinate plot is an elaborate hoax. 5 acts 18 scenes 10m 3w extras 3 interiors 4 exteriors
In Bierman, J.; Hart, J. and Johnson, S. eds. The dramatic experience
See also Bottomly, G. King Lear's wife; Bottomly, G. Gruach; Morris, T. B. A garden in Verona

About

Ashermann, O. Shakespeare

c Harding, M. The Sea King's daughter

Rubinstein, H. F. Bernard Shaw in heaven

Shaw, B. Shakes versus Shav

Sladen-Smith, F. Sweet Master William

c Totheroh, D. Master Will

Adaptations

Porter, C. Kiss me Kate

Characters—Falstaff

Boyd, A. K. Robbery at Gadshill

Parodies, Travesties, etc.

Addis, H. Sellevision

Shakespeare. Ashermann, O.

The **Shakespearean** touch. Miller, H. L.

Shall we dance? Parker, K. T.

Sharp, Anthony

Nightmare Abbey; a frolic by Thomas Love Peacock; dramatized by Anthony Sharp
Farce satirizing the views of men of letters, and progressive thinkers in 19th century England with thinly veiled caricatures of Shelley, Byron and Coleridge. Includes songs. 2 acts 6 scenes 9m 2w 2 interiors
In Plays of the year v7

Shaughnessy, Alfred

Release. Deane 1954 59p illus ("Deane's" Ser. of plays)
Young woman, sentenced to prison for murdering her husband, is released after five years, falls in love but possessive mother almost destroys chance to build a new life. 3 acts 5 scenes 5m 4w 1 interior

Shaw, Bernard

The admirable Bashville; or, Constancy unrewarded
Farcical romantic comedy. Young British prizefighter who falls in love with titled lady turns out to be son of a nobleman. Verse play. 3 acts 4 scenes 7m 2w extras 3 interiors 1 exterior
In Shaw, B. Ten short plays

Androcles and the lion
Comedy of saintliness. Based on Greek tailor's conversion to Christianity. his befriending a lion, and gladiatorial experience. 2 acts preface and prologue 3 scenes 9m 2w extras 3 exteriors
In Kronenberger, L. ed. Cavalcade of comedy
In Shaw, B. Saint Joan, Major Barbara [and] Androcles and the lion

Annajanska, the Bolshevik Empress
Farce. After a revolution daughter of former ruling family plots to regain control of her country by joining the revolutionists. 2m 1w 1 interior
In Shaw, B. Ten short plays

Shaw, Bernard—*Continued*

The apple cart. Longmans 1956 159p
A satirical comedy. To secure power, king threatens to resign his throne and go to the democratic poll. 2 acts 10m 5w 2 interiors 1 exterior

—Same

In Shaw, B. Selected plays v4

Arms and the man. [Acting ed] French 1958 83p
Satirical comedy. Romantic episode during the Serbo-Bulgarian War. 3 acts 4m 3w 2 interiors 1 exterior

—Same

In Cubeta, P. M. ed. Modern drama for analysis. 1955 edition

In Shaw, B. Plays

In Shaw, B. Selected plays and other writings

Augustus does his bit
Farce satirizing the wartime activities of a pompous, muddleheaded armchair colonel. 2m 1w 1 interior

In Shaw, B. Ten short plays

Caesar and Cleopatra; adapted by Elizabeth Jamieson. Dramatic 1957 105p illus
Comedy. The aged Roman conqueror meets the youthful Egyptian queen. 5 acts 7 scenes 17m 3w extras 2 interiors 4 exteriors

—Same

In Bierman, J.; Hart, J. and Johnson, S. eds. The dramatic experience

In Shaw, B. Four plays

Candida. Longmans 1956 122p
Domestic comedy. A clergyman is appalled to find his wife idealized by an 18-year-old poet. 3 acts 4m 2w 1 interior

—Same

In Cooper, C. W. Preface to drama

In Heffner, H. The nature of drama

In Shaw, B. Four plays

In Shaw, G. Plays

In Shaw, B. Selected plays and other writings

In A Treasury of the theatre

The Devil's disciple. Penguin 1955 89p
Pacifist New Hampshire minister turns soldier during Burgoyne's campaign against the American rebels in 1777. 3 acts 9m 3w extras 3 interiors

The doctor's dilemma
Conflict between professional ethics and personal desire, in satire on medical profession continuing Shaw's attack on inoculation and vivisection. 5 acts 8m 2w extras 3 interiors 1 exterior

In Warnock, R. Representative modern plays, British

Getting married
Shavian discussions on the inadequacies of marriage as an institution, with characters satirizing special attitudes. 7m 5w 1 interior

In Shaw, B. Selected plays v4

Great Catherine
A brief farce about an English officer meeting Queen Catharine in her highly uninhibited Court. 1 act 4 scenes 4m 4w 1 interior

In Shaw, B. Selected plays v4

Heartbreak house
Old sea captain takes a dim view of early 20th century English society, demonstrated in lives of his daughters and their guests. 3 acts 6m 4w 1 interior

In Shaw, B. Four plays

The Inca of Perusalem
Comedy. English archdeacon's daughter, posing as princess selected to marry a son of a world conqueror, succeeds in revealing the man behind the conqueror's mask. 4m 2w 1 interior

In Shaw, B. Ten short plays

Major Barbara
Salvation Army daughter changes her mind about capitalism's role in breeding poverty and converts to the views of munitions maker father. Tragic-comic irony. 3 acts and preface 8m 6w extras 1 interior 2 exteriors

In Shaw, B. Saint Joan, Major Barbara [and] Androcles and the lion

Man and superman. Longmans 1956 248p
Romantic comedy. Modernized version of the Don Juan legend portraying man as the quarry, woman as the hunter. Incidental music. 4 acts 21m 6w extras 1 interior 3 exteriors

—Same

In Shaw, G. Plays

In Shaw, B. Selected plays and other writings

In Watson, E. B. ed. Contemporary drama: fifteen plays

The millionairess
Comedy which satirizes wealth, in particular, the insidious ways of attaining it. 3 acts 6m 3w 2 interiors

In Shaw, B. Selected plays v4

Misalliance
A social comedy about class distinctions. English middle class family's mores as compared to upper classes, in parent-child relationship. 1 act 6m 3w 1 interior

In Shaw, B. Selected plays v4

Mrs Warren's profession
Young woman decides about her own life after learning about her mother's. 4 acts 4m 2w 2 interiors 2 exteriors

In Shaw, B. Plays

The music-cure
Romantic comedy. Weak-minded young socialite, upset by his injudicious purchase of stocks, falls in love with strong-minded concert pianist. Includes piano music. 2m 1w 1 interior

In Shaw, B. Ten short plays

O'Flaherty V. C.
Comedy. Experiences of Irish war hero of World War I on his leave reveal why he prefers fighting abroad to home life in Ireland. Irish dialect. 2m 2w 1 interior

In Shaw, B. Ten short plays

Pygmalion
Comedy of manners set in early 20th century London. Based on the Pygmalion legend. A British professor of phonetics transforms a Covent Garden flower girl into the semblance of a duchess. 5 acts 4m 6w extras 2 interiors 1 exterior

In Dean, L. F. ed. Nine great plays. 1956 edition

In Four modern plays

In Kronenberger, L. ed. Cavalcade of comedy

In Shaw, B. Four plays

In Watson, E. B. and Pressey, B. eds. Contemporary drama: eleven plays

Pygmalion (adaptation) See Loewe, F. My fair lady

Shaw, Bernard—*Continued*

Saint Joan
Inquisitorial court trial of Joan of Arc, her burning at the stake, and canonization in the 1920 epilogue of Shaw. 6 scenes preface and epilogue 24m 2w extras 6 interiors 1 exterior

In Shaw, B. Saint Joan, Major Barbara ₁and₁ Androcles and the lion

Shakes versus Shav
Puppet play. Shakespeare and Shaw contest each other's claim to fame as playwrights. 6 characters

In Shaw, B. Ten short plays

The shewing-up of Blanco Posnet
Man being tried as horse thief in a western frontier town decides to follow different philosophy of life. Western dialect. 7m 7w extras 1 interior

In Shaw, B. Ten short plays

The six of Calais
Comedy. Queen Philippa intercedes with her husband, King Edward III of England, to save lives of some burgesses condemned to die as part of terms of surrender of Calais to British in 1347. 8m 1w 1b extras 1 exterior

In Shaw, B. Ten short plays

Too true to be good
Shaw's opinions on religion and politics aired in farce about three reckless people who come into unlimited riches, but acquire many cares along with pleasure. 2 acts 6m 3w 1 interior 1 exterior

In Shaw, B. Selected plays v4

Why she would not
Comedy. Lady refuses to marry charming, intelligent man who proves to be very domineering. 5 scenes 5m 2w 2 interiors 2 exteriors

In Shaw, B. Ten short plays

Widowers' houses
Romance of young doctor and a widower's daughter is interrupted by widower's business (landlord) but also resolved by same. 3 acts 4m 1w 2 interiors 1 exterior

In Shaw, B. Selected plays v4

For plays about this author see Shaw, George Bernard

Shaw, David

Native dancer
Television play about girl who is torn between marriage versus career as dancer. 2m 3w

In Settel, I. ed. Top TV shows of the year, 1954-1955

Rescue
Television play. Attempted rescue of Floyd Collins from Sand Cave in Kentucky. 21m 1w

In The Best television plays v3

Shaw, George Bernard

Rubinstein, H. F. Bernard Shaw in heaven

Shaw, B. Shakes versus Shav

For plays by this author see Shaw, Bernard

She loves him yes. Gross, E. and Gross, N.

She-sickness. Carmichael, F.

She stoops to conquer. Goldsmith, O.

She walks in beauty. Kolb, K.

She who was shorn. Menander

She writes a roof. Houston, N.

Sheffield, John

The forgotten land
Son of drunkard runs away with girl to start life anew. 2 scenes 2m 1w 1 exterior

In The Best short plays of 1953-1954

The imploring flame
Juvenile delinquency in the Bronx personified by₁ girl from the age of 11 until she is 23. Background music and city noises. 4 scenes 6m 3w 4b 3g extras 1 exterior

In The Best short plays, 1952-1953

Shelby, Kermit, and Cuny, Therese Marie

Giving goes on. French 1958 20p
A mountain woman refuses to face fact that her son and daughter have lives of their own. 1 act 4w 1 interior

Sheldon, Edward

The boss
Contrast between rough politician and wife who wants to reform him. 4 acts 4 scenes 13m 4w 3 interiors

In Quinn, A. H. ed. Representative American plays

Shelley, Mary Wollstonecroft (Godwin)

Bate, S. Shelley and Mary

Shelley, Percy Bysshe

Bate, S. Shelley and Mary

Shelley and Mary. Bate, S.

Shenandoah. Howard, B.

The **shepherd** and the conqueror. Olson, E.

The **shepherd**-boy and the wolf. Moore, S. S.

The **shepherd** of Bethlehem. Knox, J.

The **shepherd** who stayed away. McGreevey, J.

The **shepherds** and the wise men. Phillips, A. L.

The **shepherd's** play. Malcolmson, A.

Sheridan, Evelyn

One bit of glory. Eldridge 1958 24p (Eldridge Popular one-act playscripts)
Old lady refuses to give her secret cake recipe to Civic Club. 1 act 6w 1 interior

Sheridan, Richard Brinsley

The critic
Satire on 18th century dramatists of London stage via device of a rehearsal within a play. 3 acts 5 scenes 20m 8w extras 2 interiors

In Sheridan, R. B. Six plays

The Duenna
Romantic comedy. Daughter's scheme results in marriage with her lover, not her father's choice, while father mistakenly marries daughter's Duenna. 3 acts 16 scenes 9m 3w extras 6 interiors 6 exteriors

In Sheridan, R. B. Six plays

The rivals; ed. by Vincent F. Hopper and Gerald B. Lahey. Barrons Educ. Ser. 1958 176p illus (Theatre classics for the modern reader)
Humorous plot built on assumed names and disguised identities in this 18th century English comedy of manners about an army officer whose sweetheart must get her aunt's consent to marry. 5 acts 17 scenes 9m 5w extras 4 interiors 4 exteriors

—Same; ed. by Alan S. Downer. Appleton 1953 99p

—Same

In Keyes, R. K. and Roth, H. M. eds. Comparative comedies, present and past

In Sheridan, R. B. Six plays

The rivals (adaptation) See Boyd, A. K. Fighting Bob

Sheridan, Richard B.—*Continued*

St Patrick's Day
Farce. Persevering Irish lieutenant succeeds in winning an English justice's daughter. 2 acts 6 scenes 5m 2w extras 2 interiors 3 exteriors
In Sheridan, R. B. Six plays

The school for scandal. Barrons Educ. Ser. 1958 172p illus
Comedy of manners. 18th century London society creates and spreads malicious gossip, but true love achieves reconciliation and marriage. 5 acts 14 scenes 12m 4w extras 8 interiors
—Same
In Kronenberger, L. ed. Cavalcade of comedy
In Sheridan, R. B. Six plays

A trip to Scarborough
Romantic comedy. Fortune hunting brother successfully plots marriage to bride intended for older brother. 5 acts 12 scenes 12m 5w extras 6 interiors 2 exteriors
In Sheridan, R. B. Six plays

Sherie, Fenn. See D'Abbes, I. jt. auth.

The **sheriff.** Arnold, J. W.

Sherman, Ralph W.

Santa's neurosis. Eldridge 1958 13p (Eldridge Christmas entertainments)
Santa consults psychiatrist because he is depressed that people are so selfish. 14 scenes 7m 6w extras choir 3 interiors

Sherriff, R. C.

Journey's end
At the battle of San Quentin in World War I British lieutenant tries to conceal his fear of combat from courageous youth who admires him. 3 acts 6 scenes 10m 1 interior
In A Treasury of the theatre

The long sunset
Events in fifth century Britain following the end of the Roman occupation. 3 acts 6 scenes 7m 2w 1b 1 interior
In Plays of the year v12

The telescope. [French's Acting ed] French (London) 1957 74p illus
Problems of young thief and the clergyman who tries to help him. Set in a modern British dockside town. 3 acts 7 scenes 5m 4w 1 interior
—Same
In Plays of the year v15

The white carnation. [Acting ed] French (London) 1953 90p illus
Fantasy. A man bids his guests goodbye outside his door at Christmastime. When he turns to go in, the house is suddenly dark and in ruins. Set in England. 2 acts 7 scenes 10m 6w 1 interior 1 exterior

Sherry, Gordon

Black limelight. [French's Acting ed] French (London) 1957 80p illus
Murder drama of suspense. Wife of a man suspected of murdering a girl in an unlighted bungalow discovers who the real criminal is. 3 acts 11m 5w 1 interior

Sherwood, Robert E. and Harrison, Joan
Rebecca
Moving picture play based on novel by Daphne Du Maurier. The shy, young second wife of a wealthy Englishman learns the truth about the mysterious death of his first wife. 5 parts 12m 4w
In Gassner, J. and Nichols, D. eds. Great film plays

Sherwood, Robert Emmet

Abe Lincoln in Illinois
Biographical account of Lincoln's career from early manhood to his election to the presidency. 3 acts 12 scenes 23m 7w 2b extras 7 interiors 3 exteriors
In Bierman, J.; Hart, J. and Johnson, S. eds. The dramatic experience

The petrified forest
Melodrama, bandits and shooting. Set in a diner in the Arizona desert country. 2 acts 18m 3w 1 interior
In Downer, A. S. ed. American drama

Small war on Murray Hill. Dramatists 1957 72p
Romantic comedy. Based on the incident in the American Revolution when Mrs Robert Murray beguiles British General Sir William Howe into lingering in her home rather than pushing on to battle. 2 acts 5 scenes 16m 8w extras 2 interiors 1 exterior

Small war on Murray Hill (condensation)
In Broadway's best, 1957

The **shewing**-up of Blanco Posnet. Shaw, B.

The **ship** of dreams. Hughes, J.

Shipmates. Fisher, A. and Rabe, O.

Shipwrecks
Hill, G. R. and Whedon, J. A night to remember
Olfson, L. The tempest
Shakespeare, W. The tempest

Shirley, Rae
Time the sad jester. Deane 1954 24p ("Deane's" Ser. of plays)
Domestic comedy. Welsh couple are visited by wife's former suitor, a poet who has become an American businessman. 1 act 4m 5w 1 interior

Shirt-tail boy. Covington, W. P.

Shoe children. Salisbury, E.

The **shoemaker** and the elves. Very, A.

Shoemakers
Dekker, T. Shoemaker's holiday
Thompson, D. The shoemaker's wife

The **shoemaker's** Christmas. Boegehold, B.

The **shoemakers'** holiday. Dekker, T.

The **shoemaker's** wife. Thompson, D.

Shoes. See Boots and shoes

Shoes for a queen. Chadwick, E.

Shojo
Short Japanese Nō verse drama in praise of the wine-spirit. 2m extras 1 exterior
In Pound, E. and Fenollosa, E. The classic Noh theatre of Japan

Sholom Aleichem. See Aleichem, Sholom

Shoot if you will. Martens, A. C.

Shore, Joseph, and Lincoln, Richard
The soldier who became a Great Dane
Farce. Soldier forced to substitute for dog in Army k-9 kennels. 8m 1 setting
In The Best short plays, 1957

Shore, Maxine
Catastrophe Clarence
Science fiction comedy. Astronomer receives visit from spaceman. 1 act 6m 1 interior
In Burack, A. S. ed. Four-star plays for boys

Shore Acres. Herne, J. A.

Short, Robin
c The red shoes. French 1954 74p illus
  Based on fairy tale by Hans Christian
  Andersen about wicked gypsy who makes
  poor orphan girl put on the magic shoes
  which dance away with her. Incidental
  music. 2 acts 3m 3w extras 2 exteriors

Shoshonean Indians
  Kissen, F. Sacajawea: guide in the wilderness

Shoub, Mac
  Ashes in the wind
    Television play. Euthanasia contemplated for an aged incurable. 3 acts 4m 5w
  In The Best television plays v3

  Thank you, Edmondo
    Television play. After World War II,
    some Italian peasants debate the priority
    of tilling a field in which they have
    discovered grave of an American soldier.
    9m
  In Best television plays, 1957

The **show**-off. Kelly, G.

The **shower** of hearts. Miller, H. L.

Shrout, Beatrice Lentz
c America sings
    Joint program for grades one through
    six. A variety of songs frequently sung
    in the United States including patriotic,
    religious and festive, accompanied by
    pantomimes. 16 scenes Large mixed cast
    1 setting
  In Birdsall, R. ed. Creative plays for
    every school month

Shulman, Max, and Smith, Robert Paul
  The tender trap. Dramatists 1956 80p
  illus
    Romantic comedy. Professional bachelor
    is finally captured in marriage by naiveté
    of determined young woman. 3 acts 4
    scenes 4m 4w 1 interior
    Trade edition published by Random
    House
  The tender trap (condensation)
  In Theatre, 1955

Shunkwan (condensation) Kwanze, M.

Shy Charlie. Hark, M. and McQueen, N.

Shyness. See Bashfulness

Shyre, Paul
  I knock at the door (dramatization) See
    O'Casey, S. I knock at the door
  Pictures in the hallway (dramatization)
    See O'Casey, S. Pictures in the hallway

Siam
      Social life and customs
  Rodgers, R. and Hammerstein, O. The
    King and I

Sicilians in the United States
  Williams, T. The rose tattoo

Sicily
  Agg, H. The happy day
      Social life and customs
  Agg, H. Silk and sawdust
  Verga, G. Cavalleria rusticana

Sick. See Sanatoriums

The **sick** fox. Carpenter, F.

Siddons, Sarah (Kemble)
  Robinson, R. Clarence Gate

Sieveking, Lance
  The strange case of Dr Jekyll and Mr
  Hyde
    Based on story by Robert Louis Stevenson about strange old doctor who had
    a dual personality. 3 acts 10 scenes 10m
    7w 3 interiors 1 exterior
  In Plays of the year v15

A **sight** for sore thoughts. Stein, H.

Sight to see. Asbrand, K.

Sigmund, Jay G. and Smith, Betty
  The silvered rope
    The suicide of Judas Iscariot; based on
    the Biblical narrative. 1 act 3m 2w 1 interior
  In Brings, L. M. comp. The golden
    book of church plays

The **sign** of Jonah. Rutenborn, G.

Signs and signboards
  Scholl, R. The golden axe

Siks, Geraldine Brain
  The Nuremberg stove. Childrens Theatre
  1956 56p illus
    Based on story by Louisa De la Ramée.
    A young Tyrolean boy takes an adventurous journey to Munich, hidden inside his family's Hirschvogel stove. Includes a ballet. 3 acts 4 scenes 8m 1w
    1b 2g extras 3 interiors

Silas Marner. Olfson, L.

Silent night (Carol)
  Marston, J. And a song was born

Silent night, lonely night. Anderson, R.

Silk and sawdust. Agg, H.

Silly, a leaf. Spamer, C.

Silver beads. Marcelline, Sister M.

The **silver** cord. Howard, S.

The **silver** idol. Waugh, J. R.

The **silver** star of Christmas. York, E. B.

The **silver** Tassie. O'Casey, S.

Silver threads among the gold. Emurian,
  E. K.

Silver wedding. Hutton, M. C.

The **silvered** rope. Sigmund, J. G. and
  Smith, B.

Simeon, the faithful servant. Day, P. F.

Simmons, Arthur
  The bruising of Satan. Epworth 1955 35p
    Easter. Mary Magdalene, David and
    Miriam, followers of Jesus, have their
    hope and courage restored by his Resurrection. 3 acts 5 scenes 4m 2w 2 interiors
    3 exteriors

Simmons, Constance
c The land of lost toys. Paxton 1958 11p
  music
    Operetta. British. Father and Mother
    Christmas, elves, fairies. 3 scenes Large
    mixed cast 1 interior 1 exterior

Simon, Neil. See Warnick, C. Heidi; Warnick, C. and Pahl, M. Adventures of
  Marco Polo

Simon and Laura. Melville, A.

A **simple** little affair. Herman, G.

Simple Simon. Brumbaugh, P.

Simple Simon. Harris, A.

Simply heavenly. Martin, D.

Simpson, Gwen Holly

A time for love. Longmans 1956 57p
> A former Navy chaplain and several nuns are in charge of a mission peopled by refugees on a South Pacific island Christmas Eve. 2 acts 3m 7w extras 1 interior

Simpson, Harold

Miss Matty in mischief. [French's Acting ed] French (London) 1954 30p illus
> Domestic comedy based on characters in the novel Cranford, by Elizabeth Cleghorn Gaskell. Much to the dismay of his sister, young man dresses in her clothes and visits his minister father pretending to be his admirer. Set in England in 1821. 1 act 2 scenes 3m 4w 1 interior

Miss Matty in society. [French's Acting ed] French (London) 1954 18p illus
> Based on characters in the novel: Cranford, by Elizabeth Cleghorn Gaskell. At a tea party, Captain Brown learns the difference between the heartless Deborah Jenkyns and her gentle sister, Matty. Set in rural England. 1836. 1 act 1m 7w 1 interior

The sin of Pat Muldoon. McLiam, J.

Sinclair, Lister

All the world's a stage
> Radio play. People from extremely different environments describe the status symbols of their societies. 16m 3w

In Goldschmidt, W. ed. Ways of mankind

But I know what I like
> Radio play. People of widely differing cultures explain the art forms of their societies. 13m

In Goldschmidt, W. ed. Ways of mankind

The case of the sea-lion flippers
> Radio play. In a dispute about pair of sea-lion flippers, elaborate code of ethics of Yurok Indians comes into play. 7m 2w

In Goldschmidt, W. ed. Ways of mankind

Legend of the long house
> Radio play. How the powerful League of the Iroquois was founded by two Indian leaders. 6m 1w

In Goldschmidt, W. ed. Ways of mankind

When Greek meets Greek
> Radio play. Contrasts different cultural values and family life in Sparta and Athens. 6m 3w 2b

In Goldschmidt, W. ed. Ways of mankind

A word in your ear
> Radio play showing relationship between language and culture by means of examples taken from languages all over the world. 11m 3w

In Goldschmidt, W. ed. Ways of mankind
See also Goldschmidt, W. jt. auth.

Sing a song of something. Martens, A. C.

Sing, America, sing. Fisher, A. and Rabe, O.

Sing me no lullaby. Ardrey, R.

Singers

Hackett, W. The way the ball bounces
Preston, E. E. The voice that failed
Rodgers, R. The sound of music
Trapp, M. A. One family sings
Wedekind, F. The tenor

The singing children. Bailey, H. F.

Singing threshold. Brabazon, F.

A single taper. Scriven, R. C.

Sinn Fein Rebellion, 1916. See Ireland— History—Sinn Fein Rebellion, 1916

Sir Galahad and the maidens. Howard, V.

Sir Thomas Wyatt. Dekker, T. and Webster, J.

Sisson, Rosemary Anne

The queen and the Welshman
> Love affair between Queen Katherine, widow of Henry V of England and Sir Owen Tudor. Set in 15th century England. 3 acts 9 scenes 9m 2w 4 interiors 2 exteriors

In Plays of the year v18

The splendid outcasts
> Events in life of Lucretia di Borgia and domineering brother Cesar di Borgia. Set in 15th century Italy. 3 acts 5 scenes 9m 3w 3 interiors

In Plays of the year v19

Sisters

Bate, S. Anniversary Day
Carter, C. A chocolate
Cusack, D. The golden girls
Garver, J. Honest to goodness
Jerome, H. Pride and prejudice
Lumsden, M. The gift
Martens, A. C. Pow wow
Raynor, M. All of a sudden
Simpson, H. Miss Matty in society
Speare, E. G. The anchor
Walden, W. Tomboy wonder

See also Brothers and sisters

Sisters and brothers. See Brothers and sisters

The sisters' tragedy. Hughes, R.

Situations vacant. Grant, N.

Siwan, Princess of Wales. See Joan, Princess of Wales

Siwan. Lewis, S.

Six characters in search of an author. Pirandello, L.

Six ladies in waiting. Spencer, G.

The six of Calais. Shaw, B.

The skeleton at the party. Pilgrim, F.

Skills to share. Fisher, A. and Rabe, O.

The skin of our teeth. Wilder, T.

Skinner, Cornelia Otis. See Taylor, S. The pleasure of his company

The sky's the limit. Greth, Le R. E.

Sladen-Smith, Frank

Sweet Master William. [French's Acting ed] French (London) 1953 30p illus
> Young William Shakespeare becomes a schoolteacher in Cotswold, but is attracted to a band of strolling players. 1 act 5m 2w 1 interior

Slander. See Gossip

Slattery, Margaret

c The circus stars' mistake
> Circus performers discover how much they need help of a schoolboy, employed for the summer. 2m 3w 1b 1 interior

In Birdsall, R. ed. Creative plays for every school month

The slaughter of the innocents. Saroyan, W.

The slave of truth. Molière, J. B. P.

Slave-trade

Dace, W. We commit this body

Slavery in the United States

Boucicault, D. The octoroon

Snow White and the seven dwarfs. Sprenger, C. H. and Attley, M.

The **snowdrop.** Spamer, C.

Snyder, William Hartwell
Another summer
Petey meets death when his companion, his grandfather, dies. 1 act 2m 5w 1b 1g 1 setting
In The Best short plays of 1953-1954
The departing
Boy's qualms on leaving home for boarding school. 1 act 3 scenes 3m 2w 1 interior
In The Best short plays of 1957-1958

Snyder, Willis
The old school bell. Bakers Plays 1955 35p illus
Comedy. When bell disappears from teacher's desk, a class of young teen-agers gets involved in series of comic episodes before mystery is solved. 1 act 2 scenes 7m 6w 1 interior

So it's Christmas again. Asbrand, K.

Soans, Jacqueline
Christmas is now. Bakers Plays 1956 15p
Little beggar girl is taken on journey by an angel to learn meaning of Christmas. 1 act 8m 5w 1g extras 1 interior

Soapera. Abstance, P. and Abstance, L.

Social adjustment
Rose, R. Dino

Social change
Burgess, C. V. The virtues of Thelma

Social distinctions. See Class distinction

Social problems
Anderson, M. Winterset
Carroll, P. V. The wise have not spoken
Carruthers, J. Fear not
Chekhov, A. The sea gull
Dimondstein, B. In the chains of life
Dimondstein, B. The life of an artist
Ibsen, H. An enemy of the people
Ibsen, H. Hedda Gabler
Ibsen, H. The wild duck
Ionesco, E. Rhinoceros
Kissen, F. Jane Addams: the good neighbor
Lantz, J. E. and Lantz, R. C. Alone
Strindberg, A. There are crimes and crimes
Swann, D. L. The crier calls
Tolstoy, L. The power of darkness
Viereck, P. The tree witch
Wilson, E. The little blue light
See also Church and social problems; Crime and criminals; Divorce; Juvenile delinquency; Migrant labor; Race discrimination; Race problems; Woman—Social and moral questions

Social reform. See Social problems

Social secretaries. See Secretaries, Social

Social settlements
Marr Johnson, D. Never say die
Rose, R. Dino

Social workers
Rose, R. Crime in the streets
Rose, R. Dino

Societies
Salverson, G. You are not alone

Society
Sinclair, L. All the world's a stage

Socrates
Aristophanes. The clouds

Softy the Snow Man. Miller, H. L.

Sognefest, Alvera
c Big top circus
Sketches show various people who perform or act or work in a circus. Includes singing and dancing. Large mixed cast 1 interior
In Birdsall, R. ed. Creative plays for every school month

Sokar and the crocodile. Barnes, E. A. and Young, B. M.

The **soldier** and the Prince of Peace. Sollitt, K. W. and Faust, J. P.

The **soldier** who became a Great Dane. Shore, J. and Lincoln, R.

Soldiers
Bucci, M. The old lady shows her medals
Büchner, G. Woyzeck
Burgess, C. V. The Army takes over
Foss, J. Courage, '53
Hayes, A. The girl on the Via Flaminia
Howard, V. The message
Kissen, F. Abraham Lincoln: with malice toward none
Rattigan, T. Adventure story
Shore, J. and Lincoln, R. The soldier who became a Great Dane
Violett, E. and Blake, L. Brewsie and Willie
See also United States. Army—Military life

Soldiers' bodies, Disposition of
c Jeffrey, H. K. and Walls, D. A. Veterans Day
Shoub, M. Thank you, Edmondo

Soldiers' graves. See Soldiers' bodies, Disposition of

Soldiers' life. See Soldiers

The **solid** gold Cadillac. Teichmann, H. and Kaufman, G. S.

Sollitt, Kenneth W. and Faust, J. Paul
The soldier and the Prince of Peace. Lorenz 1956 18p
Two Roman soldiers, one cruel the other seeking a new way of life, are stationed in Bethlehem at time of birth of Christ. 1 act 11m 2w extras 1 exterior

Solomon, King of Israel
Estes, S. In quest of power through wisdom
c Spamer, C. Solomon's Temple

Solomon's Temple. Spamer, C.

Somebody special. Heger, K.

Somebody's valentine. Newman, D.

Someone waiting. Williams, E.

Something borrowed, something blue. Wilton, A.

Something new for Halloween. Newman, D.

Something new in murder. Lathrop, D.

Something unspoken. Williams, T.

A **sometime** thing. Lineberger, J.

Sommer, Edith
A roomful of roses. ₍Rev ed₎ Dramatists 1956 80p front
Girl whose parents are divorced, suffers from loneliness and bitterness until she becomes part of a real family. 2 acts 4 scenes 3m 5w 1b 1 interior

Son-of-a-biscuit-eater. Conkle, E. P.

Son of Erin. McMullen, J. C.

Son of Stephen. Cruse, C.

Son of the revolution. Oringer, B. I.

Sondheim, Stephen. See Styne, J. Gypsy

The song and the star. Powicke, H. B.

Song for a hero. Schaefer, L.

Songs
　Crozier, E. Rab the Rhymer
　Emurian, E. K. America the beautiful
　Emurian, E. K. Battle hymn of the republic
　Emurian, E. K. The church in the wildwood
　Emurian, E. K. Columbia, the gem of the ocean
　Emurian, E. K. Dixie
　Emurian, E. K. Home sweet home
　Emurian, E. K. Silver threads among the gold
　Emurian, E. K. The Star Spangled Banner
　Emurian, E. K. Yankee Doodle
　Fisher, A. and Rabe, O. Long may it wave
　Fisher, A. and Rabe, O. Sing, America, sing
　Fisher, A. and Rabe, O. Yankee Doodle Dandy
　Howard, V. When it's moonlight on Pike's Peak
c Shrout, B. L. America sings

Songs, Popular. See Music, Popular (Songs, etc.)

Sophists (Greek philosophy)
　Aristophanes. The clouds

Sophocles
　Ajax; tr. and with an introduction by John Moore
　　Greek classical tragedy. Verse play. Ajax, unable to reconcile himself to fact that Odysseus had been chosen leader of Greek forces in Trojan War, commits suicide. 6m 2w extras 1 exterior
　In Grene, D. and Lattimore, R. eds. The complete Greek tragedies v2
　—Same; tr. by E. F. Watling
　In Sophocles. Electra, and other plays
　Antigone
　　Greek tragedy. Disaster follows refusal of Creon, King of Thebes, to permit burial of his enemy, Antigone's brother. Verse play. 1 act 5 scenes 5m 3w extras 1 exterior
　In Eleven plays of the Greek dramatists
　—Same; newly tr. by Theodore Howard Banks
　In Sophocles. Three Theban plays
　—Same; an English version by Dudley Fitts and Robert Fitzgerald
　In Cooper, C. W. Preface to drama
　In Stallman, R. W. and Watters, R. E. The creative reader
　—Same; tr. by F. L. Lucas
　In Lucas, F. L. ed. Greek drama for everyman
　—Same; tr. by Shaemas O'Sheel
　In Lind, L. R. ed. Ten Greek plays in contemporary translations

—Same; tr. by Elizabeth Wyckoff
　In Grene, D. and Lattimore, R. eds. The complete Greek tragedies v2
　In Grene, D. and Lattimore, R. eds. Greek tragedies v 1

Antigone (dramatization). See Anouilh, J. Antigone

Electra
　Greek classical tragedy. Based on the legend telling how Orestes and Electra, children of Agamemnon, avenged their father's murder. Verse play. 4m 3w extras 1 exterior
　In Eleven plays of the Greek dramatists
　—Same; by David Grene
　In Grene, D. and Lattimore, R. eds. The complete Greek tragedies v2
　In Grene, D. and Lattimore, R. eds. Greek tragedies v2
　—Same; tr. by E. F. Watling
　In Sophocles. Electra, and other plays

King Oedipus (adaptation). See Yeats, W. B. Sophocles' King Oedipus

Oedipus at Colonus; newly tr. by Theodore Howard Banks
　Tragedy, Greek classical. A conclusion to the Oedipus saga. Oedipus is pursued by Creon, but miraculously passes from this world to become the guardian spirit of Athens. Verse play. 1 act 8 scenes 6m 2w extras 1 exterior
　In Sophocles. Three Theban plays
　—Same; tr. by Robert Fitzgerald
　In Grene, D. and Lattimore, R. eds. The complete Greek tragedies v2
　In Grene, D. and Lattimore, R. eds. Greek tragedies v3
　—Same; tr. by E. H. Plumptre
　In Robinson, C. A. ed. Anthology of Greek drama. 2nd ser

Oedipus at Colonus (adaptation). See Yeats, W. B. Sophocles' Oedipus at Colonus

Oedipus Rex; tr. by Albert Cook
　Tragedy, Greek classical drama. Oedipus, King of Thebes, is powerless to throw off curse of an early crime. 4 scenes 7m 1w extras 1 exterior
　Same as: Oedipus the King
　In Lind, L. R. Ten Greek plays in contemporary translations
　—Same; an English version by Dudley Fitts and Robert Fitzgerald
　In Bierman, J.; Hart, J. and Johnson, S. eds. The dramatic experience
　In Dean, L. F. ed. Nine great plays. 1956 edition
　In Downer, A. S. The art of the play
　In Fitts, D. ed. Four Greek plays
　In Levin, R. Tragedy: plays, theory, and criticism

Oedipus the king. The Greek text tr. into English verse by Francis Storr; with an introduction by Thornton Wilder. Illus. with wood engravings by Demetrios Galanis. Heritage [1956] 159p illus
　Contains Greek and English texts on facing pages
　Same as: Oedipus Rex
　Trade edition published by Grosset

Sophocles—*Continued*

In Eleven plays of the Greek dramatists
—Same; newly tr. by Theodore Howard Banks

In Sophocles. Three Theban plays
—Same; tr. by David Grene

In Grene, D. and Lattimore, R. eds. The complete Greek tragedies v2

In Grene, D. and Lattimore, R. eds. Greek tragedies v 1
—Same; tr. by F. L. Lucas

In Lucas, F. L. ed. Greek drama for everyman

Philoctetes; tr. by Alston Hurd Chase
Greek classical drama in verse. The Greeks send Neoptolemus and Odysseus to bring the banished Philoctetes to their aid in the siege of Troy. 5m extras 1 exterior

In Fitts, D. ed. Six Greek plays in modern translation
—Same; tr. by Kathleen Freeman

In Lind, L. R. ed. The Greek plays in contemporary translations
—Same; tr. and with an introduction by David Grene

In Grene, D. and Lattimore, R. eds. The complete Greek tragedies v2

In Grene, D. and Lattimore, R. eds. Greek tragedies v3
—Same; tr. by E. F. Watling

In Sophocles. Electra, and other plays
—Same; tr. by John Rowe Workman

In Robinson, C. A. An anthology of Greek drama. 2nd ser.

The women of Trachis; tr. and with an introduction by Michael Jameson
Greek classical tragedy. Philandering Heracles returns from journey with captive women, one of whom he loves; jealous wife in attempt to win him back, mistakenly gives him robe smeared with magic ointment which causes his death. Verse play. 5m 2w extras 1 exterior

In Grene, D. and Lattimore, R. eds. The complete Greek tragedies v2
—Same; tr. by E. F. Watling

In Sophocles. Electra, and other plays

Sophocles' King Oedipus. Yeats, W. B.

Sophocles' Oedipus at Colonus. Yeats, W. B.

Sophonisba. Lee, N.

The **sorcerer's** apprentices. Olson, E.

Sorcery. See Magic

Sorell, Walter
Everyman today. Dramatists 1958 73p illus
An adaptation of the 15th century morality play in contemporary terms. 3 scenes Large mixed cast 1 interior

Sorry, wrong number. Fletcher, L.

Sotoba Komachi. Kwanze, K.

Sotoba Komachi. Mishima, Y.

Soubirous, Bernadette, Saint
Duffield, B. Christmas at Lourdes
Mary Francis, Sister. Smallest of all

A **soul** in fine array. Casey, M.

The **sound** of apples. Young, S.

The **sound** of murder. Fairchild, W.

The **sound** of music. Rodgers, R.

The South. See Southern States

South. Green, J.

South America
c Miller, H. L. Who's who at the zoo

South Pacific. Rodgers, R. and Hammerstein, O.

South Sea Islands. See Oceania

Southern dialect. See Dialect—Southern States

Southern States
Abstance, P. and Abstance, L. Cotton Road
Ford, R. Requiem for a nun
Hellman, L. The little foxes
Hellman, L. Toys in the attic
McCaslin, N. John Henry
Williams, T. Baby Doll
Williams, T. Cat on a hot tin roof
Williams, T. Suddenly last summer
Williams, T. Sweet bird of youth

Moral conditions
Williams, T. 27 wagons full of cotton

Race questions
Sartre, J. P. Respectful prostitute

Social conditions
Williams, T. Battle of angels
Williams, T. Orpheus descending

Social life and customs
Green, J. South

The **southwest** corner. Holm, J. C.

The Sower (Parable)
c Spamer, C. The parable of the sower

The **spa.** Chodorov, E.

Space flight
Eaton, J. J. and Juste, M. Atomic journey

Spafford, Horatio G.
Emurian, E. K. It is well with my soul

Spain
Benavente, J. La Malquerida [The passion flower]

History—Roman period, 218 B.C.-414 A.D.
Corneille, P. Sertorius

History—Arab period, 711-1492
Corneille, P. Le Cid
Grillparzer, F. The Jewess of Toledo
c Kramer, C. The voyage

History—House of Austria, 1516-1700
Schiller, F. von. Don Carlos

Politics and government
Vega, L. de. Fuente ovejuna

Social life and customs
Calderón. Life is a dream
García-Lorca, F. The house of Bernarda Alba
Howard, V. Don Quixote saves the day
Olfson, L. Infanta
Robinson, C. R. The white dove
Seiler, C. The wonderful adventures of Don Quixote

Spamer, Claribel

Abigail Adams
Fourteen year old Abigail meets John Adams, her future husband. 3m 3w 1 exterior

In Spamer, C. Easy sketches of famous women

c The adventurous balloon
A little breeze helps Bobby rescue his balloon from some mischievous elves. 1b extras 1 exterior

In Easy juvenile grab bag

Ah-yo-ka
Sequoya, a Cherokee Indian develops a written language for the Cherokees and begins teaching it to his daughter. 2m 1g extras 1 exterior

In Spamer, C. Easy sketches of famous women

Amelia Earhart
Four year old Amelia Earhart captures a chicken. 1w 2g 1 exterior

In Spamer, C. Easy sketches of famous women

c Andy's gun
Boy who thinks Memorial Day is boring, falls asleep and is visited by soldiers from all the wars in which the United States fought. 5m 2b 1 exterior

In Spamer, C. Easy grade school plays

c The baby Moses
Bible. Old Testament. Exodus. The baby Moses is rescued by Pharaoh's daughter. 1 act 1m 3w extras 1 interior

In Spamer, C. Bible plays for juniors

c The baptism of Jesus
Bible. New Testament. Gospels. John the Baptist baptizes Jesus. 1 act 3m extras 1 exterior

In Spamer, C. Bible plays for juniors

c The Bell that couldn't ring
The Bell wants to be independent but he learns that he has to depend on Battery and Wire. Unidentified cast 7 characters 1 interior

In Spamer, C. Easy science plays for grade school

c The bells
Little girl lost in the woods, is guided home by sounds of sleigh bells. 2m 1w 1g extras 1 interior

In Spamer, C. Juvenile treasure chest

c The boy Jesus visits Jerusalem
Bible. New Testament. Luke. The boy Jesus remains behind in the temple in Jerusalem after the Passover and worries his parents who cannot find him. 1 act 2m 1w extras 1 interior

In Spamer, C. Bible plays for juniors

c The boy who had no gravity
A boy and girl find out how important gravity is. 1m 1w 1b 1g extras 1 exterior

In Spamer, C. Easy science plays for grade school

c The bunnies' dilemma
Rabbit family decides to make people happy by painting Easter eggs. Unidentified cast 7 characters extras 1 exterior

In Spamer, C. The junior entertainment book

c The camouflage shop
Animals go to Peter Rabbit's shop to be camouflaged so they can't be seen in the forest Unidentified cast 8 characters 1 interior

In Spamer, C. Easy science plays for grade school

c The candle
Little evergreen in the forest is lonely because he is not a Christmas tree. 2b 3g extras 1 exterior

In Spamer, C. Easy grade school plays

c Carry and borrow
When a little boy and girl have trouble with their arithmetic, all the numbers come to life. 7b 6g no scenery

In Spamer, C. Easy grade school plays

Charlotte Bronte
Father asks eight year old Charlotte Bronte, her brother and four sisters a serious question. 1m 1b 5g 1 interior

In Spamer, C. Easy sketches of famous women

c The cherry tree
Trees in the orchard listen as young George Washington admits cutting down cherry tree. 1m 2b 3g 1 exterior

In Spamer, C. Easy grade school plays

c The children who forgot
Rogo, an imp, causes some Mother Goose characters to forget their identities. 1 scene 3b 2g 1 exterior

In Easy juvenile grab bag

c The chocolate bunny
Chocolate bunny in candy shop is unhappy because no one wants him, until he finds out about Easter. 6b 6g 1 interior

In Spamer, C. Easy grade school plays

c The Christ Child in the temple
Bible. New Testament. Luke. Mary and Joseph present the child Jesus to Simeon in the temple in Jerusalem. 1 act 3m 2w 1 interior

In Spamer, C. Bible plays for juniors

c Christ lives again
Bible. New Testament. Gospels. The angel tells those who seek Him at the tomb that Jesus is risen. 1 act 2m 2w extras 1 exterior

In Spamer, C. Bible plays for juniors

c Cinderella's friends
Based on Perrault's fairy tale. Some of her friends try to help Cinderella find her shoe. Verse play. 2m 2w extras no setting

In Spamer, C. Juvenile treasure chest

Clara Barton
Clara Barton the child and her first day at school. 1m 2b 3g extras 1 interior

In Spamer, C. Easy sketches of famous women

c The clock
Based on the Mother Goose rhyme, Hickory, dickory dock. Three elves repair the clock so that the mouse can run up and down on it. Verse play. Unidentified cast 8 characters no setting

In Spamer, C. Juvenile treasure chest

c The clumsy fairy
Little girl teaches fairy how to be graceful. 5g 1 exterior

In Spamer, C. Easy grade school plays

c The cold twins
Little girl takes care not to spread her cold germs to other people. Verse play. 1g extras no setting

In Spamer, C. Juvenile treasure chest

c The constable's duty
Animals are mystified when their new friend the turtle draws his head into his shell. Unidentified cast 5 characters 1 exterior

In Spamer, C. The junior entertainment book

Spamer, Claribel—*Continued*

The costume dance
  In autumn Jack gives all the leaves bright costumes. Unidentified cast 8 characters extras 1 exterior
  In Spamer, C. Easy science plays for grade school

c Crossing the street
  Good elf teaches little boy to be careful crossing streets. Verse play. 1b extras no setting
  In Spamer, C. Juvenile treasure chest

c Daniel in the lions' den
  Bible. Old Testament. Daniel. The king of Persia throws Daniel into the lions' den because he prays to God, instead of the king. 1 act 10m 1 interior
  In Spamer, C. Bible plays for juniors

c David and Goliath
  Bible. Old Testament. Samuel. David kills Goliath with his sling shot. 1 act 4m extras 1 interior
  In Spamer, C. Bible plays for juniors

Dolly Madison
  Little Dolly, later the wife of James Madison, finds it hard to accept her Quaker family's austere life. 2m 2w 1b 1g 1 interior
  In Spamer, C. Easy sketches of famous women

c Donerblitz
  All the little deer who are too small to pull Santa Claus' sleigh find a way to help him. 1m 6b 7g 1 exterior
  In Spamer, C. Easy grade school plays

c Elijah, the prophet
  Bible. Old Testament. Kings. God chooses Elijah to be His prophet. 1 act 1m 1b 1w extras 1 exterior
  In Spamer, C. Bible plays for juniors

c Elisha cures Naaman
  Bible. Old Testament. Kings. Elisha cures Naaman, a Syrian, of leprosy. 1 act 4m 2w 1 exterior
  In Spamer, C. Bible plays for juniors

c The first Christmas tree
  Christmas fairy uses magic to make first Christmas tree. 1m 3b 2g 1 interior
  In Spamer, C. Easy grade school plays

c The first jack-o'-lanterns
  Halloween play. Witch and goblin try to find something new with which to frighten people. 3b 3g extras 1 exterior
  In Spamer, C. Easy grade school plays

c The fish that wished to live on land
  Little tadpole finally becomes a frog and gets his wish to live on land. Unidentified cast 5 characters 1 interior
  In Spamer, C. Easy science plays for grade school

c Fishermen
  Verse play about several children on a rainy day who learn a game about fishing. 1w 2b 1g 1 interior
  In Spamer, C. Easy grade school plays

c The flight out of Egypt
  Bible. Old Testament. Exodus. Moses takes his people, the Israelites, across the Red Sea. 1 act 3m extras 1 interior
  In Spamer, C. Bible plays for juniors

Florence Nightingale
  When a man is about to have injured dog destroyed little Florence Nightingale nurses it back to health. 2m 2g 1 exterior
  In Spamer, C. Easy sketches of famous women

c The foolish kitten
  Based on nursery rhyme about three little kittens who lost their mittens. 3b 3g 1 exterior
  In Spamer, C. Easy grade school plays

c Friends
  A kitten, a puppy and a bird make friends after quarreling. Verse play. Unidentified cast 3 characters no setting
  In Spamer, C. Juvenile treasure chest

c Gabriel visits Mary
  Bible. New Testament. Luke. The angel, Gabriel, announces the birth of Jesus to Virgin Mary. 1 act 2m 2w 1 interior
  In Spamer, C. Bible plays for juniors

George Eliot
  Nine year old Mary Ann Evans the future novelist, starts writing a novel. 2m 1g 1 exterior
  In Spamer, C. Easy sketches of famous women

c Gideon and the angel
  Bible. Old Testament. Judges. God chooses Gideon to save Israel from the Midianites. 1 act 2m extras 1 interior
  In Spamer, C. Bible plays for juniors

c The gingerbread house
  Hansel and Gretel ask the Mother Goose characters to find someone to live in the gingerbread house. 2m 5w 2b 1g extras 1 exterior
  In Spamer, C. The junior entertainment book

c The gold spinner
  Prince kidnaps young girl so that she may spin straw into gold for him. 2m 1w extras 1 interior 1 exterior
  In Spamer, C. The junior entertainment book

c The good Samaritan
  Bible. New Testament. Luke. The Samaritan, a foreigner, is the only one who helps a wounded man. 1 act 5m extras 1 exterior
  In Spamer, C. Bible plays for juniors

c Happy New Year
  Little girl is sad because all nice things in old year are leaving, but then she meets new year. 4m 2b 1g extras 1 setting
  In Spamer, C. Easy grade school plays

Harriet Beecher Stowe
  Even as a child, Harriet Beecher Stowe knew the importance of racial equality. 1w 3b 1g 1 interior
  In Spamer, C. Easy sketches of famous women

c The hatless snowmen
  A snow elf saves snowmen from boys who are fighting over them. 4b extras 1 exterior
  In Easy juvenile grab bag

c Heavenly stars
  The stars are upset because new satellites from earth have disorganized their work. Unidentified cast 8 characters extras 1 exterior
  In Spamer, C. Easy science plays for grade school

c Helpers
  Three little girls do some housekeeping in pantomime while their mother is away. 3g no setting
  In Spamer, C. Juvenile treasure chest

c Hippety hop
  Each animal in a group decides his own type of locomotion is best for his needs. Unidentified cast 5 characters no setting
  In Spamer, C. Juvenile treasure chest

Spamer, Claribel—*Continued*

c Humpty Heart
Valentine's Day. Jack of Hearts finds a
practical way to mend the broken heart
of his brother, Humpty. 1 scene 2m 1w
6b 1g 1 exterior

In Easy juvenile grab bag

c Inside the earth
A gnome explains to two children how
volcanoes and mountains are formed. 1b
1g extras 1 exterior

In Spamer, C. Easy science plays for
grade school

c Jairus' daughter
Bible. New Testament. Gospels. Jesus
raises Jairus' daughter from the dead.
1 act 5m 3w extras 1 interior

In Spamer, C. Bible plays for juniors

Jane Welsh
Young Jane Welsh, later the wife of
Thomas Carlyle, begs to be taught
Latin. 1m 1w 1b 1g 1 interior

In Spamer, C. Easy sketches of famous
women

Jenny Lind
A famous opera star tells Jenny Lind's
mother that the little girl has a great
voice. 4m 1g 1 interior

In Spamer, C. Easy sketches of famous
women

c Jesus and the fisherman
Bible. New Testament. Luke. Jesus
chooses four of his twelve disciples.
1 act 5m extras 1 exterior

In Spamer, C. Bible plays for juniors

c Jesus is born
Bible. New Testament. Luke. The angels announce the birth of Jesus to some
shepherds in Judea. 1 act 3m extras
1 exterior

In Spamer, C. Bible plays for juniors

Joan of Arc
In the garden of her home, Joan of Arc
hears the voice of Saint Michael. 3w 1
exterior

In Spamer, C. Easy sketches of famous
women

c Jonathan's son
Bible. Old Testament. Samuel. David is
kind to Mephibosheth, the son of his
dead friend, Jonathan. 1 act 3m extras
1 interior

In Spamer, C. Bible plays for juniors

c The joy givers
One of Santa's elves is upset because
the children don't really take care of
their toys. Unidentified cast 4 characters
extras 1 interior

In Spamer, C. The junior entertainment
book

Julia Ward Howe
Ten year old Julia Ward Howe tells her
sisters she intends to write a great
hymn some day. 1w 3g 1 interior

In Spamer, C. Easy sketches of famous
women

c King Sun
King Sun proves to the planets that
they have no choice but to follow him.
Unidentified cast 10 characters 1 exterior

In Spamer, C. Easy science plays for
grade school

c The king's cooks
The king's cooks call on their fairy god-
father for help in making enough cakes
for the Prince's party. 4m 1w 2b 1g
extras 1 interior

In Easy juvenile grab bag

c The Last Supper
Bible. New Testament. Gospels. At the
Last Supper Jesus tells his disciples
that one of them will betray him. 1 act
14m extras 1 interior

In Spamer, C. Bible plays for juniors

c The laughed-at monkey
When forest animals fail to laugh at him
a runaway monkey decides to return
to the zoo. Unidentified cast 5 characters 1 exterior

In Spamer, C. Juvenile treasure chest

c Little blank book
During Book Week, the books in a book-
shop learn that children enjoy reading.
4b 4g 1 interior

In Spamer, C. Easy grade school plays

c Little boy's clock
Hours of the day teach little boy how to
tell time in relation to his routine
schedule. 1m 1w 1b extras

In Easy juvenile grab bag

c Little cloud
Little raindrops need help from cloud
and wind because they are too small to
fall to earth. Unidentified cast 3 characters and extras 1 exterior

In Spamer, C. Easy science plays for
grade school

c The little clouds
Two clouds who quarrel almost spoil a
family picnic when they spill raindrops.
Unidentified cast 4 characters no setting

In Spamer, C. Juvenile treasure chest

c The little goblins
Halloween play. Three little goblins are
unhappy because they are ugly. 4b 3g
1 exterior

In Spamer, C. Easy grade school plays

c The little greenworker
Vegetables in the garden do not realize
how important their mysterious friend
chlorophyll is to them. Unidentified cast
5 characters 1 exterior

In Spamer, C. Easy science plays for
grade school

c Little icicle
A little icicle is afraid the sun will melt
him away. Unidentified cast 4 characters
extras 1 exterior

In Spamer, C. The junior entertainment
book

c The loaves and the fishes
Bible. New Testament. Gospels. Jesus
feeds the multitude with five loaves and
two fishes. 1 act 15m 1b extras 1 exterior

In Spamer, C. Bible plays for juniors

c The lost bouquet
Mother's Day. Flower Fairy helps some
children secure a gift for Old Mother
Hubbard. 2w extras 1 exterior

In Spamer, C. Juvenile treasure chest

Louisa May Alcott
Four-year-old Louisa May Alcott gets
lost in Boston and is found by town
crier. 1m 1b 2g 1 exterior

In Spamer, C. Easy sketches of famous
women

Marie Antoinette
Young Marie Antoinette refuses to learn
to read. 1m 2w 2g 1 interior

In Spamer, C. Easy sketches of famous
women

Martha Washington
Martha Dandridge, the future wife of
George Washington, celebrates her
eleventh birthday. 2m 2w 3b 1g 1 interior

In Spamer, C. Easy sketches of famous
women

Spamer, Claribel—*Continued*

Mary Mapes Dodge
A scene from the childhood of Mary Mapes Dodge, the future author of children's books. 1m 1b 2g 1 interior

In Spamer, C. Easy sketches of famous women

c The May fairies
Two violets refuse to be in little girl's May basket because she doesn't obey her mother. 1w 3g extras 1 exterior

In Spamer, C. Easy grade school plays

c The mirror children
Little Mary discovers she has many other selves in the mirror but some of them are cross or sulky. 1 act 6g 1 interior

In Kamerman, S. E. ed. Blue-ribbon plays for girls

c Miss Muffet's lunch
Mother Goose characters help Miss Muffet get some food. Verse play. 4m 2w 1g extras no setting

In Spamer, C. Juvenile treasure chest

c The mouse and the moon
A little mouse cries for the moon because he thinks it is made of cheese. Unidentified cast 6 characters 1 exterior

In Spamer, C. The junior entertainment book

c The mystery
The platypus is upset because he isn't like any of the other animals. Unidentified cast 8 characters 1 exterior

In Spamer, C. Easy science plays for grade school

c The new book
Some children make up a book from some torn books to include in their Book Week exhibit. 8b 8g 1 interior

In Spamer, C. Easy grade school plays

c Noah's ark
Bible. Old Testament. Genesis. Noah and all the animals wait impatiently for the rainbow which will tell them the flood is over. 1 act 1m 1w extras 1 interior

In Spamer, C. Bible plays for juniors

c The Old Woman's day
Mother Goose characters decide to have Mother's Day for the old woman who lived in a shoe. Unidentified cast 7 characters 1 exterior

In Spamer, C. The junior entertainment book

c The orange tree
All the different parts of an orange tree tell why they are important. 2m 1w 1g extras 1 exterior

In Spamer, C. Easy science for grade school

c Our dumb friends
Little girl's plan to keep pets from quarreling also brings peace between her and her brother. 1b 1g 1 interior

In Easy juvenile grab bag

c The parable of the sower
Bible. New Testament. Gospels. Jesus' parable of the seeds sown on good and bad ground. 1 act 2m extras 1 exterior

In Spamer, C. Bible plays for juniors

c The parasols
The spring fairies help four little girls find Easter bouquets. 8g 1 exterior

In Spamer, C. Easy grade school plays

c The Pharaoh's dream
Bible. Old Testament. Genesis. Joseph interprets the meaning of the fat and thin cows and ears of corn in Pharaoh's dream. 1 act 3m extras 1 interior

In Spamer, C. Bible plays for juniors

c A place for all
Easter. The Easter Bunny paints some Easter eggs. 1b 1g extras 1 exterior

In Spamer, C. Juvenile treasure chest

c The playroom
A little girl's toys all wish they could be someone else. 1g extras 1 interior

In Spamer, C. The junior entertainment book

c The plight of the tree
Forest creatures tell the wood-chopper why he should not cut down their friend, the tree. Im extras 1 exterior

In Spamer, C. Easy science plays for grade school

Priscilla Alden
Sixteen year old Priscilla Alden arrives in the New World aboard the Mayflower. 4m 2w 1 exterior

In Spamer, C. Easy sketches of famous women

c Pumpkin Ghost
Halloween. When a little witch's pumpkin is taken by two children, Pumpkin Ghost helps her recover it. 4b 3g 1 exterior

In Spamer, C. Easy grade school plays

c A pumpkin's fate
Three pumpkins wait to become part of the Halloween festivities. Unidentified cast 7 characters 1 exterior

In Spamer, C. The junior entertainment book

Queen Victoria
Six year old Princess Victoria, later a queen, locks the piano and refuses to practice her music. 2m 2w 1g 1 interior

In Spamer, C. Easy sketches of famous women

c Raindrops
The raindrops want to look different, and Jack Frost changes them into snowflakes. Unidentified cast 4 characters extras 1 exterior

In Spamer, C. The junior entertainment book

c The rebellious lightning bolt
A little lightning bolt wrecks the cloud keeper's plan for rain. Unidentified cast 6 characters 1 exterior

In Spamer, C. The junior entertainment book

Rosa Bonheur
Six year old Rosa Bonheur draws pictures for her brother. 1m 1w 2b 1g 1 interior

In Spamer, C. Easy sketches of famous women

c Ruth
Bible. Old Testament. Ruth. The Moabitess. Ruth. gleans in the field of Boaz, the Israelite. 1 act 1m 3w extras 1 interior

In Spamer, C. Bible plays for juniors

c Sammy Bushytail
When the squirrels run a race gathering nuts, they are helped by all the trees. 5b 4g no scenery

In Spamer, C. Easy grade school plays

c Samson and Delilah
Bible. Old Testament. Judges. Delilah betrays secret of Samson's strength to Philistines. 1 act 4m 1w 1 interior

In Spamer, C. Bible plays for juniors

c Saul and the ghost
Bible. Old Testament. Samuel. Samuel's ghost prophesies King Saul's death. 1 act 4m 1 exterior

In Spamer, C. Bible plays for juniors

Spamer, Claribel—*Continued*

c Silly, a leaf
The leaves are satisfied being one color in autumn, but one leaf wants to be all colors. Unidentified cast 7 characters 1 exterior

In Spamer, C. The junior entertainment book

c The snowdrop
Snowdrop who does not want to melt and leave when winter is over is given green leaves by a spring fairy, and remains as a flower. 1 act 14g 1 exterior

In Kamerman, S. E. ed. Blue-ribbon plays for girls

c Solomon's Temple
Bible. Old Testament. Kings. God gives Solomon the gift of wisdom; Solomon begins to build a temple to God. 1 act 3m 2w 1 interior

In Spamer, C. Bible plays for juniors

c The stars and stripes
Little girl is visited by thirteen stars representing the states of original flag and they tell her how first flag was formed. 7b 7g 1 exterior

In Spamer, C. Easy grade school plays

c The store
Four children go to the store to buy groceries. Verse play. 1m 2b 2g 1 setting

In Spamer, C. Juvenile treasure chest
Susan B. Anthony
Sketch showing Susan B. Anthony and her sisters as children at home. 1m 3w 1g 1 interior

In Spamer, C. Easy sketches of famous women

c Tea party
Little girls have lesson in etiquette at their tea party. 4g 1 interior

In Spamer, C. Juvenile treasure chest

c The terrible grood
The birds are frightened of a big bird they have never seen. Unidentified cast 5 characters 1 exterior

In Spamer, C. The junior entertainment book

c The three bears
Based on folk tale about little girl who visits home of three bears while they are out. 1g extras 1 interior

In Spamer, C. The junior entertainment book

c The tulip garden
The crocus is chosen queen of the garden. Unidentified cast 6 characters 1 exterior

In Spamer, C. The junior entertainment book

c Valentine's party
Cupid teaches Valentine, a little boy, how to be good. 1m 2w 2b extras 1 interior

In Spamer, C. Easy grade school plays

c The visit to the moon
Some elves explore the moon. Unidentified cast 5 characters 1 exterior

In Spamer, C. Easy science plays for grade school

c The walls of Jericho
Bible. Old Testament. Joshua. Rahab, a woman of Jericho aids two Israelite spies sent by Joshua. 1 act 3m 2w extras 1 interior

In Spamer, C. Bible plays for juniors

c Washout
Halloween. Witch's magic transforms chalk drawing into real ghost. 4m 1w extras 1 exterior

In Spamer, C. Juvenile treasure chest

c The weather man
Sun, wind, snow and rain answer weather man's command to explain what they do. Unidentified cast 7 characters 1 interior

In Spamer, C. Easy science plays for grade school

c Who will kill the turkey?
In the royal palace of Thanksgiving-land no one has the heart to kill the turkey for Thanksgiving dinner. 1m 3w 2b 1g 1 interior

In Spamer, C. Easy grade school plays

c Why the evergreen trees never lose their branches
Adaptation of old nature myth. King Frost rewards evergreen trees for sheltering a bird with broken wing. Unidentified cast 9 characters 1 exterior

In Easy Juvenile grab bag

c The widow's son
Bible. New Testament. Luke. Jesus raises the dead and cures a sick man. 1 act 4m 1w extras 1 exterior

In Spamer, C. Bible plays for juniors

c The wise men
Bible. New Testament. Matthew. The three Magi bring gifts to infant Jesus. 1 act 8m 1w 1 interior

In Spamer, C. Bible plays for juniors

Spanish drama

Early to 1500
Rojas, F. de. The Celestina

Classical period—1500-1700
Vega, L. de. Fuente ovejuna

Vega Carpio, L. de. The star of Seville

Spanish folk-drama. See Folk-drama, Spanish

The **Spanish** tragedy. Kyd, T.

Spargrove, Dale
One for the book. French 1953 102p illus
Comedy. A girl whose fiance returns from South America and mysteriously postpones their marriage is justifiably suspicious when dark-eyed girl arrives and calls him her hero. 3 acts 4 scenes 4m 8w 1 interior

Spas. See Health resorts, watering-places, etc.

Speaking of murder. Roos, A. and Roos, W.

Speaking of speech. Miller, H. L.

The **spear.** Howard, V.

Speare, Elizabeth George
The anchor. Bakers Plays 1953 29p (Baker's Royalty plays)
Four sisters, separated for years meet again in their old Vermont home, but the envy felt for wealthy and beautiful one soon turns to pity. 1 act 4w 1 interior

Speech
c Miller, H. L. Speaking of speech
See also Language and languages

Speed, bonny boat. Wallace, N.

Spells. See Magic

Spence, Wall
The bridal bouquet. Bakers Plays 1953 40p illus (Baker's Royalty plays)
Romantic comedy. Snobbish girl introduces her shy, dowdy cousin to poor clerk and finds out too late that he is boss's son and heir to millions. 1 act 3m 1w 1 interior

Spence, Wall—*Continued*

Four frightened sisters. Bakers Plays 1956 36p (Baker's Royalty plays)
Mysterious curse strikes in family whenever one of the sisters announces her engagement. 1 act 5w 1 interior

A ghost of distinction. Bakers Plays 1958 40p illus (Baker's Royalty plays)
Romantic comedy. Girl falls in love with charming man who is a ghost, but who fortunately has live twin. 1 act 1m 5w 1 interior

How Betsy butted in. Bakers Plays 1954 102p illus (Baker's Edition of plays)
Mystery-comedy. Innocent youth, framed for theft, is avenged when Aunt Betsy holds a seance, and Grandpa's spirit returns to disclose key to mystery. 3 acts 5m 7w 1 interior

The locked room. Bakers Plays 1956 40p illus (Baker's Royalty plays)
Woman, embittered at being cut out of her brothers will, plots to pass off one neice, who is dying, for one who received fortune. 1 act 6w 1 interior

A message from John. Bakers Plays 1953 40p illus (Baker's Royalty plays)
Mystery. Two girls spend night in isolated cottage where they are baffled by message left by former tenant before he died. 1 act 4w 1 interior

Spencer, Gerald

Six ladies in waiting. Dramatic 1956 22p
Farce. Six ladies waiting for their husbands to come home from their night out, get into trouble trying to help a housewife who has tried to hold them up with toy gun. 1 act 6w 1 interior

Spencer, Hattie

Priscilla and John. French 1958 33p illus
Modern comedy version of the Priscilla Mullins-John Alden legend. 1 act 2m 5w 1 interior

Spewack, Bella. See Porter, C. Kiss me Kate; *also* Spewack, S. jt. auth.

Spewack, Sam

Under the sycamore tree
Satirical farce. Chief Scientist in an ant colony tries to make fellow ants take on the passionate nature of human beings. 3 acts 7 scenes 5m 3w extras 1 interior
In Plays of the year v7

Spewack, Sam, and Spewack, Bella

The festival. Dramatists 1955 78p illus
Romantic comedy. Naive young pianist who meets unscrupulous impresario in order to interest him in her young prodigy, finds herself involved in his sophisticated world. 3 acts 5m 4w 2b 1 interior

My three angels. Dramatists 1953 79p
Comedy. Based on La cuisine des anges, by Albert Husson. At Christmas time in French Guinea, three escaped convicts use their own methods to prevent owner of general store from losing his property, and to save his daughter's happiness. 3 acts 7m 3w 1 interior
Trade edition published by Random House

—Same
In Gassner, J. ed. Twenty best European plays on the American stage

My 3 angels (condensation)
In The Best plays of 1952-1953
In Theatre, 1953

Spewack, Samuel. See Porter, C. Kiss me Kate

Spielman Fred

The stingiest man in town (Scrooge) . . . music by Fred Spielman; book and lyrics by Janice Torre; adapted by Don Wilson. Harms, Inc. 1957 143p music
Christmas musical play based on A Christmas carol, by Charles Dickens. Includes words and music of songs. The experiences of Ebenezer Scrooge with three ghosts. 3 acts 21 scenes Large mixed cast 5 interiors 2 exteriors

Spies

Anderson, R. A. and Sweeney, R. L. Boris and the briefcase
Ashton, E. B. To serve a king
Badger, A. Willie's secret weapon
c Carlson, B. W. Don't tell a soul!
Chorpenning, C. B. Lincoln's secret messenger
Dunlap, W. André
Fisher, A. and Rabe, O. Not for sale
Heinlein, M. V. The panda and the spy
Howard, V. The blackbird
Howard, V. The women from Kentucky
St Clair, R. Susie and the F.B.I.
Taggart, T. Do—or die!
Trease, G. The shadow of Spain

Spigelgass, Leonard

A majority of one. French 1959 104p illus
Domestic comedy. Young man on delicate diplomatic mission to Japan is concerned with growing friendship between his Jewish mother-in-law and influential Japanese gentleman. 3 acts 6 scenes 6m 8w 4 interiors

Spinsters

Bugbee, W. N. Life starts at thirty-five
Murphy, A. The old maid
Neuenburg, E. Pinnacle
Ouzts, J. D. Just a picture

The **spirit** of Christmas. Fisher, A.

Spiritism. See Spiritualism

Spirits

Chayefsky, P. The tenth man
Giraudoux, J. The enchanted
Komparu, Z. U. Bashō
Kwanze, M. Hagoromo
Kwanze, M. Kakitsubata
Lathrop, D. A page of destiny
See also Spiritualism

Spiritualism

Coward, N. Blithe spirit
Kwanze, M. Tsunemasa
Pierce, C. W. Mum's the word
Yeats, W. B. The words upon the window-pane

Splaver, Sarah

Jill and Perry go military. Occu-Press 1955 12p (Socio-Guidrama ser)
School counselor listens to high school seniors discussion about leaving school to join the army. 2 scenes 5m 1w 1 setting

The **splendid** burden. Stanley-Wrench, M.

The **splendid** outcasts. Sisson, R. A.

Splint for a broken heart. Kirkpatrick, J.

Spook shop. Howard, V.

Spooks alive. Rose, Le R.

Spooks in books. Miller, H. L.

Spooky spectacles. Miller, H. L.

Sports. See individual sport, e.g. Baseball; Football

Spots of bother. Waugh, J. R.

Sprague, Glenn W.
c A man's point of view
Little boy who thinks it's silly to make a fuss over Father's Day, finds out what squirrels in his yard do for their fathers. 2 scenes 1w 1b 1g extras 2 exteriors
In Birdsall, R. ed. Creative plays for every school month

Sprague, Mortimer
Murder comes in threes. French 1957 91p illus
Comedy. Mysterious events involving young woman who inherited uncle's fortune reach climax when supposedly dead uncle returns. 3 acts 5m 7w 1 interior

Spreading the news. Gregory, Lady

Sprenger, Cyril H. and Attley, Marian
c Snow White and the seven dwarfs; libretto by Cyril H. Sprenger; music and lyrics by Cyril H. Sprenger and Marian Attley. Acting libretto. Paxton 1958 34p
Based on fairy tale by Jacob Grimm. Operetta. Wicked queen tries to have Snow White killed, but the seven drawfs save her. Music available separately. 3 acts 11 scenes 3m 5w extras 2 interiors 2 exteriors

Spring, Howard
The gentle assassin
Quiet middle-aged couple find their own point of view greatly contrasted with that of their rather Bohemian visitors. Set in England. 3 acts 5m 4w 1 interior
In Spring, H. Three plays

Jinny Morgan
Successful writer from poor family is torn between a sophisticated and beautiful woman and his childhood sweetheart. Set in Wales. 3 acts 5m 4w 1 interior
In Spring, H. Three plays

St George at the Dragon
Fantasy about a man who kills dragons, and a Cockney girl in a bar. 1 act 1m 2w 1 interior
In Spring, H. Three plays

Spring
c Hark, M. and McQueen, N. Spring is here
c Spamer, C. The snowdrop
c Spamer, C. The tulip garden
Strindberg, A. Easter
c Tuttle, R. Spring facts and fancies
c Very, A. King Winter
c Very, A. The Mayflower
c Very, A. Planting time

Spring daze. Hark, M. and McQueen, N.

Spring facts and fancies. Tuttle, R.

Spring fever. Ashbrand, K.

Spring flowers for Marguerite. Murch, E.

Spring is here. Hark, M. and McQueen, N.

Spring prom magic. Farrow, N.

Spunky Punky. Miller, H. L.

Spyri, Johanna
Heidi (dramatization) See Warnick, C. Heidi

The square root of wonderful. McCullers, C.

Squirrels
c Spamer, C. Sammy Bushytail
c Sprague, G. W. A man's point of view

The staff and the fiddle. Goldsmith, S. L.

The staff-room. Daviot, G.

Stafford, Kathleen
Tinker? Tailor? Soldier? [French's Acting ed] French (London) 1953 22p illus
In 16th century England Ann Gale, with mother's help, plays trick on a pompous suitor. 1 act 5m 4w 1 interior

Stage. See Acting; Actresses; Theater

Stage bore. Dias, E. J.

Stage set for Veteran's Day. Fisher, A. and Rabe, O.

Stage-stricken. Crane, B.

Stagecoach. Nichols, D.

Stalin Allee. Mannheimer, A. and Kohner, F.

Stallings, Laurence, and Anderson, Maxwell
What price glory?
An indictment of war revealed through experiences of some soldiers in World War I. 3 acts 4 scenes 26m 1w 3 interiors
In A Treasury of the theatre

The stallion. Oliver, W. I.

Stamps, Postage. See Postage-stamps

Stand-in for a murderer. Peterson, L.

Stand up to death. Parker, K. T.

Standard of living. See Cost and standard of living

Standing up for Santa. Fisher, A.

Stanley, Sir Henry Morton. See Howard, V. The spear

Stanley-Wrench, Margaret
The splendid burden. Edinburgh House 1954 96p
The responsibilities of Christians in three families: at the time of the Crucifixion, during the persecutions of Diocletian and in Africa today. Each act may be produced separately. Verse play. 3 acts 9 scenes 10m 5w extras 2 interiors

Stanton, Roma
Girl chases boy. French 1956 90p illus
Romantic comedy. Young lawyer, opposed to career girls, falls in love with young woman who has taken job as maid in the apartment he shares with a friend. 3 acts 4 scenes 4m 7w 1 interior

Star baby-sitter. Hark, M. and McQueen, N.

Star Cadets. Miller, H. L.

Star dust. Bowen, T.

A star for old glory. Fisher, A. and Rabe, O.

Star in the summer night. Mosel, T.

Star minded. Parker, K. T.

The star of Seville. Vega Carpio, L. de

Star of wonder. Preston, E. E.

The Star Spangled Banner. Emurian, E. K.

The star still shines. Neilson, P.

The star that never moves. McCaslin, N.

A star too far. Fearheiley, D.

The staring match. McNeely, J.

Stars
c Asbrand, K. The stars celebrate Christmas

Stars—*Continued*

c Floyd, B. Pinky Winky's trip to the moon

c Spamer, C. Heavenly stars

The **stars** and stripes. Newman, D.

The **stars** and stripes. Spamer, C.

The **stars** celebrate Christmas. Asbrand, K.

State of mind. Bond, N.

State of siege. Camus, A.

Statehood for Washington. Emmons, D. G.

States, Bert O.
The tall grass
> Emotional attitudes of members of family in small mining community towards new neighbors. 5m 3w 1 interior

In The Best short plays, 1959-1960

The **statue** of Saint Nicholas. Malcolmson, A.

Stealing
Corrie, J. The theft
See also Larceny

Steele, Jack
Tea for six
> Audience is invited to count how many impolite things occur when a girl invites her friends to tea. 1 act 1w 6g 1 interior

In Kamerman, S. E. ed. Blue-ribbon plays for girls

Stees, Lucille
c Red for danger
> Bert learns his lesson after he breaks safety rule and gets hurt. 1 act 1m 3w 1b 1 interior

In 'Round the year plays for the grades

Stein, Gertrude
Brewsie and Willie (dramatization) See Violett, E. and Blake, L. Brewsie and Willie

Stein, Howard
A sight for sore thoughts
> Woman can't accept the idea that husband left her because he wanted freedom. 5m 1w 1 interior

In The Best short plays, 1959-1960

Stein, Joseph. See Bock, J. The body beautiful; Hague, A. Plain and fancy; *also* Glickman, W. jt. auth.

Steinbeck, John
Of mice and men
> Based on author's novel. Migrant worker's dream of having own home is smashed when accidental murder of ranch owner's wife in Salinas Valley is perpetrated by his simple-minded friend Lennie. 3 acts 6 scenes 9m 1w 3 interiors 1 exterior

In Gaver, J. ed. Critics' choice

Sweet Thursday (dramatization) See Rodgers, R. Pipe dream

Step-in-the-hollow. MacDonagh, D.

Step lively, please. Martens, A. C.

Stephen, Saint, martyr
Estes, S. In quest of power through courage
Knox, A. He knew the Master

Stephen Foster, beautiful dreamer. Woolsey, J. and Sechrist, E. H.

The **Stephen** Foster story. Green, P.

Stephens, Cecil G.
The matter with Mildred. Bakers Plays 1958 80p
> Upset teenager takes some tranquilizer pills prescribed for her and loses her inhibitions. 3 acts 6m 4w 1 interior

More room for love. French 1956 88p illus
> Domestic comedy. Young professor pretends to be interested in student, but she finds he is really using her family for series of psychological studies. 3 acts 5 scenes 4m 4w 1 interior

Once in September. French 1957 77p illus
> Romantic comedy. Friction develops when woman is sympathetic toward her stepson's artistic ambitions, while her husband encourages her daughter's athletic prowess. 3 acts 4m 3w 1 interior

Storm cellar. French 1957 95p illus
> Young veteran who is a law student and pretty girl next door have their lives straightened out by disreputable old Uncle Mac. 3 acts 5 scenes 5m 5w 1g 1 interior

Stephens, Peter John
The changeling
> Domestic comedy. Witchcraft employed to secure return of baby spirited away from farm house. Welsh dialect. 3m 3w 1 interior

In The Best short plays, 1952-1953

Steps from beyond. Gould, J. R.

Sterling, Alma
Kissin' cousins. Bakers Plays 1957 83p (Baker's Royalty plays)
> Romantic comedy. Two girls have problems in settling their love affairs. 3 acts 4m 7w 1 interior

Stern, G. B.
Raffle for a bedspread. Methuen 1953 20p
> Comedy. The donor of bedspread for raffle to aid the British Legion wins it with her one ticket. 1 act 2 scenes 7w 1 interior

Stern, Leonard, and Zelinka, Sydney
The $99,000 answer
> Television comedy. Fate of bus driver who was sure he could win top prize in television quiz show. 5m 4w

In Writers Guild of America. The prize plays of television and radio, 1956

Stevens, Elaine
The little nuisance. Bakers Plays 1956 34p illus
> Romantic comedy. Young girl's employer takes her to dinner, causing repercussions when their respective fiances discover it. 1 act 2m 6w 1 interior

Stevens, Leslie
Bullfight. French 1959 102p illus
> Set in Mexico. A bullfighter returns home, is hailed as a hero by his family but is actually a fake and a coward. 3 acts 7m 3w extras 3 interiors 3 exteriors

Champagne complex. [Rewritten and rev] French 1955 83p illus
> Farce. Young girl, engaged to pompous and conceited man develops uncontrollable desire to take her clothes off whenever she drinks champagne. 3 acts 1m 2w 1 interior

The lovers. French 1956 73p
> Tragedy set in Middle Ages. Peasant bride is torn between the great lord who wants her and her peasant husband. 3 acts 24m 4w extras 1 exterior

The marriage-go-round. French 1959 80p illus
> Domestic comedy. Swedish house guest decides that the Dean of Women's husband is the perfect mate for her. 2 acts 2m 2w 1 interior

Stevens, Leslie—*Continued*
The marriage-go-round (condensation)
In Broadway's best, 1959
Stevenson, Burton E.
A King in Babylon. Baker & Taylor 1955
134p illus
Melodrama. Dramatization of author's novel which tells of movie-making at tomb of Sekehyen-Re, a king of ancient Egypt. 3 acts 7 scenes 9m 3w extras 1 interior 2 exteriors
Stevenson, Florence Knight
c A day with Stevenson
Highlights of Robert Louis Stevenson's life in Samoa, dramatized for primary school children. Includes songs. 2 acts 2m 1w extras 1 exterior
In Birdsall, R. ed. Creative plays for every school month
Stevenson, Robert Louis
Dr Jekyll and Mr Hyde (dramatization)
See Sieveking, L. The strange case of Dr Jekyll and Mr Hyde
Treasure Island (radio adaptation) See York, M. A. Treasure Island
About
c Stevenson, F. K. A day with Stevenson
Stewards of the soil. Emurian, E. K.
Stewardship, Christian
Holt, N. A. The willing spirit
Stick up for yourself. Carter, C.
Sticks and stones. Downing, R.
Sticks and stones. Peterson, L.
The **still** alarm. Kaufman, G. S.
The **stingiest** man in town. Spielman, F.
Stockton, Richard F.
A fabulous tale
Fantasy. Blind beggar's vision is restored on Christmas Eve. Background choral music. 1 act 7m 1w extras 1 exterior
In The Best short plays of 1957-1958
Stockyards
Brecht, B. Saint Joan of the Stockyards
Stolen goods. Kromer, H.
The **stolen** heart. Newman, D.
The **stolen** prince. Totheroh, D.
Stolen waters. Brown, L.
Stoler, Sigmund A.
End of the rainbow
Mystery. Two girls help police capture counterfeiters in fake treasure hunt. 1 act 2 scenes 2m 3w 1 interior 1 exterior
In Smith, B. and others, eds. A treasury of non-royalty one-act plays
Stone, Irving
Love is eternal (dramatization) See Sergel, R. Irving Stone's Love is eternal
Stone, Weldon
Devil take a whittler
Humorous fantasy. How the Devil helped wood-carver create his masterpiece. 1 act 7m 4w extras 1 exterior
In The Best short plays, 1957
Stood up. Dean, E.
Stop the presses! Dias, E. J.
The **store**. Spamer, C.
Stores. See Department stores

Storey, Robert
Touch it light. [French's Acting ed] French (London) 1959 90p illus
Comedy. A group of soldiers quartered in a converted cricket pavilion near the English Channel wait out World War II. 3 acts 8m 1 interior
—Same
In Plays of the year v18
The **storm** at sea. Timpany, F. P.
Storm cellar. Stephens, C. G.
A **storm** is breaking. Damico, J.
Stormalong, Alfred Bulltop
McCaslin, N. Seafaring giant
Story book Christmas. Asbrand, K.
The **story** of a well. Fisher, A. and Rabe, O.
The **story** of light. Miller, H. L.
The **story** of March 17. Pierce, G. M.
The **story** of the circle of chalk. Hui-lan-ki
Storybook Halloween. Moore, H. G.
Stout, Wilbur
In Dixon's kitchen
Young man is constantly interrupted by his sweetheart's family when he tries to propose. Set in the southern mountains. 3m 3w 1b 1 interior
In Walser, R. ed. North Carolina drama
Stoves, Earthenware
Siks, G. B. The Nuremberg stove
Stowaways
Case, T. W. Billy Adams, American
Stowe, Harriet Elizabeth (Beecher)
Spamer, C. Harriet Beecher Stowe
The **strange** case of Dr Jekyll and Mr Hyde. Sieveking, L.
The **strange** case of Mother Goose. Borgers, P. and Borgers, E.
Strange interlude. O'Neill, E.
The **strange** tale of King Midas. Howard, V.
Strange victory. Neuenburg, E.
The **stranger**. Brabazon, F.
Stranger in town. Reach, J.
Strangers at the gate. Asbrand, K. S.
Strangers in Bethlehem. Wilson, R. C.
Strangers in the land. Brand, M.
The **strangest** kind of romance. Williams, T.
Strauss, Johann
Golden butterfly; book and lyrics by Charles George; music by Johann Strauss. Denison 1954 192p music
Comedy operetta in three acts adapted and modernized from the music of "Die Fledermaus"
Complications ensue when retired veterinarian and the fiance of his wife's niece secretly accept invitations to a masked ball, supposedly sent by two feminine admirers. Includes musical scores. 3 acts 7m 5w extras chorus 2 interiors
Strawberry Circle. Wattron, F.
Street scene. Rice, E. L.
A **streetcar** named Desire. Williams, T.
Stricker, Esther B.
What is the church? Bakers Plays 1960 15p
After attending a class on Christian Church several young people try to define purpose of the church. 7m 7w extras 1 interior
Strictly Puritan. Miller, H. L.

The **strike.** Serling, R.

Strikes and lockouts

Great Britain

Burgess, C. V. Chris is sent to Coventry

Textile industry

Dreiser, T. The girl in the coffin

Strindberg, August

Comrades; tr. from the Swedish by Edith and Warner Öland
    Artist husband of a painter rebels against wife's feminism. 4 acts 4m 7w 1 interior

In Tucker, S. M. ed. Twenty-five modern plays

Creditors; tr. from the Swedish by Elizabeth Sprigge
    Psychological analysis of feminine parasitism, and of a first husband's vengence by applying mental suggestion to ex-wife's second husband. 1 act 2m 1w extras 1 interior

In Plays of the year v21

In Strindberg, A. Five plays

Crime and crime
    Psychological. When his son is found dead, the playwright, Maurice, is persecuted for crime he committed only in thought. 4 acts 8 scenes 11m 5w 1g 3 interiors 2 exteriors
    Same as: There are crimes and crimes

In Strindberg, A. Five plays

The dance of death
    Tragedy. Character study of husband and wife which is vehicle for war of the sexes. 2 parts 4 acts 7 scenes 5m 4w 2 interiors

In Strindberg, A. Five plays

The dream play; tr. by Edwin Björkman
    Fantasy symbolical of humanity's struggle toward a better world. 16 scenes Large mixed cast scenery changed frequently on darkened stage

In Watson, E. B. ed. Contemporary drama: fifteen plays
—Same; in a new translation from the Swedish by Arvid Paulson
In A Treasury of the theatre
—Same; tr. by Elizabeth Sprigge
In Strindberg, A. Six plays

Earl Birger of Bjälbo; tr. by Walter Johnson
    Earl Birger, a thirteenth century king of Sweden is forced to give up power to his shrewd and more sophisticated younger son. 5 acts 8 scenes 15m 2w extras 4 interiors 3 exteriors

In Strindberg, A. The last of the knights, The regent, Earl Birger of Bjälbo

Easter; tr. by Elizabeth Sprigge
    Christian message of Easter intensified when return of spring brings new faith and happiness to hard-pressed family in 19th century Sweden. 3 acts 3m 3w 1 interior

In Strindberg, A. Six plays
—Same; tr. by Peter Watts
In Strindberg, A. Three plays

The father; tr. from the Swedish by Edith and Warner Öland
    Tragedy. Husband driven to insanity by struggle with wife for control of daughter's destiny. 3 acts 5m 3w 1 interior

In A Treasury of the theatre
—Same; tr. by Elizabeth Sprigge
In Strindberg, A. Six plays
—Same; tr. by P. Watts
In Strindberg, A. Three plays

The ghost sonata; tr. by Elizabeth Sprigge
    Fantasy symbolical of hidden guilt and failure of lives that lack the grace of God or man. 3 scenes 8m 7w extras 2 interiors 1 exterior

In Strindberg, A. Six plays

The great highway; tr. from the Swedish by Arvid Paulson
    Symbolizes man's journey through life with its joys and sorrows until he finally finds peace in memories of past happiness. 7 scenes 12m 4w 1g extras 7 exteriors

In Modern Scandinavian plays
—Same; tr. by Elizabeth Sprigge
In Strindberg, A. Five plays

The last of the knights; tr. by Walter Johnson
    Psychological study of Sten Sture, the Younger, the naive, unsophisticated young regent of Sweden as he faces inner defeat by the unseen evil around him. Set in Sweden in the early sixteenth century. 5 acts 7 scenes 15m 3w 4 interiors 2 exteriors

In Strindberg, A. The last of the knights, The regent, Earl Birger of Bjälbo

Miss Julia; tr. by P. Watts
    Tragedy. Conflict of the sexes and of social distinctions exemplified in the relations between wealthy young woman and her man servant. Set in late 19th century Sweden. 1 act 1m 2w 1 interior
    Same as: Miss Julie

In Strindberg, A. Three plays

Miss Julie; tr. by Elizabeth Sprigge
    Same as: Miss Julia

In Strindberg, A. Six plays

The regent; tr. by Walter Johnson
    Interval in life of Gustav I Vasa of Sweden during which he sought to withdraw his country from unsatisfactory union with neighboring countries in favor of independence. 5 acts 7 scenes 8m 5w 1b extras 4 interiors 2 exteriors

In Strindberg, A. The last of the knights, The regent, Earl Birger of Bjälbo

The road to Damascus; English version by Graham Rawson. Grove 1960 285p
    A sometimes autobiographical dream trilogy interpreting Strindberg's wanderings, his marital difficulties, his religious and moral convictions. 3 parts 34 scenes Large mixed cast 12 interiors 9 exteriors

The stronger; tr. by Elizabeth Sprigge
    Social comedy. Wife vs other woman. 1 act 3w 1 interior

In Strindberg, A. Six plays

Swanwhite
    Set in a medieval stone castle. Symbolic fairy tale characters show power of love. 3 acts 11m 7w extras 1 interior

In Strindberg, A. Five plays

There are crimes and crimes; tr. from the Swedish by Edwin Björkman
    Same as: Crime and crime

In A Treasury of the theatre

Srode, Warren Chetham- See Chetham-Strode, W.

Strolling players

c Totheroh, D. Master Will

Strong, L. A. G.

It's not very nice. Deane 1954 22p ("Deane's" Ser. of plays)
    Comedy. When handsome young man has turned all the girls' heads in the village the older women call a meeting, in order to do something about it. 1 act 11w 1 interior

Summer of the seventeenth doll. Lawler, R.

Summer pavilion. Vidal, G.

Summer resorts
Manning, H. Wonderful summer
Martens, A. C. Fraidy cat

Summertime. Betti, U.

The **summoning** of Everyman. Everyman

Sun
Spamer, C. King Sun
c Very, A. The flower garden

Sun-up. Vollmer, L.

Sunday morning. Casey, B. M.

A **Sunday** school Christmas program. Mattson, J.

Sundelof-Asbrand, Karin. See Asbrand, Karin

Sunrise at Campobello. Schary, D.

The **Sun's** darling. Dekker, T. and Ford, J.

Sunstroke. Kuehl, W. A.

Supernatural
Armer, A. and Grauman, W. E. One year after
Claudel, P. The tidings brought to Mary
Conkle, E. P. The reticent one
Dunsany, Lord. The jest of Hahalaba
Greene, G. The potting shed
Howells, W. D. The impossible
Ustinov, P. The love of four colonels
Wilson, E. Cyprian's prayer

Superstition
Hark, M. and McQueen, N. Halloween luck
Parker, J. W. Sleep on, Lemuel
Wattron, F. Strawberry Circle
Williams, T. The rose tattoo
        See also Fairies; Folk-lore, American; Tragedy

Superstition. Barker, J. N.

The **suppliant** maidens. Aeschylus

The **suppliant** women. Euripides

Suppliants. Euripides

Sure as fate. Armer, A. and Grauman, W. E.

Sure cure. Fisher, A.

Suréna. Corneille, P.

Surgery, Plastic
Blackmore, P. Down came a blackbird

The **surprise.** Chesterton, G. K.

Surprise! Postance, N.

Surprise packet. Clare, N.

The **surrounding** mist. Parker, K.

Survival (after aeroplane accidents, shipwrecks, etc.)
Barrie, J. M. The admirable Crichton
Brenner, A. Survival
Hallman, E. S. Survival
Howard, V. The Swiss family Robinson—rescued
c Miller, M. Robinson Crusoe

Survival. Brenner, A.

Survival. Hallman, E. S.

Susan B. Anthony. Spamer, C.

Susan slept here. Fisher, S. and Gottlieb, A.

Susan steps out. McCoy, P. S.

Susan to the rescue. Burgess, C. V.

Susie and the F.B.I. St Clair, R.

Susie was a vampire. Neuenburg, E.

Sutherland, Dan
Art for art's sake
        Comedy. Young woman suddenly paints picture for art critic's evaluation in order to prove that her sister has wrong conception of art. 1 act 1m 3w 1 interior
        In Sutherland, D. Six more miniatures
The clean up
        Comedy. Two charwomen develop theory that their employer and his secretary staged recent robbery of firm's funds. Cockney dialect. 1 act 2w 1 interior
        In Sutherland, D. Six more miniatures
Father's economy drive
        Domestic comedy. Father has his own ideas about family's plans for his part in thrift program. 1 act 1m 3w 1 interior
        In Sutherland, D. Six more miniatures
The man who understood women
        Comedy. Young author wins bet that he can get women to do what he wants them to do. 1 act 2m 4w 1 interior
        In Sutherland, D. Six more miniatures
Scherzo in two flats
        Comedy. Young Englishman's efforts to help young woman who has locked herself out of her flat, complicated by arrival of latter's aunt. 1 act 1m 2w 1 interior
        In Sutherland, D. Six more miniatures
Trying to take things quietly
        Comedy. Lady of the house, posing as thief, gets information for police from naive young burglar. English underworld slang. 1 act 1m 2w 1 interior
        In Sutherland, D. Six more miniatures

Sutton, Thomas
Aunt Min drops in. French 1953 80p illus
        Farce. Professor lives a quiet life until the evening his daughter is hired as an extra in local tent show Biblical drama which town has banned. 3 acts 5m 6w 1 interior
        For other plays by this author see Manning, Hilda; Reach, James; Williams, Pete

Sveinbjörnsson, Tryggvi
Bishop Jón Arason; tr from the Icelandic by Lee M. Hollander
        In 16th century Iceland the conflict between Catholics and Lutherans culminates in capture and execution of Catholic bishop, Arason, and two of his sons. 4 acts 15m 2w 2b 1g 3 interiors
        In Modern Scandinavian plays

Swann, Darius Leander
The crier calls. Friendship Press 1956 15p
        Verse play. Through episodes in dream sequence, a town crier of colonial America shows two modern college students some of the problems of underdeveloped areas of the world. 3m extras 1 setting

Swann, Mona
The Little Poor Man of Assisi. St Martins 1954 91p music
        How Francisco Bernardone, the son of a wealthy clothing merchant, became St Francis of Assisi. 3 acts 7 scenes Large mixed cast 5 exteriors

Swanson, Viola Ashman
c What do you see in the manger? Augustana 1954 15p music
        Christmas service for the Church school. A nativity pantomime with choral music. Large mixed cast no scenery

Swanwhite. Strindberg, A.

Sweden

History—To 1397

Strindberg, A. Earl Birger of Bjälbo

History—1397-1523

Strindberg, A. The last of the knights

History—1523-1718

Strindberg, A. The regent

Social life and customs—1814-1905

Bergman, I. The magician
Strindberg, A. Easter

Sweeney, R. L. See Anderson, R. A. jt. auth.

Sweet bird of youth. Williams, T.

Sweet Coz. Daviot, G.

Sweet Master William. Sladen-Smith, F.

Sweet? sixteen. Greth, Le R. E.

The **sweetheart** of Broadway. Lagman, J. H.

Sweetie. Dayton, M.

Sweetness and light. Casey, B. M.

Swift, Jonathan
Gulliver's travels (dramatization) See
Howard, V. Gulliver wins his freedom
Gulliver's travels in Lilliput land (radio
adaptation) See Golden, E. Gulliver's
travels in Lilliput Land

About

Johnston, D. The dreaming dust
Yeats, W. B. The words upon the window-pane

Swindlers and swindling
Howard, V. The mayor
Nash, N. R. The rainmaker
Willson, M. The music man
See also Imposters and imposture

The **Swiss** Chalet mystery. Murray, J.

The **Swiss** family Robinson—rescued. Howard, V.

Switzerland
Murray, J. The Swiss Chalet mystery
Warnick, C. Heidi

Sydow, Jack. See Tumarin, B. jt. auth.

Sylvaine, Vernon
As long as they're happy
Domestic farce. A man has endless problems with wife and three daughters until he decides to become a Bohemian. 3 acts 5 scenes 6m 6w 1 interior
In Plays of the year v9

Symbolism
Barkentin, M. James Joyce's Ulysses in nighttown
Betti, U. The Queen and the rebels
Chekhov, A. The sea gull
Dimondstein, B. In the chains of life
Ibsen, H. The master builder
Ibsen, H. When we dead awaken
Ibsen, H. The wild duck
Li, Y. M. The grand garden
O'Casey, S. Purple dust
O'Casey, S. Red roses for me
O'Casey, S. Within the gates
O'Neill, E. The great God Brown
Saroyan, W. The time of your life
Sartre, J. P. The flies
Strindberg, A. A dream play
Strindberg, A. Ghost sonata
Strindberg, A. The great highway
Yeats, W. B. The Countess Cathleen
Yeats, W. B. The shadowy waters

Symbols of Christmas. Beneke, A.

Symphonie pastorale. George, M.

Synge, John. See Tunney, K. jt. auth.

Synge, John M.
Deirdre of the sorrows
Tragedy. Set in Ireland. Murder and suicide. The High King of Ulster wishes to marry a girl who loves another man. 3 acts 8m 3w 1 interior 2 exteriors
In Synge, J. M. The complete plays of John M. Synge
In the shadow of the glen
Old Irish peasant pretends to be dead, revives to drive his frustrated wife out of his house in company of carefree tramp. 1 act 3m 1w 1 interior
In Cerf, B. and Cartmell, V. H. eds. 24 favorite one-act plays
In Synge, J. M. The complete plays of John M. Synge
The playboy of the Western World
Folk comedy about Irish peasant life. Young braggart who thinks he killed his father is made much of in remote village to which he flees, but is ultimately deflated. 3 acts 7m 5w extras 1 interior
In Cubeta, P. M. ed. Modern drama for analysis. 1955 edition
In Kronenberger, L. ed. Cavalcade of comedy
In Synge, J. M. The complete plays of John M. Synge
Riders to the sea
Tragedy. Relentless malignity of the sea toward Irish fisherfolk and the relief which comes when the sea can do no more harm. 1 act 1m 3w extras 1 interior
In Synge, J. M. The complete plays of John M. Synge
In A Treasury of the theatre
In Tucker, S. M. ed. Twenty-five modern plays
In Warnock, R. Representative modern plays, British
In Watson, E. B. ed. Contemporary drama: fifteen plays
The tinker's wedding
Comedy about a rough Irish peasant couple and the rascally priest who is to marry them. 2 acts 2m 2w 1 exterior
In Synge, J. M. The complete plays of John M. Synge
The well of the saints
The miraculous restoration of sight to a blind Irish beggar couple does not bring them happiness. 3 acts 4m 3w 2 exteriors
In Synge, J. M. The complete plays of John M. Synge

Syphilis
Ibsen, H. Ghosts

Szogyi, Alex. See Chekhov, A. A country scandal

T

T for turkey. Hark, M. and McQueen, N.

TV or not TV. Taggart, T.

Tabitha. Ridley, A. and Borer, M. C.

Table by the window. See Rattigan, T. Separate tables

Table number seven. See Rattigan, **T. Separate tables**

Tabori, George
The Emperor's clothes (condensation)
In The Best plays of 1952-1953
Flight into Egypt. Acting ed. [Rev] Dramatists 1953 79p front
Tragedy. Experiences of family of Austrian refugees waiting for visas to America. 3 acts 13m 4w 1 interior

Tadpoles. See Frogs

Taggart, Tom
Be my guest. French 1953 81p ilus
Farce. Teenage girl pretends to be a grown up in order to entertain visiting professor. 3 acts 6 scenes 6m 6w 1 interior

Boy meets girl in Washington
Comedy. How to make love in official Washington jargon. 1m 1w 1 interior
In Taggart, T. Short and sweet

Crewcuts and longhairs. French 1954 86p illus
Farce. Not-too-intelligent high school football player has himself hypnotized in order to pass an exam but runs into complications. 3 acts 5m 5w 1 interior

Deadwood Dick. French 1953 94p illus
Old time melodrama featuring stolen gold mines, kidnapped heroines and hairbreadth escapes all based on the "dime novels" of Edward L. Wheeler which appeared in the 1870's. 3 acts 6 scenes 7m 7w extras 1 interior

Do—or die! French 1955 84p illus
Mystery. After plane crashes, a family discovers that their isolated desert home has been made focal point by network of spies. 3 acts 6m 5w 1g 1 interior

Follow simple directions
Comedy. Daddy shows Junior how to cut and assemble one of those toys on cereal box. 1m 1b 1 interior
In Taggart, T. Short and sweet

The gross story conference
Comedy. An eccentric movie producer discusses his forthcoming epic. 3m 1 interior
In Taggart, T. Short and sweet

Macbeth a la mode
Parody of Shakespeare's Macbeth as it might have been, if written by Gilbert and Sullivan. Contains words for some of Sullivan's songs. 6 scenes 2m 4w 1 interior
In Taggart, T. Short and sweet

The midnight ride of Tex O'Coco
Comic pantomime about the old West. 1m 1w extras 1 interior
In Taggart, T. Short and sweet

Morning of a private eye
Tough detective meets a pair of blondes. 1m 3w 1 interior
In Taggart, T. Short and sweet

Oily to rise
Comedy. A Texan dies and goes to heaven. 2m extras 1 interior
In Taggart, T. Short and sweet

Punky Doodle. French 1953 71p illus
Comedy. As local dowagers are putting on historical pageant a former disreputable inhabitant dies and wills the town a fortune provided they change name and erect monument to her. 3 acts 4 scenes 3m 7w 1 interior

TV or not TV. French 1955 96p illus
Domestic comedy. Television writer stays with family to study them for his new television series. 3 acts 6m 5w 1g 1 interior

Two in the balcony
Three parodies of Shakespeare's characters in Romeo and Juliet. 1m 1w 1 interior
In Taggart, T. Short and sweet

When mothers meet
Comedy. Two young mothers have brief encounter in office of school principal about disciplining their children. 3w 1 interior
In Taggart, T. Short and sweet

Taggart, Tom, and Reach, James
Dear Phoebe. French 1956 90p illus
Comedy. Young college professor's ambition for newspaper career finds him hired as advice-to-the-lovelorn editor. 3 acts 6m 7w 1 interior

Tahiti
Giraudoux, J. The virtuous island

Takasago. Kwanze, M.

Take a giant step. Peterson, L.

Take any street. Kromer, H.

Take no yuki (condensation) Kwanze, M.

Takeda, Izumo; Miyoshi, Shōraku, and Namiki, Sōsuke
The house of Sugawara (Sugawara denju tenarai kagami) tr. by Albert Miyasato and Shigeru Yamaguchi; English version by Louis M. Steed and Earle Ernst
Eighteenth century drama written for the Japanese doll theater. Murder, intrigue and love among aristocracy surrounding Japanese throne. 3 acts 4 scenes Large mixed cast 4 interiors 1 exterior
In Ernst, E. ed. Three Japanese plays

A **tale** of Chelm. See Perl, A. The world of Sholom Aleichem

The **tale** of good faith. Carpenter, F.

Talk to me like the rain and let me listen... Williams, T.

The **talking** flag. Miller, H. L.

Tall Bill and his big ideas. McCaslin, N.

The **tall** grass. States, B. O.

Tall story. Lindsay, H. and Crouse, R.

Tamayo y Baus, Manuel
Un drama nuevo (adaptation) See Howells, W. D. Yorick's love

Tamburlaine. See Timur the Great

Tamburlaine the Great. Marlowe, C.

The **taming** of the shrew. Olfson, L.

Tamura. Kwanze, M.

Tango-Monogurui (condensation) I-ami

Tanikō. Komparu, Z. U.

Tape recorders. See Recording instruments

Tarkington, Booth
Monsieur Beaucaire (radio adaptation) See Olfson, L. Monsieur Beaucaire
Seventeen (dramatization) See Kent, W. Seventeen

Tarpley, Ken. See Tarpley, V. jt. auth.

Tarpley, Vera, and Tarpley, Ken
Golden river. Row 1953 96p music
Operetta. A young man's offers of free vacation on family ranch to anyone interested in buying it, brings strange assortment of guests. Includes words and music for songs. 3 acts 5m 5w extras 1 interior

Tarpley, V. and Tarpley, K.—*Continued*
Jump over the moon. Bakers Plays 1954
79p
> Farce. A man's life is upset when his
> wife, son and daughter adopt baby
> chimpanzee to rear like a child, in the
> interest of psychology. 3 acts 5m 6w
> extras 1 interior

Ten o'clock scholar. Dramatic 1956 95p
illus
> Romantic comedy. Businessman returns
> home after long absence to resume edu-
> cation at high school where childhood
> sweetheart teaches. 3 acts 5 scenes 5m
> 9w 1 interior

Tartuffe. Molière, J. B. P.

Tashjian, Vahan
The Easter story. Bakers Plays 1953 18p
> Average citizen tells story of Christ's
> Resurrection. 1 act 8m 2w extras no
> scenery

Tasso, Torquato
Goethe, J. W. von. Torquato Tasso

A taste of honey. Delaney, S.

Tax dodging. See Tax evasion and avoidance

Tax evasion and avoidance
Bond, N. State of mind
Brown, L. This year—next year
Macrae, A. Both ends meet

Taxation
Fisher, A. and Rabe, O. Bringing up
father
See also Income tax

> Evasion and avoidance
See Tax evasion and avoidance

Taylor, Donald. See Thomas, D. The doctor
and the devils

Taylor, Douglas
Five in judgment. Dramatists 1956 25p
illus
> In a midwest farming community, two
> farmers concluding that two young men
> are responsible for a murder, get ready
> to lynch them. 1 act 7m 1w 1 interior

Taylor, Frederick
c The magic doughnuts
> When three children eat magic dough-
> nuts they wake up in Fairyland where
> they help Mother Goose characters van-
> quish wicked giant. Music for songs
> available separately. 4 scenes 11b 10g
> extras 2 exteriors

In Taylor, F. The magic doughnuts, and
The wizard's spell

c The melancholy princess. Macmillan (London) 1955 79p illus (Modern plays for
schools)
> Children's operetta based upon Mother
> Goose rhyme about Queen of Hearts.
> Music and dancing. Musical scores and
> words for songs available separately.
> 8 scenes 10m 3w extras 2 interiors 1 ex-
> terior

c The wizard's spell
> Although their mother explains that
> nursery rhymes never change, three
> children meet some Mother Goose char-
> acters and find that they do. Music for
> songs available separately. 7 scenes 12b
> 4g 2 interiors

In Taylor, F. The magic doughnuts, and
The wizard's spell

Taylor, George
Kill or cure. Deane 1955 22p ("Deane's"
Ser. of plays)
> Sam Hardcastle, feigning illness, draws
> sick pay from two companies until his
> wife uses psychological measures to
> get him back to work. 1 act 2m 2w
> 1 interior

Taylor, Samuel
The pleasure of his company; a rueful
comedy by Samuel Taylor with Cornelia Otis Skinner. Random House 1959
145p illus
> Social comedy. Irresponsible, debonair,
> globe-trotting playboy, divorced for many
> years, returns unannounced on eve of
> his daughter's wedding. 2 acts 4 scenes
> 5m 2w 1 interior

The pleasure of his company (condensa-
tion)
In The Best plays of 1958-1959
In Broadway's best, 1959

Sabrina Fair. [Acting ed] Dramatists 1955
85p illus
> Chauffeur's daughter returns from edu-
> cation in Paris to win man she loves,
> the son of her father's socialite employer.
> 4 acts 7m 7w 1 exterior
> Trade edition published by Random
> House

Sabrina Fair (condensation)
In Theatre, 1954

Taylor, Tom
The ticket-of-leave man
> Innocent man, imprisoned, manages to
> expose real criminals, with help of faith-
> ful sweetheart. 4 acts 6 scenes 8m 4w
> extras 3 interiors 3 exteriors

In Rowell, G. ed. Nineteenth century
plays

Taylor, Tom, and Reade, Charles
Masks and faces
> England. 19th century. The innocence of
> a country wife pitted against worldly,
> sophisticated men and women. 2 acts
> 3 scenes 11m 5w 2b 1g 3 interiors

In Rowell, G. ed. Nineteenth century
plays

The Taylors in the never-never land. Burgess, C. V.

Tchekhov, Anton. See Chekhov, Anton

Tea and sympathy. Anderson, R.

Tea for six. Steele, J.

Tea party. Spamer, C.

Teach me how to cry. Joudry, P.

Teachers
Adamov, A. Professor Taranne
Agg, H. Autumn term
Arthur, K. The long view
Carrière, A. It's about time
Casey, B. M. The portrait
Conkling, L. Let 'em eat steak
Crosby, M. Readin', 'ritin', and 'rithmetic
Curtis, P. D. The trial of Mr Newall
Delmar, V. Mid-summer
Erhard, T. The high white star
Garry, J. F. The bonehead case
Gethers, S. Cracker money
Gibson, M. N. Senior play
Gran, J. M. A nose for news
c Hark, M. and McQueen, N. When do we
eat?
Hayes, M. and Hayes, J. Mister Peepers
Hellman, L. The children's hour
Ionesco, E. The lesson
Kazan, M. The egghead
Martens, A. C. A dance with our Miss
Brooks
c Mason, J. "I'd be glad to"
Miller, H. L. I'll eat my hat!
Pagnol. Topaze

Teachers—*Continued*

Phillips, T. J. Miss Harper's birthday
Radin, B. A seacoast in Bohemia
Rattigan, T. The Browning version
Reach, J. Are teachers human?
Shaw, G. B. Pygmalion
Thurber, J. and Nugent, E. The male animal

Teachings of Jesus. See Jesus Christ—Teachings

The **Teahouse** of the August Moon. Patrick, J.

The **tears** of Madelon. Casey, B. M.

The **tears** of my sister. Foote, H.

Technology and civilization

Čapek, K. R. U. R.
Chayefsky, P. Printer's measure
Kaiser, G. The coral
Kaiser, G. Gas (I)
Kaiser, G. Gas—Part II

The **teddy** bear hero. Miller, H. L.

Teddy's own Santa. Matthews, E.

Tedlock, Dawn

Oil wells and wedding bells. Eldridge 1955 22p (Eldridge Popular one-act playscripts)

> Comedy. Widely assorted group of people are quarantined in hotel when one of them comes down with chicken pox. 3 scenes 5m 3w 1 interior

Teen-age. See Adolescence

The **teen** age party. Lynch, P.

Teen antics. Peavey, H.

The **Teen** Club's Christmas. Hark, M. and McQueen, N.

Teen-agers. See Adolescence; Youth

Teeth

c Fisher, A. The king's toothache

         Care and hygiene

c Weinberger, R. I. The whole tooth

Teichmann, Howard

The girls in 509. [Rev] French 1959 90p front

> Comedy. Two old ladies are discovered in hotel where they have lost contact with world after 1932, when Hoover lost the election. 2 acts 5 scenes 9m 3w 1 interior

Miss Lonelyhearts. Dramatists 1959 78p

> Based on novel by Nathanael West. Idealistic young reporter, forced to work on advice to lovelorn column, gradually becomes concerned with the personal problems of letter-writers. 2 acts 12 scenes 6m 9w 1 setting

Teichmann, Howard, and Kaufman, George S.

The solid gold Cadillac. [Rev] Dramatists 1956 71p illus

> Satirical comedy. Woman who is small stockholder outwits the four conniving directors of General Products Corporation. 2 acts 14 scenes 12m 6w 4 interiors Trade edition published by Random House

—Same

In Best American plays; 4th ser.

The solid gold Cadillac (condensation)

In Theatre, 1954

Telegraph

Blake, R. What hath God wrought

Telepathy. See Thought transference

Telephone

c O'Brien, R. Trippy answers the phone

Telephone roulette. Finney, J.

The **telescope.** Sherriff, R. C.

Television

Bremer, W. Nothing but nonsense
Lynn, K. S. Who killed Cock Robin?
Martens, A. C. What's the matter with TV?
Schulberg, B. A face in the crowd
Taggart, T. TV or not TV

Television broadcasting

c Martens, A. C. You are watching!
    See also Quiz shows

Television in advertising

Addis, H. Sellevision

Television plays

Armer, A. and Grauman, W. E. The beast lies dormant
Armer, A. and Grauman, W. E. Coral
Armer, A. and Grauman, W. E. Country cousin
Armer, A. and Grauman, W. E. In darkened rooms
Armer, A. and Grauman, W. E. Love lesson for Scotty
Armer, A. and Grauman, W. E. No time for dames
Armer, A. and Grauman, W. E. Sure as fate
Armer, A. and Grauman, W. E. Time out for dreams
Armer, A. and Grauman, W. E. To be alone
Armer, A. and Grauman, W. E. Vest pocket theatre
Armer, A. and Grauman, W. E. Whatever became of Lola Woods
Aurthur, R. A. Man on the mountaintop
Bailey, A. H. Impersonation
Bailey, A. H. The narrow man
Benjamin, J. and Kellerman, D. No man is an island
The Best television plays v3 (7 plays)
Best television plays, 1957 (7 plays)
Blake, R. What hath God wrought
Boretz, A. The trial of Poznan
Brenner, A. Survival
British Broadcasting Corporation. The television playwright (10 plays)
Burack, A. S. ed. Television plays for writers (8 plays)
Case, T. W. Billy Adams, American
Chayefsky, P. The bachelor party
Chayefsky, P. The big deal
Chayefsky, P. Holiday song
Chayefsky, P. Marty
Chayefsky, P. The mother
Chayefsky, P. Printer's measure
Chayefsky, P. Television plays (6 plays)
Chevigny, H. Daniel Webster
Costigan, J. Little moon of Alban
Costigan, J. A wind from the south
Dozier, R. A real fine cutting edge
Elward, J. Paper foxhole
Ettlinger, D. The thousand-yard look
Fenwick, R. Toys and science
Foote, H. The dancers
Foote, H. The death of the old man
Foote, H. Expectant relations

Tennant, Kylie—*Continued*

c Hamaguchi Gohei
Based on short story by Lafcadio Hearn about old man in Japanese village who saved villagers from a tidal wave. 1m 1b extras 1 exterior
In Tennant, K. The bells of the city, and other plays

c The magic fat baby
When king refuses to let his daughter marry his page, the Wise Woman's magic solves the problem. 5m 2w extras 1 interior
In Tennant, K. The bells of the city, and other plays

c The prince who met a dragon
A gnome, the guardian of the dragon's treasure, changes dragon's daughter to resemble a real princess. 3b 1g extras 1 exterior
In Tennant, K. The bells of the city, and other plays

Tennessee
McCaslin, N. The Bell Witch of Tennessee

Tennis
Porter, E. W. Callie goes to camp

Tennyson, Alfred
Becket
The struggle for power between King Henry II and Thomas à Becket, archbishop of Canterbury, in 12th century England. 5 acts 14 scenes 21m 3w 1b extras 7 interiors 7 exteriors
In Tennyson, A. Poetical works including the plays
The cup
Rivalry between two tetrarchs of Roman Empire. 2 acts 4 scenes 7m 3w 1b 2 interiors 1 exterior
In Tennyson, A. Poetical works including the plays
The falcon
Romantic comedy. Impoverished nobleman attempts to prove his love to noblewoman. Set in 19th century Italy. 2m 2w 1 interior
In Tennyson, A. Poetical works including the plays
The foresters
Robin Hood battles with Sheriff of Nottingham who wants to marry Maid Marian. 4 acts 7 scenes 12m 3w extras 3 interiors 2 exteriors
In Tennyson, A. Poetical works including the plays
Harold
Eleventh century England. The forces of King Harold II are defeated by the Normans. 5 acts 10 scenes 20m 3w extras 3 interiors 6 exteriors
In Tennyson, A. Poetical works including the plays
Idylls of the King (dramatization) See Mantle, M. Gareth triumphs
The promise of May
Nineteenth century England. Farmer's daughter loves a man who leaves her. 3 acts 3 scenes 9m 4w extras 1 interior 2 exteriors
In Tennyson, A. Poetical works including the plays
Queen Mary
Court intrigue, insurrections and religious persecutions during the reign of Mary Tudor. 5 acts 23 scenes Large mixed cast 16 interiors 3 exteriors
In Tennyson, A. Poetical works including the plays

The **tenor.** Wedekind, F.

The **tenth** man. Chayefsky, P.

Terence
The brothers
Latin comedy of manners. Tangled love affairs of two brothers, sons of strict father. 5 acts 8m 4w 1 exterior
In Casson, L. ed. Masters of ancient comedy
Phormio
Latin comedy of love and intrigue. Penniless adventurer lives by his wits. 5 acts 11m 3w 1 exterior
In Casson, L. ed. Masters of ancient comedy

Teresa, Saint
Mary Francis, Sister. La madre

The **terrible** grood. Spamer, C.

The **terrible** meek. Kennedy, C. R.

A **territory** is born. Emmons, D. G.

Terror at Black Oaks. Reach, J.

Testing ground for democracy. Flaten, M.

Tevya and his daughters. Perl, A.

Tevya and the first daughter. Perl, A.

Thane, Adele
c The Wizard of Oz. Childrens Theatre 1957 66p illus
Fairy tale fantasy. Dramatization of story by L. F. Baum. Dorothy and her dog Toto are joined by assorted friends as they travel from Kansas to visit the wonderful Wizard of Oz. Songs and dances. 3 acts 7 scenes 6m 6w 1g extras 1 interior 6 exteriors

Thank you, Edmondo. Shoub, M.

Thank you, God for everything. Hollinshead, L. M.

The **thankful** Pilgrims. Warner, L. H.

Thankful's red beads. Miller, H. L.

Thanks a million. Fisher, A. and Rabe, O.

Thanks for Thanksgiving. Newman, D.

Thanks to butter-fingers. Miller, H. L.

Thanks to the Indians. Newman, D.

Thanksgiving
Asbrand, K. Count your blessings
Asbrand, K. A day of thankful prayer
c Asbrand, K. Masquerade
c Carlson, B. W. Thanksgiving is the time
Casey, B. M. The other nine
Emurian, E. K. Thanksgiving through the ages
c Fisher, A. Mother of Tranksgiving
Fisher, A. Unexpected guests
c Hark, M. and McQueen, N. Many thanks
c Hark, M. and McQueen, N. New-fangled Thanksgiving
c Hark, M. and McQueen, N. Nothing to be thankful for
c Hark, M. and McQueen, N. T for turkey
Howard, V. Turkey for all
c A message from Thankful
c Miller, H. L. Mr Snow White's Thanksgiving
c Miller, H. L. The mystery of turkey-lurkey
Miller, H. L. Turkey turns the tables
Roberts, H. M. Old-fashioned Thanksgiving

Thirty Years' War, 1618-1648
Brecht, B. Mother Courage
Schiller, F. von. Wallenstein

This angel business. Ireland, I. A.

This dark world and wide. Horne, K. A.

This Declaration. Green, P.

This dream came true. Woolsey, J. and Sechrist, E. H.

This England. Bradley, A.

This music crept by me upon the waters. MacLeish, A.

This property is condemned. Williams, T.

This room and this gin and these sandwiches. Wilson, E.

This Thine house. Wefer, M.

This year—next year. Brown, L.

Thom, Robert
Children of the ladybug. Yale Univ. Press 1956 89p illus
  Bitterness and frustrations between members of a family. Verse play. 2 acts 5 scenes 5m 3w 1 interior

Thomas à Becket, Saint, Abp. of Canterbury
Anouilh, J. Becket; or, The honor of God
Eliot, T. S. Murder in the Cathedral
Tennyson, A. Becket

Thomas, Augustus
The witching hour
  Thought transference (mental telepathy) between a professional gambler and a man whom he believes to be a criminal. 4 acts 4 scenes 11m 3w 2 interiors
In Quinn, A. H. ed. Representative American plays

Thomas, Basil
Two of everything. Deane 1954 59p illus ("Deane's" Ser. of plays)
  Domestic comedy. Theater manager who regards his wife as a terrible actress is chagrined to find that she has accepted lead in his rival's play. 3 acts 5 scenes 4m 5w 1 interior

Thomas, Dana
Boy of mine. Northwestern Press 1953 99p
  Domestic comedy. Parents of an adopted teenage boy are hurt when he goes off to Chicago with his real mother. 3 acts 4 scenes 6m 8w 2 interiors

Thomas, Dorothy, and Slocumb, Paul
Next-to-last rites
  Planning funeral sermon before wife's death shows husband his neglect. 4m 2w 1g extras
In The Best short plays of 1954-1955

Thomas, Dylan
The doctor and the devils. New Directions 1953 138p
  Moving picture play adapted from the story-line and research by Donald Taylor. Based on Burke-Hare murder case in 19th century Scotland. Horror tale centering around a prominent lecturer in anatomy, and murder ring organized to supply corpses to medical colleges. Large mixed cast
Under Milk Wood. New Directions 1954 107p music (A New Directions Paperback)
  Radio play. A day in the life of a seacoast village in Wales. Music. Large mixed cast
  Trade edition also published by New Directions

Thomas, T. C.
Mirage. Deane 1954 31p illus ("Deane's" Ser. of plays)
  A play about Barnabas and others who might have been in Jerusalem during the crucifixion of Christ. 1 act 8m 9w 1 exterior

Thomas Jefferson: defender of liberty. Kissen, F.

Thompson, Blanche Jennings
c Pleasant dreams
  Two Girl Scouts dream of their favorite fairy tale character. 1 act 1w   12g 1 interior
In 'Round the year plays for the grades

Thompson, David
The shoemaker's wife
  Farce. When a shoemaker plays trick on his wife to test her love, the trick backfires. Time: Middle Ages. 1 act 2m 1w 1 interior
In Powers, V. E. Plays for players, and a guide to play production

Thompson, Mary Agnes
A coat of many colors
  Radio play. Discussion of the right of Americans to have free access to Communist books and teachings, based on freedoms guaranteed in Bill of Rights. Background music. 6m 2w
In Prescott, H. ed. Patrioscript
The conquered, the unconquerable, and I
  Radio play. The various duties of a citizen in a free country are explained to two immigrant girls by Spirit of Liberty. Background music. 10w
In Prescott, H. ed. Patrioscript
The witch hunters
  Radio play. Small town newspaper editor is unjustly attacked as Communist for defending freedom of the press. Background music. 12m
In Prescott, H. ed. Patrioscript
Young Doc Smith died tomorrow
  Radio play. Young man who dies in Korean War becomes, for people in his home town, a symbol of patriotism of all men who have died in American wars. Background music. 6m 2w
In Prescott, H. ed. Patrioscript

Thompson, Ruth
c The case of the misbehaving toys
  The proprietor of toy shop asks Santa to help him get toys ready for Christmas. Includes songs and dances. Large mixed cast 1 interior
In National Recreation Association. Plays, pageants and ceremonials for the Christmas season

Thon, Frederick
The island
  In Majorca, war victim's dog is run over by profiteer. 4m 1w 1 exterior
In The Best short plays of 1954-1955

Thor, with angels. Fry, C.

Thornhill, Alan
The forgotten factor. Blandford 1954 79p
  Efforts of young man to bring leaders in labor and management closer together, by showing their universal similarities regarding home and family. 3 acts 5 scenes 7m 4w extras 2 interiors

Thought transference
Thomas, A. The witching hour

The thousand flerbs. Gregory, H. and Henneberger, J.

The thousand-yard look. Ettlinger, D.

3. Ellrod, J. G.

Three actors and their drama. Ghelderode, M. de

Three and the dragon. Fisher, A.

Three bags full. De Francquen, L.

The three bears. Scott, L. B.

The three bears. Spamer, C.

The three bears (dramatization) See Spamer, C. The three bears

Three cheers for mother. Miller, H. L.

The three faces of Easter. Martens, A. C.

Three hours between planes. Winer, E.

Three little kittens. Miller, H. L.

Three little kittens (dramatization) See Spamer, C. The foolish kitten

Three little kittens go to school. Very, A.

The three Maries; Cornish cycle
    Bible. New Testament. Gospels. Easter. Ancient Cornish mystery play. The three Marys at the empty tomb and Christ's appearance to Mary Magdalene. Verse play in Middle English with modernized spelling. 3m 3w 1 exterior
    In Browne, E. M. ed. Religious drama, 2

The three Marys. Asbrand, K.

Three men on a string. Knapp, B.

Three mice for the abbot. Ridge, A.

Three needles in a haystack. McCreary, B. and McCreary, M.

Three on a bench. Estrada, D.

Three people. Gurney, A. R.

Three plays. Jonson, B.

The three sillies. Very, A.

The three sisters. Chekhov, A.

Three skits for Christmas. Emurian, E. K.

Three-way switch. See Jeans, R. Double take

Three weeks after marriage. Murphy, A.

Three wise men. See Magi

Three wishes for mother. Hark, M. and McQueen, N.

The three women of the Nativity. Russell, M.

Thrift. See Saving and thrift

Through a glass darkly. Bell, R. E.

Through a glass, darkly. Richards, S.

Through Naches Pass. Emmons, D. G.

Thunder God. Sakanishi, S. tr.

Thunder on Sycamore Street. Rose, R.

The thunderbolt. Pinero, A. W.

Thurber, James
    A Thurber carnival (condensation)
    In The Best plays of 1959-1960

Thurber, James, and Nugent, Elliott
    The male animal
    Comedy. English professor in sports-conscious midwestern college finds academic life complicated by visit of wife's former beau, a football player. 3 acts 4 scenes 8m 5w 1 interior
    In Kronenberger, L. ed. Cavalcade of comedy

A Thurber carnival. Thurber, J.

Thurston, Muriel B.
    Room for Mary
    The Warren family uses Christmas Day to show hospitality to a refugee mother and child. 1 act 6w 1 interior
    In Kamerman, S. E. ed. Blue-ribbon plays for girls

Tiberius, Emperor of Rome
    Jonson, B. Sejanus, his fall

Tick-tock. Very, A.

The ticket-of-leave man. Taylor, T.

The ticklish acrobat. Hivnor, R.

Tidal waves
    c Tennant, K. Hamaguchi Gohei

The tidings brought to Mary. Claudel, P.

Tiger at the gates. Giraudoux, J.

Tiger in the wood. Carpenter, F.

Tiger Lily. Emery, C.

Tiger on his toes. Rogers, A. B.

Tigers
    Chorpenning, C. B. Rama and the tigers

Tile stoves. See Stoves, Earthenware

Tilford, Haden
    Miss Dill from Dippyville. Bakers Plays 1953 93p (Baker's Edition of plays)
    Farce. When he is on the verge of marrying dean's pretty daughter, college professor's former wife arrives to complicate his life. 3 acts 4 scenes 3m 4w 1 interior

Time
    c Curtis, P. D. The hours on strike
    c Hark, M. and McQueen, N. Johnnie jump up
    c Jackson, M. R. Meet Father Time
    c Miller, H. L. Trouble in Tick-Tock Town
    c Spamer, C. Little boy's clock
    c Very, A. Doctor Time's office
    c Very, A. Tick-tock
    c Woolsey, J. and Sechrist, E. H. Days and days

A time for love. Simpson, G. H.

Time limit. Denker, H. and Berkey, R.

The time machine. Martens, A. C.

A time of minor miracles. Blacklock, J.

The time of the cuckoo. Laurents, A.

The time of your life. Saroyan, W.

Time out for Christmas. Fisher, A.

Time out for dreams. Armer, A. and Grauman, W. E.

Time out for Ginger. Alexander, R.

Time remembered. Anouilh, J.

Time the sad jester. Shirley, R.

Time to go. O'Casey, S.

Timeless second. Armer, A. and Grauman, W. E.

Timpany, Frederick P.
    The storm at sea. Humphries 1956 171p music
    Drama about man who is retiring from the American Presidency, and his hopes for his country. 3 acts 9 scenes Large mixed cast 4 interiors 2 exteriors

Timur the Great
    Marlowe, C. Tamburlaine the Great

The tinder box. Dillon, F.

The tiniest Christmas tree. Martens, A. C.

Tinker? Tailor? Soldier? Stafford, K.

The tinker's wedding. Synge, J. M.

Tinville, Antoine Fouquier- See Fouquier-Tinville, Antoine

The tiny closet. Inge, W.

'Tis pity she's a whore. Ford, J.

Totentanz. Schloss, M. F.

Totheroh, Dan

c Master Will. French 1957 42p
　Imaginary events in Shakespeare's childhood. The Strolling Players come to town and young Will defends them against the jokes of his playmates. 1 act 4 scenes 2m 1w 14b 2g extras 3 exteriors

c The stolen prince
　Fantasy. A prince is stolen at birth and rescued by poor fisherman and wife. Set in China. 7m 2w 2b 1g extras no scenery
In Fenner, P. and Hughes, A. comps. Entrances and exits

The stolen prince (adaptation) See Bucci, M. Chain of jade

Totheroh, Dan, and Benét, Stephen Vincent

All that money can buy
　Moving picture play based on Benét's story: The Devil and Daniel Webster. According to legend Lawyer Webster rescues the soul of a New Hampshire farmer from the Devil. 5 parts 9m 3w
In Gassner, J. and Nichols, D. eds. Great film plays

Touch it light. Storey, R.

The **touch** of fear. Christie, D. and Christie, C.

A **touch** of marble. Potter, D. S.

A **touch** of the poet. O'Neill, E.

Tourneur, Cyril

The atheist's tragedy; or, The honest man's revenge
　Jacobean tragedy. An atheist devises a complicated scheme to steal his brother's fortune. Verse play. 5 acts 21 scenes 10m 4w extras 9 interiors 4 exteriors
In Webster, J. and Tourneur, C. Four plays

The revenger's tragedy
　Jacobean tragedy. Murder of a young man's sweetheart by the old duke who has failed to seduce her creates a web of hatred and revenge. Verse play set in Italy. 5 acts 25 scenes 11m 3w extras 10 interiors 4 exteriors
In Webster, J. and Tourneur, C. Four plays

Towards zero. Christie, A.

Towie Castle. Bottomley, G.

A **town** is born. Piersel, W. G.

The **Towneley** cycle. See Towneley plays

Towneley mysteries. See Towneley plays

Towneley plays

The play of the shepherds; Wakefield cycle: secunda pastorum
　Bible. New Testament. Luke. 15th century English mystery play of Nativity which includes farce about a rogue who tried to rob the shepherds. Verse play in Middle English with modernized spelling. 5m 2w 1 setting
　Same as: The Wakefield Second shepherds' pageant
In Browne, E. M. ed. Religious drama, 2

The Wakefield Pageant of Herod the Great; The Towneley cycle
　Bible. New Testament. Matthew. 15th century English mystery play. King Herod I of Judea and Massacre of the Holy Innocents. Verse play in Middle English with modernized spelling. 3 scenes 7m 3w 2 interiors 1 exterior
In Everyman, and medieval miracle plays

The Wakefield Second shepherds' pageant; The Towneley cycle
　Same as: The play of the shepherds; Wakefield cycle: secunda pastorum
In Everyman, and medieval miracle plays

The **toymakers'** pledge. Hoggan, M. H.

Toynbee, Arnold Joseph
Buttle, M. Toynbee in Elysium

Toynbee in Elysium. Buttle, M.

Toys

c Atherton, M. Jack-in-the-box
c Chitty, A. W. I. Any old toys
　Fenwick, R. Toys and science
c Fisher, A. Time out for Christmas
c Goulding, D. J. Mr Bunch's toys
c Miller, H. L. The teddy bear hero
c Milne, A. A. Winnie-the-Pooh
　Ratcliffe, D. U. The smuggling hob
c Spamer, C. The playroom

Toys and science. Fenwick, R.

Toys in the attic. Hellman, L.

Trade-unions
　Adler, R. and Ross, J. The pajama game

Tragedy
　Aeschylus. Prometheus bound
　Alfred, W. Agamemnon
　Anderson, M. Bad seed
　Anderson, M. Elizabeth the Queen
　Anderson, M. Lost in the stars
　Anderson, M. Winterset
　Andreev, L. He who gets slapped
　Anouilh, J. Antigone
　Anouilh, J. The ermine
　Ansky, S. The Dybbuk
　Arblay, Madame d'. Edwy and Elgiva
　Armer, A. and Grauman, W. E. Sure as fate
　Arnold, J. W. The sheriff
　Barker, J. N. Superstition
　Beaumont, F. and Fletcher, J. The maid's tragedy
　Belasco, D. Madame Butterfly
　Benavente, J. La Malquerida [The passion flower]
　Bird, R. M. The broker of Bogota
　Boker, G. H. Francesca da Rimini
　Boucicault, D. The octoroon
　Broughton, J. Summer fury
　Büchner, G. Woyzeck
　Campion, C. Wayward women
　Camus, A. Caligula
　Camus, A. The misunderstanding
　Chapman, G. Bussy D'Ambois
　Chekhov, A. The sea gull
　Claudel, P. Break of noon
　Cocteau, J. The infernal machine
　Congreve, W. The mourning bride
　Conrad, J. One day more
　Corneille, P. Othon
　Corneille, P. Sertorius
　Corneille, P. Suréna
　Cox, W. N. The Scuffletown outlaws
　Coxe, L. O. and Chapman, R. Billy Budd
　Daviot, G. Barnharrow
　Daviot, G. Reckoning
　Delderfield, R. F. The Mayerling affair
　Deval, J. Tonight in Samarkand
Dryden, J. All for love

Tragedy—*Continued*

Dryden, J. and Lee, N. The Duke of Guise
Dryden, J. and Lee, N. Oedipus
Dunlap, W. André
Eaton, C. E. Sea psalm
Ervine, St J. John Ferguson
Ford, J. The broken heart
Ford, J. Five plays
Ford, J. The lover's melancholy
Ford, J. Love's sacrifice
Ford, J. Perkin Warbeck
Ford, J. 'Tis pity she's a whore
García Lorca, F. Blood wedding
García Lorca, F. The house of Bernarda Alba
García Lorca, F. Yerma
Genet, J. The maids
George, M. Symphonie pastorale
Giraudoux, J. Electra
Giraudoux, J. Judith
Godfrey, T. The Prince of Parthia
Goethe, J. W. von. Egmont
Goethe, J. W. von. Faust, part 1
Goethe, J. W. von. Torquato Tasso
Goethe, J. W. von. The Urfaust
Green, J. South
Greene, G. The living room
Grillparzer, F. The Jewess of Toledo
Grillparzer, F. Medea
Grillparzer, F. Sappho
Hauptmann, G. The rats
Hayes, A. The girl on the Via Flaminia
Hebbel, F. Maria Magdalena
Heijermans, H. The Good Hope
Hellman, L. The children's hour
Hellman, L. Watch on the Rhine
Herman, G. An echo of wings
Horne, K. A. This dark world and wide
Howells, W. D. Yorick's love
Howells, W. D. and Poel, W. A foregone conclusion
Hughes, E. W. The wishful taw
Hughes, R. The sisters' tragedy
Ibsen, H. Ghosts
Ibsen, H. Hedda Gabler
Ibsen, H. The master builder
Ibsen, H. Rosmersholm
Ibsen, H. The wild duck
Jonson, B. Sejanus, his fall
Kaiser, G. From morn to midnight
Kingsley, S. Darkness at noon
Komai, F. Cry, the beloved country
Kwanze, M. Aya no tsuzumi
Kwanze, M. J. Sumidagawa
Lee, N. Caesar Borgia
Lee, N. Constantine the Great
Lee, N. Gloriana
Lee, N. Lucius Junius Brutus
Lee, N. The massacre of Paris
Lee, N. Mithridates, King of Pontus
Lee, N. The rival queens
Lee, N. Sophonisba
Lee, N. Theodosius
Lee, N. The tragedy of Nero, Emperour of Rome
Lee, N. The works of Nathaniel Lee (13 plays)
Lessing. Emilia Galotti

Levin, R. Tragedy: plays, theory, and criticism (5 plays)
Lewis, L. The bells
Love, C. R. Proof of a man
McIlwraith, A. K. ed. Five Stuart tragedies (5 plays)
McLaughlin, M. L. The mind's construction
Maeterlinck, M. Pelléas and Mélisande
Marlowe, C. Edward the Second
Marlowe, C. The Jew of Malta
Marlowe, C. Lust's dominion
Marlowe, C. Tamburlaine the Great
Marlowe, C. The tragical history of Doctor Faustus
Massinger, P. The Roman actor
Massinger, P. and Dekker, T. The virgin martyr
Middleton, T. and Rowley, W. The changeling
Miller, A. All my sons
Miller, A. Death of a salesman
Miller, A. A view from the bridge
Mishima, Y. The damask drum
Nash, N. R. See the jaguar
O'Casey, S. Juno and the paycock
O'Casey, S. The plough and the stars
O'Casey, S. Red roses for me
O'Casey, S. The shadow of a gunman
O'Casey, S. Three plays
O'Conor, J. The iron harp
Odets, C. Golden boy
Oldfield, M. Please communicate
Olfson, L. Hamlet
Olfson, L. Julius Caesar
Olfson, L. King Lear
Olfson, L. Macbeth
Olfson, L. Romeo and Juliet
Oliver, W. I. The stallion
O'Neill, E. "Abortion"
O'Neill, E. Anna Christie
O'Neill, E. Beyond the horizon
O'Neill, E. Desire under the elms
O'Neill, E. The Emperor Jones
O'Neill, E. The hairy ape
O'Neill, E. Homecoming
O'Neill, E. Long day's journey into night
O'Neill, E. A moon for the misbegotten
Otway, T. Venice preserved
Parker, K. T. Within the family
Pirandello, L. "Henry IV"
Racine, J. Andromache
Racine, J. Berenice
Racine, J. Britannicus
Racine, J. Phaedra
Rice, E. L. Street scene
Robinson, C. R. The white dove
Rojas, F. de. The Celestina
Rowley, S. The noble Spanish soldier
Rowley, W. and others. The witch of Edmonton
Sartre, J. P. Dirty hands
Schiller, F. von. Don Carlos
Schiller, F. von. Intrigue and love
Schiller, F. von. Mary Stuart
Schnitzler, A. Light-o'-love
Schulberg, B. and Breit, H. The disenchanted
Seidelhuber, G. The lavender kite
Shakespeare, W. Othello

Treasure-trove
c Hulme-Beaman, S. B. The cruise of the
  "Toytown Belle"
  Mills, O. In the soot
  Murray, J. When the hurlyburly's done
  Olfson, L. The Count of Monte Cristo
  York, M. A. Treasure Island

Tree, Jonathan
  The fisherman
    Television play. Farcical fantasy. Jonah,
    a fisherman, tries to get a criminal into
    heaven. 4m 1w extras
  In The Best short plays, 1957

The **tree.** McMartin, E. L.

The **tree** of hearts. Miller, H. L.

The **tree** witch. Viereck, P.

Treece, Henry
  Carnival king. Faber 1955 118p
    Intrigue and treachery among powerful
    nobles surrounding the throne, ends with
    the murder of Edward II in 14th cen-
    tury Britain. 3 acts 13 scenes 18m 3w
    7 interiors 2 exteriors

Trees
c Fisher, A. On strike
c Goulding, D. J. Pagan magic
c Hark, M. and McQueen, N. A day for
  trees
c Miller, H. L. Right of adoption
c Newman, D. In honor of trees
c Spamer, C. The plight of the tree
c Spamer, C. Sammy Bushytail
c Spamer, C. Why the evergreen trees
  never lose their branches
c Very, A. The trees at school

The **trees** at school. Very, A.

Trelawny of the Wells. Pinero, A. W.

The **trial.** Crean, R. J.

Trial and error. Horne, K.

The **trial** before Pilate. Phillips, J. B.

Trial by jury. See Jury

The **trial** of Mr Newall. Curtis, P. D.

The **trial** of Poznan. Boretz, A.

Trials
  Brecht, B. The Caucasian chalk circle
  Crean, R. J. The trial
  Fields, J. and Chodorov, J. The Ponder
    heart
  Ginnes, A. S. and Wallach, I. Drink to
    me only
  Herald, H.; Herczeg, G. and Raine, N. R.
    The life of Emile Zola
  Houston, N. According to law
  Kanin, F. and Kanin, M. Rashomon
  Lawrence, J. and Lee, R. E. Inherit the
    wind
  Levitt, S. The Andersonville trial
  Manheim, M. Comedy of roses
  Miller, A. The crucible
  Raiden, E. Mr Jefferson's Burr
  Rattigan, T. The Winslow boy
  Rice, E. The winner
c Ryan, M. A. Litterbugs on trial
  Saroyan, W. The slaughter of the in-
    nocents
  Schevill, J. The bloody tenet
  Sergel, K. The remarkable incident at
    Carson Corners

c Weinberger, R. I. The whole tooth
  See also Courts-martial and courts of
  inquiry; Mock trials

Trials (Murder)
  Boretz, A. The trial of Poznan
  Christie, A. Witness for the prosecution
  Ford, R. Requiem for a nun
  Hui-lan-ki. The story of the circle of
    chalk
  Levin, M. Compulsion
  McMahon, L. E. The people versus Max-
    ine Lowe
  Reach, J. You, the jury
  Rose, R. Twelve angry men
  Williams, T. The purification

Trials (Robbery)
  Shaw, B. The shewing-up of Blanco Pos-
    net

Trick, Ormal B.
  Beneath this spire. Bakers Plays 1960
    17p
    A woman who turns old church into
    antique shop has dream in which she
    sees how much it meant to people in the
    past. Background music. 1 act 3m 9w
    choir 1 interior
  The divine miracle. Bakers Plays 1954
    15p
    Easter drama. Blind man and a woman
    who have both known suffering meet by
    chance in a church where they find hope
    through faith. 1 act 2m 4w 1 interior
  The frontier. Bakers Plays 1959 16p
    (Baker's Royalty plays)
    A couple try to cross border between
    two nations to freedom. 1 act 3m 1w 1
    interior

The **tridget** of Greva. Lardner, R.

Trifles. Glaspell, S.

Trigger, Edward
  The roaring twenties. French 1955 100p
    Comedy. After wandering brother an-
    nounces he is going to make his home
    with his sister's family, mysterious
    things happen. 3 acts 4 scenes 6m 8w
    1 interior

Trinidad
                    Festivals
  Kocher, E. Karma

A **trip** abroad. Labiche, E. and Martin, E.

The **trip** to Bountiful. Foote, H.

A **trip** to Scarborough. Sheridan, R. B.

Trippy answers the phone. O'Brien, R.

The **triumph** of the egg. Anderson, S.

The **triumph** of the egg. O'Neil, R.

Troia-nova triumphans. Dekker, T.

The **Trojan** women. Euripides

Trollope, Anthony
  Barchester Towers (dramatization) See
  Draper, J. Barchester Towers

Trollope, Frances (Milton)
  Wembley South Kenton Afternoon
  Townswomen's Guild, Drama Section.
  The sacred den

Trouble at "The Blue Lantern." Burgess, C. V.

Trouble in Tick-Tock Town. Miller, H. L.

True blue and trusted. Anderson, R. A.
  and Sweeney, R. L.

A **true** hero. Howells, W. D.

Truth
  Pirandello, L. Right you are

Truth is for the Birds. Neuenburg, E.

Truthfulness and falsehood
Kay, I. Giveaway
c Miller, M. Pinocchio
Mortimer, J. Call me a liar
Neuenburg, E. Truth is for the Birds
Osborne, S. If you ask me—
Reach, J. Open house

Try it again. Priestley, J. B.

Try! Try! O'Hara, F.

Trying to take things quietly. Sutherland, D.

Tsunemasa. Kwanze, M.

Tudor, Owen
Sisson, R. A. The queen and the Welshman

The **tulip** garden. Spamer, C.

Tully, John
Tony. Deane 1955 20p ("Deane's" Ser. of plays)
A few years after air pilot is supposedly killed in accident, his "widow" hears that he is living with his mother, and goes to nvestigate. 1 act 1m 3w 1 interior

Tumarin, Boris, and Sydow, Jack
Dostoyevsky's The brothers Karamazov. Dramatists 1958 93p illus
Based on the novel by Fyodor Dostoevsky. Complex crime story centering around three Russian brothers and probing questions of good vs. evil, guilt vs. innocence, and religion vs. atheism. 3 acts 21m 5w 1 setting

Tumpane, John D.
The gift of Tenyin. Dramatic 1956 36p illus
Christmas play. Japanese Emperor's daughter gives him gift which displeases him: a play about an Emperor (Christ) who will be the greatest one on earth. 1 act 2m 6w 1 interior

Tune in on terror. Tobias, J.

The **tunnel** of love. Fields, J. and De Vries, P.

Tunnel of Love. Richards, S.

Tunney, Kieran, and Synge, John
God and Kate Murphy (condensation)
In Broadway's best, 1959

Turgenev, Ivan
The bachelor; adapted by Miles Malleson. [Acting ed] French (London) 1953 60p illus
Dramatization by Miles Malleson of the novel about unsuccessful attempts of a kindly middle aged bachelor to marry his ward well, only for them both to realize in the end that they love each other. Set in St Petersburg in 1850. 3 acts 7m 3w 2 interiors

A month in the country; adapted into English by Emlyn Williams. French 1957 110p
Emotional conflicts among group of people at a wealthy landowner's house. Russia, 19th century. 2 acts 6 scenes 9m 5w 1 interior 1 exterior
—Same
In Gassner, J. ed. Twenty best European plays on the American stage
—Same; tr. from the Russian by Constance Garnett
In Turgenev, I. Three famous plays

A poor gentleman; tr. from the Russian by Constance Garnett
Comedy. Pensioner on young woman's estate reveals strange facts concerning her paternity. Set in 19th century Russia. 2 acts 10m 3w 2 interiors
In Turgenev, I. Three famous plays

A provincial lady; tr. from the Russian by Constance Garnett
Romantic comedy. Woman renews a flirtation with influential count in order to secure important position for her husband. Set in 19th century Russia. 1 act 5m 2w 1 interior
In Turgenev, I. Three famous plays

Turkey for all. Howard, V.

Turkey turns the tables. Miller, H. L.

Turn any stone. Allen, M.

Turn my face toward the east. Schulman, S. H.

Turn of the century. Gurney, A. R.

The **turn** of the screw. Vidal, G.

Turnbull, Agnes Sligh
Gown of glory (dramatization) See Phillips, I. Gown of glory

Turning the tables. Fisher, A. and Rabe, O.

Turning the tables. Miller, H. L.

Tuson, Neil
Moon rocket. Longmans 1955 39p illus
Set in 1985. It is thirty minutes until take-off for Hermes, first man-carrying rocket to the moon. Trouble begins when fanatical staff member takes command. 1 act 9m extras 1 interior

Tuttle, Ruth
c Spring facts and fancies
Based on the Mother Goose rhyme: Little Bo-Peep. When Bo-Peep goes to hunt her sheep she learns about all the birds and flowers that come in the spring. 2 acts Large mixed cast 1 exterior
In Birdsall, R. ed. Creative plays for every school month

Twain, Mark
Adventures of Huckleberry Finn (radio adaptation) See DuBois, G. Huckleberry Finn
The adventures of Tom Sawyer (radio adaptation) See Olfson, L. The adventures of Tom Sawyer
A Connecticut Yankee in King Arthur's court (radio adaptation) See Olfson, L. A Connecticut Yankee in King Arthur's court
A double barrelled detective story (dramatization) See St. Clair, R. Mark Twain's A double barrelled detective story
The prince and the pauper (radio adaptation) See Newman, D. The prince and the pauper
Pudd'nhead Wilson (dramatization) See Chadwicke, A. Pudd'nhead Wilson

'Twas such a night. Nichols, J.

'Twas the night before Christmas. Emurian, E. K.

Twelve angry men. Rose, R.

The **twelve** months. Very, A.

21 good neighbors. Clark, S. G.

27 wagons full of cotton. Williams, T.

Twilight crane. Kinoshita, J.

The **twin-rivals.** Farquhar, G.

Twins
　　Manning, H. Seeing double
　　Shakespeare, W. Twelfth night
　　Tobias, J. The crazy mixed-up Kidds
Two black sheep. Last, J.
Two dates for tonight. McCoy, P. S.
Two dozen red roses. Benedetti, A. de
The **two** executioners. Arrabal
Two for the seesaw. Gibson, W.
Two have dreamed. Orth, R.
Two in the balcony. Taggart, T.
Two of everything. Thomas, B.
Two of us. Verity, E. and Last, J.
Two roses. Albery, J.
Two sides of darkness. Procunier, E. R.
Two too many. Lantz, J. E. and Lantz, R. C.
The **two** woodcarvers. Ilian, C.
Two's company. Perry, M.
Tydeman, Richard
　　Duet with dowagers. Pitman (London) 1953 31p
　　　　Romantic comedy set in late 19th century England. At annual flower show, eligible bachelor, disguised as gardener, tries to avoid meeting the Dowager Countess his sister has selected as his bride. 1 act 3m 4w 1b 1 exterior
Tyler, Royall
　　The contrast
　　　　Post Revolutionary War satire. Contrast is between British sophisticated ideas of America versus unlettered but sincere homespun colonists. 5 acts 10 scenes 5m 4w extras 4 interiors 1 exterior
　　In Downer, A. S. ed. American drama
　　In Quinn, A. H. ed. Representative American plays
Tyll Ulenspiegel's merry pranks (dramatization) See Jagendorf, M. Merry Tyll
Tyranny. See Despotism
Tyson, Alec
　　Millie, the beautiful working girl; or, Pursued by a monstrous villain! Bakers Plays 1957 31p illus
　　　　Comedy melodrama. Villain attempts to force penniless servant girl to steal her employer's fortune. 3m 3w 1 interior
Tyson, Ruth Harriss
c The life of Lincoln
　　　　Pantomime. Narrator describes highlights of Abraham Lincoln's life. Background music. 6m 5w 1b 1g extras 3 interiors 3 exteriors
　　In Birdsall, R. ed. Creative plays for every school month

U

Ubu Roi. Jarry, A.
The **ugly** duckling. Milne, A. A.
Ukai. Enami, S.
Ullman, Samuel S.
　　A democratic emperor. Pan American Dramatic Press 1954 13p
　　　　Pedro II, Emperor of Brazil's part in abolishing slavery and educating youth of his country in 1871. 5m 2w 1 interior

El **gallo** (The rooster) Pan American Dramatic Press 1953 15p
　　　The natives of Central American village gather at dawn to make enough noise to awaken the sun until they find it easier getting rooster to do it. 3 scenes 4m 2w 1 exterior
Princess of the snows (Popocatepetl and Ixtaccihuatl) Pan American Dramatic Press 1953 16p
　　　Mexican legend about two volcanoes overlooking Mexico City: Popocatepetl and Ixtaccihuatl. 4 scenes 6m 2w 1 exterior
The **reward.** Pan American Dramatic Press 1953 14p
　　　A governor takes time to defend two Indians who have been accused of stealing. Set in Latin American locality during colonial times. 2 scenes 8m 2w 1 interior
The **youth,** Bolivar. Pan American Dramatic Press 1954 13p
　　　When Spanish visitors came to his family in Venezuela in 1791, Simón Bolívar, a boy of eight, began to understand tyranny of Spain over Latin American people. 1m 2w 2b 1 interior
Ulysses. See Odysseus
Ulysses in nighttown. See Barkentin, M. James Joyce's Ulysses in nighttown
Uncertain joy. Hastings, C.
Uncle Sam. Emurian, E. K.
Uncle Vanya. Chekhov, A. P.
Uncle Willie. Berns, J. and Elman, I.
Under Milk Wood. Thomas, D.
Under the monkey-bread tree. Ridge, A.
Under the skull and bones. Gow, R.
Under the sycamore tree. Spewack, S.
Underdeveloped areas
　　Swann, D. L. The crier calls
Underground movements (World War, 1939-1945) See Anti-Nazi movement
Underground railroad
　　Barbee, L. A letter to Lincoln
Unemployed
　　Swann, D. L. The crier calls
Unexpected guests. Fisher, A.
The **unexpected** guests. Howells, W. D.
An **unfair** exchange. Sakanishi, S. tr.
The **unicorn** from the stars. Yeats, W. B.
A **united** family. Prévert, J.
United Nations
　　Fisher, A. A play without a name
　　Fisher, A. and Rabe, O. The accident of birth
　　Fisher, A. and Rabe, O. Alice in Puzzle-land
　　Fisher, A. and Rabe, O. All in the UN
　　Fisher, A. and Rabe, O. Best bargain in the world
　　Fisher, A. and Rabe, O. Cavalcade of human rights
c Fisher, A. and Rabe, O. Empty bowls
　　Fisher, A. and Rabe, O. The get-together dinner
c Fisher, A. and Rabe, O. Getting in line
　　Fisher, A. and Rabe, O. Invasion from the stratosphere
　　Fisher, A. and Rabe, O. Let there be bread

United States—History—Civil War—*Cont.*

Kissen, F. Robert E. Lee: Virginia's valiant son
Levitt, S. The Andersonville trial
Vidal, G. Honor

History—Civil War—Peace

Van Doren, M. The last days of Lincoln

History—Civil War—Songs and music

Emurian, E. K. Battle hymn of the republic

History—Humor, caricatures, etc.

Emurian, E. K. Uncle Sam

History, Economic

See United States—Economic conditions

Industries

c Noon, E. F. and Daniels, E. S. Our own United States

Politics and government

Verneuil, L. Affairs of state

Politics and government—1815-1861

Chevigny, H. Daniel Webster
Emmons, D. G. A territory is born

Social life and customs

Brown, R. M. Freedom is our heritage
Lavery, E. American portrait
National Recreation Association. Children of the Americas
c Newman, D. The all-American tour

Social life and customs—Colonial period

c Field, R. Polly Patchwork
Howells, W. D. Priscilla

Social life and customs—1815-1861

Emmons, D. G. Joint occupation, joint celebration
Sergel, R. Blue stocking

Social life and customs—Civil War

Miller, H. L. Lacey's last garland
Miller, H. L. The pink parasol

Social life and customs—1865-1898

Buell, H. Fat woman picnic
Howells, W. D. A previous engagement
Wilder, T. The matchmaker

Social life and customs—20th century

Baker's Roaring twenties scrapbook
Howells, W. D. Self-sacrifice
Kent, W. Seventeen
Vidal, G. Visit to a small planet

Social life and customs—1919-1933

Mathers, A. Flapper girls

Universities and colleges

Bailey, A. H. The narrow man
Carmichael, F. Petey's choice
Conkling, L. Let 'em eat steak
Kazan, M. The egghead
Lindsay, H. and Crouse, R. Tall story
Protter, N. Follow the gleam
Richards, S. and Slocumb, P. The hobble-de-hoy
Tilford, H. Miss Dill from Dippyville

The **university** of the United States. Geiger, M.

The **unloved.** Morris, C.

Unmarried mothers

Delaney, S. A taste of honey

The **unquiet** cloister. Trease, G.

Unto thy doors. Coyle, R. W.

Unto us. Waldrop, C. L. M.

The **upholsterer.** Murphy, A.

Upholstery trade

Murphy, A. The upholsterer

Ups and downs. Murray, J.

Upson, William Hazlett

Love and Alexander Botts. Dramatic 1953 36p illus
> Romantic comedy based on author's short story. Alexander Botts, Sales Manager of the Earthworm Tractor Company, helps his secretary choose the "right man." 1 act 4m 2w 1 interior

Upstairs and downstairs. McMaster, A.

The **Urfaust.** Goethe

Ustinov, Peter

The love of four colonels. Dramatists 1953 76p illus
> Supernatural fantasy. Four officers of Allied Military Administration in Germany act out their dreams of romantic love in four short plays satirizing an 18th century social comedy, an American gangster film, a Chekhov drama, and a Shakespearean interlude. Background music. 2 acts 4 scenes 7m 2w 7 interiors
> Also published in trade edition

The love of four colonels (condensation)
In The Best plays of 1952-1953
In Theatre, 1953

Romanoff and Juliet. Random House 1958 110p illus
> Romantic comedy. In small European country the son of Russian ambassador falls in love with daughter of American ambassador. 3 acts 9m 4w 1 interior

Romanoff and Juliet (condensation)
In Broadway's best, 1958

V

Vacation in the city. Flavelle, I. B.

Vacations

Carmichael, F. Luxury cruise
c Flavelle, I. B. Vacation in the city
Hark, M. and McQueen, N. The homecoming

Vagabonds. See Rogues and vagabonds

Vagrants. See Tramps

Valency, Maurice

The Apollo of Bellac (adaptation) See Giraudoux, J. The Apollo of Bellac
Madwoman of Chaillot (adaptation) See Giraudoux, J. Madwoman of Chaillot
A supplement to Cook's voyage (adaptation) See Giraudoux, J. The virtuous island
The visit (adaptation) See Duerrenmatt, F. The visit

Valentine box. Asbrand, K.

The **valentine** box. Howard, V.

A **valentine** for Grandma. Asbrand, K.

Valentine from Mars. Atwell, R. and Virden, H.

Valentine sale. Very, A.

The **Valentine** shop
>   Story book people come to earth at midnight on St Valentine's Eve. 1 act Unidentified cast 12 characters 1 interior
>
>   *In* 'Round the year plays for the grades

Valentines
c Fisher, A. New hearts for old
c Hark, M. and McQueen, N. Cupid's post office
    Howard, V. The valentine box
c Martens, A. C. Who sent the comic valentine?
    Miller, H. L. Heart throbs
c Newman, D. The stolen heart
c Very, A. Valentine sale

Valentine's Day
    Abstance, P. and Abstance, L. The valiant Valentine
c Asbrand, K. Let's be valentines
c Asbrand, K. Valentine box
    Asbrand, K. A valentine for Grandma
c Atwell, R. and Virden, H. Valentine from Mars
c Diffin, L. T. The court of hearts
c Fisher, A. Hearts, tarts, and valentines
c Fisher, A. New hearts for old
c Hark, M. and McQueen, N. Cupies and hearts
    Hark, M. and McQueen, N. To my valentine
c Martens, A. C. Who sent the comic valentine?
    Miller, H. L. Be my "walentine"
c Miller, H. L. Crosspatch and Cupid
c Miller, H. L. The shower of hearts
    Miller, H. L. The tree of hearts
c Newman, D. Somebody's valentine
c Newman, D. The stolen heart
c Spamer, C. Humpty Heart
c Spamer, C. Valentine's party
c The Valentine shop
c Very, A. Valentine sale
c Very, A. and Brown, M. Saint Valentine's surprise
c Woolsey, J. and Sechrist, E. H. The Queen of Hearts' party

Valentine's party. Spamer, C.

Valerius. Daviot, G.

The **valiant** Valentine. Abstance, P. and Abstance, L.

Valley Forge was never like this. Howard, V.

Vanbrugh, Sir John
    The confederacy
>   Comedy of manners. Pawned necklace brings to head intrigue involving debt-ridden wife of parsimonious husband. 5 acts 9 scenes 6m 6w 3 interiors 1 exterior
>
>   *In* Kronenberger, L. ed. Cavalcade of comedy

    The relapse; or, Virtue in danger
>   Late Restoration comedy of manners. Satire on English society in the 1690's. Plot deals with marital fidelity. Includes a masque. 5 acts 20 scenes 10m 7w extras 9 interiors 2 exteriors
>
>   *In* Restoration plays

Vandenburgh, Mildred
c A "globester" trip
>   Two boys learn about many countries on their airplane trip around world. 3m 1w 1b extras 2 interiors 1 exterior
>
>   *In* Birdsall, R. ed. Creative plays for every school month

Van Doren, Mark
    The last days of Lincoln. Hill & Wang 1959 152p (A Spotlight dramabook)
>   Last few weeks before Lincoln's death when paramount issue facing the Union was terms of the surrender—should they be harsh or generous. 6 scenes 24m 4w extras 3 interiors 1 exterior

Van Druten, John
    I am a camera. Dramatists 1955 90p front
>   Adapted from "Berlin stories" by Christopher Isherwood. Four young people in Germany about 1930 including Isherwood and an actress with easy morals. 3 acts 5 scenes 3m 4w 1 interior

    —Same
>   *In* Best American plays; 4th ser.
>
>   *In* Gaver, J. ed. Critics' choice

    I remember mama
>   Matriarch guides the fortunes of immigrant Norwegian family, using the security of a mythical bank account. 2 acts 2 scenes 8m 11w 1b 2g extras 1 interior
>
>   *In* Sper, F. ed. Living American plays

    I've got sixpence. Dramatists 1953 99p front
>   Tangled lives of several cynical and desperate people who through faith find a meaning in life. 2 acts 3m 4w 1 interior

    The voice of the turtle
>   Comedy. Actress breaks wartime date with sergeant and turns him over to girl friend who falls in love with him. 3 acts 6 scenes 1m 2w 1 interior
>
>   *In* Kronenberger, L. ed. Cavalcade of comedy

Van Dyke, Henry
    The story of the Other Wise Man (dramatization) See Sergel, R. Henry Van Dyke's The Other Wise Man

The **vanishing** Easter egg. Miller, H. L.

Van Kampen, Barbara
    Dutch treat. Deane 1955 26p ("Deane's" Ser. of plays)
>   Domestic comedy. Dutch family, complete with national costume arrives to visit rather flashy American family in New York City. 1 act 4m 4w 1 interior

Vaudeville
    Styne, J. Gypsy
>   *See also* Music-halls (Variety-theaters, cabarets, etc.)

Vega, Lope de
    Fuente ovejuna; tr. by J. G. Underhill
>   Revolt of Spanish peasants against ruler of their village during reign of Ferdinand V. Includes songs. 3 acts 13 scenes 18m 4w 1b extras 8 interiors 4 exteriors
>
>   *In* Downer, A. S. ed. The art of the play

Vega Carpio, Lope de
    The star of Seville. Jarman Press 1955 172p
>   The king of Seville commands a secret murder to gain a beautiful woman. The action describes penalties extracted by code of honor, and revenge at king's court. 3 acts 49 scenes 12m 3w 8 interiors 3 exteriors

Vegetable gardening
c Zahn, M. How does your garden grow?

Vegetables
c Spamer, C. The little green worker
The **velvet** plain. Willis, C.

Vendetta
Bottomley, G. Ardvorlich's wife
Olfson, L. Romeo and Juliet

Venereal diseases
Ibsen, H. Ghosts

Venezuela
Ullman, S. S. The youth, Bolivar

Vengeance. See Revenge; Vendetta

Venice
Jonson, B. Volpone
Otway, T. Venice preserved
Zweig, S. Volpone

Venice preserved. Otway, T.

Venus observed. Fry, C.

Vera. Wilde, O.

Verdi, Giuseppe
Neuenburg, E. Strange victory

Verga, Giovanni
Cavalleria rusticana
    Tragedy. Sicilian who deserted girl he
    betrayed is killed in duel with husband
    of his former sweetheart. 9 scenes 3m 6w
    1 setting
    In Bentley, E. ed. The modern theatre
    v 1

Verity, Elma, and Allen, Vera
Appointment in Eden. Deane 1956 65p
illus ("Deane's" Ser. of plays)
    British lady helps solve some personal
    problems for women who work on her
    farm, thereby discovering that one of
    them is mother of her grandson, a war
    baby. 3 acts 6 scenes 11w 1b 1 interior

Verity, Elma, and Last, Jack
Cove Cottage. Deane 1954 30p ("Deane's"
Ser. of plays)
    Three old ladies run flourishing smug-
    gling business from their cottage until
    a lady customs officer visits them. 1 act
    4w 1 interior
Two of us. Deane 1955 26p ("Deane's"
Ser. of plays)
    Domestic comedy. Newly married couple
    have told each other that they have
    no relatives. Then the mother of each
    appears. 1 act 1m 4w 1 interior

Verne, Jules
Around the world in eighty days (dramatization) See Howard, V. Around the
world—by way of America
Around the world in eighty days (radio
adaptation) See Olfson, L. Around the
world in eighty days

Verner, Gerald
Meet Mr Callaghan. [French's Acting ed]
French (London) 1953 74p illus
    Dramatization of novel, The urgent
    hangman, by Peter Cheyney. Murder
    mystery in which a girl's eccentric
    stepfather is found murdered and prime
    suspects are her fiance's three shady
    brothers. 2 acts 7 scenes 9m 3w 1 interior

Verneuil, Louis
Affairs of state
    Romantic comedy set in Washington,
    D.C. Retired senator, still active in
    politics, promotes romance between his
    niece and rising young statesman. 3 acts
    5 scenes 4m 2w 1 interior
    In Plays of the year v8

The **Versailles** impromptu. Molière, J. B. P.

Verse drama. See Plays in verse

Verse play. See Plays in verse

Very, Alice
c Abe Lincoln goes to school
    Abraham Lincoln begs his parents to
    let him go to school to learn to read
    and write. 3 scenes 2m 3w 3b 1g 1 interior
    In Very, A. Round-the-year plays for
    children
c The callers
    Verse play about two children who find
    some bears for playmates when the
    mother bear is away. 2 scenes 1w 2b 2g
    In Very, A. Round-the-year plays for
    children
c The cat who wanted to ride on a broom
    Verse play for Halloween about how an
    airman takes a little cat for a ride. 2b
    2g extras 1 interior
    In Very, A. Round-the-year plays for
    children
c The cock and the fox
    Adaptation of story by Chaucer about
    the sly fox who raids the hen house.
    1w 3b 3g extras 1 exterior
    In Very, A. Round-the-year plays for
    children
c The dancing children
    Verse play dramatizing Indian legend
    about the seven Indian children who
    became stars in the sky. 2m 6w 8b 1g
    1 exterior
    In Very, A. Round-the-year plays for
    children
c Doctor Time's office
    Short verse play about the hours, min-
    utes, days, and months of a year and
    the arrival of New Year. 2m 15b 14g
    1 interior
    In Very, A. Round-the-year plays for
    children
c Everywhere Christmas
    Children from all over the world celebrate
    Christmas. 3m 12b 9g extras 1 interior
    In Very, A. Round-the-year plays for
    children
c The fairy circus
    Two little girls and their cats visit the
    fairies' circus in Fairyland. 3 scenes 5b
    10g extras 1 interior 1 exterior
    In Very, A. Round-the-year plays for
    children
c The flower garden
    The sun has a difficult time waking up
    the flowers in spring. Verse play. 11 un-
    identified characters extras 1 exterior
    In Very, A. Round-the-year plays for
    children
c General George
    Young George Washington goes off to
    school with his cousin to learn to be a
    surveyor. 1m 1w 8b 1g 1 interior
    In Very, A. Round-the-year plays for
    children
c Getting ready for winter
    Verse play about how all the animals
    and birds prepare for winter. 5b 4g
    extras 1 exterior
    In Very, A. Round-the-year plays for
    children
c Gifts for young Abe
    Verse play about how the spirits of
    Indians visit Abraham Lincoln's parents
    to tell them that he will be a great
    man. 3 scenes 9m 8w 1 interior
    In Very, A. Round-the-year plays for
    children

Very, Alice—*Continued*

c A golden bell for mother
Some kittens and mice can't decide on a
Mother's Day present. Verse play.
3 scenes 14 unidentified characters 3 interiors

In Very, A. Round-the-year plays for
children

c Jack and the beanstalk
Dramatization in verse of fairy tale
about beanstalk that leads up to the
giant's house. 3 scenes 2m 2w 2b 2g
extras 1 interior 1 exterior

In Very, A. Round-the-year plays for
children

c John Grumlie
A farmer thinks his wife's life is easy
until he stays at home with the children.
1m 1w 1b 1g extras 1 interior

In Very, A. Round-the-year plays for
children

c Jonathan's Thanksgiving
How a Pilgrim boy and his family celebrated first Thanksgiving. 2 scenes 3m
3w 2b 3g 1 interior

In Very, A. Round-the-year plays for
children

c King Winter
King Winter's grip on the world is
broken by the trees, birds and flowers
of spring. Large mixed cast 1 exterior

In Very, A. Round-the-year plays for
children

c The little fir tree
Adaptation of fairy tale by Hans Christian Andersen about fir tree that becomes a Christmas tree. 3 scenes 8b 7g
extras 1 interior 2 exteriors

In Very, A. Round-the-year plays for
children

c Little friends
Short verse play about the different
animals that live in the forest. 6b 5g
1 exterior

In Very, A. Round-the-year plays for
children

c The Mayflower
Several little girls discover why Fairy
May loves the Mayflower best. Verse
play. 16g extras 1 exterior

In Very, A. Round-the-year plays for
children

c Old Lady Witch's party
Jack and Jill and the Old Witch give a
party for Halloween. 12b 6g 1 interior

In Very, A. Round-the-year plays for
children

c The old woman and her pig
Dramatization of Mother Goose rhyme
about old woman who can't get her pig
over the fence. 1w extras 1 exterior

In Very, A. Round-the-year plays for
children

c Planting time
When crows steal seeds from their spring
garden, several children make a scarecrow. Verse play. 3b 3g extras 1 exterior

In Very, A. Round-the-year plays for
children

Puss-in-Boots
Fairy tale about adventures of Puss-in-
Boots and his master, Tom. 8b 1g extras

In Very, A. Round-the-year plays for
children

c The return of Columbus
Columbus' son Diego and children of
Ferdinand and Isabella eagerly await
Columbus' return from new world. 5m
1w 2b 3g extras 1 interior

In Very, A. Round-the-year plays for
children

c The shoemaker and the elves
Adaptation in verse of fairy tale by
Jacob and William Grimm about elves
who help shoemaker while he is asleep.
1m 1w 1b 1g extras 1 interior

In Very, A. Round-the-year plays for
children

c The snow girl
Peasant couple make a little snow girl
who comes to life, but when spring
comes she begins to melt. 3 scenes 1m
1w 1b 2g 1 interior

In Very, A. Round-the-year plays for
children

c Thanksgiving Eve
Short verse play about how children
help the mice and kittens celebrate
Thanksgiving. 5b 5g 1 interior

In Very, A. Round-the-year plays for
children

c Thanksgiving night
Judy has a nightmare with all the items
on her Thanksgiving dinner as characters. 1 act 1w 25g 1 interior

In Kamerman, S. E. ed. Blue-ribbon
plays for girls

c Three little kittens go to school
Short verse play for small children about
kittens and puppies in the schoolroom.
6g 3b 1 interior

In Very, A. Round-the-year plays for
children

c The three sillies
Verse play about man who comes to
court a farmer's daughter and finds
everyone there doing silly things. 5m 3w
extras 1 interior

In Very, A. Round-the-year plays for
children

c Tick-tock
Verse play. When two little girls don't
do anything on time, the clock teaches
them how. 1 act 1w 8g 1 interior

In Kamerman, S. E. ed. Blue-ribbon
plays for girls

c Too much turkey
Little boy who ate too much for Thanksgiving dinner falls asleep and is visited
by the turkey, pies and puddings. 1w
13b 13g 1 interior

In Very, A. Round-the-year plays for
children

c The trees at school
The trees tell what they do and what
they look like. Verse play. 11 unidentified characters 1 exterior

In Very, A. Round-the-year plays for
children

c The twelve months
At end of the year each of the twelve
months tell what they do during the
year. 15b 3g extras 1 interior

In Very, A. Round-the-year plays for
children

c Valentine sale
Verse play. Each of the different Valentines hopes that someone will buy it.
1b 1g extras 1 interior

In Very, A. Round-the-year plays for
children

Very, Alice, and Brown, Martha
c Saint Valentine's surprise
　　Poor little girl gets the three things
　　she wishes for most on Valentine's Day.
　　2 scenes 1m 1w 3g 1 interior
　　In Very, A. Round-the-year plays for
　　children

A **very** cold night. Winnie, D. J.

A **very** special baby. Aurthur, R. A.

Veterans
　　Kocher, E. A medal for Julien
　　Miller, H. L. A hero's homecoming
　　Roche, D. My wife's lodger
　　Suerken, E. H. John Crown's legacy

Veteran's Day
　　Fisher, A. and Rabe, O. Stage set for
　　Veterans' Day
c Jeffrey, H. K. and Walls, D. A. Veterans
　　Day
c Miller, H. L. The forgotten hero
　　Miller, H. L. A hero's homecoming
c Newman, D. The keys to peace

Veterans Day. Jeffrey, H. K. and Walls,
　　D. A.

Vice. See Degeneration

Vicky gets the vote. Miller, H. L.

Victoria, Queen of Great Britain
　　Housman, L. "A good lesson!"
　　Robinson, R. Princess Victoria's twelfth
　　birthday
　　Spamer, C. Queen Victoria

Vidal, Gore
　　Barn burning
　　　Television play. Adapted from short
　　　story by William Faulkner. Vengeful
　　　sharecropper, who deliberately burns
　　　barns is found out by his small son's dis-
　　　closure. 3m 1w 1b extras
　　　In Vidal, G. Visit to a small planet, and
　　　other television plays
　　The best man. Little 1960 168p illus
　　　American political melodrama. Two can-
　　　didates vie for their party's presidential
　　　nomination. 3 acts 7 scenes 8m 3w extras
　　　2 interiors
　　The best man (condensation)
　　　In The Best plays of 1959-1960
　　　In Broadway's best, 1960
　　Dark possession
　　　Television play. A schizophrenic woman
　　　who has killed her husband sends her-
　　　self poison pen letters. 3m 4w
　　　In Vidal, G. Visit to a small planet, and
　　　other television plays
　　The death of Billy the Kid
　　　Television play. Another version of the
　　　legend in which Pat Garrett kills his
　　　friend Billy. 9m 1w extras
　　　In Vidal, G. Visit to a small planet, and
　　　other television plays
　　Honor
　　　Television play. Self-made Southern
　　　man's romanticized sense of honor and
　　　Civil War opportunism cause him the
　　　loss of his sons. 7m 3w
　　　In Burack, A. S. ed. Television plays
　　　for writers
　　A sense of justice
　　　Television play. A supposedly disinter-
　　　ested man seeking justice fails to kill
　　　a ruthess politician when he himself
　　　realizes that he does have an interest
　　　in life. 5m 2w extras
　　　In Vidal, G. Visit to a small planet, and
　　　other television plays

Smoke
　　Television play. Adaptation of story by
　　William Faulkner. After an evil father
　　is mysteriously murdered, his sons fall
　　out with one another over inheritance
　　of land. 6m extras
　　In Vidal, G. Visit to a small planet, and
　　other television plays
Summer pavilion
　　Television play. Decadent New Orleans
　　family renews itself through the mar-
　　riage of a daughter to a Northerner.
　　3m 4w extras
　　In Vidal, G. Visit to a small planet, and
　　other television plays
The turn of the screw
　　Television play based on novel by Henry
　　James. Evil spirits of former servants
　　haunt two children who are protected
　　by a loyal governess. 1m 2w 1b 1g
　　In Vidal, G. Visit to a small planet, and
　　other television plays
Visit to a small planet. Dramatists 1959
　　77p illus
　　Fantasy satirizing contemporary Ameri-
　　can scene as viewed by visitor from
　　another planet. 3 acts 4 scenes 8m 2w
　　1 setting
　　Trade edition published by Little
—Same
　　In Vidal, G. ed. Best television plays
　　In Vidal, G. Visit to a small planet, and
　　other television plays
Visit to a small planet (condensation)
　　In The Best plays of 1956-1957
　　In Broadway's best, 1957

Vienna
Social life and customs
　　Schnitzler, A. Merry-go-round
　　Schnitzler, A. La ronde

Viereck, Peter
　　The tree witch. Scribner 1960 126p
　　　Fantasy. Shows impact of the dryad's
　　　world of creative imagination on our
　　　world of civic adjustment and mech-
　　　anized progress. 3 acts 3m 4w 3 in-
　　　teriors 1 exterior

A **view** from the bridge. Miller, A.

Vigil. Williams, E.

Villiers, George, and others
　　The rehearsal
　　　Restoration comedy. Playwright-poet in-
　　　vites two friends to rehearsal of his
　　　new play which is satire on heroic
　　　drama. 5 acts 14 scenes 17m 7w extras
　　　1 setting
　　　In Restoration plays

Villiers, George, 2d duke of Buckingham.
　　See Villiers, George

Vinci, Leonardo da. See Leonardo da Vinci

Vining, Donald
　　The one that got away
　　　Comedy. Middle-aged woman dreams of
　　　romantic places and the man she might
　　　have married. 1 act 3m 5w 1 interior
　　　In Powers, V. E. ed. Plays for players,
　　　and a guide to play production

Violett, Ellen, and Blake, Lisbeth
　　Brewsie and Willie
　　　Television play adapted from novel by
　　　Gertrude Stein. American soldiers, in a
　　　Paris café, talk about life, women, going
　　　home, etc. 6m 2w
　　　In The Best short plays of 1954-1955
　　　In The Best short plays, 1957

Virden, Helen
Let's have a covered dish. Eldridge 1958
9p (Eldridge Novelties)
Comedy. Pantomime. One woman's favorite recipe is a failure at the ladies' club's covered dish supper. 1 act 8w 1 interior
See also Atwell, R. jt. auth.
The **virgin** martyr. Massinger, P. and Dekker, T.
Virgin Mary. See Mary, Virgin
The **virtues** of Thelma. Burgess, C. V.
The **virtuous** island. Giraudoux, J.

Visions
Mary Francis, Sister. Smallest of all
Yeats, W. B. The unicorn from the stars
The **visit.** Duerrenmatt, F.
A **visit** from Washington. Martens, A. C.
Visit of Johnny Appleseed. Hark, M. and McQueen, N.
Visit to a small planet. Vidal, G.
A **visit** to Goldilocks. Miller, H. L.
The **visit** to the moon. Spamer, C.
A **visit** with the firemen. Crawford, A.
Visiting celebrity. Crane, B.
The **visitor** (Lassie) Robinson, T.
Visitor to Mount Vernon. Miller, H. L.

Vitamins
c Fisher, A. Full of vim
c Fisher, A. Hidden meanings
c Fisher, A. Leave it to Gramps
c Fisher, A. The magic formula
c Fisher, A. Murder in the kitchen
c Hark, M. and McQueen, N. Nursery rhyme diet
c Hark, M. and McQueen, N. Pleasant dreams
Vocation. See Occupations
Vocation (in religious orders, congregations, etc.)
James, H. Guy Domville
Rigney, W. J. Joe Tracy
The **voice** of liberty. Fisher, A.
Voice of the machines. Parker, K. T.
The **voice** of the turtle. Van Druten, J.
The **voice** that failed. Preston, E. E.
Voices. Fisher, A.
Voices of desire. Procunier, E. R.

Volcanoes
c Spamer, C. Inside the earth
Vollmer, Lula
Sun-up
Illiterate mountain woman has trouble comprehending the law. 3 acts 4 scenes 7m 2w 1 interior
In Quinn, A. H. ed. Representative American plays
Volpone. Jonson, B.
Volpone. Zweig, S.
Voltaire
Candide (dramatization) See Bernstein, L. Candide
Von Schiller, Friedrich. See Schiller, Friedrich von
Von Wallenstein, Albrecht Wenzel Eusebius. See Wallenstein, Albrecht Wenzel Eusebius von, Herzog zu Friedland

Vooght, Cherry
Come live with me. English Theatre 1955
32p illus (Guild lib)
Young woman and husband turn down good offer for their farm since it would mean depriving their impoverished albeit querulous mothers of a home. 1 act 8w 1 interior
Nineteen, The Beacon. English Theatre
1954 31p (Guild lib)
Lady Nelson and Lady Byron, both wives of famous and unfaithful men meet and discuss their similar, yet dissimilar lives. 1 act 6w 1 interior
Voss, B. Margaret
Our greatest gift. Bakers Plays 1957 23p
Christmas worship program traces Christmas story through the founding of the early church up to present. 26m 2w 2b 1g extras 1 interior
Vote for your hero. Hark, M. and McQueen, N.

Voting
Fisher, A. The voice of liberty
c Fisher, A. Voting Day
Fisher, A. and Rabe, O. May the best man win
c Porter, H. W. Election Day
See also Elections
Voting Day. Fisher, A.
The **voyage.** Kramer, C.

Voyages and travels
Alexander, R. Holiday for lovers
Voyages around the world
Howard, V. Around the world—by way of America
Olfson, L. Around the world in eighty days
Voysey, Michael
The amorous goldfish
Television play. A man who commits murder in order to inherit some money is eventually betrayed by his wife. 3m 9w
In British Broadcasting Corporation. The television playwright
The **vultures**; tr. from the French by Freeman Tilden. Becque, H.

W

Wagers
Randall, J. Look who's laughing
Wagner, Natalie
He is come! The Messiah! Eldridge 1953
13p (Eldridge Christmas entertainments)
Christmas pantomime with carols. Story of the Nativity from the Annunciation to Mary until the angels announce birth of Christ to the shepherds. 1 act 7m 1w extras choir 3 interiors
The **wait.** Brenner, M.
Wait and see. Miller, H. L.
Wait for morning, child. Lewis, G.
Waiters
Frost, R. Small hotel
Waiting for Gillian. Millar, R.
Waiting for Godot. Beckett, S.
The **waiting** place. Mosel, T.
Wake up, darling. Gottlieb, A.

Wake up, Santa Claus! Miller, H. L.

Wakefield Cycle
Secunda pastorum (adaptation) See Malcolmson, A. The shepherds' play

Wakefield mysteries. See Towneley plays

The **Wakefield** Pageant of Herod the Great. Towneley plays

The **Wakefield** Second shepherds' pageant. Towneley plays

Waldau, Roy S.
A cabin by the lake
Romantic comedy. Young woman succeeds in bringing suitor, overanxious about his financial affairs, to the point of proposing. 1m 1w 1 interior
In The Best short plays of 1954-1955

Walden, William
Tomboy wonder. French 1958 76p illus
When teen-ager takes medicine for her cold she suddenly becomes a female Sampson and attracts local football star. 3 acts 3m 4w 1 interior

Waldrop, Claracy L. M.
Unto us. Broadman 1957 15p illus
Nativity Christmas pageant with music. 7 tableaux 10m 2w 1 exterior

Wales
Thomas, D. Under Milk Wood

History
Lewis, S. Siwan

Social life and customs
Spring, H. Jinny Morgan
Stephens, P. J. The changeling

Walk in the light. Bailey, H. F.

Walker, Mildred
The southwest corner (dramatization) See Holm, J. C. The southwest corner

Walker, Stuart
c The seven gifts
Christmas pantomime. Many different kinds of people bring gifts to the queen. Background music. 10 scenes 16m 7w 3b 3g 1 interior
In National Recreation Association. Plays, pageants and ceremonials for the Christmas season

The **wall.** Powers, V.

Wallace, Nancy
Speed, bonnie boat. Row 1954 28p illus
Scottish girl shrewdly persuades unwilling navigator to sail his ship from Skye to her wedding appointment on mainland. 1 act 4m 3w 1 interior
—Same
In Powers, V. E. ed. Plays for players, and a guide to play production

Wallach, Ira
Phoenix '55. French 1957 39p
Five comic sketches satirizing everything from the do-it-yourself craze to the winner of a $50,000 contest. 5 acts 12m 12w 5 interiors
See also Ginnes, A. S. jt. auth.

Wallenstein, Albrecht Wenzel Eusebius von, Herzog zu Friedland
Schiller, F. von. Wallenstein

Wallenstein. Schiller, F. von

Wallenstein's camp. See Schiller, F. von. Wallenstein

Wallerstein, James S.
c Bobby and the time machine
Instead of doing his homework, a boy invents a time machine and is carried a million years into the future. 3 scenes 6m 4w 3b 4g 2 interiors
In Wallerstein, J. S. Adventure

c The cactus wildcat. French 1954 34p illus
Comedy. Girl and boy, warned that by pretending too hard things can come true, defy caution and are changed into a gypsy princess and a bandit of the Old West, respectively. 1 act 3 scenes 8m 4w extras 1 interior 1 exterior
—Same
In Wallerstein, J. S. Adventure

c Johnny Aladdin
Ten year old juvenile delinquent, fleeing from truant officer, finds a magic lamp in the city junkpile, wishes himself eventually into political action. 2 acts 12 scenes 10m 6w 6b 6g 1 interior 1 exterior
In Wallerstein, J. S. Adventure

c Raymond and the monster
Fairy tale. Village children rescue themselves and their elders from tyrannical ruler who invented a monster tax-collector. 2 acts 17 scenes 8m 8w 4b 4g 1 interior 1 exterior
In Wallerstein, J. S. Adventure

c Windigo Island
Mystery develops at summer camp when some boys and girls confront a spooky hermit. 1m 1w 6b 6g extras 1 interior 1 exterior
In Wallerstein, J. S. Adventure

Wallop, Douglass
The year the Yankees lost the pennant (dramatization) See Adler, R. and Ross, J. Damn Yankees

Walls, David A. See Jeffrey, H. K. jt. auth.

The **walls** of Jericho. Spamer, C.

Walsh, Norman
Let there be farce
Two women and a thief in the slums. 1 act 1m 2w 1 exterior
In The Best short plays of 1955-1956

Walsh, R. G.
Greg's gruesome gadgets. Eldridge 1958 74p (Eldridge 3-act playscripts)
A domestic comedy. Eccentric family and boy inventor almost ruin father's aspirations for mayoralty, but manage to capture two crooks. 3 acts 8m 10w 1 interior

The **waltz** of the toreadors. Anouilh, J.

The **wanderers.** Owen, V.

War
Aristophanes. Lysistrata
Brabazon, F. The bridge
Brecht, B. Mother Courage
Cullinan, G. The Republic of the Blind
Giraudoux, J. Tiger at the gates
Kleist, H. von. The Prince of Homburg
Miller, H. L. The judge's diary
O'Neill, E. "The sniper"
Procunier, E. R. Two sides of darkness
Smith, L. B. and Barrett, J. S. The house is still
Stallings, L. and Anderson, M. What price glory?
Zeiger, H. Five days

War and civilization
Betti, U. The burnt flower-bed
c Fisher, A. Caves of the earth

War and civilization—*Continued*
Fisher, A. Three and the dragon
Kops, B. The dream of Peter Mann
Whiting, J. Marching song
The **war** of the worlds. Duffield, B.
Warbeck, Perkin
Ford, J. Perkin Warbeck
Wardall, Clarice
Fog on the bay
Mystery. Girl and fiancé become involved in diamond theft but girl's hobby rescues them from law. 1 act 2 scenes 4m 1w extras 1 exterior
In Smith, B. and others, eds. A treasury of non-royalty one-act plays
Ware, Harlan. See Ware, L. jt. auth.
Ware, Leon, and Ware, Harlan
The man on a stick. [Rewritten and rev.] French 1957 100p
Domestic comedy. Man's second wife and her mother make life miserable for him and his daughter until a friend intervenes. 3 acts 6 scenes 4m 4w 1b 1 interior
Wareham, Ruth Cole
The miracle at Nain. Bakers Plays 1959 13p
Five women seek Jesus, each thinking she has the right reason. 5w 1 exterior
The **warm** peninsula. Masteroff, J.
Warm Wednesday. Delmar, V.
Warner, Lillian H.
c The thankful Pilgrims
Sketch of the first Thanksgiving with Thanksgiving songs and an Indian dance. 1m 1w extras 1 interior
In Birdsall, R. ed. Creative plays for every school month
Warnick, Clay
Heidi; book by William Friedberg and Neil Simon; lyrics by Carolyn Leigh; music by Clay Warnick. [Acting ed] French 1959 58p illus
A musical based on the novel by Johanna Spyri about a little girl and her life high in the Swiss Alps, on a farm with her grandfather. Music available separately. 6m 6w extras 2 interiors 3 exteriors
Warnick, Clay, and Pahl, Mel
Adventures of Marco Polo. Book by William Friedberg and Neil Simon; music by Clay Warnick and Mel Pahl; lyrics by Edgar Eager. [Acting ed] French 1959 58p illus
Musical fantasy. Story of Marco Polo's travels to court of Kublai Khan in the 13th century. Music available separately. 3 acts 17m 7w extras 2 interiors 7 exteriors
Warren, Robert Penn
All the king's men. Random House 1960 134p
Based on author's Pulitzer prize novel. Erstwhile grassroots politician uses unethical methods of political machine to get complete control of state, only to be killed by one of many he betrayed. 14m 4w extras 1 interior
Wash Carver's mouse trap. Koch, F.
Washington, George, President U.S.
Asbrand, K. Liberty Belle
c Carlson, B. W. Altogether! Heave!
Clark, B. H. Fires at Valley Forge
c Delva, J. G. The rise of a nation

Fisher, A. Washington marches on
c Graham, M. S. The promotion
Hark, M. and McQueen, N. First in peace
Kissen, F. George Washington: father of his country
c Martens, A. C. A visit from Washington
c Miller, H. L. Visitor to Mount Vernon
Miller, H. L. The Washington shilling
c Miller, H. L. Washington's leading lady
c Newman, D. Washington's gold button
c Spamer, C. The cherry tree
c Very, A. General George
Washington, Martha (Dandridge) Custis
Spamer, C. Martha Washington
Washington (State)
Emmons, D. G. Statehood for Washington
Washington marches on. Fisher, A.
The **Washington** shilling. Miller, H. L.
Washington's Birthday
Hark, M. and McQueen, N. Bake a cherry pie
c Hark, M. and McQueen, N. Enter George Washington
c Hark, M. and McQueen, N. In honor of Washington
Howard, V. Valley Forge was never like this
c Martens, A. C. A visit from Washington
Miller, H. L. February frenzy
Miller, H. L. Jump for George
c Mooar, C. H. Washington's Birthday
c Newman, D. The new Washington
c Newman, D. Washington's gold button
c Very, A. General George
c Woolsey, J. and Sechrist, E. H. George Washington serves his country
c Woolsey, J. and Sechrist, E. H. My honest friend
Washington's Birthday. Mooar, C. H.
Washington's gold button. Newman, D.
Washington's leading lady. Miller, H. L.
Washout. Spamer, C.
The **wasps.** Aristophanes
Wasserman, Dale, and Balch, Jack
Elisha and the long knives
Television play about an orphan boy on the Santa Fe Trail in the 1840's. 8m 1w
In Settel, I. ed. Top TV shows of the year, 1954-1955
Watch on the Rhine. Hellman, L.
Watch your step. Wolfe, B. S.
The **watcher** of the road. Morris, T. B.
Watermelon. Anderson, D.
Watkins, Dudley
c Frost-Bite and the eleven Fidgets. Paxton 1959 20p
Children's parody of Snow White fairy tale. 6 scenes 20m 1w 1g 2 interiors
Watkyn, Arthur
For better, for worse
Domestic comedy. Trials and tribulations of young couple in the first few months of marriage. 3 acts 5 scenes 7m 5w 2 interiors
In Plays of the year v8

Watkyn, Arthur—_Continued_
Not in the book
Comedy. Respectable Englishman with a family is approached by blackmailer who knows all about his irresponsible youth in South America. 3 acts 4 scenes 7m 1w 1 interior
_In_ Plays of the year v17

Wattron, Frank
Strawberry Circle. French 1954 89p illus
Romantic comedy. A man and his motherless children are affected in various ways by an old Indian legend concerning the meaning of wild strawberries. 3 acts 4m 4w 1b 1g 1 interior

Wattron, Frank, and Walker, Paul
Burner of the Bugle. French 1955 90p illus
Farce. Members of the staff of college paper find themselves involved in plot of the sports editor to conceal absence of a missing student. 3 acts 8m 11w 1 interior

Waugh, James R.
The burglar alarm
Comedy. A man, his family and the police get involved in a mix-up about some money he reported stolen from his office. 2 scenes 4m 2w 1 interior
_In_ Waugh, J. R. First short plays
The ebony box
Comedy. An ebony box containing money disappears and reappears several times creating a mixup of suspicion and accusations in a family. 3 scenes 3m 3w 1 interior
_In_ Waugh, J. R. Second short plays
Food for thought
Farce. Old man plays joke on two tramps. 4 scenes 5m 1 interior 1 exterior
_In_ Waugh, J. R. First short plays
The missing formula
Comedy. When absent-minded professor invents valuable formula his son outwits two thieves who try to steal it. 2 scenes 8m 2w 1 interior
_In_ Waugh, J. R. First short plays
The silver idol
Romantic comedy. Young sailor returns home with a silver idol which mysteriously grants wishes. 3 scenes 4m 2w 1 interior
_In_ Waugh, J. R. Second short plays
Spots of bother
Farce. The king sees mysterious spots before his eyes and all of his doctors cannot find the cause. 3 scenes 9m 2w 1 interior
_In_ Waugh, J. R. Second short plays
The wise counsellor
Wise counsellor uses trick to save his king from two noblemen who wish to kill him. 3 scenes 7m extras 1 interior
_In_ Waugh, J. R. Second short plays

The **way** of the world. Congreve, W.

'**Way** out West. Frankel, B. S.

The **way** the ball bounces. Hackett, W.

The **way** the wind blows. Benfield, D.

The **way** to keep him. Murphy, A.

The **way** to the inn. Newman, D.

Way, way down east. Dias, E. J.

Ways and means. Coward, N. P.

The **wayward** saint. Carroll, P. V.

Wayward women. Campion, C.

We are tomorrow. Howard, P.

"**We** bring this child unto the Lord." Bailey, H. F.

We caught the torch. Wilcox, E. M.

We commit this body. Dace, W.

We were young that year. Harris, A.

Wealth
Albery, J. Two roses
Barry, P. Holiday
Behrman, S. N. End of summer
Bulwer-Lytton, E. Money
Duerrenmatt, F. The visit
Grundy, S. A pair of spectacles
Ibsen, H. The wild duck
McMullen, J. C. Son of Erin
Shaw, B. The millionairess
Tobias, J. Be happy? go wacky!

Weather
c Hurt, F. The weather imp
c Martens, A. C. Weather or not
c Miller, H. L. Hello, Mr Groundhog
c Miller, H. L. The weatherman on trial

The **weather** imp. Hurt, F.

The **weather** man. Spamer, C.

Weather or not. Martens, A. C.

The **weatherman** on trial. Miller, H. L.

Weaver, Virginia B.
The reign of Minnie Belle
Farce. Cotton farmers strike oil in East Texas and make big plans for future. 1 act 7m 5w 1b 1 exterior
_In_ Smith, B. and others, eds. A treasury of non-royalty one-act plays

The **weavers.** Hauptmann, G.

The **weaver's** son. Fisher, A.

Webb, Chase. See Smith, B. jt. auth.

Webber, C. E.
c The barber and the donkey. Longmans 1955 31p illus music (Plays for today)
Comedy. Caliph's barber tricks woodman out of his carved, wooden saddle and in turn is tricked into contract to share a donkey. 4 scenes 4m extras 2 interiors
Be good, sweet maid
Comfortable life of prosperous business man and his mistress is changed when he is obliged to take custody of his maladjusted teenage daughter. 3 acts 7m 3w 4 interiors 2 exteriors
_In_ Plays of the year v15

Webber, John
Air sea rescue
Radio play. British Coast-guard station uses radio telephone to effect rescue of men from shipwrecked vessel. 6m
_In_ Webber, J. Over-the-air plays
A brush with the enemy
Radio play. Farce. Vacuum cleaner salesman and a brush peddler call on a housewife at same time. 3m 1w
_In_ Webber, J. Over-the-air plays
Dial 999
Radio play. Comedy. Workmen in an English furniture factory mistake a lunch parcel for a time bomb. 8m
_In_ Webber, J. Over-the-air plays
Inspector Hart's experiment
Radio play. British police inspector uses helicopter making traffic reports to effect capture of bank robbers. 7m
_In_ Webber, J. Over-the-air plays
Lights on the coast
Radio play. British Coast-guard station cooperates with the police to apprehend smugglers. 8m
_In_ Webber, J. Over-the-air plays

Webster, Daniel
Benét, S. V. The Devil and Daniel Webster
Chevigny, H. Daniel Webster
Totheroh, D. and Benét, S. V. All that money can buy

Webster, John
The Duchess of Malfi; ed. by Vincent F. Hopper and Gerald B. Lahey; with a note on the staging by George L. Hersey. Illus. by Thomas Keogh. Barrons Educ. Ser. 1960 211p illus (Theatre classics for the modern reader)
Elizabethan tragedy of revenge. Brother's family pride and avarice versus sister's marriage to commoner. Set in 16th century Italy. 5 acts 20 scenes 14m 5w 11 interiors 2 exteriors
Trade edition edited by F. L. Lucas published by Macmillan (N Y)
Same as: The Duchess of Malfy
—Same
In McIlwraith, A. K. ed. Five Stuart tragedies
In Webster, J. and Tourneur, C. Four plays
The Duchess of Malfy
Same as: The Duchess of Malfi
In Morrell, J. M. ed. Four English tragedies of the 16th and 17th centuries
The white devil; ed. by F. L. Lucas. Macmillan (N Y) 1959 [c1958] 224p
Jacobean historical tragedy. Intrigue and revenge prevail when a duke and a noblewoman conspire to murder their respective spouses. Set in 16th century Italy. Verse play. 5 acts 16 scenes 19m 5w extras 6 interiors 3 exteriors
—Same; ed. by John Russell Brown. Harvard Univ. Press 1960 (The Revels plays) 205p
—Same; or, Vittoria Corombona; general ed: Eric Bentley
In Webster, J. and Tourneur, C. Four plays
See also Dekker, T. jt. auth.
Wedding bells for Clara? Bollans, G. E.
Wedding breakfast. Reeves, T.
Weddings
García Lorca, F. Blood wedding
Herman, G. A simple little affair
Hughes, E. W. The wishful taw
Labiche, E. and Marc-Michel. An Italian straw hat
McCullers, C. The member of the wedding
Sanders, B. L. What's cookin'?
Wedekind, Frank
The tenor; tr. from the German by André Tridon
An egotistical Norwegian tenor places his career above everything including the only woman who really loved him. 5m 3w 1 interior
In A Treasury of the theatre
The **week** before Christmas! Asbrand, K.
Wefer, Marion
This Thine house. New and rev. ed. Friendship Press 1954 47p
Young minister struggles to promote program of social work in an old church whose neighborhood has changed. 1 act 9m 2w 1g extras 1 interior

Wehner, Elisabeth
Man of arts
Comedy. Retired business man gives up his artistic hobbies and goes back to business. 1 act 3m 2w 1 interior
In Smith, B. and others, eds. A treasury of non-royalty one-act plays
Weidman, Jerome. See Bock, J. Fiorello!
Weil, Rudolf. See Magito, S. jt. auth.
Weinberger, Robert I.
c The whole tooth
Little boy goes on trial because he won't take care of his teeth, and all the vegetables, fresh air and his toothbrush act as witnesses against him. 5m extras 1 interior
In Birdsall, R. ed. Creative plays for every school month
Weinstock, David
Dawn will come. French 1955 24p
Allegory. Younger members of cave-dwelling society dare to explore outside world and report their findings, only to be expelled. 1 act 6 scenes 5m extras 1 interior 1 exterior
Weiss, Harold
A bolt from heaven. Dramatic 1954 16p illus
Based on the story by Z. J. Wheeler. Using his dictaphone, the minister foils robber who demands the money collected for children's hospital fund. 1 act 2m 2w 1 interior
Weiss, M. J.
The actor
Adolescent boy's desire to become actor is thwarted by family's lack of finance. 1 act 3 scenes 2m 2w 1g 1 interior
In Weiss, M. J. Guidance through drama
Debby's dilemma
Life in a woman's college presents dating problem for an over-protected student. 1 act 4 scenes 2m 5w 2 interiors 1 exterior
In Weiss, M. J. Guidance through drama
Greetings from . . .
Activities of adolescents during World War II, hinging on parent-son view of enlistments. 1 act 3 scenes 6m 4w 3 interiors
In Weiss, M. J. Guidance through drama
Her big crush
Problem of teen-age "going steady" custom presents itself to concerned family. 1 act 2m 3w 1b 1 interior
In Weiss, M. J. Guidance through drama
Money talks
Adolescent boys ponder problem of quitting school before graduation, to get job and independence. 1 act 3 scenes 5m 4w 2 interiors 1 exterior
In Weiss, M. J. Guidance through drama
Parents are people
Teen-age daughter neglects baby-sitting job with 9 year-old brother for a blind date. 1 act 2m 3w 2b 1 interior
In Weiss, M. J. Guidance through drama
Welch, Rae
Let's get out of here
Unwed teen-age elopers evade searchers. 1 act 3m 1w 1 interior
In The Best short plays of 1957-58
A **welcome** for mother. Casey, B. M.

The **well** of Dothan. Blazer, F.

The **well** of the saints. Synge, J. M.

Welles, Robert
The man of the house
    Farce. Timid husband of lady acrobat becomes boss of home when he dons lion tamer's costume. 1 act 2 scenes 7m 3w 1 interior
In Smith, B. and others, eds. A treasury of non-royalty one-act plays

Wells, H. G.
The war of the worlds (dramatization) See Duffield, B. The war of the worlds
War of the worlds (radio adaptation) See Koch, H. Invasion from Mars

Welsh dialect. See Dialect—Welsh

The **Welsh** embassador
    Comedy. 10th century England. Two brothers of King Athelstane. one disguised as soldier and the other as Welsh ambassador. join a court conspiracy to induce King to marry his contracted wife and make their son his heir. 5 acts 15 scenes 13m 2w 1 setting
In Dekker, T. The dramatic works of Thomas Dekker v4

Welty, Eudora
The Ponder heart (dramatization) See Fields, J. and Chodorov, J. The Ponder heart

Wembley South Kenton Afternoon Townswomen's Guild. Drama Section
The sacred den; a group play. National Union of Townswomen's Guilds 1953 22p
    Publisher's letter of acceptance of her first novel helps Fanny Trollope save home from the bailiffs. Set in early 19th century England. 1 act 2 scenes 6w 1 interior

Were you there? Applegarth, M. T.

Werfel, Franz
Jacobowsky and the colonel; in the adaptation by S. N. Behrman
    Comedy. Adventures of two Polish refugees, a wily civilian and a brave but pompous Army officer, as they make their escape from Paris to England in World War II. 3 acts 6 scenes 22m 5w 1b 2 interiors 2 exteriors
In Gassner, J. ed. Twenty best European plays on the American stage
Song of Bernadette (dramatization) See Duffield, B. Christmas at Lourdes

Werner, Sally
c Home, sweet home
    Two mice find out from the other barnyard animals that their old home in the barn was the best after all. 1 act Unidentified cast 7 characters 1 exterior
In Burack, A. S. ed. Four-star plays for boys

Werry, Wilfrid
Breakdown
    Man recovering from nervous breakdown finds he was framed for a theft he didn't commit. 1 act 3m 1w 1 interior
In Richards, S. ed. Canada on stage

Wesker, Arnold
Roots. Penguin 1959 76p music
    Problems of English farm laborers in a society that has no place for them. Set in Norfolk. Includes words and music of a song. 3 acts 4 scenes 5m 4w 3 interiors

Wesley, Charles
Emurian, E. K. Charles Wesley

Wesley, Samuel
Emurian, E. K. Famous families

West, Claudine. See Jennings, T. jt. auth.

West, Nathanael
Miss Lonelyhearts (dramatization) See Teichmann, H. Miss Lonelyhearts

The **West**
Abstance, P. and Abstance, L. Gold in the West
c Carlson, B. W. Jim Bridger and his eight-hour echo
Collins, D. Summer brings gifts
c Frankel, B. S. 'Way out West
Greth, Le R. E. The dancing ghost
Howard, V. The best of the Old West
McCaslin, N. Tall Bill and his big ideas
McMahon, L. E. Half-Pint Windom rides west
c Miller, H. L. The half-pint cowboy
Payton, D. He tried with his boots on
c Seiler, C. The clown out west
Taggart, T. Deadwood Dick
Taggart, T. The midnight ride of Tex O'Coco
Tarpley, V. and Tarpley, K. Golden river
c Wallerstein, J. S. The cactus wildcat
    See also Frontier and pioneer life— The West

West Indies
O'Neill, E. The Emperor Jones

West Side story. Bernstein, L.

Western dialect. See Dialect—Western

Western night. Finch, R. and Smith, B.

Westgate, Ted
Petticoat handicap. Eldridge 1953 35p illus (Eldridge Popular one-act playscripts)
    Comedy. Radio writer. snow bound in a small town. tries to get local help when his show is due on the air that night. 1 act 5 scenes 2m 4w extras 1 interior

Westward ho. Dekker, T. and Webster, J.

Wetmore, Alphonso
The pedlar. Univ. of Ky. Lib. Associates 1955 34p
    Facsimile of farce first produced in St Louis in 1821. On the Kentucky frontier, a Yankee pedlar, distrusted because of sharp practices. is found to have heart of gold. 3 acts 12 scenes 7m 3w 3 exteriors 6 interiors

Wetzel, Donald
A wreath and a curse (dramatization) See Anderson, R. All summer long

Wexford Rebellion, 1798. See Ireland—History—Rebellion of 1798

Wharton, Edith
Ethan Frome (dramatization) See Davis, O. and Davis, D. Ethan Frome

What do you see in the manger? Swanson, V. A.

What happened in Egypt. Fisher, A. and Rabe, O.

What happened in 1776? Knight, E. M.

What happened on Clutter Street. Fisher, A.

What happened to Billy? Woolsey, J. and Sechrist, E. H.

What hath God wrought. Blake, R.

What ho! Dias, E. J.

What ho for the open road. Addis, H.

What is a patriot. Fisher, A. and Rabe, O.
What is an American? Howard, V.
What is the church? Stricker, E. B.
What make? Bayliss, A. E. M.
What makes it tick? Miller, H. L.
What, no venison? Hark, M. and McQueen, N.
What price glory? Stallings, L. and Anderson, M.
What price murder? Grable, M.
What shall we tell Caroline? Mortimer, J.
What we must all come to. See Murphy, A. Three weeks after marriage
Whatever became of Lola Woods. Armer, A. and Grauman, W. E.
What's cookin? Sanders, B. L.
What's that tune? Lynch, P.
What's the matter with TV? Martens, A. C.
What's wrong with the girls. Seiler, C.
Whedon, John. See Hill, G. R. jt. auth.
Wheeler, Edward L. See Taggart, T. Deadwood Dick
Wheeler, Z. J.
A bolt from heaven (dramatization) See Weiss, H. A bolt from heaven
Wheels within wheels. Fisher, A. and Rabe, O.
When America was young. Asbrand, K.
When daddy comes home. Asbrand, K.
When do we eat? Hark, M. and McQueen, N.
When freedom was news. Fisher, A. and Rabe, O.
When Greek meets Greek. Sinclair, L.
When it's moonlight on Pike's Peak. Howard, V.
When mothers meet. Taggart, T.
When queens cook. Kent, M.
When someone is somebody. Pirandello, L.
When the fire dies. Maher, R.
When the hurlyburly's done. Murray, J.
When the little angel sang. George, L. D.
When we dead awaken. Ibsen, H.
Wherever she may roam. Graham, A.
Which of the nine? Olfson, L.
While the sun shines. Rattigan, T.
Whirlwind courtship. Dayton, M.
Whist
Murphy, A. Three weeks after marriage
White, George
Royal gambit (adaptation) See Gressieker, H. Royal gambit
White, Joan K.
The laughing cavalier. Deane 1955 22p ("Deane's" Ser. of plays)
Romantic comedy. Gay new maid in vicar's household helps reunite daughter, a war nurse, and one of her former patients. 1 act 2 scenes 5w 1 interior
White, Natalie E.
The billion dollar saint. Dramatists 1955 55p
Farce. Fantasy about a televised football game in which St Ignatius University's team, led by St Francis of Assisi, plays barefoot and with no uniforms, thereby evoking generous world reaction. 3 acts 4 scenes 16m extras 1 interior

Seven nuns at Las Vegas. Dramatists 1954 48p
Farce. Fantasy about how on a cold snowy day in Indiana, seven nuns find themselves transported, convent and all to Las Vegas, and about their effect on the gambling resort. 2 acts 3 scenes 2m 11w 1 interior
A white butterfly. Roepke, G.
The white carnation. Sherriff, R. C.
The white Christmas. Hare, W. B.
The white devil. Webster, J.
The white dove. Robinson, C. R.
The white sheep of the family. Peach, L. du G. and Hay, I.
The white widow. Bottomley, G.
Whiting, John
Marching song
Army officer in defeated country is tried by his countrymen because his humanitarian instincts once forced him to delay an attack. 3 acts 6m 2w 1 interior
In Ring up the curtain
Whitman, Marcus
Emmons, D. G. Answering the call
Whitman, Walt
National Recreation Association. I hear America singing!
Whitney, Eli
c McMillin, M. The young whittler
Whittington, Richard
c Arlett, V. I. Young Richard Whittington
The whiz bang minstrel show. Driscoll, R.
Who are we of the United States. National Recreation Association
Who is my neighbor? Kelsey, R. W.
Who is Sylvia? Rattigan, T.
"Who is this?" Schofield, J. A. and Joudry, R. C.
Who killed Cock Robin? Lynn, K. S.
Who sent the comic valentine? Martens, A. C.
Who stole third base? Martens, A. C.
Who was that lady I saw you with? Krasna, N.
Who will hold the giant? Blyton, E.
Who will kill the turkey? Spamer, C.
The whole tooth. Weinberger, R. I.
The whole truth. Mackie, P.
The Whore of Babylon. Dekker, T.
Who's for the divide? Emmons, D. G.
Who's old-fashioned? Hark, M. and McQueen, N.
Who's scared of ghosts? Hark, M. and McQueen, N.
Who's stronger? Carlson, B. W.
Who's that knocking on my door? Martens, A. C.
Who's who at the zoo. Miller, H. L.
Whosoever believeth. Corrigan, L.
Why she would not. Shaw, B.
Why the evergreen trees never lose their branches. Spamer, C.
Why the sleepy Dormouse. Fisher, A.
Widow of Charles Dickens. Holland, N.
Widowers' houses. Shaw, B.

Widows
Asbrand, K. Candle in the window
Barry, M. H. Come live in my house
Bennett, V. E. Shadows walk softly
Bollans, G. E. The crooked courtship
Foote, H. The trip to Bountiful
Fry, C. A phoenix too frequent
Hallowell, H. The widow's choice
Jerome, P. Goin' round the hoop
Johnson, P. No weeds for the widow
Lehar, F. The merry widow
Pilgrim, F. The skeleton at the party
Scholl, R. The golden axe

The **widow's** choice. Hallowell, H.

The **widow's** son. Spamer, C.

"A **wife** for a life." O'Neill, E.

The **wife** of Martin Guerre. Bergsma, W.

Wiggin, Kate Douglas
The Birds' Christmas Carol (dramatization) See Miller, H. L. The Birds' Christmas Carol

Wilcox, Ernine M.
c A midnight ride
In the early days of the Revolution, Paul Revere rides to warn his fellow patriots that the British are on their way. 3 scenes 7m 1 interior 1 exterior
In Birdsall, R. ed. Creative plays for every school month

c We caught the torch
For their Memorial Day program a group of students decide to do all the helpful things they can for everyone in their community. 7 scenes 1m 3w 5b 5g extras 3 interiors 3 exteriors
In Birdsall, R. ed. Creative plays for every school month

Wild, Jonathan
Mayer, E. J. Children of darkness

The **wild** duck. Ibsen, H.

Wild horses. Travers, B.

Wild strawberries. Bergman, I.

Wilde, Oscar
The birthday of the Infanta (dramatization) See Olfson, L. Infanta

The Duchess of Padua
Tragedy in verse. Set in 16th century Italy. The Duchess of Padua murders her husband but makes her young lover appear to be guilty of the crime. 5 acts 10m 2w extras 2 interiors 1 exterior
In Wilde, O. Plays

A Florentine tragedy
A fragment of a play, unfinished. Love, intrigue, and violent death in medieval Florence. 1 act 2m 1w 1 interior
In Cerf, B. and Cartmell, V. H. eds. 24 favorite one-act plays
In Wilde, O. Plays

An ideal husband
Social comedy. In 19th century England British government official's marriage as well as his career are threatened by schemes of a woman eager to regain her place in society. 4 acts 9m 6w 3 interiors
In Wilde, O. Plays

The importance of being Earnest. Dramatic 1956 72p
Satirical social comedy set in England in the 1890's. The theme is an attack on earnestness, in Victorian sense. After much confusion a young man discovers who he really is. 3 acts 5m 4w 2 interiors 1 exterior
—Same. Barrons Educ. Ser. 1959 148p illus (Theatre classics for the modern reader)
—*also*
In Heffner, H. The nature of drama
In Kronenberger, L. ed. Cavalcade of comedy
In A Treasury of the theatre
In Tucker, S. M. ed. Twenty-five modern plays
In Watson, E. B. ed. Contemporary drama: fifteen plays
In Wilde, O. Plays

The importance of being Earnest (radio adaptation) See Olfson, L. The importance of being Earnest

Infanta (dramatization) See Olfson, L. Infanta

Lady Windermere's fan; ed. by Vincent F. Hopper and Gerald B. Lahey; with a note on the staging by George L. Hersey; illus. by Fritz Kredel. Barrons Educ. Ser. 1960 160p illus (Theatre classics for the modern reader)
Comedy of manners. English 19th century aristocracy. Woman with a past returns and creates a flurry in society. 4 acts 4m 6w 3 interiors
—Same
In Wilde, O. Plays

La sainte courtisane; or, The woman covered with jewels
Courtesan from Alexandria becomes a Christian convert when she visits a godly hermit. 1 act 3m 1w 1 exterior
In Wilde, O. Plays

Salomé
Tragedy. Salomé dances for Herod Antipas and as her reward claims the head of John the Baptist. 1 act 11m 2w extras 1 interior
In Wilde, O. Plays

Vera; or, The Nihilists
In 19th century Russia Vera, a Nihilist, seeking revenge for her brother's death, plots to kill the Czar. 4 acts 5 scenes 17m 1w extras 4 interiors
In Wilde, O. Plays

A woman of no importance
Social comedy. Young Englishman's courtship of rich American orphan is complicated by the reappearance of his father after a twenty-five year absence. 4 acts 8m 7w 3 interiors 1 exterior
In Wilde, O. Plays

Wilde, Percival
Legend. Bakers Plays 1953 16p
Pantomime. A miracle occurs when aged nun, whose soul has recently ascended to heaven, is granted wish to return to earth to continue her work for good of mankind. Background music of the Berlioz "Requiem." 1 act 1m 8w 1 setting

Salt for savor. Bakers Plays 1953 20p
Fantasy. Effects of a leprechaun's theft of salt from the office cleaner's lunch box. 7m 1 interior
—Same
In The Best short plays of 1953-1954

Wilder, Thornton
The happy journey
  A mother successively organizes, remonstrates with, and encourages her family who are taking a trip to see a married daughter. 1 act 2m 2w 1b 1g 1 setting
  Same as: Happy journey to Trenton and Camden
  In Cerf, B. and Cartmell, V. H. eds. 24 favorite one-act plays

Happy journey to Trenton and Camden
  Same as: The happy journey
  In Cooper, C. W. Preface to drama
  In Watson, E. B. and Pressey, B. eds. Contemporary drama: eleven plays

The long Christmas dinner
  Fantasy. Family chronicle. 4m 5w 1 interior
  In Downer, A. S. ed. American drama

The matchmaker. French 1957 120p illus
  A revised version of The merchant of Yonkers, published 1939
  Romantic farce. In the 1880's a middle-aged miserly Yonkers merchant, eager to find a young wife, invokes aid of a family friend who decides to win him for herself. 4 acts 9m 7w 3 interiors 1 exterior

—Same
  In Best American plays; 4th ser.
  In Wilder, T. Three plays

The matchmaker (condensation)
  In Best plays of 1955-1956
  In Theatre, 1956

Our town. Harper 1957 103p
  Fantasy. New Hampshire village in the early 1900's. The dead show themselves more appreciative of the wonder of life than the living. 3 acts 15m 5w 2b 2g extras no scenery

—Same
  In A Treasury of the theatre
  In Wilder, T. Three plays

The skin of our teeth
  Allegorical fantasy. Man's struggle to survive natural disasters, wars, etc. from Adam and Eve to the present. 3 acts Large mixed cast 1 interior 1 exterior
  In Cubeta, P. M. ed. Modern drama for analysis. 1955 edition
  In Hewes, H. ed. Famous American plays of the 1940s
  In Watson, E. B. ed. Contemporary drama: fifteen plays
  In Wilder, T. Three plays

Wilderness Road. Green, P.

Wilk, Max
Cloud seven. Dramatists 1958 84p illus
  Domestic comedy. Executive gets fed up with humdrum suburban life. 3 acts 16 scenes 9m 8w 5 interiors

Will. See Brain-washing

Will and testament. Holland, N.

Will-O'-Wisp. Murray, J.

Will success spoil Rock Hunter? Axelrod, G.

Will the ladies please come to order. Gibson, M. N.

The **will** to win. Rodman, H.

William of Sens. See Guillaume de Sens

William Penn: brother to all men. Kissen, F.

William Tell. Schiller, F.

Williams, Charles
Grab and grace
  Modern morality play. Man's struggle to find faith. 1m extras
  In Halverson, M. ed. Religious drama, 3

The house by the stable
  Modern morality play for Christmas. Stresses God's love for man. 2m 1w extras 2 interiors
  In Halverson, M. ed. Religious drama, 3

Williams, Emlyn
Someone waiting. Dramatists 1956 93p illus
  Mystery. Adopted youth becomes involved in scheme against his parents to avenge the unjust execution of his best friend for murder. 3 acts 5 scenes 4m 4w 1 interior
Vigil
  Two men lost on a moor and held captive by an insane man plot their host's murder but his servant forestalls them. 3m 1 interior
  In The Second book of one-act plays

Williams, Hugh, and Williams, Margaret
Double yolk
  Two plays designed to be presented together as one play: By accident and With intent. The first tells of a man who kills another in a car accident. The second describes the life of the accident victim. 2 parts 6 scenes 4m 4w 2 interiors
  In Plays of the year v21

The grass is greener
  Romantic comedy. A lord and lady who have had to open their estate to tourists in order to pay the rent are visited by an American millionaire who falls in love with the lady. Set in England. 2 acts 4 scenes 3m 2w 1 interior
  In Plays of the year v19

The happy man
  Domestic comedy. When man's wife gives birth to their fourth child, his household becomes chaotic with antagonism between the nurse, governess and nursemaid. 2 acts 4 scenes 2m 4w 1 interior
  In Plays of the year v17

Plaintiff in a pretty hat
  Romantic comedy. When impoverished young earl decides he doesn't want to marry the career girl to whom he is engaged, she sues for breach of promise. 2 acts 4 scenes 3m 2w 1 interior
  In Plays of the year v15

Williams, Mona
Invitation to breakfast. Dramatic 1955 24p illus
  On a visit to seaside cottage of her mother's friend, a young woman decides to change fiancés. 1 act 1m 3w 1 setting

Williams, Norman
A battle of wits. French 1956 29p
  An offer of marriage from an old friend saves a young Chinese widow from becoming slave to her greedy mother-in-law. 1 act 4 scenes 5m 2w 1 setting

—Same
  In Williams, N. Worlds apart

Dreams
  Dying Negro woman worries about leaving her only son. 3m 3w 1 interior
  In Williams, N. Worlds apart

The king decides
  Clash between traditional aristocracy and world of today. 4m 2w 1 interior
  In Williams, N. Worlds apart

Williams, Norman—*Continued*

The mountain
> Self-centered movie actor pretends to be grief stricken at sudden death of woman to whom he was once married. 4m 1w extras 1 interior

In Williams, N. Worlds apart

Night of storm
> Portrays historical events dealing with Alexander the Great, Philip of Macedon, rivaling wives and generals, Greek and barbarian gods. Set in Macedonia in the 4th century B.C. 4m 2w extras

In Williams, N. Worlds apart

Protest
> Elderly Japanese woman kills herself in protest against her granddaughter's disbelief in traditional way of life. Set in Japan in 1900. 1m 3w 1 interior

In Williams, N. Worlds apart

Williams, Pete

Commencement. French 1954 81p illus
> Comedy. Life in a high school centering around the principal's office and the problems he faces. 3 acts 7 scenes 7m 7w 1 interior

Williams, Roger

Fisher, A. and Rabe, O. Apostle of freedom

Schevill, J. The bloody tenet

Williams, Tennessee

At liberty
> Tragedy. Sick, dissolute showgirl contemplates gloomy future in Mississippi. 1 act 2w 1 interior

In Smith, B. and others, eds. A treasury of non-royalty one-act plays

Auto-da-fé
> In revolt against the degeneracy of his section of New Orleans, fanatical man sets fire to his mother's home. 1 act 1m 1w 1 exterior

In Williams, T. 27 wagons full of cotton and other one-act plays

Baby doll. New Directions 1956 208p
> Script for the moving picture. December-June marriage in name only, and failure in business drives husband to commit arson. 13m 3w 1b

Battle of angels
> The author's original version of his tragedy. Orpheus descending. 3 acts 5 scenes 7m 7w extras 1 interior

In Williams, T. Orpheus descending, with Battle of angels

Camino Real. New Directions 1953 161p front
> Allegory of modern times as seen in a dream outside of time and space. In the plaza of an unspecified Latin American town a tired Casanova, an aging Camille and other degenerate characters live a life of cruel revelry and terror. 1 act 16 scenes Large mixed cast 1 exterior

Cat on a hot tin roof. Dramatists 1958 85p illus
> A dying Mississippi Delta plantation owner's sons and their wives struggle for the inheritance of his rich estate. 3 acts 8m 5w 2b 2g 1 interior
> Trade edition published by New Directions

—Same

In Best American plays; 4th ser.

In Gaver, J. ed. Critics' choice

Cat on a hot tin roof (condensation)

In The Best plays of 1954-1955

In Theatre, 1955

The glass menagerie
> Mother, living in proud memory of her Southern belle past, wants crippled daughter to have suitors, but even brother's attempts to help sister fail in sordid surroundings. 2 parts 7 scenes 2m 2w 1 interior

In Cooper, C. W. Preface to drama

In Cubeta, P. M. ed. Modern drama for analysis. 1955 edition

In Downer, A. S. ed. American drama

In Gaver, J. ed. Critics' choice

In Sper, F. ed. Living American plays

In A Treasury of the theatre

In Watson, E. B. and Pressey, B. eds. Contemporary drama: eleven plays

Hello from Bertha
> Prostitute, mentally ill, tries to muster enough courage to write to a man with whom she had once lived. 1 act 4w 1 interior

In Williams, T. 27 wagons full of cotton, and other one-act plays

The Lady of Larkspur Lotion
> Comedy. Two lodgers, facing eviction from rooming house in New Orleans, describe their imaginary wealth and success. 1 act 1m 2w 1 interior

In Williams, T. 27 wagons full of cotton, and other one-act plays

The last of my solid gold watches
> Aged traveling shoe salesman regrets the passing of his generation with its emphasis on good quality. Southern dialect. 1 act 3m 1 interior

In Williams, T. 27 wagons full of cotton, and other one-act plays

The long goodbye
> Slum family's life passes in review on moving day. 1 act 7m 2w 1 interior

In Williams, T. 27 wagons full of cotton, and other one-act plays

Lord Byron's love letter
> Spinster shows tourists letter supposedly written by Lord Byron to her grandmother. Set in New Orleans during Mardi Gras. 1 act 1m 3w 1 interior

In Williams, T. 27 wagons full of cotton, and other one-act plays

Orpheus descending. Dramatists 1959 83p illus
> Tragedy. Shows corruption that bigotry breeds and also the power of love. Set in a small southern town it tells of woman storekeeper who takes in a wandering vagabond guitar player. 3 acts 7 scenes 10m 9w 1 interior

—Same

In Williams, T. Orpheus descending, with Battle of angels

Orpheus descending (condensation)

In The Best plays of 1956-1957

In Broadway's best, 1957

Period of adjustment; high point over a cavern. New Directions 1960 120p
> Comedy on marital problems: a man and his new bride drop in on his old army buddy whose wife has just left him. 3 acts 4m 5w 1 interior

Portrait of a Madonna
> Middle aged, genteel spinster's delusions concerning a youthful girlhood disappointment in love finally culminate in insanity. Some phonograph music. 1 act 4m 2w 1 interior

In Williams, T. 27 wagons full of cotton, and other one-act plays

Williams, Tennessee—*Continued*

The purification
> Tragedy in verse with musical accompaniment on the guitar. Phantom of murdered young woman appears at the trial of her husband charged with killing her because of her incestuous relations with her brother. Set in New Mexico. 1 act 3 scenes 5m 3w chorus 1 interior

In Williams, T. 27 wagons full of cotton, and other one-act plays

The rose tattoo
> Widow's grief centers on superstition concerning dead husband's tattoo. Set in Sicilian fishing village on Gulf of Mexico. Background music. 3 acts 10 scenes 9m 14w 1 setting

In Best American plays; 4th ser.

Something unspoken
> Southern dowager tries to maneuver the regency in the Daughters of the Confederacy. 1 act 2w 1 interior

In The Best short plays of 1955-1956

In Williams, T. 27 wagons full of cotton, and other one-act plays

The strangest kind of romance
> In a rooming house, the landlady throws out to starve, the pet cat of poor man who had been away because of illness. 1 act 4 scenes 3m 1w extras 1 interior

In Williams, T. 27 wagons full of cotton, and other one-act plays

A streetcar named Desire. ｢Rev. ed｣ Acting ed. Dramatists 1953 107p front
> Widowed young woman, warped by tragic marriage, comes to live with sister and brother-in-law in New Orleans where further violence causes mental breakdown. 11 scenes 6m 6w 2 interiors 1 exterior

—Same

In Gaver, J. ed. Critics' choice

In New voices in the American theatre

In Tucker, S. M. ed. Twenty-five modern plays

Suddenly last summer. New Directions 1958 90p front
> The death of a mysterious man the previous summer affects lives of a family of malicious and unbalanced people. 4 scenes 2m 5w 2 interiors
> Also available from New American Library in A Signet book

Sweet bird of youth. New Directions 1959 114p front
> Aging actress, her still youthful gigolo and the emotional tensions in a small southern town created by appearance of the ill-assorted couple. 3 acts 5 scenes 15m 7w 2 interiors 1 exterior

Sweet bird of youth (condensation)

In The Best plays of 1958-1959

In Broadway's best, 1959

Talk to me like the rain and let me listen. . .
> Woman tries to make her paramour, a drunkard, understand her reasons for wanting to leave him. Background mandolin music. 1 act 1m 1w extras 1 interior

In Williams, T. 27 wagons full of cotton, and other one-act plays

This property is condemned
> Problems of an orphaned teen-age girl after death of her sister who had earned a living for them as a prostitute. 1 act 1m 1w 1 exterior

In Williams, T. 27 wagons full of cotton, and other one-act plays

27 wagons full of cotton
> Southern degenerate gets work for his cotton gin by burning rival's plantation facilities. 1 act 3 scenes 2m 1w extras 1 exterior

In The Best short plays, 1957

In Cerf, B. and Cartmell, V. H. eds. 24 favorite one-act plays

In Williams, T. 27 wagons full of cotton, and other one-act plays

Williamson, Hugh Ross

Diamond cut diamond
> Social comedy. Contretemps ensues when young woman tries to save the marriage of man who loves her by foiling divorce plot of his wife's lover. 3 acts 2m 2w 3 interiors

In Plays of the year v7

Heart of Bruce
> Historical drama set in 14th century Scotland. Based on the idea that Robert the Bruce visited the well of St Lazarus to cure his leprosy. Includes song with musical score. 3 acts 22m 1w 2 interiors 1 exterior

In Plays of the year v20

His Eminence of England. Heinemann 1953 78p (The Drama lib)
> Life of Reginald Pole, Cardinal of England, and heir to throne after children of Henry VIII. 2 acts 7m 3w extras 2 interiors

Willie's secret weapon. Badger, A.

The willing spirit. Holt, N. A.

Willis, Cecil

The velvet plain. French 1954 140p illus
> Negro minister from New York, sent as delegate to small town in the south where he boards with white family and arouses internal strife. 2 acts 13m 9w 1 interior 1 exterior

Willis, Nathaniel Parker

Tortesa the usurer
> Setting is Italy several centuries ago. Melodrama with happy ending about young noblewoman separated from her real lover. Verse play. 5 acts 13 scenes 5m 2w extras 5 interiors 1 exterior

In Quinn, A. H. ed. Representative American plays

Wills, George

Alice in Bibleland. Philosophical Lib. 1953 54p
> Young girl finds many things that perplex her in reading the Bible. 7 scenes 2m 2w 1 interior

Wills

Coward, N. Nude with violin
Faust, E. Gone to the dogs
Gray, M. For love of a house
Holland, N. Will and testament
Jeans, R. Count your blessings
Lea, G. Aunt Martha
Murray, J. Be my ghost
Murray, J. The five buttons
Pinero, A. W. The thunderbolt
Rice, E. The winner
Savory, G. A likely tale
See also Legacies

Willson, Meredith

The music man; book, music and lyrics by Meredith Willson. Story by Meredith Willson and Franklin Lacey. Putnam 1958 157p
> Musical comedy. A drifter who arrives in town to hoodwink everybody by selling them uniforms and a brass band ends by bringing happiness to entire community. 2 acts 16 scenes 18m 9w 1b 1g extras 3 interiors 6 exteriors

Willson, Meredith—*Continued*

The music man (condensation)

In Broadway's best, 1958

Willy Velvet, homicide detective. Wimberly, R. L.

Wilson, Angus

The mulberry bush. Secker & Warburg 1956 112p

Young Englishwoman, granddaughter of snobbish family noted for liberal intellectualism and work for social reform, discovers difference between loving causes and loving people. 3 acts 6m 5w 2 interiors 1 exterior

Wilson, Don. See Spielman, F. The stingiest man in town

Wilson, Donald

Flight of the dove

Television play. A group of people on a small airplane are suddenly caught in an emergency. 7m 3w

In British Broadcasting Corporation. The television playwright

Wilson, Dorothy Clarke

Peace on Mars. Bakers Plays 1959 35p illus

American family, symbolic of man throughout the ages, exemplifies theme that man has all materials necessary to build a heaven. 1 act 4m 2w 1 interior

The return of Chandra. Bakers Plays 1954 44p

Young doctor in India regains Christian faith, when American medical missionary sacrifices the welfare of his own son to that of outcaste child. 2 scenes 3m 3w 1b 1 interior

—Same

In The Best short plays of 1954-1955

That heaven of freedom. Friendship Press 1954 39p illus music

Principal of girls' school in northern India helps two girls decide on their futures. 1 act 5w 1 interior

Wilson, Edmund

Beppo and Beth

Comedy. Sophisticated New Yorkers and how they react to stock market crash of 1929. 3 acts 6m 4w 1 interior

In Wilson, E. Five plays

The crime in the Whistler room

Fantasy portraying the artistic and moral revolt by younger generation, centered in New York City following World War I. 3 acts 6m 6w 3 interiors 2 exteriors

In Wilson, E. Five plays

Cyprian's prayer

Supernatural fantasy about a magician's daughter whose legacy is spirits she cannot manage and magical equipment she does not understand. 4 acts 4 scenes 16m 3w 3 interiors 1 exterior

In Wilson, E. Five plays

The little blue light

Fantasy about United States social and political problems. Set in the future. 3 acts 2 scenes 4m 1w 1 interior 1 exterior

In Wilson, E. Five plays

This room and this gin and these sandwiches

Artistic and moral revolt of youth after World War I. Set in Greenwich Village, New York City with off Broadway theater actors and actresses, playwrights, etc. 6 scenes 9m 3w 1 interior

In Wilson, E Five plays

Wilson, Roger C.

Easter witnesses; music by Roger C. Wilson; book by Elsie Duncan Yale. Lorenz 1956 32p music

Easter. Resurrection pageant with choral music. 7 scenes 12m 15w 6 exteriors

Strangers in Bethlehem; a Christmas pageant, by Frank L. Cross; music composed by Roger C. Wilson. Lorenz 1956 24p music

Christmas. Nativity pageant with choral music, tenor solo, medium voice solo, alto solo and quartet. 4 scenes 6m 2w 3b extras 2 interiors 2 exteriors

Wilson, Sandy

The boy friend. Dutton 1955 126p illus

Musical comedy. A British view of life in the twenties at a girls' finishing school in Paris. 3 acts 3 scenes 12m 13w 1 interior 2 exteriors

The boy friend (condensation)

In The Best plays of 1954-1955

Wilton, Amos

Something borrowed, something blue. Bakers Plays 1955 90p illus (Baker's Royalty plays)

Romantic comedy. On day before wedding, the bride's former fiancé supposedly dead for more than a year, returns to claim his bride. 3 acts 4 scenes 3m 8w 1 interior

Wimberly, Robert L.

Willy Velvet, homicide detective. Dramatic 1956 19p illus

Farce satirizing radio murder mysteries. Set in a radio station and complete with commercials and sound effects. 1 act 6m 5w 1 interior

Wincelberg, Shimon

The conqueror

After World War II Japanese family and American soldier try to understand each other. Some Japanese dialogue. 3 scenes 4m 2w 1 setting

In The Best short plays of 1954-1955

Kataki (condensation)

In The Best plays of 1958-1959

A **wind** from the south. Costigan, J.

The **windfall.** Clare, N.

Windigo Island. Wallerstein, J. S.

Windsor, Helen J.

The Emperor's nightingale; an operetta for children; words and music by Helen J. Windsor. Schirmer 1953 36p music

Adapted from fairy tale of Hans Christian Andersen. When the toy nightingale is broken the Emperor understands the unselfish love of the real nightingale. Includes words and music of the songs. 4 scenes 16m 7w extras 1 interior 1 exterior

Winer, Elihu

Three hours between planes. French 1958 22p

Based on short story by F. Scott Fitzgerald. A man returns to see his childhood sweetheart, but she confuses him with another man. 1 act 3m 1w extras 2 interiors

Wings for to fly. Green, P.

Wings over dark waters. Miller, C. L.

The **winner.** Rice, E.

Winnie, Dennis J.

A very cold night. Bakers Plays 1960 16p

The two thieves crucified with Christ appear in a modern setting and discuss Him. 1 act 3m 1 interior

Winnie-the-Pooh. Milne, A. A.

The Winslow boy. Rattigan, T.

The Winslow girl. Lathrop, D.

Winter
c Spamer, C. Little icicle
c Very, A. Snow girl

Winter sunrise. Agg, H.

Winterset. Anderson, M.

Wirz, Henry
Levitt, S. The Andersonville trial

Wisdom
Estes, S. In quest of power through wisdom

The wise children. Butler, I.

The wise counsellor. Waugh, J. R.

The wise have not spoken. Carroll, P. V.

The wise men Spamer, C.

The wish machine. Schoneman, E. T.

Wish you were here. Kober, A. and Logan, J.

Wishengrad, Morton
The danger of freedom
Radio play. As presidential candidate Thomas Jefferson continues fight for individual freedom, civil, intellectual, religious and political. Background music. 3m 1w extras
In Jeffersonian Heritage (Radio program) The Jefferson heritage

Divided we stand
Radio play. In spite of wife's illness Thomas Jefferson carries on his fight for religious freedom in Virginia. Background music and songs. 7m 2w extras
In Jeffersonian Heritage (Radio program) The Jefferson heritage

The ground of justice
Radio play. Thomas Jefferson recreates John Adams' fight for equal justice to all when he defends some British soldiers. Background music. 18m 1w
In Jeffersonian Heritage (Radio program) The Jefferson heritage

The living declaration
Radio play. Thomas Jefferson explains meaning of Declaration of Independence. Background music and a song. 4m 1w extras
In Jeffersonian Heritage (Radio program) The Jefferson heritage

The rope dancers. French 1958 80p
A mother projects her own psychological disturbances upon her child. 3 acts 5 scenes 5m 2w 2g 1 interior
Published in trade edition by Crown

The rope dancers (condensation)
In The Best plays of 1957-1958

The wishful taw. Hughes, E. W.

The wishing stream. Miller, H. L.

Wit and humor. See Satire

Witch Hazel. Martens, A. C.

Witch hunt. Atwell, R. and Virden, H.

The witch hunt. Carter, B.

The witch hunters. Thompson, M. A.

The witch of Edmonton. Rowley, W. and others

Witchcraft
Gordon, K. The broom and the groom
Martens, A. C. Witch Hazel
c Melanos, J. A. Rapunzel and the witch

Phelps, L. The Gospel Witch

Rowley, W. and others. The witch of Edmonton

Tobias, J. Be happy? go wacky!

New England
Barker, J. N. Superstition
Phelps, L. The Gospel Witch

Salem, Massachusetts
Miller, A. The crucible

United States
Chase, M. Mrs McThing
McCaslin, N. The Bell Witch of Tennessee

Wales
Stephens, P. J. The changeling

Witches' brew. Asbrand, K.

The witches' complaint. Woolsey, J. and Sechrist, E. H.

The witching hour. Johnson, P.

The witching hour. Thomas, A.

With the sunrise in his pocket. McCaslin, N.

With this sword. Jay, M. and Graham-Campbell, A.

Within the family. Parker, K. T.

Within the gates. O'Casey, S.

Witness for the prosecution. Christie, A.

Wives
Kanter, H. and others. The George Gobel show

The Wizard of Oz. Thane, A.

The wizard's spell. Taylor, F.

Wodehouse, P. G.
The mating season (dramatization) See Adler, M. D. Too much springtime

Wolfe, Betsy S.
Watch your step
Three young Christian mothers help neighbor gain faith and save her marriage. 4w 1 interior
In Applegarth, M. T., Daily, D. T. and Wolfe, B. S. Four playettes

Wolfe, Thomas
Look homeward, angel (dramatization) See Frings, K. Look homeward, angel
The return of Buck Gavin
Set in mountains of North Carolina, an outlaw is captured when he visits his sister. 2m 1w 1 interior
In Walser, R. ed. North Carolina drama

Woman
Brabazon, F. Singing threshold
Coolidge, J. T. Mrs Parker's portrait
Emery, C. Portrait of Deborah
Ibsen, H. The lady from the sea
Jay, M. and Graham-Campbell, A. With this sword
Lagman, J. H. The sweetheart of Broadway
Nash, N. R. Rouge atomique
Seiler, C. The stronger sex
Seiler, C. What's wrong with the girls
Shaw, G. B. Mrs Warren's profession
Wilson, D. C. That heaven of freedom
See also Spinsters; Widows

Clubs
See Woman—Societies and clubs

Woman—*Continued*

Dress

See Clothing and dress

Social and moral questions

Apstein, T. The beams of our house

Apstein, T. A remittance from Spain

Behrman, S. N. End of summer

Boland, B. The return

Bottomley, G. King Lear's wife

Crothers, R. He and she

Dumas, A. Camille

Hauptmann, G. The rats

Ibsen, H. Hedda Gabler

Li, Y. M. Heaven challenges

Masteroff, J. The warm peninsula

Molière, J. B. P. The learned ladies

Parker, D. and D'Usseau, A. The ladies of the corridor

Sartre, J. P. The respectful prostitute

Strindberg, A. Comrades

Strindberg, A. Miss Julie

Verity, E. and Allen, V. Appointment in Eden

Williams, T. A streetcar named Desire

Societies and clubs

Conkle, E. P. No more wars but the moon

Crane, B. Visiting celebrity

Martens, A. C. Sing a song of something

Mauermann, W. G. Just us girls

Perry, M. The fifth wheel

Williams, T. Something unspoken

The **woman** from the voe. Bottomley, G.

A **woman** killed with kindness. Heywood, T.

A **woman** of no importance. Wilde, O.

Woman of Paris. Bacque, H.

The **woman** painter. Li, Y. M.

The **woman** taken in adultery. Coventry plays

The **woman** who didn't want Christmas. Phillips, M. K.

The **women** at the tomb. Ghelderode, M. de

Women camp followers. See Camp followers

The **women** from Kentucky. Howard, V.

Women in business

Berg, D. The drop of a hat

Funt, J. The magic and the loss

Women in religion. See Convents and nunneries

Women in white. Reach, J.

Women of Trachis. Sophocles

The **women** of Troy. Euripides

Women's clubs. See Woman—Societies and clubs

Women's institutes

Delderfield, R. F. The guinea-pigs

Wonder boy. Knapp, B.

The **wonder** of a kingdom. Dekker, T.

The **wonder** world of books. Woolsey, J. and Sechrist, E. H.

The **wonderful** adventures of Don Quixote. Seiler, C.

The **wonderful** Child. Kerr, M. L.

Wonderful summer. Manning, H.

Wonderful town. Bernstein, L.

Wood-carving

c Barton, E. The third lamb

c Ilian, C. The two woodcarvers

Stone, W. Devil take a whittler

The **wooden** dish. Morris, E.

Woolsey, Janette, and Sechrist, Elizabeth Hough

c Catching the ghost

Boys camping out overnight near cemetery are frightened by what they think is a ghost. 3 acts 1m 1w 5b 1 interior 1 exterior

In Woolsey, J. and Sechrist, E. H. It's time to give a play

c Charlie's May basket

May Day. Charlie makes amends to crotchety old neighbor whose cat he had teased. 1w 3b 3g 1 interior

In Woolsey, J. and Sechrist, E. H. New plays for red letter days

c Days and days

Larry dreams of all the holidays, red letter days and forgotten days in his life. 3 acts 1w 2b extras 1 interior

In Woolsey, J. and Sechrist, E. H. New plays for red letter days

c The donkey's mission

Easter. Kenny gets a chance to keep his pet donkey after both of them are given a part in Easter pageant. 2 acts 4 scenes 1m 1w 4b 1 interior 1 exterior

In Woolsey, J. and Sechrist, E. H. New plays for red letter days

c Each star a state

Flag Day. The stars on the American flag for 48 of the states tell about themselves. Large mixed cast 1 interior

In Woolsey, J. and Sechrist, E. H. New plays for red letter days

Elizabeth Zane saves Fort Henry

During an Indian attack on Fort Henry, Ohio in American Revolution. Elizabeth Zane succeeded in getting past the Indians to secure gunpowder for the defenders of the fort. 2 acts 9m 4w extras 1 interior 1 exterior

In Woolsey, J. and Sechrist, E. H. It's time to give a play

c The feast of the dolls

On the day of the Dolls' Festival some Japanese children entertain an American visitor. 2 acts 1m 3w 1b 3g extras 1 interior 1 exterior

In Woolsey, J. and Sechrist, E. H. It's time to give a play

c Fire at the Fieldings

When their house accidentally catches fire the Fielding children learn about firemen's training and work from their neighbor, a fire chief. 2 acts 2m 1w 2b 1g extras 1 interior

In Woolsey, J. and Sechrist, E. H. It's time to give a play

c The fire demons

During Fire Prevention Week a fireman tells school children how carelessness causes most fires. 2 acts 1m 3b 3g extras 1 exterior

In Woolsey, J. and Sechrist, E. H. New plays for red letter days

First aid in the first troop

In 1912 the first American troop of Girl Scouts in America (then called Girl Guides) practices first aid. 2 scenes 6w 9g 2 interiors

In Woolsey, J. and Sechrist, E. H. New plays for red letter days

Woolsey, J. and Sechrist, E. H.—*Continued*

c George Washington serves his country
To celebrate Washington's Birthday, school class dramatizes several scenes from his life. Music and dancing. 2 acts 5 scenes 19m 3w 7b 5g extras 1 interior

In Woolsey, J. and Sechrist, E. H. New plays for red letter days

c Gifts for the elves
Christmas. The elves in Santa Claus' workshop go on a sit-down strike because no one ever gives them Christmas gifts. 1m 8b 1 interior

In Woolsey, J. and Sechrist, E. H. It's time to give a play

c The good old days
American Education Week. School children go backward in time to visit an old fashioned school, with old fashioned books. 3 acts 1m 4b 4g extras 1 setting 1 interior

In Woolsey, J. and Sechrist, E. H. New plays for red letter days

c The great Tree Council
Arbor Day. Trees such as the De Soto Oak, the Charter Oak, and the Whittier Elm tell of their part in our country's growth. 5m 4w 2b extras 1 exterior

In Woolsey, J. and Sechrist, E. H. New plays for red letter days

c A Halloween surprise package
At masked costume Halloween party at school, the jack-in-the-box costume takes the prize. 2 acts 2m 1w 2b 2g extras 2 interiors

In Woolsey, J. and Sechrist, E. H. New plays for red letter days

c I wish I were a queen
With her fairy godmother's permission, little girl tries to decide which queen of nursery rhyme or folklore fame she would like to be. 6w 3g 1 interior

In Woolsey, J. and Sechrist, E. H. It's time to give a play

c The imps' defeat
National Health Week. The Health Fairies rescue a brother and sister who have fallen under the influence of bad imps. 4 acts 1m 1w 5b 5g 1 setting

In Woolsey, J. and Sechrist, E. H. New plays for red letter days

c Jerry and the Skweegees
In a delirium at onset of measles, boy dreams that he visits an eccentric old man and his six brothers. 3 acts 12m 2w 1b 1 interior 1 exterior

In Woolsey, J. and Sechrist, E. H. It's time to give a play

c Johnny's birthday surprise
Johnny's classmates recite rhymes or sing songs for show in honor of his birthday. 2w 6b 5g 1 interior

In Woolsey, J. and Sechrist, E. H. It's time to give a play

c Juliana's birthday
Dutch provincial girl finds that her traditional native costume makes her seem different to classmates in modern Amsterdam school. 2 acts 1w 5b 3g extras 1 interior

In Woolsey, J. and Sechrist, E. H. It's time to give a play

c The legend of Babouska
Christmas pantomime. Russian folk tale about old woman who, because she was too busy cleaning her house to join the three wise men, spent the years after searching for the Christ Child, distributing gifts to children along her way. 5m 1w extras 1 exterior

In Woolsey, J. and Sechrist, E. H. It's time to give a play

c Let's travel by auto
Jackson family sets forth on automobile trip to visit relatives in Illinois. 2 acts 4 scenes 5m 1w 1b 1g 2 interiors

In Woolsey, J. and Sechrist, E. H. It's time to give a play

c Let's travel by bus
Passengers on bus, temporarily stranded by rainstorm, show kindly spirit toward each other. 2 acts 7m 6w 2b 1g 1 interior

In Woolsey, J. and Sechrist, E. H. It's time to give a play

c Let's travel by train
Railroad travel customs and manners shown in several travel-by-rail situations. 3 acts 5m 1w 1b 1g 2 interiors

In Woolsey, J. and Sechrist, E. H. It's time to give a play

c A letter is mailed
Story of postal service in United States from colonial times to present. 12m 1b 1g extras 1 interior

In Woolsey, J. and Sechrist, E. H. It's time to give a play

c Lincoln's secret journey
Lincoln's Birthday. For safety reasons Lincoln is taken secretly to Washington near end of inaugural journey, February 1861. 2 acts 13m 3w 2b 2 interiors

In Woolsey, J. and Sechrist, E. H. New plays for red letter days

c Mars calling!
Brotherhood Week. A boys' club broadcast to Mars furnishes opportunity for Americans of different racial origins to tell how they live together in peace. 2 acts 4m 1w 8b 1g extras 1 interior

In Woolsey, J. and Sechrist, E. H. New plays for red letter days

c A Mexican holiday
Two American children enjoy a week's stay with Mexican family near Mexico City. 2 acts 2m 2w 3b 3g extras 1 interior 1 exterior

In Woolsey, J. and Sechrist, E. H. It's time to give a play

Molly Pitcher, heroine of Monmouth
Incidents from life of Molly Pitcher including her firing of cannon at the Battle of Monmouth during American Revolution. 2 acts 3 scenes 5m 2w extras 1 interior 1 exterior

In Woolsey, J. and Sechrist, E. H. It's time to give a play

c Mother Goose gives advice
Be Kind to Animals Week. Children pose problems of kind treatment of animals and Mother Goose gives advice in rhyme. 1m 1w extras 1 setting

In Woolsey, J. and Sechrist, E. H. New plays for red letter days

c Mother Goose's children
Pantomime. Problems of some characters in Mother Goose nursery rhymes. 5w 6b 6g 1 interior

In Woolsey, J. and Sechrist, E. H. It's time to give a play

c Mother of the town
Mother's Day. A widow who has adopted a war orphan is voted Mother of the Year. 1m 3w 5g 1 interior

In Woolsey, J. and Sechrist, E. H. New plays for red letter days

c My honest friend
On Washington's Birthday his former army baker sends him fresh gingerbread. 2m 1b 1g 1 interior

In Woolsey, J. and Sechrist, E. H. New plays for red letter days

Woolsey, J. and Sechrist, E. H.—*Continued*

c Mystery next door
Mysterious noises next door prove to have something to do with mother's surprise birthday present. 2 acts 1m 3b 4g 1 exterior
In Woolsey, J. and Sechrist, E. H. It's time to give a play

c A Norwegian mountain mystery
Oslo children find fun and excitement at their cousins' summer farm in the mountains. 2 acts 3m 3w 3b 2g 1 interior
In Woolsey, J. and Sechrist, E. H. It's time to give a play

Paul Revere, Boston patriot
Boston Tea Party and Paul Revere's ride in the American Revolution. 2 acts 4 scenes 7m 3w 2b 2g extras 2 interiors 2 exteriors
In Woolsey, J. and Sechrist, E. H. It's time to give a play

c A picnic for father
Father's Day. A rain storm interrupts the special picnic planned for father. 3 acts 1m 2w 3b 3g 2 interiors 1 exterior
In Woolsey, J. and Sechrist, E. H. New plays for red letter days

c Pumpkin is the password
To raise money to help sick brother of one of their members. children's club opens a roadside produce stand. 3 acts 4 scenes 1m 5b 5g extras 1 interior 1 exterior
In Woolsey, J. and Sechrist, E. H. It's time to give a play

c The Queen of Hearts' party
Valentine's Day. Cinderella, Sleeping Beauty and other fairy tale characters come to the Queen of Hearts' party on Valentine's Day. 9m 6w extras 1 interior
In Woolsey, J. and Sechrist, E. H. New plays for red letter days

c Radios versus doughnuts
Boy Scout troop donates money earned for a radio to farm family whose house was destroyed by fire. 1m 14b 1 interior
In Woolsey, J. and Sechrist, E. H. New plays for red letter days

c Saint Peter and the birds
Pantomime. How St Peter turned greedy old lady into red-headed woodpecker. 3m 1w extras 1 interior
In Woolsey, J. and Sechrist, E. H. It's time to give a play

c The Santa Claus court
Fantasy. Santa Clauses from all over the world prove to St Nicholas. the patron saint of Christmas. that they represent his spirit of kindness. 10m 1w 1g 1 interior
In Woolsey, J. and Sechrist, E. H. New plays for red letter days

Stephen Foster, beautiful dreamer
The life of the 19th century American composer. Includes vocal rendition of some of his songs. 5 acts 14m 4w extras 3 interiors
In Woolsey, J. and Sechrist, E. H. It's time to give a play

c Thanksgiving Proclamation—1863
Thanksgiving Day. In 1863 President Lincoln issues a Thanksgiving Proclamation. 6m 2w extras 1 interior
In Woolsey, J. and Sechrist, E. H. New plays for red letter days

c This dream came true
Columbus Day. While young Christopher Columbus takes his first sea voyage his mother has dream about his future success. 2 acts 3 scenes 4m 2w extras 2 interiors
In Woolsey, J. and Sechrist, E. H. New plays for red letter days

c The United Nations, the hope of the world
Guide shows a boy and a girl how the agencies of the United Nations help people all over the world. 2 acts 1b 1g extras 1 setting
In Woolsey, J. and Sechrist, E. H. New plays for red letter days

c What happened to Billy?
Shows police action helpful to everyday living. street safety. and finding lost persons. 2 acts 2m 2w 4b 4g 1 exterior
In Woolsey, J. and Sechrist, E. H. It's time to give a play

c The witches' complaint
Puppet play for Halloween. To entertain Susan who is kept indoors with a cold. mother tells her a witch story. 3 scenes 1m 1w 1g extras 1 interior 1 exterior
In Woolsey, J. and Sechrist, E. H. New plays for red letter days

c The wonder world of books
Book Week. The different kinds of books invite readers. They convince children it is interesting to join the library. 1w 2b 1g extras 1 interior
In Woolsey, J. and Sechrist, E. H. New plays for red letter days

A **word** in your ear. Sinclair, L.

The **words** upon the window-pane. Yeats, W. B.

Work
Murdoch, W. Do-Nothing Dan

Worker-priests. See Priests

The **workhouse** ward. Gregory, Lady

Workhouses
c Howard, V. Oliver Twist asks for more

World, End of the. See End of the world

The **world** of Sholom Aleichem. Perl, A.

World War, 1939-1945
Behrman, S. N. Rain from heaven
Keeney, C. H. Major Milliron reports

Aerial operations
Haines, W. W. Command decision
Johnston, D. A fourth for bridge
Rattigan, T. Flare path

France
Morris, T. B. The deserted house
Werfel, F. Jacobowsky and the colonel

Great Britain
Storey, R. Touch it light

Italy
Hayes, A. The girl on the Via Flaminia

Malaya
Richardson, L. For our mother Malaya!

Naval operations
Wouk, H. The Caine mutiny court-martial

Pacific Ocean
Elward, J. Paper foxhole
Fisher, A. and Rabe, O. Flag of freedom
Laurents, A. Home of the brave
Rodgers, R. and Hammerstein, O. South Pacific

World War, 1939-1945—*Continued*

Prisoners and prisons, Japanese

Brooks, P. The only prison

Soldiers' bodies, Disposition of

See Soldiers' bodies, Disposition of

Underground movements

Morris, T. B. The deserted house

Underground movements—France

Daviot, G. The pen of my aunt

Goetz, R. and Goetz, A. The hidden river

The **world** we live in. Čapek, J. and Čapek, K.

The **world** well lost. See Dryden, J. All for love

Worlds apart. Cooper, F. A.

Worship programs

Bailey, H. F. "Better than seven sons"

Bailey, H. F. Christmas Eve candle vespers

Bailey, H. F. The Feast of the Ingathering

Bailey, H. F. A manger lowly

Bailey, H. F. The picture window frames Christmas

Bailey, H. F. The singing children

Bailey, H. F. "There was a garden"

Bailey, H. F. Walk in the light

Bailey, H. F. "We bring this child unto the Lord"

Bangham, M. D. Come to the manger

Christmas in art

Gruwell, B. G. O holy night

Hare, W. B. The white Christmas

Hein, R. Receive your King!

c Holbrook, M. A candle-lighting service

Jorgenson, E. S. The message of Christmas

Joy to the world

Kerr, M. L. His star

Lowe, E. A birthday through the centuries

Nystrom, D. Children's praises

Powicke, H. B. The song and the star

Sumerau, D. L. Make His name glorious

Voss, B. M. Our greatest gift

Worship services. See Worship programs

Woskoff, Verna

Castle in the village

> Romantic comedy. Young woman finds a husband among prospective applicants for the subletting of her apartment. 4m 3w 1 interior

In The Best short plays, 1958-1959

Wouk, Herman

The Caine mutiny court-martial. ₁Acting ed₁ French 1955 96p illus

> Based on author's novel "The Caine mutiny." Lieutenant Maryk of the United States Navy stands trial for having taken over from incompetent Captain Queeg, command of the minesweeper "Caine," caught in a typhoon during World War II. 2 acts 3 scenes 19m 2 interiors
> Trade edition published by Doubleday

—Same

In Best American plays; 4th ser.

In New voices in the American theatre

The Caine mutiny court-martial (condensation)

In The Best plays of 1953-1954

In Theatre, 1954

Nature's way. ₁Acting ed₁ French 1958 94p illus

> Romantic comedy. Young New York City couple keep their marriage together despite interference from members of "smart" theatre set. 2 acts 10m 4w 2 interiors
> Trade edition published by Doubleday

The **would**-be gentleman. Molière, J. B. P.

The **would**-be invalid. Molière, J. B. P.

Wounded, First aid to. See First aid in illness and injury

The **wounded** highwayman. Sakanishi, S. tr.

Woyzeck. Büchner, G.

Wrench, Margaret Stanley- See Stanley-Wrench, Margaret

Wright, Elizabeth McFadden

"The most heavenly hosts." Bakers Plays 1958 15p

> Traditional Christmas story. Uses Sunday school members from kindergarten through senior high. Familiar Christmas carols and Bible verses Large mixed cast

Wright, Lula

c Mr Popper's penguins

> A dramatization of book by Florence and Richard Atwater about an untidy house painter's family and their pet penguin. 2 acts 8m 3w 1b 1g extras 1 interior

In Fenner, P. and Hughes, A. comps. Entrances and exits

Wright, Robert, and Forrest, George

Kismet; a musical Arabian Night. Music and lyrics by Robert Wright and George Forrest (from themes of Alexander Borodin) Book by Charles Lederer and Luther Davis (based on the play by Edward Knoblock) Random House 1954 174p illus

> Arabian Nights fantasy. The adventures of a poet in palace and market place in ancient Baghdad. 2 acts 14 scenes Large mixed cast 6 interiors 7 exteriors

Writers. See Authors

Wuthering Heights. Jacoby, L.

Wuthering Heights. Olfson, L.

Wyatt, Sir Thomas

Dekker, T. and Webster, J. Sir Thomas Wyatt

Wycherley, William

The country wife

> Restoration comedy of manners. Young rake pursues amours under false pretenses while innocence triumphs over jealous or too trusting lovers. London setting. 5 acts 12 scenes 7m 6w extras 3 interiors 1 exterior

In Kronenberger, L. ed. Cavalcade of comedy

In Restoration plays

Wyss, Johann David

The Swiss family Robinson (dramatization) See Howard, V. The Swiss family Robinson—rescued

Y

Yaffe, James
The deadly game. Dramatists 1960 66p
Based on novel: Trapps, by Frederick Duerrenmatt. American salesman, stranded in Swiss mountain area, submits to mock trial for murder to humor his hosts, retired lawyers. 2 acts 6m 1w 1 interior
Trade edition published by Knopf

The deadly game (condensation)
In The Best plays of 1959-1960
In Broadway's best, 1960

Yankee Doodle. Emurian, E. K.

Yankee Doodle Dandy. Fisher, A. and Rabe, O.

Yankee peddler. Barnett, M.

The **Yankee** Peddler. McCaslin, N.

Yeats, W. B.
At the hawk's well
Verse play. Legendary drama from the Irish heroic age. The guardian of the well speaks to three musicians. 6m 1 exterior
In Yeats, W. B. The collected plays of W. B. Yeats

Calvary
Verse play. Christ speaks to Judas and Lazarus. 9m 1 exterior
In Yeats, W. B. The collected plays of W. B. Yeats

The cat and the moon
A blind beggar and a lame beggar consult a saint. 5m 1 exterior
In Yeats, W. B. The collected plays of W. B. Yeats

Cathleen ni Houlihan
Symbolism in the image of an old woman in the Irish Rebellion of 1798. 1 act 2m 3w 1b extras 1 interior
In Cerf, B. and Cartmell, V. H. eds. 24 favorite one-act plays
In Yeats, W. B. The collected plays of W. B. Yeats

The Countess Cathleen
Verse play. An earlier version of the author's symbolic drama Cathleen ni Houlihan. 5 scenes 5m 3w extras 2 interiors 3 exteriors
In Yeats, W. B. The collected plays of W. B. Yeats

The death of Cuchulain
Verse play. Legendary Ireland. Events which led to death of Cuchulain. 5m 4w extras no scenery
In Yeats, W. B. The collected plays of W. B. Yeats

Deirdre
Verse play on an Irish legend. Tragedy built around love an old king feels for bride of a young king. 4m 1w extras 1 interior
In Yeats, W. B. The collected plays of W. B. Yeats

The dreaming of the bones
Verse play. Young couple in a ruined abbey relate an ancient, legendary crime. 5m 1w 1 exterior
In Yeats, W. B. The collected plays of W. B. Yeats

A full moon in March
Verse play. Based on an old Gaelic legend of the queen and the swineherd whose severed head sang. 2m 2w 1 interior
In Yeats, W. B. The collected plays of W. B. Yeats

The green helmet
Legendary Irish verse play about the rivalry over the green helmet. 6m 2w extras 1 interior
In Yeats, W. B. The collected plays of W. B. Yeats

The herne's egg
Verse play. Legendary Ireland. Rivalry and death over the egg of a great bird. 6 scenes 9m 5w extras 1 interior 3 exteriors
In Yeats, W. B. The collected plays of W. B. Yeats

The hour-glass
Morality play about a wise man and a fool. 2m 1w extras 1 interior
In Yeats, W. B. The collected plays of W. B. Yeats

The King of the Great Clock Tower
Verse play. Fantasy. Execution of a poet because of his love for the queen. 4m 1w 1 interior
In Yeats, W. B. The collected plays of W. B. Yeats

The king's threshold
Verse play. An Irish romance. A poet pleads to regain his ancient rights. 10m 2w extras 1 exterior
In Yeats, W. B. The collected plays of W. B. Yeats

The Land of Heart's Desire
Irish folklore with belief in fairies and the changeling child. Verse play. 1 act 3m 2w 1g 1 interior
In Smith, B. and others, eds. A treasury of non-royalty one-act plays
In Yeats, W. B. The collected plays of W. B. Yeats

On baile's strand
Legendary Ireland. Tragic drama of kings told by a blindman to a fool. 5m extras 1 interior
In Yeats, W. B. The collected plays of W. B. Yeats

The only jealousy of Emer
Legendary drama about a woman who must renounce her love for her husband. 6m 2w 1 interior
In Yeats, W. B. The collected plays of W. B. Yeats

The player queen
Fantasy about a queen and a woman who changes places with her. 2 scenes 6m 3w extras 1 interior 1 exterior
In Yeats, W. B. The collected plays of W. B. Yeats

The pot of broth
Comedy. A tramp in search of food tells a woman he has a magic stone which will make soup if she will lend him a chicken. 2m 1w 1 interior
In Yeats, W. B. The collected plays of W. B. Yeats

Purgatory
Fantasy in verse. Old man relates his life to the son he will murder. 2m 1 exterior
In Bentley, E. ed. The modern theatre v2
In Yeats, W. B. The collected plays of W. B. Yeats

Yeats, W. B.—*Continued*

The Resurrection
Christ appears to the Apostles after the Crucifixion. 7m 1 interior
In Yeats, W. B. The collected plays of W. B. Yeats

The shadowy waters
Verse play. Symbolic fantasy. Sailors capture beautiful queen and her ship. 2m 1w extras 1 exterior
In Yeats, W. B. The collected plays of W. B. Yeats

Sophocles' King Oedipus
Modern version of Sophocles' classic Greek drama King Oedipus. 5m 3w extras 1 interior
In Yeats, W. B. The collected plays of W. B. Yeats

Sophocles' Oedipus at Colonus
Modern version of Sophocles' classic Greek drama Oedipus at Colonus. 6m 2w extras 1 exterior
In Yeats, W. B. The collected plays of W. B. Yeats

The unicorn from the stars
Tragedy. A man troubles his family with his visions. Set in 19th century Ireland. 3 acts 5m 3w 1 interior 1 exterior
In Yeats, W. B. The collected plays of W. B. Yeats

The words upon the window-pane
At a séance several people contact the spirit of Jonathan Swift. 4m 3w 1 interior
In Yeats, W. B. The collected plays of W. B. Yeats

Yellow fever. Burlingame, C.

Yelvington, Ramsey
A cloud of witnesses; the drama of the Alamo. Univ. of Tex. Press 1959 109p illus
A portrayal of concept of freedom in recreation of the siege and fall of the Alamo in Texas, 1836. Verse play. 2 acts Large mixed cast no scenery

Yerma. García Lorca, F.

Yiddish drama
Ansky, S. The Dybbuk

Yorick's love. Howells, W. D.

York, Esther Baldwin
The kindled flame
Easter. Effect of Resurrection upon Roman soldier on guard at Christ's tomb. 1 act 3 scenes 2m 2w extras 1 interior
In Brings, L. M. comp. The golden book of church plays

The silver star of Christmas
Nativity play, Shelah, handmaiden to King Herod's wife, sends warning to save the infant Jesus. 1 act 2 scenes 3m 5w 2 interiors
In Brings, L. M. ed. The modern treasury of Christmas plays

York, Marjorie Ann
Treasure Island
Radio adaptation of novel by Robert Louis Stevenson. Jim Hawkins, cabin boy on an English ship bound for an isolated island to seek buried treasure, has exciting adventures on sea and land with pirates who seize the ship. Background music including singing of: Fifteen men. 10m extras
In Burack, A. S. ed. Four-star radio plays for teen-agers

York mysteries. See York plays

York plays
The Ascension: York Tailors' play
Bible. New Testament. Gospels. 14th century English mystery play. The Ascension of Christ. Verse play in Middle English with modernized spelling. 5m 1w extras 1 setting
In Browne, E. M. ed. Religious drama, 2

The birth of Christ; York Tile-Thatchers' play
14th century English mystery play of the Nativity. Verse play in Middle English with modernized spelling. 1m 1w 1 setting
In Browne, E. M. ed. Religious drama, 2

The creation, and The fall of Lucifer; The York Pageant of the Barkers
14th century English mystery play. Biblical story from the Book of Genesis about God's creation of the world and the rebellion against God led by Lucifer, the angel of light. Verse play in Middle English with modernized spelling. Singing. 3 scenes 5m extras 1 interior 1 exterior
Same as: The creation of the heavenly beings: The fall of Lucifer
In Everyman, and medieval miracle plays

The creation of Adam and Eve; The York Pageant of the Cardmakers
Bible. Old Testament. Genesis. 14th century English mystery play. God's creation of the first man and woman. Verse play in Middle English with modernized spelling. Includes singing. 2m 1w 1 exterior
Same as: The creation of man
In Everyman, and medieval miracle plays

The creation of man; York Cardmakers' play
Same as: The creation of Adam and Eve
In Browne, E. M. ed. Religious drama, 2

The creation of the heavenly beings: The fall of Lucifer; York Tanners' play
Same as: The creation, and The fall of Lucifer
In Browne, E. M. ed. Religious drama, 2

The Crucifixion; The York Pageant of the Pinners and Painters
Bible. New Testament. Gospels. 14th century English mystery play describing in particular the part played by the soldiers assigned to crucify Christ. Verse play in Middle English with modernized spelling. 5m 1 exterior
In Everyman, and medieval miracle plays

The Crucifixion; York Butchers' play
Bible. New Testament. Gospels. 14th century English mystery play. The Crucifixion and burial of Jesus Christ. Verse play in Middle English with modernized spelling. 13m 2w 1 setting
In Browne, E. M. ed. Religious drama, 2

The fall of man; The York Pageant of the Coopers
Bible. Old Testament. Genesis. 14th century English mystery play. The eating of forbidden fruit by Adam and Eve in the Garden of Eden. Verse play in Middle English with modernized spelling. 4m 1w 1 interior 1 exterior
Same as: The fall of man: York Cowpers' play
In Everyman, and medieval miracle plays

York plays—*Continued*
The fall of man; York Cowpers' play
Same as: The fall of man; The York Pageant of the Coopers
In Browne, E. M. ed. Religious drama, 2
The Garden of Eden; York Fullers' play
Bible. Old Testament. Genesis. 14th century English mystery play. God gives the Garden of Eden to Adam and Eve for their home. Verse play in Middle English with modernized spelling. 2m 1w 1 exterior
In Browne, E. M. ed. Religious drama, 2
The judgment; The York Pageant of the Mercers
14th century English mystery play based on the New Testament accounts of the Last Judgment. Verse play in Middle English with modernized spelling. Singing. 4 scenes 14m 1 interior 2 exteriors
Same as: The last judgment
In Everyman, and medieval miracle plays
The last judgement; York Mercers' play
Same as: The judgment
In Browne, E. M. ed. Religious drama, 2
Palm Sunday; York Skinners' play
Bible. New Testament. Gospels. 14th century English mystery play. Christ's entry into Jerusalem is preceded by some of His miracles and the calling of Zaccheus. Verse play in Middle English with modernized spelling. 16m 1 setting
In Browne, E. M. ed. Religious drama, 2
The Resurrection; The York Pageant of the Carpenters
Easter. Bible. New Testament. Gospels. 14th century English mystery play about the Resurrection of Christ. Depicts the three Marys at the empty tomb and the reactions of Pilate and the chief priests to the soldiers' report. Verse play in Middle English with modernized spelling. 3 scenes 9m 3w 1 interior 1 exterior
In Everyman, and medieval miracle plays
The second trial before Pilate: The scourging and condemnation
Bible. New Testament. Gospels. 14th century English mystery play. Depicts the role of Caiaphas, the high priest, in the trial of Christ. Verse play in Middle English with modernized spelling. 11m 1 setting
In Browne, E. M. ed. Religious drama, 2
The temptation of Christ; York Locksmiths' play
Bible. New Testament. Gospels. 14th century English mystery play. During forty days in the wilderness the Devil tempts Jesus. Verse play in Middle English with modernized spelling. 4m 1 exterior
In Browne, E. M. ed. Religious drama, 2

York plays. Nativity play
The Nativity (adaptation) See Malcolmson, A. The Nativity

The York Resurrection. Johnston, R. A.

Yorkshire dialect. See Dialect—English—Yorkshire

You are not alone. Salverson, G.

You are watching! Martens, A. C.

You can't take it with you. Hart, M. and Kaufman, G. S.

"You heard me!" Bowie, L.

You, my guests! Ridley, A.

You, the jury. Reach, J.

Young, Bess M. See Barnes, E. A. jt. auth.
Young, Stanley
Mr Pickwick (condensation)
In Theatre, 1953
The sound of apples
Verse play about an imaginary episode in the life of Johnny Appleseed. 6m 3w extras 1 exterior
In The Best short plays of 1957-1958

The young and beautiful. Benson, S.

Young Doc Smith died tomorrow. Thompson, M. A.

The young Elizabeth. Dowling, J.

The young Elizabeth. Letton, J. and Letton, F.

A young lady of property. Foote, H.

Young men
Beich, A. and Wright, W. H. The man in the dog suit
Ionesco, E. Jack

Young people. See Youth

Young Richard Whittington. Arlett, V. I.

The young whittler. McMillin, M.

Young women
Benson, S. The young and beautiful
Howard, V. Happy holidays for little women
Ireland, I. A. This angel business
Molière, J. B. P. School for wives
Newman, D. Pride and prejudice
Shaughnessy, A. Release
Waldau, R. S. A cabin by the lake

The youngest shall ask. Shaber, D.

Your every wish. Goldsmith, C.

Your manners and mine. Howard, V.

Your money or your life. Howard, V.

You're a long time dead. Morgan, E.

Youth
Anderson, R. A. and Sweeney, R. L. Boris and the briefcase
Armer, A. and Grauman, W. E. Glass slipper
Asbrand, K. Easy as pie
Aschmann, H. T. As pretty does
Bailey, A. H. Impersonation
Breck, F. E. One father of mankind
Brenner, M. Bill and Sue
Burgess, C. V. Doers and viewers
Burgess, C. V. Ken changes his mind
Casey, B. M. The little things
Casey, B. M. The main road
Clapp, P. Edie-across-the-street
Conkle, E. P. Son-of-a-biscuit-eater
Davidson, W. The birds and the boys
Dean, E. Stood up
Foote, H. The dancers
Foote, H. A young lady of property
Franklin, C. Boy appeal
Friend, M. The Charleston craze
Frings, K. Look homeward, angel
Gairdner, C. C. and Pilcher, R. The dashing white sergeant
Gibson, M. N. Return engagement
Gordon, K. Money mad
Hackett, W. A dress affair

Youth—*Continued*
Hackett, W. The outgoing tide
Hackett, W. The way the ball bounces
Hale, R. and Hale, N. Lilacs in the rain
Hark, M. and McQueen, N. Romance for Dad
Hark, M. and McQueen, N. The Teen Club's Christmas
Harris, A. We were young that year
Heger, K. Somebody special
Henderson, J. A midsummer night's scream
Herlihy, J. L. and Noble, W. Blue denim
Hughes, J. The ship of dreams
Inge, W. Picnic
Joudry, P. Teach me how to cry
Kesler, H. O. The grass that's greener
Knapp, B. Wonder boy
Lamson, P. Grow up!
Lindsey, H. C. Forever Judy
McCleery, W. The family man
McCoy, P. S. Two dates for tonight
Martin, B. Eighteenth summer
Miller, H. L. Jump for George
Miller, H. L. Three cheers for mother
Miller, H. L. The vanishing Easter egg
Nail, R. Love errant
O'Neill, E. Ah, wilderness!
Peavey, H. Teen antics
Peterson, L. Take a giant step
Sergel, K. Father knows best
Sergel, K. Maudie and the opposite sex
Sergel, K. The remarkable incident at Carson Corners
Stephens, C. G. Storm cellar
Yudkoff, A. The gentleman walks outside
See also Adolescence; Church work with youth
The **youth**, Bolivar. Ullman, S. S.
Youth serves the church. Asbrand, K.
Yudkoff, Alvin
The gentleman walks outside. Dramatic 1954 24p illus
A short youth finds his blind date for the prom is a tall girl. 1 act 3m 2w extras 1 interior
Yugoslavia
Sek, M. The dawn must break
Yurok Indians
Sinclair, L. The case of the sea-lion flippers

Z

Zahn, Muriel
c How does your garden grow?
The vegetables tell how many vitamins they contain. 1 act 16 characters 1 interior
In 'Round the year plays for the grades

Zane, Elizabeth
Woolsey, J. and Sechrist, E. H. Elizabeth Zane saves Fort Henry
Zanorin. Brickenden, C.
The **zeal** of Thy house. Sayers, D.
Zeiger, Henry
Five days
Allegory of war. A prisoner and his guard show effects of their indoctrination in wartime thinking versus their natural human kindness. Drum music. 5 scenes 8m 1w 1 setting
In The Best short plays of 1955-1956
Zelinka, Sydney. See Stern, L. jt. auth.
Zembō, Motoyasu. See Komparu, Zempō
Zen (Sect)
Komparu, Z. U. The hōka priests
Ziegler, Esther. See Brydon, M. W. jt. auth.
Zimmerman, Kay
c Family Christmas
Two families who need each other get together for Christmas. 1m 1w 4b 3g 1 interior
In Birdsall, R. ed. Creative plays for every school month
Zola, Emile
Thérèse Raquin: English version by Kathleen Boutall
Love triangle in which a mother brings retribution upon her son's murderers. 4 acts 3m 4w 1 interior
In Bentley, E. ed. From the modern repertoire; ser. 3

About

Herald, H.; Herczeg, G. and Raine, N. R. The life of Emile Zola
The **zoo** story. Albee, E.
Zoological gardens
c Miller, H. L. Who's who at the zoo
Zuckerman, Albert J.
Blobo's boy
Relations between father and son affected by Congressional Committee's investigation of the father's labor racketeering. 5m 1w extras 1 setting
In The Best short plays, 1958-1959
Zuñi Indians
c Goulding, D. J. The gift of the drum
Zweig, Stefan
Volpone; tr. from the German by Ruth Langner
Adaptation of the play by Ben Jonson. Avaricious Venetian merchant's nefarious schemes to acquire wealth bring him to a bad end. 3 acts 6 scenes 20m 3w 4 interiors
In Gassner, J. ed. Twenty best European plays on the American stage

Part II

List of Collections Indexed

This is an author-title list of all collections indexed in this volume.

About time, too, and five other playlets. Carter, C.

Abstance, Polly, and Abstance, Louise
Lighthearted pantomimes. Bakers Plays 1960 79p

Addis, Hazel
On with the show; twelve numbers with words and music for group or district scout shows. Words by Hazel Addis; music by John Milner. Boy Scouts 1955 63p music
Partially analyzed

Adventure. Wallerstein, J. S.

Aeschylus
The Oresteian trilogy: Agamemnon; The Choephori [and] The Eumenides; tr. by Philip Vellacott. Penguin 1956 201p

Albee, Edward
The zoo story; The death of Bessie Smith; The sandbox; three plays, introduced by the author. Coward-McCann 1960 158p
Also published in trade edition

Allen, John
(ed.) Three medieval plays: The Coventry Nativity play; Everyman [and] Master Pierre Pathelin. Heinemann 1953 3v in 1 (The Drama lib)

American drama. Downer, A. S. ed.

Anderson, Maxwell
Four verse plays: Elizabeth the Queen; Winterset; Mary of Scotland [and] High Tor. Harcourt 1959 142p

Anouilh, Jean
Five plays. Hill & Wang 1958-1959 2v (A Mermaid dramabook)
Also published in trade edition

An **anthology** of Greek drama. Robinson, C. A. ed.

Applegarth, Margaret T.; Daily, Dorothy Tinsley [and] Wolfe, Betsy S.
Four playettes; short dramatizations for church groups. Friendship Press 1956 40p

Aristophanes
Five comedies; tr. by Benjamin Bickley Rogers; complete and unabridged; with Rogers' introductions and notes; ed. by Andrew Chiappe. Doubleday 1955 343p (Doubleday Anchor bks)
Two plays: Peace and Lysistrata; a new translation by Doros Alastos. Zeno 1953 147p

Armer, Alan, and Grauman, Walter E.
Vest pocket theatre; twenty tested television playlets. French 1955 xxxii, 131p

Arrabal
The automobile graveyard (Le cimitière des voitures) a play in two acts, and, The two executioners (Les deux bourreaux) a melodrama in one act. Tr. by Richard Howard. Grove 1960 94p (Evergreen original)
Also published in trade edition by Grove, and in both trade and paper editions by McClelland

The **art** of the play. Downer, A. S. ed.

Arthur Miller's Collected plays. Miller, A.

Artists' Theatre: four plays. Machiz, H. ed.

Asbrand, Karin
The children's program book. Bakers Plays 1958 96p music
Partially analyzed
Easy church plays for women and girls. Bakers Plays 1955 91p
Easy programs for church holidays. Bakers Plays 1953 104p music
Partially analyzed
Hark, the little angels speak (Christmas plays, exercises, recitations for youngsters) Bakers Plays 1959 80p music
Partially analyzed
Rehearsal-less fun. Bakers Plays 1958 127p music
Partially analyzed

Atwell, Rosemary and Virden, Helen
Play-time; one-act plays for children. French 1954 44p illus
Partially analyzed

Auden, W. H. and Isherwood, Christopher
Two great plays: The dog beneath the skin [and] The ascent of F6. Random House [1959] 185p (Modern Lib. Paperbacks)

The **automobile** graveyard and The two executioners. Arrabal

B

The **Bacchae,** and other plays. Euripides

Bailey, Hazel F.
Simple chancel dramas. Bakers Plays 1956 102p

Barry, Michael
(comp.) British Broadcasting Corporation. The television playwright

Beckett, Samuel
Krapp's last tape, and other dramatic pieces. Grove 1960 141p

Behrman, S. N.
4 plays: The second man; Biography; Rain from heaven; [and] End of summer. Random House [1955 c1952] 370p

The bells of the city, and other plays. Tennant, K.

Bentley, Eric
(ed.) The classic theatre; v2 Five German plays. Doubleday 1959 511p (Anchor bks)
(ed.) From the modern repertoire; ser. 3. Ind. Univ. Press 1956 527p illus
(ed.) Let's get a divorce! and other plays. Hill & Wang 1958 xx, 364p (A Mermaid dramabook)
(ed.) The modern theatre. v 1-3. Doubleday 1955 3v (Doubleday Anchor bks)

Bergman, Ingmar
Four screenplays; tr. from the Swedish by Lars Malmstrom and David Kushner. Simon & Schuster 1960 xxii, 329p illus

Best American plays; 4th series—1951-1957; ed. with an introduction by John Gassner. Crown 1958 648p

Best plays by Chekhov. Chekhov, A.

The Best plays of 1894-1899; ed. by John Chapman, and Garrison P. Sherwood. Dodd 1955 279p

The Best plays of 1952/53-1959/60; the Burns Mantle yearbook; ed. by Louis Kronenberger; illus. with photographs, and with drawings by Hirschfeld. Dodd 1953-1960 8v illus

The Best short plays, 1952/1953-1959/1960; ed. by Margaret Mayorga. Beacon 1953-1960 7v
Partially analyzed. Volumes for 1953/1954 to 1954/1955 published by Dodd. 1957/1958 volume also published in trade edition

The Best short plays. 20th anniversary edition, 1957; ed. by Margaret Mayorga. Beacon Press 1957 448p music
Partially analyzed. Also published in trade edition

Best television plays. Vidal, G. ed.

Best television plays, 1957; ed. by William I. Kaufman. Harcourt 1957 303p
Partially analyzed

The Best television plays; v3 ed. by William I. Kaufman. Merlin 1954 366p

Betti, Ugo
Three plays; tr. and with a foreword, by Henry Reed. Grove 1956 283p
Also published in trade edition

Bible plays for juniors. Spamer, C.

Bierman, Judah; Hart, James, and Johnson, Stanley
(eds.) The dramatic experience. Prentice-Hall 1958 549p illus (Prentice-Hall English literature ser)
Partially analyzed

Birdsall, Ruth
(ed.) Creative plays for every school month; illus. by Cynthia Amrine. Owen 1957 112p illus music (The Instructor activity ser)
Partially analyzed

Blue-ribbon plays for girls. Kamerman, S. E. ed.

Blue-ribbon plays for graduation. Kamerman, S. E. ed.

Bottomley, Gordon
Poems and plays with an introduction by Claude Colleer Abbott. British Bk. Centre 1953 464p front
Partially analyzed

Boyd, A. K.
An hour to play; a book of plays for school actors. Murray, J. 1956 111p

Brabazon, Francis
Singing threshold. Beacon Hill Press 1958 103p

Brecht, Bertolt
Two plays: The good woman of Setzuan, and The Caucasian chalk circle. The original English versions by Eric Bentley and Maja Apelman. Grove [1957] 192p

Breck, Flora E.
(ed.) Playlets and poems for church school (for teaching Bible truths) Wilde 1954 50p music
Partially analyzed

Brings, Lawrence M.
(comp.) The golden book of church plays. Denison 1955 476p
(ed.) The modern treasury of Christmas plays; a collection of one-act plays for church and school, ed. and comp. by Lawrence M. Brings. Denison 1955 536p illus music

British Broadcasting Corporation
The television playwright; ten plays for B.B.C. television, by Willis Hall [and others] selected by Michael Barry; introduction and notes by Donald Wilson. Hill & Wang 1960 490p illus

Broadway's best, 1957-1960; the complete record of the theatrical year, by John Chapman. Doubleday 1957-1960 4v
Partially analyzed

Browne, E. Martin
(ed.) Religious drama, 2; mystery and morality plays; selected and introduced by E. Martin Browne. Meridian Bks. 1958 317p (Living Age bks)
(ed.) Three Irish plays; introduced and ed. by E. Martin Browne. Penguin 1959 236p

Bryant, Al
(comp.) Religious plays that click. . . . Zondervan 1954 91p

Burack, A. S.
(ed.) Four-star plays for boys; a collection of fifteen royalty-free, one-act plays for all-boy casts. Plays, inc. 1957 237p
(ed.) Four-star radio plays for teen-agers; a collection of royalty-free radio dramas adapted from great literature. Plays, inc. 1959 246p
(ed.) Television plays for writers; eight television plays with comment and analysis by the authors; with a foreword by Herbert Brodkin. Writer 1957 396p

Burgess, C. V.
Talking of the Taylors. Univ. of London Press 1956 111p

The Burns Mantle yearbook. See The Best plays

C

Cahill, Edna M.
(ed.) Celebrating Christmas; plays, programs, stunts, readings, exercises (for children and adults) Bakers Plays 1954 127p
Partially analyzed

Caligula & three other plays. Camus, A.
Cameo plays: bk. 19. Arnold E.J. [1956] 95p
Camille, and other plays. Stanton, S. S. ed.

Camus, Albert
Caligula & three other plays; tr. from the French by Stuart Gilbert. Knopf 1958 302p

Canada on stage. Richards, S. ed.

The **caretaker** and The **dumb waiter.** Pinter, H.

Carlson, Bernice Wells
The right play for you; illus. by Georgette Boris. Abingdon 1960 160p illus
Partially analyzed

Carpenter, Frank
Six animal plays; with a foreword by Christopher Fry and pictures by Ronald Searle. Methuen 1953 134p illus

Carter, Conrad
About time, too, and five other playlets. [Acting ed] French (London) 1953 56p illus

Casey, Beatrice Marie
Good things for church groups. Denison 1958 366p
Partially analyzed

Casson, Lionel
(ed.) Masters of ancient comedy; selections from Aristophanes, Menander, Plautus, Terence; ed. and tr. by Lionel Casson. Macmillan (N Y) 1960 424p

Cavalcade of comedy. Kronenberger, L. ed.

Cawley, A. C.
(ed.) Everyman, and medieval miracle plays. See Everyman, and medieval miracle plays

Celebrating Christmas. Cahill, E. M. ed.

Cerf, Bennett, and Cartmell, Van H.
(eds.) 24 favorite one-act plays. Doubleday 1958 455p

Chapman, John
(ed.) The Best plays of 1894-1899. See The Best plays of 1894-1899
(ed.) Broadway's best. See Broadway's best
(ed.) Theatre, 1953-1956. See Theatre, 1953-1956

Chayefsky, Paddy
Television plays. Simon & Schuster 1955 268p

Chekhov, Anton
Best plays of Chekhov: The sea gull, Uncle Vanya, The three sisters, The cherry orchard; tr. and with an introduction by Stark Young. Modern Lib. 1956 296p (The Modern Lib. of the world's best bks)

The **children's** program book. Asbrand, K.

The **classic** Noh theatre of Japan. Pound, E. and Fenollosa, E.

The **classic** theatre. Bentley, E. ed.

Claudel, Paul
Two dramas; translations and introductions [by] Wallace Fowlie. Regnery 1960 295p illus

The **collected** plays of W. B. Yeats. Yeats, W. B.

A **comedy** and two proverbs. Musset, A. de

Comparative comedies, present and past. Keyes, R. K. and Roth, H. M. eds.

The **complete** Greek tragedies. Grene, D. and Lattimore, R. eds.

Congreve, William
Complete plays; ed. by Alexander Charles Ewald. Hill & Wang 1956 438p (A Mermaid dramabook)

Contemporary drama: eleven plays. Watson, E. B. and Pressey, B. eds.

Contemporary drama: fifteen plays. Watson, E. B. ed.

Cooper, Charles W.
Preface to drama; an introduction to dramatic literature and theater art. Ronald 1955 773p music

Cordell, Richard A. and Matson, Lowell
(eds.) The off-Broadway theatre; seven plays. Random House 1959 481p

Corneille, Pierre
Moot plays of Corneille; tr. into English blank verse with introductions by Lacy Lockert. Vanderbilt Univ. Press 1959 486p

Costigan, James
Little moon of Alban & A wind from the south; two plays. Simon & Schuster 1959 146p illus

Creative plays for every school month. Birdsall, R. ed.

The **creative** reader. Stallman, R. W. and Watters, R. E.

Critics' choice. Gaver, J.

Cubeta, Paul M.   - 808.82
(ed.) Modern drama for analysis. Rev. ed. Dryden 1955 785p illus

Curtis, P. D.
Three short humorous sketches; for boys ages 10 to 14. Paxton 1958 12p
Three short humorous sketches; for girls ages 10 to 14. Paxton 1958 12p

D

Daily, Dorothy Tinsley. See Applegarth, M. T. jt. auth.

Daviot, Gordon
Plays. Davies 1953-1954 3v

Dean, Leonard F.
(ed.) Nine great plays; from Aeschylus to Eliot. Rev. ed. Harcourt 1956 695p

Dekker, Thomas
The dramatic works of Thomas Dekker; ed. by Fredson Bowers. Cambridge 1953-1961 4v illus

Dennis, Nigel
Two plays and a preface: Cards of identity & The making of moo. Vanguard 1958 224p

Dias, Earl J.
Melodramas and farces for young actors. Plays, inc. 1956 263p

Dimondstein, Boris
Short plays, and one act plays. Literarishe Heftn 1957 79p

Don Juan, and Forced to be a doctor. Molière, J. B. P.

Downer, Alan S.
  (ed.) American drama. Crowell 1960 261p
    illus music (Reader's bookshelf of Am.
    literature)
  (ed.) The art of the play; an anthology of
    nine plays. Holt 1955 451p illus
  (ed.) Twenty-five modern plays. See
    Tucker, S. M. Twenty-five modern
    plays
The dramatic experience. Bierman, J.; Hart,
  J. and Johnson, S. eds.
The dramatic works of Thomas Dekker.
  Dekker, T.

E

Easy church plays for women and girls.
  Asbrand, K.
Easy grade school plays. Spamer, C.
Easy juvenile grab bag, by various authors.
  Bakers Plays 1955 95p
    Partially analyzed
Easy plays for church and school. Howard, V.
Easy programs for church holidays. As-
  brand, K.
Easy science plays for grade school. Spa-
  mer, C.
Easy sketches of famous women. Spamer, C.
Eight plays. Molière, J. B. P.
Electra, and other plays. Sophocles
Eleven plays of the Greek dramatists;
  Aeschylus, Sophocles, Euripides and
  Aristophanes. Grosset 1958 [1946] 376p
  (Universal lib)
Emmons, Della Gould
  Northwest history in action; a collection
    of twelve plays illustrating the epochs
    of Northwest history. Denison 1960
    287p
Emurian, Ernest K.
  More plays and pageants for many occa-
    sions. Wilde 1954 215p
  Plays and pageants for many occasions.
    Wilde 1953 192p
  Ten new plays for church and school.
    Wilde 1959 194p
Entrances and exits. Fenner, P. and Hughes,
  A. comps.
Ernst, Earle
  (ed.) Three Japanese plays from the tradi-
    tional theatre. Grove 1959 200p
    American trade edition also published by
    Grove. English trade edition published
    by Oxford
Estes, Susan
  In quest of power; twelve devotional
    dramas. Broadman 1954 91p illus
Ethel and Albert comedies. Lynch, P.
Euripides
  The Bacchae, and other plays; tr. by Philip
    Vellacott. Penguin 1954 234p
  Plays; tr. by A. S. Way; introduction by
    John Warrington. Dent 1956 2v (Every-
    man's lib)
Everyman, and medieval miracle plays; ed.
  with an introduction by A. C. Cawley.
  Dutton 1959 266p (A Dutton Everyman
  paperback)
    Trade edition published by Dent

F

Famous American plays of the 1940s. Hewes,
  H. ed.
Fanny Burney's resignation, and other plays.
  Robinson, R.
Farquhar, George
  George Farquhar; ed. with an introduction
    and notes, by William Archer. Hill &
    Wang 1959 455p (A Mermaid drama-
    book)
Favorite modern plays. Sper, F. ed.
Fenner, Phyllis, and Hughes, Avah
  (comps.) Entrances and exits; a book of
    plays for young actors; illus. by Frank
    Kramer. Dodd 1960 276p illus
First plays for children. Miller, H. L.
First short plays. Waugh, J. R.
Fisher, Aileen
  Health and safety plays and programs.
    Plays, inc. 1953 267p
    Partially analyzed
  Holiday programs for boys and girls.
    Plays, inc. 1953 374p
    Partially analyzed
Fisher, Aileen, and Rabe, Olive
  Patriotic plays and programs. Plays, inc.
    1956 418p
    Partially analyzed
  United Nations plays and programs. Plays,
    inc. 1954 285p
    Partially analyzed
Fitts, Dudley
  (ed.) Four Greek plays. Harcourt 1960
    310p (A Harvest bk)
  (ed.) Six Greek plays in modern transla-
    tion. Dryden 1955 294p
Five comedies. Aristophanes
Five modern Nō plays. Mishima, Y.
Five one-act plays. O'Casey, S.
Five plays. Anouilh, J.
Five plays. Ford, J.
Five plays. Jonson, B.
Five plays. Marlowe, C.
Five plays. Molière, J. B. P.
Five plays. Racine, J.
Five plays. Strindberg, A.
Five plays. Wilson, E.
Five Stuart tragedies. McIlwraith, A. K. ed.
Foote, Horton
  Harrison, Texas; eight television plays.
    Harcourt 1956 266p
  A young lady of property; six short plays.
    Dramatists 1955 154p
Ford, John
  Five plays; ed. with an introduction and
    notes by Havelock Ellis. Hill & Wang
    1957 427p (A Mermaid dramabook)
    Also published in trade edition
Four Christmas plays. Horn Book Magazine
Four English tragedies of the 16th and 17th
  centuries. Morrell, J. M. ed.
Four Greek plays. Fitts, D. ed.
Four modern French comedies; with an in-
  troduction by Wallace Fowlie. Putnam
  1960 256p illus (Capricorn bks)

Four modern plays: Henrik Ibsen, Hedda Gabler; Bernard Shaw, Pygmalion; Eugene O'Neill, The Emperor Jones; Arthur Miller, Death of a salesman. Rinehart 1957 338p

Four playettes. Applegarth, M. T.; Daily, D. T. and Wolfe, B. S.

4 plays. Behrman, S. N.

Four plays. Giraudoux, J.

Four plays. Ibsen, H.

4 plays. Inge, W.

Four plays. Ionesco, E.

Four plays. Shaw, B.

Four plays. Webster, J. and Tourneur, C.

Four screenplays. Bergman, I.

Four-star plays for boys. Burack, A. S. ed.

Four-star radio plays for teen-agers. Burack, A. S. ed.

Four verse plays. Anderson, M.

From the modern repertoire. Bentley, E. ed.

G

García Lorca, Federico
Three tragedies of Federico García Lorca; Blood wedding, Yerma, Bernarda Alba. Tr. by James Graham-Luján and Richard L. O'Connell. Introduction by Francisco García Lorca. New Directions 1955 212p

Gassner, John
(ed.) Best American plays. See Best American plays
(ed.) A Treasury of the theatre. See A Treasury of the theatre
(ed.) Twenty best European plays on the American stage; ed. with an introduction by John Gassner. Crown 1957 733p

Gassner, John, and Nichols, Dudley
(eds.) Great film plays; being volume 1 of a new ed. of Twenty best film plays. Crown 1959 334p

Gaver, Jack
(ed.) Critics' choice; New York drama critics' circle prize plays, 1935-55. Hawthorn Bks. 1955 661p

George Farquhar. Farquhar, G.

Ghelderode, Michel de
Seven plays; with an introduction by George Hauger. Hill & Wang 1960 304p (A Mermaid dramabook)
Partially analyzed

Gibson, William
The seesaw log; a chronicle of the stage production, with the text, of Two for the seesaw. Knopf 1959 273p
Partially analyzed

Giraudoux, Jean
Four plays; adapted and with an introduction by Maurice Valency. Hill & Wang 1958 xxi, 255p (A Mermaid dramabook)

Goethe, Johann Wolfgang von
Goethe's Faust, parts I and II; in the Sir Theodore Martin translation; introduced, revised, and annotated by W. H. Bruford. Dutton 1954 (Everyman's lib) 416p
Goethe's Faust, parts I and II. Goethe, J. W. von

Gold medal plays for holidays. Miller, H. L.

The golden book of church plays. Brings, L. M. comp.

The golden cuckoo, and other plays. Johnston, D.

Goldschmidt, Walter
(ed.) Ways of mankind, illus. by Arminta Neal. Beacon Press 1954 212p illus

Goldsmith, Oliver
Oliver Goldsmith; ed. by George Pierce Baker; introduction by Austin Dobson. Hill & Wang [1958?] 190p (A Mermaid dramabook)
Partially analyzed

Good things for church groups. Casey, B. M.

Goulding, Dorothy Jane
The master cat, and other plays. Coach House Press 1955 138p illus music

The grand garden and other plays. Li, Y. M.

Grauman, Walter E. See Armer, A. jt. auth.

Great Christian plays. Switz, T. M. and Johnston, R. A. eds.

Great film plays. Gassner, J. and Nichols, D. eds.

Greek drama for everyman. Lucas, F. L. ed.

Greek tragedies. Grene, D. and Lattimore, R. eds.

Grene, David, and Lattimore, Richmond
(eds.) The complete Greek tragedies. Univ. of Chicago Press 1959 4v
Also published in 9 volumes
(eds.) Greek tragedies. Univ. of Chicago Press 1960 3v (Phoenix bks)
A selection from The complete Greek tragedies, entered above

Griffin, Alice Venezky
Living theatre; an anthology of great plays; with a foreword by Helen Hayes. Twayne 1953 510p

Grillparzer, Franz
The Jewess of Toledo [and] Esther; tr. by Arthur Burkhard. Register Press 1953 151p
Partially analyzed

Gross, Edwin, and Gross, Nathalie
Teen theater; a guide to play production and six royalty-free plays. Foreword by Margaret C. Scoggin, with line drawings by Edwin Gross. McGraw 1953 (Whittlesey House publications) 245p

Guidance through drama. Weiss, M. J.

Gunn, John M.
(ed.) Look up and live. The seeking years

H

Halverson, Marvin
(ed.) Religious drama 1; five plays; selected and introduced by Marvin Halverson. Meridian Bks. 1957 410p (Living age bks)
Partially analyzed

A man called Jesus. Phillips, J. B.

Marlowe, Christopher
Five plays; ed. by Havelock Ellis with an introduction by John Addington Symonds. Hill & Wang 1956 344p (A Mermaid dramabook)

Marston, Millicent A.
Mimes with crowds. Arnold, E.J. [1953] 64p illus (Cameo plays, no. 18)

Martens, Anne Coulter
We're speechless; a collection of pantomimes and one-rehearsal plays. Bakers Plays 1957 95p

The master cat, and other plays. Goulding, D. J.

Masters of ancient comedy. Casson, L. ed.

Mayorga, Margaret
(ed.) The Best short plays. See The Best short plays

Melodramas and farces for young actors. Dias, E. J.

Miller, Arthur
Arthur Miller's Collected plays; with an introduction. Viking 1957 439p
A view from the bridge; two one-act plays. Viking 1955 160p

Miller, Helen Louise
First plays for children; a collection of little plays for the youngest players. Plays, inc. 1960 295p
Gold medal plays for holidays; thirty royalty-free, one-act plays for children. Plays, inc. 1958 432p
Plays for living and learning. Plays, inc. 1955 312p
Prize plays for teen-agers; a collection of one-act, royalty-free plays for all occasions. Plays, inc. 1956 504p

Miller, Madge
Miniature plays; written for The Pittsburgh Miniature Theatre. Childrens Theatre 1954 150p illus

Mimes with crowds. Marston, M. A.

Miniature plays. Miller, M.

Miracle plays. Malcolmson, A.

The **miser**; and, Coxcombs in petticoats. Molière, J. B. P.

Mishima, Yukio
Five modern Nō plays; tr. from the Japanese by Donald Keene. Knopf 1957 198p illus

Modern drama for analysis. Cubeta, P. M. ed.

Modern Scandinavian plays [by] August Strindberg [and others]. Liveright 1954 366p

The **modern** theatre. Bentley, E. ed.

The **modern** treasury of Christmas plays. Brings, L. M. ed.

Molière, Jean Baptiste Poquelin
Don Juan, and Forced to be a doctor; two comedies by Molière; English version by George Graveley. Cartmel 1953 110p
Eight plays; tr. with an introduction, by Morris Bishop. Modern Lib. 1957 399p (The Modern Lib. of the world's best bks)
Five plays; tr. with an introduction by John Wood. Penguin 1953 251p (The Penguin Classics)

The miser, and Coxcombs in petticoats; two comedies by Molière; English version by George Graveley. Cartmel 1953 109p
Six prose comedies; an English version by George Graveley. Oxford 1956 378p front
The slave of truth (Le misanthrope); Tartuffe; The imaginary invalid. New English versions by Miles Malleson. Coward-McCann 1960 269p

Moore, Stephen S.
Six playlets from Aesop's Fables. Paxton 1955 12p

Moot plays of Corneille. Corneille, P.

More plays and pageants for many occasions. Emurian, E. K.

Morrell, J. M.
(ed.) Four English tragedies of the 16th and 17th centuries. Penguin 1953 375p

Mortimer, John
Three plays. Elek 1958 158p

Mosel, Tad
Other people's houses; six television plays. Simon & Schuster 1956 242p

The **mountain** giants, and other plays. Pirandello, L.

Murphy, Arthur
The way to keep him & five other plays; ed. by John Pike Emery. N.Y. Univ. Press 1956 434p front

Murray, John
Mystery plays for young people; a collection of royalty-free one-act dramas of mystery and suspense. Plays, inc. 1956 372p

Musset, Alfred de
A comedy and two proverbs; English version by George Graveley. Oxford 1955 99p

Mystery plays for young people. Murray, J.

N

Nathan, Robert
Jezebel's husband & The sleeping beauty. Knopf 1953 209p

National Recreation Association
Pageants and programs for school, church and playground. Nat. Recreation Assn. 42p illus music
Partially analyzed
Plays, pageants and ceremonials for the Christmas season. Nat. Recreation Assn. 1953 76p

The **nature** of drama. Heffner, H.

New plays for red letter days. Woolsey, J. and Sechrist, E. H.

New voices in the American theatre; foreword by Brooks Atkinson. Modern Lib. 1955 559p (The Modern Lib. of the world's best books)

Newman, Deborah
Holiday plays for little players; a collection of royalty-free plays for children. Plays, inc. 1957 286p

Nine great plays. Dean, L. F.

Nineteenth century plays. Rowell, G. ed.

No exit, and three other plays. Sartre, J. P.

The Nō plays of Japan. Waley, A.

The Noh drama. The Japan Society for the Promotion of Science. Japanese Classics Translation Committee. Special Noh Committee

North Carolina drama. Walser, R. ed.

Northwest history in action. Emmons, D. G.

O

O'Casey, Sean
Five one-act plays. St Martins 1958 160p music
Juno and the paycock, and The plough and the stars. Macmillan (London) 1954 168p
Selected plays; selected and with foreword by the author; introduction by John Gassner. Braziller 1954 800p front music
Three plays. Macmillan (London) 1957 218p

The off-Broadway theatre. Cordell, R. A. and Matson, L. eds.

Olfson, Lewy
Radio plays from Shakespeare; ten plays by William Shakespeare adapted for royalty-free performance by Lewy Olfson. Plays, inc. 1958 193p
Radio plays of famous stories; a collection of royalty-free radio dramatizations of great stories. Plays, inc. 1956 250p

Oliver Goldsmith. Goldsmith, O.

Olson, Elder
Plays & poems, 1948-58. Univ. of Chicago Press 1958 168p

On stage tonight. Keeney, C. H.

On with the show. Addis, H.

O'Neill, Eugene
Lost plays of Eugene O'Neill. Citadel 1958 156p
Three plays. Random House 1958 376p (Modern Lib. Paperbacks)

The Oresteian trilogy. Aeschylus

Orpheus descending, with Battle of angels. Williams, T.

Other people's houses. Mosel, T.

Over-the-air plays. Webber, J.

P

Pageants and programs for school, church and playground. National Recreation Association

Parker, Kenneth T.
Parker's television plays; a collection of eight plays written for stage and television, with an introduction by Joseph Carleton Beal. Northwestern Press 1954 245p

Parker's television plays. Parker, K. T.

Patrioscript. Prescott, H. ed.

Patriotic plays and programs. Fisher, A. and Rabe, O.

Phillips, J. B.
A man called Jesus; a series of short plays from the life of Christ. Macmillan (N Y) 1959 141p

Pinter, Harold
The caretaker and The dumb waiter; two plays. Grove 1961 [1960] 121p (Evergreen original)

Pirandello, Luigi
The mountain giants, and other plays; tr. from the Italian by Marta Abba. Crown 1958 277p
The rules of the game; The life I gave you; Lazarus; introduced and ed. by E. Martin Browne. Penguin 1959 218p

Play-time. Atwell, R. and Virden, H.

Playbook: five plays for a new theatre. New Directions 1956 298p

Playlets and poems for church school. Breck, F. E.

Plays. Daviot, G.

Plays. Euripides

Plays. Shaw, G. B.

Plays. Wilde, O.

Plays and pageants for many occasions. Emurian, E. K.

Plays & poems, 1948-58. Olson, E.

Plays for happier homes. Lantz, J. E. and Lantz, R. C.

Plays for living and learning. Miller, H. L.

Plays for players, and a guide to play production. Powers, V. E. ed.

Plays of the year, v5, 1950-51; chosen by J. C. Trewin. Elek 1952 490p

Plays of the year, v7, 1951-52; chosen by J. C. Trewin. Elek 1953 526p

Plays of the year, v8, 1952-53; chosen by J. C. Trewin. Elek 1953 537p

Plays of the year, v9, 1953; chosen by J. C. Trewin. Elek 1953 584p

Plays of the year, v10, 1953/54; chosen by J. C. Trewin. Elek 1954 526p

Plays of the year, v11, 1954; chosen by J. C. Trewin. Ungar 1955 620p

Plays of the year, v12, 1954-55; chosen by J. C. Trewin. Elek 1955 562p

Plays of the year, v13, 1955; chosen by J. C. Trewin. Ungar 1956 424p

Plays of the year, v14, 1955-56; chosen by J. C. Trewin. Ungar 1957 448p

Plays of the year, v15, 1956; chosen by J. C. Trewin. Ungar 1957 443p

Plays of the year, v16, 1956-57; chosen by J. C. Trewin. Ungar 1958 432p

Plays of the year, v17, 1957-58; chosen by J. C. Trewin. Ungar 1958 429p

Plays of the year, v18, 1958; chosen by J. C. Trewin. Ungar 1959 430p

Plays of the year, v19, 1958-59; ed. by J. C. Trewin. Ungar 1959 407p

Plays of the year, v20, 1959; ed. by J. C. Trewin. Ungar 1960 432p music

Plays of the year, v21, 1959-1960; ed. by J. C. Trewin. Ungar 1961 480p

Plays, pageants and ceremonials for the Christmas season. National Recreation Association

Poems and plays. Bottomley, G.

Poetical works. Tennyson, A.

Pound, Ezra, and Fenollosa, Ernest
The classic Noh theatre of Japan. New Directions 1959 163p (A New Directions Paperbook)

Powers, Verne E.
(ed.) Plays for players, and a guide to play production; collected, arranged and ed. by Verne E. Powers, with an introduction by John Chapman and containing a special section on simplified scenery and staging by Colby Lewis. Character-illustration sketches by Jacob Landau. Cover design and introductory sketches by Rod Taenzer. Row 1957 672p illus music

Preface to drama. Cooper, C. W.

Prescott, Herbert
(ed.) Patrioscript; 13 radio plays, as originally produced by the Grinnell College Radio Players under a grant from the National Association of Educational Broadcasters, through the Fund for Adult Education, an independent agency of the Ford Foundation. Grinnell College Press 1953 275p music

Pressey, Benfield. See Watson, E. B. jt. ed.

Priestley, Florence
Six plays for girls. Methuen 1955 70p

Priestley, H. E.
Six little Punch plays. Paxton 1956 20p music

Prize plays for teen-agers. Miller, H. L.

The prize plays of television and radio, 1956. Writers Guild of America

Q

Quinn, Arthur Hobson
(ed.) Representative American plays; from 1767 to the present day; ed. with introductions and notes by Arthur Hobson Quinn. 7th ed. rev. and enl. Appleton 1953 1248p

R

Rabe, Olive. See Fisher, A. jt. auth.

Racine, Jean
Five plays; tr. into English verse, and with an introduction by Kenneth Muir. Hill & Wang 1960 xxviii, 288p (A Mermaid dramabook)

Radio plays from Shakespeare. Olfson, L.

Radio plays of famous stories. Olfson, L.

Rattigan, Terence
Collected plays. Hamilton, H. 1953 2v

Rehearsal-less fun. Asbrand, K.

Religious drama, 1. Halverson, M. ed.

Religious drama, 2. Browne, E. M. ed.

Religious drama, 3. Halverson, M. ed.

Religious plays that click. Bryant, A. comp.

Reninger, H. Willard. See Knickerbocker, K. L. jt. auth.

Representative American plays. Quinn, A. H. ed.

Representative modern plays, British. Warnock, R.

Restoration plays; with an introduction by Brice Harris. Modern Lib. 1953 xx, 674p (The Modern Lib. of the world's best books)

Rhinoceros and other plays. Ionesco, E.

Richards, Stanley
(ed.) Canada on stage; ed. and introduced by Stanley Richards. Clarke, Irwin 1960 324p

Ridge, Antonia
Six radio plays. Arnold, E.J. [1954] 96p (Cameo plays, no. 20)

The right play for you. Carlson, B. W.

Ring up the curtain; four plays. Heinemann 1955 442p

Roberts, Edward Barry
Television writing and selling; with an introduction by Ira L. Avery. Writer 1954 499p illus
Partially analyzed

Robinson, Charles Alexander
(ed.) An anthology of Greek drama. 2d ser. Rinehart 1954 398p (Rinehart Editions, 68)

Robinson, Ruth
Fanny Burney's resignation, and other plays. Macmillan (London) 1953 70p

Rodgers, Richard, and Hammerstein, Oscar
6 plays by Rodgers and Hammerstein. Random House 1955 527p
Also published by The Modern Library

Rose, Reginald
Six television plays. Simon & Schuster 1956 302p

Round-the-year plays for children. Very, A.

'Round the year plays for the grades; by various authors. Eldridge 1958 126p

Rowell, George
(ed.) Nineteenth century plays; ed. with an introduction by George Rowell. Oxford 1953 567p

The rules of the game; The life I gave you; Lazarus. Pirandello, L.

S

Saint Joan, Major Barbara [and] Androcles and the lion. Shaw, B.

Sakanishi, Shio
(tr.) Japanese folk-plays: The ink-smeared lady, and other kyogen; with illus. by Yoshie Noguchi. [New ed] Tuttle 1960 150p illus (UNESCO collection of representative works: Japanese ser)
First published 1938 by Marshall Jones Company

Two plays: Peace and Lysistrata. Aristophanes

Two saints' plays: Saint Chad of the seven wells, by Leo Lehman; followed by Man's estate, by Robert Gittings. Heinemann 1954 79p (The Drama lib)

U

United Nations plays and programs. Fisher, A. and Rabe, O.

V

Very, Alice
Round-the-year plays for children. Plays, inc. 1957 279p

Vest pocket theatre. Armer, A. and Grauman, W. E.

Vidal, Gore
(ed.) Best television plays. Ballantine 1956 250p
Visit to a small planet, and other television plays. Little 1956 278p

A view from the bridge; two one-act plays. Miller, A.

Virden, Helen. See Atwell, R. jt. auth.

Visit to a small planet, and other television plays. Vidal, G.

Voaden, Herman
(ed.) Two good plays to read and act. Longmans 1953 204p (The Heritage of literature ser)

W

Waley, Arthur
The Nō plays of Japan; with letters by Oswald Sickert. Grove [1957] 319p illus English trade edition published by Allen, G.

Wallerstein, James S.
Adventure; five plays for youth; illus. by Victor Menard. Bellamy Press 1956 195p illus

Walser, Richard
(ed.) North Carolina drama; with plays by William Norment Cox [and others] and two comedies by Paul Green; ed. with an introduction by Richard Walser. Garrett 1956 229p

Warnock, Robert
Representative modern plays, British. Scott 1953 710p illus

Watson, E. Bradlee, and Pressey, Benfield
(eds.) Contemporary drama: fifteen plays; American, English and Irish, European. Selected and ed. by E. Bradlee Watson and Benfield Pressey. Scribner 1959 577p
(eds.) Contemporary drama: eleven plays; American, English, European. Selected and ed. by E. Bradlee Watson and Benfield Pressey. Scribner 1956 341p

Waugh, James R.
First short plays. Longmans 1956 63p (Plays for today)
Second short plays. Longmans 1956 62p (Plays for today)

The way to keep him & five other plays. Murphy, A.

Ways of mankind. Goldschmidt, W. ed.

The weather imp; and, The King of Nowhere. Hurt, F.

Webber, John
Over-the-air plays. Methuen 1955 79p

Webster, John, and Tourneur, Cyril
John Webster and Cyril Tourneur (Four plays) With an introduction and notes by John Addington Symonds. General editor: Eric Bentley. Hill & Wang 1956 381p (A Mermaid dramabook)

Weiss, M. Jerry
Guidance through drama. Whiteside 1954 333p

We're speechless. Martens, A. C.

Wilde, Oscar
Plays; with an introduction by Tyrone Guthrie. Collins 1954 448p front

Wilder, Thornton
Three plays: Our town, The skin of our teeth, The matchmaker; with a preface. Harper 1957 401p

The William Saroyan Reader. Saroyan, W.

Williams, Norman
Worlds apart; six prize-winning plays. Copp 1956 203p illus

Williams, Tennessee
Orpheus descending, with Battle of angels. New Directions 1958 238p
27 wagons full of cotton, and other one-act plays. New Directions 1953 238p

Wilson, Edmund
Five plays. Farrar, Straus 1954 541p

Wolfe, Betsy S. See Applegarth, M. T. jt. auth.

Woolsey, Janette, and Sechrist, Elizabeth Hough
It's time to give a play; new plays for all occasions; illus. by Guy Fry. Macrae Smith Co. 1955 307p illus
New plays for red letter days. Macrae Smith Co. 1953 310p illus

The works of Nathaniel Lee. Lee, N.

Worlds apart. Williams, N.

Writers Guild of America
The prize plays of television and radio, 1956. Foreword by Clifton Fadiman. Random House 1957 309p

Y

Yeats, W. B.
The collected plays of W. B. Yeats; new ed. with five additional plays. Macmillan (N Y) 1953 446p front

A young lady of property. Foote, H.

Z

The zoo story; The death of Bessie Smith; The sandbox. Albee, E.

Part III

Cast Analysis

This section is designed to locate plays by number of players or readers. It is divided into four sections (1) all male cast (2) all female cast (3) mixed cast (4) puppet plays (5) unidentified cast. Under each type of cast the arrangement is from the small to the large cast of over 35 characters.

Sample entry:

MIXED CAST
7 characters (4m 3w)
Anouilh, J. The rehearsal

In the above entry a play with a mixed cast of 7 characters, 4 men and 3 women, is Anouilh's "The Rehearsal." Plays requiring extra players for non-speaking parts or chorus are indicated by "extras."

The arrangement within the cast size is from the small to the large number of men, then women, followed by boys and finally girls, *i.e.* a 4 character play for a cast of 1 man and 3 women would come before one for 2 men and 2 women, then would follow 2 men and 2 boys, and 2 men and 2 girls.

MALE CAST

1 character (1m)
Beckett, S. Act without words, I
Beckett, S. Krapp's last tape
Ghelderode, M. de. Pantagleize

1 character and extras (1m extras)
Brabazon, F. The madmen
c Carlson, B. W. Who's stronger?
Lowe, E. A birthday through the centuries
Probst, G. The experiment of a free press
c Ridge, A. Hare and the field of millet
c Ridge, A. Under the monkey-bread tree
Sakanishi, S. tr. Thunder God
c Spamer, C. The plight of the tree
c Tennant, K. The prince who met a dragon
Williams, C. Grab and grace

1 character and extras (1b extras)
c Ahrens, C. Jon's helpers
c Fowler, M. G. The enchanted pumpkin
c Spamer, C. The adventurous balloon
c Spamer, C. Crossing the street

2 characters (1m 1b)
Addis, H. Off the rocks
Taggart, T. Follow simple directions

2 characters (2m)
Albee, E. The zoo story
Beckett, S. Act without words, II
Casey, B. M. The hand of God
Casey, B. M. Myself and I
Casey, B. M. Second chance
Hughes, K. Sammy
Mankowitz, W. It should happen to a dog
Mortimer, J. The dock brief
Olson, E. The sorcerer's apprentices
O'Neill, E. Hughie

Phillips, J. B. The temptation of Jesus
Pinter, H. The dumb waiter
Probst, G. Nature's most precious gift
Sakanishi, S. tr. Gargoyle
Sakanishi, S. tr. Literate highwaymen
Sakanishi, S. tr. The melon thief
Sakanishi, S. tr. Seed of hōjō
Yeats, W. B. Purgatory

2 characters and extras (1m 1b extras)
c Tennant, K. Hamaguchi Gohei

2 characters and extras (2m extras)
Enami, S. The bird-catcher in Hades
c Fisher, A. Courting trouble
Kwanze, M. Tsunemasa
Malcolmson, A. The statue of Saint Nicholas
c Moore, S. S. The lion and the mouse
c Porter, H. W. Election Day
Sakanishi, S. tr. The Deva King Shojo
c Spamer, C. Gideon and the angel
c Spamer, C. The parable of the sower
Taggart, T. Oily to rise

2 characters and extras (2b extras)
c Carlson, B. W. It's a—!
c Moore, S. S. The travellers and the bear

3 characters (2m 1b)
Allan, D. C. Eyes that see not
Fenwick, R. Toys and science

3 characters (3m)
Anderson, B. F. Prejudice unlimited
Asbrand, K. Brotherhood
c Carlson, B. W. Not me!
Connelly, M. The traveler
Corrigan, L. Whosoever believeth

MALE CAST—*Continued*

Healey, R. M. Nobody knows
Inge, W. The tiny closet
Lardner, R. The tridget of Greva
O'Neill, E. "A wife for a life"
Pinter, H. The caretaker
Sakanishi, S. tr. A bag of tangerines
Sakanishi, S. tr. Buaku
Sakanishi, S. tr. Busu
Sakanishi, S. tr. The fox mound
Sakanishi, S. tr. Plop! Click!
Taggart, T. The gross story conference
Williams, E. Virgil
Williams, T. The last of my solid gold watches
Winnie, D. J. A very cold night

3 characters (3b)
c Blyton, E. Finding the tickets

3 characters and extras (2m 1b extras)
Fisher, A. and Rabe, O. When freedom was news
Komparu, Z. Ikuta

3 characters and extras (3m extras)
Aeschylus. The suppliant maidens
Euripides. The cyclops
c Goulding, D. J. The gift of the drum
Hiyoshi, Y. Benkei on the bridge
Komparu, Z. U. Kumasaka
Kwanze, M. Atsumori
Kwanze, M. Haku Rakuten
Kwanze, M. Suma Genji
c Miller, H. L. The rabbits who changed their minds
Sakanishi, S. tr. The magic mallet of the Devil
c Spamer, C. The baptism of Jesus
c Spamer, C. Jesus is born
c Spamer, C. Jonathan's son
Swann, D. L. The crier calls

4 characters (3m 1b)
Addis, H. St George's Day
Finch, R. From Paradise to Butte
c Nicholson, M. A. The crying clown

4 characters (4m)
Abraham and Isaac (Brome manuscript) The sacrifice of Isaac
Boyd, A. K. Fighting Bob
Boyd, A. K. Prince Arthur and Hubert
Coventry plays. Cain and Abel
Dunsany, Lord. The jest of Hahalaba
Fry, C. A sleep of prisoners
Gassner, J. The Brome Abraham and Isaac
Ghelderode, M. de. The blind men
Hallman, E. S. Survival
Howard, V. Paloma, Princess of Pluto
Howard, V. Pollywogs
Howard, V. A rest for Mr Winkle
Howard, V. Your money or your life
Olson, E. The shepherd and the conqueror
Phillips, J. B. The Transfiguration
Smith, B. and Webb, C. Mañana bandits
c Spamer, C. Saul and the ghost
York plays. The temptation of Christ

4 characters and extras (1m 3b extras)
Howard, V. Spook shop

4 characters and extras (4m extras)
c Bennett, R. The runaway pirate
Brabazon, F. The bridge
c Carlson, B. W. A bargain's a bargain
Enami, S. Ukai
Estes, S. In quest of power through courage
Estes, S. In quest of power through decision
Euripides. The Cyclops
c Fisher, A. What happened on Clutter Street
Komparu, Z. U. The hōka priests
Kwanze, K. N. Chorio
McCaslin, N. With the sunrise in his pocket
c Spamer, C. David and Goliath
c Webber, C. E. The barber and the donkey

4 characters and extras (4b extras)
c Atwell, R. and Virden, H. Witch hunt
Howard, V. Drexel
c Spamer, C. The hatless snowmen

5 characters (1m 4b)
Howard, V. Your manners and mine

5 characters (3m 2b)
c Colson, J. G. Top of the bill

5 characters (4m 1b)
Beckett, S. Waiting for Godot
Malcolmson, A. Abraham and Isaac
Phillips, J. B. The baptism of Jesus

5 characters (5m)
Abraham and Isaac (Brome manuscript) Abraham and Isaac
Addis, H. What ho for the open road
Geiger, M. The democrat and the commissar
Howard, V. The inventor's clinic
Howard, V. The message
Howard, V. Million dollar recipe
Howard, V. The publicity expert
Jones, E. M. The emerald
Jones-Evans, E. Death on the line
Kaufman, G. S. The still alarm
Keeney, C. H. Major Milliron reports
Malcolm, I. A moment of existence
Oboler, A. Night of the auk
Phillips, J. B. The calling of the disciples
Phillips, J. B. Christ the Son of God
Phillips, J. B. Jesus appears in Galilee
Sakanishi, S. tr. The ribs and the cover
Waugh, J. R. Food for thought
Yeats, W. B. The cat and the moon
York plays. The Crucifixion

5 characters (5b)
Howard, V. Herman's temptation
Howard, V. Valley Forge was never like this

5 characters and extras (5m extras)
c Fisher, A. Robots to the rescue
c Fisher, A. and Rabe, O. Thanks a million
Geiger, M. Light and liberty
c Miller, M. Robinson Crusoe
Phillips, J. B. The Lord's prayer

MALE CAST—*Continued*

Sophocles. Philoctetes
c Spamer, C. M. The good Samaritan
c Spamer, C. M. Jesus and the fishermen
c Tennant, K. The bells of the city
c Weinberger, R. I. The whole tooth
Weinstock, D. Dawn will come
York plays. The creation, and The fall of Lucifer

5 characters and extras (5b extras)

c The black mask
Howard, V. Five boys and a Santa

6 characters (1m 5b)

c Blyton, E. Mr Sly-One and the cats

6 characters (5m 1b)

c Carlson, B. W. Near mutiny on the "Santa Maria"
Cooper, F. A. Worlds apart
Phillips, J. B. The centurion's servant

6 characters (6m)

Boyd, A. K. Robbery at Gadshill
Brown, A. M. Ah, men!
Carrière, A. Mystery at the depot
Finch, R. and Smith, B. Western night
Fisher, A. and Rabe, O. Not for sale
Howard, V. The blue serge suit
Howard, V. Gizzlegump
Howard, V. The mad Doctor Zing
Laurents, A. Home of the brave
Peterson, L. Stand-in for a murderer
Phillips, J. B. The Ascension
Phillips, J. B. The healing at the Pool of Bethesda
Phillips, J. B. The healing of the man born blind
Phillips, J. B. The Last Supper
Shore, M. Catastrophe Clarence
Webber, J. Air sea rescue
Yeats, W. B. At the hawk's well

6 characters (6b)

Curtis, P. D. Picking the team
Howard, V. Turkey for all
Howard, V. The valentine box

6 characters and extras (4m 2b extras)

c Arlett, V. I. The people who came to an inn

6 characters and extras (5m 1b extras)

c Carlson, B. W. A traitor's reward

6 characters and extras (6m extras)

c Carlson, B. W. Altogether! Heave!
Dace, W. We commit this body
Dimondstein, B. In the chains of life
Estes, S. In quest of power through the Holy Spirit
Geiger, M. The university of the United States
Kwanze, M. Sanemori
Kwanze, M. Tamura
c Leuser, E. The King of the Golden River
Rose, S. The Edgar Bergen show
Vidal, G. Smoke

6 characters and extras (6b extras)

c Armstrong, J. B. No more arithmetic

7 characters (1m 6b)

Howard, V. Danger—pixies at work

7 characters (5m 2b)

c Spamer, C. Andy's gun

7 characters (6m 1b)

Curtis, P. D. The experts
Emurian, E. K. It is well with my soul

7 characters (7m)

Anderson, M. The miracle of the Danube
David takes the shoots to Jerusalem
c Holmes, R. V. King John and the Abbott of Canterbury
Howard, V. The mayor
Howard, V. When it's moonlight on Pike's Peak
Johnston, D. A fourth for bridge
Phillips, J. B. Jesus appears to His disciples
Phillips, J. B. The journey to Jerusalem
c Spamer, C. The honored ones
Webber, J. Inspector Hart's experiment
c Wilcox, E. M. A midnight ride
Wilde, P. Salt for savor
Yeats, W. B. The Resurrection

7 characters and extras (5m 2b extras)

Emurian, E. K. Charles Wesley

7 characters and extras (6m 1b extras)

Curtis, P. D. The hours on strike

7 characters and extras (7m extras)

Dozier, R. A real fine cutting edge
Emurian, E. K. Yankee Doodle
Helm, M. Fray Junípero Serra
Howard, P. The dictator's slippers
c Miller, H. L. The library circus
Waugh, J. R. The wise counsellor
York plays. The creation of the heavenly beings: The fall of Lucifer

8 characters (4m 4b)

Curtis, P. D. Fair deals

8 characters (5m 3b)

Howard, V. A hobby for Dad

8 characters (7m 1b)

c Miller, H. L. Jiminy Cinders
Phillips, J. B. Christ enters Jerusalem

8 characters (8m)

c Bateson, D. The beggar of Basra
Boretz, A. The trial of Poznan
Boyd, A. K. Half hour on the "Asia"
Clark, B. H. Fires at Valley Forge
Cullinan, G. The Republic of the Blind
Emurian, E. K. The first breakfast
Greene, N. D. The seekers
Howe, C. V. The long fall
O'Neill, E. In the zone
O'Neill, E. "The sniper"
Phillips, J. B. The gift of the Holy Spirit
Phillips, J. B. The parable of the Pharisee and the tax collector
Sayre, G. W. Final edition
Shore, J. and Lincoln, R. The soldier who became a Great Dane
Storey, R. Touch it light
Webber, J. Dial 999
Webber, J. Lights on the coast

MALE CAST—*Continued*

8 characters and extras
(7m 1b extras)

c Molloy, L. L. The fortune of Merrylegs and Tawny-Whiskers

8 characters and extras
(8m extras)

McCaslin, N. Seafaring giant
Phillips, J. B. The trial before Pilate

9 characters (1m 8b)

Howard, V. There's talent tonight
c Woolsey, J. and Sechrist, E. H. Gifts for the elves

9 characters (9m)

Clark, B. H. Fires at Valley Forge
Gogol, N. Gamblers
c Harper, J. M. The first cat on Mars
Phillips, J. B. The parable of the last judgment
Shoub, M. Thank you, Edmondo
Yeats, W. B. Calvary

9 characters and extras
(9m extras)

c Carlson, B. W. The bunyip lives again!
c Miller, H. L. Railroad rhymes and rhythms
Tuson, N. Moon rocket

10 characters (8m 2b)

c Fisher, A. Day of destiny

10 characters (10m)

Elward, J. Paper foxhole
Ridge, A. Three mice for the abbot
Sherriff, R. C. Journey's end
c Spamer, C. Daniel in the lions' den

10 characters and extras
(8m 2b extras)

c Bakeless, K. L. Most memorable voyage

10 characters and extras
(10m extras)

Aristophanes. The clouds
Bailey, H. F. Walk in the light
Estes, S. In quest of power through faith
Ettlinger, D. The thousand-yard look
Houston, N. According to law
York, M. A. Treasure Island

11 characters (11m)

Boyd, A. K. Clive's fear, unique
Phillips, J. B. The death of Jesus and the promise of the Resurrection
Phillips, J. B. Jesus returns to Galilee
Porter, J. V. Blueprint, U.S.A.
York plays. The second trial before Pilate: The scourging and condemnation

11 characters (11b)

Howard, V. Athletes all

11 characters and extras
(5m 6b extras)

c Miller, H. L. Garden hold-up

11 characters and extras
(10m 1b extras)

c Miller, H. L. Trouble in Tick-Tock Town

11 characters and extras
(11m extras)

Brabazon, F. The quest
c Howard, V. The treasure of Monte Cristo

12 characters (12m)

Burlingame, C. Yellow fever
Thompson, M. A. The witch hunters

12 characters and extras
(12m extras)

Baxter, A. M. A pageant of Christmas

13 characters (13m)

Casey, B. M. The servant of the King
Sinclair, L. But I know what I like

13 characters and extras
(13m extras)

Eliot, T. S. Murder in the cathedral
Emurian, E. K. The living dramatization of the Beatitudes
Hulme-Beaman, S. B. The cruise of the "Toytown Belle"

14 characters (14m)

Bayliss, R. G. The Gentlemen Smugglers
c Colson, J. G. Robin Hood in Sherwood Forest
Johnston, R. A. The Digby Conversion of St Paul
Rose, R. Twelve angry men
York plays. The judgment
York plays. The last judgement

14 characters (14b)

c Miller, H. L. Boys in books

14 characters and extras
(14m extras)

c Spamer, C. The Last Supper

15 characters (1m 14b)

c Woolsey, J. and Sechrist, E. H. Radios versus doughnuts

15 characters (15m)

Trease, G. Letters of gold

15 characters and extras
(15m extras)

Daviot, G. Valerius
c Delva, J. G. The rise of a nation

16 characters (16m)

Emurian, E. K. The Last Supper
Rose, R. Twelve angry men
Sapinsley, A. Lee at Gettysburg
York plays. Palm Sunday

16 characters and extras
(15m 1b extras)

c Spamer, C. The loaves and the fishes

16 characters and extras
(16m extras)

Kaiser, G. Gas—Part II
White, N. E. The billion dollar saint

17 characters (17m)

Everyman. Everyman

17 characters and extras
(13m 1b extras)

Emmons, D. G. A toehold for the U.S.A.

17 characters and extras
(17m extras)

Emurian, E. K. The Star Spangled Banner
Finian, Brother. The Light of the World

17 characters and extras
(17b extras)

c Schoneman, E. T. The wish machine

18 characters (18m)

Haines, W. W. Command decision

MALE CAST—*Continued*

19 characters (19m)
Youk, H. The Caine mutiny court-martial

**19 characters and extras
(19m extras)**
Emmons, D. G. Astor's bid for empire

**20 characters and extras
(20m extras)**
Hochwaelder, F. The strong are lonely

22 characters (22m)
Behan, B. The quare fellow

23 characters (22m 1b)
c Miller, H. L. The half-pint cowboy

**24 characters and extras
(24m extras)**
Coxe, L. O. and Chapman, R. Billy Budd

26 characters (26m)
Suerken, E. H. John Crown's legacy

27 characters (27m)
Levitt, S. The Andersonville trial
Serling, R. The strike

**27 characters and extras
(27m extras)**
Raiden, E. Mr Jefferson's Burr

FEMALE CAST

**1 character and extras
(1w extras)**
c Very, A. The old woman and her pig

**1 character and extras
(1g extras)**
c Scott, L. B. The three bears
c Spamer, C. The cold twins
c Spamer, C. The playroom
c Spamer, C. The three bears

2 characters (1w 1g)
c Quinlan, M. E. Betty gets a new dress

2 characters (2w)
Carter, C. About time too
Nash, N. R. Rouge atomique
Sutherland, D. The clean up
Williams, T. At liberty
Williams, T. Something unspoken

**2 characters and extras
(2w extras)**
c Spamer, C. The lost bouquet

**2 characters and extras
(2g extras)**
c Asbrand, K. Come to Bethlehem

3 characters (1w 2g)
Spamer, C. Amelia Earhart

3 characters (2w 1g)
Casey, B. M. God so loved the world

3 characters (3w)
Asbrand, K. Neighbors should be neighborly
Asbrand, K. A valentine for Grandma
Barrow, W. Peaceful evening
Bradley, A. This England
c Carlson, B. W. On the bat
Casey, B. M. One song for Christmas
Casey, B. M. Seventy times seven
Coolidge, J. T. Mrs Parker's portrait
Finch, R. The return
Genet, J. The maids
Malone, M. A letter for Charlotte

Spamer, C. Joan of Arc
Strindberg, A. The stronger
Taggart, T. When mothers meet

3 characters (3g)
c Spamer, C. Helpers

**3 characters and extras
(3g extras)**
c Joy, V. The milkmaid and her pail

4 characters (1w 3g)
Spamer, C. Julia Ward Howe

4 characters (3w 1g)
Posegate, E. D. Putting first things first

4 characters (4w)
Asbrand, K. More blessed to give
Asbrand, K. Spring fever
Assinder, P. The paying guest
Carter, B. The witch hunt
Carter, C. A chocolate
Casey, B. M. They say
Clapp, P. Peggy's on the phone
Daily, D. T. Displaced
Du Bois, G. His hand and pen
Gray, M. For love of a house
Houston, N. She writes a roof
Mauermann, W. G. Just us girls
Murch, E. Spring flowers for Marguerite
Neuenburg, E. Pinnacle
Osborne, S. If you ask me—
Shelby, K. and Cuny, T. M. Giving goes on
Speare, E. G. The anchor
Spence, W. A message from John
Verity, E. and Last, J. Cove Cottage
Williams, T. Hello from Bertha
Wolfe, B. S. Watch your step

4 characters (4g)
Porter, E. W. Callie goes to camp
c Spamer, C. Tea party

**4 characters and extras
(1w 3g extras)**
c Spamer, C. The May fairies

5 characters (1w 4g)
c A message from Thankful

5 characters (4w 1g)
Drapkin, I. Lucy
Spamer, C. Jenny Lind

5 characters (5w)
Allred, J. All this and Alan, too
Asbrand, K. On earth peace
Bailey, H. F. "Better than seven sons"
Bate, S. Anniversary Day
Bate, S. Escape to fear
Bate, S. Granny takes the helm
Bollans, G. E. The crooked courtship
Brenner, M. The golden land
Brenner, M. Love and Miss Dodie
Brenner, M. Middle of nowhere
Brenner, M. My Aunt Agatha
Carmichael, F. He's having a baby
Carter, B. The sermon
Clare, N. Surprise packet
Emurian, E. K. America the beautiful
Greth, Le R. E. Miss Robin Crusoe
Hagy, L. Fire in a paper
McLaughlin, M. L. The mind's construction
Martens, A. C. Cross your bridge

FEMALE CAST—*Continued*

Mills, O. Goose in the kitchen
Neuenburg, E. Fear is a murderer
Parkhirst, D. Early frost
Perry, M. The fifth wheel
Postance, N. Surprise!
Wareham, R. C. The miracle at Nain
Spence, W. Four frightened sisters
White, J. K. The laughing cavalier
Wilson, D. C. That heaven of freedom

5 characters (5g)

c Spamer, C. The clumsy fairy

**5 characters and extras
(5w extras)**

Miller, H. L. Pin-up pals
Neuenburg, E. The secret

6 characters (6w)

Agg, H. Autumn term
Agg, H. Winter sunrise
Asbrand, K. The miracle maker
Bate, S. A mouse! A mouse!
Bollans, G. E. Wedding bells for Clara?
Brenner, M. The gentle one
Brenner, M. The roof
Brenner, M. The wait
Brooks, P. Meet George
Carmichael, F. Four for the money
Carter, C. Good-bye, Aunt Mildred!
Conkle, E. P. No more wars but the moon
Cooper, D. S. And so say all of us!
De Francquen, L. The cat and the fiddle
Dennys, J. The lawn
Gehman, H. M. For the love of Pete
Gross, E. and Gross, N. Marko goes a courtin'
Holland, N. Widow of Charles Dickens
Ireland, I. A. This angel business
Johnson, P. Success story
Johnson, P. The witching hour
Last, J. Coffee for one
Last, J. Two black sheep
McConnell, J. The red cloak
McCoy, P. S. The Lieutenant pays his respects
Martens, A. C. The grandma bandit
Martens, A. C. Shoot if you will
Niggli, J. Miracle at Blaise
Phillips, M. K. A flair for fashion
Pilgrim, F. The skeleton at the party
Rees, P. Mix-up-atosis
Roberts, H. M. Old-fashioned Thanksgiving
Sheridan, E. One bit of glory
Spence, W. The locked room
Spencer, G. Six ladies in waiting
Thurston, M. B. Room for Mary
Vooght, C. Nineteen, The Beacon
Wembley South Kenton Afternoon Townswomen's Guild, Drama Section. The sacred den

6 characters (6g)

c Asbrand, K. The stars celebrate Christmas
Clark, S. G. 21 good neighbors
c Spamer, C. The mirror children

**6 characters and extras
(6w extras)**

Conkle, E. P. The reticent one
Dinner, W. and Morum, W. All this and jumble too

7 characters (1w 6g)

c Asbrand, K. Let's be valentines
Barbee, L. The Friday Foursome packs a box
Barbee, L. A letter to Lincoln
Steele, J. Tea for six

7 characters (5w 2g)

Kelsey, R. W. Who is my neighbor?

7 characters (7w)

Agg, H. The happy day
Barbee, L. Christmas for Cinderella
Barry, M. H. Come live in my house
Calitri, P. M. One love had Mary
Carmichael, F. Divorce granted
Cox, P. Myself when young
Crouch, M. Christmas in her eyes
Delderfield, R. F. The guinea-pigs
Gattey, C. N. and Bramley-Moore, Z. Mrs Adams and Eve
Jackson, M. C. Perfect understanding
Johnson, P. Ladies and females
Kirkpatrick, J. A summer for the Indians
Lathrop, D. Forever Eve
McMahon, L. E. and Sergel, R. The plum tree
Manion, D. Girl wanted
Morris, T. B. A garden in Verona
Morris, T. B. The watcher of the road
Murdoch, M. The cuckoo
Rattray, B. Night crossing
Ready, S. Peril at the post office
Richmond, S. S. Homemakers have a way
Stern, G. B. Raffle for a bedspread

**7 characters and extras
(7w extras)**

Casey, B. M. The flower of hope
Crane, B. Visiting celebrity
Holland, N. Crisis in Wimpole Street

8 characters (2w 6g)

Curtis, P. D. Acting for parts
Curtis, P. D. Autograph hunters

8 characters (3w 5g)

Brenner, M. Beacon of strength

8 characters (7w 1g)

Martens, A. C. Christmas is too old-fashioned
Martens, A. C. A cool yule
Pertwee, R. Dirty work

8 characters (8w)

Armstrong, W. F. Haunted rooms
Asbrand, K. The beautiful queen
Bottomley, G. Ardvorlich's wife
Brooks, P. The only prison
Crary, M. Beware the bear!
De Francquen, L. Three bags full
Delderfield, R. F. The Rounderlay tradition
Fernway, P. "I never said a word, but—!"
Gibson, M. N. Will the ladies please come to order
Lea, G. Aunt Martha
Martens, A. C. Quiet, please
Martens, A. C. Witch Hazel

FEMALE CAST—*Continued*

Mathers, A. Flapper girls
Priestley, F. Brown dog—black dog
Priestley, F. The mannequin parade
Raynor, M. All of a sudden
Righter, N. F. Hold onto your hat
Virden, H. Let's have a covered dish
Vooght, C. Come live with me

8 characters (8g)

c Asbrand, K. Little Christmas guest
Hill, K. Midnight burial
c Leuser, E. The little witch who tried
c Spamer, C. The parasols

8 characters and extras (1w 7g extras)

c Newman, D. Kachoo!

9 characters (1w 8g)

c Very, A. Tick-tock

9 characters (2w 7g)

c Newman, D. The stolen heart

9 characters (4w 5g)

Phillips, M. K. The woman who didn't want Christmas

9 characters (6w 3g)

c Woolsey, J. and Sechrist, E. H. I wish I were a queen

9 characters (9w)

Asbrand, K. Sight to see
Bate, S. Holiday haunts
Bennett, V. E. Shadows walk softly
Cary, F. L. Live and let love
Casey, M. A soul in fine array
Morley, O. J. Little women

9 characters and extras (9w extras)

Berg, D. The drop of a hat

10 characters (1w 9g)

c Ormandy, E. Little Ida and the flowers

10 characters (2w 8g)

Brydon, M. W. and Ziegler, E. The reluctant ghost

10 characters (9w 1g)

Curtis, P. D. Candles for sale

10 characters (10w)

Gattey, C. N. and Bramley-Moore, Z. Treasure from France
Getzinger, E. W. Not without honor
Martens, A. C. Pajama party
Ready, S. Ladies at sea
Thompson, M. A. The conquered, the unconquerable, and I

10 characters and extras (10w extras)

Garcia Lorca, F. The house of Bernarda Alba

11 characters (2w 9g)

c Mason, M. E. Mary Elizabeth's wonderful dream

11 characters (6w 5g)

c Morris, T. B. The sleeping fires

11 characters (11w)

Campion, C. On the road
Paradis, M. B. Midge rings the bell
Reach, J. Murder for the bride
Reach, J. Women in white
Strong, L. A. G. It's not very nice

11 characters and extras (11w extras)

Asbrand, K. Mothers
Priestley, F. The ballet dancer

12 characters (12w)

Atwell, R. A pound of prevention
Reach, J. Beautiful dreamers

12 characters (12g)

c Barr, J. The lazy little raindrop

12 characters and extras (12g extras)

c Fisher, A. Standing up for Santa

13 characters (1w 12g)

c Thompson, B. J. Pleasant dreams

13 characters (13w)

Campion, C. Wayward women

13 characters (13g)

c Miller, H. L. Girls in books

13 characters and extras (13w extras)

Martens, A. C. Who stole third base?

14 characters (2w 12g)

c MacLellan, E. and Schroll, C. V. A flower for Mother's Day

14 characters (14w)

Asbrand, K. Youth serves the church

14 characters (14g)

c Spamer, C. The snowdrop

14 characters and extras (14g extras)

c Duggar, F. December's gifts

15 characters (6w 9g)

Woolsey, J. and Sechrist, E. H. First aid in the first troop

16 characters and extras (16g extras)

c Very, A. The Mayflower

17 characters (17w)

Martens, A. C. Sugar and spite

17 characters and extras (17w extras)

Martens, A. C. Sing a song of something

19 characters and extras (19w extras)

McMahon, L. E. Half-Pint Windom rides west

20 characters and extras (20w extras)

Preston, E. E. The Christmas dolls' revue

26 characters (1w 25g)

Very, A. Thanksgiving night

MIXED CAST

2 characters (1m 1w)

Armer, A. and Grauman, W. E. Black star
Armer, A. and Grauman, W. E. Closing time
Armer, A. and Grauman, W. E. Coral
Armer, A. and Grauman, W. E. Country cousin
Armer, A. and Grauman, W. E. Dead weight
Armer, A. and Grauman, W. E. Glass slipper

MIXED CAST—*Continued*

Armer, A. and Grauman, W. E. The last straw
Armer, A. and Grauman, W. E. Love scores a touchdown
Armer, A. and Grauman, W. E. One year after
Armer, A. and Grauman, W. E. Sure as fate
Armer, A. and Grauman, W. E. Time out for dreams
Armer, A. and Grauman, W. E. Timeless second
Armer, A. and Grauman, W. E. To be alone
Armer, A. and Grauman, W. E. Vest pocket theatre
Armer, A. and Grauman, W. E. Whatever became of Lola Woods
Broughton, J. The last word
Casey, B. M. Important business
Gibson, W. Two for the seesaw
Grant, N. Situations vacant
Gurney, A. R. Three people
Hartog, J. de. The fourposter
Howells, W. D. The mother and the father
Howells, W. D. The parlor car
Kaufman, G. S. and MacGrath, L. Amicable parting
Lynch, P. Dutch treat
Lynch, P. Fishing hat
Malcolmson, A. The Nativity
Musset, A. de. A door should be either open or shut
Parker, D. Here we are
Sakanishi, S. tr. The aunt's sake
Taggart, T. Boy meets girl in Washington
Taggart, T. Two in the balcony
Waldau, R. S. A cabin by the lake
Williams, T. Auto-da-fé
Williams, T. This property is condemned
York plays. The birth of Christ

2 characters and extras (1m 1w extras)

Applegarth, M. T. Were you there?
Brabazon, F. The stranger
Davis, J. A. Santa's spectacles
c Goulding, D. J. Pagan magic
Kwanze, M. Kakitsubata
Moreno, R. A horse play
c Newman, D. The Pumpkineaters' pumpkin
c Peterson, M. N. Ten helpful elves
c Spamer, C. Noah's ark
Taggart, T. The midnight ride of Tex O'Coco
c Warner, L. H. The thankful Pilgrims
Williams, T. Talk to me like the rain and let me listen . . .
c Woolsey, J. and Sechrist, E. H. Mother Goose gives advice

2 characters and extras (1m 1b extras)

c Hark, M. and McQueen, N. Lincoln reminders

2 characters and extras (1m 1g extras)

c Goulding, D. J. Mr Bunch's toys

2 characters and extras (1w 1b extras)

c Hark, M. and McQueen, N. Johnnie jump up
c Ilian, C. Lazy Jack
c Miller, H. L. A February failure
c Rawe, M. S. Benny goes to Mistletonia

2 characters and extras (1w 1g extras)

c Hark, M. and McQueen, N. The five senses

2 characters and extras (1b 1g extras)

c Asbrand, K. Story book Christmas
c Asbrand, K. Witches' brew
c Atwell, R. and Virden, H. Christmas in the forest
Fisher, A. and Rabe, O. A fresco for UNESCO
c Hark, M. and McQueen, N. Christmas in the woods
c Hark, M. and McQueen, N. Meet Mr Witch
c Martens, A. C. Be nice to the Easter bunny
c Spamer, C. Inside the earth
c Spamer, C. Our dumb friends
c Spamer, C. A place for all
c Very, A. Valentine sale
c Woolsey, J. and Sechrist, E. H. The United Nations, the hope of the world

2 characters and extras (2b extras)

c Hark, M. and McQueen, N. Pleasant dreams

3 characters (1m 1w 1b)

Damico, J. A storm is breaking
c Fisher, A. Sure cure

3 characters (1m 1w 1g)

Lynch, P. Betsy's first report card

3 characters (1m 2w)

Armer, A. and Grauman, W. E. No time for dames
Casey, B. M. Sweetness and light
Casey, B. M. A welcome for mother
Finney, J. Telephone roulette
Fry, C. A phoenix too frequent
Howells, W. D. Her opinion of his story
Howells, W. D. Self-sacrifice
Ionesco, E. Maid to marry
Manning, S. A. As silent as the ocean
Mishima, Y. Hanjo
Murray, J. The door
Neuenburg, E. Strange victory
Sakanishi, S. tr. Mr Dumbtaro
Spring, H. St George at the Dragon
Stevens, L. Champagne complex
Strindberg, A. Miss Julie
Sutherland, D. Scherzo in two flats
Sutherland, D. Trying to take things quietly
Van Druten, J. The voice of the turtle
Williams, T. The Lady of Larkspur Lotion

3 characters (2m 1w)

Addis, H. The fishermen's dream
Apstein, T. Fortunata writes a letter
Armer, A. and Grauman, W. E. In darkened rooms

MIXED CAST—*Continued*

c Carlson, B. W. Jim Bridger and his eight-hour echo
Carter, C. Don't argue!
Casey, B. M. My neighbor
Casey, B. M. Sunday morning
Chekhov, A. A marriage proposal
Davies, R. Overlaid
Down, O. The maker of dreams
Gregory, Lady. The workhouse ward
Howells, W. D. The impossible
Ionesco, E. The chairs
Kay, I. Giveaway
Kennedy, C. R. The terrible meek
Kwanze, M. Kiyotsune
Lewis, G. Wait for morning, child
Lineberger, J. A sometime thing
Lynch, P. Just a little something for Christmas
Lynch, P. To open, pry cover
Lynch, P. What's that tune?
Marx, M. and others. The honeymooners
Morton, J. M. Box and Cox
O'Casey, S. The end of the beginning
O'Hara, F. Try! Try!
Perry, M. Two's company
Pound, E. and Fenollosa, E. Sotoba Komachi
Sakanishi, S. tr. The bag of parting
Sakanishi, S. tr. The family quarrel
Sakanishi, S. tr. The ink-smeared lady
Sakanishi, S. tr. An unfair exchange
Sakanishi, S. tr. The wounded highway-man
Scholl, R. The golden axe
Seidelhuber, G. The lavender kite
Shaber, D. The youngest shall ask
Shaw, B. Annajanska, the Bolshevik Empress
Shaw, B. Augustus does his bit
Shaw, B. The music-cure
Sheffield, J. The forgotten land
Thompson, D. The shoemaker's wife
Walsh, N. Let there be farce
Wilde, O. A Florentine tragedy
Wolfe, T. The return of Buck Gavin
Yeats, W. B. The pot of broth
York plays. The creation of Adam and Eve
York plays. The creation of man
York plays. The Garden of Eden

3 characters (2m 1g)
Spamer, C. George Eliot

3 characters (2b 1g)
c Martens, A. C. A visit from Washington

3 characters and extras (1m 1w 1b extras)
Asbrand, K. All that glitters
Chorpenning, C. B. Rama and the tigers
c Fisher, A. The Christmas cake
c Martens, A. C. Pictures in the fire
c National Recreation Association. The runaway sled
c Spamer, C. Elijah, the prophet
c Spamer, C. Little boy's clock

3 characters and extras (1m 1w 1g extras)
c Miller, H. L. A visit to Goldilocks
c Woolsey, J. and Sechrist, E. H. The witches' complaint

3 characters and extras (1m 2w extras)
Applegarth, M. T. Home Sweet Home
Armer, A. and Grauman, W. E. Final curtain
Kwanze, K. N. The maple viewing
c Marston, M. A. Goblin market

3 characters and extras (1m 1b 1g extras)
Bailey, H. F. The singing children
c Flavelle, I. B. Giants of the city
c Hurt, F. The King of Nowhere
c Miller, H. L. Three little kittens

3 characters and extras (1m 2g extras)
c Asbrand, K. Christmas wishes

3 characters and extras (2m 1w extras)
Brabazon, F. The moon
Casey, B. M. Dawn in the garden
Casey, B. M. The land afar
Chekhov, A. The boor
Chekhov, A. The brute
Corwin, N. The rivalry
Ionesco, E. The lesson
Kwanze, K. Kayoi Komachi
Kwanze, M. Aya no tsuzumi
Kwanze, M. Hagoromo
Kwanze, M. Nishikigi
c Marston, M. A. The robbers
Mishima, Y. Sotoba Komachi
c Spamer, C. The boy Jesus visits Jerusalem
c Spamer, C. The gold spinner
c Stevenson, F. K. A day with Stevenson
Strindberg, A. Creditors
Williams, C. The house by the stable
Williams, T. 27 wagons full of cotton
Yeats, W. B. The hour-glass
Yeats, W. B. The shadowy waters

3 characters and extras (2m 1g extras)
Spamer, C. Ah-yo-ka
c Spamer, C. The flight out of Egypt
c Spamer, C. The Pharaoh's dream

3 characters and extras (1w 1b 1g extras)
Boli, L. They found Christmas
Curtis, P. D. The angry alphabet
c Fisher, A. Many a slip
c Hastings, M. L. C. Christmas in other lands

3 characters and extras (1w 2b extras)
c Lunnon, B. S. Johnny has comicopia
c Miller, H. L. The Santa Claus twins
c Woolsey, J. and Sechrist, E. H. Days and days

4 characters (1m 1w 1b 1g)
c Carlson, B. W. Jes' too lazy!
Spamer, C. Jane Welsh

4 characters (1m 3w)
Asbrand, K. Christmas rose
Bucci, M. A pink party dress
Conkle, E. P. Granny's little cheery room
Cooney, P. The perfect aurora
Coward, N. Fumed oak
Eaton, C. E. Sea psalm
Elam, R. C. Duchess of Dogwood Lane
Emery, C. The Christmas stranger

MIXED CAST—*Continued*

Howells, W. D. An Indian giver
Mishima, Y. The Lady Aoi
Mizer, J. Golden slippers
Neuenburg, E. Distant thunder
Ouzts, J. D. Happy Pagan
Perry, M. A trap is a small place
Phillips, M. K. Grandma and mistletoe
Sutherland, D. Art for art's sake
Sutherland, D. Father's economy drive
Taggart, T. Morning of a private eye
Tully, J. Tony
Williams, M. Invitation to breakfast
Williams, N. Protest
Williams, T. Lord Byron's love letter

4 characters (1m 1b 2g)

Spamer, C. Louisa May Alcott
Spamer, C. Mary Mapes Dodge

4 characters (2m 1w 1b)

O'Neil, R. The triumph of the egg

4 characters (2m 2w)

Abstance, P. and Abstance, L. Corny confessions
Appell, D. Lullaby
Barry, S. Cupid's bow
Beckett, S. Endgame
Carmichael, F. She-sickness
Carter, C. Stick up for yourself
Carter, C. Such ado about something
Casey, B. M. Excuse for living
Casey, B. M. Green eyes
Casey, B. M. His and hers
Clare, N. The windfall
Climenhaga, J. Heathen pioneer
Courteline, G. These Cornfields
Daviot, G. The pen of my aunt
Denham, R. and Smith, C. S. A dash of bitters
Dimondstein, B. The lost victory
Easton, C. Champagne sec
Emery, C. The ant bed
Estrada, D. Three on a bench
Fleece, J. The first oyster
Getzinger, E. W. Let your light so shine
Goodchild, R. The grand duchess
Gould, J. R. The death of the hired man
Green, P. The No 'Count Boy
Halman, D. Johnny Pickup
Hark, M. and McQueen, N. Spring daze
Hawkes, J. and Priestley, J. B. Dragon's mouth
Howells, W. D. Bride roses
Howells, W. D. A previous engagement
Howells, W. D. The register
Jerome, P. Goin' round the hoop
Koch, F. Wash Carver's mouse trap
Komparu, Z. U. Bashō
Lathrop, D. The braggart
Miller, H. L. Turkey turns the tables
Morris, F. H. Reel George
Morrison, D. Mirage
Mortimer, J. What shall we tell Caroline?
Musset, A. de. Caprice
Nail, R. Love errant
Owens, R. J. Final edition
Reeves, T. Wedding breakfast
Sartre, J. P. No exit
Seiger, M. L. Blue concerto

Shaw, B. O'Flaherty V. C.
c Spamer, C. Gabriel visits Mary
Stevens, L. The marriage-go-round
Synge, J. M. The tinker's wedding
Taylor, G. Kill or cure
Tennyson, A. The falcon
Weiss, H. A bolt from heaven
Williams, T. The glass menagerie
Williamson, H. R. Diamond cut diamond
Wills, G. Alice in Bibleland
Yeats, W. B. A full moon in March

4 characters (2m 1b 1g)

c Woolsey, J. and Sechrist, E. H. My honest friend
Spamer, C. Florence Nightingale

4 characters (3m 1w)

Bangham, M. D. Come to the manger
Bayliss, A. E. M. What make?
Beckett, S. Embers
Claudel, P. Break of noon
Conkle, E. P. Son-of-a-biscuit-eater
Davidson, M. R. On the road to Egypt
Daviot, G. The Balwhinnie bomb
Dimondstein, B. The life of an artist
Green, P. Quare medicine
Herbert, F. H. The moon is blue
Howells, W. D. A true hero
Leonard, E. S. Her husband's consent
O'Casey, S. A pound on demand
Phillips, J. B. The cleansing of the Temple
Phillips, J. B. The Resurrection of Jesus
Purkey, R. A. The leprechaun
Sakanishi, S. tr. The letter "I"
Saroyan, W. Once around the block
Scriven, R. C. A single taper
Spence, W. The bridal bouquet
Synge, J. M. In the shadow of the glen
Trick, O. B. The frontier
Webber, J. A brush with the enemy
Werry, W. Breakdown
Wilde, O. La sainte courtisane

4 characters (1w 1b 2g)

Asbrand, K. Count your blessings
Conkle, E. P. Heaven is a long time to wait

4 characters (1w 2b 1g)

c Spamer, C. Fishermen

4 characters (1w 3b)

c Ruth, G. J. A birthday long ago

4 characters (2w 2g)

Asbrand, K. Reach for the moon

4 characters (2b 2g)

c Asbrand, K. Crooked dime

**4 characters and extras
(1m 1w 1b 1g extras)**

c Pottow, D. Preparing for winter
Spamer, C. The boy who had no gravity
c Very, A. The shoemaker and the elves

**4 characters and extras
(1m 3w extras)**

Asbrand, K. The Farmer in the Dell
Conkle, E. P. A bauble for the baby
Estes, S. In quest of power through obedience
Kwanze, M. Kinuta
c Marston, M. A. The riddling knight

MIXED CAST—*Continued*

c Spamer, C. The baby Moses
c Spamer, C. Ruth
Synge, J. M. Riders to the sea

4 characters and extras
(2m 1w 1b extras)

Anderson, S. The triumph of the egg
Bailey, H. F. "We bring this child unto the Lord"
Komparu, Z. U. Tanikō
Kwanze, M. J. Sumidagawa

4 characters and extras
(2m 1w 1g extras)

Cummings, E. E. Santa Claus
c Ratcliffe, D. U. Robinetta
c Spamer, C. The bells
c Spamer, C. The orange tree

4 characters and extras
(2m 2w extras)

Aeschylus. Seven against Thebes
c Bailey, H. F. Roses for the King
Fisher, A. and Rabe, O. Anonymous letter
Fisher, A. and Rabe, O. Long may it wave
Goulding, D. J. The Nativity
Kauffmann, S. The more the merrier
Kopit, A. L. Oh, Dad, poor Dad, Mamma's hung you in the closet and I'm feelin' so sad
Kwanze, M. Izutsu
Kwanze, M. Kagekiyo
Lewis, S. Siwan
McCann, K. Out of despair
MacDonald, D. M. Let nothing ye dismay
Magee, C. Radio Jerusalem, the story of Jesus
c Spamer, C. Christ lives again
c Spamer, C. Cinderella's friends
York, E. B. The kindled flame

4 characters and extras
(2m 1b 1g extras)

c Levofsky, R. A house for Duke
c Miller, H. L. New shoes
c Pierce, G. M. The story of March 17

4 characters and extras
(2m 2b extras)

Ridge, A. Emhammed of the red slippers

4 characters and extras
(3m 1w extras)

Aeschylus. The Persians
Curtis, P. D. The colours clash
Fisher, A. and Rabe, O. "Molly Pitcher"
Fisher, A. and Rabe, O. Rocket to freedom
Kinoshita, J. Twilight crane
Kleinsinger, G. Archy and Mehitabel
Kocher, E. Karma
Kwanze, M. Hachi no ki
Oliver, W. I. The stallion
O'Neill, E. The Emperor Jones
Oringer, B. I. Son of the revolution
Poverman, H. Easy money
Williams, T. The strangest kind of romance
Winer, E. Three hours between planes
Wishengrad, M. The danger of freedom
c Woolsey, J. and Sechrist, E. H. Saint Peter and the birds

4 characters and extras
(1w 1b 2g extras)

c Hark, M. and McQueen, N. Three wishes for mother

4 characters and extras
(1w 2b 1g extras)

c Graham, M. S. The promotion
c Martens, A. C. Little lost leprechaun
c Woolsey, J. and Sechrist, E. H. The wonder world of books

4 characters and extras
(2b 2g extras)

Fisher, A. and Rabe, O. Ask Mr Jefferson
c Hark, M. and McQueen, N. Rainbow colors
c Very, A. The cat who wanted to ride on a broom

5 characters (1m 1w 1b 2g)

c Fisher, A. Mother's Day off and on
c Very, A. The snow girl

5 characters (1m 1w 2b 1g)

Spamer, C. Rosa Bonheur

5 characters (1m 1w 3g)

c Asbrand, K. Our little Christmas angels
c Very, A. and Brown, M. Saint Valentine's surprise

5 characters (1m 2w 1b 1g)

Vidal, G. The turn of the screw

5 characters (1m 2w 2b)

Ullman, S. S. The youth, Bolivar

5 characters (1m 2w 2g)

Spamer, C. Marie Antoinette

5 characters (1m 3w 1b)

c Stees, L. Red for danger

5 characters (1m 3w 1g)

Spamer, C. Susan B. Anthony

5 characters (1m 4w)

Bottomley, G. Towie Castle
Chenery, M. Lesson for today
Dennys, J. Lear of Albion Crescent
Lee, W. C. Deadwood
McMahon, B. Publicity on the fifteenth
Maher, R. When the fire dies
Mosel, T. My lost saints
Nappier, P. And there was light
Neuenburg, E. Truth is for the Birds
Parker, K. T. Star minded
Priestley, F. Jane finds her cousins
Roberts, C. Mr Gaylord remembers
Sergel, R. A New England nun
Verity, E. and Last, J. Two of us

5 characters (1m 2b 2g)

c Fisher, A. Old Mr Fixit
c Spamer, C. The store

5 characters (1m 3b 1g)

c Hark, M. and McQueen, N. The stuff of heroes

5 characters (2m 1w 1b 1g)

c Carlson, B. W. Don't tell a soul!
c Fisher, A. Leave it to gramps
Fisher, A. and Rabe, O. Best bargain in the world
Fisher, A. and Rabe, O. The get-together dinner
Paige, M. C. Father trims the tree

MIXED CAST—*Continued*

5 characters (2m 1w 2g)

Hark, M. and McQueen, N. Books are bridges
c Miller, H. L. Thanks to butter-fingers

5 characters (2m 2w 1b)

Gross, E. and Gross, N. Date-time
Hark, M. and McQueen, N. Heart trouble

5 characters (2m 2w 1g)

Agnew, E. J. Beyond Good Friday
Weiss, M. J. The actor

5 characters (2m 3w)

Allred, P. and Allred, T. To the lovely Margaret
Brickenden, C. Zanorin
Campton, D. The laboratory
Camus, A. The misunderstanding
Casey, B. M. Lilies bloom at Easter
Chadwick, V. C. The invisible line
Clark, M. G. My wife, Henry
Cocteau, J. Intimate relations
Cooper, F. A. A certain star
Daviot, G. Lady Charing is cross
Daviot, G. Sweet coz
Delderfield, R. F. Smoke in the valley
Emery, C. Madame Vulture
George, L. D. When the little angel sang
Getzinger, E. W. Promise of the angels
Hallowell, H. The widow's choice
c Hark, M. and McQueen, N. Enter George Washington
Howells, W. D. Evening dress
Hughes, R. The sisters' tragedy
Joy, R. P. Hour of honor
Kimes, B. The duelling Oakes
Lathrop, D. The Winslow girl
Levin, I. Interlock
Lindsey, H. C. Forever Judy
McQuade, W. Exclusive model
c Miller, H. L. Speaking of speech
Mosel, T. The lawn party
Mosel, T. The waiting place
Murray, J. The boy next door
Murray, J. A game of chess
Olfson, L. Infanta
Ouzts, J. D. Just a picture
Phillips, T. J. Miss Harper's birthday
Powers, V. High window
Priestley, J. B. Mother's Day
Shaw, D. Native dancer
Stoler, S. A. End of the rainbow

5 characters (3m 1w 1g)

c Fisher, A. The weaver's son
Kinoy, E. Good-bye to the clown
Spamer, C. Queen Victoria

5 characters (3m 2w)

Abstance, P. and Abstance, L. Soapera
Abstance, P. and Abstance, L. The valiant Valentine
Addis, H. Sellevision
Albee, E. The sandbox
Allensworth, C. Ring once for Central
Badger, A. Before the dawn
Bannerman, H. K. My last duchess
Bayliss, A. E. M. My hat!
Becque, H. Woman of Paris
Behrman, S. N. The second man
Benedetti, A. de. Two dozen red roses

Blazer, F. The prodigal mother
Buell, H. Fat woman picnic
Burgess, C. V. A bit of peace and quiet
Burgess, C. V. Chris is sent to Coventry
Burgess, C. V. Doers and viewers
Burgess, C. V. Ken looks ahead
Burgess, C. V. Reports in the garden
Burgess, C. V. Susan to the rescue
Burgess, C. V. The Taylors in the never-never land
Burgess, C. V. Trouble at "The Blue Lantern"
Conkle, E. P. Arbie, the bug boy
Daily, D. T. The Christmas party
Daviot, G. Barnharrow
Delaney, S. A taste of honey
Emery, C. Tiger Lily
Fearheiley, D. A star too far
Finch, R. The certain man had two sons
Fisher, A. and Rabe, O. Apostle of freedom
Fisher, A. and Rabe, O. A dish of green peas
Glaspell, S. Trifles
Goethe, J. W. von. Torquato Tasso
Gould, J. R. Steps from beyond
Green, C. Janus
Hanig, D. Give us time to sing
Horne, K. A. This dark world and wide
Howard, V. The blackbird
Howells, W. D. A counterfeit presentment
Howells, W. D. Room forty-five
Ibsen, H. Ghosts
Keeney, C. H. Old Skin Flint
Kirkpatrick, J. The mind of a killer
Lamson, P. Grow up!
Lantz, J. E. and Lantz, R. C. Alone
Lantz, J. E. and Lantz, R. C. Reluctantly yours
Latham, J. and Lord, B. One in twelve
Lynch, P. The income tax
Lynch, P. Off with his head
McCourt, G. M. The curse and the crown
Mortimer, J. I spy
Mosel, T. The five dollar bill
Mosel, T. Other people's houses
Mosel, T. The presence of the enemy
Musset, A. de. It's impossible to think of everything
Niggli, J. The ring of General Macías
O'Neill, E. Long day's journey into night
Osborne, J. Look back in anger
Parker, J. W. Sleep on, Lemuel
Parker, K. T. Stand up to death
Peach, L. du G. A horse! A horse!
Priestley, J. B. A glass of bitter
Priestley, J. B. Private rooms
Raeburn, H. The greenwood
Robinson, C. R. The white dove
Rodman, H. The faith hawker
Roskam, C. Plenty of rein
Seiler, C. The stronger sex
Shaffer, P. Five finger exercise
Sigmund, J. G. and Smith, B. The silvered rope
Snyder, W. H. The departing
c Spamer, C. The Christ child in the temple
c Spamer, C. M. Solomon's Temple
Wehner, E. Man of arts
Williams, H. and Williams, M. Plaintiff in a pretty hat

MIXED CAST—*Continued*

5 characters (4m 1w)

Bailey, A. H. The narrow man
Conrad, J. One day more
Coventry plays. The Annunciation
DuBois, G. Huckleberry Finn
Emurian, E. K. Dixie
Emurian, E. K. Silver threads among the gold
Ghelderode, M. de. Three actors and their drama
Goethe, J. W. von. Iphigenia in Tauris
Holland, N. Will and testament
Housman, L. "A good lesson!"
Ionesco, E. Improvisation
Koch, F. These doggone elections
Lillington, K. The Devil's grandson
Lindsey, H. C. Mr Sweeney's conversion
McGreevey, J. The barrier
Merrill, J. The bait
O'Neill, E. A moon for the misbegotten
Pathelin. The farce of Master Pierre Pathelin
Richards, I. A. A leak in the universe
Rigney, W. J. Joe Tracy
Roskam, C. The puzzle
Roussin, A. The little hut
Shaw, B. Widowers' houses
c Spamer, C. Samson and Delilah
Thon, F. The island
Wilson, E. The little blue light
Yeats, W. B. The King of the Great Clock Tower
York plays. The fall of man

5 characters (1w 2b 2g)

c Very, A. The callers

5 characters (1w 3b 1g)

Spamer, C. Harriet Beecher Stowe

5 characters (3b 2g)

c Spamer, C. The children who forgot
c Spamer, C. Hippety hop

5 characters and extras (1m 1w 1b 2g extras)

c Chandler, R. America remembers
c Fisher, A. Long live father

5 characters and extras (1m 1w 2b 1g extras)

McCaslin, N. The legend of the Christmas candle

5 characters and extras (1m 2w 1b 1g extras)

c Hollinshead, L. M. Thank you, God for everything

5 characters and extras (1m 2w 2b extras)

c Spamer, C. Valentine's party

5 characters and extras (1m 4w extras)

Asbrand, K. The three Marys

5 characters and extras (1m 2b 2g extras)

Fisher, A. and Rabe, O. Stage set for Veterans' Day
c Miller, H. L. The mystery of turkey-lurkey

5 characters and extras (1m 3b 1g extras)

Dunbar, T. M. Girls are so useless!

5 characters and extras (2m 1w 1b 1g extras)

c Carlson, B. W. St Nicholas just the same
c Hurt, F. The weather imp

5 characters and extras (2m 2w 1b extras)

c Barnes, E. A. and Young, B. M. Sokar and the crocodile
Estes, S. In quest of power through dedication
c Hark, M. and McQueen, N. Nothing to be thankful for

5 characters and extras (2m 2w 1g extras)

Dimondstein, B. Eva

5 characters and extras (2m 3w extras)

Carrière, A. It's about time
Kelly, G. The flattering word
Melanos, J. A. Rapunzel and the witch
Mishima, Y. Kantan

5 characters and extras (3m 1w 1b extras)

c Vandenburgh, M. A "globester" trip
Vidal, G. Barn burning

5 characters and extras (3m 1w 1g extras)

c Asbrand, K. When America was young

5 characters and extras (3m 2w extras)

Abstance, P. and Abstance, L. A Hallowe'en adventure
Aguirre, I. Express for Santiago
Anouilh, J. Cecile
c Beneke, A. Symbols of Christmas
c Hark, M. and McQueen, N. In honor of Washington
Komparu, Z. U. Awoi no uye
Procunier, E. R. Two sides of darkness
c Spamer, C. M. The walls of Jericho
Yudkoff, A. The gentleman walks outside

5 characters and extras (4m 1w extras)

Abel, L. The death of Odysseus
Bailey, A. H. Impersonation
Campbell, J. G. The bleeding heart of Wee Jon
Flaten, M. Testing ground for democracy
c Goulding, D. J. The master cat
Manning, M. Passages from Finnegans wake
Mindel, J. To secure these rights
c Moore, S. S. The shepherd-boy and the wolf
c Spamer, C. Washout
c Spamer, C. The widow's son
Tree, J. The fisherman
Wardall, C. Fog on the bay
Williams, N. The mountain
Wishengrad, M. The living declaration
Yeats, W. B. Deirdre

5 characters and extras (5m extras)

Yeats, W. B. On baile's strand

5 characters and extras (1w 2b 2g extras)

c Fisher, A. A Christmas tree for Kitty
c Hark, M. and McQueen, N. A day for trees

MIXED CAST—*Continued*

5 characters and extras (3w 1b 1g extras)

Applegarth, M. T. Color blind

5 characters and extras (2b 3g extras)

c Fisher, A. Getting it straight
c Spamer, C. The candle

5 characters and extras (3b 2g extras)

c Feder, L. Gifts for mother
c Moore, S. S. The fox and the grapes

5 characters and extras (4b 1g extras)

c Miller, H. L. Spunky Punky

6 characters (1m 1w 2b 2g)

c Fisher, A. New hearts for old
Fisher, A. and Rabe, O. Bringing up father
c Hark, M. and McQueen, N. Visit of Johnny Appleseed

6 characters (1m 1w 4b)

c Woolsey, J. and Sechrist, E. H. The donkey's mission

6 characters (1m 2w 1b 2g)

c Hark, M. and McQueen, N. Cupies and hearts

6 characters (1m 2w 2b 1g)

c Hark, M. and McQueen, N. Father's Easter hat
Miller, H. L. The bashful bunny

6 characters (1m 5w)

Daviot, G. The staff-room
Foote, H. Flight
Gattey, C. N. and Bramley-Moore, Z. Mrs Griggs loses her bed
Martens, A. C. A bird in the bush
Nappier, P. Just a matter of timing
Parker, K. The surrounding mist
Sanders, B. L. What's cookin'?
Spence, W. A ghost of distinction

6 characters (1m 2b 3g)

c Spamer, C. The cherry tree

6 characters (1m 3b 2g)

c Spamer, C. The first Christmas tree

6 characters (2m 1w 1b 2g)

Fisher, A. and Rabe, O. Shipmates

6 characters (2m 1w 2b 1g)

c Carlson, B. W. Just as strong

6 characters (2m 2w 1b 1g)

c Hark, M. and McQueen, N. Bobby and the Lincoln speech
c Hark, M. and McQueen, N. Our own four walls
Hark, M. and McQueen, N. The place to begin
Keeney, C. H. Pity the poor fish
Spamer, C. Dolly Madison
Wilder, T. The happy journey

6 characters (2m 3w 1b)

Hark, M. and McQueen, N. Halloween luck
Ibsen, H. Little Eyolf
c Slattery, M. The circus stars' mistake
Weiss, M. J. Her big crush

6 characters (2m 3w 1g)

Hark M. and McQueen, N. The homecoming
Hark, M. and McQueen, N. Shy Charlie

6 characters (2m 4w)

Batson, G. House on the cliff
Batson, G. I found April
Bowen, T. Star dust
Bucci, M. The old lady shows her medals
Clandon, L. The brains of the family
Corrie, J. Colour bar
Dias, E. J. Out of this world
Emery, C. A baby for Brenda
Fields, J. and De Vries, P. The tunnel of love
Foote, H. The tears of my sister
Green, J. Gently does it
Green, J. Murder mistaken
Hall, W. Airmail from Cyprus
Howard, S. The silver cord
Howells, W. D. A likely story
Hutton, M. C. Silver wedding
Johnson, P. No weeds for the widow
Jones, P. Birthday honours
Kirkpatrick, J. Splint for a broken heart
Loos, A. Gigi
Lumsden, M. The gift
Neuenburg, E. Susie was a vampire
Parker, K. T. A cup of tea
Patton, F. G. The beaded buckle
Priestley, J. B. Try it again
Schofield, S. The old master
Sergel, R. A cup of tea
Sugarman, J. The pint pot
Sutherland, D. The man who understood women
Taggart, T. Macbeth a la mode
Trick, O. B. The divine miracle
Williams, H. and Williams, M. The happy man

6 characters (3m 1w 1b 1g)

Miller, H. L. Dolly saves the day

6 characters (3m 1w 2b)

McCaslin, N. He traveled the world

6 characters (3m 1w 2g)

c Garver, J. The Appletons and the UN
c Peterson, M. N. Happy Chanukah

6 characters (3m 2w 1b)

Covington, W. P. Shirt-tail boy
c Miller, M. Puss in Boots
Stout, W. In Dixon's kitchen

6 characters (3m 2w 1g)

Camché, N. The orphans
Cooper, F. A. If thine enemy
Rosenthal, A. Third person
Yeats, W. B. The Land of Heart's Desire

6 characters (3m 3w)

Agg, H. Red plush
Anderson, R. Silent night, lonely night
Apstein, T. A remittance from Spain
Arden, J. The party
Asbrand, K. Gifts of gold
Bate, S. Shelley and Mary
Boland, B. The return
Brampton, J. Dilemma
Braun, W. Drop dead!
Burgess, C. V. A bore for breakfast
Burgess, C. V. The virtues of Thelma

MIXED CAST—*Continued*

Carpenter, F. The setting sun
Casey, B. M. The Christmas loaf
Casey, B. M. One day for mother
Casey, B. M. The tears of Madelon
Corneille, P. Pulchérie
Coward, N. Fallen angels
Cruse, C. Son of Stephen
Dias, E. J. The sands of time
Douglas, F. Rollo
Dunlop, R. S. An overpraised season
Emery, C. Dark interlude
Emurian, E. K. Christmas traditions
Engle, J. D. The charm
Fearheiley, D. M. Mourning before morning
Garver, J. Honest to goodness
George, M. Symphonie pastorale
Greth, Le R. E. The kid from Mars
Grillparzer, F. Sappho
Hark, M. and McQueen, N. If we only could cook
Hark, M. and McQueen, N. Who's scared of ghosts?
Healy, J. The matching piece
Herlihy, J. L. and Noble, W. Blue denim
Howells, W. D. A letter of introduction
Ionesco, E. The bald soprano
Kocher, E. A medal for Julien
Krasna, N. Kind sir
Lake, G. Incident at a grave
Lantz, J. E. and Lantz, R. C. Marriage for love
Lantz, J. E. and Lantz, R. C. Two too many
Mauermann, G. A cup of kindness
Miller, H. L. "N" for nuisance
c Miller, M. Snow White and Rose Red
Morrison, D. A matter of record
Murch, E. The thin red line
Murray, J. A case for Mrs Hudson
Murray, J. Will-o'-Wisp
Parker, K. T. Within the family
Parkhirst, D. Safe harbor
Payton, D. The hanging of Uncle Dilby
Regnier, M. Paddle your own canoe
Savory, G. A likely tale
Sergel, R. The revolt of mother
Spamer, C. Abigail Adams
Stephens, P. J. The changeling
Strindberg, A. Easter
The three Maries
Tyson, A. Millie, the beautiful working girl
Waugh, J. R. The ebony box
Wilder, T. Happy journey to Trenton and Camden
Williams, N. Dreams

6 characters (3m 3g)

Schofield, J. A. and Joudry, R. C. "Who is this?"

6 characters (4m 1w 1b)

Scriven, R. C. The inward eye: boy 1913

6 characters (4m 1w 1g)

Mosel, T. The haven

6 characters (4m 2w)

Burgess, C. V. The Army takes over
Burgess, C. V. Ken changes his mind
Costa du Rels, A. The king's standards

Daviot, G. Cornelia
Fairchild, W. The sound of murder
Fisk, D. M. The secondary wife
Funt, J. The magic and the loss
Gairdner, C. C. and Pilcher, R. The dashing white sergeant
Gowan, E. P. Breeches from Bond Street
Hark, M. and McQueen, N. To my valentine
Harris, N. The dream unwinds
Howard, V. The big melodrama
Howard, V. No order in the court
Ibsen, H. Rosmersholm
c Ilian, C. The nut tree
c Ilian, C. The two woodcarvers
Ionesco, E. The leader
Keeney, C. H. Once an actor
Kwanze, M. Tōboku
Love, C R. Proof of a man
Miller, H. L. The Lincoln cupboard
Murray, J. Ups and downs
Nielson, P. Christmas unusual
O'Casey, S. I knock at the door
Olfson, L. Wuthering Heights
Payne, J. H. and Irving, W. Charles the Second
Purkey, R. A. Hangs over thy head
Relonde, M. Cheating cheaters
Shaw, B. Candida
Shaw, B. The Inca of Perusalem
Shaw, B. Mrs Warren's profession
Simmons, A. The bruising of Satan
c Spamer, C. Elisha cures Naaman
Spamer, C. Priscilla Alden
Ullman, S. S. El gallo
Upson, W. H. Love and Alexander Botts
Verneuil, L. Affairs of state
Waugh, J. R. The burglar alarm
Waugh, J. R. The silver idol
Williams, N. The king decides
Williams, T. Portrait of a Madonna
Wilson, D. C. Peace on Mars
Wincelberg, S. The conqueror

6 characters (5m 1w)

Arrabal. The two executioners
Aurthur, R. A. A very special baby
Carroll, W. Comin' for to carry
Coventry plays. The woman taken in adultery
Emmons, D. G. John Jewitt, the slave
Holmes, M. Jungle prize
Howard, V. The Pharaoh's silver
Kent, M. When queens cook
Knott, F. Dial "M" for murder
Kongō, Y. Genjō
Malcolmson, A. Saint Nicholas and the three scholars
O'Neill, E. "The movie man"
Splaver, S. Jill and Perry go military
Stein, H. A sight for sore thoughts
Yeats, W. B. The dreaming of the bones

6 characters (1w 1b 4g)

c Asbrand, K. Masquerade

6 characters (1w 3b 2g)

Miller, H. L. The magic carpet sweeper

6 characters (1w 4b 1g)

c Miller, H. L. The Christmas runaways

6 characters (2w 2b 2g)

c Miller, H. L. Mother's fairy godmother

MIXED CAST—*Continued*

6 characters (3b 3g)

Asbrand, K. Anything for father
c Fisher, A. Voices
Fisher, A. and Rabe, O. May the best man win
Schofield, J. A. and Joudry, R. C. "Many infallible proofs"
c Spamer, C. The foolish kitten

**6 characters and extras
(1m 1w 1b 3g extras)**

c Very, A. John Grumlie

**6 characters and extras
(1m 1w 2b 2g extras)**

c Newman, D. The Christmas tree surprise

**6 characters and extras
(1m 2w 3g extras)**

c Newman, D. Long ago in Bethlehem

**6 characters and extras
(1m 5w extras)**

Martens, A. C. Radiant morning

**6 characters and extras
(1m 2b 3g extras)**

Spamer, C. Clara Barton

**6 characters and extras
(1m 3b 2g extras)**

Gittings, R. Man's estate

**6 characters and extras
(2m 1w 1b 2g extras)**

Fisher, A. and Rabe, O. Johnny Appleseed's vision

**6 characters and extras
(2m 1w 2b 1g extras)**

Fisher, A. and Rabe, O. Johnny on the spot
c Woolsey, J. and Sechrist, E. H. Fire at the Fieldings

**6 characters and extras
(2m 2w 1b 1g extras)**

c Hark, M. and McQueen, N. The new broom
c Hark, M. and McQueen, N. A prize for mother
c Hondelink, M. E. Christmas cards
c Jackson, S. The bad children

**6 characters and extras
(2m 2w 2g extras)**

Fisher, A. L. The Spirit of Christmas

**6 characters and extras
(2m 3w 1b extras)**

Yeats, W. B. Cathleen ni Houlihan

**6 characters and extras
(2m 4w extras)**

Lathrop, D. Romeo and Julia
Westgate, T. Petticoat handicap

**6 characters and extras
(3m 1w 1b 1g extras)**

Asbrand, K. It happened at Christmas
Fisher, A. Caves of the earth
c Miller, H. L. Old Glory grows up
c Miller, H. L. Wake up, Santa Claus!

**6 characters and extras
(3m 1w 2b extras)**

c Miller, H. L. Visitor to Mount Vernon

**6 characters and extras
(3m 3w extras)**

Aeschylus. The Eumenides
Claudel, P. The tidings brought to Mary
Fleming, T. Miracle at midnight

Hark, M. and McQueen, N. Tomorrow is Christmas
Ibsen, H. When we dead awaken
McGreevey, J. The shepherd who stayed away
McMahon, L. E. School bus romnace
O'Brien, F. B. The guardian
Short, R. The red shoes
Sophocles. Electra

**6 characters and extras
(4m 1w 1b extras)**

Devany, E. H. The red and yellow ark

**6 characters and extras
(4m 2w extras)**

Aeschylus. Agamemnon
Anouilh, J. Medea
Betti, U. The burnt flower-bed
Casey, B. M. The lamp in the night
Estes, S. In quest of power through prayer
Euripides. The Heracleidae
Euripides. Iphigenia in Tauris
Fisher, A. and Rabe, O. Invasion from the stratosphere
Fisher, A. and Rabe, O. The story of a well
Kwanze, M. Ikeniye
Malcolmson, A. The shepherds' play
Parker, K. T. Voice of the machines
Philp, P. Love and lunacy
St Clair, R. The happy life
Williams, N. Night of storm
c Woolsey, J. and Sechrist, E. H. This dream came true

**6 characters and extras
(4m 1b 1g extras)**

c Ilian, C. Dame Robin Hood

**6 characters and extras
(5m 1w extras)**

Abstance, P. and Abstance, L. Gold in the West
Aeschylus. Prometheus bound
Emurian, E. K. I'll take you home again, Kathleen
Estes, S. In quest of power through humility
Estes, S. In quest of power through witnessing
c Fisher, A. Once upon a time
Green, P. Franklin and the King
Inge, W. Glory in the flower
c Joy to the world
Olson, E. Faust: a masque
Sartre, J. P. Respectful prostitute
c Woolsey, J. and Sechrist, E. H. The legend of Babouska
York plays. The Ascension
Zuckerman, A. J. Blobo's boy

**6 characters and extras
(1w 2b 3g extras)**

Martens, A. C. Jimmy and the same old stuff

**6 characters and extras
(2w 2b 2g extras)**

c Fisher, A. Murder in the kitchen
c Martens, A. C. The tiniest Christmas tree

**6 characters and extras
(2b 4g extras)**

c Miller, H. L. The story of light

MIXED CAST—*Continued*

6 characters and extras
(3b 3g extras)

c Hark, M. and McQueen, N. A B C for safety
c Hark, M. and McQueen, N. The book revue
c Spamer, C. The first jack-o'-lanterns
c Very, A. Planting time

7 characters (1m 1w 2b 3g)

c Hark, M. and McQueen, N. Doctor Manners

7 characters (1m 1w 3b 2g)

Asbrand, K. A day of thankful prayer
c Asbrand, K. When daddy comes home

7 characters (1m 1w 5b)

c Woolsey, J. and Sechrist, E. H. Catching the ghost

7 characters (1m 2w 1b 3g)

Asbrand, K. Christmas satellite
Miller, H. L. Lacey's last garland

7 characters (1m 3w 2b 1g)

c Spamer, C. Who will kill the turkey?

7 characters (1m 6w)

c Blyton, E. The mothers' meeting
Dinner, W. and Morum, W. Ladies' bar
Gressieker, H. Royal gambit
Harig, P. Come, fill the cup
Howells, W. D. The mouse trap
Johnson, P. H. Corinth House
Priestley, F. The Good Samaritans

7 characters (1m 1b 5g)

Spamer, C. Charlotte Bronte

7 characters (1m 3b 3g)

c Miller, H. L. The teddy bear hero

7 characters (2m 1w 2b 2g)

c Olson, E. E. Lighting the way

7 characters (2m 2w 1b 2g)

c Miller, H. L. Mr Snow White's Thanksgiving

7 characters (2m 3w 2b)

Weiss, M. J. Parents are people

7 characters (2m 3w 2g)

Stuart, A. Lace on her petticoat

7 characters (2m 4w 1b

McCullers, C. The square root of wonderful

7 characters (2m 5w)

Allen, J. Kind cousin
Bradbury, P. The come back
Coward, N. Blithe spirit
Dennys, J. Art with a capital "A"
Dias, E. J. Stage bore
Foote, H. The midnight caller
Gibson, M. N. Senior play
Greene, G. The living room
Greth, Le R. E. Sweet? sixteen
Kanter, H. and others. The George Gobel show
Kirkpatrick, J. The clubwoman's club
Kromer, H. Take any street
Sergel, R. Blue stocking
Spencer, H. Priscilla and John
Weiss, M. J. Debby's dilemma
Williams, T. Suddenly last summer

7 characters (3m 1w 1b 2g)

Fisher, A. and Rabe, O. Flag of freedom

7 characters (3m 1w 2b 1g)

McCaslin, N. St Nicholas of New Amsterdam

7 characters (3m 1w 3g)

Fisher, A. and Rabe, O. A star for Old Glory

7 characters (3m 2w 1b 1g)

Bailey, H. F. The picture window frames Christmas
c Hark, M. and McQueen, N. Hearts and flowers for mother

7 characters (3m 3w 1b)

Agg, H. Silk and sawdust
Anderson, R. All summer long
Baughman, R. K. A modern Christmas carol
Fisher, A. L. Ghosts on guard
Hark, M. and McQueen, N. Bake a cherry pie
c Hark, M. and McQueen, N. New-fangled Thanksgiving
Hark, M. and McQueen, N. Who's old-fashioned?
Wilson, D. C. The return of Chandra

7 characters (3m 3w 1g)

Hark, M. and McQueen, N. Star baby-sitter
Lantz, J. E. and Lantz, R. C. Marriage—not legal

7 characters (3m 4w)

Addyman, E. The secret tent
Barry, M. H. The nautical approach
Bell, A. Egad, what a cad!
Brenner, M. Bill and Sue
Cary, F. L. Pitfall
Casey, R. Late love
Corey, O. R. The big middle
Corrie, J. The theft
Crothers, R. He and she
Davies, R. No escape
Dimondstein, B. Mister Gultz
Donisthorpe, G. S. Fruit of the tree
Emery, C. A private affair
Federspiel, J. A. D. Behold the body
Goldman, P. Mermaid Avenue is the world
Greth, Le R. E. The ghost from outer space
Hackett, W. A dress affair
Hackett, W. The way the ball bounces
Hartley, R. Big shot
Hawse, A. The cradle
Horne, K. Trial and error
Ibsen, H. Hedda Gabler
Kirkpatrick, J. It takes a woman
Knox, A. He knew the master
Lawler, R. Summer of the seventeenth doll
Li, Y. M. Heaven challenges
McCoy, P. S. Clara paints the town
McCoy, P. S. A rumpus on rampage
MacLeod, R. Kate
McMahon, B. The Ming thing
Martens, A. C. Step lively, please
Murray, J. The five buttons
Nichols, J. 'Twas such a night

MIXED CAST—*Continued*

Olfson, L. Jane Eyre
Savory, G. A month of Sundays
Simpson, H. Miss Matty in mischief
Tilford, H. Miss Dill from Dippyville
Van Druten, J. I am a camera
Van Druten, J. I've got sixpence
Vidal, G. Dark possession
Viereck, P. The tree witch
Walden, W. Tomboy wonder
Zola, E. Thérèse Raquin

7 characters (4m 1w 2b)
Blazer, F. The well of Dothan

7 characters (4m 2w 1g)
c Hopper, V. S. Along came a blackbird
Manley, F. Best trip ever
Sebby, S. R. Easter fantasia

7 characters (4m 3w)
Anouilh, J. The rehearsal
Anouilh, J. Romeo and Jeannette
Ashermann, O. Shakespeare
Axelrod, G. Goodbye Charlie
Badger, A. The bomb
Batson, G. Murder on arrival
Conkle, E. P. Lavender gloves
Corneille, P. Suréna
Dias, E. J. Strong and silent
Dimondstein, B. Hitler's victims
Dreiser, T. The girl in the coffin
Eliot, T. S. The confidential clerk
c Fisher, A. The magic formula
Fisher, A. and Rabe, O. Turning the tables
Foote, H. The death of the old man
Hackett, W. The outgoing tide
Hamilton, P. The man upstairs
Hark, M. and McQueen, N. Cabana blues
c Hark, M. and McQueen, N. Not fit for man or beast
Heayes, N. Morning air
Holm, J. C. The southwest corner
Howells, W. D. The smoking car
Hughes, J. The ship of dreams
Kimes, B. The lost Christmas
Last, J. Mr Mason
Latham, J. L. The nightmare
McMaster, A. Upstairs and downstairs
Maeterlinck, M. The intruder
Malleson, M. Sganarelle
Masteroff, J. The warm peninsula
Maugham, W. S. The circle
Miller, H. L. The haunted clothesline
Mills, O. In the soot
Milne, A. A. The ugly duckling
Murray, J. The mystery in the lab
O'Casey, S. Bedtime story
Oldfield, M. Please communicate
O'Neill, E. "Abortion"
Owen, A. Can this be love?
Potter, D. S. A touch of marble
Prévert, J. A united family
Procunier, E. R. Voices of desire
Richards, S. Through a glass, darkly
Ridge, A. Saint Martha and the Tarasque of Tarascon

Rodman, H. A thing of beauty
Seiler, C. Nude washing dishes
Seiler, C. What's wrong with the girls
Shaw, B. Arms and the man
Stephens, C. G. Once in September
Synge, J. M. The well of the saints
Wallace, N. Speed, bonnie boat
Woskoff, V. Castle in the village
Yeats, W. B. The words upon the window-pane

7 characters (5m 1w 1b)
Boyd, A. K. Pip and the convict

7 characters (5m 2w)
Abstance, P. and Abstance, L. Cotton Road
Adamov, A. Ping-pong
Addis, H. Drama
Albee, E. The death of Bessie Smith
Arrabal. The automobile graveyard
Aurthur, R. A. Man on the mountain-top
Cox, W. N. The Scuffletown outlaws
Crozier, E. Rab the Rhymer
Dunlop, R. S. Four bells means glory!
Emurian, E. K. Columbia, the gem of the ocean
Fisher, A. and Rabe, O. What happened in Egypt
Ford, R. Requiem for a nun
Geiger, M. The return of a patriot
Greene, R. S. Decision for freedom
Mansur, F. L. Train for Sherwood
Miller, H. L. The Christmas oboe
Molière, J. B. P. The critique of The school for wives
Mosel, T. The out-of-towners
Nicholson, H. Port and a pistol
Olfson, L. As you like it
Pomerantz, E. Only a game
Powers, V. The wall
Rattigan, T. The Browning version
Rattigan, T. While the sun shines
Ringwood, G. P. The courting of Marie Jenvrin
Royle, S. and Renavent, G. Especially mother
Salverson, G. You are not alone
Saroyan, W. Hello out there
Shaw, B. Why she would not
Sladen-Smith, F. Sweet Master William
Taylor, S. The pleasure of his company
Towneley plays. The play of the shepherds; Wakefield cycle: secunda pastorum
Towneley plays. The Wakefield Second shepherds' pageant
Turgenev, I. A provincial lady
Williams, N. A battle of wits

7 characters (6m 1w)
Anderson, D. Watermelon
Arnold, J. W. The sheriff
Devany, E. H. The cow-catcher on the caboose
Howard, V. The spear
Kwanze, K. N. Funa-Benkei
Lewis, E. A screw loose
Nash, N. R. The rainmaker

MIXED CAST—*Continued*

Phillips, J. B. The boyhood of Jesus
Sinclair, L. Legend of the long house
Yaffe, J. The deadly game

7 characters (6m 1g)

Piersel, W. G. A town is born

7 characters (1w 3b 3g)

c Woolsey, J. and Sechrist, E. H. Charlie's May basket

7 characters (2w 1b 4g)

c Hark, M. and McQueen, N. The dolls

7 characters (2w 4b 1g)

c Ilian, C. A Christmas miracle

7 characters (3w 3b 1g)

c Pyle, M. T. Not on the menu

7 characters (4b 3g)

Ashton, L. S. Christmas story
c Spamer, C. The little goblins
c Spamer, C. Pumpkin Ghost

**7 characters and extras
(1m 4w 1b 1g extras)**

Fisher, A. and Rabe, O. Skills to share

**7 characters and extras
(1m 6w extras)**

O'Connell, M. O. Sister. One red rose

**7 characters and extras
(1m 3b 3g extras)**

c Woolsey, J. and Sechrist, E. H. The fire demons

**7 characters and extras
(2m 1w 2b 2g extras)**

c Jeffrey, H. K. and Walls, D. A. Veterans Day
c Woolsey, J. and Sechrist, E. H. A Halloween surprise package

**7 characters and extras
(2m 2w 1b 2g extras)**

c Carlson, B. W. Mystery of the glittering gem

**7 characters and extras
(2m 3w 1b 1g extras)**

c Newman, D. The keys to peace

**7 characters and extras
(2m 5w extras)**

Friend, M. The Charleston craze
c Jones, B. M. The magic spinning-wheel
Russell, M. The three women of the Nativity

**7 characters and extras
(3m 3w 1b extras)**

c Hastings, M. L. C. A May Day pageant

**7 characters and extras
(3m 4w extras)**

Anderson, R. A. and Sweeney, R. L. Boris and the spaceman
c Boegehold, B. The shoemaker's Christmas
Euripides. Hippolytus
Healy, J. Summer and stock
Van Druten, J. I am a camera
Vidal, G. Summer pavilion

**7 characters and extras
(3m 2b 2g extras)**

Fisher, A. and Rabe, O. The accident of birth

**7 characters and extras
(4m 1w 1b 1g extras)**

c Harris, A. Circus in the wind
Kolb, K. She walks in beauty

**7 characters and extras
(4m 2w 1g extras)**

c Spamer, C. Miss Muffet's lunch
Thomas, D. and Slocumb, P. Next-to-last rites

**7 characters and extras
(4m 3w extras)**

Anderson, R. A. and Sweeney, R. L. Boris and the briefcase
Apstein, T. The beams of our house
Brown, F. E. The educated schoolhouse
Chadwick, E. Shoes for a queen
Corneille, P. Attila
Dias, E. J. The face is familiar
Dimondstein, B. Miracle from heaven
Harris, B. K. Ca'line
Hazlewood, C. H. Lady Audley's secret
Howells, W. D. A sea change
Ibsen, H. The master builder
Jeffers, R. The Cretan woman
c Larkin, E. Mistress Betsy and the flag
Olfson, L. The adventures of Tom Sawyer
Racine, J. Britannicus
Scribe, E. The glass of water
Scribe, E. and Bayard, J. F. A. A peculiar position
Sophocles. Electra

**7 characters and extras
(4m 1b 2g extras)**

c Page, F. R. Adopted by Santa Claus

**7 characters and extras
(4m 2b 1g extras)**

c Spamer, C. Happy New Year

**7 characters and extras
(5m 1w 1g extras)**

c Miller, H. L. The weatherman on trial

**7 characters and extras
(5m 2w extras)**

Calderón. Life is a dream
Euripides. Electra
Euripides. Iphigeneia at Aulis
Euripides. Iphigeneia in Taurica
c Fisher, A. Hearts, tarts, and valentines
Gregory, H. and Henneberger, J. The thousand flerbs
Racine, J. Berenice
Sheridan, R. B. St Patrick's Day
Sophocles. The women of Trachis
c Tennant, K. The magic fat baby
Vidal, G. A sense of justice
Willis, N. P. Tortesa the usurer
Woolsey, J. and Sechrist, E. H. Molly Pitcher, heroine of Monmouth

**7 characters and extras
(6m 1w extras)**

Aeschylus. Prometheus bound
Julian, J. The Devil and the dream
Komparu, Z. Hatsuyuki
Kwanze, M. Takasago
Malcolmson, A. Herod and the magi
Smith, A. C. Greater than any man
Smith, B. Freedom's bird

**7 characters and extras
(1w 3b 3g extras)**

c Very, A. The cock and the fox

MIXED CAST—*Continued*

7 characters and extras
(1w 4b 2g extras)

Fisher, A. and Rabe, O. Pledge to the flag

c Sprague, G. W. A man's point of view

7 characters and extras
(3b 4g extras)

c Fluckey, J. O. The little blue angel

8 characters (1m 1w 3b 3g)

c Hark, M. and McQueen, N. T for turkey
c Newman, D. Christmas at the Cratchits

8 characters (1m 1w 4b 2g)

c Matthews, E. Teddy's own Santa

8 characters (1m 2w 1b 4g)

c Hark, M. and McQueen, N. Too many kittens
c Miller, H. L. Melody for Lincoln

8 characters (1m 3w 1b 3g)

c Newman, D. Washington's gold button

8 characters (1m 4w 1b 2g)

c Hark, M. and McQueen, N. When do we eat?

8 characters (1m 4w 2b 1g)

Fisher, A. Angel in the looking-glass

8 characters (1m 7w)

Priestley, F. Adventures in camp
Simpson, H. Miss Matty in society

8 characters (1m 3b 4g)

c Woolsey, J. and Sechrist, E. H. Mystery next door

8 characters (1m 5b 2g)

c Hark, M. and McQueen, N. Good neighbors

8 characters (2m 1w 2b 3g)

c Asbrand, K. S. The music mart
Fisher, A. and Rabe, O. Honest Abe Lincoln

8 characters (2m 1w 3b 2g)

c Miller, H. L. The greedy goblin

8 characters (2m 2w 3b 1g)

Spamer, C. Martha Washington

8 characters (2m 3w 1b 2g)

c Field, R. Polly Patchwork

8 characters (2m 3w 2b 1g)

Howells, W. D. The night before Christmas

8 characters (2m 4w 1b 1g)

Roos, A. and Roos, W. Speaking of murder

8 characters (2m 5w 1b)

Fuller, R. The Noël candle

8 characters (2m 6w)

Healy, J. Nero fiddles
Kirkpatrick, J. Adam's rib hurts
Kuehl, W. A. Sunstroke
Lewis, J. Return engagement
c Miller, M. The Princess and the swineherd
Stevens, E. The little nuisance
Stuart, A. A gentleman's daughters
Tumpane, J. D. The gift of Tenyin

8 characters (3m 3w 1b 1g)

Fisher, A. Abe's winkin' eye
Hark, M. and McQueen, N. What, no venison?

8 characters (3m 4w 1b)

c Barnes, E. A. and Young, B. M. The magic fishbone
Dean, E. Stood up
Hark, M. and McQueen, N. Christmas recaptured
Hark, M. and McQueen, N. Portrait of an American
Tydeman, R. Duet with dowagers

8 characters (3m 5w)

Bauer, P. The last straw
Bottomley, G. Marsaili's weeping
Broughton, J. Summer fury
Casey, B. M. High polish
Claflin, M. Saturday at the Cohens
Clark, A. W. Graves ghost
Downing, R. Sticks and stones
Grable, M. What price murder?
Hark, M. and McQueen, N. Romance for **Dad**
Home, W. D. The reluctant debutante
Ibsen, H. John Gabriel Borkman
Lathrop, D. Something new in murder
Liggat, J. Friendly relations
Lorenzen, R. F. The scarf from Smyrna
Miller, H. L. A hero's homecoming
Murdoch, W. Do-nothing Dan
Richards, S. Gin and bitterness
Roberts, M. A palm tree in a rose garden
Roos, A. and Roos, W. Speaking of murder
Vining, D. The one that got away
York, E. B. The silver star of Christmas

8 characters (4m 2w 1b 1g)

c Caplan, L. A dream of Purim
O'Neill, E. "Servitude"

8 characters (4m 3w 1b)

Hark, M. and McQueen, N. Vote for your hero
Smith, L. B. and Barrett, J. S. The house is still

8 characters (4m 3w 1g)

Miller, H. L. Mother for mayor
Schnitzler, A. Light-o'-love

8 characters (4m 4w)

Addyman, E. Over the garden fence
Anderson, R. A. and Sweeney, R. L. True blue and trusted
c Arlett, V. I. Young Richard Whittington
Ashton, L. S. The phantom postman
Banks, L. R. The killer dies twice
Berggren, J. The harp that was silent
Blackmore, P. Down came a blackbird
Casey, B. M. The love of Ruth
Casey, B. M. The main road
Casey, B. M. The other nine
Casey, B. M. A red carpet for the bishop
Collier, E. Dark lady
Corrie, J. Love and the boxer
Delderfield, R. F. **The offending hand**
Feutinger, J. Another life
Fisher, S. and Gottlieb, A. Susan slept here

MIXED CAST—*Continued*

Horne, K. The Devil was sick
Howard, V. The women from Kentucky
Inge, W. A loss of roses
Kwanze, K. Eguchi
Lathrop, D. A page of destiny
Lehman, L. Thirty pieces of silver
MacDougall, R. The facts of life
McMartin, E. L. The tree
Martens, A. C. Battle of the budget
Martens, A. C. Now it can be told
Miller, H. L. The vanishing Easter egg
Murphy, A. Three weeks after marriage
Murray, J. The impossible room
Nash, N. R. Girls of summer
Payton, D. Father says no!
Phillips, M. K. Hold that Indian
Robinson, D. F. Salt winds
Sandberg, L. M. The pastor's guiding hand
Savage, G. I won't dance!
Shaw, B. Great Catherine
Shulman, M. and Smith, R. P. The tender trap
Stephens, C. G. More room for love
Sumerau, D. L. The Christmas gifts
Van Kampen, B. Dutch treat
Williams, E. Someone waiting
Williams, H. and Williams, M. Double yolk

8 characters (5m 1w 1b 1g)

c Woolsey, J. and Sechrist, E. H. Let's travel by auto
c Woolsey, J. and Sechrist, E. H. Let's travel by train

8 characters (5m 2w 1b)

Howells, W. D. A masterpiece of diplomacy
c McMillin, M. The young whittler
Maeterlinck, M. Pelléas and Mélisande
Peterson, L. Home, sweet home

8 characters (5m 2w 1g)

Howells, W. D. Saved

8 characters (3m 3w)

Allen, M. Turn any stone
Arthur, K. The long view
Avery, I. Matilda
Behrman, S. N. Biography
Chodorov, E. Oh, men! Oh, women!
Dias, E. J. Feudin' fun
Eliot, T. S. The elder statesman
Estes, S. In quest of power through prophecy
Foote, H. The oil well
Giblin, J. My bus is always late
Gilbert, M. A clean kill
Inge, W. Bus stop
Johnston, D. The dreaming dust
King, N. The shadow of doubt
Melvyn, G. The love match
Menander. She who was shorn
Miller, H. L. Spooks in books
Miller, H. L. What makes it tick?
Mishima, Y. The damask drum
Murphy, A. The old maid
Murray, J. The case of the missing poet
Murray, J. The end of the line

O'Neill, E. Strange interlude
Osborne, J. The entertainer
Parker, K. T. Cry on my shoulder
Parker, M. M. The prodigal comes home
Popplewell, J. Dear delinquent
Rattigan, T. The deep blue sea
Robertson, T. W. Caste
St Clair, R. The promised ones
Shaw, B. Arms and the man
States, B. O. The tall grass
Strindberg, A. The father
Tedlock, D. Oil wells and wedding bells
Thom, R. Children of the ladybug
Wedekind, F. The tenor
Yeats, W. B. The unicorn from the stars

8 characters (6m 2w)

Ashton, L. S. Bethlehem's Field
Axelrod, G. Will success spoil Rock Hunter?
Chesterton, G. K. The surprise
Dias, E. J. Stop the presses!
Garry, J. F. The bonehead case
Goetz, R. and Goetz, A. The immoralist
Howard, P. The boss
Howard, V. The best of the Old West
Jackson, H. H. S. God's ambassador
Mackie, P. The whole truth
Macrae, A. Both ends meet
Miller, J. P. The rabbit trap
Molière, J. B. P. School for wives
Morgan, C. The burning glass
O'Neill, E. The hairy ape
Rodman, H. The will to win
Thompson, M. A. A coat of many colors
Thompson, M. A. Young Doc Smith died tomorrow
Ullman, S. S. Princess of the snows
Violett, E. and Blake, L. Brewsie and Willie
Whiting, J. Marching song
Yeats, W. B. The only jealousy of Emer

8 characters (7m 1w)

Foss, J. Courage, '53
Freeman, L. The answer
Green, P. This Declaration
Howard, V. I resolve
Kirn, J. The cell
Taylor, D. Five in judgment
Watkyn, A. Not in the book

8 characters (7m 1g)

Hazeltine, A. I. Madelon

8 characters (2w 6b)

c Clark, G. Columbus and a Boy Scout

8 characters (4w 2b 2g)

Martens, A. C. Mothers on strike

8 characters (4b 4g)

c Spamer, C. Little blank book

**8 characters and extras
(1m 3w 1b 3g extras)**

c Woolsey, J. and Sechrist, E. H. The Feast of the Dolls

**8 characters and extras
(1m 4w 3b extras)**

Asbrand, K. Mothers of yore

**8 characters and extras
(1m 7w extras)**

Eldridge, M. T. Conference eve

MIXED CAST—*Continued*

8 characters and extras
(2m 2w 2b 2g extras)
c Very, A. Jack and the beanstalk

8 characters and extras
(2m 6w extras)
Heger, K. Somebody special

8 characters and extras
(3m 2w 1b 2g extras)
Hark, M. and McQueen, N. All aboard
for Christmas

8 characters and extras
(3m 4w 1b extras)
Ashton, E. B. To serve a king

8 characters and extras
(3m 5w extras)
Abstance, P. and Abstance, L. Slender
Ella
Euripides. The daughters of Troy
Euripides. The women of Troy
Howells, W. D. Parting friends
Jones, T. Saben revisited
Maddern, V. and Banks, L. R. Miss
Pringle plays Portia
Racine, J. B. Phaedra
c Sprenger, C. H. and Attley, M. Snow
White and the seven dwarfs

8 characters and extras
(4m 1w 2b 1g extras)
c Spamer, C. The king's cooks

8 characters and extras
(4m 2w 1b 1g extras)
c Chitty, A. W. I. Any old toys

8 characters and extras
(4m 3w 1b extras)
Fisher, A. Three and the dragon
St Clair, R. Joy to the world

8 characters and extras
(4m 3w 1g extras)
Schulman, S. H. Turn my face toward the
east

8 characters and extras
(4m 4w extras)
Asbrand, K. Liberty Belle
c Asbrand, K. Strangers at the gate
Casey, B. M. The manger
Euripides. Hippolytus
Ferguson, J. The camp
Hellman, L. Toys in the attic
Ibsen, H. A doll's house
Malcolmson, A. Noah's flood
Martens, A. C. Nobody loves a fat boy
Mary Francis, Sister. Smallest of all
Miller, H. L. February frenzy
c Newman, D. Aladdin
Quinn, C. For want of a character
Racine, J. Andromache

8 characters and extras
(5m 2w 1b extras)
Euripides. Iphigenia in Aulis

8 characters and extras
(5m 3w extras)
Aeschylus. The Choephori
Aeschylus. Choëphoroe
Aeschylus. The libation bearers
Coyle, R. W. Unto thy doors
Dias, E. J. Way, way down east
Euripides. Hecuba
Euripides. Helen

Euripides. Ion
Ibsen, H. The lady from the sea
Labiche, E. and Delacour. Célimare
Miller, H. L. The tree of hearts
c Newman, D. The Emperor's new clothes
Parker, K. T. Double identity
Sophocles. Antigone
c Spamer, C. Jairus' daughter
Spewack, S. Under the sycamore tree
c Very, A. The three sillies
Williams, T. The purification
Yeats, W. B. The Countess Cathleen
Yeats, W. B. Sophocles' King Oedipus

8 characters and extras
(5m 2b 1g extras)
c Martens, A. C. You are watching!

8 characters and extras
(6m 2w extras)
Emurian, E. K. Battle hymn of the Re-
public
Estes, S. In quest of power through di-
vine guidance
Euripides. Heracles
Euripides. The madness of Herakles
Fisher, A. and Rabe, O. Yankee Doodle
Dandy
Kreymborg, A. There's a nation
c Lawrence, G. B. The king's shirt
Sophocles. Ajax
Sophocles. Oedipus at Colonus
c Woolsey, J. and Sechrist, E. H. Thanks-
giving Proclamation—1863
Yeats, W. B. The green helmet
Yeats, W. B. Sophocles' Oedipus at
Colonus

8 characters and extras
(7m 1w extras)
Carruthers, J. Fear not
Dimondstein, B. David and Bath-Sheba
Emurian, E. K. Stewards of the soil
Euripides. The Bacchae
Kantan
Kozlenko, W. Journey of promise
McCaslin, N. The star that never moves
MacLeish, A. The fall of the city
Mayer, E. J. Children of darkness
Miyamasu. Eboshi-ori
Murphy, A. The apprentice
O'Neill, E. The Emperor Jones
Sophocles. Oedipus Rex
Sophocles. Oedipus the King
Stockton, R. F. A fabulous tale
Wagner, N. He is come! The Messiah!

8 characters and extras
(4b 4g extras)
c Fisher, A. Full of vim
c Fisher, A. Hidden meanings
c Jackson, M. R. Meet Father Time

9 characters (1m 1w 4b 3g)
c Zimmerman, K. Family Christmas

9 characters (1m 2w 3b 3g)
c Woolsey, J. and Sechrist, E. H. A picnic
for father

9 characters (1m 3w 5g)
c Woolsey, J. and Sechrist, E. H. Mother
of the town

9 characters (1m 4w 2b 2g)
c Newman, D. Somebody's valentine

MIXED CAST—*Continued*

9 characters (1m 8w)
Hope, A. J.; Mary Francis, Sister, and Birder, D. The complaining angel
Lindsay, B. Beggars can't be choosers

9 characters (1m 5b 3g)
c Miller, H. L. The curious quest

9 characters (2m 3w 1b 3g)
McCarty, R. K. Longing for Christmas

9 characters (2m 3w 3b 1g)
c Very, A. Abe Lincoln goes to school

9 characters (2m 5w 1b 1g)
Martens, A. C. Who's that knocking on my door?
Snyder, W. H. Another summer

9 characters (2m 7w)
Asbrand, K. Candle in the window
Ashton, E. B. The beggarman's bride
Bagnold, E. The chalk garden
Bottomley, G. King Lear's wife
Martens, A. C. People to people

9 characters (3m 1w 1b 4g)
c Miller, H. L. Not for girls

9 characters (3m 2w 2b 2g)
Parr, R. Penny plain

9 characters (3m 3w 1b 2g)
Posegate, E. D. Read me a story

9 characters (3m 3w 2b 1g)
Hark, M. and McQueen, N. Mom's perfect day
Lilyers, J. The risen Christ

9 characters (3m 4w 1b 1g)
Rosten, H. The happy housewife

9 characters (3m 5w 1b)
Sommer, E. A roomful of roses

9 characters (3m 6w)
Carmichael, F. Luxury cruise
Cary, F. L. Murder out of tune
Cary, F. L. and Butler, I. The paper chain
Crean, R. J. The trial
Foote, H. A young lady of property
Jeans, R. Count your blessings
Karchmer, S. Happy birthday to you!
McCleery, W. The guest cottage
Miller, H. L. The pink parasol
Oxton, C. Late arrival
Rattigan, T. Love in idleness
Schaefer, L. The little flaw of Ernesto Lippi
Verga, G. Cavalleria rusticana

9 characters (4m 3w 2g)
Boruff, J. The loud red Patrick

9 characters (4m 4w 1b)
Hark, M. and McQueen, N. Mother's V.I.P.'s
Hastings, C. Uncertain joy
Mantle, M. Gareth triumphs
Munk, K. Egelykke
Ware, L. and Ware, H. The man on a stick

9 characters (4m 4w 1g)
Nathan, P. S. Bibi
Posegate, E. D. The Christmas star

9 characters (4m 5w)
Alexander, R. Holiday for lovers
Brown, L. Stolen waters
Bugbee, W. N. Life starts at thirty-five
Butler, I. The wise children
Carmichael, F. Inside Lester
Carmichael, F. Petey's choice
Casey, B. M. The portrait
Claiborne, R. and Banks, F. The last leaf
Delderfield, R. F. The orchard walls
Dias, E. J. Abner Crane from Hayseed Lane
Douglas, D. Just off Broadway
Duffield, B. December bride
Foote, H. Expectant relations
Howells, W. D. The Albany depot
Howells, W. D. Out of the question
Howells, W. D. and Poel, W. A foregone conclusion
Ionesco, E. The future is in eggs
Ionesco, E. Jack
Jones, G. The Mayor of Torontal
King, P. and Cary, F. L. Sailor, beware!
Kober, A. and Oppenheimer, G. A mighty man is he
Li, Y. M. The woman painter
McMullen, J. C. Deep freeze
Martens, A. C. Do-it-yourself
Maugham, W. S. The constant wife
Mills, H. The house by the lake
Osborn, P. Morning's at seven
Parker, K. T. Shall we dance?
Preston, E. E. The voice that failed
Randall, J. Look who's laughing
Ridley, A. and Borer, M. C. Tabitha
Shirley, R. Time the sad jester
Shoub, M. Ashes in the wind
Smith, B. and Webb, C. Lawyer Lincoln
Thomas, B. Two of everything
Wilder, T. The long Christmas dinner
Williams, T. Period of adjustment

9 characters (5m 2w 2g)
Wishengrad, M. The rope dancers

9 characters (5m 3w 1b)
Geiger, M. Edwin Booth
McMahon, B. Guided tour

9 characters (5m 3w 1g)
McCarty, R. K. But this I know

9 characters (5m 4w)
Addis, H. Open house
Albery, J. Two roses
Atkinson, A. Four winds
Augier, E. Olympe's marriage
Behrman, S. N. Jane
c Carlson, B. W. For soldiers everywhere
Chekhov, A. Uncle Vanya
Chown, H. Account rendered
Christie, D. and Christie, C. The touch of fear
Coward, N. Hands across the sea
Delderfield, R. F. Golden rain
Godfrey, T. The Prince of Parthia
Golden, E. Great expectations
Gray, D. Love affair
Hawse, A. Seeing the star

MIXED CAST—*Continued*

Holloway, Sister M. M. The last of the leprechauns
Howard, S. The late Christopher Bean
Howells, W. D. The garroters
King, P. Serious charge
Lockwood, L. Autumn in the air
Martens, A. C. Drag race
Mauriac, F. Asmodée
Millar, R. Waiting for Gillian
Morton, E. For heaven's sake
Murray, J. The Swiss Chalet mystery
Nicholson, N. A match for the Devil
Olfson, L. The importance of being Earnest
Osborne, J. and Creighton, A. Epitaph for George Dillon
Peach, L. du G. and Hay, I. The white sheep of the family
Roepke, G. A white butterfly
Shaughnessy, A. Release
Sherriff, R. C. The telescope
Spring, H. The gentle assassin
Spring, H. Jinny Morgan
Stafford, K. Tinker? Tailor? Soldier?
Stern, L. and Zelinka, S. The $99,000 answer
Strindberg, A. The dance of death
Weiss, M. J. Money talks
Wesker, A. Roots
Wilde, O. The importance of being Earnest

9 characters (6m 2w 1g)

c Asbrand, K. Florrie's fortune
Mary Francis, Sister. Christmas at Greccio
c Quinlan, M. E. Pete of the rancho

9 characters (6m 3w)

Alexander, R. Grand prize
Ardrey, R. Sing me no lullaby
Blacklock, J. A time of minor miracles
Bond, C. The food of love
Chodorov, E. The spa
Crane, B. Stage-stricken
Estes, S. In quest of power through wisdom
Howard, P. The man with the key
Jeans, R. Double take
Kanin, F. and Kanin, M. Rashomon
Kelly, G. The show-off
Menander. The arbitration
Olfson, L. David Copperfield and Uriah Heep
Olfson, L. King Lear
Olfson, L. Much ado about nothing
Shaw, B. The millionairess
Shaw, B. Misalliance
Shaw, B. Too true to be good

9 characters (7m 2w)

Abstance, P. and Abstance, L. Feudin' in the mountains
Anthony, R. Jackknife
Bevan, M. Inquest on Monday
Brenner, M. The physical threat
Camus, A. The just assassins
Crouch, A. Not by might
Forsyth, J. Héloïse
Gazzo, M. V. A hatful of rain

Howard, P. We are tomorrow
Howells, W. D. Samson
Howells, W. D. The sleeping car
Miller, H. A. A penny for Charon
Molière, J. B. P. The school for wives
Mosel, T. Ernie Barger is fifty
Odets, C. Awake and sing!
Olfson, L. A midsummer night's dream
Olson, E. The illusionists
O'Neill, E. Homecoming
Schnitzler, A. Countess Mizzie
Sek, M. The dawn must break
Sinclair, L. The case of the sea-lion flippers
Ustinov, P. The love of four colonels
Vollmer, L. Sun-up
Williams, T. The long goodbye

9 characters (8m 1w)

Boland, B. The prisoner
Courteline, G. The commissioner
David and Bathsheba
Euripides. The Bacchae
Kissen, F. Abraham Lincoln: with malice toward none
Kurnitz, H. Once more, with feeling
Molnar, F. The play's the thing
Olfson, L. The taming of the shrew
Orme, F. Graduation present
c Spamer, C. The wise men
Wasserman, D. and Balch, J. Elisha and the long knives
Zeiger, H. Five days

9 characters (2w 7g)

c Newman, D. The stolen heart

9 characters (3b 6g)

c Very, A. Three little kittens go to school

9 characters (4b 5g)

c Olson, E. E. The Hallowe'en party

9 characters (5b 4g)

c Spamer, C. Sammy Bushytail

9 characters (8g 1b)

c Asbrand, K. The Easter egg's dilemma

9 characters and extras (1m 1w 3b 4g extras)

c Miller, H. L. Wait and see

9 characters and extras (1m 1w 5b 2g extras)

c Fichter, H. G. To soap or not to soap

9 characters and extras (1m 8w extras)

Wilde, P. Legend

9 characters and extras (1m 3b 5g extras)

c Newman, D. Something new for Halloween

9 characters and extras (1m 4b 4g extras)

c Newman, D. A present from Abe
c Woolsey, J. and Sechrist, E. H. The good old days

9 characters and extras (1m 5b 3g extras)

c Woolsey, J. and Sechrist, E. H. Juliana's birthday

9 characters and extras (2m 1w 3b 3g extras)

c Fisher, A. Nothing ever happens!

MIXED CAST—*Continued*

**9 characters and extras
(2m 3w 1b 3g extras**

c Miller, H. L. Mary's invitation

**9 characters and extras
(2m 4b 3g extras)**

Osgood, P. E. Midwinter-Eve fire

**9 characters and extras
(3m 2w 4b extras)**

Lynch, P. The Christmas angel

**9 characters and extras
(3m 4w 2b extras)**

c O'Brien, R. Trippy answers the phone

**9 characters and extras
(3m 6w extras)**

Aschmann, H. T. As pretty does
Gross, E. and Gross, N. Dooley and the amateur hour
Pirandello, L. The life I gave you

**9 characters and extras
(4m 3w 2b extras)**

Grillparzer, F. Medea

**9 characters and extras
(4m 5w extras)**

Aristophanes. Lysistrata
Emurian, E. K. The new colossus
Euripides. The Trojan women
Olfson, L. Silas Marner
St Clair, R. Miracle of the Madonna
Shaw, G. B. Pygmalion

**9 characters and extras
(4m 2b 3g extras)**

c Moore, S. S. The miller, his son, and their ass

**9 characters and extras
(5m 2w 2b extras)**

Euripides. The Medea

**9 characters and extras
(5m 4w extras)**

Casey, B. M. The little things
Corneille, P. Don Sanche d'Aragon
Costigan, J. A wind from the south
James, H. Guy Domville
Kleist, H. von. Penthesilea
Martens, A. C. Once in a blue moon
c Martens, A. C. Who sent the comic valentine?
Obey, A. Noah
Tyler, R. The contrast
Yeats, W. B. The death of Cuchulain

**9 characters and extras
(5m 4g extras)**

c Newman, D. Mr Lincoln's beard

**9 characters and extras
(6m 2w 1b extras)**

Euripides. Alcestis

**9 characters and extras
(6m 2w 1g extras)**

McNeely, J. The staring match

**9 characters and extras
(6m 3w extras)**

Atherton, M. And it's Christmas!
Corneille, P. Sertorius
Foote, H. The trip to Bountiful
Golden, E. The Lady of the Lake
O'Neill, E. The long voyage home
Senior, E. The hunted
Sophocles. Antigone
Yeats, W. B. The player queen
Young, S. The sound of apples

**9 characters and extras
(7m 1w 1b extras)**

Duff, A. A play for Christmas Eve
Ketchum, A. Bethlehem

**9 characters and extras
(7m 2w extras)**

Boker, G. H. Francesca da Rimini
Day, P. F. Simeon, the faithful servant
Euripides. The children of Herakles
Euripides. Electra
Ferrini, V. Telling of the North Star
Scribe, E. The queen's gambit
Seneca, L. A. Oedipus
Shaw, B. The admirable Bashville
Sophocles. Ajax
Wishengrad, M. Divided we stand

**9 characters and extras
(8m 1w extras)**

Blake, R. What God hath wrought
Mindel, J. Freeing the land

**9 characters and extras
(5b 4g extras)**

c Very, A. Getting ready for winter

**9 characters and extras
(8b 1g extras)**

Very, A. Puss-in-Boots

10 characters (1m 1w 4b 4g)

c Miller, H. L. The forgotten hero

10 characters (1m 6b 3g)

c Miller, H. L. The Patriotic Teddy Bear and the UN

10 characters (2m 1w 6b 1g)

c Spamer, C. Humpty Heart

10 characters (2m 4w 4b)

Fisher, A. The voice of liberty

10 characters (2m 8w)

Chayefsky, P. The mother

10 characters (2m 4b 4g)

c Newman, D. A compass for Christopher

10 characters (3m 1w 5b 1g)

c Barton, E. The third lamb

10 characters (3m 3w 3b 1g)

c Carlson, B. W. The lady who put salt in her coffee

10 characters (3m 4w 2b 1g)

Miller, H. L. The judge's diary

10 characters (3m 5w 2b)

Peterson, L. Desert soliloquy

10 characters (3m 7w)

Asbrand, K. Easy as pie
Bottomley, G. The woman from the voe
Butler, I. Tranquil House
Foote, H. The dancers
Lisle, V. The merry matchmaker
c Marston, M. A. The roving journeyman
Taggart, T. Punky Doodle

10 characters (4m 3w 1b 2g)

c Hark, M. and McQueen, N. Junction Santa Claus

10 characters (4m 4w 1b 1g)

Anouilh, J. Ardèle
Asbrand, K. The week before Christmas!
Wattron, F. Strawberry Circle

MIXED CAST—*Continued*

10 characters (4m 5w 1b)
Gross, E. and Gross, N. She loves him yes

10 characters (4m 5w 1g)
Foote, H. The traveling lady
Hollinshead, L. M. Publican and sinner

10 characters (4m 6w)
Alexander, A. Cute as a button
Alexander, A. Right under your nose
Barry, P. Paris bound
Batson, G. Design for murder
Carmichael, F. The pen is deadlier
Chetham-Strode, W. The pet shop
Dayton, M. Sweetie
Dayton, M. Whirlwind courtship
Faust, E. Gone to the dogs
Gurney, A. R. Turn of the century
Lusk, D. Girls are better than ever
McCleery, W. The family man
Mitzman, N. and Dalzell, W. In 25 words —or death
Peavey, H. Teen antics
Perl, A. Tevya and the first daughter
Rosenthal, A. Red letter day
St Clair, R. Susie and the F.B.I.
Wilde, O. Lady Windermere's fan

10 characters (5m 1w 1b 3g)
c Miller, H. L. The wishing stream

10 characters (5m 3w 1b 1g)
Richards, S. and Slocumb, P. A dash of Santa Claus

10 characters (5m 3w 2g)
McGreevey, J. Coins of His kingdom

10 characters (5m 4w 1b)
Hark, M. and McQueen, N. Reindeer on the roof
Miller, A. All my sons

10 characters (5m 4w 1g)
Cockram, R. Shadow of the eagle
Laurents, A. A clearing in the woods
Posegate, E. D. His wonders to perform

10 characters (5m 5w)
Alexander, R. Time out for Ginger
Banks, L. R. It never rains
Blackmore, P. Mad about men
Carlton, J. Bab buys a car
Carmichael, F. The night is my enemy
Chester plays. Noah's flood
Corey, O. The Book of Job
Coventry plays. The parliament of heaven: The Annunciation and Conception
Cusack, D. The golden girls
Delmar, V. Warm Wednesday
Goodrich, F. and Hackett, A. The diary of Anne Frank
Gordon, K. The broom and the groom
Gross, E. and Gross, N. A party is born
Hark, M. and McQueen, N. G for Gettysburg
Hark, M. and McQueen, N. The Teen Club's Christmas
Howard, V. Happy holidays for little women
Last, J. Make it murder
Laurents, A. The time of the cuckoo

MacLeish, A. This music crept by me upon the waters
Miller, H. L. Be my "walentine"
Miller, H. L. A hooky holiday
Mitchell, B. E. and Rose, Le R. Mountain gal
Murray, J. Be my ghost
Orth, R. Two have dreamed
Payton, D. He tried with his boots on
Reach, J. Dragnet
Reach, J. Stranger in town
Ridley, A. You, my guests!
Roche, D. My wife's lodger
Schnitzler, A. La ronde
Taggart, T. Crewcuts and longhairs

10 characters (6m 2w 1b 1g)
Beckett, S. All that fall
c Miller, H. L. Thankful's red beads

10 characters (6m 4w)
Beers, J. Beauty and the Beast
Behrman, S. N. Rain from heaven
Beich, A. and Wright, W. H. The man in the dog suit
Belasco, D. Madame Butterfly
Brand, M. Strangers in the land
Carney, F. The righteous are bold
Colson, J. G. The green ball
Dearsley, A. P. Come back Peter
Dias, E. J. The case of the missing pearls
Dias, E. J. What ho!
Fry, C. Venus observed
George, C. Fanny, the frivolous flapper
Goldsmith, O. She stoops to conquer
Hellman, L. The little foxes
Lynch, P. Fool's paradise
Marston, J. And a song was born
Miller, H. L. Beany's private eye
Morris, E. The wooden dish
O'Neill, E. Beyond the horizon
Raeburn, H. Beginning of the way
Shaw, B. Heartbreak house
Stephens, C. G. The matter with Mildred
Weiss, M. J. Greetings from . . .
Wilson, E. Beppo and Beth

10 characters (7m 1w 2b)
c John, C. Sea shells

10 characters (7m 2w 1b)
Sherriff, R. C. The long sunset

10 characters (7m 3w)
Barnett, M. Yankee peddler
Behrman, S. N. End of summer
Boyd, A. K. The mock doctor
Goetz, R. and Goetz, A. The hidden river
Gregory, Lady. Spreading the news
c Ilian, C. Absolutely horrid
Johnston, D. The moon in the Yellow River
Kerr, W. and Kerr, J. Goldilocks
Olfson, L. A Connecticut Yankee in King Arthur's court
O'Neill, E. A touch of the poet
Percy, E. and Denham, L. The man with expensive tastes
Rattigan, T. French without tears
Spewack, S. and Spewack, B. L. My three angels

MIXED CAST—*Continued*

Towneley plays. The Wakefield Pageant of Herod the Great
Turgenev, I. The bachelor
Vidal, G. Honor
Webber, C. E. Be good, sweet maid
Wetmore, A. The pedlar
Wilson, D. Flight of the dove

10 characters (8m 2w)

c Bayliss, R. G. The burglar alarm
Glickman, W. and Stein, J. Mrs Gibbons' boys
Olfson, L. The tempest
Phillips, J. B. The arrest in the garden
Riggs, L. Roadside
Schevill, J. The bloody tenet
Ullman, S. S. The reward
Vidal, G. Visit to a small planet
Waugh, J. R. The missing formula

10 characters (9m 1w)

Curtis, P. D. The trial of Mr Newall
Hochwaelder, F. The public prosecutor
Kurnitz, H. Reclining figure
Niss, S. The penny
Steinbeck, J. Of mice and men

10 characters (1w 5b 4g)

c Mooar, C. H. Washington's Birthday

10 characters (2w 3b 5g)

c Newman, D. Memorial Day for the Blue and Gray

10 characters (5b 5g)

c Martens, A. C. Weather or not
c Very, A. Thanksgiving Eve

10 characters and extras (1m 1w 4b 4g extras)

c Martens, A. C. The magic broom

10 characters and extras (1m 6b 3g extras)

c McGee, A. Bill visits Mexico

10 characters and extras (2m 1w 3b 4g extras)

c Crank, H. P. The promise lily

10 characters and extras (2m 2w 3b 3g extras)

c Woolsey, J. and Sechrist, E. H. A Mexican holiday

10 characters and extras (2m 4w 3b 1g extras)

c Miller, H. L. The Birds' Christmas Carol

10 characters and extras (2m 5w 2b 1g extras)

c Spamer, C. The gingerbread house

10 characters and extras (3m 7w extras)

Joudry, P. Teach me how to cry
Martens, A. C. Home for Christmas
Martens, A. C. The three faces of Easter
Simpson, G. H. A time for love

10 characters and extras (4m 3w 1b 2g extras)

c Hark, M. and McQueen, N. Father keeps house
c Newman, D. The way to the inn

10 characters and extras (4m 3w 3b extras)

c Tennant, K. The ghost tiger

10 characters and extras (4m 4w 2b extras)

McCaslin, N. The Bell Witch of Tennessee

10 characters and extras (4m 5w 1b extras)

Euripides. Andromachê

10 characters and extras (4m 6w extras)

Hark, M. and McQueen, N. Miss Senior High
Shaw, B. Pygmalion

10 characters and extras (5m 4w 1b extras)

Bell, R. E. Through a glass darkly

10 characters and extras (5m 5w extras)

Asbrand, K. The Prince of Peace
Martens, A. C. The search for Wildcat McGillicuddy
Neilson, P. To hear the angels sing
Sumerau, D. L. Make His name glorious
Tarpley, V. and Tarpley, K. Golden river

10 characters and extras (6m 2w 2b extras)

Kerr, J. and Brooke, E. King of hearts

10 characters and extras (6m 3w 1b extras)

Collins, B. F. Grand jury

10 characters and extras (6m 4w extras)

Foote, H. John Turner Davis
Goldsmith, O. She stoops to conquer
Miller, C. H. Back to Bethlehem
Miller, H. L. I'll eat my hat!
Murray, W. A night in . . .
O'Casey, S. Juno and the paycock
c Palmer, K. and Palmer, W. Cinderella

10 characters and extras (6m 2b 2g extras)

c Marcus, I. H. To you the torch

10 characters and extras (7m 2w 1b extras)

c Dunbar, T. M. The Pied Piper of Hamlin

10 characters and extras (7m 3w extras)

Betti, U. The Queen and the rebels
Bond, N. Mr Mergenthwirker's lobblies
Corneille, P. Héraclius
Cullen, A. Niccolo and Nicollette
D'Alton, L. The Devil a saint would be
Euripides. Helen
Fisher, A. Luck takes a holiday
Harrington, H. The boy who knew Jesus
Jefferson, J. Rip Van Winkle
Lessing. Emilia Galotti
Maeterlinck, M. A miracle of Saint Antony
Stevens, L. Bullfight
Williamson, H. R. His Eminence of England

10 characters and extras (8m 1w 1b extras)

Shaw, B. The six of Calais

10 characters and extras (8m 2w extras)

Aristophanes. The wasps
Bird, R. M. The broker of Bogota
Carroll, P. V. The wise have not spoken
Chorpenning, C. B. Lincoln's secret messenger

MIXED CAST—*Continued*

Emurian, E. K. Three skits for Christmas
Euripides. The Phoenician maidens
Howells, J. H. Good-bye, Gray Flannel
Kromer, H. Caught between
O'Neill, E. Desire under the elms
Shaw, B. The doctor's dilemma
Tashjian, V. The Easter story

**10 characters and extras
(8m 2b extras)**

c Gow, R. Under the skull and bones

**10 characters and extras
(9m 1w extras)**

Abstance, P. and Abstance, L. The pig-skin parade
Emmons, D. G. A costly gold hunt
Vidal, G. The death of Billy the Kid

**10 characters and extras
(1w 4b 5g extras)**

c Newman, D. The new Washington

**10 characters and extras
(1w 5b 4g extras)**

c Fisher, A. Treasure hunt

**10 characters and extras
(5b 5g extras)**

c Patterson, L. The safety school

11 characters (1m 1w 5b 4g)

c Matthews, E. Mr Blanchard—Easter bunny

11 characters (1m 1w 8b 1g)

c Very, A. General George

11 characters (1m 5b 5g)

Fisher, A. and Rabe, O. A nickel and a dime

11 characters (2m 8w 1b)

McMullen, J. C. I don't believe in Christmas

11 characters (3m 3w 2b 3g)

c Very, A. Jonathan's Thanksgiving

11 characters (3m 3w 3b 2g)

c Woolsey, J. and Sechrist, E. H. A Norwegian mountain mystery

11 characters (3m 5w 3g)

c Asbrand, K. The image of Christmas

11 characters (3m 8w)

Chayefsky, P. Middle of the night
Crone, R. New girl in town
Dalzell, W. and Mitzman, N. Father's been to Mars
Parker, K. A cat has nine
Rattigan, T. Separate tables
Wilton, A. Something borrowed, something blue

11 characters (3m 3b 5g)

c Newman, D. Thanks to the Indians

11 characters (4m 2w 5b)

Robinson, T. The visitor (Lassie)

11 characters (4m 4w 2b 1g)

Hellman, L. Watch on the Rhine

11 characters (4m 7w)

Anouilh, J. The waltz of the toreadors
Bergman, I. Smiles of a summer night
Brown, L. This year—next year
Duffield, B. Christmas at Lourdes
Faust, E. Oh, to be sixteen again!

Howells, W. D. The unexpected guests
Inge, W. Picnic
Leydon, B. Johnny Jones, space cadet!
McCleery, W. The lady chooses
Manning, H. Wonderful summer
Morris, T. B. The nine days
Parish, J. Mystery, mayhem, and murder!
Pryor, C. Just my speed
Richards, S. Half-hour, please
Robinson, R. Princess Victoria's twelfth birthday
Roeder, L. Oh boy, what a girl!
Schnitzler, A. Anatol
Stanton, R. Girl chases boy
Sterling, A. Kissin' cousins
Strindberg, A. Comrades

11 characters (5m 4w 2b)

Inge, W. The dark at the top of the stairs
Spewack, S. and Spewack, B. The festival

11 characters (5m 5w 1g)

Stephens, C. G. Storm cellar

11 characters (5m 6w)

Axelrod, G. The seven year itch
Betti, U. Summertime
Blankfort, D. and Blankfort, M. Monique
Carmichael, F. More than meets the eye
Crosby, M. Readin', 'ritin', and 'rithmetic
Frost, R. Small hotel
Gottlieb, A. Wake up, darling
Graham, A. Wherever she may roam
Greth, Le R. E. The dancing ghost
Hale, R. and Hale, N. Lilacs in the rain
Hale, R. and Hale, N. Love comes in many colors
Hark, M. and McQueen, N. An ode to Spring
Howells, W. D. Five o'clock tea
Manning, H. That's my baby
Miller, H. L. Spooky spectacles
Murray, J. When the hurlyburly's done
Olfson, L. Cyrano de Bergerac
Orr, M. and Denham, R. Be your age
Reach, J. It walks at midnight
Reach, J. Open house
Schweikert, C. P. Hessie of the hills
Seidel, N. Keeping company
Sutton, T. Aunt Min drops in

11 characters (6m 1w 1b 3g)

c Flavelle, I. B. Vacation in the city

11 characters (6m 2w 2b 1g)

Bucci, M. Chain of jade

11 characters (6m 2w 3g)

c Asbrand, K. Children of the Bible

11 characters (6m 3w 2b)

Sinclair, L. When Greek meets Greek

11 characters (6m 4w 1b)

Daviot, G. The little dry thorn
McCarty, R. K. Blake's decision

11 characters (6m 5w)

Benfield, D. The way the wind blows
Benson, S. The young and beautiful
Bolton, G. Child of fortune
Conkling, L. Let 'em eat steak
Delderfield, R. F. The Mayerling affair

MIXED CAST—*Continued*

Elman, I. The brass ring
Foote, H. John Turner Davis
Greene, G. The potting shed
Lynch, P. Neglected husbands' sewing club
McMullen, J. C. Son of Erin
Marr Johnson, D. Never say die
Melville, A. Mrs Willie
Murray, J. The final curtain
Nathan, R. Jezebel's husband
Pierce, C. W. Be yourself!
Reach, J. Murder is my business
Wilson, A. The mulberry bush
Wimberly, R. L. Willy Velvet, homicide detective

11 characters (7m 3w 1b)

Hansberry, L. A raisin in the sun
Hebbel, F. Maria Magdalena
Tennyson, A. The cup

11 characters (7m 3w 1g)

c Hark, M. and McQueen, N. The princess and the rose-colored glasses

11 characters (7m 4w)

Abstance, P. and Abstance, L. Murder at the manor
Bayer, E. and Bayer, L. Third best sport
Carroll, P. V. The wayward saint
Chayefsky, P. Holiday song
Christie, A. Towards zero
Douglas, L. Crispin the tailor
Foote, H. The old beginning
Graveley, G. The mountain flock
Hayes, A. The girl on the Via Flaminia
MacDonagh, D. Step-in-the-hollow
Molière, J. B. P. The slave of truth
Rattigan, T. Flare path
Rattigan, T. The Winslow boy
Richards, S. Tunnel of Love
Serling, R. Noon on Doomsday

11 characters (8m 3w)

Fry, C. Thor, with angels
Grundy, S. A pair of spectacles
Howells, W. D. and Clemens, S. L. Colonel Sellers as a scientist
Inge, W, Come back, Little Sheba
Kimmins, A. The amorous prawn
McLiam, J. The sin of Pat Muldoon
Malleson, M. The misanthrope
Molière, J. B. P. Coxcombs in petticoats
Molière, J. B. P. The misanthrope
Molière, J. B. P. The physician in spite of himself
Molière, J. B. P. The reluctant doctor
O'Casey, S. Hall of healing
O'Casey, S, The shadow of a gunman
Parr, R. The flying machine
Pirandello, L. Lazarus
Rubinstein, H. F. Bernard Shaw in heaven
Synge, J. M. Deirdre of the sorrows

11 characters (9m 2w)

Abstance, P. and Abstance, L. The hold-up at Hoecake Junction
Anderson, R. W. Tea and sympathy
Daviot, G. The pomp of Mr Pomfret
Ervine, St J. John Ferguson

Euripides. Rhesus
c Kramer, C. The voyage
Lehman, L. Saint Chad of the seven wells
Perrini, A. Once a thief
Rutenborn, G. The sign of Jonah
Sharp, A. Nightmare Abbey
Sisson, R. A. The queen and the Welshman
Waugh, J. R. Spots of bother

11 characters (10m 1w)

O'Conor, J. The iron harp
Roffey, J. and Harbord, G. Night of the fourth
Ross, G. and Singer, C. Any other business

11 characters (1w 5b 5g)

c Childs, C. The candle in the window
c Miller, H. L. A Thanksgiving riddle

11 characters (5b 6g)

c Asbrand, K. "Come to my party"

11 characters (6b 5g)

c Miller, H. L. Mystery at Knob Creek farm

11 characters and extras (1m 3w 4b 3g extras)

c Hark, M. and McQueen, N. The house is haunted

11 characters and extras (1m 5w 5g extras)

c Fluckey, J. O. The heart of the forest

11 characters and extras (1m 5b 5g extras)

c Woolsey, J. and Sechrist, E. H. Pumpkin is the password

11 characters and extras (2m 1w 3b 5g extras)

Miller, H. L. The Washington shilling

11 characters and extras (2m 9w extras)

c Knight, C. Patch upon patch

11 characters and extras (3m 1w 3b 4g extras)

Fisher, A. The Merry Christmas elf

11 characters and extras (3m 8w extras)

Burke, N. The girl who had everything

11 characters and extras (4m 7w extras)

García Lorca, F. Blood wedding
Martens, A. C. Fraidy cat

11 characters and extras (5m 1w 2b 3g extras)

c Very, A. The return of Columbus

11 characters and extras (5m 3w 1b 2g extras)

Gibson, W. The miracle worker

11 characters and extras (5m 4w 1b 1g extras)

Cowen, W. J. Little friend

11 characters and extras (5m 4w 2b extras)

c Woolsey, J. and Sechrist, E. H. The great Tree Council

11 characters and extras (5m 6w extras)

Aske, L. Too young
Emurian, E. K. Great women of history

MIXED CAST—*Continued*

Faust, J. P. To us a son
Renno, E. L. Follow the girls
Tarpley, V. and Tarpley, K. Jump over the moon

11 characters and extras
(5m 6b extras)

Marston, M. A. The jackdaw of Rheims

11 characters and extras
(6m 2w 3b extras)

Wilson, R. C. Strangers in Bethlehem

11 characters and extras
(6m 4w 1g extras)

Moody, W. V. The faith healer

11 characters and extras
(6m 5w extras)

Grillparzer, F. The Jewess of Toledo
Hughes, G. The magic apple
Jonson, M. Greensleeves' magic
Lynch, P. The teen-age party

11 characters and extras
(7m 1w 1b 2g extras)

Emurian, E. K. 'Twas the night before Christmas

11 characters and extras
(7m 2w 1b 1g extras)

Kane, E. B. The magic word
McCaslin, N. Tall Bill and his big ideas
National Recreation Association. I hear America singing!

11 characters and extras
(7m 2w 2g extras)

McCaslin, N. The Yankee Peddler

11 characters and extras
(7m 3w 1g extras)

Anouilh, J. Thieves' carnival

11 characters and extras
(7m 4w extras)

Anouilh, J. Antigone
Daviot, G. The princess who liked cherry pie
Davis, O. and Davis, D. Ethan Frome
Stone, W. Devil take a whittler
Thornhill, A. The forgotten factor

11 characters and extras
(8m 2w 1b extras)

Ibsen, H. An enemy of the people

11 characters and extras
(8m 3w extras)

Boucicault, D. The octoroon
Congreve, W. The mourning bride
Emurian, E. K. The church in the wildwood
St Clair, R. The holy search
Vidal, G. The best man

11 characters and extras
(9m 1w 1b extras)

Jagendorf, M. The rime of the ancient mariner

11 characters and extras
(9m 1w 1g extras)

Kent, M. The Nativity

11 characters and extras
(9m 2w extras)

Euripides. The Phoenician women
Euripides. Rhesus
Lee, N. Constantine the Great
Lee, N. Mithridates, King of Pontus

Neilson, P. Room for the King
Schulberg, B. A face in the crowd
Shaw, G. B. Androcles and the lion

11 characters and extras
(10m 1w extras)

Buttle, M. Toynbee in Elysium
Ghelderode, M. de. Chronicles of hell

11 characters and extras
(1w 5b 5g extras)

c Miller, H. L. Crosspatch and Cupid

11 characters and extras
(7b 4g extras)

c Schofield, J. An indoor tree-lighting service

12 characters (1m 1w 5b 5g)

c Woolsey, J. and Sechrist, E. H. The imps' defeat

12 characters (1m 2w 2b 7g)

c Miller, H. L. Strictly Puritan

12 characters (1m 3w 1b 7g)

c Miller, H. L. Right of adoption

12 characters (1m 11w)

Ghelderode, M. de. The women at the tomb

12 characters (2m 2w 4b 4g)

Fisher, A. Unexpected guests
c Woolsey, J. and Sechrist, E. H. What happened to Billy?

12 characters (3m 2w 2b 5g)

c Newman, D. The first Thanksgiving

12 characters (3m 8w 1b)

Magary, F. A. Rest, ye merry gentlemen!

12 characters (3m 9w)

Voysey, M. The amorous goldfish

12 characters (4m 8w)

Goodhue, N. Little Nell, the orphan girl
Granby, F. Resort Hotel
Herman, G. A smell of cinnamon
LePelley, G. Absolutely murder
Mary Francis, Sister. La madre
Spargrove, D. One for the book

12 characters (5m 3w 4b)

Benchley, N. The frogs of Spring

12 characters (5m 5w 2b)

Hollinshead, L. M. In honour bound

12 characters (5m 6w 1g)

Collins, D. Summer brings gifts

12 characters (5m 7w)

LePelley, G. A is for apple
McCoy, P. S. Susan steps out
Reach, J. Ah, yesterday!
Spence, W. How Betsy butted in
Sprague, M. Murder comes in threes

12 characters (6m 3w 2b 1g)

Delmar, V. Mid-summer

12 characters (6m 5w 1g)

Taggart, T. Do—or die!
Taggart, T. TV or not TV

12 characters (6m 6w)

Cargill, P. and Beale, J. Ring for Catty
Casey, B. M. Church notices
Chase, M. Harvey
Chayefsky, P. The bachelor party

MIXED CAST—*Continued*

Chorpenning, C. B. Radio rescue
Douglas, F. It's never too late
Knapp, B. Highly seasoned
Martin, B. Eighteenth summer
Murphy, A. The way to keep him
Murray, J. A case for two detectives
Newbold, H. Joanie on the spot
Perl, A. Tevya and his daughters
Price, O. Out of the mist
Ressieb, G. Danger from the sky
Robinson, R. Fanny Burney's resignation
Sergel, K. My little Margie
Taggart, T. Be my guest
Tobias, J. The crazy mixed-up Kidds
Vanbrugh, Sir J. The confederacy
Williams, T. A streetcar named Desire
Wilson, E. The crime in the Whistler room

12 characters (6m 3b 3g)

c Crawford, A. A visit with the firemen

12 characters (7m 4w 1b)

Kazan, M. The egghead

12 characters (7m 4w 1g)

Anderson, M. Bad seed
Morris, T. B. The deserted house

12 characters (7m 5w)

Ashbery, J. The heroes
Barry, P. Holiday
Chodorov, J. and Fields, J. Anniversary waltz
Deval, J. Tonight in Samarkand
Herne, J. A. Margaret Fleming
Howells, W. D. A hazard of new fortunes
Hughes, E. Frankie and Albert
Lynn, K. S. Who killed Cock Robin?
Maurette, M. Anastasia
Melville, A. Dear Charles
Molière, J. B. P. Tartuffe
Nicholson, A. and Chorpenning, C. B. The magic horn
Shaw, B. Getting married
Synge, J. M. The playboy of the western world
Watkyn, A. For better, for worse

12 characters (8m 4w)

Behrman, S. N. The cold wind and the warm
Corneille, P. Le Cid
Draper, J. Barchester Towers
Goldsmith, C. Your every wish
c Goldsmith, S. L. The staff and the fiddle
Jackson, B. Doctor's delight
Jones, P. and Jowett, J. The party spirit
Kromer, H. Stolen goods
MacCormick, I. The small victory
Molière, J. B. P. The imaginary invalid
Rice, E. The winner
Terence. The brothers

12 characters (9m 3w)

c Bennett, R. Puss in Boots
Camus, A. Caligula
Carruthers, J. Physician in charge
Coppel, A. The gazebo
Giraudoux, J. The Apollo of Bellac
Howard, P. The real news

Menander. The grouch
Molière, J. B. P. Scapin the scamp
Murphy, A. The upholsterer
Olfson, L. Captains Courageous
Plautus. The haunted house
Sisson, R. A. The splendid outcasts
Teichmann, H. The girls in 509
Verner, G. Meet Mr Callaghan
Wilson, E. This room and this gin and these sandwiches
York plays. The Resurrection

12 characters (10m 1w 1b)

Peterson, L. Sticks and stones

12 characters (10m 1w 1g)

c Woolsey, J. and Sechrist, E. H. The Santa Claus court

12 characters (10m 2w)

Howells, W. D. Yorick's love
Kissen, F. Sam Houston: brother of the Cherokees
Musset, A. de. Fantasio
O'Casey, S. The Bishop's bonfire
Olfson, L. Hamlet
Olfson, L. Romeo and Juliet
Rednour, H. P. The oblong circle
Sartre, J. P. Dirty hands
Waldrop, C. L. M. Unto us

12 characters (10m 2b)

Ridge, A. The legend of Saint Basil

12 characters (11m 1w)

Hesketh, J. Mr Owl

12 characters (1w 5b 6g)

c Russell, S. P. Are you thrifty?

12 characters (1w 6b 5g)

c Atwell, R. and Virden, H. Valentine from Mars

12 characters (11w 1b)

Verity, E. and Allen, V. Appointment in Eden

12 characters (6b 6g)

c Palmer, K. and Palmer, W. The magic mountain
c Spamer, C. The chocolate bunny

12 characters (7b 5g)

c Seiler, C. Let's go to the moon

12 characters and extras (3m 2w 5b 2g extras)

Fisher, A. and Rabe, O. All the world around

12 characters and extras (3m 9w extras)

Trick, O. B. Beneath this spire

12 characters and extras (4m 8w extras)

c Black, F. The heartless princess
Tompkins, B. No, no, a million times no!

12 characters and extras (5m 4w 2b 1g extras)

c Miller, H. L. The Mother Goose bake-shop

12 characters and extras (6m 2w 2b 2g extras)

c Fisher, A. By order of the king

MIXED CAST—*Continued*

12 characters and extras
(6m 3w 1b 2g extras)

Hark, M. and McQueen, N. All out for Halloween

12 characters and extras
(6m 3w 2b 1g extras)

Howard, V. Johnny Appleseed in danger

12 characters and extras
(6m 4w 2g extras)

Dryden, J. All for love

12 characters and extras
(6m 6w extras)

Greth, Le R. E. Host to a ghost
Hayes, M. and Hayes, J. Penny
Lee, M. Dope!
Richards, S. and Slocumb, P. The hobble-de-hoy
Warnick, C. Heidi

12 characters and extras
(7m 1w 4b extras)

c Howard, V. Oliver Twist asks for more

12 characters and extras
(7m 2w 2b 1g extras)

c Totheroh, D. The stolen prince

12 characters and extras
(7m 3w 2b extras)

Kissen, F. Sacajawea: guide in the wilderness

12 characters and extras
(7m 5w extras)

Howard, V. David and Goliath
Mitzman, N. and Dalzell, W. Books and crooks
c Newman, D. The prize shamrock
Quinn, A. H. and Quinn, K. C. The bell of St Hildegarde
Sardou, V. and Najac, É. de. Let's get a divorce!
Strauss, J. Golden butterfly
Synge, J. M. The play boy of the western world

12 characters and extras
(8m 1w 1b 2g extras)

Siks, G. B. The Nuremberg stove

12 characters and extras
(8m 3w 1b extras)

c Jordan, L. M. and Garber, H. W. Traveler to Cathay

12 characters and extras
(8m 3w 1g extras)

Miller, H. L. Lorna Doone

12 characters and extras
(8m 4w extras)

Anouilh, J. Antigone
Congreve, W. The double-dealer
Farquhar, G. The constant couple
Giraudoux, J. The virtuous island
Heicher, M. The meaning of Christmas Day
Molière, J. B. P. The pretentious young ladies
Molière, J. B. P. Would-be invalid
Schiller, F. von. Intrigue and love
Sheridan, R. B. The rivals
Taylor, T. The ticket-of-leave man
c Wallerstein, J. S. The cactus wildcat

12 characters and extras
(9m 2w 1g extras)

Wefer, M. This Thine house

12 characters and extras
(9m 3w extras)

Aristophanes. The frogs
Büchner, G. Leonce and Lena
Corneille, P. La mort de Pompée
Corneille, P. Othon
c Howard, V. The strange tale of King Midas
Howells, W. D. Priscilla
Lee. N. Gloriana
Shaw, B. The Devil's disciple
Sheridan, R. B. The Duenna
Stevenson, B. E. A King in Babylon

12 characters and extras
(10m 1w 1b extras)

Phillips, A. L. The shepherds and the wise men

12 characters and extras
(10m 2w extras)

Labiche, E. and Martin, E. A trip abroad
Mary Francis, Sister. Counted as nine
Menander. The bad-tempered man
Wilde, O. The duchess of Padua
Yeats, W. B. The king's threshold

12 characters and extras
(11m 1w extras)

Abel, L. Absalom
Benét, S. V. The Devil and Daniel Webster
Chevigny, H. Daniel Webster
Jonson, B. The alchemist

12 characters and extras
(3b 9g extras)

c Newman, D. Thanks for Thanksgiving

12 characters and extras
(6b 6g extras)

Fisher, A. Mr Do and Mr Don't

13 characters (1m 1w 6b 5g)

c Miller, H. L. The Bar-None Trading Post

13 characters (1m 2w 3b 7g)

c Newman, D. The real Princess

13 characters (2m 4w 4b 3g)

Miller, H. L. Three cheers for mother

13 characters (2m 11w)

White, N. E. Seven nuns at Las Vegas

13 characters (2m 6b 5g)

c Woolsey, J. and Sechrist, E. H. Johnny's birthday surprise

13 characters (3m 10w)

Manning, H. Seeing double

13 characters (4m 9w)

Clapp, P. Edie-across-the-street
Erhard, T. The high white star

13 characters (4m 1w 4b 3g)

Emurian, E. K. Inasmuch

13 characters (5m 2w 4b 2g)

c Atwell, R. and Virden, H. Thanksgiving in Mother Goose land
Miller, M. Alice in Wonderland

13 characters (5m 7w 1b)

McCullers, C. The member of the wedding

MIXED CAST—*Continued*

13 characters (5m 8w)
Bowie, L. "You heard me!"
Forsythe, A. No mother to guide her
Kalen, E. Aunt Lizzie lives it up!
Morrill, K. A distant bell
Schweikert, C. Hoax of Hogan's Holler

13 characters (6m 4w 3g)
Berns, J. and Elman, I. Uncle Willie

13 characters (6m 7w)
Baker, L. G. Conspiracy at "The Crayfish"
Bottomley, G. Gruach
Gran, J. M. A nose for news
c Harris, A. The plain Princess
Henderson, J. A midsummer night's scream
Rattigan, T. Who is Sylvia?
Reach, J. Afraid of the dark
Reach, J. Are teachers human?
Reach, J. Terror at Black Oaks
Regan, S. The fifth season
Robinson, R. Clarence Gate
St Clair, R. Caught in the web
Taggart, T. and Reach, J. Dear Phoebe

13 characters (7m 5w 1b)
Asbrand, K. School daze
Schulman, A. A hole in the head
Weaver, V. B. The reign of Minnie Belle

13 characters (7m 6w)
Barrie, J. M. The admirable Crichton
Beach, L. The goose hangs high
Chadwicke, A. Pudd'nhead Wilson
De Vier, H. E. Come to the stable
Goldina, M. The courageous one
Hatlen, T. W. All in the family
Manheim, M. Comedy of roses
Mortimer, J. Call me a liar
Olfson, L. The Bishop's candlesticks
Rattigan, T. The sleeping prince
Reach, J. Patterns
Rojas, F. de. The Celestina (Univ. of Calif. Press)
Rose, R. Thunder on Sycamore Street
Sardou, V. A scrap of paper
Snyder, W. The old school bell
Tchekov, A. The seagull

13 characters (8m 1w 2b 2g)
c Mathews, J. Audubon's America

13 characters (8m 2w 3b)
Salinger, H. Great-grandfather was an immigrant

13 characters (8w 5w)
Blankman, H. By hex
Genet, J. The blacks: a clown show
Hellman, L. Another part of the forest
Hivnor, R. The ticklish acrobat
Howells, W. D. The elevator
Kissen, F. Paul Revere: patriot and craftsman
Lamkin, S. Comes a day
Maurette, M. Anastasia
Miller, A. Death of a salesman
Molière, J. B. P. The learned ladies
Murphy, A. Know your own mind
Orth, R. For heaven's sake

Payton, D. Nearly beloved
Thurber, J. and Nugent, E. The male animal

13 characters (9m 1w 3g)
c Miller, H. L. Softy the Snow Man
Schaefer, L. Song for a hero

13 characters (9m 3w 1b)
Case, T. W. Billy Adams, American

13 characters (9m 4w)
Bottomley, G. Fire at Callart
Gethers, S. Cracker money
Hawtrey, C. The private secretary
Launder, F. and Gilliat, S. Meet a body
LeRoy, W. Between two thieves
Mosel, T. Star in the summer night
Pirandello, L. The rules of the game
Travers, B. Wild horses
Ustinov, P. Romanoff and Juliet

13 characters (10m 3w)
Dias, E. J. The natives are restless tonight
Fry, C. The firstborn
Johnston, R. A. The York Resurrection
c Masters, R. and Masters, L. The mystery of the ming tree
O'Casey, S. Time to go
Turgenev, I. A poor gentleman

13 characters (11m 2w)
Brabazon, F. Happy monody
Mills, H. The little glass clock
Pirandello, L. "Henry IV"
Semple, L. Golden fleecing

13 characters (12m 1w)
Chayefsky, P. The tenth man
Dennis, N. The making of moo
Olfson, L. The Count of Monte Cristo
Sloane, A. Bring on the angels

13 characters (7b 6g)
c Fisher, A. and Rabe, O. Getting in line
c Matthews, E. On to seventh grade!
c Spamer, C. Carry and borrow

13 characters and extras (1m 1w 11b extras)
c Bornstein, M. and Cole, G. Paul in food land

13 characters and extras (1m 6b 6g extras)
Miller, H. L. The lost Christmas cards

13 characters and extras (2m 4w 3b 4g extras)
Lorenz, E. J. A Christmas gift for Hans

13 characters and extras (3m 2w 7b 1g extras)
c Asbrand, K. Hi ho! Christmas

13 characters and extras (3m 5w 2b 3g extras)
c Carlson, B. W. Thanksgiving is the time

13 characters and extras (5m 3w 2b 3g extras)
Magito, S. and Weil, R. The Snow Queen

13 characters and extras (5m 8w extras)
Greth, Le R. E. Miss President, please!
Martens, A. C. What's the matter with TV?

MIXED CAST—*Continued*

13 characters and extras
(6m 2w 2b 3g extras)

c Hoggan, M. H. The toymakers' pledge

13 characters and extras
(6m 5w 1b 1g extras)

c Tyson, R. H. The life of Lincoln

13 characters and extras
(6m 5w 2b extras)

Racine, J. Athaliah

13 characters and extras
(6m 6w 1g extras)

c Thane, A. The Wizard of Oz

13 characters and extras
(6m 7w extras)

Behan, B. The hostage
Cruse, I. R. To bear the message
Larson, V. and Magary, F. A. Message from Mars
MacAlvay, N. Beauty and the Beast
Olfson, L. Monsieur Beaucaire
Pierce, C. W. Mum's the word

13 characters and extras
(7m 4w 1b 1g extras)

Cruse, C. Healing in its wings
Hellier, E. B. He who walks in love

13 characters and extras
(7m 5w 1b extras)

Bond, N. State of mind

13 characters and extras
(7m 6w extras)

Barrie, J. M. The admirable Crichton
Casey, B. M. The promised one
Lee, N. Theodosius
Sherman, R. W. Santa's neurosis
Wycherley, W. The country wife

13 characters and extras
(8m 2w 1b 2g extras)

c Jagendorf, M. Merry Tyll

13 characters and extras
(8m 2w 3g extras)

Knox, J. The shepherd of Bethlehem

13 characters and extras
(8m 3w 1b 1g extras)

c Wright, L. Mr Popper's penguins

13 characters and extras
(8m 5w extras)

Albery, P. Anne Boleyn
Giraudoux, J. Duel of angels
Hart, M. The climate of Eden
Howard, V. The Swiss family Robinson —rescued
Olson, E. The carnival of animals
Ritchie, A. C. M. Fashion

13 characters and extras
(9m 2w 1b 1g extras)

Dunlap, W. André

13 characters and extras
(9m 4w extras)

Alfred, W. Agamemnon
Aristophanes. Ladies' day
Brecht, B. Saint Joan of the stockyards
c Brumbaugh, P. Simple Simon
Phelps, L. The Gospel Witch
Plautus. The rope
Rodgers, R. and Hammerstein, O. The King and I

Tennyson, A. The promise of May
Woolsey, J. and Sechrist, E. H. Elizabeth Zane saves Fort Henry

13 characters and extras
(10m 1w 1b 1g extras)

c Hess, M. N. Folk-o-rama U.S.A.

13 characters and extras
(10m 3w extras)

Andreev, L. He who gets slapped
Shakespeare, W. Othello
Shakespeare, W. Twelfth night
c Taylor, F. The melancholy princess

13 characters and extras
(11m 2w extras)

Jonson, B. The alchemist
McCaslin, N. John Henry
Sollitt, K. W. and Faust, J. P. The soldier and the Prince of Peace
Wilde, O. Salomé

13 characters and extras
(12m 1w extras)

Emmons, D. G. Who's for the divide?
c Kinkead, J. B. Let us adore Him

13 characters and extras
(13m extras)

Eliot, T. S. Murder in the cathedral

13 characters and extras
(3b 10g extras)

Asbrand, K. It's time for remembering

14 characters (1m 2w 6b 5g)

c The dancing school

14 characters (1m 6b 7g)

c Spamer, C. Donerblitz

14 characters (2m 2w 6b 4g)

c Miller, H. L. Vicky gets the vote

14 characters (2m 12w)

Trease, G. The unquiet cloister

14 characters (2m 9b 3g)

c Miller, H. L. Star Cadets

14 characters (3m 1w 6b 4g)

c Atwell, R. and Virden, H. Mother of the Year

14 characters (3m 5w 2b 4g)

c Newman, D. The stars and stripes

14 characters (3m 9w 1b 1g)

Heinlein, M. V. The panda and the spy

14 characters (3m 11w)

Blewett, D. Quiet night

14 characters (3m 8b 3g)

c Miller, H. L. The case of the balky bike

14 characters (4m 10w)

Gordon, K. The babbling Brooks
Kendall, K. Darling girl

14 characters (5m 3w 4b 2g)

Miller, H. L. The left-over reindeer

14 characters (5m 7w 1b 1g)

McCullers, C. The member of the wedding

14 characters (5m 9w)

Fletcher, L. Sorry, wrong number
Newman, D. Pride and prejudice
Sergel, K. Maudie and the opposite sex
Tarpley, V. and Tarpley, K. Ten o'clock scholar

MIXED CAST—*Continued*

14 characters (6m 6w 2b)
Green, J. South

14 characters (6m 8w)
Chadwicke, A. Davy Crockett
Greth, Le R. E. The sky's the limit
Knapp, B. Wonder boy
McCoy, P. S. Two dates for tonight
Payton, D. Deadly Ernest
Spigelgass, L. A majority of one
Thomas, D. Boy of mine
Tobias, J. Tune in on terror
Tolkin, M. and Kallen, L. Maybe Tuesday
Trigger, E. The roaring twenties

14 characters (7m 1w 3b 3g)
Hark, M. and McQueen, N. Aladdin steps out

14 characters (7m 6w 1b)
Asbrand, K. So it's Christmas again

14 characters (7m 7w)
Chekhov, A. The sea gull
Dighton, J. Man alive
Kesler, H. O. The grass that's greener
McCarty, E. C. The moon's still yellow
Martens, A. C. The fantastic Mr C.
Taylor, S. Sabrina Fair
Tobias, J. Coddled Egbert
Tomkins, B. Pistol-packin' Sal
Wilder, T. The matchmaker
Williams, P. Commencement

14 characters (8m 5w 1b)
Melville, A. Simon and Laura

14 characters (8m 6w)
Coward, N. Nude with violin
Gibson, M. N. Return engagement
Howard, V. The search
Locke, S. Fair game
c Newman, D. The magic goose
Owen, V. The wanderers
Rojas, F. de. Celestina (Univ. of Wisconsin Press)
Schloss, M. F. Totentanz

14 characters (9m 5w)
Chekhov, A. The three sisters
Davis, J. P. A adventure
Duncan, R. The death of Satan
Herman, G. A simple little affair
c Lewis, M. R. Dick Whittington
Lonsdale, F. Let them eat cake
Saroyan, W. The cave dwellers
Turgenev, I. A month in the country

14 characters (10m 3w 1b)
Hayes, J. The desperate hours

14 characters (10m 4w)
Adamov, A. Professor Taranne
Anouilh, J. The fighting cock
Johnston, D. The golden cuckoo
Kanin, F. and Kanin, M. His and hers
Lagerkvist, P. Let man live
Wouk, H. Nature's way

14 characters (11m 2w 1b)
Daviot, G. Reckoning

14 characters (11m 3w)
Custis, G. W. P. Pocahontas
Goldschmidt, W. and Sinclair, L. A word in your ear
Goldstone, J. S. and Reich, J. Mary Stuart
Kissen, F. Robert E. Lee: Virginia's valiant son
Lee, J. Career
Lewis, L. The bells
Moody, W. V. The great divide
Olfson, L. Quentin Durward
O'Neill, E. Anna Christie
Rose, R. Tragedy in a temporary town
Sinclair, L. A word in your ear
Terence. Phormio
Thomas, A. The witching hour

14 characters (12m 1w 1b)
Rose, R. Crime in the streets

14 characters (12m 2w)
Miller, A. A memory of two Mondays

14 characters (12m 1b 1g)
c Fisher, A. The king's toothache

14 characters (13m 1w)
Harrowing of hell. The harrowing of hell

14 characters (7b 7g)
c Miller, H. L. The Petrified Prince
c Spamer, C. The stars and stripes

14 characters and extras (1m 1w 6b 6g extras)
c Wallerstein, J. S. Windigo Island

14 characters and extras (1m 3w 5b 5g extras)
c Wilcox, E. M. We caught the torch

14 characters and extras (2m 3w 5b 4g extras)
c Miller, H. L. The Christmas umbrella

14 characters and extras (3m 2w 4b 5g extras)
c Fluckey, J. O. Davy's star

14 characters and extras (3m 11w extras)
Bailey, H. F. Christmas Eve candle vespers

14 characters and extras (4m 1w 8b 1g extras)
c Woolsey, J. and Sechrist, E. H. Mars calling!

14 characters and extras (4m 3b 1w 6g extras)
c Kerr, M. L. The wonderful child

14 characters and extras (5m 4w 3b 2g extras)
c Fisher, A. Mother of Thanksgiving

14 characters and extras (5m 7w 2b extras)
c Buzzell, A. M. "The man on the street"

14 characters and extras (6m 8w extras)
Congreve, W. The way of the world

14 characters and extras (7m 3w 2b 2g extras)
Woolsey, J. and Sechrist. E. H. Paul Revere, Boston patriot

14 characters and extras (7m 6w 1b extras)
Sartre, J. P. The flies

MIXED CAST—*Continued*

14 characters and extras
(7m 7w extras)

Apstein, T. Come share my house
Casey, B. M. The jewel beyond price
Chayefsky, P. Marty
Emery, C. Portrait of Deborah
Hayes, M. and Hayes, J. Mister Peepers
McMahon, L. Don't tell your father
Preston, E. E. The angel in the window
Shaw, B. The shewing-up of Blanco Posnet
Stricker, E. B. What is the church?
Taggart, T. Deadwood Dick
Williams, T. Battle of angels

14 characters and extras
(8m 4w 1b 1g extras)

c Miller, H. L. Pilgrim parting

14 characters and extras
(8m 5w 1b extras)

Radin, B. A seacoast in Bohemia
Strindberg, A. The regent

14 characters and extras
(8m 5w 1g extras)

Soans, J. Christmas is now

14 characters and extras
(8m 6w extras)

Hare, W. B. The white Christmas
Malango, P. The man who changed the world
Shaw, B. Major Barbara

14 characters and extras
(9m 2w 2b 1g extras)

Howard, V. Around the world—by way of America

14 characters and extras
(9m 4w 1g extras)

Mannheimer, A. and Kohner, F. Stalin Allee

14 characters and extras
(9m 5w extras)

Chayefsky, P. Printer's measure
Fisher, A. A play without a name
Fisher, A. and Rabe, O. Haym Salomon's battle
Hui-lan-ki. The story of the circle of chalk
McCaslin, N. The gift of corn
MacKaye, S. Hazel Kirke
O'Neill, E. The great God Brown
Romains, J. Dr Knock
Sheridan, R. B. The rivals
Yeats, W. B. The herne's egg

14 characters and extras
(10m 3w 1b extras)

Giraudoux, J. Judith

14 characters and extras
(10m 4w extras)

Coventry plays. Herod and the kings
Farquhar, G. The twin-rivals
Goethe. The Urfaust
c Harris, A. Simple Simon
Howard, V. Don Quixote saves the day
Pirandello, L. The mountain giants
Schulberg, B. and Breit, H. The disenchanted
Tourneur, C. The atheist's tragedy
Valency, M. The virtuous island

14 characters and extras
(11m 3w extras)

Middleton, T. and Rowley, W. The changeling
c Pennington, L. and Kaeyer, M. Our home town
The Play of Daniel
Tourneur, C. The revenger's tragedy

14 characters and extras
(12m 2w extras)

Emurian, E. K. God of our fathers

14 characters and extras
(12m 1b 1g extras)

c Woolsey, J. and Sechrist, E. H. A letter is mailed

14 characters and extras
(13m 1w extras)

Emmons, D. G. Out to win
Kawatake, M. Benten the thief

14 characters and extras
(7b 7g extras)

Fisher, A. The safety parade
c Fluckey, J. O. Santa and the space men

15 characters (2m 7w 6b)

Martens, A. C. Pow wow

15 characters (5m 1w 6b 3g)

c Goulding, D. J. Pirates!!

15 characters (5m 10w)

Rose, Le R. Headin' for a weddin'

15 characters (6m 9w)

Benavente, J. La Malquerida ₁The passion flower₁
Payton, D. It's great to be crazy
Teichmann, H. Miss Lonelyhearts

15 characters (7m 4w 1b 3g)

Humphrys, R. No trouble at all
Ratcliffe, D. U. Jingling Lane

15 characters (7m 6w 2b)

c Fisher, D. En route to the UN

15 characters (7m 7w 1g)

Gross, E. and Gross, N. Belle

15 characters (7m 8w)

McGreevey, J. A man called Peter
McGreevey, J. Papa was a preacher
Reach, J. You, the jury
Rose, Le R. Spooks alive
Sergel, R. A. A. Milne's The Red House mystery

15 characters (8m 7w)

Anouilh, J. The ermine
Bottomley, G. Deirdire
Conkle, E. P. Poor Old Bongo!
Olfson, L. The house of the Seven Gables
Ostrovsky, A. The diary of a scoundrel
Wilde, O. A woman of no importance

15 characters (9m 3w 3b)

Panetta, G. Comic strip

15 characters (9m 6w)

Crichton, K. The happiest millionaire
Howells, W. D. and Kester, P. The rise of Silas Lapham
Mitchell, L. The New York idea

MIXED CAST—*Continued*

O'Neill, E. Ah, wilderness!
Schary, D. The highest tree
Wilde, O. An ideal husband

15 characters (10m 5w)

Aiken, C. Mr Arcularis
Anouilh, J. Mademoiselle Colombe
Goldsmith, O. The good natur'd man
Herbert, F. H. A girl can tell
Li, Y. M. The modern bridge
MacKaye, P. The scarecrow
Rattigan, T. Harlequinade
Shaw, B. The apple cart
Trease, G. The shadow of Spain

15 characters (11m 4w)

Grafton, E. and Grafton, S. Mock trial
Lee, J. Career
Lindsay, K. and Lindsay, R. H. Miracle at Potter's farm
Miller, S. One bright day
Molière, J. B. P. The miser

15 characters (12m 2w 1b)

c Woolsey, J. and Sechrist, E. H. Jerry and the Skweegees

15 characters (12m 3w)

Auden, W. H. and Isherwood, C. The ascent of F6
Miller, A. A view from the bridge
O'Casey, S. Purple dust
Olfson, L. Julius Caesar
Smith, W. S. By Christ alone
Vega Carpio, L. de. The star of Seville

15 characters (13m 2w)

Camus, A. Caligula
The Welsh embassador
York plays. The Crucifixion

15 characters (14m 1w)

Gelber, J. The connection
Harrowing of hell. The harrowing of hell
Phillips, J. B. The healing of the paralyzed man

15 characters (2w 7b 6g)

c Miller, H. L. The miraculous tea party

15 characters (7b 8g)

c Miller, H. L. It's a problem

15 characters and extras (1m 5w 5b 4g extras)

c Miller, H. L. Bunnies and bonnets

15 characters and extras (4m 1w 5b 5g extras)

c Miller, H. L. Santa Claus for president

15 characters and extras (4m 11w extras)

Kissen, F. Jane Addams: the good neighbor

15 characters and extras (5m 3w 7b extras)

Euripides. Suppliants

15 characters and extras (5m 10w extras)

Bowles, J. In the summer house

15 characters and extras (6m 2w 4b 3g extras)

c Bonn, M. Magical letters

15 characters and extras (6m 5w 2b 2g extras)

Hark, M. and McQueen, N. On your own feet

15 characters and extras (6m 9w extras)

Anouilh, J. Restless heart
Badger, A. Willie's secret weapon

15 characters and extras (7m 3w 2b 3g extras)

c Seiler, C. The clown out West

15 characters and extras (7m 5w 2b 1g extras)

Jennings, T.; Slesinger, T. and West, C. The good earth

15 characters and extras (7m 8w extras)

Etherege, Sir G. The man of mode
Harris, A. The flying prince
Kesler, H. O. Million-dollar maybe

15 characters and extras (7m 4b 4g extras)

c Hark, M. and McQueen, N. Cupid's post office

15 characters and extras (8m 5w 2g extras)

Sergel, R. No star to guide them

15 characters and extras (8m 6w 1b extras)

Emmons, D. G. Through Naches Pass

15 characters and extras (8m 7w extras)

Coward, N. Quadrille
St Clair, R. Mark Twain's A double barrelled detective story
Strindberg, A. Ghost sonata
Wycherley, W. The country wife

15 characters and extras (9m 6w extras)

Ackland, R. A dead secret
c Borgers, P. and Borgers, E. The strange case of Mother Goose
Boucicault, D. The Colleen Bawn
Kao-Tong-Kia. Lute song
c Woolsey, J. and Sechrist, E. H. The Queen of Hearts' party

15 characters and extras (10m 4w 1b extras)

Emurian, E. K. Thanksgiving through the ages

15 characters and extras (10m 5w extras)

Anouilh, J. Eurydice
Bradbury, A. J. The King's anniversary
Chekhov, A. The cherry orchard
Olfson, L. Macbeth
Stanley-Wrench, M. The splendid burden

15 characters and extras (11m 4w extras)

Howard, S. Madam, will you walk?
c Howard, V. Sir Galahad and the maidens
Lindsay, H. and Crouse, R. The Prescott proposals
Molière, J. B. P. Love's the best doctor
Sheridan, R. B. The school for scandal

15 characters and extras (12m 3w extras)

Auden, W. H. and Isherwood, C. The ascent of F6

MIXED CAST—*Continued*

Dryden, J. and Lee, N. Oedipus
Nash, N. R. See the jaguar
Tennyson, A. The foresters

15 characters and extras
(13m 2w extras)
Howard, V. Gulliver wins his freedom
Kleist, H. von. The Prince of Homburg

15 characters and extras
(14m 1w extras)
Bailey, H. F. A manger lowly
McCaslin, N. Giant of the timber

15 characters and extras
(5b 10g extras)
c Very, A. The fairy circus

15 characters and extras
(8b 7g extras)
c Very, A. The little fir tree

15 characters and extras
(9b 6g extras)
Miller, H. L. The talking flag

16 characters (1m 15w)
Miller, H. L. Heart throbs

16 characters (2m 1w 8b 5g)
c Miller, H. L. The polka dot pup

16 characters (2m 14w)
Hellman, L. The children's hour

16 characters (3m 13w)
Garver, J. Father lives with seven women

16 characters (6m 10w)
Abstance, P. and Abstance, L. Aunt Vonnie on vexation
Franklin, C. Boy appeal
Reach, J. Meet me at the prom

16 characters (7m 6w 2b 1g)
c Woolsey, J. and Sechrist, E. H. Let's travel by bus

16 characters (7m 9w)
Adler, M. D. Too much springtime
Parker, D. and D'Usseau, A. The ladies of the corridor
Tobias, J. The Katz' whiskers
Tobias, J. Pick a Dilly

16 characters (7m 4b 5g)
Olfson, L. Which of the nine?

16 characters (8m 6w 1b 1g)
Anderson, W. "Me, Candido!"

16 characters (8m 8w)
Marchant, W. The desk set
Rogers, A. B. Tiger on his toes
Tobias, J. Be happy? go wacky!
Tobias, J. A boy named Beulah

16 characters (9m 7w)
Aymé, M. Clérambard
Bergh, H. Old King Cole
Bergman, I. The magician
McCreary, B. and McCreary, M. Three needles in a haystack
Martens, A. C. Hold your horsepower!
Peterson, L. Take a giant step
Pirandello, L. As you desire me

16 characters (10m 6w)
Ephron, P. "Howie"
Miller, H. L. The Shakespearean touch

Molière, J. B. P. The Versailles impromptu
O'Casey, S. The plough and the stars
Sherriff, R. C. The white carnation

16 characters (11m 4w 1g)
Strindberg, A. There are crimes and crimes

16 characters (11m 5w)
Brenner, A. Survival
Chekhov, A. A country scandal
Farquhar, G. The beaux' stratagem
Kissen, F. Thomas Jefferson: defender of liberty
Sherry, G. Black limelight

16 characters (12m 4w)
Eaton, J. J. and Juste, M. Atomic journey
Fry, C. The dark is light enough
Pinero, A. W. The magistrate
Sherwood, R. E. and Harrison, J. Rebecca

16 characters (13m 3w)
Anouilh, J. Becket
Jonson, B. Every man in his humour

16 characters (14m 2w)
Lavery, E. The magnificent Yankee

16 characters (15m 1w)
Golden, E. Gulliver's travels in Lilliput Land
Hennessy, M. A. The American spirit

16 characters (8b 8g)
c Spamer, C. The new book

16 characters (12b 4g)
c Taylor, F. The wizard's spell

16 characters and extras
(4m 8w 2b 2g extras)
Leslie, A. E. In as much

16 characters and extras
(5m 3w 4b 4g extras)
c Hark, M. and McQueen, N. Many thanks

16 characters and extras
(6m 3w 4b 3g extras)
Sheffield, J. The imploring flame

16 characters and extras
(8m 8w extras)
Hughes, E. W. The wishful taw

16 characters and extras
(9m 7w extras)
Lee, N. The Princess of Cleve
Pirandello, L. Right you are

16 characters and extras
(10m 2w 2b 2g extras)
c Mitchell, L. F. Music! Music! Everywhere!

16 characters and extras
(10m 4w 1b 1g extras)
McCaslin, N. Apples in the wilderness

16 characters and extras
(10m 6w extras)
Congreve, W. Love for love
Kops, B. The dream of Peter Mann

16 characters and extras
(11m 3w 2b extras)
Saroyan, W. The man with the heart in the highlands

MIXED CAST—*Continued*

16 characters and extras
(11m 5w extras)

c Diffin, L. T. The court of hearts
Farquhar, G. The beaux stratagem
Ford, J. Love's sacrifice
Ghelderode, M. de. Lord Halewyn

16 characters and extras
(12m 4w extras)

Farquhar, G. The recruiting officer
Ford, J. The lover's melancholy
Ibsen, H. Brand
Sheridan, R. B. The school for scandal
Webster, J. The Duchess of Malfy

16 characters and extras
(14m 2w extras)

Anderson, M. High Tor
Aristophanes. Peace
Emurian, E. K. I pledge allegiance
Ionesco, E. The killer
Jerrold, D. Black-ey'd Susan
Lee, N. Caesar Borgia

16 characters and extras
(3b 13g extras)

c Asbrand, K. Valentine box

17 characters (1m 4w 7b 5g)

c Atherton, M. Jack-in-the-box

17 characters (2m 4w 5b 6g)

c Newman, D. A gift to the world

17 characters (2m 6w 8b 1g)

c Very, A. The dancing children

17 characters (6m 4w 3b 4g)

c Wallerstein, J. S. Bobby and the time machine

17 characters (6m 6w 1b 4g)

Seiler, C. The clown and his circus

17 characters (6m 10w 1g)

Davidson, W. The birds and the boys

17 characters (7m 10w)

Sergel, C. The family nobody wanted
Sergel, K. Father knows best

17 characters (8m 5w 2b 2g)

Williams, T. Cat on a hot tin roof

17 characters (8m 8w 1b)

Preston, E. E. Star of wonder

17 characters (8m 9w)

Greth, Le R. E. The happy haunting ground
Merrill, J. The immortal husband
Thomas, T. C. Mirage

17 characters (8m 5w 4b)

Rose, R. The incredible world of Horace Ford

17 characters (9m 8w)

c Very, A. Gifts for young Abe
Wilk, M. Cloud seven

17 characters (10m 7w)

Sieveking, L. The strange case of Dr Jekyll and Mr Hyde

17 characters (11m 5w 1g)

Strindberg, A. Crime and crime

17 characters (12m 3w 1b 1g)

Cocteau, J. The infernal machine

17 characters (13m 3w 1b)

Williams, T. Baby Doll

17 characters (13m 4w)

Besier, R. The Barretts of Wimpole Street
Čapek, K. R. U. R.
Edmunds, M. Moon of my delight
Johnston, R. A. Everyman
Sheldon, E. The boss
Tabori, G. Flight into Egypt

17 characters (14m 3w)

Anouilh, J. Time remembered
Miller, H. L. Just what the doctor ordered

17 characters (15m 2w)

MacDougal, R. The gentle gunman
Shaw, B. Androcles and the lion
Ullman, S. S. A democratic emperor

17 characters (16m 1w)

Everyman. The moral play of Everyman

17 characters (5w 6b 6g)

c Woolsey, J. and Sechrist, E. H. Mother Goose's children

17 characters and extras
(1m 5w 5b 6g extras)

c Mason, J. "I'd be glad to"

17 characters and extras
(1m 8b 8g extras)

Fisher, A. and Rabe, O. Wheels within wheels

17 characters and extras
(3m 2w 7b 5g extras)

c Feder, B. Benjamin Franklin

17 characters and extras
(3m 14w extras)

Li, Y. M. The grand garden

17 characters and extras
(4m 3w 6b 4g extras)

Fisher, A. and Rabe, O. Immigrants all, Americans all

17 characters and extras
(5m 2w 6b 4g extras)

Fisher, A. and Rabe, O. What is a patriot

17 characters and extras
(6m 11w extras)

Miller, H. L. Jump for George

17 characters and extras
(7m 6w 3b 1g extras)

Marcelline, Sister M. Silver beads

17 characters and extras
(7m 7w 3g extras)

Giraudoux, J. Electra

17 characters and extras
(8m 7w 1b 1g extras)

Bailey, H. F. "There was a garden"

17 characters and extras
(8m 9w extras)

Emurian, E. K. The radiance streaming

17 characters and extras
(10m 7w extras)

Vanbrugh, Sir J. The relapse

17 characters and extras
(11m 5w 1b extras)

Jonson, B. Epicœne

17 characters and extras
(11m 6w extras)

Congreve, W. The old bachelor
Ionesco, E. Rhinoceros

MIXED CAST—*Continued*

Labiche, E. and Marc-Michel. An Italian straw hat

Lee, N. Sophonisba

Pirandello, L. When someone is somebody

17 characters and extras
(12m 2w 2b 1g extras)

Fisher, A. and Rabe, O. Our great Declaration

c Norris, J. Hiawatha

17 characters and extras
(12m 4w 1g extras)

Strindberg, A. The great highway

17 characters and extras
(12m 5w extras)

D'Abbes, I. and Sherie, F. Murder in Motley

Gillette, W. Secret Service

Lee, N. The tragedy of Nero, Emperour of Rome

Neilson, P. The star still shines

Rattigan, T. Adventure story

Sheridan, R. B. A trip to Scarborough

Sullivan, A. Ruddigore

17 characters and extras
(13m 4w extras)

Emmons, D. G. Answering the call

Gorky, M. The lower depths

Lee, N. The rival queens

17 characters and extras
(14m 2w 1b extras)

c Ryan, M. A. Litterbugs on trial

17 characters and extras
(14m 3w extras)

Anderson, M. The feast of Ortolans

Garis, R. The Inn

Ghelderode, M. de. Barabbas

Molière, J. B. P. Don Juan

17 characters and extras
(15m 2w extras)

Arblay, Madame d' Edwy and Elgiva

Emurian, E. K. Uncle Sam

Everyman. Everyman

Strindberg, A. Earl Birger of Bjälbo

17 characters and extras
(16m 1w extras)

Howard, V. The return of Rip Van Winkle

17 characters and extras
(9b 8g extras)

c Herman, S. W. Good neighbors

18 characters (1m 8b 9g)

c Miller, H. L. Who's who at the zoo

18 characters (7m 9w 1b 1g)

Harris, A. We were young that year

18 characters (7m 11w)

Pierce, C. W. Dough for dopes

18 characters (8m 8w 1b 1g)

Chase, M. Mrs McThing

18 characters (8m 10w)

Walsh, R. G. Greg's gruesome gadgets

18 characters (9m 9w)

Gordon, K. Money mad

Rouverol, A. Andy Hardy

18 characters (10m 8w)

Bolton, G. and McGowan, J. Girl crazy

Capote, T. The grass harp

Costigan, J. Little moon of Alban

Ginnes, A. S. and Wallach, I. Drink to me only

Hauptmann, G. The rats

c Miller, H. L. The real princess

18 characters (11m 7w)

Dumas, A. Camille

Heijermans, H. The Good Hope

Rodgers, R. Flower drum song

18 characters (12m 6w)

Becque, H. The vultures

Bergman, I. The seventh seal

Teichmann, H. and Kaufman, G. S. The solid gold Cadillac

18 characters (13m 3w 2b)

c Woolsey, J. and Sechrist, E. H. Lincoln's secret journey

18 characters (13m 5w)

Rowley, W. and others. The witch of Edmonton

18 characters (15m 3w)

Riskin, R. It happened one night

18 characters (16m 2w)

Anderson, M. High Tor

Christie, D. and Christie, C. Carrington, V. C.

18 characters (12b 6g)

c Very, A. Old Lady Witch's party

18 characters and extras
(1m 3w 4b 10g extras)

c Feder, L. Christmas in the melting pot

18 characters and extras
(4m 12w 2b extras)

Bielby, M. R. I was in prison

18 characters and extras
(6m 12w extras)

Davidson, W. Buy Jupiter!

Lehar, F. The merry widow

18 characters and extras
(7m 11w extras)

Dalzell, W. and Martens, A. C. Onions in the stew

Rose, R. Dino

18 characters and extras
(8m 10w extras)

Gordon, K. That's my cousin

18 characters and extras
(9m 7w 1b 1g extras)

Mattson, J. A Sunday school Christmas program

18 characters and extras
(9m 9w extras)

Bottomley, G. The riding to Lithend

18 characters and extras
(10m 8w extras)

Durrell, L. Sappho

18 characters and extras
(11m 5w 1b 1g extras)

Schiller, F. von. Don Carlos

18 characters and extras
(11m 7w extras)

Beaumont, F. and Fletcher, J. The maid's tragedy

Jerome, H. Pride and prejudice

Strindberg, A. Swanwhite

MIXED CAST—*Continued*

**18 characters and extras
(12m 5w 1b extras)**
Dillon, F. The tinder box

**18 characters and extras
(12m 6w extras)**
Adler, R. and Ross, J. The pajama game

**18 characters and extras
(13m 5w extras)**
Dekker, T. Satiromastix

**18 characters and extras
(14m 3w 1b extras)**
Duncannon, F. E. N. P. viscount. Like stars appearing

**18 characters and extras
(14m 4w extras)**
Anderson, M. Winterset
Camus, A. State of siege
Heicher, M. and St Clair, R. The lost star
Kissen, F. Benjamin Franklin: statesman and inventor
Molière, J. B. P. The middle-class gentleman
Molière, J. B. P. The self-made gentleman
Shakespeare, W. The tempest
Warren, R. P. All the king's men
Woolsey, J. and Sechrist, E. H. Stephen Foster, beautiful dreamer

**18 characters and extras
(15m 1w 1b 1g extras)**
Hark, M. and McQueen, N. First in peace

**18 characters and extras
(15m 3w extras)**
Dekker, T. Match me in London
Emurian, E. K. The Resurrection
Strindberg, A. The last of the knights

**18 characters and extras
(17m 1w extras)**
DeWitt, R. H. Arise, thy light is come!
Wilde, O. Vera

**18 characters and extras
(15b 3g extras)**
c Very, A. The twelve months

19 characters (2m 10w 3b 4g)
c Miller, H. L. Washington's leading lady

19 characters (4m 6w 4b 5g)
c Miller, H. L. The safety clinic

19 characters (8m 3w 4b 4g)
c Frankel, B. S. 'Way out West

19 characters (8m 11w)
Bottomley, G. The white widow
Miller, L. and Miller, L. 'Sno haven
Wattron, F. and Walker, P. Burner of the Bugle

19 characters (9m 3w 7g)
Giraudoux, J. The enchanted

19 characters (9m 7w 1b 2g)
Chorpenning, C. B. Abe Lincoln—New Salem days

19 characters (9m 8w 1b 1g)
Makowsky, L. The New World

19 characters (10m 9w)
Frings, K. Look homeward, angel
Pinero, A. W. The thunderbolt
Williams, T. Orpheus descending

19 characters (11m 5w 2b 1g)
Taylor, T. and Reade, C. Masks and faces

19 characters (11m 8w)
Martin, D. Simply heavenly

19 characters (12m 7w)
Hart, M. and Kaufman, G. S. You can't take it with you

19 characters (13m 6w)
Lagman, J. H. The sweetheart of Broadway
O'Casey, S. Juno and the paycock

19 characters (14m 5w)
Kaiser, G. The coral
Plautus, T. M. Mostellaria
Webster, J. The Duchess of Malfi

19 characters (15m 4w)
Lawrence, J. and Lee, R. E. The gang's all here

19 characters (16m 3w)
Sinclair, L. All the world's a stage
Wilson, E. Cyprian's prayer

19 characters (17m 2w)
Denker, H. and Berkey, R. Time limit
Odets, C. Golden boy

19 characters (18m 1w)
Olfson, L. Around the world in eighty days
Wishengrad, M. The ground of justice

**19 characters and extras
(2m 1w 14b 2g extras)**
c Totheroh, D. Master Will

**19 characters and extras
(6m 10w 1b 2g extras)**
Martens, A. C. Dr Hudson's secret journal

**19 characters and extras
(7m 3w 5b 4g extras)**
c Newman, D. The fire-safe town

**19 characters and extras
(9m 10w extras)**
c Floyd, B. Once upon a time

**19 characters and extras
(10m 7w 1b 1g extras)**
Pirandello, L. Six characters in search of an author

**19 characters and extras
(11m 8w extras)**
Schofield, J. A. and Joudry, R. C. "All hail the power of Jesus' name"

**19 characters and extras
(13m 6w extras)**
Chase, M. Bernardine
Ford, J. The broken heart

**19 characters and extras
(15m 4w extras)**
Anderson, M. Winterset
Dekker, T. Old Fortunatus
Goethe, J. W. von. Egmont
Kaiser, G. Gas (I)
Lawrence, D. H. David

**19 characters and extras
(16m 3w extras)**
Daviot, G. Dickon
Webster, J. The white devil

**19 characters and extras
(17m 2w extras)**
Otway, T. Venice preserved

MIXED CAST—*Continued*

19 characters and extras
(18m 1w extras)

Emurian, E. K. Famous fathers

20 characters (6m 14w)

Martens, A. C. A dance with our Miss Brooks

20 characters (9m 4w 4b 3g)

O'Brien, L. The remarkable Mr Penny-packer

20 characters (10m 10w)

Phillips, I. Gown of glory
Schnitzler, A. Merry-go-round

20 characters (11m 9w)

c Goldsmith, S. L. How Boots befooled the king

20 characters (12m 7w 1g)

Strindberg, A. The great highway

20 characters (12m 8w)

Knapp, B. Three men on a string

20 characters (13m 7w)

Howard, B. Shenandoah

20 characters (14m 6w)

Cross, E. W. The patriots

20 characters (15m 2w 2b 1g)

Sveinbjörnsson, T. Bishop Jón Arason

20 characters (15m 5w)

Kneale, N. Mrs Wickens in the fall

20 characters (16m 4w)

Dennis, N. Cards of identity
Kissen, F. William Penn: brother to all men

20 characters (17m 2w 1b)

Serling, R. Requiem for a heavyweight

20 characters (17m 3w)

Galsworthy, J. Loyalties
Rowley, S. The noble Spanish soldier

20 characters and extras
(8m 7w 2b 3g extras)

c Miller, H. L. May Day for mother

20 characters and extras
(10m 10w extras)

Casey, B. M. The guest at Cana

20 characters and extras
(12m 7w 1g extras)

c Klein, M. W. Ali Baba and the forty thieves

20 characters and extras
(12m 8w extras)

Duffield, B. The war of the worlds

20 characters and extras
(13m 4w 2b 1g extras)

Patrick, J. The Teahouse of the August Moon

20 characters and extras
(13m 7w extras)

Adler, R. and Ross, J. Damn Yankees

20 characters and extras
(14m 6w extras)

O'Casey, S. Within the gates
Schiller, F. von. Mary Stuart

20 characters and extras
(15m 4w 1b extras)

Barker, J. N. Superstition

20 characters and extras
(15m 5w extras)

Anouilh, J. The lark
Bernstein, L. Wonderful town

20 characters and extras
(16m 4w extras)

Aristophanes. The Acharnians
Dekker, T.; Chettle, H. and Haughton, W. Patient Grissil
Massinger, P. and Dekker, T. The virgin martyr

20 characters and extras
(17m 2w 1b extras)

Serling, R. Requiem for a heavyweight

20 characters and extras
(17m 3w extras)

Heywood, T. A woman killed with kindness
O'Casey, S. The drums of Father Ned

20 characters and extras
(14b 6g extras)

c Miller, H. L. The country store cat

21 characters (9m 12w)

Chayefsky, P. The big deal
Farrow, N. Spring prom magic

21 characters (10m 11w)

Kesler, H. O. Line of scrimmage

21 characters (11m 6w 1b 3g)

MacLeish, A. J.B.

21 characters (11m 10w)

Miller, A. The crucible
Morgan, E. You're a long time dead

21 characters (13m 6w 1b 1g)

Beloin, E. and Garson, H. In any language

21 characters (13m 6w 2b)

Daviot, G. Patria

21 characters (15m 6w)

Dowling, J. The young Elizabeth
Krasna, N. Who was that lady I saw you with?
Lindsay, H. and Crouse, R. The Great Sebastians

21 characters (16m 5w)

Anouilh, J. The lark
O'Casey, S. Red roses for me

21 characters (18m 3w)

Kingsley, S. Darkness at noon
Sherwood, R. E. The petrified forest
Treece, H. Carnival king

21 characters (19m 2w)

Middleton, T. and Dekker, T. The Roaring Girl

21 characters (11b 10g)

Fisher, A. and Rabe, O. All in the UN
c Miller, H. L. A Lincoln Museum

21 characters (13b 8g)

c Miller, H. L. Ten pennies for Lincoln

21 characters and extras
(7m 4w 4b 6g extras)

Chorpenning, C. B. Rip Van Winkle

21 characters and extras
(10m 11w extras)

Ginsbury, N. The first gentleman

21 characters and extras
(11m 10w extras)

Tolstoy, L. N. The power of darkness

MIXED CAST—*Continued*

21 characters and extras
(13m 8w extras)

Feydeau, G. and Desvallières, M. Hotel Paradiso

21 characters and extras
(14m 7w extras)

Dekker, T. The honest whore; Part 2
Kissen, F. Clara Barton: angel of the battlefield

21 characters and extras
(16m 1w 2b 2g extras)

Knight, E. M. What happened in 1776?

21 characters and extras
(16m 5w extras)

Chiari, J. Mary Stuart

21 characters and extras
(17m 4w extras)

Barasch, N. and Moore, C. Make a million
O'Neill, E. The moon of the Caribbees

21 characters and extras
(18m 3w extras)

Bulwer-Lytton, E. Money
Ibsen, H. The wild duck

21 characters and extras
(19m 2w extras)

Jonson, B. Volpone

21 characters and extras
(11b 10g extras)

c Taylor, F. The magic doughnuts

22 characters (11m 6w 3b 2g)

Rose, R. The remarkable incident at Carson Corners

22 characters (13m 6w 2b 1g)

Herman, G. An echo of wings

22 characters (13m 9w)

Willis, C. The velvet plain

22 characters (14m 8w)

Arnold, H. G. Sam Pollard

22 characters (14m 5b 3g)

Close, E. The land of the traffic goblins

22 characters (15m 6w 1g)

Giraudoux, J. Tiger at the gates

22 characters (15m 7w)

Williams, T. Sweet bird of youth

22 characters (16m 6w)

Coventry plays. Pageant of the Shearmen and Taylors—The Coventry Nativity play
Letton, J. and Letton, F. The young Elizabeth
Nash, N. R. Handful of fire

22 characters (20m 1w 1g)

c Watkins, D. Frost-Bite and the eleven Fidgets

22 characters (20m 2w)

Everyman. Summoning of Everyman

22 characters (21m 1w)

Shaw, D. Rescue

22 characters and extras
(1m 1w 11b 9g extras)

c Miller, H. L. The Bread and Butter Shop

22 characters and extras
(8m 11w 1b 2g extras)

Van Druten, J. I remember mama

22 characters and extras
(10m 12w extras)

Pirandello, L. The new colony

22 characters and extras
(12m 10w extras)

Seiler, C. The wonderful adventures of Don Quixote

22 characters and extras
(13m 9w extras)

Casey, B. M. At the foot of the Mount
Etherege, Sir G. The man of mode

22 characters and extras
(16m 6w extras)

Marlowe, C. The Jew of Malta

22 characters and extras
(17m 4w 1b extras)

Fisher, A. and Rabe, O. Champions of democracy

22 characters and extras
(17m 5w extras)

Mattson, J. M. I saw the cross
Porter, C. Kiss me Kate

22 characters and extras
(18m 4w extras)

Dekker, T. The shoemakers' holiday
Dekker, T. and Webster, J. Northward ho

22 characters and extras
(19m 3w extras)

Marlowe, C. Lust's dominion

22 characters and extras
(20m 2w extras)

Aristophanes. The birds
Jonson, B. Volpone

22 characters and extras
(21m 1w extras)

Aristophanes. The birds

22 characters and extras
(11b 11g extras)

c Fisher, A. and Rabe, O. Empty bowls

23 characters (9m 14w)

Williams, T. The rose tattoo

23 characters (10m 10w 1b 2g)

MacLeish, A. J.B.

23 characters (14m 9w)

Rodgers, R. and Hammerstein, O. Oklahoma!

23 characters (15m 6w 1b 1g)

Rose, R. An almanac of liberty

23 characters (16m 7w)

Rodgers, R. Pipe dream

23 characters (18m 5w)

Kissen, F. George Washington: father of his country
Molnar, F. Liliom
O'Casey, S. The Silver Tassie
Seiler, G. The Princess and the swineherd

23 characters (19m 4w)

Emurian, E. K. Home sweet home

23 characters (20m 3w)

Herald, H.; Herczeg, G. and Raine, N. R. The life of Emile Zola
Zweig, S. Volpone

23 characters (22m 1w)

Williamson, H. R. Heart of Bruce

23 characters and extras
(9m 3w 5b 6g extras)

Miller, H. L. The coming of the prince

MIXED CAST—*Continued*

23 characters and extras
(10m 7w 4b 2g extras)

Hare, W. B. A Christmas carol

23 characters and extras
(10m 13w extras)

McMahon, L. E. The people versus Maxine Lowe

23 characters and extras
(13m 8w 2b extras)

Tolstoy, L. Redemption

23 characters and extras
(13m 10w extras)

Brecht, B. The good woman of Setzuan

23 characters and extras
(14m 9w extras)

Richardson, H. and Berney, W. Dark of the moon

23 characters and extras
(15m 8w extras)

c Miller, H. L. The shower of hearts

23 characters and extras
(16m 7w extras)

Windsor, H. J. The emperor's nightingale

23 characters and extras
(18m 4w 1b extras)

Vega, L. de. Fuente ovejuna

23 characters and extras
(18m 5w extras)

Kingsley, S. The patriots

23 characters and extras
(20m 3w extras)

Tennyson, A. Harold

23 characters and extras
(21m 2w extras)

Jonson, B. Volpone

24 characters (6m 17w 1b)

García Lorca, F. Yerma

24 characters (8m 8w 4b 4g)

c Wallerstein, J. S. Raymond and the monster

24 characters (8m 13w 1b 2g)

Rodgers, R. The sound of music

24 characters (12m 10w 2g)

Holt, N. A. The willing spirit

24 characters (12m 12w)

Wallach, I. Phoenix '55

24 characters (14m 9w 1b)

Green, P. Wings for to fly

24 characters (16m 5w 3b)

Schary, D. Sunrise at Campobello

24 characters (17m 6w 1b)

Saroyan, W. The slaughter of the innocents

24 characters (18m 6w)

Lawrence, J. and Lee, R. E. Only in America

24 characters (19m 5w)

Camus, A. The possessed

24 characters (1w 15b 8g)

c Miller, H. L. Turning the tables

24 characters and extras
(3m 12b 9g extras)

c Very, A. Everywhere Christmas

24 characters and extras
(13m 8w 2b 1g extras)

Fisher, A. and Rabe, O. Let there be bread

24 characters and extras
(15m 5w 2b 2g extras)

Wilder, T. Our town

24 characters and extras
(15m 7w 2b extras)

Komai, F. Cry, the beloved country

24 characters and extras
(16m 4w 1b 3g extras)

Büchner, G. Woyzeck

24 characters and extras
(16m 7w 1b extras)

Peery, R. R. The glory of His coming

24 characters and extras
(16m 8w extras)

Sherwood, R. E. Small war on Murray Hill

24 characters and extras
(17m 7w extras)

Chapman, G. Bussy D'Ambois
Villiers, G. and others. The rehearsal
Warnick, C. and Pahl, M. Adventures of Marco Polo

24 characters and extras
(18m 6w extras)

Clinton-Baddeley, V. C. Jack and the beanstalk

24 characters and extras
(19m 5w extras)

Anderson, M. Elizabeth the Queen
Emmons, D. G. Statehood for Washington
Lee, N. Lucius Junius Brutus
Moross, J. The golden apple
Webster, J. The white devil

24 characters and extras
(20m 4w extras)

Dekker, T. and Middleton, T. The honest whore; Part I
Dryden, J. and Lee, N. The Duke of Guise

24 characters and extras
(21m 3w extras)

Dekker, T. and Webster, J. Sir Thomas Wyatt
Ford, J. Perkin Warbeck
Shakespeare, W. Romeo and Juliet

24 characters and extras
(23m 1b extras)

Coxe, L. O. and Chapman, R. Billy Budd

25 characters (12m 13w)

Wilson, S. The boy friend

25 characters (17m 8w)

Hartke, G. V. The little world of Don Camillo

25 characters (20m 5w)

Morris, C. The unloved

25 characters and extras
(11m 14w extras)

Sergel, R. Henry Van Dyke's The Other Wise Man

25 characters and extras
(13m 11w 1b extras)

Carrière, A. Danbury Fair

25 characters and extras
(13m 12w extras)

c Parkhirst, D. The Clown Prince of Wanderlust

MIXED CAST—*Continued*

25 characters and extras
(17m 8w extras)
Giraudoux, J. The Madwoman of Chaillot

25 characters and extras
(19m 6w extras)
Magnau, K. Goodbye, Texas—Broadway, hello!
Nichols, D. Stagecoach

25 characters and extras
(20m 5w extras)
Dekker, T. and Webster, J. Westward ho
Massinger, P. The Roman actor

25 characters and extras
(21m 3w 1b extras)
Tennyson, A. Becket

25 characters and extras
(21m 4w extras)
Marlowe, C. Tamburlaine the Great; Part I
Shakespeare, W. Romeo and Juliet

26 characters (4m 22w)
c Hourihane, U. Lucinda and the birthday ball

26 characters (10m 16w)
Fitch, C. The girl with the green eyes

26 characters (11m 2w 6b 7g)
c Miller, H. L. Paul Revere rides again

26 characters (12m 14w)
Bergman, I. Wild strawberries

26 characters (13m 13w)
Sergel, K. The remarkable incident at Carson Corners

26 characters (15m 10w 1g)
Kent, W. Seventeen

26 characters (17m 8w 1g)
Galsworthy, J. Escape

26 characters (18m 7w 1g)
Lamphere, E. A. Crosses on the hill

26 characters (18m 8w)
Saroyan, W. The time of your life

26 characters (21m 2w 3b)
Emmons, D. G. Joint occupation, joint celebration

26 characters (21m 5w)
Bergsma, W. The wife of Martin Guerre
Tumarin, B. and Sydow, J. Dostoyevsky's The brothers Karamazov

26 characters and extras
(11m 7w 5b 3g extras)
Harding₀ M. The Sea King's daughter

26 characters and extras
(16m 9w 1g extras)
Feydeau, G. Keep an eye on Amélie!

26 characters and extras
(21m 5w extras)
Dekker, T. The wonder of a kingdom
Lee, N. The massacre of Paris

26 characters and extras
(23m 1w 2b extras)
Sayers, D. The zeal of Thy house

26 characters and extras
(24m 2w extras)
Shaw, B. Saint Joan

27 characters (10m 6w 11b)
Pagnol. Topaze

27 characters (12m 15w)
Wilson, R. C. Easter witnesses

27 characters (15m 5w 4b 3g)
Emurian, E. K. Famous families

27 characters (18m 9w)
O'Casey, S. Pictures in the hallway

27 characters (20m 7w)
c Hauser, W. The big decision

27 characters (26m 1w)
Stallings, L. and Anderson, M. What price glory?

27 characters (1w 13b 13g)
c Very, A. Too much turkey

27 characters and extras
(18m 8w 1g extras)
c Hark, M. and McQueen, N. Christmas Eve news

27 characters and extras
(19m 8w extras)
Bissell, R.; Burrows, A. and Bissell, M. Say, darling
Dekker, T. and Ford, J. The Sun's darling

27 characters and extras
(20m 5w 1b 1g extras)
Richardson, L. For our mother Malaya!
Rodgers, R. and Hammerstein, O. South Pacific

27 characters and extras
(21m 6w extras)
Bock, J. The body beautiful
Shaw, B. Man and superman

27 characters and extras
(25m 2w extras)
Marlowe, C. Tamburlaine the Great; Part II

28 characters (10m 6w 6b 6g)
c Wallerstein, J. S. Johnny Aladdin

28 characters (22m 5w 1b)
Werfel, F. Jacobowsky and the colonel

28 characters and extras
(13m 15w)
Kesler, H. O. Dream a little dream

28 characters and extras
(14m 8w 6b extras)
c Palmer, C. K. Hop o' my thumb

28 characters and extras
(19m 5w 3b 1g extras)
Baden, R. The Christmas Eve visitor

28 characters and extras
(20m 8w extras)
Sheridan, R. B. The critic

28 characters and extras
(21m 7w extras)
Jonson, B. Bartholomew Fair

28 characters and extras
(22m 6w extras)
Styne, J. Bells are ringing

28 characters and extras
(24m 4w extras)
Stevens, L. The lovers
Van Doren, M. The last days of Lincoln

28 characters and extras
(26m 2w extras)
Marlowe, C. Edward the Second

MIXED CAST—*Continued*

28 characters and extras
(27m 1w extras)

Dekker, T. If this be not a good play, the Devil is in it

29 characters (16m 7w 3b 3g)

c Walker, S. The seven gifts

29 characters (17m 12w)

Giraudoux, J. Ondine

29 characters and extras
(16m 13w extras)

Merrill, B. New girl in town

29 characters and extras
(18m 9w 1b 1g extras)

Willson, M. The music man

29 characters and extras
(18m 11w extras)

Hague, A. Plain and fancy

29 characters and extras
(23m 6w extras)

Dekker, T. The Whore of Babylon

30 characters (14m 16w)

Sergel, R. Irving Stone's Love is eternal

30 characters (15m 8w 5b 2g)

Fields, J. and Chodorov, J. The Ponder heart

30 characters (19m 10w 1g)

Herne, J. A. Shore Acres

30 characters (20m 10w)

Perl, A. The world of Sholom Aleichem

30 characters (21m 8w 1b)

Lindsay, H. and Crouse, R. Tall story

30 characters (21m 9w)

O'Casey, S. Red roses for me

30 characters (15b 15g)

c Miller, H. L. Hello, Mr Groundhog

30 characters and extras
(16m 14w extras)

Rodgers, R. and Hammerstein, O. Carousel

30 characters and extras
(17m 13w extras)

Rodgers, R. Me and Juliet

30 characters and extras
(22m 8w extras)

Ford, J. 'Tis pity she's a whore

30 characters and extras
(23m 7w extras)

Lawrence, J. and Lee, R. E. Inherit the wind

30 characters and extras
(25m 5w extras)

Pushkin, A. Boris Godunov

31 characters (1m 15b 15g)

c Miller, H. L. A travel game

31 characters (2m 15b 14g)

c Very, A. Doctor Time's office

31 characters and extras
(21m 7w 2b 1g extras)

Cannan, D. and Bost, P. The power and the glory

31 characters and extras
(25m 6w extras)

Anderson, M. Mary of Scotland

31 characters and extras
(26m 2w 2b 1g extras)

Voss, B. M. Our greatest gift

31 characters and extras
(27m 4w extras)

Carter, A. P. Operation Mad Ball

31 characters and extras
(28m 3w extras)

Marlowe, C. The tragical history of Doctor Faustus

32 characters (20m 12w)

Brecht, B. The threepenny opera

32 characters and extras
(17m 10w 3b 2g extras)

Chorpenning, C. B. The prince and the pauper

32 characters and extras
(23m 7w 2b extras)

Sherwood, R. E. Abe Lincoln in Illinois

32 characters and extras
(24m 8w extras)

Fisher, A. and Rabe, O. Cavalcade of human rights

Newman, D. The prince and the pauper

33 characters and extras
(26m 7w extras)

Jonson, B. Bartholomew Fair

34 characters (26m 8w)

Anderson, M. Lost in the stars

34 characters and extras
(19m 3w 7b 5g extras)

c Woolsey, J. and Sechrist, E. H. George Washington serves his country

34 characters and extras
(21m 13w extras)

Ansky, S. The Dybbuk

34 characters and extras
(30m 4w extras)

Shakespeare, W. Antony and Cleopatra

35 characters (22m 3w 5b 5g)

c Clark, I. S. The Christmas Tree Forest

35 characters and extras
(32m 3w extras)

Jonson, B. Sejanus, his fall

Large cast

c Asbrand, K. Christmas snowman
Auden, W. H. and Isherwood, C. The dog beneath the skin
Bailey, H. F. The Feast of the Ingathering
Baker's Roaring twenties scrapbook
Bangham, M. D. "Come, see the place..."
Bangham, M. D. Come to the manger
Barkentin, M. James Joyce's Ulysses in nighttown
Bean, V. I created Santa Claus
Becque, H. The weavers
Bernstein, L. Candide
Bernstein, L. West Side story
Bock, J. Fiorello!
Brabazon, F. Singing threshold
Brecht, B. The Caucasian chalk circle
Brecht, B. Mother Courage
Bremer, W. Nothing but nonsense
Brown, R. M. Freedom is our heritage

MIXED CAST—*Continued*

Čapek, J. and Čapek, K. The world we live in
Carlson, M. M. Christmas in many nations
Christie, A. Witness for the prosecution
Christmas in art
c Christmas old—Christmas new
Church, R. The prodigal
c Close, E. Germs versus Fairy Good-Health
Connelly, M. Green pastures
Coward, N. Cavalcade
Dekker, T. Britannia's honor
Dekker, T. London's tempe
Dekker, T. The magnificent entertainment given to King James
Dekker, T. Troia-nova triumphans
Driscoll, R. The whiz bang minstrel show
Duerrenmatt, F. The visit
c Early, L. S. Everywhere, Christmas
Emmons, D. G. Ours to the forty-ninth
Fisher, A. On Halloween
Fisher, A. Voting Day
Fisher, A. Washington marches on
Fisher, A. and Rabe, O. Cavalcade of human rights
Fisher, A. and Rabe, O. Sing, America, sing
c Floyd, B. Pinky Winky's trip to the moon
c Fluckey, J. He said he was Santa
c Gilbert, J. Community Easter parade
c Gill, M. L. Treasure hunt
Goethe, J. W. von. Faust, part 1
Goethe, J. W. von. Faust, part II
Green, P. The confederacy
Green, P. The founders
Green, P. The lost colony
Green, P. The Stephen Foster story
Green, P. Wilderness Road
Gruwell, B. G. O holy night
Halloween assembly
c Hark, M. and McQueen, N. The Santa Claus parade
Hatcher, H. B. The holy Nativity
Hein, R. Receive your King!
c Henry, V. May day in the woods
Herman, G. Brighten every corner
Hill, G. R. and Whedon, J. A night to remember
c Howard, D. Christmas doings
Howard, V. What is an American?
Ibsen, H. Peer Gynt
Ingebretson, A. Sister; Miller, J. Sister, and Roberts, M. Sister. The living Saviour
Jarry, A. Ubu Roi
Jay, M. and Graham-Campbell, A. With this sword
Jorgenson, E. S. The message of Christmas
Kaiser, G. From morn to midnight
Kerr, M. L. His star
Kielland, T. Queen Margaret of Norway
Kromer, H. They made a path
Kyd, T. The Spanish tragedy
Lavery, E. American portrait
Lawrence, J. and Lee, R. E. Auntie Mame
Levin, I. No time for sergeants
Levin, M. Compulsion
Loewe, F. My fair lady
Lord, D. A. Joy for the world

Marlowe, C. The tragical history of Doctor Faustus
c Marston, M. A. A Christmas carol
c Marston, M. A. The Pied Piper of Hamelin
c Marston, M. A. The time machine
Martens, G. M. The hopeful travellers
Miller, C. L. Wings over dark waters
c Miller, H. L. The busy barbers
Millet, M. Dangerous Jack
c Moore, D. O. Christmas comes to Santa's workshop
Nathan, R. The sleeping beauty
National Recreation Association. Children of the Americas
National Recreation Association. Who are we of the United States
c Noon, E. F. and Daniels, E. S. Our own United States
Nu, U. The people win through
Nystrom, D. Children's praises
Powicke, H. B. The song and the star
Protter, N. Follow the gleam
Rice, E. L. Street scene
Rodgers, R. and Hammerstein, O. Allegro
Rome, H. Fanny
Rostand, E. Cyrano de Bergerac
Russell, M. A fashion revue
c Salisbury, E. Shoe children
Schiller, F. von. Wallenstein
Schiller, F. von. William Tell
c Shrout, B. L. America sings
Simmons, C. The land of lost toys
Smith, M. G. For God so loved the world
c Sognefest, A. Big top circus
Sorell, W. Everyman today
Spielman, F. The stingiest man in town
Strindberg, A. A dream play
Strindberg, A. The road to Damascus
Styne, J. Gypsy
Swann, M. The Little Poor Man of Assisi
c Swanson, V. A. What do you see in the manger?
Takeda, I.; Miyoshi, S. and Namiki, S. The house of Sugawara
Tennyson, A. Queen Mary
Thomas, D. The doctor and the devils
Thomas, D. Under Milk Wood
c Thompson, R. The case of the misbehaving toys
Timpany, F. P. The storm at sea
Trapp, M. A. One family sings
c Tuttle, R. Spring facts and fancies
c Very, A. King Winter
Wilder, T. The skin of our teeth
Williams, T. Camino real
c Woolsey, J. and Sechrist, E. H. Each star a state
Wright, E. M. "The most heavenly hosts"
Wright, R. and Forrest, G. Kismet
Yelvington, R. A cloud of witnesses

PUPPETS

2 characters

Priestley, H. E. Introducing Judy
Priestley, H. E. Punch and the showman

3 characters

Priestley, H. E. Bathing the baby
Priestley, H. E. The dog Toby
Priestley, H. E. Punch and the doctor

PUPPETS—*Continued*

6 characters

Priestley, H. E. Au revoir

Shaw, B. Shakes versus Shaw

UNIDENTIFIED CAST

3 characters

c Spamer, C. Friends

3 characters and extras

c Spamer, C. Little cloud

4 characters

c Spamer, C. The little clouds

4 characters and extras

c National Recreation Association. Santa Claus visits Mars

c Posso, M. E. Santa was so tired!

c Spamer, C. The joy givers

c Spamer, C. Little icicle

c Spamer, C. Raindrops

5 characters

c Carpenter, F. Doctor Fox

c Carpenter, F. The tale of good faith

c Spamer, C. The clock

c Spamer, C. The constable's duty

c Spamer, C. The fish that wished to live on land

c Spamer, C. Hippety hop

c Spamer, C. The laughed-at monkey

c Spamer, C. The little green worker

c Spamer, C. The terrible grood

5 characters and extras

c Fisher, A. Catch as catch can

c Moore, S. S. The hare and the tortoise

6 characters

c Carpenter, F. The magic owl

c Carpenter, F. The sick fox

c Carpenter, F. Tiger in the wood

c Fisher, A. Why the sleepy Dormouse

c National Recreation Association. The St George play

c Spamer, C. The mouse and the moon

c Spamer, C. The rebellious lightning bolt

c Spamer, C. The tulip garden

6 characters and extras

c Carlson, B. W. Litterbug convention

7 characters

c Asbrand, K. Light up the world

c Carpenter, F. A day of good deeds

c Spamer, C. The bell that couldn't ring

c Spamer, C. The Old Woman's day

c Spamer, C. A pumpkin's fate

c Spamer, C. Silly, a leaf

c Spamer, C. The weather man

c Werner, S. Home, sweet home

7 characters and extras

c Spamer, C. The bunnies' dilemma

8 characters

c Chitty, A. W. I. The bath-room folks party

c Fisher, A. The not-so-crooked man

c Fisher, A. On strike

Fisher, A. and Rabe, O. Of gods and men

c Halloween trial

c Hark, M. and McQueen, N. Off the shelf

c Miller, M. Pinocchio

c Spamer, C. The camouflage shop

c Spamer, C. The mystery

8 characters and extras

c Spamer, C. The costume dance

c Spamer, C. Heavenly stars

9 characters

c Holbrook, M. A candle-lighting service

c Moore, H. G. Storybook Halloween

c Spamer, C. Why the evergreen trees never lose their branches

9 characters and extras

c Blyton, E. Who will hold the giant?

c Mattice, I. A bomb for Santa

c Newman, D. Bunny of the year

10 characters

c Spamer, C. King Sun

10 characters and extras

c Newman, D. The all-American

11 characters

c Very, A. The flower garden

c Very, A. The trees at school

12 characters

c Ringe, M. The land of good health

c The Valentine shop

13 characters

c Blossom, L. The safety elves

Fisher, A, and Rabe, O. Alice in Puzzleland

c Milne, A. A. Winnie-the-Pooh

13 characters and extras

c Newman, D. In honor of trees

14 characters

c Hark, M. and McQueen, N. Nursery rhyme diet

c Very, A. A golden bell for mother

14 characters and extras

c Miller, H. L. The broken broomstick

15 characters

c Jones, C. B. Thanksgiving at Mother Hubbards

c Newman, D. Roses for mother

16 characters

c Austin, C. L. Mrs Santa proves a point

c Zahn, M. How does your garden grow?

17 characters

c Hark, M. and McQueen, N. Mind your P's and Q's

c Miller, H. L. A school for scaring

17 characters and extras

c Oh, can you help the princess?

18 characters

c Miller, G. and Livingston, S. A march of dimes

18 characters and extras

c Newman, D. The best part of Christmas

19 characters

c Jones, C. Clean-up time

19 characters and extras

c Hark, M. and McQueen, N. Spring is here

20 characters

c Manthorn, R. A. A Christmas box

21 characters and extras

c Newman, D. Election Day in the U.S.A.

c Newman, D. Happy holidays

28 characters

c Fisher, A. Time out for Christmas

Part IV

Directory of Publishers

Abingdon. Abingdon Press, Hdqrs, 201 8th Av, S, Nashville 2, Tenn.

Allen, G. George Allen & Unwin, Ruskin House, 40 Museum St, London, W.C. 1

Anti-Defamation League. Anti-Defamation League of B'nai Brith, 515 Madison Av, N.Y. 22

Appleton. Appleton-Century-Crofts, Inc, 60 E 42d St, N.Y. 17

Arnold, E.J. E. J. Arnold and Son, Ltd, Butterley St, Hunslet Lane, Leeds 10, England

Art Craft. The Art Craft Play Company, Drawer 1830, Cedar Rapids, Iowa

Augsburg. Augsburg Publishing House, 426 S 5th St, Minneapolis 15

Augustana. See Fortress Press

Baker, W.H. Walter H. Baker Company, 100 Summer St, Boston 16

Baker & Taylor. Baker & Taylor Company, 1405 N Broad St, Hillside, N.J.

Bakers Plays. See Baker, W.H.

Ballantine. Ballantine Bks, Inc, 101 5th Av, N.Y. 3

Banner. Banner Play Bureau, Inc, 619 Post St, San Francisco 9

Barrons Educ. Ser. Barron's Educational Series, Inc, 343 Great Neck Rd, Great Neck, N.Y.

Beacon Hill Press. See Nazarene

Beacon Press. Beacon Press, Inc, 25 Beacon St, Boston 8

Bellamy Press. The Bellamy Press, 152 W 42d St, N.Y. 18

Bethany Press. The Bethany Press, 2640 Pine Blvd, St Louis 66

Blackwell. Basil Blackwell & Mott, Ltd, 49 Broad St, Oxford, England

Blandford. Blandford Press, Ltd, 167 High Holborn & Grape St, London, W.C. 1

Boy Scouts. The Boy Scouts Association, 25 Buckingham Palace Rd, London, S.W. 1

Braziller. George Braziller, Inc, 215 Park Av, S, N.Y. 3

British Bk. Centre. British Book Centre, Inc, 122 E 55th St, N.Y. 22

Broadman. The Broadman Press, Sunday School Board, Southern Baptist Convention, 127 9th Av, N, Nashville 3, Tenn.

Bugbee. The Willis N. Bugbee Company, 428 S Warren St, Syracuse 2, N.Y.

Cambridge. Cambridge University Press, Bentley House, 200 Euston Rd, London N.W. 1

Campfield Press. The Campfield Press, St Albans, Hertfordshire, England

Cape, J. Jonathan Cape, Ltd, 30 Bedford Sq, London, W.C. 1

Cartmel, W. Cartmel & Sons, 6-8 Victoria St, St Albans, Hertfordshire, England

Childrens Theatre. Children's Theatre Press, Cloveriot, Anchorage, Ky.

Christopher. Christopher Publishing House, 1140 Columbus Av, Boston 20

Citadel. Citadel Press, 222 Park Av, S, N.Y. 3

Clarke, Irwin. Clarke, Irwin and Company, Ltd, Clarwin House, 791 St Clair Av, W, Toronto 10

Coach House Press. Coach House Press, Inc, 53 W Jackson Blvd, Chicago 4

Collins. William Collins Sons & Company, Ltd, (Collins Clear-Type Press) 215 Park Av, S, N.Y. 3

Collins (London) William Collins Sons & Company, Ltd, (Collins Clear-Type Press) 14 St James's Pl, London, S.W. 1

Columbia Univ. Press. Columbia University Press, 2960 Broadway, N.Y. 27

Constable. Constable & Company, Ltd, 10-12 Orange St, London, W.C. 2

Copp. The Copp Clark Publishing Company, Ltd, 495-517 Wellington St, W, Toronto 2B

Coward-McCann. Coward-McCann, Inc, 200 Madison Av, N.Y. 16

Criterion Bks. Criterion Books, Inc, 6 W 57th St, N.Y. 19

Crowell. Thomas Y. Crowell Co, 201 Park Av, S, N.Y. 3

Crown. Crown Publishers, 419 Park Av, S, N.Y. 16

Davies. Peter Davies, Ltd, 23 Bedford Sq, London, W.C. 1

Deane. H. F. W. Deane & Sons, The Year Book Press, Ltd, 31 Museum St, London, W.C. 1

Dell. Dell Publishing Company, 750 3d Av, N.Y. 17

Denison. T. S. Denison & Company, 309-321 5th Av, S, Minneapolis 15

Dent. J. M. Dent & Sons, Ltd, Publishers, Aldine House, 10-13 Bedford St, London, W.C. 2

De Wolfe & Stone. Felix De Wolfe and Richard Stone, 4/5 William IV St, Strand, London, W.C. 2

Dodd. Dodd, Mead & Company, Inc, 432 Park Av, S, N.Y. 16

Doubleday. Doubleday & Company, Inc, 575 Madison Av, N.Y. 22

Dramatic. Dramatic Publishing Company, 179 N. Michigan Av, Chicago 1

Dramatists. Dramatists Play Service, Inc, 14 E 38th St, N.Y. 16

Dryden. See Holt

Dutton. E. P. Dutton & Co, Inc, 201 Park Av, S, N.Y. 3

Edinburgh House. Edinburgh House Press (United Council for Missionary Education) 2 Eaton Gate, Sloane Sq, London, S.W. 1

Eldridge. Eldridge Publishing Company, Franklin, Ohio

Elek. Elek Books, Ltd, 14 Great James St, London, W.C. 1

English Theatre. English Theatre Guild, Ltd, Ascot House, 52 Dean St, London, W. 1

Epworth. The Epworth Press, Publishers (Frank H. Cumbers) 25-35 City Rd, London, E.C. 1

Eucharistic Crusade of the Knights and Handmaids of the Blessed Sacrament. The Eucharistic Crusade of the Knights and Handmaids of the Blessed Sacrament, 3115 S Grand Blvd, St Louis 18

Evans. Evans Brothers, Ltd, Montague House, Russell Sq, London, W.C. 1

Faber. Faber & Faber, Ltd, 24 Russell Sq, London, W.C. 1

Farrar, Straus. Farrar, Straus & Co, Inc, 19 Union Sq, W, N.Y. 3

Formative Press. Formative Press, Box 9771, Philadelphia 40

Fortress Press. Fortress Press, 2900 Queen Lane, Philadelphia 29

French. Samuel French, Inc, 25 W 45th St, N.Y. 36

French (Canada) Samuel French (Canada) Ltd, 27 Grenville St, Toronto 5

French (London) Samuel French, Ltd, 26 Southampton St, Strand, London, W.C. 2

Friendship Press. Friendship Press, 475 Riverside Drive, N.Y. 27

Garden City Bks. Garden City Books, 575 Madison Av, N.Y. 22

Garrett. Garrett & Massie, Inc, 1901 Roane St, Richmond 15, Va.

Globe Bk. Globe Book Company, Inc, 175 5th Av, N.Y. 10

Great-Concord Publishers. Great-Concord Publishers, Grand Central Annex, Box 1001, N.Y. 17

Grinnell College Press. Grinnell College Press, Grinnell College, Grinnell, Iowa

Grove. Grove Press, Inc, 64 University Pl, N.Y. 3

Hamilton, H. Hamish Hamilton, Ltd, 90 Great Russell St, London, W.C. 1

Harcourt. Harcourt, Brace and World, Inc, 750 3d Av, N.Y. 17

Harms, Inc. Harms, Inc, 488 Madison Av, N.Y. 22

Harper. Harper & Row, Publishers, Inc, 49 E 33d St, N.Y. 16

Hartmus Handpress. Hartmus Handpress, 4390 Mission St, San Francisco 12

Harvard Univ. Press. Harvard University Press, Publishing Dept, Kittredge Hall, 79 Garden St, Cambridge 38, Mass.

Hastings House. Hastings House, Publishers, Inc, 151 E 50th St, N.Y. 22

Hawthorn Bks. Hawthorn Books, Inc, Publishers, Route 9W, Englewood Cliffs, N.J.

Heinemann. William Heinemann, Ltd, 15-16 Queen St, Mayfair, London, W. 1

Heritage. Heritage Press, 595 Madison Av, N.Y. 22

Heuer. Heuer Publishing Co, 231-235 Dows Bldg, Cedar Rapids, Iowa

Hill & Wang. Hill & Wang, Inc, 141 5th Av, N.Y. 10

Holt. Holt, Rinehart & Winston, Inc, 383 Madison Av, N.Y. 17

Horizon Press. Horizon Press, Inc, 156 5th Av, N.Y. 10

Horn Bk. Horn Book, Inc, 585 Boylston St, Boston 16

Houghton. Houghton Mifflin Company (Riverside Press, Cambridge) 2 Park St, Boston 7

Humphries. Bruce Humphries, Inc, Publishers, 48 Melrose St, Boston 16

Ind. Univ. Press. Indiana University Press, 10th & Morton Sts, Bloomington, Ind.

Jarman Press. Jarman Press, 916 Preston Av, Charlottesville, Va.

Kenyon House Press. Kenyon House Press, Kenyon House, Alexander St, London, W. 2

Knopf. Alfred A. Knopf, Inc, 33 W 60th St, N.Y. 23

Lawrence, Lawrence & Wishart, Ltd, 81 Chancery Lane, London, W.C. 2

Li, Yu-chu Man-kuei. See Wong, Mrs Bing-Fang

Lippincott. J. B. Lippincott Company, E. Washington Sq, Philadelphia 5

Literarishe. Literarishe Heftn Publishing, 10143 Mountair Av, Tujunga, Calif.

Little. Little, Brown & Company, 34 Beacon St, Boston 6

Liveright. Liveright Publishing Corporation, 386 4th Av, N.Y. 16

Longmans, See Longmans, Inc. and Longmans, Ltd.

Longmans, Inc. See McKay

Longmans, Ltd. Longmans, Green & Company, Ltd, 48 Grosvenor St, London, W. 1

Lorenz. Lorenz Publishing Company, 501 E 3d St, Dayton 1, Ohio

Lund. Percy Lund, Humphries & Co, Ltd, 12 Bedford Sq, London, W.C. 1

McClelland. McClelland & Stewart, Ltd, 25 Hollinger Rd, Toronto 16

McGraw. McGraw-Hill Book Co, Inc, 330 W. 42d St, N.Y. 36

McKay. David McKay Company, Inc, 119 W 40th St, N.Y. 18

Macmillan (London) Macmillan & Co, Ltd, 10 St Martin's St, London, W.C. 2

Macmillan (N Y) The Macmillan Company, Publishers, 60 5th Av, N.Y. 11

Macrae Smith Co. Macrae Smith Company, Lewis Tower Bldg, 225 S 15th St, Philadelphia 2

Meridian Bks. Meridian Books, Inc, c.o. World Publishing Company, 119 W 57th St, N.Y. 19

Merlin. Merlin Press, Inc, 250 W 57th St, N.Y. 19

Methuen. Methuen & Company, Ltd, 36 Essex St, Strand, London, W.C. 2

Michael Houghton. Michael Houghton, 49A Museum St, London, W.C. 1

Miller, J.G. J. Garnet Miller, Ltd, 13 Tottenham St, London, W. 1

Modern Lib. Modern Library, Inc, 457 Madison Av, N.Y. 22

Murray, J. John Murray, Publishers, Ltd, 50 Albermarle St, London, W. 1

N.Y. Univ. Press. New York University Press, Inc, Washington Sq, N.Y. 3

Nat. Educ. National Education Association of The United States, 1201 16th St, N.W, Washington 6, D.C.

Nat. Recreation Assn. National Recreation Association, 8 W 8th St, N.Y. 11

National Union of Townswomen's Guilds. National Union of Townswomen's Guilds, 2 Cromwell Pl, London, S.W. 7

Nazarene. Nazarene Publishing House, 2923 Troost Av, Kansas City 41, Mo.

Nelson. Thomas Nelson & Sons, 18 E 41st St, N.Y. 17

New Am. Lib. The New American Library of World Literature, Inc, 501 Madison Av, N.Y. 22

New Directions, New Directions, Norfolk, Conn.

Noble. Noble and Noble Publishers, Inc, 67 Irving Pl, N.Y. 3

Northwestern Press. Northwestern Press, 315 5th Av, S, Minneapolis 15

Occu-Press. Occu-Press, 489 5th Av, N.Y. 17

Owen. F. A. Owen Publishing Company, Dansville, N.Y.

Oxford. Oxford University Press, 16-00 Pollitt Drive, Fair Lawn, N.J.

Pan American Dramatic Press. Pan American Dramatic Press, 5562 Netherland Av, N.Y. 71

Partridge Press. Partridge Press, Jubilee Terrace, Leeds 6, England

Paxton. W. Paxton & Co, Ltd, Paxton House, 36-38 Dean St, Soho, London, W. 1

Peasant Jugoslavia Ltd. Peasant Jugoslavia Ltd, 100 Oslo Ct, London, N.W. 8

Penguin. Penguin Books, Ltd, Bath Rd, Harmondsworth, Middlesex, England

Philosophical Lib. Philosophical Library, Inc, 15 E 40th St, N.Y. 16

Pitman. Pitman Publishing Corp, 20 E 46th St, N.Y. 17

Pitman (London) Sir Isaac Pitman & Sons, Ltd, Pitman House, Parker St, Kingsway, London, W.C. 2

Plays, inc. Plays, Inc, 8 Arlington St, Boston 16

Prentice-Hall. Prentice-Hall, Inc, Route 9W, Englewood Cliffs, N.J.

Putnam. G. P. Putnam's Sons, Inc, 200 Madison Av, N.Y. 16

Random House. Random House, Inc, 457 Madison Av, N.Y. 22

Register Press. Register Press, Yarmouth Port, Mass.

Regnery. The Henry Regnery Co, 14 E Jackson Blvd, Chicago 4

Reynolds. Reynolds & Co (Music Publishers) Ltd, London, W. 1

Rinehart. See Holt

Rodale. Rodale Books, Inc, 6th & Minor Sts, Emmaus, Pa.

Rodeheaver. Rodeheaver-Hall-Mack Co, Winona Lake, Ind.

Ronald. The Ronald Press Co, 15 E 26th St, N.Y. 10

Row. See Harper

Ryerson Press. Ryerson Press (United Church Publishing House) 299 Queen St, W, Toronto 2B

Sagamore. Sagamore Press, Inc, 11 E 36th St, N.Y. 16

Scarecrow. Scarecrow Press, Inc, 257 Park Av, S, N.Y. 10

Schirmer. G. Schirmer, Inc, 4 E 49th St, N.Y. 17

Scott. Scott, Foresman & Company, Educational Publishers, 433 E Erie St, Chicago 11

Scribner. Charles Scribner's Sons, 597-599 5th Av, N.Y. 17

Seabury. The Seabury Press, 815 2d Av, N.Y. 17

Secker & Warburg. Martin Secker & Warburg, Ltd, 14 Carlisle St, Soho Sq, London, W. 1

Sheed. Sheed & Ward, Ltd, 33 Maiden Lane, London, W.C. 2

Shoe String. The Shoe String Press, Inc, 965 Dixwell Av, Hamden 14, Conn.

Sierra Press. Sierra Press, Box 96, Long Island City 4, N.Y.

Simon & Schuster. Simon and Schuster, Inc, Publishers, 360 5th Av, N.Y. 20

St Anthony Guild. St Anthony Guild Press, 508 Marshall St, Paterson 3, N.J.

St Martins. St Martin's Press, Incorporated, 175 5th Av, N.Y. 10

Stacey Publications. Stacey Publications, 9 Houndsden Rd, London, N. 21

Stanford Univ. Press. Stanford University Press, Stanford, Calif.

Staples Press. Staples Press, Ltd, 151 High St, Aldershot, Hampshire, England

Sterling. Sterling Publishing Company, Inc, 419 Park Av, S, N.Y. 16

Swallow, A. Alan Swallow, 2679 S York St, Denver 10

Taplinger. Taplinger Publishing Company, Inc, 119 W 57th St, N.Y. 19

Theatre Arts. Theatre Arts Books, 333 6th Av, N.Y. 14

Thunder Pub. Thunder Publishing Company, 257 S Spring St, Los Angeles 12

Tuttle. Charles E. Tuttle Company, 28-30 S Main St, Rutland, Vt.

Twayne. Twayne Publishers, Inc, 31 Union Sq, W, N.Y. 3

Ungar. Frederick Ungar Publishing Company, 131 E 23d St, N.Y. 10

Univ. of Ark. University of Arkansas, Bureau of Research, Fayetteville, Ark.

Univ. of Calif. Press. University of California Press, Berkeley 4, Calif.

Univ. of Chicago Press. University of Chicago Press, 5750 Ellis Av, Chicago 37

Univ. of Ky. Lib. Associates. The University of Kentucky Library Associates, Lexington, Ky.

Univ. of London Press. University of London Press, Ltd, Little Paul's House, Warwick Sq, London, E.C. 4

Univ. of N.C. Press. University of North Carolina Press, Box 510, Chapel Hill, N.C.

Univ. of Tex. Press. University of Texas Press, 2211 Red River St, Austin 12, Tex.

Univ. of Wash. Press. University of Washington Press, 11 Thomson Hall, Seattle 5, Wash.

Univ. of Wis. Press. University of Wisconsin Press, 430 Sterling Ct, Madison 6, Wis.

Vanderbilt Univ. Press. Vanderbilt University Press, Kirkland Hall, Nashville 5, Tenn.

Vanguard. The Vanguard Press, 424 Madison Av, N.Y. 17

Viking. The Viking Press, Inc, 625 Madison Av, N.Y. 22

Vintage. Vintage Books, Inc, 33 W 60th St, N.Y. 23

Vosper, M. Marjorie Vosper Ltd, 32 Shaftesbury Av, London, W. 1

Wartburg Press. See Augsburg

Washington Sq. Press. Washington Square Press, 32 Washington Pl, N.Y. 3

Weidenfeld. George Weidenfeld & Nicolson, Ltd, Publishers, 20 New Bond St, London, W. 1

Whiteside. Whiteside, Inc, Publishers, 425 Park Av, N.Y. 16

Wilde. W. A. Wilde Company, 10 Huron Drive, Natick, Mass.

Winthrop College. Winthrop College, College Store, Box 132, Rock Hill, S.C.

Wong. Mrs Bing-Fang Wong, 4101 Lakeshore Av, Oakland 10, Calif.

World Pub. The World Publishing Company, 2231 W 110th St, Cleveland 2

Writer. The Writer, Inc, 8 Arlington St, Boston 16

Yale Univ. Press. Yale University Press, 149 York St, New Haven 11, Conn.

Yoseloff. Thomas Yoseloff, Inc, Publishers, 11 E 36th St, N.Y. 16

Zeno. Zeno, Booksellers, 6 Denmark St, London, W.C. 2

Zondervan. Zondervan Publishing House, 1415 Lake Drive, S.E, Grand Rapids 6, Mich.